March 20–23, 2017
Yokohama, Japan

Association for
Computing Machinery

Advancing Computing as a Science & Profession

TEI'17

Proceedings of the Tenth International Conference on Tangible, Embedded, and Embodied Interaction

Sponsored by:

ACM SIGCHI

Association for
Computing Machinery

Advancing Computing as a Science & Profession

The Association for Computing Machinery
2 Penn Plaza, Suite 701
New York, New York 10121-0701

ISBN: 978-1-4503-4676-4 (Digital)

ISBN: 978-1-4503-5450-9 (Print)

Additional copies may be ordered prepaid from:

ACM Order Department
PO Box 30777
New York, NY 10087-0777, USA

Phone: 1-800-342-6626 (USA and Canada)
+1-212-626-0500 (Global)
Fax: +1-212-944-1318
E-mail: acmhelp@acm.org
Hours of Operation: 8:30 am – 4:30 pm ET

Printed in the USA

TEI'17 Chairs' Welcome

Welcome to ACM TEI'17, the 11th-anniversary edition of the International Conference on Tangible, Embedded and Embodied Interactions, hosted at Keio University Graduate School of Media Design, known as Keio Media Design or KMD, in Yokohama, Japan, from March 20th to March 23rd, 2017.

This year's conference marks TEI's eleventh anniversary and the first time in Asia.

Welcome to Japan, a country of futuristic innovation with the blend of diverse culture and aesthetics!

The ACM International Conference on Tangible, Embedded and Embodied Interaction (TEI) addresses issues of human-computer interaction, novel tools and technologies, interactive art, and user experience. The work presented at TEI has a strong focus on how computing can bridge atoms and bits into cohesive interactive systems. The intimate size of this single-track conference provides a unique forum for exchanging ideas and presenting innovative work through talks, interactive exhibits, demos, hands-on studios, posters, art installations and performances.

The 11th TEI conference one year after the ten-year anniversary should set an outlook about the future directions of the community and the research. Therefore, we feel it is significant that the conference is hosted in Asia. In this new chapter, we are creating and experiencing the future together at TEI 2017. Related to past and future there is a fitting Japanese pro-verb: 温故知新 (On-ko-chi-shin). It means "you need to recall the past to understand the future" in English. We modified it slightly, as a tagline for our theme: "recall your past to grasp the future". More than most other academic venues in the interaction area, the TEI community understands that our mind is embodied, so to design the future we need to grasp it. We welcome contributions and experiences that touch our future lives, wellbeing, productivity etc.

TEI'17 hosts a four-day program, starting on Monday March 20th with the Graduate Student Consortium and a series of Studios that engage participants in making tangible interfaces and interactions. The main program starts with an opening keynote on Tuesday March 21st by Natalie Jeremijenko, followed by talks on tangible applications for domains ranging from health to ideation in the morning and poster, demonstration and work-in-progress sessions in the afternoon, in which projects from Student Design Challenge, with the theme of Reality from Sci-Fi are on display for audience interaction and judging. Wednesday's sessions discuss frameworks and principles for tangible interaction, present projects that make science tangible, and introduce new materials and fabrication techniques. On Thursday March 23rd, we have Seiichi Saito from Rhizomatiks giving a keynote, followed by talk sessions about novel experiences, and body and aesthetics.

This year we received 151 submissions to the Papers track. A total of 41 papers were selected after a double-blind peer review process of at least three reviewers and a meta-reviewer, resulting an acceptance rate of 27%.

For the Work-in-Progress track we received 87 submissions, which were subjected to a double-blind peer review process of two reviewers each. This resulted in 39 accepted submissions, making for an acceptance rate of 44.8%.

We thank all the authors, all the chairs and members of the organizing committee, the program committee and external reviewers, the local organizing committee, the sponsors, supporters and partners, and the TEI steering committee, together, we make TEI what it is, an exciting venue for sharing research and work on creative innovations. Let's invent the future with Tangible, Embedded and Embodied Interactions!

General Co-Chairs

Masa Inakage
Keio University (Japan)

Hiroshi Ishii
Massachusetts Institute of Technology (USA)

Ellen Yi-Luen Do
National University of Singapore (Singapore) & Georgia Tech (USA)

Program Co-Chairs

Jürgen Steimle
Saarland University (Germany)

Orit Shaer
Wellesley College, Massachusetts (USA)

Kai Kunze
Keio University (Japan)

Table of Contents

Session: Fabrication and New Materials

Session: Novel Experiences

Session: Body and Aesthetics

Session: Demos and Posters

Session: Works in Progress

Student Design Challenge

Studios

TEI'17 Conference Organizing Committee

General Chairs:	Masa Inakage, *Keio University (Japan)* Hiroshi Ishii, *Massachusetts Institute of Technology (USA)* Ellen Yi-Luen Do, *National University of Singapore (Singapore)*
Program Chairs:	Jürgen Steimle, *Saarland University (Germany)* Orit Shaer, *Wellesley College, Massachusetts (USA)* Kai Kunze, *Keio University (Japan)*
Proceedings Chairs:	Roshan Peiris, *Keio University (Japan)*
Work in Progress Co-Chairs:	Liwei Chan, *Keio University (Japan)* Andrea Bianchi, *KAIST (Korea)*
Demo Chair:	Kouta Minamizawa, *Keio University (Japan)*
Arts and Performance Chair:	Yasuaki Kakehi, *Keio University (Japan)*
Graduate Student Consortium Chairs:	Jelle van Dijk, *University of Twente (Netherlands)* Wendy Ju, *Stanford University (USA)* Yasuto Nakanishi, *Keio University (Japan)*
Student Design Challenge Chairs:	Cheng Xu, *Motorola Mobility, Chicago (USA)* Peter Bennett, *University of Bristol, Bristol (United Kingdom)* Pedro Lopes, *Hasso Plattner Institute, Potsdam (Germany)*
Studio Co-Chairs:	Katrin Wolf, *University of Art and Design Berlin (Germany)* Tsutomu Terada, *Kobe University (Japan)*
Local Co-Chairs:	Charith Fernando, *Keio University (Japan)* Roshan Peiris, *Keio University (Japan)* Yuta Sugiura, *Keio University (Japan)*
Treasurer:	Maki Sugimoto, *Keio University (Japan)*
Web Chair:	Charith Fernando, *Keio University (Japan)*
Social Media Chair:	Paul Strohmeier, *DIKU - Datalogisk Institut Københavns Universitet (Denmark)*
Sponsorship Chair:	Chihiro Sato, *Keio University (Japan)*
Student Volunteer Chair:	MHD Yamen Saraiji, *Keio University (Japan)*

Steering Committee (current):

Albrecht Schmidt, *Universität Stuttgart (Germany)*
Ali Mazalek, *Georgia Tech (USA) & Ryerson University (Canada)*
Alissa Antle, *Simon Fraser University (Canada)*
Andreas Butz, *LMU (Germany)*
Audrey Girouard, *Carleton University (Canada)*
Bart Hengeveld, *Eindhoven University of Technology (the Netherlands)*
Brygg Ullmer, *Louisiana State University (USA)*
Caroline Hummels, *Eindhoven University of Technology (the Netherlands)*
Elise van den Hoven, *University of Technology Sydney (Australia) & TU/e (the Netherlands)*
Ellen Yi-Luen Do, *Georgia Institute of Technology (USA)*
Eva Hornecker, *Bauhaus-Universität Weimar (Germany)*
Hiroshi Ishii, *MIT Media Lab (USA)*
Lian Loke, *University of Sydney (Australia)*
Martin Kaltenbrunner, *UFG (Austria)*
Nicolas Villar, *Microsoft Research (UK)*
Rob Jacob, *Tufts University (USA)*
Ron Wakkary, *Simon Fraser University (Canada)*
Saskia Bakker, *Eindhoven University of Technology (the Netherlands)*
Sergi Jorda, *UPF (Spain)*
Wendy Ju, *Stanford University (USA)*
Ylva Fernaeus, *KTH (Sweden)*

Steering Committee (current):

Hans Gellersen, *Lancaster University (UK)*
Jamie Zigelbaum, *Zigelbaum + Coelho (USA)*
Mike Fraser, *Unversity of Bristol (UK)*
Shahram Izadi, *Microsoft Research (UK)*

Program Committee:

Dzmitry Aliakseyeu, *Philips Research Europe (Netherlands)*
Alvaro Cassinelli, *University of Tokyo, (Japan)*
Liwei Chan, *National Taiwan university (Taiwan)*
Enrico Costanza, *University of Southhampton (United Kingdom)*
Audrey Desjardins, *Simon Fraser University (Canada)*
Tanja Doering, *University of Bremen (Germany)*
Florian Echtler, *Bauhaus University Weimar (Germany)*
Sean Follmer, *Stanford University (USA)*
Mike Fraser, *University of Bristol (United Kingdom)*
Audrey Girouard, *Carleton University (Caneda)*
Bart Hengeveld, *Technische Universiteit Eindhoven (Netherlands)*
Juan David Hincapie-Ramos, *University of Manitoba (Canada)*
Mike Horn, *Northwestern University (USA)*
Jörn Hurtienne, *University of Würzburg (Germany)*
Martin Kaltenbrunner, *University of Art and Design Linz (Austria)*
Rohit Ashok Khot, *RMIT University (Australia)*

Program Committee (continued):

Andrew Kun, *University of New Hampshire (USA)*
Manfred Lau, *Lancaster University (United Kingdom)*
Geehyuk Lee, *KAIST (South Korea)*
Kris Luyten, *Hasselt University (Belgium)*
Ali Mazalek, *Georgia Institute of Technology (USA)*
Amon Millner, *Olin College of Engineering (USA)*
Martin Murer, *University of Salzburg (Austria)*
Masashi Nakatani, *Hokkaido University (Japan)*
Ian Oakley, *Ulsan National Institute of Science and Technology (South Korea)*
Evan Peck, *Bucknell University (USA)*
Roshan Peiris, *Keio University (Japan)*
Michael Poor, *Baylor University (USA)*
Claudia Rebola, *Rhode Island School of Design (USA)*
Michal Rinott, *Shenkar - Engineering. Design. Art (Israel)*
Michael Rohs, *University of Hannover (Germany)*
Enrico Rukzio, *University of Ulm (Germany)*
Jelle Saldien, *Ghent University (Belgium)*
Wolfgang Stuerzlinger, *Simon Fraser University, SIAT, (Canada)*
Ehud Sharlin, *University of Calgary (Canada)*
Beat Signer, *Vrije Universiteit Brussel (Belgium)*
Sri Subramanian, *University of Sussex (United Kingdom)*
Yuta Sugiura, *Keio University (Japan)*
Jakob Tholander, *MobileLife@Stockholm University (Sweden)*
Manfred Tscheligi, *ICT&S Center, University of Salzburg (Austria)*
Daniel Wessolek, *Bauhaus-University Weimar (Germany)*
Andy Wilson, *Microsoft Research (USA)*
Raphael Wimmer, *University of Regensburg (Germany)*

Sponsor: SIGCHI

Reviewers

Abdelrahman Yomna
Achenbach Attila Victor
Adamczyk Piotr
Aggarwal Deepti
Agrawal Harshit
Alexander Jason
Aliakseyeu Dzmitry
Alt Florian
Amores Judith
Anderson Fraser
Antle Alissa
Ardaud Guillaume
Arif Ahmed Sabbir
Arnold Peter
Ashbrook Daniel
Aslan Ilhan
Büschel Wolfgang
Baba Tetsuaki
Baehr Benjamin
Bailly Gilles
Banerjee Amartya
Barker Matthew
Barreto Mary
Bateman Scott
Bates Oliver
Beaudouin-Lafon Michel
Bellucci Andrea
Bendor Roy
Bennett Peter
Bianchi Andrea
Boa Duncan
Bongers Bert
Booth Tracey
Brady Corey
Branton Chris
Brewer Robin
Briot Audrey
Brock Anke
Brockmeyer Eric
Brown Mark
Bucci Paul
Burstyn Jesse
Buruk Oğuz Turan
Byrne Richard
Cabral Mota Roberta
Calvo Andres
Carrascal Juan Pablo
Cartwright Stephen
Cassinelli Alvaro
Catala Alejandro
Chan Liwei
Chang Jack Shen-Kuen
Chattopadhyay Debaleena
Chen Yi-Ling
Chen Yingjie
Chi Peggy
Choi Judeth Oden
Chow Ka Nin
Chu Jean Ho
Coelho Marcelo
Conradie Peter
Coros Stelian
Costanza Enrico
Coutrix Celine
Couture Nadine
Cramer Emily
Cuadra Andrea
Cuykendall Shannon
D'Angelo Sarah
Döring Tanja
Dörk Marian
Dade-Robertson Martyn
De Raffaele Clifford
De Vos Ellen
Dekel Amnon
Delbressine Frank
Desjardins Audrey
Devendorf Laura
Dippon Andreas
Dobbelstein David
Doering Christopher
Donnarumma Marco
Dumas Bruno
Dunne Lucy
Eady Alex
Echtler Florian
Edge Darren
England David
Ens Barrett
Essen Harm van
Essl Georg
Esteves Augusto
Fan Kevin
Feng Mi
Ferguson Jamie
Fernando Charith
Finn Patrick
Fjeld Morten
Flannery Louise
Fox Tyler
Fröhlich Peter
Franinovic Karmen
Frankjær Raune
Fraser Mike
Freeman Dustin
Frens Joep W.
Froehlich Jon
Fuchsberger Verena
Fuentes Carolina
Fukushima Shogo
Güldenpfennig Florian
Garzotto Franca
Geiger Shachar
Geurts Luc
Giacaman Nasser
Gilleade Kiel
Giordani Alice
Girouard Audrey
Goikhman Alisa
Gomes Antonio
Gong Jun
Good Judith
Grah Thomas
Grundgeiger Tobias
Gu Jiseong
Gugenheimer Jan
Guinness Darren
Guminski Karin
Gundersen Kara
Gupta Aakar
Hachisu Taku
Haesen Mieke
Hakkila Jonna
Han Gyeol
Hanamitsu Nobuhisa
Harley Daniel
Harrison Chris
Hashida Tomoko
He Liang
Heller Florian
Hemmert Fabian
Hendriks Gerard
Hengeveld Bart
Heo Seongkook
Higuchi Keita
Hincapié-Ramos Juan David
Hirsch Matt

Ho Hsin-Ni
Holmquist Lars Erik
Holzinger Andreas
Honnet Cedric
Hook Jonathan
Horn Mike
Hornecker Eva
Hoshi Takayuki
Houben Steven
HSIAO Chiao-Yin
Huang Chung-Ching
Huang Da-Yuan
Huang Da-Yuan
HUANG Yi-Ching
Huber Stephan
Huo Ke
Hurtienne Jörn
Iacovides Ioanna
Ikematsu Kaori
Ion Alexandra
Isbister Katherine
Israel Johann Habakuk
Jang Sujin
Jansen Yvonne
Jenkins Tom
Jetter Hans-Christian
jo kazuhiro
Jonsson Martin
Jude Alvin
Jung Heekyoung
Kadomura Azusa
Kakehi Yasuaki
Kaltenbrunner Martin
Kammer Dietrich
Kangas Jari
Kao Hsin-Liu Cindy
Karnik Abhijit
Karunanayaka Kasun
Kaul Oliver Beren
Kawahara Yoshihiro
Kay Judy
Khot Rohit Ashok
Kim Han-Jong
Kim Hyungil
Kim Hyunyoung
Kim Hyunyoung
Kim Jeeeun
KIM SuKyoung
Kim Sunjun
Kim Sunyoung
Kirshenbaum Nurit
Klinkhammer Daniel
Knibbe Jarrod
Knouf Nicholas
Koike Hideki
Koizumi Naoya
Kono Michinari
Kranz Matthias
Kratz Sven
Krischkowsky Alina
Kubota Akihiro
Kukka Hannu
Kun Andrew
Kunze Kai
Kwak Matthijs
Kwon Hyosun
Löchtefeld Markus
Löffler Diana
Laaksolahti Jarmo
Laput Gierad
Lau Manfred
Ledo David
Lee Austin
Lee DoYoung
Lee Geehyuk
Lee Jaeyeon
Lee Jaeyeon
Lee Ji-Hyun
Lee Juyoung
Lee Leila Hyelip
Lee Sung-Hee
Lee Uichin
Lee Woohun
Lee Yeoreum
Lee Yi-Chieh
Leigh Sang-won
Leithinger Daniel
Leong Zeina Atrash
Letondal Catherine
Leventhal Laura
Levy Pierre
Li Jiannan
Li Nico
Liang Rong-Hao
Liao Yi-Chi
LIN YU-TZU
Lindlbauer David
Long Kiel
Loparev Anna
Lucero Andrés
Luyten Kris
Maquil Valérie
Marsh William
Marshall Mark
Martelaro Nikolas
Martinez Diego
Marzo Asier
Mason Jon
Matthies Denys J.C
Maurer Bernhard
Mazalek Ali
McIntosh Jess
McMillan Donny
McNaney Roisin
McPherson Andrew
Megard Christine
Mellis David
Memoli Gianluca
Merritt Tim
Millner Amon
Miyashita Homei
Moradinezhad Reza
Mosher Matthew
Mott Martez
Murer Martin
Nakagaki Ken
Nakamaru Satoshi
Nakamura Hiromi
Nakatani Masashi
Nakazawa Jin
Nam Tek-Jin
Nanayakkara Suranga
Neate Timothy
Nebeling Michael
Neustaedter Carman
Neutelings Ineke
Nguyen Linh Chi
Nisi Valentina
Nojima Takuya
Normark Maria
Nowacka Diana
Nylander Stina
Oakley Ian
Obiorah Mmachi
Oehlberg Lora
Ogata Masa
Oh Hyunjoo
Oh Hyunjoo
Oh Seoyoung
Omirou Themis
Ortega Michael
Otero Nuno
Ou Jifei
Outram Benjamin
Panëels Sabrina
Park Young-Woo

Parmentier Davy
Pauchet Sylvain
Payne Jennifer
Pearson Jennifer
Peck Evan
Peek Nadya
Peiris Roshan
Personal Melodie
Perteneder Florian
Petersen Mariane Graves
Petrelli Daniela
Pfeuffer Ken
Pietrzak Thomas
Plaumann Katrin
Pohl Henning
Pon Aura
Poor Michael
PORTAZ Maxime
Posch Irene
Preßler Jan
Price Sara
Przybylla Mareen
Ramakers Raf
Ranasinghe Nimesha
Rasmussen Majken Kirkegaard
Rebola Claudia
Regal Georg
Reinhardt Daniel
Reiterer Harald
Rendl Christian
REY Stéphanie
Riener Andreas
Rinott Michal
Rivière Guillaume
Robinson Simon
Rohs Michael
Roseway Asta
Rossito Chiara
Roudaut Anne
Roumen Thijs
Rukzio Enrico
saakes daniel
Sahoo Deepak
Sakamoto Daisuke
Saldien Jelle
SALEM Ben
Sapounidis Theodosios
Savage Valkyrie
Schaefer Michael
Schneider Jan
Schneider Oliver
Schoessler Philipp
Schroeter Ronald
Schwappach Florin
Scott Michelle
Sean Follmer
Seitinger Susanne
Seo Jinsil Hwaryoung
Seo Kyoungwon
Seong Young-Ah
Seyed Teddy
Sharlin Ehud
Shibley Noah
Shiloh Michael
Signer Beat
Simbelis Vygandas
Simeone Adalberto
Simpson Emma
Sinclair Mike
Sirkin David
Smit Dorothé
Solovey Erin
Somanath Sowmya
Song Youngeun
Spelmezan-new Daniel
Spiel Katharina
Sridhar Priyashri
Strohmeier Paul
Stusak Simon
Subramanian Sri
Sugiura Yuta
Suh Jihoon
Tabard Aurelien
Takashima Kazuki
Tan Haodan
Tanenbaum Josh
Tang Anthony
Therón Roberto
Tholander Jakob
Thudt Alice
Tiab John
Todi Kashyap
TOLIAS Evangelos
Trullemans Sandra
Tsai Hsin-Ruey
Tsaknaki Vasiliki
Tscharn Robert
Tscheligi Manfred
Tse Edward
Tseng Tiffany
Tsukada Koji
Ueoka Ryoko
Ullmer Brygg
Umanski Daniil
Valdes Consuelo
Vallgårda Anna
van Rheden Vincent
Vanacken Davy
Varsanyi Petra
Vatavu Radu-Daniel
Vega Katia
Velloso Eduardo
Verame Jhim
Vi Chi
Vibol Yem
Villanosa Krystal
Vo Dong-Bach
Voida Stephen
Vossoughi Shirin
Wakita Akira
Wang Johnty
Warren Jillian
Watanabe Yoshihiro
Weibel Nadir
Weichel Christian
Weigel Martin
Weiler Jennifer
Wessolek Daniel
Wiberg Mikael
wilde danielle
Willemse Christian
Williamson Julie
Wilson Andy
Wimmer Raphael
Withana Anusha
Wolff Annika
Wolfgang Stuerzlinger
wyffels Francis
Xambó Anna
Yamanaka Shota
Yamaoka Junichi
Yang Xing-Dong
Yao Lining
Yasu Kentaro
Yeo Hui-Shyong
Yoo Sanghyun
Yoon Dongwook
Yoon Sang Ho
Zhu Kening
Zoran Amit
Zuckerman Oren

The Blue Studio: Designing an Interactive Environment for Embodied Multi-Stakeholder Ideation Processes

Philémonne Jaasma
Eindhoven University of Technology
Eindhoven, The Netherlands,
p.g.jaasma@tue.nl

Dorothé Smit
University of Salzburg
Salzburg, Austria
dorothe.smit@sbg.ac.at

Jelle van Dijk
University of Twente
Enschede, The Netherlands,
jelle.vandijk@utwente.nl

Thomas Latcham
Interactive RI.SE ICT
Umeå, Sweden
thomaslatcham@hotmail.com

Ambra Trotto
Interactive RI.SE ICT
& Umeå University
Umeå, Sweden
ambra@tii.se

Caroline Hummels
Eindhoven University of Technology
Eindhoven, The Netherlands,
c.c.m.hummels@tue.nl

ABSTRACT
This paper describes the process of designing the Blue Studio: an interactive space for embodied multi-stakeholder ideation processes. Inspired by *embodied sensemaking* – the way people make sense of things through external expression and interaction with other people – we iteratively designed material, interactive and spatial interventions in the Blue Studio and evaluated them with multi-stakeholder participants in various studies. Thereupon, we analyzed the impact of the design interventions, based on the seven principles to design for embodied sensemaking and highlighted opportunities for refining our interactive space for embodied ideation. Based on the insights gained, a final design of the Blue Studio was realized and evaluated on functionality.

Author Keywords
Ideation; Embodied Ideation; Interactive Ideation Space; Tools for Multi-Stakeholder Ideation.

ACM Classification Keywords
H.5.m. Information interfaces and presentation; H.5.3. Group and Organization Interfaces.

INTRODUCTION
Complex societal challenges, such as sustainability, the refugee crisis and inclusive and affordable health care systems, have gathered multi-disciplinary stakeholders in creative collaborations to ideate on future solutions [4], as these complex challenges often require more than the expertise of a single person or organization. Designers can support these ideation sessions by creating tools for stakeholders to express themselves and to generate future-proof ideas.

TEI '17, March 20-23, 2017, Yokohama, Japan
© 2017 ACM. ISBN 978-1-4503-4676-4/17/03…$15.00
DOI: http://dx.doi.org/10.1145/3024969.3025002

Creative spaces
There have been various attempts at enriching group ideation sessions using interactive technology, e.g., by using vertical or horizontal large, interactive displays (e.g. [10], [24]), sometimes in combination with tangible objects (e.g. [31]; [14]; [7]), or by offering creative and interactive spaces (e.g. [26], [16], [30]). Some of the existing tools focus on representing, storing, searching and retrieving ideas and insights, which is not the same as a technology that would actively, in real-time, support the *process* of collaborative ideation ([1]). Recently, Lucero [17] has made the first efforts towards what he calls 'funky-design-spaces', holistic design studios that support the creation of mood boards. Amongst his considerations for tools for mood board making, he lists involving the senses, flexible and intuitive interaction with provided tools, and the need for a holistic interactive space. A design space should invite exploration and stimulate users to move around the room.

Figure 1. The current version of the Blue Studio

In multi-stakeholder ideation settings, the added value of implementing interactive technology may well lie in making the participants value and coordinate their shared stakes, which, according to van Dijk [28], [29], must evolve through actual, face-to-face contact between the stakeholders in a joint activity, in our case ideation sessions. The development of the 'Blue Studio' (see figure 1), as described in this paper, is an exploration into the design of an interactive space that aims at facilitating this face-to-face process of shared value making and coordination during multi-stakeholder ideation, for which we use the concept of embodied sensemaking. In this paper, we first elucidate this concept of embodied sensemaking. Thereupon, we describe three iterations of design interventions in, and user studies of the Blue Studio, followed by our insights gained in relation to the seven principles of designing for embodied sensemaking [11]. Finally, we describe how these insights have been applied to the final design iteration in the Blue Studio. With this contribution, we hope to feed a conversation and inspire future work about the role of interactive artifacts and environments in mediating ideation in multi-stakeholder groups.

Multi-Stakeholder Ideation through Embodied Sensemaking

The creative collaborative process of a multi-stakeholder ideation session can be seen as an unfolding process of 'embodied sensemaking' ([11], [13]). Embodied sensemaking describes the way people collaboratively create shared insight in a creative and improvisational manner. This is not a special-purpose activity: embodied sensemaking is the normal, mundane way in which people in everyday practices make sense of things. It is to be contrasted with rational, cognitivist models in which an understanding or idea originates and develops completely as an inner, mental process, prior to, and essentially detached from, any following expression of such an idea in an external medium. Instead, theories of embodied sensemaking hold that in the majority of everyday practices people make sense of things *through* external expression and *through* embodied interaction with other people [6]. Embodied sensemaking is thus grounded in the way people use their embodied skills in appropriating, configuring and transforming objects and materials in their environment (including nonverbal expression and posture of their own body), a process by which they develop and express their thoughts [13]. Such skillful, expressive evolution of creative insight is inherently social in nature, because it plays out not in a person's private mind but in the public world [23]. Additionally, drawing on Gibson's notion of affordance [9], Gaver [8] argued that collaboration is affected by the digital and physical media through / in which people collaborate ('media spaces').

When designers create tools for collaborative ideation sessions, these tools function as external media that enable participants to develop and express their thoughts in a way that allows for other people to join in on the sensemaking process and contribute to it. To support designers in creating such tools (artefacts), Hummels and Van Dijk [11] have translated available theory on embodied sensemaking into seven concrete principles, shown in table 1, to take into account when designing for embodied sensemaking.

Social Situatedness	Insight emerges as co-constituted in the interaction between people and against the background of a social setting in which people always already relate to one another [23].
Scaffolds	Physical objects and spaces serve as binding anchors, both for individual reflective conversations as well as for fusing individually sensemaking efforts into a collective, participatory phenomenon [28].
Traces	Evolving traces of creative expressions can themselves come to function as scaffolds [30].
Interactive Imagery	The ambiguous, sensuous nature of our creative expressions, for example in sketches collages or moodboards, may empower our capacity for imagining new, unthought-of possibilities [16].
Dialogical System	Expressions of thought are not "*communication [... in the sense of] the transmission of information but rather [function in] the co-ordination of behavior between living organisms through mutual structural coupling*" [3].
1st person perspective	As said people do not contribute as detached 'generators of information' but engage in the meaning-making process while interacting with their whole, embodied selves [18]. This calls for a design that acknowledges the importance of personal engagement, empathy and maybe even intimacy.
Catalyzing Engage-ment	Bodily involvement e.g. by using body storms, tinkering sessions or enactment [2], [22] elicit a direct engagement and a (pro)active, empathic and responsible attitude propelled by personal experiences. Moreover, bodily encounters seem to lower the threshold to merge the perspectives from people with different backgrounds [12].

Table 1. Seven principles to design for embodied sensemaking based on Hummels & Van Dijk [11].

In the current project, we have applied these principles in the design of the "Blue Studio" to enhance embodied sensemaking during collaborative ideation in multi-stakeholder teams. In the section *Insight*, which is placed after the description of the approach and design iterations, we reflect on our design iterations using these principles.

APPROACH

The design-research project took place in one of the meeting rooms in Sliperiet. The meeting room, named the "Blue Studio", was initially a meeting room with dark-blue painted walls, a grey vinyl floor, a white suspended ceiling and no windows. The furniture consisted of a round table with several chairs and a blue dry-erase board integrated in the wall. The ambition of the project partner was to transform this room into a creative place where the visitors of Sliperiet - multi-disciplinary stakeholders of innovative projects - could gather to spark new ideas and inspiration.

We used an ongoing Research through Design process [33] to transform the Blue Studio from a dark meeting room into a space that mediates embodied ideation. The final Blue Studio space was iteratively designed: over the course of 10 months, several (interactive) design interventions were integrated in the meeting room and subsequently evaluated in user studies with multi-stakeholder groups. We obtained insights for further iterations through an analysis of video recordings of the entire ideation session and a semi-structured interview conducted after each user study. Ultimately, the process resulted in the final design of the Blue Studio, which has been evaluated in three sessions.

DESIGN ITERATIONS IN THE BLUE STUDIO

In this section we describe three iterations of design interventions in the Blue Studio, as well as the user study setup of each iteration, and the findings from the observations and interviews.

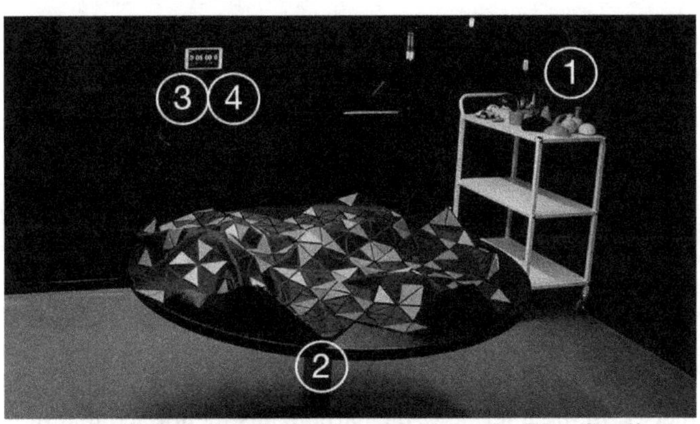

Figure 2: The first design interventions the Blue Studio

Iteration 1: Objects and Landscape

The following design interventions (see figure 1) were developed and implemented in the space: the Embodied Ideation Toolkit (EIT) [21] (1 in figure 1) designed to boost imagination and explore scenarios through enactment, a flexible surface suspended from the ceiling by fishing wire (2), serving as a dynamic landscape for the participants to build on; a time indicator placed on the wall (3) to be started by participants themselves, that could inform them of the time left. Finally, the 'Voice Commander' (4) (or 'VC'): a voice transformer that allowed the researchers to instruct the participants during the session without physically being present in the Blue Studio.

Study setup 1

The first user study was a 15-minute pilot test with a group of four university lecturers (1 male 3 female) of different disciplines, whose motivation to participate was that they were looking for ideas for a new educational program that they were working on. We invited the participants into the Blue Studio for an ideation session without disclosing any information about the space or the process of using it. While in the Blue Studio we only used the VC to instruct the participants on a few steps: how to start the timer; to inform them they could pick objects from EIT that were of interest to them; to ask them to explain why they had picked an object; and to ask them to build a storyline of their ideas with the objects they had picked.

The session was monitored from a separate space and video recorded for later analysis. After the session, we briefly interviewed the participants about their experiences. Finally, we instructed the participants to record their generated ideas in a *Future Narrative*: a one-minute video, based on One-Shot-Video technique [TII website Stockholm] and performance theory, in which participants use the space and the objects in it to act out a scenario that demonstrates the ideas they generated during the session ("twice behaved behavior", [20]), as a means to preserve, enrich [25] and reflect on their collaborative sensemaking process.

Study setup 2

The second user study was a 30-minute session with three (male) participants from different professions: mechanical engineering, software engineering and academia. They had recently become the new management team of the local FabLab, but were not yet familiar with each other. Their motivation to participate was that they had the shared task to develop a vision for the FabLab.

Before entering the Blue Studio, the participants collectively defined and recorded their challenge in five minutes in the Grey Room, a small room adjacent to the Blue Studio. After that, the participants entered the Blue Studio, where they were given a minute to explore before the VC reminded them to keep their challenge in mind and to set the timer to 20 minutes. The participants used that time to create ideas using the objects from the EIT in combination with the flexible surface in the space. After finishing the ideation session in the Blue Studio, the participants moved back into the Grey Room, where they reflected on their challenge and the session's outcomes. Following this reflection, they recorded the Future Narrative as a short video conclusion. Finally, the participants were interviewed about their experiences.

Findings

The space and tools influenced the embodied sensemaking process in several ways. When looking at the physical aspects of the space, the round shape of the surface triggered the participants to stand around it in a circle and they hardly moved from their positions, focusing all their attention on creating ideas in the center of the room while forgetting about the other objects in the corner. Moreover, because the VC introduced the flexible surface as a 'landscape', it led to a very direct translation in its use, i.e. a literal landscape with roads, mountains and roundabouts. The participants did use the EIT objects in their ideation: they attributed meaning and behavior to objects or related them to a representation of the elements of their ideas. However, they mentioned that the objects from the EIT did not feel like they were 'part of the room'.

Considering the aspect of time, it became clear from the interviews after both sessions that time played a crucial role in embodied sensemaking. The awareness of having little time to ideate and the presence of a timer stimulated the participants to not overthink their ideas and instead share them immediately with each other. They indicated that it felt safe to do so, in the playful rush of the space. In the second study, participants appreciated the opportunity to take some time to reflect on their ideation session.

Even through the instructing researcher was not physically present in the room but connected through a remote VC, participants were very willing to follow instructions from the VC. While it only intervened four times, the participants noted that the VC supported them in remaining focused and oriented on completing their challenge. Another contribution to their focus was the dark color of the walls and the lack of windows. Day-to-day hassle felt far away while being in the space, as the participants indicated.

Design Directions

The first iteration gave useful insights for further iterations. The space requires more interventions outside of the center of the room to stimulate movement and embodied exploration of the space. The objects need reconsideration both in spatial terms (size, expansion qualities, interaction possibilities in the room) and in material terms to function as an integrated part of the room. Participants appreciate a form of guidance in the space, e.g., time pressure or a commanding voice, while at the same time we should remain the element of surprise to stimulate participants to step out of their comfort zone and share new ideas.

Iteration 2: Constructional Puzzle Pieces & Integrated Dry-Erase Board

In the second iteration (see figure 3), we removed the flexible surface from the middle of the room. We decided to preserve the EIT objects and extend them with triangular wooden 'puzzle pieces' (1 in figure 3) fitted with slots and magnets, that could connect to each other and be constructed into bigger 3D structures. Some of these 3D structures were already built, while the remaining puzzle pieces were scattered throughout the room. Participants could use the prepared structures and the remaining pieces as a multi-faceted stage for their ideas, as an alternative to the 'landscape' in the first iteration. The dis-embodied VC was removed from the set-up all together. Instead, participants received a brief at the start that informed them about three phases of the ideation session in the Blue Studio. Moreover, the timer was replaced with a lamp (2) that was slowly dimmed throughout the session as a more indirect yet continuous indication of time passing. Finally, the space was equipped with a video-recording tablet (3) and a spotlight (4) that illuminated near the end of the session as an invitation to start recording their future narrative.

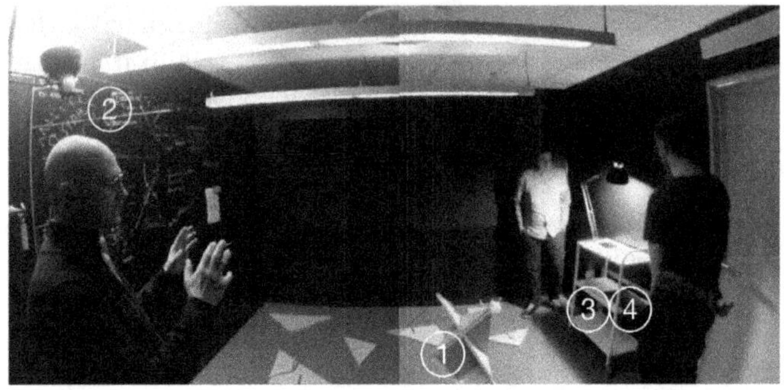

Figure 3: Second design iteration & third user study in the Blue Studio

Study setup

The design interventions of the second iteration in the Blue Studio were evaluated with three (male) participants: a manager, a student volunteer and a PhD researcher. Their motivation to participate was to generate ideas for their shared task of promoting and maintaining the FabLab. The ideation session in the Blue Studio took thirty minutes. At the end of the ideation session, participants used the tablet to record a Future Narrative to summarize their ideas. The study was concluded with an interview.

Findings

Upon entering the Blue Studio, the participants were immediately drawn to the integrated dry-erase board (figure 3, left wall) and neglected the other materials. We then realized that we had forgotten to remove the markers, as we had done in the first iteration, and we removed them halfway the session (after 15 minutes). After seven minutes, the participants spontaneously started to include the physical materials in the Blue Studio to act out their written ideas and explore them further. They also used the prepared 3D structures in the room as a stage for their ideas, but they were hesitant to build new structures using the remaining puzzle pieces. In the interview, the participants mentioned that they were unsure 'where to start' in the Blue Studio and began using the dry-erase board and markers because these were familiar to them, as opposed to the other materials in the space. However, the use of these other materials helped them to create shared understanding by overcoming the limitations of language and jargon. The participants indicated that while using the objects to talk and explore, they figured out that they oftentimes meant the same things, but expressed them differently. The participants also positively experienced the removal of the markers, as the focus on building shifted their ideation from divergent, explorative ideas to convergent, concrete ideas. Finally, the spotlight, used to highlight the tablet at the end of the session, was immediately recognized by participants as an indicator to conclude their creative session and they quickly picked up the tablet to film their Future Narrative.

Design Directions

Altogether, the second iteration shed light on the opportunities for more interactive materials or triggers in the space to seduce participants to overcome the hurdle of physically engaging with the space, its objects and each other, and not gravitating towards the known dry-erase board, the affordances of which are less supportive for embodied sensemaking [28]. Consequently, we permanently removed the markers from the Blue Studio. The use of directive lighting (spotlight on tablet for filming) appears to be effective in guiding participants in the space without being as intrusive as a VC. Further design opportunities for embodied sensemaking may lie in explorations into interactive technology as mediator of ideation, which was done in the 3rd iteration.

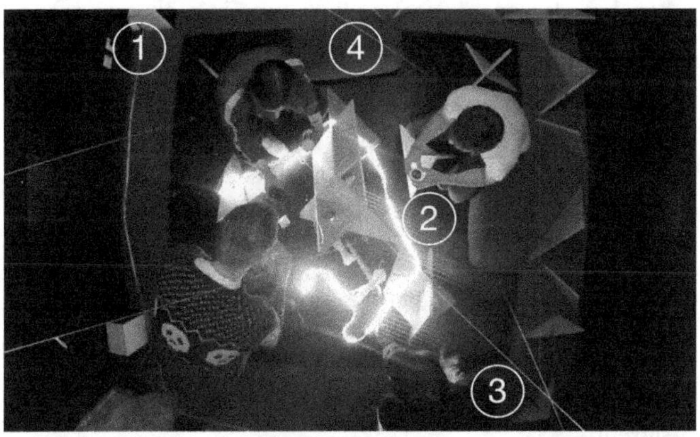

Figure 4: Third design iteration & user study in the Blue Studio

Iteration 3: Interactive Ambient Effects

In the third iteration (see figure 4) of the Blue Studio we kept the EIT objects, the puzzle pieces and spotlight of iteration 2, but expanded their connection possibilities with spatial interactions and ambient effects, as to explore the effect of interactive materiality [22] as mediator for embodied sensemaking in ideation. The ambience of the space was influenced by dynamic light and sound. A soundscape (1 in figure 4) increased in intensity and volume throughout the session to build up a climax and make the participants aware of the approaching end of the session. The interactive light that was offered consisted of an RGB lamp in loop mode and a controllable RGB LED strip (2). Additional spatial interactions were created with diagonal wires from the floor to the ceiling (3) that would influence the soundscape when manipulated. The final intervention in this iteration was the addition of pillows (4) to allow for sitting while interacting with the puzzle pieces and EIT objects.

Study setup

The third iteration was evaluated with a group of four (all male): three students from creative programs and one software engineer. Their motivation to participate was to develop a business plan for the local FabLab. The study had the same structure and timing as the study in iteration 2.

Findings

The participants built a high structure with the puzzle pieces and used all artifacts and the LED strip to build a story around it: e.g., the LED strip illuminated the 'desired situation' and some secluded puzzle pieces represented 'each project partner being on its own island'. After ten minutes the participants discovered that they could influence the soundscape by manipulating the wires. They also related the RGB lamp's changing colors to their own actions, while it was, in fact, in a standard loop. The pillows were not used by all participants, but some used them to sit or lie down and take a break. As in iteration 2, the directional spotlight proved to be very effective: within a minute after the spotlight illuminated the tablet, the participants were filming their future narrative.

The participants indicated that they were intrigued to discover their effect on the space and that they enjoyed exploring the interactivity. They indicated that they felt free in exploring, because the space reacted to them - this felt like a reward. At the same time, they felt in control of what was happening, as they attributed the space's behavior to their own actions and appropriated the effects in their Future Narrative. The soundscape was described as 'a subtle indication of time passing by', and was experienced (both positively and negatively) as an element of a 'gameshow' in which a puzzle had to be solved within a set time. The participants explained that being able to sit or lie down on the pillows provided them with a (literally) new perspective on their built structure, and brought them to new ideas. Some felt that the pillows and the dim lighting gave a 'cozy' atmosphere to the space.

Design Directions

The implementation of digital effects to the participants' actions (e.g., manipulating wires) contributed to the playful character of the space, inviting the participants to try things out and explore other effects throughout the space. The EIT objects were still a separate element in the space and in order to integrate them they should not only be bigger but also be able to actuate effects in the space. The inspiration and added value of embodied sensemaking for ideation seems to lie in the interplay between the objects, the space and the participants. We concluded that the final design of the Blue Studio requires refinement of the design interventions: careful implementation of connection possibilities and effects (sensors and actuators) between the objects, space and people in it. We used a more careful analysis of our iterations based on the seven principles of embodied sensemaking to steer these refinements.

Figure 5: Wide-angle impression of final design of Blue Studio

INSIGHTS

Over the course of the development of the Blue Studio, we observed several strengths of the Blue Studio and its effect on the people using it for their ideations. The gained insights are clustered by the seven principles to design for embodied sensemaking [11] that inspired the design interventions. These insights were the guideline for the final design of the Blue Studio.

Social Situatedness

The evaluations showed that, due to the unfamiliarity of the space and its materials, people who normally took the lead in meetings did not necessarily take the lead in the Blue Studio. Individuals who had never met before felt free to share their ideas with each other in the Blue Studio. Participants indicated that they felt that the 'normal rules' did not apply in the Blue Studio, as the (darkness of the) space, the (non-descriptive) materials and the (unexpected, ambient) effects created an alien environment in which every person had to re-establish their role in the group in the space.

Scaffolds

In all iterations the EIT objects were scaffolds for ideation. The magnets in these and other objects, such as the puzzle pieces, provided anchors for building a narrative. Participants were able to switch quickly between verbally expressing their ideas and thoughts, and constructing their ideas using the EIT objects and puzzle pieces provided to them. The studies did show that it is beneficial to have scaffolds of different sizes and orientation to enable making connections in and with the entire space. Therefore, the floor, walls and ceiling of the Blue Studio should also function as scaffolds.

Traces

Building with the EIT objects and puzzle pieces, the landscape cloth or the LED strips allowed participants to physically create traces in the space. We observed that longitudinal objects were helpful for participants to create a narrative, literally moving in space from one subject to another. Finally, offering the tablet enabled to participants to create a video as a trace of the outcome of the ideation session, which was appreciated by participants.

Interactive Imagery

The Blue Studio offered various ways for participants to express themselves creatively and because the objects were not familiar and had an open script of use, they triggered imagination. Connecting the objects into new combinations was a popular way to not only generate ideas, but moreover to elaborate on each other's ideas. Unexpected connections of physical objects and unexpected effects of these connections often directly impacted the ideation, e.g. in taking a second look at things, opting for another train of thought, or uttering new ideas, e.g., "What if our product would be modular?"

Dialogical System

Participants did not necessarily 'solve' their challenge during sessions, but always mentioned an increase in shared understanding as a result of the session. The unfamiliarity of the space, and the absence of direct guidance or fixed steps to be followed in the space, makes the participants depend on one another to 'figure it out'. We observed that in some sessions, participants started to examine the room individually, but in all sessions they soon set out on a common mission to explore the capabilities of the space. In exploring, they did not only share their findings with each other, but also spent most of their time in gathering around interactive points (e.g., lights or audio strings) and experimenting with those together. While doing this, they were establishing a common understanding of the Blue Studio and exploring the possible functions of a certain interactive point. It was in this manner that the participants in user study 3 convinced themselves of their impact on the color of the lamp, which was actually displaying colors in a continuous loop. During the evaluations, the objects helped to strengthen communication and dialogue. Or, previously described, the objects supported participants to talk while exploring the topic hands-on and figuring out that they oftentimes meant the same things, but expressed them differently.

1st Person Perspective

The Blue Studio can hardly be understood or used without engaging with it physically: trying out and exploring what happens. This was a threshold for some participants, but once over that threshold (stimulated, e.g., by the Voice Commander or other participants in the session), they became engaged with their whole embodied selves. Managers could not maintain their 'managing role' as that role provides no benefit in the Blue Studio; no managerial expertise is needed to connect objects together, or build puzzle structures. To illustrate, one participant with a managerial background, initially refused to kneel down to fiddle or build with objects. However, within minutes, he started pointing at objects or specific parts of the structure, and soon thereafter, he was on his knees building the additions to the structure that he was thinking of. The element of triggering engagement could be further refined in the final design, especially in the interior design of the space itself and in the script that guides the participants, e.g. when entering the Blue Studio.

Catalyzing Engagement

When participants discovered the ability to connect objects to one another and combine them with the puzzle pieces, the landscape cloth, the wires or LED strips, they commenced an exploration of the characteristics of the space, and even of the other participants in the space. They connected objects they were holding to objects others were holding or built structures together. Furthermore, as the room is quite small and the structures (e.g. puzzle pieces, wires) were quite prominent, there were often unintended or even funny moments of participants bumping into one another, which contributed to a more relaxed relation between participants.

FINAL DESIGN OF THE BLUE STUDIO

Following the explorations in the Blue Studio, a final design (figure 5) was drawn up and realized. To amplify the alien atmosphere of the room, the walls, floor and ceiling were covered by (vaulted) wooden or steel triangular panels, integrating interactive elements, such as capacitive sensors, LED strips, a sound installation, and magnetic switches. The extended EIT objects, granting exploration of these interactive elements, were visibly spread throughout the space. The extended toolkit included larger objects than the original toolkit (figure 6), which invites people to build spacious structures and to physically connect to each other in the Blue Studio.

Phases of Ideation in the Blue Studio

To help users of the Blue Studio orient themselves, a session in the Blue Studio always consists of three pre-programmed phases, integrating two of the phases of the creative process as defined by Kneller [15]: idea generation and idea selection. The remaining two phases (problem definition and idea verification) take place before and after the session, respectively. One Blue Studio session amounts to just under 30 minutes. During the session, an ambient soundscape supports the phases of the Blue Studio. Moreover, an Instruction Board was developed and placed on the wall, indicating the time participants have spent in the Blue Studio, and the phase of their ideation session.

Orientation phase (duration: 2 to 5 minutes): during the first phase, the Blue Studio 'introduces' itself to its participants. The LED strips in the floor light up in a specific pattern, leading the participants past all of the interaction possibilities in the Blue Studio, prompting them to experience the interactions they can trigger by connecting objects to specific spots on the walls, or simply by touching the walls. Participants learn how their actions change the lighting scheme and the ambient soundscape of the room.

Idea generation phase (duration: 20 minutes): after the participants have explored all of the interaction opportunities of the room, the lighting scheme and soundscape of the Blue Studio change to indicate the beginning of a new phase. During the second phase in the Blue Studio, participants will tackle the creative challenge they have set before they entered the Blue Studio. Now familiar with the behavior of the room, participants can use the interaction possibilities and the Embodied Ideation Toolkit and the environment to support their ideation.

Idea selection phase (duration: up to 2 minutes): when the time for the ideation has run out, the participants are guided to one of the wooden panels in the wall, which will open up. In this panel, participants find a tablet that runs an app that invites them to film a 'future narrative': the conclusion of their creative session visualized in a scenario using the objects from the toolkit and interaction opportunities of the Blue Studio. Upon completion, the resulting video is sent to all participants of the creative session.

Evaluation of the final Blue Studio design

The final design of the Blue Studio was evaluated through three ideation sessions with two different participant groups. These three sessions were organized to evaluate both the technical and conceptual functionality of the Blue Studio, in order to prepare it for real-life, multi-stakeholder ideation sessions. The Instruction Board was still under development in the first two sessions, and only used in the third evaluation session.

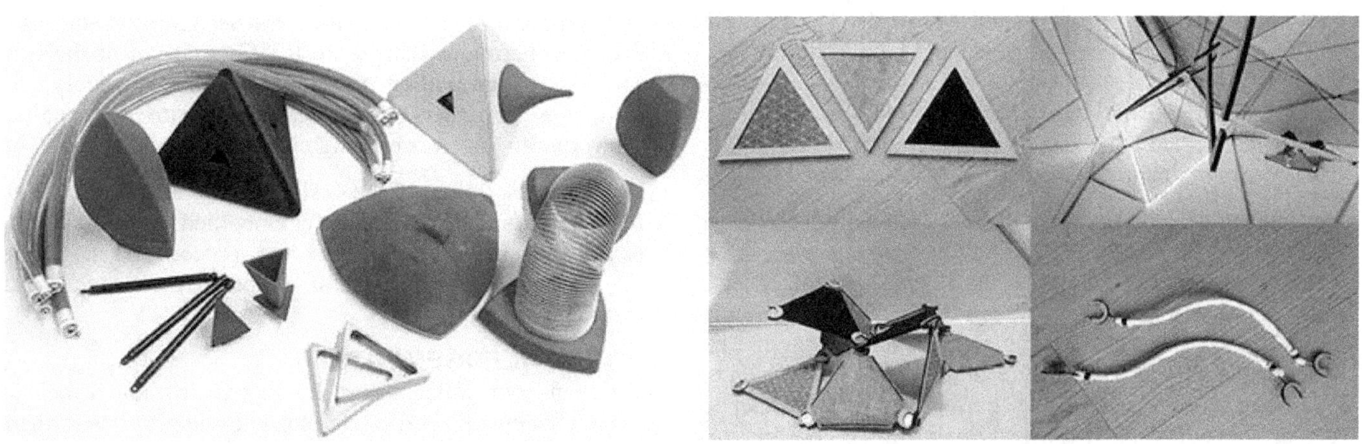

Figure 6: Original Embodied Ideation Toolkit (left) and several objects (right) that extend it in the Blue Studio

Final Evaluation Setup

The final design of the Blue Studio was put to the test in several conclusive evaluations aimed at exploring the functionality of the technological and conceptual interventions in the space. The first evaluation was performed by 4 employees of Sliperiet. The goal of this session was to familiarize the employees of Sliperiet with the Blue Studio, next to assessing the technical functioning of the Blue Studio. The second was performed by five employees of Sliperiet. They were asked to focus on the functionality of the room during the session. During the third evaluation, employees of Sliperiet (two of whom had participated in study 2, and two of whom had not yet experienced the final design of the Blue Studio) used the Blue Studio in a session that focused more on the conceptual functionality of the room, rather than the technical functionality.

Findings

The final design of the Blue Studio was informed and supported by three explorative design iterations. It was inspired by and evaluated through the seven principles to design for embodied sensemaking [11]. The cavernous atmosphere, created by the (vaulted) triangular floor, wall and ceiling elements, and the ambient soundscape were designed to invoke a feeling of being removed from the 'real world', which allowed participants to relinquish existing social constructions and instead re-establish their role in a creative context (*social situatedness, dialogical systems*). The objects in the (extended) EIT turned out to be well-suited as *scaffolds* for ideation during creative sessions. The large objects that were added in the final design support the connection of participants to each other and to the interactive possibilities of the room (*interactive imagery*). The EIT, in combination with the interactive lighting plan of the Blue Studio, can be used as traces that participants can refer back to throughout the session, and that can be recorded in the future narrative at the end of the session - which, in itself, also serves as a *trace* of the session. The relatively small space and the lack of familiar setting limits the possibility for participants to lean on others and 'free ride' [5] during a session. Instead, participants seemed to be compelled to physically interact with the room (*catalyzing engagement*) and take an embodied *first person perspective* throughout the session, as we had hoped for by grounding the design of the Blue Studio in the principles for embodied sensemaking.

During the three final evaluations in the Blue Studio, several issues came to the fore. Most of these issues were of a technical nature, e.g.: some of the magnets in the objects were not strong enough to trigger the sensors that allow participants to interact with light and sound in the room. The panel that should have opened up at the end of the session to reveal the tablet for recording the future narrative, opened too early or not at all. A few LED strips in the floor did not respond to triggers from the participants. Throughout our user studies in the different iterations, we found that participants felt supported by the interaction possibilities that were *ready at hand* in the Blue Studio, but any malfunctions would pull participants back into the 'real world' [32], making the interaction possibilities *present at hand*: no longer acting as an extension of the body or as a scaffold [27] but rather as an obtrusive artifact. The three evaluations of the final design, also revealed some issues of a conceptual nature. The orientation phase and idea selection phase of the Blue Studio were experienced as being too short and the transition to filming as too abrupt. The Blue Studio should already guide participants towards a future narrative at the end of the idea generation phase. The Instruction Board, developed after the first two evaluations of the final design, helped participants to gain overview of the structure of the session and to prepare for recording their future narrative in a timely manner.

Related to this, it was noted that, although the element of surprise when entering the Blue Studio was perceived as a positive influence on the creativity of the participants, too little information about the nature of the session and the intended use of the Blue Studio had an adverse effect on the engagement of the participants. Participants enjoyed exploring the interactive possibilities of the room, but if the process or goal of the creative session were unclear, participants became anxious or agitated, which vitiated the creative atmosphere during the session. We believe that further design interventions may help preventing this situation, e.g., clearer instructions and expectation management before the session, the introduction of the Instruction Board, and a longer and more directive introductory phase in the Blue Studio.

CONCLUSION

With the design of the Blue Studio, we aimed at creating an unfamiliar environment that counterbalances rational decision making processes by inviting participants to use all of their embodied senses to ideate and explore a challenge, and therewith we strived to engage people in embodied sensemaking to generate unexpected ideas.

The seven principles to design for embodied sensemaking [11] supported the reflection on the design interventions in the three iterations that led to the final design of the Blue Studio. By grounding the interventions in theory, the principles provided the researchers with an analytic viewpoint to discover missing elements in the design.

With the description of the design process and its relation to the seven principles to design for embodied sensemaking, we have provided insights into the process of designing physical, interactive spaces for embodied, multi-stakeholder ideation processes.

ACKNOWLEDGEMENTS

We thank our colleagues at Interactive Institute Umeå for their conceptual and technological support. We thank directors and staff of Sliperiet for their open-mindedness to take on this project and their support in funding and facilities. Finally, we thank all participants of the user studies and evaluation sessions.

REFERENCES

1. Ernesto Arias, Hal Eden, Gerhard Fischer, Andrew Gorman, and Eric Scharff. 2000. Transcending the individual human mind—creating shared understanding through collaborative design. *ACM Trans. Comput.-Hum. Interact.* 7, 1, 84-113. http://dx.doi.org/10.1145/344949.345015
2. Colin Burns, Eric Dishman, William Verplank, and Bud Lassiter. 1994. Actors, hairdos & videotape—informance design. In *Conference Companion on Human Factors in Computing Systems* (CHI '94) ACM, 119-120. http://dx.doi.org/10.1145/259963.260102
3. Fritjof Capra. 2002. *The Hidden Connections. A Science for Sustainable Living.* Harper Collins, London.
4. Elke den Ouden. 2012. *Innovation design: Creating value for people, organizations and society.* London: Springer
5. Michael Diehl and Wolfgang Stroebe. 1987. Productivity loss in brainstorming groups: Toward the solution of a riddle. *Journal of personality and social psychology.* 497 – 509.
6. Paul Dourish. 2004. *Where the action is: the foundations of embodied interaction.* MIT press, Cambridge, MA, USA.
7. Florian Geyer, Ulrike Pfeil, Anita Höchtl, Jochen Budzinski, and Harald Reiterer. 2011. Designing reality-based interfaces for creative group work. In *Proceedings of the 8th ACM conference on Creativity and cognition* (C&C '11). ACM, 165-174. http://dx.doi.org/10.1145/2069618.2069647
8. William W. Gaver. 1992. The affordances of media spaces for collaboration. In Proceedings of the 1992 ACM conference on Computer-supported cooperative work (CSCW '92). ACM, New York, NY, USA, 17-24. DOI=http://dx.doi.org/10.1145/143457.371596
9. James J. Gibson. 2014. *The ecological approach to visual perception: classic edition.* Psychology Press.
10. Otmar Hilliges, Lucia Terrenghi, Sebastian Boring, David Kim, Hendrik Richter, and Andreas Butz. 2007. Designing for collaborative creative problem solving. In *Proceedings of the 6th ACM SIGCHI conference on Creativity & cognition* (C&C '07). ACM, 137-146. http://dx.doi.org/10.1145/1254960.1254980
11. Caroline Hummels and Jelle van Dijk. 2015. Seven Principles to Design for Embodied Sensemaking. In *Proceedings of the Ninth International Conference on Tangible, Embedded, and Embodied Interaction* (TEI '15). ACM, 21-28. http://dx.doi.org/10.1145/2677199.2680577
12. Philemonne Jaasma, Ambra Trotto and Caroline Hummels. 2014. Bodystorming vs brainstorming: the influence of the body On codesign processes. In E. Stolterman, J. Redström, A. Valtonen & H. Wiltse (Eds.), Poster: DRS2014 Design's big debates: pushing the boundaries of design research: Umea, Sweden, 16-19 June 2014, pp. 1737.
13. Hanne de Jaegher and Ezequiel Di Paolo. 2007. Participatory sense-making: An enactive approach to social cognition. *Phenomenology and the Cognitive Sciences*, 6(4), 485-507.
14. Scott R. Klemmer, Mark W. Newman, Ryan Farrell, Mark Bilezikjian, and James A. Landay. 2001. The designers' outpost: a tangible interface for collaborative web site. In *Proceedings of the 14th annual ACM symposium on User interface software and technology* (UIST '01). ACM. http://dx.doi.org/10.1145/502348.502350
15. George F. Kneller. 1978. *Arte e ciencia da criatividade* Trans. J. Reis. Sao Paulo, Brazil.
16. Andrés Lucero, Kirsikka Vaajakallio, and Peter Dalsgaard. 2011. The dialogue-labs method: process, space and materials as structuring elements to spark dialogue in co-design events. *CoDesign*, Taylor & Francis, 1-23.
17. Andrés Lucero. 2015. Funky-Design-Spaces: Interactive Environments for Creativity Inspired by Observing Designers Making Mood Boards. In *Human-Computer Interaction*, pp. 474-492. Springer International Publishing.
18. Maurice Merleau-Ponty. 1962. *Phenomenology of perception.* Trans. Colin Smith.
19. One-Shot Video. https://www.tii.se/node/10395 Accessed: 26-10-2016.
20. Richard Schechner. 1985. *Between Theater and Anthropology.* Philadelphia: University of Pennsylvania Press.
21. Dorothé Smit, Doenja Oogjes, Bruna Goveia de Rocha, Ambra Trotto, Yeup Hur, and Caroline Hummels. 2016. Ideating in Skills: Developing Tools for Embodied Co-Design. In *Proceedings of the TEI '16: Tenth International Conference on Tangible, Embedded, and Embodied Interaction*(TEI '16). ACM, 78-85. http://dx.doi.org/10.1145/2839462.2839497
22. Jelle Stienstra, Miguel Bruns Alonso, Stephan Wensveen, and Stoffel Kuenen. 2012. How to design for transformation of behavior through interactive materiality. In *Proceedings of the 7th Nordic Conference on Human-Computer Interaction: Making Sense Through Design* (NordiCHI '12). ACM, 21-30. http://dx.doi.org/10.1145/2399016.2399020
23. Lucy Suchman. 1987. Plans and Situated Actions: The Problem of Human-Machine Communication. NewYork: Cambridge University Press.
24. Lucia Terrenghi, Torsten Fritsche, and Andreas Butz. 2006. The EnLighTable: design of affordances to support collaborative creativity. In *International*

Symposium on Smart Graphics. 206-217. Springer Berlin Heidelberg.

25. Victor Turner. 1982. *From Ritual to Theatre: Human Seriousness of Play*. New York: PAJ Publisher.
26. Kirsikka Vaajakallio. 2008. *Design Dialogues Studying co-design activities in an artificial environment. Copenhagen working papers*
27. Jelle van Dijk. 2013. Creating traces, sharing insight: explorations in embodied cognition design. *Doctoral Dissertation.*
28. Jelle van Dijk and Remko van der Lugt. 2013. Scaffolds for shared understanding. AI EDAM, Special Issue on Design Communication, 27, 107–117.
29. Jelle van Dijk, Jirka van der Roest, Remko van der Lugt, and Kees C.J. Overbeeke. 2011. NOOT: a tool for sharing moments of reflection during creative meetings. In *Proceedings of the 8th ACM conference on Creativity and cognition* (C&C '11). ACM, 157-164. http://dx.doi.org/10.1145/2069618.2069646
30. Jelle van Dijk and Gerrit Willem Vos. 2011. Traces in creative spaces. In *Proceedings of the 8th ACM conference on Creativity and cognition* (C&C '11). ACM, 91-94. http://dx.doi.org/10.1145/2069618.2069634
31. Brygg Ullmer and Hiroshi Ishii. 1997. The metaDESK: models and prototypes for tangible user interfaces. In *Proceedings of the 10th annual ACM symposium on User interface software and technology* (UIST '97). ACM 223-232. http://dx.doi.org/10.1145/263407.263551
32. Peter-Paul Verbeek. 2000. *Materializing Morality.Design Ethics and Technological Mediation.* University of Twente. https://www.utwente.nl/bms/wijsb/organization/verbeek/materializingmorality.pdf
33. John Zimmerman, Jodi Forlizzi, and Shelley Evenson. 2007. Research through design as a method for interaction design research in HCI. In *Proceedings of the SIGCHI Conference on Human Factors in Computing Systems* (CHI '07). ACM, 493-502. http://dx.doi.org/10.1145/1240624.1240704

Polipo – a Tangible Toy for Children with Neurodevelopmental Disorders

Victoria Tam
Massachusetts Institute of Technology
Cambridge (US)
vtam@alum.mit.edu

Mirko Gelsomini
Politecnico di Milano, M.I.T.
Milano (IT), Cambridge (US)
mirko.gelsomini@polimi.it

Franca Garzotto
Politecnico di Milano
Via Ponzio 34/5, Milano (IT)
franca.garzotto@polimi.it

ABSTRACT
The paper presents Polipo, a tangible toy created for children with Neurodevelopmental Disorders (NDD). Designed in collaboration with therapists, and tested with six children for five weeks, Polipo offers various opportunities for tangible interaction and a range of multisensory stimuli aimed at promoting the development of fine motor skills. One of the most distinguishing attributes of Polipo is its strong customization capability. The system provides a means for therapists to personalize luminous and sound stimuli; it is equipped with a set of add-ons that therapists can easily and quickly adjust on the basic structure to extend the physical affordances of the tool, offering new tactile stimuli and new manipulation experiences. These design solutions, and the promising results of the on-the-ground trials, highlight the potential of Polipo to address the unique learning needs of each single child with NDD.

Author Keywords
Human-centered design; disability; children; usability; personalization; toys, fine motor skills, neurodevelopmental disorder

ACM Classification Keywords
K.4.2 Social Issues: Assistive technologies for persons with disabilities.

INTRODUCTION
Neurodevelopmental Disorder (NDD) is an umbrella term for a wide spectrum of disability, including intellectual disability, ADHD (Attention Deficit Hyperactivity Disorder), and ASD (Autistic Spectrum Disorder), among others. These disorders emerge during the developmental period and progressively affect, at varying degrees of severity, mental, emotional, physical, social, and cognitive capabilities as an individual grows. Early interventions can help alleviate symptoms of NDD [19] and the use of interactive technology can effectively complement more traditional therapeutic approaches for NDD children [21].

TEI '17, March 20-23, 2017, Yokohama, Japan
© 2017 ACM. ISBN 978-1-4503-4676-4/17/03...$15.00
DOI: http://dx.doi.org/10.1145/3024969.3025006

Polipo is a novel interactive toy (Fig. 1) that encourages children with NDD to practice fine motor skills through various manipulative actions and offers multisensory stimuli to promote engagement, sense of control, and cause-effect understanding.

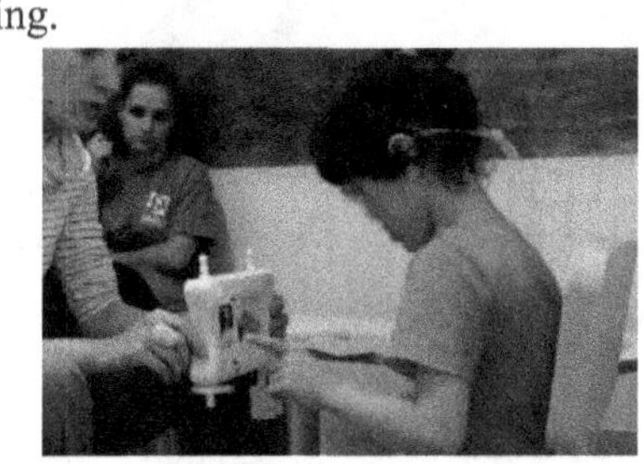

Fig. 1. A LED light indicates which function needs to be performed and encourages the child to interact with Polipo.

Interaction with Polipo is largely guided by a therapist, who can direct the child's focus and control, promote his understanding of stimuli, and strike a balance between giving a child autonomy and mediating. Even though this interactive toy is focused on practicing fine motor skills, it weaves in an interactive experience between both the child and toy, and the child and therapists. It is appropriate as a tool for promoting socialization with the therapist and peers and enhance basic cognitive skills such as attention.

Polipo enables the customization of the basic physical and digital affordances and interaction capabilities of the toy in a unique way. Therapists easily and smoothly modify or expand the physical components and the digital content of the tool, thereby curating their own set of audio stimuli, increasing the difficulty of each of Polipo's physical functions, or adding new ones. The therapists are also able to monitor each subjects' individual progression and to personalize their play experience. This is achieved by taking into account his or her specific and evolving needs in the behavior (s)he may exhibit during the use of the tool.

Integrating all the above features in a single simple interactive toy is the novelty of Polipo. Polipo has been designed in cooperation with therapists, and its potential for children with NDD has been evaluated in an exploratory study involving six children with NDD in a therapeutic center. The lessons learned from the design and evaluation activities offer an original contribution to tangible interaction design, highlighting the challenges that must be faced when creating tangibles for children with multiple disabilities and offering insights to help designers of tangible interactive toys for this target group.

RELATED WORK

There are various methodologies in the realm of traditional therapy for children with NDD that exploit play with physical objects [2]. Many of them apply the Montessori method, which highlights simplicity and learning through exploration, and promotes learning through repeated tasks and free play at one's own pace. Montessori toys reflect this approach, which also emphasizes the use of natural materials: the majority of Montessori toys are made of wood with simple parts such as wheels or different shapes (Fig. 2). The simple design of the toys also allows therapists to be creative in the games they design in order to tailor the level of difficulty to each child.

Fig. 2. Example of Montessori toys

Fig. 3. Left: The Bop-It!; Right: Fisher-Price Tablet

While the task repetition can be effective in terms of predictability and relaxation, additional stimuli such as light and sound can be helpful in motivating children with NDD to complete a certain task, as discovered by Mandil et al. in their research with children with cerebral palsy [13].

Multisensory stimuli are often offered by existing toys in the commercial marketplace that therapists use with their children (even if they are not specifically designed for children with NDD). These toys typically have more features than typical Montessori tools to stimulate a variety of senses, such as digital sounds and lights. Increased sensory engagement can help to enhance the conceptual foundation that Montessori toys provide [19]. One such example is the Bop-It! toy, created by Hasbro (Fig. 3a). The original Bop It! has three functions, the bop it, pull it, and twist it. A voice calls out various commands that you need to follow and increases its speed as the game goes on. Another example is the Fisher-Price Smart Tablet (Fig. 3b), which attempts to bring learning to life for 3-6 year olds. The different game modes include music mode and typing mode, allowing children to experience a wide range of educational material. The color changing LCD screen enhances game play and adds to the excitement of learning.

A variety of digitally enhanced toys have also been created in the research arena. Verhaegh et al. [12] prototyped TagTiles, adding sensor technology and computing to traditional toys, and pinpoint that this approach offers promising opportunities for learning as it introduces a dimension of excitement and novelty to the traditional toy. Several researchers have explored the learning effects of different types of game-based activities that exploit tangible interaction, highlighting that interacting with physical objects helps children construct mental representations of the world around them, promote various cognitive skills, prompt spontaneous engagement and facilitate social play [27, 28, 29]. The learning potential of playing with tangibles is grounded on theoretical approaches that emphasize two main aspects: i) the role of play in human development and evolution [31]; ii) the relationship between physical activity and cognitive processes, and the formative role of embodiment in the development of different levels of cognitive skills [32].

There is some empirical evidence [3, 24] that tangible interaction brings a strong educational potential for disabled children, as it fosters the development of memory capability, perceptual skills, and sense of control. Garzotto and Bordogna [3] have developed low-tech paper-based materials (PCS - Picture Communication Symbol cards - enriched with RFID tags linked with multimedia resources) for children with severe cognitive, linguistic, and motor disabilities. A pilot study with 2 children with severe intellectual and motor impairments has shown that the systems promoted the above skills more effectively than traditional educational tools.

Limited prior research on tangible interaction has focused specifically on fine motor skills and its importance in performing children's everyday tasks. For instance, Chia and Saakes [10] designed interactive training chopsticks that pair with an augmented mirror. The system guides children through practicing the fine motor skills required to handle chopsticks and uses gameplay to provide encouragement. An example of system that uses more conventional forms of interaction is PointAssist [11], a software developed that assists individuals with motor impairments in pointing tasks on the computer, helping them to practice with sequential fine-grained movements that can then be generalized in daily activities.

Several authors pinpoint that, because individuals with disabilities have unique needs that evolve over time, the educational value of technology for children with disability is directly related to its ability to adapt to the needs of its user [2]. Empowering therapists to modify the technology they use is a fundamental requirement in the field of assistive technology [22]. As reported in the study of Phillips et al. [23], technologies for persons with disability that cannot be easily customized, or can be customized by professionals only, are more often abandoned.

Unfortunately, the existing tangibles designed for children with disability, or adopted in therapeutic contexts, seldom meet this requirement. Most of them are "closed", i.e., their functionality is pre-programmed and can be changed only by developers. In Bop-It!, for example, features such as the volume of the voice commands and the various game modes are set and cannot be changed. Hengeveld at al. [24] developed LinguaBytes – a tangible play-and-learning environment to stimulate communication skills of toddlers with multiple disabilities and with a developmental age between 1 and 4 years. The authors acknowledge the importance of customization and their modular system comes with a large database of curated words. Still, those who work with children but are not skilled programmers cannot easily extend and adapt LiguaBytes. The paper-based tangible system described in [3] is integrated with a simple web based tool that enables therapists to tag new cards and link cards to new digital materials [25].

Polipo enables the customization of both the physical components and the digital content of the tool, and integrates these features in a unique way. Therapists can curate their own set of audio stimuli, increase the difficulty of each of Polipo's physical functions eventually adding new ones to personalize the experience and to monitor each child's individual progression.

THE DESIGN OF POLIPO

General Design requirements

The design process for Polipo started with observations of children with NDD at an inclusion school in Cambridge, MA to gain a better understanding of the types of needs that existed, the current therapeutic practices and the physical toys adopted to deal with them. We decided to focus on fine motor skill development because it is a key component (along with gross motor skills) in the path to independence and self-care [11]. Fine motor movements refer to the coordination of small muscles in the fingers and hands. These movements are integral to completing daily tasks and will continue to play an important role throughout a child's lifetime. A child lacking well-developed fine motor skills may struggle with tasks in the classroom such as learning to write. At the same time, developing these skills has proven to help children gain confidence in other areas of their emotional, social, and cognitive development [18]. In the context of treatment, each child's fine motor skill level can inform how their therapy can be structured in order to optimize the child's development.

Observations of various therapy sessions at the inclusion school also highlighted that physical toys often act as social facilitators—in other words, a medium to develop a child's affection towards her/his therapist and to motivate the communication between a child and the adult, and eventually to trigger social interaction with peers [17]. The idea of social connection was a recurring theme among therapists, as individuals with NDD tend to suffer from communication deficits or social isolation [14].

As a result, the overall goal for Polipo is to improve *fine motor skills*, with the understanding that continued play with the toy will also encourage children to develop *social and cognitive skills*.

An additional orthogonal element that emerged very clearly was that therapists deal with a diverse set of disabilities, and even children with the same diagnosis have extremely diversified needs and behavior. As discussed in the previous section, the final product would have to be *highly adaptable* in order to offer features that are appropriate for the specific and evolving profile of each child, to appeal to a wide audience and to promote its adoption in therapeutic contexts.

Discussions with therapists throughout the initial design phase yielded several key insights into achieving the above goals. The main takeaways were to build in a *cause and effect model* for game play, incorporate the concept of *grading*, and create the conditions for *social play* to extend the effectiveness of the toy. In order to increase the "universality" of the toy, therapists proposed to design the toy for low functioning children, which are those who suffer from the most severe impairments induced by NDD. The cause and effect strategy is especially effective for this segment because it provides immediate reward and satisfaction. For example, therapists suggested having parts of the toy light up or vibrate, then require the child to touch it. They provided suggestions about the type of feedback as well, citing that a negative noise for any mistakes can be frustrating. We incorporated the visual stimuli component by using lights to draw the child into the toy. In order to support a range of abilities, the concept of grading was introduced. Grading is the modification of any activity to support an individual. Activities can be graded to make them harder or easier and can take various forms, from changing the amount of steps, assistance, or time given to complete a certain task. [8] This concept drove the creation of the various add-ons and branches of Polipo.

Physical Design

The physical design of Polipo (Fig. 4) is partially inspired by Bop-It! (Fig. 3a) and is quite simple, with *one main body* which houses the *four different functions*. The outlining shape of the body is curved to evoke a playful and approachable design that is kid-friendly. In addition, because the therapist would be holding the toy the entire time, curved edges were included to make it more comfortable to hold for an extended period of time. The width of the toy was also designed for ease of holding.

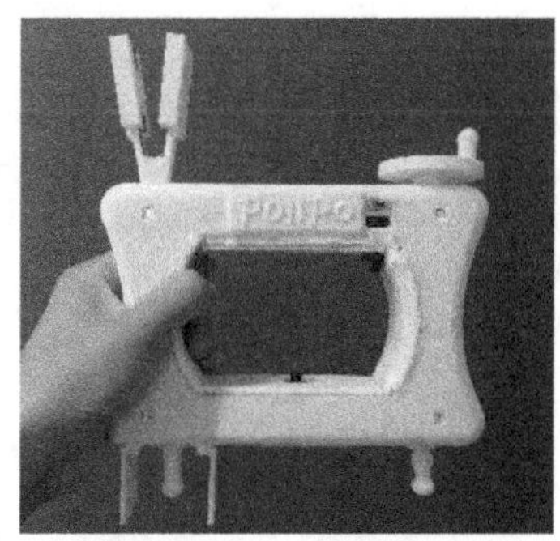

Fig. 4. Front view of Polipo.

Each of the functions was chosen with help from the therapists. Fine motor skills are typically practiced with the intention of applying those skills to real world applications. The four functions are the *pincher, knob, piston, and slider*. They were chosen to represent functions that the children might encounter in everyday life [15]. Additional components called "add-ons" can be added to Polipo for more variety. Each function except for the slider comes with a set of add-ons that change the difficulty of the task.

Therapists shared that the pincer grasp is an integral part in a child's physical development. The grasp allows the child to pick up and place small objects in a controlled manner using the one or more fingers and the thumb. In addition, it enables children to perform many functions independently such as feeding themselves, holding pencils and utensils, or fastening closures on clothing [7]. The *pincher* was therefore included to encourage children to practice this important action. In its base form, it closely represents a clothespin. The resemblance to a household object helps children to learn to form connections between what they are practicing in therapy and what they see in their everyday lives.

The pincher (Fig. 5a) comes with two options for additional attachments. One is a wide rectangular shape that provides room for more than one finger on one side (Fig. 5b). The wider surface area decreases the amount of force required to complete the function. This attachment increases the surface area from 1 cm wide to 3 cm wide on each side of the pincher. The other type of attachment is a half done in the shape of an ellipse (Fig. 5c). When attached to the pincher, its smooth form fits into the shape of the child's hand. This allows for a better grip and also decreases the force required to successfully complete the function.

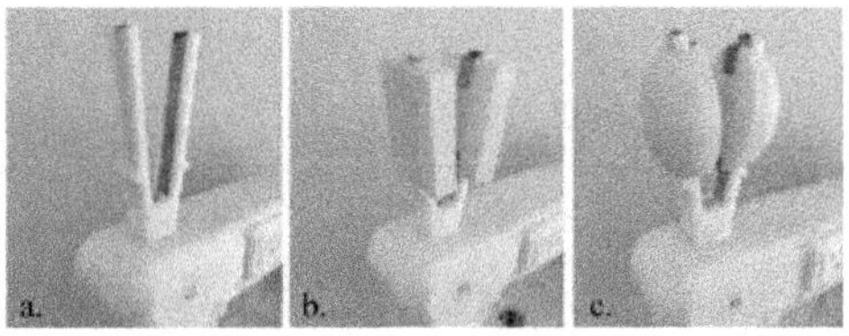

Fig. 5. The pincher and its attachments.

The *knob* is meant to help children practice grasping and rotating small objects. For example, it can mimic the action of opening a door knob or the cap of a water bottle. The base knob itself is small (Fig. 6a), with a diameter of 2.5 cm and allows for a 90 degree turn. There are a series of additional add-ons in the shape of discs that can modify the amount of strength and the type of grip required to successfully rotate the knob. They are all circular in shape with a few variations. There are two discs with ridges on the edge, a medium one at 3 cm in diameter and a larger one that has a diameter of 5 cm (Fig. 6b, 6c). The ridges provide tactile stimuli to encourage interaction from the child. A third option is a larger disc with a smooth diameter (Fig. 6d).

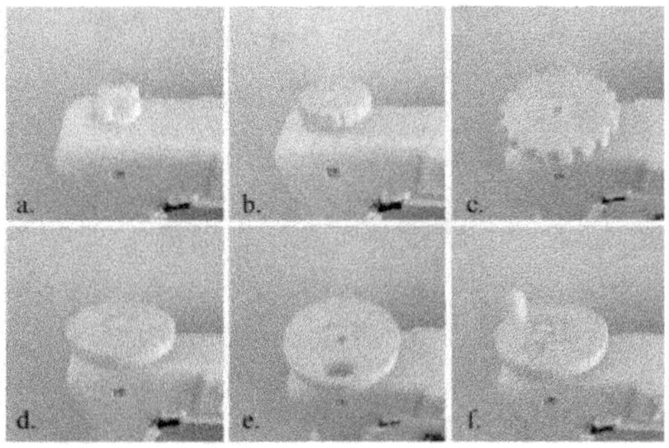

Fig. 6. The base knob and accompanying attachments.

The smooth edge makes it more difficult to grasp, thus making it harder for the child. Another option features a finger-sized hole in the disc (Fig. 6e). It allows the child to isolate one finger to guide the disc to turn to practice finger isolation, an important ability in the development of fine motor skills. The last option is a disc with a small vertical protrusion on the top (Fig. 6f). This small protrusion makes it easier for children with less developed control to wrap their fingers around the handhold, as opposed to the entire disc itself.

The *piston* function (Fig. 7a) requires the child to grasp the body of the piston and pull upwards. It provides another opportunity to practice finger isolation while exercising the pulling action. The function simulates picking up small objects and requires strength from the wrist and forearm as well. It has a small hole at the top of the cylinder for further customization. A therapist can choose to thread string or a paperclip to create different form factors to increase or decrease the level of difficulty of the action. This function also comes with a set of attachments for the body of Polipo, rather than the piston itself. There is a set of rails on either side of the piston to which the therapist can attach borders. There are four different sets of borders that increasingly modify the difficulty of the task. There are two heights for the borders, 3.5 cm (Fig. 7b, 7c) and 5 cm (Fig. 7d, 7e). For each height, there is a narrow and wide option. The narrow borders create a space of 3 cm around the piston, while the wide borders create a space of 4 cm. The purpose of the borders is to allow for a gradual increase in difficulty, to encourage the child to use fewer fingers to complete the action.

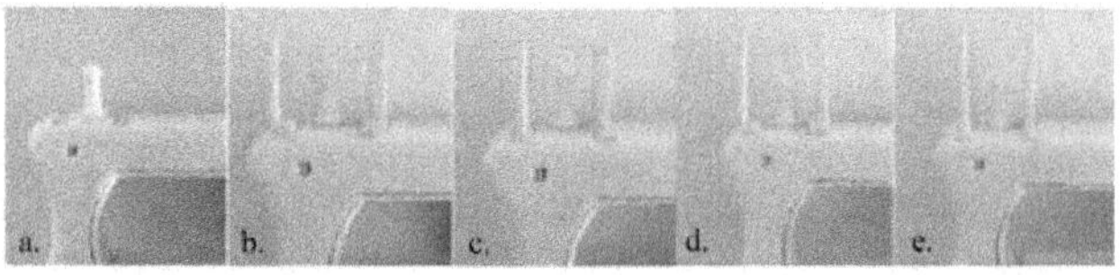

Fig. 7. The piston with short, tall, wide, and narrow borders

Digital Design

The digital side of Polipo was designed to enable additional customization—concerning visual and auditory stimuli—according to the needs of the children and the observations of the therapists.

The first feature is the 8 LED lights placed around the body. Each function has a designated light on either side of the toy so that the therapist can rotate and reorient the toy as needed. A different colored light is assigned to each of the four functions to distinguish them from one another. A single-colored blinking light indicates a function that is waiting to be completed. Once the function is completed, all 8 lights illuminate in a flashing rainbow display to reward the child, which lasts for 15 seconds. Many aspects of the lights can be modified and adjusted depending on the child, including the color of each function's designated light, the duration and aesthetic of the light display reward, and whether the light is blinking or solid.

When a function is completed successfully, a short sound clip is triggered in addition to the light display. The sounds are mp3 files that can also be modified as needed. The original sounds were generic celebratory sounds such as bells ringing or an upbeat drum beat. They were later modified at the request of the therapist to use familiar songs. To move between functions, there is a button in the middle of the toy. It allows the therapist to cycle through the four functions consecutively. The lights, sound, and manual manipulation are all connected by and controlled through an Arduino Nano.

EXPLORATORY STUDY

Goal and research variables

The goals of the exploratory study were to investigate in an ecological context the opportunities offered by Polipo as a therapeutic tool, to explore the learning benefits that this interactive toy can bring to children with severe and multiple disability in the NDD spectrum, and to derive suggestions for re-design.

The study was carried out at L'Abilità, a rehabilitation center in Milan specializing in NDD. Every year, the center hosts over 150 children aged 2-17 years with different forms of NDD. They attend L'Abilità either on a daily or a weekly base to perform educational and rehabilitation activities with the support of different specialists (special educators, psychologists, neuro-psychiatric doctors, speech therapists, motor therapists).

The evaluation approach is aligned with the therapeutic practice at the center. Together with therapists, we identified the main variables to investigate during the study, which are briefly described below:

V1) Communication: Uses gestures to ask for help
V2) Comprehension: Responds to commands with the appropriate action
V3a) Attention: Is oriented towards the toy
V3b) Attention: Stays focused and follows verbal cues and gestures
V3c) Attention: Is attracted by visual and auditory stimuli
V4a) Interest: Expresses appropriate emotions
V4b) Interest: Shows willingness to engage in repetition
V5) Sensory: Reacts appropriately to objects
V6) Total number of functions attempted
V7) Functions completed independently with help, or incomplete

The research variables were defined according to current assessment methods adopted at the center and were organized in 5 groups.

Eight variables are clustered into four groups (Communication, Comprehension, Attention, Interest, and Sensory) which correspond, in the therapeutic jargon, to main "areas of intervention" or "areas of development"; they are associated to classes of skills (in the cognitive, emotional, or motor sphere) that therapists attempt to promote during regular therapy with traditional toys. These variables can be defined as "behavioral" in that they are operationalized in terms of behavioral signals and are scored on the basis of the children's observed behavior. The metrics for these variables is: (1) for "absent", (2) for "sometimes", (3) for "often", and (4) for "always."

Two variables (V6 and V7) are related to Performance, i.e., how the child uses the functions available in Polipo, and allows for comparison over time. V6 is the total number of functions attempted during a session, whether it was successful in execution or not. (The highest number of functions completed was 24). V7 measures the number of functions that are completed successfully – independently or with the help of the therapist, or are not completed.

Procedure

Trials for Polipo were scheduled over a span of *five weeks* with *one session per week* for *six* children. The children, aged 5-10, were all non-verbal and had varying abilities. There were two with autism, three with intellectual disability, and one with Down's syndrome.

The children involved come to the center once a week for a 90-minute session. They played with Polipo for 5-10 minutes during their weekly session. The length of play with Polipo depended mostly on the behavior, willingness, and attention span of the child. While each child has their own dedicated therapist that they work with each week, one main therapist used Polipo with all the children regardless of who their main therapist was.

To start each session, the therapist chose one of the four functions of Polipo (Fig. 8). She would usually choose the easiest one for that particular child so (s)he could gain confidence at the outset. The therapist would then choose the order of subsequent functions. A session would end after about 10 minutes or if a child started to get distracted or tired, whichever came first.

Fig. 8. Child playing with Polipo

The Polipo designer sat in a corner of the room to observe and complete a quantitative form throughout each session focusing on Performance and manually measuring variables V6 and V7. She recorded each function that was chosen, the type of add-on it had (if any), and whether the function was completed alone, with help, or not at all. The form also includes a section for notes and observations. Each session was video recorded.

After each session, the therapist would re-watch the session from the video recording and filled out a form organized around the behavioral variables on the five key areas of development (Communication, Comprehension, Attention, Interest, and Sensory). The therapist scored each child on each of these variables using the metrics described in the previous section. The therapist also assigned values based comparison to previous performance. Additional qualitative observations were expressed in the Notes section.

Main Results

Children's progresses were measured with respect to the set of variables described above, and comparing the results between the various sessions. The series of graphs in Fig. 9-10 represent each of the 6 children and their progress in each category of variables.

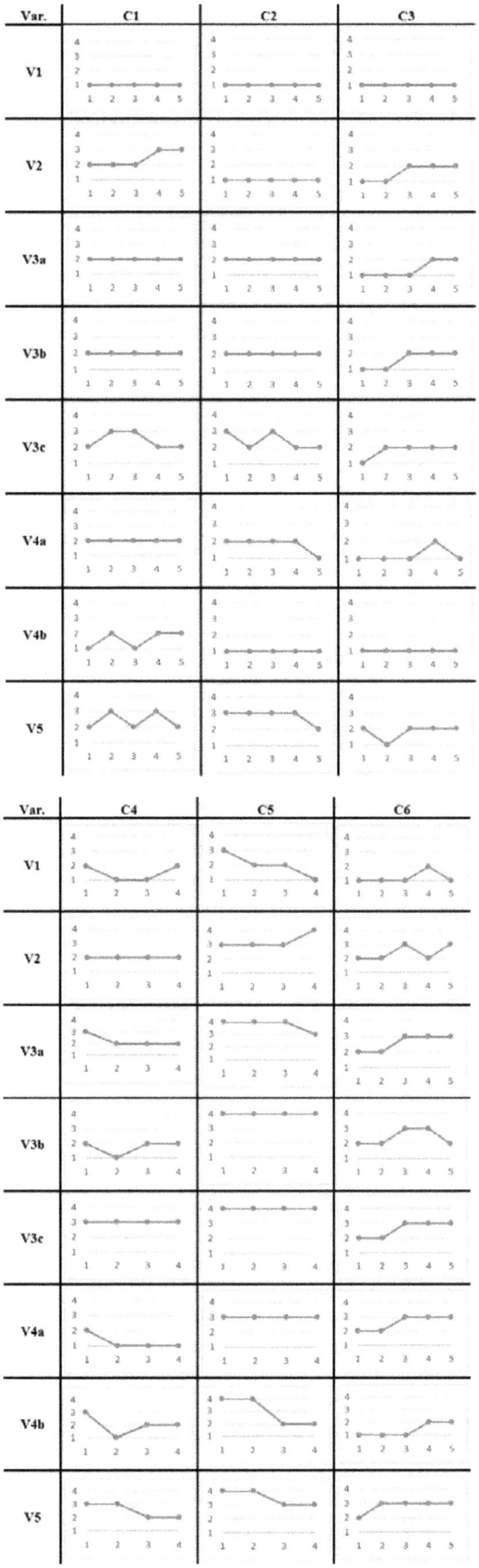

Fig. 9-10. Results on the key areas of development/intervention

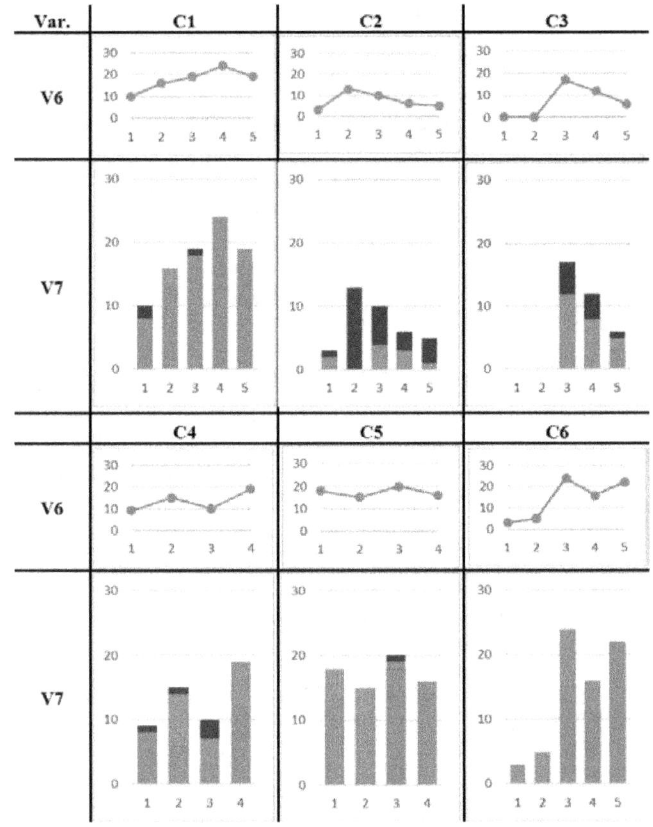

Fig. 11. Results on Performance Variables

Fig. 11 indicates for each child, the total number of functions attempted in a given session (V6). The graphs for V7 show the number of functions that each child completed independently (green), with help (orange), or did not complete (purple) in each session.

From children's observations by therapist and designer it clearly emerged that the children exhibited a diverse range of fine motor skill abilities which resulted in varied usage of each of the four functions.

For example, with the pincher, some were not strong enough to use just two fingers, and would instead use the palm of their hand. For others, it was easier to use their thumb to push the slider than to hold it with two fingers. The adaptability of Polipo with its add-ons allowed therapists to customize the toy at the beginning of each session according to the child's needs or performance the previous week.

We observed that over time, the children became familiar with the cause and effect nature of the toy. It encouraged them to persist in trying a function a few times even if they did not get it on the first try because they wanted the auditory and visual reward that came with successful completion. In some instances, even when the therapist intervened to try to get them to complete the pincher function using the more difficult pincer grip, as described in an earlier section, they were motivated to attempt it because they wanted the corresponding stimuli. Once they had a better grasp of the reward mechanism, they would be more willing to continue to play with the toy.

Discussion

While some children show upward behavioral progress throughout the five weeks, the majority of the results are up and down. Concerning performance, we note improvements for all children (but one), even if with ups and downs. Several children's total task numbers stayed within a range and others increased as their comfort and familiarity with the toy grew over time.

It is worth noticing that the therapists tried to progressively decrease the amount of help they gave the children. This made it more difficult for children to accomplish the tasks. Even if some children were able to progress with less help as they became more comfortable and confident with using Polipo, the decrease of therapist's support partially explains the relatively small increase (or the decrease) of performance values along the various sessions for some subjects.

The empirical results of this exploratory study are preliminary and circumscribed, and should at present be taken with caution. As in most empirical research involving subjects with severe and multiple disabilities, causality is hard to measure, and it is almost impossible to isolate all the potentially confounding variables the have certainly may influence an observed process of improvement.

Individuals with NDD tend to have unpredictable behavior; One time it could go smoothly and the next, could be something completely opposite [6]. The measured effects in this study were certainly affected by individual characteristics such as their attention span, interest, and ability. Contingent factors such as children's physical and psychological state during the sessions, or the proposed task, may also have influenced the behavior.

In addition, we can only compare within session behaviors, and we do not know the degree to which the benefits that we measured during the sessions with Polipo, can be translated to other contexts and moments of the participants' life.

Finally, the length of the study was too short to claim the effectiveness of using Polipo in the therapeutic practice. As indicated by the specialists, children's assessment of the benefits of therapeutic interventions is normally done after at least one year of treatment.

Lessons Learned

The exploratory study has highlighted a number of issues about the various design features of Polipo, and the way of using this tool in the therapeutic practice. We have distilled them into a set of "lessons learned". Some of them were implemented within the trials, with the designer discussing and iterating on the design with the therapist who was in charge of the trials, and others will guide the design of the future versions of Polipo.

Lesson 1: Light and Music

Both music and light rewards were an important factor that greatly enhanced the enjoyment of the child and provided motivation to complete each function. Still, the LED light did not seem to be as engaging as we intended, possibly due to its location on the side of the toy. While flashing lights could serve as a positive reinforcement for some kids, it would also be a distraction for others [13]. The therapist suggested that an option be added to switch *off* the lights. The need for this option emerged from the first session of the trial and was immediately integrated into the toy. In addition, the music reward seemed more captivating than the flashing lights. A suggestion that the therapist made in the very beginning was to use songs that are familiar to the children as the reward tune. The therapist provided a list of seven songs that were familiar to all the children and a 15 second clip from the main chorus was incorporated into the toy. These songs replaced generic celebratory sounds that were previously programmed in the toy. The songs have been used extensively in other parts of the child's therapy so they helped to provide a sense of familiarity when the children approached the toy for the first time.

Lesson 2: Augmented Communication

One "addition" that was built after the first session was a small poster created using the Augmentative and Alternative Communication (AAC) method. AAC is a visual communication technique for persons with severe communication impairments that relies on visual symbols and images as language elements [33]. The most used low tech tools for this form of communication are the so-called PCS (Picture Communication Symbols) systems. They employ single tangible picture cards that represent objects, activities, people, events, as well as more abstract concepts like feelings or relationships. These cards are used by a person with communication impairments to form a message, or as supplementary visual prompts by caregivers.

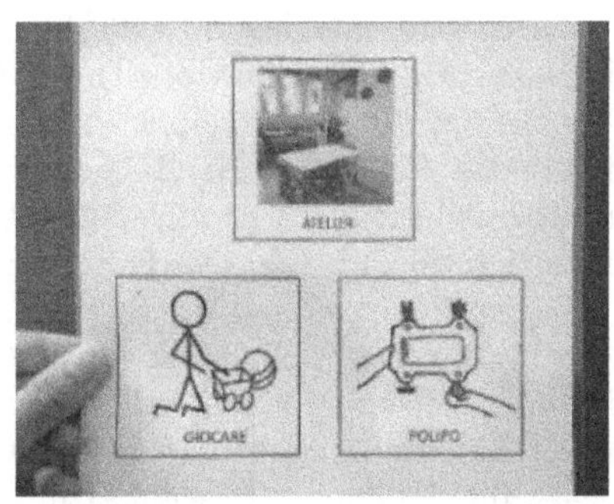

Fig. 12. The poster created to communicate playing with Polipo. (Legend: giocare = play)

The poster (Fig. 12) had a picture of Polipo and the room where the session would take place. It was used to transition the children between activities. The pictures would help the children build recognition of the toy over time. Because this pictorial communication system is used throughout the therapy sessions, children are familiar with it.

Moreover, the therapists were able to turn Polipo into another opportunity to practice communicating with the images. As the weeks went on, the therapist tried to reduce the amount of aid given to the child. This prompted the creation of images for each of the four functions. The images showed the therapist's hand in position on each function. The child had to choose which of the four functions they wanted to play with first. One by one, the respective pictures were stuck on to the toy right beneath the actual function. The child had to then process and understand the picture before completing the function.

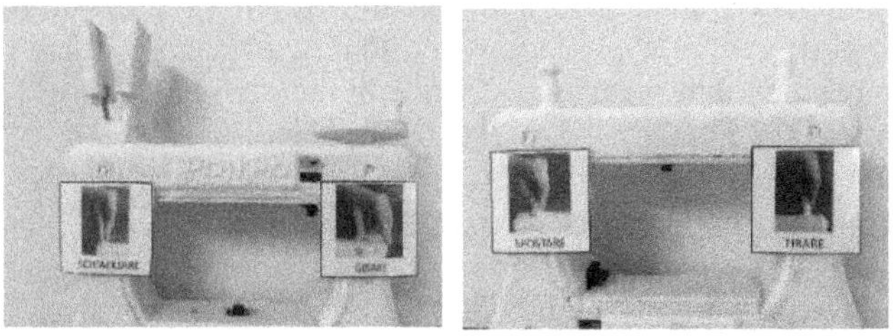

Fig. 13. Images of each function shown to the child, and the images stuck to the toy during play (Legend: girare = turn; schiacciare = pinch; tirare = pull; spostare = slide)

Lesson 3: Functions

One of the limitations we saw with Polipo during testing is that children would get distracted and touch *all* the functions, regardless of which one they were supposed to do. It might be more appropriate, at least in the initial state of therapy, to provide one function at a time. Functions should also be very robust because of the unpredictable actions and movements of the children.

Lesson 4: Socialization

Communication and social interaction played a bigger role than the designer had envisioned during the design process. While Polipo was developed first and foremost as a toy for individual use, therapists created new, unique ways to engage each child in social relationships and created opportunities to enforce the children's communication with the therapist and engage each child in social behavior. The children were encouraged for example to ask for help when needed, to wait for their turn or to pass Polipo to a friend. The therapists could also wait until the child looks at them and gives eye contact before allowing a turn with the toy. Turn taking and eye contact are two important skills that, when mastered, have been linked to improved social interaction [34]. With the evolution of Polipo from being a toy designed for solo play to one that can be used with peers, the therapist played a central role, directing the flow of interactions to maximize the child's exploitation of the experiential opportunities offered by Polipo, and promoting the use of the toy as a tool for socialization [4].

Lesson 5: Customization

The relevance of customization as a means to personalize interventions to the specific profile and needs of each subject has been discussed in earlier sections. A further element emerging from our study is that customization is also important to seamlessly integrate technology into an existing therapy program. With Polipo, the reward songs customized by therapists were listened to on a regular basis in other moments of the therapy. This on the one hand helped the children become acquainted with the toy faster. On the other hand, it supported a smooth integration of the different moments of the therapeutic program, and enforced memorization.

CONCLUSIONS AND FUTURE WORK

Designing interactive technologies that can be effective in the treatment of children with NDD and can be truly adopted in a therapeutic context is a challenging issue, because of the unique requirements of this target group. Polipo is a novel interactive toy that has been designed in cooperation with a therapeutic team and is simple, provides multisensory stimuli (tactile and auditory), and is highly customizable in its physical and digital components. An exploratory study at a care center highlights that Polipo can be integrated in the current therapeutic practice as a tool to develop fine motor skills and basic cognitive functions skills, and to promote social connection with the therapists and peers. The lessons learned from the design of Polipo and the evaluation activity reported in the paper can benefit designers of similar tangibles for children with severe and multiple disability.

The first item in our research agenda is to perform a wider and more systematic empirical study to validate the results of the preliminary exploratory study on Polipo. We have planned a controlled study that will involve 10 therapists and at least 50 children with NDD for 6 months in two different care centers. We will aim for as homogeneous as possible of a clinical profile of the children in order to mitigate the confounding effects of individual impairments. This future study will also enable us to evaluate the usability of the customization features of Polipo, their flexibility and their fit to personalization requirements of therapists. The work with Polipo leaves many opportunities and avenues for further technical developments and design extensions. Our first study pinpointed the need of reducing the effort of gathering data that concern children's behavior during the use of the tool. This data (currently collected manually) is useful for therapists, parents, and researchers in tangibles for children with disability as they help to monitor progression, to complement therapeutic assessment, and to perform design oriented empirical research. We will extend Polipo to automatically keep track of children's interactions and will integrate the toy with an application that will support the analysis and interpretation of relevant data. To enhance the children's experience, we are integrating Polipo with an external display to show a real-life equivalent of whichever function is being practiced, similar to what Hengevel's Phonotron can do [8]. For example, if the knob is being practiced, an image or animation of a doorknob or a water bottle will show up. This would help children increase association and generalization capability by connecting their practice with Polipo to daily life, thus extending the learning potential of this tool.

ACKNOWLEDGMENTS

This work has been partially supported by the Research and International Exchange Program MISTI and Roberto Rocca Doctoral Fellowship. The authors are grateful for the therapists, children and families at L'Abilità for their participation and support during the design and evaluation activities.

REFERENCES

1. Brederode, B., Markopoulos, P., Gielen, M., Vermeeren, A. and De Ridder, H., 2005, June. pOwerball: the design of a novel mixed-reality game for children with mixed abilities. In Proceedings of the 2005 conference on Interaction design and children (pp. 32-39). ACM.
2. Brodin, J., 1999. Play in Children with Severe Multiple Disabilities: play with toys-a review. International Journal of Disability, Development and Education, 46(1), pp.25-34.
3. Garzotto, F. and Bordogna, M., 2010, June. Paper-based multimedia interaction as learning tool for disabled children. In Proceedings of the 9th international Conference on Interaction Design and Children (pp. 79-88). ACM.
4. Hanline, M.F. and Fox, L., 1993. Learning within the context of play: Providing typical early childhood experiences for children with severe disabilities. Research and Practice for Persons with Severe Disabilities, 18(2), pp.121-129.
5. Hengeveld, B., Hummels, C., Overbeeke, K., Voort, R., van Balkom, H. and de Moor, J., 2009, February. Tangibles for toddlers learning language. In Proceedings of the 3rd International Conference on Tangible and Embedded Interaction (pp. 161-168). ACM.
6. Norton, P. and Drew, C., 1994. Autism and potential family stressors. The American Journal of Family Therapy, 22(1), pp.67-76.
7. Rule, A.C. and Stewart, R.A., 2002. Effects of practical life materials on kindergartners' fine motor skills. Early Childhood Education Journal, 30(1), pp.9-13.
8. Vining Radomski, M. and Trombly Latham, C., 2008. Occupational therapy for physical dysfunction.
9. Zuckerman, O., Arida, S. and Resnick, M., 2005, April. Extending tangible interfaces for education: digital montessori-inspired manipulatives. In Proceedings of the SIGCHI conference on Human factors in computing systems (pp. 859-868). ACM.
10. Chia, F.Y. and Saakes, D., 2014, November. Interactive training chopsticks to improve fine motor skills. In Proceedings of the 11th Conference on Advances in Computer Entertainment Technology (p. 57). ACM.
11. Salivia, G. and Hourcade, J.P., 2013, April. PointAssist: assisting individuals with motor impairments. In Proceedings of the SIGCHI Conference on Human Factors in Computing Systems (pp. 1213-1222). ACM.
12. Verhaegh, J., Fontijn, W. and Hoonhout, J., 2007, February. TagTiles: optimal challenge in educational electronics. In Proceedings of the 1st international conference on Tangible and embedded interaction (pp. 187-190). ACM.
13. Mandil, M., Jamil, N., Gupta, S., Ahirrao, S. and Sorathia, K., 2015, December. PhysiTable: Tangible Interactive System for Physical Rehabilitation of Children with Cerebral Palsy. In Proceedings of the 7th International Conference on HCI, IndiaHCI 2015 (pp. 149-153). ACM.
14. Hengeveld, B., Voort, R., Hummels, C., Overbeeke, K., de Moor, J. and van Balkom, H., 2008, June. LinguaBytes. In Proceedings of the 7th international conference on Interaction design and children (pp. 17-20). ACM.
15. Caro, K., Martínez-García, A.I., Tentori, M. and Zavala-Ibarra, I., 2014, October. Designing exergames combining the use of fine and gross motor exercises to support self-care activities. In Proceedings of the 16th international ACM SIGACCESS conference on Computers & accessibility (pp. 247-248). ACM.
16. Hengeveld, B., Hummels, C., Overbeeke, K., Voort, R., van Balkom, H. and de Moor, J., 2009, February. Tangibles for toddlers learning language. In Proceedings of the 3rd International Conference on Tangible and Embedded Interaction (pp. 161-168). ACM.
17. Case-Smith, J., 1995. The relationships among sensorimotor components, fine motor skill, and functional performance in preschool children. American Journal of Occupational Therapy, 49(7), pp.645-652.
18. Morrison, C.D., Bundy, A.C. and Fisher, A.G., 1991. The contribution of motor skills and playfulness to the play performance of preschoolers. American Journal of Occupational Therapy, 45(8), pp.687-694.
19. Dawson, G., 2008. Early behavioral intervention, brain plasticity, and the prevention of autism spectrum disorder. Development and psychopathology, 20(03), pp.775-803.
20. Bauminger, N. and Kasari, C., 2000. Loneliness and friendship in high-functioning children with autism. Child development, 71(2), pp.447-456.
21. Guha, M.L., Druin, A. and Fails, J.A., 2008, June. Designing with and for children with special needs: an inclusionary model. In Proceedings of the 7th international conference on Interaction design and children (pp. 61-64). ACM.
22. Hurst, A. and Tobias, J., 2011, October. Empowering individuals with do-it-yourself assistive technology. In The proceedings of the 13th international ACM SIGACCESS conference on Computers and accessibility (pp. 11-18). ACM.
23. Phillips, B. and Zhao, H., 1993. Predictors of assistive technology abandonment. Assistive technology, 5(1), pp.36-45.
24. Hengeveld, B., Voort, R., Hummels, C., de Moor, J., van Balkom, H., Overbeeke, K. and van der Helm, A., 2008. The development of LinguaBytes: an interactive tangible play and learning system to stimulate the language development of toddlers with multiple disabilities. Advances in Human-Computer Interaction, 2008, p.1.
25. Garzotto, F. and Gonella, R., 2011, June. An open-ended tangible environment for disabled children's

learning. In Proceedings of the 10th International Conference on Interaction Design and Children (pp. 52-61). ACM.

26. Bakker, S., van den Hoven, E. and Antle, A.N., 2011, January. MoSo tangibles: evaluating embodied learning. In Proceedings of the fifth international conference on Tangible, embedded, and embodied interaction (pp. 85-92). ACM.
27. Manches, A., O'Malley, C. and Benford, S., 2009, February. Physical manipulation: evaluating the potential for tangible designs. In Proceedings of the 3rd International Conference on Tangible and Embedded Interaction (pp. 77-84). ACM.
28. Marshall, P., 2007, February. Do tangible interfaces enhance learning?. In Proceedings of the 1st international conference on Tangible and embedded interaction (pp. 163-170). ACM.
29. Price, S., Rogers, Y., Scaife, M., Stanton, D. and Neale, H., 2003. Using 'tangibles' to promote novel forms of playful learning. Interacting with computers, 15(2), pp.169-185.
30. Price, S., Sheridan, J.G. and Pontual Falcao, T., 2010, January. Action and representation in tangible systems: implications for design of learning interactions. In Proceedings of the fourth international conference on Tangible, embedded, and embodied interaction (pp. 145-152). ACM.
31. Bruner, J.S., Jolly, A. and Sylva, K., 1976. Play: Its role in development and evolution.
32. Wilson, M., 2002. Six views of embodied cognition. Psychonomic bulletin & review, 9(4), pp.625-636.
33. Beukelman, D. and Mirenda, P., 2005. Augmentative and alternative communication: Supporting children and adults with complex communication needs.
34. Mundy, P., Sigman, M., Ungerer, J. and Sherman, T., 1986. Defining the social deficits of autism: The contribution of non-verbal communication measures. Journal of child psychology and psychiatry, 27(5), pp.657-669.

Design Directions for Media-Supported Collocated Remembering Practices

Mendel Broekhuijsen[1,2]
m.j.broekhuijsen@tue.nl
[1]Eindhoven University of Technology
Dept. of Industrial Design
Eindhoven, the Netherlands

Elise van den Hoven[2,1,3,4]
elise.vandenhoven@uts.edu.au
[2]University of Technology Sydney
School of Design, DAB &
School of Software, FEIT
Sydney, Australia

Panos Markopoulos[1,2]
p.markopoulos@tue.nl
[3]DJCAD University of Dundee
Dundee, UK

[4]ARC Centre of Excellence in Cognition and its Disorders

ABSTRACT
Since the widespread adoption of digital photography, people create many digital photos, often with the intention to use them for shared remembering. Practices around digital photography have changed along with advances in media sharing technologies such as smartphones, social media, and mobile connectivity. Although much research was done at the start of digital photography, commercially available tools for media-supported shared remembering still have many limitations. The objective of our research is to explore spatial and material design directions to better support the use of personal photos for collocated shared remembering. In this paper, we present seven design requirements that resulted from a redesign workshop with fifteen participants, and four design concepts (two spatial, two material) that we developed based on those requirements. By reflecting on the requirements and designs we conclude with challenges for interaction designers to support collocated remembering practices.

Author Keywords
Interaction design; design research; collocated sharing; PhotoUse; design requirements; remembering; storytelling.

ACM Classification Keywords
H.5.m. Information interfaces and presentation (e.g., HCI): Miscellaneous.

INTRODUCTION
Sharing memories has been an essential part of people's social interaction for millennia. Traditionally, shared remembering and storytelling occur when people are collocated (e.g. [10,15]), and despite increased opportunities for remote memory sharing, *collocated remembering* remains a popular activity. In such settings, the narratives about one's life are frequently supported by personal media, such as photos. Since the widespread adoption of domestic digital photography at the start of the century, people create many digital photos with the purpose to use them as support for shared remembering and storytelling [10,36], among other purposes (see e.g. [9,22]). Photos can be instrumental for memory sharing because of their ability to cue memories related to our lives, our autobiographical memories [6,18]. Although autobiographical memory serves several functions in our lives [4], for our research we are interested in the social function of autobiographical memory, e.g., bonding, maintaining relationships and making friends [4].

In the last decades the advances in media capture and media sharing technologies have changed the practices surrounding digital photos (e.g. [10,20,31,34]). For example, we transitioned from viewing photos in carefully curated and preserved family albums, to the use of digital collections, often with chaotic structures, that are distributed over different devices such as smartphones, computers, and cloud storages. While the practices change, the *purpose* of sharing practices is still primarily to share memories or tell stories [36]. Frohlich et al. made the distinction between these two kinds of conversations: *shared remembering* occurs when all individuals have been present at the original event; *storytelling* occurs if a person shares memories of events the others did not attend [10].

In our research, we are interested in the changing practices around digital media for remembering purposes. Although much research was done in the early days of digital photography two decades ago, the tools that are available today for media-supported shared remembering and storytelling still have many limitations. One of the issues, for example, is screen size: smartphones have a limited screen size, making it hard to view content with multiple people at once. Another issue is privacy: people are reluctant to pass their phone or tablet around to share their photos, because of the personal nature of other content on the smartphone. Another issue is access to photo collections: many collections are distributed over several devices and cloud services, and not available at all times. Although storage is getting cheaper, the solid state drives

TEI '17, March 20-23, 2017, Yokohama, Japan
© 2017 ACM. ISBN 978-1-4503-4676-4/17/03…$15.00
DOI: http://dx.doi.org/10.1145/3024969.3024996

used in smartphones, tablets, and modern laptops are still expensive, as is consumer cloud storage. Therefore, users often don't have access to their entire collection. Even if they do have everything stored in the cloud, a slow or costly (mobile) internet connection can severely hinder the experience. Last but not least, since most people do not curate their photos, interacting with their collection is mostly limited to scrolling through the entire collection in chronological order, which can ruin the viewing experience for both the sharer and the recipient. Therefore, the objective of our research is to explore spatial and material design directions to *better* support the use of personal photos for collocated shared remembering and storytelling.

RELATED WORK

In this section, we will discuss related work in the fields of Psychology and Human-Computer Interaction that relates to mediated remembering and collocated photo sharing.

Collocated Remembering

One of the primary purposes of sharing memories is to engage with each other socially. Nelson [27] even argues, that our autobiographical memory system only exists *because* of its function in interpersonal communication. Van House [34] also argues that shared reminiscing reinforces shared past experiences, thus strengthening relationships in the present. Part of shared remembering is the notion of *cross-cueing*, or *interactive cueing* [35], where one person's memory and conversation triggers the memory of others. However, our autobiographical memory can also be triggered by external triggers, also referred to as *memory cues* [17,18,33]. Upon encountering a memory cue, such as a digital photo, our memories are reconstructed [13], and the resulting memory is influenced by, e.g., the timing of the cue, the context, (social) situation and emotional state of the person (e.g. [16]).

Media Tools

Tools to support cueing and remembering are naturally changing along with the changing media types and media collection dynamics. Especially smartphones allow people to collect high-quality photos with a device they always carry with them, while before cameras used to be taken out only for holidays or special events. The opportunity to take photos has increased dramatically and therefore also the volumes of photos.

The technologies for photo sharing can be distinguished by their intended purpose. First, tools for managing and organising digital photos (e.g. [20,31]), which are essential for making the right content available for sharing. Secondly, technologies for remote photo sharing (e.g. [8,10,34]). Thirdly, tools that support viewing of photos. For *remote* photo sharing, there are many commercial tools available, such as Whatsapp instant messaging (whatsapp.com), and social platforms like Facebook (facebook.com). There are only a few technologies specifically designed for *collocated* sharing, e.g. streaming devices such as the Apple TV (apple.com/tv), which allow users to show content from portable devices onto a large (TV) screen. However, generally speaking, all devices with a display and some storage capability can be used to display photos. Although we can use these commercial photo sharing tools, they are not specifically designed to support shared remembering practices, but rather focus on *individual* collection management and retrieval. Even digital photo frames are used as decoration rather than for interactive co-viewing of photos, while they were intended to support collocated viewing.

In research, we have seen more promising examples of collocated photo sharing solutions. The variety of examples includes *4 Photos* [28], a concept for shared viewing of Facebook content during dinner, and *Shoebox* [2], a combination of a photo display and a storage device, placed in the living room. We have also seen tools that, for example, enable projection of multiple photos on the wall [30], playful interactions with photographic content [26] and new software solutions that combine several existing devices to create a shared viewing experience [23]. These examples also make better use of the context and space in which they are used. Specific media tools to support storytelling can be found in research as well (e.g. [1,25]). Various commercial tools offer a narrative structure: either automated, e.g. *Stories* in Google Photos (google.com/photos/about), Facebook's *Year in Review* (facebook.com/yearinreview) or more dedicated applications such as ICDL's StoryKit (childrenslibrary.org). These tools show promising directions for storytelling, but they also do not specifically support collocated shared remembering, because they focus on digital devices only, and they are geared towards a single person's activities, their photos and their interaction with the story.

Media Practices

Along with the technology, the practices around photo sharing are changing. In the early days of digital photography, Frohlich et al. [10] investigated the photo sharing activities that take place in the home, with the goal to identify opportunities for new photo technologies, which they termed *Photoware*. There they made a distinction between collocated sharing and remote sharing, and between synchronous and asynchronous sharing. A few years later, Kirk et al. [20] introduced a model outlining common photo activities leading to sharing, called *Photowork*. More recently, Lindley et al. [22] emphasised the influence of technology on social practices surrounding digital photos and vice versa. Moreover, Van House [34] argued that the experience of collocated sharing of photos and stories enacts the relationships between owner and viewer. New photo (sharing) technologies are being adapted by users to support these sharing activities [34] better. Our prior research emphasises that the complex set of practices, which we termed *PhotoUse*, should not be studied or addressed in isolation [5]. The holistic perspective also facilitates the design of tools that support sophisticated experiences such as media supported remembering.

Design Challenge

Despite the efforts in research to innovate the experience of collocated photo sharing, commercial tools have many limitations in their support for shared viewing. Therefore, our design challenge was to identify the limitations of current tools and to explore the opportunities for tools that are *better* at supporting collocated remembering practices.

In the remainder of this paper, we will outline a redesign exercise with 15 participants that led to design requirements for photo sharing tools, followed by an iterative design process to integrate the requirements into four concepts. We conclude with a discussion on the challenges for designing tools for future media-supported collocated remembering practices and possible ways to address the challenges.

REDESIGN SESSION

To understand the participants' ideas, needs and desires for the future of photo sharing we did a redesign exercise with them, because co-creation methods allow people to express themselves through showing and discussing what they create (e.g. see the work by Sanders and Stappers [32]). We based the redesign method on the method described by Frohlich et al. [11]. They used a light-weight method that asks participants what they want to *keep*, *lose* or *change* in existing designs. We applied this method because the participants had no prior experience with design methods.

Participants

The participants had to be familiar with each other (which was important for the redesign exercise), they had to own a digital camera or a smartphone, and they had to be well acquainted with digital photography, online sharing services and social platforms. Each participant had to own a collection of at least 2.000 digital photos, which ensured that they had experience with sharing from a large collection. The convenience sample of 15 participants were male Dutch university students, between the age of 18 and 25. They were all enrolled in different courses (mainly law, business and medicine), none of them STEM or design-related. We recruited participants via a student fraternity. Apart from the unbalanced gender, all fraternity members matched the requirements, and the existing social bonds between them made them especially suitable for our study.

Procedure

We organised one redesign session, lasting about 2 hours 15 minutes, roughly divided into three parts: a warm-up exercise, a group analysis of current photo sharing scenarios, and the actual redesign exercise. We held the session in a house where 4 of the 15 participants live, and so it was a familiar environment for all participants.

Warm-up

The warm-up with the whole group consisted of 15 minutes of introducing the background of the research, followed by 30 minutes of practising the design process through a redesign case. We formulated the design case as *"the use of a smartphone for collocated sharing of a personal photo to support storytelling at home"*. First, we asked each participant to show a single photo to another participant using their smartphones and to tell a story related to the photo. Afterwards, each participant had to indicate from this sharing scenario what aspects they liked (wanted to *keep*), what they did not like (*lose*), and what aspects they would want to change (*change*). They wrote these aspects down, and we briefly discussed all of them in the group.

Listing Photo Sharing Scenarios

After the first analysis, we asked the participants to come up with as many examples of other collocated photo sharing scenarios, to write those on notes and to discuss them in the group. This exercise was used to prioritise the scenarios that were most common for this group. The overview of collocated photo sharing scenarios can be found in Table 1. We assigned the first four scenarios to the four groups.

Redesign Exercise

The resulting list provided the scenarios that the participants redesigned in groups of 3-4 in the second part of the session, lasting 90 minutes. In the first 45 minutes, each group analysed the existing tools that are used in their scenario. They used the same method as they had practised as a group, with the goal to identify issues with the existing technologies and practices and to think of points for improvement. In the last 45 minutes, the participants were asked to come up with new concepts that could support their improved scenarios of collocated photo sharing. They made sketches, and presented the concepts to each other.

Scenario	Example	Redesign
Looking together at photos on a *portable device*	Smartphone, Nintendo DS	Group A
Looking together at photos on a *fixed display*	TV, PC, laptop	Group B
Looking together at photos that are printed in a *paper photo album*	Printed photos in an album, holiday album	Group C
Looking together at photos on a *projection*	Projector	Group D
Looking together at photos on a *tablet*	Tablet	N/A
Putting a photo on the *wall* as decoration	Collage	N/A
Looking at photos in a *photo frame*	Frame with digital or printed photo	N/A
Looking together at *printed photos*	Printed photo, polaroid	N/A

Table 1: Overview of collocated photo sharing scenarios that participants came up with, of which four were redesigned

Data Gathering & Analysis

The group sessions were audio recorded, just as each group discussion. The audio ensured that we captured the richness of the discussion. The most informative parts of the session were the discussions of the limitations and the valued aspects of current tools and practices for each scenario. In our analysis of the recordings, we focussed on identifying the issues for the different areas of interest, primarily the experience of sharing, but also on other areas such as curation and organising, and technical limitations of the technology. To support the audio, we encouraged participants to write all the aspects of their analyses on post-it notes, which we used afterwards to help generate an overview of the values, issues and opportunities for each collocated photo-sharing scenario. We used selective transcription [12] to gather the data from the audio. We looked for details about specific aspects of the scenarios that the participants talked about, as well as the pros and cons of the tools that were part of these scenarios. We collected the quotes that best described the different discussion points, and we used thematic clustering [7] to identify the themes that persisted between groups.

DESIGN REQUIREMENTS

In this section we will provide an in-depth description of the seven requirements (*R1-R7*) that we were able to formulate after analysing the recordings and notes from each group about the desired *experience of sharing*.

R1. Facilitate Spontaneity

Any tool that supports photo sharing should be simple and quick, to be able to illustrate parts of an on-going conversation spontaneously. Especially for augmenting a story, showing a *single* photo should not be cumbersome or interrupt the flow of a discussion or social activity in which photo sharing is embedded. As group A and B put it:

"People are looking for simple. The simpler, the better" - Group A

"[A tool] should be easy enough so that you can show just a single photo. Because when you are with friends, that is how you tell stories" - Group B

Participants especially did not want to boot a laptop just to show a single photo. Even less popular is to connect the laptop or phone to a projector or television, because too many devices are required to show the photos, and most of the time these devices need proprietary cables or are not compatible with each other. The participants discussed ideas for universal applications that run cross-platform and enable instant viewing of a single photo from a mobile device on external displays. A universal interface for all devices would help to smooth the process, along with compatibility across platforms, devices and media formats.

R2. On-the-fly Content Control

Privacy is important, and the participants specifically wanted to hide certain photos from certain audiences. Most groups suggested to apply censoring, hiding or locking specific photos to address different audiences. Moreover, most groups agreed that it would be helpful if selecting shared content *on-the-fly* would be possible. Most participants had experience with accidentally showing a photo to the wrong person. A common cause was that the next photo in the camera roll was not appropriate, and people either scroll to the next photo themselves, or they give their phone to a friend, who scrolls to the next photo. When showing personal photos to multiple people, this issue is even more amplified: on a big screen a photo can be exposed to multiple people at once. In group B a private queue with "delay" was hence part of the concept, to enable the presenter to preview what would show next using a second screen, a solution very similar to what is already used for e.g. MS PowerPoint presentations.

R3. Seamless Embedding in Narrative Structure

Tools for sharing should facilitate *storytelling*, to support, guide and influence the narrative. Participants often want to share several photos and structure the narrative around them. Not only can the narrative be supported with better guidance from the photos, but it can also influence the narrative. When people are telling a story, it is problematic if they skip a photo that is important for the chronology of the narrative. On the other hand, because taking digital photos is free, people take multiple snaps to capture a moment, so that they can be sure to have a good one. This creates the need for them to select later the 'best' snap, which they often neglect to do. In viewing poorly or non-curated photo collections it is very common to see multiple instances of the same moment. During storytelling, this can be cumbersome. As participants in group B summarised:

"If you want to show a holiday, you want chronology, and no duplicates" - Group B

R4. Tailoring to Audience

Tools for sharing should *tailor* the content to the *audience* because different contexts require different photo selections. Group D argued that the audience would lose interest if the content was not appropriated to them:

"[When telling a story] some people were present at the time, and others were not. So you have to explain everything [...] and so some people lose interest. [...] It should be possible for the presenter to adjust what he presents while presenting" - Group D

The need for context-specific selections also holds for individual photo viewing. Because of the growing size of the photo collections on our smartphones, not every photo is relevant and participants were looking for more control:

"I want to be able to determine how [many photos] of certain events I want to see. So how many photos from India, perhaps just a few, but at some point, I want to be able to see more. They should be in [my collection], but not in my album". - Group C

In the group discussion, automated "highlights" of events were mentioned that are offered by e.g. Facebook's *Year in Review*. However, for the participants, it was not clear what caused a photo to become a highlight, and they did not always agree with the system's automated selection.

R5. Support Multi-User Content and Interaction

Photo sharing tools intended for multiple users should support *multi-user* content and interaction. Some of the sharing tools that were discussed also included a discussion on collocated use of tools. One of the opportunities was to *merge* content from different users of the system.

"[Think of a] photo album that brings the content of two people together, similar to Facebook's "other people that were here as

well", because a photo album is usually very one-sided, as in one guy is blabbering, and the others just listen. So if you now want to do this with one other person, your content is merged. Not photos from random people, but from the people that you are with". - Group C

Another way to better support multiple users is through multi-user interaction with the content itself:

"Other people should also be able to join in on the presentation" - Group D

R6. Show Photos in Context

Photo sharing tools should provide support for *contextualised* photo viewing. One of the interesting discussions that was especially held in group C covered the aspects of thematic photos. In group C, all participants agreed that the value of the paper photo album was that you can see multiple photos at the same time. The smartphone typically displays a single photo, which does not provide the best support for stories because every photo appears to be as significant as any other.

"A photo shows the situation, but without the context" - Group C.

Combining photos with related content to support the narrative is a typical practice when organising a traditional paper-based photo album, but this thematic or contextual aspect is not so much present in digital sharing. Although one can create digital folders or albums to group photos, their presentation is usually per single photo, and the few technologies that offer so-called *panels* for slideshows are hardly used. An automated storytelling aid, such as Google's *Stories* feature, was also mentioned as an interesting direction for the thematic display of information.

R7. Photo Sharing should be Personal and Intimate

Photo sharing should be more like a *special event*, to enhance the social experience. Sharing stories, especially after the holidays, is often part of a valuable get-together and viewing photos used to be at the heart of these gatherings. The family album is viewed together, in a homely atmosphere. Group C (given the task to redesign the experience of the photo album) was especially keen on ensuring these intimate qualities in the experience.

"It should stay homely, intimate, not become too slick" - Group C.

It appears that the charm of a *physical* photo album is partly because it is a tangible object, partly because it is a dedicated object for photo viewing, and partly because a book affords intimate sharing practices (sitting on the couch together). Group B shared the view of group C that in certain circumstances it is important to set the stage for sharing photos, and that you need to take the time to enjoy photo sharing properly.

Long-standing Design Challenge

Since we selected a convenience sample, we must be careful with generalising our findings from the redesign sessions, especially because of the unbalanced gender and the affinity with technology of this group. However, the requirements that we found all resonate with prior research in this domain: in line with our first requirement on usability, Van House [34] indicated that easy and spontaneous access to content is important, as did [29]. Participants in the study of Van House [34] also requested more flexible control over who sees which photo on online photo sharing services, similar to the desire underneath our second requirement. Bergman et al. [3] also worked on software tools for temporary hiding photos, which they called *demoting.* Our fourth requirement to adapt content to audiences is also in line with Van House, who stressed the importance of flexibility in photo sharing and flexible content as a way to support the performative nature of storytelling [34]. The fact that many valuable findings and requirements from the past decades have not made their way into commercial tools for photo sharing motivated us to investigated the current state of user needs. We see the novelty of our findings in the fact that these requirements still surface when talking to a group of young adults, who were all toddlers around the time of the first studies into digital photo sharing practices. E.g., Frohlich et al. did their research between 1998 and 2000, and Van House's study took place between 2005 and 2006, around the introduction of Facebook and the iPhone. So much has changed for digital photography. But the technological capabilities of current sharing tools and available high-bandwidth internet connections make it also feasible for designers to address the long-standing issues, while that was not possible two decades ago. Moreover, by listing the requirements all together in this paper, designers can also attempt to address them holistically in new concepts.

DESIGN DIRECTIONS

With our research, we aim to tackle this long-standing design challenge by addressing the user experience requirements, as formulated in the previous section. We used those requirements as input for the development of several concepts that we believe illustrate promising design directions for media-supported collocated remembering.

In an iterative design process (Figure 1), done mainly by the first author, the approximately ten ideas that came directly from the redesign session were matured towards detailed concept sketches in three iterations: I) the seven requirements guided the selection and clustering of early ideas. Some of the concepts also addressed other photography practices besides collocated photo sharing, such as curation and remote sharing, but those were excluded from this paper. II) also in consultation with fellow design researchers, we selected and combined those concepts to get to the four presented here. III) we detailed, described and visualised the four concepts. Because we are interested in holistic solutions for photo practices [5], the concepts are deliberately addressing multiple requirements. Two concepts incorporate more spatial aspects; two concepts incorporate more material aspects into the interaction. In Figure 2 we have mapped the concepts (labelled C1-C4) onto the requirements (R1-R7).

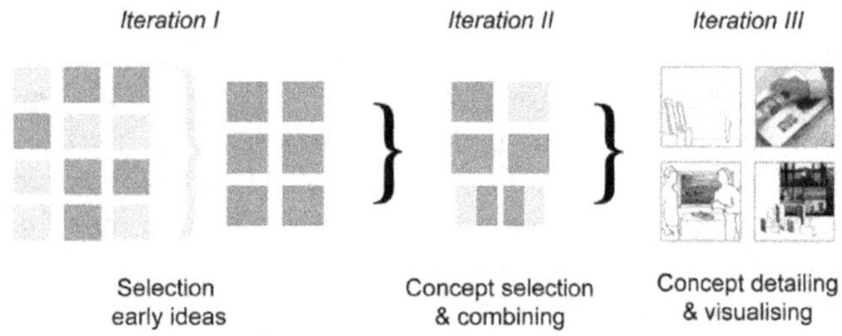

Figure 1: Iterative design process

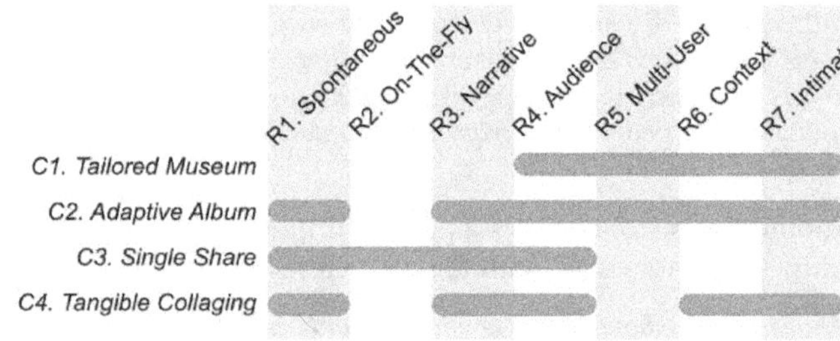

Figure 2: Mapping of the four concepts on the left (C1-C4) and seven requirements on the top (R1-R7)

C1. Tailored Museum

The goal of *Tailored Museum* (Figure 3) is to facilitate shared remembering in an interactive space with photographic content projected onto the walls. The concept is a combination of the concept presented by Group 1 and a website that was launched by Intel in 2011, called the *Museum Of Me* (museumofme.intell.com). In the Museum of Me, all the content from Facebook was used to create a personalised virtual museum, focused on a single user's content. Instead of focusing on a single person, *Tailored Museum* focusses on the relationship between *multiple* individuals. The concept offers a unique, overwhelming experience: people are invited to come with their friends or family to an empty villa or an abandoned factory. Upon entering, the users will put their mobile phones on a docking station and their entire (online) photo collections will appear on the inner walls of the building. Every room displays a different period of the visitors' lives, e.g. childhood, high school, university, etc. To support social remembering, the collections of the people that enter together will be *merged* in rooms that show shared life-time periods (e.g. student years) and *contrasted* side by side in the other rooms to allow visitors to discuss their parallel lives. Some rooms will be private and only accessible by the owner of the content. Interaction within the Tailored Museum is done with a combination of motion tracking, and speech and gesture analysis to determine what photos are addressed and how they relate to the people and the narrative. The relevant photos will be enlarged, allowing to review the conversation that emerged in the museum.

Figure 3: C1. *Tailored Museum*, a novel way of sharing photos in a museum setting, where the combined collections of the visitors who go in together are merged and contrasted

C2. Adaptive Album

Adaptive Album (Figure 4) is an intelligent paper photo album that adapts its content to the social situation and available time for viewing. The goal is to aim for an intimate and instant experience. This concept is largely based on the concept that was described by Group C:

"It should be simple, choose a photo with the press of a button, if you open the book you want to see the photos instantly, you should not first need to select them, because it depends on the moment if you want 10 or 20" - Group C.

"Selecting photos takes too long, so that should be done automatically, and if you view photos often or longer [on other devices], they should be included in the book, and those you view on your phone go automatically into the book, or even these kinds *of photos are included in the book more often." - Group C*

Adaptive Album provides the users with an "old fashion" family album experience, but the content is adaptable to the situation. To start the experience, you have to trigger content generation via speech. E.g., ask the book for "Holidays with Simon", or "Italy 2015", and the content will appropriate itself to the audience that is facing it, based on face recognition. While viewing the photos, you can easily enlarge photos (by pinching), or delete photos from the album (swiping it off the page) and the photo composition will reconfigure itself. Turning the page will change the topic within the event (e.g. the next day of the trip). Both the material sensation of a heavy book that is held by multiple people, and the use of high-quality pages aim to enhance the intimate setting and the perceived value of the content.

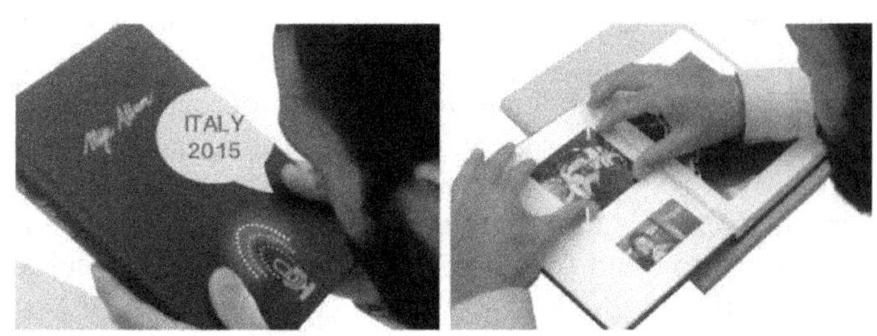

Figure 4: C2. *Adaptive Album*, an interactive paper photo album displaying the combined content of the audience

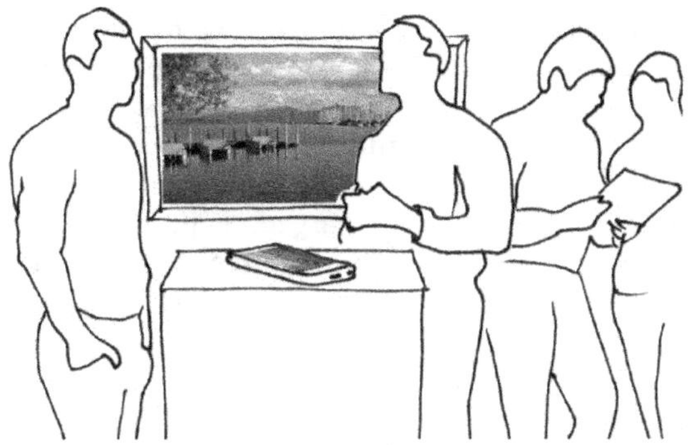

Figure 5: C3. *Single Share*, a smartphone showing a relevant photo is placed on top of a special dock, and the content is instantly displayed on a large screen

C3. Single Share

Single Share (Figure 5) is an easy photo sharing device for the home environment. As soon as you lay a smartphone on a dedicated spot on the living room table, the photo that is visible on the phone's screen is shown on the wall. Very important for the feeling of spontaneous sharing is that you do not need to configure anything and that any phone can be used with the system, setting this concept apart from configuration-intensive systems such as Apple TV.

"You should just put your phone somewhere and be instantly connected, no screen or wall needed, and no cables" - Group D

The photo that is shared on the wall is of high quality, similar to a piece of art. The most important value of this design is the ease with which people can casually bring up a photo to support their narrative. Moreover, the act of putting the device down emphasises the importance of the uninterrupted face to face communication.

C4. Tangible Collaging

Tangible Collaging (Figure 6) combines the requirements of showing content within its context, with the ability to influence the content on the fly. The concept consists of a high-quality screen and a table-top with interactive building blocks that enable the user to construct a collage on the screen. The purpose of the concept is to co-construct the story with the friends that are together, but it also provides the users with an interface for their digital content, enabling them to leave out parts that are irrelevant.

The physicality of the interaction is an important aspect of the experience because it allows for a playful way to literally build up the story and group photos per topic. Contextualising the content through a collage also means that every session can be tailored to the audience. The blocks can be reused, repurposed and reordered, while the story is saved for later retrieval. *Tangible Collaging* enables users to arrange and tinker in the physical space, and have the result in the digital space, enabling more control over sharing and co-constructing stories.

Figure 6: C4. *Tangible Collaging*, tangible collaborative manipulation of digital content using interactive building blocks

DISCUSSION

None of the concepts have been implemented or evaluated. Rather than developing any one of these ideas into a final prototype, the aim of this study was to step back and reflect on the requirements, ideas and the rationale behind them and to identify general design directions, that will be addressed in future design projects. In this section, we reflect on the implementation of the requirements into the design concepts. In our aim to include as many of the requirements as possible in each of the concepts, we realised that there are some trade-offs that designers need to consider when designing for media-supported collocated remembering.

Digital Experience vs. Physical Experience

Requirement R7 about the need to (re-)create a personal and intimate experience around photo sharing reflects a general desire to partly model photo sharing experiences after printed photo practices. Although we agree that some of the personal and intimate sharing experience is getting lost with the digitisation of practices, we do not believe designers should aim at replicating the practices from three decades ago. Instead, designers should merely understand and acknowledge the qualities from earlier practices, but use new media types to fuel the design of tools to support *new* kinds of experiences. While most current systems that support collocated photo sharing still approach photos as objects in hierarchically managed collections [14], a different perspective is needed for designers to reinvent the practices around evolving media collection. We believe a first step is to consider photo collections as flexible streams of information which are transformed dynamically to match the fluid and emergent needs of users, their context and activities. With the concepts that we presented in this paper we want to illustrate that photo practices can be designed to support new kinds of intimate and personal qualities, based on metadata and other features that are unique for digital photos, allowing e.g. merging and contrasting photo sets in chronological order, or offering a tailored viewing experience based on face detection. Such experiences would not have been possible before and can be offered only by leveraging the features that are unique to digital photographic material.

On the other hand, designers must also acknowledge the distraction of digital interfaces and devices in face to face interaction. Tangible interaction such as flipping pages (C2) or arranging blocks (C4) can limit distraction in collocated communication and even stimulate collaboration.

Digital Overview vs. Device Mobility

In line with research on graspable, tangible and hybrid interfaces (e.g. [19,21]), the goal of the *Tangible Collaging* concept was to bridge the gap between our physical capabilities and our digital possessions. Interacting with printed photos is very different from interacting on-screen with the digital photos [10]. Especially the limited screen size makes it hard to keep a good overview of the collection, and so in *Tangible Collaging* we separated the interaction and the visual representation. Currently, an overview of a complete photo collection can only be achieved by considerably increasing the size of the screen. Many people believe that, because of the digitisation of photo collections, curation will become easier. However, it does not seem feasible yet to provide the user with an appropriate overview of their entire collection.

In all our concepts we explored the use of screens for *displaying* content only, not as an *interface* for overviewing and selecting from large collections. We consider one of the big challenges for designers to find solutions to bring better overview in the digital space, without losing mobility of the devices. Some potential directions for solutions could be small projectors integrated into smartphones. Another solution is to leverage public screens (interactive walls in shopping malls, advertisement screens in the street, etc.) to display personal content temporarily. Augmented-, Virtual- or Mixed Reality technology might be an interesting next step (e.g. Microsoft's HoloLens (microsoft.com/microsoft-hololens/)), as long as designers at the same time innovate existing archiving structures and folder hierarchies, because otherwise, the digital files are as hard to navigate as books in an attic. Another direction for creating a better overview could be to innovate the interaction with digital elements on the screen. E.g., by using smart clustering (based on e.g. visual similarity), overlapping elements, stacked views (similar to e.g. [24]), summarising information, or other ways to manipulate large quantities of information.

Dedicated Tool vs. Multifunctional Device

One of the main threats for media-supported remembering is that digital items are hidden behind the technology on which they are stored [29]. Even a tablet or a smartphone usually needs up to 10 steps before a single photo can be displayed. In the age of physical photos, the family album had a dedicated function for showing these photos, and opening the book immediately started the (sharing) experience. Because of their form factor, tablets and other personal devices can be used for intimate sharing, but there is also a lot of distraction from other functions of the devices, both private and professional, which are not relevant to the experience of photo viewing.

The concepts *Adaptive Album* and *Single Share* lower the technological threshold for shared remembering, addressing the need for easy and quick access. However, there is a trade-off between a multifunctional device which offers photo viewing alongside other apps, and a dedicated device that needs to be carried, charged, kept up to date and synchronised. We see three directions for possible solutions: a) dedicated tools, as some of the concepts in this paper; b) tools that extend existing devices, that need charging but maintenance is done in parallel with the main device, similar to smartwatches; c) applications that are capable of dedicating a device temporarily to the task at hand, e.g. unlocking the smartphone in a certain way renders it into a dedicated photo viewer, and none of the other applications or tasks on the smartphone will be able to distract the user for the duration of the activity.

System Automation vs. Manual Tailoring

Context-aware recommender systems can be interesting to introduce to collocated photo-sharing activities, to automate some of the retrieval tasks that currently encumber social interaction. Such an approach would be challenging, as photographic content selection to support remembering depends on the social dynamics, context, intentions of participants, etc. But the alternative to letting people do this manually is not desirable either. Even automated folders based on user-defined hashtags or keywords is just a small step, because for it to work people need to be very consistent with their tagging, which becomes difficult over time. Perhaps the solution can be found in combining the social capabilities of people to *inform* systems about required content, with technologies for automatically annotating data and retrieving photos, in response to user activities and interactions with the system.

CONCLUSION

In this paper, we have presented a design exploration into support for collocated remembering practices. Based on a redesign exercise we formulated seven requirements, which guided the development of four concepts to illustrate new directions for media-supported shared remembering. We concluded with a discussion of four trade-offs that surfaced after reflecting on the process. We believe that acknowledging the trade-offs described in this paper can help designers to address the long-standing design challenges and inspire the innovation of new tools for collocated media supported remembering practices.

ACKNOWLEDGMENTS

This research was supported by STW VIDI grant number 016.128.303 of The Netherlands Organisation for Scientific Research (NWO), awarded to Elise van den Hoven. The study was approved by the UTS Research Ethics Committee under REF NO. 2015000007. We would like to thank the members of O.M.S.G. Plutarchus for their contribution and enthusiasm during the redesign workshop.

REFERENCES

1. Marko Balabanović, Lonny L Chu, and Gregory J. Wolff. 2000. Storytelling with digital photographs. In *Proceedings of the SIGCHI conference on Human Factors in Computing Systems*. ACM Press, New York, New York, USA. 564-571 http://doi.org/10.1145/332040.332505
2. Richard Banks and Abigail Sellen. 2009. Shoebox: mixing storage and display of digital images in the home. In *Proceedings of the 3rd International Conference on Tangible and Embedded Interaction*. ACM, New York, New York, USA, 35–40. http://doi.org/10.1145/1517664.1517678
3. Ofer Bergman, Simon Tucker, Ruth Beyth-Marom, Edward Cutrell, and Steve Whittaker. 2009. It's Not That Important: Demoting Personal Information of Low Subjective Importance Using GrayArea. In *Proceedings of the SIGCHI conference on Human Factors in Computing Systems*. ACM Press, New York, New York, USA. 269–278. http://doi.org/10.1145/1518701.1518745
4. Susan Bluck, Nicole Alea, Tilmann Habermas, and David C Rubin. 2005. A TALE of Three Functions: The Self–Reported Uses of Autobiographical Memory. *Social Cognition* 23, 1: 91–117. http://doi.org/10.1521/soco.23.1.91.59198
5. Mendel Broekhuijsen, Elise van den Hoven, and Panos Markopoulos. (*in press)*. From PhotoWork to PhotoUse: Exploring Personal Digital Photo Activities. *Behaviour & Information Technology*. Taylor & Francis. http://dx.doi.org/10.1080/0144929X.2017.1288266
6. Martin A. Conway and C. W. Pleydell-Pearce. 2000. The construction of autobiographical memories in the self-memory system. *Psychological Review* 107, 2: 261–288. http://doi.org/10.1037/0033-295X.107.2.261
7. J. Corbin and A. Strauss. 2008. *Basics of qualitative research: Techniques and procedures for developing grounded theory*. Los Angeles, California: Sage Publications, Inc.
8. Andy Crabtree, Tom Rodden, and John Mariani. 2004. Collaborating around collections: informing the continued development of photoware. In *CSCW '04: Proceedings of the 2004 ACM conference on Computer supported cooperative work*. ACM, New York, New York, USA. http://doi.org/10.1145/1031607.1031673
9. Jose Dijck van. 2008. Digital photography: communication, identity, memory. *Visual Communication* 7, 1: 57–76.
10. David M. Frohlich, Allan Kuchinsky, Celine Pering, Abbe Don, and Steven Ariss. 2002. Requirements for photoware. In *CSCW '02: Proceedings of the 2002 ACM conference on Computer supported cooperative work*. ACM, New York, New York, USA, 166–175. http://doi.org/10.1145/587078.587102
11. David M. Frohlich, Christopher Sze Chong Lim, and Amr Ahmed. 2014. Keep, lose, change: Prompts for the re-design of product concepts in a focus group setting. *CoDesign* 10, 2: 80–95. http://doi.org/10.1080/15710882.2013.862280
12. Nigel Gilbert. 2008. *Researching social life*. Sage Publications Ltd.
13. R. Kim Guenther. 1998. *Human Cognition*. Prentice Hall, Upper Saddle River, New Jersey.
14. Richard Harper, Siân E. Lindley, Eno Thereska, et al. 2013. What is a file? In *CSCW '13: Proceedings of the 2013 conference on Computer supported cooperative work*. ACM, New York, New York, USA. http://doi.org/10.1145/2441776.2441903
15. Celia B. Harris, Amanda J. Barnier, John Sutton, and Paul G. Keil. 2014. Couples as socially distributed cognitive systems: Remembering in everyday social and material contexts. *Memory Studies* 7, 3: 285–297. http://doi.org/10.1177/1750698014530619
16. Celia B. Harris, Anne S. Rasmussen, and Dorthe Berntsen. 2013. The functions of autobiographical memory: an integrative approach. *Memory (Hove, England)* 22, 5: 559–581. http://doi.org/10.1080/09658211.2013.806555
17. Elise van den Hoven and Berry Eggen. 2009. The effect of cue media on recollections. *Human Technology: an International Journal on Humans in ICT Environments* 5, 1: 47–67.
18. Elise van den Hoven and Berry Eggen. 2014. The cue is key: Design for real-life remembering. *Zeitschrift für Psychologie* 222, 2: 110–117. http://doi.org/10.1027/2151-2604/a000172
19. Elise van den Hoven, Joep Frens, Dima Aliakseyeu, Jean-Bernard Martens, Kees Overbeeke, and Peter Peters. 2007. Design research & tangible interaction. In *Proceedings of the 1st international conference on Tangible and Embedded Interaction*. ACM Press, New York, New York, USA, 109–115.
20. David S. Kirk, Abigail Sellen, Carsten Rother, and Kenneth R. Wood. 2006. Understanding photowork. In *Proceedings of the SIGCHI Conference on Human Factors in Computing Systems*. ACM, New York, New York, USA, 761. http://doi.org/10.1145/1124772.1124885
21. David S. Kirk, Abigail Sellen, Stuart Taylor, Nicolas Villar, and Shahram Izadi. 2009. Putting the physical into the digital: issues in designing hybrid interactive surfaces. In *Proceedings of the 23rd British HCI Group Annual Conference on People and Computers: Celebrating People and Technology*. British Computer Society, 35–44.
22. Siân E. Lindley, Abigail C. Durrant, David S. Kirk, and Alex S. Taylor. 2009. Collocated social practices

surrounding photos. *International Journal of Human-Computer Studies* 67, 12: 995–1004. http://doi.org/10.1016/j.ijhcs.2009.08.004

23. Andres Lucero, Jussi Holopainen, and Tero Jokela. 2011. Pass-them-around: collaborative use of mobile phones for photo sharing. In *Proceedings of the SIGCHI conference on human factors in computing systems*. ACM Press, New York, USA, 1787–1796.
24. Richard Mander, Gitta Salomon, and Yin Yin Wong. 1992. A "Pile" Metaphor for Supporting Casual Organization of Information. In *CHI '92: Proceedings of the SIGCHI Conference on Human Factors in Computing Systems*. ACM Press, New York, New York, USA
25. Daniel Meadows. 2003. Digital storytelling: Research-based practice in new media. *Visual Communication* 2, 2: 189–193.
26. Bernt Meerbeek, Peter Bingley, Wil Rijnen, and Elise van den Hoven. 2010. Pipet: a design concept supporting photo sharing. In *Proceedings of the 6th Nordic Conference on Human-Computer Interaction: Extending Boundaries*. ACM Press, New York, USA, 335–342.
27. K. Nelson. 1993. The psychological and social origins of autobiographical memory. *Psychological science* 4(1), 7-14.
28. Kenton O'Hara, John Helmes, Abigail Sellen, Richard Harper, Martijn ten Bhömer, and Elise van den Hoven. 2012. Food for talk: phototalk in the context of sharing a meal. *Human–Computer Interaction* 27, 1-2: 124–150. http://doi.org/10.1080/07370024.2012.656069
29. Daniela Petrelli and Steve Whittaker. 2010. Family memories in the home: contrasting physical and digital mementos. *Personal and Ubiquitous Computing* 14, 2: 153–169. http://doi.org/10.1007/s00779-009-0279-7
30. Daniela Petrelli, Simon Bowen, and Steve Whittaker. 2014. Photo mementos: Designing digital media to represent ourselves at home. *International Journal of Human-Computer Studies* 72, 3: 320–336. http://doi.org/http://dx.doi.org/10.1016/j.ijhcs.2013.09.009
31. Kerry Rodden and Kenneth R. Wood. 2003. How do people manage their digital photographs? In *CHI '03: Proceedings of the SIGCHI Conference on Human Factors in Computing Systems*. ACM Press, New York, New York, USA, 409–416. http://doi.org/10.1145/642611.642682
32. Elizabeth B. N. Sanders and Pieter Jan Stappers. 2008. Co-creation and the new landscapes of design. *CoDesign* 4, 1: 5–18.
33. Abigail Sellen and Steve Whittaker. 2010. Beyond total capture. *Communications of the ACM* 53, 5: 70–77. http://doi.org/10.1145/1735223.1735243
34. Nancy A. Van House. 2009. Collocated photo sharing, story-telling, and the performance of self. *International Journal of Human-Computer Studies* 67, 12: 1073–1086. http://doi.org/10.1016/j.ijhcs.2009.09.003
35. Daniel M. Wegner, T. Giuliano, and P. T. Hertel. 1985. Cognitive interdependence in close relationships. *Compatible and incompatible relationships*. Springer New York. 253-276.
36. Steve Whittaker, Ofer Bergman, and Paul Clough. 2010. Easy on that trigger dad: a study of long term family photo retrieval. *Personal and Ubiquitous Computing* 14, 1: 31–43. http://doi.org/10.1007/s00779-009-0218-7

Wobble: Shaping Unobtrusive Reminders for Prospective Memories in the Home Context

Jan Zekveld[1], **Saskia Bakker**[1], **Annemarie Zijlema**[2,1] **and Elise van den Hoven**[2,1,3,4]

[1] Department of Industrial Design, Eindhoven University of Technology, the Netherlands,
[2] Faculty of Engineering and Information Technology, University of Technology Sydney, Australia,
[3] Duncan of Jordanstone College of Art & Design, University of Dundee, United Kingdom,
[4] ARC Centre of Excellence in Cognition and its Disorders, Sydney, Australia,
j.e.zekveld@alumnus.tue.nl, s.bakker@tue.nl, annemarie.f.zijlema@student.uts.edu.au, elise.vandenhoven@uts.edu.au

ABSTRACT
Reminders are designed to support remembering actions or intentions to be performed later in time. Most technologies that have a reminding functionality do so by asking attention (e.g., by using auditory alerts or vibration patterns) from users at a certain point in time or location. Because of their obtrusive nature, the reminders of many (digital) prospective memory aids we use on a daily basis are hard to ignore, regardless of our ability and motivation to perform the reminded action or intention. In this paper, we present Wobble: an interactive cone-shaped artefact for reminding in the home environment. Wobble was designed to investigate peripheral reminders. Our results imply that wobble is best suitable for reminding intentions that do not require direct action but can be carried out over a period of time, which is a type of reminding currently not met by most electronic memory aids.

Author Keywords
Prospective Memory; Future Intention; Tangible Interaction; Persuasive Technology; Research Through Design; Peripheral Reminding; Multi-modal Interaction.

ACM Classification Keywords
H.5.m. Information interfaces and presentation (e.g., HCI):Miscellaneous;

INTRODUCTION
Prospective memory is used to remember future intentions [13]. An example of a future intention is: 'return a borrowed book'. To remember these future activities or intentions we make use of memory aids, which can be both analog and digital. Analog memory aids lose their novelty over time due to 'familiarity'. This makes them gradually lose their ability to stand out when they are supposed to remind the user of the cued intention. The majority of digital memory aids ask users' attention at a certain point in time or at a specific location. Reminders presented by these memory aids are designed to attract attention for example by using auditory alerts or vibrating patterns, which makes them hard to ignore- regardless of the user's ability to put it into practice. However, reminders for intentions, are more likely to be brought into practice when the user is able to perform the activity when reminded. Also, reminders for activities that cannot be executed when perceived by the user ('mismatched' reminders) can cause frustration or annoyance [4]. The success of an executed (future) intention can be defined as a product of a user's *ability* and *motivation* at the time of perceiving the reminder (or: '*trigger*', 'cue') [4]. The frustration and annoyance caused by mismatched reminders is an issue which existing digital memory aids do not address. We believe reminders should not be designed to force the user to focus on each reminder (e.g., by simply designing very obtrusive reminders). Instead we believe that reminders that are easier to ignore than traditional reminders can be presented more often, and may be picked up by users when they are more open to be reminded. To evaluate these sorts of reminders we build on the concept of 'peripheral interaction' [2]. We aim to apply peripheral interaction to the design of a reminding application and explore how unobtrusive reminders for cued intentions are experienced in the home context. In addition we are interested in how a tangible approach to creating memory cues influences the ability to recall cued intentions. We explored this concept using research-through-design [5][20], in which we iteratively created an interactive prototype called 'Wobble'. We evaluated Wobble in a user study and present generalized insights for the design of unobtrusive memory aids.

TEI '17, March 20-23, 2017, Yokohama, Japan
© 2017 ACM. ISBN 978-1-4503-4676-4/17/03 $15.00
DOI: http://dx.doi.org/10.1145/3024969.3024984

THEORETICAL BACKGROUND AND RELATED WORK
This paper explores a tangible artifact to support reminding in the periphery of attention. In this section we discuss theories of prospective memory, in which our design is grounded, and we discuss related work in the area of peripheral interaction.

Figure 1. Wobble prototype.

Prospective Memory Cues

People often use memory cues to remember intentions and actions that need to be performed at a point of time in the future. To discern remembering future intentions (prospective memory) from remembering past experience (retrospective memory), we call these cues 'prospective memory cues'. Future intentions are remembered when prospective memory cues [3] are triggered. They can be created intentionally by people (using memory aids) but can also spontaneously come to mind [13]. Depending on the specifics of the intention the memory cues can be event-based, time-based or location-based. Various memory aids have been designed to support the prospective memory for a diverse range of situations, locations and intentions. For example, the apps Wunderlist [19] and Any.Do [1] have been designed for the purpose of reminding by enabling users to create lists. These applications overlap with the old-fashioned pen and paper list making, but differ in their ability to actively remind the user at a predefined moment in time. Differently, Google Now [7], Cues [14] and Place-it's [17] are applications that actively remind users of tasks at relevant locations, using GPS technology.

Calm Technology and ambient displays

While the above-mentioned reminding applications are designed to attract the user's attention (using alerting notifications), ambient displays [11] or peripheral displays [12] are designed to inform people without alarming or intruding. Such ambient displays find their origin in the vision of Calm Technology, described as "that which informs but doesn't demand our focus or attention" [18], and characterized by information shifting back and forth between the center and periphery of attention. The prototype ReMind [10] unobtrusively prompts users to perform an action by a rotating wall-mounted disk, on which tangible tokens are placed to represent specific intentions. Move-it Sticky Notes [15] enhances physical sticky notes with technology which allows them to move in order to subtly draw attention. The design presented in this paper adds to these existing works, by exploring a combination of sound and movement to create subtle reminders, and by relying on a portable and open-ended design which is hypothesized to be particularly suitable in the home-context, where the timing of tasks and activities are generally more flexible compared to the office context.

PERIPHERAL REMINDING ARTEFACT: WOBBLE

Wobble (depicted in Figure 1) is an open-ended memory aid that produces reminders designed to be perceived in the periphery of attention. It is a research instrument created to explore peripheral interaction in the domain of prospective memory (retrieval). Wobble both allows for creating memory cues and provides the reminder.

Wobble is a cone-shaped tangible artefact that produces reminders by physically rotating. When Wobble rotates it generates a subtle sound as a consequence of the friction with the surface it is positioned on. These reminders are hypothesized to be more subtle than traditional reminders since wobble produces a softer, more calm sound. Additionally, subtlety may be realized by the location at which the sound is generated, which is not necessarily produced near the user (as memory aids on mobile phones are). Its tangible design allows Wobble to be placed in different locations, depending on the user's wishes. Wobble provides multiple unobtrusive reminders over a longer period of time, in contrast to just one obtrusive reminder at one specific moment. Because of their subtlety, Wobble's reminders are likely easier to ignore or to 'miss' than reminders with a more alarming character.

Reminders that are presented both visually and auditory are more likely to be perceived when one modality is overshadowed by a more dominant information source. The multi-modality of Wobble's reminder has another advantage: when a user is able to link the perceived visual and auditory information to the same event, the perception of the reminder is strengthened [6].

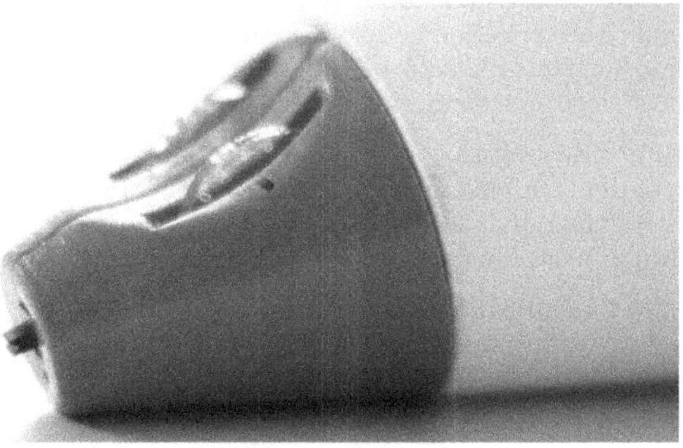

Figure 2. Close-up of Wobble's tip and user interface.

Wobble allows for tangible creation of prospective memory cues and its reminder's relevance can be set using location (where Wobble becomes active) and time (when Wobble is set to become active). This portability allows the user to increase the likelihood that reminders are noticed at relevant locations. The desired timing is determined using Wobble's tangible user interface [9]. Wobble's tip includes an on/off-button and two scroll wheels, which can be rotated to set Wobble's behavior. Scroll wheel 1 allows the user to determine in how many hours the reminder should become active (varying from 0 to 24). Scroll wheel 2 can be used to determine the frequency with which Wobble becomes active in the period until the final reminder. This value varies between 1 time per 2 hours to 4 times per hour.

A prototype was made for evaluating Wobble's reminders in a user study. The (15 cm long) Wobble prototype exists of two robust parts that encapsulate the electronics required for functioning. These parts are connected by a geared axis. Weight is strategically added to ensure Wobble rotates around its (blue) tip. A LightBlue Bean microcontroller [16] enables Wobble to function independently. The rotation of Wobble is realized using a small, silent stepper motor. The home-context is less often explored in relation to prospective memory cue retrieval than other contexts. We believe Wobble's reminders are suitable for many actions or intentions people want to be reminded of in the home-context. Firstly because the multi-modal reminders allow users to be reminded while other sources of information are more dominant. Also Wobble can be relocated, allowing users to set reminders in various parts of the house.

USER STUDY

To gain insights in the use of Wobble as an external memory aid and the related experience in the home context, a user study was to conducted. Since the home is a dynamic context, that differs from person to person both in physical setup and in present routines, we believe the experience of Wobble can only be evaluated when deployed in the real context of use. We therefore decided to conduct an 8-day field study in the participants' own home environment.

In a one-on-one meeting, the study was explained to the participants. Wobble and a diary booklet were handed out and demonstrated. Wobble's functionality was explained as an open-ended memory aid, designed to support remembering future intentions. After demonstrating the Wobble prototype was handed over to the participant for a period of 8 days. During this period the participant was free to interact with Wobble in whatever way they thought would suit the purpose of a memory aid.

3 participants were selected to evaluate Wobble. Participant A was a 33-year-old woman, who lived with her 5 and 6-year-old sons. Participant B was a 32-year-old man, who lived together with his girlfriend and owned a cat. The third participant (Participant C) was a 25-year-old man, who lived together with his fiancée. All three participants had a full-time job for which they left the house during weekdays. We handed out a diary booklet that explained Wobble's functionality and contained a section in which the participant was asked how Wobble was set and how its reminders were perceived. Participants were asked to answer these questions one day after they had used Wobble, to minimise the influence the act of filling in the questions had on the study. If the participants did not use Wobble during one day of the study, they were asked to leave the fields related to that day empty. The user evaluation concluded with a semi-structured interview to gain in depth insights on the experience of using Wobble. The interview contained questions such as "How did you use Wobble and on what time interval did you set it?". Additionally, we asked why Wobble was used the way it was used, and how Wobble's reminder was experienced in comparison to those of other memory aids. The diary booklets were used as base for the semi-structured interviews, to help participants to recall the intentions cued with Wobble.

Figure 3. Wobble during the user study.

FINDINGS

The data gained through the interviews was analysed using 'affinity diagramming' [9]. The answers to the interview questions were transcribed and clustered to find common themes within the data. The following clusters were found:

Usage of Wobble and examples of cued future intentions

In the 8-day period Participant A used Wobble 5 times, Participant B and C used Wobble 7 times. None of the participants used Wobble more than once per day. Content-wise the future intentions cued with Wobble in this study were low in complexity. The participants used Wobble to remind themselves to execute relatively simple activities such as 'administer anti-biotics to the cat'. Participants did not use Wobble to remind themselves of intentions that involve multiple consecutive activities (e.g., making a holiday planning). All participants stated they used different memory aids to be reminded of these more complex intentions during the study. Participants B and C stated that in some cases Wobble helped to remind them to execute activities which they "probably would have forgotten otherwise". Participant B stated Wobble worked especially well for intentions related to activities out of his daily routine, that were not strictly linked to a specific point in time and did not rely on a narrow time window to be executed. These time-based intentions were allocated a few hours in which they needed to be executed.

Experience of Wobble's reminders

Participant B and C indicated to experience Wobble as a valuable addition to the existing set of memory aids and indicated to appreciate the subtlety of Wobble's reminders. Participant B for example stated that the subtle reminders "allow Wobble to get the user's attention without being pushy". However, in some cases, participants also stated that the reminders "could be more dominant" to make them easier to notice.Participant B and C explicitly stated they appreciated that Wobble's reminders would become active not only once but multiple times. According to them, this allowed for "snoozing" when not able or motivated to put an intention into practice. In that case Wobble's reminders could be ignored, without being afraid to forget to put the intention into practice afterwards. Participant B for example indicated that he 'snoozed' (ignored) Wobble while playing a video game, counting on it to become active again later.

Prompt to action

For Participant A Wobble's reminders were insufficient to recall the cued intentions. Participants B and C indicated to have no problems recalling their cued intentions, but that they would see value in increasing the amount of information that can be stored in Wobble to "make Wobble suitable for cueing more complicated intentions."

Location of use

We learned that Wobble was mainly used in the living room or kitchen. It was usually placed on large surfaces such as the kitchen table (see Figure 3), cupboard or the floor, where it could freely rotate without risking a situation in which people would step on it. Participants B and C placed Wobble on the terrace floor when sitting outside multiple times. Participant A stated that Wobble did not work for her because she is "always on the run". She indicated that she usually writes down the things she needs to do on post-it notes, which are stuck to the kitchen door.

DISCUSSION

The goal of the study was to evaluate the use and experience of Wobble as an open-ended prospective memory aid. In this section we discuss the implications of the study's findings. Participants indicated that they had failed to notice some reminders they were 'supposed' to perceive; they were near Wobble when it was active, but did not notice the reminder. This for example happened when the participant was engaged in other activities.

We also found cases in which Wobble's reminders *were* perceived while a participant was for example playing a video game. The fact that in both cases the reminders did not result in a negative experience or frustration might be an indicator of Wobble's ability to provide reminders subtle enough to be ignored when irrelevant or when the participant is occupied.

We found that the intentions for which the participants used Wobble's were often not linked to a specific point in time at which the intention needed to be executed.

We find it interesting to see how the irrelevant reminders resulted in participants ignoring reminders, knowing the reminder would return later in time. The idea of users choosing to (for the moment) ignore a reminder created an interaction that current reminding applications do not facilitate. The moment a participant 'snoozes' Wobble he can estimate how his ability or motivation to perform the to-be-executed activity relate to each other in a future scenario. Wobble currently does not allow for indicating the purpose of a reminder through writing. For Participant A contextual information alone was insufficient to recall cued intentions. For Participants B and C this information was sufficient, but still only relatively uncomplicated intentions were cued. Therefore we think Wobble might benefit from a link to systems (e.g., existing mobile phone applications or online calendars) to allow users to digitally insert more information on the cued intention. This additional information could make it easier to recall the cued intention while maintaining the tangible user interface. This could also help to present the reminders for these systems less alarming than their current reminders. In our user study Wobble was mainly used in the living room or kitchen, placed on large surfaces. This might have to do with Wobble's dimensions, which make it unsuitable to place on smaller surfaces such as the windowsill. However, the fact that the participants allocated Wobble to the kitchen and living room (and sometimes outside to the terrace) indicate that Wobble's portability is used as a means to determine (anticipated) relevance.

Since Wobble's tangibility seemed successful, even with its current dimensions, a future direction in this research should use a smaller prototype, to further enhance this ability. During the user study we found that the 'interim-reminders' did remind the user of the to-be executed intention, but often did not prompt the participants to action. Such 'snoozing' might sound as procrastination rather than a prompt to action. However, being able to ignore the reminder allowed participants to find a future moment in which they expects to be both motivated and able to perform an activity too. Participants B and C considered Wobble a valuable addition to the existing set of memory aids, since Wobble reminded them of their future intentions without being pushy. Therefore Wobble does not replace the post-it notes or mobile phone applications, but could be used as an addition to these existing memory aids by providing reminders that do not ask attention obtrusively. This means Wobble can also be beneficial in cases where participants are unable to perceive the reminder, or if they are interrupted while executing the activity.

CONCLUSION

The aim of the work presented in this paper was to explore tangible interaction to support people's prospective memory in the periphery of attention. Following a research-through-design process we designed a memory aid called 'Wobble', an artefact that offers peripheral reminding, and evaluated it with three participants in the home context. In particular, we explored how timing and location supported reminding. We hypothesized that peripheral reminders, perceived when being open to perform the intention the reminder was set for, and easily ignored when engaged in other activities, improve the likelihood of an intention being carried out and decrease the times people get disturbed (and frustrated by) reminders.

The results of our study indicate that the series of multiple subtle reminders presented by Wobble seemed to support participants to execute activities which they stated they 'would probably have forgotten otherwise'. Wobble was used mainly to cue intentions related to relatively uncomplicated intentions that did not rely on a specific time window to be executed. This work contributes to the field of prospective memory aids with reminding applications by exploring how peripheral interaction can be applied in the domain of reminding applications in the home context.

ACKNOWLEDGEMENTS

This research was supported by STW VIDI grant number 016.128.303 of the Netherlands Organization for Scientific Research (NWO), awarded to Elise van den Hoven. We thank the participants who took part in the user study.

REFERENCES

1. Any.do Inc, Any.do, 2016. www.any.do/
2. Bakker, Saskia, Elise van den Hoven, and Berry Eggen. "Peripheral interaction: characteristics and considerations." *Personal and Ubiquitous Computing* 19.1 (2015): 239-254.
3. Einstein, Gilles O., and Mark A. McDaniel. "Normal aging and prospective memory." *Journal of Experimental Psychology: Learning, Memory, and Cognition* 16.4 (1990): 717.
4. Fogg, Brian J. "A behavior model for persuasive design." *Proceedings of the 4th international Conference on Persuasive Technology*. ACM, 2009.
5. Frayling, Christopher. "Research in art and design." (1993).
6. Gaver, William W. "What in the world do we hear?: An ecological approach to auditory event perception." *Ecological psychology* 5.1 (1993): 1-29.
7. Google Inc, Google Now, 2016. www.google.com/intl/nl/landing/now/
8. Hanington, Bruce, and Bella Martin. *Universal methods of design: 100 ways to research complex problems, develop innovative ideas, and design effective solutions.* Rockport Publishers, 2012.
9. Ishii, Hiroshi, and Brygg Ullmer. "Tangible bits: towards seamless interfaces between people, bits and atoms." *Proceedings of the ACM SIGCHI Conference on Human factors in computing systems.* ACM, 1997.
10. Laschke, Matthias, et al. "Overcoming procrastination with ReMind." *Proceedings of the 6th International Conference on Designing Pleasurable Products and Interfaces.* ACM, 2013.
11. Mankoff, Jennifer, et al. "Heuristic evaluation of ambient displays." *Proceedings of the SIGCHI conference on Human factors in computing systems.* ACM, 2003.
12. Matthews, Tara, et al. "A toolkit for managing user attention in peripheral displays." *Proceedings of the 17th annual ACM symposium on User interface software and technology.* ACM, 2004.
13. McDaniel, Mark A., and Gilles O. Einstein. "Strategic and automatic processes in prospective memory retrieval: A multiprocess framework." *Applied cognitive psychology* 14.7 (2000): S127-S144.
14. Normak, Henri 2011, Cues. Retrieved August 20 2016 from http://thenextweb.com/apps/2011/09/19/want-location-based-reminders-on-your-iphone-try-cues/#gref/
15. Probst, Kathrin, et al. "Move-it: interactive sticky notes actuated by shape memory alloys." *CHI'11 Extended Abstracts on Human Factors in Computing Systems.* ACM, 2011.
16. PunchThrough, LightBlue Bean, 2016. www.punchthrough.com/bean/
17. Sohn, Timothy, et al. "Place-its: A study of location-based reminders on mobile phones." *International Conference on Ubiquitous Computing.* Springer Berlin Heidelberg, 2005.
18. Weiser, Mark, and John Seely Brown. "The coming age of calm technology." *Beyond calculation.* Springer New York, 1997. 75-85.
19. Wunderlist Inc, Wunderlist 2016, www.wunderlist.com/
20. Zimmerman, John, Erik Stolterman, and Jodi Forlizzi. "An analysis and critique of Research through Design: towards a formalization of a research approach." *Proceedings of the 8th ACM Conference on Designing Interactive Systems.* ACM, 2010.

Window-Shaping: 3D Design Ideation by Creating on, Borrowing from, and Looking at the Physical World

Ke Huo, Vinayak, Karthik Ramani *
School of Mechanical Engineering, Purdue University
West Lafayette, IN 47907, USA
{khuo, vinayak, ramani}@purdue.edu

ABSTRACT
We present, *Window-Shaping*, a tangible mixed-reality (MR) interaction metaphor for design ideation that allows for the direct creation of 3D shapes on and around physical objects. Using the *sketch-and-inflate* scheme, our metaphor enables quick design of dimensionally consistent and visually coherent 3D models by borrowing visual and dimensional attributes from existing physical objects without the need for 3D reconstruction or fiducial markers. Through a preliminary evaluation of our prototype application we demonstrate the expressiveness provided by our design workflow, the effectiveness of our interaction scheme, and the potential of our metaphor.

ACM Classification Keywords
H.5.1 Information Interfaces and Presentation: Multimedia Information Systems; H.5.2 Information Interfaces and Presentation: User Interfaces; I.3.7 Computer Graphics: Three-Dimensional Graphics and Realism

Author Keywords
Design ideation; Sketch-based 3D modeling; Mixed reality; Augmented reality

INTRODUCTION
The physical environment often serves as a means for inspiring, contextualizing, and guiding the designer's thought process for expressing creative ideas. In early design processes, physical objects are frequently used as references to explore the space of novel designs [31, 35, 10]. Recent works [30, 36, 40] have shown that *through-the-screen* Augmented Reality (AR) and Mixed Reality (MR) can play a vital role in bridging the gap between the physical and digital worlds for creative expression of ideas. However, most of these approaches use the physical environment mainly as a dormant container of digital artifacts rather than as a source of inspiration for facilitating quick digital prototyping for design ideation. The key potential value that AR/MR systems brings to design, is the integration of *reflection-in-action* [31] (creating on the physical world), *design inspiration* [11] (borrowing from the physical world) and *reflection-on action* [12] (looking at the physical world). In this paper, we explore this value through re-purposing the physical environment as a reference, context, and source of inspiration for quick idea generation in early design.

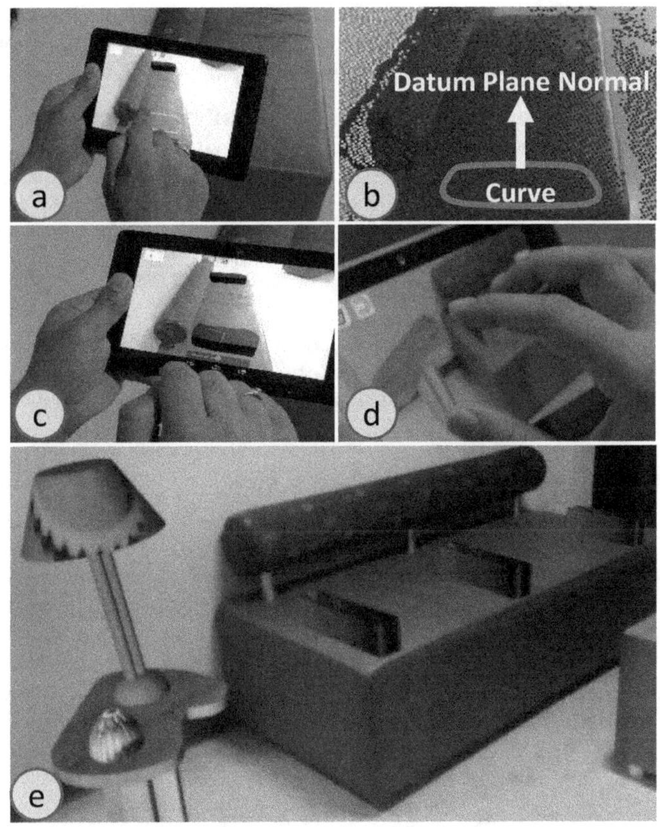

Figure 1. Users simply draw a curve on the screen (a), that is mapped to a 3D planar curve using the point cloud (b). The 3D curve is inflated into a 3D model (c). Users manipulate the shapes through a multi-touch interaction scheme (d). *Window-Shaping* enables quick creation of virtual artifacts for augmenting the physical environment by borrowing dimensional and textural attributes from objects (e).

We present *Window-Shaping*, an approach that integrates sketch- and image-based [21, 24] 3D modeling approaches within a mixed-reality interface to develop a new design workflow (Figure 1). Using the Google Tango device, *Window-Shaping* leverages the RGB-XYZ (i.e. image and point-cloud)

*School of Electrical and Computer Engineering (by courtesy)

TEI '17, March 20-23, 2017, Yokohama, Japan

DOI: http://dx.doi.org/10.1145/3024969.3024995

representation of a scene allowing users to create planar curves on physical surfaces and *inflate* them into 3D shapes. Using *Window-Shaping* we demonstrate design scenarios including the use of everyday objects and low-fidelity mock-ups as design references, and exploration of novel designs by combining physical references from multiple sources. *Window-Shaping* both complements and extends existing approaches [36, 18, 38] through presenting a new interaction metaphor wherein a new virtual 3D object is created as an extension of its physical context without the need for reconstructing the 3D model of the physical scene. We make two contributions:

Tangible In-Situ Design Workflow: We offer a novel combination of an existing modeling scheme with synchronized RGB-XYZ information to enable creative design exploration with the physical environment in context.

Dimensionally consistent and visually coherent design: We offer the capability of creating and visualizing 3D shapes directly on the surface of any object with the desired dimensions and locations. Further, by mapping the background texture of the users' sketch inputs, we allow users to re-purpose existing textures in new creations.

RELATED WORKS

Our main focus in this work is on a novice-friendly interaction metaphor allowing design directly in 3D for *early stage design ideation.* We discuss the relevant works selectively.

Design in Context

Most of the existing approaches for digital design focus on modeling from scratch rather that on allowing novice users to draw inspiration from existing physical artifacts - a frequent activity in creative idea generation. Importantly, we use the physical environment as a dimensional and visual reference. Although many works infer the design context in various forms, such as static images [19, 39, 4], registered bundle photographs [25], and 3D models [33, 36, 5, 8], they do not allow for modeling directly in 3D space. *Window-Shaping* focuses on creation of new geometry in an augmented 3D scene through a hand-held interface. Our approach uses RGB-XYZ representation of the physical environment.

Content Creation with AR

Virtual content creation using an AR-based system has also been explored. Previous works integrated instrumented tangible tools for operations such as modifying virtual models [1]. Nuernberger et al. [22] interpreted 2D drawing annotations using cues from 2D images and 3D geometry. *SnapToReality* [23] took a step further by extracting 3D edge and planar surface constraints from the environment and using them for precise alignment. Lau et al. [18] attached fiducial markers onto physical primitives and stamped the corresponding virtual shapes together to create shapes. Leveraging the merging mobile AR techniques, Xin et al. [38] presented *Napkin Sketch* as a system for creating 3D wire-sculptures on a napkin. Recently, *MixFab* [36] integrated scanned 3D model towards design using mid-air gestures in MR environments. While we draw inspirations from these approaches, our aim is to allow users to design directly on physical objects without being constrained by set-ups or being limited by the mobility.

Geometric Design with Hand-Held Devices

Previous explorations on 3D sketching using hand-held devices tended to separate the input devices from the display [28, 7]. Following a similar approach, Vinayak et al. [34] and Piya et al. [26] demonstrated systems that utilized smartphones as multi-touch controllers. Further, past works approached an immersive design environment by incorporating projection-based [15] or see-through head mounted displays [29]. Other works such as *(T)ether* [17] leveraged both touch inputs and mid-air gestures for modeling using a tracking infrastructure in conjunction with instrumented wearables and a tablet. *Paper3D* drew inspiration from papercraft and used multi-touch gestures for casual 3D modeling. In these works, the 3D shapes were created in either an empty physical space or in a virtual environment thus neither the dimensionality nor the visual appearance might pertain to their designated environment. While *Napkin Sketch* and *Second Surface* [14] started to merge the mobile AR technique, the physical reference in their works was limited to smaller working volumes and their outcomes were 3D wire or drawings. We concentrate on enabling the creation and editing of 3D models on arbitrary physical surfaces using a simple multi-touch interaction scheme.

WINDOW-SHAPING

The *Window-Shaping* interface comprises a hand-held Google Tango device, that serves as a local interface between the physical environment and the user. The simultaneous localization and mapping (SLAM) algorithm available with the Tango API allows for the acquisition of a point-cloud of the scene with respect to the global coordinate system. The resulting RGB-XYZ data allows users to implicitly define planes on any physical surface by simply drawing on the physical scene. Any touch input on the device screen can be *unprojected* on the physical environment to obtain a 3D point along with its normal in the global (world) coordinate system (Figure 1). This essentially helps users define a plane at any recognized point on a physical surface. Below, we describe the design goals, modeling metaphor, and user interactions.

Design Choices

We build towards the broad theme of "*effortless integration of physical objects into the design process*" [37]. The primary objective of our work is to support quick design ideation by allowing users to (a) quickly create 3D geometry in reference to physical artifacts, (b) borrow shape and appearance from physical artifacts to re-purpose them for design exploration, and (c) inspect the virtual artifacts in the physical context from different views in order to make design modifications. Our interface design choices are described below.

Appropriate Use of Interaction Modality:

The use of Google Tango tablet allows for both spatial (3D) and multi-touch (2D) interactions. While touch-based interactions allow for precise control and 2D sketching operations, spatial mobility allows for *reflection-on-action* by enabling users to inspect their creations from multiple views with respect to the physical environment. Thus, we use well-established multi-touch interactions for enabling content creation, editing, and rigid transformations. For inspection, we

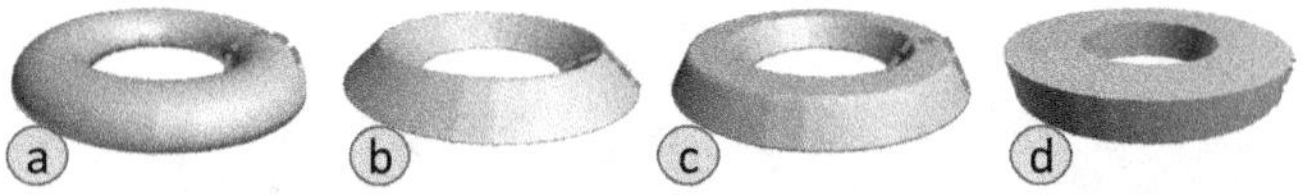

Figure 2. Geometric primitives with different inflation functions in *Window-Shaping* include: a. Circular, b. Conical, c. Tapered, and d. Linear.

make use of the natural spatial movement. With the augmentation from the see-through video and captured RGB-XYZ information, the traditional 2D interactions go beyond planes, and are enhanced with a third dimension. Further, this three dimensional extension of touch interactions provides a tangible and immersive experience for the design ideation.

Consistent dimension and appearance:
The appearance of designers' creations is an important factor in reflecting their intent. Our metaphor enables users to both use physical objects as contextual references as well as re-purpose them at different physical locations. Further, our approach allows copying the texture of physical references for a consistent rendering of the newly created 3D shapes. Further, the editing operations are designed such that the changes maintain the consistency of visual appearance.

Geometric Modeling Scheme:
We aim for flexibility in terms of the expressive power of the modeling scheme while retaining the simple interactions for shape creation. Multi-touch inputs naturally allow for 2D curve input. Thus, we employ a *sketch-and-inflate* modeling scheme in *Window-Shaping*. First, a user sketches the silhouette (and holes) of the shape with which a closed mesh is generated. Then we inflate the mesh using a distance transform function [24] to obtain an inflated 3D shape. We provide users with four inflation functions (primitives) for expressive shape creation(Figure 2). The main advantages of this approach are that it: (a) has been demonstrated to be particularly simple for novice users [13], (b) allows for creation of complex topological structures with a simple set of interactions, and (c) has a simple and natural 2D parametrization that allows for texture mapping.

User Interactions

Shape Creation and Editing

Projective Sketching: *Window-Shaping* allows for direct one finger drawing on the tablet screen. Once finalized, the sketched curve is mapped on the physical scene and is converted and rendered in the scene as a 3D inflated mesh (Figure 3(a, b)). The first curve drawn by the user is by default the boundary curve. Multiple *hole* curves can then be drawn inside the boundary.

Placing Curve Templates: As an alternative to direct drawing, we also provide a set of curve templates (Figure 3(c,d)). Users can simply place the selected curve on any surface of a physical or virtual object using a single-tap gesture. The curve is placed on a fitted 3D plane around the single-tapped location. The curve template feature allows for quick exploration of complex ideas with minimal interaction effort.

Capturing Outlines: *Window-Shaping* also allows users to extract the outline of the object from the scene in *the image space*.

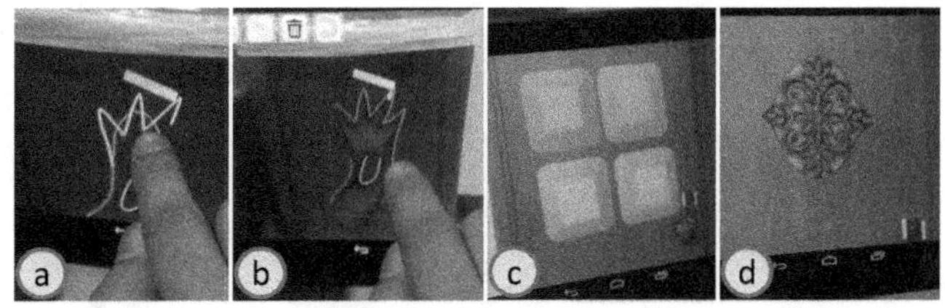

Figure 3. The user sketches boundary and hole curves on a physical object, edits the sketched curves to add local details(b), and obtains an inflated circular shape (b). The user creates a tapered inflated shape with a template, inflates it, patterns it (c), explores complex features(d).

Users draw a region of interest (ROI) which is automatically converted into a contour using the GrabCut algorithm [27]. This enables users to directly employ the visual representation (outline shape and texture) of a physical object and re-purpose it in 3D form in their own designs.

Editing Curves: Using the over-sketching interaction technique [3], we provide simple and quick curve editing (Figure 3(a)), which enables users to add details and improve the appearance. Moving the tablet closer to a desired region allows for precise virtual operations in screen-space. On the other hand, moving away from a physical surface allows for a better overview, which is valuable for coarse operations such as placing shapes and curve templates on desired locations.

Inflating and Deflating: We implement a three-finger gesture for inflating or deflating a 3D mesh. Here, pinching (bringing fingers closer) effects in pulling the shape out of the screen as well as spreading (moving fingers apart) result in pushing the shape into the screen.

Manipulating Shapes

Rotations & Scaling: Two-finger rotate and pinch/spread are used for rotating and scaling the shape respectively. These gestures can be applied either directly to the 3D shape or to the underlying curve of the shape. The two-finger interaction constrains all rigid transformation to the plane of the curve.

Translation: The in-plane translation is performed by dragging a shape using one finger. This allows for precise placement of the shape on the plane defined by its underlying curve. In order to provide consistent dimensional perception, we project the finger movement onto the underlying plane instead of using constant mapping between the pixel space and the physical space.

Placement: Shape placement allows users to directly transfer a selected 3D shape to any point in the scene by using a one-finger tap gesture. Here the 3D shape is both translated to the specified point and re-oriented along the normal at this point. Here users can place a new virtual object on the physical scene as well as on an existing virtual object. This maintains a perceptual depth consistency during interactions.

Auxiliary Operations: In addition to geometric operations, we provide operations such as copying/patterning and deleting a shape. Users can select and make a copy/pattern of the shape by using a single-tap gesture.

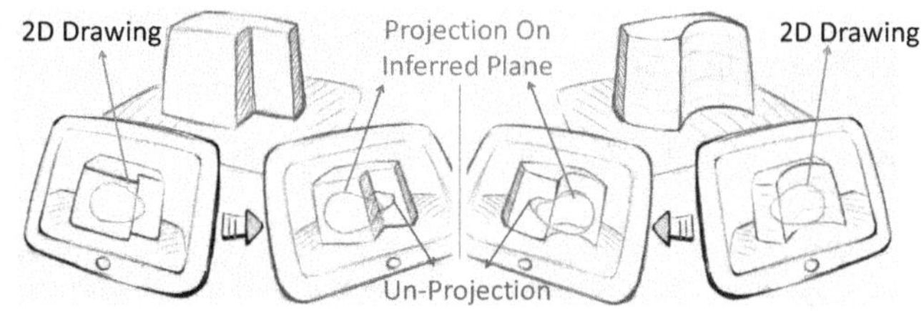

Figure 4. Illustration of plane inference: Un-projection of a 2D drawing results in a discontinuous curve (red) and a projection on the inferred plane(green)

Appearance Control

During the over-sketching operation, we automatically update the texture image to maintain the visual consistency. We also provide the option to explicitly update the texture during rigid transformations. This is helpful to users when they are experimenting with different backgrounds for the same shape.

IMPLEMENTATION

Hardware & Software

Our hardware comprises a Google Tango 7 inch tablet with the NVIDIA Tegra K1 processor and 4GB RAM, running Android 4.4 KitKat OS. The tablet captures the RGB image ($60Hz$) and depth data ($5Hz$) from the built in 4MP color camera and depth sensor respectively. The Tango SDK [9] provides functionality for synchronizing these two cameras, allowing us to compute a point cloud (XYZ) of the scene such that each point is mapped to a unique pixel in the RGB image. We prototyped our metaphor using the Android SDK and the geometric modeling methods in C++ using the Android NDK (JNI) with OpenGL Shading Language for rendering.

2D Curve Processing

We require all curves to be closed, oriented, and preferably smooth while preserving the features. To meet these requirements, we first apply an exponential smoothing filter [32] to each point on the curve as the user is drawing them. We then check the curve for closure based on the distance between the end-points, discarding an open curve as an invalid input. For a closed curve, we perform an equidistant curve re-sampling [16] and orient the boundary curve counter-clockwise (i.e. positive area) with the holes oriented clockwise (negative area).

3D Planar Curve Computation

Given the processed curve on the screen, we first query the 3D points corresponding to each curve-point. For each 3D point we compute its normal by fitting a plane using its neighborhood. Based on the standard deviation of the distances between adjacent points on the 3D curve, we categorize the curve as either continuous or discontinuous. For a continuous curve, we estimate its plane by averaging the position and normals of these points. This, however, results in unpredictable planes for discontinuous curves (Figure 4). In this case, we first divide the curve into segments belonging to the same plane using euclidean distances and normal differences and then select the largest segment to identify the plane.

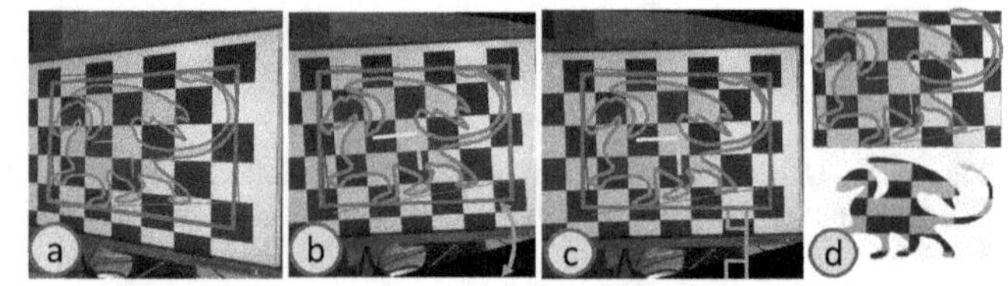

Figure 5. Creating a texture: (a) projecting the bounding rectangle (blue) of the 3D planar curve (red), (b) image skewing, (c) rotation correction, and (d) image cropping.

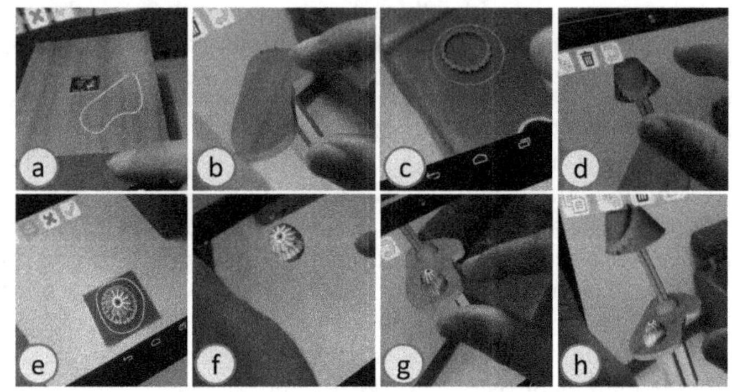

Figure 6. Furniture design: A virtual side-table is created by borrowing the texture from a physical table (a, b). The surrounding objects are then used to explore the lamp design (c, d) and *GrabCut* is applied to capture the outline and texture(e, f) to form a decorative object(g, h)

Mesh Generation

Given the processed boundary and hole curves, the mesh generation is performed in three steps: (a) computing two symmetrically aligned open (*half*) meshes bounded by curves (boundary and holes) through constrained delaunay triangulation (CDT), (b) topologically stitching these two open meshes to create a closed mesh, and (c) inflating the *top half mesh* using the distance transform function [24]. We implement CDT using the poly2tri library [6]. For the round, conical and tapered primitives, we sample the interior region of the curve with a uniform equilateral point configuration and add the sample as Steiner points to obtain a regularly sampled triangulation. Further, this modeling scheme has a simple and natural 2D parametrization which allows for texture mapping.

Texture Computation

We implement texture generation using openCV in four steps (Figure 5). We first compute the bounding rectangle of the 3D planar curve and project the bounding box on the image space. Then, we apply a skew transformation on this image with the constraint that the projected bounding rectangle is axis-aligned with the image. We rotate the skewed image to correct the residual angle between the rectangle and the image. Finally, we crop the image using this projected bounding rectangle to obtain the texture image.

USE CASES

The design work flow and interactions in Window-Shaping, can potentially be adapted to different kinds of design contexts. Below, we identify four such design patterns.

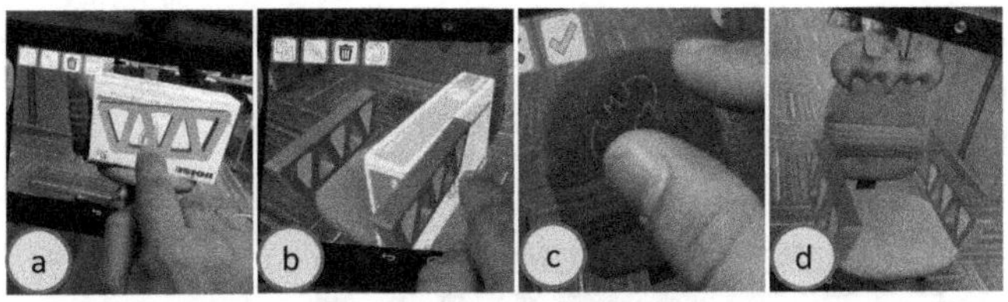

Figure 7. Chair armrest design: A *truss*-like shape is created on a metal shelf and placed as an armrest on the sides of a chair (a). A box is used here to appropriately position and orient the armrest with respect to the seat (b). Using a template (c), the back-rest is re-designed (d)

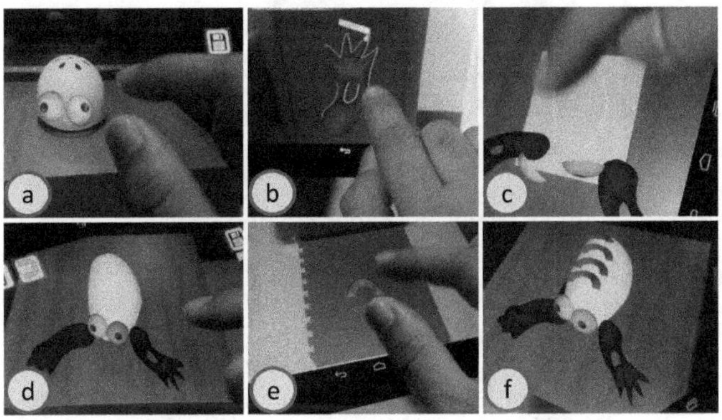

Figure 8. Creature design: The eyes (a), limbs (b), and body (c) are created using a helmet, a trash can, and a piece of white paper as visual references respectively. They are then assembled on a table (d) and the details (the scales of the creature) are created from a mat sheet and patterned on the body (e, f).

Designing on Physical Objects: The most important design capability offered by *Window-Shaping* is creating new geometric features on existing objects. These existing objects can be both physical and virtual objects. For instance, in an interior design scenario, a user could add complementary features to a piece of furniture (Figure 1, Figure 6(a,b)) and also create virtual additions to the scene by adding new assemblies to the surrounding area (Figure 6(g, h)).

Re-purposing Physical Objects: By re-purposing, we mean the use of both the shape and the appearance of a physical object to create a new design feature. The aforementioned GrabCut algorithm allows users to capture outlines of existing objects from the scene for shape creation. The captured outline shape and texture serve as design inspiration for direct use in an existing mixed-reality scene(Figure 6(e, f)).

Physical Objects as Spatial References: In situations where users desire to *fill in a blank space* to augment a physical product, it can be helpful to use a physical object to define a reference plane (Figure 7). Using objects as references enables a tangible and spatially coherent way of designing in context.

Physical Objects as Visual References: The appearance can serve both aesthetic and functional purposes (such as material specification). In *Window-Shaping*, users can experiment with the appearance of a 3D model. Such experiments can be performed either by transferring the virtual shape to a new location and re-texturing or by simply changing the background texture of a sketched curve (Figure 8).

USER TRIALS

We conducted a preliminary evaluation for eliciting user feedback regarding the utility, experience, potential, and limitations of our workflow in creative design activity.

Participants

We recruited 8 (2 female, 6 male) participants (26 – 30 years old) with 5 engineering students and 3 students from non-engineering fields (science, management, etc). Of these, 4 participants had no prior knowledge of AR or MR interfaces, 3 were familiar with the concept of AR/MR, and 1 had used AR interfaces for gaming. Three participants had no prior knowledge of computer-aided design (CAD) or 3D modeling.

Procedure

We conducted user trials (45 – 60 min. per trial) with the *Window-Shaping* prototype application. We first introduced participants to the broader idea behind *Window-Shaping* and demonstrated the user interactions in *Window-Shaping* through practical use-cases (10 min.). Following this, we invited the users to perform four design tasks. We gave the users the option to either use a capacitive stylus or direct finger touch for tablet interactions.

(T1) Designing with physical mock-ups where the participants were given a cubiodal box and were asked to create the face of a creature. **(T2) Re-purposing objects** through which we introduced the grab-cut feature to the participants and asked them to create a 3D new part using *GrabCut* and add it to the face. **(T3) Using an object as a spatial reference** the participants were asked to design the handle of a chair using a cubiodal for placing the handle on the sides of the chair. **(T4) Using objects as visual references**, the users added details to the back rest and seat and explored the texture of the handles.

The participants were allowed to move around in the surrounding environment, create their feature on an arbitrary object and then transfer the feature back on the design. While we guided the participants through the interactions, we encouraged them to define their own strategy for completing the design tasks. At the end of the tasks, they were asked, through answering a questionaire, about their experience in using the interface (Figure9(a, b, c)). We also asked them to explain their reasons along with the Likert scales. Moreover, we asked three open-ended questions regarding the usability, potential use scenarios, and desirable capabilities.

Findings

Although we constrained the design tasks, we found that the resulting creations (Figure 9(d)) had reasonable diversity across users. Most of the users were able to quickly understand the modeling mechanism and successfully perform the trial tasks within the given time. Below, we discuss the main insights we gained from our observation and the feedback from the users.

Validation of Interactions

All participants responded favorably to the ease of use offered by direct drawing and creating fine details and a majority preferred drawing more than using available curve templates (Figure 9(a)). Interestingly, there was a distinction between the engineering and non-engineering students in terms of the

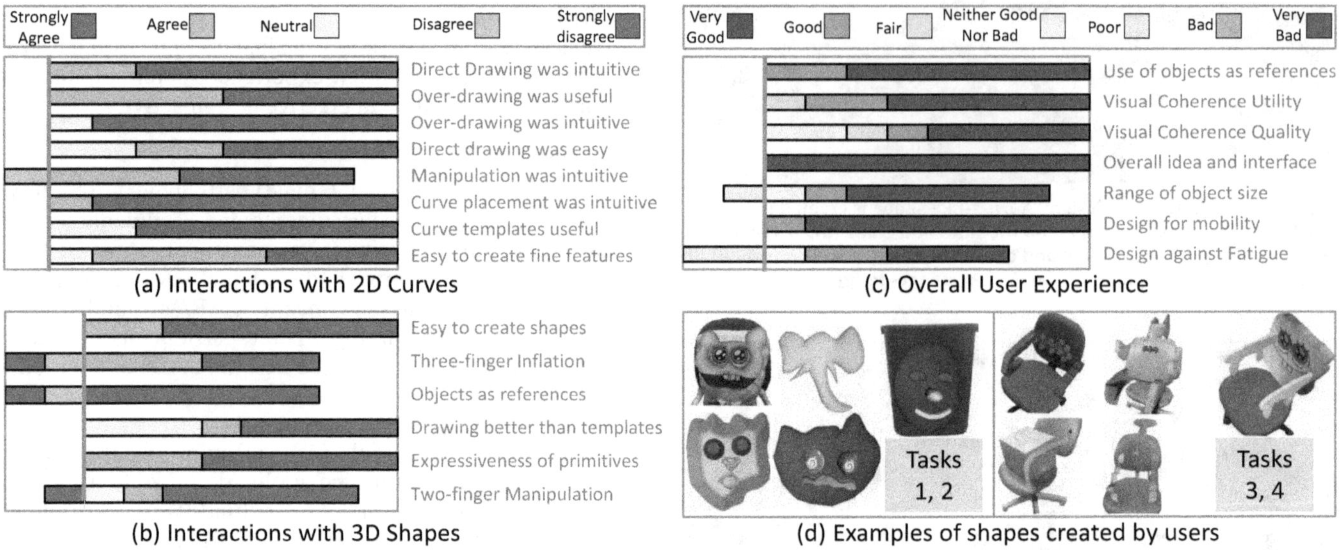

Figure 9. User feedback on interactions (a, b) and overall experience (c), and designs generated in trial tasks (d).

curve creation. Engineering students expressed a need for interactions such as mirroring, symmetric curve creation and editing. A user suggested: "*to enter some numeric values of the extrusion lengths*". In contrast, one non-engineering user commented on the curve templates provided: "*I did not use these features. It was intuitive to create something by myself*".

Most users found the interactions for placing (one finger tap) and manipulating (two finger rotate-scale) the curves and shapes to be intuitive. A user noted: "*Very similar to existing gestures on smartphones and tablets, so very intuitive*". Regarding shape inflation, while 6 out of 8 users agreed on the intuitiveness of the 3-finger gesture, 2 users expressed negative response to it. According to one user, "*It was intuitive, but the direction could be inverted*". This was contrary to our assumption in which pinching increased the inflation and spreading decreased the inflation magnitude similar to in the physical action of deforming clay.

Mobility & Fatigue

One of the most important aspects enjoyed by all users was the capability to move around in physical space during the design process. This mobility offered the flexibility for users to borrow geometric and visual features from various locations (user comment: "*this help(s) you also to create shapes everywhere at any time*"). During the trial tasks, we observed that the users walked frequently within our constrained space to look for existing objects as references, to perform spatial inspection from different angles, and to design new shapes on reference planes. Further, some of the users naturally moved the device close to the object while creating detailed features on the curves. One user said: "*Bringing it [the tablet] closer did help a lot.*" This strongly suggests a positive outcome of our approach towards enhancing design ideation by increasing the reflection in and on the action.

While we expected this outcome, we were also interested in knowing how this mobility in our interface affected user fatigue. Six users agreed that using our system did not cause physical stress or fatigue that could adversely affect the design task itself. We believe this to be a result of the balance between the size ($119.77 \times 196.33 \times 15.36$ *mm*) and the weight (0.82 *lbs*) of the Tango tablet [9]. However, we did notice that our system caused fatigue specifically in the process of adding details to the curves for some users. A female user mentioned: "*While getting precise details for a long time it may cause the arm to be a bit tired.*". Last, although we offered the users two choices between using a stylus and their fingers for touch inputs, we got no particular comments on this through the survey.

Design Workflow

Users responded favorably in terms of the expressiveness, engagement, and enjoyment provided by *Window-Shaping*. In particular, the user feedback strongly validated our primary goal – quick design ideation through dimensionally consistent and visually coherent shape modeling. In the given design contexts, all users except one agreed that our geometric primitives were expressive and allowed for sufficient scope for creative exploration. As expected, users generally favored the fact that our system allows capturing the background textures and can be used in real time. A user reported "*[without using our system] it will be difficult specially for getting textures or for placing the features on the desired position.*" Also, users tended to inspect the dimensionality of the creations from different perspectives. One user stated: "*The scale of the object with respect to the surroundings could be easily found.*"

Utility & Potential

Users confirmed *Window-Shaping's* utility as a quick ideation tool both for individuals and design teams. As one user said: "*The tool is definitely very useful for tinkering and showing new ideas to others.*" In particular, users with prior CAD experience appreciated the value of designing with a real scene in context. One user commented: "*You can visualize the components in the real world much more clearly than any CAD software.*" Another user pointed to the potential for collaborative design: *"I can see this being very useful in design collaboration where several people work on it at the same time. Very useful in modifying existing products and brainstorming what features to add.*". Participants also proposed some novel applications such as *"It's useful for topography when we need to study the landforms of some region*" and "*design your garden before planting*".

Discussions & Limitations

User Interaction: Drawing while holding the device resulted in a lack of precise control. The participants found the curve editing to be more challenging in comparison with tasks such as placement. This primarily affected the addition of curve details. We believe this can be addressed through filtering out hand jitters by using the device IMU data and the camera image. Long term usage of the device may cause potential fatigue. Nonetheless, depth sensing technologies are emerging with more light-weight mobiles, such as *Lenovo Phab 2 Pro* [20]. Further, the texture capturing could be better implemented by allowing users to control the object segmentation. While users liked the idea of using physical objects as references, they pointed out a need for a mechanism to explicitly define a reference plane. This issue can be easily addressed by introducing *virtual plane* and *3D widget* elements into our interface. While previous work has shown better drawing accuracy for styli in comparison to fingers [2], it will be worthwhile to conduct more controlled experiments with a mobile system such as ours in terms of accuracy, fatigue, and stimulation.

Advanced AR Environment: While the robustness of the tracking provided by the Tango was impressive, our current implementation did not allow for object awareness. This resulted in shifting of the users' creations due to the frequent device movement. Introducing object tracking will reduce the tracking artifact when dealing with featureless scenes. Even though our interface offers mobility in a large indoor environment, it is currently difficult to create or borrow geometric and textural features from smaller objects. At this stage, the point cloud quality is limited by the low accuracy of the depth camera. Another issue in our current implementation is occlusion management with real objects. To address this issue, usually a fine model of the object and a high resolution of the depth data are required. With constant hardware improvements to the depth camera and mobile computational power in the future, we believe this issue will be easier to resolve.

Modeling Scheme: We restricted our implementation to the use of planar curves for inflating shapes. Although the current modeling scheme allows for reasonable expressive capabilities, there is a need to investigate the usage of 3D curves as well as different shape representations such as swept primitives, skeleton-based models, and volumetric representations. Towards a more complete and refined application, additional standard operations such as undo and redo will certainly enhance the modeling work-flow. Further, improvements in point-cloud acquisition will also allow us to extract and use manifold constraints (e.g. corners, edges, curvature) from the environment. The assembly mating relationships and kinematic constraints could then be leveraged for designing functional objects.

CONCLUSIONS

Window-Shaping reveals an untapped design space that emerges from the combination of multi-touch interactions, sketch-based geometric design, and mixed-reality interface towards bridging the gap between physical and digital space in early phase design exploration. Given the users' positive reactions, we believe that the proposed concept has potential towards a richer space of MR-based design work-flows for advanced in-situ modeling, collaborative idea generation, and fabrication-aware design. Although through the preliminary evaluations, we obtain overall positive feedback on the interface, the limitations of the current implementation need to be addressed before *Window-Shaping* reaches its broader potential. Based on the findings from our preliminary evaluations, we plan to improve the interaction metaphors against the jitter, accuracy and fatigue issues, and adding advanced geometric features into the existing modeling approach. Further, we plan to study how experience, performance, and creative outcomes will change with respect to different user groups such as artists, engineering designers, and young participants. Finally, it will be worthwhile to find how the interactions behind *Window-Shaping* could be extended to applications in domains such as architecture, education, animation, and engineering design and analysis.

ACKNOWLEDGMENTS

We thank the reviewers for their valuable feedback and comments. This work was supported partially by the NSF Awards No. 1538868 (CMMI) and 1632154 (PFI). Any opinions, findings, and conclusions or recommendations expressed in this material are those of the author(s) and do not necessarily reflect the views of the National Science Foundation.

REFERENCES

1. Ryan Arisandi, Mai Otsuki, Asako Kimura, Fumihisa Shibata, and Hideyuki Tamura. 2014. Virtual Handcrafting: Building virtual wood models using ToolDevice. *Proc. IEEE* 102, 2 (2014), 185–195.

2. Sriram Karthik Badam, Senthil Chandrasegaran, Niklas Elmqvist, and Karthik Ramani. 2014. Tracing and sketching performance using blunt-tipped styli on direct-touch tablets. In *Proceedings of the 2014 International Working Conference on Advanced Visual Interfaces*. ACM, 193–200.

3. Thomas Baudel. 1994. A mark-based interaction paradigm for free-hand drawing. In *Proc. of UIST*. ACM, 185–192.

4. Tao Chen, Zhe Zhu, Ariel Shamir, Shi-Min Hu, and Daniel Cohen-Or. 2013. 3Sweep: Extracting Editable Objects from a Single Photo. *ACM Transactions on Graphics (TOG) - Proceedings of ACM SIGGRAPH Asia 2013* 32, 6 (Nov. 2013), 195:1–195:10.

5. Xiaowu Chen, Bin Zhou, Feixiang Lu, Lin Wang, Lang Bi, and Ping Tan. 2015. Garment modeling with a depth camera. *ACM Transactions on Graphics (TOG)* 34, 6 (2015), 203.

6. Vid Domiter and Borut Žalik. 2008. Sweep-line algorithm for constrained Delaunay triangulation. *International Journal of Geographical Information Science* 22, 4 (2008), 449–462.
7. Michele Fiorentino, Raffaele de Amicis, Giuseppe Monno, and Andre Stork. 2002. Spacedesign: A mixed reality workspace for aesthetic industrial design. In *Proceedings of the 1st International Symposium on Mixed and Augmented Reality*. IEEE Computer Society, 86.
8. Madeline Gannon, Tovi Grossman, and George Fitzmaurice. 2015. Tactum: A Skin-Centric Approach to Digital Design and Fabrication. In *Proceedings of the 33rd Annual ACM Conference on Human Factors in Computing Systems*. ACM, 1779–1788.
9. Google. 2016. Tango Developer Overview. (Jan 2016). `https://developers.google.com/tango/developer-overview`
10. Nicolai Brodersen Hansen and Peter Dalsgaard. 2012. The productive role of material design artefacts in participatory design events. In *Proceedings of the 7th Nordic Conference on Human-Computer Interaction: Making Sense Through Design*. ACM, 665–674.
11. Scarlett R. Herring, Chia-Chen Chang, Jesse Krantzler, and Brian P. Bailey. 2009. Getting Inspired!: Understanding How and Why Examples Are Used in Creative Design Practice. In *Proceedings of the SIGCHI Conference on Human Factors in Computing Systems (CHI '09)*. ACM, New York, NY, USA, 87–96.
12. Caroline Hummels and Joep Frens. 2009. The reflective transformative design process. In *CHI'09 Extended Abstracts on Human Factors in Computing Systems*. ACM, 2655–2658.
13. Takeo Igarashi, Satoshi Matsuoka, and Hidehiko Tanaka. 2007. Teddy: a sketching interface for 3D freeform design. In *Acm siggraph 2007 courses*. ACM, 21.
14. Shunichi Kasahara, Valentin Heun, Austin S Lee, and Hiroshi Ishii. 2012. Second surface: multi-user spatial collaboration system based on augmented reality. In *SIGGRAPH Asia 2012 Emerging Technologies*. ACM, 20.
15. Daniel F Keefe, Daniel Acevedo Feliz, Tomer Moscovich, David H Laidlaw, and Joseph J LaViola Jr. 2001. CavePainting: a fully immersive 3D artistic medium and interactive experience. In *Proceedings of the 2001 symposium on Interactive 3D graphics*. ACM, 85–93.
16. Per-Ola Kristensson and Shumin Zhai. 2004. SHARK^2: A Large Vocabulary Shorthand Writing System for Pen-based Computers. In *Proceedings of the 17th Annual ACM Symposium on User Interface Software and Technology (UIST '04)*. ACM, New York, NY, USA, 43–52.
17. David Lakatos, Matthew Blackshaw, Alex Olwal, Zachary Barryte, Ken Perlin, and Hiroshi Ishii. 2014. T(Ether): Spatially-aware Handhelds, Gestures and Proprioception for Multi-user 3D Modeling and Animation. In *Proceedings of the 2nd ACM Symposium on Spatial User Interaction (SUI '14)*. ACM, New York, NY, USA, 90–93.
18. Manfred Lau, Masaki Hirose, Akira Ohgawara, Jun Mitani, and Takeo Igarashi. 2012. Situated Modeling: A Shape-stamping Interface with Tangible Primitives. In *ACM Conference on Tangible, Embedded and Embodied Interaction (TEI '12)*. 275–282.
19. Manfred Lau, Greg Saul, Jun Mitani, and Takeo Igarashi. 2010. Modeling-in-context: User Design of Complementary Objects with a Single Photo. In *Proceedings of the Seventh Sketch-Based Interfaces and Modeling Symposium (SBIM '10)*. Eurographics Association, 17–24.
20. Lenovo. 2016. Phab 2 Pro. (Jan 2016). `http://shop.lenovo.com/us/en/tango/`
21. Andrew Nealen, Takeo Igarashi, Olga Sorkine, and Marc Alexa. 2007. FiberMesh: Designing Freeform Surfaces with 3D Curves. In *ACM SIGGRAPH 2007 Papers (SIGGRAPH '07)*. ACM, New York, NY, USA, Article 41.
22. Benjamin Nuernberger, Kuo-Chin Lien, Matthew Turk, and others. 2016a. Interpreting 2D gesture annotations in 3D augmented reality. In *2016 IEEE Symposium on 3D User Interfaces (3DUI)*. IEEE, 149–158.
23. Benjamin Nuernberger, Eyal Ofek, Hrvoje Benko, and Andrew D Wilson. 2016b. SnapToReality: Aligning Augmented Reality to the Real World. In *Proceedings of the 2016 CHI Conference on Human Factors in Computing Systems*. ACM, 1233–1244.
24. Luke Olsen, Faramarz Samavati, and Joaquim Jorge. 2011. NaturaSketch: Modeling from Images and Natural Sketches. *IEEE Comput. Graph. Appl.* 31, 6 (Nov. 2011), 24–34.
25. Patrick Paczkowski, Min H Kim, Yann Morvan, Julie Dorsey, Holly E Rushmeier, and Carol O'Sullivan. 2011. Insitu: sketching architectural designs in context. *ACM Trans. Graph.* 30, 6 (2011), 182.
26. Cecil Piya, Vinayak, Yunbo Zhang, and Karthik Ramani. 2016. RealFusion: An Interactive Workflow for Repurposing Real-World Objects towards Early-stage Creative Ideation. In *Proceedings of Graphics Interface 2016*. ACM.
27. Carsten Rother, Vladimir Kolmogorov, and Andrew Blake. 2004. "GrabCut": Interactive Foreground Extraction Using Iterated Graph Cuts. *ACM Trans. Graph.* 23, 3 (Aug. 2004), 309–314.
28. Emanuel Sachs, Andrew Roberts, and David Stoops. 1991. 3-Draw: A Tool for Designing 3D Shapes. *IEEE Computer Graphics and Applications* 11, 6 (1991), 18–26.

29. Steven Schkolne, Michael Pruett, and Peter Schröder. 2001. Surface drawing: creating organic 3D shapes with the hand and tangible tools. In *Proceedings of the SIGCHI conference on Human factors in computing systems*. ACM, 261–268.

30. Rajinder S. Sodhi, Brett R. Jones, David Forsyth, Brian P. Bailey, and Giuliano Maciocci. 2013. BeThere: 3D Mobile Collaboration with Spatial Input. In *Proceedings of the SIGCHI Conference on Human Factors in Computing Systems (CHI '13)*. ACM, New York, NY, USA, 179–188.

31. Hyunyoung Song, François Guimbretière, Chang Hu, and Hod Lipson. 2006. ModelCraft: Capturing Freehand Annotations and Edits on Physical 3D Models. In *Proceedings of the 19th Annual ACM Symposium on User Interface Software and Technology (UIST '06)*. ACM, New York, NY, USA, 13–22.

32. Yannick Thiel, Karan Singh, and Ravin Balakrishnan. 2011. Elasticurves: Exploiting stroke dynamics and inertia for the real-time neatening of sketched 2d curves. In *Proc. of UIST*. ACM, 383–392.

33. Anton van den Hengel, Anthony Dick, Thorsten Thormählen, Ben Ward, and Philip H. S. Torr. 2007. VideoTrace: Rapid Interactive Scene Modelling from Video. In *ACM SIGGRAPH 2007 Papers (SIGGRAPH '07)*. New York, NY, USA, Article 86.

34. Vinayak, Devarajan Ramanujan, Cecil Piya, and Karthik Ramani. 2016. MobiSweep: Exploring Spatial Design Ideation Using a Smartphone As a Hand-held Reference Plane. In *Proceedings of the TEI '16: Tenth International Conference on Tangible, Embedded, and Embodied Interaction (TEI '16)*. ACM, New York, NY, USA, 12–20.

35. Shahtab Wahid, Stacy M. Branham, D. Scott McCrickard, and Steve Harrison. 2010. Investigating the Relationship Between Imagery and Rationale in Design. In *Proceedings of the 8th ACM Conference on Designing Interactive Systems (DIS '10)*. ACM, New York, NY, USA, 75–84.

36. Christian Weichel, Manfred Lau, David Kim, Nicolas Villar, and Hans W. Gellersen. 2014a. MixFab: A Mixed-reality Environment for Personal Fabrication. In *Proceedings of the 32Nd Annual ACM Conference on Human Factors in Computing Systems (CHI '14)*. ACM, New York, NY, USA, 3855–3864.

37. Christian Weichel, Manfred Lau, David Kim, Nicolas Villar, and Hans W Gellersen. 2014b. MixFab: a mixed-reality environment for personal fabrication. In *Proceedings of the 32nd annual ACM conference on Human factors in computing systems*. ACM, 3855–3864.

38. Min Xin, Ehud Sharlin, and Mario Costa Sousa. 2008. Napkin Sketch: Handheld Mixed Reality 3D Sketching. In *Proceedings of the 2008 ACM Symposium on Virtual Reality Software and Technology (VRST '08)*. ACM, New York, NY, USA, 223–226.

39. Youyi Zheng, Han Liu, Julie Dorsey, and Niloy J Mitra. 2016. SmartCanvas: Context-inferred Interpretation of Sketches for Preparatory Design Studies. In *Computer Graphics Forum*, Vol. 35. Wiley Online Library, 37–48.

40. Fabio Zünd, Mattia Ryffel, Stéphane Magnenat, Alessia Marra, Maurizio Nitti, Mubbasir Kapadia, Gioacchino Noris, Kenny Mitchell, Markus Gross, and Robert W. Sumner. 2015. Augmented Creativity: Bridging the Real and Virtual Worlds to Enhance Creative Play. In *SIGGRAPH Asia 2015 Mobile Graphics and Interactive Applications (SA '15)*. ACM, New York, NY, USA, Article 21, 7 pages.

Designing for Embodied Being-in-the-World: Two Cases, Seven Principles and One Framework

Jelle van Dijk
University of Twente
Enschede, Netherlands
jelle.vandijk@utwente.nl

Caroline Hummels
Eindhoven University of Technology,
Eindhoven, Netherlands
c.c.m.hummels@tue.nl

ABSTRACT
How may we design coherent, physical-digital hybrid artifacts as meaningful, mediating elements in a persons' embodied 'Being-in-the-World? We explore this question through two cases, one of designing for a person with autism spectrum disorder and one for people with dementia. We reflected in an iterative way on how the designs evolved, and on how our theoretical lens, grounded in embodied theory, helped to shape the designs. In the final round of reflection, we compared both case studies, looking for overall commonalities, which formed the basis for the resulting design framework that we introduce in this paper. The framework consists of seven principles, of which three support embodied activity in the here-and-now, three support developmental processes over a longer time-scale, and finally the idea of a reflective process to connect them.

Author Keywords
Embodied Being-in-the-World; assistive technology; empowerment; tangible interaction; ubiquitous computing

ACM Classification Keywords
H.5.2. Information interfaces and presentation (e.g., HCI): Theory & Methods; K.4.2. Computers and society: Assistive technologies for persons with disabilities

INTRODUCTION
Over the past years we have explored the value of Embodied theories for design [16], with embodied cognition [10, 52], ecological psychology [24], phenomenology [43, 19, 55], situated cognition [53, 25, 47] and pragmatism as our main sources [15, 49]. Especially concerning 'physical-digital hybrids', as e.g. in Tangible Interaction, Augmented Reality, Ubiquitous- and Wearable computing, we see merit in taking an Embodied approach (and with us [18; 37, 54, 41]). Physical-digital hybrids (hereafter: 'hybrids') by nature invite a rethinking of the traditional distinction between 'digital' and 'physical'. Such rethinking may benefit from grounding in appropriate theory. Embodied theories may help designers in understanding how in the concrete interaction between a person and a technological artifact, the 'material' and 'immaterial' aspect are really part of one 'lived' experience.

TEI '17, March 20 - 23, 2017, Yokohama, Japan.

ACM 978-1-4503-4676-4/17/03…$15.00
DOI: http://dx.doi.org/10.1145/3024969.3025007

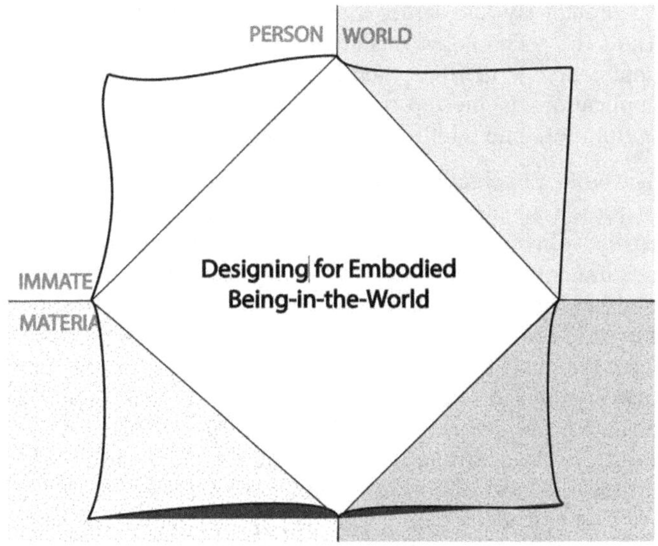

Figure 1. Opening up traditional Cartesian splits reveals a design space focused on 'Embodied Being-in-the-World'

In this paper we ask what it concretely means to design hybrids that cater such integrated experiences, and how to actually go about it in practice. Building on [16], and the design principles in [34], and by reflecting on two new case studies, we now offer a coherent design framework for designing hybrid interactive artifacts to become meaningful, mediating elements in what phenomenologists call our Embodied Being-in-the-World [19;16].

BEYOND CARTESIAN SPLITS
Our proposal concerns a qualitatively different role for hybrids, one that goes beyond more conventional forms of tangible- and embodied interaction. In particular, we are not just proposing to design 'embodied' or 'tangible' *interfaces* to, for example, digital personal applications, or to digital social- or communication applications. Neither is our take on embodiment to be understood as designing technologies in support of the *physical body*, such as for example a responsive leg-prosthesis. And neither do we mean

intelligent physical environments that respond to our physical bodies' location or movements (e.g. the room that automatically plays your favorite song when entering it).

Instead, the perspective we promote aims to overcome two, strongly related, lingering 'Cartesian' splits: 1) the separation of 'immaterial' from 'material' (c.f. the mind-body problem in philosophy [43, 19, 52]); and 2) the distinction between an (inner) person and an (outside) world (c.f. phenomenology's critique of the subject-object distinction in science [43])[1]. We plotted these splits as axes in Figure 1 resulting in a conceptual space with four quadrants. By and large, the quadrants represent the four kinds of technology mentioned earlier: personal digital applications in the top-left, social communication applications in the top-right, physical body support in the bottom-left, and intelligent spaces in the bottom-right.

The bulk of interactive technology today can be placed in one of these four quadrants, or, alternatively, a device may be easily split up into component parts that each occupy a quadrant. However, there are many (especially classical) tools and artifacts that seem to question this Cartesian frame. For example, the hammer [29] and the blind man's cane [43] have famously been used to argue against a strict separation between person and world, or between body and mind: the artifact is both an extension of the body as well as an object in the world, and through skillful, bodily interactions with artifacts, a world of meaning opens up for us in experience [43]. Or consider a family table. A physical platform to carry objects, but also an object mediating social coordination between people (see [23]). It makes no sense to split the table into its 'physical' or 'social' aspect: it is both, and the *way* in which the table supports physically is inherently tied into the *way* in which it mediates socially [25]. There are many examples challenging the Cartesian splits..Is our car a 'space' that we occupy, or our 'extended body'? Is a whiteboard a place to express individual thoughts, or a platform for collaborative sensemaking? Is a roundabout an object constraining physical movement, or a social norm that actors respond to?

The TEI community has contributed both theoretically and practically to developing alternatives to the strict separation of the physical and digital [35, 33, 18, 3, 30, 54, 37, 22, 41]. In this sense we may see TEI as being critical of traditional Cartesian intuitions in HCI [22, 18]. Several researchers are developing design frameworks based on embodied interaction, all with their own specific focus, such as collaboration [32, 33] or somaesthetic design [31]. In addition to all this work, we see the necessity to develop a framework for hybrids that dives more deeply into the consequences of radically *rejecting* the Cartesian split. This is our response to 'classic' tangible interaction where the purpose of physical artifacts ('tangibles') is to *represent* digital information [35, 3], which theoretically means *bridging* the Cartesian split, rather than actually *rejecting* it.

In Figure 1 we illustrate our approach by 'opening up' the Cartesian splits to reveal a new design space in its center, aimed explicitly and univocally at designing for a person's Embodied Being-in-the-World. As we will show in detail through analysis of two design cases, the center space contains three core aspects: Embodied skills [24], socially situated coordination [53] and our embedding in a *Lifeworld* [1]. Through ongoing reflective practice [49] these aspects develop into our personal identity, our social relations, and gradually transform our lifeworlds (Figure 4). Hybrid technologies allow for designing artifacts that support one or more of these core aspects, in effect supporting a person's Embodied Being-in-the-World.

DESIGNING FOR EMBODIED WELL-BEING

The theoretical reflections that have led to the framework are grounded in two design case studies, to which we turn now. In recent years we have sought design challenges that would in a strong and critical sense ask us to scrutinize in detail what lies in the embodied design space occupying the center of figure 1. In this paper, we do so by reflecting on two design cases, aimed at designing technology supporting everyday, routine activities of people with Autism Spectrum Disorder (Case 1) and people with Dementia (Case 2). The context and specific challenges in these projects helped us to reflect on how the theory could guide the design process and the designs. One driving question in both projects was how to respect the lives and personally developed ways of doing of the people involved, knowing that they cannot manage without some form of care. The question "How to design technological assistance without thereby compromising the identity and authenticity of the person?" helped us to get grip on what it means to design for someone's 'being'. It raised further questions, e.g.: What could interactive technology be for people that slowly but certainly loose their cognitive and motor skills, or for people that have a completely different understanding of the world and their social interactions? What do we mean with 'empowerment' and 'self-management'? What could our world look like if autism was seen as simply another way of being in the world and not as a disorder? What could our world look like if we would design for the extreme, e.g. if we all would have dementia or we would see dementia as a blessing? Consequently, we might not focus on steering our designs towards remedy, compensation, adjustment or delay of progression of cognitive and motor impairments as is often done in interactive technology design [42; 26; 51; 38; 40], but on respecting everyone's unique embodied being in the world. Could designing for 'Embodied-being-in-the-World' (the center of Figure 1) offer a new perspective for not only these two target groups, but in the end for all of us? So, can the

[1] Actually these splits are often taken together as 'The Cartesian split'. We make no strong claims on whether it is better to talk about one or two splits; the purpose of the sketch in Figure 1 is to provide a background against which we can introduce our alternative as one rejecting all such strict separations between mind, body, social world and physical world.

lessons learned from these challenging cases, be applied to our everyday HCI artifacts?

The aim in both cases is to *empower* people in living their own everyday lives, that is, to design artifacts that enable people to be most fully themselves in their own familiar world. The first case focuses on independent living in the home environment and the second case focusing on living respectfully and situated towards and in a care home.

CASE STUDY CONTEXT AND APPROACH

In each of the case studies we reflected in iterative fashion on the way the design evolved, how our embodied theoretical lens helped to shape this evolution, and how, in turn, the practicalities of the design challenge and context critically 'talked back' [49] to the theory, demanding us to be ever more precise about the theory's contribution in making concrete design decisions. All levels of design were considered: from discussions about overall function and purpose all the way to the detailed shaping of interaction design and form-giving. Taken together, our cases explore the embodied design space both in-depth, iterating one specific design concept (MyDayLight, see below), as well as more broadly, by developing a collection of different designs (Sensuous Dementia, see below). In the final reflections we compared the two case studies by looking for overall commonalities, which formed the basis for the resulting design framework as presented below. But let us first introduce the two case studies.

CASE 1: DAILY ROUTINES AND AUTISM SPECTRUM DISORDER

Over the course of two years, in four main projects (each resulting in experienceable prototypes), 24 bachelor students and 3 master students designed for- and with Max (not his real name), a 31 year-old high functioning person with Autism Spectrum Disorder (ASD[27]), who lives in an independent living facility. All projects included interviews, observation, co-design activities and prototype evaluations with Max and three of his professional caretakers.

The supported living facility has the aim to help Max manage his own life to the greatest extent possible. This is challenging mostly when Max is free to make is own plans (e.g. on a day off). Max is easily distracted by recurring worries [7] or becomes preoccupied with 'irrelevant' details [2]. Planned tasks remain unfinished, leading to frustration and a sense of personal failure. Unfinished business in his apartment itself may be a source of new distractions, creating a feedback loop where the chaos in his head becomes reflected in the chaos in his apartment and vice versa. With Max and his caregivers, we developed MyDayLight: a ubiquitous, interactive light system that helps in structuring daily activities (Figure 2). It works as follows. If Max wants to do the dishes each day at 11AM, he plans this task in a calendar on a tablet and assigns it to a tangible 'Highlight' (for example, one that Max placed in the kitchen). At 11AM, the kitchen Highlight will light up. This cues Max's attention to the kitchen, prompting him to do the dishes. Once the time is up, the Highlight fades out. With each planned task, another light-cue in an associated physical location lights up.

Figure 2. MYDAYLIGHT (fourth prototype), including the Highlight and the Reflector overview

Figure 3. Sensuous Dementia: *For the time being* (upper left), *The Richness of Tea* (upper right), *Warm Place* (lower left) and *Orchestra of Senses* (lower right)

Max is free to place Highlights where he wants, creating a visual web 'highlighting' task-relevant areas in his apartment. By turning a Highlight, where turn-right means 'I am feeling ok" and turn-left means "I am not feeling ok", a visual pattern emerges in the Reflector overview (Figure 2) to help Max and his caregiver to reflect on the day, learn, and make new plans.

CASE 2: DAILY ROUTINES AND DEMENTIA

In the first phase (2,5 months) of this 3-year Transformative Homes for Sensuous Dementia project, 19 ID Master students under guidance of 10 creative experts developed 4 experienceable prototypes of situations in a transformative home with people with dementia and their (formal and informal) caregivers (Figure 3). Designs were iteratively developed and evaluated after 8 weeks during an exhibition with 50 external stakeholders (care institutions, insurance companies, home automation industry, design firms, citizens). The designs approach dementia from the experience in the here and now, exploring the uncultivated space of using people's sensorial skills to empower them, given that cognitive and motor skills appear to be deteriorating over time [8, 44, 56]. The approach ran opposite to many technologies designed for dementia, as we did not try to revive memory and reminiscence, or delay deterioration of cognitive skills [42, 26, 51].

Most of the designs focus on the care home, but the first concept can also be used in a regular home. The four concepts were prototyped for experience, though sometimes simplified for technical reasons. They are (see Figure 3):

1) *For the Time Being*: An integrated "clock" in the house that does not tell time, but shows/offers valuable objects via a spotlight, inviting to do the related activities at a specific time.
2) *The Richness of Tea*: A new tea ritual where caregivers and people with dementia enjoy making tea together and take time for each other. The orientation of the spotlight and of the rotating display can be adjusted according to the stage of the tea ritual.
3) *Warm Place*: A playful way to use heating spots in the care home, i.e. an interactive heat lamp that adjusts its heights in relation the place of ones hands, and a warm tactile rice-box, to create sensory moments of comfort in interaction with others.
4) *Orchestra of Senses*: a set of playful instruments that use smell, touch, sight and sound to raise the appetite, forming an embodied activity bridging to actual dinner.

DESIGNING FOR EMBODIED-BEING-IN-THE-WORLD: A FRAMEWORK

The main insights from the two projects formed the basis for our design framework, illustrated in figure 4. We reflected both on the design process itself, as on the use evaluations. For MyDayLight, use evaluations are primarily based on an in-depth, one week long ethnographic study with a fully working prototype (the third version) placed in Max' home, followed by daily visits with situated interviews, observations of all daily client-caregiver meetings, and a final group interview with Max, his parents, and one caregiver. Insights from the Sensuous Dementia projects are based on the qualitative feedback from the 50 stakeholders present at the interactive exhibition, and on 5 user tests done in care homes with the Richness of Tea.

We distinguish between how artifacts support embodied activity in the here-and-now, and how they may spur a developmental process over a longer time-scale. While we present the framework as a list of separate principles, we emphasize that these are strongly interrelated: e.g., to engage in social coordination is part of our skillful dealing with the world, and skillful dealing is always already socially situated. The principles we list here are meant to be integrated through design into a complete system in context, that will give rise to a unified, lived experience.

Embodied Interactions in the here-and-now

We first discuss embodied interaction in the here-and-now:

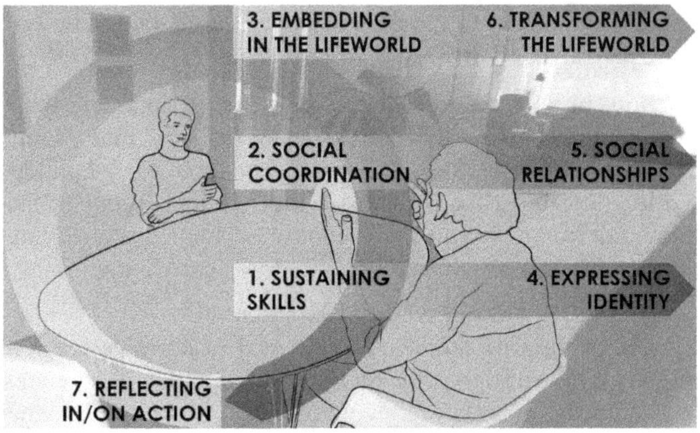

Figure 4. A design framework: Designing for Embodied Being-in-the-World

1. Sustaining Skills

Skillful action, mediated by the use of tools, is something we do with our whole body. Tools do not only produce a desired 'output' behavior – the ultimate effect emerges from the way a person skillfully uses the tool. Skill is 'know-how' – it is acting intelligently, though in an embodied way, enabling a person to deal successfully with circumstances, without a detached 'cognitive' phase of observing, interpreting, internal processing and action-planning. In acting skillfully there is no separation, nor a linear ordering, of action and perception: they unfold in parallel and become *coupled*, and the tool functions as a binding element this coupling process [19].

Our designs contain aspects of tools supporting skills, i.e., mediating and sustaining action-perception couplings. For example MyDayLight does not provide 'information messages' to the user that need to be interpreted in order to decide what to do. Instead, the light cues, situated in a context, help the user to attend to relevant aspects of that context, upon which one 'sees what needs to be done'. The design challenge became to find how technology would mediate in the evolution of a person's skill in utilizing the familiar structure ones' apartment in order to guide appropriate action. The third prototype used for testing contained a regular Google Calendar for setting time and day for each lamp. However Max experienced difficulties in setting the *exact time* for each task: at various moments he refused to set a task, because, in his words, he didn't know *for sure* that he would actually want to do that task *at that precise time*, the next day. Google Calendar actually biased the interaction again towards thinking of the device as a tool for precise planning of future events, rather than as setting a rough-and-ready *cue* that would guide, but not specify, the actual time and manner in which the task would be done.

For the Time Being offers personally relevant tools needed to maintain certain skills and interests. It is both the offering of the tool as a reminder of the activity, as well as the way of offering the tool that addresses action-perception loop. So instead of reminding a person to read a book or do her embroidery via a calendar, time sheet or verbally, For the

Time Being offers the tools directly to the person by putting them into the spot light. For the Time Being uses the affordances of the tools and offers the activity itself.

2. Scaffolding Social Coordination

Whatever we do, we do it against the background of having to negotiate our own position over and against other human beings in our social world, and our actions, decisions and the way we make sense of things in action is socially contextualized [39, 53, 25]. The manipulation of physical objects (which relates to skills in 1.), plays a crucial part in this ongoing 'social coordination'. People use the public world of objects and artifacts, including their own physical bodies, as *scaffolds* [13] for participatory sensemaking [36].

The Richness of Tea includes a table full of scaffolds for making and drinking tea. The lamp in the middle can be operated by the host (caregiver, family member, ...) and successively highlights the four activities related to the ritual (exploring and selecting the ingredients; crushing and mixing the tea leaves; playing with and selecting sugar; pouring water and drinking the tea). By turning the display, the person with dementia and the host go through the journey of making and drinking tea, while enjoying the richness of the sensorial sensations of interacting with the ingredients. The design and the ritual create a physical and social place for taking time for each other, as the caregivers indicated during the 5 user tests performed in care homes. Currently, there is place nor time in care homes to evoke attentive, empathic relaxation with inhabitants. So, the scaffolds are used in the moment to make meaning together.

We observed how Max and his caregivers were together discussing how to program the lamp as part of their regular daily meeting. We learned that these talks were not purely instrumental to programming the lamp but also functioned to share mutual perspectives on 'what would be the right thing to do' – which in effect meant a process of bringing together Max's first-person experience, and the caregivers' professional, third-person perspective, on Max and his ASD challenges. This is why we reframed the graphical user interface on the tablet to be not just a representation of task plans – but a REFLECTOR instead: a shared space for a person with ASD and his caregiver, to look at, point at, refer to, in order to collaboratively make sense of the current state of affairs, and how to improve it.

Whenever we engage in action-perception cycles with a physical object, this object is always already socially situated. So, when a person sees a MyDayLight light becoming active in the kitchen, he may feel the need to do the dishes, but this need always includes some sense of what it means to do those dishes *in relation to others,* for example in relation to the care-giver with which we had discussed the plan to do the dishes the day before. So the scaffolds are used for looking back at moments of social interaction.

When looking at For the Time Being, the rotating platform /cabinet offers an opportunity for the family or caregivers to suggest activities. So, social coordination between the care-taker and (informal) care-giver is facilitated by the scaffolds placed at the platform. These activities can be activities for the person with dementia, but also for social activities, e.g. placing cups for drinking tea together, placing a book for reading a story for the person with dementia, or placing the telephone to make a phone call with friends or family members. So, the scaffolds are used for anticipating social interaction.

3. Embedding in the Lifeworld

The physical- as well as social world that people inhabit we call the 'lifeworld' [50, 1]. People do not act in the void, they do so against a meaningful background of things and people that forms a 'context-of-practice' [39]. Because lifeworlds co-evolve with our skills and routines, the things in our lifeworlds are always already meaningful to us. Thus, within the lifeworld things pop up as relevant to our current activity, and by acting in the world we leave traces in the world that we may later encounter and think with.

Orchestra of Senses is developed for people with dementia living in care homes. They often get ready-made food presented in front of them at a fixed time slot, but which might not be aligned with their appetite or expectations, since their connection with their lifeworld is often distorted. Moreover, there is often no perceivable preparation phase; by taking away the process of cooking, dementia patients tend to forget to eat and they tend to lose their appetite [28]. Orchestra of Senses tries to restore this relation by offering a ritual to recreate a connection with their dinner. By playing with the set of sensorial instruments their olfactible, haptic, visual and auditory senses are triggered towards dining, thus aiming to raise their appetite and restoring part of the relationship with their lifeworld.

In MyDayLight the lamps by themselves convey little information – instead what they do is to highlight the particular organization of already meaningful things in the users' own apartment. These things are meaningful cues because the environment has developed alongside with the skills, routines and habits of the person: this is *his* environment. In case of a person with ASD (and to some extent for all of us), the cues we perceive do do not always coincide with what we had rationally planned to do. In this case a person becomes distracted and defocused. Instead of 'overruling' bottom up triggers by providing explicit notifications on a screen, MyDayLight functions as a (self-developed) situated filter, drawing attention to those aspects in the user's own lifeworld that *help* rather than *confuse.*

Long-term developments

The second set of principles that make up our framework deals with long-term effects of interacting with physical-digital hybrids in embodied ways. While the principles below are grounded in theoretical reflections on the design evolution, they are in some sense more speculative, as working prototypes have not been tested for longer than one week, and the transformative effects we propose would typically take weeks, months, or even years to evolve, as the artifacts are gradually appropriated within a person's daily routines and take up position within the larger physical- and social setting that makes up the lifeworld.

4. Forming and expressing identity

Skills, tools, and the lifeworld relate to identity. Exercising ones' skills, being reliant on ones' tools, in ones' familiar context, in a way means expressing who one is. Developing ones' skills, building social relations and growing a lifeworld goes hand in hand with forming an identity.[19]

Riemer and Johnston [46], conclude that much IT poses a threat to identity because it lacks the quality of what Heidegger [29] calls 'equipment':

"Use of equipment is at the heart of our human way of being, ... and constitutive of self ... [I]ndividuals express their ... identities through the equipment they use. Replacing this equipment might in the worst case equate to tearing apart one's (professional) lifeworld, one's existence, which was built on the basis of what one does and therefore how (in what way) one 'is'" [46, p.10.]

Likewise, Lave [39] argues how becoming 'knowledgeably skillful' is part of developing an identity as a member of a community [39]. This means for assistive technologies at least that the user should experience using an assistive tool as 'something I do with the tool', which then also means a way to 'express myself', rather than 'something the tool does for me' [17]. This means also to not replace existing routines and 'ways of being' with technologies based on externally defined, normative accounts of 'how things should be done' [6, 53]. In the many conversations we had with Max, using 'his' lamp clearly seemed to help him take up a more autonomous position regarding his own life – managing tasks became something that *he* was doing, rather than being a response to the caregiver's demands.

The change or loss of identity for people with dementia is still under debate, since the topic is not sufficiently explored [9] and/or there is no agreement on the process of sense of identity, since some researchers claim a disintegration of the self as the disease progresses [e.g. 14], other researchers claim that the sense of self persists [e.g. 21], and others indicate their might be two sides of sense of identity: one quite stable and the other varying over time and with experience. [20]. When taking Dreyfus' stance that 'exercising ones' skills becomes the expression of who one 'is' [19], it implies that the sense of self will be effected, especially since their cognitive and motor skills are deteriorating over time [8, 44, 56].

One of the people with dementia that participated in our study experienced a kind of sense of identity loss, since he couldn't remember to go cycling which was one of his most important hobbies; he was a cyclist and by not cycling he (sometimes) felt a great loss. Others were very attached to certain objects in their environment since they allowed them to do certain valuable activities and use their skills.

For the Time Being tried to address this sense of identity in two ways. Firstly, by offering valuable objects over the day that invite to keep using, maintaining or even developing specific skills, and thus being invited regularly to express who one is through one's skills. Secondly, For the time being can also be used to deal with the changes of skills over time, especially during the earlier phases of dementia. For the Time Being invites people with dementia in the early phases to create rituals when they still have most of their skills for the time that their skills will be challenged or deteriorate. Which skills are important for them, their life, their identity, and how would they like to incorporate them in their everyday living through For the Time Being? This way, it also makes For the Time Being a tool for reflection (see principle 7).

5. Social relationships

When people socially coordinate their activities in situ, this creates *roles* people take within communities of practice on the long run [39].

In MyDayLight the different roles that the person with ASD, caretaker and parents played were explicitly discussed. One of the aims of the project was to help, through the device, transform existing roles to ones in which people with ASD would be more autonomous in their own lives and caretakers would 'carefully coach' rather than 'take care of things'. Max actually used the system mostly to plan meetings with other people and less for daily chores. He anticipated on social implications of programming the lamp, which gave him some sense of control over the future event. For example he'd say: "For Sonja I choose a nice violet color for the couch-lamp, so I'll put her in a beautiful light when she sits there tomorrow'.

Next to the roles of people, we also looked at social relationships and attachments. Attachment may be radically embodied, and social baseline theory [45, 4] might support this premise. [5] Attachment in an embodied context can be seen through the lens of affordances as relations, in this case between two living bodies. For example, attachment can emerge and be strengthened by a person's body to provide support (e.g., softness, body heat and body trunk one can cling to) and his/her capacity to elicit the type of support needed by someone else (e.g., eliciting soft caresses and huddling or holding behaviors) [12]. Moreover, literature shows that one's health correlates with the intensity of empathy and helpfulness of the social network a person is embedded in [5]. Warm Place specifically focuses on jointly playing with the installations while stimulating body heat through the warmness of the rice and the lamp. The Richness of Tea targeted at empathy and helpfulness by affording through the tea ritual to take time for each other. Finally, For the Time Being aimed at using both physical and social affordances to trigger empathy and helpfulness. The family and caregivers can suggest activities through the objects, they can put valuable objects and potential events in the spotlight, and they can do the activities together with the person with dementia. While the disease is advancing, this design aims at supporting attachment by keep on doing things together, especially when verbal communication is getting more troublesome.

6. Transforming the Lifeworld

In 3. we discussed how the lifeworld forms an active element in the way people perceive and act in the world. This lifeworld however itself changes as people gradually reconfigure the space they inhabit [6]. At this point we have to speculate about actual long-term outcomes. Over time, using MyDayLight the user may decide now and then to put lights in different locations, trying out, improvising, and deciding to plan new tasks, at various moments in time, up to the point the system works well with the given configuration of the apartment. In a future study, next to investigating where people put their lamps, we plan to investigate what *names* users give to the lamps, and *how many* lamps they feel they need in order to manage an activity, or set of activities. While gradually configuring the system, other elements in the apartment (furniture, tools, etc.) may also be replaced to have them 'work better' with the lamps (e.g. put everything that belongs to one task in the same location, [1]). The technology does not prescribe such reconfigurations nor does it create a completely new, artificial environment next to the apartment itself (as in a virtual management tool on a screen). Rather, it would catalyze a process by which a person gradually adapts his own space to whatever works best for him.

Considering dementia a gradual adaptation of the lifeworld is a necessity, as the person in question gradually changes in her capabilities due to the disease. The user test of The Richness of Tea revealed that the ritual and the scaffolds need to be adjusted over time. Whereas in the earlier phases of dementia a variety of scaffolds can stimulate sensorial pleasure and social connectedness, in the later phases it might cause confusion and dangerous behavior (e.g. burning by touching a heated tea pot, or getting confused due to too much visual stimulation), thus the table should offer less and/or different scaffolds in a later phase. Moreover, although not implemented yet, The Richness of Tea could register the interaction during a tea ritual and visualize the changes in interaction over a longer period of time in order to enable the host to adjust the ritual over time. The table could even suggest alterations regarding time or light focus based on the patterns of change.

7. Reflecting in- and on action

Finally, as the overall process by which existing couplings, between people and tools (skills), between people (social relations) and between people and the overall setting (lifeworlds) change, we offer the process of reflection as grounded in action. This basically pragmatist, Schönean-Deweyan process is to be contrasted with a rational, theory-based approach in which one first *thinks* about what should ideally be the right sort of behavior, then executes it, and then afterwards evaluates whether the activities conformed to the model or not and, if not, what should be done about it. In contrast, reflective practice means that one at times temporarily steps back from an essentially *ongoing* activity, one takes a distanced perspective, one looks at what is there to be seen (which is not something one was looking for based on some previous idea) and this looking with a distance may then evolve into a 'new way of looking at things', which subsequently invites new sorts of actions (which may help to overcome the hurdles that emerged from the old way of looking).

In MyDayLight the process of reflection on action was quite explicitly implemented by creating a 'reflector' interface that should help caretaker and person with ASD to reflect on the day and on that basis discuss future actions. This design move itself instantiated a reframing of the original idea of the tablet interface as a calendar in which to plan future actions as just one aspect of a larger process that is focused on *reflection*: on taking a step back and looking at how things are going. From our user evaluations it became apparent that in this reflection the exact time at which a task was executed, and its duration, are actually much less important than is the *mood* experienced during execution of tasks. In other words, in self-management may be more important to focus on how one feels, than on whether one is actually performing according to plan. This is why in the final prototype we included the option turning the lamp to the left or right, thereby indicating a positive or negative mood. This action itself already invites a 'mini-moment of reflection'. It also adds to a gradually emerging visual pattern of colored dots in the calendar, to be used for looking back on the day later on.

For the Time Being incorporated reflection on action in a fairly implicit way. Initially, the platform and objects can work as a reflection mechanism for caretaker and caregivers, but over time it slowly but certainly becomes a reflection mechanism for the caregivers. There is not a separate visualization to stimulate reflection on action as was designed for MyDayLight, but the reflection goes initially through the change of scaffolds over time: the amount and kinds of objects that change. The platform could register what has been used and in which way, and leave traces over time on the platform when put in reflection mode.

DISCUSSION

A framework for reframing

Working from an Embodied perspective means a repeated revisiting of implicit 'mainstream' assumptions, at various levels of detail, each time again reframing the design challenge. For example, in MyDayLight, we initially considered *informing* the user on what to do, e.g. using icons in the tablet interface, text-messages on the lamps, and so on. Taking an embodied perspective however helped us in the later prototypes to emphasize the users' own skills, and rely on the meaning present in the social- and physical context, instead of predetermining meanings in designed representations.

A similar shift happened in the Sensuous Dementia project in hindsight, when evaluating with users during the exhibition. For example, the students designing For the Time Being did not initially distinguish between actual use objects and placeholder/representations of such objects. A mini chair (a representation) was used as well as a real book and someone's embroidery (actual products), while actual use objects of course have very different immediate affordances for action than its representations. Objects were also placed on every "hour" of the platform, which made for a total of 12. At the exhibition it became clear that this configuration ignored social coordination in actual practices, where meaning is created based on the pace of the day, the needs and interest of the person with dementia, relationships and activities with caregivers etc., having no intrinsic relation to the structure of a clock face.

One of the reasons for developing this framework is to make such considerations explicit and open for reflection to students of design, such that reframing becomes possible. The aim is to question possible Cartesian presuppositions and offer an embodied alternative. For example, the framework would have invited the students to think about objects and activities that can not be placed on a platform, such as the bike of the cyclist. In similar fashion the framework may also help health-care organizations and professional health-tech designers to becomes sensitive to alternative mediating roles for assistive technology that fits a person's lifeworld and skills and thus may less likely to be abandoned in practice [11]. For example, it may help health care organizations to focus less on wanting to 'control the situation', and instead 'facilitate' people's means for maintaining self-control.

What we mean when we talk about embodiment

The framework we present can be used by designers exploring ways to connect more deeply and intimately to people's situated, embodied practices. However it also invites to go beyond other known uses of the term 'embodiment' in design. Some of these other views have perhaps been more readily applied in tangible- and embodied interaction design in the past, as they typically demand a less radical departure from the Cartesian frame we introduced in the introduction (Figure 1). Here, we briefly contrast some of these approaches to our own.

First, our framework has little to do with the superficial interpretation of 'embodied' as meaning just anything involving physical bodies. Interactive bracelets, -clothes, even prostheses or implants are not (necessarily) 'Embodied' in our interpretation. Consider for example our embedding in the *lifeworld,* which deals with the social- and physical *environment* much more than with our *body*.

Second, we move beyond the popular notion of *distributed cognition* as well [13,16]. Our framework targets a level of person-world engagement that comes 'prior' to the evolved practice of creating and using 'external representations'. External representations are of course also part of our embodied practices, and such elements are also part of our designs. But our framework focuses first and foremost on supporting skillful couplings and social coordination, which in fact form the ground upon which something like 'using representations' becomes possible at all [53]. We invite designers to connect to this deeper level of Embodiment.

Third, the previous point entails we will ignore the use of bodily *metaphors* to *re-present* digital information [3; 35, 16]; or re-presenting in artifacts metaphors of the human body [48]. All of this may be tremendously important for designing information representations, but our intention is not to design information representations: our intention is to design for Embodied Being-in-the-World, which concerns skills, social coordination and action-based reflection.

Fourth: neither do we propose to design artifacts that enforce specific behaviors, by clever use of constraints and affordances. We carefully design to cater embodied practices, yet our systems always remain open, because the artifact must be *incorporated*, which happens in use. In our cases, this also meant not to aim at technology taking over deteriorating cognitive skills of people with dementia, nor to create technology that would specify or train specific desired behaviors to people with ASD. An anecdote from the MyDayLight project serves to illustrates this. When the first prototype was presented, the caretaker suggested enthusiastically to Max to take the 'task-list' (an existing paper list to-do list that the caregiver had earlier created for Max), and 'program it into the lamp'. 'Absolutely not', Max replied, 'we are not going to put *your* task-list into *my* lamp'. This reply showed to us that the product, even in this early design phase, started to help Max to take up a new, more autonomous position, transforming the social relation.

As a last remark, our framework is not meant to critique other embodied approaches as being invalid accounts, for Embodied Theory is itself an umbrella term for many related, but also often fiercely discussed notions. What we intend to show with these studies is that there is more to embodiment than designing tangible metaphors, or to distribute digital information in a physical space, and that 'tangible', 'wearable' or 'ubiquitous' design does not *necessarily* mean a design for Embodied Being-in-the World. Of course, we are not alone in this initiative; there are several examples of strong embodied designs at the various TEI conferences. But we do hope to offer, to those who wish to take this path, seven concrete principles in one coherent framework, to help designers appreciate what a strong sense of Embodiment may offer, and to provide inspiration and guidance during their design process.

ACKNOWLEDGMENTS

This research is supported by SIA-RAAK and the city of Eindhoven. We gratefully thank Max, all involved students, Jorge Alves Lino, Ambra Trotto and all coaches involved in the Sensuous Dementia project, Philadelphia Care organization, Ordina, Philips and 3TU Design United.

REFERENCES

1. Philip Agre and Ian Horswill. 1997. Lifeworld analysis. J. of Artificial Intelligence Research, 6: 111-145.
2. Catherine Ames and Sue Fletcher-Watson. 2011. A review of methods in the study of attention in autism, Developmental Review, Volume 30, Issue 1, March 2010, Pages 52-73,
3. Saskia Bakker, Alissa N. Antle, and Elise Van Den Hoven. 2012. Embodied metaphors in tangible interaction design. Pers and Ubiquitous Comp 16(4): 433-449.
4. Lana Beckes and James Coan. 2011. Social baseline theory: the role of social proximity in emotion and economy of action. *Soc. Pers. Psychol. Compass* 5, 976–988. doi: 10.1111/j.1751-9004.2011.00400.x
5. Lana Beckes, Hans IJzerman and Mattie Tops. 2015. Toward a radically embodied neuroscience of attachment and relationships. *Front. Hum. Neurosci.* 9:266. doi: 10.3389/fnhum.2015.00266
6. Margot Brereton. 2013. Habituated objects: everyday tangibles that foster the independent living of an elderly woman. Interactions 20(4): 20-24.
7. A. Bruggink, S. Huisman, R. Vuijk, V. Kraaij and Nadia. Garnefski. 2016. Cognitive emotion regulation, anxiety and depression in adults with autism spectrum disorder, Research in Autism Spectrum Disorders, Volume 22, February 2016, Pages 34-44
8. Aron S Buchman and David A Bennett. 2011. Loss of motor function in preclinical Alzheimer's disease. In: *Expert Rev Neurother*. 2011 May ; 11(5): 665–676. doi:10.1586/ern.11.57.
9. Lisa and Linda Clare. (2010). The impact of dementia on self and identity: a systematic review. Clinical Psychology Review, 30, 113 - 126.
10. Paolo Calvo and Anthony Gomila (Eds.). 2008. Handbook of cognitive science: An embodied approach. Amsterdam: Elsevier.
11. Stefan Parry Carmien and Gerhard Fischer. 2008. Design, adoption, and assessment of a socio-technical environment supporting independence for persons with cognitive disabilities. *Proc of CHI '08*. ACM, New York, NY, USA, 597-606.
12. Anthony Chemero. (2009). *Radical Embodied Cognitive Science.* Cambridge, MA, MIT Press.
13. Andy Clark. 1997. Being there: Putting brain, body, and world together again. Cambridge (MA): MIT
14. Daniel Davis. 2004. Dementia: sociological and philosophical construction. Social Science & Medicine, 58, 369–378.
15. John Dewey. 1916. Democracy and education. New York: Macmillan.
16. Jelle van Dijk, Remko van der Lugt, and Caroline Hummels. 2014. Beyond distributed representation: embodied cognition design supporting socio-sensorimotor couplings. In Proc of TEI '14. ACM, New York, NY, USA, 181-188. http://doi.acm.org/10.1145/2540930.2540934
17. Jelle van Dijk and Fenne Verhoeven. 2016. Designing for Embodied Empowerment of people with an Autistic Spectrum Disorder. Presented at: *Autism and Technology: Beyond Assistance & Interventions Workshop held May 7th at CHI 2016* in San Jose, California. Last retrieved August 7, 2016: http://igw.tuwien.ac.at/chi16-autismtechnology/
18. Paul Dourish. 2001. Where the action is: The foundations of embodied interaction. Cambridge (MA): MIT.
19. Hubert L. Dreyfus. 1991. Being-in-the-world: A commentary on Heidegger's Being and Time, Division I. Cambridge (MA): MIT.
20. Marie-Lou Eustache, Mickael Laisney, Aurelija Juskenaite, Odile Letortu, Herve Platel, et al..Sense of identity in advanced Alzheimer's dementia: a cognitive dissociation between samenessand selfhood? *Consciousness and Cognition*, Elsevier, 2013, pp.1.<inserm-00874387>
21. Sam Fazio and David Mitchell. 2009. Persistence of self in individuals with Alzheimer's disease: Evidence from language and visual recognition. Dementia, 8, 39-59.
22. Ylva Fernaeus, Jakob Tholander and Martin Jonsson. 2008. Towards a new set of ideals: consequences of the practice turn in tangible interaction." *Proceedings of the 2nd international conference on Tangible and embedded interaction.* New York: ACM
23. William Gaver, Bowers, J., Andy Boucher, Law, A., Pennington, S., Nicholas Villar. .2006. History Tablecloth: Illuminating Domestic Activity. Proc of DIS, '06, 199-208.
24. James J. Gibson. 1979. The ecological approach to visual perception. London: Lawrence Erlbaum (repr. in 1986).
25. Charles Goodwin. 2000. Action and embodiment within situated human interaction. *Journal of pragmatics*, 32, 1489-1522.
26. Gary Gowans, Jim Campbell, Norm Alm, Richard Dye, Arlene Astell and Maggie Ellis. 2004. Designing a Multimedia Conversation Aid for Reminiscence Therapy in Dementia Care Environments Proceeding CHI EA '04 CHI '04 Extended Abstracts on Human Factors in Computing Systems, p. 825-836. ACM New York.
27. Francesca Happé, Autism: cognitive deficit or cognitive style?, Trends in Cognitive Sciences, Volume 3, Issue 6, 1 June 1999, Pages 216-222
28. Hasselkus, B.R. 2006. The World of Everyday Occupation: Real People, Real Lives. The American Journal of Occupational Therapy, 60 (6), 2006.
29. Martin Heidegger. 1927. Sein und Zeit. *Tübingen: Max Niemayer Verlag.*
30. Bart Hengeveld, Caroline Hummels, Balkom, van, H., Voort, R. & Moor, de, J. 2013. Wrapping up LinguaBytes, for now. TEI'13 Proceedings of the 7th International Conference on Tangible, Embedded and

Embodied Interaction (pp. 237-244). New York: ACM. In Scopus Cited 5 times.

31. Kristina Höök, Martin Jonsson, Anna Ståhl, Jakob Tholander, Toni Robertson, Patrizia Marti, Dag Svanaes, Marianne Graves Petersen, Jodi Forlizzi, Thecla Schiphorst, Katherine Isbister, Caroline Hummels, Sietske Klooster, Lian Loke, George Poonkhin Khut. 2016. Moved to be moved. In: CHI EA '16. Proceedings of the 2016 CHI Conference Extended Abstracts on Human Factors in Computing Systems. Pp. 3301-3308.
32. Eva Hornecker. A Framework for the Design of Tangible Interaction for Collaborative Use. Paper at the Danish HCI Symposium, University of Aalborg, Nov. 16. *HCI Lab Technical Report no 2004/1. pp.57-61.* Retrieved November 17, 2016 from http://www.ehornecker.de/Papers/DanishHCI.pdf
33. Eva Hornecker and Jacob Buur. 2006. Getting a grip on tangible interaction: a framework on physical space and social interaction. *Proc. of Human Factors in Comput. Sys. '06,* Apr. 22-27, 437-446, New York: ACM.
34. Caroline Hummels and Jelle Van Dijk. 2015. Seven principles to design for embodied sensemaking. *Proceedings of the 9th International Conference on Tangible, Embedded and Embodied Interaction (TEI '15)*, January 16 - 19 2015, Stanford, CA, USA, pp. 21-28; New York: ACM
35. Hiroshi Ishii. 2008. Tangible bits: beyond pixels. In *Proceedings of the 2nd int. TEI Conference* (Bonn, Germany, February 18 - 20). New York: ACM, xv-xxv.
36. Hanne De Jaegher and Ezequiel Di Paolo. 2007. Participatory sense-making: An enactive approach to social cognition. *Phenomenology and the Cognitive Sciences*, 6(4), 485- 507
37. Scott Klemmer, Björn Hartman and Leila Takayama. 2008. How bodies matter: five themes for interaction design. *Proceedings of the 2nd int. TEI Conference* (Bonn, Germany, February 18 - 20). ACM, New York.
38. Xabier Laiseca, Eduardo CAstillejo, Pablo Orduña, Aitor Gómez-Goiri, Diego López-de-Ipiña and Ester González Aguado, E. 2011. Distributed Tracking System for Patients with Cognitive Impairments. In J. Bravo, R. Hervás, & V. Villarreal, *Ambient Assisted Living* (pp. 49-56). Torremolinos-Málaga: Springer Heidelberg Dordrecht London New York.
39. Jean Lave. 1991. Situating learning in communities of practice. In Lauren Resnick, John Levine and Stephanie Teasley (Eds.), *Perspectives on socially shared cognition*, pp. 63-82. Washington, DC: APA.
40. Clayton Lewis. 2006. HCI and Cognitive Disabilities. *Interactions*, (May + June)14-15.
41. Lian Loke and Toni Robertson. 2013. Moving and making strange: An embodied approach to movement-based interaction design. *ACM Trans. Comput.-Hum. Interact.* 20, 1.
42. João Martins, José Carilho, Oliver Schnell, Carlos Duarte, Francisco M. Couto, Luís Carriço and Tiago Guerreiro. 2014. Friendsourcing the unmet needs of people with dementia. *Proceedings of the 11th Web for All Conference.* ACM
43. Maurice Merleau-Ponty. 1962. *Phenomenology of Perception*, trans. Colin Smith. New York: Humanities Press.
44. Helen Nairn. 1995. Discover the difference activities can make. Journal of Dementia Care 3, 16–18.
45. Dennis Proffitt. 2006. Embodied perception and the economy of action. Perspect. Psychol. Sci. 1, 110–122. doi: 10.1111/j.1745-6916.2006. 00008.x
46. Kai Riemer, and Robert B. Johnston. 2014. Rethinking the place of the artifact in IS using Heidegger's analysis of equipment. *European Journal of Information Systems* 23(3): 273-288.
47. Philip Robbins & Murat Aydede (Eds.). 2009. The Cambridge Handbook of Situated Cognition. Cambridge: Cambridge University Press
48. Thomas van Rompay and Geke Ludden. 2015. Types of Embodiment in Design. *IJdesign*, 9(1): 1-11.
49. Donald A. Schön. 1983. The reflective practitioner: How professionals think in action. Basic books.
50. Alfred Schutz, 1967. The phenomenology of the social world. Northwestern University Press.
51. Panote Siriaraya and Chee Siang Ang. 2014. Recreating Living Experiences from Past Memories through Virtual Worlds for People with Dementia. In: *Proceedings of the 32nd Annual ACM Conference on Human Factors in Computing Systems*, pp. 3977-3986.
52. John R. Stewart, Olivier Gapenne, and Ezequiel A. Di Paolo. 2010. Enaction: Toward a new paradigm for cognitive science. MIT Press, 2010.
53. Lucy A. Suchman, 1987. Plans and situated actions: the problem of human-machine communication, Cambridge university press.
54. Dag Svanæs. .2013. Interaction Design for and with the Lived Body: Some Implications of Merleau-Ponty's Phenomenology. ACM Transactions on Computer-Human Interaction. vol. 20 (1).
55. Peter Paul Verbeek. 2005. What Things Do – Philosophical Reflections on Technology, Agency, and Design. Penn State: Penn State University Press
56. Lawrence Whalley. 1997. Early Onset Dementia. In S. Hunter (Ed). *Dementia: Challenges and new directions.* Jessica Kingsley Publishers., p. 71-78.

What a Life! Building a Framework for Constructive Assemblies

Joanne Leong[1], Florian Perteneder[1], Hans-Christian Jetter[2], Michael Haller[1]

[1] Media Interaction Lab, University of Applied Sciences Upper Austria

[2] University of Applied Sciences Upper Austria

ABSTRACT

Constructive assemblies are tangible user interfaces (TUIs) that involve the interconnection of modular parts. As such, they offer a unique means to support us in our various and diverse activities. However, little information is available for understanding the intricacies of taking a modular, constructive assembly approach to TUI design. Based on an analysis of extensive data collected from interviews with eight world-class TUI experts, we propose a descriptive, conceptual framework to facilitate systematic investigation and critical consideration of constructive assemblies. The paper presents a lifecycle model for constructive assemblies and discusses their main design qualities and associated parameters. We demonstrate how this can be used to structure critical discussions by applying the principles to existing works and the design of our own constructive assembly.

Author Keywords

Tangible Interface; Tangible Interaction; Framework; Design; Constructive Assembly

ACM Classification Keywords

H.5.2. User Interfaces

INTRODUCTION

Constructive assemblies are tangible user interfaces (TUIs) that involve the interconnection of modular physical, interactive *units* to formulate larger constructions that are automatically or manually put-together [7,17,28]. The modularity of such TUIs inherently allows for varying degrees of versatility in how they are used. As such, constructive assemblies have appeared and been leveraged in many domains ranging from storytelling and education to rapid prototyping and the manipulation of digital content, as pictured in Figure 1. However, despite the wealth of examples of successful constructive assemblies, we observe that there is a lack of guidelines for this topic which can serve to aid designers in systematically investigating constructive assemblies and creating new ones.

TEI '17, March 20 - 23, 2017, Yokohama, Japan

ACM 978-1-4503-4676-4/17/03…$15.00

DOI: http://dx.doi.org/10.1145/3024969.3024985

Figure 1. Examples of constructive assemblies: Tern [15] **a tangible programming exhibit at the Boston Museum of Science (left); Tiles that Talk** [6] **a system to aid students in prototyping interactive, networked systems; GaussBricks** [21] **a system of magnetic building blocks for use on portable displays (right).**

This absence motivated us to speak with experts in the field to elicit key thoughts and design cornerstones for constructive assemblies. In this paper, we present our findings from an in-depth analysis of interview data gathered through an extensive expert study. Summarizing, the main contributions of this paper are as follows:

- A *discussion of the benefits and risks* of a constructive assembly approach to TUI design
- A *lifecycle model* that outlines different phases that constructive assemblies can transition between, and how these phases are interconnected
- An outline of *central design themes* for constructive assemblies and a discussion of *parameters* that can be manipulated to achieve a desired balance of these qualities
- Three *case studies* based on examples from literature and our own design example, which demonstrate how these principles can be applied to elicit critical design thinking and discussion and can be used to shape future design iterations.

RELATED WORK

State of the Art for Constructive Assemblies

The category of TUIs referred to as *Constructive Assemblies* was explicitly identified by Ullmer and Ishii in 2000 [34], and was later reiterated as being one of seven promising directions for the development of new TUIs [17]. They are typically defined as TUIs which consist of interactive units that can be either manually or automatically connected to form more complex structures [7,17,28].

Constructive assemblies have been created for a variety of use cases. They were originally created for the purposes of modelling and simulation [1,2,4,9,10], but have since been leveraged for numerous other domains. For instance, constructive assemblies have been heavily used for hands-on education

[23,25–27,30,33,35,37], storytelling and other forms of entertainment [3,5,12,13], rapid prototyping [6,20,38], interactive public exhibits [15], and input devices for working with digital displays and content [11,21,36]. Furthermore, advancements in fabrication and actuation have spurred efforts to explore the boundaries of what is technologically feasible for this category of TUIs, and has thus been a central topic for recent works such as Changibles and Kinetic Blocks [28,29]. In research, a constructive assembly consisting of identical units has also been used as a medium with which to explore the concept of emergent interfaces and its associated parameters [7]. However, while there are numerous successful examples of constructive assembly TUIs, we observe that there is a lack of conceptual description, formalization and theory to guide their design. In this work, our aim is to address this gap by presenting a framework for such TUIs.

Positioning our Framework

Many conceptual frameworks for TUIs have been established, which differ in their focus and conceptual origin [24,31]. Some prominent examples include the Model-View-Controller pattern presented by Ullmer and Ishii [34], the containers, tokens and tools concept from Holmquist et al. [14], the tokens and constraints concept within the TAC paradigm introduced by Shaer et al. [32], and the 2D taxonomy of embodiment and metaphor by Fishkin [8]. Frameworks have also been established to understand TUIs within the scope of greater contexts and domains (e.g. within a social context [16], within the context of learning [22,37], and within the scope of reality-based interaction [18]). Given the large number of frameworks that have been created for TUIs, it can be challenging both to understand what a framework offers with respect to others, and to isolate a framework that best serves one's needs.

Fortunately, Mazalek and Van Den Hoven [24] created a map of TUI frameworks that brings frameworks into one conceptual space and helps readers to navigate between them. We use their definition of framework (i.e. a skeletal structure that can contain guidelines and can be used by designers to select a course of action in different stages of their design processes) and use their map to situate our work with respect to others. We identify our framework as being of the ***designing*** type, which covers the ***interactions*** and ***physicality*** facets of this space. This is because our work focuses on highlighting design considerations to guide the formation of new constructive assemblies, and aims to establish a better understanding of both user-interactions and physical affordances pertaining to constructive assemblies. In this work, we achieve this by conducting interviews with several TUI experts in order to gain insight on constructive assemblies. Later in this paper, we ground our framework by discussing our concepts in the context of examples from literature and our own design example.

STARTING POINT: CONSTRUCTIVE ASSEMBLIES

Constructive assemblies present an interaction paradigm shaped by their transient and ever adapting physical forms. Looking at examples in literature, we hypothesized a basic perspective of constructive assemblies involving three stages, as illustrated in Figure 2. A *creation* phase marks the beginning of a lifecycle, where interactive components or *units* are put-together to form an interactive whole or *assembly*. The assembled whole then typically serves a purpose to the user in a *usage* phase. The *destruction* phase closes one lifecycle, where the assembly is then disassembled into its constituent parts. A cycle can be established by recycling the disassembled components into the design of a new assembled whole.

Figure 2. Basic interaction phases of constructive assemblies.

This initial concept was the starting point from which we decided to talk with experts to investigate and distill a more refined model of our interactions as users with constructive assemblies. We surmised that a refined model of the lifecycle would provide a framework for deeper and more structured critical discussion of constructive assemblies.

EXPERT STUDY

We talked to experts with the intention of eliciting key thoughts surrounding constructive assemblies and collecting responses that could ground our understanding of these TUIs.

Expert Study Participants

We consulted 8 experts (4 female) in the field of TUIs to conduct an expert study. The experts (E1-E8) interviewed came from both academic and industry backgrounds, and were based in world-renown facilities and institutions across North America and Europe. The group of experts with academic experience consisted of several leading researchers (professors and post-docs) who have extensive experience in the field of TUIs, and have on average 46 publications, many of which have been accepted to top-tier HCI conferences such as TEI, CHI and UIST. Those with industry experience work in large-scale international companies and have experience developing tangible interfaces that have been incorporated into products for end-users. Moreover, a few of the interviewed experts had experience in steering both academic and commercial endeavors to create TUIs for various contexts and scenarios.

Interview and Data Analysis Procedure

Each expert was asked a series of questions in a semi-structured interview process. The interviews were between one half to two hours in duration. Prior to the interviews, themes of interest and sample questions catered to the backgrounds of the experts were prepared. Interviewees were asked questions that fell into four general categories: *general design considerations*, *constructive assemblies*, *TUI special issues* and *user-involvement*. These questions were used as a loose structure for the interview process. Follow-up questions were asked to clarify and elicit more detailed explanations of the concepts that interviewees raised. Interviewees were encouraged to draw upon their past projects and experiences in creating TUIs as part of their responses. All interviews were transcribed and sectioned into quotes for a bottom-up, open coding approach to data analysis. Affinity diagrams were built, and groupings emerged that highlighted an array of problems, qualities, benefits and drawbacks, opportunities and risks, and approaches to creating constructive assemblies. The results of this qualitative analysis are explained in the following result sections.

RESULT 1: BENEFITS AND DRAWBACKS

All the experts that were consulted emphasized that the design of a TUI must always depend on the specific target problem and the goal you want to reach. In light of this, many experts pointed out a number of benefits and risks that can offer some assistance in determining whether a constructive assembly approach is suitable for a given problem.

There is a wide array of potential benefits for taking a constructive assembly approach to TUI design. Two experts were quick to express that the design space for constructive assemblies is, *"much wider"* (E6) and that they are *"versatile [and] endless in possibilities"* (E4). E4 added that they can be *"accessible to users"*; the notion of putting together pieces such as blocks is an experience many of us can relate to as children. Furthermore, positive implications for *performance*, *lifespan* (E1) and *attachment* (E6) were identified. One expert noted that a modular approach opens the doors to *optimization* and *customization*, leading to prolonged use of the TUI and increased *emotional attachment* (E1). Many experts expressed that constructive assemblies can be "*very beneficial*" to learning (E1, E5, E7, E8); amongst the reasons listed were that they can provide *"enjoyment"*, and are *"more motivating [and] more engaging"* (E7). Two experts also added that the simple process of building meant users would develop an inherit understanding of the assembly, thereby circumventing the need to explicitly learn the tool (E1, E8). Another expert noted that they can *"encourage a kind of thinking [or] mindset"* (E6).

Experts cautioned that constructive assemblies could result in a *"very rectangular"* (E6) aesthetic that could be likened to the look of the video game Minecraft (E4). Particular technical concerns were also raised. E5 noted that having modular components could result in assemblies that are *"too bulky,"* or that may *"accidentally fall apart."* This expert also noted that the constant need to *"plug them together"* could in itself be a disadvantage to other types of TUIs. Furthermore, E8 pointed out that users may have limited capacities to effectively use the modules for construction, likening it to: *"giving them all the parts of a fishing rod, and they don't know what to do with it."*

RESULT 2: LIFECYCLE MODEL

In discussion with experts, it became clear that a more sophisticated model was needed to describe the lifecycle of constructive assemblies. Based on the interviews, we now augment our earlier hypothesized model of a three-phased lifecycle for constructive assemblies, which had consisted of a *creation phase*, *usage phase* and *destruction phase*. Figure 3 depicts the more complex and refined picture of the lifecycle that emerged from speaking with our TUI experts.

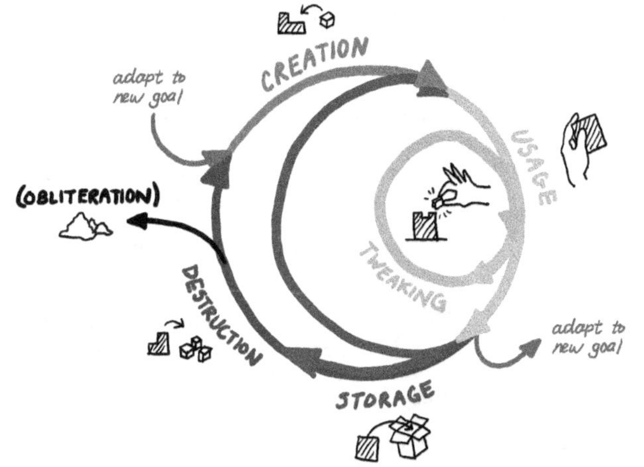

Figure 3. The constructive assembly lifecycle.

Lifecycle Phases

The refined model of a lifecycle for constructive assemblies consists of the following phases: ***creation, usage, tweaking, storage, destruction, and obliteration.*** A summary of the terminology is provided in Table 1.

In both the creation and usage phases, users can reflect on the design and assess whether the current state of the assembly is in alignment with their goal. Four of the experts referred to this concept with phrases such as *"trial and error"* (E5) and *"trying it out."* E2 explicitly pointed out a *"reflective phase."* In the proposed model, this concept is presented under both creation and usage. Users can evaluate the assembly in increments as they add additional pieces or evaluate an assembly as a whole after they believe their goal has been reached.

Conversations with experts resulted in three new phases being introduced to the lifecycle: a *tweaking phase*, a *storage phase*, and an *obliteration phase.* Three experts suggested that users interacting with constructive assemblies can *"enter a phase of rapid iterative testing and evaluation [and] adjustment,"* (E8) where the user is *"building on the fly,"* (E1) modifying the construction, and trying to *"improve it"* (E5). E8 referred to this as a *"constant tweaking,"* inspiring the name for the ***tweaking phase***. Experts also referred to a stage where the constructed whole may simply be *"standing around"* because users may choose to *"not take them apart"* and *"keep it for a later specialized session of that type"* (E8). We refer to this as the ***storage phase***.

The possibility for the constructed wholes to be thrown away (E2) or *"disappear* or *break"* (E4) was also mentioned, suggesting that the components in the assembly enter a state where they can no longer be used, and can more extensively make the system, as an assembly, unusable. We refer to this phase then as the ***obliteration phase***.

Phase Transitions

Each arrow represents a phase in the constructive assembly lifecycle, where the phases *"entwine [and] flow into each other"* (E8). This blending of phases is visualized by the overlapping of certain arrows. Entry points and exit points for the

Table 1. Lifecycle phase descriptions.

Phase	Description
Creation	When a user has a goal in mind, and pieces together the modular components in incremental steps to achieve this goal. While building, users usually evaluate their construction.
Usage	The user interacts with the constructed whole, and evaluates it in the process.
Tweaking	The user adds, modifies, or removes components in order to improve the construction.
Storage	A constructed whole is kept, but not used.
Destruction	The phase in which users take-apart the assembly into its constituent parts.
Obliteration	The phase in which the pieces of the constructive assembly are no longer functional.

lifecycle are marked by gray arrows leading in and outwards of the circle. These correspond with users adapting their goals. For instance, a user's goal may transition from simply trying to game a system and find out its limitations (E1), to trying to get it to do *"what you want it to do"* (E8).

Closing the loop

The cycle is created with the overlapping of the destruction and creation phases. While it may be that the modular components are not ultimately re-appropriated for use in new constructions, many experts' comments referred to the possibility of repurposing and reusing modules (E1,E2,E3,E5,E8). Furthermore, two experts saw destruction and creation as tightly interlinked, where destruction was seen as a *"prerequisite for another construction phase"* (E1) and saw disassembly as being motivated by assembly (E8).

Value of Lifecycle Concept

Knowing and considering the opportunities and challenges that are highlighted when considering TUIs from the perspective of their lifecycle can help us focus our overall design approach. Directing emphasis towards a particular phase of the lifecycle can help designers achieve specific design goals. For instance, if the TUI should engage a user to explore a multitude of ideas in high-frequency design cycles, a crucial aspect to the design will be to ensure the system consists of components that can be easily taken apart and are interchangeable.

RESULT 3: DESIGN THEMES AND PARAMETERS

In conversations with experts, many different aspects of consideration for constructive assemblies were discussed. Through the coding of conversations followed by affinity diagramming, we found a number of themes to emerge from the interview data. In this section, we first outline these themes, and propose an overarching structure for how they relate to one another. We then discuss each theme in greater detail.

Overview of Themes and Parameters

The analysis of the expert interviews revealed an intricate, interconnected network of design attributes for constructive assemblies, visualized in Figure 4. Attributes can be organized into a two-tier hierarchy: **themes** and **parameters**. We view **themes** (e.g. efficiency vs. exploration, and constrained vs. expressive) as higher-level attributes that primarily characterize the user experience, and can be *indirectly* influenced by the TUI designer through the *direct* manipulation of lower-level **parameters** (e.g. number of modules, module granularity). Themes cannot be considered in isolation from one another; rather, they are closely interrelated through a web of the parameters. By tuning parameters, designers can help shift their systems to better meet their design intentions. Four themes emerged from speaking with experts, which take on the form of bipolar axes:

- ***Efficiency vs. Exploration*** describes the extent to which users are encouraged to arrive at a specific configuration versus try out different physical arrangements of modules
- ***Repulsion vs. Attachment*** refers to the degree to which a user is inclined to either dispose of or keep the modules of a constructive assembly or assembled wholes
- ***Constrained vs. Expressive*** refers to the size of the design space covered by the constructive assembly
- ***Novice vs. Expert*** describes the extent to which the constructive assembly is geared towards novices or experts in the target problem domain.

The tight coupling of parameters and themes can be illustrated as follows. For instance, increasing both the number of possible connections and modular granularity (i.e. making modules smaller) would increase the complexity of the assembly. This would make it more difficult for novice users to handle, but would boost the degree of expressiveness of the constructive assembly. If this expressiveness is wielded skillfully by the user to create assemblies that are aesthetically pleasing, they may feel stronger attachment to their constructions. Consequently, these users would be more hesitant to disassemble them and would experiment less with different configurations.

Theme 1: Efficiency vs. Exploration

Efficiency and exploration represent two sides of the same coin. This theme (see Figure 5) captures this concept and describes to what degree a system encourages users in trying out different physical configurations versus arriving at a specific configuration of modules.

In general, making modules robust (E1, E8), cheap (E1) and easy to attach and detach from one another (E1) was said to encourage exploration. Furthermore, limiting the number of modules in a set can *"force people to modify it and destroy it"* (E1) and thereby drive exploration by necessity. Emphasis on physical over digital representations was said to encourage

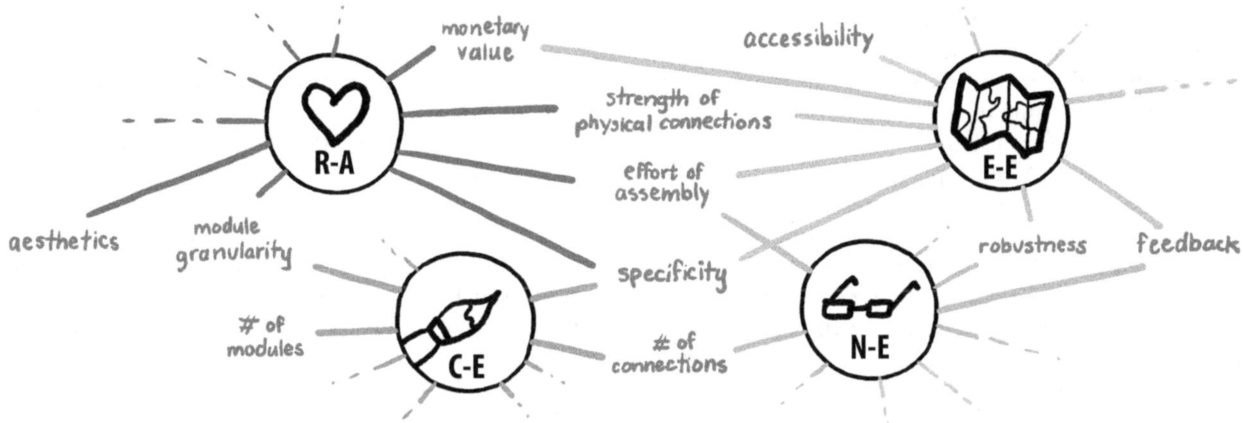

Figure 4. A figurative depiction of the network of the themes for constructive assemblies [Efficiency vs. Exploration (E-E), Repulsion vs. Attachment (R-A), Constrained vs. Expressive (C-E), and Novice vs. Expert (N-E)] and some of their associated parameters.

exploration since *"anything physical will be modified or will be used for something different"* (E1), while making physical modules more generic would have a similar effect and be a catalyst for *"creative misuse"* (E1). In contrast, working opposite to these suggestions would push a design towards the efficiency side of the axis.

Experts pointed out that a user's personality and mentality are also influential, albeit they lie outside the designers' control. *"Revolutionary thinking"* (i.e. thinking in a cycle of construction and deconstruction) and an attitude of *"not getting too precious about individual constructions"* motivates users to explore (E6), but there is ultimately *"variation within the users"* where some are *"super proactive and reconfigure a simple interface all the time"* while others are *"very lazy" (E8).*

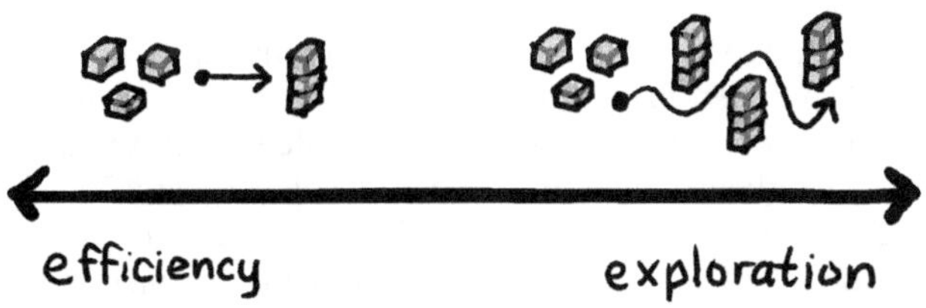

Figure 5. Efficiency vs. Exploration Axis.

Prevalence in Literature

The target problem to be addressed by the constructive assembly determines where the design should be situated along the axis. For instance, this theme has played an important role in past constructive assemblies such as with the caterpillar for storytelling in [3], or in Triangles [13] where designers intended for users to experiment with different configurations and topologies. In contrast, a constructive assembly designed to be used as a rig for 3D character animation [11] seeks to position itself on the efficiency side of this axis.

Theme 2: Repulsion vs. Attachment

This theme (see Figure 6) refers to the level of emotional attachment a constructive assembly fosters. Users can develop attachment to either the system as a material, or to constructed wholes. As mentioned by E6, *"people don't feel bad making a thing and breaking it apart. But they do feel really precious about the material itself,"* referring to how users have *"strong emotional reactions"* to supergluing LEGO® bricks such that blocks cannot be reclaimed (E6).

In general, it appears that user attachment to constructions largely hinges on whether they anticipate them to stay intact; weak physical connections and low material value and quality hampers feelings of attachment. E6 mentioned that people are *"much less precious"* about traditional building blocks *"because they don't hold themselves together,"* and see cheap Popsicle sticks as *"entirely fungible [and] completely disposable."* Conversely, having an aesthetic look and a more specific rather than general purpose nature can foster attachment. As stated by E2, *"if you have a beautifully designed object, you will form a very strong connection with it."* Stated by E6, *"people are going to have a more personal relationship with a specific teddy bear, as opposed to blocks that could be anything."* Additionally, the mere act of building was identified as a process that can impart significance to an assembled whole (E2, E7).

Figure 6. Repulsion vs. Attachment Axis.

Beyond designers' control, we can recognize that some people simply like to keep their constructions (E5). Time can also play a factor wherein attachment can develop retrospectively: *"a lot of the love for LEGO is retrospective ... you remember afterwards all this time you spent doing things..."* (E6).

Prevalence in Literature

We observe that existing constructive assemblies do not span broadly across this design axis. With regards to attachment to constructive assemblies as a material, designers have predominantly strived to foster higher levels of emotional attachment, for instance, by leveraging *aesthetics* and incorporating a variety of pleasant colors [11,15,27].

The observed gaps along this axis can be exploited as new areas for research. In fact, we suspect that as the fabrication of modular and interactive pieces becomes cheaper and easier, more examples of one-time or 'disposable' constructive assemblies will emerge. For instance, we can consider a constructive assembly kit to help people physically express their ideas, which fosters low levels of attachment such that people dispose of it after use – like scrap paper. Conversely, with regards to fostering high levels of attachment for assembled wholes, one can envision assemblies for creating personalized robots as companions. In this case, the underlying design intention may be for people to keep assembled creations largely intact rather than completely disassemble them.

Theme 3: Constrained vs. Expressive

This theme (see Figure 7) refers to the size of the space of possibilities the constructive assembly can accommodate, and touches upon the degrees of freedom a system has.

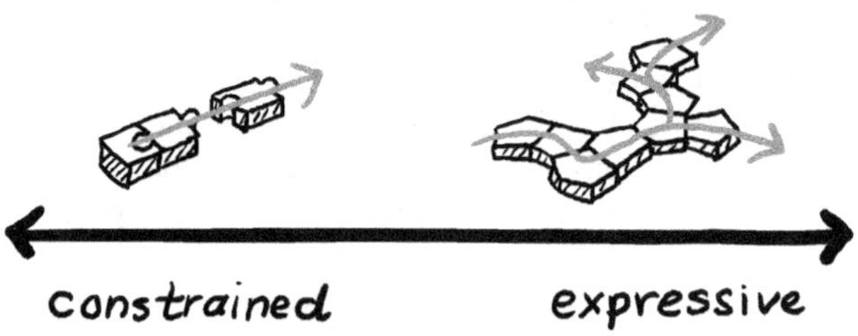

Figure 7. Constrained vs. Expressive Axis.

On the whole, a design can be made more expressive by introducing more physical and digital degrees of freedom. Specific examples include increasing the number of types of modules or the number of possible physical connections. Whilst not a constructive assembly, the reacTable [19] (an interactive surface, tabletop TUI for live music performance), was mentioned as allowing users to "*express their musical intention*" due the fact that it allows for "*many combinations ... and so many configurations, which is virtually endless*" (E4). Increasing granularity (i.e. reducing module size) can also extend the expressive capacity of the system by offering users a finer degree of control and more means of physical manipulation: "*Clay is expressive and dynamic. You can hammer with a fist on it and make something with it, whereas you wouldn't do that with LEGO bricks*" (E4). Additionally, "hacking" can be seen as a user attempt to expand the expressiveness, for which designers can explicitly choose to support (E1), and the growing access to prototyping tools can help to fuel this (E4).

On a superficial level, it may seem that this theme mirrors the efficiency vs. exploration theme. However, we highlight the distinction that this theme concerns the design space covered by the constructive assembly system, whereas the other focuses on the degree to which the system encourages users to explore possible configurations within the design space afforded by the system. Whether designers aim for a more constrained or expressive system depends on the target problem. Expressivity can work to cater to different tastes (E3) and working needs (E1), whereas more constrained systems can aid users in arriving at desirable topologies sooner.

Prevalence in Literature

Many works from literature lean towards high expressivity, as in Triangles [13] or the emergent interfaces assembly in [7]. As the ability to quickly connect and disconnect pieces is generally conducive for experimentation and creativity, many designers wish to exploit this by designing their system to have a broad space within which users can explore different topologies [27]. However, designers have also worked to constrain their systems – oftentimes to teach topics that involve strict rules or syntax. Constraints help to enforce users to recognize and internalize these strict rules; constructive assemblies for teaching programming [15,25] or for producing code [6] for instance can be situated on the constrained side of the axis.

Theme 4: Novice vs. Expert

This theme (see Figure 8) refers to the extent to which the constructive assembly is designed to cater to novice or expert users in a target domain. Experts generally felt that existing work has a tendency to target novices and "*address a very early stage of [skill] development,*" (E4). Short projects, small teams, (E2) and a desire to limit the scope of work (E4) were said to be reasons for this.

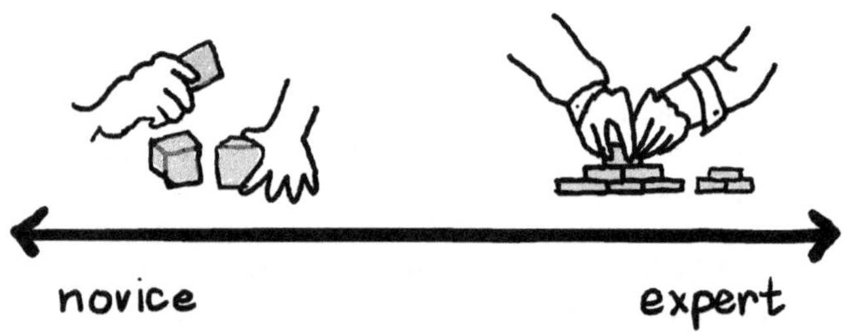

Figure 8. Novice vs. Expert Axis.

In general, experts expressed differing opinions on handling the novice-expert user spectrum. E5, E6, and E7 commented that tools should not be designed to handle both novices and experts. Conversely, comments from E1, E2, E3 and E5 suggested that it would be ideal for a TUI to cater and adapt to both. Hiding advanced functionality, allowing advanced functionality to be added (E1), and allowing learning aids to be removed (E1, E5) were suggested as ways to bridge the gap between different levels, in which case care should be taken to ensure that functionality is not then overlooked by users (E3).

Furthermore, novices and experts were said to have different sets of needs and desires. Novices value robustness and functional transparency, such that *"...no unexpected things can happen" (E1).* E4 and E5 underlined the importance of feedback, as it "*helps [users] make sense of the response"* (E5). In some cases, physical rather than digital interactions were said to be helpful for novices, as many people are comfortable with modifying physical materials (E1). However, E2 and E4 cautioned against making constructive assemblies too simple. *"Easy is one thing people strive for, but for very wrong reasons. [...] maybe it should be harder, not easier than using another, because most of the rewarding experiences we have are not easy ones"* (E2). Experts, on the other hand, were said to appreciate the ability to build constructions which do specific things (E1, E4), increase performance, and speed-up common actions (E1). Systems should also have enough depth such that experts can continue to *"discover new combinations [and] learn new things"* (E4).

Prevalence in Literature

This is a prominent theme and topic for discussion in the design of constructive assemblies. We note that in practice, no TUI targets a discrete level of expertise; rather, they always cater to a range of skill levels. However, in general, the bulk of systems focus on catering to novice users e.g. [6,35]. We suspect that the reason is two-fold. First, physical interfaces afford physical gestures or manipulations that many people are capable of performing and are used to doing in their everyday lives. Secondly, we suspect that this may be because many TUIs rely on a 1:1 representation of pieces and concepts, and thus rapidly become increasingly cumbersome to use as higher and more expert levels of complexity are approached. On the high end of the spectrum, we observe that few works have focused predominantly on catering to experts. This may begin to change however, as one work (a constructive assembly for 3D character animation [11]) has shown a significant breakthrough in tackling the practicality-complexity trade-off issue. It demonstrated how software can be effectively used to make constructive assemblies useful and appealing to expert users.

UTILITY OF THE FRAMEWORK: CASE STUDIES

In this section, we motivate the utility of the lifecycle model and the network of themes and parameters as a tool for critical reflection of existing constructive assemblies and as an aid to find directions for future iterations in their design. We examine two examples from literature through the lens of our framework, and also explore the concepts in the context of our own design case for a constructive assembly. In selecting these examples, we adhere to the definition of constructive assemblies in [7,17,28] as TUIs that have traditionally been inspired from LEGO and involve the interconnection of modular interactive elements that are manually or automatically put together to create more complex structures. Furthermore, these cases were chosen to include classical and modern examples that cover a diverse range of design goals and intentions, in order to demonstrate the broad applicability of the framework.

Case 1: Topobo

Topobo [27], is designed to teach children physics concepts, by enabling them to experiment in making biomorphic forms which can record and replay motion (see Figure 9, left). Its ***lifecycle*** comprises *construction (*piecing together modules), *usage* (observing assembled creations), *tweaking* (adding, removing, or programming pieces), and *destruction* (disassembling creatures). In evaluation, users who did incremental tweaking as opposed to constructed entire creations before programming had greater success in making creatures that were balanced and could walk. As visualized in Figure 10, left, the system supports high degrees of ***exploration***; generally, the *immediacy* of the interface in responding to user-manipulation encourages rapid experimentation and tweaking. However, a software bug of one module had detracted from this as it sometimes caused erratic behavior and gave people the fear of broken parts. The system appeals to a fairly high degree of ***attachment***, as it *reflects qualities of the user;* creatures tend to exhibit "emotionally engaging motions" as they mirror users' body movements. It is also highly ***expressive*** as it supports a wide breadth of possible topologies given a *high number of modules* (13) which were furthermore *programmable* to have unique motion patterns. The system primarily supports ***novices*** as pieces are generally *robust,* have *guides and scaffolding* integrated into them, and have a *simple* one-button interface for programming. However, the depth of expression afforded by the system expands its reach beyond novice users to also reach slightly more expert users.

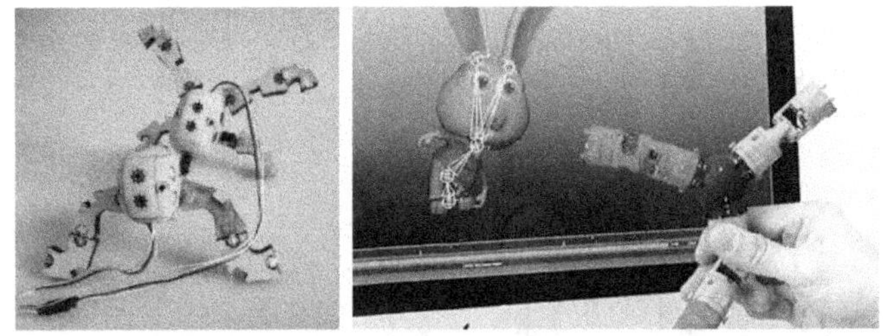

Figure 9. Examples of constructive assemblies: an early version of Topobo [28] (left), and a tangible and modular input device for the animation of 3D characters [10] (right).

Case 2: Tangible and Modular Animation Rig

This system uses a constructive assembly as a physical input device and rig for posing and animating 3D characters [11] (see Figure 9, right). The ***lifecycle*** for this assembly is straightforward, and comprises *creation* (assembling of an entire rig according to a software-generated suggestion), *usage* (repositioning the rig into different poses), optionally *storage* (keeping the rig intact for subsequent sessions), and *destruction* (disassembling the rig into constituent pieces for use in new rigs.) As seen in Figure 10, middle, this work focuses on supporting ***efficiency***. Software is used to bypass user experimentation, such that users can arrive at an effective configuration of modules to model a 3D character. The system features modules with pleasing *aesthetics,* fostering a moderate degree of ***attachment*** not for particular configurations but for the system as a tool. The system also features a high degree of ***expressiveness***, which is necessary for it to accommodate a large design space of possible 3D characters. This is achieved by designing modules to support a high *number of connections*, which are also *physically dynamic* and afford *movement.* It caters well to both ***novice and expert*** users. Direct manipulation makes interaction fairly *simple* which is good for novices, while it also offers experts a significant *speed-up* through the use of computational optimization and modelling.

Case 3: Designing an Emotion Music Player

We implemented a constructive assembly (see Figure 11) to allow users to find and play music that complements their changing moods. Different vertical configurations of colored LEGO bricks atop a monitor, detected with a depth-sensing camera, determine what music is played. To use the system, users first map colors to moods using an onscreen editor (e.g.

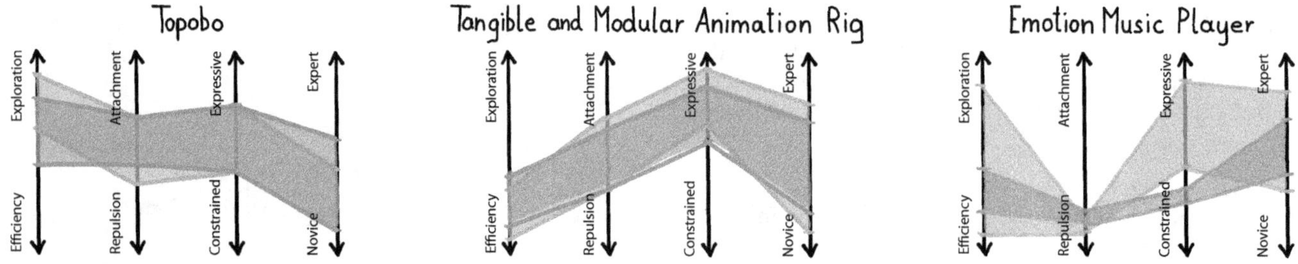

Figure 10. Mapping examples of constructive assemblies along the four design axes. Blue marks the current system's qualities; green indicates a direction for future iterations of the respective systems.

yellow to 'happy', green to 'relaxed'). Thereafter, adding or removing blocks to a stack increases or decreases a specific mood's weighting respectively. The system has a ***lifecycle*** comprising *creation* (assembly of stacks), *usage* (listening to the triggered music), *tweaking* (adding or removing blocks), *storage* (keeping a configuration constant while away from the desk) and *destruction* (disassembly of the stacks). The system should span both ***efficiency and exploration***, where users can find new music tracks that correspond with their mood. However, the limited number of colors hinders the ease with which a user can navigate the broad search space of music. This mismatch can be detected along the first axis of Figure 10, right. Offering *more physical means* to interact with music search parameters may improve this. The *generic* appearance discourages ***attachment*** to particular configurations and instead encourages users to experiment with different ones. As the current implementation only offers two *degrees of freedom* (colors, number of blocks), it appears to have an insufficient degree of ***expressiveness*** to cover the music space (see Figure 10, right). Introducing more (e.g. width or color sequences) could help to close the gap between the prototype and the design intentions. While the system is intended to appeal to a broad spectrum of users, it could be improved to better cater to both novices (as it has low *functional transparency* or unclear mapping between emotions and colors) and experts (as it lacks a means to formulate *specific* search queries).

Figure 11. Emotion Music Player: users assemble stacks of blocks to control music to match their changing moods.

Case Studies Discussion

We applied our framework to different cases based on examples from literature and our own design study. The diversity of the examples covered highlight the framework's broad applicability, and the case studies illustrate how the framework can be used to critically analyze works that have very different design intentions, in order to provide directions for improvement that align appropriately with these intentions.

Applying the lifecycle model can help break down user-interactions to study them in greater depth. For instance, we can observe that Topobo's strength lies in supporting rapid *tweaking*. In contrast, the *storage phase* of the animation rig could be enhanced with the ability to reinstate past poses, since users are likely unable to complete animation tasks in a single session. The design axes helped to frame design choices and isolate both where designs succeed and fall short of their intentions (as illustrated in Figure 10). They also help to pinpoint parameters which may help push the design of a system closer towards its intended purpose.

CONCLUSION AND FUTURE WORK

While many established frameworks enhance our overall understanding of TUIs, few works have focused on highlighting key considerations for taking a constructive assembly approach to TUI design. In this paper, based on an analysis of data elicited through extensive interviews with world-class academic and industry TUI experts, we presented a framework for constructive assemblies. We presented benefits and drawbacks, established a lifecycle model, and unveiled key design themes pertaining to constructive assemblies alongside their associated design parameters. We applied our framework to our own work and examples from literature, and demonstrated its utility for supporting critical reflection and discussion of design choices and their implications. While one can consider it a limitation that systems cannot be precisely quantified along the four themes, the process of mapping them along the axes helps to focus one's attention on adjusting qualities that have a direct impact on the user experience for the system. Given its utility, we would like to, in future, continue using it for critical reflection to drive the improvement of constructive assembly designs. Moreover, we see that there may be opportunities to expand this framework; as more instances of constructive assemblies arise, it could be refined to contain more attributes, which in turn could further strengthen its utility for designers and practitioners making such TUIs. As some of the presented concepts appear to have use beyond constructive assembly TUIs, it would also be interesting to explore its applicability in a broader context for future research.

ACKNOWLEDGEMENTS

We thank our experts for their time in interviews, the authors who allowed us to picture their work, and Kathrin Probst for her valuable feedback and idea to present charts. This work received the funding support of NCBiR, FWF, SNSF, ANR, and FNR in the framework of the ERA-NET CHIST-ERA II.

REFERENCES

1. R. Aish. 1979. 3D input for CAAD systems. Computer-Aided Design 11, 2: 66–70. http://doi.org/10.1016/0010-4485(79)90098-8
2. Robert Aish and Peter Noakes. 1984. Architecture without numbers — CAAD based on a 3D modelling system. Computer-Aided Design 16, 6: 321–328. http://doi.org/10.1016/0010-4485(84)90116-7
3. Mike Ananny. 2002. Supporting children's collaborative authoring: practicing written literacy while composing oral texts. 595–596. Retrieved September 23, 2015 from http://dl.acm.org/citation.cfm?id=1658616.1658739
4. David Anderson, Jonathan S. Yedidia, James L. Frankel, et al. 2000. Tangible Interaction + graphical interpretation: a new approach to 3D modeling. Proceedings of the 27th annual conference on Computer graphics and interactive techniques - SIGGRAPH '00, ACM Press, 393–402. http://doi.org/10.1145/344779.344960
5. Richard Borovoy. 1996. Dr. LEGOHead, Ph.D.: a real-world story construction environment. 552. Retrieved September 23, 2015 from http://dl.acm.org/citation.cfm?id=1161135.1161220
6. David Bouchard and Steve Daniels. 2015. Tiles that Talk: Tangible Templates for Networked Objects. Proceedings of the Ninth International Conference on Tangible, Embedded, and Embodied Interaction - TEI '14, ACM Press, 197–200. http://doi.org/10.1145/2677199.2680607
7. Alexandru Dancu, Morten Fjeld, Catherine Hedler, et al. 2015. Emergent Interfaces. Proceedings of the 33rd Annual ACM Conference Extended Abstracts on Human Factors in Computing Systems - CHI EA '15, ACM Press, 451–460. http://doi.org/10.1145/2702613.2732509
8. Kenneth P. Fishkin. 2004. A taxonomy for and analysis of tangible interfaces. Personal and Ubiquitous Computing 8, 5: 347–358. http://doi.org/10.1007/s00779-004-0297-4
9. J.H. Frazer, J.M Frazer, and P.A Frazer. 1980. Intelligent physical three-dimensional modeling system. Computer Graphics Conference, vol. 80, 359–370.
10. John Frazer. 1995. An Evolutionary Architecture. Architectural Association, London.
11. Oliver Glauser, Wan-Chun Ma, Daniele Panozzo, Alec Jacobson, Otmar Hilliges, and Olga Sorkine-Hornung. 2016. Rig animation with a tangible and modular input device. ACM Transactions on Graphics 35, 4: 1–11. http://doi.org/10.1145/2897824.2925909
12. Jennifer W. Glos and Justine Cassell. 1997. Rosebud. CHI '97 extended abstracts on Human factors in computing systems looking to the future - CHI '97, ACM Press, 359. http://doi.org/10.1145/1120212.1120433
13. Matthew G. Gorbet, Maggie Orth, and Hiroshi Ishii. 1998. Triangles. Proceedings of the SIGCHI conference on Human factors in computing systems - CHI '98, ACM Press, 49–56. http://doi.org/10.1145/274644.274652
14. Lars Erik Holmquist, Johan Redström, and Peter Ljungstrand. 1999. Token-Based Access to Digital Information. Proceedings of the 1st international symposium on Handheld and Ubiquitous Computing, Springer-Verlag, 234–245.
15. Michael S. Horn, Erin Treacy Solovey, and Robert J. K. Jacob. 2008. Tangible programming and informal science learning. Proceedings of the 7th international conference on Interaction design and children - IDC '08, ACM Press, 194. http://doi.org/10.1145/1463689.1463756
16. Eva Hornecker and Jacob Buur. 2006. Getting a grip on tangible interaction. Proceedings of the SIGCHI conference on Human Factors in computing systems - CHI '06, ACM Press, 437. http://doi.org/10.1145/1124772.1124838
17. Hiroshi Ishii. 2008. Tangible bits: beyond pixels. Proceedings of the 2nd international conference on Tangible and embedded interaction - TEI '08, ACM Press, xv. http://doi.org/10.1145/1347390.1347392
18. Robert J.K. Jacob, Audrey Girouard, Leanne M. Hirshfield, et al. 2008. Reality-based interaction. Proceeding of the twenty-sixth annual CHI conference on Human factors in computing systems - CHI '08, ACM Press, 201. http://doi.org/10.1145/1357054.1357089
19. Sergi Jordà, Günter Geiger, Marcos Alonso, and Martin Kaltenbrunner. 2007. The reacTable. Proceedings of the 1st international conference on Tangible and embedded interaction - TEI '07, ACM Press, 139. http://doi.org/10.1145/1226969.1226998
20. Yoshifumi Kitamura, Yuichi Itoh, Toshihiro Masaki, and Fumio Kishino. 2000. ActiveCube: a bi-directional user interface using cubes. KES'2000. Fourth International Conference on Knowledge-Based Intelligent Engineering Systems and Allied Technologies., IEEE, 99–102. http://doi.org/10.1109/KES.2000.885768
21. Rong-Hao Liang, Liwei Chan, Hung-Yu Tseng, et al. 2014. GaussBricks. Proceedings of the 32nd annual ACM conference on Human factors in computing systems - CHI '14, ACM Press, 3153–3162. http://doi.org/10.1145/2556288.2557105

22. Paul Marshall. 2007. Do tangible interfaces enhance learning? Proceedings of the 1st international conference on Tangible and embedded interaction - TEI '07, ACM Press, 163. http://doi.org/10.1145/1226969.1227004
23. Fred Martin and Mitchel Resnick. 1993. LEGO/Logo and Electronic Bricks: Creating a Scienceland for Children. In Advanced Educational Technologies for Mathematics and Science, David L. Ferguson (ed.). Springer Berlin Heidelberg, 61–89. http://doi.org/10.1007/978-3-662-02938-1_2
24. Ali Mazalek and Elise van den Hoven. 2009. Framing tangible interaction frameworks. Artificial Intelligence for Engineering Design, Analysis and Manufacturing 23, 3: 225. http://doi.org/10.1017/S0890060409000201
25. Timothy S. McNerney. 2004. From turtles to Tangible Programming Bricks: explorations in physical language design. Personal and Ubiquitous Computing 8, 5: 326–337. http://doi.org/10.1007/s00779-004-0295-6
26. Hyunjoo Oh and Mark D. Gross. 2015. Cube-in. Proceedings of the Ninth International Conference on Tangible, Embedded, and Embodied Interaction - TEI '14, ACM Press, 383–386. http://doi.org/10.1145/2677199.2680597
27. Hayes Solos Raffle, Amanda J. Parkes, and Hiroshi Ishii. 2004. Topobo. Proceedings of the 2004 conference on Human factors in computing systems - CHI '04, ACM Press, 647–654. http://doi.org/10.1145/985692.985774
28. Anne Roudaut, Rebecca Reed, Tianbo Hao, and Sriram Subramanian. 2014. Changibles. Proceedings of the 32nd annual ACM conference on Human factors in computing systems - CHI '14, ACM Press, 2593–2596. http://doi.org/10.1145/2556288.2557006
29. Philipp Schoessler, Daniel Windham, Daniel Leithinger, Sean Follmer, and Hiroshi Ishii. 2015. Kinetic Blocks. Proceedings of the 28th Annual ACM Symposium on User Interface Software & Technology - UIST '15, ACM Press, 341–349. http://doi.org/10.1145/2807442.2807453
30. Eric Schweikardt and Mark D. Gross. 2006. roBlocks. Proceedings of the 8th international conference on Multimodal interfaces - ICMI '06, ACM Press, 72. http://doi.org/10.1145/1180995.1181010
31. Orit Shaer. 2009. Tangible User Interfaces: Past, Present, and Future Directions. *Foundations and Trends in Human–Computer Interaction* 3, 1–2: 1–137. http://doi.org/10.1561/1100000026
32. Orit Shaer, Nancy Leland, Eduardo H. Calvillo-Gamez, and Robert J.K. Jacob. 2004. The TAC paradigm: specifying tangible user interfaces. *Personal and Ubiquitous Computing* 8, 5: 359–369. http://doi.org/10.1007/s00779-004-0298-3
33. Hideyuki Suzuki and Hiroshi Kato. 1995. Interaction-level support for collaborative learning. *The first international conference on Computer support for collaborative learning - CSCL '95*, Association for Computational Linguistics, 349–355. http://doi.org/10.3115/222020.222828
34. B. Ullmer and H. Ishii. 2000. Emerging frameworks for tangible user interfaces. *IBM Systems Journal* 39, 3.4: 915–931. http://doi.org/10.1147/sj.393.0915
35. Peta Wyeth and Helen C. Purchase. 2002. Tangible programming elements for young children. *CHI '02 extended abstracts on Human factors in computing systems - CHI '02*, ACM Press, 774. http://doi.org/10.1145/506443.506591
36. Jamie Zigelbaum, Michael S. Horn, Orit Shaer, and Robert J. K. Jacob. 2007. The tangible video editor. *Proceedings of the 1st international conference on Tangible and embedded interaction - TEI '07*, ACM Press, 43. http://doi.org/10.1145/1226969.1226978
37. Oren Zuckerman, Saeed Arida, and Mitchel Resnick. 2005. Extending tangible interfaces for education. *Proceedings of the SIGCHI conference on Human factors in computing systems - CHI '05*, ACM Press, 859. http://doi.org/10.1145/1054972.1055093
38. littleBits Electronics. Retrieved July 31, 2015 from http://littlebits.cc/

Un-Crafting: De-Constructive Engagements with Interactive Artifacts

Martin Murer[1], Verena Fuchsberger[1], Manfred Tscheligi[1,2]
[1]Center for Human-Computer Interaction, University of Salzburg, Salzburg, Austria
[2]AIT Austrian Institute of Technology, Vienna, Austria
firstname.lastname@sbg.ac.at

ABSTRACT
Crafting interactive artifacts is typically associated with synthesizing, making, constructing, putting things together. In this paper, we discuss how these activities can be contrasted with de-synthesizing activities that revolve around decomposition, dissection, and taking things apart. Based on framings that emphasize how related practices are valuable in engineering processes, we aim to unlock the potential of de-constructive engagements with interactive technologies as a material driven (design) practice. We propose *un-crafting* as a framework of four modes of taking interactive artifacts apart (i.e., un-crafting for material exposition, material inspiration, material inquiry, and material exploration) aiming to pinpoint de-constructive episodes inherent to design processes, as well as to encourage the refinement of respective techniques and methods.

ACM Classification Keywords
H.5.m. Information Interfaces and Presentation (e.g. HCI): Miscellaneous

Author Keywords
Crafting; Deconstruction; Disassembly; Interaction Design; Making; Material; Un-Crafting.

INTRODUCTION
A young girl, not ten years old, spending much of her upbringing in the backwoods of northern Quebec, satisfying her curiosity about the world through pocketbook mysteries, carefully dissecting insects or cutting open her doll's head to figure out the mechanism of its rolling eyes. Since the childhood of famous Canadian science fiction author Margret Atwood, lively recounted during a keynote at CHI 2014 [2], taking things apart has had a lasting impact on her imagining of new things. Similarly, design pioneer Don Norman, as a boy, "wanted to know what makes things work. From his toys to the family radio, he tried to take them apart and figure them out" [12].

TEI '17, March 20 - 23, 2017, Yokohama, Japan

ISBN 978-1-4503-4676-4/17/03. . . $15.00
DOI: http://dx.doi.org/10.1145/3024969.3024993

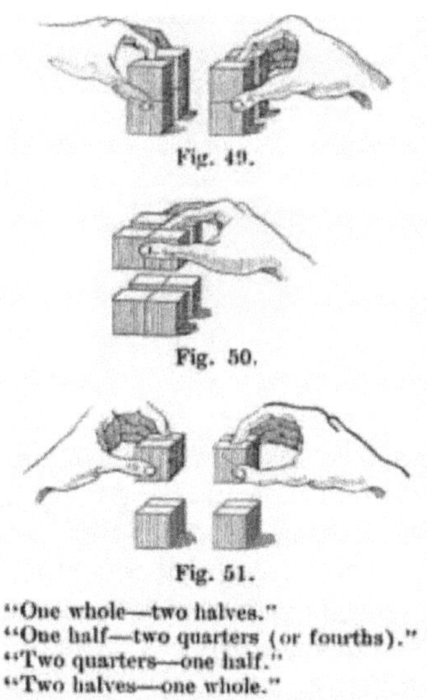

Figure 1. Fröbel's Third Gift, part of a series of educational toys, a cube composed of eight cubes, accompanied by detailed instructions for the educator. It aimed to enable children to get ideas on early number through the acts of taking it apart, putting it back together, and recombining its pieces. Image taken from [53, p. 100]

Episodes like these and similar personal encounters with dissecting are often originating from curiosity, i.e., to figure out and understand the world.

Already what can be considered the first educational toys (see figure 1) aimed to harvest this curiosity by emphasizing the value of disassembling as inherent counterpart to constructing with building blocks. This particular set of educational material laid the foundation of many of today's popular construction kits, such as LEGO or Lincoln Logs, and continually inspires the development of novel (computational) construction kits (e.g., [18]). Current building and construction kits (e.g., [10, 18, 19, 26, 36]) not only target learning but are essential elements of design and research practice.

However, most available tools and (constructive) design approaches (e.g., [20, 46, 47]), as well as the related theoretical discourse, typically emphasize construction, leaving aside the potential of the inherent de-constructive counterpart. Nevertheless, activities that focus on dissecting the physical world

Figure 2. The *Third Gift* as it was deployed by game manufacturer Milton Bradley to Kindergartens in the late 19th century. The *Fröbel Gifts* are considered to be fundamental for the development of construction kits, from LEGO to computational construction kits. [35] Image courtesy of *The Strong* (www.museumofplay.org), Rochester, New York, USA

are inherent in many interaction design practices as well, e.g., during tinkering, harvesting of components from broken appliances, refactoring an existing prototype, etc. Given the complex nature of today's products, taking them apart to figure them out is particularly challenging, and tremendously different from, e.g., taking apart a LEGO construction. Nevertheless, de-constructive practices continue to provide a rich potential for human engagement with the objects that surround us, for instance during repair and reuse (e.g., [17]) or as part of an artistic practice (e.g., [25]). With this paper, we aim to foreground how de-constructing is an inevitable element of constructing things with elaborating *how interaction design may render its de-constructive practices visible; how we can articulate and frame these moments of* un-crafting.

In order to elaborate a conceptual framework for how to approach de-constructive engagements with interactive artefacts, we first trace the roots of un-crafting in constructionist thinking and how it informs interaction design research, and proceed by illustrating how de-construction is already part of education. Based on a respective framework of reverse engineering and product dissection, we then propose an *un-crafting framework* which consists of four engagements with the forms and functions of interactive artifacts: *material exposition*, *material inspiration*, *material inquiry*, and *material exploration*. Finally, we discuss the potential of un-crafting in interactive system design, i.e., for material engagements and dissections of the interactive, and what it might contribute to collaborative sense making.

BACKGROUND

Taking things apart, as a *de-constructive* approach to interactive artifacts in education, research, and design practice, can be rooted in a tradition that is of high relevance and visibility in contemporary interaction design research: constructionist thinking. Below, we will highlight how constructionist thinking led to early educational toys and the further development and refinement of *constructive* approaches and methods in (mainly STEM) education, as well as to a plethora of related construction kits used in education and design practice that emphasize the act of making things as a bridge between "creative physical and conceptual exploration" [37, p. 252]. Thereafter, we articulate how engineering education has adapted de-constructive approaches (e.g., reverse engineering or product dissection) for applying them as educational program.

Historical Foundations

Many accounts for disassembling practices are related to childhood and curiosity, as described already in the 19th century by educator Edward Wiebe:

> A prominent desire in the mind of every child is to divide things, in order to examine the parts of which they consist. This natural instinct is observable at a very early period. The little one tries to change its toy by breaking it, desirous of looking at its inside, and is sadly disappointed in finding itself incapable of reconstructing the fragments. [52, p. 11]

In his 1869 *Guide to Kinder-Gartners*, Wiebe articulates the Kindergarten movement, a program of preschool education envisioned by the German educator Friedrich Fröbel, who, through his observations of young learners, had noticed that children have "observing and destructive as well as unifying and creative instincts" [35]. Consequently, taking objects apart, putting them back together, observing and analyzing them, imitating existing and creating new objects were essential parts of his educational vision. Based on the fundamental idea that all education should begin with a development of the "desire for activity innate in the child" [52, p. 11], Fröbel developed his Kindergarten program to encourage children to learn through self-directed play, facilitated by a sequence of educational toys he entitled *gifts* and *occupations*.

This "Fröbel Gifts" are still at use in various educational settings and are considered fundamental to both the development of construction kits, as well as their formal, structured application in education [35]. Especially the third Gift, depicted in Figure 1 and Figure 2, takes up on dissection, taking apart, disassembling:

> In it the child receives a whole, whose parts he can easily separate, and put together again at pleasure. Thus he is able to do that which he could not in the case of the toys – restore to its original form that which was broken – making a perfect whole. And not only this – he can use the parts also for the construction of other wholes. [52, p. 11]

The epistemological potential of such acts of decomposing, dissecting, and disassembling have, since then, been discussed quite regularly. It's not surprising that they found their way into various strands in education. User interface researcher Ted Selker once expressed a similar observation. Being interviewed about the current state of engineering education, he stated that processes of taking things apart and building things have been proven to facilitate the ability to learn conceptually and not just procedurally, as they allow the development of intuition needed to make useful and creative connections [7].

Constructionist Thinking

With regards to understanding computational technology no longer as just a tool but as material that can be "messed around with", Seymour Papert is considered to be one of the first proponents of such a perspective [50]. His constructionist theory holds that learning as a "construction in the head" happens especially well when

> it is supported by construction of a more public sort 'in the world' — a sand castle or a cake, a Lego house or a corporation, a computer program, a poem, or a theory of the universe. [34, p. 142]

Asserting that meaning-construction happens especially well when it is accompanied by an external material resource is fundamentally related to what Fröbel called 'making the inner outer and the outer inner' and Piaget later described as 'assimilation and accommodation' [16]. Thereby, assimilation is considered a mental operation, which changes representations of the world to fit individual ways of thinking, while accomodation means to adapt individual ways of thinking to fit the world [34]. Constructionist theory though goes beyond Piaget's constructivism in its emphasis on *building* external and sharable artifacts [19], on constructing "things in the world" that can be "shown, discussed, probed, and admired" [34]. Knowledge is considered as experience, i.e., it is actively constructed and reconstructed through direct interaction with the environment [1]. Designing and creating things, and especially those that are meaningful to the learner and others around them, are likely to provide "the best learning experiences" [40].

Construction in Education

Based on Papert's understanding of computers as materials, a plethora of educational construction kits has since been developed in this tradition. Many of those efforts explicitly see LEGO construction kits as a model for what they are trying to achieve with computational technology [40]. Following this programatic agenda, Mitchel Resnick, a disciple of Papert heading the Lifelong Kindergarten group at the MIT Media Lab, and his colleagues, have designed manifold creative tools and instruments that aim at engaging people in creative learning. For instance, their programmable bricks [39] ultimately led to the development of the LEGO mindstorms, as one of the most prominent computational thinking tools. Taking things apart is part of what they envision their users to do with the tools they provide:

> In designing creativity support tools, we put a high priority on 'tinkerability' we want to encourage users to mess with the materials, to try out multiple alternatives, to shift directions in the middle of the process, to take things apart and create new versions. [39]

Nevertheless, while taking things apart – as a complementing practice to putting things together – is not excluded in the constructionist tradition, it is though arguably not part of their core program, with its emphasis on the construction, on the synthesizing of elements into a new thing.

Constructionist thinking and respective construction kits are commonly accepted as being beneficial for education (and especially STEM education). While many construction kits, computational thinking tools and related platforms may have initially targeted education in, e.g., engineering or computational thinking, the boundaries between education and interaction design (research) practice are continuously blurring: research on tangible and embedded interaction is contributing largely to the development and refinement of the according tools (e.g., [3, 5, 11, 41, 44, 56]); likewise the tools (with platforms such as Arduino or RaspberryPi being the most prominent ones) play a crucial role in various design processes. Deconstruction, however, has been a less visible paradigm, with only a few accounts of how deconstruction can be a means for education (and, hence, also for design processes), which we will discuss in the following.

De-Construction in Education

In contemporary engineering education, constructionist modes of learning are complemented by what one may call *deconstructive* modes of learning, and by the respective methods and approaches that harvest the potential of taking things apart.

Practices that involve disassembling of existing artifacts, e.g., appliances, have a long tradition in engineering. While since adopted in manifold engineering realms such as software, reverse engineering has its origins in the analysis of hardware. The practice of deciphering designs from finished products is considered to be commonplace and regularly applied in industry

> to improve your own products, as well as to analyze a competitor's products or those of an adversary in a military or national-security situation. [6, p. 13]

Consequently, typical questions reverse engineering aims to answer are: *How does it work? What is it made of? How was it manufactured?*

Product dissection got introduced to (undergraduate) engineering in the early 1990s and since got pervasive [27]. Its roots lay in a course entitled *Mechanical Dissection* initiated at Stanford University by Sheri D. Sheppard (see e.g., [45]). In line with constructionist thinking, product dissection in engineering education facilitates hands-on activities [27].

Reverse engineering and product dissection have been used interchangeably, though they carry at least subtle differences. Ogot and colleagues [32] differentiate between them two, as their aims, roles, and outcomes differ. The distinction they propose is that dissection can be simply defined as "disassembling and reassembling an [...] artifact", while reverse engineering is typically goal oriented and, as phrased by Wood and colleagues,

> initiates the redesign process wherein a product is predicted, observed and disassembled, analyzed, tested, 'experienced', and documented in terms of functionality, form, physical principles, manufacturability, and assemblability. [55]

As a related approach to de-constructive modes of learning for STEM education, Griffin and colleagues propose *Deconstruction Kits*, designed to promote learning as they are taken apart [13]. They envision deconstruction kits based on the building blocks of construction kits of various kinds: games, mobile apps, stories, circuits, animations, simulations, etc. In particular, they propose three distinct types of deconstruction kits: DEBUG'EMS are intentionally broken, COMPLETE'EMS are incomplete, and EXPLORE'EMS are designed to be taken apart and explored. They further argue that deconstruction kits may effectively complement constructionist learning tools as there is a

> ying/yang interplay of the two learning modalities of Constructionism (learning by building) and Deconstructionism (learning by taking apart). [13, p. 4]

Besides those examples of application in formal education, an endless number of educational programs exist that facilitate taking things apart.[1] However, systematic descriptions of de-constructive programs and techniques, as well as their characteristics, have not been provided yet.

DE-CONSTRUCTION IN INTERACTION DESIGN: FROM CRAFTING TO UN-CRAFTING

Craft has become a central concern in HCI and interaction design research, with a variety of suggested approaches. For instance, Fernaeus and colleagues held a studio on handcrafting electronic accessories using 'raw' materials at a recent TEI conference (Conference on Tangible, Embedded and Embodied Interaction) [9]. Perner-Wilson et al. engaged with handcrafting textile interfaces [36], Mellis et al. discussed crafting circuits with paper, conductive ink and electronic components [26], and Tsaknaki et al. investigated leather as a material for crafting interactive and physical artifacts [47]. A studio workshop at the TEI conference 2015 addressed how disassembling computational things can yield a potential for design practice and coined *Un-Crafting* as

> the thoughtful, reflective process of disassembling [...] something which could be developed into a practice that – not unlike other studio crafts – requires particular skills, involves specific ways of reflection, and develops and according set of terms and framings. [30]

Hence, disassembly can be considered an elaborate art of its own; one that – as any craft – entails its distinct routines, practices, exercises, and working styles, and – ultimately – may lead to a strive for mastership. Several artists have arguably mastered that craft, for instance contemporary photographer Todd McLellan who created a series of photographs of 50 design classics, ranging from iconic Apple computers to chainsaws, all carefully taken apart and laid out in stunning compositions [25].

> I have been refining the art of disassembly since childhood. As a kid, I was caught in my room taking apart my toys with a hammer, and in secondary school I almost completely disassembled my 1985 Hyundai Pony car. If an object interested me, it would soon be in pieces. [25, p. 10]

[1]The *toy take apart* at the Tinkering Studio of San Francisco's Exploratorium [8] might be one of most visible examples.

If we understand interaction design as a practice of giving form to computational material [48], un-crafting can be one means to unveil the paradigms that might have directed the form-giving of a particular artifact. On a conceptual level, Hallnäs and Redstörm [14] proposed a methodological exercise that aims to unravel the relations between function and form by turning the traditional form follows function paradigm upside down:

> "Whereas 'form follows function' suggests that design expression somehow is 'derived" from functionality, the idea that 'function resides in the expression of things' suggests that we could try to discover functionality in expressions and rediscover the hidden aesthetical choices in the expressiveness of things in use. [15]

Framed as *Deconstructivist Interaction Design*, Murer and colleagues contrasted this methodological exercise with *deconstructivist* phases in related design disciplines (e.g. architecture) in order to "facilitate the differentiation of an expressional vocabulary in interaction design" [28, p. 1]. Un-crafting exercises are thought to support this program with tangible material explorations that untangle form and function of artifacts through taking them apart. As articulated by Jackson and Kang [17], uncovering the expressiveness of things is essentially linked to whether an object is functioning (or broken, respectively), a state that though can be altered purposefully by means of creative breakdowns:

> A typewriter is always a typewriter while a typewriter; once broken, [...] can be just about anything. In this way, function can constrain and obscure, locking objects into a world of necessary dependencies that limits the kinds of relations we may imagine with them (though rarely as completely as designers may imagine or perhaps hope). This is mostly to the good – technologies are designed to function and we want them to. But it also sets limits to practice and imagination that designers would do well to bear in mind, and that acts of creative breakdown, repair, and repurposing may liberate. [17, p. 457]

Jackson and Kang argue how "the wider problematic of breakdown, obsolescence and repair [...] deserves deeper consideration among the panoply of HCI concerns." [17, p. 458] Based on a program of ethnographic work with artists, who feature found and broken technologies as central methods and topics of their work, they discuss how (collaborative) acts of building with broken and discarded technologies can challenge or extend our notions of design.

Reflecting on the 'lives' of technologies that extend beyond the functions and contexts they where originally designed for, they argue that processes of creative breakdown and reuse can be one means to unleash these, as well as suggest alternate relationships with technologies.

> Within this world of creative material engagement [...] acts of maintenance, repurposing and repair constitute important and undervalued moments. 'Broken' things push back on human action and possibility in ways that ex-nihilo conceptions of creativity and design may miss. And activities of repurposing and repair may call out

> forms of long-run relationships between humans and objects that tend to disappear under the up-front design orientations of the HCI field. [17, p. 452]

Maestri and Wakkary discuss an exploratory study that aims to unveil the role creativity plays in repair [24]. Their study shows evidence of repair as

> not only an act of restoration, but also as an act of creativity that entails the repurposing and resourcing of objects. [24, p. 81]

Another account of *un-crafting* has been described by Murer et al. [29], reporting on an collaborative design exploration revolving around a mystery device, that details how unveiling the device's function through the collaborative act of taking it apart led to the emergence of common ground, as well as *shared material knowledge*. This temporary knowledge about the materials that emerged through the disassembling, together with the resulting "trove of materials", created a shared material resource that prompted the design team into a material oriented exploration of simple movement sensors (the core component of the device they took apart).

> In this case there was no real design situation in the traditional sense of having a design brief, but rather what would emerge halfway into the process was something of a *material brief*. [29, p. 472]

The above interpretation of a *material brief* resonates with *bricolage* in its interpretation as an interaction design practice, articulated by Vallgårda and Fernaeus as a way of making "which draws on what is already there both culturally and materially." [49, p. 173] While they do not explicitly mention material gained from disassembling as resources of the bricoleur, they refer to repurposing and hacking what is already there, scrape materials, and discarded projects – all of which inherently imply taking apart. Bricolage might well incorporate – or start from – an activity of taking something apart.

FRAMING UN-CRAFTING

As described earlier, un-crafting, breakdown, and repair (among others) are substantial activities in interaction design. In contrast to synthesizing activities, however, they are rarely emphasized in contemporary design practice and the according research. In order to systematically depict these distinct activities of un-crafting, we present a preliminary framework for artifact disassembling. It is conceptually based on a framework addressing disassemble/analyze/assemble (DAA) in engineering education by Ogot and colleagues [32]. In the following, we will describe the foundation of this framework that classifies disassemble/analyze/assemble activities in engineering education into four distinct categories: *expose, inspire, inquire, and explore*.

The first two activities (i.e., expose and inspire) are based on *product dissection*, revolving around *how questions* (e.g., how does the device work?), and are considered to be suitable for students in 1st and 2nd year courses. *Expose* activities aim to familiarize students with physical artifacts in a structured way and address, for instance, learning the related engineering vocabulary and terminology. *Inspire* activities are less structured and promote learning through self-discovery.

> While Expose activities use DAA to teach students about the artifacts themselves, Inspire activities use artifacts to inspire learning about related topics such as computer aided design (CAD), force transmission, or Design for X. [32, p. 125]

The latter two activities (i.e., inquire and explore) are based on *reverse engineering*, aiming at answering *why questions* (e.g., why did designers choose this material?) and are considered to be suitable for 3rd and 4th year courses. *Inquire* activities aim to reinforce engineering principles through hands-on activities in a structured way. The activities focus on the artifact and the design considerations it entails, manifested for instance, in form of reverse engineering a blueprint from a product. *Explore* activities are less structured and aim to uncover the design rationales that led to the particular implementation of a product so that those findings can then be used to design a new product that builds on that finding.

> While Inquire activities focus on the artifact itself, Explore activities use DAA to help students develop new ideas and insights. [32, p. 128]

The framework for un-crafting described in the following is conceptually based on this framework and proposes four different un-crafting engagements, i.e., dedicated ways of engaging with tangible interactive artifacts by taking them apart.

The Un-Crafting Framework

Our framework for un-crafting (depicted in figure 3) differentiates four modes of un-crafting, characterized by a distinct *purpose* of the exercise, i.e., material exposition, material inspiration, material inquiry, and material exploration. The four modes frame design exercises that, while not mutually exclusive in any practical design situation, are distinct with regards to the their *focus* (*on* the artifact / *motivated by* the artifact) and their *orientation* (*divergence* / *convergence*):

Focus refers to what is in the center of attention. For instance, in a repair situation the broken artifact is in focus, while the artifact motivates the (new) focus when remixing components gained from disassembly.

Orientation refers to the direction the exercise entails. Divergent modes of un-crafting are opening up, meandering around questions such as *How does this thing work? What is it made of?* Convergent modes of un-crafting are characterized by questions revolving around rationales and questions, such as *Why is this artifact designed as it is? Why did the designer choose a particular material?* Accordingly, the latter requires a different level of pre-conceptions about the object at hand.

The four modes of the framework may serve two distinct purposes (i.e., analytical and constructive) in the realm of interaction design: First, they may be applied *analytically* to pay attention to specific forms of un-crafting with specific purposes, foci and orientations. Here, the framework may be used to render activities visible, which are otherwise hidden in

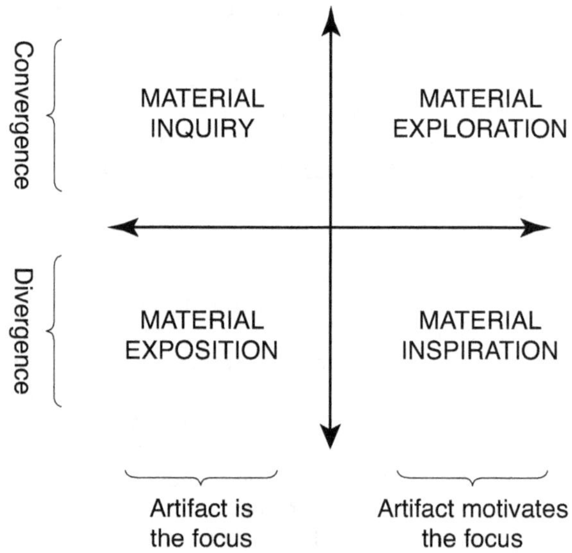

Figure 3. Un-crafting: The proposed organizational framework for disassembling in interaction design, conceptually based on [32]. While not mutually exclusive in any practical instantiation, the four quadrants classify modes of working that are distinct in their *focus* (*on* the artifact / *motivated by* the artifact) and their *orientation* (*divergence / convergence*).

or overshadowed by synthesizing, constructive activities. The four modes may be used as analytic lenses to reflect on, and describe, designs and design activities. Second, in both design practice as well as in educational exercises, the four modes may be used in a *constructive* way to create material knowledge that is neither exclusively focusing on function, nor on form, but on their interrelations. In the following paragraphs, the four modes are described in detail, including their epistemological goals and potentials. Although the framework is also intended to serve an analytical purpose, the following description of the four modes will be based on practical exercises in order to provide comprehensive exemplary activities.

Un-crafting for Material Exposition

This exercise exposes the artifact's components and how they relate to each other. Un-crafting for material exposition is an open-ended exercise and does not require specific preconceptions about the particular artifact it focuses on. An everyday example of un-crafting for material exposition is the (sometimes unconscious) disassembly of a retractable click pen, an exercise used in engineering education as well.[2] Material exposition is moreover the necessary first step to understand the inner workings of the system at hand, e.g., during repair of a broken appliance. The resources that can be gained from material exposition are twofold: a trove of materials and exposed material properties. First, it leaves one with a trove of material ready to be reassembled, reused, stored, or discarded. Second, material exposition allows to unveil the material properties of the single components.

[2]For instance, [4] provides a curricular activity around the disassembly of a click pen that targets K-12 education.

Un-crafting for Material Inspiration

Un-crafting for material inspiration studies how a particular composition of materials forms an interactive artifact. It is based on the assumption that each single component gained from disassembly carries a *material history* that emerges from the previous relations to other components in the artifact that was disassembled. Un-crafting for material inspiration is related to *sketching with hardware* in its emphasis on articulating and expressing the rules governing those interrelations. It allows for a creative engagement with the components gained in integration with those particular interrelations. A component that was gathered from disassembly is essentially different from an allegedly *identical* component gathered from a different source, e.g., a well sorted repository of materials. This material history encoded in the object also translates to the practical level of crafting with the particular component (for instance, a screw carries the torque that was needed to be removed from a casing).

Un-crafting for Material Inquiry

Un-crafting for material inquiry focuses on the details of a particular material through dissecting one ore multiple artifacts, for instance, taking apart several computer keyboards to inquire how the different spring mechanisms of their keys relate to the different feel and sound. As an inquiry into the details of the material, related to reverse engineering, this exercise is concerned with the identification of the underlying design rationales encoded in the object at hand.

Un-crafting for Material Exploration

Un-crafting for material exploration studies the relations between the function and form of an artifact through disassembling it and re-mixing its material components into a new composition. According design exercises include: taking apart an artifact and altering its physical form while leaving its functionality intact; taking apart an interactive artifact and creating a new one that puts the complete trove of components (i.e., all of them) to use; rendering an object unusable (in respect to the originally intended purpose).

Many practical design (research) situations incorporate multiple instances of one or more of the four modes of un-crafting, conducted in a particular sequence or in process of shifting attention back and forth between them. Moreover, a practical design situation may well meander between constructive and de-constructive operations, between putting things together and taking them apart.

DISCUSSION

With the four modes of material engagements, we introduced in the un-crafting framework we provide an initial tool that may be either applied as an analytical lens to dissect processes of taking interactive artifacts apart or used in constructive design exercises facilitating a particular design process. As un-crafting shares multiple roots with current practices and theoretical discourses in interaction design research, we will in the following provide reflections on three particular areas that we hope those modes of engagement will contribute to: how to foster material engagements in interaction design research, how to dissect the interactive, and, finally, the collaborative breakdowns required in interdisciplinary design work.

Material Engagements

Many concepts and approaches in contemporary interaction design are inspired and informed by Donald Schön's work on design practice (e.g., [42, 43]) and Seymour Papert's approaches to the material (e.g., [34]). They all express a desire to engage with the physical and digital world as part of design and research, emphasizing the inevitable role of design practice and craftsmanship. Material engagements fulfill bridging functions between design and research, and between thinking and making, by connecting the conceptual space (of knowledge) and the lived space (of the body) [37]. *Critical making*, a concept provided by Ratto, is a specific mode of materially productive engagement. Therein, material production (i.e., making things) is considered as part of an explicit practice of concept elaboration. Critical thinking and physical making are reunited in order to satisfy the desire to theoretically and pragmatically connect these two modes of engagement with the world [37].

In recent years, approaches to material engagements have increasingly been proposed. For instance, Sundström and colleagues developed *Inspirational Bits*, i.e., an approach to become familiar with digital design materials in HCI. Inspirational bits are quick-and-dirty, fully working systems in both hardware and software, which are "built with the aim of exposing one or several of the dynamic properties of a digital material" [46, p. 1561]. With these *Inspirational Bits,* they foreground technologies as a design material, inspiration by exploring the properties of a technology, a constructive view on limitation, sketching the material, and detailed material system descriptions.

Although the un-crafting exercises that we propose in this paper are not to be understood as fully developed methods, techniques, or programs (such as, e.g., Inspirational Bits [46]), they are points of departure for analyzing tangible systems, allowing experiential engagements with an artifact's material by dissecting it. Contrasting Ratto's notion of *critical making*, un-crafting could well be rephrased as *critical un-making*. Both critical making and un-crafting relate to Papert's visions of constructionism in their goals of making concepts more apprehensible through linking abstract concepts (of, e.g., interaction, materials) to bodily engagements with artifacts and materials. Further, both seek to integrate material engagements with critical thinking. While critical making focuses on constructive engagements, un-crafting emphasizes moments of taking apart as epistemological moments, either for material exposition, material inspiration, material inquiry, and material exploration.

Dissecting the Interactive

Dissecting hardware, dissecting software, and dissecting the physical become increasingly incorporated in engineering and interaction design. However, when it comes to computation, it is hard to dissect it; thus, its underlying principles and mechanisms, as well as the considerations inscribed into computation are difficult to understand in a given computational "thing". Consequently, efforts to *un-craft* computation are arguably important:

> The soul of the creator is imbued in the machine, and as users we glean wisdom from understanding its workings. To disassemble is to learn, to mend, and to move forward." [25, p. 43]

What Kyle Wiens, co-founder and CEO of iFixit, an online repair community providing product teardowns and repair manuals as well as a vendor of spare parts and related tools, expresses in this quote is a desire to learn from the wisdom of the creator that is embodied in an artifact and its composition of components. Similar to how the artifact incorporates the "soul of the creator", the material components gathered from taking it apart entail invisible traces to their previous role in a composition. This material history – that is only to be grasped through the tangible act of taking a component *out* of a composition – may also influence the design process of a new or adapted artifact. Regarding bricolage, Vallgårda and Fernaeus emphasize that

> The treasury of the bricoleur, whether it is an IKEA store, old inherited furniture, or the scrape materials from other lab activities, will inevitably set the aesthetic tone of the result. [49, p. 178]

Similarly, un-crafting exercises, as proposed and differentiated in the aforementioned framework, might inscribe certain aesthetic tones and settings into the envisioning of a new design, especially affecting those activities, where the (disassembled/analyzed/assembled) artifact motivates a new, alternative focus.

Collaborative Breakdowns

If we, in Schön's terms, understand designing as "a communicative activity in which individuals are called upon to decipher one another's design worlds," [43] it is crucial how this collaborative "world making" can be facilitated. Considering design from this constructivist perspective (Schön's work has many associations to constructivism, in particular to Goodman's notion of "worldmaking", as Kinsella describes [21]), its de-constructive moments not only play out in individual design activities, but also in collaborative actions, which are often essential in design projects that require a multitude of skills and disciplines to be united.

Taking a thing apart in a team might allow to develop common ground and a *shared material understanding* [29]. In relation to "collaborative imagining" (a concept provided by Keith Murphy [31] that addresses the semiotic resources that collaborative imagination is based on, such as talk, gestures, and material objects), Murer et al. unveiled the value of un-crafting in a design exercise:

> In the process of taking an unknown device apart, it is those semiotic resources that unfold. We have identified several distinct occasions where there were mismatches in language, practices, assumptions and understanding. However, through the practice of working collaboratively with exploring these materials, such mismatches were bridged at the levels of language and understanding. [29, p. 471]

Another particular concept that is related to *un-crafting* is the notion of breakdown as means of "revealing the nature of the world around us" [23, p. 25] in its relation to the physical act of breaking an artifact down. We envision, especially in collaborative design situations, that un-crafting can be also understood as a form of engagement, which creates breakdowns that are inherently related to the material at hand and, thus, support the creation of shared *design worlds*.

> Computers do not exist, in the sense of things possessing objective features and functions, outside of language. They are created in the conversations human beings engage in when they cope with and anticipate breakdown. [54, p. 78]

The (collaborative) repair of breakdowns that was caused by ambiguity is thought to construct common ground, and hence shared understanding [33]. Similar to *distributed constructionism*, i.e., more than one person being involved in construction activities [38], de-constructive activities may also be of value for collaborative learning and meaning-making (or, in Schön's and Goodman's terms, "world making" [21]), especially when it comes to the role of breakdown or repair. However, further work is required to create an understanding of the mechanisms of collaborative un-crafting and how it contributes to knowledge building.

With the framework provided in this paper and its goal to contribute to (collaborative) material engagements, we aim to stimulate the discourse on how constructionist thinking can promote not only synthesizing activities inherent to many design processes, but also de-synthesizing acts. We hope that these acts of un-crafting, which we depicted in form of four modes as part of an un-crafting framework, will eventually find their way into existing or novel theories, as well as propel the creation of dedicated design tools, approaches, and methodologies.

CONCLUSION

Construction, making, and building are increasingly emphasized as essential parts of interaction design processes, as design is no longer an "abstract enterprise separate from or prior to making (along with related dichotomies of thinking versus doing, mind versus matter, subject versus object, and so on)" [22, p. 2]. In this paper, we argue that not only activities of crafting are relevant to interaction design, but also *un-crafting* as a means to understand the materials we work with.

This paper started by describing Fröbel's Gifts, which sought to reflect children's curiosity in learning about the material world, and which inspired a variety of learning tools and kits in engineering and design. The third gift specifically focuses on taking apart – an exercise that is important in design processes as well. Though inherent to (constructive) design processes in various forms, a systematic account of these practices has not been provided yet; a gap, which we aim to fill with this paper. By describing an organizational framework (based on a framework of disassemble/analyze/assemble activities for engineering education), we propose four distinct material engagements with interactive artifacts, that can be described on two dimensions, i.e., focus (on the artifact or motivated by the artifact) and orientation (convergent or divergent).

We intend that the *un-crafting* framework presented in this paper can serve several purposes: First, it may help to identify how existing design practices and techniques already imply taking things apart as inherent to them. Second, we hope that this framework may stimulate the further development and articulation of distinct practices, methods, and techniques revolving around disassembling that, similar to what was achieved in engineering, allow for an engagement with interactive artifacts and their constituting materials that supports linking abstract conceptions with their material realities. Both modes of working, i.e., disassembling as it is inherent to design practices and as an interaction design practice of its own, are thought to be beneficial to design research endeavors, as well as design education. In particular, we hope that this framing will contribute to the ongoing discourse around material engagements in interaction design.

> Every time we touch a piece of bendy aluminium or soft copper, our brain builds a library of the physicality of that object, and the possibilities for it [...] [7, p. 128]

Not least, we hope that an emphasis on un-crafting may allow to carry over some of the passionate engagement to contemporary design research projects that young learners reveal when being confronted with a thing that is mystical, magical, or unfamiliar in its form or function. However, the prevalent interaction paradigm that, for instance, touch based technologies follow, is a result of a history we do not necessarily want to pursue, as

> claiming that Pictures Under Glass is the future of interaction is like claiming that black-and-white is the future of photography. It's obviously a transitional technology. And the sooner we transition, the better. [51]

Relating these trends in computation back to the introductory reflections on learning and materials (such as the Fröbel Gifts), it becomes arguably harder to engage with the technology that surrounds us today through taking it apart, as the technology itself gets more and more complex and, thus, is rendered inaccessible to any kind of disassembly. "Something important is lost when kids don't have – or don't take – the opportunity to explore the world with their hands." [7, p. 127]

Aiming to explore the potential and consequences of computational form from an interaction perspective calls for a critical assessment of current artifacts in order to unveil their underlying assumptions, paradigms and interpretations. We see *un-crafting* as one means supporting that endeavor.

ACKNOWLEDGMENTS

The financial support by the Austrian Federal Ministry of Science, Research and Economy and the National Foundation for Research, Technology and Development is gratefully acknowledged (Christian Doppler Laboratory on "Contextual Interfaces").

REFERENCES

1. Edith Ackermann. 1996. Perspective-taking and object construction: two keys to learning. *Constructionism in practice: designing, thinking, and learning in a digital world, Lawrence Erlbaum, Mahwah, NJ* (1996), 25–35.
2. Margaret Atwood. 2014. Robotics in My Work and Life. In *CHI '14 Extended Abstracts on Human Factors in Computing Systems (CHI EA '14)*. ACM, New York, NY, USA, 13–14. DOI: http://dx.doi.org/10.1145/2559206.2580094
3. Ayah Bdeir and Paul Rothman. 2012. Electronics As Material: LittleBits. In *Proceedings of the Sixth International Conference on Tangible, Embedded and Embodied Interaction (TEI '12)*. ACM, New York, NY, USA, 371–374. DOI: http://dx.doi.org/10.1145/2148131.2148220
4. Tufts University Center for Engineering Educational Outreach. 2016. Hands-on Activity: Disassemble a Click Pen. (2016). https://www.teachengineering.org/activities/view/disassemble_a_click_pen.
5. Joshua Chan, Tarun Pondicherry, and Paulo Blikstein. 2013. LightUp: An Augmented, Learning Platform for Electronics. In *Proceedings of the 12th International Conference on Interaction Design and Children (IDC '13)*. ACM, New York, NY, USA, 491–494. DOI: http://dx.doi.org/10.1145/2485760.2485812
6. Elliot J. Chikofsky and James H. Cross II. 1990. Reverse Engineering and Design Recovery: A Taxonomy. *IEEE Softw.* 7, 1 (Jan. 1990), 13–17. DOI: http://dx.doi.org/10.1109/52.43044
7. Tom Clynes. 2015. *The Boy who Played with Fusion: Extreme Science, Extreme Parenting, and how to Make a Star*. Houghton Mifflin Harcourt.
8. Exploratorium. 2014. Toy take apart. (2014). http://tinkering.exploratorium.edu/sites/default/files/Instructions/toy_take_apart_0.pdf.
9. Ylva Fernaeus, Martin Murer, Vasiliki Tsaknaki, and Jordi Solsona Belenguer. 2013. Handcrafting Electronic Accessories Using 'Raw' Materials. In *Proceedings of the 8th International Conference on Tangible, Embedded and Embodied Interaction (TEI '14)*. ACM, New York, NY, USA, 369–372. DOI: http://dx.doi.org/10.1145/2540930.2567906
10. Connie Golsteijn, Elise Hoven, David Frohlich, and Abigail Sellen. 2014. Hybrid Crafting: Towards an Integrated Practice of Crafting with Physical and Digital Components. *Personal Ubiquitous Comput.* 18, 3 (March 2014), 593–611. DOI: http://dx.doi.org/10.1007/s00779-013-0684-9
11. Sidhant Goyal, Rohan S. Vijay, Charu Monga, and Pratul Kalita. 2016. Code Bits: An Inexpensive Tangible Computational Thinking Toolkit For K-12 Curriculum. In *Proceedings of the TEI '16: Tenth International Conference on Tangible, Embedded, and Embodied Interaction (TEI '16)*. ACM, New York, NY, USA, 441–447. DOI: http://dx.doi.org/10.1145/2839462.2856541
12. gqpzhang. 2013. Donald A. Norman–2006 Benjamin Franklin Medal. Video. (1 February 2013). Retrieved January 2, 2015 from https://www.youtube.com/watch?v=Wl2LkzIkacM.
13. Jean Griffin, Eliot Kaplan, and Quinn Burke. 2012. Debug'ems and other deconstruction kits for stem learning. In *Integrated STEM Education Conference (ISEC), 2012 IEEE 2nd*. IEEE, 1–4.
14. Lars Hallnäs and Johan Redström. 2002a. Abstract information appliances: methodological exercises in conceptual design of computational things. In *Proceedings of the 4th conference on Designing interactive systems: processes, practices, methods, and techniques (DIS '02)*. ACM, New York, NY, USA, 105–116. DOI:http://dx.doi.org/10.1145/778712.778730
15. Lars Hallnäs and Johan Redström. 2002b. From use to presence: on the expressions and aesthetics of everyday computational things. *ACM Trans. Comput.-Hum. Interact.* 9, 2 (June 2002), 106–124. DOI: http://dx.doi.org/10.1145/513665.513668
16. Dorothy W. Hewes. 2001. Speculation on a Conversation Between Piaget and Froebel. (2001). http://www.froebelfoundation.org/speculationhewes.html.
17. Steven J. Jackson and Laewoo Kang. 2014. Breakdown, Obsolescence and Reuse: HCI and the Art of Repair. In *Proceedings of the SIGCHI Conference on Human Factors in Computing Systems (CHI '14)*. ACM, New York, NY, USA, 449–458. DOI: http://dx.doi.org/10.1145/2556288.2557332
18. Yasmin B. Kafai, Kylie A. Peppler, Quinn Burke, Michael Moore, and Diane Glosson. 2010. FrÖBel's Forgotten Gift: Textile Construction Kits As Pathways into Play, Design and Computation. In *Proceedings of the 9th International Conference on Interaction Design and Children (IDC '10)*. ACM, New York, NY, USA, 214–217. DOI: http://dx.doi.org/10.1145/1810543.1810574
19. Yasmin Bettina Kafai and Mitchel Resnick. 1996. *Constructionism in practice: Designing, thinking, and learning in a digital world*. Routledge.
20. Elvin Karana, Bahar Barati, Valentina Rognoli, and Anouk Zeeuw van der Laan. 2015. Material Driven Design (MDD): A Method to Design for Material Experiences. (2015). http://www.ijdesign.org/ojs/index.php/IJDesign/article/view/1965
21. Elizabeth Anne Kinsella. 2006. Constructivist underpinnings in Donald Schön's theory of reflective practice: echoes of Nelson Goodman. *Reflective Practice* 7, 3 (2006), 277–286. DOI: http://dx.doi.org/10.1080/14623940600837319

22. Terry Knight and Theodora Vardouli. 2015. Computational making. *Design Studies* 41, Part A (2015), 1 – 7. DOI: http://dx.doi.org/10.1016/j.destud.2015.09.003 Special Issue: Computational Making.

23. Timothy Koschmann, Kari Kuutti, and Larry Hickman. 1998. The Concept of Breakdown in Heidegger, Leont'ev, and Dewey and Its Implications for Education. *Mind, Culture, and Activity* 5, 1 (1998), 25–41. DOI: http://dx.doi.org/10.1207/s15327884mca0501_3

24. Leah Maestri and Ron Wakkary. 2011. Understanding repair as a creative process of everyday design. In *Proceedings of the 8th ACM conference on Creativity and cognition (C&C '11)*. ACM, New York, NY, USA, 81–90. DOI:http://dx.doi.org/10.1145/2069618.2069633

25. Todd McLellan. 2013. *Things Come Apart: A Teardown Manual for Modern Living*. Thames & Hudson.

26. David A. Mellis, Sam Jacoby, Leah Buechley, Hannah Perner-Wilson, and Jie Qi. 2013. Microcontrollers As Material: Crafting Circuits with Paper, Conductive Ink, Electronic Components, and an "Untoolkit". In *Proceedings of the 7th International Conference on Tangible, Embedded and Embodied Interaction (TEI '13)*. ACM, New York, NY, USA, 83–90. DOI: http://dx.doi.org/10.1145/2460625.2460638

27. Deborah Moore-Russo, Katie Grantham, Kemper Lewis, and Susan M Bateman. 2010. Comparing Physical and Cyber-Enhanced Product Dissection: Analysis from Multiple Perspectives. *International Journal of Engineering Education* 26, 6 (2010), 1378.

28. Martin Murer, Verena Fuchsberger, and Manfred Tscheligi. 2015. Deconstructivist Interaction Design: Interrogating Expression and Form. In *Proceedings of The Fifth Decennial Aarhus Conference on Critical Alternatives (AA '15)*. Aarhus University Press, 33–36. DOI:http://dx.doi.org/10.7146/aahcc.v1i1.21313

29. Martin Murer, Mattias Jacobsson, Siri Skillgate, and Petra Sundström. 2014. Taking Things Apart: Reaching Common Ground and Shared Material Understanding. In *Proceedings of the SIGCHI Conference on Human Factors in Computing Systems (CHI '14)*. ACM, New York, NY, USA, 469–472. DOI: http://dx.doi.org/10.1145/2556288.2557267

30. Martin Murer, Anna Vallgårda, Mattias Jacobsson, and Manfred Tscheligi. 2015. Un-Crafting: Exploring Tangible Practices for Deconstruction in Interactive System Design. In *Proceedings of the Ninth International Conference on Tangible, Embedded, and Embodied Interaction (TEI '15)*. ACM, New York, NY, USA, 469–472. DOI: http://dx.doi.org/10.1145/2677199.2683582

31. Keith M Murphy. 2005. Collaborative imagining: The interactive use of gestures, talk, and graphic representation in architectural practice. *Semiotica* 2005, 156 (2005), 113–145.

32. Madara M. Ogot, Gul E. Okudan, Timothy W. Simpson, and John S. Lamancusa. 2008. A framework for classifying disassemble/analyse/assemble activities in engineering design education. *Journal of Design Research* 7, 2 (2008), 120–135. DOI: http://dx.doi.org/10.1504/JDR.2008.020852

33. Jonathan Ostwald. 1996. *Knowledge construction in software development: The evolving artifact approach.* Ph.D. Dissertation. University of Colorado.

34. Seymour Papert. 1993. *The Children's Machine: Rethinking School in the Age of the Computer.* ERIC.

35. Eric Parkinson. 1999. Re-constructing the Construction Kit – Re-constructing Childhood: A Synthesis of the Influences which have Helped to Give Shape and Form to Kit-based Construction Activities in the Primary School Classroom. *International Journal of Technology and Design Education* 9, 2 (1999), 173–194. DOI: http://dx.doi.org/10.1023/A:1008837418448

36. Hannah Perner-Wilson, Leah Buechley, and Mika Satomi. 2011. Handcrafting Textile Interfaces from a Kit-of-no-parts. In *Proceedings of the Fifth International Conference on Tangible, Embedded, and Embodied Interaction (TEI '11)*. ACM, New York, NY, USA, 61–68. DOI:http://dx.doi.org/10.1145/1935701.1935715

37. Matt Ratto. 2011. Critical Making: Conceptual and Material Studies in Technology and Social Life. *The Information Society* 27, 4 (2011), 252–260. DOI: http://dx.doi.org/10.1080/01972243.2011.583819

38. Mitchel Resnick. 1996. Distributed Constructionism. In *Proceedings of the 1996 International Conference on Learning Sciences (ICLS '96)*. International Society of the Learning Sciences, 280–284. http://dl.acm.org/citation.cfm?id=1161135.1161173

39. Mitchel Resnick, Brad Myers, Kumiyo Nakakoji, Ben Shneiderman, Randy Pausch, Ted Selker, and Mike Eisenberg. 2005. Design principles for tools to support creative thinking. (2005).

40. Mitchel Resnick and Brian Silverman. 2005. Some Reflections on Designing Construction Kits for Kids. In *Proceedings of the 2005 Conference on Interaction Design and Children (IDC '05)*. ACM, New York, NY, USA, 117–122. DOI: http://dx.doi.org/10.1145/1109540.1109556

41. Matthew Schmidtbauer, Samuel Johnson, Jeffrey Jalkio, and AnnMarie Thomas. 2012. Squishy Circuits As a Tangible Interface. In *CHI '12 Extended Abstracts on Human Factors in Computing Systems (CHI EA '12)*. ACM, New York, NY, USA, 2111–2116. DOI: http://dx.doi.org/10.1145/2212776.2223761

42. Donald A. Schön. 1983. The reflective practitioner: How professionals think in action. (1983).

43. Donald A. Schön. 1992. Designing as reflective conversation with the materials of a design situation. *Knowledge-Based Systems* 5, 1 (1992), 3–14.

44. Eric Schweikardt and Mark D. Gross. 2006. roBlocks: A Robotic Construction Kit for Mathematics and Science Education. In *Proceedings of the 8th International Conference on Multimodal Interfaces (ICMI '06)*. ACM, New York, NY, USA, 72–75. DOI: http://dx.doi.org/10.1145/1180995.1181010

45. Sheri D. Sheppard. 1992. Mechanical Dissection: An experience in how things work. *Proceedings of the Engineering Education: Curriculum Innovation & Integration* (1992), 6–10.

46. Petra Sundström, Alex Taylor, Katja Grufberg, Niklas Wirström, Jordi Solsona Belenguer, and Marcus Lundén. 2011. Inspirational bits: towards a shared understanding of the digital material. In *Proceedings of the SIGCHI Conference on Human Factors in Computing Systems (CHI '11)*. ACM, New York, NY, USA, 1561–1570. DOI: http://dx.doi.org/10.1145/1978942.1979170

47. Vasiliki Tsaknaki, Ylva Fernaeus, and Mischa Schaub. 2014. Leather As a Material for Crafting Interactive and Physical Artifacts. In *Proceedings of the 2014 Conference on Designing Interactive Systems (DIS '14)*. ACM, New York, NY, USA, 5–14. DOI: http://dx.doi.org/10.1145/2598510.2598574

48. Anna Vallgårda. 2014. Giving Form to Computational Things: Developing a Practice of Interaction Design. *Personal Ubiquitous Comput.* 18, 3 (March 2014), 577–592. DOI: http://dx.doi.org/10.1007/s00779-013-0685-8

49. Anna Vallgårda and Ylva Fernaeus. 2015. Interaction Design As a Bricolage Practice. In *Proceedings of the Ninth International Conference on Tangible, Embedded, and Embodied Interaction (TEI '15)*. ACM, New York, NY, USA, 173–180. DOI: http://dx.doi.org/10.1145/2677199.2680594

50. Anna Vallgårda and Johan Redström. 2007. Computational composites. In *Proceedings of the SIGCHI Conference on Human Factors in Computing Systems (CHI '07)*. ACM, New York, NY, USA, 513–522. DOI:http://dx.doi.org/10.1145/1240624.1240706

51. Bret Victor. 2011. A brief rant on the future of interaction design. *WorryDream.com* (2011).

52. Edward Wiebé. 1869. *The paradise of childhood: a manual for self-instruction in Friedrich Froebel's educational principles, and a practical guide to kinder-gartners*. M. Bradley & Company.

53. Edward Wiebé, Milton Bradley, and Henry Wolcott Blake. 1907. *Quarter century edition of The paradise of childhood: A practical guide to kindergartners*. Milton Bradley Company.

54. Terry A. Winograd and Carlos Fernando Flores. 1986. *Understanding computers and cognition: A new foundation for design*. Intellect Books.

55. Kristin L. Wood, Daniel Jensen, Joseph Bezdek, and Kevin N. Otto. 2001. Reverse Engineering and Redesign: Courses to Incrementally and Systematically Teach Design. *Journal of Engineering Education* 90, 3 (2001), 363–374. DOI: http://dx.doi.org/10.1002/j.2168-9830.2001.tb00615.x

56. Kuan-Ju Wu and Mark D. Gross. 2010. TOPAOKO: Interactive Construction Kit. In *CHI '10 Extended Abstracts on Human Factors in Computing Systems (CHI EA '10)*. ACM, New York, NY, USA, 3619–3624. DOI: http://dx.doi.org/10.1145/1753846.1754028

Texture Metaphors and Tangible Interaction: No Smooth Relationship?

Jörn Hurtienne
Julius-Maximilians-Universität
Würzburg, Germany
hurtienne@acm.org

Daniel Reinhardt
Julius-Maximilians-Universität
Würzburg, Germany
daniel.reinhardt@uni-wuerzburg.de

ABSTRACT
Conceptual Metaphor Theory is able to predict how physical object properties can trigger associated abstract content. Based on prior research on texture metaphors, we hypothesised that even incidental sensations of texture can influence the subjective evaluation of user experience and the interpretation of an ambiguous social situation. In three studies users interacted with smooth and rough versions of cases of mobile devices (Study 1), trackpads (Study 2) and tangibles for interactive gameplay (Study 3). Despite convincing evidence collected in earlier studies, the results confirmed none of the hypotheses in any of the three studies. Possible reasons and their relevance for the use of metaphors in HCI and tangible interfaces are discussed and conclusions for further applications of rough/smooth metaphors are drawn.

Author Keywords
Image schemas; conceptual metaphors; embodied cognition; replication; texture manipulation.

ACM Classification Keywords
H.5.m. Information interfaces and presentation (e.g., HCI): Miscellaneous.

INTRODUCTION
Texture perception is a relevant part of tactile object perception and the rough-smooth dimension is the most salient dimension in texture perception (together with hard-soft, [10, 11, 28, 29]). Apart from their immediate physical qualities, variations on the rough-smooth dimension can also communicate abstract qualities. Humans consistently rate, for example, rough textures as unpleasant and smooth textures as pleasant [6, 7, 23]. Across cultures, Germans [15] and Canadians [22] reliably associate smooth tangibles with the attributes *polite*, *safe*, *continuous*, *unproblematic*, and *boring*, and they associate rough tangibles with the attributes *impolite*, *dangerous*, *interrupted*, and *problematic*. These relationships between physical roughness and abstract concepts are not mere semantic associations. Research in social psychology has shown that some of these associated attributes are subconsciously transferred to other items than the rough or smooth object itself [1, 26]. Thus the texture of the object could prime judgements of abstract properties of other items. Such findings are exciting and highly relevant for designing tangible interactions. By varying the roughness of tangible tokens (that are used to manipulate digital content) designers could then implicitly shape the perception of abstract properties of the digital content.

Inspired by this possibility, we devised a series of three studies in which we investigated whether the abstract meaning associated with rough or smooth tangible objects would subconsciously transfer to the evaluation of digital content. More specifically, we extended the prior findings in the literature to hypothesise that incidental rough/smooth sensations can also influence subjective ratings of user experience. In addition, we attempted to conceptually replicate the prior research that showed that incidental rough/smooth sensations influenced the interpretation of ambiguous social situations. In the following sections we give more background on the underlying theory and prior research before reporting on the three studies and discussing the results.

PRIOR WORK ON CONCEPTUAL METAPHORS
Predicting associations between concrete and more abstract domains is the hallmark of conceptual metaphor theory. The theory originates from cognitive linguistics where it was found that metaphors are an abundant phenomenon rather than rare embellishments to otherwise literal speech [18]. Most of these are so-called 'dead metaphors' that we do not consciously recognise as metaphors anymore. Expressions like *the inflation rose by 5%* or *prices are falling*, for example, are not about literal up-down movements, but about increasing or decreasing quantities. Cognitive linguists found that a large number of similar metaphorical expressions systematically mapped the vertical dimension to quantities of all sorts. Such systematic mappings have shown to be surprisingly consistent across even unrelated languages. So the linguists concluded that dead metaphors cannot only be interpreted as a matter of language, but must be seen as a matter of thought. But how do the connections between simple physical attributes and their abstract connotations come about? Repeated co-

TEI '17, March 20-23, 2017, Yokohama, Japan
© 2017 ACM. ISBN 978-1-4503-4676-4/17/03…$15.00
DOI: http://dx.doi.org/10.1145/3024969.3024986

experience of physical attributes with abstract judgments lead to repeated co-activation of these concepts in the mind. The high frequency of co-activations leads to their subconscious representation in the mind. For example, the repeated experience of rising and falling levels of liquids in containers or growing and shrinking piles of objects and their association with judgments of quantity eventually form the *conceptual* metaphor MORE IS UP – LESS IS DOWN. In this notation MORE and LESS represent the target domain, and UP and DOWN represent the source domain of the metaphor. Conceptual metaphors can be instantiated in language, graphic representations, behaviour and user interfaces. A growing number of studies in social psychology and HCI shows the validity of conceptual metaphors for human judgement and behaviour [12, 19, 20, 24]. Conceptual metaphors were shown to inspire many population stereotypes of physical-to-abstract mappings. When conceptual metaphors are instantiated in tangible and graphical interfaces, they enhance usability, intuitive use, and judgments about the innovativeness of these interfaces (for a recent review see [12]).

Examples of metaphors using the rough-smooth dimension as a source domain include [15]:

1. UNPROBLEMATIC IS SMOOTH – PROBLEMATIC IS ROUGH, as in *Don't interfere with the smooth running of our lives. Top management faces a potentially rough ride.*
2. CONTINUOUS IS SMOOTH – INTERRUPTED IS ROUGH, as in *The smooth movement of the robot arm. This illustrates the somewhat uneven pattern of evolution.*
3. POLITE IS SMOOTH – IMPOLITE IS ROUGH, as in *The mercenaries - a numerous, rough and uncultivated set. He pacified the customer with a smooth apology.*
4. BORING IS SMOOTH – DANGEROUS IS ROUGH, as in *He always creates those smooth contour-less designs. Rough driving claims thousands of victims each year.*
5. PLEASANT IS SMOOTH – UNPLEASANT IS ROUGH, as in *The nomad life is rough and hazardous. This makes the whiskeys much smoother.*

The conceptual reality of these five metaphors was confirmed in previous studies [15, 22]. In these, participants responded to abstract words by selecting one of two objects that best represented the concept denoted by the word. Objects were smooth and rough Lego bricks [15] or smooth and heavily scratched foam cubes [22]. The results indicated that, on average, 80% [15] and 97% [22] of the participants' responses were consistent with the metaphors. The difference between the results could be explained that in [15] the roughness of the Lego bricks could only be determined by touch while in [22] the roughness of the foam cubes was also clearly visible. The multisensory availability of roughness cues can thus enhance the number of metaphor-consistent responses.

While [15] and [22] confirmed that people semantically associate abstract concepts with rough and smooth objects, they did not investigate whether these physical-abstract associations can also be automatically triggered and transferred beyond the current object. The former condition would be necessary to claim intuitive use (briefly defined as the subconscious application of prior knowledge in interaction, e.g. [12]). The latter condition is necessary to claim any usefulness for designing tangible tokens representing independent digital content.

Both concerns were addressed in an experiment in social psychology ([1], n = 64). Participants completed a five-piece puzzle, either a version with pieces covered in rough sandpaper (rough condition) or a -ersion with the pieces uncovered (smooth condition). They then read a passage describing an ambiguously valenced social interaction and answered questions about the 'social coordination' in this interaction (i.e. whether the interaction was adversarial or friendly, competitive or cooperative, a discussion or an argument, and whether people were on the same side or on opposite sides) and about the 'relationship familiarity' (i.e. about the closeness of the relationship and whether the interaction style was formal or casual). Following metaphors 1 and 3 above, it was expected that participants who completed the rough puzzle would rate the interaction as more difficult and harsh than would participants who completed the smooth puzzle. No effect of the rough-smooth variation was expected for 'relationship familiarity'. The results were consistent with the hypotheses. The rough-smooth manipulation had an effect on 'social coordination', $d = .58$, and no effect on 'relationship familiarity'. Thus, the rough-smooth manipulation specifically triggered the proposed metaphors and did not result in an overall change in participant's response behavior.

This study was conceptually replicated in a slightly different setting using passive tactile stimulation (rough: sandpaper, smooth: paintbrush) or no stimulation [26]. Again participants were first stimulated with the smooth or rough prime and then interpreted ambiguous social scenarios similar to [1] and using the same questions as in [1]. As expected, when primed with a rough stimulus, participants rated the interaction more difficult and harsh than when primed with a smooth stimulus or when they were not primed. Again, no effect was found for 'relationship familiarity'.

ROUGH-SMOOTH IN INTERACTION DESIGN

If incidental haptic sensations have an influence on abstract judgments, like [1] and [26] (and previous research on metaphors in general) suggest, then tangible interaction designers would be able to manipulate the intuitive flow of information from tangible tokens to the digital content represented by the token. But it would also mean that we would have to rethink the results of evaluation studies to factor in the importance of hardware properties.

Thus, we extended the previous results with our own hypotheses. The rough-smooth conceptual metaphors inspired us to expect incidental smooth/rough cues to also influence subjective ratings of user experience. We expected that rough and smooth stimuli would influence ratings of the hedonic quality, the pragmatic quality and the attractiveness of digital content. These user experience dimensions can be measured with the AttrakDiff, a widely used questionnaire that further differentiates hedonic quality into 'stimulation' and 'identity' [8, 9]. Thus, in line with the conceptual metaphors above, we expected that a rough object (compared to a smooth object) would result in

- lower ratings of pragmatic quality (e.g. the product is more complicated, confusing, and cumbersome to use), as inspired by metaphor 1;
- higher ratings of hedonic quality/stimulation (e.g. the product is more challenging, less dull), as inspired by metaphor 4;
- lower ratings of hedonic quality/identity (e.g. the product is less integrating, less presentable), as inspired by metaphor 3; and
- lower ratings on attractiveness (e.g. the product is less pleasant, likeable, or appealing), as inspired by metaphor 5.

As a manipulation check that allows comparing our results with the earlier studies, we also investigated the influence of rough-smooth primes on the judgment of ambiguous social situations, following [1]. In particular, we expected that a rough object (compared to a smooth object)

- would prime lower ratings of 'social coordination' when interpreting an ambiguous social situation, and
- would have no effect on ratings of 'relationship familiarity' – to show the selectivity of the effect.

The rationale of the following studies was not so much a direct replication of [1] or [26], but to look for similar effects in the context of interaction design. Thus we were looking for rough-smooth manipulations that were plausible to be realised in a dynamic context of interacting with technology rather than using the static rough-smooth stimuli used in [1] and [26].

STUDY 1: ROUGH AND SMOOTH CASES

The first study set out to create very incidental haptic sensations to see whether subtle rough-smooth variations can lead to changes in user experience. To be incidental the haptic sensation of rough and smooth textures needed to be uninformative to the actual tasks our participants solved. The study was announced as a usability test of a calendar app on a smart mobile device. The device (an iPod Touch 5G) was either in a rough or a smooth case. Solving the tasks required several turns between landscape and portrait mode so that the movement between the case and the skin of the hand holding the device was maximised. Both sets of hypotheses were tested.

Participants

Forty-eight participants (about two-thirds of them female) were recruited from a German university campus. Most of these were students of human-computer interaction and media communication. Participants were reimbursed for their time in form of partial course credit. The age of the participants ranged from 18 to 35 years. All participants were familiar with mobile digital devices and used calendar apps on their mobile devices at least three times per month. They were all naive to the subject of investigation.

Materials and Procedure

Participants were told that they would be taking part in two unrelated studies; the first involving a usability test of a smartphone app and the second involving a pre-test of another study. Each participant was asked to complete a short demographic questionnaire before being instructed on the tasks. Then they were randomly assigned either to the rough or to the smooth condition. In the rough condition, the iPod Touch had a plastic casing covered in a rough fabric; in the smooth condition, an identical iPod had an identical casing covered in a smooth fabric (Figure 1).

The first part required the participants to perform 19 tasks (e.g., opening the app or setting a reminder) using the "CalenMob – Google Calendar Client" application by Appxy that was unknown to the participants. After finishing the tasks, participants completed the AttrakDiff questionnaire [8, 9] administered on the iPod using EFS Survey by Questback GmbH. They then answered several questions about the app, what calendar apps they regularly use and which kind of smartphone they own.

In the second part, participants read a vignette on the iPod that was adapted from [1, 16] describing an ambiguous social interaction between two individuals. The vignette described both positive (e.g. kidding around) and negative interaction components (e.g. exchanging sharp words). After reading, participants rated whether the social interaction was: adversarial/friendly, competitive/cooperative, a discussion/argument, and whether the interlocutors had mutual or opposite interests, using 0-9 scales (adapted from [16]). These responses were averaged to form the composite measure 'social coordination'. To test whether the rough-smooth priming would extend to a theoretically unrelated measure ('relationship familiarity'), participants also rated how well the interlocutors knew each other and whether the nature of the interaction was business-like or casual, again using 0-9 rating scales. These responses were averaged to form the composite measure 'relationship familiarity'. After the participants had completed both parts of the study, they were debriefed and thanked for their participation.

Results and Discussion

Independent samples *t*-tests, $\alpha = .05$ were used to assess the effects of the two experimental conditions (rough vs. smooth) on the dependent variables. To correct for multiple testing, all tests were Bonferroni corrected. Effect sizes are reported as Cohen's *d*.

Figure 1. Mobile Devices used in Study 1 with cases covered in rough (left) and smooth fabric (right).

The experimental conditions had no influence on any of the dependent variables, except on relationship familiarity: rough M = 4.94, SD = 1.24; smooth M = 4.46, SD = .94; $t(46) = 1.51, p = .036, d = .44$:

- AttrakDiff pragmatic quality: rough M = 4.55, SD = .37; smooth M = 4.59, SD = .53; $t(46) = .28$, $p = .779, d = .09$.
- AttrakDiff hedonic quality 'stimulation': rough M = 3.99, SD = .48; smooth M = 4.02, SD = .31; $t(39.83) = .22, p = .831, d = -.07$.
- AttrakDiff hedonic quality 'identity': rough M = 4.53, SD = .41; smooth M = 4.38, SD = .46; $t(46) = 1.19$, $p = .239, d = -.34$.
- AttrakDiff attractiveness: rough M = 4.62, SD = .70; smooth M = 4.41, SD = .52; $t(46) = 1.18$, $p = .246$, $d = -.34$.
- Social coordination: rough M = 3.26, SD = .55; smooth M = 3.30, SD = .76; $t(46) = .22, p = .828, d = .06$.

The rough and smooth texture manipulation of the iPod cases had no significant effects, neither on the evaluation of the software nor on the judgement of the ambiguous social interaction, except on relationship familiarity where no difference was expected. The effect sizes were small on average.

Some methodological limitations of the study need to be considered that could have brought about the null effect. First, the difference between the smooth and the rough case was quite subtle, at least when compared to [1] who used sandpaper for the rough prime. Previous studies have shown that people give more metaphor-consistent answers when roughness cues are strong and multimodal [22]. Although the rough-smooth manipulation could be more contrasting, it remained within the range of practical applicability, because it is hard to imagine a smart device covered in sandpaper or similar material. This lack of extremity in roughness, however, may have led to diminished effects. Second, the sample size may have been too small to find an effect. In this study, sampling stopped when the pre-scheduled time in the field was reached. Instead, it would be more desirable to calculate sample sizes according to the expected effect sizes. Finally, manipulating the roughness on the back of the device may be too subtle a manipulation as it is too unrelated to the actual task. The roughness of the case may have hardly been noticed by the participants despite aiming for maximum interaction with the case – within the limits of the cover story. It may have been that this still was not enough interaction. Constant (instead of occasional) finger movements across the texture might, therefore, be desirable. Study 2 aimed to take this into account while still presenting a realistic interaction scenario.

STUDY 2: ROUGH AND SMOOTH TRACKPADS

The results of Study 1 suggested that there was not enough interaction with the smooth and rough textures at the back of the device. Therefore, in Study 2 the rough/smooth manipulation was changed. When solving a task at a laptop computer, participants used a rough or smooth version of a trackpad. Participants played a game that required them to constantly move the cursor so that they were constantly interacting with the manipulated surface of the trackpad. The dependent measures were the same as in Study 1. The sample size was calculated to 72 using an effect size that would be practically relevant (d = .60, power = .80).

Participants

Seventy-six university students (48 female, 28 male), were recruited from the campus of a German university. They participated in the study in exchange for partial course credit or 5 Euros. The ages of the participants ranged from 18 to 29 years (M = 21.20, SD = 2.58) and their backgrounds were mainly in human-computer interaction and media communication. All participants were naive as to the subject under investigation and did not take part in Study 1.

Materials and Procedure

As in Study 1, participants were told they would be taking part in two unrelated experiments: a usability test of a computer game and a pre-test for another study. The whole experiment was implemented as an online survey using EFS Survey by Questback and was conducted in a university lab. Participants sat down in a chair in front of a 22-inch monitor, a keyboard and an Apple Magic Trackpad. The first task required participants playing the game 3D Logic by Alex Matveev that was directly embedded within the online survey.

Participants were randomly assigned to the rough or smooth condition. In the rough condition, the sensitive surface of the Magic Trackpad was covered with a rough transparent plastic film. In the smooth condition, the trackpad was covered with a smooth transparent plastic film (that made the trackpad smoother than in its original state, Figure 2). Pilot tests ensured that the functioning of the trackpad was not impaired by the covers.

Figure 2. Rough (left) and smooth surface (right) of the Apple Magic Trackpads used in Study 2.

After a short instruction, participants played the game for five minutes and then completed the AttrakDiff questionnaire to evaluate the game. They also answered several questions about their familiarity with similar games, their PC and smartphone use. Then, participants received the same vignette of the social interaction as in Study 1 and answered the same questions. After the participants had completed both parts of the study, they were debriefed and thanked for their participation. No participant reported any awareness of the true purposes of the experiment.

Results and Discussion

The same types of analyses as in Study 1 were conducted. The experimental conditions had no influence on any of the dependent variables:

- AttrakDiff pragmatic quality: rough $M = 4.00$, $SD = .69$; smooth $M = 4.11$, $SD = .87$; $t(74) = .51$, $p = .611$, $d = .14$.
- AttrakDiff hedonic quality 'stimulation': rough $M = 4.55$, $SD = 1.03$; smooth $M = 4.56$, $SD = 1.00$, $t(74) = .64$, $p = .949$, $d = -.01$.
- AttrakDiff hedonic quality 'identity': rough $M = 4.33$, $SD = .56$; smooth $M = 4.46$, $SD = .85$; $t(74) = .82$, $p = .412$, d = .18.
- AttrakDiff attractiveness: rough $M = 4.74$, $SD = .90$; smooth $M = 4.73$, $SD = 1.06$; $t(74) = .07$, $p = .947$, $d = -.01$.
- Social coordination: rough $M = 4.18$, $SD = 1.13$; smooth $M = 4.10$, $SD = 1.27$; $t(74) = .31$, $p = .757$, $d = -.07$.
- Relationship familiarity: rough $M = 5.13$, $SD = 1.48$; smooth $M = 5.33$, $SD = 1.44$; t(74) = -.59, $p = .557$, $d = -.14$.

To summarize, the rough and smooth texture manipulation of the trackpads had no effects, neither on the evaluation of the software nor on the judgement of the ambiguous social interaction. Thus, a more direct and continuous interaction with the rough or smooth texture was not effective. The effect sizes were even smaller than in study 1 and far from practical relevance. A possible reason could be that the rough trackpad in the rough condition was not as strong as the sandpaper in [1]. It is also possible that the roughness manipulation was not salient enough, because in Studies 1 and 2 the graphical interface provided so many additional stimuli that the rather subtle roughness manipulation got lost in the noise. Another explanation may relate to habituation effects: the rough-smooth manipulation was always present throughout all phases and tasks, and the contact with the manipulated textures was much longer in these studies than in the study of [1]. Nevertheless, these studies already suggest a reduced scope of the automatic activation and subconscious transfer of rough-smooth metaphors in tangible interaction. The positive outcome is that the results of a widely used user experience questionnaire remain unaffected by small changes in the texture of input devices.

STUDY 3: ROUGH AND SMOOTH TANGIBLE TOKENS

Maybe trackpads and cases of mobile devices are objects too generic to elicit specific effects. Manipulating the texture of more conspicuous objects could potentially produce better results. In Study 3, therefore, we moved closer to [1] who employed smooth and rough puzzle pieces as a prime and then immediately presented the vignette about the ambiguous social situation and asked questions about it. To transfer this paradigm into a plausible case of tangible interaction we used the Newton app for Osmo. Osmo is a commercial tangible user interface, which uses an Apple iPad´s camera to use physical objects as input devices. Newton is an interactive game in which physical objects are used to guide falling on-screen balls into targeted zones (https://www.playosmo.com/en/newton/). Participants played this game either with rough or smooth tangible objects, where the rough manipulation was close to sandpaper, as in [1].

In this study, we focused on replicating the effects obtained by [1, 26] and therefore did not include tests of the perceived hedonic and pragmatic qualities of the tangible game. As the usability cover story in Studies 1 and 2 may have added unnecessary complexity, omitting this step from the procedure makes way for a potentially more straightforward chain of causality.

Participants

Seventy students were recruited at a German university campus (53 female, 17 male). The participants' ages ranged from 18 to 28 years (M = 20.76, SD = 1.88) and their backgrounds were in human-computer interaction and media communication. All participants were naive as to the subject under investigation and did not take part in Studies 1 or 2. Participants were reimbursed for their time in form of partial course credit.

Materials and Procedure

Participants were told that they would be taking part in an experiment involving interpersonal perception and that the researchers were interested in people's evaluations of social situations. Prior to interpreting the vignette of the social situations used in Studies 1 and 2, participants played the first five levels of the Newton game on the Osmo iPad suite. As in the original priming task of Ackermann et al., the game was presented as a measure of cognitive abilities such that the researchers could determine the link between these abilities and the social impressions. The first levels of the Newton game are designed for beginners and can be easily completed. There was no time limit for finishing the five levels.

To play the game, the participants used two flat wooden triangles (Figure 3). Participants were randomly assigned to one of two experimental conditions in which they either used rough or smooth versions of these triangles. The rough triangles were coated with a mixture of acrylic paint and fine sand. This was done to mimic the sandpaper used in [1], but with a more natural feel and more fluid transitions on the edges. The smooth triangles were coated with acrylic paint only. Following [1] participants were instructed not to pick up the pieces while playing, which helped to maximize the tactile contact with the tangibles and ensured the use of mainly lateral movements. The tangibles were placed on a white sheet of paper in order to ensure their accurate tracking by the camera.

After completing the game, participants read the vignette and indicated their impressions about the nature of the interaction on a paper questionnaire. The scenario and questions were identical to those used in Study 1 and 2. The whole experiment lasted about 15 minutes, with no considerable variance between the participants.

Results and Discussion

The same types of analyses as in Study 1 were conducted. The experimental conditions had no influence on any of the dependent variables:

- Social coordination: rough $M = 3.65$, $SD = 1.32$; smooth $M = 3.48$, $SD = 1.31$; $t(68) = .55$, $p = .587$, $d = -.13$.
- Relationship familiarity: rough $M = 5.01$, $SD = 1.73$; smooth $M = 4.86$, $SD = 1.87$; $t(68) = .35$, $p = .669$, $d = .08$.

Again, the manipulation of the haptic stimuli failed to elicit a metaphorical effect of rough and smooth texture manipulations. This was the closest (although not a direct) replication of [1] that was realistic in the context of tangible interaction. Although the contrast between the rough and smooth stimuli was stronger than in Studies 1 and 2 and the experimental procedure was decluttered from simultaneously testing other hypotheses this did not help to elicit a significant effect. It seems that interacting with digital content has overshadowed any effect that might have been present. By receiving another null effect using the paradigm of [1], time seems to be ripe to conclude that one should be sceptical about rough-smooth manipulations influencing the interpretation of ambiguous social situations – at least in the context of tangible interaction. We take up this point in the next session.

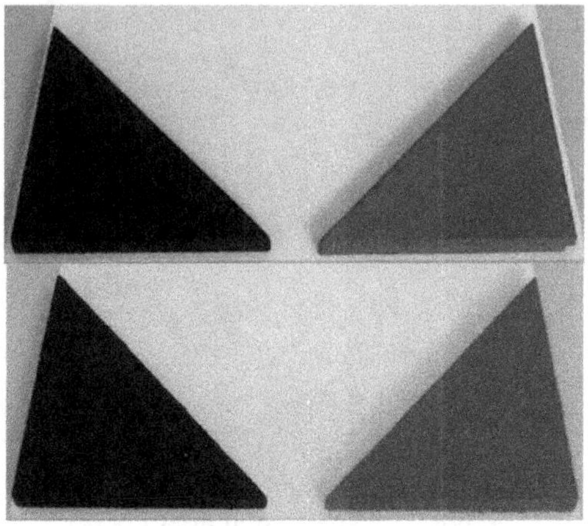

Figure 3. Smooth (above) and rough (below) tangibles used for playing a tangible game in Study 3.

GENERAL DISCUSSION

Taking the results of the three studies together, it seems that – in a context of tangible interaction – the predictions of the automatic activation of the rough-smooth metaphors under study cannot be confirmed. Incidental haptic sensations do not seem to influence the evaluation of user experience as measured with the AttrakDiff questionnaire and they do not influence the interpretation of an ambiguous social situation. Although we failed to produce a significant effect in study after study, these findings do not mean that there is no effect at all. Many interpretations of the results are possible. They inspire a search for alternative explanations as well as thoughts about their broader implications. In this exercise, it helps to compare the present studies with the results of prior research.

First of all, the effect might be too small to be picked up by our (relatively small) sample sizes or it may not have been elicited at all by our experimental setup. We deem the second possibility more likely, as our sample sizes were similar to or larger than those in [1] or [26]. When transferring the experimental paradigm into the context of human-computer interaction, the interaction became much more complex and more dynamic than with the simple puzzle in [1] or even just touching the stimuli as in [26]. Any metaphorical associations triggered by the rough/smooth manipulations could have gone lost in the noise of stimuli generated by the dynamic user interfaces (calendar, games) used in our studies. Indeed, pointing out this boundary condition seems to be the most important outcome of our study: the automatic triggering of conceptual metaphors should not be expected to readily occur in dynamic interactive environments.

Second, the exposure of the user to the tactile stimuli was much longer in our studies than in [1] or [26]. Participants might have habituated to the stimuli. By the time the responses on the dependent variables were collected, any metaphorical associations might have worn off (i.e. already been deactivated), even when the physical stimuli were still present (as in Studies 1 and 2).

Third, in contrast to [1] (and most tangible interaction), there was a spatial divide between the incidental haptic sensations and the visual feedback on the task at hand. Further research needs to clarify whether a better overlap of the visual and haptic perception spaces would result in a facilitated mental integration (cf. [27]) of the haptic sensation with the digital content and whether metaphoric effects would, therefore, be more likely to occur.

Fourth, our studies used different materials than [1] and [26] to instantiate the rough and smooth stimuli. While the original studies used sandpaper for rough stimuli and plain paper or paintbrushes for smooth stimuli, we used rough and smooth variations of textile and plastic film (Studies 1 and 2) and a self-produced acrylic-paint-sand coating versus a simple acrylic-paint coating (in Study 3). The major concern is that the contrast between the rough and smooth stimuli was too gentle. However, with the aim to stay realistic we wanted to use textures that were not conspicuous and matched the product's character. Not every object can be clad in sandpaper and satisfy aesthetic requirements at the same time. In study 3, however, we used a rough stimulus very close to sandpaper, but no differences could be obtained between conditions. To enhance the impact, future studies could go beyond static stimuli and include surfaces that can dynamically change perceived roughness (i.e. Sprout I/O in [5] or Revel [2]).

Fifth, several other differences between the original studies and our replication attempts might have caused a difference in results. In [1] the study was (presumably) conducted in the US whereas our studies were conducted in Germany. Conceptual metaphors can differ between languages and cultures [3, 4], but more often they do not [17, 25]. Previous research has shown a correspondence in population stereotypes of rough-smooth metaphors between Canadian and German participants [15, 22]. Furthermore, [26] produced a successful conceptual replication of [1] also with German participants. Thus, language and culture differences probably do not qualify as an explanation of the differences in effect sizes. Both the samples in [1] and our studies were drawn from a university community, but participants in [1] probably had a more heterogeneous background than the participants in our studies. Our participants were possibly more tech-savvy that may have affected the results. The digital content could have drawn even more attention than would be normal. The dependent measures were comparable in these studies. In the vignette about the social interaction only the names and the type of sports were adapted to the German context. How other differences regarding participant remuneration, cover stories used, and the administration of dependent measures could have affected the results (if at all) is difficult to ascertain.

What are the broader implications of our results? In line with the qualifications stated above, these null findings cannot refute the validity of conceptual metaphor theory at large. A number of studies in social psychology have shown that conceptual metaphors exist and that these are relevant for behaviour [19, 20, 24]. Conceptual metaphors have also been shown to be useful in user interface design. They have shown to underlie population stereotypes of physical-to-abstract mappings [13, 14, 21], including rough-smooth metaphors [15, 22]. User interfaces instantiating conceptual metaphors were shown to be more intuitive to use, more innovative, and more inclusive regarding different age groups than comparable solutions (for a review see [12]). Thus, the current state of knowledge would speak against a generalisation of our non-significant results to assume a failure of the usefulness of conceptual metaphor theory in human-computer interaction or tangible user interfaces at large.

CONCLUSION AND OUTLOOK

Our studies could not show an automatic metaphoric effect of incidental rough-smooth cues when applied to interactive technology. Thus, they tell us to be sceptical about the transferability of social psychological findings on metaphoric effects to tangible interactions. The design space and constraints may change the context in which these metaphors are valid to an extent that the effects cannot be detected anymore. Metaphorical effects may drown in a sea of a multitude of other stimuli impinging on the user when interacting with novel technology. Further studies thus should clarify the boundaries of applying conceptual metaphors in tangible interaction.

There are two options for further studies: either enhance the ecological validity by moving closer to realistic application contexts or to move closer to a direct replication of [1] and [26]. In the first case one would conduct studies that enhance the contrast between rough and smooth stimuli, let the haptic and visual perception space overlap and shorten the exposure time to the rough/smooth stimuli before collecting dependent measures. One would, however, not touch the crucial element of tangible user interfaces: their interactivity. In the second case, one would relinquish interactivity in order to move very close to a direct replication of the original studies in terms of the participant sample structure, procedures for participant recruitment and remuneration, the design of instructions and tasks as well as stimuli, measures and the procedures of data analysis. One would also need to employ much larger sample sizes for enhanced statistical power. At the current state of knowledge about the applicability of texture metaphors, both roads need to be taken.

ACKNOWLEDGEMENTS

We would like to thank our students Philipp Arnolds, Joe Bucher, Margarita Grinko, Matthias Sierzega and Elisabeth Tsechanski for conducting the studies and collecting data.

REFERENCES

1. Joshua M. Ackerman, Christopher C. Nocera, and John A. Bargh. 2010. Incidental Haptic Sensations Influence

Social Judgments and Decisions. *Science* 328, 5986: 1712–1715. http://doi.org/10.1126/science.1189993

2. Olivier Bau and Ivan Poupyrev. 2012. REVEL: Tactile Feedback Technology for Augmented Reality. *ACM Trans. Graph.* 31, 4: 89:1–89:11. http://doi.org/10.1145/2185520.2185585
3. Daniel Casasanto, Lera Boroditsky, W. Phillips, et al. 2004. How deep are effects of language on thought? Time estimation in speakers of English, Indonesian, Greek, and Spanish. In *Proceedings of the 26th Annual Meeting of the Cognitive Science Society*, K. Forbus, D. Gentner and T. Regier (eds.). Lawrence Erlbaum, Mawah, NJ, 186–191.
4. Daniel Casasanto. 2014. Experiential origins of mental metaphors: Language, culture, and the body. In *The power of metaphor: Examining its influence on social life*, Mark J. Landau, Michael D. Robinson and Brian P. Meier (eds.). American Psychological Association, Washington, DC, US, 249–268.
5. Marcelo Coelho and Jamie Zigelbaum. 2010. Shape-changing interfaces. *Personal and Ubiquitous Computing* 15, 2: 161–173. http://doi.org/10.1007/s00779-010-0311-y
6. Gosta Ekman, Jan Hosman, and Brita Lindstrom. 1965. Roughness, smoothness, and preference: A study of quantitative relations in individual subjects. *Journal of Experimental Psychology* 70, 1: 18–26. http://doi.org/10.1037/h0021985
7. Roberta Etzi, Charles Spence, and Alberto Gallace. 2014. Textures that we like to touch: An experimental study of aesthetic preferences for tactile stimuli. *Consciousness and Cognition* 29: 178–188. http://doi.org/10.1016/j.concog.2014.08.011
8. Marc Hassenzahl, M. Burmester, and F. Koller. 2003. AttrakDiff: Ein Fragebogen zur Messung wahrgenommener hedonischer und pragmatischer Qualität. In *Mensch & Computer 2003. Interaktion in Bewegung.*, J. Ziegler and G. Szwillus (eds.). B.G. Teubner, Stuttgart, Leipzig, 187–196.
9. Marc Hassenzahl. 2008. The Interplay of Beauty, Goodness, and Usability in Interactive Products. *Hum.-Comput. Interact.* 19, 4: 319–349. http://doi.org/10.1207/s15327051hci1904_2
10. Mark Holliins, Richard Faldowski, Suman Rao, and Forrest Young. 1993. Perceptual dimensions of tactile surface texture: A multidimensional scaling analysis. *Perception & Psychophysics* 54, 6: 697–705. http://doi.org/10.3758/BF03211795
11. Mark Hollins, Sliman Bensmaïa, Kristie Karlof, and Forrest Young. 2000. Individual differences in perceptual space for tactile textures: Evidence from multidimensional scaling. *Perception & Psychophysics* 62, 8: 1534–1544. http://doi.org/10.3758/BF03212154
12. Jörn Hurtienne. 2016. How Cognitive Linguistics Inspires HCI: Image Schemas and Image-Schematic Metaphors. *International Journal of Human–Computer Interaction.* https://doi.org/10.1080/10447318.2016.1232227
13. Jörn Hurtienne and Oliver Meschke. 2016. Soft Pillows and the Near and Dear: Physical-to-Abstract Mappings with Image-Schematic Metaphors. *Proceedings of the TEI '16: Tenth International Conference on Tangible, Embedded, and Embodied Interaction*, ACM, 324–331. http://doi.org/10.1145/2839462.2839483
14. Jörn Hurtienne, Christian Stößel, Christine Sturm, et al. 2010. Physical gestures for abstract concepts: Inclusive design with primary metaphors. *Interacting with Computers* 22, 6: 475–484. http://doi.org/10.1016/j.intcom.2010.08.009
15. Jörn Hurtienne, Christian Stößel, and Katharina Weber. 2009. Sad is Heavy and Happy is Light: Population Stereotypes of Tangible Object Attributes. *Proceedings of the 3rd International Conference on Tangible and Embedded Interaction*, ACM, 61–68. http://doi.org/10.1145/1517664.1517686
16. Aaron C. Kay, S. Christian Wheeler, John A. Bargh, and Lee Ross. 2004. Material priming: The influence of mundane physical objects on situational construal and competitive behavioral choice. *Organizational Behavior and Human Decision Processes* 95, 1: 83–96. http://doi.org/10.1016/j.obhdp.2004.06.003
17. Zoltan Kövecses. 2005. *Metaphor in culture: universality and variation.* Cambridge University Press, Cambridge ; New York.
18. George Lakoff and Mark Johnson. 1980. *Metaphors we live by.* University of Chicago Press, Chicago.
19. Mark J. Landau, Brian P. Meier, and Lucas A. Keefer. 2010. A metaphor-enriched social cognition. *Psychological Bulletin* 136, 6: 1045–1067. http://doi.org/10.1037/a0020970
20. Mark Landau, Michael D. Robinson, and Brian P. Meier (eds.). 2014. *The power of metaphor: Examining its influence on social life.* American Psychological Association, Washington, DC, US.
21. Diana Löffler, Lennart Arlt, Takashi Toriizuka, Robert Tscharn, and Jörn Hurtienne. 2016. Substituting Color for Haptic Attributes in Conceptual Metaphors for Tangible Interaction Design. *Proceedings of the TEI '16: Tenth International Conference on Tangible, Embedded, and Embodied Interaction*, ACM, 118–125. http://doi.org/10.1145/2839462.2839485
22. Anna Macaranas, Alissa N. Antle, and Bernhard E. Riecke. 2012. Bridging the Gap: Attribute and Spatial Metaphors for Tangible Interface Design. *Proceedings of the Sixth International Conference on Tangible,*

Embedded and Embodied Interaction, ACM, 161–168. http://doi.org/10.1145/2148131.2148166

23. D. R. Major. 1895. On the Affective Tone of Simple Sense-Impressions. *The American Journal of Psychology* 7, 1: 57–77. http://doi.org/10.2307/1412037
24. Brian P. Meier, Simone Schnall, Norbert Schwarz, and John A. Bargh. 2012. Embodiment in Social Psychology. *Topics in Cognitive Science* 4, 4: 705–716. http://doi.org/10.1111/j.1756-8765.2012.01212.x
25. Christoph Neumann. 2001. Is Metaphor Universal? Cross-Language Evidence From German and Japanese. *Metaphor and Symbol* 16, 1–2: 123–142. http://doi.org/10.1080/10926488.2001.9678890
26. Michael Schaefer, Claudia Denke, Hans-Jochen Heinze, and Michael Rotte. 2013. Rough primes and rough conversations: Evidence for a modality-specific basis to mental metaphors. *Social Cognitive and Affective Neuroscience*: nst163. http://doi.org/10.1093/scan/nst163
27. C.D. Wickens and C.M. Carswell. 1995. The Proximity Compatibility Principle: Its Psychological Foundation and Relevance to Display Design. *Human Factors: The Journal of the Human Factors and Ergonomics Society* 37: 473–494.
28. Bodo Winter. 2016. *The Sensory Structure of the English Lexicon*. University of California Merced, Merced, CA. Retrieved from https://escholarship.org/uc/item/885849k9
29. M. Yoshida. 1968. Dimensions of tactual impressions. *Japanese Psychological Research* 10: 157–173.

Interactive Architecture: Exploring and Unwrapping the Potentials of Organic User Interfaces

Sara Nabil[1], Thomas Plötz[1,2], David S. Kirk[3]

[1]Open Lab
Newcastle University
Newcastle upon Tyne, UK
s.nabil-ahmed2@ncl.ac.uk

[2]School of Interactive Computing
Georgia Institute of Technology
Atlanta, GA, USA
thomas.ploetz@gatech.edu

[3]Faculty of Engineering & Environment
Northumbria University
Newcastle upon Tyne, UK
david.kirk@northumbria.ac.uk

ABSTRACT

Organic User Interfaces (OUIs) are flexible, actuated interfaces characterized by being aesthetically pleasing, intuitively manipulated and ubiquitously embedded in our daily life. In this paper, we critically survey the state-of-the-art for OUIs in interactive architecture research at two levels: 1) Architecture and Landscape; and 2) Interior Design. We postulate that OUIs have specific qualities that offer great potential for building interactive interiors and entire architectures that have the potential to –finally– transform the vision of smart homes and ubiquitous computing environments (calm computing) into reality. We formulate a manifesto for OUI Architecture in both exterior and interior design, arguing that OUIs should be at the core of a new interdisciplinary field driving research and practice in architecture. Based on this research agenda we propose concerted efforts to be made to begin addressing the challenges and opportunities of OUIs. This agenda offers us the strongest means through which to deliver a future of interactive architecture.

ACM Classification Keywords

H.5.m Information Interfaces & Presentation (e.g. HCI): Misc.; J.5 Computer Applications: Arts & Humanities – Architecture

Author Keywords

Organic user interfaces; Tangible user interfaces; Shape changing interfaces; interactive architecture; kinetic building skins; ambient displays

INTRODUCTION

Organic User Interfaces (OUIs) arguably represent the flexible, adaptive and malleable version of both Tangible User Interfaces (TUIs) and Shape-changing interfaces (SCIs). Initially introduced as 'organic tangible interface' or 'organic TUI' [33], OUI evolved offering radical new materialities and form factors that underpin both input and output interactions, coinciding with Ishii's vision for the future of UI as 'Radical Atoms' [34]. Therefore, over recent years OUIs have seen increased interest amongst HCI [11], Ubicomp [76] and TEI research communities [24].

TEI '17, March 20 - 23, 2017, Yokohama, Japan

ISBN 978-1-4503-4676-4/17/03...$15.00

DOI: http://dx.doi.org/10.1145/3024969.3024981

Figure 1. Examples of OUI Architecture: a) Kinetic sun-shade: Al Bahr Towers by Aedas Architects, Abu Dhabi 2012; Photo credit: Aedas.com. b) Climactive skin: Hygroscopic Envelope Prototype, 2010 [64]; Photo credit: Steffen Reichert. c) Shape-changing: Hoberman Arch by Chuck Hoberman, Salt Lake 2002 [28]; Photo credit: hoberman.com.

By definition, OUIs are non-planar interfaces taking any 3D shape and morphing either actively or passively, to support direct physical interaction [31, 33, 65, 76]. So, OUIs enable manipulative and bodily input (like TUIs) and kinetic interactions (like SCIs) facilitating flexible form and change of appearance as output, which matches their intended function and supports intuitive interaction. However, OUI conceptually depends on the 'shape' of the interface being the 'key' for interaction; that is: the physical 'form' conveys its function and invites users to familiar interactions such as deformable/non-deformable hand manipulations in addition to body gestures and movements, including hand, head, eye tracking, etc. [51] as means of user input; and multi-sensory auditory, visual or haptic feedback as means of output interaction. Early examples of OUIs range from surface computing, volumetric (spherical [3], polygonal [52], cylindrical [4], etc.) and bendable computers to flexible displays or paper computers [1]. Similarly OUI can utilize flexible, deformable, skin-changing and shape-changing materials in order to cover, embed and surround real-world objects and environments.

The concept of OUI builds on organic electronics or 'Transitive Materials' [11, 34] allowing displays/ devices to be malleable & actuated in an aesthetically pleasing way. Examples of such flexible and controllable displays include flexible Organic Light Emitting Diodes (OLED), Electrophoretic displays (EPDs), and Electroluminescent Lighting (EL). In addition to flexible displays, OUI can be designed using all ranges of flexible conductive materials; from paper or fabric to wood and glass that has embedded thin & flexible electronic sensors, microcontrollers and actuators, such as muscle wires, metal powder, conductives (thread, fabric and paint), optical fibres, thermochromic color-changing pigments and e-textiles. Such materials and technologies pave the way for rethinking user interfaces that can be embedded into everyday objects. Accordingly, OUI have great potential for radically new applications, e.g., dynamic artwork, pattern-changing fabrics, reactive architectural facades or even entire interactive spaces.

Examples of OUIs that have specifically explored new materialities include FuSA [53] the furry display, ClothDisplays [42], Hairlytop [56] and uniMorph [27] a curved actuated interface that enables designers to print custom responsive OUIs in various flexible and dynamic forms. In addition, one of the key potentials of OUI is their malleability, as seen in Follmer et al. [17], who introduced a technique for enabling programmatic control of a material's stiffness enabling actuated manipulations and deformations as both input and output interactions. Several other possibilities of deformable display materials have been motivating researchers for the past few years creating leading to innovative ideas and novel flexible design materials [2].

These kinds of interactive technology have enormous potential to not only change the nature of our interactions with technology but also to change the very environments we inhabit. Computational processes and interactivity will become increasingly embedded within the environment (as per the vision of ubiquitous computing). However, those environments will also increasingly react to our presence through embedded sensing, now with the additional potential to change form and function on demand. Accordingly, technologies such as 'Reactive Architecture' [68] and 'Kinetic Architecture' [39] offer substantial scope for redefining current architecture (see Figure 1). However, such architectural interventions are quite rare, and commonly only possible as new builds (thereby ignoring existing building stock) and largely neglect interior design, focusing more on dynamic structural features or interactive service layers within the building fabric.

We believe that OUIs have significant potential for opening up a new architectural design space for the development of interactive architecture and interior design. In this paper we make a case for this and encourage researchers & practitioners to adopt OUIs as key technology for future developments in this area. We begin by examining the state-of-the-art in OUI to lay out the play-of-possibilities that they offer, before looking at current applications in interactive architecture/ interior design. We then formulate a manifesto, i.e., our vision for the role of OUIs in architectural design and then finally present an articulation of the future challenges for researchers and practitioners to realize this radical pervasive computing agenda.

OUI: THE STATE-OF-THE-ART

Through contextualizing OUI with regards to the state-of-the-art we can formulate the research agenda for OUI as means for interactive architecture and interior design. In this section, we explore a specific subset of OUI application areas to demonstrate the general concept of Organic User Interfaces and to highlight advantages and benefits of designing interactive architectural spaces. We divide potential OUI applications into two levels matching the common classic design disciplines: 1) Architecture and Landscape; 2) Interior Design. Although, we do realize that both levels are not mutually exclusive or complementary, but are inter-related in many aspects, we tackle each level as to present OUI potentials from a holistic large-scale experience to the smallest ornamental detail. The first level focuses on the entire architecture of buildings and planning the landscape/environment around them, where OUI buildings could be reactive to people, environment or other buildings. The second level includes reactive surfaces, context-aware spaces within buildings and interactive interior elements.

OUI Architecture

Architectural history demonstrates early adoptions of 'Organic Architecture' emphasizing how organic designs (from buildings to ornamental details) could be flowing in harmony and blended naturally with our environment whilst fulfilling their essential structural, functional and aesthetic purposes [58, 41]. Decades ago, architect Frank Lloyd Wright's philosophy of 'Organic Architecture' focused on nature-inspired organic designs for buildings to be "not only convenient but charming" imagining both the exterior of buildings, the interior areas together with furniture and decorative accessories all integrated into a design that serves and contributes to users' values concerning usability and comfort. Although how literal the term 'organic' was used back then do refer to non-rectlinear architectural designs, OUI takes it further to focus on impacting aesthetics of interactive architecture or 'architecture as user interface' that should live, grow and adapt with users along their lifetime. We believe that Wright's ideas emphasizes the motivation and need for OUI architecture harvesting the value of designing any building or artefact -even a digitally augmented one- in real-world affordances and aesthetics.

Evident ecent literature of architecture ('Dynamic Buildings' [40], 'Interactive Architecture' [36, 18, 25] and 'Responsive Landscapes' [8]) and practice (Diller & Scofidio, Jean Nouvel, Chuck Hoberman, Ned Kahn) architects started envisioning the future of architecture using smart materials that can sense, react and integrate with their architectural designs. Some authors even proposed the integration of physical computing, robotics and sensor technologies. However, collaboration with HCI communities, UI and UX designers and researchers to fully realise the potential of these novel interfaces is still quite limited. For example, 'Kinetic Facades' [49] started to be adopted in architecture as means for energy-efficiency using flexible sun-shade envelopes that cover several buildings nowadays around the world. This is one kind of interaction with the environment. OUI Architecture concept incorporates a broader meaning and understanding of dynamic architecture in a way that would be more interactive and organic. For example, climactive architectural skins that react to environmental changes such as sun light/shadow, temperature, humidity, rain, wind, etc to create dynamic forms that would essentially change how people perceive and feel their surroundings. Figure 1 shows different examples for OUI Architecture.

In HCI, recent studies around architecture such as 'Kinetic Organic Interfaces' (KOI) [39] and 'Proactive Architecture' (ProA) [57] have developed notions of responsive actuated buildings with mass customization designed in entirely new aesthetic (curved surfaces, bent lines, organic designs, and unusual innovative structures) and responsive to both users and its surrounding environment (temperature, wind, solar radiation, etc), emphasizing the need and possibility for buildings to be dynamic and interactive enough in order to change physical form autonomously thereby reflecting context-awareness. Oosterhuis et al. describe the concept of proactive architecture as buildings that are "organic, ever-changing vehicles for processing and displaying information" [57].

Similarly, studies of 'Adaptive Architecture' [5, 68] attempted to create a self-sustaining, user oriented and real-time interactive 'skin' where building designs involve entire dynamic facades that are flexible in two opposite curvatures during their movement, with embedded sensors (light, energy, humidity) and actuators to generate kinetic adaptations that respond to, store and regulate environmental factors (sun, wind, precipitation) enhancing comfort level, social interaction and environmental conditions within the living environment. ExoBuilding [68] is an example of adaptive architecture, exploring potential biofeedback relationships between buildings and users.

Alternatively, the term 'Interactive Architecture' has been used. For example, Acacia [44] is a platform developed for the design of interactive building facades using organic smart materials allowing interactivity between users, buildings and the environment. In this sense, responsive architectural facades are thought to bring opportunities that redefine building skins offering impactful values being both architecturally aesthetic and interactive surfaces at the same time. Similarly, other researchers [50, 61, 39] have been motivated to study and design interactive architectural facades using OUI arguing how the visibility and size of building facades together with possible embedded capabilities create potential for utilizing them as public displays or interactive architectural surfaces.

Others envisioned 'Display Buildings' [69, 21] where buildings and cities will become gigantic multi-dimensional, frameless displays and entire architectural surfaces can become interactive media facades using huge screens in building scale, wrapped around surfaces that are possibly curved facades. Schoch [69] suggested that architects should design interactive buildings that can significantly change its appearance, using novel materials, describing such interface as changing 'curtain' covering the entire building than a distinct display.

More sustainable designs has considered the use of organic and natural materials that are responsive to different environmental conditions. Responsive materials such as hydromorphic, hygromorphic [47, 32] , photomorphic [14] or thermomorphic materials can sense changes in moisture, humidity, light or temperature respectively and autonomously react by changing their physical shape or colour. For example, Climactive wood [47, 13] that is physically programmed to respond to rain through shape-changing hygromorphic natural thin wood (see Figure1.b) and SynthMorph [62] that uses synthetic biological materials such as morphological bacteria [63] as construction elements for shape-changing architectural structures. Such OUI Architecture does not require electronic or mechanic control, or even energy-consumption but are engineered to autonomously react to certain environmental conditions creating novel dynamic spatial experiences.

Again, we refer to OUI Architecture as not just 'literally' organic in form or materialism, but as user interfaces that are ambient, and dynamic in a way that allows buildings and architectural structures (from bridges to sculptures) to react, express or heal us through changing their appearance or shape similar to the way humans and animals are able to communicate by simple speechless gestures or subtle reactions. OUI architectural designs can shift the appearance of exterior facades/skins, physically transform position, orientation, colour, lighting or curvature of either small modules or large blocks. Such organic interactions can be subtle, slow transformations, or reactive to people's needs and contextual situations. Think of a stadium that autonomously reacts to spectators' cheers or a bridge that illuminates in a way that expresses its traffic load or rain-sensitive convertible pedestrian walkways, or city skyline towers that can together chant a silent melody to celebrate.

OUI Interior Design

Although interior spaces are typically of static nature that require an interior designer and/or architect to facilitate any changes to their appearance and function, the idea of dynamic interiors has recently gained popularity. Interior elements such as surfaces (walls, floors, ceilings) and openings (doors, windows) can be augmented with digital technology to enhance both their aesthetic impact and potential dynamic functionalities. Examples of interactive interior walls are Smartwall [16], LivingWall [7] and LivingSurface [78], while GravitySpace [6] is an interactive floor. However, ceilings seem to be neglected from similar interaction design in spite of all opportunities and potentials that could potentially be addressed especially in bedrooms where users lie down facing their normally plain ceilings.

In general, research on building interactive surfaces and walls has taken two approaches: either wall-sized emissive displays or subtle ambient designs. Wall-sized displays are either light-emissive (i.e. LED displays) or projection-based, while subtle tactile designs focus on embedding interactivity in normal coating, lighting or different finishing materials, such as wood panels, ceramic tiles, wallpaper, ..etc. An example for the first approach is Smartwall [16] where the wall display is divided into large pixel-like, reconfigurable cells that users can select

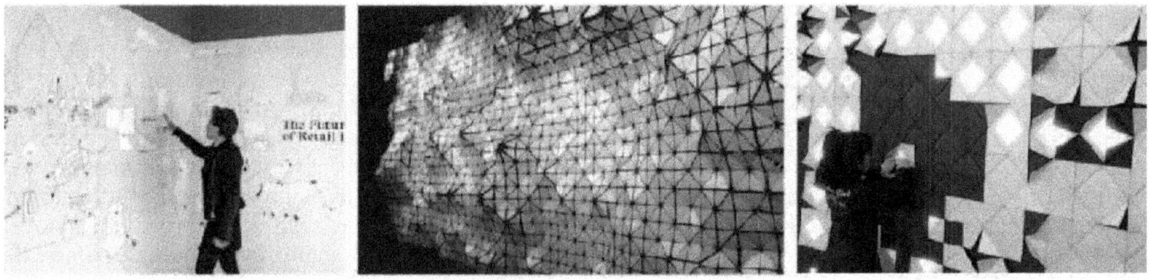

Figure 2. Examples of OUI Interior. Left to right: a) Engaging Retail Space, Dalziel & Pow, 2015 [dalziel-pow.com] b) Aegis Hyposurface, Mark Goulthorpe, 2000; Photo credit: Mark Burry c) Light-Form interactive wall, Francesca Rogers, 2010; Photo courtesy: Daniele Gualeni Design Studio.

and/ or drag each cell representing a certain function, utilizing room dividers and interior walls in user interaction design. Similarly, GravitySpace [6] is an interactive floor designed for smart rooms using real-time tracking, detecting multiple users, their positions/ orientations, and furniture through the pressure-sensitive, back-projected floor.

On the other hand, LivingWall [7] is an interactive wallpaper that uses conductive paint layers connected to microcontrollers and LEDs for interactivity. Users not only interact with it by touching it, but also through walking beside it, which creates a playful experience for interactive interior and a large ambient dynamic wallpaper. Likewise, LivingSurface [78] is a shape-changing surface that interacts with users through its non-emissive material that rather changes its physical shape in response to sensed user physiological data, reflecting their internal body processes such as heart rate and blood volume pulse. The shape-changing interaction of LivingSurface is designed using cutouts in the wallpaper that is actuated to form different interesting 3D shapes. Actuation is deployed in a back layer embedded with hidden servo-motors, vibration motors and small fans controlled using Arduino microcontrollers. The same effect could be implemented without motors using non-mechanical linear actuators such as muscle wire or Shape-Memory Alloys (SMA) that are light-weight thin wires with strong and silent actuation capabilities.

We believe that non-emissive responsive surfaces are much more appropriate to be widely adopted in our environments as they do not constantly stand out and capture attention like with emissive wall displays. Therefore, non-emissive materials and ambient ubiquitous interaction are more appropriate to designing and creating entire interactive interior spaces rather than just a single actuated surface or wall. Still, some examples have used lighting techniques in ambient interactivity such as Light-Form by Francesca Rogers (see Figure2.c) and Luminous by Philips [59] creating interesting playful experiences. Figure 2 shows examples of interactive interiors.

Likewise, other interior elements that range from furniture and decorative art to soft furnishing such as cushions, curtains and carpets can be transformed into OUI devices employing haptic interactions they already afford, serving both beauty and function. Previous work on interactive furniture includes interactive tabletops [35] and shape-changing furniture such as EmotoCouch [48] and shape-changing bench [26]. Other interior elements have also been investigated in OUI research creating haptic interior artefacts such as interactive Tablecloths [20, 72], interactive curtains [19, 71], wall art [75], lampshade [37] and other interior 'Soft User Interfaces' [70].

The above examples form rich inspiration for artists, designers and architects, but only scratch the surface of possibilities for promising smart and dynamic interiors yet to come. General benefits of interactive interiors have been discussed in related prototype installations [20, 46, 48]. By generalizing the concept, we come closer to the vision of ubiquitous computing where technology quite literally weaves into the fabric of everyday life [77], providing inhabitants with potential benefits at both the emotional and physical level. The emotional and psychological effect of changing interiors, e.g., colours, lights, shapes and textures, can have significant impact on inhabitants, potentially leading to improved quality of life through novel, possibly serendipitous experiences and sensory stimulations.

A MANIFESTO FOR OUI ARCHITECTURE

Although previous work on OUI has mentioned art and architecture as interesting applications of OUI, e.g. [12, 31, 65, 76], no systematic research has been undertaken investigating, questioning and discussing how 'OUI Architecture and Interior' can be designed, perceived and lived with. This is a missed opportunity, as instead of having our built environments as static structures built from static materials, designing them as OUIs can create dynamic, responsive and thus context-aware architecture. OUI Architecture can be actuated to modify its appearance, spaces and surfaces as a response to interaction with users, other devices (or buildings), and the surrounding environment. All of which emphasizes the motivation, opportunities and potentials of designing architectural elements that can be interactive, responsive and, consequently, have the potential for fundamentally changing the way architecture and interior design is done leading to radically different ways of interacting with the built environment.

In the sections above we have identified the potential of OUI for substantially opening up a design space that offers new opportunities for Interactive Architecture and Interior Design. Adopting this direction would emphasize how technology can support future architecture in a way that is beyond contemporary techniques of Computer-Aided Design (CAD), Computer-Aided Manufacturing (CAM) and Computer-Aided Engineering (CAE) applications.

In the following we present a manifesto outlining the key considerations for OUIs as a core technology underpinning our vision for the future of architecture and interior design.

1. **Ubiquitous Interaction**: OUI interaction is defined as intuitive and familiar affordance of everyday objects in our physical world[23, 22, 30]. This allows to employ both explicit and implicit interactions we perceive and perform on a daily basis into the fabric of future interactive spaces, fulfilling Weiser's vision of ubiquitous computing [77]. OUI explicit input interactions could range from physical hand manipulations (both deformable and non-deformable) to in-air gestures, body motions and speech [22] resembling more intuitive human-physical and human-human interactions [65]. Implicit input may be triggered by other activities, motion or presence, psychological or physiological sensing or environmental stimuli. Output interactions range from simple visual and haptic feedback such as light, sound or motion to richer sensory and morphological actuation, e.g., skin-change or shape-change. In this sense, people will engage effortlessly through their normal daily interactions with real-world objects and environment, and step into immersive experiences of a ubiquitous dynamic world.

2. **Context-Awareness**: With OUIs, architectural and interior designs can be context-aware for both occupants and the surrounding environments. A user's environment can be seamlessly embedded with technology that captures, analyses and understands different situations and contexts changing around. Earlier work on smart environments has led to robust but not necessarily non-intrusive sensing and inference systems (e.g., [66, 67]). Morphological natural or manufactured responsive materials [47, 32] that sense changes in humidity or temperature and react -by transforming their shape or colour- are rich materials for context-aware building envelopes and fabrics, at no energy cost. Equally, there is clear potential to leverage the strength of the emergent Internet of Things (IoT) to support this seamless networking of OUIs (e.g., [74, 38]). This furthers the vast potential to leverage interaction with everyday objects as sources of data and user input to interactive environments and offers opportunities for interactive interfaces to be based on our interactions with familiar objects. For example, OUI Walls can expect user actions and therefore emerge hidden parts or layers, i.e. bring out a hidden shelf when user holds something needs to put down; or bring out a hidden seat when user seams tired and looking to sit down. In this sense, a new generation of context-aware smart buildings and smart homes can emerge, i.e., rooms that can change their size based on occupants and context of use, decorations that can change their skin based on temporal or social events, and exteriors that can be interactive as well.

3. **Dynamic Nature**: Advances in organic smart materials will allow interfaces to be malleable, deformable, change colour or shape, and be actuated, giving us unprecedented opportunities to design dynamic architecture and interior designs that are not necessarily static like most contemporary designs. OUIs will offer the flexibility of dynamically changing structures and spaces, either on demand (passively) or autonomously (actively). Changing tastes or interests will be accommodated instantaneously. And likewise with exterior architecture, which no longer has to be fixed, using smart OUI materials, a building will be able to alter its facade or even dynamically reconfigure its internal spaces to suit the needs of inhabitants. Essentially, this vision requires re-thinking current architectural methodologies in different ways as it is not that obvious yet, but would also solve historical dilemmas for architects such as orientation towards sun light, view and natural ventilation through dynamic adaptive architecture. Some are already considering buildings that rotate with the sun [49]. So we can foresee the future of having skin-changing and shape-changing architecture being feasible, practical and efficient.

4. **Seamless and Seamful Sensing**: Possibly complete houses and entire buildings can be embedded with intelligence through technology to allow seamless and spatial data sensing. Such embedded intelligence when employed in our everyday objects, furniture and surfaces will allow them to do much more than they already afford. OUIs can eventually replace current health sensor devices in a ubiquitous and seamless implicit interaction [60, 29]. The simplest example could be a duvet/blanket that can measure heart rate, blood pressure, etc. or a sofa arm that senses stress levels. A bigger picture is where –through OUI spaces– architects can design buildings that are able to capture different neurophysiological and psychological data for both the analysis and better understanding of user behaviour and user experiences within interior spaces, buildings and landscapes. On the other hand, seamful ubiquity [9] is also necessary for solving issues of ambiguity and uncertainty of interaction and sensing that might occur in some seamless systems [10]. For example, to design interactive interior spaces, we don't have to achieve completely seamless interaction in every surface and object but could exploit the representation of seams allowing the user to understand the edges of connectivity. Not only is this approach useful for user interaction regarding awareness, ambiguity and control challenges of ubiquitous interaction [15]. It will also provide flexibility for designing both public and private spaces in terms of social concerns such as privacy and personal data. Therefore, incorporating both seamful interation and implicit or seamless data collection through proper appropriation can together support a better user experience and simpler acquiring of the information and knowledge needed to improve the quality of living experience. In addition, such appropriation will support efficient management of urban flows aimed by researchers of smart cities and smart grids, who are already open to such opportunities through big data capabilities and tackling personal data protection challenges[45, 73].

5. **Visualizing the Unseen**: OUI buildings open frontiers for visualizing hidden data in new ways by translating the unseen data into visual, peripheral and tangible representations in the space. For example, displaying energy consumption of a house or a building through colour-changing interior elements. Another application might be for office buildings where the OUI space can visualize employees' satisfaction or engagement through sensing work loads, social interaction or stress levels and giving feedback through ambient texture-changing OUIs. Applications for healthcare spaces (patient rooms, senior homes, etc) can be similarly designed

to give biofeedback to certain health conditions and thresholds through peripheral OUIs. Even gentle breezes can be sensed and interpreted by wind-responsive architecture [43] or an actuating force, such as the work of Ned Kahn [54] (facades of flexible metal panels moving with wind force revealing impressive patterns of wind turbulence).

6. **Aesthetic Computers**: Concomitant with the third generation of computing is the desire to explore how computational devices can be made more aesthetically engaging. The rise of lifestyle brands such as Apple demonstrate consumers' desires for aesthetically pleasing products. OUI provides a design space allowing both researchers and designers to collaborate and innovate around new, dynamic forms of decorative artefacts, harvesting the potential of creating aesthetic computers that can exist in any shape. These devices embed both digital technology -with all its capabilities- and decorative beauty -with all its artistic values- together in one integral interface that can live, engage and influence people's lives over years. Using this paradigm, a lace tablecloth, a shaggy cushion or a Persian rug can become a computational device. Furthermore, aesthetic interaction -which is similarly important and impactful- aligns well with OUI interactions being more intuitive, familiar and manipulative than earlier user interface paradigms. Additionally, OUI can provide a user-friendly interface alternative for complex embedded systems in simple metaphors. For example, tangibilizing power utilization trends through colour-changing tangible clouds hanging as decorative elements.

7. **Sustainability**: OUI architecture contributes to sustainability on four different levels. First, less need for re-design or refurbishment, if interiors and/or exteriors of spaces and buildings are able to change their appearance (colour, shape, pattern, state, texture, etc) either autonomously or responding to occupants' interactions and/or needs. Second, OUI materials such as flexible bendable OLEDs, energy-efficient RGB LEDs and other organic electronics and polymers offer low-power alternatives and energy-efficient technologies [17, 50, 76] that do not compromise energy sustainability. Third, OUI responsive materials that sense and react to changes in humidity, light or heat requires zero energy consumption and can be physically programmed to solely act as sensing, processing and actuating complete system of adaptive architecture. Finally, we've got a missed opportunity of utilizing wasted energy sources that are literally pouring, facing and blowing towards every architectural structure anyway. Such natural resources can be either directly utilized as actuating stimuli [54, 47] creating natural behavioural patterns or employed in a more complicated processes. Nature powers of wind, sun radiation, wasted rain water (storm drain) and even greywater drains are all considered nature's gift to sustainable architecture researchers and should inspire interaction designers as well.

8. **Expressiveness**: Both personalization and playfulness are two important aspects of interaction design in general and in OUI design in particular. OUI interactive and manipulative interfaces have been found to be playful and enjoyable by users. Ubiquitous computing environments are believed to add a pleasure dimension leading to more user-friendly architectural design [50]. OUI interactions such as air gestures and direct hand manipulations are not only intuitive but pleasurable as well. This explains how children nowadays often enjoy playing with technology more than ever before. In her study of interactive architecture in a pleasure-based methodology, Mounajjed [50] stated that "accommodating aesthetic elements that appeal to the emotions is critical to the development of a user-centric design", where the pleasure factor influences the behavioral patterns of users. Therefore, OUI interactions accommodate pleasure as both a cause and an effect in where it encourages user participation and enhances the user experience in an enjoyable and pleasurable flow, influencing their emotions and visceral responses. On the other hand, expressing personalization -in some cases- is beneficial. When tangible art pieces and decorative surfaces become OUIs that are digitally aware of occupants' presence, and perhaps identity, then profiling and real-time customization can be easily implemented so that the same artefact or room can look differently for different occupants as they use a space. Moreover, OUI materials can help transform the same object into different other personalized appearances that suit its owner/user.

9. **Expand Creativity**: Art and architecture are about inspiration, questioning and creativity, provoking people's curiosity and thinking differently. When augmenting an artifact with actuated capabilities, allowing it to dynamically transform, creativity fosters conversations that alter meanings and aesthetics conveyed each time it generates a new form or appearance. OUI Architecture enables such creativity in different designs not only in residential interiors, but also in public spaces such as museums, galleries and showrooms. Commercial spaces are also a candidate for designers who consider technology in their installations to incorporate tangible and tactile interactions to draw innovative, surprising, experimental and engaging user interaction experiences. For example, retail designers Dalziel and Pow recently designed the 'EngagingSpace' at Retail Design Expo 2015 (Figure 2.a) where they installed an interactive animated space to engage visitors in an entertaining novel user experience through simple tactile interactions with interactive wallpaper. In this sense, we have to promote that technology should not be means to performing tasks, solving problems and improving efficiency and productivity only, but rather as well support us to be human, expanding the unique human abilities of vision, creativity and imagination and thus enhancing our quality of living and potentials.

10. **Tangible Decor**: Because domestic environments are required to be both comfortable and beautiful for a lifetime, architecture and interior design (including furniture, decorative accessories, fabrics, e.g., curtains, linens, upholstery) need to serve and contribute to the usability values of occupants in simple synthetics and impacting aesthetics that could live with occupants for years, interact and adapt with them along their lifetime. Domestic decorations can be designed and manufactured as OUIs with slow technology that allows them to respond and interact with occupants calmly and seamlessly over the years, manifesting their physical

pre-existing function and form, in addition to all their potential contribution to enhancing the quality of domestic living, being embedded computers; moreover, provoking inspiration, anticipation and self-reflection. Another important aspect of home decoration is the problem of habitual blindness. Over long periods of time, decorative home artefacts tend to lose their ability to 'stand-out' as they do when first brought-in and blend in a way that stops attracting our attention by time [20] losing a lot of their intended aesthetic values. OUI decorative artifacts that change their appearance, create subtle movements or form alterations, avoid blindness towards them, and create a renewable sense of awareness and perception of these decorative elements and thus a charming atmosphere influencing people's perception of value and meaning of such artefacts over time [55].

WAY FORWARD

We have explored the need, motivation and opportunities OUI provide for developing interactive architecture, both exterior and interior. However, the vision of OUI as key technology for interactive architecture requires substantial efforts to become a reality, which effectively defines the research agenda for the field. In what follows we outline what we have identified as the most important aspects that future research on OUI for interactive architecture has to address.

a) **Radical Interdisciplinarity**: Bridging the gap between involved parties, e.g., computer scientists, material physicists, architects, interior designers, OUI and UX researchers is an essential requirement for realizing the vision of OUI for interactive architecture. More than in any other domain truly interdisciplinary collaborations are essential meaning that where researchers and practitioners from different core subject areas need to go out of their way and work together on creating what eventually will turn into an entirely new research area. Such radical interdisciplinarity needs to be formalized and -more importantly- "lived" in everyday practice of researchers and practitioners. Staying in -certainly comfortable- silos of core disciplines will not lead to the realization of OUI-based architecture be it related to either interiors or exteriors. Although it may sound obvious to some, we have identified this as a key problem for the development of this research area: both architecture and HCI researchers and academics work separately from one another, yet with the same vision. What is ultimately necessary is that, for example, classical architects not only utilize new materials and technologies but rather also actively contribute to their research and developments. Conversely, core technical research disciplines need to engage in thinking like architects and appreciate OUI from a UX and general user perspective. As such a new generation of researchers and practitioners will be able to develop and employ radically new methods, tools, and materials and thus be able to transform both architecture and interaction technologies.

b) **Appropriation and Retrofitting**: An interesting design space emerges not only for designing new buildings with embedded OUIs, but also for retrofitting existing buildings and interior spaces. This requires less structural intervention and allows new OUI layers to cover entire pre-existing interior or exterior surfaces. Considering that interior elements (furniture, decorative accessories and soft furnishings etc) can be appropriated as interactive surfaces through the design of OUIs there is a broad space through which interior designers and OUI researchers can come to collaborate. Similarly, utilizing OUI in architectural exterior facades creates numerous possibilities for exploration. The design space for OUI in architecture is unique in the sense that it bears an intrinsic conflict of conceiving, designing, and developing new objects that effectively implement Organic User Interfaces vs the need for altering, adapting and extending existing objects that are not necessarily straightforward to modify. Especially the latter is the predominant case for existing buildings, which requires retrofitting and approaches of opportunistic modification.

c) **Tackling Scalability**: Addressing scalability of OUI is a fundamental challenge for the field. Scalability hereby refers to moving on from prototypical or exemplary developments to large scale uptake of OUI in everyday scenarios of interactive architecture & interior design. Scalability of large interfaces, e.g., building exteriors, is much more challenging than small-sized interior interfaces. Designing OUIs in ways to be skinned on architectural structures requires many different considerations and functional testing than just lab research. Such considerations are required due to the large scale and reliability required for building envelopes in addition to surviving different environmental conditions. As any newly introduced building material, OUI architectural skin materials must prove durability in terms of sun, rain, wind and fire resistance. If designed as a structural material (holding some building weight), it needs to be tested for load resistance as well, as architecture is non-risk tolerant. Other considerations that require further research and testing are lifespans, vandalism and maintenance approaches of such subtle materials. Once OUI materials are proved to stand such testing and be produced into building components with qualified and quantified specs for architects and structural engineers, pioneers can start using them with confidence and we can start witnessing a new era of responsive and organic architecture as reality.

d) **Re-defining the User**: As somehow different than usual interfaces, defining who would be users of OUI architecture is rather vague and not straightforward. Traditionally, users of an indoor interface system are thought of as the inhabitants, while users of an outdoor interface are considered as the public passing-by. On the other hand, architects and interior designers may consider their users as the contractors, project owners or funding bodies of the designed building/space. In either cases, rethinking who is the user is an important point to be tackled and explored by OUI research when it comes to entire buildings as application/ design space. This is crucial from both perspectives: HCI and Architecture disciplines, both depend on building their design 'concept' on defining the users. More importantly, defining the actual users will essentially push forward a user-centric design and a post-occupancy testing or long-term evaluation of such designs/interfaces that can potentially constantly change, transform and react.

e) **Immersive Interaction Design**: as much as OUI Architecture sounds revolutionary and promising, it also triggers the need for essentially a new generation of interaction design. When re-defining architecture as user interfaces, we need to start reconsidering many interaction design fundamentals. User interaction will be immersive rather than focused, when interacting with spaces rather than devices or building-sized interfaces rather than tabletops. Crowd interaction would replace the traditional 'multiuser' notion, and would require creative methods and tools to study and evaluate. Even with small decorative OUIs, HCI research needs to create and evaluate new arrays of interaction techniques that are immersive, playful and engaging, together with designers. Several challenges require careful design for OUI interactions that would need to be ubiquitous and ambient but not entirely hidden, intuitive but not basic or mundane, surprising and enchanted but at the same time not -perceived as- completely random. Moreover, as OUI Architecture is realized, opportunities for social actions in these interactive spaces would also become an important topic in HCI. But what are the consequences of shifting users' expectations for their surroundings? When would embedded OUIs be appropriate? When would 'smart' be needed? How can we design long-term interactions?

f) **Ethical and Behavior-Shaping**: when building interiors and exteriors that can dynamically transform their shape or appearance either autonomously or interactively, new challenges for ethics and security will emerge. Sensing environments in general are advanced systems that involve complex scenarios and thus are potentially subject to 'hacking' activities as well. Special security procedures might need to emerge to protect one's wallpaper or moving furniture. An essential step forward for OUI Architecture would be considering BIM (Building Information Management) as means of embedding security techniques into OUI software not only for creating anti-hacking systems but defining who has the rights to interact -thus change- the physical appearance and form of interior elements or exterior facades. We are aware that such implications are applicable for any embedded system, yet we need to highlight this here as it would require new methodologies and considerations impacting people in their very own bedrooms. Another challenge is designing the appropriate skin-changes of the original architectural design and their possible emotional effects on residents. In theories of architecture, different colors, materials and textures have definite meanings, feelings and uses, thus consequently emotional effects on the building occupants and often the entire surrounding ecosystem. In OUI Architecture, the materials and methods of sensing, actuation and interaction will be an essential part of the architectural design, requiring careful studies in each context to control and avoid any implications that might result on families either physiologically or psychologically. When designing for domestic spaces, more challenges emerge on different technical, social and ethical levels. Since some early challenges of domestic ubiquitous computing [15] have been resolved, it seems that it is a matter of continuous studies and research to find ways to overcome more.

g) **Sustainability Dilemma**: Currently, sustainability research predominantly focuses on exploring means of building resource-efficient, energy-conservative and environment friendly architecture through Green Building and Sustainable Architecture practices. OUI exteriors can contribute to sustainable buildings through 'modularity' where component-parts can be replaced easily. In addition, any kinetic interaction employed in the interface can contribute to energy-harvesting in a way that allows micro-scale energy production that will support self-sustainable buildings. Not only buildings, but other architectural structures from bridges, tunnels and motorways to narrow streets, parks and transportation facilities. Together they form the urban glue in which indeed shapes our daily lives, is a rich space for OUI, converting them from mute structures to possible 'urban actors'. Yet, creating new urban actors would raise more sustainability challenges, and opportunities.

CONCLUSION

Technology is converging to bring together a new generation of devices and interactions built around smart OUI materials. The vision of smart homes and ubiquitous computing environments (calm computing) has never been closer to realization. Previous visions of interactive architecture have been just that, visions, largely unrealizable at a scale that would actually impact people in an everyday context (being largely restricted to specific experimental builds). The advances in networked technology and new materials mean that it is now possible to make architectural interventions at both the exterior and interior scale, in affordable and sustainable ways. Older building stock can be retrofitted with technology to dynamically alter spaces and make environments responsive in ways not possible before. No longer do we need to make the case for building entirely new reactive architecture when older buildings can be adapted with technology to make them smart. The imminent proliferation of smart home controls is making the general populace more switched on to the idea of technologically enhanced and reactive environments. Now is therefore the time to invest in thoroughly exploring a new future of interactive, dynamic and reactive architecture. This requires a fundamental attack from multidisciplinary and interdisciplinary researchers to begin to address the challenges and opportunities of OUIs, which offer us the strongest means through which to deliver a future of interactive architecture. In this paper we have sought to outline some of those challenges and to begin to galvanize a community that might seek to explore how OUIs can fundamentally alter the way we live.

REFERENCES

1. Eric Akaoka, Tim Ginn, and Roel Vertegaal. 2010. DisplayObjects: Prototyping Functional Physical Interfaces on 3D Styrofoam, Paper or Cardboard Models. In *Proceedings of the fourth international conference on Tangible, embedded, and embodied interaction - TEI '10*. Cambridge, Massachusetts, USA, 49. DOI: http://dx.doi.org/10.1145/1709886.1709897

2. Jason Alexander, Viljakaisa Aaltonen, Johan Kildal, Andrees Lucero, Kasper Hornbæk, and Sriram Subramanian. 2012. Interaction with Deformable

Displays. In *MobileHCI*. San Francisco, CA, USA. DOI: http://dx.doi.org/10.1145/2371664.2371723

3. Hrvoje Benko, Ad Wilson, and Ravin Balakrishnan. 2008. Sphere: Multi-touch Interactions on a Spherical Display. *UIST '08* (2008). DOI: http://dx.doi.org/10.1145/1449715.1449729
4. Gilbert Beyer, Florian Alt, Jörg Müller, Albrecht Schmidt, Karsten Isakovic, Stefan Klose, Manuel Schiewe, and Ivo Haulsen. 2011. Audience Behavior Around Large Interactive Cylindrical Screens. In *SIGCHI Conference on Human Factors in Computing Systems ACM CHI*. Vancouver, BC, Canada, 1021–1030. DOI: http://dx.doi.org/10.1145/1978942.1979095
5. Nimish Biloria and Valentina Sumini. 2007. Performative Building Skin Systems: A Morphogenomic Approach Towards Developing Real-Time Adaptive Building Skin Systems. *International Journal of Architectural Computing* 07, 04 (2007). DOI: http://dx.doi.org/10.1260/1478-0771.7.4.643
6. Alan Branzel, Christian Holz, Daniel Hoffmann, Dominik Schmidt, Marius Knaust, Patrick Luhne, Rene Meusel, Stephan Richter, and Patrick Baudisch. 2013. GravitySpace: Tracking users and their poses in a smart room using a pressure-sensing floor. In *SIGCHI Conference on Human Factors in Computing Systems*. Paris, France. DOI: http://dx.doi.org/10.1145/2470654.2470757
7. Leah Buechley, David Mellis, Hannah Perner-Wilson, Emily Lovell, and Bonifaz Kaufmann. 2010. Living Wall: Programmable Wallpaper for Interactive Spaces. In *Proceedings of the international conference on Multimedia*. Firenze, Italy, 1401–1402. DOI: http://dx.doi.org/10.1145/1873951.1874226
8. Bradley E Cantrell and Justine Holzman. 2015. *Responsive Landscapes: Strategies for Responsive Technologies in Landscape Architecture*. Routledge.
9. Matthew Chalmers. 2003. Seamful Design and Ubicomp Infrastructure. 4. http://citeseerx.ist.psu.edu/viewdoc/download?doi=10.1.1.61.6779
10. Matthew Chalmers and Ian MacColl. 2003. Seamful and Seamless Design in Ubiquitous Computing. In *Proc. Ubicomp 2003 Workshop At The Crossroads: The Interacton of HCI and Systems Issues in Ubicomp*. Seattle, WA, USA, 8. DOI:http://dx.doi.org/10.1.1.104.9538
11. Marcelo Coelho, Ivan Poupyrev, Sajid Sadi, Roel Vertegaal, Joanna Berzowska, Leah Buechley, Pattie Maes, and Neri Oxman. 2009. Programming Reality: From Transitive Materials to Organic User Interfaces. In *CHI 2009 Workshops*. Boston, MA, USA. DOI: http://dx.doi.org/10.1145/1520340.1520734
12. Sandra Coelho. 2011. Art Evolves through Technology: Haptic after the Hegemony of Visual Art. In *LNICST*, Vol. 101. 171–176. DOI: http://dx.doi.org/10.1007/978-3-642-33329-3{_}21
13. David Correa, Oliver David Krieg, Achim Menges, and Steffen Reichert. 2013. HYGROSKIN: A Climate Responsive Prototype Project Based on the Elastic and Hygroscopic Properties of Wood. In *ACADIA 2013 Adaptive Architecture*. 33–42.
14. Michael Dickey, Ying Liu, and Jan Genzer. 2012. Light-induced folding of two-dimensional polymer sheets. *SPIE* (2012), 3–4.
15. W.K. Edwards and R.E. Grinter. 2001. At Home with Ubiquitous Computing: Seven Challenges. In *Proceedings of the 3rd international conference on Ubiquitous Computing*. 256–272. DOI: http://dx.doi.org/10.1007/3-540-45427-6
16. Nicholas Farrow, Naren Sivagnanadasan, and Nikolaus Correll. 2014. Gesture Based Distributed User Interaction System for a Reconfigurable Self-Organizing Smart Wall. In *Proceedings of the 8th International Conference on Tangible, Embedded and Embodied Interaction - TEI '14*. Munich, Germany. DOI: http://dx.doi.org/10.1145/2540930.2540967
17. Sean Follmer, Daniel Leithinger, Alex Olwal, Nadia Cheng, and Hiroshi Ishii. 2012. Jamming User Interfaces: Programmable Particle Stiffness and Sensing for Malleable and Shape-Changing Devices. In *Proceedings of UIST'12*. Cambridge, Massachusetts, USA, 519. DOI: http://dx.doi.org/10.1145/2380116.2380181
18. Michael Fox and Miles Kemp. 2009. Interactive Architecture: Adaptive World. *Architectural Design* Novak (2009), 256. DOI: http://dx.doi.org/10.4018/978-1-61350-180-1.ch015
19. Markus Funk, Stefan Schneegaß, Michael Behringer, Niels Henze, and Albrecht Schmidt. 2015. An Interactive Curtain for Media Usage in the Shower. *Proceedings of PerDis'15* (2015). DOI: http://dx.doi.org/10.1145/2757710.2757713
20. William Gaver, John Bowers, Andy Boucher, Andy Law, Sarah Pennington, and Nicholas Villar. 2006. The History Tablecloth: Illuminating Domestic Activity. *Dis 2006* (2006). DOI:http://dx.doi.org/10.1145/1142405.1142437
21. Sven Gehring, Elias Hartz, and Markus Löchtefeld. 2013. The Media Façade Toolkit: Prototyping and Simulating Interaction with Media Façades. In *UbiCompâĂŹ13*. Zurich, Switzerland. DOI: http://dx.doi.org/10.1145/2493432.2493471
22. Atef Ghalwash and Sara Nabil. 2013. Organic User Interfaces: Framework, Interaction Model and Design Guidelines. *International Journal of Ad hoc, Sensor & Ubiquitous Computing (IJASUC)* 4, 4 (2013). DOI: http://dx.doi.org/10.5121/ijasuc.2013.4404
23. Audrey Girouard, Roel Vertegaal, and Ivan Poupyrev. 2011. Second International Workshop on Organic User Interfaces. In *Proceedings of the fifth international conference on Tangible, embedded, and embodied interaction - TEI '11*. Funchal, Portugal, 381. DOI: http://dx.doi.org/10.1145/1935701.1935791

24. Audrey Girouard, Roel Vertegaal, and Ivan Poupyrev. 2013. Special Issue: Organic User Interfaces. *Interacting with Computers* 25, 2 (2013). DOI: http://dx.doi.org/10.1093/iwc/iws001

25. Ruairi Glynn. 2014. Animating Architecture: Coupling high-definition sensing with high-definition actuation. *Architectural Design* 84, 1 (2014), 100–105. DOI: http://dx.doi.org/10.1002/ad.1707

26. Erik Grönvall, Sofie Kinch, Marianne Graves Petersen, and Majken K. Rasmussen. 2014. Causing Commotion with a Shape-Changing Bench. In *Proceedings of CHI'14*. Toronto, ON, Canada. DOI: http://dx.doi.org/10.1145/2556288.2557360

27. Felix Heibeck, Basheer Tome, Clark Della Silva, and Hiroshi Ishii. 2015. uniMorph - Fabricating Thin-Film Composites for Shape-Changing Interfaces. In *Proceedings of UIST'15*. Charlotte, NC, USA. DOI: http://dx.doi.org/10.1145/2807442.2807472

28. Hoberman Associates - Transformable Design - Hoberman Arch. 2002. Hoberman Arch. (2002). http://www.hoberman.com/portfolio/hobermanarch.php?projectname=HobermanArch

29. Jesse Hoey, Thomas Ploetz, Dan Jackson, Andrew F Monk, Cuong Pham, and Patrick Olivier. 2011. Rapid specification and automated generation of prompting systems to assist people with dementia. *Pervasive and Mobile Computing (PMC)* 7, 3 (2011), 299–318.

30. David Holman, Audrey Girouard, Hrvoje Benko, and Roel Vertegaal. 2013. The Design of Organic User Interfaces: Shape, Sketching and Hypercontext. *Interacting with Computers* 25, 2 (2013). DOI: http://dx.doi.org/10.1093/iwc/iws018

31. David Holman and Roel Vertegaal. 2008. Organic User Interfaces: Designing Computers in Any Way, Shape or Form. *Commun. ACM* 51, 6 (2008), 48. DOI: http://dx.doi.org/10.1145/1349026.1349037

32. Artem Holstov, Ben Bridgens, and Graham Farmer. 2015. Hygromorphic Materials for Sustainable Responsive Architecture. *Construction and Building Materials* 98 (2015), 570–582. DOI: http://dx.doi.org/10.1016/j.conbuildmat.2015.08.136

33. Hiroshi Ishii. 2008. The Tangible User Interface and its Evolution. *Commun. ACM* 51, 6 (2008). DOI: http://dx.doi.org/10.1145/1349026.1349034

34. Hiroshi Ishii, Dávid Lakatos, Leonardo Bonanni, and Jean-Baptiste Jb Labrune. 2012. Radical Atoms: Beyond Tangible Bits, Toward Transformable Materials. *Interactions* XIX, February (2012), 38–51. DOI: http://dx.doi.org/10.1145/2065327.2065337

35. Hiroshi Ishii, Daniel Leithinger, and Sean Follmer. 2015. TRANSFORM: Embodiment of "Radical Atoms" at Milano Design Week. In *CHI'15 Extended Abstracts*. Seoul, Republic of Korea. DOI: http://dx.doi.org/10.1145/2702613.2702969

36. Taysheng Jeng. 2012. Interactive Architecture: Spaces that Sense, Think and Respond to Change. *Computational Design Methods and Technologies: Applications in CAD, CAM and CAE Education: Applications in CAD, CAM and CAE Education* (2012), 257.

37. Heekyoung Jung, Youngsuk L Altieri, and Jeffrey Bardzell. 2010. SKIN : Designing Aesthetic Interactive Surfaces. *Proceedings of the fourth International Conference on Tangible, embedded, and embodied interaction* (2010), 85–92. DOI: http://dx.doi.org/10.1145/1709886.1709903

38. Aftab Khan, James Nicholson, Sebastian Mellor, Daniel Jackson, Karim Ladha, Cassim Ladha, Jon Hand, Joseph Clarke, Patrick Olivier, and Thomas Plötz. 2014. Occupancy Monitoring using Environmental & Context Sensors and a Hierarchical Analysis Framework. In *Proc. ACM BuildSyS*. Memphis, TN, USA. DOI: http://dx.doi.org/10.1145/2674061.2674080

39. Chin Koi Khoo and Flora D. Salim. 2013. Lumina: A Soft Kinetic Material for Morphing Architectural Skins and Organic User Interfaces. In *Proceedings of UbiComp'13*. Zurich, Switzerland, 53. DOI: http://dx.doi.org/10.1145/2493432.2494263

40. Branko Kolarevic and Vera Parlac. 2015. *Building Dynamics: Exploring Architecture of Change*. 304 pages. DOI:http://dx.doi.org/10.4324/9781315763279

41. Hanno-Walter Kruft. 1994. *A History of Architectural Theory: From Vitruvius to the Present*. Princeton Architectural Press.

42. Julian Lepinski and Roel Vertegaal. 2011. Cloth displays: interacting with drapable textile screens. *Proceedings of the fifth international conference on Tangible, embedded, and embodied interaction* (2011). DOI: http://dx.doi.org/10.1145/1935701.1935765

43. Lorenzo Lignarolo, Charlotte Lelieveld, and Patrick Teuffel. 2011. Shape Morphing Wind-Responsive Facade Systems Realized With Smart Materials. In *Adaptive Architecture Conference*. London, UK, 1–14.

44. Daniel Cardoso Llach, Avni Argun, Dimitar Dimitrov, and Qi Ai. 2014. Acacia: A Simulation Platform for Highly Responsive Smart Facades. In *SimAUD Symposium on Simulation for Architecture and Urban Design*. Tampa, Florida, USA.

45. Antoni Martinez-Balleste, Pablo Perez-Martinez, and Agusti Solanas. 2013. The pursuit of citizens' privacy: A privacy-aware smart city is possible. *IEEE Communications Magazine* 51, 6 (2013), 136–141. DOI: http://dx.doi.org/10.1109/MCOM.2013.6525606

46. Rupert Meese, Shakir Ali, Emily-Clare Thorne, Steve D Benford, Anthony Quinn, Richard Mortier, Boriana N Koleva, Tony Pridmore, and Sharon L Baurley. 2013. From Codes to Patterns: Designing Interactive Decoration for Tableware. In *Proceedings of CHI'13*. Paris, France, 931–940. DOI: http://dx.doi.org/10.1145/2470654.2466119

47. Achim Menges and Steffen Reichert. 2012. Material Capacity: Embedded Responsiveness. *Architectural Design* 82, 2 (2012), 52–59. DOI: http://dx.doi.org/10.1002/ad.1379

48. Sarah Mennicken, A.J. Bernheim Brush, Asta Roseway, and James Scott. 2014. Finding Roles for Interactive Furniture in Homes with EmotoCouch. In *Ubicomp'14*. Seattle, WA, USA. DOI: http://dx.doi.org/10.1145/2638728.2641547

49. Jules Moloney. 2011. *Designing Kinetics for Architectural Facades: State Change.*

50. Nadia Mounajjed and Imran A Zualkernan. 2011. From Simple Pleasure to Pleasurable Skin: An Interactive Architectural Screen. In *DPPI '11*. Milano, IT. DOI: http://dx.doi.org/10.1145/2347504.2347537

51. Sara Nabil and Atef Ghalwash. 2013. Perspectives and Application of OUI Framework with SMaG Interaction Model. In *AmI 2013 (Ambient Intelligence) Workshops - Communications in Computer and Information Science CCIS*, Vol. 413 CCIS. Dublin, Ireland. DOI: http://dx.doi.org/10.1007/978-3-319-04406-4{_}29

52. Sara Nabil and Atef Ghalwash. 2015. Organic Interactive Displays: A Bridge from History. *The 5th International Symposium on Frontiers in Ambient and Mobile Systems (FAMS 2015) - Procedia Computer Science* 52 (2015). DOI:http://dx.doi.org/10.1016/j.procs.2015.05.109

53. Kosuke Nakajima, Yuichi Itoh, Takayuki Tsukitani, Kazuyuki Fujita, Kazuki Takashima, Yoshifumi Kitamura, and Fumio Kishino. 2011. FuSA2 Touch Display: A Furry and Scalable Multi-touch Display. In *Proceedings of ITS'11*. Kobe, Japan. DOI: http://dx.doi.org/10.1109/VR.2012.6180852

54. Ned Kahn Studios. 2016. Wind | Ned Kahn. (2016). http://nedkahn.com/wind/

55. William T. Odom, Abigail J. Sellen, Richard Banks, David S. Kirk, Tim Regan, Mark Selby, Jodi L. Forlizzi, and John Zimmerman. 2014. Designing for Slowness, Anticipation and Re-visitation: A Long Term Field Study of the Photobox. In *Proceedings of the 32nd annual ACM conference on Human factors in computing systems - CHI '14*. Toronto, ON, Canada, 1961–1970. DOI: http://dx.doi.org/10.1145/2556288.2557178

56. Yoshiharu Ooide, Hiroki Kawaguchi, and Takuya Nojima. 2013. An Assembly of Soft Actuators for an Organic User Interface. In *Proceedings of the adjunct publication of the 26th annual ACM symposium on User interface software and technology - UIST '13 Adjunct*. St. Andrews, UK. DOI:http://dx.doi.org/10.1145/2508468.2514723

57. Kas Oosterhuis and Nimish Biloria. 2008. Interactions with Proactive Architectural Spaces. *Commun. ACM* 51, 6 (2008). DOI:http://dx.doi.org/10.1145/1349026.1349041

58. David Pearson. 2001. *New Organic Architecture: The Breaking Wave*. Univ of California Press.

59. Philips Lighting. 2016. Philips Luminous Patterns. (2016). http://www.lighting.philips.com/main/systems/packaged-offerings/retail-and-hospitality/luminous-patterns.html

60. T Ploetz, P Moynihan, Cuong Pham, and P Olivier. 2010. Activity Recognition and Healthier Food Preparation. In *Activity Recognition in Pervasive Intelligent Environments*. Atlantis Press.

61. Ingrid Maria Pohl and Lian Loke. 2012. Engaging the Sense of Touch in Interactive Architecture. In *Proceedings of the 24th Australian Computer-Human Interaction Conference on - OzCHI '12*. Melbourne, VIC, Australia, 493–496. DOI: http://dx.doi.org/10.1145/2414536.2414611

62. Carolina Ramirez-Figueroa, Martyn Dade-Robertson, and Luis Hernan. 2013. Adaptive Morphologies: Toward a Morphogenesis of Material Construction. In *ACADIA 2013 Adaptive Architecture*. Cambridge, ON, Canada, 21–23.

63. Carolina Ramirez-figueroa, Luis Hernan, Aurelie Guyet, and Martyn Dade-robertson. 2016. Bacterial Hygromorphs: Experiments into the integration of Soft Technologies into Building Skins. In *ACADIA 2016 Posthuman Frontiers, Programmable Matter*. Acadia Publishing Company, 244–253.

64. Steffen Reichert, Achim Menges, and David Correa. 2015. Meteorosensitive Architecture: Biomimetic Building Skins Based on Materially Embedded and Hygroscopically Enabled Responsiveness. *CAD Computer Aided Design* 60 (2015), 50–69. DOI: http://dx.doi.org/10.1016/j.cad.2014.02.010

65. Jun Rekimoto. 2008. Organic Interaction Technologies: From Stone to Skin. *Commun. ACM* (2008), 38–44. DOI: http://dx.doi.org/10.1177/1464700109355214

66. J Richarz, T Ploetz, and Gernot A Fink. 2008. Real-time Detection and Interpretation of 3D Deictic Gestures for Interaction With an Intelligent Environment. In *Pattern Recognition, ICPR 2008 19th International Conference on IEEE.*

67. B Schauerte, J Richarz, T Ploetz, C Thurau, and Gernot A Fink. 2009. Multi-Modal and Multi-Camera Attention in Smart Environments. In *Proc. ICMI*. 261–268.

68. Holger Schnadelbach, Ainojie Irune, David Kirk, Kevin Glover, and Patrick Brundell. 2012. ExoBuilding: Physiologically Driven Adaptive Architecture. *ACM Transactions on Computer-Human Interaction* 19, 4 (2012). DOI:http://dx.doi.org/10.1145/2395131.2395132

69. Odilo Schoch. 2006. My Building is my Display. In *Proceedings of the the 24th Conference on Education and Research in Computer Aided Architectural Design in Europe: Communicating Space(s) (eCAADe'06)*. Volos, Greece, 610–616.

70. Yuta Sugiura, Gota Kakehi, Anusha Withana, Calista Lee, Daisuke Sakamoto, Maki Sugimoto, Masahiko Inami, and Takeo Igarashi. 2011. Detecting shape deformation of soft objects using directional photoreflectivity measurement. In *Proceedings of UIST '11*. Santa Barbara, CA, USA, 509. DOI:http://dx.doi.org/10.1145/2047196.2047263

71. Tomomi Takashina, Kotaro Aoki, Akiya Maekawa, Chihiro Tsukamoto, Hitoshi Kawai, Yoshiyuki Yamariku, Kaori Tsuruta, Marie Shimokawa, Yuji Kokumai, and Hideki Koike. 2015. Smart Curtain as Interactive Display in Living Space. In *SIGGRAPH Asia 2015 Posters*. Kobe, Japan. DOI:http://dx.doi.org/10.1145/2820926.2820971

72. Sarah Taylor and Sara Robertson. 2014. Digital Lace: A Collision of Responsive Technologies. In *In ISWC'14 Adjunct: Proceedings of the 2014 ACM International Symposium on Wearable Computers*. New York: ACM, 93–97. DOI:http://dx.doi.org/10.1145/2641248.2641280

73. Omer Tene and Jules Polonetsky. 2013. Big data for all: Privacy and user control in the age of analytics. *Northwestern Journal of Technology and Intellectual Property Volume* 11, 5 (2013), 240–273. http://heinonlinebackup.com/hol-cgi-bin/get

74. Edison Thomaz, Vinay Bettadapura, Gabriel Reyes, Megha Sandesh, Grant Schindler, Thomas Ploetz, Gregory D Abowd, and Irfan Essa. 2012. Recognizing Water-Based Activities in the Home Through Infrastructure-Mediated Sensing. In *Proceedings of the 2012 ACM Conference on Ubiquitous Computing*. ACM.

75. Kohei Tsuji and Akira Wakita. 2011. Anabiosis: An Interactive Pictorial Art Based on Polychrome Paper Computing. In *Proceedings of the 8th International Conference on Advances in Computer Entertainment Technology*. Lisbon, Portugal, 80:1–80:2. DOI: http://dx.doi.org/10.1145/2071423.2071521

76. Roel Vertegaal and Ivan Poupyrev. 2008. Organic User Interfaces. *Commun. ACM* 51, 6 (2008), 26. DOI: http://dx.doi.org/10.1145/1349026.1349033

77. Mark Weiser. 1991. The Computer for the 21st Century. *Scientific American* 265, September 1991 (1991), 94–104. DOI:http://dx.doi.org/10.1145/329124.329126

78. Bin Yu, Nienke Bongers, Alissa van Asseldonk, Jun Hu, Mathias Funk, and Loe Feijs. 2016. LivingSurface: Biofeedback through Shape-changing Display. In *Proceedings of the TEI '16*. Eindhoven, Netherlands, 168–175. DOI: http://dx.doi.org/10.1145/2839462.2839469

Tangible mtDNA: A Tangible Tabletop System for Exploring Genetic Mutations on Mitochondrial DNA Cancer Data

Roozbeh Manshaei[1], Nauman Baig[1], Sean DeLong[1], Shahin Khayyer[1], Brien East[1], Ali Mazalek[1,2]
Synaesthetic Media Laboratory
Ryerson University[1], Toronto, Ontario, Canada
Georgia Institute of Technology[2], Atlanta, GA, USA
{roozbeh.manshaei, nauman.m.baig, sean.delong, skhayyer, beast, mazalek}@ryerson.ca

ABSTRACT
Rapid growth in the volume of cancer DNA sequencing data has not been matched by an increase in our ability to understand, explore, and interpret this data. There is a need for new tools that can enhance analyses in order to enable us to interpret the data, discover new or unexpected information, and ultimately form insights. We present Tangible mtDNA, an active tangible and tabletop system that allows multiple users with diverse expertise to collaborate in exploring and understanding mitochondrial DNA sequencing data in breast cancer patients. Five expert biologists evaluated the system and found it to be effective for data exploration and useful in supporting understanding, collaboration and discussion of DNA datasets.

Author Keywords
Tangible interaction; tabletop interaction; active tangibles; bioinformatics; visualization; genetic mutations; cancer; clinicopathological features; collaboration; exploration.

ACM Classification Keywords
H.5.2 Information Interfaces and Presentation (e.g., HCI): User Interfaces—*input devices and strategies*, *interaction styles*, *user-centered design*; I.6.7 Simulation and Modeling: Simulation Support Systems—*environments*.

INTRODUCTION
Big data is one of the largest challenges faced by modern computational researchers [9]. It is a collective term to define massive datasets that are computationally analyzed for revealing initially unapparent trends. Various fields utilize large data sets. Bioinformatics and epigenetics are two major fields that revolve around the collection and analysis of Big Data, specifically genomic data [23]. Genomic analysis allows researchers to make hypotheses about the expressions and interactions of certain genes based on the DNA sequence [19]. A large portion of genomic data used within human cancer research is genomic mutation data [2]. This data is analyzed to observe the effects of mutations on gene expression and is later used to produce effective drugs and cancer therapies [35]. The data of interest primarily consists of physiological and pathological measurements named ClinicoPathological (CP) features [16]. Challenges arise when the acquired data contains multiple CP features (such as age, Alkaline Phosphatase (ALP), Hemoglobin (HB) levels, Lymph Node Metastasis (LNM)) with an enormous quantity of samples, all of which lack significance when considered independently. Visualizing the large sample sets of data while allowing manual filtering and comparison of the samples can provide users with an opportunity to paint a bigger picture about the significance of certain CP features on various genes within the DNA sequence.

TEI '17, March 20-23, 2017, Yokohama, Japan
© 2017 ACM. ISBN 978-1-4503-4676-4/17/03...$15.00
DOI: http://dx.doi.org/10.1145/3024969.3025005

In recent years, there has been a growing interest in the use of tangible and embodied interaction (TEI) and tabletop interaction techniques to support the exploration and interpretation of large genomic datasets [29]. Tangible and tabletop interfaces have proved to be effective in supporting collaboration, distributed cognition, and reflection [34], making them good candidates for addressing the above-mentioned challenges. To this end, we formed an interdisciplinary team of seven researchers: four biomedical engineers with significant experience in bioinformatics tools, a hardware engineer, and two HCI researchers with expertise in tangible and tabletop interaction methods.

In this paper, we present Tangible mtDNA, a TUI-based system for exploring large sets of genomic mutation data. The system employs active tangibles, programmable physical objects with integrated display, sensing, or actuation technologies [34], in combination with an interactive tabletop for the manipulation and visualization of the data and its parameters. The research contributions of this work are three-fold. First, the system introduces novel visualizations and interactions to encourage collaborative exploration of CP feature effects on mutation trends; users of varying expertise are provided with a common language for understanding and discovery. Second, the system contributes to the use of active tangibles for data exploration; active tangibles provide fast and efficient methods for manipulating and filtering data through a combination of tangible and gestural interactions, both on and off the table. Third, the visualization of gene-based and patient-based networks through clustering methods that are accessed via tangible and tabletop interactions provides insight into the relationships between mitochondrial genes or between patients based on mutation patterns.

BACKGROUND

Importance of Mitochondrial DNA

Mitochondria are organelles present within most eukaryotic cells and have the key role of energy conversion and the production of Adenosine Triphosphate (ATP) [33]. They do this through the process of cellular respiration, an operation of oxidizing food molecules into a usable form of chemical energy such as ATP. For this reason, mitochondria are essentially known as the powerhouse or energy-factory of the cell [20]. In addition to the production of ATP, mitochondria have other crucial functions and direct effects on different parts of the body, such as the maintenance of homeostasis within the cell through the regulation of chemicals and ions [25]. Also, the different functions of mitochondria have different effects on different organelles within the cell itself, such as the nucleus and cell wall [11]. For this reason, a change in the mitochondrial anatomy or physiology can have major effects and be the cause of various diseases. Diseases linked to a dysfunctional mitochondria include: Cardiomyopathy, Huntington's, Alzheimer's, Arthritis, breast and prostate cancers [24].

In order to understand the cause of such diseases and develop appropriate treatments, it is important to understand the relation of mitochondria to these diseases and determine what mutation within the mitochondrial chromosome is at its root. Upon finding this, researchers and scientists can identify those parts of the mitochondrial DNA along with the pathways as targets, and create treatments that target those pathways [36]. We believe that a visualization platform that employs tangible interaction can be an effective tool for performing complex analyses on diseased mitochondrial DNA (mtDNA) data, thereby supporting the formation of insights [30]. The aim of this project is to develop a tangible platform that facilitates collaborative analysis of mtDNA sequence data to understand its effects on diseases such as breast cancer.

Exploration of Genetic Mutations

Mutations are processes by which a person's DNA sequence is permanently altered. These can occur at certain regions of the DNA sequence called genes, in which case they are referred to as genetic mutations [6]. Genes are segments of a DNA sequence that code for specific proteins. These proteins are responsible for different functions of tissues and traits within the human body [1].

Genetic mutations occur during the process of DNA replication and are of two types within the human body: hereditary and acquired [14]. Inherited mutations are passed from a parent to their child through reproductive sperm cells. These mutations remain in every cell since birth and are passed on from generation to generation. Acquired mutations are not passed on through reproductive cells, rather they occur later on during the person's life. These kinds of mutations are usually the result of a person's habits and lifestyle. They occur only in certain cells of the human body and can also be caused by environmental factors such as radiation and chemicals.

Most mutations are neutral, meaning that they have no effect on the expression of the genes on the human body. However, some can be beneficial or harmful based on their location [18]. Beneficial mutations are those that have a positive effect on the human body by allowing it to adapt to a change in the environment. Harmful mutations lead to a genetic disorder, which causes negative effects on the body. For example, a significant mutation in the gene that codes for the protein that is essential in the functions of the heart can lead to a fatal heart disease such as Arrhythmia (irregular beating of the heart) [15]. Thus, exploring genetic mutations and their effects is a crucial step in determining cures for a variety of diseases caused by genetic disorders.

A large amount of time is devoted to collecting large samples of data from patients affected by different diseases. However, much of the data is irrelevant (false positives) or is incomprehensible due to its complexity and large magnitude [3]. Thus, in order to interpret and understand the data, it needs to be simplified using computer processing and visualization methods. Tangible mtDNA, as an interactive display of CP-based mutation data, attempts to enhance the data's readability, and allow efficient analysis that may lead to effective theories and results.

RELATED WORK

In recent years, the importance of GUI visualization techniques has been emphasized in the understanding and accessibility of complex biological data. A comprehensive review done by Schroeder et al. [27] provides a selection of effective and common genomics visualization tools, and also discusses their limitations. One of the limitations is that current visualization tools are focused only on visualizing data and organizing the interface, rather than on exploring relationships and making interpretable comparisons between the different samples of data [31, 37]. Also, current tools focus largely on single user interaction and do not provide platforms for collaborative exploration [7, 22].

Based on these limitations, Shaer et al. [30] have described the challenges of using TEIs for the study of genomic data and have also suggested potential solutions to those challenges for the TEI community. Their paper acts as a turning point within the field, providing guidelines for using TEIs to enhance the exploration of and collaboration around genomic data. The paper discusses three main challenges that need to be solved: (i) Addressing a diverse audience: from the general public to experts, (ii) Increasing the amount of collaboration while exploring large-scale data using representations and interaction techniques, and (iii) Facilitating the investigation and manipulation of heterogeneous data (of different depths and layers) through the use of computational methods. They also suggest potential solutions: (a) Developing interactive and informative systems to enhance the user's exploration and understanding of complex problems. (b) Using common TEI systems such as tabletops and other large surfaces to visualize biological data, (c) Using the combination of tangible artifacts, tabletops, personal devices and interactive displays to enable large collaborations between users, and (d) Targeting diverse audiences, including biologists, engineers, mathematicians, computer scientists, etc.

There are relatively few TEI and/or tabletop systems that have been developed to address the challenges described by Shaer et al. [30]. The G-nome Surfer [28] is a multi-touch tabletop interface for browsing gene expression data. However, the system does not support tangible interaction and was designed for non-experts, focusing more on the learning of biological concepts rather than on exploration and analysis of data by experts. Furthermore, the ability to explore and directly compare information freely is limited. SynFlo [21] is a tangible museum exhibit that allows visitors to engage in a bio-design activity through passive and active tangibles. The piece encourages collaboration between children, students, and parents. The focus is on teaching concepts of synthetic biology rather than on exploration and investigation by experts. Eugenie [13] is a multi-touch and tangible interface for browsing big datasets. Users explore 3,000 biological parts by forming queries through tangible interactions. Eugenie's limitations include restricted table space, along with users' lack of understanding of the system's designed interactions. Sparse Tangibles [4] is a system for collaborative gene network exploration of a database of around 50 organisms. It employs an interactive tabletop and custom active-tangibles, aiming to assist expert users in better understanding experimentally extracted gene interactions and deciding about new experiment designs. The system provides a limited number of filters and computational methods for exploration and does not support the comparison of organisms in terms of interactions.

Other work by Valdes et al. [34] explored the design of gestural interactions with active tangibles for the manipulation of large datasets and provided a vocabulary of user-defined gestures for interacting with active tangibles. The work served as an inspiration for the design of our system's gestures. However, the focus of their study was on single user interaction. No exploration of a collaborative scenario was considered, and there was no exploration of interactions for the comparison between datasets.

Although not focused on the exploration and analysis of large data sets, a number of researchers have investigated the use of tangible interaction to support scientific practices and education. For example, Fjeld et al. [10] developed a tangible and augmented reality (AR) system for chemistry education; Gillet et al. [12] developed a tangible and AR system for visualizing the 3D structure of proteins; and Schkolne et al. [26] developed a tangible and virtual reality system for DNA molecule design. Other work has looked at supporting wet lab practices, such as the eLabBench [32] and Labscape [5].

In contrast to previous work, our system allows users to access large-scale cancer sequencing datasets along with associated CP features, compare the DNA sequences of large numbers of cancer patients, and explore the relationships between CP features and mutation patterns, all while supporting the collaborative exploration of the data. It also enables users to use clustering as a computational method for further exploration.

TANGIBLE MITOCHONDRIAL DNA

Tangible mtDNA is a tangible tabletop interaction system that visualizes a set of mitochondrial genetic mutation data of affected cancer patients. The system uses an interactive tabletop, which supports interaction via multi-touch and active tangibles on its surface. The system also supports off-screen interaction through the active tangibles, which include a multi-touch screen and additional sensors. Interactions with the active tangibles include stacking, shaking, and on-screen gestures on and off the tabletop.

A User Scenario

Jane and Ramesh are collaborating to understand the effect of mitochondrial gene mutations on breast cancer. Typically, they do this by performing independent analyses of the data and then coming together to discuss their observations. With the Tangible mtDNA system, they can perform their analyses in a hands-on manner, together or in parallel, and discuss them immediately. This supports the formation of insights by allowing them to develop a shared conceptual model of relationships within the data in real time. This scenario describes part of their work process, in which they visualize a set of mutation data of a specific mitochondrial gene, ND5. The users want to compare the dataset based on two parameters: Hemoglobin (HB) and Alkaline Phosphatase (ALP) levels. The data to be displayed is first sorted by the HB levels of patients and then compared to the same dataset sorted by their ALP values.

Table 1. Scenario overview

Step	Goal	Interaction	Representation
1	Find potential patterns	Users **SELECT** on table to sort data by different clinical features.	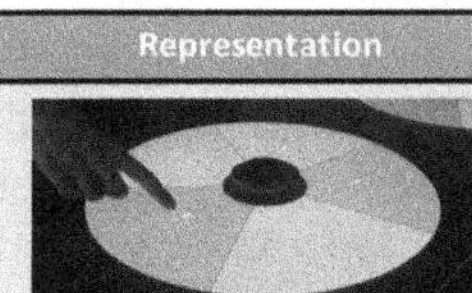
2	See relationships	Users **STACK** tangibles to compare data cross identified features of interest.	
3	Test ideas on relationships	Users **SELECT** on tangible to cluster data by genes or patients	

To accomplish this, Jane begins by placing the first tangible onto the tabletop display, which shows a menu of the different clinical features by which the data can be sorted. She selects the HB feature by tapping on the screen (Table 1, Step 1). The platform extracts the preprocessed mutation data sorted by HB and displays it on the tabletop screen, while transitioning into the second layer. This layer shows the several regions of mtDNA such as all the genes, overlaps and introns, scaled and organized based on their sizes and arrangements in the nucleotide sequence. She taps on the ND5 gene, which prompts the system to transition to the third layer of the interface. This layer displays the number of mutations for the different patients sorted by their HB levels. Along with the scalar quantity of mutations, the platform also displays the specific locations of the mutations with respect to the length of the gene. This gene contains large numbers of mutations and one location is common among most patients. She is interested in this trend, and notes this gene for later analysis.

The users now have the dataset sorted by HB and want to compare it with the dataset sorted by ALP. Ramesh places another active tangible on the table and selects ALP from the first layer. He is then provided with the second layer, where he selects the same gene as for the HB sorting, ND5. He then picks up the object and stacks it on top of the first active tangible, which shows the two gene layers alongside each other (Table 1, Step 2). The users observe the variation in trends between the two sorted datasets and draw conclusions as to whether ALP and HB are dependent or independent in their effects on the mutation data.

Next, the users want to see any relationships of the ND5 gene with other genes based on mutation trends in order to gain an understanding of which other mitochondrial genes might be related. To do so, Jane selects the 'Gene-based clustering' option on her active tangible by tapping on the screen. Then she selects a quantity of 15 clusters using a slider and presses 'cluster' (Table 1, Step 3). The system displays a network of clustered genes on the tabletop. The genes are grouped into nodes based on K-means clustering. Seeing that genes *CYTB, TRNC,* and *TRNB* are grouped into the same node as ND5, the users make note of these genes with similar mutation patterns. Then, Ramesh selects the 'Patient-based clustering' option on his tangible. He selects 6 clusters on the slider, and applies the clustering. The users note that patients 54, 70 and 82 are clustered together, and thus have similar gene mutation trends. Finally, both users shake the active tangibles to clear any cached selections.

Interaction Techniques

Tangible mtDNA incorporates several types of tangible interaction techniques that provide an enhanced level of interactivity to the users as they explore and analyze genetic mutation patterns. It encompasses basic user interaction techniques that are common to most user interfaces, along with query construction methods via interactions with the active tangibles. These types of interactions allow the user to perform several functions within Tangible mtDNA, such as navigate through, manipulate, and compare the data. The interactions involved as well as their applications within Tangible mtDNA are further discussed below.

Basic Interactions and Visualizations

Most interactions are on-screen interactions which include tapping, swiping, dragging, rotating, and pinching. These interactions are implemented on both the interactive tabletop, as well as on the active tangibles. The user interface on the active tangibles consists of a mobile menu that provides users with options for filtering and selecting data. The multi-touch tabletop displays the different interactive visualizations such as doughnut charts.

Mobile menu navigation: The swiping gesture is used as the primary means of navigation between different pages on the mobile menu. It is also used to confirm selections and, if needed, to return and alter selections. So if users want to return and change a selection, they may do so by swiping down, which takes them back to the previous selection page. This interaction is familiar from mobile devices and helps make the user's experience as fluid as possible.

Clinical feature selection: As the user places the active tangible on the table, the tabletop screen shows the first layer of visualization, namely the clinical feature selection menu. This layer consists of a doughnut chart, which is divided into different segments based on the number of CP features available. In this case, we consider five CP features, and thus there are five segments within the chart. Each segment has a unique color and is labeled based on a CP feature (see Figure 1). The distinct coloring allows the user to differentiate between the options and makes the interface more visually appealing. The doughnut chart is displayed around the tangible as it is placed on and moved around the tabletop screen. Rotating the active tangible causes the chart to rotate as well. In order to select the CP feature, the user needs to tap an on-screen CP segment. Based on the user's selection, the system extracts the appropriate mutation data sorted by that CP feature and displays it on the table, around the active tangible.

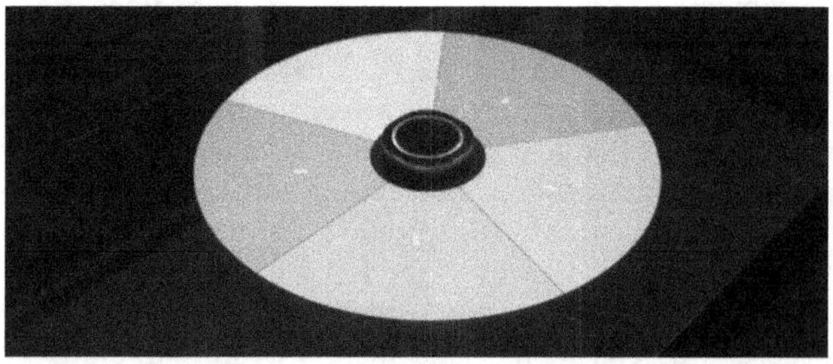

Figure 1. When an active tangible is placed on the multi-touch surface, available CP features are displayed in the form of a doughnut chart surrounding the tangible.

Gene selection: Upon selection of the CP feature, the visualization transitions into the second layer, namely the gene selection menu. This layer consists of a doughnut chart visualizing the mutation data and acts as a selection menu for the genes. The doughnut is partitioned based on the number of regions (genes, gene overlaps, and introns) within the mtDNA (see Figure 2). It is linearly scaled according to the mtDNA region nucleotide lengths, therefore the size of each segment is relative to the sequence size of each region within mtDNA. The regions are labeled on the outside of the arc according to their biological names. Gene overlaps and introns do not have a specific naming convention, thus they are labeled as *'IN'* for introns and *'OV'* for overlaps.

The chart (see Figure 2) is also divided into multiple arcs based on the number of patients in the data sample. Each arc represents a patient that is affected by breast cancer and has at least one genomic mutation within mtDNA. Furthermore, every arc within each region has a certain color based on the number of mutations within that gene for that particular patient. The color scale ranges from yellow to red; an arc with a yellow color represents a single mutation in that gene, whereas red represents maximum number of mutations. Since only the mutations related to genes and overlaps have been reported in the database, the intron regions are given a gray color to distinguish them from other regions. Patient arcs that do not have any mutations for certain genes are made transparent, giving them the same black appearance as the background.

Users can also select a specific gene for individual viewing by simply tapping on that specific region. This takes them to the third layer.

Figure 2. The second visualization layer shows mtDNA regions and the number of mutations for each patient in those regions.

Mutation locations: The third layer of Tangible mtDNA visualizes the genomic mutation data for the specific gene selected by the user. In addition to showing the mutation frequency for each patient, this layer also includes the specific location of each mutation within the nucleotide sequence of the region. This is marked by red dots on the arc (see Figure 3). Each dot represents a mutation and is placed on the arc based on its relative location in the nucleotide sequence. By noting the locations of mutations, users can identify certain mutations trends within genes, which can be helpful for gene-targeted research.

If there is a mass of mutations in a certain area that is difficult to view, the user can also pinch on that area of the screen to zoom in on that location. This will allow them to see large samples of mutation data, at a closer detail.

In addition, this layer of Tangible mtDNA has an implemented dynamic DNA sequence bar which displays a fraction of the nucleotide sequence (see Figure 3). There is a pointer placed at the top of the doughnut chart, which acts as a marker for the DNA sequence bar. So as the active tangible is rotated, the bar displays the fraction of the gene sequence that the marker is pointing to.

Figure 3. The third visualization layer shows the location of mutations and the nucleotide fraction at the pointer location.

Query Construction and Visualization

Tangible mtDNA uses interactions with the active tangibles to allow users to manipulate and interact with the data. Specifically, the interactions allow users to construct queries to the dataset using gestures such as stacking and shaking of the tangibles. Current user interfaces within the biology research field are limited to using physical buttons, sliders, and other touch interactions within a GUI. Tangible mtDNA expands the user's interaction possibilities by providing opportunities to interact with the data using tangible interaction. By stacking and shaking the active tangibles, users are able to filter, compare, and manipulate the data for fast and efficient analysis.

Figure 4. After stacking two tangibles, the second layer shows mtDNA region mutation counts in parallel.

CP features comparison: A significant feature of Tangible mtDNA is the use of stacking for query construction. Specifically, users can compare the same mutation dataset sorted by different CP features. This is done by selecting two different CP features through the tangibles, and stacking them. This prompts the tabletop interface to display both visualizations in parallel (see Figure 4).

This function allows users to see the difference between the orders of the mutation data when the same set of patients is sorted by two different CP features. Users can then observe certain trends and make inductions about the features and their effects on genomic mutations. They can also navigate through layers two and three during the query.

Figure 5. Users exploring the result of gene-based (left) and patient-based (right) clustering.

Mutations similarity patterns clustering: Along with the CP features comparison, Tangible mtDNA can also perform the clustering of data in order to observe any gene-gene or patient-patient relationships based on the mutation data sample. Users can perform this function using the mobile menu implemented on the active tangibles.

The menu provides the user with two options for the basis of the clustering: gene-based and patient-based. The users choose an option and select the number of clusters using a slider. Upon selection, the tabletop interface performs the clustering of data and displays a force-directed network consisting of either gene or patient nodes depending on the chosen basis of clustering. Tangible mtDNA uses K-means clustering on the mutation patterns. K-means clustering was selected because it is a simple and efficient method that displays meaningful results quickly. This is helpful in keeping the program fast and responsive [17].

Selecting different clusters: Upon selecting the basis for clustering, the mobile menu prompts the user to select the number of clusters for the K-means clustering. Each cluster consists of a centroid, a reference iteratively extracted from the mutation trends. K-means clustering finds the nearest mutation patterns to each centroid, and places them within that cluster. This is further explained below.

Gene-based clustering: If the user selects gene-based clustering, the data is clustered according to similarities between genes based on their mutation trends. Using the selected cluster number, the clustering function randomly selects the K number of centroids from the dataset. These data points act as the center of a cluster and each gene is assigned to a cluster depending on how close or similar it is to other genes assigned to that cluster. Essentially, each cluster acts as a class of gene mutation trend similarities. By seeing these similarities, researchers working with a specific gene might identify other genes following the same mutation pattern as the target gene (see Figure 5, left side).

Patient-based clustering: This follows the same procedure as gene-based clustering. However, instead of comparing mutation patterns between genes, it performs the clustering between patients. The interface displays all the patients in clusters depending on the similarity in mutation patterns among patients (see Figure 5, right side). This interaction might aid physicians or researchers working with known patient datasets in applying successful treatments to new patients with similar mutation trends.

TECHNICAL IMPLEMENTATION

Tangible mtDNA is a mainly web-based platform made using front-end web development tools such as HTML, CSS, and JavaScript. There are back-end tools involved as well, such as Node.js and Python scripts, used to handle, process, and transfer project-related data. There are several reasons for implementing the system using web-based development tools: (i) Most current generation devices support HTML/JavaScript and are web-page friendly; (ii) JavaScript has a large collection of libraries that allow for easy and productive development; and (iii) It requires the least amount of client-side tools, and can run solely on a web browser. We describe the implementation of the different system components, including the active tangibles, the interactive tabletop, and the communication processes.

Active Tangibles

We use a platform called "Actibles" developed in our lab for the active tangibles in this system. Actibles are hand-held devices that support tangible interactions both on and off interactive tabletop surfaces. They employ LG G smartwatches as their core. These come with an IPS LCD Display, 9 Axis sensors, 512 MB RAM, and 4GB internal storage[1]. Each smartwatch is contained within a 3D printed custom case that includes additional hardware and sensors to support query-based interactions such as stacking, rotating, shaking, and bumping. Further technical details are described by East et al. [8].

The Actibles also include a Wi-Fi module, which can send and receive data packets through the UDP protocol. This allows for a more direct and versatile form of communication between the tangibles and the Node.js server. More specifically, the Wi-Fi connection is used to send any interaction information, such as stacking and bumping, to the server. The Node.js[2] server acts as a communication link between the active tangibles and the interactive tabletop display.

Mobile-friendly JavaScript/HTML5 web-pages were implemented on the smartwatches using jQuery mobile[3] to display the mobile menus and read any events such as swipe, touch, and shake. In order to detect the Actibles on the interactive tabletop, unique fiducial markers were attached to the bottom of each one. These markers are read by the IR

[1] http://www.lg.com/us/smart-watches/lg-W100-lg-watch

[2] https://nodejs.org/

[3] https://jquerymobile.com

sensors within the tabletop display and transmitted to the server using the TUIO protocol.

We utilize the sensors in the actibles to support on and off the table tangible interactions within the mDNA system. In our current implementation, stacking of the actibles is used to produce a complementary representation that facilitates comparison of the existing data, while shaking the tangibles clears any cached selections. We also leverage the web capabilities and touch display of the actibles' smartwatch core to create a dynamic menu that allows operations to be performed on cached selections, such as the ability to cluster data by patients or genes.

Interactive Tabletop

The interactive tabletop used within Tangible mtDNA is the MultiTaction Cell Ultra-Thin Bezel (MT553UTB) display[4]. The MT553UTB is a 55-Inch-High Definition LCD display that features several built-in infrared cameras for touch and marker detection. The display has its own internal computer running the Linux OS. It includes a Hybrid Tracking Engine[5] that allows for several interaction methods such as multi-finger touch, hold, drag, as well as fiducial marker tracking using the MultiTaction Codice markers[6].

The MultiTaction display is connected to a computer running the Windows 10 OS. A web browser is used to open the HTML5/JavaScript web-pages of the Tangible mtDNA system, which display the tabletop visualization interface. The system predominantly uses the Data Driven Documents (D3.js[7]) library, which stores data using Document Object Model (DOM) elements and JSON[8] files, and visualizes it using Scalable Vector Graphics (SVG).

Communications

To communicate between the devices, a Node.js server is used in conjunction with Socket.IO[9]. Socket.IO is a JavaScript library that allows for real-time bidirectional communication between devices via web-browsers. When a device-based event such as tap or swipe occurs on a device, Socket.IO broadcasts a message, which is received by the central Node.js server. The server handles the message appropriately by communicating with the tabletop. Instead of a TUIO server, a client-based Node.js server is used as it allows us to broadcast custom events. Although the server is located on the same computer that drives the tabletop display, it runs separately from the tabletop interface.

EXPERT FEEDBACK

Five experts from the biological research field were invited to the lab to provide feedback on the Tangible mtDNA system. All of the experts were from a distinguished clinical research facility and were familiar with genomic data and its importance within cancer research.

One expert (P1) was a male with a MD/PhD degree and 10 years of background in clinical research. The other four experts were two male (P2 and P3) postdoctoral researchers and two females, a PhD student (P4) and a biologist (P5), all within the same field. They arrived as a group. Upon arrival, they were introduced to the system components, including the interactive tabletop and active tangibles.

Next, the experts were asked to collectively assemble around the tabletop and the overall concept of the Tangible mtDNA system was presented to the group, along with the data querying, processing and visualization techniques involved. They were then seated in the common area and were invited one at a time to interact with and experience the system. Finally, they were all assembled as a group and were asked to provide their feedback about the system in a focus group format. The entire session lasted about two hours and the participants were compensated for their time with a $10 cash incentive.

Overall the experts found the concept to be novel and important to the exploration of genetic mutations. They mentioned that the system was unique, intuitive, and effective for navigating through data. In particular, they highlighted certain aspects of the system such as data exploration, data comparison and clustering. They also compared it to other systems and discussed the learning and collaborative aspects of the system.

Data Exploration, Comparison and Clustering

P1 expressed that the system could be helpful in creating a common language between biologists, bioinformaticians, computer scientists and others in related interdisciplinary fields. P2 and P4 added that this system was useful in explaining DNA sequencing results for non-scientists. The other two highlighted that using the system assisted in investigating large-scale genetic mutation data. However, they all suggested that the system would be more practical if it provided more information regarding the patients (like patient identification) and the mutation data (such as precise mutation positions and the type of each mutation). Also, they suggested that indicating the normal range of clinical features within the visualization could improve their understanding of the relationships between CP features.

The experts found that the stacking gesture could simplify the comparison of genetic mutation data based on CP features, as it allowed them to align two visualizations together with respect to their nucleotide sequences so they could compare mutation trends in parallel rather than separately. In regards to clustering, P1 emphasized that if treatment data was available within the database, patient-based clustering could provide valuable information for applying suitable treatments to new patients. Other

[4]https://www.multitaction.com/

[5]https://cornerstone.multitouch.fi/sites/default/files/generated-content/taction-guide/adjustingtracking.html

[6]https://www.multitaction.com/products/codice

[7]http://d3js.org

[8]http://json.org

[9]http://socket.io

participants confirmed the importance of patient-based clustering as they were able to understand similarities of genetic mutation patterns among patients. In addition, P2 and P4 found that gene-based clustering was interesting and it sparked their curiosity. Although this clustering has been previously applied on gene expression data [17], Tangible mtDNA was the first time they encountered its use on DNA mutation patterns. Overall they found this to be the best feature of our system, because it allowed them to explore an unexpected direction of genetic mutations.

Comparison to Other Systems

The majority of the participants (P1, P2, and P3) said they use static visualization systems for similar data, and they found this dynamic and interactive visualization to be very unique. They commented that the combination of tangible interaction and a large display potentially allows for the representation of an almost limitless amount of data. Therefore, it could provide the opportunity to explore mutations inside the entire genome based on different patients. On the other hand, other systems they work with allow for more statistical analyses (such as survival analysis) so they suggested incorporating those within our system to make it more practical for them to use. Overall, the experts primarily criticized the system's lack of statistical tools and computationally-intense methods of analysis that they are currently familiar with.

Collaboration and Learning

P1, P4 and P5 felt that our system is superior to traditional interfaces as it provides a higher level of engagement, allows users to convey complex genomic concepts, and enhances their learning process. All of them found that the system promotes collaborative exploration and discussion. They thought that the collaborative discussion could reduce misunderstandings about their hypotheses and the rapid prototyping of data queries could help them make informative decisions when designing new experiments. When asked about whether they would recommend this system to their colleagues, experts P1 and P3 were not sure, however, experts P2, P4, and P5 said that if more statistical analyses were added to the system, they would recommend its use. P1 and P3 thought a specific question for exploration needed to be defined before using the system.

CONCLUSION AND FUTURE WORK

We presented a novel tangible and tabletop visualization system for the exploration of mtDNA mutation data within a breast cancer dataset. The system aims to support the needs of biologists and physicians by allowing them to collaboratively investigate large-scale cancer data. With the system, users can discover genetic mutation information, compare the effects of CP features on mutation patterns, and manipulate clustering parameters to find similarities between genes or patients based on mutation trends.

Although tangible and tabletop interfaces have proved effective in supporting collaboration, there remain many technical and interaction design questions as to how they can best handle the size and complexity of real world datasets in order to support the formation of shared insights in areas such bioinformatics. Tangible mtDNA is a platform that materializes a single shared problem space among its users, within a scientific domain where such platforms are uncommon. The tools that biologists, bioinformaticians, and computer scientists typically use are designed for a single user, and while collaboration is necessary, it happens outside these tools. Our work demonstrates how web-based technologies can be used as a foundation for developing tangible tabletop systems that support collaboration around big data applications. Building on the results of Valdes et al. [34], we also show how active tangibles that leverage web-based technologies can easily interface and embody big data, and provide ways to extend the interactions beyond the tabletop display surface.

Upon conducting an informal user study with five biological and clinical experts, we found that the system is intuitive, is effective for information navigation, and facilitates learning and collaboration between users. Based on the experts' suggestions, we aim to provide additional details about the genetic mutations such as their types and precise locations. We also intend to add a filter for 3D protein structure prediction, which is important for clinicians and biologists as it assists them in designing drugs and enzymes. Finally, we plan to add survival analysis techniques to the system by considering event-related information pertaining to each patient.

The current system is designed to allow exploration solely for mtDNA and breast cancer data. We intend to expand it to support the study of the whole human genome, which would allow users to observe the effects of breast cancer on other chromosomes as well. One of the challenges with this addition will be the need to deal with extremely big data, which makes navigation tedious and time consuming for the user, and also poses challenges for visualization. To address these challenges, we will explore methods of directly locating and showing specific genes of interest. Also, to make the system more universal, we intend to include mutation datasets from different types of cancers. This would facilitate the comparison of mutation patterns from multiple diseases, and could lead to users making hypotheses about disease-disease and gene-disease relationships as well. As observed mutation trends can provide a means for users to make optimized decisions, a clinician could, for example, decide on an appropriate treatment plan for patients using the obtained similarities from disease-disease relationships.

ACKNOWLEDGEMENTS

This work has been supported in part by NSF grant IIS 1320350, NSERC, the Canada Foundation for Innovation, the Ministry of Research and Innovation of Ontario, and the Canada Research Chairs program. We also thank MultiTaction for their support. And we thank Dr. Julia Hopkins and Dr. Paul Boutros from Ontario Institute for Cancer Research, Dr. Matthew Kyan from York University, and Dr. Ahmed Sabbir Arif from Ryerson University for their insights and expertise.

REFERENCES

1. Alberts, B. (2008). Molecular Biology of the Cell with CD. *Garland.*
2. Alexandrov, L.B., Nik-Zainal, S., Wedge, D.C., Aparicio, S.A., Behjati, S., Biankin, A.V., ... & Boyault, S. (2013). Signatures of mutational processes in human cancer. *Nature*, 500(7463), 415-421.
3. Alyass, A., Turcotte, M., & Meyre, D. (2015). From big data analysis to personalized medicine for all: challenges and opportunities. *BMC medical genomics*, 8(1), 33.
4. Arif, A.S., Manshaei, R., Delong, S., East, B., Kyan, M., & Mazalek, A. (2016, February). Sparse Tangibles: Collaborative Exploration of Gene Networks using Active Tangibles and Interactive Tabletops. *In Proceedings of the TEI'16: Tenth International Conference on Tangible, Embedded, and Embodied Interaction* (pp. 287-295). ACM.
5. Arnstein, L., Hung, C. Y., Franza, R., Zhou, Q. H., Borriello, G., Consolvo, S., & Su, J. (2002). Labscape: A smart environment for the cell biology laboratory. *IEEE Pervasive Computing*, 1(3), 13-21.
6. Brooker, R.J. (1999). Genetics: analysis & principles. *Addison-Wesley.*
7. Cerami, E., Gao, J., Dogrusoz, U., Gross, B.E., Sumer, S.O., Aksoy, B.A., ... & Antipin, Y. (2012). The cBio cancer genomics portal: an open platform for exploring multidimensional cancer genomics data. *Cancer discovery*, 2(5), 401-404.
8. East, B., DeLong, S., Manshaei, R., Arif, A., & Mazalek, A. (2016, November). Actibles: Open Source Active Tangibles. In *Proceedings of the 2016 ACM on Interactive Surfaces and Spaces* (pp. 469-472). ACM.
9. Fan, J., Han, F., & Liu, H. (2014). Challenges of big data analysis. *National science review*, 1(2), 293-314.
10. Fjeld, M., Fredriksson, J., Ejdestig, M., Duca, F., Bötschi, K., Voegtli, B., & Juchli, P. (2007, April). Tangible user interface for chemistry education: comparative evaluation and re-design. *In Proceedings of the SIGCHI conference on Human factors in computing systems* (pp. 805-808). ACM.
11. Friedman, J. R., & Nunnari, J. (2014). Mitochondrial form and function. *Nature*, 505(7483), 335-343.
12. Gillet, A., Sanner, M., Stoffler, D., & Olson, A. (2005). Tangible interfaces for structural molecular biology. *Structure*, 13(3), 483-491.
13. Grote, C., Segreto, E., Okerlund, J., Kincaid, R., & Shaer, O. (2015, January). Eugenie: Multi-Touch and Tangible Interaction for Bio-Design. *In Proceedings of the Ninth International Conference on Tangible, Embedded, and Embodied Interaction* (pp. 217-224). ACM.
14. Hardman, J. (2007). Breast Cancer Answers: Understanding and Fighting Breast Cancer. *Cancer Nursing Practice*, 6(2), 16-18.
15. Hsiao, P.Y., Tien, H.C., Lo, C.P., Juang, J.M., Wang, Y.H., & Sung, R.J. (2013). Gene mutations in cardiac arrhythmias: a review of recent evidence in ion channelopathies. *Appl Clin Genet*, 6, 1-13.
16. Huang, Q., Su, X., Bella, A.E., Luo, K., Jin, J., Zhang, S., ... & Fu, J. (2015). Clinicopathological features and outcome of gastric metastases from primary lung cancer: A case report and systematic review. *Oncology letters*, 9(3), 1373-1379.
17. Liu, P., & Si, Y. (2014). Cluster analysis of RNA-sequencing data. In Statistical Analysis of Next Generation Sequencing Data (pp. 191-217). *Springer International Publishing.*
18. Loewe, L., & Hill, W.G. (2010). The population genetics of mutations: good, bad and indifferent. *Philosophical Transactions of the Royal Society B: Biological Sciences*, 365(1544), 1153-1167.
19. McLysaght, A., & Hurst, L. D. (2016). Open questions in the study of de novo genes: what, how and why. *Nature Reviews Genetics.*
20. Opalińska, M., & Meisinger, C. (2015). Metabolic control via the mitochondrial protein import machinery. *Current opinion in cell biology*, 33, 42-48.
21. Okerlund, J., Segreto, E., Grote, C., Westendorf, L., Scholze, A., Littrell, R., & Shaer, O. (2016, February). SynFlo: A Tangible Museum Exhibit for Exploring Bio-Design. *In Proceedings of the TEI'16: Tenth International Conference on Tangible, Embedded, and Embodied Interaction* (pp. 141-149). ACM.
22. Perez-Llamas, C., & Lopez-Bigas, N. (2011). Gitools: analysis and visualization of genomic data using interactive heat-maps. *PloS one*, 6(5), e19541.
23. Robinson, J.T., Thorvaldsdóttir, H., Winckler, W., Guttman, M., Lander, E.S., Getz, G., & Mesirov, J.P. (2011). Integrative genomics viewer. *Nature biotechnology*, 29(1), 24-26.
24. Schaefer, A. M., McFarland, R., Blakely, E. L., He, L., Whittaker, R. G., Taylor, R. W., ... & Turnbull, D. M. (2008). Prevalence of mitochondrial DNA disease in adults. *Annals of neurology*, 63(1), 35-39.
25. Schinzel, R., & Dillin, A. (2015). Endocrine aspects of organelle stress—cell non-autonomous signaling of mitochondria and the ER. *Current opinion in cell biology*, 33, 102-110.
26. Schkolne, S., Ishii, H., & Schroder, P. (2004, October). Immersive design of DNA molecules with a tangible interface. *In Proceedings of the conference on*

Visualization'04 (pp. 227-234). IEEE Computer Society.

27. Schroeder, M.P., Gonzalez-Perez, A., & Lopez-Bigas, N. (2013). Visualizing multidimensional cancer genomics data. *Genome medicine*, 5(1), 1.
28. Shaer, O., Kol, G., Strait, M., Fan, C., Grevet, C., & Elfenbein, S. (2010, April). G-nome surfer: a tabletop interface for collaborative exploration of genomic data. *In Proceedings of the SIGCHI Conference on Human Factors in Computing Systems* (pp. 1427-1436). ACM.
29. Shaer, O., Strait, M., Valdes, C., Wang, H., Feng, T., Lintz, M., ... & Liu, S. (2012). The design, development, and deployment of a tabletop interface for collaborative exploration of genomic data. *International Journal of Human-Computer Studies*, 70(10), 746-764.
30. Shaer, O., Mazalek, A., Ullmer, B., & Konkel, M. (2013, February). From big data to insights: opportunities and challenges for TEI in genomics. *In Proceedings of the 7th International Conference on Tangible, Embedded and Embodied Interaction* (pp. 109-116). ACM.
31. Speir, M.L., Zweig, A.S., Rosenbloom, K.R., Raney, B.J., Paten, B., Nejad, P., ... & Heitner, S. (2016). The UCSC Genome Browser database: 2016 update. *Nucleic acids research*, 44(D1), D717-D725.
32. Tabard, A., Hincapié-Ramos, J. D., Esbensen, M., & Bardram, J. E. (2011, November). The eLabBench: an interactive tabletop system for the biology laboratory. *In Proceedings of the ACM International Conference on Interactive Tabletops and Surfaces* (pp. 202-211). ACM.
33. Taylor, R.W., & Turnbull, D.M. (2005). Mitochondrial DNA mutations in human disease. *Nature Reviews Genetics*, 6(5), 389-402.
34. Valdes, C., Eastman, D., Grote, C., Thatte, S., Shaer, O., Mazalek, A., ... & Konkel, M.K. (2014, April). Exploring the design space of gestural interaction with active tokens through user-defined gestures. *In Proceedings of the SIGCHI Conference on Human Factors in Computing Systems* (pp. 4107-4116). ACM.
35. Vogelstein, B., Papadopoulos, N., Velculescu, V.E., Zhou, S., Diaz, L.A., & Kinzler, K.W. (2013). Cancer genome landscapes. *science*, 339(6127), 1546-1558.
36. Weinberg, S. E., & Chandel, N. S. (2015). Targeting mitochondria metabolism for cancer therapy. *Nature chemical biology*, 11(1), 9-15.
37. Zhang, J., Finney, R., Edmonson, M., Schaefer, C., Rowe, W., Yan, C., ... & Liu, H. (2010). The Cancer Genome Workbench: identifying and visualizing complex genetic alterations in tumors. *NCI Nature Pathway Interaction Database*, 10.

BacPack: Exploring the Role of Tangibles in a Museum Exhibit for Bio-Design

Anna Loparev[1], Lauren Westendorf[1], Margaret Flemings[1], Jennifer Cho[1], Romie Littrell[2], Anja Scholze[2], Orit Shaer[1]

[1]Wellesley College
Wellesley, MA, USA
{aloparev, lwestend, mfleming, jcho7, oshaer}@wellesley.edu

[2]The Tech Museum of Innovation
San Jose, CA, USA
{rlittrell, ascholze}@thetech.org

ABSTRACT

We present BacPack, a tangible museum exhibit for exploring bio-design. BacPack utilizes tangible tokens on a large multitouch table display to allow visitors the opportunity to participate in a playful bio-design activity—engineering bacteria for sustaining life on Mars. To understand the role of tangible tokens in facilitating engagement and learning with the exhibit, we developed and evaluated two versions of BacPack: one with tangible tokens and one that consists of only multitouch interaction. Results from an evaluation in the Tech Museum of Innovation indicate that tangible tokens provide additional opportunities for collaborative problem solving and impact learning through support for tinkering and experimentation. We discuss design considerations for exhibits that facilitate creative engagement and exploration with biology.

Author Keywords

Tangibles; museum; children; bio-design.

ACM Classification Keywords

H.5.m. Information interfaces and presentation: User Interfaces---input devices and strategies, interaction styles.

INTRODUCTION

Biology has become a powerful technology in today's world, driving innovation in domains ranging from health, to agriculture, energy, and space travel. Considering the transformative impact of biology, it is important to expose the public to the burgeoning fields of synthetic biology, bioengineering, and biological design, inspiring the next generation of innovators to explore these cutting-edge fields. Our goal is to create educational activities that spark imagination and allow people of all ages to personally engage in creative problem solving with biology.

However, creating interactive and exploratory educational activities in biology is challenging due to the long time scales of living cells, the complexity of the topic, and the unique behaviors of biological systems, many of which occur at the nanometer level and are subject to unintuitive physics [19]. The unique aspects of biology—invisible medium, unintuitive behavior, slow response, and prescriptive experimental design—conflict with the goals of exploratory design-based activities, which require a tangible and responsive medium, and foster open-ended inquiry. Our approach combines virtual simulation with tangible tokens to bring the time and size scales of biology into the range of an effective exploratory learning activity.

In this paper, we present BacPack, an interactive museum exhibit that introduces core synthetic biology concepts to visitors through tangible and multitouch interaction. Similar to our previous work on SynFlo [18], BacPack bridges the size and time scales of biology by combining tangibles, animation, and simulation. However, while we designed SynFlo to allow users to experience the steps and actions of the experimental *process* of engineering living cells, BacPack focuses on highlighting the *application* of bio-design for solving real-world problems. BacPack engages users in problem solving through the design of bacteria, which are helpful for sustaining a research mission on Mars, providing a collaborative platform for creative engagement with digital biological creations.

This paper presents two primary contributions: (1) The design and implementation of a novel museum exhibit that utilizes tangible and tabletop interaction to engage the public in bio-design; and (2) Findings from an evaluation in the Tech Museum of Innovation focused on identifying the role of tangible interaction with passive tokens versus that of multitouch interaction with digital tokens in facilitating collaborative engagement and learning. We also share lessons from the iterative design and evaluation of our exhibit, including a discussion of design considerations for an exhibit that enables people to engage in creative problem solving with biology.

TEI '17, March 20-23, 2017, Yokohama, Japan
© 2017 ACM. ISBN 978-1-4503-4676-4/17/03...$15.00
DOI: http://dx.doi.org/10.1145/3024969.3025000

RELATED WORK

Constructionist Learning

We designed and evaluated BacPack in collaboration with the Tech Museum of Innovation, whose philosophy is to "inspire the innovator in everyone" by encouraging people to learn by exploring and creating. The museum's philosophy and our design of BacPack draw upon Papert's Constructionist educational framework [19]. Constructionism asserts that children learn deeply when building their own meaningful projects in a community of learners, and when reflecting on the process. This framework is rooted in Piaget's [20] constructivism – which conveys the idea that children build knowledge through experience, emphasizing "learning by doing." Constructionism is often applied to learning in synthetic biology, where learners construct knowledge by solving real-world problems using a toolkit of biological parts [12, 22]. More generally, providing opportunities and tools to design, tinker with, and build has become an accepted framework for creative learning [21]. In the design of BacPack, we follow this approach—engaging users in designing and building (virtual) bacteria for solving real problems related to sustaining manned missions to Mars.

Tabletop and Tangible Interactions for Learning of Biological Concepts

Several projects have demonstrated the potential of applying TEI approaches to learning biological concepts. G-nome Surfer [23] and GreenTouch [25] are tabletop applications for collaborative exploration of genomic and phenology databases, which support open-ended inquiry. However, these applications are designed for formal learning at the college level. The DeepTree exhibit [6] is a multitouch tabletop interface that allows users to explore an interactive visualization of the Tree of Life, while Fishing with Friends [5] is a multiplayer exhibit where visitors play in a simulated fishing environment to learn about overfishing. Another application is Build-a-Tree, an interactive tabletop game for natural history museums [8].

A number of games have been written to engage players in the design of new organisms [Spore, Cubivore, Graffiti Kingdom], but few act as a platform for non-scientists that simulates tinkering and creating with actual biological material outside a wet laboratory setting. Most related to our work are the museum exhibits TrapIt! [13] and SynFlo [18], both deployed in the Tech Museum. TrapIt! [13] uses a touchscreen to control light beams that interact with live cells. Previously, our team designed SynFlo [18], through which museum visitors can experience the steps and actions of the biological engineering experimental process. With SynFlo, visitors use active tangible tokens (Sifteo cubes) embedded in authentic labware to imitate gestures scientists make in the lab, allowing them to experience the scientific workflow. While SynFlo and TrapIt! support collaborative, playful, and prolonged experiences exploring biological *phenomena* and *processes*, we designed BacPack to emphasize real world *applications*, encouraging visitors to engage creatively in problem solving through *design*.

Tangible Interaction for Learning

Much research has highlighted the benefits of tangible interaction for learning [3, 9, 15]. For example, Antle et al. [3] compared a tangible user interface to a mouse-based interface for jigsaw puzzle solving. They found that the tangible interface led to a higher success rate with faster success times, more communication, and more time spent actively interacting with the system. Similarly, Horn et al. [9] compared tangibles to a mouse-based graphical user interface in a museum exhibit, showing that using tangibles resulted in more participation. Horn et al. [7] also discussed several tangible and non-tangible versions of interactive learning tools and concluded that it is often a combination or hybrid of the two styles that is most effective. In the evaluation of SynFlo [18], we compared the use of abstract active tangible tokens (blocks) with the use of active tokens embedded in concrete authentic tangibles (labware). We found that the affordance of authentic tangibles encourages adult involvement and learning through observation compared to free exploration facilitated by the abstract tangibles. The evaluation of BacPack focuses on a different question – what is the role of passive tangible tokens in facilitating collaboration and learning in a problem solving and bio-design task, compared to multitouch interaction with digital tokens.

Ma et al. [14] compared tangible and graphical versions of an exhibit and found that while the tangible version attracted more visitors, there was not necessarily a difference in the visitors' experience with the exhibit. However, their exhibit utilized only three tangibles that needed to be shared among visitors. BacPack utilizes a set of 22 tangibles, which represent biological building blocks (genes); selecting and combining tangibles is a key phase in the BacPack activity. Our investigation focuses on understanding the role of tangibles in facilitating creative engagement and learning with the exhibit.

APPLICATION DOMAIN AND DESIGN GOALS

Synthetic Biology

Synthetic biology is an interdisciplinary field that combines engineering and biology. The field applies basic engineering principles such as standardization, abstraction, and modularity to the design of living organisms with new properties. Complex genetic programs are composed from standardized biological parts called BioBricks, which are used like "Lego Bricks". Synthetic biology aims to provide solutions to a wide range of real-world problems in areas such as agriculture, medicine, energy, and space travel.

Biological Design for Resource Utilization in Space

The premise of BacPack is that museum visitors take on the role of astronauts on an extended scientific mission on Mars. Visitors engineer bacteria that can help the astronauts by consuming resources that exist on Mars (e.g. soil, CO_2, biomass) and producing products that are required for sustaining human life on Mars (e.g. water, nutrients, O_2). This concept draws upon a known research paper, which quantifies the utility of synthetic biology techniques to harness available resources on manned exploration missions to Mars [17]. The paper discusses the importance of using synthetic biology to make Mars missions more viable by decreasing the amount of materials required to be sent to Mars. The authors propose to identify which molecules could be utilized to create desired products. BacPack mirrors this investigation by allowing visitors to experiment with biological designs of bacteria that consume different input molecules and produce desired output.

Design and Learning Goals

We designed BacPack in close collaboration with synthetic biologists and educators. The exhibit aims to introduce core concepts of synthetic biology to a general audience. We defined the following learning goals for BacPack: (L1) Demonstrate the principles of abstraction and modularity—genetic materials with documented functionality are used as standard biological parts, and are combined to create new biological systems; (L2) Facilitate the design and construction of genetic programs that include distinct input and output, and where output from one program serves as input to a different program; (L3) Communicate the basic steps of a synthetic biology protocol: constructing a genetic program, adding the program to a plasmid, inserting plasmid to a bacterial cell, testing for expected behavior; and (L4) Engage visitors in creative problem solving of critical challenges related to survival on Mars.

Our design goals for BacPack were informed by these learning goals and influenced by the Museum's constructionist educational philosophy: G1) Allowing people of all ages to design with biology; G2) Facilitating the development of inquiry skills through a hands-on playful experience; and G3) Providing opportunities for collaborative learning.

DESIGN ITERATIONS AND RATIONALE

Iterative Design

The current prototype of the exhibit, BacPack 2.0, is a result of an 18-month iterative design process. The premise of the exhibit is that museum visitors take on the role of an astronaut working in a research lab on Mars. The astronaut is tasked with engineering new bacteria, which could help the mission team to survive on Mars. The engineered bacteria consume resources that are available on Mars—such as CO_2, soil, and poop—and produce essential products—such as O_2, water, and biomass. The exhibit consists of an interactive tabletop combined with tangible tokens (see Figure 1a). The interactive tabletop is divided into two areas: a wet lab (on Mars) with four workbench stations, and the Mars landscape, which includes a biodome where astronauts make required products.

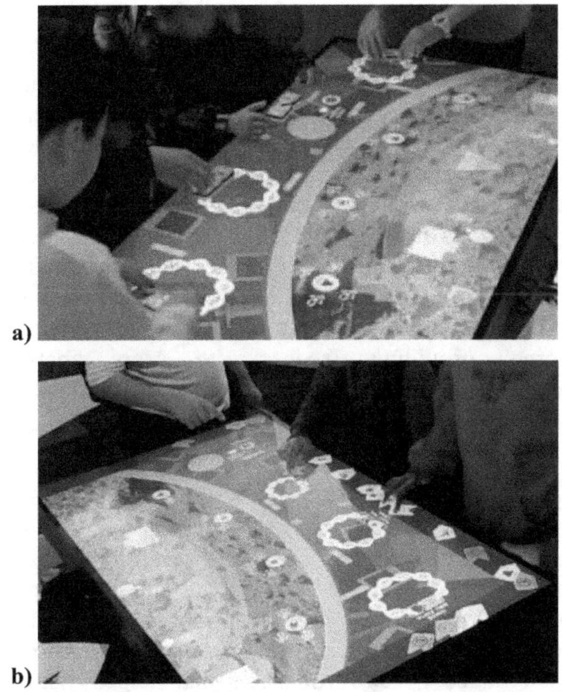

Figure 1. BacPack 2.0 (a), genes are represented by tangible tokens that visitors can place on the screen to make a selection. BacPack 2.1 (b), genes are represented by digital tokens dispersed along the edges of the screen. Visitors touch and drag the representations to make a selection.

Museum visitors use 22 tangible representations of BioBricks (i.e. genes) from the Registry of Standard Biological Parts [12] to design and engineer the bacteria. The goal of the activity is to increase the capacity of needed products. The quantity of products in the biodome is gradually reduced over time. Visitors are required to pick two genes, an input gene that consumes a particular resource, and an output gene that produces a product. These two genes are combined into a genetic program. Some combinations of input and output genes are more effective than others (i.e. produce more of the desired product). Figure 2 shows some of the possible combinations of resources and products.

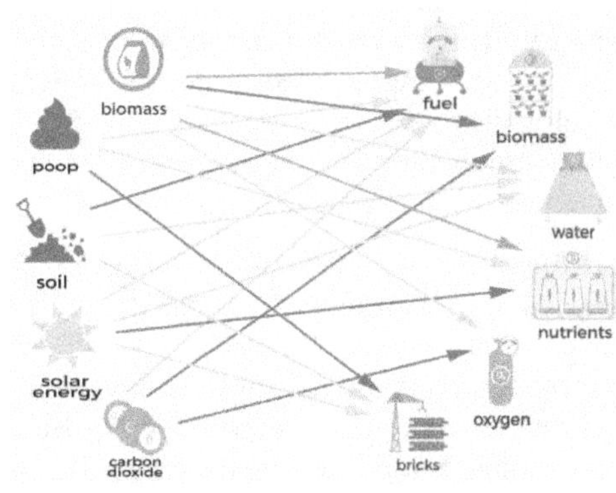

Figure 2. Subset of possible resource and product combinations; Color coded based on how many units are produced by each combination: green = 3 units, yellow = 2 units, red = 1 unit. Green combinations are most efficient.

Visitors then insert the genetic program into a digital plasmid by placing and wiggling/shaking the two genes on the screen surface. The visitors add the digital plasmid to a bacterial cell using a drag gesture, which results in multiplication of the cells and the growth of a colony of bacteria containing the genetic program. The visitors release the bacteria to Mars by dragging the petri dish with the colony towards the open Martian landscape. The bacteria gather around the resources they are consuming and produce a product that is added to products available in the biodome. An astronaut figure moves around the biodome, providing feedback to users about the effectiveness of the bacteria they created and indicating what products are most urgently needed.

To date, we have developed and evaluated three different prototypes of BacPack in the museum. The first prototype was designed as a facilitated exhibit that combines a digital lab and an actual web lab. The digital portion of the exhibit was similar in general to the current prototype but emphasized the process (i.e. lab protocol) rather than the design aspects of engineering bacteria. The wet lab portion was facilitated by two volunteers that helped visitors go through the experimental lab protocol of engineering bacteria. Based on an evaluation in the museum we decided to eliminate the wet lab activity, as it requires two facilitators and is time consuming. Instead, we redesigned the digital BacPack exhibit to encourage creative engagement by focusing visitors on the design of genetic programs rather than on the detailed protocol of inserting new genetic material into a bacterial cell. We abstracted some of the experimental protocol steps and eliminated virtual labware (e.g. beakers and flasks), and redesigned tangibles so that they are easier to grab and include a visual reference to DNA. We introduced a digital representation of a plasmid (i.e. ring of DNA), which carries the genetic program created by the users into the bacterial cell, as the main focus of the tabletop interaction. We also added a history tab with information about genetic programs created by previous visitors to inform and inspire current users.

Following further evaluation, we introduced more narrative in the activity using an astronaut character to motivate visitors by highlighting needed products. The astronaut character helps visitors start the activity and aids visitors in design optimization by providing concrete feedback about the effectiveness of their genetic program.

To explore the role of the tangible tokens in facilitating engagement and learning, we created an alternative prototype of the exhibit, BacPack 2.1, in which the tangibles were replaced with 22 digital tokens that could be moved and rotated via touch. Figure 1b shows BacPack 2.1. The Observational Study section describes the procedure and results of comparing these prototypes in the museum.

Implementation
BacPack was developed on the 55" MultiTaction Cell. It was programmed in JavaScript using the Multitouch Cornerstone 2 SDK. Tangibles were assembled from laser-cut acrylic layers and incorporated into the design using the MultiTaction fiducial markers.

Design Rationale
We encountered several challenges in the design of BacPack, which are common when designing museum exhibits for direct interaction with biological entities. Here we describe the choices we made to address them. Our design choices were informed by user feedback we received through our iterative design process as well as by other museum exhibits [13, 18] and by frameworks for learning with interactive surfaces and tangibles [1, 2].

Supporting social scalability – Based on the museum philosophy and on exhibit design principles [11, 24] our exhibit aimed not only to accommodate multiple people but also to enhance visitors' experience through collaboration. BacPack provides four virtual workbenches where visitors can work in parallel on different biological designs. The application invites all users to release their engineered bacteria to a common environment (i.e. Mars landscape) and observe the impact. Users are encouraged to collaborate on solving pressing problems (e.g. lack of oxygen) as well as to draw upon bio-designs (i.e. genetic programs) created by previous visitors. The tangible bio bricks provide multiple access points [10], allowing visitor groups to collaborate while working within the same station.

Overcoming time and size scales - Bio-design activities typically require time on the scale of days in order to allow for cell transformation. In the exhibit, we chose to implement a virtual workbench on an interactive surface, where animation is used to bridge the time scale from days to seconds through simulation. To represent genes (i.e. sequences of DNA with specified functionality) we draw upon the metaphor of BioBricks, which is widely used within bio-design [12]. BioBricks embody three engineering principles that are important in synthetic biology: abstraction, standardization, and modularity. We decided to use tangible representation for BioBricks in order to allow for physical interactions that support experimentation and learning [4]. The form factor of the tokens reinforces the metaphor of BioBricks; the shapes of the tangibles reflect the symbols used for depicting genes in real bio-designs. The touch-based gestural interactions (wiggling, dragging) were implemented to mimic physical aspects of laboratory work that include manipulating liquids through shaking, and pouring.

Fostering strategy development – The goal of the exhibit, survival on Mars through efficient utilization of resources, aims to encourage problem solving and strategy development. We chose to provide tangible tokens to encourage tinkering and experimentation with BioBricks and bio-design. To further help visitors develop a strategy within the activity's short time span, we provide users with contextual hints (through the astronaut character), as well as a dynamic simulation of resource depletion and production.

Facilitating learning in informal settings - Interactions with museum exhibits are typically short and casual. To allow visitors to learn even from a brief experience, we designed BacPack so that initial success could be achieved within a short time frame. We designed the core activity—creating a genetic program, inserting it to a cell, and releasing to Mars—to be quick and exciting, yet at the same time visitors are exposed to core principles of bio-design. The visibility of the tangible and gestural interactions allows for learning through observation before or while visitors actively engage with the exhibit. The use of physical actions (grabbing, combining, placing) and gestural interaction (wiggling, dragging) facilitates *learning through doing,* helping visitors to develop a conceptual model that is connected to the processes and applications of bio-design. Visitors that engage with the exhibit for extended periods are exposed to additional layers of complexity. The exhibit does not present formal game levels but rather allows visitors to discover the complex relationships between resources, genetic programs, and the Martian environment.

OBSERVATIONAL STUDY

To understand how our design decisions influenced interactions with the exhibit, we conducted an observational study in the Tech Museum of Innovation. To explore the role of the passive tangible tokens in facilitating engagement and learning in a problem solving and bio-design task, compared to multitouch interaction with digital tokens, we tested two different prototypes: BacPack 2.0 (Figure 1a), which uses tangible tokens, and BacPack 2.1 (Figure 1b), which supports multitouch digital tokens.

Procedure

We deployed BacPack in the Tech Museum of Innovation over four days. We ran the study on two weekend days (Saturday, Sunday) and two weekdays (Tuesday, Wednesday) for a total of 4 hours with BacPack 2.0 (tangible tokens) and 3.5 hours with BacPack 2.1 (virtual tokens). Both interfaces were tested on each day. For each visitor group, a facilitator seated behind the tabletop invited the visitors to build bacteria for Mars. The facilitator then pointed to the tokens around the table, explaining that they were genes to be selected from, and that these genes would tell their bacteria what to do. The facilitator then encouraged the visitors to choose two genes and insert them into the plasmid. The facilitator would step in to help visitors when needed.

After visitors completed the activity, the facilitator conducted a debrief - asking child visitors their age, questions to assess their understanding of the biological process, and to rank on a scale of 1 to 10 how difficult they thought the exhibit was and how much they enjoyed interacting with it. We used a video camera on a tripod to record the interaction on and around the tabletop surface.

Data Analysis

Video recordings were split into segments by the facilitator based on visitor group. We used Atlas.ti to analyze 16:16:42 hours of clips using a video coding scheme informed by existing frameworks [1, 13, 18] and developed iteratively based on interactions found while observing the videos. Based on emerging themes, we eventually consolidated our observations into 12 codes, each representing a different higher-level theme. Inter-coder reliability among three coders based on 62% overlap was very good with an intraclass correlation coefficient of 0.98. Video coding data was analyzed using SPSS. Independent samples t-tests were used to compare means between groups and chi-square tests for independence were used to determine significance between conditions for categorical variables.

Results

Participation

Over the four days of the study, 103 visitor groups interacted with the exhibit, accounting for 193 users varying in age from 4 through adulthood. We alternated between the tangible and multitouch versions in an attempt to observe a similar number of groups between the two prototypes. However, because the number of visitors in the museum varied dramatically even throughout a single day due to the large number of organized group visits, our data includes an uneven split across the two versions: 65 groups interacted with the tangible version of BacPack but only 34 with the non-tangible version.

Several groups and individuals were excluded from video coding measures due to camera obstruction or a lack of meaningful engagement due to young age. However, demographic measures are still reported for these groups. Additionally, four groups sought out and interacted with both versions of the exhibit and thus were excluded from comparative analyses. Table 1 describes group composition per condition. There were no significant differences in group composition, nor group size, age, or gender ratio.

Holding Time and Progress

We measured holding times from the time the first visitor in a group approached the exhibit to the time that the last visitor in that group left the exhibit. In both versions of the exhibit the average holding time was more than 4 minutes, indicating that our exhibit could facilitate active prolonged engagement (APE) [11]. In both versions about 20% of the groups interacted with the exhibit for more than 7 minutes. There were no significant differences in holding times between the two versions. Figure 3 shows a histogram of holding times for visitor groups per condition.

In both versions of the exhibit, almost all groups (tangible: 56/59 groups, 95%; multitouch: 31/34 groups, 91%) completed the activity successfully at least once - deploying engineered bacteria to Mars and watching their impact. Table 2 summarizes success and holding times by condition.

Group Composition	BacPack 2.0 (Tangible Tokens)	BacPack 2.1 (Multitouch Tokens)
One child	24	9
One adult	13	11
One child + one adult	5	1
Multiple children only	15	9
Multiple adults only	2	1
Group size	N = 65, M = 1.24 (1.45)	N = 34, M = 2.03 (1.45)
Total adults (18+)	29 (13 female)	21 (6 female)
Total children	86 (59 female)	48 (30 female)
Age (children)	N = 38, M = 10.55 (2.25)	N = 53, M = 10.49 (2.83)
Total groups	67	36

Table 1. Group composition by condition

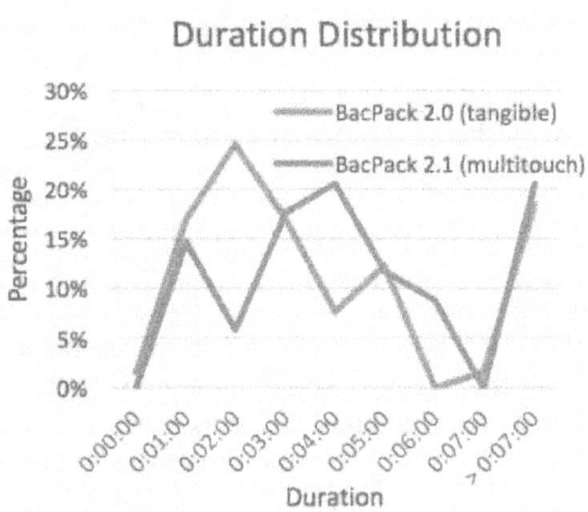

Figure 3. Histogram of holding times for visitor groups per condition

Apprehendability

To assess the apprehendability of the exhibit, we looked at temporal and subjective measures. We measured time to first touch as the time passed from a visitor's initial approach to the exhibit to first active interaction with the exhibit. On average visitors time to first touch was 15.7 seconds, and average time to first success was 1:16.02 minutes. There were no significant differences in these measures between the two versions of BacPack (Table 2).

In the debrief, we asked visitors to rate (on a scale of 10) how difficult it was to interact with the exhibit (see Table 2), users from both conditions generally responded that the exhibit was not very difficult to figure out and interact with. However, one 8-year-old who engaged with the tangible version explained in more detail that he felt the functionality was really easy but that the concept was really hard.

	BacPack 2.0 (Tangible Tokens)		BacPack 2.1 (Multitouch Tokens)		
	N	M (SD)	N	M (SD)	p
Minutes to first success	56	1:14.81 (0:51.15)	31	1:18.20 (0:43.15)	.742
Minutes to first touch	59	0:17.25 (0:46.88)	34	0:32.71 (1:52.12)	.355
Overall holding time (Minutes)	59	4:44 (5:52)	34	4:40 (3:14)	.961
Enjoyment	51	7.41 (2.01)	42	7.07 (2.26)	.436
Difficulty	50	3.40 (2.45)	39	3.64 (2.35)	.641

Table 2. Success and interaction by condition, as well as attitudes of users on a 10 point Likert scale

Enjoyment

Many visitors expressed enthusiasm towards the exhibit. Four groups even returned to try a version of BacPack they had not seen yet. Responding to debrief questions, users of both versions of BacPack reported positive enjoyment, and there was no significant difference between the two conditions (see Table 2).

Strategy

To identify cases when visitors applied basic strategy to their bio-designs and problem solving, we looked at verbal utterances among group members. In one group (G3, tangibles, 38:07 minute visit), we saw the following exchange: A: "We need more biomass." B: "Wait. What do we need? What is this? [Points to biomass on Mars.]" A: "Biomass" B: "Oh. We need biomass?" A: "Yeah." B: "Produce, if there is biomass, OK, I've got this." We also encountered children conveying their current state and the state of the system to the group: "We've got a bunch more bricks coming. Uh oh. We need water." (G7, multitouch, 22:06 minute visit).

In addition to verbal utterances, we also looked at physical indicators such as searching for particular genes around the exhibit (rather than simply combining any two available genes). Although in both conditions about half of users physically moved their hands or actively looked around their vicinity as they decided which genes to use (tangible: 55%, 57/103; multitouch: 53%, 35/66), significantly more people physically reached outside of their immediate area to acquire tokens in the multitouch condition (42%, 28/66) than in the tangible condition (27%, 28/103). From observations, we saw that reaching for distant tokens located on the bezel in the tangible condition often meant reaching around the table or physically walking to a new location, while for multitouch tokens users could reach directly across the table surface, which could potentially explain the disparity. However, the need to reach further to access tangible tokens created opportunities for collaborative engagement, as described in the next section.

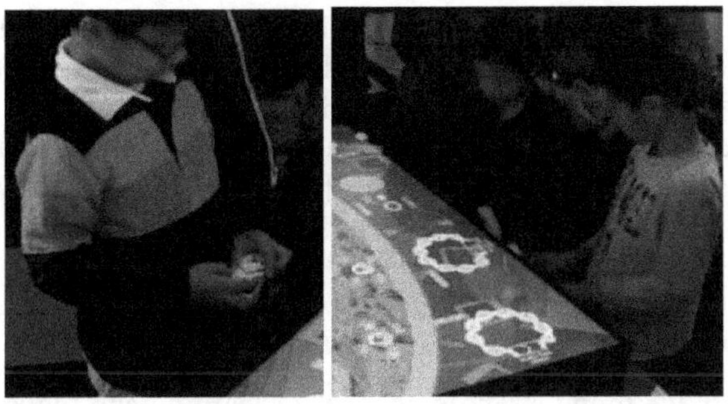

Figure 4. (left) A child holds two tangible tokens up to each other in the air. He performs this action four times in a row, each with a different token in his left hand, before deciding on a combination to place on the screen. (right) A child passes a pair of tangible tokens to a child at a neighboring station.

While visitors were free to manipulate tokens in both versions of BacPack, we found that only the tangible version exhibited epistemic exploratory action. Visitors would pick up physical tokens and experimentally place them next to others in the air, trying different combinations, before committing to a particular combination of genes and placing it on the surface (Figure 4).

In some groups (4%, 4/107), visitors actively engaged with multiple stations at once. In one group (E1, multitouch and tangibles, 24:02 minute visit), a visitor stood in front of one station and occasionally reached over to the neighboring station to complete a round there. When the exhibit started to get more crowded, she moved to the neighboring station permanently. In another group (OP, tangibles, 22:06 minute visit), a visitor stood between two stations and alternated during the time an animation played.

Collaborative Engagement

The exhibit supported multiple visitors while facilitating parallel work, peer support, and rich collaborative engagement. In 47% (48/103) of the groups (tangible: 45%, 30/67; multitouch: 47%, 16/34, and 2/4 who tried both versions) visitors worked in parallel. We also found evidence for peer support and for learning through observation. In about 30% (30/101) of groups we saw learning through observation, where visitors watched a parent or peer at least briefly before starting to interact with the exhibit. Throughout the interaction with the exhibit, in about 45% (18/40) of groups we identified peer support in the form of physical intervention (e.g. pointing to a particular object or area on the tabletop), as well as direct assistance (e.g. to help touch input). Such peer support was more prominent with the tangible version (54%, 14/26) than the multitouch version (29%, 4/14), although the difference was not statistically significant.

In general, we identified several peer collaboration patterns: working together (handing pieces, giving verbal suggestions or instructions both within and between stations); working in parallel (side by side independent work, occasionally helping a peer or reaching over to a different station to acquire a token); and sharing a station (interacting together within the same station).

One interesting subset of collaboration scenarios occurred during gene selection. Sometimes support during selection arose from a parent who offered a potential gene or pair of genes to a child actively engaged in the exhibit. In one case (G1, tangible, 5:18 minute visit), a father walked around the table to pass a tangible token to his daughter at the other end, who in turn offered it to her brother, the one actively interacting with the exhibit. Support can also come from peers. In one case (G2, tangible, 5:14 minute visit), a girl asks another across the table what tangibles are visible from the other's vantage point.

We also found fluidity in support roles. For example, in one group (G2), a father walks over to the exhibit and start interacting. His son quickly takes over the station and the father takes on a support role. His daughter, who had been working at her own station, eventually comes over to take over for her father as the son's main supporter. Another example includes a group of 7 school-aged girls (G5, multitouch, 10:21 minute visit) who initially had to double-up on some stations. As some group members lost interest, the others began to spread out until each had her own station. Although they had the opportunity to work in parallel, they chose to continue to verbally strategize.

	BacPack 2.0 (Tangible Tokens)		**BacPack 2.1 (Multitouch Tokens)**		**Overall**	
	N	**Count**	**N**	**Count**	**N**	**Count**
Mars	35	11	20	12	55	23
Bacteria	35	14	20	4	55	18
DNA	35	3	20	0	55	3
Plasmid	35	1	20	1	55	2
Make	35	7	20	9	55	16
Gene	35	8	20	2	55	10
Combine	35	1	20	1	55	2
Product / Resource Names	35	2	20	1	55	3

Table 3. Dialogue analysis: open answers that include the term

Learning

To assess learning, we asked visitors open-ended questions after they completed interacting with the exhibit, getting visitors to describe the exhibit in their own words. We quantified the number of relevant biology and domain terms used (Table 3). Interestingly, in the multitouch version we see more use of the terms "Mars", "plasmid", "make", and "combine", while in the tangible version we see more "bacteria", "DNA", and "gene". In particular, visitors who used the multitouch tokens used the terms "Mars" (χ^2 (2, N = 55) = 4.27, p = 0.039) and "make" (χ^2 (2, N = 55) = 3.86, p = 0.050) significantly more than those who encountered the tangible tokens. There were no significant differences for the other five terms. However, the differences in terminology used suggest that the two versions result in somewhat different learning outcomes: the tangible version focuses on the design problem and the elements of the genetic program, and the multitouch version highlights process and context.

Aside from using relevant terms, visitors showed a grasp of the learning goals through their overall response to post-task questions. For example, "[The goal is] Helping to survive on Mars" (multitouch, age 9); and "I'm making bacteria to go on Mars, so I choose something and make something else. Yeah. Telling you what we need" (tangibles, age 9). Visitors were also able to describe aspects of the process. For example, "I found that the poop is the best thing to make water and the energy" (tangibles, age 11). We also found some evidence for inquiry and reflection during the interaction. Children sometimes read the science-term-laden text on screen out loud and occasionally asked the facilitators questions like "Why are we sending bacteria to Mars?" (tangibles, age 9).

DISCUSSION

We performed an on-site evaluation of two versions of the BacPack museum exhibit: BacPack 2.0 (tangible tokens) and BacPack 2.1 (multitouch tokens). Our investigation focused on how our design choices support the exhibit's learning and design goals. In particular, we were interested in the role of the tangible tokens in supporting engagement and learning in a bio-design task compared to the use of multitouch digital tokens.

In both versions of the exhibit, visitors of all ages collaborated with friends, family, and strangers, sometimes for extended periods of time and overall expressing a positive impression of their experiences (G1, G3). Despite the general perception that the activity was relatively easy, it proved challenging enough to provide opportunities for collaboration not just among active users, but also from visitors who were observing the interaction and serving a supportive role like parents and caretakers. While we did not find statistically significant quantitative differences between the two prototypes of BacPack, we identified several more nuanced qualitative differences between the tangible and multitouch prototypes.

First, we observed that in general the exhibit was able to effectively facilitate a variety of collaboration styles and fluid role switching. In particular, the tangible tokens created opportunities for collaboration beyond those afforded by the multitouch only version. For example, because the tangible tokens were spread around the bezel, often out of immediate reach for a particular user, people asked for help from other users. Placing the tangible tokens around the interactive surface also encouraged observers (e.g. parents) to reach out to the tokens and suggest them to users.

Second, we found that the tangible tokens allowed users to tinker and experiment independent of the steps needed to progress through the exhibit in ways that we did not observe with the multitouch users, thus facilitating physically distributed learning [16]. We identified several epistemic actions taken by users on the tangible prototype that are similar to those outlined by Antle et al. [1] including *spatial arrangement of tokens* and *comparing alternative combinations of tokens.*

Third, we found strong evidence for learning and inquiry in both versions of the exhibit (G2). However, we did see differences between the tangible and multitouch prototypes in the learning concepts visitors retained, as evidenced by the terminology used and comments visitors made in the debrief. With the tangible version, visitors more readily used terminology like "gene" and "bacteria" and contributed comments about the combination of genes they made, the process of inserting a genetic program to the bacterial cells, and the effect of particular gene combinations (L1, L2, L3, L4). Visitors who engaged with the multitouch version focused more on "Mars" commenting more broadly on the impact of made products on Mars (L3, L4). We hypothesize that through physical interaction with the tangible tokens, visitors developed a conceptual model that explained the role of genes and bacteria, which are represented by the tangible token interactions.

Taken together, these findings, while not conclusive, indicate that tangible tokens provide further support for learning as well as more opportunities for collaboration.

CONCLUSION AND FUTURE WORK

TEIs play a major role in creating educational activities that spark imagination and allow people of all ages to experience creative problem solving with biology. We presented BacPack, a tangible museum exhibit for exploring bio-design, which utilizes tangible tokens on a large multitouch table display to allow visitors to participate in a playful bio-design activity - engineering bacteria for sustaining life on Mars. We discussed design considerations for interactive exhibits, which foster creative engagement with biology, and investigated the role of tangible tokens in facilitating collaborative learning in such exhibits. We showed that tangible tokens provide additional opportunities for collaborative problem solving and impact learning through physical interaction and support for tinkering and experimentation.

Future work will continue to draw upon TEIs to provide young children with educational activities that encourage creative problem solving with biology, support open-ended inquiry, and facilitate collaborative exploration of concepts previously considered too complicated for children.

ACKNOWLEDGMENTS

This work is partially funded by NSF IIS-1149530 and NSF IIS-1563932.

REFERENCES

1. Alissa N. Antle. Scratching the Surface: Opportunities and Challenges from Designing Interactive Tabletops for Learning. In Victor R. Lee (ed) *Learning Technologies and the Body: Integration and Implementation, Education Research Series, Routledge* (Taylor & Francis) (2015), 55-73.
2. Alissa N. Antle and A.F. Wise. Getting down to details: Using learning theory to inform tangibles research and design for children. In *Interacting with Computers*, 25, 1 (2013), 1-20.
3. Alissa N. Antle, Milena Droumeva, and Daniel Ha. 2009. Hands on what?: comparing children's mouse-based and tangible-based interaction. In *Proceedings of the 8th International Conference on Interaction Design and Children* (IDC '09). ACM, New York, NY, USA, 80-88.
4. Sanjay Chandrasekharan. 2009. Building to discover: A common coding model. *Cognitive Science*, 33: 1059-1086.
5. Sarah D'Angelo, D. Harmon Pollock, and Michael Horn. 2015. Fishing with friends: using tabletop games to raise environmental awareness in aquariums. In *Proceedings of the 14th International Conference on Interaction Design and Children* (IDC '15). ACM, New York, NY, USA, 29-38.
6. Michael Horn, Brenda Phillips, Margaret Evans, Florian Block, Judy Diamond, and Chia Shen. 2015. Visualizing the tree of life: Learning around an interactive visualization of biological data in museums. In Proceedings of the *National Association for Research in Science Teaching Annual International Conference* (NARST '15).
7. Michael Horn, R. Jordan Crouser, and Marina U. Bers. 2012. Tangible interaction and learning: the case for a hybrid approach. *Personal and Ubiquitous Computing* 16, 4: 379-389.
8. Michael Horn, Zeina Atrash Leong, Florian Block, Judy Diamond, E. Margaret Evans, Brenda Phillips, and Chia Shen. "Of BATs and APEs: an interactive tabletop game for natural history museums." In *Proceedings of the SIGCHI Conference on Human Factors in Computing Systems*, pp. 2059-2068. ACM, 2012.
9. Michael Horn, Erin Treacy Solovey, R. Jordan Crouser, and Robert J.K. Jacob. 2009. Comparing the use of tangible and graphical programming languages for informal science education. In *Proceedings of the SIGCHI Conference on Human Factors in Computing Systems* (CHI '09). ACM, New York, NY, USA, 975-984.
10. Eva Hornecker, Paul Marshall, and Yvonne Rogers. 2007. From entry to access: how shareability comes about. In *Proceedings of the 2007 conference on Designing pleasurable products and interfaces* (DPPI '07). ACM, New York, NY, USA, 328-342.
11. Thomas Humphrey, Joshua Gutwill, and Exploratorium APE Team. "Fostering active prolonged engagement." *San Francisco, CA: The Exploratorium* (2005).
12. International Genetically Engineered Machine (iGEM). Retrieved August 2, 2015 from http://igem.org/About
13. Seung Ah Lee, Engin Bumbacher, Alice M. Chung, Nate Cira, Byron Walker, Ji Young Park, Barry Starr, Paulo Blikstein, and Ingmar H. Riedel-Kruse. 2015. Trap it!: A Playful Human-Biology Interaction for a Museum Installation. In *Proceedings of the 33rd Annual ACM Conference on Human Factors in Computing Systems* (CHI '15). ACM, New York, NY, USA, 2593-2602.
14. Joyce Ma, Lisa Sindorf, Isaac Liao, and Jennifer Frazier. 2015. Using a Tangible Versus a Multi-touch Graphical User Interface to Support Data Exploration at a Museum Exhibit. In *Proceedings of the Ninth International Conference on Tangible, Embedded, and Embodied Interaction* (TEI '15). ACM, New York, NY, USA, 33-40.
15. Paul Marshall. 2007. Do tangible interfaces enhance learning?. In *Proceedings of the 1st international conference on Tangible and embedded interaction* (TEI '07). ACM, New York, NY, USA, 163-170.
16. Taylor Martin and Daniel Schwartz. 2005. Physically Distributed Learning: Adapting and Reinterpreting Physical Environments in the Development of Fraction Concepts. *Cognitive science* 29, 4: 587-625.
17. Amor A. Menezes, John Cumbers, John A. Hogan, and Adam P. Arkin. "Towards synthetic biological approaches to resource utilization on space missions." *Journal of The Royal Society Interface* 12, no. 102 (2015): 20140715.
18. Johanna Okerlund, Evan Segreto, Casey Grote, Lauren Westendorf, Anja Scholze, Romie Littrell, and Orit Shaer. SynFlo: A Tangible Museum Exhibit for Exploring Bio-Design. In *Proceedings of the Tenth International Conference on Tangible, Embedded, and Embodied Interaction (TEI '16)*, pp. 141-149. ACM, 2016.
19. Seymour Papert. 1980. *Mindstorms: Children, Computers and Powerful Ideas*. New York: Basic books.
20. Jean Piaget. 1954. *The construction of reality in the child.* New York: Basic Books.
21. Mitchel Resnick, Brad Myers, Kumiyo Nakakoji, Ben Shneiderman, Randy Pausch, Ted Selker, and Mike Eisenberg. 2005. Design Principles for Tools to Support Creative Thinking. Technical Report: *NSF*

Workshop Report on Creativity Support Tools. Washington, DC.

22. Orit Shaer, Consuelo Valdes, Sirui Liu, Kara Lu, Kimberly Chang, Wendy Xu, Traci L. Haddock, Swapnil Bhatia, Douglas Densmore, and Robert Kincaid. 2013. Designing Reality-Based Interfaces for Experiential Bio-Design. *Personal and Ubiquitous Computing* 18, 6: 1515-1532.
23. Orit Shaer, Megan Strait, Consuelo Valdes, Heidi Wang, Taili Feng, Michael Lintz, Michelle Ferreirae, Casey Grote, Kelsey Tempel, and Sirui Liu. 2012. The design, development, and deployment of a tabletop interface for collaborative exploration of genomic data. *International Journal of Human-Computer Studies* 70, 10: 746-764.
24. Scott S. Snibbe and Hayes S. Raffle. "Social immersive media: pursuing best practices for multi-user interactive camera/projector exhibits." In *Proceedings of the SIGCHI Conference on Human Factors in Computing Systems*, pp. 1447-1456. ACM, 2009.
25. Consuelo Valdes, Michelle Ferreirae, Taili Feng, Heidi Wang, Kelsey Tempel, Sirui Liu, and Orit Shaer. 2012. A collaborative environment for engaging novices in scientific inquiry. In *Proceedings of the 2012 ACM international conference on Interactive tabletops and surfaces* (ITS '12). ACM, New York, NY, USA, 109-118.

Toward Wearable App Design for Children's In-the-World Science Inquiry

Sharon Lynn Chu
Texas A&M University
The StoryLab
sharilyn@tamu.edu

Brittany Garcia
Texas A&M University
The StoryLab
brinni@tamu.edu

ABSTRACT

Little is understood on how to design wearables for education, especially for children. We explore how smartwatches may allow children to see the world through the lens of science. In our study, 20 children are tasked to record stories related to specific scientific concepts in their daily life and drawing from their embodied experiences using a commodity smartwatch. Our findings describe the types of 'science stories' that the children capture through the smartwatch, and how the stories relate to science. From our findings, we elicit seven areas of future research needed to catalyze the design of wearable apps to support informal science learning for children.

Author Keywords
Wearables; Children; Science learning; Smartwatch; Storytelling; Narrative.

ACM Classification Keywords
H.5.m. Information interfaces and presentation (e.g., HCI): Miscellaneous.

INTRODUCTION

The problem of poor college graduation rates from STEM majors and low percentages of 'ready' students entering STEM degrees is well-documented [1]. This is often because students are psychologically disengaged from the process of learning in STEM subjects. According to many models of academic motivation, such as Jones' MUSIC model [2], usefulness is a key factor for student success in science that is difficult for educators to address. Usefulness refers to how students perceive how what they are learning is useful to them and to their future. In science, a lack of perceived usefulness often comes from a lack of personal or cultural relevance of the content to be learned to the student; the science is decontextualized with respect to actual contexts of use [3]; and students are only passive recipients of science content.

TEI '17, March 20-23, 2017, Yokohama, Japan
© 2017 ACM. ISBN 978-1-4503-4676-4/17/03...$15.00
DOI: http://dx.doi.org/10.1145/3024969.3025008

Yet, the child's experiences in the world outside the classroom is rich and full of experiences that implicitly or explicitly relate to science [4, 5]. This paper is positioned in the tradition of research looking at how 'out-of-school experiences' or 'everyday experiences' may help children to understand and learn about science. While much research in HCI and educational technologies have looked at how to design technologies to support such informal science learning for children, the introduction of wearable technologies presents a new opportunity to fulfill this research goal with an approach that is perhaps more interactive, mobile and immediate for students. Little is understood currently on the potential of wearables to support science learning.

Our work posits that wearables may provide a 'technological lens' by which children may view their world through science. In this paper, we present a study that explored how children make use of smartwatches as a means to record science episodes in their daily life in the form of stories. Rather than showing the effectiveness of a particular approach, the primary objective of our study was to describe and interpret first the type of science-based observations or stories that children derive from their embodied 'in-the-world' experiences, and second the children's experience using a smartwatch as a tool for science learning. Based on our findings, we advance areas where research is needed to move forward the broader agenda of how wearables may support children's informal science learning and inquiry.

Our research addresses elementary school-aged children in the 3rd to 5th grade (8 to 11 years old). A major rationale for this target population is that especially in STEM fields, early motivation is critical: "research clearly shows that early childhood experiences serve as a major influence on academic interest ... [and] lead to a positive commitment toward science that is enduring." [6].

In the rest of this paper, we first present the context and motivation for our work, followed by related work on science learning through wearables. We then describe our theoretical foundation in embodied narrative-based learning, and our study with 20 children, before presenting our findings. Finally, we discuss various areas for future research on wearables for science learning.

CONTEXT AND MOTIVATION

The motivation for our research is two-fold: one track arises from the problems of children gaining a proper understanding of science in the classroom, and the promise of informal science education; and the second track is shaped by the lack of research in how wearables may be used to support children's learning and development.

Informal Science Learning

Learning science entails understanding real-world concepts that address the physical, material and social environment around us. Creating a connection between the outside world in instruction that is situated in a classroom however is challenging. Much literature attempt to tackle this problem. Bouillon and Gomez [7] for example report that "schools are in communities but often not *of* communities". They further argue that the disconnect in classroom-based instruction may lead to students perceiving learning at school as distinct from learning about life and how to function in everyday settings. This has been referred to as a failure in the enculturation of students into the science way of thinking [4]. Informal science education, sometimes called "casual learning, extended learning, or free-choice learning" [8] has been posited as providing approaches to address such scientific enculturation. Although we do not present a comprehensive review of science enculturation in informal learning here, it has been studied in contexts such as the home (e.g., [9]), field trips (e.g., [10], or summer camps (e.g., [11]). Braund and Reiss [12] for example proposed an evolutionary model of learning that attempts to integrate "more sites of valid data gathering and knowledge production" (museums, science centers, zoos, etc.) beyond the school science laboratory.

We are particularly interested in informal science learning in terms of everyday experiences. In a key report entitled "Learning science in informal environments: People, Places and Pursuits" [13] commissioned by the US National Research Council, the committee reported that while no comprehensive study has been conducted to date, "the sheer number of hours in which individuals encounter scientific information outside school over the life span is far greater than the number of hours of science education in formal classroom environments". The report lays out six strands reflecting the goals and practices of informal science learning: *Strand 1* – Experience excitement, interest, and motivation to learn about phenomena in the natural and physical world; *Strand 2* – Come to generate, understand, remember, and use concepts, explanations, arguments, models, and facts related to science. *Strand 3* – Manipulate, test, explore, predict, question, observe, and make sense of the natural and physical world; *Strand 4* – Reflect on science as a way of knowing; on processes, concepts, and institutions of science; and on their own process of learning about phenomena; *Strand 5* – Participate in scientific activities and learning practices with others, using scientific language and tools; and *Strand 6* – Think about themselves as science learners and develop an identity as someone who knows about, uses, and sometimes contributes to science.

Wearables for Learning

Advances in miniaturization, processing power, sensing and battery life have led wearable computing to be commercializable as useful products [14]. Wearables present an opportunity to look at informal science learning from a perspective that is anchored in children's everyday life. Barfield and Caudell [15] define a wearable as a "fully functional, self-powered, self-contained computer that is worn on the body ... (and) provides access to information, and interaction with information, anywhere and at anytime". Wearables typically possess three main capabilities: sensing (observing physical environments); analysis (analyzing observations); and communication (relaying information to other machines) [16]. Examples of modern wearable devices include smartwatches (e.g., Apple Watch [17]), wristbands (e.g., Nike Fuelband [18]), intelligent glasses (e.g., Google Glass [19]) and other less common device forms such as the Purple smart locket [20]). To date, relatively little research has been conducted on the design, use and effectiveness of wearables, especially for learning. Arguably, the most common uses of wearables currently is for health purposes, notably fitness trackers that track heart rate and calorie usage (e.g., [21]), and as a proxy to send and receive phone calls and messages.

From responses to an online survey of 66 experts in higher education, Bower and Sturman [22] identified 14 affordances of wearable technologies to support education and learning. They classify the 14 affordances into 3 categories: A. capabilities of wearables that may have pedagogical uses, e.g., providing in-situ contextual information; recording of information; first-person view; B. capabilities of wearables that may enhance educational quality, e.g., enhancing engagement and focus; enhanced sense of presence; and C. capabilities of wearables that may affect logistic and other aspects, e.g., hands-free access; eliminating boundedness to physical spaces. All in all, wearables afford "interactive, communicative and functional capabilities between users, environment, information and digital data in unique ways" [23]. They differ from mobile devices such as smartphones, PDAs, etc. in terms of key characteristics including portability, intrusiveness, screen space, and media capabilities. They are attached to the wearer, and are thus constantly available whenever and wherever needed.

RELATED WORK

We reviewed the literature that has addressed the use of wearable technologies to support learning. We note that we are not including literature on electronics or microprocessor-based wearable artifacts, such as the LilyPad Arduno [24], that are also sometimes referred to as wearables. We draw out three points of relevance here that helps to situate our work. First, wearables have been proposed to support more often the teacher, rather than the student. De Freitas et al. [25] give three scenarios by which wearables can be used in education: 1) To deliver lecture materials, assignments, and assessments to the learner on the move; 2) To encourage collaborative learning and other work without a physical campus; and 3) To facilitate the collection and compilation of experience during field trips. Similarly, Llorente and Morant [26] advance new classroom paradigms for the applications of wearables in "presentation slide control and student response monitoring" and "examination and student metric extraction in the lab".

Second, more work on wearables appear to have addressed formal learning environments than informal settings. For example, Park et al. [27] built a wearable platform to track the child's interactions with the physical world to provide "coherent information, which can readily assist the teachers in evaluating and assessing the progress of children's learning process and their social behavior". Scholl, Wille and Laerhoven [28] proposed a wristband combined with Google Glass to support middle school science 'wet labs' by displaying step-by-step lab protocols on the wristband. There have been work in the literature on the more established movement of ubiquitous computing investigating learning experiences in informal contexts, such as Hall and Bannon's [29] work in museums. The use of wearable sensors and RFID-enabled devices has been explored with regard to the physical activity of children (e.g., Consolvo et al. [30], Lee and Drake [31]), and much less with respect to learning of specific content.

And third, the use of wearables to support learning has been closely tied to mostly quantitative data. This may be because wearable and mobile technologies have been often harnessed in the context of the the 'quantified self' (QS) movement. Self-quantification began as a hobbyist activity, defined as a "highly tailored set of data practices that build upon (and are also constrained by) the specifics associated with one's lives and circumstances" [32]. Collected sensor data for instance is then displayed on dashboards or in specific types of data visualizations for the user to consult. Discussing the challenges of and opportunities for integrating self-quantification into the learning sciences, Lee [33] highlights three characteristics of the QS movement: 1) it typically involves continual and longitudinal collection of data; 2) it entails frequent intermediate reviews of data; and 3) there is a privileging of unexpected findings in activities.

We did not find up to date research that look empirically at the use of wearables to collect more qualitative data. Although it makes use of mobile technologies instead of wearables per se, one particularly relevant work is that of Pauw et al. [34]. They call their approach 'life-relevant science learning' and designed a mobile social media app, 'ScienceKit', that allows children to "capture moments of interest in their daily lives with multimedia and connect them to science inquiry by making claims, posing questions, and designing experiments". However, their study was conducted with only 7 learners in a summer camp called 'Kitchen Chemistry' focusing on cooking, whereby the children could record moments of interest only during the time that they were in the sessions. Moreover, much of the children's activity during the camp seemed to have been moderated by facilitators. Part of their findings nevertheless are useful for the purpose in our work. They detail three types of learners' experiences through ScienceKit: 1) the use of ScienceKit to mostly engage in pre-planned scientific inquiry. E.g., a child's video entry detailing his thought processes, hypotheses, and observations during an experiment mixing oil and water using eggs as an emulsifier; 2) the use of ScienceKit to connect with peer-groups while engaging in scientific inquiry. E.g., two children recording videos interviewing one another or the facilitator about what they are doing at the moment with brownies and measurement tools; and 3) the use of ScienceKit to move from interest-driven inquiry to more complex academic-like inquiry. E.g., a child initially posting about an observation he made during breakfast: "Some [strawberries] probably got more care than others. Some are bigger than others.", leading him to later review the ingredients lists on labels.

Moving beyond Pauw et al. [34], our work explores the type of science stories that children would capture in-the-wild given the affordances of wearables.

THEORETICAL FOUNDATION

Learning from Everyday Experiences

The use of wearables allows for science reflections to be grounded in children's everyday life. Various theoretical paradigms that capture different aspects of the importance of everyday experiences for learning have been proposed. Situated learning theory [35] suggests that learning happens in "authentic contexts: 'ordinary practices of the culture', or "what students face in the real world" [36]. In an ethnographic case study of a female child from 4th to 6th grade, Bricker and Bell [37] detail the situated events related to science in her daily experiences. They conclude that "many of Brenda's school experiences also represented missed opportunities to create linkages to out-of-school practices, which might have deepened and furthered Brenda's interests and expertise development".

In embodied learning, the idea of embodiment entails that "cognitive processes are deeply rooted in the body's interactions with the world" [38]. Learning is not only about symbols and symbol manipulation, but must ground itself in experience [39] in a physical-spatial, temporally dynamic, social-cultural, and affective world [40]. Particularly for children, Hedges [41] advanced that they are natural "life-theorizers" who "develop working theories for making sense of the natural, social, physical, and material worlds".

Contextual learning acknowledges the diversity in students' experiences and background knowledge. New knowledge is constructed from experiences, and each new experience leads either to assimilation or accommodation in the student's mental representations [42]. Within this framework, Bouillion and Gomez [7] have proposed the notion of "connected science" that uses a curricular design grounded in context characterized by 4 features: a 'real world' community-based problem, partnerships of the school with the community or business, problem-based learning, and student-developed products.

Science Discourse

In our work, children relate their everyday experiences with science concepts by capturing discourse using wearables. We analyze discourse about science through the lens of the concept of narrative intelligence. Narrative intelligence posits that "we organize our experience and our memory of human happenings mainly in the form of narrative – stories, excuses, myths, reasons for doing and not doing, and so on" [43, 44]. We advance that there is much potential in students understanding science through telling their own stories about the world – hence their 'science stories'. While children may not be able to express science concepts using scientific terms yet, their personal stories may be founded on implicit science understanding and reveal their mental models of the concepts. We note that we adopt a broad perspective on storytelling here as entailing any "structured narration of experience" [45] that detail "human attempts to progress to a solution, clarification or unraveling of an incomplete situation" [46].

Our understanding of science stories is grounded in the Vygotsky's [47] distinctions between two main types of concepts: *Spontaneous* concepts are formed through a synthesis of direct experiences with the world by engaging in inductive processes, such as "pattern recognition, comparisons made between multiple events, reflection on activities, and the use of analogical reasoning" [48]. While spontaneous concepts rely on one's common-sense and everyday understanding, *scientific* concepts are handed to a child typically in formal learning environments by teachers and senior students. Beyond concrete phenomena, scientific concepts are the abstracted generalizations that a child learns, for example, the formal definition of a concept from a textbook. The majority of discourse told in the classroom engage the paradigmatic mode of thought, conveying scientific concepts. We hypothesize that science storytelling through wearables is characterized by students telling stories about science in the moment grounded in their concrete daily experiences interacting with the world. Such storytelling may thus add a new dimension to informal science learning, making it more personally-relevant, contextualized, and interactive.

STUDY DESCRIPTION

The specific questions that we addressed in our study were: *RQ 1: What kinds of science stories do children capture using smartwatches?*;

RQ 2: What is the relationship of science stories captured through smartwatches with informal science learning?' and

RQ 3: What is the general experience of children using smartwatches to contemplate science in-the-wild?.

Our study involved 20 child participants (12 boys and 8 girls) aged 8 to 11 (mean age = 9.25). Their demographics were as follows: White (85% (n = 17); Hispanic: 10% (n = 2); Asian: 5% (n = 1) For the study, we made use of the Samsung Gear Neo 2, a standard commercially-available smartwatch, synced with a Samsung Galaxy tablet. The smartwatch battery has a run time of continuous use of up to 72 hours. The 'voice memo' app that allows for voice and sound recording was used as a simple means of allowing storytelling on the smartwatch. Figure 1 shows pictures of the watch with the app opened. The voice memo app comes pre-installed on the smartwatch, and allows for recordings of up to 5 mins each. The recordings are transferred automatically to the tablet via bluetooth when the smartwatch is within range.

The participants were recruited through an announcement on the university student, staff and faculty listservs. Children were registered for the study on a first-come, first-served basis upon the return of a signed consent form from their parents. In our study, the smartwatch acts as a lens to view the world through science, i.e., children are told to record only stories related to a science concept. The study took place over three consecutive days as follows:

Day 1: **1.** The child arrived at a lab space at a scheduled time after their school time. He/she was given a brief description of the study, and provided minor's assent to participate in the study; **2.** The child watched a 5 mins-long video providing basic facts about a science concept (the concept of either friction or gravity was randomly chosen. For friction, aspects such as what is friction, what influences friction, etc. would be covered) suitable for the children's age range and cognitive level. A focus science concept was given to the children to give us a common baseline in analysis when looking for similarities, patterns and differences; **3.** The child filled in a basic demographic questionnaire; **4.** A researcher introduced the smartwatch and explained to the child how to use the voice memo app to do a recording; **5.** The child was given some time to practice creating recordings; **6.** When the researcher was confident that the child knew how to use the smartwatch and the voice memo app, the child was instructed on the requirements of the study (he/she has to collect stories related to the science concept over the course of Day 2 and Day 3). The child was told explicitly that there is no right or wrong answer to the science stories that they could collect. He/she was then given the smartwatch to take home.

Figure 1. Smartwatch used

Day 2: The child used the smartwatch to record stories as he/she saw fit. No interaction between the child and the researcher took place.

Day 3: 1. The child met the researcher at a lab; 2. The child was interviewed about his /her experience in the study, with the smartwatch, and with storytelling; 3. The smartwatch was taken back, the child was debriefed;

4) the researcher ensured that the recordings were transferred to the tablet.

DATA COLLECTION AND ANALYSIS

A total of seventy-nine smartwatch stories were obtained from the 20 children. All the story recordings were fully transcribed and entered into a spreadsheet for analysis. Basic statistics were first calculated for the stories, including the number of stories per child, and the length of stories per child. A qualitative open coding process was performed by two coders independently on the transcribed stories to identify the (explicit or implied) context in which the story was recorded, the story theme, the type of story, and the role that the child appears to have taken during the recording of the story. The coders also identified how the story addressed the science topic given, i.e., the story's relation to the science concept. The average intercoder reliability for all of these categories was 81.22%. The two coders discussed the cases of disagreement, and agreed on a common code for each case.

We then conducted three further analyses that were based on specific frameworks: first, the stories were coded using the 3-act story model to determine their narrative structure. The 3-act model of introduction, middle and end/resolution is the most basic story structure dating back to Aristotle (see [49]); second, Vygotsky's framework (see Theoretical Foundation section) of spontaneous and scientific concepts were used to analyze the stories. All the concepts contained within each story were identified, and then each concept as spontaneous or scientific. For instance, a story excerpt stating "Another force was at work to stop you, friction makes things stop" would be coded as having one scientific concept. Conversely, "Friction let my pencil stop rolling" would be coded as having one everyday concept; and third, the six strands of informal science learning from the key report by the National Research Council [13] (see Context and Motivation section) was used to analyze the stories.

The post-interviews about the children's experience with the smartwatch were audio-recorded. The recordings were fully transcribed, and a qualitative coding process was performed on the transcripts using the MaxQDA software using the following method: descriptive codes were generated. Essentially, each meaningful idea unit is assigned a code describing the idea, or an in-vivo code using the interviewee's own words is assigned if no better code could be generated [50]; the descriptive codes were then grouped into categories, and then into high-level themes.

STUDY FINDINGS

RQ 1: Kinds of wearable stories

Basic story profile: Using the smartwatch, an average of 4.45 science stories were recorded per child over two days. The average length of a story was 41.79 words, which amount to about 3 lines of typed text. A child covered an average of 1.15 themes per science story. Most of the stories had a full 3-part narrative structure (45.6%), followed by 33.3% having only 2 parts, 13.3% having no narrative structure, and 7.8% having a hybrid overall structure.

Recording contexts: We were able to identify the context of recording for 39.6% of the science stories. The identified contexts of recording were classified into 4 main categories, shown in Figure 2:

i) *At home:* 16.5% of the identified contexts were in the home. Three specific home contexts were seen: a) the living room. Instances of stories were "I found one of my scientific research when Luke was sliding on the maroon leather couch…", "So when I shuffle my feet across the carpet in our living room it creates friction…"; b) the kitchen. Story examples were "So I had an egg on the counter and it started rolling and then it stopped because of friction", "On Saturday uh my mom was cooking and the way that she was cooking our dinner, she was kind of making smoke…"; and c) the backyard. For example, stories were "When I kick my ball in the tall grass of our backyard it did not go very far because there was too much friction…", "I tested out my friction experiment with my soccer ball in the tall grass of my backyard and the ball…there was too much friction…".

ii) *At school:* 3.3% of the science stories were taken at school. Two specific school contexts were found: a) the sports field. E.g., "Today on Thursday we are running outside for PE and I noticed that we are running and it was friction…"; and b) the school yard. E.g., "Today what I noticed was that in recess everyone was playing and the balls were dropping, everyone was running and having fun but without even floating…".

iii) *In a vehicle:* 11% of the science stories were done in a vehicle, typically a car or a bus, when the child was being transported to school, an activity, etc. Example stories are "I heard the car rolling around the pavement which counts as friction.", "The bus slowed down to a stop with friction."

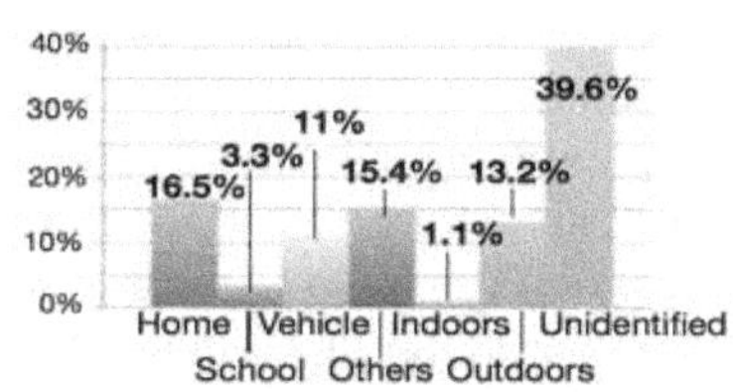

Figure 2. Recording contexts found

iv) *Others:* Other specific recording contexts were seen to a lesser extent. These included the library (e.g., "The library has a bridge across to it and is being held up by both the library and the walkway across from the other side of it"; at a desk (e.g., "My pencil falls off my desk, my papers fall off my desk, my notebook falls off my desk,…"); at a sports venue (e.g., "When I pivoted on the basketball court I did not slide because I had friction on my shoes."); on the pavement (e.g., I saw a bike that was riding around the pavement which counts as friction."); at a park (e.g., "When I was at the park I was testing out if the bigger rock was going to go down on the ground faster than the little rock…"); on a hill (e.g., "When I was walking up the hill I noticed that it was harder to walk up the hill and that was friction."); and at an after-school club (e.g., "Today when I was in kids club and...we were doing this thing where there was an experiment about trying to make fake blood out of corn starch and corn syrup, red dye, and blue dye").

In the rest of the stories, we were able to identify the recording context as being either outdoors (13.2%) or indoors (1.1%), but no specific context was identifiable.

Story types: Five story types were found in terms of the form in which children recorded their stories (Figure 3 left):

i) *Accounts of personal experiences.* These stories (34.78% of all stories) were about the children relating their current or past designed or ad hoc experience (e.g., "I was sliding my finger on my kindle which makes it friction because I was sliding the finger on the kindle");

2) *Observations of happenings.* These stories (42.39%) were about an event that the child observed (e.g., "When my dog rides in the front seat of the car and my mom slams on the brakes his paws have little friction so he flies straight into the window. Poor Shadow.");

3) *Narration from a predefined text.* These stories (13.04%) are read from an existing text not original from the child, perhaps from a textbook or a website (e.g., "My third story is about the Triceratops, most common large plant eating dinosaurs of the late Cretaceous period in western North America where the Triceratops, they were found Nowhere else in the world. The word which means horned faced fits with these massive four leg dinosaurs."); and

4) *Working through a thought experiment or a question of interest.* In these stories (9.78%), the children first pose a question or an issue that they proceed to solve by voicing out their problem-solving steps (e.g., "When I need to move something from one place to another...how could I do it? Well first I could use a piece of wood, put it on there and start dragging it, but that would not work very well because too much friction. But if I use a sled it would be better but still too much friction. Finally, my last option is a wagon which is the greatest one to use because it has wheels which will create the right amount of friction.").

Recording roles: We found that the children adopted 5 main types of roles when recording the smartwatch stories:

i) *Observer.* This was the most prominent role adopted in 40.2% of the stories (Figure 3 right). The child analyzes the environment around him/her, and proffers an observation. They adopt an etic perspective, and reflect on something that they saw happen or that was brought to their attention. E.g., "While I'm sitting on the couch I'm noticing my mom's water bottle and it's been sitting out for a while and I'm noticing the condensation on the water bottle because the water has been like evaporating and has been not evaporating condensing on the outside of the water bottle."

ii) *Actor.* 29.35% of the stories illustrated this role. The child analyzes his/her own actions that he/she is currently doing, or has recently done either by themselves or with others, and proffers an observation. E.g., "For my first story as we're sitting here playing Mario Cart 8 we're having to use science because we're having to figure out the best combinations of speed, acceleration, handling traction and weight to be the

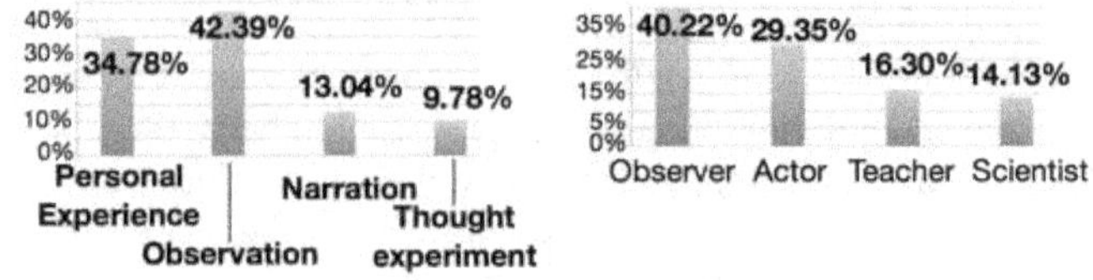

Figure 3. Types of stories recorded (left); Roles children adopted (right)

best or just what we like in a race."

iii) *Teacher.* We saw this role in 16.3% of the stories. The child adopts the role of someone tasked to explain a phenomenon akin to an instructor, and explains the subject of the recording in detail as if he/she is teaching someone about the topic. E.g., "If you have gears and they're not running so good if they're not turning right and they won't work, what you do is you get oil and you put it in there so there is less friction so they'll run better but if you don't have oil then there is too much friction and they won't run."

iv) *Scientist.* In this role (14.13%), the child adopts a problem-solving stance toward the world. He/she brainstorms about phenomena, raises questions, and comes up with solutions to the problems that the child either observed or was given. E.g., "If you have a pile of bricks and you're trying to move them from one place to another and you put a piece of wood on the ground and put the bricks on top of that piece of wood and you start to pull or push the wood it wouldn't work because there is too much friction touching the ground from the wood to the ground so what you need is some wheels to put it on there so there is less friction and then you can pull it easier because of the wheels."

v) *Hybrid.* The roles described are not mutually-exclusive. For instance, children often combined an actor and a scientist role when they conducted self-generated experiments in which they were taking part, but that allowed them to walk through a problem and generate a possible solution. Such a hybrid role is illustrated in the example story: "So what I did was I had my skateboard and I pushed with myself on it, not very fast but it took 9 seconds to go to a full stop. And then I pushed it without me on it and it took ten seconds to stop."

RQ 2: Relationship with science learning

Vygotsky's framework was used to identify instances of spontaneous and scientific concepts in the children's stories. On average, a story contained 1.59 spontaneous concepts and 0.18 scientific concepts. 89% of the stories had only spontaneous concepts (e.g. "The socks were smooth and the wood was nice and smooth and there must have been less friction which is why I was gliding easily."). Surprisingly, no stories had only scientific concepts. Children would typically accompany a scientific concept with a spontaneous concept, for example, "If it weren't for friction everyday would be like walking down ice. [spontaneous concept] Friction happens when two surfaces are in contact and are trying to move passed each other, they catch and rub and slow each other down. [scientific concept]".

Relation to science: We found that the stories related to the science concept in 3 ways:

i) *the story emphasizes a characteristic or form related to the concept.* 59.3% of the stories addressed the science concept in that manner. An example would be a story that describes a 'type of friction': "I found one of my scientific research when Luke was sliding on the maroon leather couch it was friction but he glided very easily so I figured the leather couch must have been smooth even though he was a little rough so it must have been an in-between friction. Not a lot but not really a little";

ii) *the story describes an aspect of the process of the concept.* Only 1.1% of the story illustrated this approach. For example, the following story describes a process relating to gravity: "If you have a pulley and you are trying to lift something up that's crazy heavy all you need to do is have something heavier than the thing that you are trying to pull up. And once you like your strength so what you do is you pull one end of the rope and what you what it'll do is it'll lift up the other end."; and

iii) *the story relates the cause and/or effect of the concept.* 39.6% of the stories were in this category. For example, in the short story "So I was on the trampoline and I went up and gravity forced me down", the child related that the result of gravity was that she was pulled back down.

Goals of informal science learning: Our coding process of the science stories using the six strands of informal science learning as a framework revealed that the children engaged mostly (57.14% in Figure 4) in Strand 2. They were able to utilize what they know about science and apply it to understand what is around them. Strand 3 was also fairly common (32.97%). The children "manipulate[d], test[ed], explore[d]...and ma[de] sense of the natural and physical world". Strand 1 ("experience[ing] excitement, interest, and motivation to learn about phenomena in the natural and physical world) was scarcely seen (4.4%) explicitly in the recordings. We do not believe that this meant that the children were not excited or interested, but rather than they did not capture this metacognitive state verbally.

Moreover, only a few stories (4.4%) engaged Strand 4, where the children "reflect[ed] on science as a way of knowing". Even fewer stories (1.1%) discussed the children "partici-

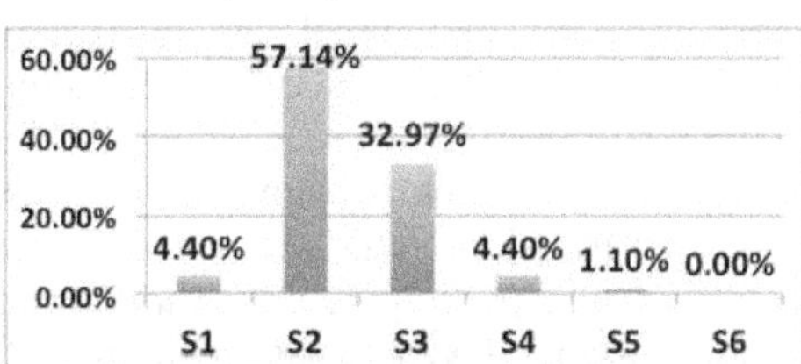

Figure 4. Strands of informal science learning results

pat[ing] in scientific activities and learning practices with others" (Strand 5). The most evident one was of a child participating in a science afterschool club. We did not find any instance of Strand 6 ("think about themselves as science learners and develop an identity as someone who knows about, uses, and sometimes contributes to science"). Although the activity of recording science stories in-the-wild may have helped to create a sense of science identity in the child, this was not apparent in the story analysis.

RQ 3: General user experience

Our coding of the interview transcripts from the children revealed numerous interesting themes with respect to the smartwatch storytelling experience:

A. Device awareness: Many of the children mentioned that they were bothered by others, including their friends and adults, asking about the smartwatch ("it was kind of annoying how many people asked me, is that your watch, why do you have that watch?");

B. Multi-function interface: Other functions of the smartwatch were accessible to the children during the study, although we did not mention any during the study briefing. While the variety of functions led to children accidentally pushing buttons that they did not mean to push, they also keenly explored other watch functions (e.g., steps, timer, stopwatch, music, heart rate, background settings);

C. Appropriateness for in-situ storytelling: There were indications that the smartwatch was suitable for anytime, anywhere storytelling. Particularly, children appreciated that they "can run in it" and that voice recording facilitated their storytelling because they "didn't have to write them down";

D. Perceptions of smartwatch science storytelling: The smartwatch for storytelling seemed to have encouraged reflection in the children on science-related issues, forcing them to figure out what to say ("kind of see what you could say about science like what you did and things"). Example quotes from the children are: "I didn't know that there was science in even more places than I thought that there was" and "science can um you may just look at something and go like oh it's just an object but science is really around you".

DISCUSSION

We were interested in whether children can use wearables, specifically smartwatches, to view their world and daily embodied experiences through the lens of science anytime, anywhere, and if so, how they would engage in the task. Understanding the types of stories that they capture and how the stories may or may not relate to science informs us on what needs to be paid attention to in the design of wearables apps to support science understanding for children. Wearable technology has opened up a whole new vista of possibilities with regard to informal science learning that was not conceivable with older technology, both in terms of research and practical applications. The higher cost and greater complexity of older technologies (e.g., smartphones, augmented reality, PDAs) has limited many prior studies to controlled settings (i.e., a child using the technology within a (set of) fixed location(s) and within a fixed timeframe), for example, Clegg et al. [51] providing children with tablets when they came in for a summer workshop.

The smartwatch stories that we obtained from the children were rich and fascinating. The types of stories from the smartwatches were akin to the 'micro-stories' common in microblogging (e.g., Twitter) and Web 2.0., but were slightly longer with somewhat of a narrative structure. The children adopted different roles as they captured science stories. While the data we collected did not allow us to derive any causal explanations for this, one hypothesis to explore would be the differences in personal epistemologies toward science among the children (see [52]) that may link to the types of roles that they adopt for science stories.

We saw that even with basic oral storytelling on the watch, the children began to see that many aspects of their everyday environment relate to science. They recorded science reflections in contexts where they would not have been able to without the watch (e.g., playing outdoors) either because of practical reasons (e.g., with mobile phones), or because they would not have been as 'science-aware'.

From our findings, we outline seven areas that merit much further research for the design of wearables apps that may effectively support children's informal science learning:

1) Encouraging in-situ reflection. Structures are needed in the smartwatch design to encourage scientific reflective acts by children. The task of smartwatch recording by itself was successful in having children take greater notice of their surroundings, as is evident by the high number of stories of the observation type. We were rather dissatisfied however that we did not see deeper or more extensive scientific analysis or inquiry. In the Quantified Self movement, statistics are typically presented on a dashboard that the user consults and reflects on after the fact. A relevant question thus is *how may the smartwatch be designed to encourage deeper scientific reflection and inquiry in the moment or immediately after the fact?*

2) Maintaining focus on science. In our study of two recording days, simple verbal instructions were sufficient to maintain the child's focus of recording on science. We do not know however whether this focus would endure over a longer study period. A relevant question is *what kinds of design features may help to ensure that the scope of recordings are related to a scientific concept of focus?*

3) Diversifying contexts of scientific inquiry. The primary contexts of recording were reflective of where children typically spend most of their time, i.e. at home and at school. There were instances of other contexts, but these were not as common as we expected. Looking at varied contexts through the lens of science has the potential to generate much richer understandings in terms of the presence of different artifacts, possible comparisons, etc. A relevant question is *how may the smartwatch be designed to enable scientific reflection and inquiry in diversified contexts?*

4) Involving others. Our study revealed that wearables are uncommon for children, although the health-focused activity trackers, FitBits, are increasingly seen on children. Adults question the use and appropriateness of wearables for children. The children even found the involvement of others as an intrusion or a "bother". There was a missed opportunity for them to see others as possible participants in their science inquiry. Much of the educational potential identified in microblogging is tied to the social and peer learning opportunities that it provides since all posts are viewable by one's followers [53]. A relevant question is *what kinds of structures are needed in the design of a smartwatch to encourage social or collaborative scientific inquiry and discussion in-place?*

5) Increasing motivation to record. A child recorded on average around 4 to 5 stories over two days. A challenge of sustained engagement has been noted with smartwatch use [54]. Users typically reported to discontinue use after the novelty factor wears off and the feel of the smartwatch recedes into the background. A relevant question thus is *what kinds of motivational design affordances can lead children to use the smartwatch as an educational tool for science learning over long periods of time?*

6) Leading to mindset formation. The smartwatch science storytelling task was successful to a certain extent in our study to help the children realize that science is useful in daily life. Nevertheless, the children relied mostly on their existing knowledge of the given scientific concept to observe, analyze and reflect on phenomena. Evidence of the children affirming themselves as a scientist with the possibility of contributing to knowledge was absent. While this may be due to the short duration of our study, a relevant question is *how may the smartwatch be designed to encourage children to see themselves as scientists with the ability to contribute new knowledge about the world?*

7) Eliminating usability issues. Various issues related to the usability of the smartwatch in terms of learning support were found. Notably, the children were distracted by other smartwatch functions, such as the footstep count, and accidental touches of the smartwatch on the move resulted in unwanted recordings.

CONCLUSION

We put forth that wearable technologies may enable a new form of informal science learning for children that we have only begun to explore. Our study using the basic audio recording function of a commodity smartwatch provided an initial picture of the kinds of science stories that children may use wearables for, and elucidated the potential of smartwatches to encourage children to see their world through science. It would be interesting to see whether the kinds of science stories that children capture change with the use of more multimedia-based functions. Our study was limited by the sample of students who participated, the short duration of the study, and the design idiosyncrasies of the specific smartwatch that we used. However, our findings allowed us to articulate directions for research in children's wearables for learning that future work may explore by bringing to bear many other relevant areas of HCI, such as critical design, reflective design, notification systems, etc.

REFERENCES

[1] Stem Education & Workforce. (2013). *STEM Crisis Page Stats and References*. Available: https://nms.org/Portals/0/Docs/STEM Crisis Page Stats and References.pdf

[2] B. D. Jones, "Motivating Students to Engage in Learning: The MUSIC Model of Academic Motivation," *International Journal of Teaching and Learning in Higher Education,* vol. 21, pp. 272-285, 2009.

[3] National Center for Science and Engineering Statistics, "Elementary and Secondary Mathematics and Science Education," National Science Foundation2014.

[4] M. Andrée, "Ways of using 'Everyday Life'in the science classroom," in *Research and the quality of science education*, ed: Springer, 2005, pp. 107-116.

[5] K. Mayoh and S. Knutton, "Using out-of-school experience in science lessons: reality or rhetoric?," *International Journal of Science Education,* vol. 19, pp. 849-867, 1997.

[6] J. Osborne, S. Simon, and S. Collins, "Attitudes towards science: A review of the literature and its implications," *International Journal of Science Education,* vol. 25, pp. 1049-1079, 2003/09/01 2003.

[7] L. M. Bouillion and L. M. Gomez, "Connecting school and community with science learning: real world problems and school–community partnerships as contextual scaffolds*," *Journal of research in science teaching,* vol. 38, pp. 878-898, 2001.

[8] S. Hsi, "Technology for Informal and Out-of-School Learning of Science," *Encyclopedia of Science Education,* pp. 1053-1055, 2015.

[9] H. T. Zimmerman, "Participating in science at home: Recognition work and learning in biology," *Journal of Research in Science Teaching,* vol. 49, pp. 597-630, 2012.

[10] Y. Song, L.-H. Wong, and C.-K. Looi, "Fostering personalized learning in science inquiry supported by mobile technologies," *Educational Technology Research and Development,* vol. 60, pp. 679-701, 2012.

[11] K. A. Riedinger, "Identity development of middle school students as learners of science at an informal science education camp," 2011.

[12] M. Braund and M. Reiss, "Towards a more authentic science curriculum: The contribution of out-of-school learning," *International Journal of Science Education,* vol. 28, pp. 1373-1388, 2006.

[13] P. Bell, B. Lewenstein, A. W. Shouse, and M. A. Feder, *Learning science in informal environments: People, places, and pursuits*: National Academies Press, 2009.

[14] R. Rawassizadeh, B. A. Price, and M. Petre, "Wearables: has the age of smartwatches finally arrived?," *Communications of the ACM,* vol. 58, pp. 45-47, 2014.

[15] W. Barfield and T. Caudell, "Basic concepts in wearable computers and augmented reality," *Fundamentals of wearable computers and augmented reality,* pp. 3-26, 2001.

[16] V. Dibia, "An Affective, Normative and Functional Approach to Designing User Experiences for Wearables," in *International Conference on Information Systems SIGHCI 2014 Proceedings, Auckland, New Zealand*, 2014.

[17] Apple. (2015, September 20th). *Apple Watch: To wear it is to love it*. Available: http://www.apple.com/watch/

[18] Nike. (2015, September 20th). *Nike+Fuelband.*

[19] Google. (2012, September 20th). *Glass*. Available: https://www.google.com/glass/start/

[20] Startefact. (2015, September 20th). *Purple: A locket for the 21st century*. Available: https://www.artefactgroup.com/content/work/purple-a-wearable-locket-for-the-21st-century/

[21] C. Boletsis, S. McCallum, and B. F. Landmark, "The Use of Smartwatches for Health Monitoring in Home-Based Dementia Care," in *Human Aspects of IT for the Aged Population. Design for Everyday Life*, ed: Springer, 2015, pp. 15-26.

[22] M. Bower and D. Sturman, "What are the educational affordances of wearable technologies?," *Computers & Education,* vol. 88, pp. 343-353, 2015.

[23] R. E. Gomez, T. Flanagan, and R. M. Davis, "Designing experiences with wearables: A case study exploring the blurring boundaries of art, design, technology, culture and distance," in *Proceedings of the 6th IASDR (The International Association of Societies of Design Research Congress)*, 2015, pp. 805-820.

[24] L. Buechley, M. Eisenberg, J. Catchen, and A. Crockett, "The LilyPad Arduino: using computational textiles to investigate engagement, aesthetics, and diversity in computer science education," in *Proceedings of the SIGCHI conference on Human factors in computing systems*, 2008, pp. 423-432.

[25] S. De Freitas and M. Levene, "Evaluating the development of wearable devices, personal data assistants and the use of other mobile devices in further and higher education institutions," *JISC Technology and Standards Watch Report,* pp. 1-21, 2003.

[26] R. Llorente and M. Morant, "Wearable Computers and Big Data: Interaction Paradigms for Knowledge Building in Higher Education," in *Innovation and Teaching Technologies*, ed: Springer, 2014, pp. 127-137.

[27] S. Park, I. Locher, A. Savvides, M. B. Srivastava, A. Chen, R. Muntz, *et al.*, "Design of a wearable sensor badge for smart kindergarten," in *Wearable Computers, 2002.(ISWC 2002). Proceedings. Sixth International Symposium on*, 2002, pp. 231-238.

[28] P. M. Scholl, M. Wille, and K. Van Laerhoven, "Wearables in the wet lab: a laboratory system for capturing and guiding experiments," in *Proceedings of the 2015 ACM International Joint Conference on Pervasive and Ubiquitous Computing*, 2015, pp. 589-599.

[29] T. Hall and L. Bannon, "Designing ubiquitous computing to enhance children's learning in museums," *Journal of Computer Assisted Learning,* vol. 22, pp. 231-243, 2006.

[30] S. Consolvo, K. Everitt, I. Smith, and J. A. Landay, "Design requirements for technologies that encourage physical activity," in *Proceedings of the SIGCHI conference on Human Factors in computing systems*, 2006, pp. 457-466.

[31] V. R. Lee and J. Drake, "Quantified recess: design of an activity for elementary students involving analyses of their own movement data," in *Proceedings of the 12th international conference on interaction design and children*, 2013, pp. 273-276.

[32] V. R. Lee, "What's happening in the" Quantified Self" movement?," *ICLS 2014 Proceedings,* pp. 1032-1036, 2014.

[33] V. Lee, *Learning technologies and the body: Integration and implementation in formal and informal learning environments* vol. 135: Routledge, 2015.

[34] D. Pauw, T. Clegg, J. Ahn, E. Bonsignore, J. Yip, and J. Uchidiuno, "Navigating connected inquiry learning with ScienceKit," in *Eleventh International Conference on Computer Supported Collaborative Learning, Gothenburg, Sweden, June*, 2015, pp. 7-11.

[35] J. Lave and E. Wenger, *Situated Learning : Legitimate Peripheral Participation*, 1st ed. Cambridge: Cambridge University Press, 1991.

[36] H.-S. Lee and N. Butler, "Making authentic science accessible to students," *International Journal of Science Education,* vol. 25, pp. 923-948, 2003.

[37] L. A. Bricker and P. Bell, "“What comes to mind when you think of science? The perfumery!”: Documenting science-related cultural learning pathways across contexts and timescales," *Journal of Research in Science Teaching,* vol. 51, pp. 260-285, 2014.

[38] M. Wilson, "Six views of embodied cognition," *Psychonomic bulletin & review,* vol. 9, pp. 625-636, 2002.

[39] S. Harnad, "The symbol grounding problem," *Physica D: Nonlinear Phenomena,* vol. 42, pp. 335-346, 1990.

[40] F. Quek, "Embodiment: We're Just Human," in *CHI 2011 Workshop on Embodied Interaction: Theory and Practice in HCI*, Vancouver, British Columbia, 2011.

[41] H. Hedges, "Vygotsky's phases of everyday concept development and the notion of children's “working theories”," *Learning, Culture and Social Interaction,* vol. 1, pp. 143-152, 2012.

[42] J. Piaget and B. Inhelder, *Memory and intelligence.* London: Routledge and Kegan Paul, 1973.

[43] J. Bruner, "The Narrative Construction of Reality," *Critical Inquiery,* vol. 18, pp. 1-21, 1991.

[44] J. S. Bruner, *Actual minds, possible worlds*: Harvard University Press, 2009.

[45] R. A. Mar, "The neuropsychology of narrative: Story comprehension, story production and their interrelation," *Neuropsychologia,* vol. 42, pp. 1414-1434, 2004.

[46] J. Szurmak and M. Thuna, "Tell me a story: The use of narrative as a tool for instruction," *Indianapolis, IN,* pp. 546-552, 2013.

[47] L. S. Vygotsky, Ed., *Thought and Language, (Edited and translated by E. Hanfmann and G. Vakar)* Cambridge: MIT Press, 1987, p.^pp. Pages.

[48] P. Wellings, "Title," unpublished|.

[49] T.-Y. Mou, T.-S. Jeng, and C.-H. Chen, "From storyboard to story: Animation content development," *Educational Research and Reviews,* vol. 8, p. 1032, 2013.

[50] J. Saldaña, *The coding manual for qualitative researchers*, 2nd ed.: Sage, 2012.

[51] T. Clegg, E. Bonsignore, J. Yip, H. Gelderblom, A. Kuhn, T. Valenstein*, et al.*, "Technology for promoting scientific practice and personal meaning in life-relevant learning," in *Proceedings of the 11th International Conference on Interaction Design and Children*, 2012, pp. 152-161.

[52] D. L. Medin and M. Bang, "The cultural side of science communication," *Proceedings of the National Academy of Sciences,* vol. 111, pp. 13621-13626, 2014.

[53] F. Gao, T. Luo, and K. Zhang, "Tweeting for learning: A critical analysis of research on microblogging in education published in 2008–2011," *British Journal of Educational Technology,* vol. 43, pp. 783-801, 2012.

[54] V. Dibia. (2015). *An Affective, Normative and Functional Approach to Designing User Experiences for Wearables*. Available: http://dx.doi.org/10.2139/ssrn.2630715

FoldMecha: Exploratory Design and Engineering of Mechanical Papercraft

Hyunjoo Oh[1] Jeeeun Kim[2] Cory Morales[2] Mark D. Gross[1,2] Michael Eisenberg[2] Sherry Hsi[3]
[1]ATLAS Institute [2]Computer Science
University of Colorado Boulder
Boulder Colorado USA
{hyunjoo.oh, jeeeun.kim, cory.morales, mdgross, duck}@colorado.edu
[3]Concord Consortium
Emeryville CA USA
shsi@concord.org

ABSTRACT

We present *FoldMecha*, a computer-aided design (CAD) system for exploratory construction of mechanical papercraft. FoldMecha enables students to (a) design their own movements with simple mechanisms by modifying parameters and (b) build physical prototypes. This paper describes the system, as well as associated prototyping methods that make the construction process easier and more adaptable to widely different creations. The paper also discusses a week-long workshop that we held with six teenagers using FoldMecha. The teens successfully designed and built their own mechanisms, and adapted them to a variety of creations. Throughout the workshop, they progressively achieved an advanced level of skill and understanding about mechanical movements.

Author Keywords

Computer-aided design (CAD); tangible learning; learning by making; exploratory construction

ACM Classification Keywords

H.5.2 [Information interfaces and presentation]: User Interfaces – Input devices and Strategies, Interaction styles; K.3.1 [Computers and Education]: Computers Uses in Education

INTRODUCTION

What distinguishes tangible interaction from screen-based interaction is physical embodiment. Many instances of tangible interaction employ sensors and actuators embedded into pre-existing physical objects or environments, and therefore require little expertise in physical design and construction. In many others, on the other hand, the design and construction of the physical embodiment is essential to the interaction.

Conventional CAD tools are well-suited to designing physical embodiments of simple and static objects–e.g., embedding electronics into an object of furniture. However, when the device itself has mechanical behavior, conventional tools challenge even experienced designers. Despite the reduced burdens of calculation, modeling, and hand skills that current CAD tools provide, designing and building mechanical models still remains demanding. It requires understanding mechanical movements, visualizing relationships between component mechanisms, and accurately predicting the behavior of these mechanical systems.

We developed *FoldMecha*, an experimental software system to design movements for mechanical papercrafts. Exploratory construction is a springboard for creative learning [16], and the FoldMecha tool is intended to support this type of playful construction. Using FoldMecha, beginners can (a) design movements by modifying individual components; (b) download parts to cut, (c) build mechanical prototypes using the assembly instructions, and (d) apply those prototypes in their own creations. Our mechanisms are implemented in paper because paper is lightweight, malleable, aesthetically appealing, and inexpensive, and it can be worked with simple craft tools. In developing FoldMecha and associated fabrication methods, we considered accessibility (whether students can use FoldMecha and the methods) and adaptability (whether the tool and methods are sufficiently open to support novel and original designs).

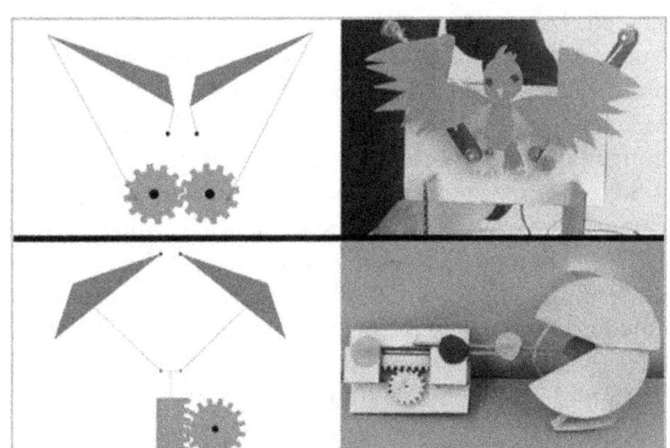

Figure 1. FoldMecha supports users to design mechanical movements by changing parameters, construct the physical models using the parts and folding nets the system generates, and adapt the movements to implement their creative ideas.

TEI '17, March 20-23, 2017, Yokohama, Japan

DOI: http://dx.doi.org/10.1145/3024969.3024991

In the remainder of this paper, we first describe design and fabrication using FoldMecha, and the philosophy behind its development. We then describe a mechanical papercraft workshop with six middle school girls in which we evaluated the accessibility and adaptability of the system and prototyping methods. We conclude with findings from the workshop and reflect on how the tool and methods support our design goal.

RELATED WORK

In developing FoldMecha we draw on three areas of related work: computer-aided design for crafting, construction kits, and learning by making. We describe prominent work in these fields that influenced the design of FoldMecha.

Computer-aided design for crafting

Working with physical materials—learning "through one's hands"—need not be opposed to computation [4]. In the area of mechanical crafting, researchers have built computational tools to both elicit and support a designer's intent by simulating a (presumed) target construction on the screen, and by producing materials for the physical, hands-on phase of construction. A widely used approach is automatic (computer-driven) configuration of mechanical designs. For instance, to synthesize motions into mechanical toys, Zhu *et al.* [23] enabled users to simulate mechanical toys. The user specifies geometry and motion of the toy, then the system selects an appropriate configuration of assemblies from its library to optimize part parameters. In a similar vein, Megaro *et al.* [9] and Coros *et al.* [3, 20] helped users to create a design by drawing the desired movement as a 2D curve on the computer screen. Other software like AutoGami also supports users in selecting movement types to apply to movable papercraft design. The system then actuates the papercraft using shape memory alloy wire and selective inductive power transmission [22]. In these automatic-configuration systems, users *specify* desired behaviors, and the system *generates* a mechanism to produce that behavior; the designer need not be concerned with how the behavior is produced. In contrast, in developing FoldMecha, we aimed to support open-ended creative work, where novice users explore and understand the relations of various local components that generate a mechanical movement, and then incrementally specify their design. In this sense, our system is a bottom-up system that does not automate synthesis but assists the experimental design and learning process. FoldMecha can be seen as an application (in the mechanical realm) of the ideas of Schulz *et al.* [19], whose system enabled users to select a 3D model from an expert-authored database and customize it by modifying parameters. Although FoldMecha similarly supports beginners by providing a set of parameterized templates, we focus on mechanical craft applying certain movements. Whereas previous work simulated static objects, in FoldMecha interactive simulations animate how the movement changes by varying local components.

Construction kits

Diverse construction kits enable designers to experiment with or—as Schön poetically puts it—to engage in a "reflective conversation with the materials of a design situation" [18]. For instance, fischertechnik [5], Capsela [2], MOSS [10], and Tinkerbots [21] afford direct manipulation of the components of a mechanical assembly. A designer can configure components of a mechanism and investigate the behavior of the ensemble. When the parameters of the kit components match the designer's goals, construction kits are an effective way to work. Yet the very features of a construction kit that make it a fast and easy way to explore a design space also make it suboptimal for some tasks. Components are of specific sizes and functions; they assemble only on a modular grid and the kit is a closed system. In this sense, making mechanical movements with a construction kit is a devil's bargain: designers can quickly build complex configurations as long as they stay within the system, but they cannot customize the kit of parts. FoldMecha addresses this issue by supporting users at a more fundamental level. In FoldMecha, users design their own mechanical behavior and generate parts to build and customize it using craft tools and materials.

Learning by making

The iterative process of design and engineering–in short, making–enables one to imagine, play, create, tinker, share, reflect, and learn relevant concepts. Ratto [15] described "critical making" as a theoretical and pragmatic method to connect critical thinking and physical making. He stated the importance of bridging bodily experience with abstract knowledge—wrestling with technical prototypes and exploring various configurations and alternatives. Keune *et al.* [7] also highlighted how material artifacts promote learning. They described the flexibility of artifacts, which is linked to pliability, accessibility, and mobility and is important to support boundary crossing. Similarly, Resnick and Rosenbaum [17] presented design guidelines for tinkerable kits: immediate feedback, fluid experimentation, and open exploration. They described tinkering as a playful style of designing and making things (regardless whether physical or virtual) to learn to improvise, adapt, and iterate. Inspired by these frameworks, and to enable open-ended exploration, we developed the FoldMecha software, in which users design mechanical movements by changing parameters in order to imagine and build various physical creations. We believe that this process can provide opportunities to understand the basics of mechanical movement, but also support creative learning.

FOLDMECHA DESIGN AND FABRICATION PIPELINE

FoldMecha is a bottom-up computational system to support interactive exploratory design and engineering for moveable mechanical paper crafts. Figures 2 and 3 summarize the FoldMecha workflow.

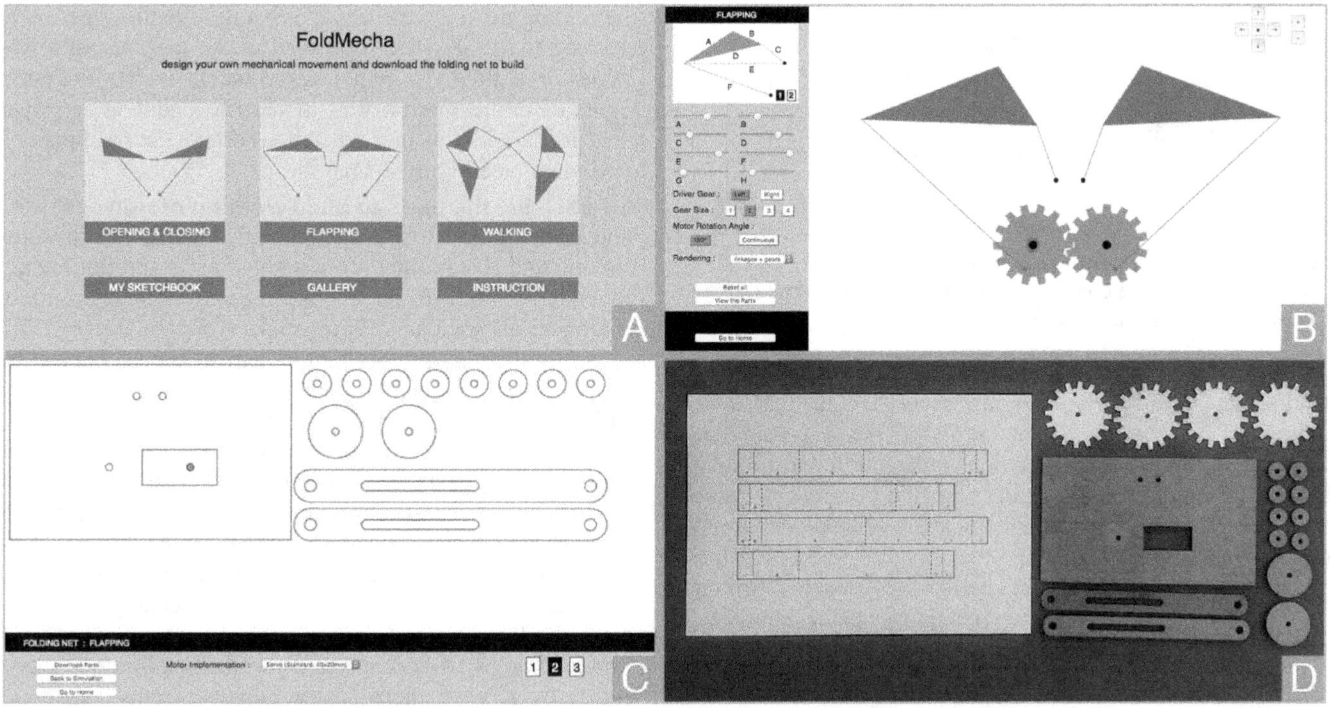

Figure 2. User workflow in flapping movement: (A) The splash page catalogs individual movements; (B) Simulation interacting with local parameters; (C) System-generated parts (D); Cut and printed parts and folding net for physical construction.

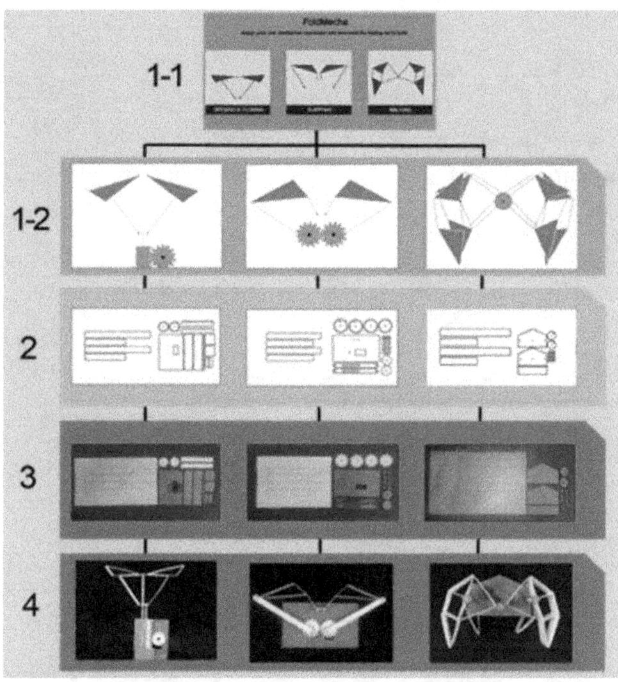

Figure 3. Steps in making a paper machine: (1-1) select a movement; (1-2) change parameters; (2) customize parts; (3) print and cut the files; (4) build working prototypes.

1. Parameterized individual movements

FoldMecha's splash page (figure 2-A) shows an animated catalog of three individual movements: opening-closing, flapping, and walking. Choosing one brings a user to that movement's design page, which shows a parameterized simulation, with options and parameters on the left panel (figure 2-B). The opening-closing movement is made with linkages connected to a rack and pinion mechanism, a pair of gears that convert rotation into linear motion. The flapping movement is made with linkages connected to two identical interlocking gears that turn in opposite directions. The walking movement is a variant on Theo Jansen's 'Strandbeest' mechanism [6]: a strut configuration comprising two triangles and two quadrilaterals.

Users can explore a variety of designs for arms (opening and closing), wings (flapping), or legs (walking) using sliders to vary geometric parameters of the linkages. In the walking movement, users can add pairs of legs, which the Jansen mechanism uses to generate a crab-like motion. In specifying each movement, users select a gear size from 1 to 4 by pressing buttons. Larger gears generate more dynamic movement. The user can also add a motor to drive the mechanism, leading to further options. For instance, in the opening and closing movement, the user must select the motor type (continuous or alternating 180° rotation), which adjusts the gear design (see Figure 4). The continuous rotation version has teeth removed from the pinion gear, allowing the rack to drop suddenly on each full turn when the untoothed section of the gear comes around. In the flapping movement, which includes two gears, users must specify which gear drives and which is driven; this determines a location to embed a motor in the following step. In all movements, users can also set rendering parameters (whether to display both gears and linkages, only gears, or only linkages).

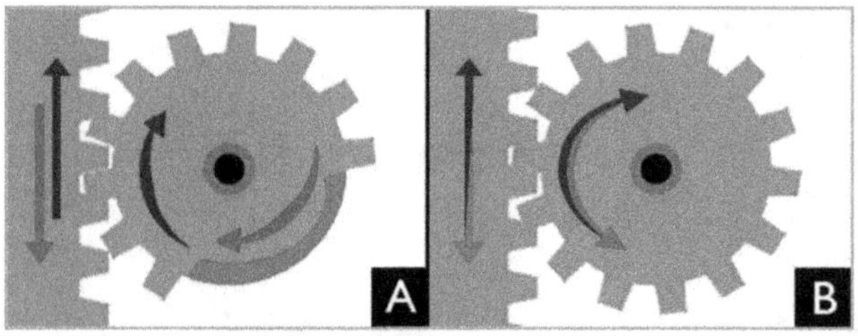

Figure 4. Motor type affects gear design. Depending on the motor, FoldMecha changes the simulation and parts: (A) continuous rotation (B) 180° alternating rotation of gears.

2. Customize the parts and folding net

After selecting and parameterizing, users view the parts and folding net by pressing "View the Parts" (see Figure 2-C). Here, users specify conditions for construction and modify the parts and folding net, deciding about motor implementation, motor size, and thickness of linkages (arms, wings, or legs). Specifying the opening and closing movement entails setting the number of linkages, which modifies the bottom part of the arms. For instance, choosing three linkages makes the bottom figure an equilateral triangle; choosing five produces a regular pentagon.

In order to simplify construction, we produce paper folding net templates. Once the design is done, FoldMecha generates a drawing of folding net strips with marked folding locations. Then users print, cut, and fold the strips following instructions to build the basic linkage modules [11, 12]. Figure 5 shows the folding instructions to form paper strips into an arm, a wing, and a leg.

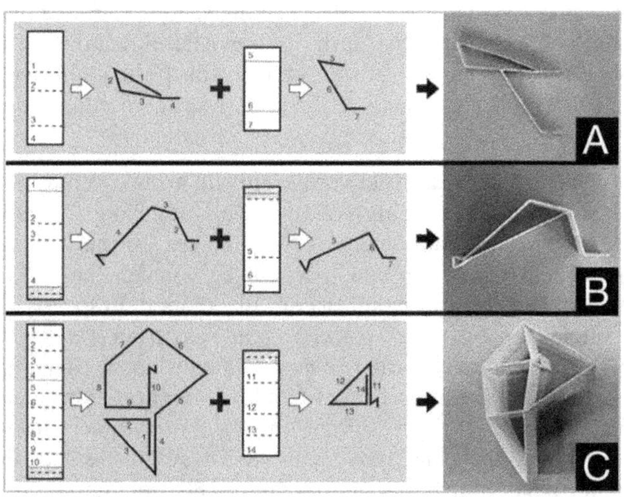

Figure 5. Dashed and dotted lines indicate mountain and valley folds respectively. Folding generates moving joints and unfolded faces become linkages: (A) an arm for opening and closing, (B) a wing for flapping, and (C) a leg for walking.

3. Print and cut PDF files

Once all parts have been specified, the user requests PDF files by pressing "Download Parts". The system generates three separate files: gears for 'high resolution' rigid material such as mat board that can be accurately cut; parts and stands for any rigid material such as cardboard; and stick figures of the folding net to create linkages using foldable paper. After creating the PDF files, the user can cut parts using a laser cutter or a hobbyist paper cutter such as the Silhouette Cameo. For the latter, hand skills are needed to attach layers of gears carefully as these machines do not cut rigid paper or cardboard (see Figure 2-D).

4. Assemble the parts to build working prototypes

The critical part of building mechanical crafts lies in setting moving and fixed joints. To assemble parts and folding nets generated in FoldMecha, the user employs simple craft tools and materials such as lollipop sticks (or wood dowels). The assembly instruction provided as part of the accompanying learning materials explains how to adjust lollipop sticks in multiple places to connect the various parts and the stand. For instance, the assembly instruction for the flapping movement suggests applying lollipop sticks to stand to connect linkages and other parts to connect with gears and linkages, and to attach gears to the stand (see Figure 6). Also, the assembly instruction suggests attaching two layers of gear parts to strengthen the gear teeth. Especially in building gears for flapping and walking movements, this sandwich structure helps to add a space to attach lollipop sticks to gears. Even with these instructions, students still found opportunities to play and tinker with their papercrafts and make adaptations and refinements to their originally conceived idea.

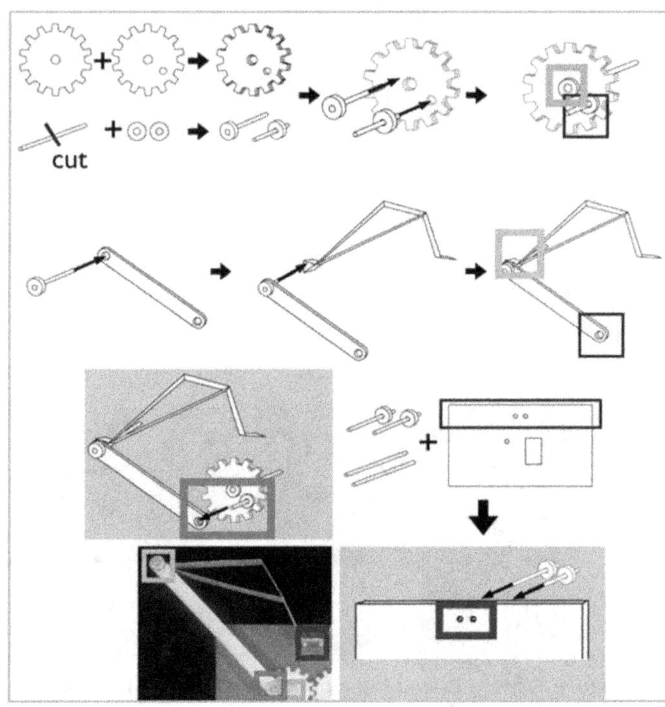

Figure 6. Craft-friendly materials enhance accessibility and adaptability. Lollipop sticks connect gears and linkages.

Design rationale

Our goal is to develop a design tool and methods to support exploratory construction of mechanical papercraft for beginners. To this end, our design decisions respond to two questions of accessibility and adaptability:

1) *Accessibility*: Can students use FoldMecha to construct mechanical papercraft?
2) *Adaptability*: Can they use FoldMecha to be inventive and go beyond examples they are given?

FoldMecha to see the big picture of movements

We wanted users to explore and understand relationships between component mechanisms and their impact on the whole movement. Therefore interactive simulation is a key strategy to engage and support the users. In addition, by providing parts and folding nets for construction, FoldMecha reduces the burdens of calculating and modeling. We also considered generality (abstractness) of movement modules to be applied to widely different ideas.

Prototyping methods to ease and diversify constructions

We tried to simplify the construction process to reduce any barriers to hands-on prototyping, for example, printing paper strips with marked folding lines to generate linkages. We also considered easy manipulation by craft tools and materials. This availability of the craft materials is essential to support iterative construction and encourage active integration with individual and personal creations.

MECHANICAL PAPERCRAFT WORKSHOP

We conducted three workshop sessions with six middle school girls to evaluate the accessibility and adaptability of FoldMecha and associated prototyping methods. We recruited students (ages 11-14) from a university based summer camp program. None had relevant previous experience in mechanical design. In prior workshops, a "rhythm board" was provided to control the speed of servos and solenoids without the need for prior knowledge of electronics or programming [13]. In this workshop basic Arduino coding was introduced and included in the workshop lessons.

Workshop structure

Our workshop met on five consecutive days in 4-5 hour sessions. On the first day we showed examples of mechanical papercraft to introduce the week-long curriculum and engaged students in a warm-up exercise learning to control a 180-degree range servo motor using a microcontroller and to change the speed and the rotation range by modifying example code in Arduino [1]. Then on each of the following two days, we introduced a specific movement theme: open-close movement using a rack and pinion mechanism—a pair of gears that convert rotational motion (by a pinion gear) to linear motion (by a rack gear), and flapping movement using two identical interlocking rotational gears. Then for the last two days, students designed their own machines, combining movements they learned. We included only 180-degree-range servomotors. After each session we asked students to reflect on what they learned, how their creations work, their inspirations in applying each movement to their own creations, and challenges they faced.

We divided the studio into several stations: A design station with laptop computers to design parts in FoldMecha and program microcontrollers in Arduino to control servomotors, a glue-gun station, and a cutting-station. A shared material table provided various craft materials (color papers and pens, tapes, wood dowels, glittery glues, et cetera). We also provided a wireless ink-jet printer, a white board and a projector connected to the instructor's desktop computer.

During the workshop, participants used individual laptops, with FoldMecha and Arduino installed. After finishing the design of their movements, participants transferred files to the instructor's computer, which we printed on A3 paper. Each file showed the file names and the selected gear size; we provided the selected gears (which we had precut). Then participants attached their case and parts to cardboard, and cut their parts by hand; they also cut and folded the printed linkage paper files. We provided printed instructions to assemble each movement (both open-close and flapping) as well as video instruction only for flapping movement.

Results

First session: building an open-close movement

During the first (open-close movement) session every participant used FoldMecha to design a movement. Five students among six built working mechanical papercrafts and four applied the movement to make wings, mouth or leaves; two students struggled to imagine and find an application for the open-close movement.

Second session: building a flapping movement

Likewise, in the second session, all participants started by designing movements in FoldMecha. Students took more time in design than in the first session as they started thinking about what to build (how to apply the movement). Some students started by selecting a gear size and modifying linkage proportions to reflect a specific machine they planned to build. Every participant built a working mechanical papercraft.

In the workflow of the second session, participants were more confident and fluent in using FoldMecha and craft tools (box-cutters, glue-guns, etc.). Also, in the second session we provided video instruction along with the printed instructions (building a flapping movement) and minimized individual explanations. The video instruction was more helpful, as students watched it at their own pace.

Third session: inventing your own machine

For the last two days, students invented, designed and built their own machines by combining mechanical components. Figure 8 shows what students built. Machines A and B are complete and machines C, D, E, and F are works-in-progress. In (A) a fish swims in the sea: as the motor-driven pinion gear turns, the rack gear produces linear motion that makes the fish's fins connected to linkages move back and forth. In (B) a Tyrannosaurus-rex opens and closes its mouth as its baby jumps up and down: the rack produces

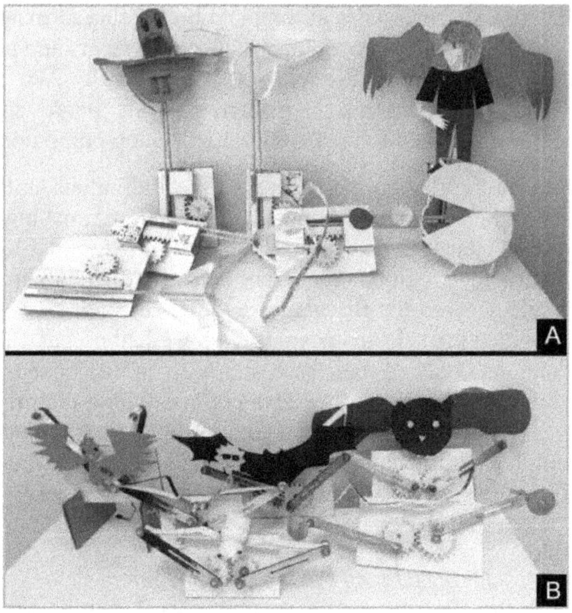

Figure 7. Participants applied movements to working mechanical papercraft: (A) open-close, and (B) flapping.

linear motion, using linkages to open and close the T-rex's mouth while the baby T-rex attached to the other side of the rack jumps. Machine (C) is a pterodactyl, animated by a rack gear connected with two pinion gears and two additional gears one for each side. (The student planned to add a pair of wings to the two bottom rotational gears and attach the head of the pterodactyl to the rack). Machine (D) is a big bird: the student planned to add a pair of wings to the flapping movement and attach the rack and pinion at the front to combine up and down motion with flapping. (E) is a woman waving her arms: two identical gears interlock with arms attached to the linkages. (The student planned to attach the body to the center). In the Dancing Ballerina (F): the motor-embedded pinion gear produces linear motion on the right side rack while another pinion gear rotates in the opposite direction, triggering another linear motion on the left side. (The student planned to attach the body of the ballerina on the center with arms on each rack moving up and down.) Throughout the two days, students were deeply engaged in the design process and presented presented their ideas confidently. In the reflection interviews, those who didn't complete their constructions emphasized that the they were presenting work in progress and explained the rest of their ambitious plans.

WORKSHOP FINDINGS

Open-close is a better designed module than flapping

FoldMecha aims to support beginners to design and build their own constructions by adapting and applying mechanical movements. Therefore, the range of outcomes was the criterion to gauge adaptability, whether each movement module was sufficiently flexible to diverse designs. By this criterion, the open-close movement is a better module than the flapping movement. Students interpreted the open-close movement in more ways than the flapping movement (see Figure 7). Five students applied the flapping motion as wings and made a kind of bird (bat, gull, owl, etc.) whereas students interpreted the open-close movement into more dynamically different ways such as a Pac-man mouth, angel wings or a bluebird. That is, abstractness of a movement was linked to creative interpretations.

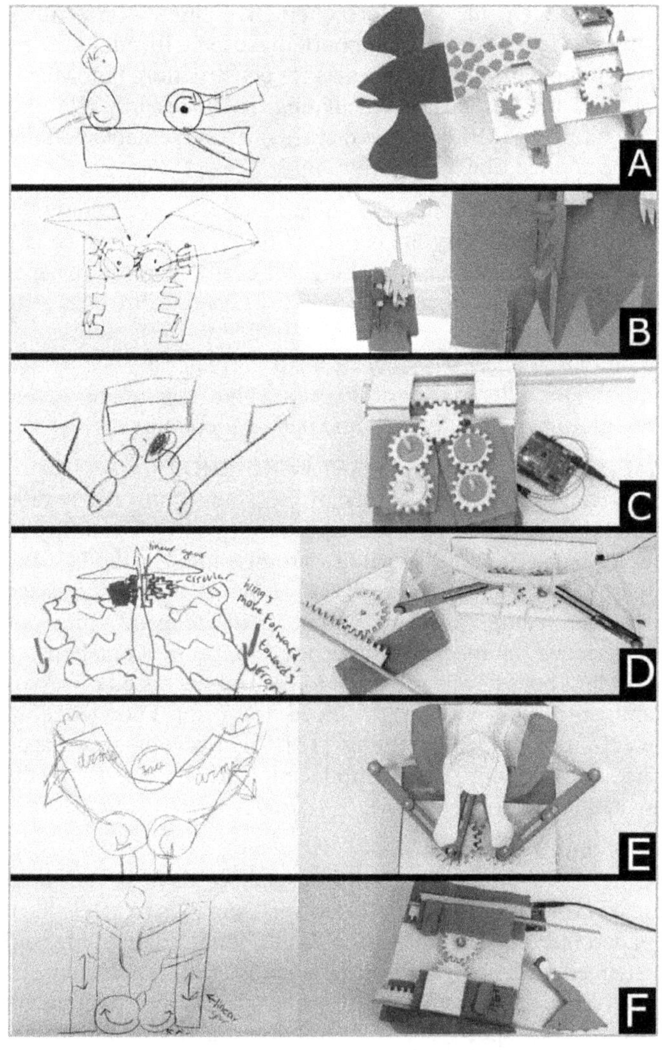

Figure 8. The third session combined multiple mechanical components to create their own mechanical inventions: idea sketches (left) and the workshop outcomes (right).

Craft materials enhance accessibility and adaptability

The material properties of mat board (used for gears) and cardboard enabled students to experiment as they built their own mechanical movements; this was important especially in the third session. Students cut and glued mat board and cardboard, modifying the parts in order to build the movement, which was more complicated than the first two movements and lacked assembly instructions. For instance, one student, an 11-year-old girl, realized that the given rack gear was too short to interlock two rotational gears (see Figure 8-A), and attached two rack gears next to a long wood dowel and cut it to the length she needed. Also students who employed two rack gears (Figure 8-B, 8-F) needed to customize the case to add a track to keep a rack gear in position to interlock with a pinion gear. Both students successfully built the movement by attaching extra cardboard to match the height of gears.

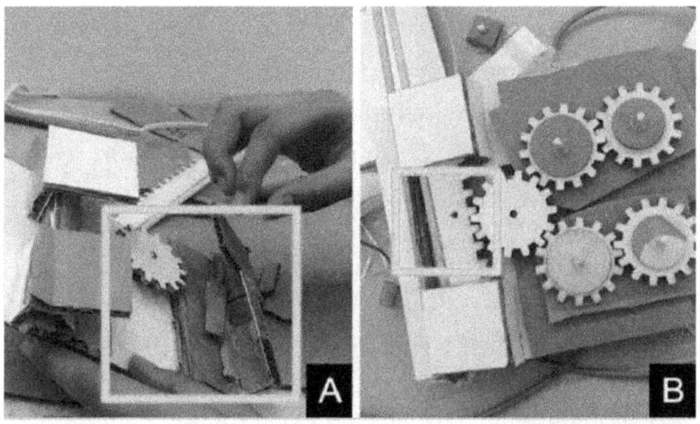

Figure 9. Craft materials encouraged tinkering to build mechanical movements: (A) adding a track by attaching small cardboard pieces to interlock two rack gears with the center pinion gear, and (B) adding another hole to set a wood dowel.

Expressivity of craft materials increases adaptability

Our FoldMecha workshop on building mechanical papercraft aimed to integrate mechanical design with rich crafting expression. Student integrated mechanical movements with drawing (Figures 10-A, E, F), decorating (Figure 10-B), outlining with glittery glue (Figure 10-C), and attaching to other objects made of tape with beads (Figure 10-D) or wood dowels (Figure 10-F). As their expressive explorations were closely linked to the tools and materials available in the studio, we expect that providing more tools and materials would have increased the spectrum of expressivity of the outcomes. Also, the one-week workshop format could limit student opportunities to mix, combine, and adapt multiple movements to create even more expressive forms and thus we plan to explore longer periods of design exploration.

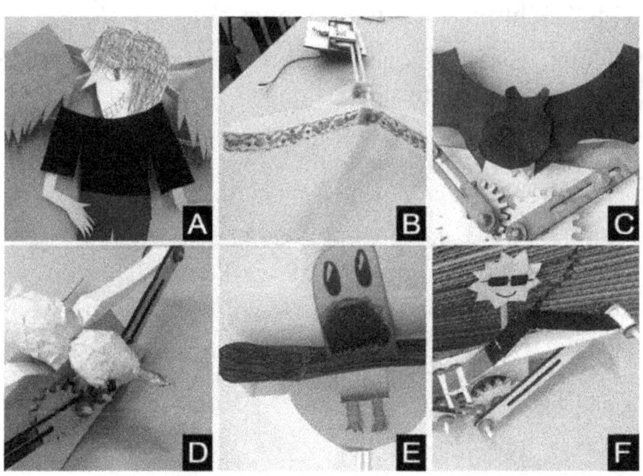

Figure 10. Craft materials invite expressions such as drawing, coloring, cutting, and attaching additional objects.

Digital tool for a big picture of mechanical movement and physical prototyping to strengthen understanding

Different media supported learning in its own affordances. As author Malcolm McCullough [8] writes, "Whereas hands feel their way one piece at a time, eyes see wholes, and compare many objects simultaneously" (p. 31). Design with interactive simulation in FoldMecha initiated understanding mechanical movements by modifying local parameters that impact the whole movement. Physical prototyping specified and strengthened this understanding. Using FoldMecha, students observed how varying gear sizes or linkage lengths affects the movement and this influenced their design decisions. Specifically, during the second (flapping movement) session, a 13-year-old girl who decided to build a bat selected size 4 gears and designed a long linkage. She said that she made design decisions "to make the bat fly more dynamically" like the bats that she saw on her family vacation. At the same time, some students did not quite understand the relation between pulling and pushing in the physical world: A common mistake on the first day was to attach the rack to the case, and then wonder how to make it move. As students built physical movements by hands-on prototyping, they returned to the FoldMecha application and compared their prototypes to the simulation. One 12-year-old girl who built a Pac-man figure using the open-close movement on the first day reflected, "I might have needed to select a bigger gear to be able to entirely close the mouth of the Pac-man."

Gradual shift from beginning to advanced level

The weeklong workshop enabled students to gradually attain an advanced level of skill. They not only started describing the movements, which they planned to build in more detail by confidently taking specific poses and gestures; they also illustrated how to implement these movements mechanically. Reflecting on the third session, one student described her project by distinguishing forward from vertical flapping and illustrated how she planned to connect the linear movement by a rack and pinion to the flapping movement to create a bird-like flying forward and up-and-down movement (See Figure 11-A). Another girl, a dancer, presented a machine to make a ballerina jump and take a stretching arm pose (Figure 11-B). Another made rotational hand-gestures to describe how she made the arms of her construction wave, and talked about how she wants to add more gears to connect the legs (Figure 11-C).

Overall, this progress influenced students to spend more time planning and to stick with their initial ideas. In the first two sessions, rather than change their mechanical design structure to build what they planned, they instead changed their ideas to use the mechanism they had chosen. However, in the third session they designed the completed movement more quickly and avoided drastic modifications to the basic movement structure.

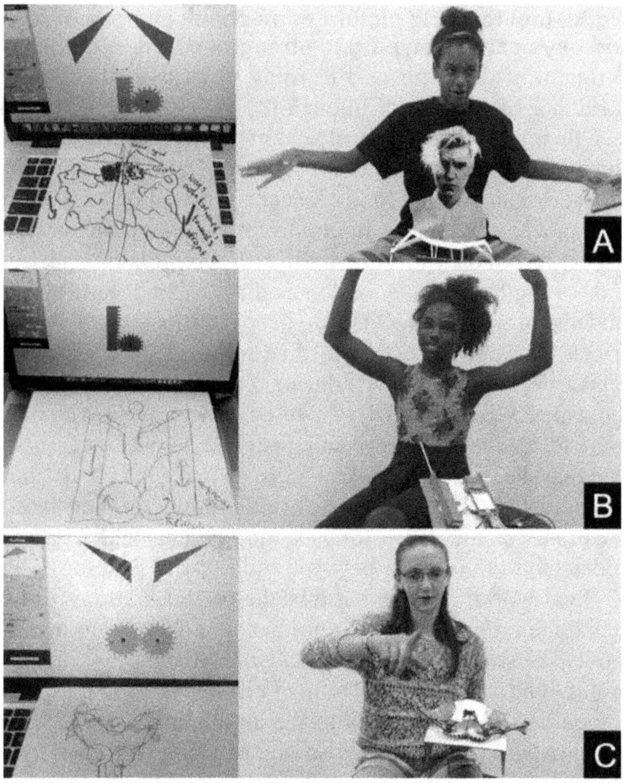

Figure 11. In the final session students presented project ideas more accurately by taking specific poses and gestures to describe the machines they designed.

CONCLUSION

FoldMecha is a computer-aided design system that supports exploratory construction of mechanical papercraft. It enables beginners to design their own movements by varying component parameters and build physical prototypes using the system-generated parts and folding nets. We developed simple folding nets to build linkages and employed craft materials for the parts to make the prototyping process easy to follow and tinker. This accessibility also increased adaptability to be integrated with various expressive creations. We conducted a week-long workshop with six middle school students to test the accessibility and adaptability of the FoldMecha design tool and its prototyping methods. Students were highly engaged in the design process and successfully designed and built their own mechanical papercrafts and actively adapt to a variety of creations. They also showed gradual progression on their understanding about mechanical movements.

We believe that consciously designed tools and methods can widen the gate of exploratory construction that ultimately promotes "powerful ideas" (in Papert's [14] famous phrase) for young learners. This paper presents our progress in developing FoldMecha and associated prototyping methods, to address how to lower the burdens of design and engineering for novices (accessibility) and how to extend the diversity of creations (adaptability).

ACKNOWLEDGMENTS

We thank Nichole Pinkard and her students and staff of the digital youth divas (http://digitalyouthnetwork.org/divas/) for their active participation and kind support. This material is partly based upon work supported by the National Science Foundation under Grant No. IS1451463.

REFERENCES

1. Arduino: https://www.arduino.cc
2. Capsela: https://en.wikipedia.org/wiki/Capsela
3. Coros, S., Thomaszewski, B., Noris, G., Sueda, S., Forberg, M., Robert W. Sumner, Wojciech Matusik, and Bernd Bickel. 2013. Computational design of mechanical characters. *ACM Trans. Graph.* 32, 4, Article 83 (July 2013).
4. Eisenberg, M.; Eisenberg, A.; Gross, M.; Kaowthumrong, K.; Lee, N.; and Lovett, W. 2002. Computationally-Enhanced Construction Kits for Children: Prototype and Principles. International Conference of the Learning Sciences (ICLS), 79-85.
5. Fischertechnik: http://www.fischertechnik.de/
6. Jansen, Theo: http://www.strandbeest.com/
7. Keune, A., Gomoll, A., and Peppler, K. 2015. Flexibility to learn: Material artifacts in makerspaces. Paper presented at the fifth annual FabLearn Conference: Equity and Diversity in Making. Palo Alto, CA: Stanford University.
8. McCullough, M. 1996. *Abstracting Craft: The Practiced Digital Hand.* MIT Press, Cambridge, MA
9. Megaro, V., Thomaszewski, B., Gauge, D., Grinspun, E., Coros, S., and Gross, M. 2015. ChaCra: an interactive design system for rapid character crafting. In *Proceedings of the ACM SIGGRAPH/Eurographics Symposium on Computer Animation* (SCA '14). Eurographics Association, Aire-la-Ville, Switzerland, Switzerland, 123-130.
10. MOSS: http://www.modrobotics.com/moss/
11. Oh, H., Eisenberg, H., Gross, M.D., and Hsi, S. 2015. Paper mechatronics: a design case study for a young medium. In *Proceedings of the 14th International Conference on Interaction Design and Children* (IDC '15). ACM, New York, NY, USA, 371-374.
12. Oh, H., Gross, M.D., and Eisenberg, M. 2015. FoldMecha: Design for Linkage-Based Paper Toys. In *Adjunct Proceedings of the 28th Annual ACM Symposium on User Interface Software & Technology* (UIST '15 Adjunct). ACM, New York, NY, USA, 91-92.
13. Oh, H., Harriman, J., Narula, A., Gross, M.D., Eisenberg, M., and Hsi, S. 2016. Crafting Mechatronic Percussion with Everyday Materials. In *Proceedings of the TEI '16: Tenth International Conference on*

Tangible, Embedded, and Embodied Interaction (TEI '16). ACM, New York, NY, USA, 340-348.

14. Papert, S. 1980. *Mindstorms: Children, copmuters, and powerful ideas*. Basic Books, Inc.
15. Ratto, M. 2011. Critical Making: Conceptual and Material Studies in Technology and Social Life. The information society, 27:4, 252-260.
16. Resnick, M. 2007. All I really need to know (about creative thinking) I learned (by studying how children learn) in kindergarten. In *Proceedings of the 6th ACM SIGCHI conference on Creativity & cognition* (C&C '07). ACM, New York, NY, USA, 1-6.
17. Resnick, M., & Rosenbaum, E. Designing for Tinkerability. in Honey, M., & Kanter, D. eds. Design, Make, Play: Growing the Next Generation of STEM Innovators, Routledge, 2013, 163-181
18. Schön, D.A. 1992. Designing as reflective conversation with the materials of a design situation. *Knowledge-Based Systems* 5(1), March 1992, Pages 3-14.
19. Schulz, A., Shamir, A., Levin, D. I. W. Pitchaya Sitthi-amorn, and Wojciech Matusik. 2014. Design and fabrication by example. *ACM Trans. Graph.* 33, 4, Article 62 (July 2014), 11 pages.
20. Thomaszewski, B., Coros, S., Gauge, D., Megaro, V., Grinspun, E., and Gross, M. 2014 Computational design of linkage-based characters. ACM Trans. Graph. 33, 4, Article 64 (July 2014), 9 pages.
21. Tinkerbots: https://www.tinkerbots.com/
22. Zhu, K. and Zhao, S. 2013. AutoGami: a low-cost rapid prototyping toolkit for automated movable paper craft. In Proceedings of the SIGCHI Conference on Human Factors in Computing Systems (CHI '13). ACM, New York, NY, USA, 661-670.
23. Zhu, L., Xu, W., Snyder, J., Liu, Y., Wang, G., and Guo, B. 2012. Motion-guided mechanical toy modeling. *ACM Trans. Graph.* 31, 6, Article 127 (November 2012).

UTAP - Unique Topologies for Acoustic Propagation: Designing Algorithmic Waveguides for Sensing in Interactive Malleable Interfaces

Jan Rod[2],[*] **David Collins**[2,3],[*] **Daniel Wessolek**[2],
Thavishi Illandara[2], **Ye Ai**[2], **Hyowon Lee**[2], **Suranga Nanayakkara**[2]
[1] Keio University, Graduate School of Media Design, Tokyo, Japan. janrod@kmd.keio.ac.jp
[2] Singapore University of Technology and Design, Singapore
{david_collins, thavishi, daniel, ye_ai, hlee, suranga}@sutd.edu.sg
[3] Massachusetts Institute of Technology, Cambridge, MA, USA

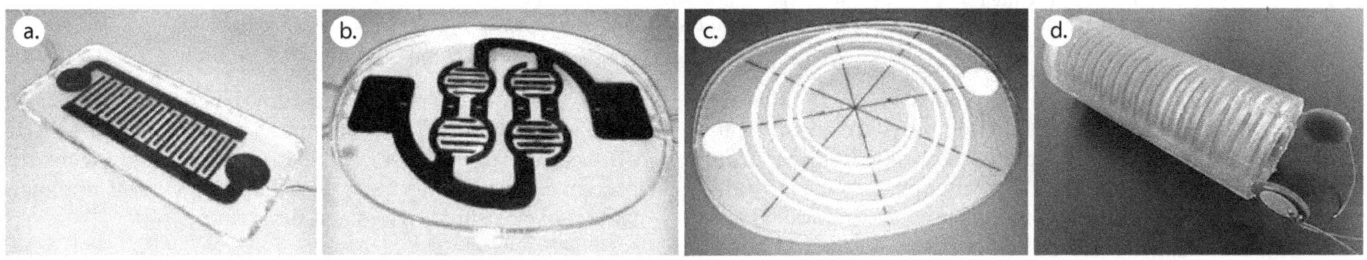

Figure 1. Systematic approach towards building malleable tangible interfaces: Using algorithmically produced acoustic waveguides, our interfaces can sense deformation positions, different force levels, as well other deformations including bending and twisting. In this figure we show prototype interfaces tested and evaluated within this paper.

ABSTRACT

Construction and sensing within malleable interfaces is usually limited by a number of constraints. Building the interface from diverse combinations of conductive and nonconductive soft materials, such as fabrics or foams combined with various sensors, complicates the manufacturing process and offers limited options in shaping. In this paper we propose *"Unique Topologies for Acoustic Propagation"* (*UTAP*), a novel approach for algorithmic design of malleable tangible interfaces. A fundamental feature of our approach is the implementation of algorithmically generated topologically distinct lattices that, attached to piezoelectric (PZT) transducers, allow us to sense and recognize changes in a modulated acoustic signal on deformation and classify it into different interaction states. Our systematic approach to manufacturing malleable interfaces opens possibilities to design shapes that allow implementation in a wide range of potential use cases. We demonstrate the UTAP approach on multiple interfaces assembled using laser cut and 3D printed lattices in conjunction with silicon compound moulding. Finally, we present a technical evaluation of our method based on studies of four distinct interface designs, assessing performance in sensing and localising simple deformations such as pressing on single and multiple spots, as well as different force levels and actions, including bending and twisting.

TEI 2017, March 20–23, 2017, Yokohama, Japan.
 ISBN 978-1-4503-4676-4/17/03 ...$15.00.
http://dx.doi.org/10.1145/3024969.3024987

Author Keywords
Malleable interfaces, acoustic sensing, deformable objects

ACM Classification Keywords
H.5.2. Information Interfaces and Presentation (e.g. HCI): Input devices and strategies

INTRODUCTION

Malleable interfaces offer new interaction possibilities where tangible objects can take advantage of the extensive manipulatory abilities of human hands [4]. Sensing and differentiating deformations in malleable interfaces has, however, been a challenge and often imposes limits on the potential such interfaces offer. In this paper we present a novel, systematic technique for building soft, malleable tangible interfaces containing algorithmically-generated topologically distinct lattices with unique acoustic properties that allow for sensing of unique acoustic responses with different types of deformation (see Figure 2 for system structure overview). These lattice structures are affixed to piezoelectric (PZT) transducers that serve both as emitters and sensors of acoustic frequency sweeps optimized for given combinations of lattice dimensions, type of materials used and frequency responses of the transducers. Since different interactions produce unique changes in the acoustic signal profile, we classify and subsequently recognize them using machine learning.

[*]These authors contributed equally to this work.

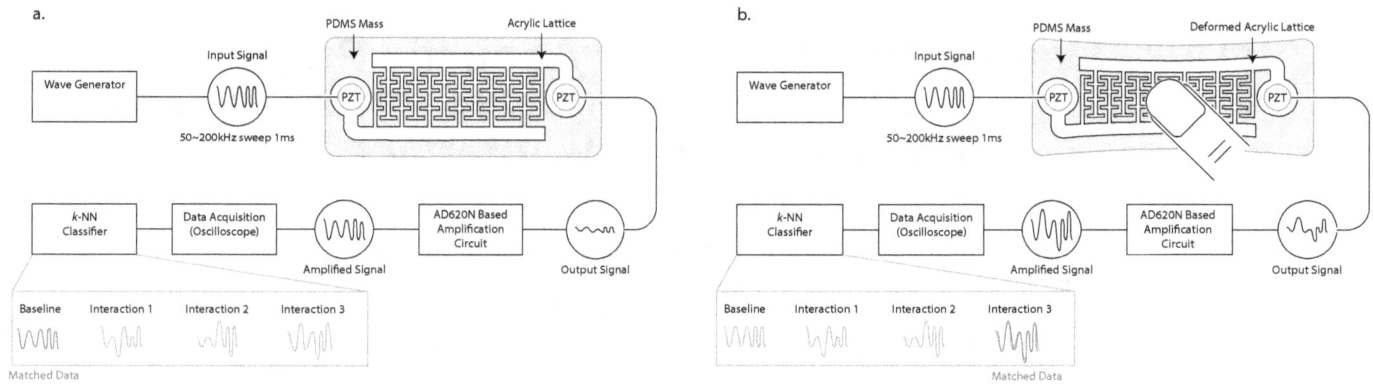

Figure 2. System architecture presented in a use case with one of our interfaces in two states. (a) Baseline state - no interaction, and (b) pressed, deformed state where output signal is matched to one of pre-existing states system was taught during supervised machine learning.

We tested UTAP approach on four different interface types (see Figure 1a-d) moulded from polydimethylsiloxane (PDMS) with laser cut acrylic and 3D printed lattice structures. The results show that our technique is precise in detecting single and multiple simultaneous deformation locations, up to five different applied pressure levels and bending/twisting deformations of the entire interface.

We envision usage scenarios where tangible interaction is desirable and current sensing technologies (e.g. computer vision, pressure and flex sensors, capacitive touch sensing and radar) do not provide optimal solutions in the suitable combinations of sensing capabilities (force, location, duration), tangible properties and freedom in creating desired form that fit a particular use case. This sensing approach is readily scalable, with any number of interaction states being detected with only one single-channel sensing element.

The contribution of this paper consist of:

- Description of a novel approach to designing algorithmic waveguides for acoustic sensing in malleable interfaces - ***Unique Topologies for Acoustic Propagation (UTAP)***
- Proof of concept ***implementation of various malleable interfaces*** moulded from a silicone elastomer with embedded topologically distinct acrylic lattice structures
- Technical ***validation of our sensing method*** for various deformation using four different interfaces

OVERVIEW OF RELATED RESEARCH

Sensing Techniques on Hard Surface

Sensing interactions between machines and humans is one of the most prominent areas of research in the field of Human Computer Interaction (HCI). A number of approaches have been demonstrated for sensing touch interactions on hard surfaces, including optical sensing [22, 5], capacitive sensing [35, 36], time domain reflectometry [47], acoustic sensing [29, 8] and various types of pressure sensing [37], both on displays as well as other types of hard surfaces that serve as Human Machine Interfaces (HMI). A similar set of techniques is available for tracking of hand motions in the air where no surface is present at all, where the computer recognizes hand gestures, and can be built around use of optical sensors with both high [1] and low spatial resolution [48], laser rangefinding [10] or, recently, radar waves [2]. A few of these approaches have been applied to sensing techniques used in malleable interfaces, together with various implementations of pressure sensors and flex sensors [40].

Sensing on Malleable Interfaces

Elastic, soft and malleable materials are becoming increasingly popular and are used to build interfaces that are tangible and can support diverse types of rich interactions including squeezing for physical therapy applications [3, 6, 30] and enhancing interactions with plush toys [16]. Other explorations are looking into how to enhance interactions with existing systems and devices [24] as well as envision completely novel ones [15, 45, 49].

Construction and sensing within malleable interfaces, however, is usually limited by fabrication constraints. Building the interface from combinations of conductive and non-conductive materials, such as fabrics or foams, complicates the manufacturing process [32] and offers limited options in shaping the resulting interface. Using large number of pressure sensors placed on the surface [41] or embedded into the a soft structure during moulding [40] affords substantial sensitivity, but requires en-masse integration of sensor components and multichannel processing. Some promising methods limit the spatial extent of sensing, usually into 2.5 dimensions, such as camera based optical sensing [14], though this requires it to be placed on (or part of) a transparent hard flat surface, also a limitations of some other approaches, including those utilizing ferromagnetic fluids [25, 23], or piezoelectric foils [39, 38].

Applications of Acoustics

Acoustic sensing has been implemented in previous HCI work to understand types of interactions [29, 42], augment mobile phones with tangible interfaces [27], or to discover surroundings of a given device using ultrasound of [28]. Distinguishable acoustic properties of simple interactions have been researched for passive understanding of scratching and touching on surfaces [18, 21], as well as recognizing an object or part of a touching finger [19], or even interactions on human skin [20]. However, the majority of contemporary research utilizes passive acoustics, where the possibilities of active acoustics and its properties for enhanced sensing of different interactions remains relatively unexplored. Some recent work shows that active acoustic sensing approach can substitute pressure sensing [34], or understand different configurations of object assemblies and different user interactions [33]. We acknowledge that our sensing pipeline is analogous to the Touch & Activate system [33], in as much as it also uses frequency sweeps, realtime Fast Fourier Transformation ((FFT), analysis of changes in the frequency domain, and machine learning to recognize different states. Our principal contribution lies in formalising the integration and design of the topologically distinct waveguides that allow for custom designed soft interfaces supporting a variety of interactions, specifically in malleable interfaces. Our approach also overcomes some of the limitations of Touch & Activate system, which was limited to sensing on hard surfaces and with non-symmetric objects. By integrating a waveguide material within a malleable interface, we permit the use of soft materials (with higher acoustic attenuation constants) and the decoupling of the interface shape from the ability to sense interaction locations. While our UTAP approach could sense specific interaction locations on a soft sphere surface, for example, Touch & Activate could not.

Active acoustic methods outside of the HCI field have been widely used in a number of different sensing and actuation technologies over a number of length scales, where acoustic fields are capable of imaging and/or manipulating objects from cells [12, 11] to macro-scale structures [31]. These dimensions can be accessed via the wide range of acoustic frequencies that can be generated, with the acoustic wavelength given by

$$\lambda = c/f, \tag{1}$$

where c is the sound speed in the material and f is the applied frequency. For readily generated frequencies on the order of 10^2–10^9 Hz and materials with $c \sim 10^3$ ms^{-1}, this corresponds to wavelengths meters to microns. This high degree of resolution, combined with the ability for acoustic fields to interact with structures embedded within the bulk of a material, has made acoustic fields useful for sensing applications including non-destructive testing [26] and ultrasonic imaging [13]. While 2D or 3D imaging using acoustic fields typically requires an array of combined mode acoustic actuators/sensors with sufficient temporal resolution for time-of-flight measurements, we propose localization through the use of spatially varying waveguide structures embedded within the sensing material; when these structures vary non-symmetrically, position can be inferred from the signal received at a single sensing transducer along the axes where symmetry is broken by the waveguide elements.

SENSING METHOD

The sensor localization in interfaces built using UTAP method operates as such: (1) a broadband transducer vibrates (2) an acoustic waveguide that is used to preferentially conduct acoustic energy along transducer-side structure elements, whereafter (3) acoustic energy preferentially transmits to sensing-side elements at local resonance conditions and (4) the acoustic energy continues to propagate through sensing-side waveguide material and (5) couple into the piezoelectric sensing transducer. A simple operational amplifier circuit can be used to enhance sensing sensitivity. Preferential propagation through the waveguide material occurs when the acoustic attenuation coefficient in the waveguide material, α_w, is higher than that of the intervening medium α_m and there is a significant acoustic reflection coefficient between the two materials (the acoustic energy is largely contained within the waveguide, as is the case with the hard acrylic embedded in a deformable silicone elastomer used in this work). The attenuation and reflection coefficients are given by

$$\alpha = \alpha_0 \omega^\gamma, \tag{2}$$

$$R = \left(\frac{z_2 - z_1}{z_2 + z_1}\right)^2, \tag{3}$$

where the acoustic displacement follows the form $\xi = \xi_0 e^{-\alpha x}$, ω is the angular frequency, α_0 and γ are material specific factors (though $\gamma = 2$ for typical non-viscoelastic materials including the acrylic waveguide material used here), and z_1, z_2 are the acoustic impedances of the pre- and post-interface mediums, with $z_i = \rho_i c_i$. Acoustic transmission between nearby waveguide structures is optimized at resonance (with $f = f^*$), a condition that occurs when the compression wave emanating from the transmitting waveguide element coincides with and reinforces that reflected from the receiving one, specifically at integers of half-wavelengths (i.e., $N = 1/2, 1, 3/2 \cdots, f^* = c/(N\lambda)$).

A straightforward implementation embedded resonating elements utilizes structures based on chirped interdigital transducers (IDTs), where the spacing between alternating transmitting and sensing IDT elements varies from one end of the structure to the next. As each of these spacings corresponds to a specific frequency as per Eqn. 1, localization across the spatial extent occurs in the frequency domain, as shown in Figure 3a and 3b. The range of appropriate IDT element spacings for a given frequency range bounded by f_{min} and f_{max} is given by

$$\begin{aligned} \lambda_{max} &= c/f_{min}, \\ \lambda_{min} &= c/f_{max}. \end{aligned} \tag{4}$$

These λ_{max} and λ_{min} values indicate the maximum and minimum realizable IDT spacings, respectively. Though multiple half-integer values of λ are capable of generating resonant conditions between oscillating elements, the smallest one (and the one which yields the highest spatial resolution) is $N = 1/2$: accordingly, the IDT finger spacings should vary between $\lambda_{max}/2$ and $\lambda_{min}/2$. To generate a structure whose spacings vary along a linear axis (i.e. Figs 1a,d) the spacings simply vary from one IDT finger-pair to the next with a defined increment. Starting from the finger position $x_0 = 0$ at the end with the largest IDT spacing and given an increment value ϵ, the centre positions of subsequent fingers are given

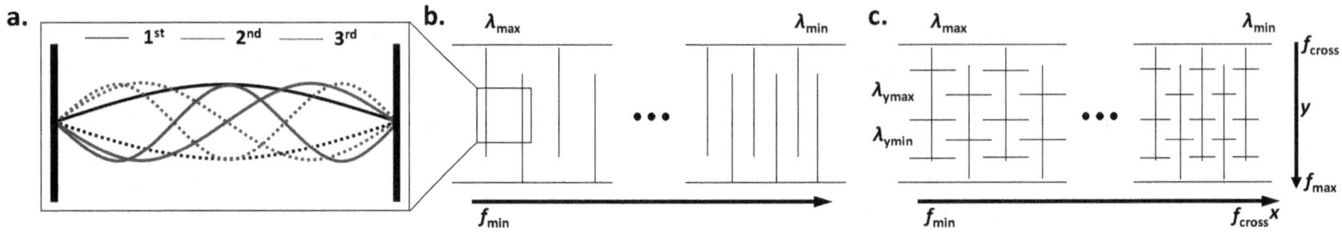

Figure 3. Functional principle of UTAP. (a) The transmission of acoustic energy is maximized when the distance between the transmission and sensing elements corresponds to an integer number of half wavelengths for a given frequency - the first, second and third harmonic resonance modes are shown. (b) Smaller wavelengths, represented by λ, correspond to higher frequencies. By varying λ between transmitting and sensing waveguide elements across a spatial extent, perturbations in the spatial domain can be mapped to the frequency domain, permitting the localization of interaction when a user deforms the waveguide elements. (c) This approach can be extended into two dimensions, where one of two transducers emits a broadband acoustic signal through a stiff waveguide material that is sensed by the other transducer affixed to a interleaved sensing waveguide. Each x, y position corresponds to a unique set of frequencies: the x position to $f_{min} < f_x < f_{cross}$ and the y position to $f_{cross} < f_y < f_{max}$.

by

$$\begin{aligned} x_1 &= x_0 + \lambda_{max}/2 - \epsilon + w/2, \\ x_2 &= x_1 + \lambda_{max}/2 - 2\epsilon + w/2, \\ x_3 &= x_2 + \lambda_{max}/2 - 3\epsilon + w/2, \\ &\ldots, \end{aligned} \tag{5}$$

until $x_n - x_{n-1} \leq \lambda_{min}/2$, where w is the width of the waveguide finger elements and n is the last finger index. To find the value of ϵ appropriate for a given length L of the sensing device that spans finger-spacings in the range of λ values, a simple script can be composed that increments the ϵ value from an arbitrarily small value (i.e., 1e-6 m) until $x_n \leq L$. When the material containing the waveguide structures is deformed by user interaction at a given location, the position information is encoded in the change in acoustic transmission coefficient at acoustic frequencies that transmit across the deformed elements. Though this is the theoretical optimum sensing range, it is somewhat indicative, however, as localization only requires that each point on an interaction surface has a unique fingerprint of acoustic transmission from the transmission to sensing side in the frequency domain, similar to capacitive sensing work [35].

This can occur outside the indicated IDT spacing range in Eqn. 4, with some acoustic energy transmitting/reflecting due to second-order effects including off-resonance transmission, acoustic interactions within the waveguide material, acoustic reflections with the spatial extents of the bounding media and, of course, deformations induced by user interactions. Nevertheless, Eqn. 4 offers a good first-order guide to the relationship between waveguide element spacings and the appropriate frequency range applied, and where the sensing is more robust and the response in the frequency domain more easily interpreted when the frequency sweeps occur within the range in Eqn. 4.

This method can utilize any surface manifold by integrating topologically distinct structures along its boundaries, such that the fingerprint of acoustic behaviour is unique to each location. However, in the example given in Eqn. 5, the structure spacings vary linearly between the maximum spacing and the minimum one; while only a unique, non symmetric environment is required for position sensing, a linear gradation is more likely to be fault tolerant (indicating a nearby position rather than a far away one) than one where the spacing increments occur randomly. In the case of a of a planar interface for sensing along two dimensions this is readily realized by creating IDT structures, potentially in two-dimensions across the x-y plane, as shown in Figure 3c. Both x and y position sensing are independently retained when there is no overlap in the frequency ranges corresponding to the wavelengths in each direction, and where the crossover frequency f_{cross} simply corresponds to the a coordinate shift from the x-dimension to y-dimension in Eqn. 5.

IMPLEMENTATION

A schematic overview of our system is shown in Figure 2. A PZT transducer is affixed to the IDT transmission and sensing lattice components. The lattices are completely encompassed by a malleable material. The actively powered transmission transducer is actuated by a frequency-swept signal that is generated by a function generator. The acoustic signal that is captured by the sensing-side transducer is captured with an oscilloscope and uploaded in real-time to a computer for analysis and classification, using a supervised machine learning algorithm. Due to the differences in the acoustic profile that occur when the lattice is deformed, the system can recognize various (prior trained) states. Subsequently, these interaction states can be mapped to particular functions on a target system.

We have built four interfaces using PDMS moulding with lattice structures to test our sensing method. The lattice structures were produced by two different techniques. The first technique uses a laser cutter, is simple and can be replicated using a hobby equipment, while the second one, using additive manufacturing, is geared towards building more complex structures. Using the first method, we also demonstrate various approaches towards designing the lattice structures that confer spatial localization, namely a 1D grid, specific malleable regions, as well as continuously converging spiral IDT elements.

For the purpose of evaluating feasibility of algorithmic production of the IDT lattices, we created a script written in Matlab programming language that generates spacing coordinates to define a unique position in three-dimensional space for each of the topological features following Eq. 5 within given parameters: generating the point cloud in one, two or three dimensions, overall size of the interface and initial spacing parameters related to invariable characteristics of used material (fixed thickness of the acrylic). These coordinates are written into a CSV file. Subsequently, we import these coordinates into a CAD software (Autodesk Inventor) and use them to drive placement of the pre-designed IDT fingers (cf. Fig. 4). In this early stage, we finalize the outer shape of the interface manually to give it a desired shape. To demonstrate the versatility of the approach, we have constructed four diverse interfaces, where Fig. 1a shows the simplest linear deformation sensing. As more closely spaced elements yield greater position selectivity, the range of spacings chosen (centre positions 3.75 mm to 5 mm, spacing between elements 1.75 mm to 3 mm with a $w = 2$ mm finger width) were the smallest routinely realizable given the fabrication procedure (where elements may shift slightly during elastomer curing). These spacings, given fundamental mode resonance (N=1, half-wavelength spacing) gives values of $f_{min} = 72$ kHz and $f_{max} = 123$ kHz as per Eqn. 4, well within the actuation and sensing range of working frequencies of our piezo elements. To design a system with a representative length L within 100 mm given these values for $\lambda_{max}/2$ and $\lambda_{min}/2$, Eqn. 5 can be used to define the waveguide finger spacings along the x-axis, and where a simple script was utilized to increase the increment (ϵ in Eqn. 5) between finger pairs until $x_n \leq L$, where x_n is position of the last element. In the sensing device here this process gives an increment of 0.06 mm. The interface in Fig. 1b demonstrates the versatility of variable waveguide spacing where the lattices can be shaped to form deformable areas mimicking functionality of buttons. Interface Fig. 1c then further expands on the versatility of the embedded waveguide approach using converging spirals, where variable spacing is accomplished via continuously converging elements rather than discretely incremented positions. The interface Fig. 1d is then an attempt to evaluate three-dimensional shape that is better geared towards supporting bending and twisting interactions, and is indicative of the range of interfaces that can be produced using this approach. These design choices were made to show versatility and robustness of our approach in this early stage of our research.

For the transducer instrumentation we experimented with PZTs with 27 mm diameter from different manufacturers to test the universal applicability of our approach, all inexpensive designs (< 0.20 US$) used in, for example, alarm buzzers. Different piezo transducers have varying amplitude responses for given applied frequencies, which needs to be reflected when defining appropriate frequency sweeps for each specific application and material combination. We have tested the frequency responses for each batch of PZTs that we acquired and selectively worked with those that had good response in a higher frequency spectrum. In our technical evaluation, we use frequency sweeps in the 50 kHz to 200 kHz range (with a 1 ms sweep period), where we achieved best frequency response with our chosen PZT transducer and which covers our frequencies dictated by the algorithm used for producing the IDT interfaces. This range is well above the range of human hearing (approx. 50 Hz to 20 kHz). Though specialized transducers should be able to readily generate higher frequency displacements more effectively, the use of non-optimal transducers in the case here demonstrates the robustness of this method and its applicability to low-cost position sensing.

Interface Construction

We present and evaluate four lattice designs (three produced using 2D laser cutting and one produced using additive manufacturing), some of which enable malleability of the whole surface others with specifically designed malleable regions (Cf. type (a) and type (b) in Figure 1).

Our tested IDT lattice structures are fabricated from acrylic using simple 2D laser cutting as well as additive manufacturing for more complex 3D interfaces. For 2D laser cutting, we used 2 mm material as an attempt to compromise between stiffness and lateral acoustic wave propagation; thicker material results in a higher acoustic amplitude at the sensing transducer, while a thinner material is more readily deformable (and can be used for smaller scale interfaces - i.e. watch size).

Prototype IDTs fabricated using additive manufacturing (VeroCyan RGD843 and VeroMagenta RGD851 materials on Stratasys Objet 3D printer) have the same 2 mm thickness to achieve comparable acoustic conductivity at the desired scale of the interface. We subsequently attach two piezo transducers directly to the transducer pads on the IDT using epoxy glue, resulting in good acoustic coupling between the transducer's brass disc and the acrylic structure. Using simple moulds, we encase the whole structure in PDMS curable elastomer material (sylguard 184, Dow Corning, USA). First, we pour and cure a thin 1 mm layer of PDMS that will form the top of the interface. Once the initial layer is cured, we insert and position the lattice and pour another layer of PDMS over it (See Figure 4 for a construction diagram). The resulting interface can conceivably be much larger (or smaller), but here range in size between that of a smartphone and a tablet computer. For the 3D printed lattice, we have designed a specific mould that held both IDTs in correct position to assure accurate spacing along all three axes. Based on the lattice design implemented, finalized interface can be pressed, bent and twisted depending on desired interaction.

Acoustic Sweep Sensing and Interaction Recognition

Due to the specific properties of each construction methods and also specific response frequencies of the PZT elements, we explore the responsive frequencies of each interface after the construction and discover frequencies that give consistent specific responses to different interactions. Subsequently we use this data to construct the acoustic frequency sweeps. For example, the interface built using laser cut lattice and PDMS moulding, given the acoustic properties of acrylic (velocity ca. 2600 m/s and acoustic impedance of 3.1e6 Rayls) and PDMS (velocity ca. 1076 m/s and acoustic impedance of 1.1e6 Rayls), lattice features on the order of cm to mm and our transducer element response, we utilize frequencies within a range of 50 to 200 kHz.

The output signal is then amplified using a custom circuit built around two AD620 instrumentation amplifiers. Subsequently, we capture a fixed window of data points using an

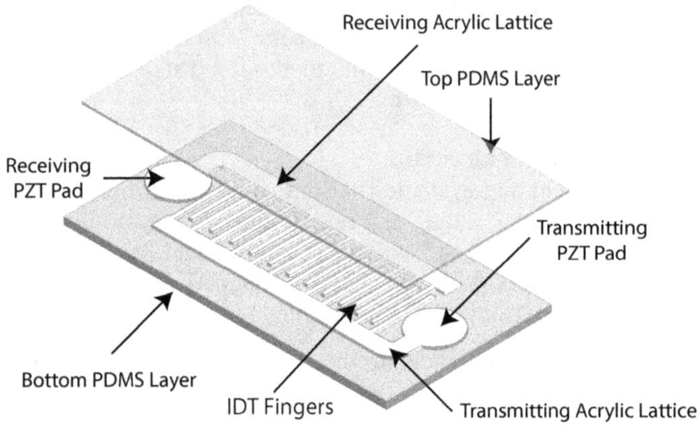

Figure 4. Overview of a malleable interface construction using laser cut IDT lattice and PDMS moulding.

oscilloscope, from where it is transferred to a computer. We then perform an FFT analysis on selected frequency range resulting in 750 data points in each sample we further use for interaction recognition. Interaction recognition is achieved using simple k-Nearest Neighbour (k-NN) supervised machine learning algorithm from WEKA machine learning toolkit [17] with $k = 1$ to train the system acoustic profile of a baseline state with no interaction happening and various states where certain interaction occurs. Both in test and live setup, we observe deformations in the acoustic spectrum and match them with previously trained states to recognize different types of deformations.

Our system can also to be used in live environment, using continuous capture of the acoustic signal and analysis on the fly using the same (k-NN) algorithm. The current implementation of this system uses a fixed data window capture from an oscilloscope tethered to a computer and has a recognition frequency around 10 Hz due to the equipment limitations (mainly upload delay from our oscilloscope and delay introduced by performing the FFT analysis on the fly), however due to the material resistance and relaxation timescales in a thick material, individual interactions occur over timescales longer than 1/10s, thus this speed is sufficient for our early implementation and evaluation of the UTAP approach. Subsequent implementations may make use of specialized FFT microchips to perform higher refresh-rate sensing.

EVALUATION AND RESULTS

To evaluate our sensing technique, we have conducted separate experiments using three types of interfaces constructed to measure the accuracy in sensing different types of deformations. Specifically, we have measured ability of the UTAP approach to sense individual *local deformations* (i.e. pressing with human finger and other objects), *multiple local deformations* occurring at the same time (i.e. pressing with multiple fingers), five different *force levels*, as well as *bending* and *twisting* actions.

Evaluation Methodology

For each of the experiments, we create our training set capturing 100 samples of data from the oscilloscope for each of the pre-defined states. A state is defined as a deformation, such as pressure applied by a human digit on a certain area of the interface, or a bend performed by a user holding the interface in a specific way. This was also performed for the baseline state when the interface is not deformed at all. We recreate each of the states and capture a testing data set with 50 samples of each state. All of the interactions are performed by one of the researchers actuating the designated interaction area to first collect the training samples and later presses on the same areas to collect the test samples. Provided the deformations are happening in the same location, the precision will not change from user to user, or even between a human digit and other similarly shaped object deforming the interface with similar force, since the deformation is sensed by varying frequency response of the waveguides. Particular type of actuator used is irrelevant as fair as it produces given deformation. This was tested by authors, but is not part of results reported in this paper. To prevent loss of accuracy through undesired acoustic interactions between the interfaces and the surface they are placed on, we have placed each of the interfaces onto a styrofoam block to acoustically isolate them where necessary. Data sets are captured to a computer using oscilloscope and FFT function is performed on each data sample. The resulting FFT features (750 data points) are then compared using the k-NN algorithm with $k = 1$. We present results from four separate studies carried out on four different interfaces seen in Figures 1(a), (b), (c) and (d). Respective state configurations are described within the sections. We have focused on evaluating different types of interactions as well as different types of lattice structures.

Results

1-Dimensional Interface

This interface shown in Figure 1(a) is built to detect deformations using a 1-dimensional lattice structure - i.e. the change in spacing of the IDTs occurs on one axis, allowing us to sense deformations along that dimension. We trained it to recognize 7 deformation regions along the lateral axis of the interface (labeled P1 - P7), as well as different types of deformations: bending upwards (B1), bending downwards (B2), twisting left (T1) and twisting right (T2). Bending states were achieved by supporting the interface with a hard object on each end (B1) and then bending it using a human digit pressing on the middle part, as well as supporting it in the middle and pressing on the outer ends (B2). Twisting was achieved by supporting the interface in diagonal corners and pressing on the unsupported corners to create a lateral left (T1) and right (T2) twist The results can be seen in the form of confusion matrix in Figure 6(a). The overall accuracy of 92 % points to a high degree of sensed state specificity. Some states were mis-classified as neighbouring states due to relatively higher density of trained regions. Note that the bending and twisting deformations have 100 % recognition rate. The overall accuracy increases with a smaller number of trained interaction states (99 % for three trained locations).

Multipoint Interface

The Multipoint interface (Figure 1(b)) demonstrates the potential to sense deformations in multiple isolated regions. In addition to sensing deformations in each of the regions, our

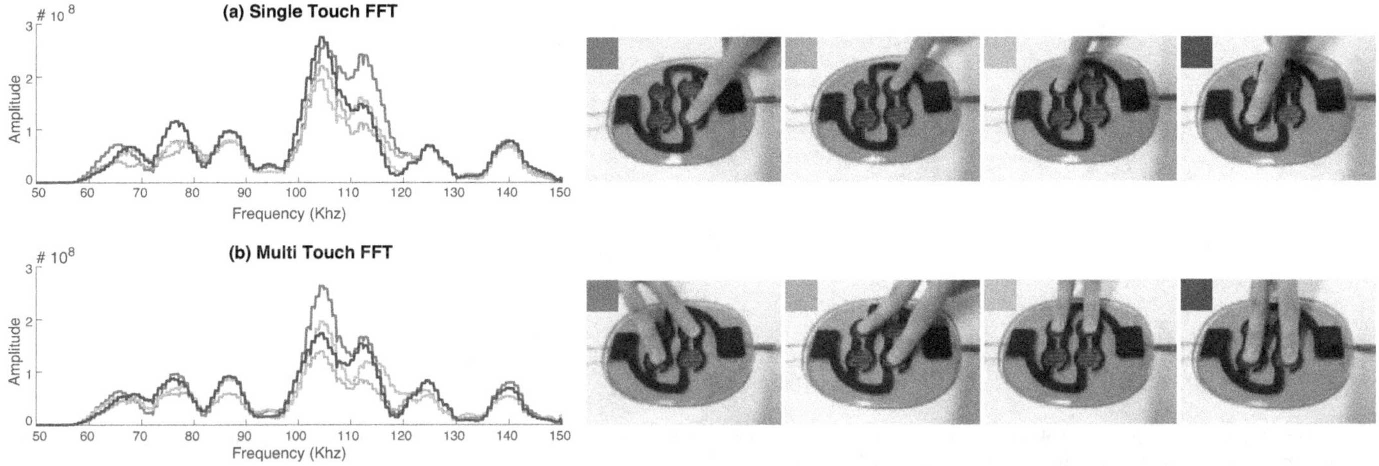

Figure 5. Sample comparison of FFT differences between interaction states. Figure (a) shows differences for single points pressed states as seen in corresponding photographs, figure (b) displays multiple points pressed at the same time. All results are averages of 50 data samples for each state compared to normalized common baseline. Plot cropped to range of 50 kHz to 150 kHz. Note that the PZTs have similar frequency response profiles, thus the profile of each interaction state may also appear similar.

aim was to use the distinct regions for straightforward evaluation of different combinations of deformations within the defined regions (labeled P1 to P4), as well as different pressures (F1 to F2), where each multiple deformation (i.e. P1P3 means simultaneous deformation of *point 1* and *point 3*) or pressure level is defined as a dedicated state (i.e. P1F1 means *point 1, force level 1*). Results can be seen in Figure 6(b) with overall accuracy of 95.7%. In addition, we present averaged normalized FFT curves for some states in Fig. 5 for purpose of illustrating the differences in frequency spectrum. Interestingly, our system can recognize five different force levels (F1 to F5) in one region of the interface with an accuracy of 90% (cf. Figure 6(e)). For this particular study, force levels were consistently produced using a digit analogue (a rounded object with diameter of 10 mm resembling a human digit) with applied mass/force increments of 0.8 kg / 78N.

Spiral Interface
The spiral interface seen in Figure 1(c), is an attempt to evaluate a lattice in the form of 2 converging spirals. Similar to the other lattice structures, this interface can yield deformation localization through a distinct fingerprint of local topological features, here as the effective distance between transducer and sensing elements continuously changes from the outside to the inner part of the sensing interface rather than the discrete changes in the other tested interfaces. We have trained it with 11 different deformation points (labeled P1 to P11) distributed along the spiral converging inwards to the center of the interface. The results can be seen in the form of confusion matrix in Figure 6(c). Here we can observe one state which tended to be misclassified, arguably due to lack of significantly pronounced geometrical features. Overall results, however, were nonetheless indicate 94.8% accuracy.

Interface Using Lattice Fabricated by Additive Manufacturing
The spiral interface seen in Figure 1(d), is an attempt of basic evaluation of a lattice fabricated using additive 3D manufacturing. Oval shape of the interface is geared towards evaluating bending and twisting. We have defined two bend states, up and down (B1 and B2) as well as twist clockwise and counterclockwise (T1 and T2). The results can be seen in Figure 6(d). The overall result is 90.0% of successful recognition. We can observe that the twisting states, while generally recognized, have significantly lower successful recognition rate. The reason for the lower performance is lesser deformation of the lattice structure occurring during twisting, since the "ribs" of the lattice structure do not displace significantly. The potential strategies to increase twist sensing accuracy would be to design additional features that would increase displacement of the whole lattice during twisting interaction, thus changing the acoustic profile of such interaction in a more significant manner.

Discussion
Our results show that the UTAP approach is precise in detecting different deformation locations and states. The theoretical spatial precision of UTAP is very high with ability to detect deformations at the same time. However, the geometrical properties of lattices used together with a rudimentary method of training the machine learning algorithm decrease the precision in our particular implementation of the system. While the difference in waveguide topology between spiral and rectilinear waveguide elements complicates a direct comparison between multipoint interfaces, a spiral interface is beneficial from the standpoint of being simple to design though may suffer from poor spatial resolution and weak signal due to the continuous (rather than discrete) nature of spacing increment, which limits the robust recognition of discrete states, and the long waveguide transmission path over which acoustic energy is transmitted, especially towards the spiral centre. Interestingly, UTAP can also detect different force levels, which we classify as different states of deformation in the same region. The consistent performance points towards good system trainability and present a solid basis for further exploration of this technique. Some of the practical limitations of UTAP are further discussed in-depth within the following section.

a.

Performed \ Classified	BL	P1	P2	P3	P4	P5	P6	P7	B1	B2	B3	B4
BL	49	0	1	0	0	0	0	0	0	0	0	0
P1	0	50	0	0	0	0	0	0	0	0	0	0
P2	0	0	50	0	0	0	0	0	0	0	0	0
P3	0	0	1	49	0	0	0	0	0	0	0	0
P4	0	0	0	0	47	3	0	0	0	0	0	0
P5	0	0	0	0	0	50	0	0	0	0	0	0
P6	0	0	0	0	0	8	41	1	0	0	0	0
P7	0	0	0	0	0	0	0	50	0	0	0	0
B1	0	0	0	0	0	0	0	0	50	0	0	0
B2	0	0	0	0	0	0	0	0	0	50	0	0
T1	0	0	0	0	0	0	0	0	0	0	50	0
T2	0	0	0	0	0	0	0	0	0	0	0	50

b.

Performed \ Classified	BL	P1F 1	P1F 2	P2F 1	P2F 2	P3F 1	P3F 2	P4F 1	P4F 2	P1P 4	P2P 3	P1P 3	P2P 4
BL	50	0	0	0	0	0	0	0	0	0	0	0	0
P1F1	0	48	2	0	0	0	0	0	0	0	0	0	0
P1F2	0	0	50	0	0	0	0	0	0	0	0	0	0
P2F1	0	0	0	50	0	0	0	0	0	0	0	0	0
P2F2	0	0	0	8	42	0	0	0	0	0	0	0	0
P3F1	0	0	0	0	0	35	15	0	0	0	0	0	0
P3F2	0	0	0	0	0	2	48	0	0	0	0	0	0
P4F1	0	0	0	0	0	0	0	49	1	0	0	0	0
P4F2	0	0	0	0	0	0	0	0	50	0	0	0	0
P1P4	0	0	0	0	0	0	0	0	0	50	0	0	0
P2P3	0	0	0	0	0	0	0	0	0	0	50	0	0
P1P3	0	0	0	0	0	0	0	0	0	0	0	50	0
P2P4	0	0	0	0	0	0	0	0	0	0	0	0	50

c.

Performed \ Classified	BL	P1	P2	P3	P4	P5	P6	P7	P8	P9	P10	P11
BL	50	0	0	0	0	0	0	0	0	0	0	0
P1	0	49	0	0	0	0	0	0	0	0	1	0
P2	0	0	42	0	0	0	8	0	0	0	0	0
P3	0	0	0	49	1	0	0	0	0	0	0	0
P4	0	0	1	0	47	0	2	0	0	0	0	0
P5	0	0	0	0	0	32	18	0	0	0	0	0
P6	0	0	0	0	0	0	50	0	0	0	0	0
P7	0	0	0	0	0	0	0	50	0	0	0	0
P8	0	0	0	0	0	0	0	0	50	0	0	0
P9	0	0	0	0	0	0	0	0	0	50	0	0
P10	0	0	0	0	0	0	0	0	0	0	50	0
P11	0	0	0	0	0	0	0	0	0	0	0	50

d.

Performed \ Classified	BL	B1	B2	T1	T2
BL	47	0	0	0	3
B1	0	50	0	0	0
B2	0	0	50	0	0
T1	0	0	0	38	12
T2	0	0	0	10	40

e.

Performed \ Classified	BL	F1	F2	F3	F4	F5
BL	50	0	0	0	0	0
F1	0	41	6	3	0	0
F2	0	3	41	6	0	0
F3	0	1	2	43	4	0
F4	0	0	2	3	45	0
F5	0	0	0	0	0	50

Figure 6. Experiment results: Tables (a) to (e) show resulting confusion matrices of each tested deformation for corresponding interfaces in displayed in Figure 1. Label explanations in the main text, BL = Baseline state.

LIMITATIONS

While in principle UTAP allows for very precise deformations measurement in wide scope of interface shapes and designs, there are some practical and theoretical limitations that impact the method and the interface fabrication. Furthermore, due to the PZT transducers being enclosed in the bulk matter of the interface, UTAP allows for creating interfaces with low instrumentation footprint, even though the interface still needs to be wired to the rest of the instruments, rendering some handheld operations slightly more cumbersome.

General Limitations of UTAP

Though there is no inherent theoretical limit in the spatial resolution that can be realized using UTAP, in this implementation the limited frequency range permitted with the transducers implemented and the laser-cutting manufacturing method used results in detection resolution on the order of the cm-scale features utilized. As the manufacture of smaller components and higher frequency transducing and data recording elements is substantially more cost intensive, this technique is likely optimal for low cost sensing applications that require relatively coarse resolution (with respect to a touchscreen, for example). The sensed state is also sensitive to the conditions during which the training data capture was undertaken; in the case of our setups described herein, the interfaces were acoustically isolated on styrofoam blocks for consistent testing conditions between measurements. Measurement of deformation states does not necessarily require this, though future work on the recognition engine is needed to automatically update and recognize different states irrespective of boundary conditions. The spatial limits of the sensing area are a function of the spatial sensitivity required; lower frequencies result in correspondingly lower attenuation and greater signal transmission, but require larger waveguide spacings to robustly sense discrete states. Hence, larger interfaces have an inherent tradeoff with spatial resolution, though the particular limits for a given implementation are a function of practical considerations including sensitivity of the sensing transducer and the applied power. Using our systems here as a first-order example, however, we have shown that cm-scale spatial resolution is possible in 10 to 20 cm scale interfaces.

Materials and Manufacturing

Acoustic attenuation occurring in soft materials negatively influences the signal strength and the possible distances between the two IDT parts of each lattice structure (i.e. if the lattices are too far, the signal will be excessively attenuated). Depending on the strength of the signal that we inject into the interface, our method is suitable for hand-held scale interfaces. Increasing the size demands for stronger signal injected into the interface as well as stronger amplification of sensed signal. However, unlike other similar approaches using acoustic sensing, employing UTAP to design and fabricate custom lattices allows for more control over shape and distribution of the materials with different acoustic properties (and different elastic moduli) - e.g. embed the IDTs which have better acoustic conductivity and lower attenuation coefficient into a “core” of the interface and have a larger mass of soft malleable material on the top, which would still allow to sense deformations but on a significantly larger scale - such as pillow or plush toy.

The cheap, affordable PZT transducers that we use in this proof of concept have variable frequency response across the acoustic spectrum that often differs from one PZT transducer to another. Prior to specifying the actual frequencies for the sweep, we test the frequency response of the transducer pair to see in which frequencies they perform well.

Real Time Interaction Sensing

In our current configuration of the real time sensing the speed of the recognition is around 10 Hz. This limitation is given by limitations of data capture and transfer speed from oscilloscope to the computer as well as FFTs performed on each data window which is later cropped to 750 data points that are used as input for the WEKA machine learning. The real time sensing can be improved to perform at higher frequency (around 50 Hz) using real-time hardware based FFT digital signal processing and implementing faster machine recognition pipeline, such as Sci-Kit Learn library for Python.

FUTURE WORK

Our system at present serves as a proof of concept for our UTAP method and demonstrates some early approaches to building malleable interfaces. There is a number of improvements we plan to address in continuation of the work, improving the system setup to increase speed recognition, as well as exploring the potential for an automatic, algorithm driven generative method for creating the lattice automatically for any given 3D shape. While foundations for this work are laid out in this paper, additional work is needed to optimize features and properties of the IDT structures and to explore the possibilities this research opens.

Our current system implementation works in real time, however with a slower recognition rate that is sub-optimal for real use. In the future, we expect to improve system hardware pipeline, integrating it into standalone, wireless, inexpensive battery powered module that can be configured for a wide variety of interaction interfaces, which would allow us reduce the form factor of the system to allow for fabricating standalone interfaces. Additional configurability of custom built hardware also allows to experiment with switching cycles of the PZT elements between transmitting and receiving. In such configuration, it is possible to acquire deformed acoustic signal from both IDT structures in one cycle (i.e. in first half-cycle, PZT A transmits a signal and PZT B receives, in the second half-cycle PZT B transmits and PZT A receives, creating symmetric deformation profile) and thus with more information, increase the precision of the system.

We plan to explore a number of potential applications, building specialised interfaces across different scales for use cases we have mentioned earlier, such as custom made rehabilitation devices and testing them for real rehabilitation scenarios in post-traumatic hand/body rehabilitation or post-stroke rehabilitation. We also plan to take popular interaction strategies and modalities used today in our day-to-day use of IT devices, and explore how these could be augmented, enhanced or even replaced when the malleable sensing material we propose in this paper is extensively adopted in their design.

Furthermore, there are other interesting trajectories to explore, such as implementation of actuation properties into the interface, or implementing light-conductive elements that would allow the interfaces to be infused with controlled light to complement the sensing functionality to turn our interfaces to outputs, as well as inputs. Our IDT structures would then gain another functionality as light conductive elements, similar to 3D printed conductive light tubes [9, 46]. Multi-material additive manufacturing methods are suitable for such enhancements. Looking further ahead, we can imagine our method to be used to and sense interactions in greater custom shaped surfaces, such as 3D artificial skin.

POSSIBLE APPLICATIONS

Our technique has multiple potential applications. Soft tangible interfaces provide additional modalities to hard touch-enabled surfaces and enable various types of interactions that take advantage of highly advanced motoric properties of human hands.

Since our method of interface construction is universal, it can be used for specialized single purpose applications to support specific, very narrow and specialised interactions, as well as to build more generic ones, that can be used and re-trained repeatedly for different purposes. For example, we envision that our method could be used to construct interfaces that require tracking of specific interactions in rehabilitation, such as hand injury requiring repeated exercises on particular muscle groups and mobility of different fingers (e.g. [44]). Another potential application might be post-stroke rehabilitation that often includes training focusing on regaining motor abilities (e.g [3, 7]) to replace current generation of unsuitable "hard" tangible devices. In a general computing applications, we can devise a supportive interfaces for tasks such as 3D modelling where a soft interface can simulate clay and mirror sensed interactions on a modeled object on the screen (e.g. [43, 32]).

A separate group of possible applications is to enhance user experience of interactive devices with malleable, soft components. The hard, sharp and delicate buttons and controllers on our modern IT devices have much room for improvement in offering interactivity. For example, we envision game controllers with flexible handles, or add-ons to other mobile, hand-held devices such as smartphones and tablets where the casing, grips, handles or even the main body of the devices support additional input mechanisms through more natural and intuitive gripping or squeezing action. Importantly, this scalable approach to interaction with malleable interfaces requires only a single sensing channel to measure and detect several different action states using inexpensive sensing and receiving transducers. In most of these application areas, our approach could offer a significant benefits for cost-effect manufacturing of interactive device.

CONCLUSION

In this paper we have presented UTAP, unique topologies for acoustic propagation, a systematic approach towards designing algorithmic waveguides for building malleable tangible interfaces. As this method achieves localization through algorithmic design of integrated waveguides and measurements in the frequency domain, only one sensing element is required. The use of a cheap, off-the-shelf sensor here demonstrates that this localization technique can be applied more cost-effectively than conventional multi-channel sensing devices. Using algorithmically created acoustic waveguides, our system can sense various deformations, such as pressing, bending and twisting, as well as different force levels, a combination of sensing modalities that are not afforded by comparable techniques. We have demonstrated and tested four different types of the interfaces build using laser-cut acrylic lattices moulded into malleable PDMS structures. Our results show that UTAP is a reliable technique with high accuracy.

UTAP, as presented in this paper, is an initial exploration of this technique and we expect it to significantly expand to investigate the implications for building interfaces of novel shapes, allowing for rich interactions, ultimately taking advantage of endless potential and sensomotoric abilities of our human bodies.

REFERENCES

1. Leap Motion Device. `https://www.leapmotion.com`. Accessed: 11-03-2016.
2. Project Soli, Google ATAP. `https://www.google.com/atap/project-soli/`. Accessed: 11-03-2016.
3. Alankus, G., Lazar, A., May, M., and Kelleher, C. Towards customizable games for stroke rehabilitation. In *Proceedings of the SIGCHI Conference on Human Factors in Computing Systems*, CHI '10, ACM (New York, NY, USA, 2010), 2113–2122.
4. Amunts, K., Schlaug, G., Jancke, L., Steinmetz, H., Schleicher, A., Dabringhaus, A., and Zilles, K. Motor cortex and hand motor skills: structural compliance in the human brain. *Hum Brain Mapp 5*, 3 (1997), 206–215.
5. Augsten, T., Kaefer, K., Meusel, R., Fetzer, C., Kanitz, D., Stoff, T., Becker, T., Holz, C., and Baudisch, P. Multitoe: High-precision interaction with back-projected floors based on high-resolution multi-touch input. In *Proceedings of the 23Nd Annual ACM Symposium on User Interface Software and Technology*, UIST '10, ACM (New York, NY, USA, 2010), 209–218.
6. Balaam, M., Rennick Egglestone, S., Fitzpatrick, G., Rodden, T., Hughes, A.-M., Wilkinson, A., Nind, T., Axelrod, L., Harris, E., Ricketts, I., Mawson, S., and Burridge, J. Motivating mobility: Designing for lived motivation in stroke rehabilitation. In *Proceedings of the SIGCHI Conference on Human Factors in Computing Systems*, CHI '11, ACM (New York, NY, USA, 2011), 3073–3082.
7. Boulanger, C., Boulanger, A., de Greef, L., Kearney, A., Sobel, K., Transue, R., Sweedyk, Z., Dietz, P. H., and Bathiche, S. Stroke rehabilitation with a sensing surface. In *Proceedings of the SIGCHI Conference on Human Factors in Computing Systems*, CHI '13, ACM (New York, NY, USA, 2013), 1243–1246.
8. Braun, A., Krepp, S., and Kuijper, A. Acoustic tracking of hand activities on surfaces. In *Proceedings of the 2Nd International Workshop on Sensor-based Activity Recognition and Interaction*, WOAR '15, ACM (New York, NY, USA, 2015), 9:1–9:5.
9. Brockmeyer, E., Poupyrev, I., and Hudson, S. Papillon: Designing curved display surfaces with printed optics. In *Proceedings of the 26th Annual ACM Symposium on User Interface Software and Technology*, UIST '13, ACM (New York, NY, USA, 2013), 457–462.
10. Cassinelli, A., Perrin, S., and Ishikawa, M. Smart laser-scanner for 3d human-machine interface. In *CHI '05 Extended Abstracts on Human Factors in Computing Systems*, CHI EA '05, ACM (New York, NY, USA, 2005), 1138–1139.
11. Collins, D. J., Morahan, B., Garcia-Bustos, J., Doerig, C., Plebanski, M., and Neild, A. Two-dimensional single-cell patterning with one cell per well driven by surface acoustic waves. *Nature communications 6* (2015).
12. Danworaphong, S., Tomoda, M., Matsumoto, Y., Matsuda, O., Ohashi, T., Watanabe, H., Nagayama, M., Gohara, K., Otsuka, P. H., and Wright, O. B. Three-dimensional imaging of biological cells with picosecond ultrasonics. *Applied physics letters 106*, 16 (2015), 163701.
13. Fenster, A., Downey, D. B., and Cardinal, H. N. Three-dimensional ultrasound imaging. *Physics in medicine and biology 46*, 5 (2001), R67.
14. Follmer, S., Johnson, M., Adelson, E., and Ishii, H. deform: An interactive malleable surface for capturing 2.5d arbitrary objects, tools and touch. In *Proceedings of the 24th Annual ACM Symposium on User Interface Software and Technology*, UIST '11, ACM (New York, NY, USA, 2011), 527–536.
15. Follmer, S., Leithinger, D., Olwal, A., Cheng, N., and Ishii, H. Jamming user interfaces: Programmable particle stiffness and sensing for malleable and shape-changing devices. In *Proceedings of the 25th Annual ACM Symposium on User Interface Software and Technology*, UIST '12, ACM (New York, NY, USA, 2012), 519–528.
16. Geurts, L., Deville, J., Abeele, V. V., Saldien, J., and Vanderloock, K. Skweezee studio: Turn your own plush toys into interactive squeezable objects. In *Proceedings of the 8th International Conference on Tangible, Embedded and Embodied Interaction*, TEI '14, ACM (New York, NY, USA, 2013), 377–380.
17. Hall, M., Frank, E., Holmes, G., Pfahringer, B., Reutemann, P., and Witten, I. H. The weka data mining software: An update. *SIGKDD Explor. Newsl. 11*, 1 (Nov. 2009), 10–18.
18. Harrison, C., and Hudson, S. E. Scratch input: Creating large, inexpensive, unpowered and mobile finger input surfaces. In *Proceedings of the 21st Annual ACM Symposium on User Interface Software and Technology*, UIST '08, ACM (New York, NY, USA, 2008), 205–208.
19. Harrison, C., Schwarz, J., and Hudson, S. E. Tapsense: Enhancing finger interaction on touch surfaces. In *Proceedings of the 24th Annual ACM Symposium on User Interface Software and Technology*, UIST '11, ACM (New York, NY, USA, 2011), 627–636.
20. Harrison, C., Tan, D., and Morris, D. Skinput: Appropriating the body as an input surface. In *Proceedings of the SIGCHI Conference on Human Factors in Computing Systems*, CHI '10, ACM (New York, NY, USA, 2010), 453–462.
21. Harrison, C., Xiao, R., and Hudson, S. Acoustic barcodes: Passive, durable and inexpensive notched identification tags. In *Proceedings of the 25th Annual ACM Symposium on User Interface Software and Technology*, UIST '12, ACM (New York, NY, USA, 2012), 563–568.

22. Hofer, R., Naeff, D., and Kunz, A. Flatir: Ftir multi-touch detection on a discrete distributed sensor array. In *Proceedings of the 3rd International Conference on Tangible and Embedded Interaction*, TEI '09, ACM (New York, NY, USA, 2009), 317–322.

23. Hook, J., Taylor, S., Butler, A., Villar, N., and Izadi, S. A reconfigurable ferromagnetic input device. In *Proceedings of the 22Nd Annual ACM Symposium on User Interface Software and Technology*, UIST '09, ACM (New York, NY, USA, 2009), 51–54.

24. Kato, H., and Kato, T. A camera-based tangible controller for cellular phones. In *Proceedings of the 11th International Conference on Human-Computer Interaction with Mobile Devices and Services*, MobileHCI '09, ACM (New York, NY, USA, 2009), 63:1–63:2.

25. Koh, J. T. K. V., Karunanayaka, K., Sepulveda, J., Tharakan, M. J., Krishnan, M., and Cheok, A. D. Liquid interface: A malleable, transient, direct-touch interface. *Comput. Entertain. 9*, 2 (July 2011), 7:1–7:8.

26. Kohl, C., Krause, M., Maierhofer, C., and Wöstmann, J. 2d-and 3d-visualisation of ndt-data using data fusion technique. *Materials and Structures 38*, 9 (2005), 817–826.

27. Laput, G., Brockmeyer, E., Hudson, S. E., and Harrison, C. Acoustruments: Passive, acoustically-driven, interactive controls for handheld devices. In *Proceedings of the 33rd Annual ACM Conference on Human Factors in Computing Systems*, CHI '15, ACM (New York, NY, USA, 2015), 2161–2170.

28. Laput, G., Chen, X. A., and Harrison, C. Sweepsense: Ad hoc configuration sensing using reflected swept-frequency ultrasonics. In *Proceedings of the 21st International Conference on Intelligent User Interfaces*, IUI '16, ACM (New York, NY, USA, 2016), 332–335.

29. Lopes, P., Jota, R., and Jorge, J. A. Augmenting touch interaction through acoustic sensing. In *Proceedings of the ACM International Conference on Interactive Tabletops and Surfaces*, ITS '11, ACM (New York, NY, USA, 2011), 53–56.

30. Löwe, M., Yosha, O., Krause, A., Wettach, R., and Krüger, N. Valeo: Alienation gesture-enhanced tactile pain logging. In *Proceedings of the Fourth International Conference on Tangible, Embedded, and Embodied Interaction*, TEI '10, ACM (New York, NY, USA, 2010), 213–216.

31. Marzo, A., Seah, S. A., Drinkwater, B. W., Sahoo, D. R., Long, B., and Subramanian, S. Holographic acoustic elements for manipulation of levitated objects. *Nature communications 6* (2015).

32. Murakami, T., and Nakajima, N. Direct and intuitive input device for 3-d shape deformation. In *Proceedings of the SIGCHI Conference on Human Factors in Computing Systems*, CHI '94, ACM (New York, NY, USA, 1994), 465–470.

33. Ono, M., Shizuki, B., and Tanaka, J. Touch and activate: Adding interactivity to existing objects using active acoustic sensing. In *Proceedings of the 26th Annual ACM Symposium on User Interface Software and Technology*, UIST '13, ACM (New York, NY, USA, 2013), 31–40.

34. Ono, M., Shizuki, B., and Tanaka, J. Sensing touch force using active acoustic sensing. In *Proceedings of the Ninth International Conference on Tangible, Embedded, and Embodied Interaction*, TEI '15, ACM (New York, NY, USA, 2015), 355–358.

35. Poupyrev, I., Harrison, C., and Sato, M. TouchÉ: Touch and gesture sensing for the real world. In *Proceedings of the 2012 ACM Conference on Ubiquitous Computing*, UbiComp '12, ACM (New York, NY, USA, 2012), 536–536.

36. Rekimoto, J. Smartskin: An infrastructure for freehand manipulation on interactive surfaces. In *Proceedings of the SIGCHI Conference on Human Factors in Computing Systems*, CHI '02, ACM (New York, NY, USA, 2002), 113–120.

37. Rekimoto, J., and Schwesig, C. Presenseii: Bi-directional touch and pressure sensing interactions with tactile feedback. In *CHI '06 Extended Abstracts on Human Factors in Computing Systems*, CHI EA '06, ACM (New York, NY, USA, 2006), 1253–1258.

38. Rendl, C., Greindl, P., Haller, M., Zirkl, M., Stadlober, B., and Hartmann, P. Pyzoflex: Printed piezoelectric pressure sensing foil. In *Proceedings of the 25th Annual ACM Symposium on User Interface Software and Technology*, UIST '12, ACM (New York, NY, USA, 2012), 509–518.

39. Rendl, C., Kim, D., Fanello, S., Parzer, P., Rhemann, C., Taylor, J., Zirkl, M., Scheipl, G., Rothländer, T., Haller, M., and Izadi, S. Flexsense: A transparent self-sensing deformable surface. In *Proceedings of the 27th Annual ACM Symposium on User Interface Software and Technology*, UIST '14, ACM (New York, NY, USA, 2014), 129–138.

40. Slyper, R., Poupyrev, I., and Hodgins, J. Sensing through structure: Designing soft silicone sensors. In *Proceedings of the Fifth International Conference on Tangible, Embedded, and Embodied Interaction*, TEI '11, ACM (New York, NY, USA, 2011), 213–220.

41. Smith, R. T., Thomas, B. H., and Piekarski, W. Digital foam interaction techniques for 3d modeling. In *Proceedings of the 2008 ACM Symposium on Virtual Reality Software and Technology*, VRST '08, ACM (New York, NY, USA, 2008), 61–68.

42. Tanaka, Y., Fukuda, T., Fujiwara, M., and Sano, A. Tactile sensor using acoustic reflection for lump detection in laparoscopic surgery. *International Journal of Computer Assisted Radiology and Surgery 10*, 2 (2015), 183–193.

43. Vanderloock, K., Vanden Abeele, V., Suykens, J. A., and Geurts, L. The skweezee system: Enabling the design and the programming of squeeze interactions. In *Proceedings of the 26th Annual ACM Symposium on User Interface Software and Technology*, UIST '13, ACM (New York, NY, USA, 2013), 521–530.

44. Wang, H.-S., Hsu, C., Chiu, D., and Tsai, S. N. Using augmented reality gaming system to enhance hand rehabilitation. In *2010 2nd International Conference on Education Technology and Computer*, vol. 3 (June 2010), V3–243–V3–246.

45. Weigel, M., Lu, T., Bailly, G., Oulasvirta, A., Majidi, C., and Steimle, J. iskin: Flexible, stretchable and visually customizable on-body touch sensors for mobile computing. In *Proceedings of the 33rd Annual ACM Conference on Human Factors in Computing Systems*, CHI '15, ACM (New York, NY, USA, 2015), 2991–3000.

46. Willis, K., Brockmeyer, E., Hudson, S., and Poupyrev, I. Printed optics: 3d printing of embedded optical elements for interactive devices. In *Proceedings of the 25th Annual ACM Symposium on User Interface Software and Technology*, UIST '12, ACM (New York, NY, USA, 2012), 589–598.

47. Wimmer, R., and Baudisch, P. Modular and deformable touch-sensitive surfaces based on time domain reflectometry. In *Proceedings of the 24th Annual ACM Symposium on User Interface Software and Technology*, UIST '11, ACM (New York, NY, USA, 2011), 517–526.

48. Withana, A., Peiris, R., Samarasekara, N., and Nanayakkara, S. zsense: Enabling shallow depth gesture recognition for greater input expressivity on smart wearables. In *Proceedings of the 33rd Annual ACM Conference on Human Factors in Computing Systems*, CHI '15, ACM (New York, NY, USA, 2015), 3661–3670.

49. Yao, L., Niiyama, R., Ou, J., Follmer, S., Della Silva, C., and Ishii, H. Pneui: Pneumatically actuated soft composite materials for shape changing interfaces. In *Proceedings of the 26th Annual ACM Symposium on User Interface Software and Technology*, UIST '13, ACM (New York, NY, USA, 2013), 13–22.

Flexy: Shape-Customizable, Single-Layer, Inkjet Printable Patterns for 1D and 2D Flex Sensing

Nirzaree Vadgama
Saarland University
Saarland Informatics Campus
Saarbrücken, Germany
nirzaree.svnit@gmail.com

Jürgen Steimle
Saarland University
Saarland Informatics Campus
Saarbrücken, Germany
steimle@cs.uni-saarland.de

Figure 1. Flexy enables designers and makers to easily, quickly and cheaply realize thin physical objects in custom shapes that feature an embedded deformation sensor. This enables a wide range of interactive applications with deformable surfaces.

ABSTRACT
We contribute a new technique for fabricating highly customized 1D and 2D flex sensing surfaces on thin and flexible substrates. It enables designers and makers to easily, quickly and inexpensively realize thin physical objects in custom shapes with an embedded deformation sensor. The deformation sensor is digitally designed and then fabricated with a single layer of conductive material in a single pass, using an off-the-shelf inkjet printer. We establish a design space and investigate how to realize flex sensing surfaces of highly varied geometries. In a technical evaluation, we demonstrate the technical feasibility of such sensors and investigate their response. Lastly, we demonstrate the practical applicability for tangible interfaces by presenting five example applications.

Author Keywords
Flexible sensor; conductive inkjet printing; deformable input devices; digital fabrication; rapid prototyping.

ACM Classification Keywords
H.5.m. Information interfaces and presentation.

INTRODUCTION
Flexible and deformable user interfaces are of increasing interest to the HCI research and interaction design communities. Advances in sensing and output technologies and miniaturization of electronics enable very thin, lightweight, and deformable form factors [19, 15, 20, 29, 12]. These open up a new space of intuitive physical interactions [9, 21, 33, 35, 26, 16, 30]. Moreover, varied and highly custom form factors allow for physical interactions that are tailored to the specific shape of the user interface [27, 32].

An important question for realizing interactive prototypes is how to sense deformations. Using external optical sensing limits mobility [14, 35]. Creating prototypes with commercially available flex sensors results in rather thick and not very deformable prototypes [21, 23, 37]. Printed deformation sensors offer the benefit of a very slim form factor and high deformability. However, existing approaches are either very complicated to fabricate and interface for HCI researchers and designers [29] or they are restricted to sensing of only coarse and discrete deformations [15].

We contribute a new technique for fabricating highly customized 1D and 2D flex sensing surfaces. It enables designers and makers to easily, quickly and inexpensively realize thin physical objects in custom shapes featuring an embedded deformation sensor. The technique is based on conductive inkjet printing [19] and on the basic sensing principle of resistive strain gauges.

While conductive inkjet printers are now getting widely used in HCI labs, it is unclear thus far if and how well this inexpensive and fast printing technology would allow for resistive sensing of deformations. In addition, printing and patterning approaches offer a lot of freedom in how conductive traces can be laid out. This enables an unprecedented geometric variety of sensor layouts, including highly varied sizes, arrangements, and shapes of sensors.

TEI '17, March 20 - 23, 2017, Yokohama, Japan

ACM 978-1-4503-4676-4/17/03$15.00
DOI: http://dx.doi.org/10.1145/3024969.3024989

This has the potential to open up a new design space for deformable user interfaces of very custom shapes.

In this paper we investigate the design space of easy-to-fabricate resistive flex sensors to support 1D and 2D flex sensing on deformable surfaces. Based on this design space, we will demonstrate how to realize flex sensing surfaces of highly varied geometry. Moreover, the design space allows to provide recommendations for interface designers on how to design such flex sensors for their interface prototypes.

In a technical evaluation, we demonstrate the technical feasibility of such sensors, investigating the response of these sensors for various dimensions and various types of deformations. Lastly, we demonstrate the practical applicability for tangible interfaces by presenting five example applications.

The main contributions of this paper are as follows:

1) We present a shape-customizable single layer pattern for flex sensing and introduce a design space. The pattern can sense single as well as multi-axial bending deformations. The design can be customized by adapting parameters of several primitives; this results in a wide range of geometries that can be augmented with the pattern. The flex sensor is fabricated through fast and inexpensive conductive inkjet printing.

2) We present spatial arrangements of the sensor design in 1D & 2D for sensing surface deformations, in varied sensor geometries. For sensing more complex deformations of a 1D surface, a linear array of sensing units is presented. A radial array enables sensing of 2D deformations on a surface.

3) We contribute results from a technical evaluation and present a set of practical application examples to demonstrate the feasibility of the approach.

RELATED WORK

Embedded flex sensors are commonly constructed using fabric, fiber optic or functional ink materials [6]. Fabric-based flex sensors are constructed by sandwiching a piezoresistive material between layers of conductive fabric [2]. Such a sensor design is primarily designed for pressure sensing; however it can also measure pressure as a function of flexion, thereby acting as a flex sensor. An optical bend sensor [9, 17] consists of pairs of light emitters and receivers, which are connected by an optical fiber. The intensity of the received signal varies in proportion to fiber bending. Shapetape [9], a bendable and twistable input strip, extends this principle by using fiber optic bend sensors spaced at regular intervals.

Functional ink-based deformation sensors [15, 19, 25, 29, 30, 24] are interesting for rapid prototyping since they can be easily fabricated through printing. Most commercial flex sensors based on conductive ink are printed as a linear pattern of carbon-based ink on a polyimide substrate with terminal connections of more conductive material, usually silver [1, 7]. The sensors function as analog resistors whose resistance depends on the magnitude of surface flexion. These sensors exhibit a large change in resistance in the permissible bending range due to the carbon-based ink material. Also, each sensor can only sense bending along a single axis. For sensing multi-axial deformations, multiple sensors need to be laid out on the substrate which would not be possible for highly curved or narrow shapes.

Prior work has investigated deformation sensing of paper substrates using an array of commercial strain gauges [11]. Commercial strain sensors are easy to interface, but not to customize and they are not very conformal to different surface shapes.

FlexSense [29] captures bending deformations of an A4-sized flexible sheet using screen-printed piezoelectric sensors. The surface deformation is reconstructed in high fidelity through machine learning techniques. However, the sensor has a fixed geometry and involves a multi-step, multi-material screen printing process. DefSense [8] investigates computational design of 3D deformable input devices of highly custom shapes. However, the approach builds on use of resistive wires and manual assembly. In contrast, our approach addresses sensors on thin surfaces that are printed in one pass.

As one of the instant fabrication techniques, we leverage conductive inkjet printing [19], a technique for printing conductive traces directly on a paper substrate that requires no post-processing steps. Using such single layer printed patterns, various sensing modalities have been investigated, including touch sensing, pressure and proximity sensing [15]. In conjunction with other electronic components, interesting functional prototypes have been reported in [18]. Novel interaction capabilities such as robustness against cutting [26] and deformability [15] arise, since sensors are directly printed on thin and flexible substrates. In this work, we investigate flex sensing on custom shapes using inkjet-printed patterns.

BASIC PRINCIPLE

Electrical conductivity of certain conductive materials changes with surface flexion. When such a material is subject to tensile (outward) bending, conductive particles within the material move apart from each other, increasing the overall resistance. Similarly, when the material is under compressive (inward) bending, conductive particles move closer to each other and hence overall resistance decreases [6]. The higher the magnitude of flexing, the higher is the change in resistance.

Commercial flex sensors use proprietary carbon-based ink [1, 7]. Recent work on embedded 3D printed strain gauges for flex sensing [25] used carbon conductive grease material. Graphite bounded with clay, as in pencil cores, also exhibits resistance change to flexion as demonstrated in [22]. Silver nanoparticle ink used for conductive inkjet printing also exhibits a change in resistance to flexing [19]; however it shows a smaller response range than the more resistive carbon-based ink.

The most basic design of a flex sensor is just a single line of conductor, whose resistance is measured from its two ends. The line can also be laid out in a U shape, resulting in two parallel lines responding to flexing with a higher response than a single line. Eventually, an even longer line can be laid out in a zig-zag pattern of parallel lines to maximize the sensing lines subjected to bending in the parallel direction. Figure 2(a) illustrates the standard design. The sensor design senses bending predominantly along the direction of the parallel sensor lines, referred as the longitudinal axis. We will demonstrate how to build upon this basic principle to realize customized sensor surfaces.

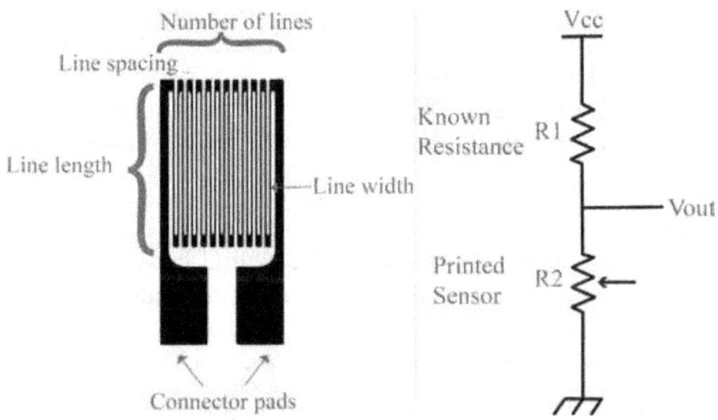

Figure 2. (a) Standard resistive flex sensor design, (b) Schematics of a voltage divider circuit

DESIGNING AND FABRICATING A SENSING SHEET

The first step towards making a sensor sheet consisting of a single sensor or an array is preparing a digital design in any 2D vector graphics application, such as Adobe Illustrator.

The design is then fabricated using printing. We focus on conductive inkjet printing [19], however the design can also be screen-printed using appropriate ink material [28, 24]. We used Mitsubishi NBSIJ–MU01 [5] silver nanoparticle ink. We successfully used a Canon iP100 photo inkjet printer and an Epson L220 inkjet printer for printing the designs. White and transparent PET films [5] were used as substrates for printing conductive traces. Other substrates such as resin coated paper and glossy photo paper can also be used, as reported in [19]. [19] reports the thickness of silver layer on paper is around 300 nm, and the cost of printing a one meter conductive trace of 1mm width is approximately 5 US cents.

The designs are printed in a single print step, as the design consists of a single material, both for active sensing as well as end connectors. The ends of the sensor design are generally made slightly wider to attach connecting wires. We connected the printed sensors to measurement circuit using thin flat cables adhered to the design with copper tape.

The change in resistance of the sensor can be measured directly with a resistance meter or can be read by a microcontroller using a voltage divider circuit, as shown in Figure 2(b). For single sensors and small sensor arrays, we used an Arduino Uno and for arrays requiring more I/O pins an Arduino Mega. In Figure 2(b), the resistance of the printed sensor (R2) is calculated by:

$$R2 = \left(\frac{Vcc}{Vout} - 1\right) * R1$$

where R1 is a known resistance, V_{cc} is the supply voltage and V_{out} is the measured voltage output. The known resistance value is generally chosen to be close to the flat state resistance of the printed design. For instance, for a printed design with flat state resistance of 500Ω, a known resistance R1 of 470Ω was used.

In scenarios involving either very low resistance change of the sensor pattern or when requiring high accuracy of sensing, resistance can be measured by high resolution measurement devices as in [3, 22] or circuits such as a wheatstone bridge with amplifier as in [11, 24].To increase robustness of the printed sensor, laminate of clear tape can be applied. This avoids moisture contact and silver being rubbed off. Other thinner laminate coating alternatives are reported in [19]. For short term usage, no laminate is required.

DESIGN PRIMITIVES

The possibility to design a flex sensor in a vector graphics application opens up a wide space for customizing the shape. It enables novel opportunities for tangible interfaces. In this section, we give an overview of the design primitives and how these affect sensing. The design of a flex sensing geometry has the following primitives: i) number of sensing lines, ii) line length, iii) line width, iv) line spacing, v) composition and vi) connecting traces. The resistance of the pattern depends on the sensor dimensions by

$$R = \rho \frac{L}{A} \quad (1)$$

where L is the sensor length, A is the cross-sectional area and ρ is resistivity of the sensing material. The cross-sectional area is determined by line width and line thickness. Line thickness can be customized by printing a pattern multiple times.

Number of sensing lines The overall change in resistance of the pattern to flexing depends on the number of sensing lines. With more sensing lines, the resistance change to flexing is higher as compared to fewer sensing lines. Our sensor designs typically have 10 to 30 sensing lines. In designs where the entire shape is encased by a continuous sensor, such as crescent and leaf designs (Figure 1) the total sensing lines are more however intermediate tapping lines can be inserted to measure a more granular response.

Line length Sensor resistance measurement indicates the average strain across the active sensing area, hence the active line length can be matched with the target deformation curvature. Typically, the line length of our sensors varies between 2cm and 5cm.

Line width Line width can be customized depending on the sensing material. For more conductive materials such as silver nanoparticle ink, wider sensing lines result in a lower sensor response and are generally not preferred as more material is consumed with no advantage in sensing response. Instead, for applications that require less response range, fewer thin sensor lines can be drawn instead of a larger number of wide lines. However, commercial flex sensors are printed typically as a single wide line, as they use carbon-based ink. The typical width of our sensor designs varies between 300µm and 500µm.

Line spacing This primitive caters to the linear and angular spacing between the sensor lines. Each of the sensor lines need not be parallel to each other and can be placed at different angular orientations. This enables sensing multi-axial deformations. Intermediate tapping can be done for multi-axial sensing designs depending on the required sensing granularity. Figure 3 illustrates an omni-directional circular sensor.

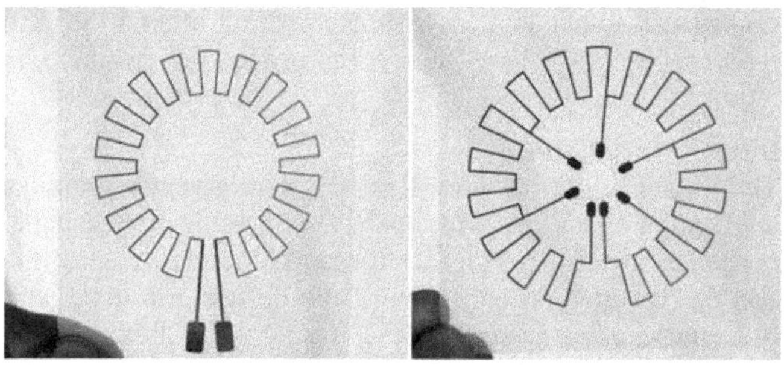

Figure 3. An omni-directional flex sensor design (right) with intermediate tapping

The linear spacing between the sensor lines is also customizable. Generally, the linear spacing between the sensor lines is kept much smaller than the sensor length. If the spacing is larger, then the change in resistance to flexing across sensor length is attenuated within the material laid out in perpendicular direction. In our standard design, the line spacing is slightly less than twice the line width. In other designs, the maximum spacing is 1mm except in designs such as the fish fin, where we used a considerably wider spacing to mimic the visual appearance of a caudal fin.

Composition This primitive captures how multiple sensing units within a geometry are laid spatially. Multiple sensing units can be laid on 1D & 2D surfaces in different geometries as described in the next section. Linear and angular spacing between each of the sensing units can be customized for different application scenarios. For instance, two sensing units in a bird shape design are slightly curved to fit the wing shape better. As another example, five sensing units arranged in a flower shape allow for multiple points of interaction on a single flower-shaped sensor. (Figure 1)

Connecting traces These traces connect the sensor design to the area on the substrate where contacts are tethered to a microcontroller. The connecting traces are generally quite wide to have less resistance, and typically curved to avoid resistance change due to any uni-axial flexion.

In the next section, we discuss sensor geometries for 1D & 2D, along with interesting custom shape geometries.

SPATIAL 1D & 2D SENSOR GEOMETRIES

A single sensor can only sense uni-radial flexing, hence to sense more complex flex deformations, multiple sensors can be arranged in different spatial arrangements. For a one-dimensional sensing strip, multiple sensing units can be arranged linearly with some spacing. For two-dimensional surfaces we propose a circular arrangement, with individual sensor units oriented in different directions. The total response of surface deformation is simply the integration of individual sensing unit responses.

Apart from these generic arrangements, the sensor geometries can be customized to suit a wide variety of custom 2D shapes. We illustrate six example patterns (Figure 1, Figure 9): inchworm, bird wing, flower, leaf, crescent and fish fin.

Inchworm: An inchworm design illustrates the simplest sensor design. The design spans the central body shape of a paper inchworm and can sense its curvature while it is being moved. The sensor consists of a U-shaped line design. *(design dimensions: length = 62mm, line width = 0.5mm)*

Bird wing: This design illustrates a composition of multiple sensing units. A flex sensor spanning each of the wings can capture flexion during wing flapping. Sensing lines in each unit span the wings partly and are slightly curved to better fit to the wing shape. *(design dimensions: length = 45mm, width = 0.35mm, curved at 8°)*

Flower: This design illustrates a circular arrangement of individual sensing units. The example design consists of five petals connected through a central unit. Each of the sensing units consists of varying line lengths to conform to the petal shape and is connected to the central connector. *(design dimensions: length1 = 29.78mm, length2 = 35.36mm, length3 = 36.46mm, width =0.33mm)*

Leaf design: This design illustrates alignment of the sensing lines at an angle to better fit the target shape. A single sensor runs through the entire leaf shape. Intermediate tapping points can be added for granular sensing response. *(design dimensions: leaf length: 80mm, width: 35mm, sensing lines aligned at 45°)*

Crescent design: This design illustrates embedding a flex sensing within an extremely curved surface. Length of the sensing lines is continuously varied to adapt to the crescent shape. *(design dimensions: length of crescent: 77 mm, width of crescent: 22mm, line width: 0.35mm)*

Fish design: This design illustrates how a sensor can mimic the visual appearance of the interactive object. We illustrate a sensor placed around the caudal fin (tail) of the fish. The sensor can sense the back and forth wavy movement of the tail. It has fewer sensing lines with varying spacing between them. *(design dimensions: length of fin =30mm, width of fin = 44mm, line width = 0.5mm)*

SPECIAL CASE OF FOLD SENSING

A fold is an extreme case of bending, resulting in an axial crease on the surface. Such a deformation causes a much higher increase in the sensor resistance. When the fold is released, the resistance value stays still considerably higher than the flat state resistance due to the permanent physical deformation of the substrate and the sensor. A fold can be sensed once through such a sharp increase in the sensor resistance. Due to the large change in resistance at a fold, the sensor pattern can be minimized to a single line design (Figure 4).

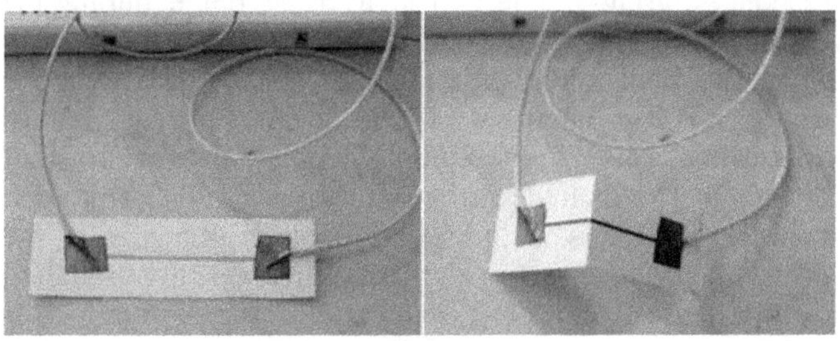

Figure 4. Sensing folding through single line sensors. (left) flat line, sensor released after a sharp fold at the center

An inkjet-printed trace (*length = 4cm and width = 0.5mm*) on a sheet of paper had a flat state resistance of 63Ω. In a completely folded state, the resistance was 356Ω (565% increase). After the sensor was released from the pinched state, the resistance still stayed at 231Ω (366% of flat state). These inexpensive and simple line sensors can be arranged at to-be-folded axes on a deformable surface for sensing the sequence of folds for a single use, as we illustrate in the applications section.

CHARACTERIZATION AND EVALUATION

In this section, we investigate sensor response in different deformation scenarios through a set of technical experiments. We then relate the findings to answer practical questions from an interface designer's perspective: what is the sensor response at different bending curvatures, how does it compare to a commercial flex sensor, how does the sensor behave for repetitive deformations, and how does the response vary with sensor dimensions?

Depending on the applied deformation, sensor response falls in two categories: static and dynamic. In static deformation, the sensor moves from one state to another slowly, and it has time to settle at a state before being deformed to another state. In dynamic deformation, the sensor is deformed at a higher speed and it does not have time to settle at a particular state.

We conducted two experiments to understand the sensor response for static and dynamic deformations. We printed sensors of two sizes relevant for practical usage scenarios, as illustrated as inset in Figure6. (***large sensor**: total length (l)* *61.4 mm, sensor line length (sl) 39 mm, no. of lines (n) 22, line width (w) 0.35 mm, spacing(s) 0.65 mm,* ***small sensor**: 55% scaled version of the larger sensor*). Three sensors of each of the sizes were printed.

In the first experiment, we 3D-printed 7 cylinders of different curvatures (with diameter between 3-10 cm). We bent the sensors across each of them, with printed side up (tensile bending) and printed side down (compressive bending). Each sensor was flexed across a cylinder, resistance was measured and then the sensor was brought back to flat state and the process was repeated for consecutive cylinders.

Figure 5 shows the normalized (R/R_{flat}) response of both the sensor sizes for tensile (outward) flexing. As expected, the sensor resistance increases from the flat state value with increasing curvatures (smaller bend radii). A third-degree polynomial curve fitted best to each of the responses (large sensor: $R^2 = 0.9883$, small sensor: $R^2 = 0.9921$).

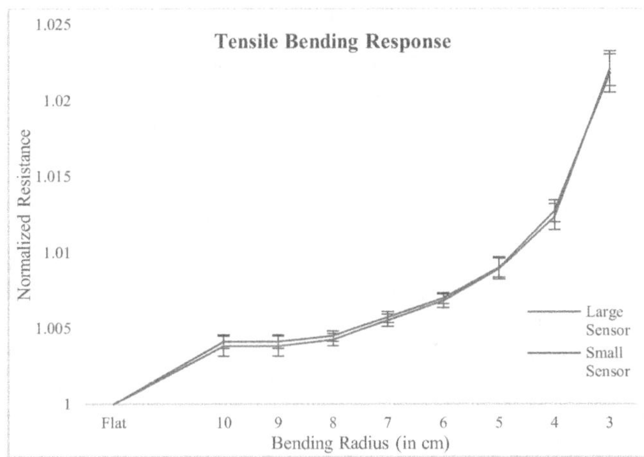

Figure 5. Sensor response to tensile bending

Figure 6 shows the response of sensors to compressive bending. The sensor resistance decreases from flat state for increasing curvatures, as expected. Each response can be well represented by a polynomial of third degree as it does for tensile bending (large sensor: $R^2 = 0.9957$, small sensor: $R^2 = 0.9927$).

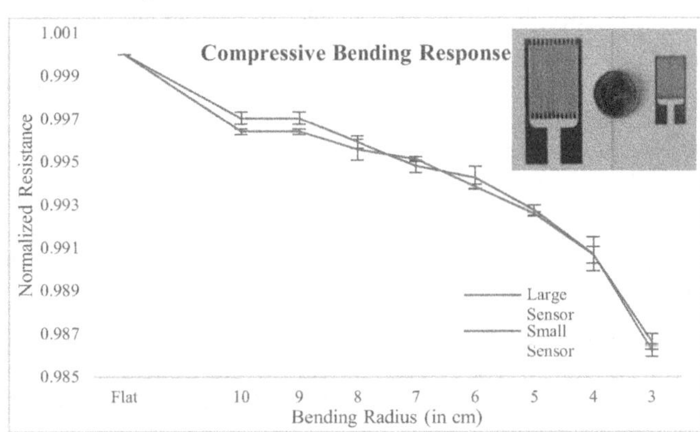

Figure 6. Sensor response to compressive bending

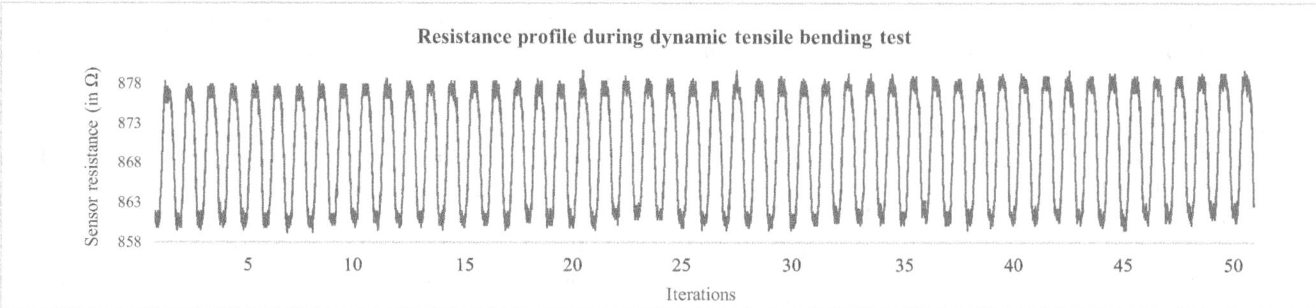

Figure 7. Sensor response during 50 iteration dynamic tensile bending test

These findings show that the sensors have a continuous response for flexing in both directions. A third-degree polynomial yields a robust mapping function of resistance to curvature in the measured range. Hence, for a sensor to be used for static deformations, the mapping can be stored beforehand, and then the measured resistance values can be used for a lookup of surface curvature.

We also find that normalized sensor response (R/R_{flat}) for tensile and compressive bending for both the sensor sizes is quite similar. Tensile bending response is slightly higher ($\Delta R/R_{flat}$ = 2.213% (large sensor), $\Delta R/R_{flat}$ = 2.18% (small sensor)) than compressive bending response ($\Delta R/R_{flat}$ = 1.34%(large sensor), $\Delta R/R_{flat}$ = 1.38% (small sensor)).

To compare the response of our design to a commercial flex sensor, we took a 2.2 inch carbon ink-based sensor [7] and flexed it across different diameter cylinders, with printed side up and down. The sensor datasheet reports a tolerance of 30% for the resistance values. Flat state resistance of the sensor was around 21.6kΩ and the resistance at 2cm tensile radius of curvature was 58.8kΩ ($\Delta R/R$ = 172.0%). The bending response of this sensor also followed a third order polynomial (R^2 = 0.996) during tensile bending. The compressive bending response of the sensor was slightly irregular and there was no monotonous reduction in the resistance from flat state resistance. The resistance at 2cm compressive bending curvature was 19.52 kΩ ($\Delta R/R$ = 11.5%). This is in-line with findings from other experiments on commercial flex sensors, which have also indicated a non-linear relation between sensor resistance and bending radius [34]. Our findings indicate that in tensile bending the range of the commercial sensor is considerably higher, related to use of carbon-based sensing material compared to silver ink. However, its response range is considerably lower and slightly irregular in compressive bending.

The next experiment was conducted to understand the sensor response for repetitive dynamic deformations. We measured the sensor response for deformations generated by a simplistic rack and pinion based dc motor setup. We took a substrate containing a large sized sensor. Both the ends of the substrate were mounted to revolute joints, to allow movement during flexion. One of the ends was kept steady while the other moved linearly through the motor, generating repetitive flexion of the substrate. The sensor was flexed fifty times from flat state to a curvature of 2.96 cm at a speed of ~0.25Hz. Figure 7 shows the running average of the sensor response during the test. The average range during the iterations was found to be 16.39Ω (standard deviation: 0.43). Since the deviation in the range and flat state resistance is small, no re-calibration of the sensor is required for applications where the acceptable error is above the observed deviation. The slight deviation in this case could be attributed to multiple factors including mechanical properties of the print paper sheet, minor irregularities in the dc motor motion and properties of the silver nanoparticle ink. Factors such as speed and extent of deformation and number of iterations also affect the sensor behavior in dynamic deformations. A detailed characterization of dynamic behavior of the sensor is beyond the scope for the present work.

Sensor dimensions affect the sensor response following equation (1), within the resolution limits of the printer. Normalized sensor response for uniformly scaled sizes described earlier has been observed to be identical. Our experience indicates that when the sensor lines are very thin (≤ 250μm), the line width of closely spaced parallel lines is not very uniform when printed, i.e. few lines are slightly wider than others in prints. Sensors printed with such dimensions still work, however the resistance relation to dimensions as given by equation (1) now depends on the actual printed width of each of the lines. We achieved best sensing results with the standard design.

EXAMPLE APPLICATIONS

In this section, we showcase application scenarios using a single sensor as well as multi sensor 1D and 2D arrays. In the design of these application cases, we have favored simplicity over complex functionality, to showcase how creative makers who might have only little programming skills can leverage the easy-to-use printing framework for creating their custom flex sensors.

Curvature measurement of objects

A single sensor is well-suited to measure curvature of objects and surfaces within its responsive range. We took five objects with diameters ranging from 1.5cm to 8cm. The sensor was calibrated to an accuracy of 1cm and could correctly classify the curvature of the test objects (Figure 8).

Figure 8. Curvature measurement using a single sensor

Animating virtual entities through direct physical input

In this application example, we describe usage of i) a single sensor and ii) a linear 1D array. A flex sensor can be used as a direct physical input for animating virtual entities. Locomotion patterns of certain species involve flexion and we can emulate them through the sensors. We have created *Inchi*, a virtual inchworm that can be animated through direct physical input.

Radius of the motion loop can be regulated through the extent of flexion of the sensor. Since we have a bi-directional sensor, we can also associate inward and outward bending to movement of *Inchi* in forward and reverse directions (Figure 9).

Figure 9. Inchi, a virtual inchworm animated with a single flex sensor

A printed sensor containing an array of two sensing units is used to animate an emoticon. Physical shape of the sensor sheets is mapped to one of the various moods: *neutral, happy, sad, confused* (Figure 10).

Interactive paper craft

Kids can design interactive paper crafts that contain flex sensors in custom shapes. Specific deformation gestures can be mapped to audio output. For instance, flexing a bird wing can generate a flapping sound, moving the tail of a fish can generate a wave sound, humming bees can be heard when flexing the petals of a paper flower.

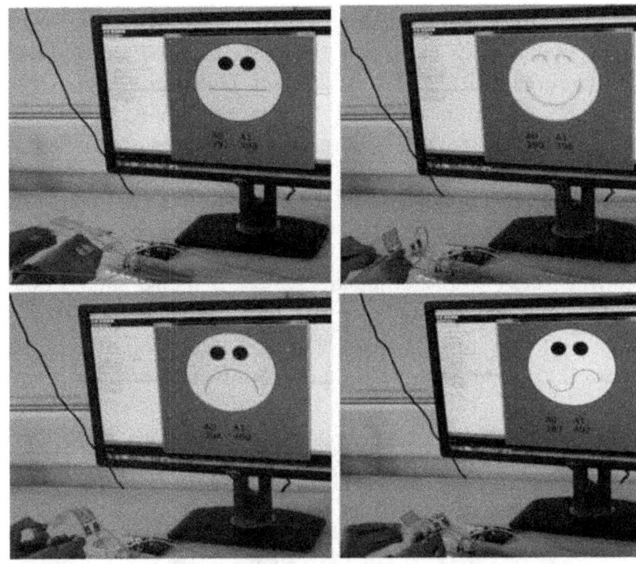

Figure 10. A two sensor linear array animating four moods of an emoticon (clockwise from top): i) neutral ii) happy iii) confused iv) sad.

Multimodal I/O sheet

We can integrate other sensing modalities such as touch sensing [15] and output capabilities such as LEDs along with flex sensing on a single printed sheet. Such an I/O surface allows users to build interactive objects with multimodal interaction capabilities. Figure 11 shows a sample bow shaped sheet containing two flex sensors on the side and a touch sensor in between. Each flex sensor is accompanied by a resistor to form a voltage divider. Each of the sensors have a corresponding led that glows when the sensor is interacted with (flexed or touched).

In Figure 11, left flex sensor has been bent resulting in turning the left led on. The components are adhered to the printed connectors using a conductive Z tape [19].

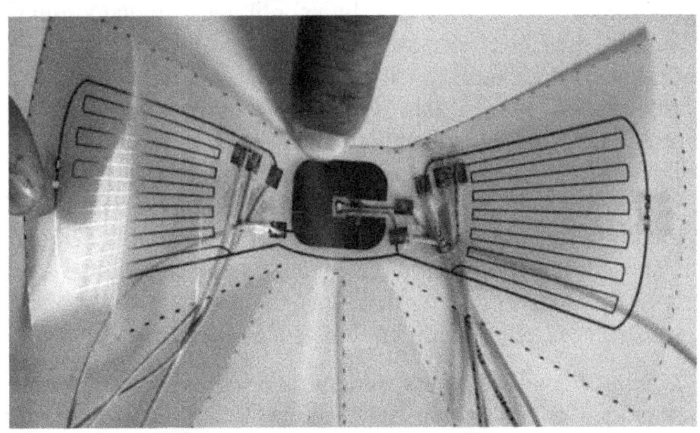

Figure 11. Printed IO Sheet with touch, flex inputs and LEDs

Origami training tool

In this application case, we showcase two different 2D sensor geometries. We leverage the fold sensing ability of the design. Making an origami model involves a one-time usage of specific paper surface. Inkjet-printed sensor arrays can act as an affordable guidance tool. Novice users can be interactively guided towards the correct sequence of folds and be corrected if a step is skipped. One can alternatively use plain graphite, drawn with a pencil, to pattern it on thinner origami paper. A graphite line (*2cm x 0.4cm*) on a sheet of origami paper had a flat state resistance of 47.7kΩ. In completely folded state resistance was 124.8kΩ (261.6% increase).

We illustrate two origami shapes: boat and airplane. A boat shape can be made with box pleat folds (folds at 90° and 45°) [10]. Figures12(a-b) show the respective front and back sensor lines arrangements for a boat shape fold on an origami sheet. Figures 12(c-d) show the sensor lines wired with copper tape and flat cables. For the airplane design, sensors can be laid out in a radial 2D arrangement, as shown in Figure 12(e and f).

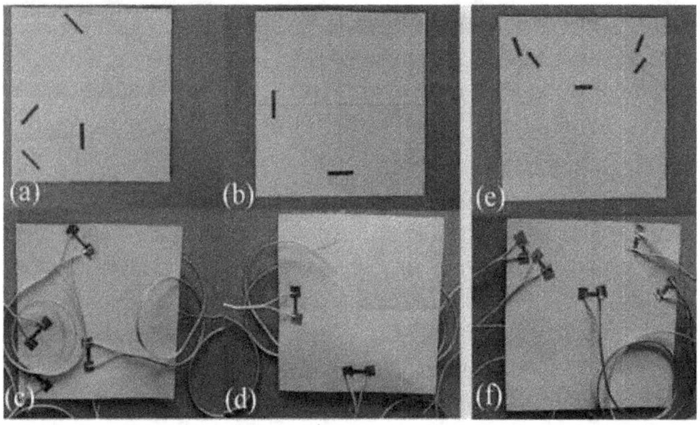

Figure 12. Line sensor arrangement for boat and airplane shapes: Boat (a-b) Sensor placement (front and back) with respective wiring (c-d); Airplane (e) Sensor placement with respective wiring (f).

DISCUSSION

Generality of the design: The presented sensor design (also referred to as a meander line/continuous folded/sinuous pattern) has been investigated in several other electronic design architectures such as printed inductors [36] and antennas [31]. Certain styles of decorative art and architecture also inculcate such continuous line pattern [4]. Locomotion patterns in species such as fishes, snakes, worms [13] involve generation of flexion waves along the length of the body for propulsion. Wind current over sand dunes and water current on soil create meander patterns over time. Our investigation related to flex sensing in highly deformable substrates is yet an additional instance of its generality.

Limitations: Connectors remain a challenge for printed sensors. Connection wires add weight to the sensing surface and can affect its deformation. Even with printed connector traces, we eventually need to wire them for connection to the controller and in cases such as multi-modal IO sheet with close spacing between the connector pads, connections become quite tricky. For fold sensing of complex patterns, printed connectors can also be challenging as they would be accidentally folded while making the origami shape. Silver nanoparticle ink demonstrates a small resistance change to flexing due to its high conductivity, which in turn requires the design to have multiple thin sensing lines for a measurable, repetitive response. This leads to a slightly wider flex sensing design compared to commercial flex sensors which are relatively narrower. Scalability of sensor designs is essentially limited by the effective printing resolution (we recommend a trace width above 250 μm when using our printer) and by the number of analog input pins of the microcontroller.

Directions of future work: Design of an automated tool for generating sensor designs including printed connectors, for user-defined shapes and materials will be an interesting direction for future research. Exploration of different connection mechanisms for printed sensors, such as vias to connect different layers of a printed sheet would be interesting. Once a wider set of functional materials can be printed with inexpensive printers, it will be relevant to explore their characteristics for custom-designed flex sensors. Advances in 3D printing of functional materials will make 3D printed designs a further interesting avenue for future work.

CONCLUSION

In this work, we presented the design and fabrication of shape-customizable flex sensing patterns. The sensor can be designed digitally and printed. It offers the unique advantages of visual customizability, single and multi-axial flex sensing, single material and single step fabrication, and low cost. Moreover, it is easy to interface with for non-experts. We also presented different spatial arrangements of the sensor in 1D and 2D and showed how they can be used for tangible user interfaces. We believe that the design and fabrication guidelines will aid HCI researchers, practitioners, designers and makers to quickly, easily and cheaply realize deformable sensors and in-turn open new avenues of interactivity.

ACKNOWLEDGEMENTS

This work has been partially funded by the German Research Foundation under award number EXC 284: Multimodal Computing and Interaction. We would like to thank Virendra Ashiwal, Narayan Rangarajan and Mayuresh Sarpotdar for their valuable and timely technical feedback and support.

REFERENCES

1. Flexpoint bend sensor. Retrieved January 22, 2017 from http://www.flexpoint.com/.
2. How to make a fabric bend sensor. Retrieved January 22, 2017 from http://www.kobakant.at/DIY/?p=20.
3. Keithley 2400 source meter. Retrieved January 22, 2017 from http://www.tek.com/keithley-source-measure-units/keithley-smu-2400-series-sourcemeter.
4. Meander pattern. Retrieved January 22, 2017 from https://en.wikipedia.org/wiki/Meander_(art).
5. Mitsubishi silver nano inkjet system. Retrieved January 22, 2017 from http://diamond-jet.com/silvernanoinkjetsystem.aspx.
6. Sensor wiki flexion. Retrieved January 22, 2017 from http://www.sensorwiki.org/doku.php/sensors/flexion.
7. Spectra symbol bend sensor. Retrieved January 22, 2017 from http://www.spectrasymbol.com/flex-sensor.
8. Moritz Bächer, Benjamin Hepp, Fabrizio Pece, Paul G. Kry, Bernd Bickel, Bernhard Thomaszewski, and Otmar Hilliges. Defsense: Computational design of customized deformable input devices. In *Proceedings of the 2016 CHI Conference on Human Factors in Computing Systems*, CHI '16, 3806–3816. http://doi.acm.org/10.1145/2858036.2858354
9. Ravin Balakrishnan, George Fitzmaurice, Gordon Kurtenbach, and Karan Singh. Exploring interactive curve and surface manipulation using a bend and twist sensitive input strip. In *Proceedings of the 1999 Symposium on Interactive 3D Graphics*, I3D '99, 111–118. http://doi.acm.org/10.1145/300523.300536
10. Nadia Benbernou, Erik D. Demaine, Martin L. Demaine, and Aviv Ovadya. A universal crease pattern for folding orthogonal shapes. *CoRR*, abs/0909.5388, 2009. http://arxiv.org/abs/0909.5388
11. Chin-yu Chien, Rong-Hao Liang, Long-Fei Lin, Liwei Chan, and Bing-Yu Chen. Flexibend: Enabling interactivity of multi-part, deformable fabrications using single shape-sensing strip. In *Proceedings of the 28th Annual ACM Symposium on User Interface Software & Technology*, UIST '15, 659–663. http://doi.acm.org/10.1145/2807442.2807456
12. Artem Dementyev, Hsin-Liu (Cindy) Kao, and Joseph A. Paradiso. Sensortape: Modular and programmable 3d-aware dense sensor network on a tape. In *Proceedings of the 28th Annual ACM Symposium on User Interface Software &Technology*, UIST '15, 649–658. http://doi.acm.org/10.1145/2807442.2807507
13. Kelly M. Dorgan, Chris J. Law, and Greg W. Rouse. Meandering worms: mechanics of undulatory burrowing in muds. In *Proceedings of the Royal Society of London B: Biological Sciences*, 280(1757), 2013. http://dx.doi.org/10.1098/rspb.2012.2948
14. David T. Gallant, Andrew G. Seniuk, and Roel Vertegaal. Towards more paper-like input: Flexible input devices for foldable interaction styles. In *Proceedings of the 21st Annual ACM Symposium on User Interface Software and Technology*, UIST '08, 283–286. http://doi.acm.org/10.1145/1449715.1449762
15. Nan-Wei Gong, Jürgen Steimle, Simon Olberding, Steve Hodges, Nicholas Edward Gillian, Yoshihiro Kawahara, and Joseph A. Paradiso. Printsense: A versatile sensing technique to support multimodal flexible surface interaction. In *Proceedings of the SIGCHI Conference on Human Factors in Computing Systems*, CHI '14, 1407–1410. http://doi.acm.org/10.1145/2556288.2557173
16. Daniel Groeger, Elena Chong Loo, and Jürgen Steimle. Hotflex: Post-print customization of 3d prints using embedded state change. In *Proceedings of the 2016 CHI Conference on Human Factors in Computing Systems*, CHI '16, pages 420–432. http://doi.acm.org/10.1145/2858036.2858191
17. Gero Herkenrath, Thorsten Karrer, and Jan Borchers. Twend: Twisting and bending as new interaction gesture in mobile devices. In *CHI '08 Extended Abstracts on Human Factors in Computing Systems*, CHI EA '08, pages 3819–3824, New York, NY, USA, 2008. http://doi.acm.org/10.1145/1358628.1358936
18. Y. Kawahara, S. Hodges, Nan-Wei Gong, S. Olberding, and J. Steimle. Building functional prototypes using conductive inkjet printing. *Pervasive Computing, IEEE*, 13(3):30–38, July 2014. http://doi.org/10.1109/MPRV.2014.41
19. Yoshihiro Kawahara, Steve Hodges, Benjamin S. Cook, Cheng Zhang, and Gregory D. Abowd. Instant inkjet circuits: Lab-based inkjet printing to support rapid prototyping of ubicomp devices. In *Proceedings of the 2013 ACM International Joint Conference on Pervasive and Ubiquitous Computing*, UbiComp '13, 363–372. http://doi.acm.org/10.1145/2493432.2493486
20. Johan Kildal, Susanna Paasovaara, and Viljakaisa Aaltonen. Kinetic device: Designing interactions with a deformable mobile interface. In *CHI '12 Extended Abstracts on Human Factors in Computing Systems*, CHI EA '12, 1871–1876. http://doi.acm.org/10.1145/2212776.2223721

21. Byron Lahey, Audrey Girouard, Winslow Burleson, and Roel Vertegaal. Paperphone: Understanding the use of bend gestures in mobile devices with flexible electronic paper displays. In *Proceedings of the SIGCHI Conference on Human Factors in Computing Systems*, CHI '11, 1303–1312. http://doi.acm.org/10.1145/1978942.1979136
22. Cheng-Wei Lin, Zhibo Zhao, Jaemyung Kim, and Jiaxing Huang. Pencil drawn strain gauges and chemiresistors on paper. *Scientific Reports*, 4:3812, January 2014. http://dx.doi.org/10.1038/srep03812
23. J. Lo and A. Girouard. Fabricating bendy: Design and development of deformable prototypes. *IEEE Pervasive Computing*, 13(3):40–46, July 2014. http://doi.org/10.1109/MPRV.2014.47
24. Joanne Lo, Doris Jung Lin Lee, Nathan Wong, David Bui, and Eric Paulos. Skintillates: Designing and creating epidermal interactions. In *Proceedings of the 2016 ACM Conference on Designing Interactive Systems*, DIS '16, 853–864. http://doi.acm.org/10.1145/2901790.2901885
25. Joseph T. Muth, Daniel M. Vogt, Ryan L. Truby, Yig˘it Mengüç, David B. Kolesky, Robert J. Wood, and Jennifer A. Lewis. Embedded 3d printing of strain sensors within highly stretchable elastomers. *Advanced Materials*, 26(36):6307–6312, 2014. http://dx.doi.org/10.1002/adma.201400334
26. Simon Olberding, Nan-Wei Gong, John Tiab, Joseph A. Paradiso, and Jürgen Steimle. A cuttable multi-touch sensor. In *Proceedings of the 26th Annual ACM Symposium on User Interface Software and Technology*, UIST '13, 245–254. http://doi.acm.org/10.1145/2501988.2502048
27. Simon Olberding, Sergio Soto Ortega, Klaus Hildebrandt, and Jürgen Steimle. Foldio: Digital fabrication of interactive and shape-changing objects with foldable printed electronics. In *Proceedings of the 28th Annual ACM Symposium on User Interface Software &Technology*, UIST '15, 223–232. http://doi.acm.org/10.1145/2807442.2807494
28. Simon Olberding, Michael Wessely, and Jürgen Steimle. Printscreen: Fabricating highly customizable thin-film touch-displays. In *Proceedings of the 27th Annual ACM Symposium on User Interface Software and Technology*, UIST '14, 281–290. http://doi.acm.org/10.1145/2642918.2647413
29. Christian Rendl, David Kim, Sean Fanello, Patrick Parzer, Christoph Rhemann, Jonathan Taylor, Martin Zirkl, Gregor Scheipl, Thomas Rothländer, Michael Haller, and Shahram Izadi. Flexsense: A transparent self-sensing deformable surface. In *Proceedings of the 27th Annual ACM Symposium on User Interface Software and Technology*, UIST '14, 129–138. http://doi.acm.org/10.1145/2642918.2647405
30. Christian Rendl, David Kim, Patrick Parzer, Sean Fanello, Martin Zirkl, Gregor Scheipl, Michael Haller, and Shahram Izadi. Flexcase: Enhancing mobile interaction with a flexible sensing and display cover. In *Proceedings of the 2016 CHI Conference on Human Factors in Computing Systems*, CHI '16, 5138–5150. http://doi.acm.org/10.1145/2858036.2858314
31. Analisa Russo, Bok Yeop Ahn, Jacob J. Adams, Eric B. Duoss, Jennifer T. Bernhard, and Jennifer A. Lewis. Pen-on-paper flexible electronics. *Advanced Materials*, 23(30):3426–3430, 2011. http://dx.doi.org/10.1002/adma.201101328
32. Martin Schmitz, Mohammadreza Khalilbeigi, Matthias Balwierz, Roman Lissermann, Max Mühlhäuser, and Jürgen Steimle. 2015. Capricate: A Fabrication Pipeline to Design and 3D Print Capacitive Touch Sensors for Interactive Objects. In *Proceedings of the 28th Annual ACM Symposium on User Interface Software & Technology* (UIST '15). 253-258. http://dx.doi.org/10.1145/2807442.2807503
33. Carsten Schwesig, Ivan Poupyrev, and Eijiro Mori. Gummi: A bendable computer. In *Proceedings of the SIGCHI Conference on Human Factors in Computing Systems*, CHI '04, 263–270. http://doi.acm.org/10.1145/985692.985726
34. Lisa Simone ,Derek G. Kamper. Design considerations for a wearable monitor to measure finger posture. *Journal of NeuroEngineering and Rehabilitation*, 2(1):5, 2005. http://dx.doi.org/10.1186/1743-0003-2-5
35. Jürgen Steimle, Andreas Jordt, and Pattie Maes. Flexpad: Highly flexible bending interactions for projected handheld displays. In *Proceedings of the SIGCHI Conference on Human Factors in Computing Systems*, CHI '13, 237–246. http://doi.acm.org/10.1145/2470654.2470688
36. Victor Torres, Ruben Ortuno, Pablo Rodriguez-Ulibarri, Amadeu Griol, Alejandro Martinez, Miguel Navarro-Cia, Miguel Beruete, and Mario Sorolla. Mid-infrared plasmonic inductors: Enhancing inductance with meandering lines. *Sci. Rep.*, 4:–, January 2014. http://dx.doi.org/10.1038/srep03592
37. Jun-ichiro Watanabe, Arito Mochizuki, and Youichi Horry. Bookisheet: Bendable device for browsing content using the metaphor of leafing through the pages. In *Proceedings of the 10th International Conference on Ubiquitous Computing*, UbiComp '08, 360–369. http://doi.acm.org/10.1145/1409635.1409684

Bendy: Exploring Mobile Gaming with Flexible Devices

Jessica Lo[1,2]
[1]Eindhoven University of Technology
Eindhoven, The Netherlands
j.m.lo@tue.nl

Audrey Girouard[2]
[2]Carleton University
Ottawa, Canada
audrey.girouard@carleton.ca

ABSTRACT
We explore the use of bend gestures in gaming with flexible devices and investigate the size differences between smartphones and tablets. We conducted a study asking users to select bend gestures for nine tasks derived from gaming, grouped by navigation, action, and deformation. Our results suggest pairing opposing tasks, such as navigating left and right, by gesture location. We saw low consensus for action tasks, and strong association between the location of the gestures and the location of the visual, relating to the Simon Effect. We suggest guidelines for the design of game controls for flexible devices. We implemented the proposed gestures into six games using an interactive flexible prototype in our second study. Our results are similar between sizes, yet with an overall user preference for the smaller prototype. We observed that hand positioning is an important usability issue to consider when designing flexible devices.

Keywords
Deformable user interface; deformable prototype; flexible display; bend gestures; mobile games

ACM Classification Keywords
H.5.2 [Information interfaces and presentation]: User Interfaces.

INTRODUCTION
We use deformation to interact with everyday objects, allowing for a rich set of possibilities involving many degrees of freedom with intuitive interactions [27]. Flexible devices benefit from these attributes by connecting reality based interactions with virtual experiences, which embody engaging interactions [7–9]. This element of embodied engagement is a natural fit for games on mobile devices, which are hampered to engage by touch-only interactions.

Mobile games are designed to be short, simple and competitively engaging, which makes them the most used mobile application [31]. However, there are limitations due to small screen sizes such as the use of on-screen game controls and finger occlusion [33], an inherent issue of touch input. By leveraging the use of deformation as an input method and the success of mobile games, we envision an input modality that could potentially create new and innovative gameplay. In addition, we view bend interactions to complement touch input as well as potentially resolve its limitations. While deformable interactions may offer many new creative possibilities, we begin our exploration through the use of simple binary bend gestures with basic gaming tasks inspired by classic arcade games.

TEI '17, March 20-23, 2017, Yokohama, Japan
© 2017 ACM. ISBN 978-1-4503-4676-4/17/03…$15.00
DOI: http://dx.doi.org/10.1145/3024969.3024970

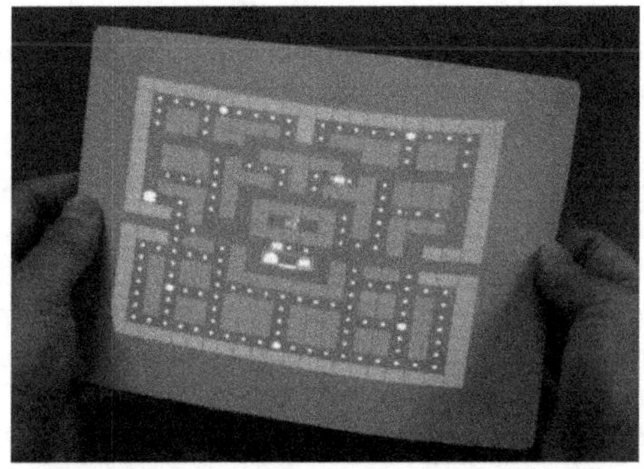

Figure 1. Bendy explores bend gestures for novel game input. The user plays Pacman by bending the flexible prototype.

We present an explorative study into the interactions of mobile gaming using an interactive flexible prototype called Bendy (Figure 1). We aim to understand and explore the use of bend gestures when playing games on a flexible device. This work contributes to deformable interactions research in two folds: an analysis of bend gestures for gaming, and a qualitative examination of user experiences in gaming with a flexible prototype. We also examine differences between two common mobile sizes: smartphones and small tablets.

We conducted a study where participants were presented with a series of simple game tasks and asked to select a bend gesture for each. We quantified and used the results to inform the design of the bend gestures for six simple games. We built the Bendy prototype to provide users with an interactive experience and gathered feedback regarding their user experience and the usability of the bend gestures. We conclude by reporting insights found and propose guidelines for designing games with mobile flexible devices.

RELATED WORK
We surveyed deformable interaction research, and mobile game input modalities.

Deformable Interactions
Deformable user interfaces use the physical deformation of an object as a form of input [12], ranging from simple bends

[25,30] to complex deformations [11,12]. Lahey et al. [14] defined bend gestures as the "physical, manual deformation of a display surface to form a curvature for triggering an action on a computer display". Ahmaniemi et al. [1] suggested that their full potential occurs when they are mapped to continuous, bipolar input. The authors note that some discrete actions such as page turning also have strong value when performed with bends. They found bending to be well-suited for clearly-directional manipulations. Researchers have applied flexible devices to applications such as ebook readers [35,36], smartphones [14,28], tablets [30], media players [12] or to perform music [32].

We only found four instances of deformation in games, two presenting concepts and two evaluating simple games. Cobra [38] introduced flexible displays in a gaming context through the use of bend gesture input. They proposed a portable system comprised of a shoulder-mounted pico-projector connected to a laptop, which recognized user input from the flexible device. Their preliminary exploration did not expand on game interactions and omitted a user evaluation. Similarly, Nguyen et al. created foam-based prototypes that capture local pressure points and deformation in BendID [20] and Softii [19]. They indicated using their prototype with a 3D racing game but provided no detail other than a picture. In terms of experimentation, Ahmaniemi et al. [1] included a task to control the vertical position of a moving ball, which they qualified as a simple game. They reported participants suggesting games as an area with potential for bend gestures. Daliri and Girouard [6] used a simple game task to evaluate visual feedback guides. Users moved a character along a four by four grid while eating fruits. Grounded in prior work, our research extends beyond conceptual exploration [19,20,38] or extremely simple games [1,6] and examines gaming with flexible devices in detail.

Mobile Game Input

The most popular game input on current mobile devices is touch, which has two common interaction problems: screen occlusion, which is created by fingers reaching for a target on a screen; and the *"fat fingers"* problem, which is the ambiguity of the selection point [33]. In addition, the small display size of mobile devices often limits game interaction, as it is restrictive to use on-screen game controls.

Several comparative studies have explored the use of other input modalities versus touch input. Zaman et al. [39] compared the use of touchscreen-based controls on the Apple iPhone versus physical controls on the Nintendo DS for the game Assassin's Creed. They found users' performance and preference were significantly higher when using physical buttons. This suggests that designers need to consider alternative input methods for touchscreen devices. Chehimi and Coulton [5] explored the use of accelerometers in a 3D space shooter game and found the response from users to be positive and intuitive. Browne and Anand [4] evaluated usability and user experience of a side-scrolling shooter game for the iPod Touch using three inputs: accelerometer, simulated touch button and touch gestures. Users preferred the accelerometer-based interface and it also exhibited the best performance measures. Browne and Anand recommend that the physical properties of gestures should be directly translated into the virtual properties. While using the accelerometer has been widely accepted, tilting or shaking the mobile device can obstruct the field of view. These works illustrate the necessity of exploring other input modalities, which offer ways of improving touch input's shortcomings.

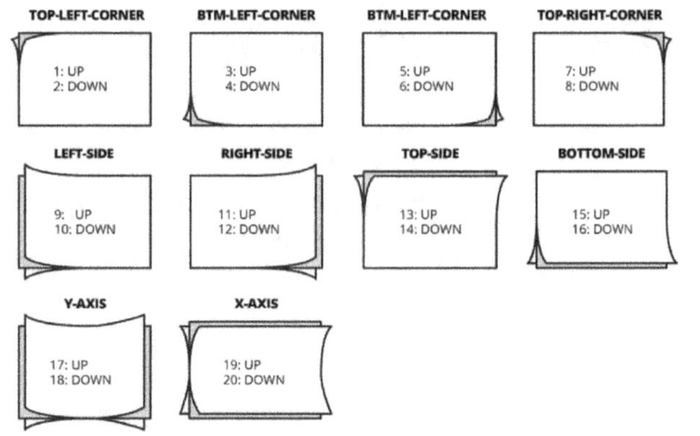

Figure 2. Bendy's bend gesture interaction language.

BENDY PROTOTYPE

We designed and built an interactive flexible prototype to investigate the use of twenty bend gestures with simple games. We used the fabrication technique for deformable prototypes outlined by Lo and Girouard [17]. To achieve our research goals, we assessed the requirements for the prototype based on size, material stiffness, and interaction.

Bend Gesture Interaction Language

Our interaction language uses the bend gesture classification scheme proposed by Warren et al. [34] involving location and direction. Gestures can be performed in ten locations using four corners, four sides, or along the x or y-axis in both directions, resulting in a set of twenty gestures (Figure 2). The nomenclature used in this paper to describe gestures first states the location and secondly the direction. The four corners are described as follows: *top-right, bottom-right, top-left or bottom-left corner*. Side bends are designated as *top, bottom, left or right side*. Central bends are described by the parallel axis of which they are bent. The *up* direction indicates a gesture performed toward the user and the *down* direction is performed away from the user.

Hardware and Apparatus

Bendy is comprised of three layers: a flexible plastic substrate, FlexPoint bidirectional bend sensors augmented with a flexible circuit, and a silicone enclosure (Figure 3, left). The prototype is cast in a material with a shore hardness of 30A, which is equivalent to a soft rubber gasket [22], as users feel more comfortable and engaged with less stiff materials [13]. This prototype has enough resilience to return to a neutral state after repeated deformations.

Researchers thus far have evaluated two sizes for flexible devices: smartphones [12,14] and large tablets [15,30], and

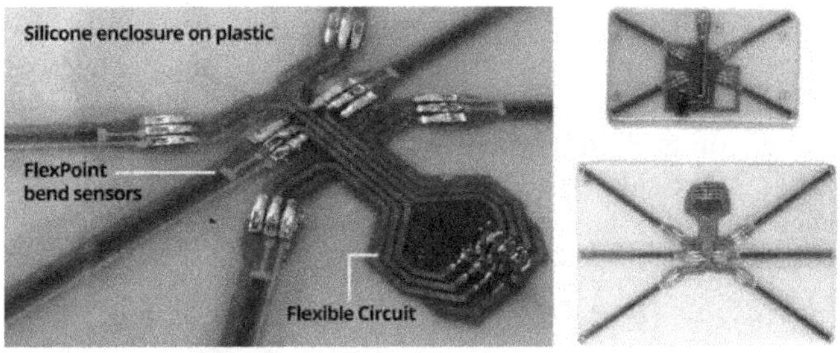

Figure 3. Bendy's three layers: the plastic substrate, the flexible circuit and the silicone enclosure.

prior work found small devices to be better than larger ones [16]. However, researchers have not studied sizes in between. As smartphones get bigger and tablets get smaller, we investigate the differences between smartphone, referred to as small (120 mm x 72 mm) and mini tablet size, called medium (170 mm x 120 mm), illustrated in Figure 3, right.

We simulated the display by projecting onto the surface of the prototype using a pico-projector. The animations in study one used the whole prototype, while the games were centered with a border of approximately 5 mm for the small prototype and 10 mm for medium prototype. We placed a fiducial marker on the back of the prototype and positioned a web camera to detect its location using reacTIVision [10]. We integrated this position data in the Processing applications to keep the projection within the frame of the prototype. We did not correct for the perspective deformation of the projection. Participants were asked to hold the prototype in front of the projector at a fixed distance. We adjusted the projector for each participant so that the display size remained consistent.

Sensors were strategically positioned for each prototype to detect the twenty bend gestures. There are four sensors in each four corners for both prototypes, two sensors centered on the left and right sides for the medium prototype, and one sensor horizontally in the middle of the small one. We detected gestures using the combination of activated sensors: corner bends required single sensor activation; top and bottom side bends required both corner sensors to be activated; left and right bends required all three sensors on that side to activate. We detected y-axis bends when all six sensors were activated, and the x-axis bends when only the four corner bends were activated.

We connected the sensors to an Arduino Uno microcontroller and implemented a digital smoothing algorithm to remove outliers. We set activation threshold values for every sensor so the angle for classifying a deformation as a bend would be approximately 30°. We sent the bend gesture output continuously to the Processing game applications. In Bendy, the gestures detected are binary in nature, that is each gesture is on or off, based on a threshold. However, they are in fact continuous; if users maintained the bend past the threshold, the system will recognize many gestures in a row. We used this bend gesture recognition in our second study. For our first study, bend gestures were recorded manually.

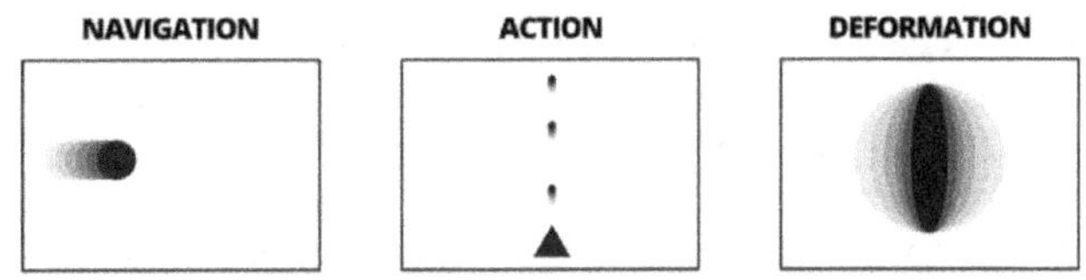

Figure 4. An example of our three gaming interactions.

STUDY 1: DECONSTRUCTING GAMING INTERACTIONS

Bend gestures are a novel interaction language for users and as a result, there are many intricacies to be examined. In the context of gaming, how would you navigate Mario and avoid enemies? What bend gestures would you use to shoot invading enemies? The main research goal of this study is to elicit bend gestures from users given these types of basic gaming interactions with our flexible prototype Bendy.

We conducted a study using simple gaming interactions represented by a simplified visual animation and asked users to select a bend gesture for each from our defined set of twenty (Figure 2). We simplified the graphic representation to remove visual bias. By using a simple *cause* and *effect* methodology, we observed user behaviours given the visual feedback *(effect)* of the system and asked users to select a bend gesture *(cause)*. This process provided a dialogue between the system and the behaviour enabling them.

We proposed a set of three tasks for each of three interaction categories: navigation, action, and deformation (Figure 4).

Navigation Tasks. We selected three navigation tasks to observe how participants would navigate on a 2D plane: left and right only, up and down only, and in all four directions. For the left/right and up/down tasks, we wanted to test if the location of the visual would influence the bend gesture performed. To investigate the relationship, we consider the stimulus-response compatibility principle, the Simon Effect [26]. Stimulus-response compatibility [23] is where the rate of information transfer is dependent on the association of stimulus and response. Simon found faster response times due to spatial correspondence, that is when the stimulus and response occur in the same location. For this task, the Simon Effect is relevant because the location of stimuli (visual) may influence the location of the response (gesture). We hypothesized that participants would select gestures relative to the location of the visual. Therefore, we used location as a variable condition for the left/right and up/down tasks. The visual was presented in three locations: top, center, bottom and left, center, right respectively. Within these tasks, we instructed participants that they could select gestures independently of each other, which meant they could repeat gestures should they see fit. The third navigation task combined all four directions and participants were asked to select four unique bend gestures. We designed this task to test how participants would map bend gestures given the condition they could not be collocated.

Action Tasks. We selected three tasks commonly found in gaming: shooting, jumping and rotating. This set of tasks represent a subset of arcade-style game actions that have no binding characteristics with respect to real-world deformable actions. We hypothesized that participants will have low consensus in transforming these tasks into bend gestures. In addition, participants were required to select separate bend gestures to navigate left and right. We included navigation in each task to test how participants would map action bend gestures given a situation where they could not be collocated with navigation bend gestures. These constraints reflect the constraints of real games. For example, a button on a game controller cannot move left and jump at the same time.

Deformation Tasks. We deviated from common game interactions and generated a set of three tasks embodying deformable characteristics found in real-world interactions, to leverage the properties of the flexible device. We devised a spring task where an object is pulled back and sprung forward by release, similarly to a catapult. The elasticity task explored compressing and stretching vertically and horizontally. This second task is like squeezing a sphere of soft material, such as a silicone ball or a water balloon. The final task manipulates magnitude by increasing and decreasing the size of an object. We hypothesized that these three tasks would achieve a higher level of consensus due to their relative closeness to real-world actions.

To summarize, we have made two hypotheses toward our research: (1) Participants will achieve a higher level of consensus if the tasks embody deformable characteristics and hold true for the converse and (2) the location of bend gestures will map relative to the location of the visual.

Participants

We recruited 24 participants (15 females) with an average age of 27.2 years old and were all right handed. Participants had no prior experience with bend gestures on flexible devices. Participants on average reported playing games occasionally (3.63/7) and had average gaming experience (3.54/7). Participants were given $10 compensation.

Methodology

In our pilot study, we observed participants were unsure of how to interact with the prototype. In addition, we expected our participants would be novice users. We iterated our study to include a short demonstration of the twenty bend gestures. As a result, participants were able to quickly grasp the full range of possible bend gestures and familiarize themselves with the prototype. We presented the nine tasks randomly and the conditions within each task were also at random. After viewing the visual, participants were asked to respond by performing a bend gesture. The researcher asked participants to repeat the bend gesture to confirm their decision. The researcher manually recorded the bend gestures selected. The procedure was repeated for both prototype sizes in a counterbalanced order.

Results

Each participant contributed 37 gestures for each prototype size for a total of 1,776 gestures. From the collected bend gestures, we calculated an agreement score [37], which represents the degree of consensus amongst participants. The value varies between 0 and 1, with a higher number indicating a stronger agreement. For example, for the navigation task, left, 15 participants chose left-side-down, 7 chose right-side-up, 1 chose top-left-corner-down and 1 chose top-right-corner-up. The agreement score for this task:

$$A_{left} = \left(\frac{15}{24}\right)^2 + \left(\frac{7}{24}\right)^2 + \left(\frac{1}{24}\right)^2 + \left(\frac{1}{24}\right)^2 = 0.48$$

The agreement scores are graphed in descending order for the medium prototype (Figure 5). In both sizes, the deformation tasks ranked the highest, whereas the action tasks ranked the lowest. Therefore, we omitted the graph for the small prototype. Table 1 summarizes the results for agreement score and the selected gesture for each task (i.e. the bend gesture with the largest frequency). We also identified tasks with conflicting results indicated by X. We define conflict as gestures that occur in equal frequencies or received a low agreement score ($A < 0.2$). Figure 6 illustrates the most selected and conflicting gestures for all tasks.

Navigation Tasks

(1) Up + Down. The most selected gesture sets are the same for both sizes. If the visual was located on either the right or left, participants mapped the gestures to the corners. When the visual was presented in the center, participants chose to bend the top-side-down to perform the up task. A conflict occurred in both sizes for the down task when the visual was in the center. Participants performed either the top-side-up or bottom-side-down gesture.

To evaluate for the Simon Effect, we complied the gestures per location: left, center, and right. We conducted a Chi-square test for association between the location of the gesture and visual location. We found a significant association between them for both sizes (small χ^2 (4) = 108.677, p < .001 and medium χ^2 (4) = 138.739, p < .001). Participants performed the gestures in the location of the visual stimuli.

(2) Left + Right. On the small prototype, participants selected to use the left and right sides down to perform navigate left and right, respectively. The location of the visual stimuli did not affect the gesture location.

The gestures performed on the medium prototype did not result in the same set. For the navigate left task, when the visual was in the bottom and center location, participants

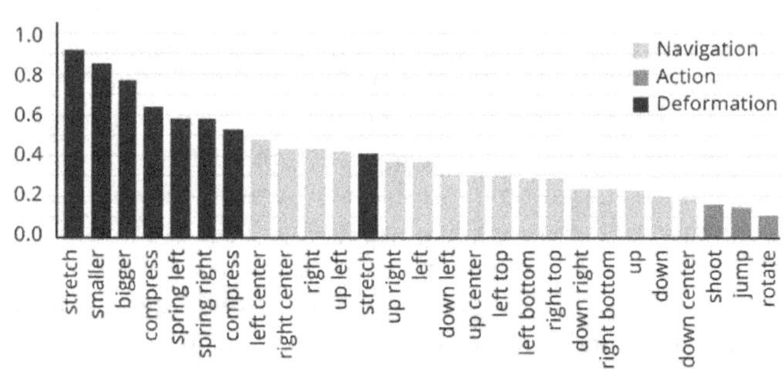

Figure 5. Agreement scores for the medium prototype.

Table 1. Agreement scores of both sizes and selected gesture represented by numbers in reference to Figure 2.

	Event	Variable	Agreement		Selected	
			Small	Medium	Small	Medium
Navigation	down	center	0.25	0.19	X	X
		left	0.21	0.31	4	4
		right	0.28	0.24	6	6
	up	center	0.32	0.30	16	16
		left	0.27	0.42	2	2
		right	0.34	0.37	8	8
	left	bottom	0.32	0.29	10	10
		center	0.46	0.48	10	10
		top	0.28	0.30	10	2
	right	bottom	0.24	0.24	12	6
		center	0.46	0.43	12	12
		top	0.28	0.29	12	X
	down		0.20	0.20	15	X
	left		0.37	0.37	10	10
	right		0.42	0.43	12	12
	up		0.21	0.23	X	16
Action	rotate		0.15	0.11	X	X
	shoot		0.13	0.16	X	X
	jump		0.14	0.15	X	X
Deformable	spring	left	0.70	0.58	10	10
		right	0.70	0.58	12	12
	elasticity	hcompress	0.58	0.53	19	19
		vcompress	0.66	0.92	13	13
		hstretch	0.18	0.41	X	20
		vstretch	0.77	0.64	14	14
	magnitude	bigger	0.71	0.77	14	14
		smaller	0.78	0.85	13	13

selected to use left-side-down. When the visual was at the top, they selected top-left-corner-down. For the navigate right task, participants selected the bottom-right-corner-down when the visual was presented on the bottom. When the visual was presented at in the center participants choose right-side-down. A conflict occurred when the visual was presented in the top location. Participants equally selected top-right-corner-down or right-side-down.

We compiled the gestures performed according to location: top, center, and bottom and conducted the same Chi-square test. We found a significant association between the location of the gesture performed and visual stimulus location for both sizes (small χ^2 (4) = 33.222, p < .001 and medium χ^2 (4) = 90.937, p < .001). The significance found for the left/right task is unlike the one found in the up/down task. The association is regardless of the location of the visual, the gesture was performed in the center, which suggests using the using side bends to navigate left and right. While we did observe a slight difference with the medium prototype, a significant amount of gestures was still performed in the central location. This might suggest our results would not apply for much larger devices.

(3) 4-Way Navigation. For both sizes, the bend gestures for the left and right tasks are left-side-down and right-side-down. When it came to selecting gestures for the up and down tasks for both prototype, the conflict found earlier is also evident in this task. Participants struggled to reach a consensus whether to pair this task by location or direction.

Action Tasks

The agreement scores for all three action tasks ranked the lowest for both prototype and resulted in the largest number of unique gestures performed. There was no consensus for any gesture, though we noted a slight preference to map actions to the top-right-corner.

Deformation Tasks

(1) Spring. Both prototype sizes exhibited the same gesture-task pairings: the left side down gesture pulling the spring to the left. To manipulate the target line, participants used the top left-corner-down to move it up and the bottom-left-corner-down to move it down.

(2) Elasticity. Participants selected an x-axis gesture to compress/stretch an object along the horizontal axis and a y-axis gesture to compress/stretch along the vertical axis. Bend gestures for compression were performed in the up direction, and bend gestures for stretch were performed in the down direction. When asked to stretch the object on the small prototype along the horizontal axis, participants received a low agreement score value (0.18) as 10 participants performed the x-axis-down, and 9 participants performed y-axis-down.

(3) Magnitude. In both sizes, the bend gestures to increase and decrease the magnitude were y-axis-down and y-axis-up respectively.

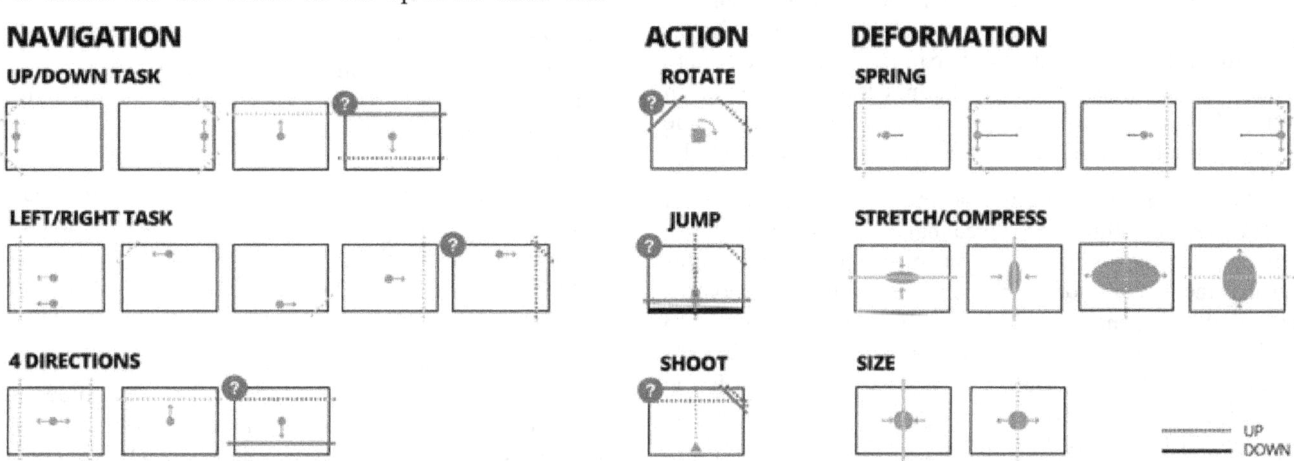

Figure 6. Most selected (blue) and conflicting (red) bend gestures for each task for medium prototype.

Discussion

We discuss our findings and suggest guidelines for designing gestures for gaming with flexible devices. Overall, we observed few differences in performance between the sizes.

Gestures for Navigation on a 2D Plane

Participants paired gestures with opposing tasks, a finding supported by prior work [14,25]. While we did not present the navigation tasks in pairs, most participants (85%) selected paired gestures by location. For instance, to go left and right, participants used the left and right side of the prototype. Only a few (4%) chose to pair gestures by direction: a few chose to move left and right by using only the right-side-up and right-side-down gestures.

In addition, participants demonstrated a common perception that governed how to move the virtual objects. They either "pushed" or "pulled" the object in the desired direction. For instance, a participant would use the left-side -down to "pull" the object to the left; whereas another participant might bend the right-side-up to "push" the object to the left. We analyzed the navigation tasks and observed 56% utilized the "pull" concept, whereas 25% performed the "push" concept, and the remaining 19% showed no particular pattern. We also observed that participants remained consistent in their responses once they perceived they were "pushing" the object, therefore inherently influencing how they selected bend gestures for subsequent tasks. For example, if a participant perceived to "pull" the object, they performed the down gesture in order to do so therefore most of their resulting gestures were in the down direction. Given these observations we suggest pairing opposing tasks by gesture location and using the down direction over up.

For the up/down tasks, participants performed the gesture in the stimulus location, which validates our hypothesis to be true and indeed adheres to the Simon Effect. While this holds true, during the study we observed that bending the prototype using the top and bottom sides were not only very awkward, but also required participants to reposition their hands. The combination of these observations presents an ergonomic concern for implementing the top and bottom side bends as gestures for gaming. In addition, we predict given the gaming context where time and challenge are a factor, performing these gestures would be unfavourable and lead to negative experiences. We suggest duplicating the gestures on both sides of the device to minimize the top/bottom side gestures. We tested this implementation in our second study.

For the left/right navigation task, the majority performed a central gesture. While we noticed that an increase in distance between visuals might compel users to the select gestures towards the visual's location (given the medium prototype's result), the evidence was not significant enough for us to implement into our design. We recommend for flexible devices that fall within our range in size to use the left and right side down for left/right navigation tasks. Our results support this finding as 45% of the gestures created for both sizes utilized these bends.

Gestures for Action Tasks

The action tasks ranked the lowest in user agreement and with the highest average of unique gestures performed. Our participants noted that these types of actions are dissimilar from deformable action and do not utilize the flexible properties of the device, which contributed to their inability to select a bend gesture. Despite participants having trouble to reach a consensus, we observed that many participants assimilated the top corners of the prototype to game console controls and would comment, "I would use it like a trigger button." In addition, several prior works note that the top corners are favourable for assigning frequent tasks [14]. For action tasks, we suggest assigning them to the top corners on both sides, maintaining symmetry, if this does not conflict with navigation gestures. Otherwise, we do not recommend assigning bends to such tasks.

Gestures for Deformation Tasks

Tasks that share deformable characteristics are easily translated into gestures for flexible devices (high user agreement and lowest number of gestures performed). Even for participants with no previous experience with flexible devices, selecting these gestures appeared effortless. Bending downward translated into increasing the surface of an object, while upwards mapped to decreasing.

We encourage designing games that leverage deformation, for example, stretching a bow to shoot targets, or flicking the device to hurl balls of paper into a trash can. The closer the interaction mimics a real-world deformable action, the easier it is for users to conceptualize and use the gestures.

STUDY 2: IMPLEMENTING BENDS IN ARCADE GAMES

We extend our exploration of gaming with flexible devices by further examining the gestures from the first study in an in-game context. We used the main findings from the first study and implemented the gestures with six games. We selected classic arcade-style games because of their simple game controls (e.g. navigation controls, rotation, sling, shoot), all of which could be done using binary input. We aimed to determine an overall preference for prototype size, evaluate the design of the game controls and observe behavioural patterns.

Games and Action Mapping

We used the results from the first study to guide our design for the game controls in this study using the following principles: use down gestures, pair opposing tasks by location, and map action tasks to the top-right-corner. We balanced each game to ease the play for the participant: the pace was decreased, and game life was unlimited to allow for sufficient opportunity for participants to experience the controls. Figure 7 illustrates the games and their bend gesture mapping.

The goal of Pong [2] is to return the ball to the opponent's side using a vertical right paddle. The researcher played using the keyboard to control the left paddle. We used the results from the up/down navigation task. The goal of Bricks [3] is to deflect the ball using a horizontal paddle and

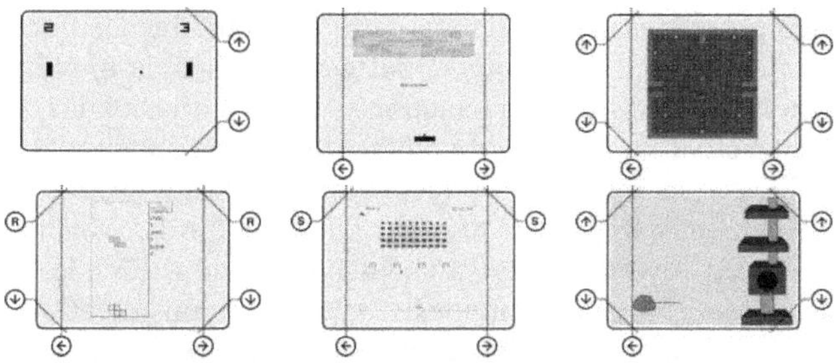

Figure 7. Games and their bend gesture mapping: Pong, Bricks, Pacman (top row), Tetris, Space Invaders, and Fat Cats (bottom row). Arrows indicate navigation actions, R indicates rotating the block and S indicates shooting.

eliminate the "bricks" above. We implemented the results suggesting the use of the central left and right side bends. In PacMan [18], the player navigates a character through a maze to eat all the pac dots, while avoiding the enemies. We identified navigating up/down to have usability concerns and therefore implemented the up/down tasks to the four corners to test how participants would fare using this mapping. Tetris [21] is a puzzle-based game where the user manipulates the position of the geometric shapes to form horizontal lines. In Space Invaders [29], the player controls a space ship by moving it horizontally, while shooting at the descending aliens above. For these two games, we remained consistent in assigning left and right side bends to navigate. We assigned the action task to the top right and left corners given the feedback from the first study that participants perceived the prototype to mimic that of a game controller.

Fat Cats was inspired by the popular game Angry Birds™ [24]. The objective of the game is to spring the cat toward the scratching post aiming for one of three target levels. We applied our results from the spring task and assigned the left-side-down gesture to launch the Fat Cat. Participants used the top and bottom corners down to move the target line.

Participants
We recruited 12 participants (4 females) with an average age of 24.3 years old with no prior experience with flexible devices. 10 participants were right handed, 1 left handed and 1 ambidextrous. We offered a $10 compensation. They reported playing games occasionally (4.51/7) and had an average gaming experience (4.08/7).

Methodology
We gave participants a brief introduction to flexible devices, bend gestures as input for gaming, and the prototype setup. To familiarize participants with the prototype, they completed a tutorial prior to playing the games. We designed a within-subjects experiment to evaluate perceptual differences between the two differently sized prototypes. The order of the six games was randomized and the prototype size was counterbalanced. Participants played each game until they reported confidence in evaluating the controls. We asked participants to rate the controls by indicating on a seven-point Likert scale (strongly disagree to strongly agree) given the statement "The controls were physically easy to perform". We also evaluated intuitiveness and asked them to rate the statement "The controls were mentally intuitive to use". To determine an overall preference for size, participants indicated their preference after each game and chose an overall size preference after playing all the games. We conducted a semi-structured interview and encouraged a "think out loud" protocol to solicit responses and gather additional insights regarding the user experience.

Results
We evaluated the user experience of gaming with flexible devices. We transcribed their responses and summarized them into descriptive codes. For example, the participant's comment "I like the smaller prototype because it was easier to grasp" would be translated to the codes: *small prototype* and *ergonomics*. This process was iterative until a finalized set reported the feedback gathered. We formulated the results from the second study and discuss our findings.

Preference for the Small Prototype
When asked to indicate their overall preference, 75% preferred using the small prototype. All participants commented on the distance between the controls and how it affected their performance. "The smaller one is better because the distance is closer, making them [controls] easier to access." (P9) The smaller distance enabled participants to "brace the entire device" (P4) and perform all the required gestures with minimal repositioning of the hands.

All four female participants reported the medium prototype to be more difficult to use due to having smaller hands. Three male participants indicated the medium one was "slightly more comfortable" because it fitted their hand size better. Overall, the small prototype provided a better user experience: it was easier to use and increased game performance.

Reducing Hand Repositioning to Perform Gestures
All participants commented on the repositioning of their hands to perform the gestures and preferred maintaining a close proximity to their grasp position. Almost all the participants (10/12) struggled with the game Pong and suggested the gestures be collocated by direction instead of location to reduce repositioning of the hands.

Observable Patterns of the Simon Effect
Our first study suggested for navigation tasks, there is a significant association between visual location and gesture location. Therefore, we implemented this finding into three games: PacMan, Tetris, and Space Invaders. Our implementation tested whether the Simon Effect would hold true if applied to games. For example, if PacMan was on the left, the participants would be more inclined to use the left top and bottom corners to move him up and down. In Tetris, if the puzzle piece was on the right, the participants would use the top right corner to rotate. Similarly, if the space ship in Space Invaders was on the left, participants would use the top-left-corner to shoot. However, we observed a very interesting pattern. All the participants used both sides of the prototype during PacMan, however, only some (7/12) during

Tetris and very few (3/12) during Space Invaders. During Space Invaders, half of the participants commented on the top-right-corner being similar to a game console controller: "It's like using the buttons on my Xbox to shoot, which makes sense" (P7). It could be that the action of "shooting" as a repetitive trigger was easily relatable to the form factor of a flexible device. For future works, if the game tasks involve navigating in all four directions, the Simon Effect is indeed applicable. However, it should be carefully considered when designing other types of games.

Discussion

We implemented user-selected gestures as game controls and found overall positive results. Evaluating controls in this context allowed us to further uncover and extrapolate important insights that did not arise during the first study.

While the results from the first study strongly indicated that participants paired opposing tasks by location, the results of this study challenged this guideline, particularly for the up/down task in Pong. Pong received the most feedback, with participants suggesting to collocate the gestures to a single location for ease of use. Our evaluation proves to be beneficial in highlighting an important usability requirement: hand repositioning. While the result contradicts our suggested guideline, we may resolve the usability issue by increasing the size of the bend gesture and minimizing hand repositioning. The results also revealed user motivations whilst playing games that we did not account for previously. Because of the gaming nature, participants often expressed concern for performance and efficiency and that the game controls should not influence these two factors. This leads to interesting future work to see how game challenge would influence bend gestures. Overall, while this somewhat limits the validity of the first study, it mainly highlights the necessity to evaluate user-selected gestures in context.

In the second study, we observed participants using the deformable prototype like they would a game controller. As gestures were continuously generated while users were bending the prototype, participants tended to maintain the gesture in directional actions, similarly to holding the left side of the D-Pad to move left, while they naturally used more of a "flicking" motion to perform action tasks such as shooting or rotating a block. We found that participants did not use both sides of the display as often as we had expected. The Simon Effect appeared more prevalent in the navigation type game (e.g., PacMan) and less in the action games (e.g., Tetris and Space Invaders). This observation holds particularly true in the 2D shooter game where participants formed a strong association with the top-right-corner as the "trigger" button. It further strengthens participants strongly associate gaming with flexible devices to game controllers.

Limitations

Both studies were based on an explorative process and our hardware, software, and methodologies were designed to fit our goals. We were limited by technological feasibility in available hardware. In lieu of using a flexible display, we used projection. We made efforts to maintain the position of the display on the prototype, but we were unable to reduce distortion during bend interactions. We also do not know the influence of the border around the display on our results. In addition, the bend gesture recognition software used in the second study limited us to using binary controls, which we mitigated by choosing arcade-style games. While we outputted gestures continuously, hence our consideration of them as being continuous gestures, this still restricted the use of finer metrics. There is room to improve bend interaction sensing with higher-fidelity prototypes that use of the full potential of bend gestures [1], and an additional study with games using continuous controls is warranted.

CONCLUSION

With Bendy, we explored mobile gaming on flexible devices. We began our exploration by conducting a first study where users were asked to select bend gestures for tasks in three interaction categories: navigation, action, and deformation. Our results provided a set of bend gestures for the navigation and deformation tasks. We found that the action tasks scored lowest in user agreement and the deformation tasks ranked highest. Additionally, we compared two common mobile device sizes and found similar bend gestures were selected for each, leading us to suggest designers can select the same gestures for different size mobile devices (small and medium). Finally, we were interested in observing the Simon Effect with bend gestures and we found a strong association between the locations of the gesture and that of the visual stimuli. Our preliminary investigation also highlighted interesting interaction paradigms such as users pairing opposing tasks to gestures by location, "push" and "pull" mental models, and experimenting with various hand positions.

We evaluated Bendy using six simple arcade-style games that implemented the guidelines for our first study. We found participants preferring the small prototype due to increased ease of use and performance. We observed hand positioning as an important usability requirement to consider: participants were unanimously concerned with having to reposition their hands from their holding positions to perform bend gestures. Through two studies with the Bendy prototype, we show that the use of bend gestures for gaming with mobile devices is a novel and viable input modality.

To expand our work, we will explore additional gaming interactions using different flexible form factors and improved gesture recognition algorithms. Further works would include designing games using real-world metaphors, such as flicking a device to toss paper into a trash can. Finally, an evaluation of the combination of touch and bend is also warranted.

ACKNOWLEDGEMENTS

This project was funded by NSERC (RGPIN 402494-2011) as well as by the GRAND Network of Centers of Excellence.

REFERENCES

1. Teemu T. Ahmaniemi, Johan Kildal, and Merja Haveri. 2014. What is a device bend gesture really good for? *Proceedings of the SIGCHI Conference on Human Factors in Computing Systems*, 3503–3512. http://doi.org/10.1145/2556288.2557306
2. Atari. 1972. *Pong*. Game [Various]. (November 29, 1972). Atari, Sunnyvale, CA, USA.
3. Atari Arcade. 1976. *Breakout*. Game [Various]. (April 1976). Atari, Sunnyvale, CA, USA.
4. Kevin Browne and Christopher Anand. 2012. An empirical evaluation of user interfaces for a mobile video game. *Entertainment Computing* 3, 1: 1–10. http://doi.org/10.1016/j.entcom.2011.06.001
5. Fadi Chehimi and Paul Coulton. 2008. Motion controlled mobile 3D multiplayer gaming. *Proceedings of the 2008 International Conference in Advances on Computer Entertainment Technology - ACE '08*, 267. http://doi.org/10.1145/1501750.1501813
6. Farshad Daliri and Audrey Girouard. 2016. Visual Feedforward Guides for Performing Bend Gestures on Deformable Prototypes. *Proceedings of Graphics Interfaces 2016*, 209–216. http://doi.org/10.20380/GI2016.27
7. David Holman and Roel Vertegaal. 2008. Organic User Interfaces : Design Computer in Any Way, Shape, or Form. *Communications of the ACM* 51, 6.
8. Hiroshi Ishii. 2008. The tangible user interface and its evolution. *Communications of the ACM* 51, 6: 32. http://doi.org/10.1145/1349026.1349034
9. Robert JK Jacob, Audrey Girouard, Leanne M Hirshfield, et al. 2008. Reality-based interaction: a framework for post-WIMP interfaces. *Proceeding of the twenty-sixth annual CHI conference on Human factors in computing systems - CHI '08*, ACM Press, 201. http://doi.org/10.1145/1357054.1357089
10. Martin Kaltenbrunner and Ross Bencina. 2007. reacTIVision: A Computer-Vision Framework for Table- Based Tangible Interaction. *Proceedings of the 1st international conference on Tangible and embedded interaction - TEI '07*, ACM Press, 69. http://doi.org/10.1145/1226969.1226983
11. Johan Kildal, Andrés Lucero, and Marion Boberg. 2013. Twisting Touch : Combining Deformation and Touch as Input within the Same Interaction Cycle on Handheld Devices. *Proceedings of the 15th international conference on Human-computer interaction with mobile devices and services - MobileHCI '13*, 237. http://doi.org/10.1145/2493190.2493238
12. Johan Kildal, Susanna Paasovaara, and Viljakaisa Aaltonen. 2012. Kinetic device: Designing Interactions with a Deformable Mobile Interface. *ACM SIGCHI conference on Human Factors in Computing Systems Extended Abstracts*, 1871. http://doi.org/10.1145/2212776.2223721
13. Johan Kildal and Graham Wilson. 2012. Feeling it: the roles of stiffness, deformation range and feedback in the control of deformable ui. *Proceedings of the 14th ACM international conference on Multimodal interaction - ICMI '12*, ACM Press, 393. http://doi.org/10.1145/2388676.2388766
14. Byron Lahey, Audrey Girouard, Winslow Burleson, and Roel Vertegaal. 2011. PaperPhone: Understanding the Use of Bend Gestures in Mobile Devices with Flexible Electronic Paper Displays. *Proceedings of the SIGCHI Conference on Human Factors in Computing Systems*, 1303–1312. http://doi.org/10.1145/1978942.1979136
15. Sang-Su Lee, Sohyun Kim, Bipil Jin, et al. 2010. How users manipulate deformable displays as input devices. *SIGCHI Conference on Human Factors in Computing Systems*, 1647–1656. http://doi.org/10.1145/1753326.1753572
16. Sang-su Lee, Youn-kyung Lim, and Kun-Pyo Lee. 2012. Exploring the effects of size on deformable user interfaces. *Proceedings of the 14th international conference on Human-computer interaction with mobile devices and services companion - MobileHCI '12*, ACM Press, 89. http://doi.org/10.1145/2371664.2371682
17. Jessica Lo and Audrey Girouard. 2014. Fabricating Bendy: Design and Development of Deformable Prototypes. *IEEE Pervasive Computing Special Issue on Fabrication and Printing* 13, 3: 40–46. http://doi.org/10.1109/MPRV.2014.47
18. Namco. 1980. *Pacman*. Game [Various]. (May 22, 1980). Namco, Tokyo, Japan.
19. Vinh Nguyen, Pramod Kumar, Sang Ho Yoon, Ansh Verma, and Karthik Ramani. 2015. SOFTii : Soft Tangible Interface for Continuous Control of Virtual Objects with Pressure-based Input. *Proceedings of the Ninth International Conference on Tangible, Embedded, and Embodied Interaction - TEI '15*, ACM Press, 539–544. http://doi.org/10.1145/2677199.2687898
20. Vinh P. Nguyen, Sang Ho Yoon, Ansh Verma, and Karthik Ramani. 2014. BendID: Flexible Interface for Localized Deformation Recognition. *Proceedings of the 2014 ACM International Joint Conference on Pervasive and Ubiquitous Computing - UbiComp '14 Adjunct*, 553–557. http://doi.org/10.1145/2632048.2636092
21. Alexey Pajitnov and Vladimir Pokhilko. 1984. *Tetris*. Game [NES]. (6 June 1984). Nintendo, Kyoto, Japan.

22. Plastic World. 2016. Alumilite Flex 30. Retrieved January 19, 2016 from http://plasticworld.ca/store/index.php?main_page=product_info&cPath=7_43&products_id=152

23. Robert W Proctor and T.G. Reeve. 1989. *Stimulus-response compatibility: An intergrated perspective*. Elsevier.

24. Rovio Mobile. *Angry Birds*. Game. (11 December 2009). Rovio Entertainment, Keilaniemi, Espoo, Finland.

25. Carsten Schwesig, Ivan Poupyrev, and Eijiro Mori. 2004. Gummi: A Bendable Computer. *Proceedings of the 2004 conference on Human factors in computing systems - CHI '04*, 263–270. http://doi.org/10.1145/985692.985726

26. J. Richard Simon. 1969. Reactions toward the source of stimulation. *J Exp Psychology* 8, 1: 174–176. http://doi.org/10.1037/h0027448

27. Jürgen Steimle, Andreas Jordt, and Pattie Maes. 2013. Flexpad. *Proceedings of the SIGCHI Conference on Human Factors in Computing Systems - CHI '13*, ACM Press, 237. http://doi.org/10.1145/2470654.2470688

28. Paul Strohmeier, Jesse Burstyn, Juan Pablo Carrascal, Vincent Levesque, and Roel Vertegaal. 2016. ReFlex: A Flexible Smartphone with Active Haptic Feedback for Bend Input. *Proceedings of the TEI '16: Tenth International Conference on Tangible, Embedded, and Embodied Interaction*, 185–192. http://doi.org/10.1145/2839462.2839494

29. Taito Corporation. 1978. *Space Invaders*. Game [Various]. (July 1978). Taito, Tokyo, Japan.

30. Aneesh Tarun, Peng Wang, Paul Strohmeier, Audrey Girouard, Derek Reilly, and Roel Vertegaal. 2013. PaperTab: Tablets as Thin and Flexible as Paper. *CHI '13 Extended Abstracts on Human Factors in Computing Systems on - CHI EA '13*, 2881. http://doi.org/10.1145/2468356.2479559

31. The Nielsen Company. 2011. *The State Of Mobile Apps*.

32. Giovanni Maria Troiano, Esben Warming Pedersen, and Kasper Hornbæk. 2015. Deformable Interfaces for Performing Music. *Proceedings of the 33rd Annual ACM Conference on Human Factors in Computing Systems - CHI '15*, ACM Press, 377–386. http://doi.org/10.1145/2702123.2702492

33. Daniel Vogel and Patrick Baudisch. 2007. Shift: a technique for operating pen-based interfaces using touch. *Proceedings of the SIGCHI conference on Human factors in computing systems - CHI '07*, ACM Press, 657. http://doi.org/10.1145/1240624.1240727

34. Kristen Warren, Jessica Lo, Vaibhav Vadgama, and Audrey Girouard. 2013. Bending the rules: Bend Gesture Classification for Flexible Displays. *Proceedings of the SIGCHI Conference on Human Factors in Computing Systems*, 607–610. http://doi.org/10.1145/2470654.2470740

35. Jun-ichiro Watanabe, Arito Mochizuki, and Youichi Horry. 2008. Bookisheet: Bendable Device for Browsing Content Using the Metaphor of Leafing Through the Pages. *Proceedings of the 10th international conference on Ubiquitous computing - UbiComp '08*, 360. http://doi.org/10.1145/1409635.1409684

36. Doug Wightman, Tim Ginn, and Roel Vertegaal. 2011. BendFlip: Examining Input Techniques for Electronic Book Readers with Flexible Form Factors. In *Proceeding INTERACT'11 Proceedings of the 13th IFIP TC 13 international conference on Human-computer interaction*. 117–133. http://doi.org/10.1007/978-3-642-23765-2_9

37. Jacob O. Wobbrock, Meredith Ringel Morris, and Andrew D. Wilson. 2009. User-defined gestures for surface computing. *Proceedings of the 27th international conference on Human factors in computing systems - CHI 09*, ACM Press, 1083. http://doi.org/10.1145/1518701.1518866

38. Zi Ye and Hammad Khalid. 2010. Cobra: Flexible Displays for Mobile Gaming Scenarios. *Proceedings of the 28th of the international conference extended abstracts on Human factors in computing systems - CHI EA '10*, 4363. http://doi.org/10.1145/1753846.1754154

39. Loutfouz Zaman, Daniel Natapov, and Robert J. Teather. 2010. Touchscreens vs. traditional controllers in handheld gaming. *Proc. Futureplay*: 183. http://doi.org/10.1145/1920778.1920804

End-User Prototyping of Cross-Reality Environments

Andrea Bellucci, Telmo Zarraonandia, Paloma Díaz, Ignacio Aedo
Dept. of Computer Science, Universidad Carlos III de Madrid
Leganés, Madrid, Spain
{andrea.bellucci, telmo.zarraonandia, paloma.diaz, ignacio.aedo}@uc3m.es

ABSTRACT
Building physical spaces interconnected with virtual worlds is a complex task that requires high technical knowledge and hours of programming and, as a matter of fact, is relegated to the work of expert professionals. The goal of this research is to lower the development threshold through the design of an end-user toolkit that provides a visual integrated environment for the rapid prototyping of cross-reality interactions. A user study with 8 participants showed the effectiveness of our approach and uncovered design opportunities and challenges for supporting the development of cross-reality environments.

Author Keywords
Cross-Reality; End-User Development; Prototyping.

ACM Classification Keywords
H.5.2. User Interfaces: Prototyping

INTRODUCTION
Tangible and Ubiquitous Computing are in pursuit of the seamless integration of the technological medium with the physical environment in order to achieve an embodied digitality: the boundaries between the *real* and the *virtual* world become so uncanny that they define just one aspect of a single hybrid, intertwined reality. Milgram and Kishino [24] foresaw that technological advances can make our experience of the world less unequivocal; it will be difficult to draw a neat separation between the predominance of physical components over virtual ones and vice versa. Clark [8] pushed this vision one step further, claiming that the next-generation human minds will not be worried by the "digital/physical divide" but instead they will recognize physicality and virtuality as a blended medium of self-expression. Current technologies are indeed mature enough to provide the hardware substratum for the materialization of cross-reality environments, in which physical and virtual objects co-exist and interact in real time. Examples of off-the-shelf Input/Output (I/O) devices are: depth cameras for body movement recognition (e.g., Microsoft Kinect RGB-D camera [23]), head mounted virtual reality display (e.g., Oculus Rift [29]), and microcontrollers that make it easier to integrate networked sensors and actuators in the physical space [11, 22, 35]. There have been great advances also with respect to the software, as demonstrated by tools for the creation of 3D content (e.g., Google SketchUp [9], Blender [4]), databases of user-generated 3D models (e.g., Google Sketchup 3D Warehouse), virtual worlds engines (e.g., Unity [36]), and toolkits for the rapid prototyping of spatially-aware interaction [21], physical computing [11], tangible interaction [15] and for managing sensors data from networked smart objects [3].

TEI 2017, March 20–23, 2017, Yokohama, Japan.
© 2017 ACM ISBN 978-1-4503-4676-4/17/03...$15.00.
http://dx.doi.org/10.1145/3024969.3024975

The development of cross-reality interactions, however, is not evolving at the same pace. Assembling cross-reality environments is still a challenging task that requires, in most cases, knowledge of electronics and the underlying hardware, be familiar with hardware drivers, communication protocols and many hours of programming work. Cross-reality applications are packed with opportunities, e.g., novel visitor experiences in museums [27], but they are currently missed in large part because of the technical complexity. To promote the dissemination and consolidation of cross-reality environments, it is therefore incumbent to provide toolkits that ease their arrangement. By lowering the skill barriers, such toolkits can shift implementation efforts from low-level technical details to more sophisticated design nuances [10].

The main contributions of this research are: (i) exposing the complexities of developing across virtual and physical reality when adding interactive elements and (ii) introducing XRT (X-Reality Toolkit) as a system for approaching those complexities. Current research has focused on providing solutions to isolated problems such as designing the virtual world or building interactive physical objects. Moreover, the support to end users with low technical skills is very limited. The main novelty of our toolkit resides in empowering end users with limited technical knowledge, such us interaction designers or TEI researchers, to rapidly build low-cost functional prototypes of environments that combine interactions between electronic-incorporated objects and 3D virtual worlds and, thus, to test designs in a real context and identify problems sooner [7]. Designers will also be encouraged to explore different alternatives, thanks to the easiness of modifying the behavior of existing interactive components and/or integrating new components in their designs. XRT provides an authoring tool and a runtime environment to build and test cross-reality applications. The authoring interface integrates different visual tools in the same development environment aiming to make it easier to edit virtual and physical entities as well as their interweaving. Based on a first user study with 8 participants, we show the effectiveness of the proposed approach. Results uncover opportunities and challenges for the development of tools that support the creation of cross-reality interactions.

RELATED WORK

The related research comes from the areas of End-User Development (EUD), cross-reality, virtual environments, and physical computing.

End-User Development

EUD is a socio-technical paradigm that provides tools and techniques to allow end users, who are acting as non-professional software developers, to write a program to create, modify or extend a software system. There is a large body of research on EUD [17, 18, 26]. As reported by Lieberman et al. [18], techniques to support end users in the programming task include: scripting languages, domain-specific languages, programming-by-demonstration, tailoring, configurability, visual languages and natural programming environments. In particular, our toolkit makes use of visual metaphors for the composition of sensor-based tangibles and for the definition of cross-reality behaviors. It also exploits the programming-by-demonstration technique for defining sensor triggers.

The definition of who is an end user is tightly coupled with his/her intent [17]; that is, the kind of non-professional activities of programming/configuring performed by a user to accomplish his/her task. Different class of people might have different goals and, thus, perform different programming activities and use different tools. With our toolkit we aim to address the needs of TEI researchers and designers with limited or no textual programming skills and knowledge of electronics who want to quickly build prototypes of cross-reality environments.

Cross-Reality

Cross-reality or xReality (also dubbed "dual reality" [19]), is an extension of mixed-reality [24] that emphasizes on transferring data between both worlds, the virtual and the real, via the interplay of pervasive sensors/actuators networks and online virtual worlds [19]. Both worlds are complete unto themselves. However, they are also enriched by their ability to mutually reflect, influence, and merge into one another. Cross-reality is bi-directional: sensed data from one world can be used to enrich the other world and the other way around. TwinSpace [30] has been developed to explore the fusion of technologically-augmented physical spaces with virtual worlds. It focuses on an architecture and a common data model to make the interplay between both worlds possible. Fusality [27] is an open framework and software architecture to build distributed mirror worlds. It provides tools to create a 3D reconstruction of a real world environment through laser scanning and to fuse virtual and real sensory data. Both tools are a promising approach for building cross-reality applications. However, it is not clear to what extent they can be exploited by an end user, what kind of support they provide for prototyping sensor-based interaction, and the generalizability of such tools, e.g., which kind of cross-reality applications can be built beyond the use cases provided.

3D Virtual Environments

Several technologies can support the development of 3D virtual environments. Most online virtual worlds and sandbox games, like Second Life [33] or Minecraft [25], offer tailoring mechanisms and provide users with editors to build interactive 3D virtual spaces. These tools do not require a specific knowledge of 3D modelling or programming skills, but the resulting designs are platform specific, and can not be used in a different system. 3D creation suites like Blender [4] or Autodesk 3ds Max [1] offer a more interoperable solution for modelling general purpose 3D environments and objects animations. These designs, in fact, can be exported to game engines such as Unity [36], which provide a whole programming environment for developing interactive 3D experiences. However, these engines require high technical skills and specific training. Our end-user tool exploits the Unity engine and provides a visual interface for the definition of the virtual world, thus aiming to bypass the technical barrier.

Physical Computing

Research has long focused on the development of toolkits that facilitate the creation of physical interaction. Arduino [22] is a vivid example: an open-source electronics prototyping platform based on flexible, easy-to-use hardware and software. It still requires some knowledge of electronics and programming. Integration of sensors and actuators into a prototype, in fact, requires to build the electronic circuit, which connects the sensors with the Arduino micro-controller, and to program the software on the microcontroller to make sense of the data gathered. Phidgets [11], .NET Gadgeteer [38] and iStuff [2] are other toolkits that aim to lower the complexity of building devices made up of components like sensors, lights, switches, displays, communications modules, or motor controllers, by providing libraries of ready-to-use physical widgets. They are programmed using classical textual languages and therefore they are not suitable for novice users. Our toolkit builds on the top of the Arduino platform for the implementation of networked sensors and actuators and provide visual interfaces to support the hardware design.

Together with hardware toolkits, many solutions have been built to ease the development of physical-digital interaction. d.tools [13] is one of the first attempts to introduce EUD techniques in a physical interaction authoring tool, such as the use of visual programming via a visual statechart editor. The system was later extended by Examplar [14], which exploits the programming-by-example technique to enable interaction via sensors data. Other environments embraced visual programming for prototyping physical interaction. For instance, Scratch4Arduino [30] exploits the Scratch visual programming language to program the Arduino hardware through the composition of logical blocks on the screen [32]. Node-RED [28] is another visual tool that implements a data-flow language to interweave smart things. It provides high configurability and extensibility and it is powered by crowd-based development, which allows to reuse behaviors programmed by other users. However, users still need to have programming knowledge to create useful programs.

Physical systems need to provide unified access to different devices that *"may have radically different interfaces, yet perform essentially the same function"* [34]. TUI-VR [15] proposes an object-oriented approach for giving comprehensive support to different technologies and integrating tangible interfaces with virtual environments. Nevertheless, it only provides a software API and configurability through XML, which imposes a restriction to the range of possible users.

CROSS-REALITY CHALLENGES

Building cross-reality environments is a complex and tiresome task, mostly due to the technical and design challenges imposed by merging the physical with the virtual world. Among such challenges, our toolkit has been designed to address the following issues, which arise from the state of the art, as well as our experience in the development of systems that bridge the real and the virtual world [3, 39, 40].

(1) Designing and building the virtual world. Building complex and rich virtual worlds without proper training and extensive experience might result difficult. This is due to the complexity and the wide variety of tasks required for designing a 3D virtual space, which include 3D modelling, system control, viewpoint handing, space navigation, model selection, and different types of model manipulations and transformations like resizing, rotating or positioning [12]. In addition, populating the world and defining the interactions between avatars and virtual objects might be a tedious task.

(2) Augmenting the physical world by means of networked sensors and actuators. This task introduces both hardware and software threats. A recent study [5] on the problems end users encounter in physical computing programming showed that, to be successful, users are expected to be sufficiently proficient at both programming and building electronic circuits. The knowledge of electronics required to build interactive objects is in part subsidized by the availability of hardware toolkits. Regarding the software, low-level programming against a particular technology is a highly specialized task and developers have been found to struggle with debugging and program construction [5].

(3) Managing the communication between the two worlds. Developers need to create the technical infrastructure that makes the interplay between the two worlds possible. This involves (a) the definition of common communication protocols, (b) manage different network interfaces (e.g., WiFi, NFC, Bluetooth, Zigbee, etc.), (c) process real-time raw sensors data, and (d) create bidirectional channels for input and output.

(4) *Defining a mapping between the two worlds.* Developers need to define and implement a strategy to determine *"exactly how the real and virtual will interact and map onto each other"* [19]. This task is difficult because there are many possible mappings (e.g., direct mapping, distorted mirroring or subjective perceptions [19] to cite some) and such mappings require to define interaction rules among physical and virtual objects accordingly, in order to generate the desired behavior.

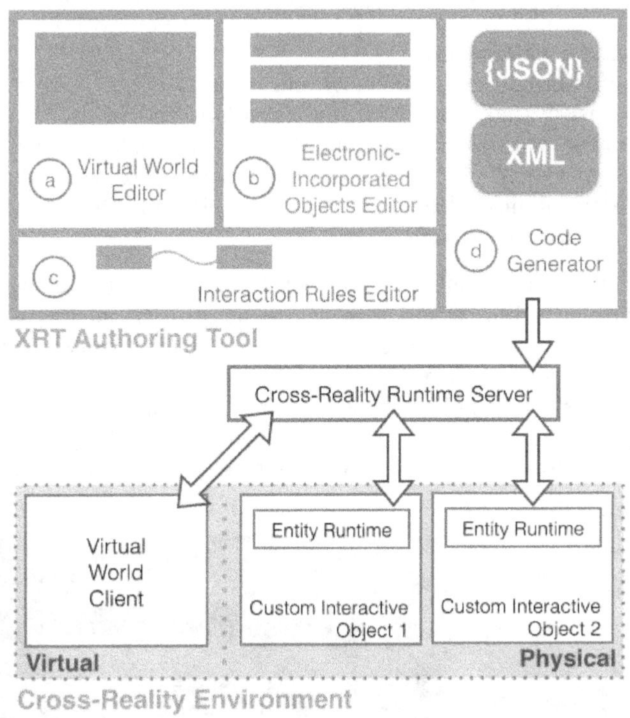

Figure 1. The software architecture of the X-Reality Toolkit.

X-REALITY TOOLKIT

The design of the system has been informed by the insights gathered during a TEI 2014 workshop we run to explore the development of physical/digital cross-device interactions [3] as well as workshops focusing on understanding the end-user programmability of virtual worlds [39].

To develop cross-reality environments and cope with the aforementioned challenges, the X-Reality Toolkit (XRT) provides a web-based authoring tool and a runtime environment. Figure 1 shows the software architecture to create cross-reality environments. The XRT authoring tool provides an integrated development environment for end users to visually design and build the virtual world as well as the electronics of interactive objects and to define the interaction between the two worlds (Figure 2). The authoring tool comprises: The *Virtual World Editor*, the *Electronic-Incorporated Objects Editor*, the *Interaction Rules Editor*. The runtime environment encloses the logic to run the cross-reality environment as designed by the user. The runtime environment includes: The *Cross-Reality Runtime Server*, the *Virtual World Client* and the *Entity Runtime* that runs on the custom-defined electronic-incorporated objects.

The toolkit has been developed to allow a wide range of physical-digital interactions following an event-driven approach. Events generated from sensors in the real world (e.g., detecting the presence of a person in a room) are broadcasted to the virtual world. Correspondingly, events in the virtual world, for instance an avatar approaching a specific object, can activate actuators in the real world (e.g., turn on/off an LED for visual feedback).

System walkthrough

We describe the functionality and components of XRT by means of a user story that illustrates how an end user can build a cross-reality environment using the toolkit as well as to what degree each component addresses the aforementioned challenges. This example shows only one of the possible workflows.

Assume an exhibition developer at an archeological museum, Bill, would like to create a new interactive exhibition to enable cross-reality user experiences for visitors of the virtual tour as well as in-situ. He decides to use XRT to quickly develop a prototype for one of the rooms of the museum. One of the feature of his design will allow virtual and physical visitors to know when someone else from the other world is watching the same piece (a Nefertiti bust). He decides that, in order to provide feedback to visitors, a light will turn on and off both in the real world as well as in the virtual world depending on the presence of people near the piece. To this end, he will have to connect and program a microcontroller to turn on and off a lamp in the real world and also program the behavior of virtual and physical distance sensors. We demonstrate how the different tools provided by XRT help Bill in this task.

Virtual World Editor

Bill starts by creating the 3D virtual scenario that represents the exhibition room. To carry out this task he uses the Virtual World Editor (Figure 2, a), which addresses the *Challenge 1: Design and build the virtual world.* This tool gives access to a warehouse that contains 3D models of different objects as well as *settings*. Settings are 3D models that serve as an initial background for the 3D scene and range from empty terrains or floors to more elaborate environments like a forest, empty rooms or entire buildings. The user can select and use a *setting* instead of modelling the scene from scratch. Finding the right objects or themes in a huge collection of elements is not always straightforward. To support the end user to quickly build 3D scenes, XRT provide *theme templates*. A theme template provides a collection of settings and 3D objects that are thematically connected (e.g., a school, a farmhouse, etc.), thus facilitating the management and retrieval of 3D models. In our case Bill uses a theme for designing generic indoor environments.

Once the setting for the scene has been defined, Bill starts exploring the virtual scene and populate it. As aforementioned, this process can be cumbersome for novice

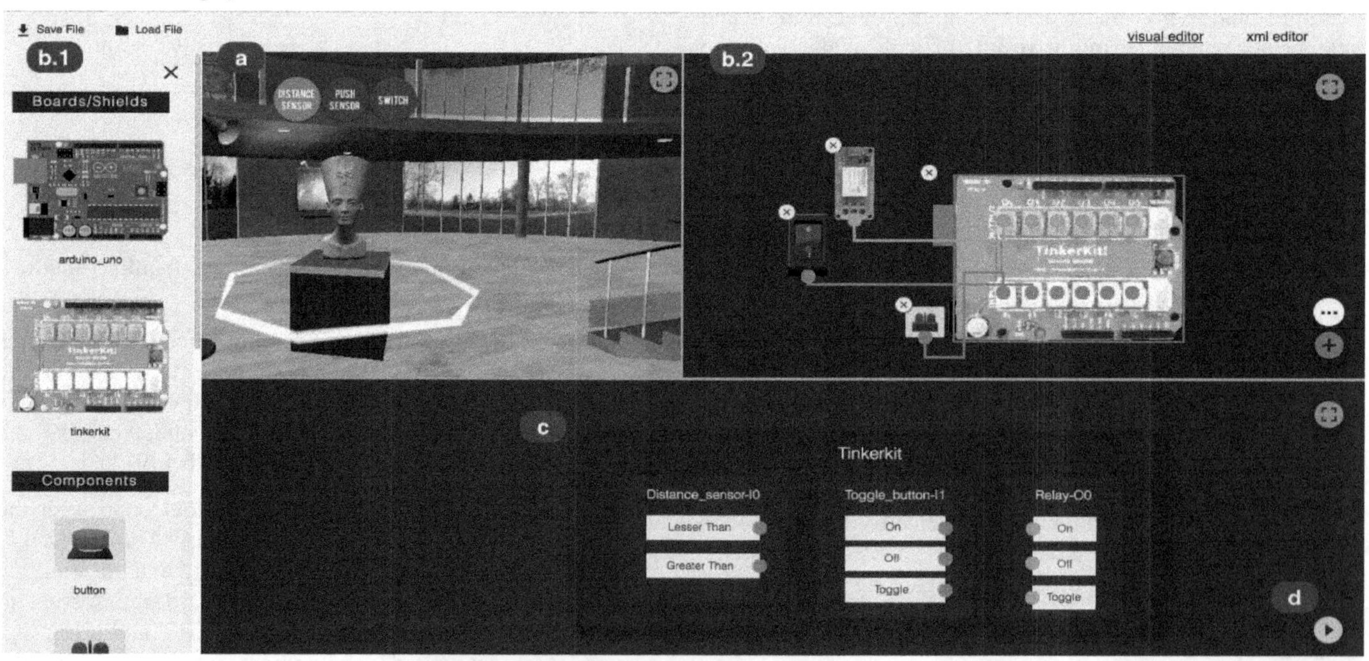

Figure 2. The authoring tool. Users can (a) edit the virtual world by adding new objects and actions (Virtual World Editor), (b.1) select boards and components and (b.2) design interactive objects (Electronic-Incorporated Objects Editor), (c) define the interplay between the virtual and physical world via visual data-flow syntax (Interaction Rules Editor), and (d) create the runtime environment.

task, XRT implements an approach similar to Minecraft and other game sandboxes; Bill can edit existing elements (e.g., rotate, shrink/enlarge, etc.) as he walks around the environment using a first-person perspective. The Virtual World Editor provides two menus: the *3d models menu*, that gives access to the toolkit's 3D models warehouse, and the *transformations menu* (Figure 3), which allow to remove an object or to modify its size, orientation or position. Using the first menu Bill navigates the selected theme template to search for a podium and a lamp that could match with the real ones in the museum. Luckily, he finds good candidates and he will just have to adjust their size and colour (using the *transformations menu*) to have perfect digital 3D replicas. As for the Nefertiti bust, Bill had already captured a 3D model of the bust with a 3D scanner.

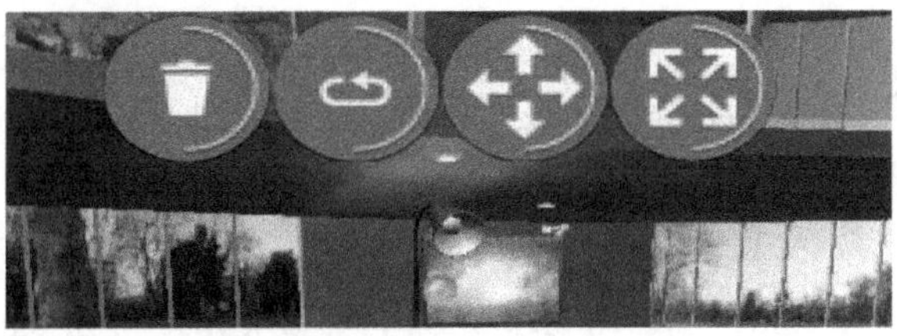

Figure 3. The transformations menu. It allows to remove, rotate, move or resize the selected object.

Once the whole virtual scene is composed, the next step is to add interactive capabilities to its elements. To support this task, the toolkit provides a *behaviours menu* that allows to associate pre-defined actions/triggers to the objects in the scene. For instance, Bill programs the podium with a *proximity sensor* trigger, that will activate an action according to the distance from the podium. Next to this, Bill assigns a *switch* behaviour to the lamp, a special behaviour which allows him to specify an alternative state for the object. In this case he selects the lamp turned on from the 3D models available for this object (Figure 4). The design of the virtual world is stored in a XML descriptor file, and automatically updated anytime the user edits the world. The XML descriptor is used by the Virtual World Client to run the interactive 3D scene.

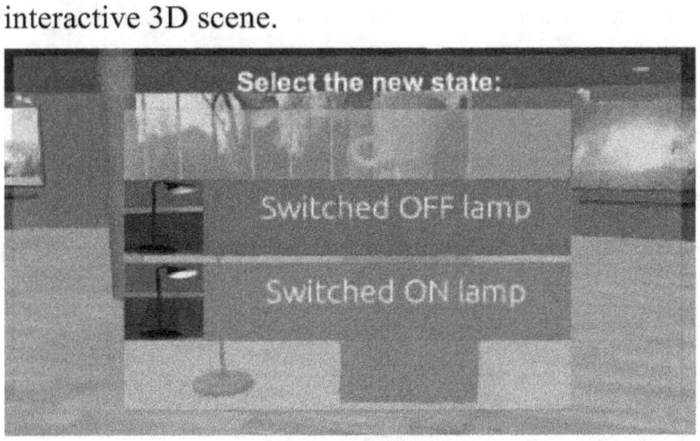

Figure 4. Select an alternative state for the object among the available 3D models.

Electronic-Incorporated Objects Editor

Next, Bill starts building the interactive objects that will be used to interact with the physical world. He will need to use two Arduino-based boards: one will be attached to a lamp to turn the light on or off via a relay, and a second one will be used to sense the distance of the visitors from the piece (via a distance sensor). Bill will place this second device on the pedestal, near the piece. The Electronic-Incorporated Objects Editor supports Bill in this task. It copes with *Challenge 2: Augmenting the physical world* by providing a visual tool to build custom interactive objects through the combination of sensors and actuators on microcontroller boards. The user interface allows to choose a microcontroller board and to attach sensors and actuators by drag-and-drop from a palette of components, as shown in Figure 2 (b.1). The editor panel is zoomable and scrollable. However, the screen may get cluttered if the cross-reality environment requires to design many electronic-incorporated objects. To cope with this problem, the editor allows to hide and "minimize to tray" selected objects and retrieve them at a later time.

```xml
<object
    id='923c63e1-6a36-44dd-b830-73c1886c5b1b'
    name='Tinkerkit-1'
    type='arduino'
    board='arduino_uno'
    shield='tinkerkit'>
    <input>
        <I0 port='I0'>
            <component
                id='18525ab2-99c8-46dc-ae9e-1757a80e18e5'
                name='distance-1'
                type='distance'
                data_type='discrete'
                data_range='0,1023'/>
        </I0>
    </input>
    <output>
        <O0 port='O0'>
            <component
                id='3097cd94-d43a-4e21-905a-b3a597bee4af'
                name='relay-1'
                type='relay'
                data_type='boolean'/>
        </O0>
    </output>
</object>
```

Figure 5. Example of the XML file for the definition of an electronic-incorporated object with a relay (output) and a distance sensor (input) built on top of the Tinkerkit shield.

The user interface aims to relieve end users from the complexity of the electronic design by providing visual hints that guide the user to correctly connect the components in the right place. The visual design serves as a visual reference that users can exploit at the moment of the physical design, e.g., when the user physically connects the sensors to the board. A different color code has been used for output and input components (Figure 2, b.2). The specification of the interactive objects are defined through an XML-based language in terms of their components (Figure 5). This approach provides the backbone for the development of physical-digital interactions that are independent of the underlying hardware. The XML file is dynamically created while the user is interacting with the interface. It describes the input and output components of each interactive object, and it provides the references (e.g., device and components ids) for the definition of interaction rules between physical and virtual objects. The XML description of the interactive objects is automatically parsed to generate the logic of the Cross-Reality (XR) Runtime Server to manage physical I/O on host devices (Figure 2, d).

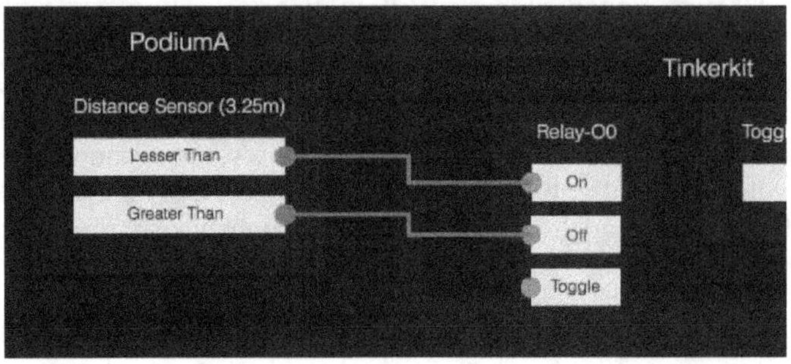

Figure 6. Example of a trigger-action rule in the toolkit: turning on and off a relay depending on the distance from a virtual object (the podium in the walkthrough scenario).

Interaction Rules Editor

The Interaction Rules Editor addresses *Challenge 4: Defining a mapping between the two worlds* by providing a visual scrollable and zoomable state-chart editor for programming the cross-reality behavior of virtual and physical elements. The two previous tools —the Virtual World Editor and the Electronic-Incorporated Objects Editor— provide a coherent definition of all the objects in the cross-reality environment in terms of XML-based descriptions of their components and attributes. The Interaction Rules Editor exploits these descriptions to produce a third kind of XML descriptor that stores the logic for connecting physical spaces with their virtual counterparts by means of high-level interaction policies that synchronize sensors and actuators in the physical room with digital entities in the virtual world.

Two kind of rules are supported at the current stage of implementation: direct mapping and trigger-action [37]. For direct mapping rules, there is a one-to-one mapping of the input value into the output value. For instance, a rotary potentiometer provides values from the range *[0,1023]*. If a user wants to link potentiometer values with the orientation of a virtual object, a mapping from *[0,1023]* to *[0,359]* will provide the correct outcome. Trigger-action rules allow users to define interactive behaviors in the form *if something happens* (the trigger), *then do something* (the action) [37]. If a sensor event matches with the trigger of the rule, then the corresponding output is propagated to the target object. On the target object, an actuator (e.g., a servomotor in case of an augmented physical object), or a specific action (e.g., "rotate" in case of a virtual object), will produce a change to some attributes of the physical or virtual object. In our example Bill programs both a virtual and a physical distance sensor —the one associated with the virtual podium and the one attached to the real podium— to turn on and off the light of the lamp, in the virtual and real world accordingly, depending on a specific distance value (Figure 6 and Figure 7).

At this early stage of development, we decided to adopt a trigger-action approach for programming since it had already been shown to allow the implementation of a wide variety of smart behaviors [37]. In addition, a trigger-action syntax is simpler for non-technical users to understand and use when compared to more advanced programming approaches such as block-based languages [32].

To support end users in programming sensor-based interaction, the authoring tool allows the definition of trigger values by demonstration [14, 18]; that is, instead of introducing a numeric value for specifying the distance from the podium, Bill can come nearer/go away from the podium in the first-person perspective to set the distance value. Similarly, Bill can set the trigger value for the physical distance sensor by "showing" the system the desired distance (Figure 7).

Cross-Reality (XR) Runtime Server

The XR Runtime Server is a central component that manages the interplay between the physical and virtual world, thus addressing the *Challenge 3: Managing the communication between the two worlds*. After Bill has defined (i) all the elements of the virtual world, (ii) the augmented objects in the real world, and (iii) their cross-reality behavior, then the cross-reality environment is set up and ready to run. The web-based interface provides a button to run and test the actual configuration (Figure 2, d), which will launch a session instance on the server. All the XML-based descriptions are stored in the runtime server, which parses these files and creates the logic of the cross-reality environment in terms of data structures that hold the description of physical and virtual objects as well as their interactions.

Figure 7. The user interface of the authoring tool for defining trigger values by demonstration. In the case of a physical distance sensor, the user clicks the "show me the distance" button (on the left) and then shows the desired distance to the sensor (center). She then clicks on the "Set distance" button to set the value of the distance trigger (right).

The server acts as a central communication unit for the virtual world that runs in the Virtual World Client and the electronic-incorporated objects in the real world (Entity Runtime). When the server receives events from sensors, it controls if the event meets a specific trigger by checking a look-up table that stores sources, triggers, destinations and actions of the interaction rules. Once an interaction rules is found in the table, the server generates a message with the corresponding output to be routed to (a) the Virtual World Client that will update the state of a virtual object or (b) an interactive physical object that will activate an actuator according to the received outcome. The server also acts as a bridge for different connections (*Challenge 3*) by providing a network-independent routing mechanism. Users do not need to know or to program the communication among different networked objects because the server automatically handles all the connections transparently thus achieving agnosticism of low-level communication protocols.

IMPLEMENTATION

XRT is built on top of Node.js to host the authoring tool, which has been implemented using HTML5 and JavaScript. The Virtual World Editor and the Virtual World Client are extensions of the GREP (Game Rules scEnario) Platform [39]. This system provides a set of tools to allow the definition of digital serious games, which can be exported as XML files and interpreted by the platform to generate 3D games. The original GREP capabilities have been extended to support the definition of cross-reality behaviors and the communication with the XRT Runtime Server, e.g., exchanging messages between virtual and real world. The Virtual World Editor and the Virtual World Client are built as web plugins on top of the Unity game engine. An implementation of the Firmata protocol runs in the Arduino-based tangibles (the Entity Runtime in Figure 1), which allows to execute the cross-reality environment without deploying any code on the interactive objects. All the logic to handle the devices' behavior is implemented in the runtime server, which uses WebSocket and JSON to exchange message between the virtual world and the objects in the real world. The current implementation support WiFi, Bluetooth Low Energy, nRF24 and USB Virtual Serial communication interfaces. We have implemented and tested proxies for three Arduino-based devices, the Arduino UNO board, the Tinkerkit [35] shield that is used in combination with an Arduino UNO board and BLE-enabled LightBlue Bean/Bean+ [20].

Current technical limitations

At this stage of development, the setup of a cross-reality environment is limited to only one 3D world instance as well as one user. Real-time distributed interactions with multiple avatars is a work-in-progress feature. The toolkit allows to build custom Arduino-based objects. At the moment, other kind of microcontrollers such as the Raspberry PI or off-the-shelf devices such as tablet or smartphones are not supported. Cross-reality behaviors are implemented in the form of simple trigger-action rules. Other forms of end-user programmability, such as scripting, block coding [30], or advanced composition of behaviors are not supported in the current implementation.

USER STUDY

We conducted an empirical user study, using the 'think-aloud' protocol, to evaluate the effectiveness of our toolkit. We wanted to learn whether our toolkit provides an easy platform to quickly prototype application scenarios that interweave the virtual and the physical world. We chose not to include a baseline condition (e.g., a control group) since there is no similar tool, to the best of our knowledge, that allows this kind of development.

Participants and setup

We recruited 8 adult participants (2 females, age M=33, SD=7.63) from the Computer Science department at our university: 4 HCI/Interaction Design researchers, 2 PhD. students in HCI and 2 undergraduate students in Computer Science. Participants received no compensation. Overall participants had an average previous knowledge of virtual reality authoring tools (M=3.5, SD=1.41 on a 7-point Likert scale question) and a less than average experience with physical computing (M=3.25, SD=0.85) and electronics (M=2.5, SD=0.70). The user study was conducted in a quiet lab environment using a 27-inch (1900x1200) iMac running OS X and Google Chrome browser. We provided an external mouse and keyboard, one Arduino, a Tinkerkit shield and the sensors needed to complete the proposed task.

Procedure and task

At the beginning of the session, participants were asked to complete a background questionnaire that was used to gather information about their demographics and their previous experience with virtual reality, electronics and physical computing. Then, a researcher introduced the X-Reality Toolkit to the participants and proposed a simple training task —turn on a LED when the user hits a specific object in the virtual world (collision detection sensor). This served as a tutorial session to show the main functionality of the toolkit.

Participants were then asked to perform a task to develop a cross-device environment with our toolkit, similar to the walkthrough scenario. We choose 15 minutes as maximum time length according to a pilot study. Participants were given a task instruction sheet with a brief description of the goals to satisfy. The task asked participants to edit a virtual scene by adding a pedestal, a sculpture on the pedestal, and a lamp. The 3D model of a museum room was already provided. In the real world the same situation was reproduced, with a lamp, a pedestal and the 3D-printed reproduction of the physical sculpture. Participants were also asked to program cross-reality interactivity. Specifically, they were asked to implement the following behaviors: (1) turn on/off the light in the virtual world when a button in the real world is pressed, and (2) turn on/off the lamp in the real world when a user in the virtual world come closer/go away from the virtual sculpture. The experiment was not fully controlled as it was designed in a way that participants were free to choose different authoring strategies and workflows to complete the task. On average, a user session lasted 45 minutes in total.

Data collection

We collected quantitative data such as the time to complete the task and participant self-assessment on their physical computing skills, on a 7-point scale from complete beginner (1) to expert (7), including their expertise with electronics, Arduino and sensor-based interaction. Participants were also asked to provide post-test feedback in the form of Likert-scale answers to the ten-items SUS questionnaire [6] as well as a debriefing interview. We audio- and video-recorded the participants during the task as well as video-recorded the screen activity.

EXPERIMENTAL RESULTS AND DISCUSSION

Seven out of eight participants successfully completed the task in the given time (M=7.40 minutes, SD=1.11 minutes). The only participant who did not complete the task said he was *"confused by the functionality and interaction modalities of the authoring tool"* (P8). He *"expected that, for any virtual object, the toolkit would automatically create an Arduino-based physical object."* SUS score reported an average usability for the toolkit (M=69.79, SD=21.30). In particular, participants expressed interest in using the toolkit and reported they would use it frequently (M=4.13, SD=1.05) and that most people would learn how to use it quickly (M=3.90, SD=1.26). One of the participants said: *"I see potential in this toolkit"* (P2). They also found that the functionalities of the system were well integrated (M=4.5, SD=0.70).

The results show that users with no particular technical knowledge were able to setup the cross-reality environment and complete the task in a reasonable amount of time. This can be due to many factors: participants reported that they did not need special knowledge to complete the task, they did not need to program or deploy any code on host devices, the user interface helped in the physical design and ensured participants they were connecting the sensors to the right sockets. Participants also found it easy to use the programming-by-demonstration approach for sensor-based interaction. Participants commented: *"It [the toolkit] was easy to use. It took me very little time to learn how to use it and it shortens the time to prototype cross-reality interactions"* (P1); *"I like the integration of virtual and physical authoring through the rules editor"* (P3).

The user study identified the weaknesses of the current implementation and opportunities for future development.

Interaction. Even if participant praised the integration of elements in the interface, they found it cumbersome to use mouse-based interaction to both edit the virtual world as well as the Arduino-based objects. In particular, the virtual world requires to perform a variety of actions (e.g., controlling the camera orientation, navigate the 3D scene, object manipulation, selection of menu options, etc.) that may benefit from exploring alternative interaction paradigms. Allowing the user to edit the virtual world through gesture-based interaction with immersive virtual-reality technology (e.g., Oculus Rift) is a possibility [40].

Mapping. Three out of eight participants thought that the toolkit should allow to create instances of mirrored-worlds in such a way that for any object added to the virtual world, an electronic-incorporated object is automatically created that replicates the behavior of the virtual object in the real world. That was a serendipitous discovery: the toolkit could be extended to provide additional end-user support depending on the cross-reality mapping the want to achieve. For instance, in the case of mirror worlds, it would be interesting explore the trade-offs of providing the functionality suggested by the participants.

Trigger-action rules. The user study also highlighted the need for unambiguous trigger-action interpretation. For instance, the task asked to turn on the light in the real world when the user approaches the virtual sculpture. Four out of eight participants were not sure whether or not the rule would automatically revert the lamp to its original state (off) when the condition does not hold true. Participants also reported that the trigger-action rule system would benefit from providing a higher degree of programmability such as rule composition with conditional operators and constraints as well as more complex programming operators (e.g., loop statements).

CONCLUSIONS AND FUTURE WORK

The need of advanced programming skills together with hardware and electronics knowledge are major barriers that prevent non-expert users from building cross-reality environments. In this paper we introduced an end-user toolkit that aims to ease such development. Results from the user study show the potential of our approach: end users with limited knowledge of sensor-based interaction were able to quickly setup a cross-reality environment without requiring any textual programming.

Our current work focuses on exploring immersive virtual world editing and potential user interfaces for improving the definition of rules (e.g., a visual block syntax [30]). We are also extending the toolkit to support devices such as Augmented Reality wearables and a wide range of sensors, including depth sensors to enable spatial interactions in the physical world. Lastly, after fixing the usability issues we encountered during the evaluation, we plan to make the toolkit available as an open-source project for the HCI/TEI community to use, learn from and contribute to.

ACKNOWLEDGMENTS

This work has been funded by the CREAx project (TIN2014-56534-R). We thank David Suarez and Juan Escudero for helping with the development of the toolkit.

REFERENCES

1. AutoDesk 3DS Max. 2016. Retrieved July 19, 2016 from http://www.autodesk.es/products/3ds-max/overview.
2. Rafael Ballagas, Meredith Ringel, Maureen Stone, and Jan Borchers. 2003. iStuff: a physical user interface toolkit for ubiquitous computing environments. In *Proceedings of the SIGCHI Conference on Human Factors in Computing Systems* (CHI '03), 537-544. DOI=http://dx.doi.org/10.1145/642611.642705
3. Andrea Bellucci, Paloma Díaz, Ignacio Aedo, and Alessio Malizia. 2014. Prototyping device ecologies: physical to digital and viceversa. In Proceedings of the 8th International Conference on Tangible, Embedded and Embodied Interaction (TEI '14). ACM, New York, NY, USA, 373-376. DOI=http://dx.doi.org/10.1145/2540930.2567905
4. Blender. 2016. Retrieved July 19, 2016 from https://www.blender.org/.
5. Tracey Booth, Simone Stumpf, Jon Bird, and Sara Jones. 2016. Crossed Wires: Investigating the Problems of End-User Developers in a Physical Computing Task. In *Proceedings of the 2016 CHI Conference on Human Factors in Computing Systems* (CHI '16), 3485-3497. http://dx.doi.org/10.1145/2858036.2858533
6. John Brooke. 1996. SUS-A quick and dirty usability scale. *Usability evaluation in industry*, 189, 194, 4-7.
7. Scott Carter, Jennifer Mankoff, Scott R. Klemmer, and Tara Matthews. 2008. Exiting the cleanroom: On ecological validity and ubiquitous computing. *Human–Computer Interaction*, 23, 1, 47-99. http://dx.doi.org/10.1080/07370020701851086
8. Arthur Clark. 2004. Natural-Born Cyborgs: Minds, Technologies, and the Future of Human Intelligence. Oxford University Press.
9. Google Sketchup. 2016. 3D modeling for everyone. Retrieved July 19, 2016 from https://www.sketchup.com/es.
10. Saul Greenberg. 2007. Toolkits and interface creativity. Multimedia Tools and Applications 32, 2, 139–159.
11. Saul Greenberg and Chester Fitchett. 2001. Phidgets: easy development of physical interfaces through physical widgets. In *Proceedings of the 14th annual ACM symposium on User interface software and technology* (UIST '01), 209-218. http://dx.doi.org/10.1145/502348.502388
12. Chris Hand. 1997. A survey of 3D interaction techniques. In *Computer Graphics Forum*, Blackwell Publishers, 16, 5, , 269-281
13. Björn Hartmann, Scott R. Klemmer, Michael Bernstein, Leith Abdulla, Brandon Burr, Avi Robinson-Mosher, and Jennifer Gee. 2006. Reflective physical prototyping through integrated design, test, and analysis. In *Proceedings of the 19th annual ACM symposium on User interface software and technology* (UIST '06), 299-308. http://dx.doi.org/10.1145/1166253.1166300
14. Björn Hartmann, Leith Abdulla, Manas Mittal, and Scott R. Klemmer. 2007. Authoring sensor-based interactions by demonstration with direct manipulation and pattern recognition. In *Proceedings of the SIGCHI Conference on Human Factors in Computing Systems* (CHI '07), 145-154. http://dx.doi.org/10.1145/1240624.1240646
15. Johann Habakuk Israel, Oliver Belaifa, Adrienne Gispen, and Rainer Stark. 2010. An object-centric interaction framework for tangible interfaces in virtual environments. In *Proceedings of the fifth international conference on Tangible, embedded, and embodied interaction* (TEI '11), 325-332. http://dx.doi.org/10.1145/1935701.1935777
16. Scott Klemmer and James A. Landay. 2009. Toolkit Support for Integrating Physical and Digital Interactions. *Human-Computer Interaction, 24*, 3, 315–366. http://dx.doi.org/10.1080/07370020902990428
17. Andrew J. Ko, Robin Abraham, Laura Beckwith, Alan Blackwell, Margaret Burnett, Martin Erwig, Chris Scaffidi, Joseph Lawrance, Henry Lieberman, Brad Myers, Mary Beth Rosson, Gregg Rothermel, Mary Shaw, and Susan Wiedenbeck. 2011. The state of the art in end-user software engineering. *ACM Comput. Surv.* 43, 3, Article 21 (April 2011), 44 pages. http://dx.doi.org/10.1145/1922649.1922658
18. Henry Lieberman, Fabio Paternò, Marcus Klann, Volker Wulf, 2006. End-User Development: An Emerging Paradigm. In *End User Development*. Springer Netherlands, 1–8.
19. Joshua Lifton and Joseph A. Paradiso. 2010. Dual Reality: Merging the Real and Virtual. *Facets of Virtual Environments*, Volume 33 of the series Lecture Notes of the Institute for Computer Sciences, Social Informatics and Telecommunications Engineering, 12-28.
20. LightBlue Bean. 2016. Retrieved July 19, 2016 from https://www.punchthrough.com/bean.
21. Nicolai Marquardt, Robert Diaz-Marino, Sebastian Boring, and Saul Greenberg. 2011. The proximity toolkit: prototyping proxemic interactions in ubiquitous computing ecologies. In *Proceedings of the 24th annual ACM symposium on User interface software and technology* (UIST '11), 315-326. http://dx.doi.org/10.1145/2047196.2047238
22. David A. Mellis, Massimo Banzi, David Cuartielles, and Tom Igoe. 2007. Arduino: An open electronic prototyping platform. In *CHI'07 Extended Abstracts on Human Factors in Computing Systems.* (CHI EA'07), 1–11.

23. Microsoft Kinect. 2016. Retrieved July 19, 2016 from http://www.xbox.com/es-ES/xbox-one/accessories/kinect-for-xbox-one#fbid=lyd_jW8qoq_

24. Paul Milgram and Fumio Kishino. 1994. A taxonomy of mixed reality visual displays. *IEICE TRANSACTIONS on Information and and Systems* 77(12), 1321–1329.

25. Minecraft. 2016. Retrieved July 19, 2016 from https://minecraft.net/.

26. Bonnie A. Nardi. 1993. A small matter of programming: perspectives on end user computing. MIT press.

27. Nicholas F. Polys, Benjamin Knapp, Matthew Bock, Christina Lidwin, Dane Webster, Nathan Waggoner, and Ivica Bukvic. 2015. Fusality: an open framework for cross-platform mirror world installations. In *Proceedings of the 20th International Conference on 3D Web Technology* (Web3D '15), 171-179. http://dx.doi.org/10.1145/2775292.2775317

28. Node-RED. 2016. Retrieved July 19, 2016 from http://nodered.org.

29. Oculus Rift. 2016. Retrieved July 19, 2016 from https://www3.oculus.com/en-us/rift/

30. Eric Rosenbaum, Evelyn Eastmond, and David Mellis. 2010. Empowering programmability for tangibles. In *Proceedings of the fourth international conference on Tangible, embedded, and embodied interaction* (TEI '10), 357-360. http://dx.doi.org/10.1145/1709886.1709974

31. Derek F. Reilly, Hafez Rouzati, Andy Wu, Jee Yeon Hwang, Jeremy Brudvik, and W. Keith Edwards. 2010. TwinSpace: an infrastructure for cross-reality team spaces. In *Proceedings of the 23nd annual ACM symposium on User interface software and technology* (UIST '10), 119-128. http://dx.doi.org/10.1145/1866029.1866050

32. Mitchel Resnick, John Maloney, Andrés Monroy-Hernández, Natalie Rusk, Evelyn Eastmond, Karen Brennan, Amon Millner, Eric Rosenbaum, Jay Silver, Brian Silverman, and Yasmin Kafai. 2009. Scratch: programming for all. Commun. ACM 52, 11 (November 2009), 60-67. DOI=http://dx.doi.org/10.1145/1592761.1592779

33. Second Life. 2016. Retrieved July 19, 2016 from http://secondlife.com/.

34. Russell M. Taylor, II, Thomas C. Hudson, Adam Seeger, Hans Weber, Jeffrey Juliano, and Aron T. Helser. 2001. VRPN: a device-independent, network-transparent VR peripheral system. In *Proceedings of the ACM symposium on Virtual reality software and technology* (VRST '01). ACM, New York, NY, USA, 55-61. http://dx.doi.org/10.1145/505008.505019

35. Tinkerkit. 2016. Retrieved 19 July, 2016 from https://github.com/TinkerKit.

36. Unity. 2016. Retrieved July 19, 2016 from http://unity3d.com/.

37. Blase Ur, Elyse McManus, Melwyn Pak Yong Ho, and Michael L. Littman. 2014. Practical trigger-action programming in the smart home. In *Proceedings of the SIGCHI Conference on Human Factors in Computing Systems* (CHI '14), 803-812. http://dx.doi.org/10.1145/2556288.2557420

38. Nicolas Villar, James Scott, Steve Hodges, Kerry Hammil, and Colin Miller. 2012. .NET gadgeteer: a platform for custom devices. In Pervasive Computing, Volume 7319 of the series Lecture Notes in Computer Science, Springer Berlin Heidelberg, 216-233.

39. Telmo Zarraonandia, Paloma Diaz, and Ignacio Aedo. 2016. Using combinatorial creativity to support end-user design of digital games. *Multimedia Tools and Applications*, 1-26. http://dx.doi.org/10.1007/s11042-016-3457-4

40. Telmo Zarraonandia, Paloma Diaz, Ignacio Aedo and Alvaro Montero. 2016. Inmersive End User Development for Virtual Reality. In *Proceedings of International Working Conference on Advanced Visual Interfaces* (AVI 2016), 346-347.

Virtual Lemonade: Let's Teleport Your Lemonade!

Nimesha Ranasinghe[1], Pravar Jain[1], Shienny Karwita[1], Ellen Yi-Luen Do[1,2]
Keio-NUS CUTE Center, Interactive & Digital Media Institute, National University of Singapore[1]
School of Industrial Design & School of Interactive Computing, Georgia Institute of Technology[2]
{nimesha, pravar, shienny, ellendo}@nus.edu.sg, ellendo@gatech.edu

ABSTRACT
This paper presents a novel methodology to digitally share the flavor experience of a glass of lemonade (or other similar beverages) remotely. The proposed method utilizes a sensor to capture valuable information (primarily, the color and the corresponding pH value) of the lemonade and a customized tumbler to virtually simulate these properties using plain water. Thus, the system consists of three main components: 1) the lemonade sensor, 2) the communication protocol, and 3) a customized tumbler, acting as the lemonade simulator. Initially, the sensor captures the color and the pH value of the lemonade and encodes this information based on an established communication protocol for wireless transmission. On receiving the information from the sensor, the lemonade simulator overlays the color of the drink on plain water using an RGB Light Emitting Diode (LED) and simulates sour taste sensations on the user's tongue via electrical stimulation. An experimental study was conducted to evaluate this novel approach of digitally teleporting a glass of lemonade: 1) to assess the pre-taste perceptions based on the user's visual perceptions of the colors (real vs. virtual lemonade) and 2) to assess the taste sensations (real vs. virtual lemonade). By simulating the experience of drinking a glass of lemonade through the digital reconstruction of the beverage's main visual and taste factors, the results from these experiments will be able to justify the feasibility of teleporting a glass of lemonade using this novel methodology.

ACM Classification Keywords
H.5.1. Multimedia Information Systems: Artificial, augmented, and virtual realities

Author Keywords
Teleport; virtual lemonade; virtual reality; food teleportation; beverage communication; multimodal interaction

INTRODUCTION
Social sharing of beverages among friends and loved ones is a common practice among humans. However, thus far, it has not been possible to digitally share beverages remotely, for example, over the Internet. Three of the main challenges encountered in this action are: 1) being a chemical sense, the sense of taste is one of the least understood and most subjective human senses, 2) the need for complex sensing technologies, similar to an electronic tongue, to detect the chemical composition of the beverage, and 3) the impracticalities of transferring or storing chemicals in an interactive system [19].

TEI 2017, March 20–23, 2017, Yokohama, Japan.

http://dx.doi.org/10.1145/3024969.3024977

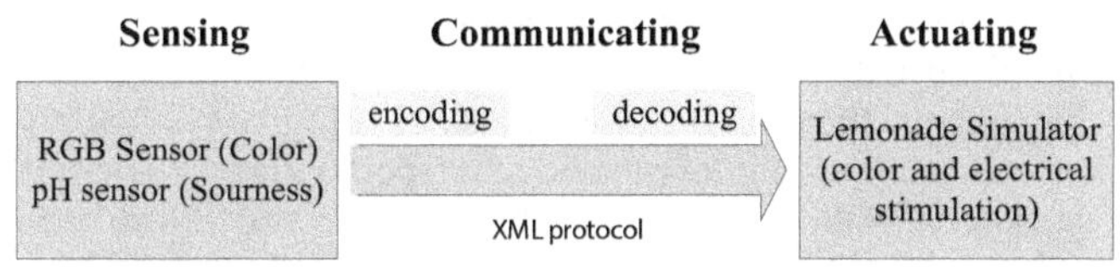

Figure 1. The system architecture of the lemonade sharing platform highlighting the three main modules.

As a solution, this paper introduces a new method and a digital platform for remotely sharing a glass of lemonade by sensing, communicating, and simulating its flavor information. The proposed method is based on the following two concepts: 1) usually, on seeing a glass of lemonade we create a pre-taste in our mind based on the beverage's color, fizziness, temperature, and other such attributes [15], 2) on drinking it, we perceive the multisensory experience of flavor, which includes the factors mentioned above, as well as taste sensations (primarily sourness in the case of lemonade), 3) additionally, it is noticed that the visual cues such as the color of lemonade may influence a cross-modal effect on the perceptions of different sensory channels (e.g. brighter yellow colors may provoke a strong sour taste sensation) [17]. Based on these phenomena, we hypothesize that, by capturing and simulating the color and sourness of a glass of lemonade, we can digitally teleport its flavor.

Therefore, in this proposed platform, as illustrated in Figure 1, we digitally sense, transfer, and simulate two of the most important attributes of a glass of lemonade: the color and the degree of sourness. To sense these two attributes, an RGB color sensor and a pH sensor are used. For the purpose of simulation, we have developed a customized tumbler that overlays different colors on plain water using an RGB LED and delivers controlled electrical pulses on the user's tongue to digitally simulate varying levels of sourness. Utilizing these stimulation methods enables us to further study the human perception of sourness with different colored beverages and to optimize the digital simulation of these factors.

A user experiment was conducted to assess and compare users' experiences of real and virtual lemonades regarding the perception of sourness. It was designed specifically to compare two aspects: 1) preconception of sourness based on the color and 2) perception of sour taste sensations between the real and virtual lemonades. The key highlights of the results suggest that there is no statistically significant difference between the real and virtual lemonades with regards to the perception of sourness when both the pre-taste and actual taste feedbacks are combined. However, in general, it was noted that a significantly higher perception of the sour taste was associated with the real lemonade when compared to the virtual lemonade.

In the rest of this paper, we first present a review of related literature on the crossmodal perception of taste sensations, the electrical stimulation of sour taste and the digital communication of flavors. Based on these existing works, we then introduce a new digital method to teleport a glass of lemonade remotely. Following this, we describe the execution and results of the user experiment that investigating how participants experience real and simulated lemonades using the proposed system. Finally, before concluding the paper, we discuss the experimental results and propose several future works based on the limitations of this approach.

RELATED WORK

Digital interactions related to food and beverages have been identified as an extremely challenging area in the Human-Computer Interaction (HCI) domain. Due to physical and perceptual factors, it is even more difficult to realize digital interactions related to food and beverages when the interaction takes place remotely from the physical food or beverage source. This section reviews existing pieces of literature that relate to the three most important aspects of this challenge: pre-perception of flavors based on the color of a beverage, simulating taste sensations, and communication of flavors.

Pre-perception of Flavors Based on Colors

Pre-perception of taste sensations (pre-taste) is mainly recognized as a cross-modal interaction between colors and taste sensations. A very useful research work conducted by Narumi et al. [10] experimentally studied this phenomenon in interactive systems. They describe an experiment with a pseudo-gustatory display based on the virtual color of a real drink. Here, a wireless LED module attached to the bottom of a transparent plastic cup is used to superimpose the virtual color of a customized drink. Studies with this methodology examined the cross-sensory effects of visual feedback and flavor interpretation of real drinks, and results from this suggested that different colors may induce a perception of different flavors, even with the same drink.

Similarly, there are a number of research works that have reported the influence of food and beverage colors on flavor perception [15, 16]. These studies are mainly concerned with exploring associations of food and beverage colors with the perception of flavors (such as lemon, banana, and the like) or basic taste sensations (such as sour, sweet, salty, bitter, and umami) and their intensity levels. These studies have assessed colors that people commonly associate with specific taste sensations. For example, it has been found that yellow and green are commonly linked to sour sensations while red to sweet sensations. They have also noticed slight differences in perceptions based on participant's culture and geographical region.

Also, several studies have highlighted that individuals usually have a preconception that brightly colored meals and beverages will be more palatable, and that the color of the food and drink generally contributes to their decision of overall acceptability [17, 4]. Similarly, individuals usually get confused when they taste colorless solutions with different flavors simply due to the lack of color information. These observations and phenomenon underline the importance of crossmodality in flavor perception and the influence that color can have on this aspect of eating and drinking.

Flavor Simulation

Recently, there has been an active growth in attention towards researching the simulation of taste sensations in interactive systems. Ranasinghe et al. presents Digital Taste Interface to simulate primary taste sensations based on electrical and thermal stimulation of the human tongue in [11, 14]. Based on their experimental results, sour, salty, bitter, and sweet (minor) tastes are simulated through electrical and thermal stimulation on the human tongue.

FunRasa is an interactive drinking platform which enhances drinking experience by combining techniques of overlaying different colors on the beverage and stimulating the tongue using electrical pulses through a 3D printed straw. They also report similar preliminary results where the participants perceived enhanced sourness, saltiness, and bitterness [12]. Similarly, Taste+ has several utensils such as spoon and bottle to augment the flavors of food and beverages [13]. Again, the perception of sour, bitter, and salty sensations were reported during these studies with varying levels of intensities and accuracies.

Alternatively, Nakamura et al. demonstrate the use of electricity for augmented gustation in [8]. They apply an electric current through isotonic drinks (which contains electrolytes) and food (juicy vegetables, fruits, and cheese) to change their taste perceptions. In this study, the main concern is the change of voltage levels to augment the sensations of food items. However, applying an electric current through isotonic drinks could elicit chemical reactions (through the process of electrolysis), which could be harmful in certain situations. They have also explored and measured the latency between presentation and perception using visual and electric taste stimuli in [9].

Apart from the research works described above, several interactive systems explore other important sensory aspects during the consumption of a beverage such as sounds, temperature, and vibrations. Straw User Interface, proposed by Hashimoto et al. [5], allows users to experience virtual drinking through an interactive system. The drinking experiences are generated by referencing prerecorded data of actual sounds, pressures, and vibrations produced by drinking from a normal straw.

"Affecting Tumbler" [18] also focuses on altering the flavor perceptions of a beverage by applying thermal sensations on the skin around the nose to simulate skin temperature changes. User studies with this system suggested that the flavor richness and aftertaste strength were significantly improved by heating up the skin around the nasal region.

Communication of Flavors

Scientists and designers, as well as sci-fi novelists, have long been anticipating the remote communication of flavors to create novel interactions. In Taste/IP [11], the authors presented a novel methodology to introduce the concept of taste messaging. They have developed a mobile application to formulate a taste message while defining a new extensible markup language (XML) format called the TasteXML (TXML) to communicate the taste message. However, this work does not have a complete teleportation capability as they were transferring only the basic taste sensations such as sourness and saltiness.

Another important aspect to consider when teleporting a flavor sensation is the sensing of the flavors. Several sophisticated electronic tongue systems have been developed to analyze and sense the chemical composition of various beverages such as wine and tea [7, 6]. Most of these taste sensors are developed with multichannel electrodes using lipid membranes as a transducer of taste substances. Similar to the human gustatory system, these sensors identify taste sensations based on recognizing response patterns of electric signals that transform information about the available taste substances in a beverage [20].

Teleporting Lemonade

The method presented in this paper to digitally teleport a lemonade is primarily inspired by the research works as mentioned above. While these works address various challenges to simulate or augment taste sensations, they have not been adapted to the unique requirements of teleporting a beverage. We have combined some of the approaches mentioned above into a single piece of technology to develop an interactive platform that simulates lemonade drinking experiences electronically and remotely.

There is deep history and meaning rooted in the preparation and serving of beverages during social gatherings. This often catalyzes conversations and brings people together to celebrate occasions. With the advent of telepresence and virtual reality technologies, the prospect of remotely interacting with friends and family in a social context becomes ever more feasible. However, the ability to establish a feeling of presence in such scenarios can be restricted by a lack of co-experiencing other interactions, such as sharing beverages. Moreover, recent research works have shown that sharing a taste experience with another person, even without verbally communicating, amplifies their taste experiences [1]. Thus, the main motivation behind our research is to develop a technology that enables the remote digital sharing of beverages, in-order to enrich our everyday digital interactions. We are also motivated to study human multisensory perception when consuming beverages and hypothesize that the experience of consuming a glass of lemonade can be effectively simulated by overlaying only the visual (color) and taste (sourness) sensory information on plain water.

In this paper, lemonade is selected to demonstrate the concept of digitally sharing and simulating beverages due to the following reasons: 1) It is a common beverage in most cultures, 2) Sourness (acidity) - the primary taste sensation associated with lemonades can be readily measured using pH sensors, and effectively simulated using the electrical stimulation on the tongue as demonstrated by [14, 13, 8], and 3) Lemonade is available in numerous colors such as yellow, green, and cloudy white, which can be detected using an RGB color sensor and simulated using an RGB LED.

The applications of this work extend not only towards virtual flavor technologies, but also in entertainment and well-being. Users may use such devices during social gatherings for multisensory interactions, for example, by toasting drinks users could share the flavors of their drinks with others. In the future, we envision a cloud repository for people to share digital signatures of their beverages. This concept may also impact personal well-being by encouraging people to drink virtually flavored water rather than artificial soft drinks.

METHOD

This section describes the implementation and technical details of the proposed platform. As explained, this platform incorporates three modules to teleport a glass of lemonade: the sensor, actuator, and communication protocol. The main modules of this platform are illustrated in Figure 1.

The Lemonade Sensor

As displayed in Figure 2, the lemonade sensor has two main components. It utilizes an RGB color sensor (ISL29125 from SparkFun[1]) and an analog pH sensor (SEN0161 from DFRobot[2]) to capture the color and sourness of the beverage respectively. As established in previous related work, it is important to simulate beverage color accurately as it directly affects the user's flavor perceptions. Moreover, at present, there are hundreds of different artificial lemonade drinks in the market, available in various colors such as red and blue apart from the traditional yellow, cloudy, or green variants. Additionally, a Bluetooth Low Energy (BLE) enabled Arduino board is used in the control module to handle the Bluetooth communication.

The pH sensor captures the level of sourness of the lemonade (measuring the degree of acidity) and correlates this value with five groups: barely detectable, mild, medium, strong, and very strong. We have experimentally developed this range by diluting 15ml of squeezed lemon juice with different amounts of distilled water - barely detectable: 50ml, mild: 30ml, medium: 15ml, strong: 5ml, and very strong: 0ml. To develop this range, we asked participants to rank the solutions on the above scale while recording the pH values of the solutions as reported in Table 1.

As shown in Figure 3, based on the current design, the user has to submerge the sensor and press the push-button to capture and send the information to the simulator. The sensor is designed in such a way that it can be easily mounted on a glass of lemonade during use, and the control module is attached separately to improve the portability.

[1] www.sparkfun.com
[2] www.dfrobot.com

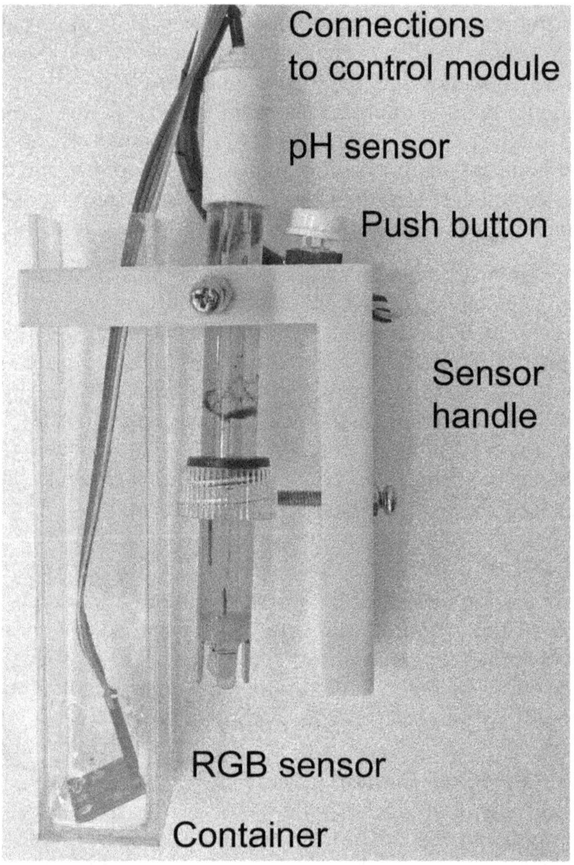

Figure 2. Different components of the lemonade sensor. Once submerged, the pH sensor captures the pH value while RGB sensor captures the color.

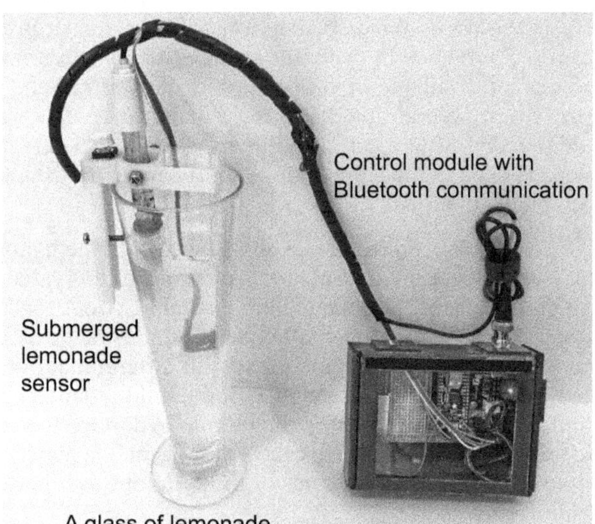

Figure 3. Once the lemonade sensor is submerged, it captures the information of the beverage. The control module sends this information to the simulator via Bluetooth.

Communication Protocol

Communication between the sensor and simulator is established via Bluetooth and an XML based protocol is utilized to encode the data as explained in [11]. Once the lemonade sensor captures the color and pH information, the control module formulates the XML message and transfers it to the simulator. An example message formulated from a yellow colored lemonade with strong sour taste is displayed below:

<lemonade>
<color r=239, g=239, b=31 />
<sourness>strong</sourness>
</lemonade>

Group	pH range	Magnitude of current
barely-detectable	2.84 and above	$60\mu A$
mild	2.52 - 2.84	$80\mu A$
medium	2.38 - 2.52	$120\mu A$
strong	2.25 - 2.38	$160\mu A$
very-strong	2.17 and below	$180\mu A$

Table 1. pH values are mapped with different magnitudes of current.

The Lemonade Simulator

As shown in Figure 4, a customized tumbler has been developed to simulate the lemonade experience on plain water. The tumbler has an RGB LED with a light diffusing mechanism at the bottom to provide different color stimuli and a ring of silver electrodes attached to the mouthpiece to simulate sourness by electrically stimulating the user's tongue. Users simply touch the silver electrodes using their tongues while drinking to simulate the sourness. To simulate the sour taste, controlled electrical pulses (frequency: 800Hz, magnitude of current: $60\mu A$ - $180\mu A$) were used [12, 13]. The mapping of pH values to magnitudes of current is shown in Table 1. Due to limitations of the human taste system when perceiving small step changes in taste intensity, and the subjective nature of taste, one-to-one mapping between pH values and magnitudes of current was not considered.

When using this tumbler, the users only consume plain water but the experience of the lemonade flavor is simulated using the crossmodal effects as mentioned above. In addition to the RGB LED at the bottom of the tumbler, the control module has a constant current source to output controlled electrical pulses and a BLE enabled Arduino board handles the Bluetooth communication and control signals. We also used white colored diffuse-papers in every tumbler as the plain water is too clear to diffuse the light properly.

EXPERIMENTAL EVALUATION

We have conducted a user experiment to evaluate the effectiveness of this approach by comparing different aspects of the real vs. virtual lemonades. Three common lemonade colors - green, yellow, and cloudy were chosen to compare the pre-taste and actual taste aspects between real and virtual lemonades. Our main hypothesis is that the participants will have a similar degree of flavor experience in real as well as virtual lemonades because of the crossmodal effects.

Participants

Thirteen (13) participants (5 male and 8 female), aged between 20-30 (AVG = 22.76, M = 22, SD = 2.01), were recruited for this experiment. Participants were randomly recruited from

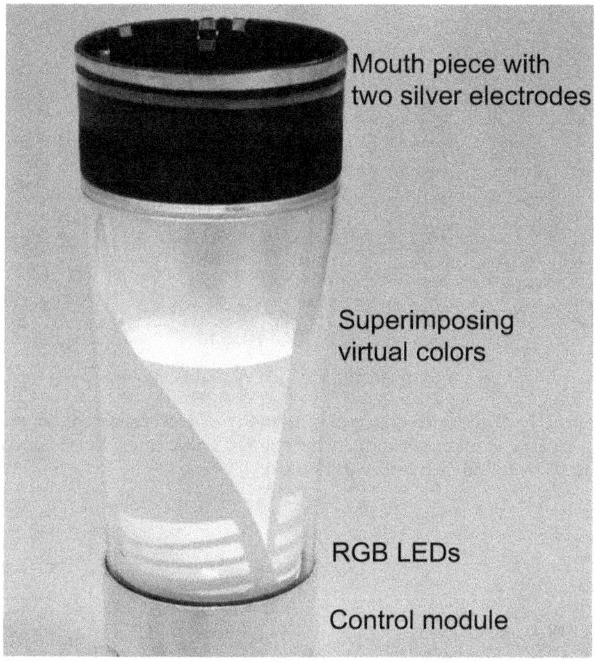

Figure 4. Different components of the lemonade simulator. It stimulates the user's tongue using electrical stimulation and superimposes virtual colors onto the water to simulate lemonades

the university staff and students and had no prior experience with the concept or the prototypes before being tested. All participants were in good health (without known problems like cold, fever, or a runny nose), non-smokers, and reported no taste or smell problems. Furthermore, all of them were familiar with using technology such as computers and mobile phones.

In general, certain medical conditions and medications, as well as consuming spicy and hot food, may temporarily interfere with the sensitivity of the sense of taste. Therefore, they were instructed not to consume spicy, alcoholic, too hot or too cold - food or beverages at least one hour before the experiments as these may alter their perceptions. The experiments were conducted in the morning between 10 AM - 12 PM and afternoon between 2 PM - 6.30PM to avoid breakfast and lunch periods. Furthermore, as some loss of taste sensation also occurs due to the normal aging process, we selected a particularly focused age group spanning 20 to 30 years [2].

Apparatus

The experiments were conducted in two quiet private meeting rooms (with approximately similar ambient light and temperature settings) inside the laboratory. One room was used to conduct the experiments with the real lemonade (as displayed in Figure 5) and the other with the virtual lemonade (as shown in Figure 6). To prepare the three colored lemonade solutions, we used the Florida's Natural Lemonade[3] (pH = 2.34) with tasteless food coloring agents. In this way, we preserved the same taste for all the three lemonades but applied different colors for each. Furthermore, all lemonades, real and virtual were presented in vessels that were identical in physical form.

[3]https://www.floridasnatural.com/our-juices/lemonade.php

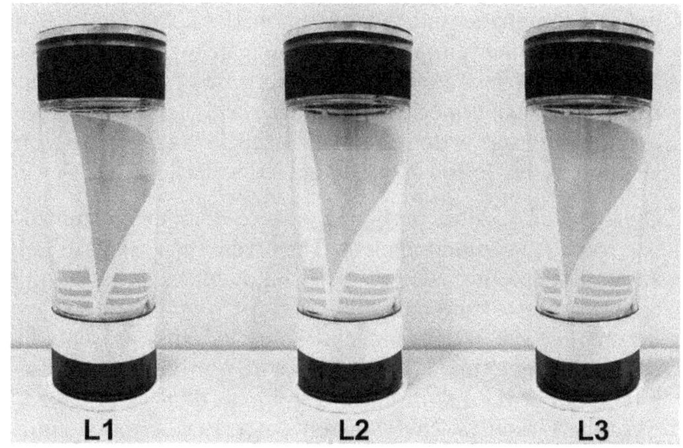

Figure 5. The real lemonades prepared in three commonly available colors (green, cloudy, and yellow).

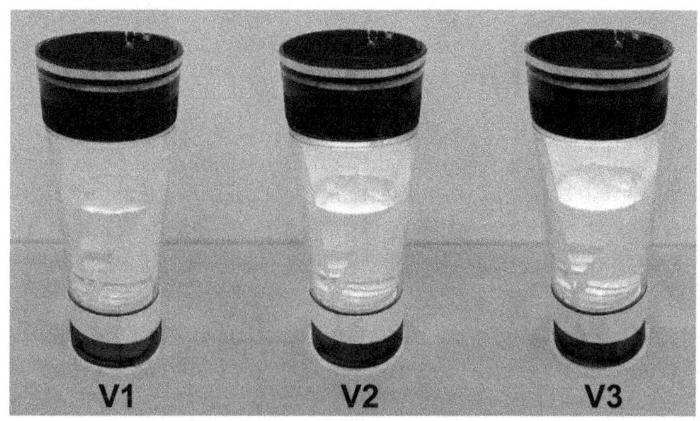

Figure 6. The three commonly available colors of lemonades (green, cloudy, and yellow) are simulated by overlaying respective colors using LEDs.

To simulate the virtual sour taste, the lemonade simulator was configured with the settings related to the strong level (frequency: 800Hz, magnitude of current: 160μA).

Experimental Method

As mentioned, this experiment was focused on studying the effectiveness of simulating a virtual lemonade remotely by capturing and sharing the color and pH levels of a real lemonade in three different colors: yellow, cloudy, and green. In this study, we mainly focused on studying two aspects of the experience: pre-taste of sourness based on the colors (appearance) and perception of actual taste sensations.

Before the formal experiment, for each participant, we conducted a short training session (using an empty tumbler with no real or artificial stimuli) to get them familiar with the apparatus. Then, during the experiment, each participant was randomly presented with 12 different stimuli in two sessions - six stimuli based on real lemonade (two stimuli per lemonade: color and taste) and similarly six other based on virtual lemonades. The real and virtual lemonades were arranged in two separate meeting rooms (to counterbalance) to simulate a remote sharing scenario. The experiment was conducted in two similarly structured separate sessions (one session per room) for real lemonade and virtual lemonades. The fact that the beverages in the tumblers were lemonades was not disclosed to the participants along with the purpose of this experiment. Before each experiment, mouth-pieces and the electrodes were rinsed using tap water, then sterilized using 70% isopropyl alcohol swabs, followed by deionized water [3].

During each session, participants were randomly assigned to one room (to counterbalance). They were then asked to judge and rank the lemonades on the level of sourness based on its color (pre-taste) and next, based on the sourness (after drinking). Three colored lemonades were randomly presented (to counterbalance) one after another with minimum five-minute intervals between stimuli during which they were asked to rinse their mouth with deionized water. Furthermore, similar tumblers were used for all the stimuli to prevent bias and for counterbalancing. At the end of the first session, participants were rested for a minimum of five minutes before the next session. They were asked to rank the intensity of sourness on a six-point scale of no-taste, barely-detectable, mild, medium, strong, and very-strong.

Results and Discussion

As presented in Figures 7, 8, and 9, we analyzed the results of perceiving the sourness based on three aspects: pre-taste (primarily based on the color), taste of sourness, and as a combined measurement (perception of sourness based on color and taste).

Pre-taste of sourness based on the color

Paired-Samples T-Tests were conducted between the real and virtual lemonade scores for the three colored beverage groups regarding the pre-perception of sourness. The results suggest that there is no significant difference in the scores for the pairs of green L1 - V1 [$t(12)=0.519$, $p > 0.5$, SD=0.26, SE=0.07] and yellow L3 - V3 [$t(12)=-1.723$, $p > 0.1$, SD=0.28, SE=0.078] (as in Figures 5 and 6). This finding suggests that the participants had a similar preconception of sourness based on green and yellow beverages. However, there is a significant difference in the scores for cloudy L2 - V2 [$t(12)=-0.208$, $p < 0.05$, SD=0.408, SE=0.113], which suggests that the participants perceived a higher intensity of sourness in the virtual lemonade than the real lemonade based on their colors. This may be due to the white color of the LED which is much brighter than the cloudiness in the real lemonade; the participants might associate higher intensity of sourness because of the intensity of the color as explained in [17]. The normalized and averaged results based on the pre-taste of sourness are displayed in Figure 7.

Perception of sour taste

Similarly, Paired-Samples T-Tests were conducted between real and virtual lemonade scores for the three colored beverage groups to compare the participant's perception of sour taste. In this phase, visual information of the drink was intentionally overlapped with its taste information to mimic the normal setting, wherein the preconception of taste based on visual information, along with the color and taste of the beverage at the time of consumption, contribute to the overall flavor experience. However, when the participants taste the sourness of real and virtual lemonades, as the paired-samples t-tests suggest,

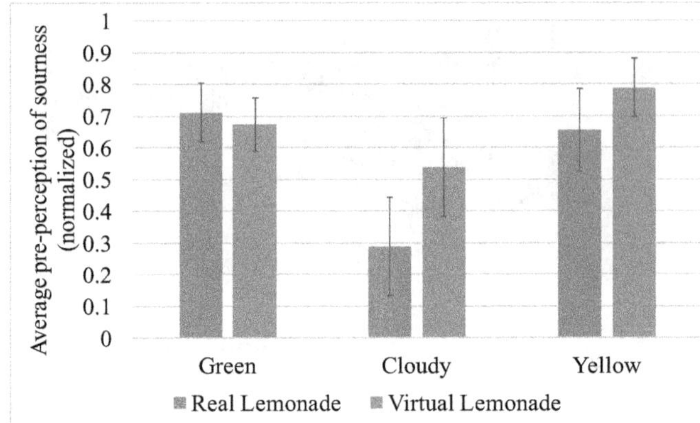

Figure 7. Normalized average intensity scores reported for the pre-perception of sourness of the three colored lemonades. Error bars represent 95% confidence interval (N = 13).

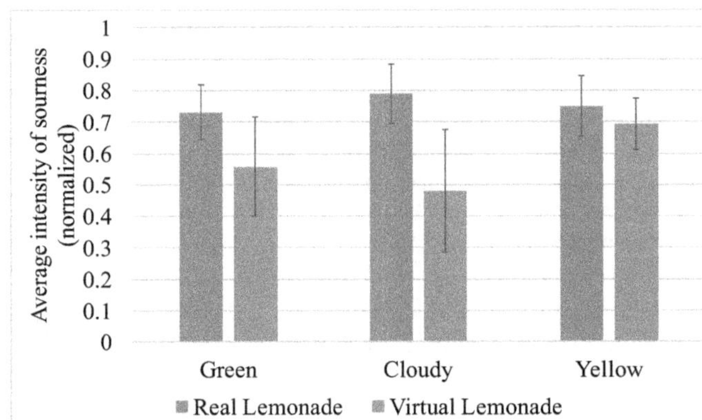

Figure 8. Normalized average intensity scores reported for the sour taste of the three colored lemonades. Error bars represent 95% confidence interval (N = 13).

there is a significant difference in the scores for both pairs of green L1 - V1 [$t(12)=2.25$, $p < 0.05$, SD=0.27, SE=0.076] and cloudy L2 - V2 [$t(12)=3.593$, $p < 0.05$, SD=0.308, SE=0.085]. As reported in Figure 8, in both of these occasions the intensity of the real sour taste was much stronger than the virtual sourness produced by the simulator. We suspect two possible reasons: 1) The perception of the sourness and its intensity through electrical stimulation on the tongue may be weakened because of the plain water or 2) Participants may perceive mixed sensations, for example, higher sweetness or saltiness due to the color change and crossmodal effects as also noticed in [21]. One suggestion to increase the perception - the intensity of virtual sour taste - is to utilize a slightly stronger electrical pulse, for instance - apply the electrical stimuli as in very-strong category when the sourness of the real beverage falls only in the strong category (as in Table 1). Nevertheless, there is no significant difference in the scores for yellow L3 - V3 [$t(12)=0.762$, $p > 0.05$, SD=0.272, SE=0.075], which confirms that the sour taste perception of yellow colored real and virtual lemonades are similar.

Overall perception (combined measurement)

Finally, we compare the overall perception of real and virtual flavor experience (combined measurements of pre-perception

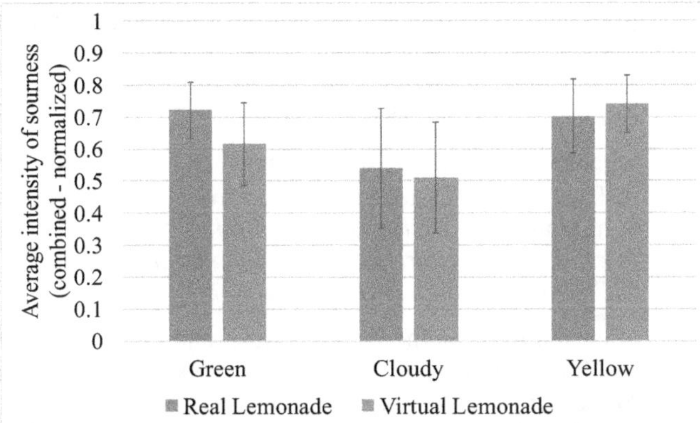

Figure 9. Normalized average intensity scores reported for combined pre-perception and sour taste for the three colored lemonades. Error bars represent 95% confidence interval (N = 13).

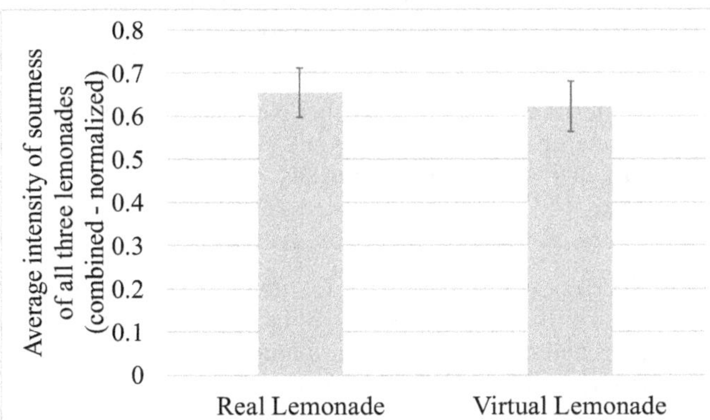

Figure 10. Normalized average intensity scores reported for overall all the real and virtual lemonades. Error bars represent 95% confidence interval (N = 13).

of the sourness and the sour taste). As mentioned earlier, we hypothesize that by simulating only the color and basic taste information (i.e. sourness) participants will have a similar degree of flavor experience in virtual lemonades due to the crossmodal effects. Paired-Samples T-Tests were conducted between real and virtual lemonades of the three colored beverage groups to compare the participant's perception of lemonade flavors. Interestingly, the paired-samples t-tests suggest that there are no significant difference in the scores for green L1 - V1 [t(25)=1.958, p > 0.05, SD=0.275, SE=0.054], cloudy L2 - V2 [t(25)=0.324, p > 0.05, SD=0.454, SE=0.089], and yellow L3 - V3 [t(25)=-0.679, p > 0.05, SD=0.288, SE=0.056] lemonades when compared in terms of their overall perception of sourness. Furthermore, as can be seen in Figure 9, the mean values are approximately equivalent when compared with the overall flavor perception of the three lemonades.

To further confirm this result, another Paired-Samples T-Test was conducted between the overall perceptions of all real and virtual lemonades (combining both factors: pre-perception and taste of the sourness, as well as the three colored lemonades - green, cloudy, and yellow). As depicted in Figure 10, the results show that the overall perception of sourness between real and virtual lemonades are not statistically significant, thus in general participants perceive a similar flavor experience in real and virtual lemonades [t(77)=0.809, p > 0.05, SD=0.349, SE=0.039]. These results also confirm that, although there are several aspects we need to study further (for example, the results of varying perceptions of sour taste in cloudy and green color lemonades), in general teleportation of lemonades may be achieved by transferring only the color information and pH values (which matched to the degree of sourness).

LIMITATIONS AND FUTURE WORK

Designing technologies to share flavor experiences remotely is challenging, mainly due to the lack of fundamental knowledge on the multisensory perception of flavor experiences. However, in this work, we utilized the unique opportunity of crossmodal perception to simulate the flavor experience of lemonades.

One of the main limitations of this work is that at its present stage, we are only focused on the primary taste attribute of lemonades, i.e. the perception of sour sensations. Hence, future work would concentrate on other sensations including the sweetness, saltiness as well as bitterness. More importantly, we intend to study how crossmodal effects might change the perception of these sensations and their intensities.

Future studies should also focus on more variables such as the change in color intensities and the properties of electrical stimulation to study their effect on the overall flavor perception in humans. Moreover, other modalities such as smell, temperature and other properties of beverages such as fizziness should be included to simulate more varieties and realistic virtual experiences.

During the user experiments, most participants found the experience of flavor sharing pleasant and surprising. However, on several occasions elicited taste sensations and their intensities were found to be subjective mainly in terms of their intensities. One possible solution to overcome this limitation is to calibrate the stimuli (intensity of color and properties of the electrical stimuli) of the lemonade simulation according to users' perceptions. This phenomenon is common in natural (or chemical based) flavor perception as well [22].

CONCLUSION

In conclusion, we presented a novel method to teleport the flavor experience of a glass of lemonade. The platform consists of three stages: sensing (which captures the RGB color and the pH value of the beverage), communication (the XML protocol to encode the data), and simulating (a custom built tumbler to overlay the color and stimulate the tongue using electrical pulses to simulate the sourness and control its intensity). Furthermore, we conducted experiments to determine the effectiveness of this approach and evaluate the crossmodal effects on flavor perception, which employs the overlaying of colors and stimulating the tongue to simulate varying degrees of sourness. The results of this experiment recommend that, in general, the proposed platform could teleport and simulate lemonades with an approximately similar perception of sourness when compared to real lemonades.

However, being an exploratory study, this work merits further investigations in multiple directions including studying of other aspects of flavor experiences to share remotely. More work is required to be done before introducing a digital platform to share any beverage remotely both in terms of technology as well as usability of this platform. Once introduced, their interactions could revolutionize the domain of digital interactions. Further experimentations with this work will help us in developing social food and beverage sharing platforms with multisensory experiences in the future. We believe that this research on digitally sharing of lemonades will enable cross-disciplinary, novel, and innovative application possibilities in the future.

ACKNOWLEDGMENTS

This research is supported by the National Research Foundation, Prime Minister's Office, Singapore under its International Research Centres in Singapore Funding Initiative.

REFERENCES

1. Erica J Boothby, Margaret S Clark, and John A Bargh. 2014. Shared experiences are amplified. *Psychological science* 25, 12 (2014), 2209–2216.
2. JM Boyce and GR Shone. 2006. Effects of ageing on smell and taste. *Postgraduate medical journal* 82, 966 (2006), 239–241.
3. R.J. Dobrin. 1984. Liquid cleaner-disinfectant composition for use in wiping down dental operatories. (Aug. 7 1984). US Patent 4,464,293.
4. Cynthia N DuBose, Armand V Cardello, and Owen Maller. 1980. Effects of Colorants and Flavorants on Identification, Perceived Flavor Intensity, and Hedonic Quality of Fruit-Flavored Beverages and Cake. *Journal of Food Science* 45, 5 (1980), 1393–1399.
5. Yuki Hashimoto, Naohisa Nagaya, Minoru Kojima, Satoru Miyajima, Junichiro Ohtaki, Akio Yamamoto, Tomoyasu Mitani, and Masahiko Inami. 2006. Straw-like user interface: virtual experience of the sensation of drinking using a straw. In *Proceedings of the international conference on Advances in computer entertainment technology*. ACM, 50.
6. A Legin, A Rudnitskaya, L Lvova, Yu Vlasov, C Di Natale, and A D'amico. 2003. Evaluation of Italian wine by the electronic tongue: recognition, quantitative analysis and correlation with human sensory perception. *Analytica Chimica Acta* 484, 1 (2003), 33–44.
7. Andrey Legin, Alisa Rudnitskaya, Yuri Vlasov, Corrado Di Natale, Fabrizio Davide, and Arnaldo D'Amico. 1997. Tasting of beverages using an electronic tongue. *Sensors and Actuators B: Chemical* 44, 1 (1997), 291–296.
8. Hiromi Nakamura and Homei Miyashita. 2011. Augmented gustation using electricity. In *Proceedings of the 2nd Augmented Human International Conference*. ACM, 34.
9. Hiromi Nakamura and Homei Miyashita. 2012. Development and evaluation of interactive system for synchronizing electric taste and visual content. In *Proceedings of the SIGCHI Conference on Human Factors in Computing Systems*. ACM, 517–520.
10. Takuji Narumi, Munehiko Sato, Tomohiro Tanikawa, and Michitaka Hirose. 2010. Evaluating cross-sensory perception of superimposing virtual color onto real drink: toward realization of pseudo-gustatory displays. In *Proceedings of the 1st Augmented Human International Conference*. ACM, 18.
11. Nimesha Ranasinghe, Adrian David Cheok, and Ryohei Nakatsu. 2012. Taste/IP: the sensation of taste for digital communication. In *Proceedings of the 14th ACM international conference on Multimodal interaction*. ACM, 409–416.
12. Nimesha Ranasinghe, Kuan-Yi Lee, and Ellen Yi-Luen Do. 2014. FunRasa: an interactive drinking platform. In *Proceedings of the 8th International Conference on Tangible, Embedded and Embodied Interaction*. ACM, 133–136.
13. Nimesha Ranasinghe, Kuan-Yi Lee, Gajan Suthokumar, and Ellen Yi-Luen Do. 2016. Virtual ingredients for food and beverages to create immersive taste experiences. *Multimedia Tools and Applications* 74, 24 (2016), 1–19.
14. Nimesha Ranasinghe, Ryohei Nakatsu, Hideaki Nii, and Ponnampalam Gopalakrishnakone. 2012. Tongue Mounted Interface for Digitally Actuating the Sense of Taste. In *Wearable Computers (ISWC), 2012 16th International Symposium on*. IEEE, 80–87.
15. Charles Spence, Carmel A Levitan, Maya U Shankar, and Massimiliano Zampini. 2010. Does food color influence taste and flavor perception in humans? *Chemosensory Perception* 3, 1 (2010), 68–84.
16. Charles Spence, Xiaoang Wan, Andy Woods, Carlos Velasco, Jialin Deng, Jozef Youssef, and Ophelia Deroy. 2015. On tasty colours and colourful tastes? Assessing, explaining, and utilizing crossmodal correspondences between colours and basic tastes. *Flavour* 4, 1 (2015), 1.
17. Jennifer A Stillman. 1993. Color Influences Flavor Identification in Fruit-flavored Beverages. *Journal of Food Science* 58, 4 (1993), 810–812.
18. Chie Suzuki, Takuji Narumi, Tomohiro Tanikawa, and Michitaka Hirose. 2014. Affecting tumbler: affecting our flavor perception with thermal feedback. In *Proceedings of the 11th Conference on Advances in Computer Entertainment Technology*. ACM, 19.
19. Kiyoshi Toko. 2000a. *Biomimetic sensor technology*. Cambridge University Press.
20. Kiyoshi Toko. 2000b. Taste sensor. *Sensors and Actuators B: Chemical* 64, 1 (2000), 205–215.
21. Xiaoang Wan, Andy T Woods, Jasper JF van den Bosch, Kirsten J McKenzie, Carlos Velasco, and Charles Spence. 2014. Cross-cultural differences in crossmodal correspondences between basic tastes and visual features. *Frontiers in psychology* 5 (2014), 1365.
22. Massimiliano Zampini, Emma Wantling, Nicola Phillips, and Charles Spence. 2008. Multisensory flavor perception: Assessing the influence of fruit acids and color cues on the perception of fruit-flavored beverages. *Food quality and preference* 19, 3 (2008), 335–343.

LaserViz: Shared Gaze in the Co-Located Physical World

Vincent van Rheden[1,2], Bernhard Maurer[1], Dorothé Smit[1], Martin Murer[1], Manfred Tscheligi[1,3]
[1] Center for Human-Computer Interaction, University of Salzburg, Salzburg, Austria
[2]Department of Industrial Design, Eindhoven University of Technology, Eindhoven, the Netherlands
[3]AIT Austrian Institute of Technology, Vienna, Austria
[vincent.vanrheden, bernhard.maurer, dorothe.smit, martin.murer, manfred.tscheligi]@sbg.ac.at

ABSTRACT
Gaze is an important aspect in social communication. In this paper, we present a first exploration of visualizing gaze in the co-located physical world. LaserViz augments gaze in the physical world by means of an eye-tracking enabled wearable device that laser beams the gaze position to real world objects. Based on an initial prototype, we explored the effects of shared gaze through a collaborative, as well as a competitive, scenario in a co-located setting. This paper discusses the insights and implications following these explorations for the concept of shared gaze in the co-located physical world.

Author Keywords
Gaze Visualization; Collaboration; Gaze Interaction; Shared Gaze

ACM Classification Keywords
H.5.m. Information Interfaces and Presentation (e.g. HCI): Miscellaneous

INTRODUCTION
Gaze is, amongst others, a crucial factor in interpersonal communication [16, 19]. Seeing where another person is looking communicates task relevant spatial information easily [2, 13, 15] and can deliver information about a person's relation to the environment [6]. We frequently use our gaze for, e.g., addressing a person in conversation, spatial referencing, and pointing, which makes it important for establishing shared attention and intention over an object or area of interest in a shared environment. When two people speak about an object of joint attention, this object is the third component that shapes the "triadic" relation [27]. When establishing the consensus of what is actually the shared interest, the listening person can aim to determine the location of the object by reading the face and eye direction of the speaker and mapping this spatially to make an educated guess about the location of the object.

TEI '17, March 20 - 23, 2017, Yokohama, Japan

ACM 978-1-4503-4676-4/17/03...$15.00
DOI: http://dx.doi.org/10.1145/3024969.3025010

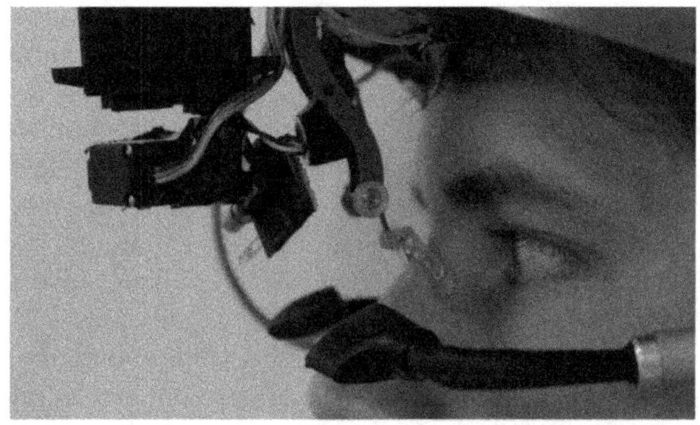

Figure 1: LaserViz Prototype © Center for HCI, Salzburg

Required parameters are missing or incorrect. While hand movements are often explicitly used to point to objects, head motion and gaze yield implicit cues to objects that are in a person's focus of attention as the person turns and looks toward the object of interest [3]. In HCI, the visualization of gaze is a commonly utilized approach for, e.g., remote communication, using gaze as an explicit way of pointing and directly visualizing the exact point of interest.

We argue that making gaze explicit in the physical world could carry similar advantages by transferring gaze direction and visualizing it at the corresponding location of visual attention. We, thus, transfer the bodily, social quality of gaze from the user's body to the physical world. We argue that this could benefit shared attention on a non-verbal layer and making the visualized gaze a shared embodied resource for collaboration.

In this paper, we present a first implementation of a prototype that explores the implications of shared gaze in the physical world. In this first exploration, we limit our interest to exploring the implications of augmenting gaze in the co-located physical world as an extension of our normal co-located communication modalities (e.g., verbal communication). Additionally, we will explore the effect of continuously visualizing gaze, to assess the impact of an augmented gaze visualization that is "always on".

In this paper, we describe work related to shared gaze and wearable computers, after which we present our concept, LaserViz (Figure 1) and the technological implementation of our prototype. We then introduce two explorative scenarios leading to reflections, in which we discuss insights and implications for shared gaze in the co-located physical world. Finally, we present our next steps in future work.

RELATED WORK

In this section, we introduce two areas closely related to our concept: *shared gaze* and *wearable computers,* as the previous work in these areas has led to the prototype used in the explorations presented in this paper.

Shared Gaze

Shared gaze is a natural and efficient method of communication that can significantly improve cooperative performance [26]. Usually it refers to the concept of capturing the gaze of a person and visualizing it on a shared interaction space. In tasks requiring rapid communication of spatial information, gaze may even be more efficient than speech [6]. Shared gaze is used in a wide range of application domains, both in remote situations such as enhancing mediated interaction [4] and collaborative search [5], and collocated situations such as gameplay [23] and providing tourist information [25]. In this work, the point where a person looks is visualized on the screen of (another) person through a cursor (e.g., a circle).

Recently, interest has emerged for using gaze visualization to direct to off-screen applications, e.g., in the automotive context [28, 29, 12, 22] and in a city environment [24]. Still, these implementations have been onscreen, e.g., a driving simulator. Akkil et al.[1] introduced GazeTorch, a tool for remote collaboration in which the gaze of the remote collaborator is projected on top of the physical space of the worker.

Until now, there have been no implementations of shared gaze that focus on co-located communication with the visualization of gaze off-screen, in the physical world.

Wearable Computers

In an early definition, Mann stated that a wearable computer is always 'on', part of the user, and under the user's complete control [20]. Research in the field of wearable computers has largely focused on how wearable systems can enhance a single user's interaction with the world around them (see [25, 10]). Research has been conducted on collaboration, focusing on sharing information through various modality channels in various ways [7,20,21,9,14,17,21,18] including pointing [11]. Fussel et al. found that displaying a remote pointer significantly improved communication and shared awareness [11].

While remote collaboration has been an important area in work related to wearable computers, both shared gaze and co-located collaboration have not yet been covered in this field. Our contribution lies in a first exploration of co-located shared gaze and presenting initial implications

CONCEPT

We propose LaserViz, a wearable system capable of sharing one's gaze location with others in the co-located physical world. Figure 2 illustrates this concept, in which person A (Figure 2, A) wears the LaserViz prototype to capture his gaze direction and projects it on the actual

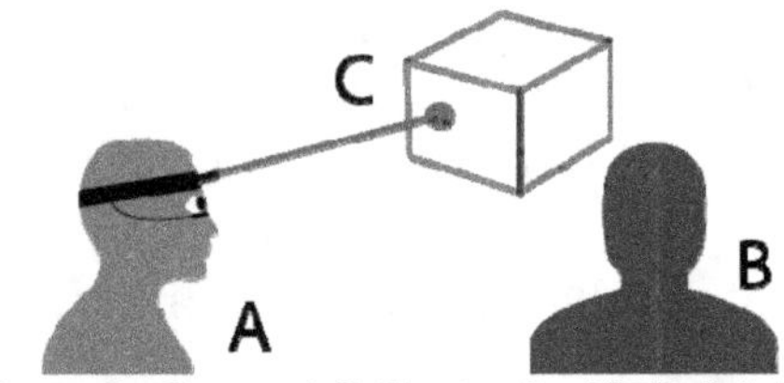

Figure 2: Concept © Center for HCI, Salzburg

Figure 3: Technical Setup © Center for HCI, Salzburg

object of interest (the box, Figure 2, C), visualizing the actual point he is looking at (Figure 2, C). This visualization, or the augmented gaze cursor (the red dot, Figure 2, C), makes the point of interest explicit for a second person (Figure 2, B). With LaserViz, we create a new non-verbal communication layer that usually wouldn't be possible in physical settings, i.e., seeing exactly where another person is looking at.

Technical Setup

To explore the effects of our concept, we constructed a prototype. It consisted of a head-mounted eye-tracker (http://www.ergoneers.com) (Figure 3, A) capable of precisely tracking the gaze direction of both eyes, a laser pointer (Figure 3, B) on a pan/tilt mechanism constructed of two servos (Figure 3, C and D); and a portable computer. The chosen laser pointer was low power and not able to do any (permanent) damage to one's eyes when accidentally looking into the beam. The pan/tilt mechanism was mounted on the frame of the eye-tracker in such a way that the laser-pointer was as much in line with the eyes as possible but did not occlude the wearer's sight. The X and Y values of the pupils, read from the eye-tracker, were captured via a TCP-based Processing (https://processing.org) sketch and fed into an Arduino (https://www.arduino.cc) sketch to map the X and Y values to the corresponding servomotors.

EXPLORATIVE SCENARIOS

With this prototype, we explored two different scenarios and reflected on the experiences we had while using the prototype. Our main goal was to explore how shared gaze impacts co-located scenarios, the inherent social dynamics, and potential collaboration strategies that would emerge. Therefore, we explored two scenarios in which shared gaze was an additional interaction modality to our normal communication. Both scenarios were chosen to reflect

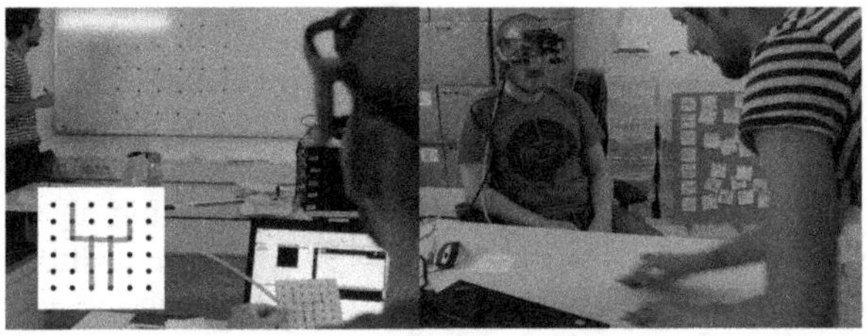

Figure 4: Left: Collaborative Scenario with shape-drawer standing in front of the white board. Right: Competitive Scenario with players facing each other. ©Center for HCI, Salzburg

everyday activities, i.e., 1) a collaborative work-like situation and 2) a competitive leisure activity. Each scenario consisted of two roles, taken by two researchers, and an object in a collocated physical space, which was the subject of communication. In the first scenario (i.e., collaborative), one researcher was dependent on the information of the other researcher who was wearing the prototype. In the second scenario (i.e., competitive), the wearer of the prototype needed to balance intentional and unintentional gazing. As the calibration of the prototype was a very tedious process, only one researcher was wearing the prototype throughout the whole exploration. The duration of the overall exploration was limited to two repetitions for the collaborative and four repetitions for the competitive scenario (25 minutes in total).

Collaborative Scenario

In this scenario, one researcher took the role of the *shape-drawer* and the other researcher the role of the *information-giver* (Figure 2). The task of the shape-drawer was to draw a shape on a whiteboard with a 6x6 grid, following the instructions of the information-giver. The information-giver, wearing the prototype, has the to-be-drawn shape on a sheet of paper. The task was to put the shape on the whiteboard as fast as possible without making a mistake. We explored how the prototype would affect our communication and did not restrict ourselves in terms of other (non)verbal communication. However, the whiteboard was positioned in a way that the shape-drawer could not have face-to-face contact with the information-giver when looking at the whiteboard to draw the shape.

Reflections

We noticed that the communication became easier and faster over time and we needed less words and eye contact to establish a shared understanding. However, we did note that it was sometimes difficult to distinguish between the moments where the information-giver was looking at the whiteboard (intended gaze movement) and the moments where the information-giver was looking at the paper with the original drawing (unintended gaze movement). When reflecting on the exploration, the researcher that drew the shapes indicated that these moments triggered him to seek eye contact with the information-giver to confirm his intention. The information-giver reflected that he became more aware of his gaze direction and, therefore, tried to make his gaze as meaningful as possible by pointing at task-relevant locations instead of, e.g., randomly looking around while thinking or looking for a long time at the sheet of paper that visualized the intended shape.

Competitive Scenario

In the competitive scenario, we played a form of the well-known 'cup game', a game that is played by two people: the *mixer* and the *guesser*. The mixer places a ball underneath one of three upside down cups and then quickly shuffles them on a table so the guesser has a hard time remembering/deciding which cup contains the hidden ball. In our scenario, we simulated this using three cards: two identical cards and one 'special' card. The task of the mixer was to prevent the guesser from picking the correct card by mixing the cards as best as he could. The task of the guesser was to follow the special card and, in the end, pick the special card, for which he could utilize the GazeVis. Four rounds of the game were played, during which the prototype-wearing researcher performed each role twice.

Reflections

While reflecting on the experiences of the competitive scenario, the researcher not wearing the prototype indicated that the laser point was easier to find and follow in comparison to the collaborative scenario. This could have been the result of the increased brightness of the point due to the shorter range in this scenario, or the fact that the two researchers were facing each other and, therefore, the location of the laser point could be read from the wearer's face direction.

In both roles, the researcher wearing the prototype initially experienced a disadvantage, as the information about his gaze was used by the other participant to win the game. This happened either by inferring the location of the 'special' card based on the wearer's gaze, or by mixing the cards until the wearer of the prototype lost track of it himself. However, during the second round, the wearer tricked the guesser by consciously looking at a card that was *not* the 'special' card, resulting in a wrong answer by the guesser. Afterwards, the researcher wearing the prototype reflected that he deliberately used gaze to indicate the wrong card when mixing or guessing, but that it was very challenging to maintain the visual attention to a point outside of the intended focus.

DISCUSSION

In this section, we discuss limitations and reflections of the presented scenarios, followed by the insights and implications resulting from our exploration.

First, our prototype had its limitations. Once calibrated, it was fairly accurate at a fixed distance to the object of interest it was calibrated for (leaving aside the offset that resulted from the fact that the laser pointer was not perfectly in line with the eyesight). Switching towards a setting with an object at a different distance increased inaccuracy substantially.

Though the tasks of the presented scenarios were simple, they already resulted in rich initial reflections. More complex (spatial) scenarios with, e.g., limited eye contact or verbal communication could result in even more rich insights. The study would have benefited from a bigger amount of people experiencing the prototype and from a longer duration of the scenarios to potentially trigger more complex gaze-behavior-strategies to develop. Therefore, insights of our exploration are mainly a first direction for future research.

Despite the aforementioned limitations of the exploration, the advantages of gaze (visualization) are evident in a social or collaborative atmosphere. In triadic settings where collaborators don't share the same point of view or cannot look at each other's face due to, e.g., physical constraints, our approach can be a means to regain a certain sense of a shared view and understanding.

Accuracy and visibility

At some point in the collaborative scenario, the shape-drawer could rely on the visualization of the gaze alone, rather than creating verbal or face-to-face understanding, increasing the efficiency and effectiveness of the collaboration. However, if the pointer does not immediately become apparent to the collaborating person, or if the visualization is inaccurate, the aforementioned advantages of gaze visualization dissipate.

Social Cues

Implementing shared gaze in co-located settings bear consequences for the social conventions of face-to-face contact. Seeing where the other person looks amplifies the focus on the object of interest. This would result in a decrease of attention on the other person's non-verbal social cues (facial expressions, gestures, posture, etc.) that can indicate, e.g., emotion, confirmation, or attention.

Intended and Unintended Gaze

Our explorations showed that when wearing the gaze visualization prototype, the awareness of your own gaze increases. This resulted in more explicit behavior of the wearer of the prototype, i.e., avoiding meaningless gaze or intentionally adjusting the focus point of the gaze. The wearer of the prototype reported a notion of unintentionally sharing important information, even when this was unwanted. This issue of intentional and unintentional conveying of information was amplified by the gaze visualization being "always-on".

Asymmetry

In the explorations described in this paper, the relation between the two participants was asymmetrical, i.e., one person was wearing the gaze visualization prototype, while the other person was observing the visualized gaze. The attention dilemma and unintended sharing of information was, therefore, one-sided. In the competitive scenario, this resulted in an obvious strategic disadvantage for the wearer of the prototype.

Attention Dilemma

Another insight we gained is that of an emerging *attention dilemma.* While wearing the prototype, your gaze is continually externalized in the physical world (i.e., the system is "always on"). When the wearer is using his gaze as a means of communication, this results in an inhibition of one of the natural uses of gaze, i.e., perceiving the world. In practice, this results in difficulties, for example, when needing to look at a drawing you are trying to convey via gaze. This notion of this attention dilemma was an interesting finding as it could be utilized for e.g., gameplay purposes.

CONCLUSION & FUTURE WORK

In this paper, we explored LaserViz, a concept of shared gaze augmented in the physical world in co-located situations. We devised a prototype and conducted a first exploration through two everyday scenarios: a collaborative and competitive scenario. Based on the experiences with the prototype, we abstracted implications for the concept itself and the future development of the concept.

We argue that the concept adds value in collaborative and social situations, as we could clearly deduce meaning from the gaze visualization. Gaze visualization may increase efficiency in spatially related tasks by adding a non-verbal communication layer, speeding up the process of creating shared understanding in conjunction with verbal communication and specifically in situations in which verbal communication is not possible.

Apart from the previously mentioned advantages of the concept, the shift of focus on the location of the gaze brings two issues: a decreased focus on face-to-face social cues and the emerging *attention dilemma* as a result the system being "always on". Another interesting side effect from the system being "always on" is the observed interplay between intended and unintended gaze; the wearer of the prototype makes his behavior more explicit to avoid confusion (or to conceal the direction of his attention).

This first iteration of the presented concept offers new opportunities for design to utilize the positive aspects of the new layer of communication that visualized gaze offers. We aim to continue exploring and evaluating future scenarios in which, e.g., verbal communication is limited. We intend to improve the prototype (in terms of accuracy, visibility, and portability) to make it suitable for longer studies with more participants and validate our current preliminary results.

The prototype in this exploration utilized a laser-pointer as visualization tool for gaze. In a future iteration, we aim to explore a visualization tool that is flexible in terms of visualization and can dynamically change (graphical) appearance (i.e., shape, size or color). This could allow the wearer to control the cursor deliberately or undeliberately by, e.g., translating facial expression to communicate emotion through the gaze visualization. Finally, in this paper, we discussed an asymmetrical setup in which only one person's gaze was visualized. A future step is to explore situations in which multiple people wear a gaze visualizer at the same time.

REFERENCES

1. Deepak Akkil, Jobin Mathew James, Poika Isokoski, and Jari Kangas. 2016. GazeTorch: Enabling Gaze Awareness in Collaborative Physical Tasks. In *Proceedings of the 2016 CHI Conference Extended Abstracts on Human Factors in Computing Systems* (CHI EA '16). ACM, New York, NY, USA, 1151-1158. http://dx.doi.org/10.1145/2851581.2892459
2. Michael Argyle and Mark Cook. 1976. Gaze and mutual gaze. Cambridge University Press.
3. Gérard Bailly, Stephan Raidt, Frédéric Elisei. 2010. Gaze, conversational agents and face-to-face communication. *Speech Commun.* 52, 598–612.
4. Gary Bente, Felix Eschenburg, and Nicole C. Krämer. 2007. Virtual gaze. a pilot study on the effects of computer simulated gaze in avatar-based conversations. In *Proceedings of the 2nd international conference on Virtual reality* (ICVR'07), Randall Shumaker (Ed.). Springer-Verlag, Berlin, Heidelberg, 185-194.
5. Susan E. Brennan, Xin Chen, Christopher A. Dickinson, Mark B. Neider, Gregory J. Zelinsky, Coordinating cognition: The costs and benefits of shared gaze during collaborative search, Cognition, Volume 106, Issue 3, March 2008, Pages 1465-1477, ISSN 0010-0277, http://dx.doi.org/10.1016/j.cognition.2007.05.012.
6. Jean-David Boucher, Ugo Pattacini, Amelie Lelong, Gerard Bailly, Frederic Elisei, Sascha Fagel, Peter F Dominey, Jocelyne Ventre-Dominey. 2012. I Reach Faster When I See You Look: Gaze Effects in Human-Human and Human-Robot Face-to-Face Cooperation Frontiers in Neurorobotics, 6, 3.
7. British Telecom. (1993). CamNet Promotional Video.
8. DesFaccount. 2016. Gaze Video 1. (26 July 2015). Retrieved August 9, 2015 from https://vimeo.com/176442499
9. Mikael Drugge, Marcus Nilsson, Roland Parviainen, and Peter Parnes. 2004. Experiences of using wearable computers for ambient telepresence and remote interaction. In *Proceedings of the 2004 ACM SIGMM workshop on Effective telepresence* (ETP '04). ACM. 2-11. http://dx.doi.org/10.1145/1026776.1026780
10. Steven Feiner, Blair MacIntyre, Tobias Höllerer, and Anthony Webster. 1997. A touring machine: Prototyping 3D mobile augmented reality systems for exploring the urban environment. *Personal Technologies*, 1(4), 208–217.
11. Susan R. Fussell, Leslie D. Setlock, Jie Yang, Jiazhi Ou, Elizabeth Mauer, and Adam Kramer. 2004. Gestures over video streams to support remote collaboration on physical tasks. *Human–Computer Interaction*, 19(3), 273–309. http://dx.doi.org/10.1207/s15327051hci1903_3
12. Magdalena Gärtner, Alexander Meschtscherjakov, Bernhard Maurer, David Wilfinger, and Manfred Tscheligi. 2014. "Dad, Stop Crashing My Car!": Making Use of Probing to Inspire the Design of Future In-Car Interfaces. In *Proceedings of the 6th International Conference on Automotive User Interfaces and Interactive Vehicular Applications* (AutomotiveUI '14). ACM, New York, NY, USA, , Article 27 , 8 pages. http://dx.doi.org/10.1145/2667317.2667348
13. Charles Goodwin. 1981. Conversational organization: Interaction between speakers and hearers. Academic Press.
14. Bjørn Hestnes, Svein Heiestad, Peter Brooks, and Lasse Drageset. 2001. Real situations of wearable computers used for video conferencing and for terminal and network design. In *Wearable Computers. Proceedings. Fifth International Symposium on.* 85-93.
15. Adam Kendon. 1967. Some functions of gaze direction in social interaction. Acta Psychologica, 26, 22–63.
16. Chris L. Kleinke. 1986. Gaze and eye contact: a research review. Psychological bulletin 100, 1, 78.
17. Gerd Kortuem, Martin Bauer, and Zary Segall. 1999. NETMAN: The design of a collaborative wearable computer system. *Mobile Networks and Applications*, 4(1), 49–58.
18. Robert E. Kraut, Mark D. Miller, and Jane Siegel. 1996. Collaboration in performance of physical tasks: effects on outcomes and communication. In *Proceedings of the 1996 ACM conference on Computer supported cooperative work* (CSCW '96), Mark S. Ackerman (Ed.). ACM, 57-66. http://dx.doi.org/10.1145/240080.240190
19. Kristine Lund. 2007. The importance of gaze and gesture in interactive multimodal explanation. Language Resources and Evaluation 41, 3-4, 289–303.
20. Steve Mann. 1997. Wearable computing: A first step toward personal imaging. *Computer*, 30(2), 25–32.
21. Steve Mann. 2000. Telepointer: Hands-free completely self-contained wearable visual aug- mented reality without headwear and without any infrastructural reliance. In *The Fourth International Symposium on Wearable Computers.* 177-178.
22. Bernhard Maurer, Sandra Trösterer, Magdalena Gärtner, Martin Wuchse, Axel Baumgartner, Alexander Meschtscherjakov, David Wilfinger, and Manfred Tscheligi. 2014. Shared Gaze in the Car:

Towards a Better Driver-Passenger Collaboration. In *Adjunct Proceedings of the 6th International Conference on Automotive User Interfaces and Interactive Vehicular Applications* (AutomotiveUI '14). ACM. 1-6. http://dx.doi.org/10.1145/2667239.2667274

23. Bernhard Maurer, Ilhan Aslan, Martin Wuchse, Katja Neureiter, and Manfred Tscheligi. 2015. Gaze-Based Onlooker Integration: Exploring the In-Between of Active Player and Passive Spectator in Co-Located Gaming. In *Proceedings of the 2015 Annual Symposium on Computer-Human Interaction in Play* (CHI PLAY '15). ACM, New York, NY, USA, 163-173. http://dx.doi.org/10.1145/2793107.2793126
24. Mark B. Neider, Xin Chen, Christopher A. Dickinson, Susan E. Brennan, and Gregory J. Zelinsky. 2010. Coordinating spatial referencing using shared gaze. *Psychonomic Bulletin & Review.* 17, 5, 718-724.
25. Ken Pfeuffer, Yanxia Zhang, and Hans Gellersen. 2015. A collaborative gaze aware information display. In Adjunct Proceedings of the 2015 ACM International Joint Conference on Pervasive and Ubiquitous Computing and Proceedings of the 2015 ACM International Symposium on Wearable Computers (UbiComp/ISWC'15 Adjunct). ACM, New York, NY, USA, 389-391. http://dx.doi.org/10.1145/2800835.2800922
26. Bradley J. Rhodes. 1997. The wearable remembrance agent: A system for augmented memory. *Personal Technologies*, 1(4), 218–224.
27. Michael Tomasello, Malinda Carpenter, Josep Call, Tanya Behne and Henrike Moll. 2005. Understanding and sharing intentions: The origins of cultural cognition. Behavioral and Brain Sciences, 28, pp 675-691 doi:10.1017/S0140525X05000129
28. Sandra Trösterer, Martin Wuchse, Christine Döttlinger, Alexander Meschtscherjakov, and Manfred Tscheligi. 2015. Light my way: visualizing shared gaze in the car. In *Proceedings of the 7th International Conference on Automotive User Interfaces and Interactive Vehicular Applications* (AutomotiveUI '15). ACM, New York, NY, USA, 196-203. http://dx.doi.org/10.1145/2799250.2799258
29. Sandra Trösterer, Magdalena Gärtner, Martin Wuchse, Bernhard Maurer, Alexander Meschtscherjakov, and Manfred Tscheligi. 2015. Four Eyes See More Than Two: Shared Gaze in the Car. In *Proceedings of International Conference on Human-Computer Interaction* (INTERACT 2015).

Bio-Sensed and Embodied Participation in Interactive Performance

Asreen Rostami[1], Donald McMillan[1], Elena Márquez Segura[2], Chiara Rossito[1], Louise Barkhuus[3]

[1]Stockholm University
Sweden
{asreen, donald.mcmillan, chiara}@dsv.su.se

[2]Uppsala University &
University of California, Santa Cruz, USA
elena.marquez@ucsc.edu

[3]ITU
Denmark
barkhuus@itu.dk

ABSTRACT

Designing for interactive performances is challenging both in terms of technology design, and of understanding the interplay between technology, narration, and audience interactions. Bio-sensors and bodily tracking technologies afford new ways for artists to engage with audiences, and for audiences to become part of the artwork. Their deployment raises a number of issues for designers of interactive performances. This paper explores such issues by presenting five design ideas for interactive performance afforded by bio-sensing and bodily tracking technologies (i.e. Microsoft Kinect) developed during two design workshops. We use these ideas, and the related scenarios to discuss three emerging issues namely: *temporality of input, autonomy and control*, and *visibility of input* in relation to the deployment of bio-sensors and bodily tracking technologies in the context of interactive performances.

Author Keywords

Interactive performances; Bio-Sensing; Audience Engagement; Bodily tracking; Biodata.

ACM Classification Keywords

H.5.m. Information interfaces and presentation (e.g., HCI): Miscellaneous;

INTRODUCTION

The number of readily available body sensor technologies opens up a wealth of new possibilities for interactive performances in terms of audience interaction and interactive storytelling. While bio-sensing has made it into commercial products for areas like health and medical monitoring [22,55,64], entertainment areas are still exploring more readily available scenarios for the use of sensors in performances. Experiments with implementing different types of sensors and embodied interaction in performances are not new [6], and many theaters and play houses have great success in long-running interactive performances both with and without technology, such as *Sleep No More* (www.sleepnomore.com), *La Mama* (www.lamama.org) and *RATS Theater* (ratsteater.se). As this type of artistic productions are setting out to deploy bio-sensors technologies, a variety of scenarios can be explored to envision different design possibilities exploiting, for instance, audience members' physiological states through heart rate, qualities of breathing [8], or abstractions of emotional states using galvanic skin response (GSR) [26].

By taking advantage of these technologies, participation in interactive performances can evolve from consciously deciding to send a message [12], or moving to a certain location [46], to harnessing the feedback loop of bio-processes. With this move comes a change in the agency of the audience participator. Some bio-mechanical features are easier to control than others, and some are more influenced by the current lived experience of the person being sensed. As the role of the artists can be moved more and more behind the curtain to direct audience peer-production of the content of a piece, the lines between performer, audience member, and director become blurred, and the process of designing and developing experiences changes.

In this paper we use the term "interactive performance" in its broadest sense, encompassing theatre, street performances, dance, and interactive video performances. Interactive simply denotes elements of audience interaction either with (i.e. [39]) or without digital technology. Interacting with a performance through technology can range from sending text [12], physical navigation, physical contact [65], to controlling our breathing [9].

To explore the role of sensor-based interaction modalities in the context of interactive performances, we carried out two design workshops. Participants included choreographers and dancers, interaction designers, engineers, HCI researchers, theatre directors, and actors. The variety of the participants' backgrounds was purposely selected to reflect the diversity of expertise and professional roles required in the design and implementation of interactive performances. The two workshops used techniques of brainstorming [40] and bodystorming [32,50] to enable the participants to discuss the embodied aspects inherent in their artistic expression and creation.

TEI '17, March 20 - 23, 2017, Yokohama, Japan

ACM 978-1-4503-4676-4/17/03...$15.00
DOI: http://dx.doi.org/10.1145/3024969.3024998

This paper presents five scenarios illustrating five design ideas of interactive performances based on bio-sensing and bodily tracking technologies. We first provide examples of the role such technologies could play in the context of various performance. We then expand our discussion by addressing three main issues emerging from the suggested designs, namely: i) *Temporality of input* – the extent of the feedback loop between audience action and its influence on the performance, ii) *Autonomy and Control* – that is the degree to which audience members, performers and directors can act upon the performance; iii) *Visibility of Input* – that is the degree to which the use of such sensors can make audience's actions socially visible.

These issues reflect paramount conceptual and interactional aspects inherent in the design and production of interactive performances that creative teams – often characterized by heterogeneous backgrounds and professional skills (ranging from artistic directors to technology experts) – might have to tackle when introducing sensor-based and bodily tracking technologies.

BACKGROUND

Several artists, designers and researchers within HCI have focused on creating interactive performances, both for the value of the performance themselves, but also for studying them for better understanding audience impact [6,28], technology infrastructure [8], and theoretical aspects of interactive theatre [19]. More recently the focus on participation-through-technology in interactive performances has been seen as a way to understand other people and engage in a dialogue with them [12, 34]. In the following sections, we introduce previous research on participatory and interactive performances, embodied interaction, as well as investigation of bodily tracking and bio-sensing technologies envisaged to facilitate interactivity. These different areas of research constitute the background of our work.

Participatory Performances

Much of the current participatory live-artwork is body-focused, both in terms of both interaction modalities (e.g. using bio-sensors as input), and of purposes of the art piece (e.g. bodily aesthetic experiences). An example is Loke's installation, *Surging Verticality* [30]. Here, mediation of a 'human aide' and soundscape was used to guide and augment the experience of "feeling gravity through the skeleton", for the participant. Other works from this project, *Thinking Through the Body* [66], included *Drawing Breath*, visualising the breathing of the audience, and *Cardiomorphologies*, which used their heart rate. Mentis and Johansson's interactive-improvisational dance performance explored the use of movement as input: A Kinect sensor capturing movement qualities of the audience modified the music, which in turn influenced the dancers on stage [36]. Alaoui et al. [3] and Grønbæk et al. [21] used movement qualities as a modality for interaction to promote a more explorative and expressive experience of artwork.

Embodiment and Interactive Technologies

Embodied interaction can be seen as one's cyclical, iterative process of action and reaction with one's physical and social worlds. It influences and is influenced by emotion, space, context, and time. Since the introduction of the concept of embodied interaction [18], we have witnessed a wealth of movement-based technologies [24,52] and practices of designing technology from an embodied perspective [18,37,53]. In the field of performance, and especially interactive performance, we note that the deep and intertwined connection between experience and body – how certain physical states and actions can cause, and are caused by, certain emotional states [62] – can be an important tool in the design of curated performances. Benford et al. for example, in *Breathless* have looked at how negative physical and emotional experiences can be used as building blocks for interaction by "embedding the breath sensors into a gas mask which is used to drive a large powered swing" [9]; in the arts, examples of causing negative emotions are more common [1]. Schiphorst in her *exhale: (breath between bodies)* [49] has combined body movements and wearable technology to design a participatory performance. Feedback from these inputs that are influencing performance is rarely observable as a one-to-one reaction from the performers to the action. Cafaro et al. [11] show that interactive schema that support a 1:1 correspondence between movement and concept (such as those presented in [3,4]) are easy to understand; however, as the complexity of the correspondence increases, the development of the vocabulary of embodied interaction becomes more nuanced, more difficult to understand, and more difficult to design. To ameliorate this scholars have drawn on other disciplines, for example Loke and Robbertson [31] present a method that extends traditional perspectives in HCI of designing from the perspective of the observer and the technology, to a first person perspective. Larssen et al. [27] move past functionality or appearance and explore design with a focus on the tactile dimension and our kinaesthetic sense.

Bodily Tracking

Bodily tracking has been used in a number of fields and is much more prevalent since the introduction of the Microsoft Kinect in 2010, which provided high quality tracking at a low price. From full body gait analysis to measure strides and intervals for health purposes [20] to designing a dance performance [13,36] or creating real time feedback to improve user's posture or movement habits [61]. In a study more related to everyday life activities, Panger [43] focuses on bodily interaction in the kitchen where different body parts and body gestures can send different commands in order to navigate through the recipe, set the cooking time, and finally play music.

In relation to the performance art and particularly dance we can find several tools and applications [35,45] that can be used for choreographic creation [15] or teaching ballet lessons by combining movement sequences which were performed by ballet teachers and captured with a 3D motion capture system [58].

Bio-Sensing as Input

Sensors that detect the physical state of the body have been around for a long time, but only recently have they been small enough and non-invasive enough to be designed for wearable technologies such as a sensor bracelet [42] that can capture the skin and ambient temperature to diagnose certain medical problems. Recent work by Howell et al. [23] use skin conductance sensor in a form of a dynamic thermochromic t-shirt to detect and display the sudden arousal of the wearer in different social interaction such as embarrassment, joy, or sadness. With this approach as an attempt to engage *affect-as-interaction* [10] with design practice, the authors study the conversations that took place between the participants and used them to frame 'biosignal' displays as social cues rather than categorizing them just as bio-sensing technologies. In another domain Simbelis et al. [51] attempt to capture and share the living body with others. They present interactive work, in which a machine transforms and interprets bio data (pulse, movement, etc.) from a participant's body to a colorful painting.

Another study [25] using Galvanic Skin Response (GSR) which measures conductivity on the skin influenced by sweat, measured cognitive load and trust of their participants in a text-chat platform. In [60] authors use GSR to measure psychophysiological engagement of their participants in the audience during a live performance as a method to monitor their reaction to different scenes and plots. Unlike the mentioned studies, which tried to detect the audience-participant response, Tennent et al. [56] capture such data from actors, and transfer it to the audience in order to enhance the show and give a richer sense-making experience to the viewers.

METHODS

The work presented stems from two related workshops carried out with six months in between. The aim of the first workshop was to broadly explore the role of novel digital technologies in the context of interactive performances, including theatre and everyday public performances (i.e. commuting as a social act). The second workshop was more narrowly focused on envisioning design ideas and novel interaction modalities for an interactive movie where the main protagonist is a dancer. Both workshops provided a context to reflect on issues emerging from the participation modalities envisioned, and not merely the interactional qualities of the enabling technology. Our material for analysis was the outcome from the workshops rather than the workshop process itself.

In the sections below we detail the procedure of each workshop and how they relate to each other before describing our data collection and data analysis methods.

Workshop one: Envision

The goal of the first full-day design workshop was to brainstorm and develop design ideas for various interactive performances (from theatre to street performance). It was organized by three of the authors of this paper. A total of twenty people were asked and volunteered to participate in this workshop, thus reflecting a variety of backgrounds including three interaction designers, two computer scientists, eight HCI and media technology researchers, two theatre and movie directors, two professional actors, and three artists. The participants were chosen to represent a wide variety of backgrounds, as well as skills and professional roles that are involved in interactive performances, from designing, script writing, production and actual performance.

The workshop started with an introduction to its goals and methods. In order to gain a common ground, we provided participants with six theme cards highlighting two central aspects of interactive performances: *"art"* and *"technology"*. The theme *art* included *"participation"*, *"story-telling"* and *"temporality"*. Participation and story-telling were chosen as two main aspects of interactive performances. These first two themes relate to various modalities enabling members of the audience to contribute to the performance. The latter one encompasses the narrative strategies that can be employed to tell a story. In the context of interactive performances, technology is constitutive of story-telling [7], rather than being an additional layer to the narration. Temporality was relevant as it addresses how technology can redefine the traditional, sequential experience of interactive performance.

The *technology* category included *"kinetic interaction"* (i.e. responsive material, kinetic actuators, and proximity sensors), *"taste and scent interaction"* (i.e. edible interaction, smell-based interaction) and *"biometrics"* (galvanic skin response, hormone levels, and heart rate) as examples of technologies that could be incorporated to design novel ideas of interactive performance. Such technologies were chosen as they are available, but not widely explored in the context of interactive performances (they have however been used in other domains such as fitness [57], wellbeing [42], robotics [63], etc.).

All the themes were briefly presented to the participants with the aid of some concrete examples of each. For the theme art, concrete examples of interactive performances were

Figure 1: Stills from the movie LIV, shown to participants.

discussed, each one highlighting one of the themes introduced above. In the second case, elements of kinetic interaction, taste and scent interactions and of biometrics were introduced independently of an application area; the potential of the technology was discussed abstractly, while the participants were invited to think of concrete deployments in the context of a performance. During the second phase the participants were divided into three groups, with a distribution of backgrounds and skills in each group. Each group had one organizer as facilitator. Drawing from ideation techniques and brainstorming methods [40], we gathered some simple design tools (playdough, fabrics, pen and paper and etc.) to enable participants to create, sketch and describe their ideas in a hands-on workshop activity. This phase lasted three hours.

During the group activities, participants were asked to first choose and design their performance space, for example if it is an indoor or outdoor performance, a staged or street performance, a play or everyday activity and so on. They were then asked to develop possible interaction modalities in the context of the selected performance space and a relevant example scenario to be presented to the other groups during the final workshop activity.

Workshop two: Move:ie

Continuing a longstanding collaboration with a prominent interactive performance director, Rebecca Forsberg, this second workshop focused on design ideas for a performance entailing a short movie. This performance was targeted at children and centered around the protagonist's love for dancing. Thus, unlike the previous workshop in which participants were encouraged to think about different forms of performances, for this workshop we focused on different application scenarios for interacting with a movie.

We chose to employ a more evocative way of brainstorming that used physical artefacts, including body, playthings, textiles, and art and craft material as design resources [31,32,50]. Considering children as one of the target groups of the short movie, we provided probes and tools (toys, playdough, balloons, pieces of a local outdoor game, fabrics, etc.) that could induce creative thinking [15,20] and inspire participants. These probes can encourage and be powerful evocative elements, and suggest novel uses and functionalities in a similar way to Djajadiningrat et al.'s unusual artefacts [16].

For this workshop, we recruited eight participants including three researchers with embodied interaction background, two HCI researchers, one interaction designer, one professional choreographer and the director of the short movie. Similarly, these were chosen to represent a wide set of people engaged in different stages of interactive performances. It was organized by two of the authors, one (the first author) overlapping with the previous workshop.

The workshop began with the organizers introducing the movie and its characters, thus enabling participants to become familiar with the story, and to think of possible themes related to it (Figure 1). After introducing the concept of bodystorming [32,50], participants were divided into two groups with a distribution of backgrounds and skills in each group. Each group had one organizer as a facilitator. The participants' attention was drawn towards the characteristics of the movie (e.g. playfulness, being together, dance, collaboration and etc.), the space around them, and the probes and artefacts that had been provided. Participants were asked to elaborate on the presented ideas by role playing possible scenario(s) [41]. They were encouraged to think about variations of ideas by changing the rules, artefacts, audience participation and/or performer interaction, the participant's roles, or the method of engagement. For the final step of the workshop, we asked participants to create a video prototype of each finalised idea to present to the other group.

Data Collection

Throughout the two workshops we documented activities by direct and participatory observation. The main data that we collected was video recording, which we made use of for the final idea presentations in each workshop as well as the smaller tasks and exercises. With one organizer always present in each group, we were able to take notes as well as still pictures to document the process and to remember details when discussing the workshops later. We also collected the artifacts generated during the workshops including drawings, paper models and playdough models. Our data for analysis resulted in 5+ hours of video and 50+ still pictures, along with our notes and the artifacts.

Data analysis

Our unit of analysis was the ideas generated throughout the workshops. We used qualitative thematic analysis methods, such as categorization and comparison, to analyse these ideas. The authors conducted several round of analysis in which the presentation videos from the workshops were watched alongside the artefacts and notes taken at the time. We started with the authors collaboratively coding and categorising the ideas generated; they were then themed and categorized in terms of several characteristics: 1) if they were temporally bound or not, 2) could work as a game with rules and competition, 3) if they included play objects, 4) could count as performance or be part of a performance, 5) if they involve audience participation, or 6) if the interaction could be categorised as bodily sensing or bio-sensing. We excluded ideas that were not adhering to a broad definition of interactive performance as introduced above. It should be noted that for the purposes of this paper, we have decided to analyse the workshop material to highlight the conceptual and interactional aspects that might emerge from the actual implementation of the designs suggested, rather than the concrete technological issues inherent in them. This is relevant as the issues addressed apply to a variety of interactive performances beyond the concrete use situations instantiated in the scenarios presented.

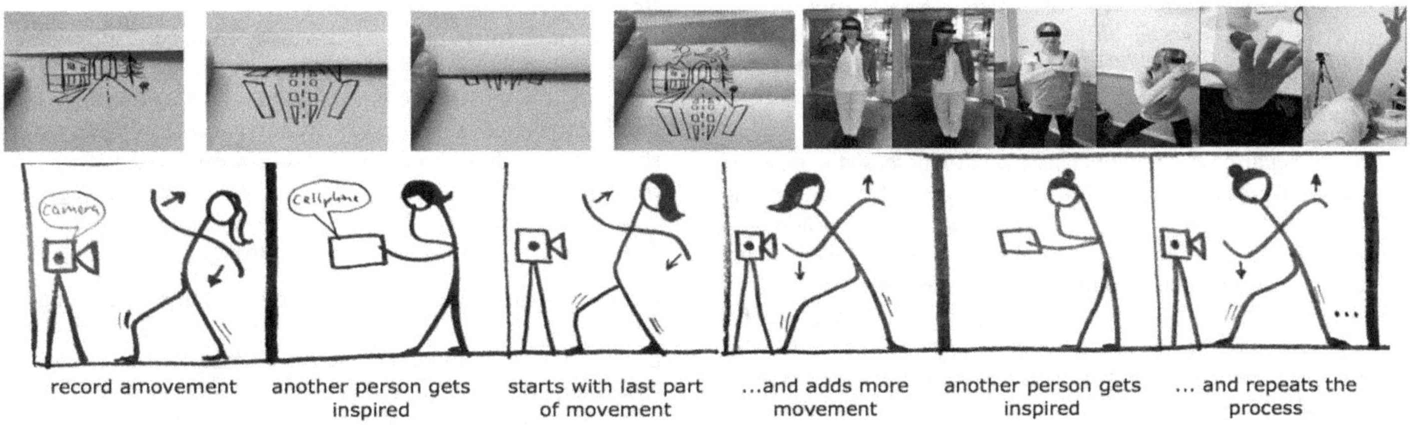

Figure 2: Movement Chain. Top Left: The inspiration, Top Right: Stills from the video produced during the workshop. Bottom: Explanation of the creation of the dance video

RESULTS

We begin with the description of five design ideas and the related scenarios produced during the group activities at the workshops. Five scenarios were selected from the 17 presented by participants at both workshops, as exemplars of the range of use of, and interaction with, bio-sensors and bodily tracking envisaged by our participants. These scenarios constitute the base to discuss relevant issues emerging from the influences of bodily sensing and bio-sensing.

Scenario 1: Data Director

In this idea, designed in the first workshop, the navigation through the plot of a movie, or a stage show would be directed, at least partly, by the biometric data sensed from the audience. With certain biological states shown as indicators of psychological ones [29], these could be used as triggers to automatically adjust a performance, or information that a director could take advantage of:

> *"For example, you have got some sort of argument and you could keep the argument script going and going until you see the heart rate of the audience reached the certain point and then you could break a glass and go to the next scene" Participant3, Workshop1*

Possible implementations could employ the detection of heart rate as in indicator of excitement, or the detection of GSR as an indication of the stress levels of the audience. One scenario that was discussed in the group who came with this idea was the horror trope of walking along a dark path with menacing music, just waiting for the antagonist to appear. Using bio-feedback, this tension building scene could be extended until the desired level of excitement was reached by a percentage of the audience, and only then would the footage of the antagonist's appearance be shown.

This system was not envisaged to necessarily be fully automatic, but could allow for a human director to interpret the incoming data from the audience and either trigger scenes or give direction to the actors on stage. The feedback loop between the performance and the audience's emotional and physiological states is, in this example, happening in real time. As the director watches the audience calm down during an interlude scene, he can judge the most impactful time to re-engage with the plot, then watch the change this has in the audience to time the next transition. However, the use of previously collected or repurposed data was also considered. For example, by tracking locations as well as physiological data the director could make assumptions on the community connections and preferences of audience members by locating the tell-tale signals of favourable and unfavourable emotional responses. It was supposed that this could then be used to, for example, play on the fears and assumptions of a suburban audience for whom the less than desirable area of the theatre causes a stressful response.

Scenario 2: Movement Chain

This idea, designed by a group from workshop 2, is inspired by the popular parlour games of additive writing or drawing with limited knowledge of the previous players' additions, and where the full composition is only revealed at the end.

In this scenario, it is the physical position of the previous player that one must connect with at the start of a turn instead of the final line of the previous player's story or the bottom edge of their drawing. One player records a movement and the next must start their movement from the final position of the player before them in the chain, adding another phase to the choreography before passing on to another player. The role of the bodily tracking technology in this idea is that of mediator, in the sense that it is used to record the movements of each player and to indicate when the starting position is close enough for the chain to 'link.' The final output would be a multi-party dance video which would showcase the combinatory choreography (Figure 2).

Scenario 3: Voice of the City

The Voice of the City was developed while a group of participants in the first workshop was exploring location-based audio stories. In this iteration of a location based story, access to the different parts of the narrative isn't only restricted by location, but also by the audience member's physical and emotional state.

"We decided to see the city as our theatre, where we could be playful, serious and empathetic [...]you can go to some places and you have an app, and you just hear some noise, but if you stand still there you can register what the city is telling you" Participant8, Workshop1

This scenario was perceived as a way to increase the emotive power of traditional location based stories. In one scenario presented by the participants, instead of simply attaching a piece of narrative to a location, the audio would be presented as 'of the city' and would only become clear and audible once the listener has waited, still, in a certain place for enough time to move themselves outside the normal flow of the city dwellers. This would be tracked using bio-sensors to encourage a moment of mild meditation in the middle of the city. Expanding this to other narratives, the audience member could be restricted to matching the heart rate chosen by the artist or lowering their galvanic skin response at a certain location. Although it was noted that this may not lend itself to all genres, as a tool for influencing the emotional state of the listener the artists involved saw a number of areas of possible application and an advance over relying solely on location such as in *I seek the nerves under your skin* [33].

Scenario 4: Bob the Blue Ghost

This idea was to enable navigation through the performance individually, rather than something shared by the whole audience as was described in Scenario 1 (Data Director), while still socially attending a performance as part of an audience. Elements of the performance would be hidden from the audience by default, and only shown to them when their bio data matched a certain threshold.

This scenario could take the form of an audio track delivered through headphones or visually, using augmented reality (e.g. a head mounted display). Audience members would then experience the performance differently depending on their physiological readings. The example scenario made by this group, which included a professional actor and a director, can be seen in Figure 3 (left). Bob, a blue ghost that was a figment of the imagination of one of the characters on stage, would only be visible and audible to any audience member when their heart rate was very slow. Described as a 'window on madness' the seemingly irrational behaviour of the main character would be explained, to some extent, when Bob was visible. One interesting opportunity the director saw was to use the invisible ghost in a highly emotive way, quickly pushing the audience back out of the head of the main character as their emotions raised their heart rate.

Figure 3: Left, Bob the Blue Ghost (and some of his friends). Right, Magical Dance Key being performed

Scenario 5: Magical Dance Keys

The interaction in this scenario centred around providing additional content to the movie described in workshop 2. To increase the sense of connection to the characters in the movie, audience members who wanted access to these extra scenes would have to perform the corresponding 'Key' in front of a Kinect or similar device at home. These keys, given this scenario's connection to a movie about dance, were to dance the same steps as the central protagonist.

In expanding this idea, the workshop participants envisaged an alternative, physical installation that would display its content for an amount of time once someone performs the movements, rewarding insider knowledge or fandom in a public setting (Figure 3, Right). Either instantiation was seen as a way to encourage the viewer to watch closely the movements on screen and, through performing and perfecting them themselves, to have a stronger connection to the characters and the story.

EMERGING ISSUES IN BIO-SENSING AND BODILY TRACKING PERFORMANCES

The following sections are structured around three central issues emerging from our analysis that further extend the contemporary discourse on interactive performances, namely; *Temporality of input, Autonomy and control* and *Visibility of input.*

Temporality of Input

In traditional interactive performances, and in traditional methods for interacting with systems, the act of providing input is highly temporally bound. The press of a key causes a letter to appear in the word processor in much the same way as sending a text message causes a text to appear on a stage like, for instance, in the performance Ada [12] . On the contrary, the passive nature of the input relied upon in bio-sensed and bodily tracking systems gives rise to the possibility of providing input on different temporal scales.

Interactive Sensing

Bodily sensing and bio-sensing have, on the surface, different temporal properties. Bodily sensing, in the way that it was envisaged in the scenarios at the workshops, was immediate. This means, it followed the deliberate movements elicited by the system or performers, and provided output immediately to the user. Bio-sensing was also seen as something to be connected to the ongoing artwork, although the interaction timescales were slower to be in line with the biological limits apparent in the lowering of a heart rate, for example. In using the sensors in this way, the person being sensed still has a large degree of autonomy in that they enter the space where they are being sensed, or put on the wearable provided as part of the installation, and the effect that their input is having on the interaction can be learned through manipulation and experimentation.

Long term Sensing

It is interesting to point out that with an increase in mobile sensing and the growth of personal informatics with movements such as the quantified self [54], it is possible to now sense, or make use of sensed data, from outwith the time of the performance. This leads to possibilities such as the use of audience members' routines, and the everyday patterns of interactions between them as an input for interacting within the performance. For instance, the number of times one was in proximity to any other member of the audience before the performance can be calculated from the location traces of the participants, which may be stored by any number of services. However, at the point of interaction and effect, no explicit agency is required from the audience to participate as the actions have already taken place.

With the rise in both the use and the complexity of the sensing of fitness trackers, bodily movement will start to be tracked in the same way as location is currently. This will allow the physical limits of audience members to be known by the system and adaptively pushed by the artist. The yoga instructor may be given a physically different movement to perform than the middle-aged researcher, however the *experience* may be analogical. This also opens the possibility of an audience's interaction taking place after the performance. With access to behavioural patterns, the current performance could be built upon the behavioural change measured in those who have already been to the installation and shown to those currently visiting.

Autonomy and Control

The scenarios presented above can be used as examples to show the range of influence that the designer of the interactive performance can have on the audience members' interaction (summarized in Table 1).

Balancing Artist and Audience Autonomy

Action in a traditional interactive performance goes hand in hand with agency and control; the audience member chooses when to interact and how that interaction is directed (i.e. clapping). This is preserved in the bodily movement sensing scenarios; "*Magical Dance Keys*" and "*Movement Chain*". However, this is blurred in those that are based on bio-data. Even with data collection that is temporally bound to the audience member's interaction with the performance, as we move towards more passive and bodily sensing the control that participants have over their input drops. Inversely, the control that the artist has over the audience's input increases, as we see in "*Data Director*" and "*Voice of the City*". Take heart rate as an example; while there are techniques to regulate one's heart rate this is much more difficult than pressing a button or changing location. It is also open to more external manipulation – excitement can raise the heart rate or the beat of a drum can be used to synchronize it [62]. Galvanic Skin Response is becoming a common sensor to include in wearables, something very difficult for the user to consciously control.

Biosensing	Voice of the City Data Director	Bob the Blue Ghost
Voice of the City	Magical Dance Keys	Movement Chain
Data Director	*Artist*	*Audience*
Bob the Blue	**Locus of Control**	

Table 1: Classifying scenarios according to who has primary control over the input

As highlighted in Better than Life [17] the implicit rules of interaction between performer and audience can be built on-the-fly. These come in part from the understanding built up by audience members through the control they have [48], and where their attention is in the 'split centre' of the mixed reality performance (from the stage cue for two actors to have equal prominence, splitting the audience attention) [59]. This provides another axis for artist: the demonstration and transgression of these rules of interaction can be balanced against the understanding of how each audience member can influence the performance.

Visibility of input

The act of giving input to an interactive system is traditionally a physical movement (such as pressing a button) or the production of sound (clapping or voicing commands) [47]. These types of action are well understood in daily life and negotiating their visibility to others is done fluidly [38]. One may move a mobile device out of the visual range of another to type a message, or move oneself out of audible range to conduct a voice search. The individual actions involved in providing input to bio-sensing and bodily tracking systems can have different communicative abilities with respect to the system and others around the user. It is this aspect that reflects on how visible to others the action of interaction is. Drawing on example from the performances and projects that we studied in the background section and the scenarios produced in two workshops, we try to describe and classify them in terms of *Visibility of Input*.

Socially Sharing Highly Personal Data

The interactions included in Figure 5 can be looked at from the perspectives of both the impact each interaction has upon the performance it was directed towards, and also the social investment and the amount of personal performance that is imbued in the act of interacting. We can see the contrast between the personal and mostly non-visible interactions afforded by the bio-sensors (on the left side) with the very visible and, as a result, mostly collaborative interactions using the bodily tracking sensors (on the right side). Breathless [9] is one exception, where the normally low-visibility act of breathing is amplified by the system so that it can be heard by the audience, shown as a linear trace on a large screen, and turned into a highly visible physical action – that of swinging on a swing.

This lack of scenarios could stem from the lack of social practices around sharing biometrics. While we all learn to negotiate our visual privacy around our body and our movements, we do not learn to negotiate the sharing of our

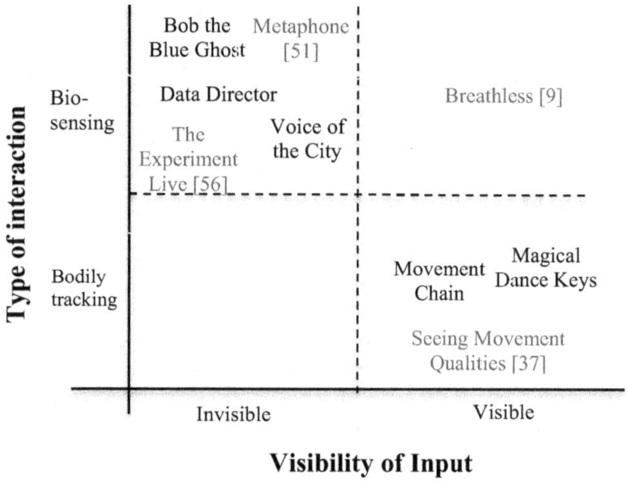

Figure 5: Classifying scenarios and example performances (projects and performances from the background in red)

GSR, heart rate, or breathing in the same way [14,23]. This lack in current practice may be a factor in limiting the interactions around such information to aggregate and hidden ones. As the range of sensed data available to us, and thus available for sharing with others, increases, so will our social practices around them deepen. Now that they are in genesis and flux exploring them with art would be timely and produce interesting, impactful results. One avenue of future work we hope to pursue is design work focused on this emerging field leading to the production of performances and installations to expose the general public to these issues.

Reconfiguring boundaries

The ideas presented, and the technology upon which they are based, all in some way alter the boundaries between the creative team and the audience. On one hand it could be said that the act of interaction by an audience member within an interactive performance is already under the control of the creative team to a greater (i.e. Stage Hypnotism) or lesser (i.e. improvisational theatre) extent. The environment, emotional cues, and information on the plot and characters are all under the control of the artists and are used in the manipulation of the emotional and psychological state of the audience – traditional interaction can then be seen as both a means to probe the effectiveness, and further the impact of this manipulation.

Asking the audience to 'boo' the protagonist is an act that is socially obligated in situ, reinforces the emotional commitment to the hero, and at the same time provides a window on the engagement level of the audience for the artists. By changing the act of interaction from active, as in the example above, to passively being sensed these three aspects of interaction can be disconnected from each other. It is this disconnection between action and reaction, between cause and effect, that opens the possibility for the artists to manipulate, blur, and play with boundaries between traditional roles. For example, in the *Bob the Blue Ghost* scenario, each audience member takes part of the role of director by directly influencing through their bodily functions the modalities of the experience they are able to perceive, but the director still has influence through the choice of triggers and thresholds, as well as through traditional means of influencing the psychological, and as result the physiological, state of the audience.

Tracking Invisible Bodily Movements

The least populated areas of the graph in Figure 5 are those where the inherent visibility of the input is challenged. Opportunities to take advantage of low-visibility physical movements exist, but they are technologically more difficult to harness than larger movements. Designing systems that respond to micro-expressions [44], the involuntary, short, and small movements in facial muscles that signal emotional states, is hampered by the current need to have a high quality, well lit video of the face of the users. The current need for high quality video in the detection of fidgeting [2] and other small bodily movements at a distance similarly limits the current application of these types of movement as an input. However, as both the quality and quantity of cameras that can be trained on an audience increases alongside the complexity and robustness of algorithms to detect such small movements the inclusion of low-visibility bodily movements will become viable. What is interesting here is that the concerns around autonomy and control with bio-sensed data are echoed and, because of the short time scale of the actions being detected, amplified.

CONCLUSIONS

In this paper we have presented five design ideas and related scenarios for interactive performance systems centred on bio-sensing and bodily movement interaction modalities. The ideas were generated during two design workshops which various experts in digital technology and interactive performance participated in. These ideas provide a base for the exploration of novel opportunities for audience participation in interactive performances. We use these ideas to present three key issues concerning such interactive performances; *the temporality of input, the audience's degree of agency and control,* and *the visibility of the interaction itself.* At a time when the deployment of sensor-based devices is quickly making its way into a range of use applications (i.e. including health and medical monitoring), this paper draws attention to potential developments and issues that might emerge when designing for artistic experiences. The issues discussed constitute three paramount conceptual and interaction aspects inherent to triggering reflection on the role of the audience (i.e. from spectator to participant), and on the reconfiguration of boundaries between members of the audience, creative production teams, and performing artists.

ACKNOWLEDGMENT

We are grateful to Rebecca Forsberg, director and scriptwriter for the movie LIV 2015 StellaNovan filmproduktion. We would like to thank our participants in both workshops. We are thankful to Charles Windlin for drawing figure 2 and his contribution to our workshop.

REFERENCES

1. Marina Abramovic and Klaus Peter Biesenbach. 2010. *Marina Abramović: The artist is present*. The Museum of Modern Art.
2. Lars Adde, Jorunn L. Helbostad, Alexander Refsum Jensenius, Gunnar Taraldsen, and Ragnhild Støen. 2009. Using computer-based video analysis in the study of fidgety movements. *Early Human Development* 85, 9: 541–547. https://doi.org/10.1016/j.earlhumdev.2009.05.003
3. Sarah Fdili Alaoui, Baptiste Caramiaux, Marcos Serrano, and Frédéric Bevilacqua. 2012. Movement Qualities As Interaction Modality. In *Proceedings of the Designing Interactive Systems Conference* (DIS '12),761–769. https://doi.org/10.1145/2317956.2318071
4. Alissa N. Antle, Milena Droumeva, and Greg Corness. 2008. Playing with the Sound Maker: Do Embodied Metaphors Help Children Learn? In *Proceedings of the 7th International Conference on Interaction Design and Children* (IDC '08), 178–185. https://doi.org/10.1145/1463689.1463754
5. Saskia Bakker, Alissa N. Antle, and Elise Van Den Hoven. 2012. Embodied Metaphors in Tangible Interaction Design. *Personal Ubiquitous Comput.* 16, 4: 433–449. https://doi.org/10.1007/s00779-011-0410-4
6. Louise Barkhuus and Tobias Jørgensen. 2008. Engaging the Crowd: Studies of Audience-performer Interaction. In *CHI '08 Extended Abstracts on Human Factors in Computing Systems* (CHI EA '08), 2925–2930. https://doi.org/10.1145/1358628.1358785
7. Louise Barkhuus and Chiara Rossitto. Acting with Technology: Rehearsing for Mixed-Media Live Performances. In *Proceedings of the 34th Annual ACM Conference on Human Factors in Computing Systems* (CHI'16). https://doi.org/10.1145/2858036.2858344
8. Steve Benford, Martin Flintham, Adam Drozd, Rob Anastasi, Duncan Rowland, Nick Tandavanitj, Matt Adams, Ju Row-Farr, Amanda Oldroyd, and Jon Sutton. 2004. Uncle Roy All Around You: Implicating the city in a location-based performance. *Proc. Advances in Computer Entertainment (ACE 2004)* 21: 47.
9. Steve Benford, Chris Greenhalgh, Gabriella Giannachi, Brendan Walker, Joe Marshall, and Tom Rodden. 2012. Uncomfortable Interactions. In *Proceedings of the SIGCHI Conference on Human Factors in Computing Systems* (CHI '12), 2005–2014. https://doi.org/10.1145/2207676.2208347
10. Kirsten Boehner, Rogério DePaula, Paul Dourish, and Phoebe Sengers. 2007. How emotion is made and measured. *International Journal of Human-Computer Studies* 65, 4: 275–291. https://doi.org/10.1016/j.ijhcs.2006.11.016
11. Francesco Cafaro, Leilah Lyons, Raymond Kang, Josh Radinsky, Jessica Roberts, and Kristen Vogt. 2013. Framed Guessability: Using Embodied Allegories to Increase User Agreement on Gesture Sets. In *Proceedings of the 8th International Conference on Tangible, Embedded and Embodied Interaction* (TEI '14), 197–204. https://doi.org/10.1145/2540930.2540944
12. Teresa Cerratto-Pargman, Chiara Rossitto, and Louise Barkhuus. 2014. Understanding Audience Participation in an Interactive Theater Performance. In *Proceedings of the 8th Nordic Conference on Human-Computer Interaction: Fun, Fast, Foundational* (NordiCHI '14), 608–617. https://doi.org/10.1145/2639189.2641213
13. Alexis Clay, Gaọl Domenger, Julien Conan, Axel Domenger, and Nadine Couture. 2014. Integrating augmented reality to enhance expression, interaction amp; collaboration in live performances: A ballet dance case study. In *2014 IEEE International Symposium on Mixed and Augmented Reality - Media, Art, Social Science, Humanities and Design (ISMAR-MASH'D)*, 21–29. https://doi.org/10.1109/ISMAR-AMH.2014.6935434
14. Franco Curmi, Maria Angela Ferrario, Jen Southern, and Jon Whittle. 2013. HeartLink: Open Broadcast of Live Biometric Data to Social Networks. In *Proceedings of the SIGCHI Conference on Human Factors in Computing Systems* (CHI '13), 1749–1758. https://doi.org/10.1145/2470654.2466231
15. Scott deLahunta and Frédéric Bevilacqua. 2007. Sharing descriptions of movement. *International Journal of Performance Arts and Digital Media* 3, 1: 3–16. https://doi.org/10.1386/padm.3.1.3_1
16. J. P. Djajadiningrat, William W. Gaver, and Joep W. Frens. 2000. Interaction Relabelling and Extreme Characters: Methods for Exploring Aesthetic Interactions. In *Proceedings of the 3rd Conference on Designing Interactive Systems: Processes, Practices, Methods, and Techniques* (DIS '00), 66–71. https://doi.org/10.1145/347642.347664
17. Nicky Donald and Marco Gillies. 2015. Novel Dramatic and Ludic Tensions Arising from Mixed Reality Performance as Exemplified in Better Than Life. In *Interactive Storytelling*, Henrik Schoenau-Fog, Luis Emilio Bruni, Sandy Louchart and Sarune Baceviciute (eds.). Springer International Publishing, 297–308. Retrieved November 16, 2016 from http://link.springer.com/chapter/10.1007/978-3-319-27036-4_28
18. Paul Dourish. 2004. *Where the action is: the foundations of embodied interaction.* MIT press.
19. Magy Seif El-Nasr. 2007. Interaction, narrative, and drama: Creating an adaptive interactive narrative using

performance arts theories. *Interaction Studies* 8, 2: 209–240. https://doi.org/10.1075/is.8.2.03eln
20. Moshe Gabel, Ran Gilad-Bachrach, Erin Renshaw, and Assaf Schuster. 2012. Full body gait analysis with Kinect. In *2012 Annual International Conference of the IEEE Engineering in Medicine and Biology Society*, 1964–1967. https://doi.org/10.1109/EMBC.2012.6346340
21. Kaj Grønbæk, Karen Johanne Kortbek, Claus Møller, Jesper Nielsen, and Liselott Stenfeldt. 2012. Designing Playful Interactive Installations for Urban Environments – The SwingScape Experience. In *Advances in Computer Entertainment*, Anton Nijholt, Teresa Romão and Dennis Reidsma (eds.). Springer Berlin Heidelberg, 230–245. Retrieved August 9, 2016 from http://link.springer.com/chapter/10.1007/978-3-642-34292-9_16
22. Daniel Hernández, Gabriel Villarrubia, Alberto L. Barriuso, Álvaro Lozano, Jorge Revuelta, and Juan F. De Paz. 2016. Multi Agent Application for Chronic Patients: Monitoring and Detection of Remote Anomalous Situations. In *Highlights of Practical Applications of Scalable Multi-Agent Systems. The PAAMS Collection*, Javier Bajo, María José Escalona, Sylvain Giroux, Patrycja Hoffa-Dąbrowska, Vicente Julián, Paulo Novais, Nayat Sánchez-Pi, Rainer Unland and Ricardo Azambuja-Silveira (eds.). Springer International Publishing, 27–36. Retrieved August 5, 2016 from http://link.springer.com/chapter/10.1007/978-3-319-39387-2_3
23. Noura Howell, Laura Devendorf, Rundong (Kevin) Tian, Tomás Vega Galvez, Nan-Wei Gong, Ivan Poupyrev, Eric Paulos, and Kimiko Ryokai. 2016. Biosignals As Social Cues: Ambiguity and Emotional Interpretation in Social Displays of Skin Conductance. In *Proceedings of the 2016 ACM Conference on Designing Interactive Systems* (DIS '16), 865–870. https://doi.org/10.1145/2901790.2901850
24. Katherine Isbister and Kaho Abe. 2015. Costumes As Game Controllers: An Exploration of Wearables to Suit Social Play. In *Proceedings of the Ninth International Conference on Tangible, Embedded, and Embodied Interaction* (TEI '15), 691–696. https://doi.org/10.1145/2677199.2688813
25. Ahmad Khawaji, Jianlong Zhou, Fang Chen, and Nadine Marcus. 2015. Using Galvanic Skin Response (GSR) to Measure Trust and Cognitive Load in the Text-Chat Environment. In *Proceedings of the 33rd Annual ACM Conference Extended Abstracts on Human Factors in Computing Systems* (CHI EA '15), 1989–1994. https://doi.org/10.1145/2702613.2732766
26. Nicholas D. Lane, Mashfiqui Mohammod, Mu Lin, Xiaochao Yang, Hong Lu, Shahid Ali, Afsaneh Doryab, Ethan Berke, Tanzeem Choudhury, and Andrew T. Campbell. 2011. Bewell: A smartphone application to monitor, model and promote wellbeing. In *in Intl. ICST Conf. on Pervasive Computing Technologies for Healthcare*.
27. Astrid Twenebowa Larssen, Toni Robertson, and Jenny Edwards. 2007. The Feel Dimension of Technology Interaction: Exploring Tangibles Through Movement and Touch. In *Proceedings of the 1st International Conference on Tangible and Embedded Interaction* (TEI '07), 271–278. https://doi.org/10.1145/1226969.1227024
28. Celine Latulipe, Erin A. Carroll, and Danielle Lottridge. 2011. Love, Hate, Arousal and Engagement: Exploring Audience Responses to Performing Arts. In *Proceedings of the SIGCHI Conference on Human Factors in Computing Systems* (CHI '11), 1845–1854. https://doi.org/10.1145/1978942.1979210
29. Christine Laetitia Lisetti and Fatma Nasoz. 2004. Using Noninvasive Wearable Computers to Recognize Human Emotions from Physiological Signals. *EURASIP J. Appl. Signal Process.* 2004: 1672–1687. https://doi.org/10.1155/S1110865704406192
30. Lian Loke and George Poonkhin Khut. 2011. Surging Verticality: An Experience of Balance. In *Proceedings of the Fifth International Conference on Tangible, Embedded, and Embodied Interaction* (TEI '11), 237–240. https://doi.org/10.1145/1935701.1935747
31. Lian Loke and Toni Robertson. 2013. Moving and Making Strange: An Embodied Approach to Movement-based Interaction Design. *ACM Trans. Comput.-Hum. Interact.* 20, 1: 7:1–7:25. https://doi.org/10.1145/2442106.2442113
32. Elena Márquez Segura, Laia Turmo Vidal, Asreen Rostami, and Annika Waern. Embodied Sketching. In *Proceedings of the 34th Annual ACM Conference on Human Factors in Computing Systems* (CHI'16). https://doi.org/10.1145/2858036.2858486
33. Joe Marshall. 2009. I Seek the Nerves Under Your Skin. In *Proceedings of the Seventh ACM Conference on Creativity and Cognition* (C&C '09), 477–478. https://doi.org/10.1145/1640233.1640364
34. John McCarthy and Peter Wright. 2015. *Taking [A]part*. MIT Press.
35. W. Scott Meador, Timothy J. Rogers, Kevin O'Neal, Eric Kurt, and Carol Cunningham. 2004. Mixing Dance Realities: Collaborative Development of Live-motion Capture in a Performing Arts Environment. *Comput. Entertain.* 2, 2: 12–12. https://doi.org/10.1145/1008213.1008233
36. Helena M. Mentis and Carolina Johansson. 2013. Seeing Movement Qualities. In *Proceedings of the SIGCHI Conference on Human Factors in Computing Systems* (CHI '13), 3375–3384. https://doi.org/10.1145/2470654.2466462
37. Helena M. Mentis, Jarmo Laaksolahti, and Kristina Höök. 2014. My Self and You: Tension in Bodily Sharing of Experience. *ACM Trans. Comput.-Hum. Interact.* 21, 4: 20:1–20:26. https://doi.org/10.1145/2617945

38. Don Norman. 2013. *The Design of Everyday Things: Revised and Expanded Edition*. Basic Books, New York, New York.
39. Leif Oppermann, Clemens Putschli, Constantin Brosda, Oleksandr Lobunets, and Fabien Prioville. 2015. The Smartphone Project: An Augmented Dance Performance. In *Proceedings of the 33rd Annual ACM Conference on Human Factors in Computing Systems* (CHI '15), 2569–2572. https://doi.org/10.1145/2702123.2702538
40. Alex F. Osborn and Lee Hastings Bristol. 1979. *Applied Imagination: Principles and Procedures of Creative Thinking*. Charles Scribner's Sons, New York.
41. Antti Oulasvirta, Esko Kurvinen, and Tomi Kankainen. 2003. Understanding contexts by being there: case studies in bodystorming. *Personal and Ubiquitous Computing* 7, 2: 125–134. https://doi.org/10.1007/s00779-003-0238-7
42. Martin Ouwerkerk, Pierre Dandine, Dennis Bolio, Rafal Kocielnik, Johanna Mercurio, Henk Huijgen, and Joyce Westerink. 2013. Wireless Multi Sensor Bracelet with Discreet Feedback. In *Proceedings of the 4th Conference on Wireless Health* (WH '13), 6:1–6:8. https://doi.org/10.1145/2534088.2534104
43. Galen Panger. 2012. Kinect in the Kitchen: Testing Depth Camera Interactions in Practical Home Environments. In *CHI '12 Extended Abstracts on Human Factors in Computing Systems* (CHI EA '12), 1985–1990. https://doi.org/10.1145/2212776.2223740
44. Tomas Pfister, Xiaobai Li, Guoying Zhao, and Matti Pietikäinen. 2011. Recognising spontaneous facial micro-expressions. In *2011 International Conference on Computer Vision*, 1449–1456. https://doi.org/10.1109/ICCV.2011.6126401
45. Michalis Raptis, Darko Kirovski, and Hugues Hoppe. 2011. Real-time Classification of Dance Gestures from Skeleton Animation. In *Proceedings of the 2011 ACM SIGGRAPH/Eurographics Symposium on Computer Animation* (SCA '11), 147–156. https://doi.org/10.1145/2019406.2019426
46. Omer Rashid, Ian Mullins, Paul Coulton, and Reuben Edwards. 2006. Extending Cyberspace: Location Based Games Using Cellular Phones. *Comput. Entertain.* 4, 1. https://doi.org/10.1145/1111293.1111302
47. Stuart Reeves. 2011. *Designing Interfaces in Public Settings*. Springer London, London. Retrieved August 8, 2016 from http://link.springer.com/10.1007/978-0-85729-265-0
48. Joseph Butch Rovan, Robert Wechsler, and Frieder Weiss. 2001. Seine hohle Form: Artistic Collaboration in an Interactive Dance and Music Performance Environment. *Crossings: eJournal of Art and Technology* 1, 2. Retrieved November 16, 2016 from http://crossings.tcd.ie/issues/1.2/Rovan/
49. Thecia Schiphorst. 2005. Exhale: Breath Between Bodies. In *ACM SIGGRAPH 2005 Electronic Art and Animation Catalog* (SIGGRAPH '05), 62–63. https://doi.org/10.1145/1086057.1086087
50. Dennis Schleicher, Peter Jones, and Oksana Kachur. 2010. Bodystorming As Embodied Designing. *interactions* 17, 6: 47–51. https://doi.org/10.1145/1865245.1865256
51. Vygandas Šimbelis, Anders Lundström, Kristina Höök, Jordi Solsona, and Vincent Lewandowski. 2014. Metaphone: Machine Aesthetics Meets Interaction Design. In *Proceedings of the SIGCHI Conference on Human Factors in Computing Systems* (CHI '14), 1–10. https://doi.org/10.1145/2556288.2557152
52. Bart Simon. 2009. *Wii are Out of Control: Bodies, Game Screens and the Production of Gestural Excess*. Social Science Research Network, Rochester, NY. Retrieved January 17, 2016 from http://papers.ssrn.com/abstract=1354043
53. Dag Svanaes. 2013. Interaction Design for and with the Lived Body: Some Implications of Merleau-ponty's Phenomenology. *ACM Trans. Comput.-Hum. Interact.* 20, 1: 8:1–8:30. https://doi.org/10.1145/2442106.2442114
54. Melanie Swan. 2012. Sensor Mania! The Internet of Things, Wearable Computing, Objective Metrics, and the Quantified Self 2.0. *Journal of Sensor and Actuator Networks* 1, 3: 217–253. https://doi.org/10.3390/jsan1030217
55. Emmanuel Munguia Tapia, Stephen S. Intille, William Haskell, Kent Larson, Julie Wright, Abby King, and Robert Friedman. 2007. Real-Time Recognition of Physical Activities and Their Intensities Using Wireless Accelerometers and a Heart Rate Monitor. In *2007 11th IEEE International Symposium on Wearable Computers*, 37–40. https://doi.org/10.1109/ISWC.2007.4373774
56. Paul Tennent, Stuart Reeves, Steve Benford, Brendan Walker, Joe Marshall, Patrick Brundell, Rupert Meese, and Paul Harter. 2012. The Machine in the Ghost: Augmenting Broadcasting with Biodata. In *CHI '12 Extended Abstracts on Human Factors in Computing Systems* (CHI EA '12), 91–100. https://doi.org/10.1145/2212776.2212787
57. Jakob Tholander and Stina Nylander. 2015. Snot, Sweat, Pain, Mud, and Snow: Performance and Experience in the Use of Sports Watches. 2913–2922. https://doi.org/10.1145/2702123.2702482
58. Bin Umino, Jeffrey Scott Longstaff, and Asako Soga. 2009. Feasibility study for ballet e-learning: automatic composition system for ballet enchaînement with online 3D motion data archive. *Research in Dance Education* 10, 1: 17–32. https://doi.org/10.1080/14647890802697171
59. Jordan Beth Vincent, Kim Vincs, and J. McCormick. 2015. Splitting centre : directing attention in trans-media dance performance. *ISEA 2015 : Proceedings of*

the 21st International Symposium on Electronic Art: 1–1.

60. Chen Wang, Erik N. Geelhoed, Phil P. Stenton, and Pablo Cesar. 2014. Sensing a Live Audience. In *Proceedings of the 32Nd Annual ACM Conference on Human Factors in Computing Systems* (CHI '14), 1909–1912. https://doi.org/10.1145/2556288.2557154
61. Qiao Wang, Pavan Turaga, Grisha Coleman, and Todd Ingalls. 2014. SomaTech: An Exploratory Interface for Altering Movement Habits. In *Proceedings of the Extended Abstracts of the 32Nd Annual ACM Conference on Human Factors in Computing Systems* (CHI EA '14), 1765–1770. https://doi.org/10.1145/2559206.2581339
62. Lisa N. Woodside, V. K. Kumar, and Ronald J. Pekala. 1997. Monotonous Percussion Drumming and Trance Postures: A Controlled Evaluation of Phenomenological Effects. *Anthropology of Consciousness* 8, 2-3: 69–87. https://doi.org/10.1525/ac.1997.8.2-3.69
63. Kuan-Ju Wu, Mark D. Gross, and Mark Baskinger. 2012. Giffi: A Gift for Future Inventors. In *Proceedings of the Sixth International Conference on Tangible, Embedded and Embodied Interaction* (TEI '12), 335–336. https://doi.org/10.1145/2148131.2148209
64. Yan Zhang, Lei Wang, Jing Zhu, Yadong Hu, Wanli Xing, and Jing Cheng. 2011. Real-time monitoring of extracellular matrix-mediated PC12 cell attachment and proliferation using an electronic biosensing device. *Biotechnology Letters* 34, 2: 397–404. https://doi.org/10.1007/s10529-011-0773-7
65. Touching a Stranger: Designing for Engaging Experience in Embodied Interaction. *International Journal of Dsign*. Retrieved January 17, 2016 from http://www.ijdesign.org/ojs/index.php/IJDesign/article/view/976
66. Thinking Through the Body | Body-focussed Interactive Art and Somatics. Retrieved January 17, 2016 from http://thinkingthroughthebody.net/

Torrent: Integrating Embodiment, Physicalization, and Musification in Music-Making

Aura Pon, Eric Pattison, Lawrence Fyfe, Laurie Radford, Sheelagh Carpendale
University of Calgary
Calgary, Canada
{aapon; eric.pattison; ljfyfe; lradford; sheelagh}@ucalgary.ca

ABSTRACT
In this paper, we present *Torrent, for Flutes and Water*. *Torrent* is an embodied electroacoustic music composition written to commemorate a catastrophic local flood and the spirit of the citizens who united to overcome it. To create this music, we designed and built an interactive computer system to make audible and physical that which is usually hidden but ever-present in music-making: the musicians' muscle tension as they perform, think about, and feel their music. The *Torrent* system *musifies* and *physicalizes* the flutists' muscle tension as live water sounds and movement that accompany the musicians as they perform. Semi-structured interviews and surveys were conducted to understand the experiences of the performers and audience during one performance. The use of embodiment, as integral to the music itself, aspires to emphasize means and end, body and mind, effort and achievement in the struggle of people united against the elements.

Author Keywords
Electroacoustic Music; Embodied Interaction; Physicalization; Musification; Electromyography.

ACM Classification Keywords
H.5.2. Information interfaces and presentation: User Interfaces, H.5.5. Information Interfaces and Presentation: Sound and Music Computing.

INTRODUCTION
Torrent, for Flutes and Water, an electroacoustic music composition inspired by a local catastrophic flood, uses technology to explore musical embodiment through physicalization and musification (see Figure 1). As discussed by Leman, music is increasingly mediated by technology [15]. However, where music-making historically necessitated an inseparable connection between human physical expression and sound through direct connection with a physical sound production mechanism [22], the flexibility of digital technology in music-making [13] is a double-edged sword when

Figure 1. *Torrent, for Flutes and Water* in performance.

it comes to this connection. In music-making with digital technology, the power to design the coupling of action to sound can lead to music that is disembodied from human presence and action, or, conversely, to music that is more linked to human intentionality and body expression than ever before. We chose to leverage and illuminate the rich expression of the human music-maker in this musical research project. We designed and built an interactive system for augmenting the flute music of *Torrent*. The muscle tension of flutists as they play their flutes is used to create live water sounds that accompany the flutists. This musification and physicalization of the flutists' internal states helps this unusual sonic augmentation of the water sounds become embodied and connected to the presence of the flutists.

This project leverages biosensing technology, that is, sensors that measure biological responses or behavior. Biosensing is increasingly being demonstrated as a way to capture a person's expressivity with emphasis on their intentions and internal states, in contrast with more traditional measurements of the final physical output of gestures [5].

We present the related work, the concept and objectives of this project, and our realization. We then discuss feedback from some members of the ensemble and audience, and close with our reflections and future work.

RELATED WORK
The *Torrent* project is an artistic work that incorporates biofeedback to highlight music-making processes in musical and physical form towards a more embodied music experience. It is inspired by artistic works with similar elements, as well as by particular music controllers designed to

TEI '17, March 20 - 23, 2017, Yokohama, Japan

ACM 978-1-4503-4676-4/17/03...$15.00
DOI: http://dx.doi.org/10.1145/3024969.3024974

incorporate mental or corporeal expression. It builds upon research projects that seek to incorporate philosophical ideas of embodiment and embodied cognition into design.

Chafe et al.'s Brain Stethoscope is a device that translates brain activity during epileptic seizures or normal daily life into sound [6]. The sonic mapping of electroencephalography (EEG) data facilitates timely detection of seizures. It can be used to record and present a musified version of a seizure that can then be experienced by a listener [6]. While inspired by this work, *Torrent*'s musification serves to integrate live data into a composition and live performance, actuated through the medium of water as opposed to sound synthesis. Water serves to enhance the embodied interaction instead of focusing on the presentation of sensor data.

Park's *Eunoia I* and *II* are performance art installations that transform the artist's brainwaves into sounds and cymatic ripples on trays of water. The installations present the artist's inner thoughts and emotions in a medium the audience can experience. Sonic content corresponding to different emotions is played through speakers mounted beneath metal trays of water when triggered by the corresponding brainwaves sensed by an electroencephalography (EEG) headset worn by the artist [17]. *Torrent* also seeks to present a multi-sensory experience of otherwise hidden processes, while at the same time integrating these elements into the pre-meditated aesthetic experience of a music composition, and using the water sounds in themselves to leverage people's familiarity and connotations with water.

Donnarumma's doctoral work [9] provides profound insights into the overt and hidden connections between the human body and music-making as explored through muscle sensing, such as in his *Music for Flesh II* and other compositions that use his Xth Sense biosensing instrument to amplify and process the sounds of muscle movement to make music [8]. *Torrent* is inspired by Donnarumma's work, while differing in its use of water as a mediator of muscle data, and in its integration of this musified data with instrumental music. Also, it highlights muscle tension as part of the action of playing a flute, rather than revealing this corporeal action as an isolated music-controlling gesture.

Tanaka and collaborators have an oeuvre of technical and artistic works that use the BioMuse, a musical instrument using multiple physiological biosensing technologies for control of computer media such as digital audio, video, and computer graphics. He specifically has written about his experience of applying the SEMG aspect of the instrument to articulate musical gesture. From this, he reflected insightfully on the philosophical meaning of this ability to enact physical interaction with an otherwise intangible medium [19]. *Torrent* takes inspiration from Tanaka's work while seeking to create an original artistic instance of SEMG exploration that integrates flutes and water within an electroacoustic music composition.

TORRENT PROJECT

We are exploring how to reintegrate expressive physicality into digital music. Many instances of digital music require little bodily involvement, which may change or minimize the role of embodiment and embodied cognition in music creativity and expressivity. To incorporate bodily expressions into music-making with technology, we employ embodiment, physicalization, and musification in this musical project. In this section, we explain how we applied these ideas in an electroacoustic music composition for flute choir and live electronics.

Concept

The impetus in creating *Torrent* was to integrate flute and water sounds in a composition to commemorate the catastrophe of the June 2013 Calgary flood and the spirit of the citizens who united to overcome it. The nature of this integration arose from the following research objectives:

1) Pertaining to musician: foster an embodied connection between a musician's musical intentions, their emotional connection to their music, their bodily actions in music-making, and the sonic content of the music;
2) Pertaining to audience: foster relationships between the musician's presence on stage and the sonic content of the music, especially the digital sonic content not derived physically from an acoustic musical instrument;
3) To illuminate the hidden or otherwise imperceptible processes of music-making to the musicians and audience alike.

To meet these objectives, we investigated possible biological control signals which convey a flutist's mental and physical state as they listen to and perform music, as a way to control live water sounds, and therefore connect the flutists to such sounds foreign to the stage. We chose muscle tension, as measured by surface electromyography, as one visceral and feasible measure of the flutists' inner processes in music-making (see Electromyography below). We composed a musical score and built an interactive system in tandem that integrated music for flute choir with live water effects by connecting musical tension with the musicians' physical muscular tension. Four flutists – Piccolo, Flute 1, Alto Flute 1, and Bass Flute 1 – henceforth referred to as the *sensored* players, each wore electromyography sensors, and from each, muscle tension data was processed to control the turning of one of four propellers in a bin of water as they and the rest of the flute ensemble play their individual scored parts. The way the water ripples caused by their muscle contractions interact in the common bin of water is metaphorically similar to both how the flute soundwaves interact in space and how the flutists mutually respond to each other in the complex system of music performance. These water sounds were amplified and output to four speakers surrounding the audience, serving as an accompaniment to the flute choir, conveying the flutist's tensions, and integrating water sounds into the composition. An overview video of the project can be found at https://vimeo.com/177136590.

Electromyography

The sensing method we chose is surface electromyography (SEMG), which is a non-invasive technique for measuring the electrical voltage generated by the neural activity that commands muscle contraction and relaxation cycles [3]. It is important to note that SEMG does not report movement or position, but rather, captures the neural intention to engage muscles, which might – or might not, result in movement [20]. "This intention may or may not manifest itself in legible media output, creating space for ambiguity and interpretation, and within this, the fragile fleeting hints of intimacy" [19, p. 2], where such "intimacy" could refer to this unique insight into a performer's internal states. Research shows a correlation between muscle contraction and a listener's response to music [7]. The flutists' right upper trapezius area was chosen as the site for placement of the electromyographic electrodes. The upper trapezius is part of the area of Primary Control [2] that is viewed as the origin of how a person controls the rest of their body. It is also reportedly an area of higher tension for flute players [16], and was an accessible area for our researchers to mount electrodes prior to performances.

Embodiment, Physicalization, and Musification

The water, a physical element with properties familiar to all people, serves as a physicalization and musification of this muscle tension data, which is an expression of the flutists' thoughts, emotions, and actions as they perform the music. We use the term *physicalization*, as described by Jansen et al., to mean a physical artifact whose geometry or material properties encode data [11]. *Musification* is a type of sonification where the data is not just converted to sound, but rather, various constraints are created and applied in order to create a musical performance using the data [21].

By experiencing the actions of the water, we hope audience members and music-makers alike will viscerally experience the underlying but normally hidden processes of music-making. Too often in music-making as well as other human activities, people are focused only on end results, while the manner in which the results are achieved is treated as less significant. We are inspired by the Alexander Technique philosophy, which values mindfulness in the means whereby a person uses himself or herself to achieve an end [1, 2]. Whether for fostering musician proprioception or encouraging listener contemplation of the forces involved in music-making, capturing this muscle tension energy and making it externally perceivable is part of our quest for integration of intention and action.

We united the metaphorical tension of the musical content with the physical bodily tension as manifest in the flutists, and in turn with the perceived metaphorical tension of the turbulent water sounds and water movement. In this way, we sought to reinforce the embodied way people relate abstract concepts, and especially musical concepts, with bodily experiences familiar to them [12,14]. The system investigates embodied interaction in the sense suggested by Dourish: "The primary characteristic of technologies supporting embodied interaction is that they variously make manifest how they are coupled to the world, and so afford us the opportunity to orient to them in a variety of ways" [10, p. 154]. The flutist SEMG data, a force intangible and somewhat incomprehensible to us, is coupled to the water, which has properties and behavior we understand, therefore offering an opportunity to orient ourselves to this force during experiencing *Torrent.*

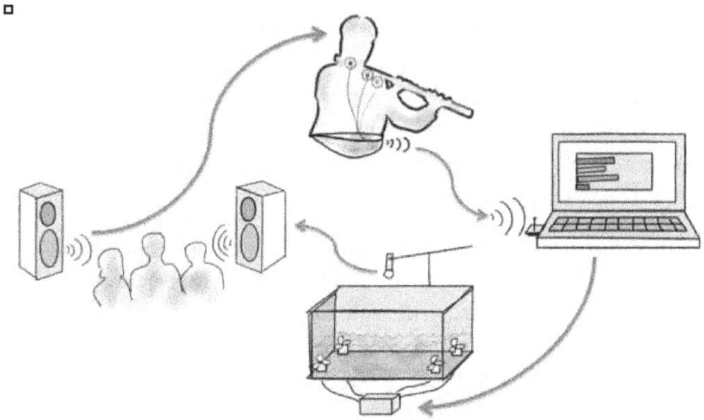

Figure 2. The *Torrent* System, showing data flow.

Finally, beyond being purely informational, we intend for the water to be an integrated component of the overall aesthetic experience of this music composition.

REALIZATION

We composed a musical score, and designed and built a custom hardware and software system (Figure 2) for *Torrent* to fulfill our previously stated goals of embodiment, physicalization and musification. In the process we had to address several practical and logistical considerations. The design had to consider costs and set-up time, given the limited access to the performance spaces prior to the performance. Above all, the system had to maintain safety and comfort for the flutists, and integrate as seamlessly as possible into the flutists' normal performance practice. The flutists needed to be uninhibited from focusing on performing and operating their instruments, so that the system could access their natural responses to the music and capitalize on their performing expertise. While maintaining this unobtrusiveness, the interactive system acts to mesh with the flutists' actions and extend their field of influence into the digital realm, towards the ideal of apparent "non-mediation," or seemingly seamless integration of a tool and the person using it, as discussed by Leman [15].

Music Composition

The musical score was written with several compositional objectives relating to the artistic and research goals of the project. The form, texture, and harmonic content of the music strive to metaphorically evoke the emotions and forces involved in the local flood, as well as take inspiration from the sounds and movement of the local river. The composer paid attention to the flow of sonic tension and relaxation, and how this related to the possible bodily tension level the flutists might have in performing and listening to the specific musical material. By doing this, the composer aimed to synchronize the music's sonic tension with the flutists' muscular tension, thus revealing links with the audible water turbulence.

The composer also sought to integrate the water with the flute music in a dramatic manner that balanced the importance of both flute and water sounds. The introduction of the piece starts with only flute sounds. Each motor is then turned on in sequence as each sensored player enters playing a solo. A middle section is characterized by restrained, quiet tension and features the water in bursts with the sounds underwater captured via a hydrophone transducer (see Implementation section). The climax of the piece features the flutes abruptly ending on a dissonant high-tension chord. Only the water sounds remain audible as the members of the flute ensemble cease playing and relax their bodies and arms. This results in a calming of the water sounds and leads to a serene, harmonious mix of both flute and water in the final section of the piece.

Hardware

The hardware consists of the sensors, the motors, the water container, and the audio system, detailed below.

Sensors

The hardware system begins with the collection of muscle tension data in the sensor system. The four performers need to be able to move freely as they played their flutes and be unencumbered by the electromyography sensors, so the sensor apparatus is contained wirelessly in wearable, black waist packs with a total weight of 475 grams each. (Figure 3A). Within each is a container holding an Advancer Technologies V3 Muscle Sensor board with a 3-electrode cord to adhere to the musician's muscles (Figure 3B), and an Arduino Mega microcontroller. The V3 Muscle Sensor outputs an amplified, rectified and smoothed signal; details on this processing are not published by Advancer Technologies [25]. The Mega samples the sensor at approximately 750 ms and transmits the data for processing wirelessly via an XBee shield and 1mW chip antenna Xbee module set at 9600 baud and an XBee 1mW coordinator connected to a computer. The sensor board is powered by two 9V batteries, and the Mega by either 5 AA batteries or a Lithium-Polymer Ion rechargeable battery and connected via USB.

Motors

Four model boat propellers mounted on 12V pump motors, each corresponding to one of the four SEMG sensors, actuate the water physicalization (Figure 3C). The motors are powered by two switching power supplies and controlled by two Sabertooth 2x5 motor controllers in Simplified Serial Mode at 9600 baud, and an Arduino Mega, which receives control messages via USB (Figure 3D).

Water Container

The water and all four frame-mounted propeller motors are contained in one 30"L x 22"W x 17"H transparent storage

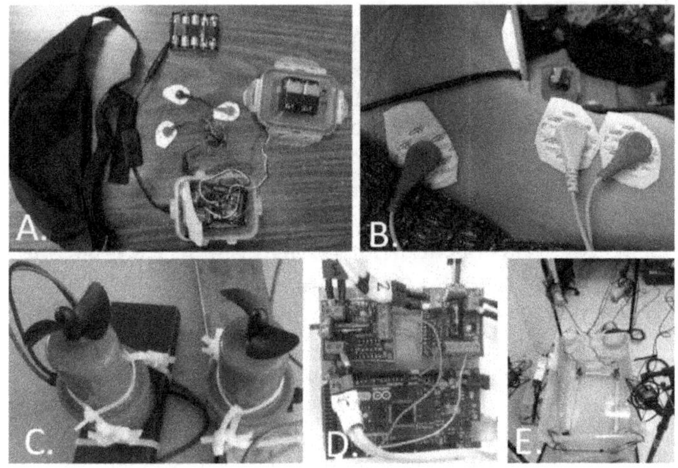

Figure 3. The hardware components of the *Torrent* System.

bin sitting in a custom-built movable cart (Figure 3E). The water is filled to 1 inch above the propellers for maximum sound level. We explicitly decided to have all the propellers located in the same water bin, so the ripples each created would interact and mutually influence each other, paralleling the action of the sound waves of each flutist in the performance space. For performances, we positioned a bright LED worklight beneath the bin (see light glowing through bin in Figure 1) to cast ripples of the water movement on the ceiling.

Audio System

The water sounds of each propeller are amplified via a condenser microphone (Figure 3E) and routed to one of four speakers surrounding the audience using a Roland Octa-Capture Audio Interface. The underwater sounds of all four propellers were captured by a submerged hydrophone microphone and routed to all the speakers in a middle section of the composition.

Software

We created and used three types of software for processing sensor data and generating and distributing motor control messages. All software can be found on Github [18].

Arduino Software

Within the Arduino 1.6.7 IDE, software was written for the Arduino Megas within the sensor packs to receive sensor data and transmit it wirelessly via XBee to the laptop computer. Also, software on the Arduino Mega connected to the motor controllers receives serial control messages to set the propeller motor speeds.

Processing Software

Within the Processing 3.0.1 environment, we created a program to perform the following functions: 1) receive the sensor data, 2) visualize the data dynamically in a bar graph (see Figure 4), 3) simulate the data in emergency cases if a sensor is malfunctioning, 4) allow the administrator input to adjust the way the data is mapped to motor speeds via modes and settings, 5) receive Open Sound Control network messages [23] to also allow control of the same ad-

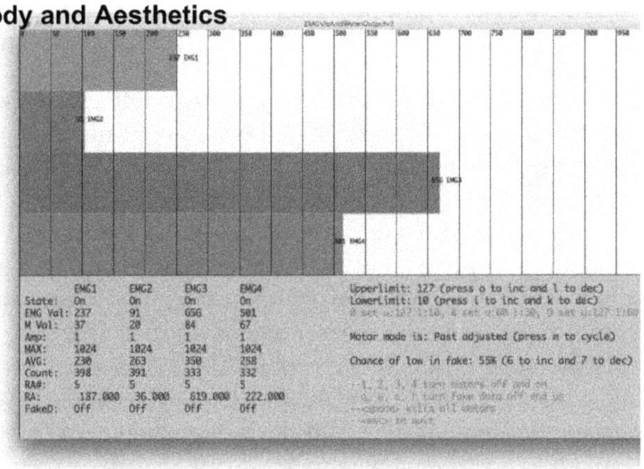

Figure 4. EMG data Visualization

ministrator functions as per 4) above from within MaxMSP, and 6) send speed control messages to the propeller motors. This program offers a choice of three mapping modes that control how the sensor data is translated into motor movement. ***Normal*** mode is a straight scaling of sensor data 0-1024 to motor range of 10-127. ***Burst*** mode enables the sensor data to proportionally relate to the speed and number of short high-speed bursts occurring in each two second period, for the purposes of creating a more granular sonic texture that still varied with tension. ***Past-Adjusted*** mode takes a running average of the last 5 readings from the sensor to determine the motor speed, resulting in motor behavior that shows more general trends in the musician's muscle tension. We also have the ability to manually adjust the maximum and minimum outputs of the motor. This is sometimes necessary for balancing the motors' ranges with the flutists' loudness. This function can also be automatically controlled by the loudness of the flute ensemble as measured in MaxMSP.

MaxMSP

We used MaxMSP 6 to route the audio input from the 5 microphones (4 condensor, 1 hydrophone) to the 4 surrounding speakers, and monitor sound levels. We also designed a new feature for the second performance that allowed the audio levels from the flute players and the current section of the composition to influence the selection of the mapping modes. This feature aspired towards an autonomous system that determined its behavior from the ever-changing context of the live performance.

Performance

Two concert performances by a local flute choir took place in January and June 2016 in two different concert halls. A third performance by the same ensemble occurred at a Maker Faire in August 2016. A fourth is planned for June 2017.

FEEDBACK AND OBSERVATIONS

Throughout the development and performances of *Torrent*, we have worked closely with both the performers and the audience to shed light on the experience of *Torrent* and to refine our research objectives. Here we report on audience and performer feedback collected following its second performance, together with our reflections, as self-reflection is an important part of practice-based artistic research [4]. All surveys and interview questions can be found on Github [18].

Audience Survey

To connect with the audience and gain their feedback, we verbally introduced the piece at the beginning of the second performance, distributed program notes regarding the concept and implementation, and offered paper surveys following the performance. The verbal introduction indicated a link between the performers and the water without disclosing the use of muscle tension. The program notes included more information such as details about the electromyography sensors. The paper surveys asked nine questions regarding audience perceptions, experiences, and connections made between the water sounds, flute music, and flutists, such as "Describe your experience in listening to and watching *Torrent.*" The surveys were available for audience members to complete voluntarily shortly following this second performance. Nine anonymous paper surveys were completed, providing a sampling of perspectives on the audience experience. More would have been ideal but the completion rate was a function of how many people remained and volunteered following the evening concert. Even though this is only a small sample of the audience, the data collected is detailed and insightful.

Use of Water

In general, the survey results conveyed that the people found *Torrent* an engaging experience. Four people wrote about how the presence and action of the water was visually stimulating, which three regarded as positive while one person found it distracting. Some people commented on the calming or pleasant quality of the sound of the water, which one found to "balance out the tension in the flute music," while another wondered that this might seem incongruent with the relationship of the piece to the devastation of the flood, noting reflectively: "Water is soothing yet powerful." Five expressed this type of sentiment: "I loved how the rushing water sounds intersected with the music."

Water-Flute Connection

Despite the mention of the muscle tension sensors in the written program notes, eight people seemed unsure of the actual connection of the water sounds to the flutists. One person thought the connection was ambiguous, and another thought the main function of the water was as an ambient background sound to remind listeners of the historical context of the piece. Still, the remaining people said that the water was very responsive and the two entities complemented each other well. Notably, they perceived various connections of activity level, loudness, energy level, flute air stream, shapes of phrases, and tempo of the music as ways that the water seemed to relate to the flutists and the music they were playing. "We see the energy of the flutists in the water," wrote one person. None of these hypotheses would be entirely incorrect, as all these attributes could be related to each other as well as to muscle engagement. When asked what they thought or felt about this connection between the flutists and the water, the one person who indicated awareness that the flutist muscle tension was controlling the water stated: "It felt a bit revealing. Like I could see things that the flutists couldn't manipulate directly and maybe did unintended."

Performer Feedback

Three days following the second performance, we collected 10 anonymous paper surveys from the ensemble that contained seven questions regarding their experiences, such as "Describe your experience of knowing or hearing that your actions affect the water sounds." We also conducted verbal, semi-structured interviews, recorded by video camera, with three sensored players, three non-sensored players, and the conductor, asking a flexible list of questions such as "What connection did you hear between the water and the music you were playing, if any?" This post-performance feedback was diverse but had some general trends. Overall, all the performers were very positive about the experience, in that they appreciated the music aesthetically, found working with the technology engaging, and appreciated the process of working on and performing the piece.

Personal Connection

Amongst the performers there was some expression of feelings of personal connection to the piece, especially among the sensored players. One of the sensored players conveyed that she especially loved the concept of the piece, as it is a personal topic for everyone in their city. "[*Torrent*] had a literal representation with the water, but it was also connected to us [through the sensors]...I felt it was a little more personal by that kind of involvement, especially for the nature of the piece. Every piece presents a different opportunity for a performer to get engaged, but this way, especially because of the subject matter, it really made you a part of it, and it made it very personal and very involving." Other players commented: "It made the piece that much more personal to me, knowing that I was helping to create such a symbolic element of the piece." "It felt good to know that whatever I'm doing affects the water 'music'." The non-sensored players conveyed a less personal but still engaged interest: "[It was] eye-opening to hear the effect of the internal dialogue through sensors and water." "Interesting to hear how others are feeling while playing alongside them."

Effect of the Water

The ensemble members varied in how they related to and were influenced by the water and its sounds. Aside from the conductor, who was very aware of all sounds in the piece, all of the performers conveyed to varying degrees that, due to focusing on playing the flute music, they were not always directly aware of the water except at certain points where the water was more exposed in the music. This is unsurprising, given that music performance requires a "flow state" that may block out distractions [24]. The sensored players had mixed reactions about how the water affected them. Two of these players said that hearing the water and knowing they were controlling it generally did not change how they performed, because they neither felt the sensors on their bodies nor listened to the water very much, especially as they were trying to limit distractions. When asked if they would prefer that the water be more present for them, they declined for fear of distraction or fear of the water reaction becoming "staged." A third sensored player had a slightly differing reaction of increased body and self-awareness: "It made me more nervous and yet more excited. I was more aware of myself at times and what I was doing with my body." In general, the unsensored players described the immersiveness of the water sounds and would have liked to hear them even more.

Characterization of the Water

While the members of the ensemble from whom we gained feedback understood the water as an expression of the four sensored players, when in the "performance zone," they seemed to regard the water as another entity or member of the ensemble. The unsensored players expressed that because they did not have a direct relationship with the water, they all regarded the water as another, albeit special, member of the ensemble "like having a famous soloist join for a concerto", and that it was interesting to adjust to it like another player. Two of the sensored players indicated they were detached from the water sound and so also tended to regard it as another sound of the ensemble, while a third saw it as both an expression of themselves and as its own entity. They all seemed to agree the water added another dimension to their experience and the piece did not feel complete without it.

Music-Water Connection

As we strove to set up relationships between the water sounds and the musical content, we were naturally interested in whether the players perceived such a connection. All participants cited sections of the piece where it seemed to them that the tension and relaxation of the water matched the music. Referring to a build-up to a fast section, someone said, "You can really get this frenetic sense [from the fast moving water]". "It was an energy, an energetic carpet underneath what was going on, so as the music got more excited, I did feel the water was with us." One person commented on the parallels of the water physicalization with the subject matter of the piece: "The level of tension in the performers was unpredictable, just like the flood waters, so I think it's neat that the water will never be the same in performance."

Use of Technology

Though the ensemble members had limited or no experience using computer technology in music performance, the *Torrent* technology was not perceived as cumbersome or invasive in how they individually or collectively performed music. The sensored players felt "special" or "honored" that they were the selected few to be contributing to the piece in this way. Two sensored players did not feel exposed or self-conscious by it as they were barely aware they were wearing the sensors due to the lightness and comfort of the sensor packs. One said they felt it promoted more self-awareness, as previously stated. Those without sensors expressed that they would have liked to have sensors and see how the results might differ, though one expressed minor trepidation at having the sensors for fear that it would be a distracting element.

In comparing the experience of *Torrent* to other music without electronics that they perform, they had a mix of perspectives. One thought the latter felt less personal and more "static" in comparison to *Torrent.* Two players related it to times they perform with other extra-musical elements, such as dancers or a photo slideshow. One person countered that she was more aware of the water than she would be of a slideshow, and compared to a dancer, it felt more novel. Plus, the dance was the dancer's contribution, whereas the water was originating from the group. One non-sensored player expressed that it created a more involved performance, and made her focus more on the body-music connection. For all, the technological aspect did not interfere with the experience that they were making music, and they communicated that it enhanced it and made it feel novel.

Overall, the members spoke highly of the experience and expressed its uniqueness and immersive qualities. They all expressed particular eagerness to view a video made of the performance so they could experience the overall effect that was difficult to obtain from a performing musician's perspective.

Researcher Observations

Our observations during rehearsals and performances reinforced the testimonials of the ensemble members. The ensemble members appeared to be enjoying their experience in rehearsing and performing the piece while still always maintaining an intense focus on the task of enacting the music. In more relaxed periods of rehearsals, the sensored players were observed playfully trying to deliberately control their motors with their muscle movements. It was interesting to observe how the water sounds generally varied with the individual performing contexts at the time. Each run-through of the piece assumed unique profiles of water behavior, with the sensored players averaging higher or lower muscle tension at different times such as in performances versus rehearsals, or from day to day. This contextual nature of the system seemed especially reinforced when one sensored player left the stage during the dress rehearsal while still wearing her sensor to deal with a mechanical problem with her flute. Her water sounds were completely different and ill-fitting with the music compared to the other sensored performers who continued to play on stage.

REFLECTIONS AND FUTURE WORK

As demonstrated in the three performances of *Torrent*, we successfully created a system that translated bodily expression into water sound and movement, and integrated this into an electroacoustic music composition for flute choir. In comparing the performances against our research objectives, the audience and performer testimonials seem to indicate that, to some extent, they experienced relationships between the water, the music, and the flutists' presence and internal actions, and the water represented a part of the bodily music-making process that was normally hidden. The exact nature of the embodied experience for the ensemble members and audience still remains somewhat elusive to define. While ensemble testimonials are mixed about the effect the water had on their playing or mental state, this does not preclude the possibility that there was an effect. The water movement and sounds may have many associations for people that may render a visceral experience that escapes conscious awareness. On the other hand, methods to objectively study such an effect may defy the aesthetic goals and integrity of the composition and thus tamper with the crucial contextual nature of the performance—as mutually influencing and influenced by the performers. Further, a seamless integration of the water with the ensemble was necessary to preserve the players' focus and performance practice. The ensemble and authors felt this integration was achieved.

We can improve some aspects of the performance to move towards a more complete experience and especially towards meeting our research objectives. We have gradually realized the importance of the visual aspect of the water in people's awareness of what is happening, and would like to make it more visible to the audience and performers such as by projecting a live video feed of the water's surface on a large screen. Though logistics and resource limitations may forbid it, ideally all the flutists would be connected to the water so that the water serves as a true representation of their collective efforts and experiences. Towards this, we are taking steps to have at least the sounds of the ensemble influence certain modes of the motor movement.

The feedback and design lessons learned from this project have been incredibly rich and require continued study and contemplation as we move forward in our research. Our explorations and that of other researchers reveal much potential in the integration of meaningful performance data into an instrumental performance, both in the possible data to capture from the music-making process, and in how to physically represent this data in an aesthetic way. Overall, the authors, performers, and audience members with whom we worked found *Torrent, for Flutes and Water* to be a unique musical experience that wove together meaning, physicality, and sound towards expressing its themes.

ACKNOWLEDGEMENTS

We thank the Social Sciences and Humanities Research Council, Natural Sciences and Engineering Research Council, Alberta Innovates Technology Futures, and SMART Technologies for their support, Lucie Jones and the Mount Royal Chamber Flutes for their outstanding dedication to this project, Jim Akeson and Johnty Wang for equipment and technical advice, and the University of Calgary iLab, Leacock Theatre and Rosza Centre for workshop and performance spaces.

REFERENCES

1. Pedro de Alcantara. 1997. *Indirect Procedures: A Musician's Guide to the Alexander Technique.* Clarendon Press, Oxford.
2. F. Matthias Alexander. 1932. *The Use of the Self.* E.P. Dutton & Co., Inc.
3. Yves Blanc and Ugo Dimanico. 2010. Basics of Surface Electromyography Applied to Physical Rehabilitation and Biomechanics. *Open Rehabilitation Journal* 3: 84–93.
4. Linda Candy. 2011. Research and Creative Practice. In *Interacting: Art, Research and the Creative Practitioner.* Libri Publishing Ltd., Oxford, 33–59.
5. Baptiste Caramiaux, Marco Donnarumma, and Atau Tanaka. 2015. Understanding Gesture Expressivity Through Muscle Sensing. *ACM Trans. Comput.-Hum. Interact.* 21, 6: 31:1–31:26.
6. Chris Chafe, Juan-Pablo Caceres, and Michael Iorga. 2013. Sound synthesis for a brain stethoscope. *The Journal of the Acoustical Society of America* 134, 5: 4053–4053.
7. Elliott Dainow. 1977. Physical Effects and Motor Responses to Music. *Journal of Research in Music Education* 25, 3: 211.
8. Marco Donnarumma. 2012. Music for Flesh II: Informing Interactive Music Performance with the Viscerality of the Body System. In *Conference on New Interface for Musical Expression (NIME-12).*
9. Marco Donnarumma. 2016. Configuring Corporeality: Performing Bodies, Vibrations and New Musical Instruments. University of London, Goldsmiths.
10. Paul Dourish. 2004. *Where the Action Is: The Foundations of Embodied Interaction.* MIT press.
11. Yvonne Jansen, Pierre Dragicevic, Petra Isenberg, Jason Alexander, Abhijit Karnik, Johan Kildal, Sriram Subramanian, and Kasper Hornb\a ek. 2015. Opportunities and Challenges for Data Physicalization. In *Proceedings of the 33rd Annual ACM Conference on Human Factors in Computing Systems* (CHI '15), 3227–3236.
12. Mark Johnson. 1987. *The Body in the Mind: The Bodily Basis of Meaning, Imagination, and Reason.* University of Chicago Press, Chicago.
13. Sergi Jordà. 2004. Instruments and Players: Some Thoughts on Digital Lutherie. *Journal of New Music Research* 33, 3: 321–341.
14. Steve Larson. 2012. *Musical Forces: Motion, Metaphor, and Meaning in Music.* Indiana University Press.
15. Marc Leman. 2008. *Embodied Music Cognition and Mediation Technology.* Mit Press.
16. Karen Lonsdale. 2011. Understanding Contributing Factors and Optimizing Prevention and Management of Flute Playing-Related Musculoskeletal Disorders.
17. Lisa Park. Eunoia. *LISA PARK.* Retrieved July 7, 2016 from http://www.thelisapark.com/
18. Aura Pon, Eric Pattison, Lawrence Fyfe, Laurie Radford, and Sheelagh Carpendale. GitHub - mindbodymusic/torrent. Retrieved November 8, 2016 from https://github.com/mindbodymusic/torrent
19. Atau Tanaka. 2012. BioMuse to Bondage: Corporeal Interaction in Performance and Exhibition. In *Intimacy Across Visceral and Digital Performance*, Maria Chatzichristodoulou and Rachel Zerihan (eds.). Palgrave Macmillan UK, 159–169.
20. Atau Tanaka. 2015. Intention, Effort, and Restraint: The EMG in Musical Performance. *Leonardo* 48, 3: 298–299.
21. Federico Visi, Giovanni Dothel, Duncan Williams, and Eduardo Miranda. 2014. Unfolding| Clusters: A Music and Visual Media Model of ALS Pathophysiology. In *Proceedings of SoniHED Conference: Sonification of Health and Environmental Data. York, United Kingdom.*
22. David Wessel and Matthew Wright. 2002. Problems and Prospects for Intimate Musical Control of Computers. *Computer Music Journal* 26, 3: 11–22.
23. M. Wright. 2005. Open Sound Control: An Enabling Technology for Musical Networking. *Organised Sound* 10, 3: 193–200.
24. William J. Wrigley and Stephen B. Emmerson. 2013. The Experience of the Flow State in Live Music Performance. *Psychology of Music* 41, 3: 292–305.
25. Advancer Technologies Muscle Sensor V3. *Advancer Technologies, LLC: Muscle Sensor v3.* Retrieved from http://www.advancertechnologies.com/p/muscle-sensor-v3.html

Collective Loops — Multimodal Interactions Through Co-located Mobile Devices and Synchronized Audiovisual Rendering Based on Web Standards

Norbert Schnell
Benjamin Matuszewski
Jean-Philippe Lambert
Sébastien Robaszkiewicz
UMR STMS
IRCAM-CNRS-UPMC
Paris, France

Oussama Mubarak
Dominique Cunin
Samuel Bianchini
EnsAD (PSL Research University) EnsadLab / Reflective Interaction Group
Paris, France

Xavier Boissarie
Gregory Cieslik
Orbe
Paris, France

ABSTRACT
As an interdisciplinary group of developers, researchers, and designers, we are currently exploring collaborative co-located applications that invite users to engage with interactive audiovisual media using the mobile devices they carry with them. This work simultaneously investigates basic concepts of collaborative interactions and user experience, together with technical concepts and features. Allowing for rapid prototyping, easy deployment, and spontaneous participation, these explorations are entirely based on established and upcoming web standards such as *WebSockets*, *WebGL*, and *Web Audio API*.

After an overview of basic concepts common to these applications, this paper describes *Collective Loops*, a prototypical interactive audiovisual installation that instantiates these concepts and allows for discussing important details in the design and implementation of applications of its kind. The final part of the article summarizes the incremental design and validation of two versions of the *Collective Loops* installation presented at public events.

INTRODUCTION
Collective Loops is a prototypical audiovisual installation the users are asked to join with a mobile device. It essentially consists of three elements that are combined to create a consistent audiovisual environment:

- multimodal mobile interaction (i.e. touch and gestures)
- audiovisual rendering on individual mobile devices (i.e. smartphones or tablets)
- shared visual rendering in the environment (i.e. a floor projection)

The installation can be seen as a mobile multiplayer game. However, the users' mobile devices are not only used as multimodal interfaces to a virtual or augmented environment, but also contribute to the audiovisual rendering in a shared space. As a digital musical system, the installation is a collaborative instrument that invites users — with or without musical training — to play together.

Co-located Mobile Interaction and Web Standards
Mobile devices have become a powerful multimodal platform that enables a wide range of applications of different categories such as social networking and communication, games and entertainment, education, business and productivity. They are ubiquitous in the hands and pockets of users of all profiles who often invest multiple hours per day in mobile-based activities and have developed considerable knowledge and skills in the interaction with these devices. Consequently, it becomes more and more interesting to support not only individual mobile interactions, but also collaborative interactions between co-located users. During the past years, many authors have explored novel interactions between co-located users based on mobile devices (see for example [17, 23, 10]).

The introduction of new standardized web APIs such as *WebSockets*,[1] *WebRTC*,[2] *WebGL*,[3] *WebAudioAPI*[4] currently opens new opportunities not only for raising the level of sophistication in existing application categories, but also to explore novel scenarios and metaphors [4] across mobile platforms. Furthermore, on mobile devices, a set of forthcoming Javascript APIs (i.e. *DeviceOrientation* and *DeviceMotion*) enables the development of web applications that allows for interactions based on motion [12].

Currently, more and more artists and production companies discover the potential of these technologies and start to explore novel kinds of participative artworks and public events.

Collaborative and Mobile Music Performance
Many collaborative music systems created over the past two decades extend the paradigms of traditional music instruments and ensembles [3]. Novel musical instruments like the *reacTable* [11] allow professional performers and novices to

[1] https://www.w3.org/TR/websockets/
[2] https://www.w3.org/TR/webrtc/
[3] https://www.khronos.org/registry/webgl/specs/latest/
[4] https://www.w3.org/TR/webaudio/

TEI'17, March 20–23, 2016, Yokohama, Japan

DOI: http://dx.doi.org/10.475/123_4

collaborate on music making through a shared graphical and tangible interface. Interactive sound installations like the *Piano Staircase* [21] and *Urban Musical Game* [22] enable users to spontaneously collaborate on music making through embodied interactions independently of their musical skills.

Before the appearance of smartphones, mobile phones have been used in musical performance as early as 2001 in Golan Levin's performance *Dialtones (A Telesymphony)* [6]. Smartphones have been used for example in Atau Tanaka's *MubuFunkScatShare* performance, where members of the audience are invited on stage to spontaneously improvise together by shaking smartphones [25]. Since 2008, mobile phone ensembles like the *Stanford Mobile Phone Orchestra* (MoPhO) have explored a large range of different interaction metaphors, including gestural interactions between the performers on stage and distributed in the audience [27, 20].

While these ensembles are composed of semi-professional performers generally using custom-build software for many of the performed pieces, many available mobile music applications target users without musical knowledge and training. Popular music applications like Apple's *GarageBand for iOS* [2] and Korg's *iElectribe* [14] combine digital instruments and DJing tools with automation and sequencing features to support the musical performance of experts and novices. To support collaborative music performance, some applications allow for connecting multiple mobile devices over a local network to synchronize musical parameters, and sequences [1].

Collaborative Graphics and Graphical Interfaces

Many projects have emerged in the past two decades on interfaces that support co-located multi-user interaction. Some of them focused on real-time abstract visual representations of audience actions such as *Evoke* [7] in which a video projection on the facade of a building reacts to the crowd's voices, and *Unnumbered Sparks* [5], a light floating sculpture acting as a canvas reacting to individual interactions on mobile phones. Other projects have, on the other hand, focused on interfaces for the visual analysis of data to ease collaboration of small teams in a working environment, as in the study conducted by Petra Isenberg et al. on data analysis on interactive tabletop displays [9], or the *iFloor* project [15].

Recent research has explored how co-located collaboration can be supported through multi-display groupware (MDG) environments [26, 18], and how to encourage a crowd to interact with a shared public display using their individual devices [13].

DESIGN CONCEPTS

The *Collective Loops* installation has been created as a proof of concept and prototype application of an early version of a software platform dedicated to collaborative mobile applications.[5]

[5]While the *CoSiMa* platform – that also includes a set of authoring tools – is still under development, the web-based framework *Soundworks*, providing the platform's basic services through a Javascript API, has been released under the *BSD 3-Clause* open source license at `https://github.com/orgs/collective-soundworks`.

This platform is designed to support a range of applications including:

- mobile-based collaborative music performances and participative concerts
- massive multi-user interactive installations
- extended audioguides and soundwalks

Collaborative, Co-located, Situated, Distributed

In our explorations, we are particularly interested in applications based on collaborative interactions where users are co-located within a delimited space (e.g. a gallery space, a concert hall, a museum, a district of a city).

Generally, such applications redefine the existing environment by the superposition of interactive elements. This includes the distributed rendering of individual and shared sound and graphics on the users' mobile devices and embedded into the space (e.g. graphic displays and projections, loudspeakers and other acoustic elements). The audiovisual rendering on the mobile devices may address users individually, but also contribute to a shared environment. While individual audio rendering requires headphones, certain applications — such as *Collective Loops* — use the devices inbuilt speakers to create a sound environment from a multitude of distributed audio sources. A mobile device may also contribute to the visual environmental by emitting light via the screen and flashlight.

To create a coherent environment the users can engage with, all of these interactive elements have to be appropriately coordinated.

Rendering the "Magic Circle"

An important motivation for the design of audiovisual elements embedded into an existing environment may be the creation of a privileged context that fertilizes collaborative play and experimentation. This context can be created by sophisticated augmented reality techniques, but also — as in *Collective Loops* — through a simple projection on the floor. In both cases, the application transcends the existing elements of the environment (e.g. the displays in a museum, the walks of a park) to create a symbolic *play-ground*.[6]

This transformation can be achieved by visual elements, but also by acoustic ones. For example, in extended soundwalk and audioguide applications that were previously created, individual audio rendering through headphones was used to emphasize situations of shared interactions and collaboration. In these applications, the synchronized presence of individualized sounds have been associated to particular zones or to the users' mutual proximity, using GPS- and Bluetooth-based localization. The *Collective Loops* installation literally features a "magic circle" in form of a symbolic musical representation around which users gather to play.

A familiar HCI for Unfamiliar HHI Experiences

The interactions with mobile devices through touch screens and motion sensors can often leverage the knowledge and

[6] The "magic circle" mentioned in the title of this section refers to Johan Huizinga's generalized notion of "play-grounds" that he defines as "*temporary worlds within the ordinary world, dedicated to the performance of an act apart.*" [8]

skills which users have acquired in the use of other applications provided on the same devices. For example, most mobile users are familiar with the manipulation of more or less abstract shapes and virtual objects on a touch screen as well as the dynamic adaptation of displayed graphical content to the device's orientation and other motion-based interactions inviting for tilting or shaking the device. More generally, users usually appreciate that they can bring their own device — this well-known extension of their (embodied) cognition — into interactions that, unlike other applications, allow for engaging with other users around within unfamiliar experiences.

The idea that users could spontaneously pull their smartphone out of their pocket to engage together with others in collective experiences has become an important motivation in the design of our applications — especially considering that in many other situations mobile users tend to isolate themselves from their environment.

In addition to engage with technology and through technology with other users, in co-located mobile applications, users may at the same time interact through the usual modalities of face-to-face interaction. These different levels of interaction permanently coexist and have to be taken into account in the design. For example, looking at a graphical interface on a mobile device does not prevent the users from listening to each other and from collaborating musically. However, complex graphical interfaces constantly calling for the users' attention, may strongly interfere with desired interactions between users and their perception of the environment. On the other hand, motion-based interfaces, which the users can use blindfolded, are generally compatible with other visually engaging interactions.

Just a Web Page

The use of web standards for the implementation of such applications could be solely justified by the need for a convenient environment for the rapid prototyping and deployment of complex experimental systems that run partially on the users' mobile devices. However, the most important advantage of implementing the client side of these applications using web standards lies in the user experience that they enable. To join the experience, users simply pull their mobile device out of their pocket and visit a web page. There is nothing to install and nothing undesired remains on the users' devices after they have left the experience.

In addition, web technologies allow designers to test ideas not only at dedicated events, but also through informal exchanges at virtually any occasion. The ubiquity of the web platform — anywhere and on anybody's device — is particularly helpful in the exploration of novel interactions.

APPLICATION FEATURES AND USER EXPERIENCE

As a prototypical application, *Collective Loops* enables co-located users with handheld mobile devices to collaboratively interact within an audiovisual environment. Once connected to the installation a device becomes a graphical interface and motion controller that enable its user to interact with complementary audiovisual elements. These elements are synchronously rendered on the users' devices and in the environment.

The installation features an 8-step loop sequencer that is collectively embodied and collaboratively controlled by up to 8 users who can spontaneously join and leave the installation at any time.[7] Apart from some signage (i.e. a poster or display on the wall) explaining how to connect to the installation, the installation environment consists solely of a circle of a diameter of about 2 to 4 meters divided into 8 sectors [8] projected on the floor of an empty space (see Figure 1). One-by-one, the sectors are highlighted (i.e. changing their color) in an anti-clockwise motion of steady tempo, and the selected sounds on that sector are played on the corresponding mobile device.

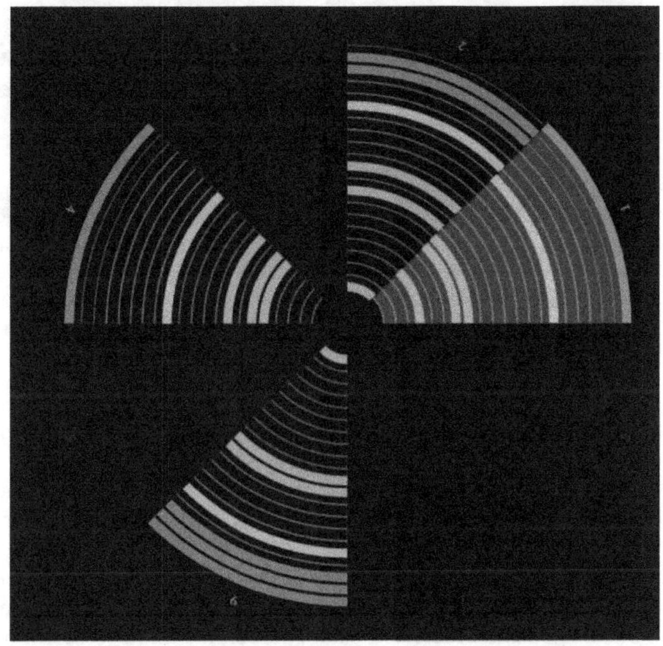

Figure 1. Representation of a segmented circle projected on the floor with 4 connected users (i.e. in sectors 1, 2, 4 and 6). Each circle sector displays the sounds selected through the corresponding mobile interface. The highlighting of the sectors — here in sector 1 — jumps counterclockwise from sector to sector in a steady tempo. When a sector is highlighted the selected sounds are played on the corresponding mobile device.

To join the installation, visitors have to connect their smartphone (or other handheld mobile device) to a given local Wi-Fi access point and visit a given URL with a recent browser.[9] Once connected, the users choose an available position on the graphical interface appearing on their mobile device. The interface corresponds to the circle of 8 sectors projected on the floor whereby only the available sectors are displayed (see Figure 2, left).[10]

[7] We describe here the second version of the application (see section 5 for an overview of the different versions of the installation).

[8] In different variations of the installation, the circle could also be divided into, for example, 12 or 16 sectors. However, too many sectors may result in less clear interactions.

[9] Since the installation uses forthcoming web standards, it requires relatively recent smartphones running Android ≥ 4.2 or iOS ≥ 7 and recent versions of *Chrome* or *Safari*. We are currently testing devices using *Firefox* on different mobile platforms as well as *Edge* on Windows Mobile.

[10] In the case that none of the sectors are available, a message is displayed informing the users that all sectors are taken and asking them to try to connect again later.

Figure 2. Screenshot of the mobile graphical interfaces for selecting an available sector (beat) when connecting to the installation (left) and for controlling the sounds played in the loop sequence at the selected sector (right).

After having chosen a sector, the users symbolically enter the circle and start playing. The floor projection invites them to stand around the circle to create a circular trajectory of the sounds produced by the mobile devices.[11] The second graphical interface on the mobile devices enables the users to control the sounds associated to their sector (see Figure 2, right). Twenty-one horizontal lines on the interface represent different pitches of drum, bass, and marimba sounds that can be selected and deselected within predefined limits (3 marimba pitches out of 12, 1 out of 6 bass pitches, and 3 out of 3 drum sounds). The selected sounds are graphically emphasized on the mobile interface as well as on the corresponding sector of the circle on the floor (see Figure 1). Each time the sector is highlighted, the currently selected sounds are played on the loudspeakers of the corresponding mobile device. The audio rendering on the users' devices generates a musical sequence of 8 beats that changes according to the users' selection, leaving silences at sectors which are not associated to any user. The pitches of the sounds fit a whole-tone scale (i.e. adjacent pitches are separated by a major second), which allows for creating perpetuate melodics of a static but pleasantly meditative character.

Complementary to the graphical interaction, the users can control the sound intensity through a gesture of tilting their device between the horizontal and vertical position.[12] The sound is damped when the users tilt their device towards themselves and opens up again when moving back into a horizontal position. At the user's disconnection from the installation (e.g. by closing the web page or by leaving the range of the Wi-Fi network), the corresponding sector is removed from the circle and becomes available for the next user who connects to the installation.

Invited by a symbolical space, the users enter a collective listening experience where their relationships are metaphorically articulated through the musical relationships between the sounds emitted by their mobile devices (see also [24]).

TECHNICAL FOUNDATIONS

Platform and Setup

As mentioned in section 2, the implementation of the *Collective Loops* installation is based on a platform dedicated to the production of co-located multimedia experiences that is currently under development. The current version of the platform is entirely based on web technologies. On the client side, the platform provides a set of modules for interaction, and audio-visual rendering that are built on top of a set of services such as network messages and network distributed states, audio synchronous scheduling, and clock synchronization. The graphic rendering modules are based on *Mobilizing.js*[13] that provides a convenient programming interface for *WebGL* graphics rendering. The audio rendering modules essentially use the *WavesJS* audio components[14] implemented with the Web Audio API. The server side of the platform is based on *Node.js*.[15]

The web applications that run inside a standard browser on the users' mobile phones are implemented as clients of our platform. Using a slightly different URL than the users, the floor projected graphics are also implemented as a web client running in a browser in full-screen mode on a dedicated computer. This way, all parts of the installation's audiovisual rending can easily communicate and synchronize through the services provided by the platform.

Apart from the mobile devices — contributed by the users — the overall technical setup of the installation essentially consists of the following elements (see Figure 3):

- a computer running the web server
- a computer running the web client for the floor projection
- a video projector projecting on the floor
- a Wi-Fi access point

In addition, the server runs a DHCP and a DNS to handle the network access of the mobile clients connected to the Wi-Fi access point and to provide an easy to communicate URL for the mobile web clients.

Synchronization and Dataflow

The synchronization between different clients through the server relies on three elements.

Firstly, the clients are synchronized to a common reference clock using an NTP-like protocol [19] that is built on top of standard web APIs [16]. The reference clock is provided by the server, as a high-resolution time.[16] Since for many

[11] Since the installation does not imply automatic localization, the users' interaction does not depend on whether they are actually placed around the floor projected circle or not.

[12] The effect is implemented through a low-pass filter.

[13] http://www.mobilizing-js.net/en

[14] http://wavesjs.github.io/audio/

[15] https://nodejs.org/

[16] https://nodejs.org/api/process.html#process_process_hrtime

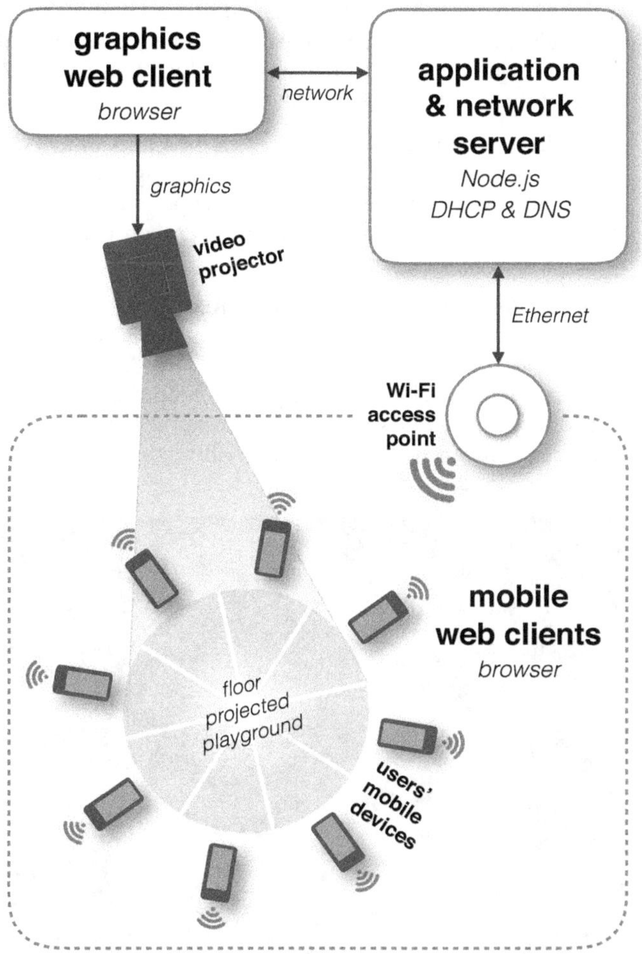

Figure 3. Schematic overview of the *Collective Loops* technical setup.

audiovisual applications precise audio timing and synchronization is critical, the platform's synchronization module uses the clock of an *AudioContext*[17] on the client side. Given that the clients' common logical scheduling time is permanently synchronized to the server time, the clients can generate synchronized events. These synchronized events can either be autonomously generated by the clients themselves or initiated by the server.

Secondly, all events sent between the clients and the server carry precise time-tags that can be used to precisely schedule events in time, which is of particular importance for audio rendering.

Finally, the precise timing and synchronization of perceivable audiovisual events across different rendering clients has to take into account the local latencies of the audio and graphics subsystems. For example, generating an audio event on a mobile phone may take up to a few hundred milliseconds between the moment the event's rendering is initiated (i.e. using a Web Audio API method) and the moment the event is actually produced by the loudspeakers. To achieve synchronized control of multiple clients, the server has to anticipate the transmission of events sufficiently so that the clients can compensate network and local rendering latencies.

Since the scheduling of events in *Collective Loops* is based on a common synchronized time, it does not require any further communication with the rest of the system, apart from the synchronization protocol itself. To realise the synthesis of the sound events on the right beat of the 8-step sequence loop, the events scheduled by the mobile clients have only to take into account the beat phase. This phase can be calculated locally from the common synchronized time[18] using the index of the sector chosen by the user (see Figure 4).

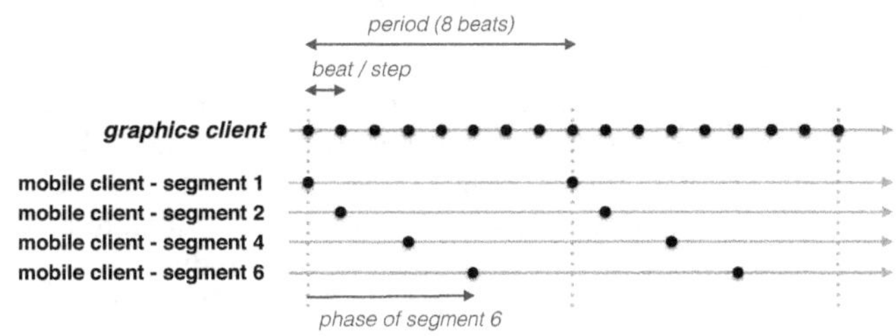

Figure 4. Distributed scheduling according to a common reference time. The figure shows scheduled events over time for each mobile clients and the shared visualisation, on top of their logical synchronized timelines.

The clients send messages — through the server — to communicate their current state to the shared graphics client. The floor-projected graphic rendering mirrors the state of each mobile client in the corresponding sector of the circle by highlighting selected pitches and by modulating the luminosity according to the sound intensity (i.e. controlled through the mobile device's tilt).

While the control of the audio synthesis and local graphical interface is directly connected to the touch and device orientation (i.e. for the tilting gesture) events to achieve minimum latencies, the rendering of the floor projection is controlled over the network with a much higher but tolerable latency.

ITERATIVE DESIGN AND VALIDATION

Executed in a multidisciplinary team, the design and development of our platform and the *Collective Loops* prototype follow an iterative and incremental process, and co-creation sessions are held every few weeks.

While many other applications of its genre (see Section 2) are tedious to test since they only work through the participation of many users (e.g. participative concerts), *Collective Loops* can be very easily deployed and simulated in virtually any context. Nevertheless, many aspects of the installation's design can only be validated through the participation of users.

[17] `https://developer.mozilla.org/en/docs/Web/API/AudioContext`

[18] We simply assume that the sequence has started at time 0 of the common synchronized time. Given the (constant) tempo, the next time of an event on a particular beat can be easily calculated at any time.

First Version and Public Test

A first stable version of *Collective Loops* was completed in early June 2015. As the second version described above in section 3, this version implemented an 8-step loop sequencer visualized by a floor projected circle of 8 sectors. However, in this version the installation could accommodate up to 24 users, three per sequencer step. The users' mobile devices where limited to a single sound, therefore each step could superpose three sounds of different users with different instruments that where displayed in distinctive colors on the corresponding sector of the circle on the floor. The sectors and instruments were randomly attributed to the users joining the installation. The pitch of the emitted sounds — of constant intensity — could be controlled through a 12-note pentatonic scale by tilting the device back or forth from horizontal into vertical position.

A first full-scale test of this version was performed during an open days event in June 2015. The public was invited to participate using their own mobile phones, but could also borrow pre-configured devices in case theirs was not compatible. The test lasted 6 hours and gathered over 200 individuals of all ages from a large variety of profiles. Most of the participants had little or no experience with music software.

Figure 5. A group of users engaging with the first version of the installation at an open days event in June 2015.

We conducted a qualitative user study during the experimentation that included interviews and questionnaires. This study allowed us to evaluate several design choices. The questionnaire included three general questions (age, gender, and profession), three questions related to the participant's previous musical experience, and eight questions regarding their experience with *Collective Loops*. The main goal of this study was to understand and assess the difficulties encountered by participants to follow the impact of their actions and the actions of the other participants in the installation.

A total of 13 questionnaires were filled by participants varying in age from 13 to 56. Moreover, we conducted 16 interviews with participants ranging from 12 to 60 years old. Most of them noted that the pitch control of the generated sound (i.e. by tilting the device) was not very intuitive, and that they had spent a non-negligible amount of time figuring out how to manipulate the device. Certain participants even believed that the pitch was related to their physical location and tried to move around or even jump to alter it.

Regardless of this difficulty, most participants enjoyed the experience and found the project interesting and engaging. Some, however, considered that their scope of action was too limited, dissuading them from prolonging their participation.

Improvements and Second Public Test

Drawing on the first test, we developed a second version of *Collective Loops* with an improved design. As described in section 3, in this version, the sequencer loop was also divided into 8 steps, but unlike in the first version the users could manually select a sector of the circle through a user interface on the mobile device (see Figure 2, left).

Figure 6. A group of users engaging with the second version of the installation at the occasion of an international forum in November 2015.

Instead of controlling the pitch of a single sound by tilting the mobile device, the user can select multiple pitched sounds on a whole-tone scale mixing 3 different instruments through a multi-touch graphical user interface (see Figure 2, right). The tilting interaction that controlled the note pitch in the first version, here controls the sound intensity, which as a continuous parameter fits better the participant's gesture. Furthermore, to create a more engaging musical experience, especially when only a few users are connected to the installation, we added a polyrhythmic echo effect to the audio rendering.

Since the sound levels of the inbuilt loudspeakers of the users' mobile devices appeared rather weak in the first test, we decided to hand out a 3-Watt loudspeaker to each participant. The loudspeakers where connected to the mobile devices with a short mini-jack cable that allowed the users to hold the loudspeaker in one hand and the mobile device in the other, while interacting with the graphical user interface using their thumb (see Figure 7).

To evaluate the new design choices, we scheduled a second public test in November 2015 during an international forum

Figure 7. A user holding a mobile device in one hand and a mobile loudspeaker in the other while interacting with the installation.

dedicated to research and innovation in the field of musical and acoustic systems. The audience of the forum was invited to participate in the installation and asked to volunteer in a user study by filling out a questionnaire. In addition to questionnaires, which mainly inquired about the users' individual and collective experience, we collected video recordings and detailed system logs to measure the project's ability to spur and endorse user collaboration.

Approximately 100 individuals participated in this test, and 68 filled out a questionnaire. Unlike during the first test, most of the participants of this second test had prior experience with musical composition software. The average interaction time per user was approximately 11 minutes, with an average of 3 simultaneous users.

From the collected data, we discovered that the new user interface was more intuitive and required less time to adopt, making the individual experience more enjoyable. Contrary to the first version, most participants spent very little time understanding the impact of their actions thought the individual devices on the collective environment. Besides the aesthetic aspect, the new graphical interface design managed to achieve its primary goal of supporting the acoustic interaction through a direct relationship between the actions performed on the smartphones and their representation on the shared interface.

However, the collective and collaborative aspects of the installation were still not fully taken advantage of. Some participants noted that although the floor-projected interface allowed them to easily identify their choices as well as others', it tended to draw all their attention and discouraged face-to-face interactions with other users. The prominence of the shared graphical interface even inspired users to select specific pitches in order to collaboratively create graphical patterns, such as spirals and circles.

In addition to making the acoustic output more enticing even with a small number of participants, the polyrhythmic echo effect and the low-pass filter added in this version appear to have succeeded in improving the user experience by making it more dynamic and increasing the participants' impact on the emitted sounds. Nevertheless, especially participants with a musical background wanted more control over some system parameters such as the pitch scale and the tempo of the sequencer.

CONCLUSIONS AND FUTURE WORK

We have presented *Collective Loops*, an interactive audiovisual installation inviting co-located users to collaboratively interact through the mobile devices that they carry with them. The installation has been described as a distributed audiovisual environment composed of a floor projection and the users' mobile devices, which synchronize and communicate through the network services of a dedicated web-based platform.

Beyond its interaction design and technical foundations, we have presented the installation as a prototypical application in the sense that (1) it has actually been designed as a prototype application of a platform that we are currently developing, and (2) that it shares fundamental concepts and characteristics with a set of applications that are emerging as a genre from our own design practice. In this sense, the presentation of the application has been a pretext to discuss the current state of our investigations concerning the foundational concepts of the genre of applications our platform is intended to support. Instead of delivering a complete definition of this genre, we have briefly summarized conceptual key elements of the applications it embraces (i.e. (1) collaborative co-located situated distributed interaction, (2) creating efficient digital playgrounds from few elements, (3) using mobile device as a familiar interface to join unfamiliar experiences of manifold interactions, (4) using web technologies to enable ubiquitous and ongoing experimentation with users).

Finally, we have reported on two experimental showings of the installation that coincide with two main stages of the iterative design process it went through. We have summarized some conclusions we could draw from recorded observations, interviews, and questionnaires that have been collected at these occasions.

All in all, *Collective Loops* has perfectly fulfilled its role as a prototype application and significantly enlightened our understanding of many conceptual and technical aspects. As an application that initially was intended to provide a testbed for a first version of our platform, it has also confirmed the efficiency of its genre and the underlying technical concepts. Firstly, this efficiency concerns the development and deployment of the installation. Secondly, we have been delighted that even a prototypical interactive installation like *Collective Loops* that neither provides very sophisticated possibilities of musical composition and performance, nor generates very exciting music altogether, finally succeeds to create a very pleasant point of attraction where people spontaneously meet and play together. Our next prototypes will try to reproduce and even beat the efficiency of *Collective Loops* in this sense.

One of the most important revelations of this work has been an idea of modularity that does not only apply to the functional modules used to create an application, but also to individual elements of interaction and rendering distributed over the environment. Especially in the context of applications that already consist of a highly distributed network of synchronized communicating devices (i.e. the users' mobile devices) it is evident that all other interactive elements (i.e. sensors, displays, actuators) could be developed as individual (web) clients that use the same services provided by the platform.

ACKNOWLEDGEMENTS

Collective Loops has been developed in the framework of the *CoSiMa* (http://cosima.ircam.fr/) project coordinated by Ircam and supported by the French National Research Agency (ANR-13-CORD-0010). We would like to thank our project partners for their contributions to the development of the installation and its showings, especially Christophe Aubry (ID Scènes), Christophe Domino (ESBA TALM), as well as Uroš Petrevski and Jean-Louis Frechin (NoDesign). We are also grateful to Viviane Gal, Filipe Pais, Olive Ryorp, Élodie Tincq, and Jules Zimmermann for their help with the user study.

REFERENCES

1. Ableton. 2015. Link – Play Together. http://www.ableton.com/en/link/.
2. Apple Inc. 2011. GarageBand for iOS. http://www.apple.com/ios/garageband/.
3. Tina Blaine and Sidney Fels. 2003. Contexts of Collaborative Musical Experiences. In *NIME Proceedings*. Montreal, Quebec, Canada.
4. Kevin Curran. 2012. The Future of Web and Mobile Game Development. *International Journal of Cloud Computing and Services Science (IJ-CLOSER)* 1, 1 (2012), 25–34.
5. Janet Echelman and Aaron Koblin. 2014. Unnumbered Sparks. http://www.unnumberedsparks.com/.
6. Golan Levin et al. 2001. Dialtones, a Telesymphony. http://www.telesymphony.com/.
7. Usman Haque. 2007. Evoke. http://www.haque.co.uk/evoke.php.
8. Johan Huizinga. 1949. *Homo Ludens*. Routledge & Kegan Paul Limited.
9. Petra Isenberg, Danyel Fisher, Meredith Ringel Morris, Kori Inkpen, and Mary Czerwinski. 2010. An Exploratory Study of Co-located Collaborative Visual Analytics Around a Tabletop Display. In *Visual Analytics Science and Technology (VAST), 2010 IEEE Symposium on*. IEEE, 179–186.
10. Pradthana Jarusriboonchai, Sus Lundgren, Thomas Olsson, Joel Fischer, Nemanja Memarovic, Stuart Reeves, PawełWoźniak, and Olof Torgersson. 2014. Personal or Social?: Designing Mobile Interactions for Co-located Interaction. In *Proceedings of NordiCHI '14: Fun, Fast, Foundational*. ACM, New York, NY, USA, 829–832.
11. Sergi Jordà, Martin Kaltenbrunner, Günter Geiger, and Ross Bencina. 2005. The reacTable. In *ICMC Proceedings*.
12. Ville Karavirta and Lasse Hakulinen. 2012. Educational Accelerometer Games for Computer Science. In *mLearn (CEUR Workshop Proceedings)*, Vol. 955. CEUR-WS.org, 216–219.
13. Nima Kaviani, Matthias Finke, and Rodger Lea. 2009. Encouraging crowd interaction with large displays using handheld devices. In *Crowd Computer Interaction Workshop at CHI*.
14. Korg Inc. 2010. iElectribe for iPhone. http://www.korg.com/us/products/software/korg_ielectribe_for_iphone/.
15. Peter Gall Krogh, Martin Ludvigsen, and Andreas Lykke-Olesen. 2004. "Help Me Pull That Cursor" A Collaborative Interactive Floor Enhancing Community Interaction. *Australasian J. of Inf. Systems* 11, 2 (2004).
16. Jean-Philippe Lambert, Sébastien Robaszkiewicz, and Norbert Schnell. 2016. Synchronisation for Distributed Audio Rendering over Heterogeneous Devices, in HTML5. In *Web Audio Conference*.
17. Andrés Lucero, Jaakko Keränen, and Tero Jokela. 2010. Social and Spatial Interactions: Shared Co-located Mobile Phone Use. In *CHI EA*. ACM, New York, NY, USA, 3223–3228.
18. Sus Lundgren, Joel E. Fischer, Stuart Reeves, and Olof Torgersson. 2015. Designing Mobile Experiences for Collocated Interaction. In *CSCW Proceedings*.
19. Mills, Delaware, Martin, Burbank, and Kasch. 2010. *Network Time Protocol Version 4: Protocol and Algorithms Specification*. Standards Track RFC 5905. Internet Engineering Task Force (IETF).
20. Jieun Oh, Jorge Herrera, Nicholas J. Bryan, Luke Dahl, and Ge Wang. 2010. Evolving The Mobile Phone Orchestra. In *NIME Proceedings*. Sydney, Australia.
21. Michel Peeters, Carl Megens, Elise van den Hoven, Caroline Hummels, and Aarnout Brombacher. 2013. Social Stairs: Taking the Piano Staircase towards Long-Term Behavioral Change. In *Persuasive Technology*. Lecture Notes in Computer Science, Vol. 7822. Springer Berlin Heidelberg, 174–179.
22. Nicolas Rasamimanana, Frédéric Bevilacqua, Julien Bloit, Norbert Schnell, Emmanuel Fléty, Andrea Cera, Uros Petrevski, and Jean-Louis Frechin. 2012. The Urban Musical Game: Using Sport Balls As Musical Interfaces. In *CHI EA*. ACM, New York, NY, USA, 1027–1030.
23. Thomas Reitmaier, Pierre Benz, and Gary Marsden. 2013. Designing and Theorizing Co-located Interactions. In *CHI Proceedings*. ACM, New York, NY, USA, 381–390.
24. Christopher Small. 1998. *Musicking: The Meanings of Performing and Listening*. University Press of New England.
25. Atau Tanaka, Baptiste Caramiaux, and Norbert Schnell. 2013. MubuFunkScatShare: Gestural Energy and Shared Interactive Music. In *CHI EA*. ACM, New York, NY, USA, 2999–3002.
26. James R. Wallace, Stacey D. Scott, Taryn Stutz, Tricia Enns, and Kori Inkpen. 2009. Investigating teamwork and taskwork in single- and multi-display groupware systems. *Personal and Ubiquitous Computing* 13, 8 (2009), 569–581.
27. Ge Wang, Georg Essl, Deutsche Telekom, and Henri Penttinen. 2008. MoPho: Do Mobile Phones Dream of Electric Orchestras. In *ICMC Proceedings*. 29.

Learning from the Crackle Exhibition

Kristina Andersen
STEIM
Amsterdam, Netherlands
kristina@tinything.com

Nicholas Ward
University of Limerick
Limerick, Ireland
nicholas.ward@ul.ie

ABSTRACT
This paper describes the Crackle exhibition, an interactive exhibition presented at the Stedelijk Museum in Amsterdam in 1975. We propose that it can be seen as a foreshadowing of aspects of the current state of the art of TEI avant la lettre; and that there might not only be value in examining historical work to construct a longer historical framework for TEI, but that the methods used in the construction of this exhibition might be useful in constructing new visions that foreshadow into the future from our current technological position. We present a detailed description of the exhibition based on documentation and interviews with the people who built it, and suggest that the current state of disappearing computers and embedded computational ability in everyday devices form an opportunity to imagine novel interaction paradigms that may transcend the digital in a similar way as the Crackle exhibition in 1975 transcended the electrical.

ACM Classification Keywords
H.5.m. Information Interfaces and Presentation (e.g. HCI): Miscellaneous

Author Keywords
Tangible Interaction; Magic; Performance; Ideation; Exhibitions

INTRODUCTION
With this paper we want to respond directly to the Japanese proverb: 温故知新 (On-ko-chi-shin), "you need to recall the past to understand the future" included in this year's call for participation. We would like to suggest an extension to which 'past' is pertinent to the TEI community, and in doing so propose that an analysis of a broader selection of prior work may yield useful insights into both the design process and the characteristics of interactive devices.

TEI '17, March 20 - 23, 2017, Yokohama, Japan.

ACM ISBN 978-1-4503-4676-4/17/03 ...$15.00.
http://dx.doi.org/10.1145/3024969.3024997

Figure 1. Interactive crackle objects.

In support of this proposition we present a description and analysis of a very specific moment in the past; namely the development and presentation of an exhibition of interactive works in 1975. This exhibition involved the development of 20 interactive (electric) pieces loosely connected by the theme of the family home. It was developed by Michel Waisvisz in collaboration with engineers at STEIM (the STudio for Electro-Instrumental Music, an independent electronic music research centre based in Amsterdam, Netherlands), on a commission from The Stedelijk Museum Amsterdam. The exhibition was entitled, 'The Crackle Exhibition, an exhibition of musical instruments, theater props, artifacts and domestic appliances' and ran from the 26 September to the 2nd of November in 1975 (See Figure 1).

THE CRACKLE CONTEXT
By 1975 Michel Waisvisz had already been working on concepts of 'crackle' for a number of years. Broadly speaking he would touch the electronic boards of radios and other sound producing devices, creating 'crackling' sounds that where a direct result of the 'wet' fingers connecting various parts of the circuits.

Describing the process in an article from 2004 [12], he writes: "Some time in the early-sixties I started touching the inside of my fathers short-wave radio receivers. Before that with my brother René I had given 'concerts' at home by placing our fingers on circuit boards of transistor radios that were 'wrongly', but usefully, interconnected with wires. The little electrical shocks were nice and the changes in the sound were exciting and magic mind-openers. Through touch I was able to start playing with short wave sounds in a way that would later become 'sound music'."

He goes on to state: "During this development process we started extending the concept to a whole range of theatrical instruments and playable objects. All sorts of household objects were wired and would become musical 'Crackle' instruments: One could play music by pouring tea into wired cups or by sticking connected spoons and forks in the mouth... Floors, bicycles, chairs, bedsheets, clothes, cuckoo-clocks, books, string instruments and plants were wired and connected to 'Crackle' circuits and would be played in music theatre performances."

These objects went on to form the content of the 1975 'Crackle' exhibition, which we will describe in this paper. The exhibition can be seen as a snapshot of a particular set of tangible, touchable electronic devices at this particular moment in time.

A TEI CONTEXT

Since the pioneering work of Fitzmaurice and Ishii [5], the term tangible user interface (TUI) has gained use outside of the HCI community in product design, architecture, computer science and interactive arts. Whereas the early definition of a TUI specifically emphasises the idea of physically interacting with and representing data, the notion of tangibly interacting with a digital device has been expanded to form the basis of a general approach to digital interface design.

Hornecker and Buur use the phrase 'Tangible Interaction' to encompass, 'a broad range of systems and interfaces relying on embodied interaction, tangible manipulation, physical representation of data, embeddedness in real space, and digitally augmenting physical spaces' [7]. Within this field they distinguish three different viewpoints: a data centered view, pursued in Computer Science and HCI and most easily seen to include the notion of TUIs as defined by Ishii; an expressive movement centered view from industrial and product design; and a space centered view, influenced by architecture and the arts.

In expanding and contextualising tangible interaction in this way, a narrative or story is shaped. One which evolves from the problematising of the GUI and WIMP paradigm of interaction, to the development of graspables, and later to the expanded notion of tangible.

But this move lands us in a funny space. The objects we are concerned with, and the scenarios of their use, are diverse. As a field of research it is united more by a particular sense of interaction experience, connected with a concern for the "whole human" , embodied, intelligent, empathetic and messy [13], than by any focus on digital devices or computationally enabled interaction. This broadness calls upon us to recognize that perhaps there has been something overlooked in how tangibility has been considered beyond the digital and pushes us to look further outside of HCI for inspiration and knowledge.

THE CRACKLE EXHIBITION: METHOD AND MATERIALS

We base our description and analysis of the Crackle exhibition on material archived at STEIM and the Stedelijk in Amsterdam and in depth interviews with Johan den Biggelaar and Nico Bes, who both worked on the development of the exhibition as technicians based at STEIM. In the following we will describe the objects in the exhibition and attempt a contemporary reading of the technologies they imply.

For the exhibition 20 interactive objects were delivered. They were placed in a gallery at the Stedelijk arranged in the form of a traditional house or living space (See Figure 2). Many of the exhibits presented a novel or everyday object, that had been 'crackled', i.e. given an additional interactive function with a sound output. It is worth noting that these objects were all essentially variations on the same theme: They are all touchable devices that produce sound based on combining analogue electronic circuits with finger contacts. The objects were humorous and lighthearted, aimed at bringing novel or artistic interaction techniques and technology to a wide audience of non-experts and children as well as artists and performers. Alongside these crackled everyday items were presented variations and prototypes of the popular hand-held electronic musical instrument known now as the cracklebox.

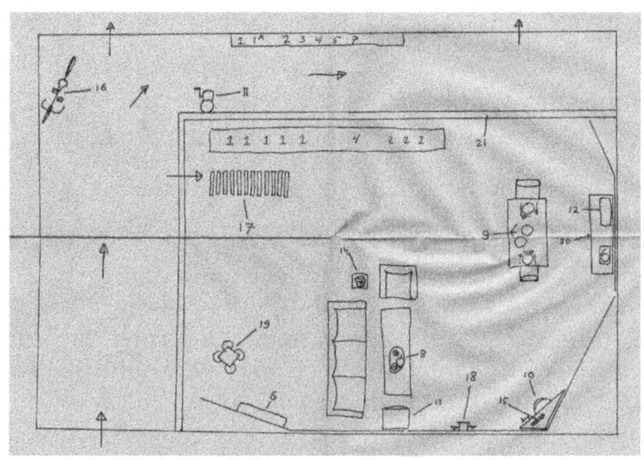

Figure 2. Plan of the exhibition.

In the following we present a selection of these objects, grouped by input modality.

Crackle Synth and Crackle Boxes

The crackle box had already been in development since the 1960's. Dissatisfied with the interfaces on commercial synthesisers Michel Waisvisz developed an alternative input for the commercially available Putney synthesiser, which used the direct contact of the skin of the performer on a conductive contact to enable nuanced analogue control [12].

This work evolved into a large standalone synthesizer which included a similar direct contact interface. Four of these devices, coupled with a bespoke battery powered speaker were included in the exhibition.

A further version of the device, entitled the 'mini-kracker', was developed which integrated a small speaker, battery power, synth and interface into a small box (exhibit 1a). This is the device which later became the crackle box. These pieces were laid out on a counter top for visitors to perform with (See Figure 3).

Figure 3. Girl playing with crackle box.

Blowing Crackle and Crackle Candles

The exhibition contained two pieces, numbered 5 and 15 in the exhibit plan, which responded to users breath. The blowing crackle was a version of the mini crackle box, which used a piezo electric film sensor placed in a tube as a breath sensor, in addition to 4 finger touch inputs. The breath sensor speaker, crackle synth circuit, and 4 touch sensors were arrranged in a tube. The player blew through the tube whilst playing the touch sensors.

The second of these was a candelabra with five electric candle-style bulbs. Embedded in the stalk of this was a Thermistor which was configured so that when air was blown over the thermistor, the candle-bulbs brightened: the reverse of the expected output (See Figure 4).

Crank Fire and Crank Power

These two exhibits, numbered 9 and 10 in the exhibit plan, were based around turning a crank. In the first an electric fire's heat was controlled by the turning of a crank. When a visitor turned the crank the fire warmed up. In the second the crank was connected so as to power a range of different household items including a vacuum cleaner, coffee grinder and a fan. When turned all of these items came to life generating quite the racket [den Biggelaar, personal communication].

Raay Kraaker and Crackle Radio

The Raay kraaker was inspired by the ideophone works of Dick Raaymaker [10]. In these a speaker is essentially

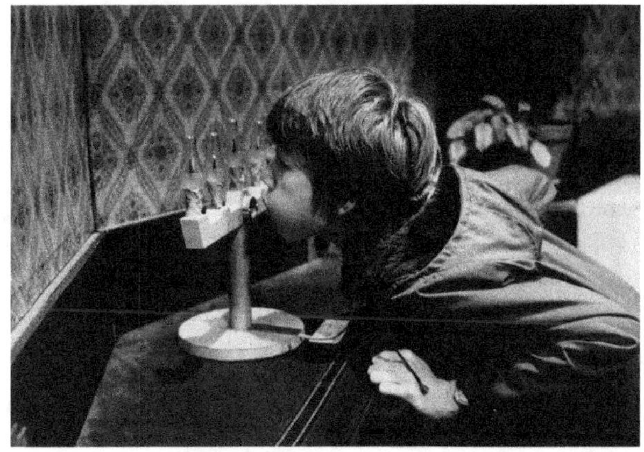

Figure 4. Boy blowing out electric candle bulbs.

connected directly to a battery. However, the circuit contains a 'switch', where one contact is a metal strip on the speaker cone and the other is a metal pin. This 'switch' is closed by touching the pin against the speaker which causes current to flow and the speaker to move, thereby breaking or disturbing the contact. The metal pin bounces against the metal strip on the loudspeaker cone. In the Raay Kraaker both pin and strip are also connected to a crackle circuit. Variations on the sound and behaviour are obtained by holding the stylus tighter or looser in the hand and by a switch that reverses the direction of the cone movement.

The Crackle Radio integrated the above Raay Kraaker setup in a radio. In addition to the interaction by touching the pin to the contact on the speaker, the radio also intermittently received "a radio program on cracking issues" (See Figure 5).

Figure 5. Tuning the crackle radio.

Crackle Clock

The Crackle clock, exhibit 18 in the exhibit plan, is special since it is not interactive, in the sense that it does not require user input or touch. The clock contained a very simple circuit, again inspired by Dick Raaymakers ideophone [10]. In this case the weights of the clock were replaced with batteries. The batteries were connected to two speakers embedded in the clocks decorative front, one on each side of the clock face. The connection however was broken by a switch consisting of the minute hand and a brush contact placed at each numeral. Every five minutes the clock would begin to 'crackle' in a manner that sonified the second by second ticking motion of the minute hand as it brushed across each numeral (See Figure 6).

Figure 6. The crackle clock with batteries for pendulum.

Crackle Television

The crackle television, exhibit 13, consisted of a TV with a simple video synthesizer which generated visuals similar to Lissajou curves [4]. Sitting in the chair and putting ones feet on the table switched on the TV. A remote control was created using the same type of touch sensor as the crackle box but embedded in a free standing ashtray. This enabled the user to choose between watching a recorded program on crackle subjects and creating electronic images via the simple video synthesis circuit (See Figure 7).

Figure 7. Watching the crackle television.

Light Kraaker

Exhibit number 6 consisted of a hand-held tube, approximately eight inches long, which contained a simple sound synthesizer including a speaker and battery. The synthesiser' s output was modulated by a light dependent resistor embedded in the end of the tube. Accompanying this was a wall hung light box which illuminated a graphical score. The user could explore the score and create sound by placing the tube to their ear and then moving the other end along the pattern on the lightbox (See Figure 8).

Figure 8. Listening to the images.

Kraak Telefon

The Kraak Telefon, exhibit 14, made use of a tape delay system connected to a telephone. When a user spoke into the receiver they would hear themselves several seconds later (See Figure 9).

Crackle Bicycle

The crackle bicycle, labeled 16 in the plan, was placed on a stand in the gallery, just outside of the living room

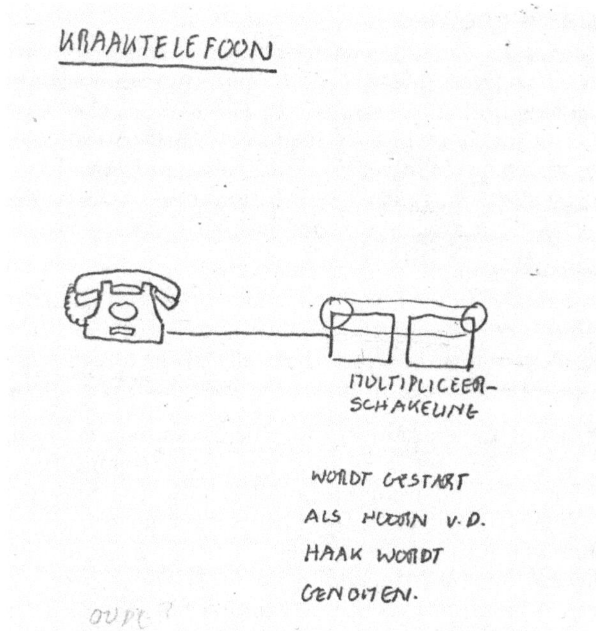

Figure 9. Sketch of the crackle telephone.

Figure 10. Crackle bicycle.

space. Six speakers were attached to the bicycle frame pointing out in different directions (See Figure 10). Each speaker was connected to a dynamo arranged so that it connected to the tire and was driven, when the wheel was spun. A small panel with buttons was mounted on the handlebar (perhaps to allow selection of different speakers). The catalogue for the exhibition proposes that,"in the dark you can find your way by listening to the reflections of the speaker sound."

UNDERSTANDING THE EXHIBITS

Several of the works in the exhibition had been developed by Michel Waisvisz over the years preceding the exhibition, and in the period that followed he continued to elaborate these ideas. An exhibition in Bourges in France in the summer of 1975 presented the crackle boxes, the crackle bicycle and the crackle clock. An exhibition of some of the crackle boxes were also installed at NINT [2]. The plate, knife and fork appeared in Utrecht at Hoogt in February 1977 [12]. The final version of the crackle boxes are still on sale from STEIM today (http://steim.org/product/cracklebox/).

As mentioned above these exhibits can be seen as a series of improvisations around the theme of "touching electronics". Throughout the development process the central aim was to disrupt and challenge the"do not touch" exhibition mentality of the museum, and instead trust the audience with fragile equipment and allow things to break and be repaired [den Biggelaar, private correspondence].

The work process was fast and iterative, the team is described by the surviving members as essentially riffing on the theme with an underlying ethos of building every idea, even the silly ones. As such humour and laughter is central in both how the work was developed, and in how the the work was presented.

This riffing on a small set of circuits (the business end) and a small set of input (the interface) essentially foreshadows the separation of interface and the engine, so common in digital systems, and establishes a diverse, yet arguably similar, set of interactions.

Exhibits such as the Dinner Service and Teapot (See Figure 11) - with their wires exposed and the sound generator separate - present examples of systems defined by a clear and explicit separation of the interface and engine: a paradigm that came to define the characteristics of computer based music performance much later and of course one which defines interaction with desktop computing in general. But also alongside these, several exhibits showed a real concern for the type of interaction enabled by totally self contained and encapsulated devices: the mini kraaker, cuckoo clock, candelabra and crackle radio for example. Taken together then, we see within the exhibition a foreshadowing of both the concerns that lead to the development of TUI for desktop and also the possibilities and challenges that arise when computation becomes embedded, mobile and hidden.

Figure 11. Crackle dinner.

Technology as a Magical Unknown

With the current fulfillment of the much anticipated 'disappearance' of the computer [1], technologies are shrinking to become barely visible [3], and any new technological ability must now be believed rather than understood, and as a consequence, technological advances increasingly require suspension of disbelief in a manner similar to Hayes' definition of naive physics [6]. At the same time the so-called internet of things is providing us with a vast array of everyday objects with an additional digital layer [9].

Add to this the emergence of micro or nano-computing, AI and robotics, and it is appears that we are at a point where our notions of technology are about be re-framed in a manner that might recall the transition from the electronic to the digital in the 70's and 80's [8]. In order to understand what this might mean, for the way we will interact with our environments in the future, we suggest looking further backwards towards the experimental art and everyday technology objects of the past.

Histories of Objects

Øritsland and Buur [14] demonstrate the value of revisiting technological objects in their review of products designed by Danfoss. Through an analysis of control devices designed over the course of the 20th century, they explore the question of interaction style, showing how in this case the products became less and less embodied over time and thus manifesting a similar move from physical to digital.

In a similar manner we might consider the crackle exhibition as a cultural foreshadowing of the impending move towards the tangible and touchable everyday devices we would now recognize as IoT [9].

FORESHADOWING

The value of looking back at these examples of early interactive work may not lie in extensive analysis of technologies and interactions. In the case of the 'Crackle' exhibition, it is already becoming hard to find the people who were involved in building it, and even harder to find visitors and gather impressions of how the exhibition worked as a audience experience.

Instead we might look at these kinds of art exhibits from the past as examples of visionary objects. The artist' desire to express something that cannot yet be done, drives the creation of objects, that effectively foreshadows aspects of mainstream interactive works 40 years later.

Oppenheimer famously described scientists as 'living always at the "edge of mystery" - the boundary of the unknown' and Rebecca Solnit echoes this sentiment in A Field Guide to Getting Lost: 'scientists transform the unknown into the known, haul it in like fishermen; artist get you out into that dark sea' [11]. These exploratory art works can be said to be examples of objects retrieved from such 'dark seas'.

CONCLUSION

We believe that the 'Crackle' exhibition presents us with a couple of recommendations for how we might construct such exploratory visionary objects.

The first recommendation is to, instead of working on a particular technological opportunity, focus on the artistic vision or desire, regardless of whether it is actually build-able or 'timely'. We might know which experience we desire, but not how it will manifest exactly.

The second recommendation is to use absolutely any technology available to construct the effect of such an artistic vision, even if we might have to use theatricality and messy solutions to arrive at a desired experience.

The third and most obvious strategy is to build multiple variations on a given theme. Essentially the crackle process teaches us to build every idea, no matter how silly or difficult, in a similar way to how we might approach a brainstorm. This is effective, when the envisioned object cannot yet be build; none of the crackle exhibits fulfilled the artistic and technological desires of the team, but together the 20 objects began to draw an outline of what that desire might be.

And finally we take away an appreciation for the light-heartedness and humor present in these 'crackled' objects. We cannot predict and truly envision the technology and paradigm shifts to come, but we can build and iterate and take the silly deadly serious. Who knows, something might come from it...

ACKNOWLEDGMENTS

We would like to thank the archives of Michel Waisvisz and the Stedelijk; as well as Johan den Biggelaar and Nico Bes for helping us with the interpretation of the material.

REFERENCES

1. 2003. The Disappearing Computer. (2003). http://www.disappearing-computer.eu/
2. 2016. History - Science Center NEMO. (2016). https://www.nemosciencemuseum.nl/en/about-nemo/organization/nemosciencemuseum/history/
3. 2016. National Nanotechnology Initiative. (2016). http://www.nano.gov/
4. H. Martyn Cundy and A. P. Rollett. 1981. *Mathematical Models* (3rd edition ed.). Tarquin Publications, Norfolk.
5. George W. Fitzmaurice, Hiroshi Ishii, and William A. S. Buxton. 1995. Bricks: Laying the Foundations for Graspable User Interfaces. In *Proceedings of the SIGCHI Conference on Human Factors in Computing Systems (CHI '95)*. ACM Press/Addison-Wesley Publishing Co., New York, NY, USA, 442–449. DOI: http://dx.doi.org/10.1145/223904.223964
6. Patrick J Hayes. 1978. The naive physics manifesto. In *Expert Systems in the Microelectronic Age*, D. Michie (Ed.). Edinburgh University Press, Edinburgh, 242–270.
7. Eva Hornecker and Jacob Buur. 2006. Getting a Grip on Tangible Interaction: A Framework on Physical Space and Social Interaction. In *Proceedings of the SIGCHI Conference on Human Factors in Computing Systems (CHI '06)*. ACM, New York, NY, USA, 437–446. DOI: http://dx.doi.org/10.1145/1124772.1124838
8. Kevin Kelly. 2010. *What Technology Wants.* Penguin Group, New York, USA.
9. Robert Kranenburg. 2007. *The Internet of Things. A critique of ambient technology and the all-seeing network of RFID.* Network Notebooks 02, Institute of Network Cultures, Amsterdam.
10. Joke Mulder, Arjen; Brouwer. 2008. *Dick Raaymakers: A Monograph.* V2 publishing, Rotterdam.
11. Rebecca Solnit. 2006. *A Field Guide to Getting Lost* (reprint edition ed.). Penguin Books, New York.
12. Michel Waisvisz. 2004. Crackle.org - Cracklebox. (2004). http://crackle.org/CrackleBox.htm
13. Peter Wright and John McCarthy. 2008. Empathy and Experience in HCI. In *Proceedings of the SIGCHI Conference on Human Factors in Computing Systems (CHI '08)*. ACM, New York, NY, USA, 637–646. DOI: http://dx.doi.org/10.1145/1357054.1357156
14. Trond Are Øritsland and Jacob Buur. 2000. Taking the best from a company history - designing with interaction styles. In *Proceedings of the 3rd conference on Designing interactive systems: processes, practices, methods, and techniques (DIS '00)*. ACM, New York, NY, USA, 27–38. DOI: http://dx.doi.org/10.1145/347642.347658

Tacit Narratives: Surfacing Aesthetic Meaning by Using Wearable Props and Focusing

Claudia Núñez-Pacheco
University of Sydney
148 City Road NSW, Australia
claudia.nunezpacheco@sydney.edu.au

Lian Loke
University of Sydney
148 City Road NSW, Australia
lian.loke@sydney.edu.au

ABSTRACT
Although not always consciously collected, bodily information shapes the way we construct meaning. By paying attention towards the subtle changes of the soma, it is possible to access part of the ongoing source of meaning and self-knowledge contained in the inner self. In this paper, we describe how the use of wearable devices to amplify direct perception in conjunction with the somatic technique *Focusing* can facilitate the articulation of the tacit dimension of people's experiences. The perceptible feedback generated by wearable props opens up a dialogue space between the soma and intellect, acting as a facilitator to connect people with unknown aesthetic aspects of their personal stories. Beyond mere amplification of sensation, wearable technology can potentially assist in the ongoing human process of meaning-generation.

Author Keywords
HCI; wearables; aesthetics of interaction; somaesthetics; Focusing; experience; meaning.

ACM Classification Keywords
H.5.m. Information interfaces and presentation (e.g., HCI): Miscellaneous.

INTRODUCTION
As a natural occurrence, our bodies constantly collect sensory information from the interaction with the world. Although not consciously collected, bodily information shapes the way we construct meaning [12,21]. By paying attention towards the subtle changes of the soma, it is possible to access part of the ongoing source of meaning and self-knowledge contained in the inner self. Under this principle, wearable technology in conjunction with somatic techniques, can offer novel ways to access the tacit dimension of self-knowledge, helping to reveal aesthetic aspects of our experiences that would normally remain unexplored. To access these non-explicit dimensions, some strategies promoting spaces for inner self-dialogue are necessary. In line with the principles of slow technology [14, 15] and beyond the goals of efficiency and promptness of action pursued by traditional approaches, we believe that the philosophical aims of *reflection,* and *focus* should be values of interest embodied by technologies promoting self-exploration. A focus on a more reflective approach can offer fresh ways of understanding how the lived body interacts with artefacts, products and spaces [22].

TEI '17, March 20 - 23, 2017, Yokohama, Japan

ACM 978-1-4503-4676-4/17/03...$15.00
DOI: http://dx.doi.org/10.1145/3024969.3024979

In this paper, we describe how the use of wearable devices to amplify direct perception in conjunction with the somatic technique Focusing [8,13] can facilitate the articulation of the tacit dimension of people's experiences. Focusing is a psychosomatic technique that uses body scanning and heightened attention towards the inner self as a doorway to access personal discoveries. It can be facilitated in one-to-one sessions or through group exercises. In our Focusing exercises, participants are prompted to sense, experience and filter out personal narratives through their bodily senses, related to things they love and make them feel inspired. Additionally, we include wearable props to add layers of richness to participants' somatic dimension, eliciting a transformative process of their personal stories. By using these artefacts, we explore aesthetic opportunities emerging from sensing direct stimuli on the lived body, as an active source of meaning-generation. The perceptible feedback generated by wearable props opens up a dialogue space between the soma and intellect, acting as a facilitator to connect people with unknown aesthetic aspects of their personal stories.

Beyond the act of understanding the self, a focus on the lived body can open up opportunities to devise artefacts that have not yet been invented, as proposed by Wilde and Anderson [33,34] in their OWL project. In this example, participants were asked to use placebo objects as props [4] to pay attention to the lived body in unfamiliar ways, with the purpose of imagining new technology possibilities. In a similar vein, we also use props as explorative tools, in our case to inquiry about the process of meaning-generation through the body as a way of accessing the unknown, promoting values such as reflection and curiosity.

Meaning-generation is a multifaceted human process that implies *sensing, acknowledging, and reflecting* [12, p12]. The combination of Focusing with the stimuli generated by our artefacts, facilitates this tri-faceted process by eliciting an interactive exchange between the bodily dimension and the device's output, as articulated in our previous research on the cycle of self-awareness occurring in the lived body when interacting with wearable devices [24]. Drawing on Dreyfus' interpretation of Heidegger's literature and the importance of deliberate attention to access curiosity [3], our initial hypothesis was that simple and subtle stimuli applied on the body could be a helpful tool to enhance our focus on experiential aspects of the self, as also suggested by the following literature [5,7,17]. Apart from enhancing bodily focus, in this paper we describe how using gentle stimuli (such as heat and vibration) could shape the way personal stories are perceived.

In this paper, we introduce our explorations with props and the somatic technique, Focusing into two modalities: workshop and one-to-one sessions. We document how our participant's narratives are shaped by the utilisation of simple stimuli and an enhanced focus on bodily self-awareness. As a result, beyond perception-amplification, the use of simple stimuli contributes to the generation of fresh meaning, arising from the tacit dimension of people's experiences. Our method has proven useful to: 1) bridge the tacit and the tangible dimensions, by integrating perceptible stimuli into memories, 2) Mapping the body terrain, as sensations move around the body and finally 3) the use of devices work either as a mirror of the sense of self, or as scaffolding for new meaning generation.

Our objective is not the introduction of "readily easy to interact" devices in the first place, but rather understanding how the use of Focusing in conjunction with wearable stimuli could potentially work as a coherent system for self-observation. Our primary contribution is the provision of artefacts as wearable props that contribute to the task of self-knowledge by recognising the interactional nature of the body as a valid constructor of meaning, facilitating spaces for authentic self-dialogue.

The body as a generative tool of meaning

Although the interest in the body has flourished as a relevant topic in HCI academia, the lived body is not a prevailing topic in theory and practice [16]. The sensory-aesthetic aspects of the lived body, including intuition and meaning-construction (which have a strong felt component) [21], are rarely discussed as potential materials or inspiration for design. Current technologies for bodily exploration tend to follow normative conventions of well-being leaning towards control and rationalisation of behaviour [26]. Still relevant nowadays, as a result of the emergence of the *new health consciousness movement* during the 70's [1], the care of the self is linked with concepts of moral responsibility, deepening the perception of the body as a battlefield. Bodily intuition – or what some might identify as "gut feelings" – seems to be understood as a problem to be fixed [35], instead of a natural occurrence with potential for creative action. In this scenario, it is not strange that ideas emerging from pragmatic aesthetics, and particularly from *Somaesthetics* have gained so much interest in part of the HCI community, by offering an alternative view from Cartesian ways that tend to see the body as in need of being controlled and monitored. In our perspective, we embrace the *somaesthetic* philosophy, by placing the lived body as the core element of our perceptual realm, thus shaping the way we understand our being in the world.

In the following section, we introduce the three key theoretical references informing this research: Shusterman's proposal of *Somaesthetics* [29,30], Gendlin's *philosophy of the implicit* [10,11], materialised through his practical method *Focusing* [8,13], and Dewey's ideas on the art of experience [2], to understand how aesthetic experiences emerge from everyday acts, however also acknowledging the challenges of documenting the aesthetic qualities of such experiences.

Somaesthetics and the Phenomenology of carrying forward: Acknowledging the somatic dimension

Devoted to the aesthetic appreciation of the experiential body, Somaesthetics [29,30] is a philosophical proposal that places the importance of *bodily cultivation* and *improvement* at the centre of the philosophical activity. This aim for improvement should be driven by subjective appreciation instead of being shaped according to an ideal representation of how a human body should be [29,31]. Instead of engaging in the traditional philosophical critique on the unreliability of our senses, Shusterman has contributed with a theoretical framework advocating for the self-improvement of our bodily responses towards the experiential pursuit of happiness, virtue and political agency [30]. In order to do so, it is important to engage in self-examination, cultivating somatic self-awareness towards a better understanding of the self. The importance of somatic awareness is not only useful to overcome potentially harmful behaviour, but also to control the image we project to the external world in a more purposeful way [29].

As we have done, some designers, researchers and design schools have put into practice the idea of the body as a generative source of ideas and meaning, by placing the lived, self-agentic body at the centre of the discourse. From the standpoint of somaesthetics–one of our main theoretical references–Lee, Lim and Shusterman [23] materialised some principles emerging from practical and pragmatic dimensions of somaesthetics into the design ideation process, by advocating for the utilisation of the lived body as a crafting material for shaping design. Schiphorst [28] transferred somaesthetic principles into four themes represented through the artistic installation Soft(n), which explored the somaesthetics of touch: a) experience as sensory and aesthetic; b) poetics of interaction as the centrality of the senses as meaning-constructors, c) the importance of embodiment and its application to physical materials, and d) the semantics of caress or meaning of touch. Höök et al. [17] proposed a general framework of aesthetic qualities embodied by somaesthetical design: a) artefacts should subtly direct the user inwards, b) these should make spaces for reflection, c) interactive devices provide feedback that make sense with the rhythm of the body, and d) these should also facilitate the articulation of experiences.

It is important to note that experience-articulation is a complex task that generally relies on our use of recurrent representational patterns. These patterns refer to language conventions and readily available expression of feelings, which have been in part culturally determined and shaped by our interaction with the social world. As a way to access meaning beyond those patterns, Gendlin [10,11] proposed a *new phenomenology of carrying forward*, which in a similar manner to Shusterman's Somaesthetics also places the subjective body as the centre of interest. Gendlin's approach however, deals with the importance of exploring our tacit, implicit dimension through directing our attention towards manifestations emerging from the inner body as a source of ongoing meaning-making.

Attentive sensing of bodily signals can be a door to access the implicit [12], the ambiguous space between the conscious and unconscious dimensions [13, p.1]. This implicit force is latent, bodily and contains information preceding our representational reality. As a relatable example, we can refer to the act of writing a manuscript, which was also used by Gendlin [10]. For instance, when trying to verbalise your ideas to others about the content of a paper, you might be able to articulate a few points of what you plan to write down. You know these statements are shallow and insufficient compared with what you will express on your manuscript, however you are still able to *sense* that *you know* what the content is going to be. It is an imprecise and slightly unsettling physical sensation that embodies the tension between certainty and uncertainty. The knowledge exists as such, but it remains encapsulated in the implicit, in a non-representational form. We capture this idea in our research, understanding that an important part of the information we collect in our daily lives is awaiting to be articulated. The act of acknowledging our feelings and sensations is just the first step towards an endless source of self-discovery and meaning.

Emerging directly from these concepts, *Focusing* [8,13] is a technique to access the tacit dimension of experience. In our methodology section, we will describe how Focusing guided experiences for groups are designed, and how these should be conducted. By practicing Focusing, we aim to access part of our tacit dimension, materialised by the articulation of the *felt-sense*. Different than culturally recognised emotions, felt-senses are blurry manifestations of feelings, emotions, sensations and metaphors, which are hard to put into words, however facilitated through the guided exercises. Felt-senses contain a bodily quality, as in our previous example, the *feeling of knowing* the content of my paper well, even though it has not yet been written. By establishing a dialogue between body and representational intellect, where the body directs the conversation, we obtain rich, complex and interesting narratives as a result, containing sometimes bits of information people did not notice before the sessions.

Based on these philosophical inspirations, our work aims to acknowledge the role of the body in the generation of meaning. According to Gendlin [10], the implicit dimension never becomes entirely explicit, but rather by attending to our senses in regard to a situation, we consciously *carry part of this implicit dimension* along with us. This idea is particularly relevant to our research, because since the implicit is never revealed in its totality, the inner self becomes a source for endless inspiration, curiosity and aesthetic searching.

Dewey's experience

Returning to the idea of the encapsulated meaning contained by the soma, the implicit dimension is not an inaccessible state of consciousness, but rather a natural and ongoing process. As with the tension of sensing we know something despite its uncertain reality (such as in the example of the manuscript), everyday situations offer plenty of these instances.

As accessing the implicit dimension is something that occurs naturally, aesthetic experiences are important elements in the art of living. The pragmatist philosopher John Dewey [2] introduced the radical notion of aesthetic experiencing as not exclusive and enclosed to the appreciation of fine arts, but actually a part of everyday phenomena. According to Dewey, aesthetic experiences generate a *sense of unity* encapsulated by the event itself [2,p.28]. Aesthetic experiences are also characterised by having a commencement and an outcome, and leaving a lasting sensation of meaningfulness and memorability. For example, dining out with friends can be recognised as a meaningful event by those who lived the experience. Third wave HCI has brought valuable contributions towards Deweyan perspectives in terms of aesthetics of experience [36,37], and how to transfer aesthetic qualities into everyday interactions with artefacts [6,25]. Despite being recognised as meaningful, the task of describing the aesthetic qualities of events is generally quite complex, because an important part of the sense of *meaningfulness* and *completeness* cannot be expressed in its full complexity through common representational language. Dining with friends can be a meaningful experience for a series of reasons, however our descriptions possibly fall short to articulate the deep meaning of these interactions.

The use of the Focusing technique offers a possible way to fill this gap, by acknowledging the sentient body as the door for accessing the tacit dimension, adding new layers of information to more traditional ways of describing phenomena. As we will see in some of the narratives obtained in our studies, this method assists in surfacing out aesthetic qualities of experience through the materialisation of felt-senses, which essentially contain feelings, sensations, memories, thoughts and creative manifestations, sensed as a whole [13]. As such, experiencing the felt-sense generates the sense of "closure" of having an aesthetic experience, revisiting memories and building up fresh meaning in the process.

The exercise of reflecting on experiences that are already important for us does not prevent our senses to generate new meanings and discoveries, therefore extracting new aesthetic qualities. Meaning-generation is an ongoing process [9,10], which evolves at the rhythm of our bodies, emotions, intellect and personal experiences. As pointed out by Shusterman [30], one of the reasons to engage in the act of cultivation resides in the fact our bodies are in constant change, which opens up opportunities for permanent learning and curiosity.

In the following section, we will describe how the use of Focusing, combined with artefacts as props can help us to access the implicit, aesthetic qualities and unfold the emergence of discoveries through people's personal stories.

THE STUDY

We will now describe the method employed to obtain narratives emerging from bodily sensing. In our study, we wanted to find out whether the use of simple stimuli such as heat and vibration would have an effect on people's stories. Before starting the study, we hypothesised that our selection of stimuli could either become *distracting* or *enhancing* in regard to the sensations experienced by our participants. However, after a closer look, we discovered the transformative power of introducing wearable scaffoldings to extract aesthetic meaning.

As physical representations of open-ended questions, our props use basic technology such as vibration motors attached to microcontrollers, as well as non-technological means and materials. The way we use our props shares a few similarities with technology probes [18], specifically in regard to 1) their exploratory quality beyond strict functionality and 2) the deliberate use of limited functionality, allowing the user to interact with open-ended artefacts and complete with their own meaning. Their simplicity is intended to stimulate primary sensations and also support a broad provision of responses. The cyclical nature of the Focusing process reinforces and brings aesthetic qualities from the tacit dimension to the surface of people's consciousness, while wearable devices act as physical handles to reveal unexpected aspects from personal stories. The process of documentation of participants' personal accounts becomes particularly relevant for acknowledging the aesthetic quality of stories and meaning through sensing.

METHOD

The studies were conducted in two main formats: one-to-one interactions, and a group workshop. Our main interest was to analyse the written narratives emerging from the exercises, in order to understand the levels of engagement with people's inner exploration. Seventeen participants have produced a total number of 21 narratives.

One-to-one interactions

In our first iterations, our main interest was to understand whether the use of heat and vibration was useful to acknowledge, anchor and amplify the presence of the felt sense, or on the contrary, if the stimuli would remove people from their inner focus. Two devices were tested, being attached to a glove-like portable pouch, called the Sense Pouch: 1) a small microcontroller (Arduino Mini Pro) with a vibration motor activated by a soft push button (Figure 1). Participants were asked to select their preferred intensity of vibration before commencing with the exercises. Additionally, 2) a small hot water bag emitting a perceived heat of around 50C was also used. Considering the bodily quality of the felt-sense is generally sensed in the upper torso, our handcrafted devices were designed to fit on the hand, and to be placed on the area where sensations were more distinct. To avoid potentially distracting stimuli, pouches were crafted with insulating materials facing the palm of the hand.

A total of five participants were recruited for this first iteration, involving participation in two sessions each. Only one participant–a scholar visiting from abroad–was unable to attend the two sessions due to time limitations. As a result, nine narratives were collected.

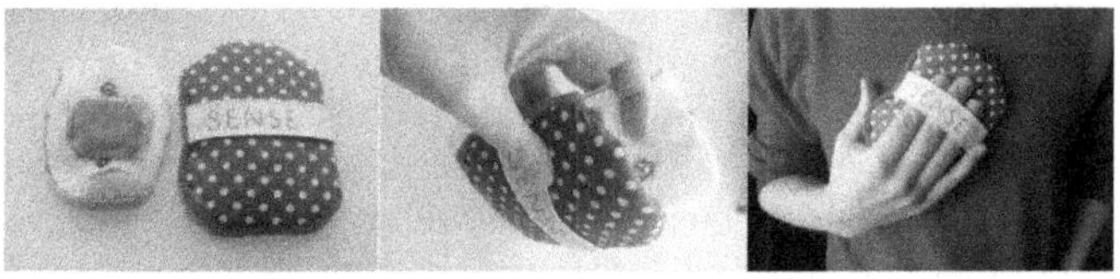

Figure 1- The *Sense pouch* could either contain a vibratory device or a water bag

Sessions were conducted as one-to-one Focusing interviews. As part of the inclusion criteria, we recruited participants with some experience in somatic practices. We used mindfulness meditation as a theoretical reference point to introduce Focusing, by highlighting their similarities and differences. Both practices use body scanning techniques and emphasise the importance of acknowledging and adopting a non-judgemental attitude [27], however whereas in mindfulness meditation the attitude leans towards the act of *letting go* and staying present, in Focusing the approach is *staying with*, as described in the protocol:

"Focusing is similar to meditation, but while in meditation you internally might say 'oh... I am getting distracted by this thought... just acknowledge it and let it go', in Focusing you adopt a curious attitude, something more like: 'oh, a thought or sensation is popping up. Come here and let's have a chat. I won't judge you".

Additionally, we explain the Focusing process as *filtering out ideas through the body*, which means paying attention to the senses before commencing the intellectual dialogue.

After introducing Focusing, participants were asked to think of an object, memory, situation or activity they loved and made them feel inspired. This part of the exercise is inspired by Simon's *love exercise* [32, p.5], which is generally taught to beginner Focusers to stimulate a strong connection with their somatic dimension. The Focusing guided exercise is centred on the topic selected by the participant. The facilitation process of guided exercises can be broken down into three stages: *body scanning, felt-sensing and closing* (Figure 2). We start the exercise by asking participants to close their eyes and follow a brief body scanning, to help them to sensitise their process of filtering out their experiences through the body. Still keeping their eyes closed, participants go through the process of felt-sensing. To facilitate inner conversation, they are guided through a series of questions related to the process of bringing their stories to the process. Participants can keep these stories to themselves, or conversely articulate the experienced sensations through a process of "sensing aloud". What the participant says is carefully listened to and reflected back by the facilitator, enabling either confirmation of what is said, or a further inner search for the term, metaphor or gesture making more sense. This technique is also known as *active listening* or *reflective listening* [20], and is useful to: a) gain empathy towards the participant, b) connect with their personal stories on a deeper level and c) to help the participant to articulate the implicit quality of what is sensed.

In the guided interview, we ask our participants: "why do you think this object or situation is so important to you?", whilst pointing out that this idea of "thinking" is also allowing the situation to be sensed as a whole through the body. During this part of the process, they are instructed to pay attention to their bodily responses, and to place the felt-sense pouch on those areas where the sensations are perceived. After allowing the sensations to set for a moment, we also ask them to define such experiences, by prompting them to find a word, phrase or metaphor representing the tacit dimension of their sensing process. Such a representation or *handle* has to be sensed back, in order to understand whether it makes sense or not. The wearable output is also used as a handle, to highlight or anchor where the felt sense is perceived. After some minutes of inner dialogue and open interaction with the device, participants are informed that the exercise will come to its end in a couple of minutes, before guiding them through a brief body scanning, to close the cycle by gently opening the eyes in their own time.

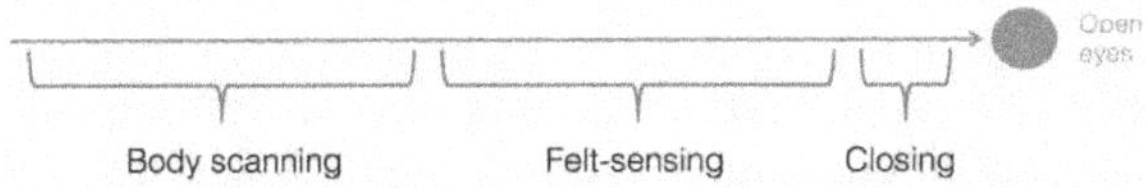

Figure 2- Break down of the Focusing process

After the facilitation is finished, participants were asked to describe and document their Focusing experience in a one-page document. The rules for the documentation process are simple: a) avoid evaluative language, b) descriptive language is desired, c) whilst grammar and traditional writing conventions are not relevant, metaphors are encouraged. The idea of the documentation was to describe the object or situation inspiring love, and how it was felt-sensed through the experience. Additionally, they were asked to complete a body map, highlighting those body areas more actively engaged in the exercises. They were also encouraged to draw symbols and metaphors representing their felt-senses.

Group Workshop of Somatic Evaluation

As part of the contents taught in the studio component of our Master of Interaction Design program, we run a workshop on *somatic evaluation methods*, involving the use of Focusing integrated with other more traditional evaluation tools. A total of twelve students participated in this activity. Since Focusing applied as an ideation method had been introduced in lectures and experienced in some of our tutorials, students were already familiar with the structure of the somatic guided exercises.

Students were instructed to wear two types of devices (see Figure 3), one producing gentle vibration (a glove containing a small button and a vibration motor operated at 3v), and a second non-digital prototype generating a moderate amount of heat (a scarf-like pouch with a small hot water bag inside, emitting a temperature of around 50C). From some considerations emerging from previous iterations, we decided to change the original pouch to allow a more active engagement of the hands during the process.

From a group of twelve students, five wore vibration gloves and seven wore scarfs with water bags. In the first part of the exercise, they were asked to assess the stimulus generated by the device by applying it on different body parts located at the upper torso, which is the area where the felt sense is generally perceived [8]. Aspects such as comfort and wearability were assessed, by completing Likert scales numbered from 1 to 9, where the higher the number, the subtler and more positive the assessed feature. After this initial assessment, the *love exercise* was conducted with the class. Different than in the one-to-one protocol where reflective listening was performed, students were instructed to keep emerging sensations to themselves, and document their ideas, sensations and felt-senses in their answer sheets. The rules for documentation and use of language were the same as in the one-to-one sessions.

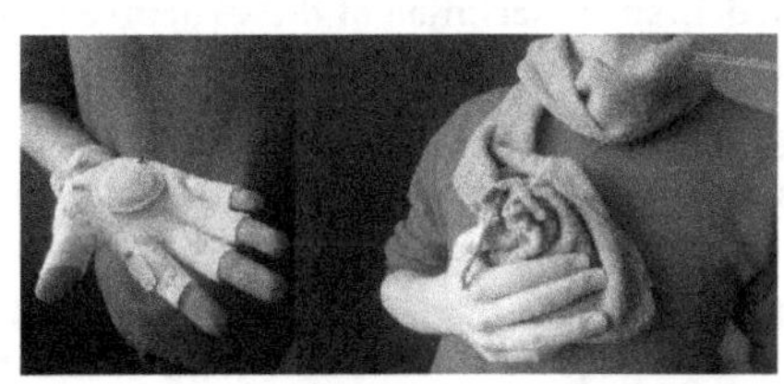

Figure 3- Wearable props used in the workshop: Vibration glove and scarf with water bag

RESULTS

The data obtained in this research can be analysed from multiples perspectives, however this paper focuses on how the use of Focusing and the stimuli generated by the wearable devices influenced the quality of experiences and narratives of our participants.

One-to-one sessions versus group Focusing

In both Focusing modalities, participants connected with their inner dimension in different ways, similar to what Ihde [19] describes in terms of embodiment as *body one* and *body two*. While experiences described as being immersed in the situation are recognised as experienced by the *body one* or the sensorial body, a third person description of phenomenological experiencing is part of the construction of the *body two*, which can be understood as a representationally constructed body. In the same vein, we found two predominant ways of describing embodied experience:

a) Documenting different experiential qualities of the experience as being there

One-to-one sessions demonstrated to be more intimate, reflected in the experiential quality of participant's documentation. The quality of describing the experience as "being there" can be explained by the intimate effect of personalised reflective listening, as well as the inclusion criteria to recruit participants, which in the case of the workshop was not applied. As an example of this (table 1), one of the participants reflected on a happy memory where she and her boyfriend went hiking on a rainy weekend, and described her sensations as she was immersed in the experience. During the session, she wore the vibratory prototype, which in her opinion helped to pinpoint the area where different sensations were emerging.

Dream state - A sense of nostalgia - Memory bubble - Peaceful, calm, carefree, content - Floating sensation - Warm, radiating. Loving and feeling loved, secure. Taking myself to a familiar place - A simple time... perfection, complete.

Table 1. Participant description of *being there*

The experience was different from the last one in terms of the effect at the bodily experience, which in this case lasted longer even when the exercise almost ended. The vibration I felt on my chest was normal in the start, but when I started visualising the scenario, which makes me happy, the vibration felt like spreading to a larger surface area than before. Also it started feel as if my body had become more sensitive to vibration (...)

Table 2. Participant description of the structure of felt-sensing in evaluative language

b) Documenting the structural elements of the experience, by using evaluative language

Even though half of the participants from our workshops also described their stories from the previously described experiential perspective, the other half "evaluated" the session without going into much detail about the source of happiness, despite the fact anonymity of responses was ensured. In the example in table 2, the participant describes the structure of his felt-sensing, by describing the structural elements of the experience, and comparing his session with a Focusing exercise conducted in a previous tutorial activity.

Despite the differences, the collected narratives from our workshop explicitly articulated an enhanced connection with body and emotions, as shown in figures 4 and 5.

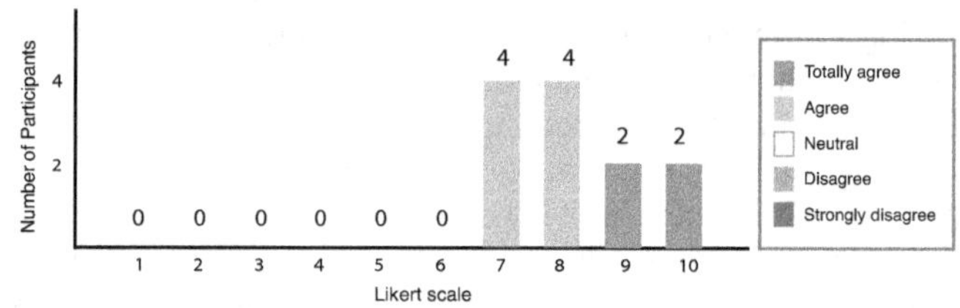

Figure 4. Question 1 (Q1) "The guided experience was more intense that solely thinking about the situation"."

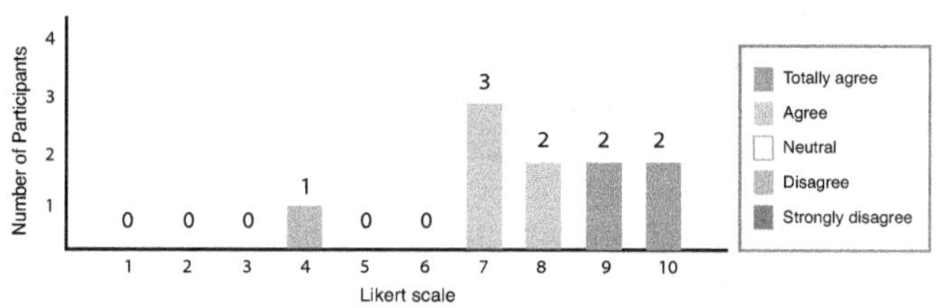

Figure 5. Question 2 (Q2) "The guided experience was useful to discover a new dimension of my experience

General themes

Beyond the utilisation of experiential versus evaluative language in the resulting narratives, the use of our artefacts influenced the course of felt-sensing, and in some cases, the articulation of stories and therefore, the process of meaning-making. Some predominant themes emerged from the analysis of the narratives obtained from the application of the *Love exercise*. In these, the stimuli generated by the devices had different effects in people's bodily self-awareness. In this paper, we do not focus on the subtle differences between vibration and heat, but rather in how the aesthetic qualities of people's narratives are transformed by using Focusing and wearable stimuli.

a. Device stimuli can bridge the tacit with the tangible dimensions

This theme refers to how the use of tangible stimuli and Focusing works as a handle to explore the tacit dimension, giving memories an enhanced bodily character. As a result, apart from its intellectual quality, the process of meaning-generation is perceived as a somatic experience. The use of wearable stimuli assisted in the generation of two main effects: 1) amplification of sensations, leading to the acknowledgement and confirmation of the source of happiness, and 2) the sensation of "being there", transported to the situation or memory. This act of being transported was not only intellectual or creative, but also somatic. In

How the body is mapped	Body language keywords	Possible interpretation
Participant places device on a specific part of the upper torso and stays there.	Calm. Smiley face. Head facing up, like imagining. The device is carefully being held.	Felt-sensing what is loved.
Participant places the device on different parts around the torso, taking some few seconds on each pause.	Slightly frowning, as expressing concentration. Careful movements.	Searching or following the felt sense, as it moves and changes.
Participant places the device on different parts around the torso before staying on one spot.	Slightly frowning, as expressing concentration at first. Then the facial expression changes to calm.	After searching and tracking sensations, the participant finds the felt sense.
Participant places the device on different body parts, taking some few seconds on each pause. Sometimes devices are placed up and down, following a linear trajectory.	Calm, Neutral Rapid movements.	Instead of felt-sensing, the participant is focused on the perceptual qualities given by the prop.
Participant places the device on areas where the felt sense is not generally perceived.	Calm, neutral.	The participant might be trying to match a specific physical memory with the stimulus (i.e. recalling riding a bike and the effort on legs makes the participant to place device on calves)

Table 3: Observations of body language and meaning

our methodology section, we described how participants were instructed to *filter their sensations out through the body* before jumping into thoughts and ideas. As a result of this distillation process, some participants experienced sensing their memories on specific body parts. For instance, participant OM1 pointed out: *"Through reminding the happy moment with my [significant object], I realised that the memory comes from the body part it had contact with. I could remember something from the body part straight away."*

The aesthetic merging between the worlds of the tacit dimension of memories and the tangible interaction with objects appeared in several of our narratives. It is important to note how aesthetic experiences are ongoing building relations between artefacts and people [36]. Even in more evaluative narratives such as in table 2, the participant describes how vibration was feeling normal, until imagining his happy situation made the sensation spread on his chest. Some of the adjectives collected in this process of immersing and recalling are: *spreading, expanded, amplifying, transported, thought enhancing, grounded.* Participant OM2 who reflected on playing cricket with his friends pointed out: *"Heat helps generate feeling that you are "breathing into" the materiality of the body. E.g. The muscles, which tell a certain story about body, habits and past events"*. By applying the stimulus in combination with Focusing, somaesthetical qualities can be directly accessed through the exploration of the tacit.

b. Devices can function as tools for mapping the body geography of felt-sensing manifestations

As previously discussed, the felt sense is an inner state that not only contains feelings and memories, but also a strong bodily component [13]. When sustained self-awareness is purposely practiced, we can start noticing that these somatic sensations change and move around the body. Our devices were useful to map the body's terrain, helping participants to keep track of these series of inner movements as expressed in table 4.

WM3: *"The experience was perhaps more profoundly felt with the hot water bag. It was possible to more accurately notice parts of the experience. The hot water was also a way to follow awareness/ sensations as it felt and moved through the body"*
OF1: *"The device served as a 'detector'. It helped me detect a part of my body that reacted the most to the experience. It enhanced the sensations and brought meaningful links to what the concert signified for me" (Vibration)*

Table 4: Some examples of devices mapping the body

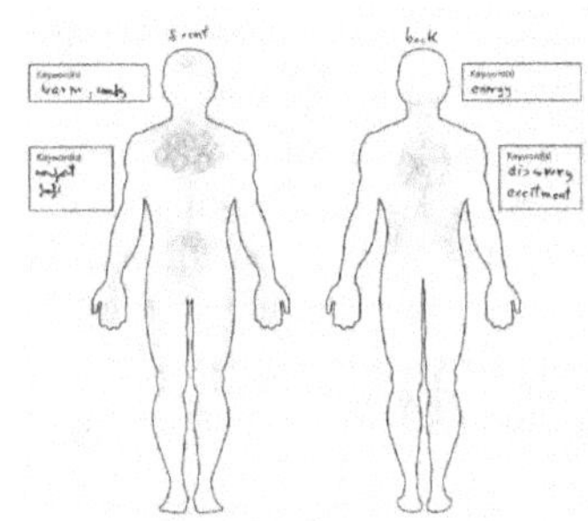

Figure 6: Body map from participant WF9. Keywords: Comfort, safe, discovery, excitement

Different ways of mapping the felt-sense were observed, expressed through various forms of body language (table 3). Beside the narratives, through the observation of participant's body language it is possible to determine whether a participant is felt sensing, exploring the relationship between body and thought or in the process of generating meaning. Body maps are also useful to complement these observations, as observed in figure 6, where the participant WF9 expressed to have perceived the feeling of happiness accentuated by using the heat prop on chest and abdomen. During the session, our participant was smiling, and holding the prop as described in the first row in table 3. After the workshop finished, the participant still expressed her satisfaction in regard to the idea of using heat to access memories. Although portability of devices is important to facilitate inner dialogue, flow, and to follow the felt-sense's movement, the process of meaning generation experienced through the body, in part transcends these design considerations.

In previous research [24], we have discussed about how to build a sense of self, where trust on perceptible feedback was fundamental to build a space for inner observation. When feedback is immediate and spaces for unreliability are less obvious (such as in the case of the stimulus generated by water bag), disagreements between the user's expectation and the perceptible feedback still might occur. These disagreements do not prevent the body to find its way in the process of meaning-generation, as we will discuss in the following theme.

c. Mirror or scaffolding: Devices provide open-ended clues for the body to complete with meaning

Höök et al.'s framework on somaesthetical qualities [17] introduces one interesting point about designing feedback that makes sense to the rhythms of the body. Since we have applied our devices to obtain information from the tacit, non-explicit dimension of our reality, such manifestations remain partially unknown until acknowledged. In the practice of Focusing, the body finds its way to generate meaning, even beyond our immediate, conscious understanding. As Gendlin points out [9], the body already *knows its situation,* and by paying attention we get in contact with the interactional nature of our implicit dimension. As an example of this ongoing meaning generation, the use of reflective listening in Focusing facilitates two possible responses: a) the meaning is mirrored to the participant/focuser, confirming and reinforcing the inner state of felt-sensing, or b) the wording might not be the one that *feels right*, stimulating the search for a new, fresh term representing the inner meaning more accurately. In Focusing, this active searching is a process that occurs continuously, as experiencing is interactional [20].

Similar to the act of reflective listening, the devices' stimuli contain sensory information, which can work either as a *mirror that reflects back*, or as *scaffolding* for new meaning-searching. In table 5, vibration was useful to accentuate the participant's felt-sense, acting as a mirror.

My happy situation is the moment I came back from work, or finishing a big project, and got back to home, laying down on my bed. My body feels melting and I feel satisfied. When I used the vibration on my body, it emphasised this melting "feeling" [...]. The pleasure comes from the satisfaction of "finishing something", kind of a sense of accomplishment, other comes from finding all my stress goes away, no more deadlines, no more plans I need to worry about, I enjoy the "stress relieving" feeling. Is emphasised both physically and mentally.

Table 5- Male participant (WM01)- vibration as a mirror

In some cases, the stimuli of our devices *did not feel right* in the subjective process of our participants, however these dissonances had a transformative character in the interactional construction of the aesthetic experience. These cases were observed indistinctively by using heat or vibration. We can see this process exemplified in the following narrative, as in the example in table 6.

"The thought that I had chose was my last visit to Watson's Bay – a beautiful beach. Now, I usually felt in these sessions the deeper meaning that I gathered was usually something familiar or close to the heart. Not this time. This time I felt the sensation of isolation and noise [...] I started questioning my reason for being there. The device felt like a foreign object from a different world- alive but strange. Its texture informed me on a furry animal, but its fluidity suggested something otherworldly. The creature had to move, but I did not know if it was defending or tucking me away! I realised then that I was staring at my own mortality. For the calming and chaotic nature of the beach was my personal symbol of death and inevitability. It was a calming and chaotic duality I had been observing all this time."

Table 6 – Male participant W13 – Heat as scaffolding

These narratives show how the complexity of human experience takes shape when open spaces of self-dialogue are facilitated. This process of self-dialogue can be insightful and pleasurable, as well as deep and sometimes confronting. Aesthetic aspects of interaction do not need to be solely focused on pleasure, as it would embody a reductionist understanding of the richness of our humanness [25]. Open stimuli can also act as a metaphor, shaped by the inner somatic process of the participant. In the light of our results, we also conclude that our initial interest of assessing artefacts under the sole dichotomy of distracting-enhancing to the practice of Focusing was simplistic. We consider important to facilitate spaces for the body to generate its own critical meaning, in concordance with its natural way of being in the world.

CONCLUSION

In line with the philosophical thinking proposed by Shusterman, Gendlin and Dewey, this paper introduced the use of Focusing in combination with wearable stimuli as a path to access inner knowledge. The relevance of this approach is that it makes evident the importance of the body in the meaning-making process. By means of practical exercises, it is possible to access the tacit dimension, surfacing out aesthetic qualities of people's memories and allowing the body to find its way in the generation of new meaning. We recognise that the exploration with our simple artefacts is just the first step in the generation of more sophisticated solutions. Beyond our specific method, we creatively envision other applications for this approach, such as facilitating sensorial ways of delivering storytelling, potential technology applications on body-based therapies (including somatic psychotherapy), and the creation of systems to promote the existence of ritual spaces to facilitate instances for creative self-dialogue.

ACKNOWLEDGMENTS

This work was funded by CONICYT/ Programa Formación de Capital Humano Avanzado, Folio 72140272. Additionally, we wanted to thank the Design Research Society (DRS) for supporting this research.

REFERENCES

1. Crawford, Robert. 1980. Healthism and the medicalization of everyday life. *International journal of health services* 10 (3):365-388.
2. Dewey, John. 1934. Art as experience Vol. 30, ALA Booklist.
3. Dreyfus, Hubert. L. 1991. Being-in-the-world: A commentary on Heidegger's Being and Time, Division I. *The MIT Press.*
4. Dunne, Anthony, and Fiona Raby. 2001. Design noir: The secret life of electronic objects: *Springer Science & Business Media.*
5. Fogel, Alan. 2013. Body Sense: The Science and Practice of Embodied Self-Awareness. *Norton Series on Interpersonal Neurobiology: WW Norton & Company.*
6. Forlizzi, Jodi, and Katja Battarbee. 2004. Understanding experience in interactive systems. *Proceedings of the 5th conference on Designing interactive systems: processes, practices, methods, and techniques.*
7. Friedman, N. 2004. The integration of focusing with other body-centered intervention. Accessed 30/08/2013.
8. Gendlin, Eugene T. 1978. Focusing. *Random House Digital, Inc.*
9. Gendlin, Eugene T. 1993. Three assertions about the body. *The Folio* 12 (1):21-33.
10. Gendlin, Eugene T. 2004. The new phenomenology of carrying forward. *Continental Philosophy Review* 37 (1):127-151.
11. Gendlin, Eugene T. 2012. Implicit Precision. Knowing Without Thinking: *Mind, Action, Cognition and the Phenomenon of the Background*:141.
12. Gendlin, Eugene T. 1962. Experiencing and the creation of meaning: *Free press of Glencoe New York.*
13. Gendlin, Eugene T. 1996. Focusing-oriented psychotherapy: A manual of the experiential method. *Guilford Press.*
14. Hallnäs, Lars, Patricija Jaksetic, Peter Ljungstrand, Johan Redström, and Tobias Skog. 2001. Expressions: towards a design practice of slow technology. *Proceedings of the human–computer interaction conference (Interact '01),* Amsterdam, The Netherlands.
15. Hallnäs, Lars, and Johan Redström. 2001. Slow technology, designing for reflection. *Personal and ubiquitous computing* 5 (3):201-212.
16. Höök, Kristina, Anna Ståhl, Martin Jonsson, Johanna Mercurio, Anna Karlsson, and Eva-Carin Banka Johnson. 2015. Somaesthetic design. *Interactions* 22 (4):26-33.
17. Höök, Kristina, Martin Jonsson, Anna Ståhl, and Johanna Mercurio. 2016. Somaesthetic Appreciation Design. *Proceedings of the SIGCHI Conference on Human Factors in Computing Systems (CHI'16),* San Jose, CA, USA.
18. Hutchinson, Hilary, Wendy Mackay, Bo Westerlund, Benjamin B. Bederson, Allison Druin, Catherine Plaisant, Michel Beaudouin-Lafon, Stéphane Conversy, Helen Evans, and Heiko Hansen. 2003. "Technology probes: inspiring design for and with families." *Proceedings of the SIGCHI conference on Human factors in computing systems.*
19. Ihde, Don. 2002. Bodies in technology. Vol. 5. *University of Minnesota Press.*
20. Ikemi, Akira. 2011. Empowering the implicitly functioning relationship. *Person-Centered & Experiential Psychotherapies* 10 (1):28-42.
21. Johnson, Mark. 2013. The body in the mind: The bodily basis of meaning, imagination, and reason: *University of Chicago Press.*
22. Larssen, Astrid Twenebowa, Toni Robertson, and Jenny Edwards. 2007. The feel dimension of technology interaction: exploring tangibles through movement and touch. *Proceedings of the 1st international conference on Tangible and embedded interaction.*
23. Lee, Wonjun, Youn-kyung Lim, and Richard Shusterman. 2014. Practicing somaesthetics: exploring its impact on interactive product design ideation. *Proceedings of the 2014 conference on Designing interactive systems.*
24. Núñez-Pacheco, Claudia, and Lian Loke. 2014. Crafting the body-tool: a body-centred perspective on wearable technology. *Proceedings of the 2014 conference on Designing interactive systems.*
25. Petersen, Marianne Graves, Ole Sejer Iversen, Peter Gall Krogh, and Martin Ludvigsen. 2004. Aesthetic Interaction: a pragmatist's aesthetics of interactive systems. *Proceedings of the 5th conference on Designing interactive systems: processes, practices, methods, and techniques.*
26. Purpura, Stephen, Victoria Schwanda, Kaiton Williams, William Stubler, and Phoebe Sengers. 2011. Fit4life: the design of a persuasive technology promoting healthy behavior and ideal weight. *Proceedings of the SIGCHI Conference on Human Factors in Computing Systems.*
27. Rome, David I. 2014. Your Body Knows the Answer. Using Your Felt Sense to Solve Problems, Effect Change, and Liberate Creativity. First edition ed. Boston, United States: *Shambhala Publications.*

28. Schiphorst, Thecla. 2009. soft (n): Toward a Somaesthetics of Touch. *CHI'09 Extended Abstracts on Human Factors in Computing Systems.*
29. Shusterman, Richard. 1999. Somaesthetics: A disciplinary proposal. *The Journal of Aesthetics and Art Criticism* 57 (3):299-313.
30. Shusterman, Richard. 2011. Somaesthetics - Thinking Through the Body and Designing for Interactive Experience. *In The Encyclopedia of Human-Computer Interaction, 2nd Ed., edited by Mads and Dam Soegaard, Rikke Friis.* Aarhus, Denmark: The Interaction Design Foundation.
31. Shusterman, Richard. 2016. Personal communication. March 3rd
32. Simon, Bebe. 2015. How I Teach Focusing: Discovering the Gift of Your Inner Wisdom: *MILL CITY PressINC.*
33. Wilde, Danielle, and Kristina Andersen. 2009. Doing things backwards: the OWL project. *Proceedings of the 21st Annual Conference of the Australian Computer-Human Interaction Special Interest Group: Design: Open 24/7.*
34. Wilde, Danielle, and Kristina Andersen. 2010. Part science part magic: analysing the OWL outcomes. *Proceedings of the 22nd Conference of the Computer-Human Interaction Special Interest Group of Australia on Computer-Human Interaction.*
35. Wolf, Gary. 2010. The data-driven life. *The New York Times* 28:2010.
36. Wright, Peter, and John McCarthy. 2004. Technology as experience: *MIT Press Cambridge*, MA.
37. Wright, Peter, Jayne Wallace, and John McCarthy. 2008. Aesthetics and experience-centered design. *ACM Transactions on Computer-Human Interaction (TOCHI)* 15 (4):18.

Designing and Making the Datacatchers: Batch Producing Location-Aware Mobile Devices

Andy Boucher, William Gaver
Interaction Research Studio
Goldsmiths, University of London
London, UK
initial.surname@ gold.ac.uk

ABSTRACT

In this paper we describe the Datacatcher, a location-aware, tangible and embodied mobile device that displays a continuous stream of statements about its location that are drawn from a large number of data sources and which speak to sociopolitical issues. We describe how the design and our underlying research interests emerged and changed over the course of three distinct phases of development: the device's conceptual design, its refinement to a final design, and the final detailing leading to batch production of 130 of the devices. We discuss the Datacatcher as resonant with many current issues in HCI, including augmented reality, environmental issues, political systems and using data as a design material.

Author Keywords

Design; research through design; batch-production; mobile device; location; Big Data

ACM Classification Keywords

H.5.m. Information interfaces and presentation (e.g., HCI): Miscellaneous.

INTRODUCTION

In this paper, we describe the development of the Datacatcher, a tangible and embodied mobile device that displays data about its location drawn from a number of online sources (Figure 1). It was designed and built by our university-based research group, with funding from a successful EU research proposal. We trace the trajectory of the project from the background concerns that gave rise to the initial concept, through the process of refining the conceptual design, developing the hardware, software and product design, the batch production of 130 highly finished and fully functional research devices and their deployment to participants in a subsequent field trial.

TEI '17, March 20 - 23, 2017, Yokohama, Japan

ACM 978-1-4503-4676-4/17/03…$15.00
DOI: http://dx.doi.org/10.1145/3024969.3024971

In describing this project, we emphasise two perspectives. First, we offer the Datacatcher as an innovative design that offers an engaging interactive experience on its own terms, and moreover as a design that resonates with disciplinary concerns ranging from augmenting the physical world with online information to designing for political engagement [4], to questioning the value of digital devices vs. apps, to extending our understanding of environmental HCI. Here we offer the Datacatcher as a case study, an 'ultimate particular' [15,20] that embodies a constellation of stances with regards to these issues. Second, we describe the project as an example of research through design, responding to observations that the complex processes involved in designing devices should be better represented in the HCI literature [3,14,18,23].

In the following, then, we describe the project as a series of stages: initial conceptualisation, developing the concept to a design, refinement and production. Finally, we reflect on how our research intentions emerged over the course of design, and the lessons we learned in the process.

BACKGROUND AND INITIAL CONCEPT

The Datacatcher was developed as part of our long-term research, in which we take a design-led approach to developing new technological artefacts. We do not intend the things we make to become commercial products, but instead build them as *research devices* (c.f. [16]) that investigate new possibilities for technology, and that also help reveal peoples' values and practices in targeted

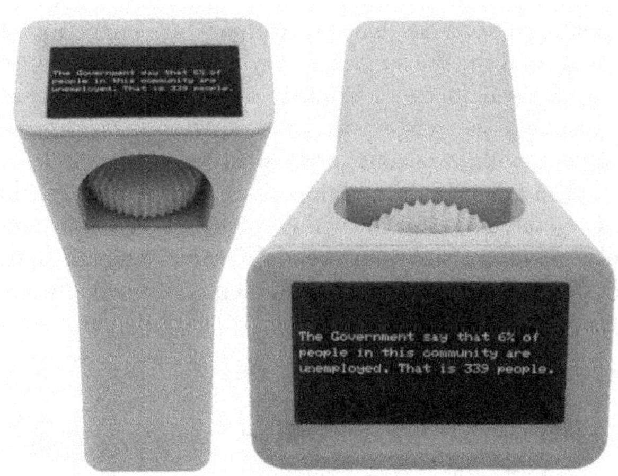

Figure 1: Two views of a batch produced Datacatcher

domains. In particular, the Datacatcher was the final design of a 5-year research programme concerned with exploring batch production and deployment as a method of pursuing a form of 'third-wave HCI' (c.f. [13]) that stresses the situated, holistic and interpretative nature of interactions with technology. The project was guided by two main objectives. The *domain objective* was to take a third-wave sensibility to issues of clear social importance (i.e., the Datacatcher was initially conceived as addressing environmental issues). The *methodological objective* was to explore the prospects for using batch production of hundreds of devices, and batch deployment to similar numbers of people, as a means to explore the diversity of interpretations, orientations and practices that might emerge, as this is a core interest of third-wave HCI.

From this perspective, the identity of the device we developed – what it was about – was shaped by our concern to explore socially important issues. At the outset of this project, we built on previous work we had done trying to extend notions of environmental HCI. Dissatisfied with the instrumental and prescriptive nature of many designs in the field at the time, and influenced by the critiques and arguments of colleagues such as [2,5,19,21] we had already produced designs to balance aesthetic and resource-oriented views of the home's microenvironment [10], to provide feedback about electricity consumption at a community level in the form of a graph painted directly on a neighbourhood street [1], and to gather and condense online discourse about energy-related issues as a way of reflecting and disrupting the understandings of a number of existing UK energy communities [11].

At the outset of this phase, then, our thinking was informed by a growing perception that, rather than conceiving and acting on environmental issues directly, it is important to understand them as continuous with, and a manifestation of, larger individual and cultural patterns. The development of this view on environmental issues also resonated with some of our more personal, 'lived' political concerns: about the inequality that cocoons the rich and exposes the rest, the lack of responsibility and sense of entitlement fuelled by an imbalanced access to resources, the surveillance and deprivation excused by invocations of terrorism and austerity, and the consumerist envy and egocentric thinking that goes hand in hand. From this (academically sketchy) perspective, our impact on the environment, and our seeming inability to ameliorate or even focus on it, is a 'natural' outcome of the sociopolitical patterns of our time. Thus a viable route for designing to protect the environment would involve pointing out evidence of inequality, consumerism, and so forth, with potentially explicit links to environmental measures.

This was the backdrop for a conversation between two of the team members in which the initial concept for the Datacatcher emerged. Discussing what might be useful for exploring environmental problems as a symptom of consumerism, one of us said something like: *"what would be fascinating is some kind of device that would let you see how much money people earn in the buildings right in front of you, and how much their homes are worth, and what kinds of environmental impacts they make."* This speculative notion marked the first beginnings for mining data to orientate local sociopolitical conditions.

CONCEPTUAL DIRECTION

Considering that research issues that we wanted to explore, we developed a fairly open brief for a design that would 'Provide politically relevant information (in some sense) in response to the device's location (in some sense) using web sourced data sets'. From this, then, the team engaged in intense exploration of ideas in the form of sketches, notes and conversations, exploring through and against the edges of the brief. We developed the most promising ideas in relatively systematic and considered – if often quite spare – treatments collected together in a series of design workbooks [6].

Over time, a brief for a device emerged as we settled on countless small decisions (or preferences) about how we would proceed. As a team, we felt a milestone was reached when we felt confident that the as-yet-unnamed system would:

- be handheld,
- use a black and white, e-reader-like outdoor legible screen, and
- have a battery that lasts days,
- eschew power hungry GPS in favour of GPRS cell phone technology to approximate location and to
- connect to a remote server providing data scraped from
- government sites, credit agencies, the UK census, Twitter™, Wikipedia™, etc, and
- allow participants to contribute their own opinions.

Form and affordances

By this point the team had already fabricated some test hardware using the .Net Gadgeteer platform [22], had evaluated a low-power Sharp memory LCD screen (a larger version of that used in the first generation Pebble watch [17]), that was to be used in the final design, and investigated batteries capable of powering the device for requisite periods of time, so we had a fair idea of the packaging requirements for a device. This allowed the team to explore dozens of eventual configurations, which led to speculations about how the device might be used (At home? Carried by hand? Mounted on a car dashboard? Attached to objects by a built-in strap? Perhaps left in a public space as a form of electronic graffiti?). Figure 2 shows a small sample of the sketches produced around this time; the co-definition of form and anticipated uses continued through to the final specification of the device.

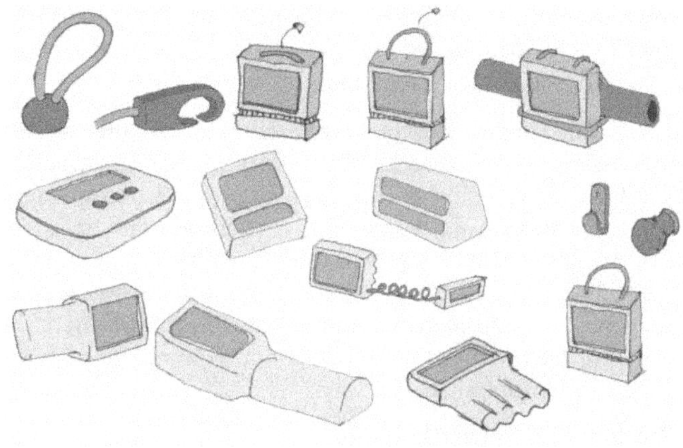

Figure 2: sketches of possible forms

Data, Treatment and Voice

We decided fairly quickly that the system would scrape existing information from the Internet, similarly to previous designs we had produced [7,8,9,12]. Now we set about exploring a wide range of sources for sociopolitically relevant information. For example, the team collected every scrap of public data for a given postcode in London, gathering information about poverty, energy prices, test results, population and demographics, house prices, businesses, historical figures, events tweets, MP activity, meetings, blogs, news, gang activity and songs which mentioned the place. This was useful in gauging available information and assessing valuable sources.

Two issues arose in the process. First, data sources define 'location' at different resolutions and with overlapping boundaries, raising the question of how we could indicate what 'here' means. Second, most sources take the form of databases that return numbers or short phrases in response to queries, and we wanted the device to display natural language outputs. We started to explore how this might be achieved by simulating sentences and trying cut-up techniques to explore possibilities for algorithmic production. We also started to experiment with different 'voices' for the system, ranging from brief summative 'area glimpses' to formulations which were optimistic or complaining, and considered 'curating' the tone of outputs to, for instance, reflect stock market movements.

Interaction and Participation with Data

Another line of thought concerned moving the experience beyond passive reception of information towards more active involvement. For instance, a recurring idea concerned a 'significant moment' button that would allow people to tag messages they thought interesting, perhaps for broadcast to other devices or to allow later review. Similarly, 'less-like-this' and 'more-like-this' buttons might allow people to shape the sorts of information they received or perhaps request more detail.

Over time, these ideas settled into two new modes for the device. First, we decided that people should be able to scroll through the history of previously received messages, allowing them to review a timeline of information about areas they had been. Second, we formulated a series of 20 questions and multiple-choice answers that people could use to register and share their opinions of the local area, with the results added to the corpus of content available to the devices.

Changing Conceptual Direction

As the project progressed, the conceptual direction for the design of the device evolved. Our initial motivation was to build a system that would illuminate how environmental practices are entangled in sociopolitical issues such as inequality, privilege and consumerism. As we explored the design space, however, this began to shift. To begin with, we were influenced by the availability of data as a design material. In exploring what we could find about specific areas, it became clear that while some environmentally relevant data was available (e.g. about energy consumption, sources for heating, pollution levels), this was overwhelmed by information about other topics (income, housing prices, crime). Conceptually, we were enthusiastic about providing a broader view onto the sociopolitial realities of local neighbourhoods as relevant for thinking about issues beyond the environment. Thus the Datacatcher evolved from an environmentally-centred design to take on a broader sociopolitical ambit.

Second, as we began to explore the large corpus of datasets from private and public bodies that tag and categorise location, we began to become increasingly interested in Big Data as a subject of interest in its own right. We discovered, for instance, that credit rating agencies have classified each household in the UK with one of 64 categories that predict who they vote for, the newspaper they read, the car they drive, their career prospects and their disposable income. We saw how health statistics reveal that life expectancy can vary drastically from London borough to borough, and indicate areas where people don't eat enough fruit and vegetables. It became clear that as a material for design, data is never neutral, but always reflects assumptions and motives that themselves can be seen as political. This raised questions for us about how Big Data represents us, and about whether a tension might exist between how this data represents local populations and how people might understand themselves. Thus we saw the Datacatcher as implicitly raising issues about data, as well as about the sociopolitical textures of the UK.

MAKING: REFINEMENT AND PRODUCTION

As our work converged around a set of common ideas and decisions, the project shifted towards implementation as we our efforts turned towards constructing a working system – the data mining and processing, the device electronics, the form and interaction design. This shift was also marked by the choice of Datacatcher as name for the device, which both summarised our thinking and helped guide development.

The Datacatcher was a challenging device to produce in low (hundreds) volume. We faced innumerable issues and challenges in bringing together the electronics, software, housing design and interactivity, and a full account of this process would be lengthy, confusing and tedious. In general, however, the first emphasis was on the data that it was to display, the second on the electronics and software that allowed it to do so, and the third on the design of the housing for the emerging behaviour of the device.

Sourcing and Presenting Sociopolitical Data

Through our experiments mining localised data, we settled on a total of fourteen different online and offline UK sources, many of which provided dozens of separate data sets, to give us access to hundreds of individual data streams for use by the system. Data from public bodies like the Office for National Statistics, the Department of Energy and Climate Change, and crime statistics from the police were supplemented with commercial data from Twitter and property index site Zoopla. Several sources, such as data from the credit agency Experian, were available to us only because we work for a university.

Server-side code translates data returned by these sources into meaningful and legible sentences for delivery by the Datacatchers. For instance, health-ranking indices for different postcodes were turned into messages such as '*The census shows that 25% of people around these parts are smokers*'. Each of these translations is built around a crafted sentence structure that accepts an automatically inserted variable. In total, there are there are around 600 individual template sentences for each UK postcode. Many of them sought to draw attention to the agencies behind the data, for instance by starting sentences with "they say", as in "they say people around here are not happy".

Determining Location and Transferring Data

The design of the Datacatcher's hardware is similar to a GPRS phone, handling connectivity to a server to provide cell information, receive messages, and send any answers to poll questions. Each device connects to a local cell phone tower, opening a GPRS connection to the server that queries the location of the tower ID which is used as a proxy for the device's location.

The Datacatcher server preforms all of the system processing – e.g., data mining and sentence construction. We have used a similar approach in previous designs (e.g. [8]), but instead of supplying content to one or a few devices, the Datacatcher server generates hundreds of individual feeds that react in real time to location changes. This was a significant challenge, the scale of which was difficult to appreciate at the outset but required considerable expertise to implement reliably.

Product and Form Sketches

The form design evolved alongside technical development. Figure 3 shows a small sample of the dozens of form studies and models that we produced. The left panel shows a selection of early models, in which we pursued early concerns with different usage scenario including, for instance, ways of attaching the device to others, or possibilities for tabletop versions, and even a version in which the screen is mounted within a mirror to emphasise the data's link to the surrounding environment.

The designs on the right, in contrast, reflect refinement much later in the cycle. At this point we had decided to mount the screen on the end of the device, so that in use attention would be on the content rather than the object. The physical size of these form studies increased as we began to appreciate the power requirements of the system, gradually increasing battery capacity in each iteration. The figures also show the evolution of a cutout section, originally conceived as a means of attachment, to eventually become a recess for the control dial and space to hang the device on the thumb.

A Handle for a Battery

We investigated several different options for powering the device. We hoped to use a small and light power pack, but also wanted the device to last days on a single charge. We discovered the modem demanded a 1.4A current whenever

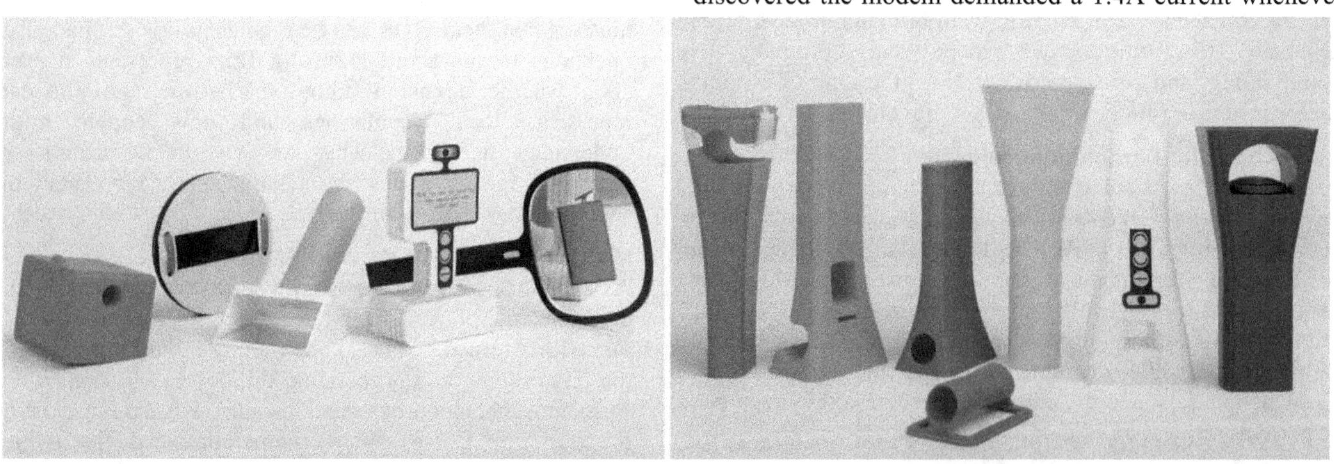

Figure 3: Evolution of the Datacatcher's form. Left panel shows early explorations, right panel shows convergence on final form.

we opened a GPRS connection (frequent due to code glitches), so we decided to use a large power cell with around four times the capacity of a smart phone. Our first form designs were of a similar size to a pager, but the chosen battery was bigger than initially anticipated, so the form evolved and a handle was created to house the power unit. Some observers have compared the final design to a torch (US 'flashlight'), however the intention is not to create a pointing device, but rather to allow the bulk of the battery and electronics to disappear behind the screen so that, in use, only the messages appear to the viewer.

App vs device

Of course, our considerations of form would have been rendered irrelevant had we decided to produce the design as an app. This question was often raised during our development cycle, but there were several reasons why we considered that a standalone device would be superior. Overall we felt the design would best work conceptually as a system that would continuously collect data as it is carried around, and we wanted to avoid having our design compete for attention, screen space, processor and battery power with other apps that sit in a landscape of iOS/Android mediated entertainment, lifestyle or wayfinding systems. Designing the device also allowed us to investigate different affordances, aesthetics and cultural connotations, than would be possible in an app housed on a smartphone or tablet mediated by consumer operating systems.

In addition, while an app could be distributed to thousands, our ambition was build a system for around a hundred participants whose experiences we could manageably observe. It was therefore advantageous to technically ring fence the system hardware. For our small team, building a server that could reliably talk to a few hundred identical devices was just about possible. Developing an app to run on a multitude of versions of different operating systems (and future updates) would have been more resource intensive, not only during development, but also through the field study and in any future uses of the system.

Finally, many of us felt that the endless landscape of similar-appearing apps is flattening and uninspiring, and wanted to explore and indeed insist on the continuing viability of stand-alone computational products in the current technological landscape.

Technical Description:

The Datacatcher uses an entirely bespoke electronic design. It was prototyped and developed using modules from the .NET Gadgeteer platform [22], which were later rationalised and combined onto a single board that is based on the architecture of the open source GHI Electronics FEZ Cerberus Mainboard. The Datacatcher's PCB measures 100 x 40mm and its main features include an ARM 32bit 168MHz STM32F427VIT6 microcontroller and a SIMCom SIM900 quad-band GSM/GPRS module, with battery management and charging utilising the Maxim MAX1508 chip. There are two Gadgeteer sockets for two peripherals: a rotary encoder (Alps EC11J) and display unit. The screen is a 2.7-inch memory-LCD display manufactured by Sharp (LS027B7DH01) with a resolution of 400 x 240 pixels.

The footprint of the PCB was broadly based on that of the rechargeable battery, a Panasonic PA-L46 lithium-ion. This is a large unit (in comparison to say two AAA cells) that occupies much of the Datacatcher's physical volume but outputs 4500 mAh at 3.6V, which is enough to power the device for several days of continuous use. Cell phone radio is handled by the FXP.07 quad-band GSM flexible PCB antenna manufactured by Taoglas. Data service is provided by a machine-to-machine SIM capable of roaming across different UK carriers for the strongest signal. Each Datacatcher connects to an Amazon web server that utilises the Google Maps API to geo-locate the cell tower that the SIM is connected to, information which is used to build a feed of local data that is delivered back to the device in messages groups of 20. The server-code was written in JavaScript using a service oriented architecture consisting of multiple node.js processes communicating via Redis.

Thumb Dial Interaction

The interface for the Datacatcher is via a thumb dial (figure 4) which interfaces all the devices functions. The dial is attached to a 20 step rotary encoder which includes a push down switch. The default mode of the Datacatcher is to display messages, paged individually to the screen every eight seconds (see figure 5 for example screen modes). Rotating the dial anti-clockwise from this default mode enters the timeline, where all previously collected messages can be viewed chronologically. In this mode, additional metadata surrounds the original message that identifies the location, time/date stamp and message source. Clicking the thumb dial holds the historic message on screen indefinitely, otherwise the Datacatcher springs back to the default mode after a period of no interaction. Spinning the thumb dial quickly in timeline mode accelerates scrolling through the history, ensuring that it is relatively easy to navigate to a particular time point.

Rotating the dial clockwise from the default mode enters the poll question mode. Once this mode is entered 20

Figure 4. Datacatcher Thumb Dial

questions (see Table 2) about the local area can be scrolled through left and right. Clicking the thumb dial again when viewing a question reveals a set of multiple choice answers, which can also be scrolled left and right. Clicking again confirms an answer, otherwise the display springs back to the main questions. Answered questions are returned to the server and enter the corpus of data that may be delivered back to a Datacatcher in the same location at a later time (phrased appropriately for ownership 'earlier you thought ... here' or 'someone previously thought... here') As with the timeline, after a period of no interaction the Datacatcher will return to the default message mode.

Physical Construction

The Datacatcher casing is constructed from two nylon components made via additive manufacturing using selective laser sintering (SLS). These parts are an internal chassis that includes the display bezel and an outer sleeve that forms the skin of the device. The majority of components including the screen, battery, antenna and PCB clip into the internal chassis, whereas the rotary encoder is secured by two self-tapping screws for strength and reliability. The assembled chassis slides into the outer sleeve, which locks shut with a clip and there is one self-tapping screw to prevent these two parts detaching. The push-fit dial is also made with SLS. It attaches to the Alps encoder and is locked in place with cyanoacrylate glue.

Batch Production

Our team is experienced in making technically sophisticated research devices, yet producing 130 high fidelity and robust devices raised some challenging issues. It was a method that involved many people, materials and processes, and the sheer scale introduced problems that we had not envisaged or encountered before. Our solutions to these issues further shaped the Datacatchers' eventual identity and, ultimately had effects on the way our research played out.

For instance, our choice of the manufacturing technique used to produce the case had decisive effects on the device's eventual form. We considered using injection moulding, but that would have made the cutout section we had been developing impossible to achieve. Instead we chose to use additive manufacturing as that allowed dramatically different possibilities for form design. Even here though, however, the particular manufacturing technology used turned out to influence the design, and it took a great deal of work (including specifying the exact orientation of each part during printing) to achieve the same fit and finish we had with prototypes built on our own fused deposition modelling (FDM) machine on the SLS machines used by the contractor we hired to batch produce them.

A simpler but more dramatic effect was made when we discovered that a crucial component of the devices was in short supply. We had decided early in our design process to use a particular memory-LCD part (Sharp LS027B7DH01) for the display, because of its resolution, legibility and – importantly – its low power requirements. But when we came to order the planned 250 units, we discovered that Sharp had sold out and were not planning to produce more for months. This led to a worldwide search for the last remaining units, but even so reduced our planned production of Datacatchers from 250 to an eventual 131. This didn't affect the realisation of the devices itself, but it did impact on the scale of and plans for the field trial.

The Emergence of the Datacatcher

Over the course of figuring out how to make and ultimately batch produce the Datacatchers, their specific identity became fixed in detail. From the space of possible forms and use scenarios explored through the models on the left of Figure 3, the final design emerged. Along the way the identity of the device coalesced, shifted and sharpened under a large number of influences.

One of the major influences on the Datacatchers' evolution was our increasing focus on making the Datacatchers' aesthetically appealing and engaging in their interaction. Arguably, this is irrelevant if we think of the device narrowly as a way of only exploring our domain objectives. But this was crucial for a device that we would ask people to use for extended times in their everyday lives: we couldn't rely on them to share our research interests, but instead had to produce devices that would be rewarding in their own right. Our concern to achieve an appealing design impacted every aspect of the design development, shaping the devices as much as our intentions to expose issues of sociopolitics and big data did.

Thus our initial research concerns and the desire to produce an engaging design joined to shape the Datacatchers. But many other factors played important parts. As we have described, these included technical issues ranging from the capacity of batteries to print orientation of parts. They also included the nature of data available, and the resolution of that data both geographically and in time. Moreover, many other design details resulted from our engagement with infrastructures, networks, data and materials. The UK cell phone network, Google Maps Geolocation API, data licensing, postcode revisions, global supply chains, database formats, nylon dyeing methods, University lawyers, UK mail regulations for lithium batteries, quirky cell phone hardware: these all had impact on details of the final design and interaction. In many respects the final design is a result of thousands of small decisions that work around problems and issues [20].

These influences did not simply constrain or compromise our initial concept. They also suggested new possibilities and led the design in new directions. Notably, the decision to use additive manufacturing to produce the Datacatchers' housings allowed a form design that would have been difficult or impossible to achieve in other ways. The sheer scale and scope of data available led us to expose a range of topics and to create flows of messages in a far more flexible way than we had anticipated. As the Datacatcher evolved, then, so did our understanding of what it could be.

DATACATCHER: TANGIBLE INTERACTION WITH COMPLEX DATA

Figure 5 shows Datacatchers displaying a variety of live and historical messages as well as a few of the poll questions. Once switched on, the Datacatcher displays user instructions while it connects to the cellular network and server. In its default operation, it streams messages about its local surroundings at the rate of one every eight seconds. Turning the dial anticlockwise scrolls through previous messages, and also shows the data sources (e.g. 'UK Census') and the location and time they were displayed ('Greenwich, 14 November, 15:42'). Turning the dial clockwise accesses a series of poll questions that can be answered by scrolling through multiple-choice options and selected a response with by clicking the dial. Table 1 shows a few of the hundreds of potential messages presented by the devices, and some of the poll questions and possible answers are shown in Table 2.

DISCUSSION

In this account, we have exposed the complexity behind the Datacatcher's seeming simplicity. Technically, we believe this is of interest to other small teams seeking to produce sophisticated systems. Our team is experienced in producing low-volume runs of embodied devices, but the Datacatcher was extremely challenging: We batch produced devices in numbers far greater than we have attempted before. The server handles far more data sources than any other system we have built. It talks to more devices than any server that we have constructed previously.

Conceptually, the Datacatcher is equally complex. As we have described, it emerged from considerations of environmental problems and orientations, of sociopolitical issues in current society, of locative media and of apps vs. computational products. It was enabled by the availability of data to illuminate some of those issues, and conversely raises questions and doubts about how Big Data is collected and used to represent communities and individuals. Bringing together all this complexity to produce such a simple-seeming device is, we suggest, one of the achievements of the Datacatchers' design.

Field Study – Giving Away 130 Devices

Our emphasis in this paper has been on the design process that led to the Datacatchers. A full account of the field trial that followed is available in another paper [12]; here we briefly summarise its highlights.

We employed a commercial design consultancy to deploy the devices to volunteers recruited at street markets, and hired two teams of documentary filmmakers to capture participants' experiences in a collection of short documentary films which are available to view on a Vimeo channel [24].

Source	Message
Census	The census says that 10,300 people in Lewisham are unemployed.
Experian	They say residents in Deptford have smaller carbon footprints than nearby in East Dulwich.
National Archives	Low level of happiness around here
Police	941 crimes in July
Fix My Street	"Dog fouling in the mornings" is a local issue
Zoopla	A 6+ bed house will cost £9,794,000 to buy
Experian	A credit agency says people who live in the vicinity are young, well paid, mostly single professionals, who have chosen flats suitable for commuting to urban Jobs
Census	43% of people in this community are White.
Participant Poll	9/10 of us were happy in this location recently
Wikipedia	Deptford Market, a street market in Deptford High Street sells a range of goods, and is considered one of London's liveliest street markets.
Google	More places of worship here in Deptford than nearby in Southwark.
Participant Poll	3/6 of us described poverty we were recently as "growing".

Table 1. Sample Datacatcher sources and messages

Sample Poll Questions and Answers
What are the dogs like here? *handbag / working / family / weapons / fighting / blow-dried*
How do you feel here? *scared / unsafe / on guard / comfortable / secure / nannied / smug*
What is the air quality like? *mountain fresh / good / poor / toxic*
What are the politics around here? *friendly fascist / neo-liberal / weekend radical / anarchy rules / not bothered*
Are the buildings here? *chocolate box / social / brutal / imperial / fascist / innovative / faux*
Poverty here is? *endemic / growing / hidden / nowhere / frowned upon*
Around here, the revolution will... *start /pass through / avoid / miss / be televised / be quashed / overturn everything*

Table 2. Sample poll questions and answers

Participants Impressions

Most participants expressed positive impressions about the the Datacatchers' design: 'Absolutely everybody who saw it was completely intrigued by the design, the shape of it and stuff… it is a really beautiful design…' (participant 102). This extended to the aesthetics of interacting with it: 'It's really satisfying when you use the wheel, because you get that lovely clicking feel… as opposed to just flicking through a bunch of messages' (p019).

Participants reported that the Datacatcher's design often prompted social interactions with bystanders: 'It immediately gets people asking questions.' (p026). As one participant explained: 'People around the office were kind of like, "Wow, what's that? Is this like a toy? What is this device?" So the design, the colour, the shape, that was quite a good talking point' (p009). Moreover, what started as discussions about the Datacatcher's appearance would often merge to conversations about the issues it raised: '…so in a group we had discussions around "Is this useful or is this just an interesting fact? Or what does this mini survey tell us about the area?" So it was a great, I think the social value, the entertainment factor was great' (p035). In part, such discussions were valued as drawing attention to rarely discussed issues: 'You start discussing the facts and it brings you to bigger issues in the area that normally in your day to day life are not really brought to attention' (p065).

In sum, participants' responses indicated that the Datacatchers successfully raised many of the issues we intended, and were appreciated in their own right as well.

Conclusion

The Datacatcher was successfully manifested from a complex set of ideas and design challenges. Moreover, we believe that the many conceptual issues that we addressed in its creation can be discerned in the final device itself. The data sources we chose provide environmentally relevant information, for instance about the sources of energy people use at home, or the modes of transportation they use, or local pollution levels. They also provide information about sociopolitical issues, including local income levels and housing prices, educational achievement, access to healthcare and ethnic makeup. Viewing the device while travelling, or revisiting messages by scrolling through the device's history, effectively reveals the very different sociopolitical backdrops of peoples' lives. Finally, by revealing the sources of the messages, and through the use of phrasing, the device provides resources for beginning to appreciate the extent of information held by Big Data, the ways it represents people, the questions it asks and the ways it couches its answers.

At the same time, a Datacatcher is not a set of ideas, but a physical device. It has weight in the hand, and a solid feel that gives it a kind of presence. It is, in Nelson and Stolterman's terms, the result of 'a process of moving from the particular, general and universal to the *ultimate particular* – the specific design' ([15] p. 33). Artefacts such as a Datacatcher are ultimate particulars because they are *real*. None of their details are unspecified or left to the imagination; they are fully resolved, perhaps the only undeniable fact to emerge from our design research [20].

ACKNOWLEDGEMENTS

This research was supported by the European Research Council's advanced investigator award no. 226528, 'Third Wave HCI'. Special thanks to the Interaction Research Studio Datacatcher team: Nadine Jarvis, Dave Cameron, Mark Hauenstein, Liliana Ovalle & Sarah Pennington. All figures © Interaction Research Studio.

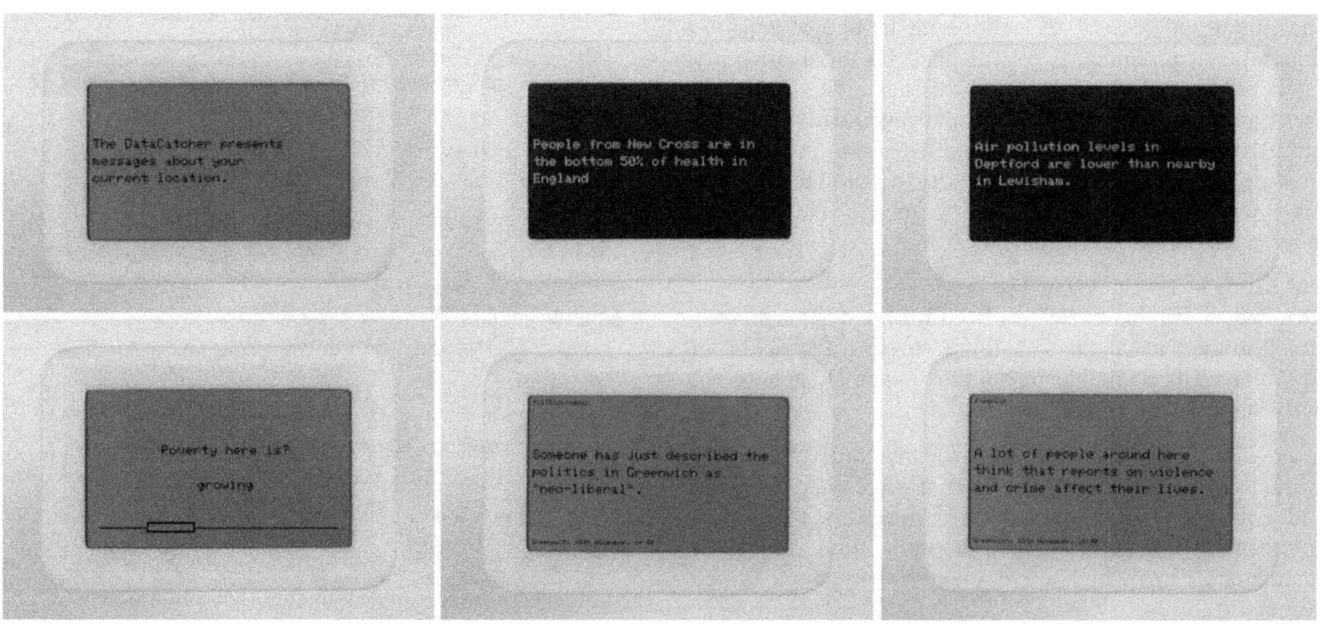

Figure 5. Clockwise from top left: start up screen, live feed messages from the NHS, the Environment Agency, credit agency message stored in the timeline, Participant Poll broadcast and Participant Poll question.

REFERENCES

1. Boucher, A., Cameron, D. and Jarvis, N. (2012). Power to the people. *In Proc. of DIS 2012. ACM, New York, 2012.*
2. Brynjarsdottir, H., Hakansson, M., Pierce, J., Baumer, E., DiSalvo, C., and Sengers, P. (2012). Sustainably unpersuaded. *In Proc. of CHI 2012. ACM, New York, 2012.*
3. Dalsgaard, P. and Halskov, K. (2012). Reflective Design Documentation. *In Proc of the DIS 2012. ACM, New York, 2012. 428–37.*
4. DiSalvo, C. (2012). Adversarial design. *Cambridge, Mass.: MIT Press.*
5. Dourish, P. 2010. HCI and environmental sustainability. *In Proc. of DIS 2010. ACM, New York.*
6. Gaver, W. (2011). Making Spaces: How Design Workbooks Work. *In Proc. CHI '11, ACM, New York, 1551-1560.*
7. Gaver, W., Boucher, A., Law, A., Pennington, S., Bowers, J., Beaver, J., Humble, J., Kerridge, T., Villar, N. and Wilkie, A. (2008). Threshold devices. *In Proc. of CHI 2008. ACM, New York, 2008.*
8. Gaver, W., Blythe, M., Boucher, A., Jarvis, N., Bowers, J. and Wright, P. (2010). The prayer companion. *In Proc. of CHI 2010. ACM, New York, 2010.*
9. Gaver, W., Wright, P., Boucher, A., Bowers, J., Blythe, M., Jarvis, N., Cameron, D., Kerridge, T., Wilkie, A. and Phillips, R. (2011). The Photostroller. *In Proc. of CHI 2011. ACM, New York, 2011.*
10. Gaver, W., Bowers, J., Boehner, K., Boucher, A., Cameron, D., Hauenstein, M., Jarvis, N. and Pennington, S. (2013). Indoor weather stations. *In Proc. of CHI 2013. ACM, New York, 2013.*
11. Gaver, W., Michael, M., Kerridge, T., Wilkie, A., Boucher, A., Ovalle, L. and Plummer-Fernandez, M. (2015). Energy Babble. *In Proc. of CHI 2015. ACM, New York, 2015.*
12. Gaver, W., Boucher, A., Jarvis, N., Cameron, D., Hauenstein, M., Pennington, S., Ovalle, L., Bowers,J., Pike, J., Beitra, R. (2016). The Datacatcher: Batch Deployment and Documentation of 130 Location-Aware, Mobile Devices That Put Sociopolitically-Relevant Big Data in People's Hands: Polyphonic interpretation at Scale. *In Proc. of CHI 2016. ACM, New York, 2016.*
13. Harrison, S. Tatar, D., and Sengers, P. (2007). The three paradigms of HCI. *In Proc. of CHI 2007. ACM, New York, 2007.*
14. Koskinen, I., Binder, T. and Redström, J. (2009). Lab, Field, Gallery, and Beyond. *Artifact, 2, 1 (2009), 46--57.*
15. Nelson, H. G., & Stolterman, E. (2003). The design way: Intentional change in an unpredictable world: Foundations and fundamentals of design competence. Educational Technology. *MIT Press. 2012*
16. Odom, W., Wakkary, R., Youn-kyung Lim, YK., Desjardins, A,. Hengeveld, B., and Banks, R. 2016. From Research Prototype to Research Product. *In Proc. of CHI 2016. ACM, New York, 2016.*
17. Pebble Smart Watch. https://en.wikipedia.org/wiki/Pebble_(watch)
18. Pierce, J. (2014). On the Presentation and Production of Design Research Artifacts in HCI. *In Proc. of DIS 2014. ACM, New York, 2014. 735–744*
19. Shove, E. (2003). Comfort, cleanliness and convenience. *Oxford, England: Berg.*
20. Stolterman, E. (2008). The nature of design practice and implications for interaction design research. *International Journal of Design, 2(1), 55-65.*
21. Strengers, Y. (2013) Smart Energy Technologies in Everyday Life: Smart Utopia*? Palgrave MacMillan.*
22. Villar, N., Scott, J. and Hodges, S. (2011). Prototyping with microsoft .net gadgeteer. *In Proc. TEI 2011. ACM, New York, 2011.*
23. Zimmerman J., Stolterman, E. and Forlizzi. J. (2010). An analysis and critique of Research through Design: towards a formalization of a research approach. *In Proc. of DIS 2010, ACM Press, 310-319.dfvd*
24. Datacatcher documentaries can be viewed at: www.vimeo.com/channels/Datacatcher

Data Flow, Spatial Physical Computing

Alvaro Cassinelli
cassinelli.alvaro@gmail.com

Daniel Saakes
saakes@kaist.ac.kr

Department of Industrial Design. KAIST

Figure 1. With *Spatial Physical Computing (SPC)* data processing modules are deployed in space and programmed with simple physical actions. Our prototype modules are battery powered and communicate wirelessly to form long range smart sensor/actuator networks. An example scenario is shown on the left: a proximity sensor generate events as a door opens, and a non-collocated accumulator module counts and display them.

ABSTRACT

Latest hardware improvements on transceivers supporting Low Power Wide Area Networks (LPWAN) make it feasible to connect small battery powered devices hundred of meters or even km away. In this paper, we propose a physical computing paradigm fully exploiting this novel technology. *Spatial physical computing* (SPC) leverages not only natural manipulation typically used on TUI and construction kits but also integrates the necessary deambulation (around a building or a city) in the process of creating, testing and tuning a distributed smart sensor/actuator network. The overall system is a compound of (an unlimited) set of independent data-processing nodes supporting an event-driven data-flow programming scheme. We demonstrate in a few examples how such networks can be deployed - spatially programmed - through intuitive physical actions, and discuss the unique qualities and challenges of Spatial Physical Computing.

ACM Classification Keywords

H.5.2 Information Interfaces and Presentation (e.g. HCI): Graphical user interfaces.

Author Keywords

Programming; Spatial; Tangible; Physical Computing

TEI '17, March 20-23, 2017, Yokohama, Japan

© 2017 ACM. ISBN 978-1-4503-4676-4/17/03. . . $15.00

DOI: http://dx.doi.org/10.1145/3024969.3024978

INTRODUCTION

Whereas we traditionally relied on hardwired physical connections for home automation - such as for lighting and audio/video - we will be less likely to use cables to *program* interactive scenarios in our future homes. Advances in low-power computing and wireless communication make it possible to turn everyday objects into smart networked items. Although this introduces flexibility in terms of system architecture, the invisible connections are difficult to make and monitor. A common approach in home automation is to use an abstract, screen based representation of the network and sensor states. Unfortunately, this just transposes the mapping problem from the real world to the GUI interface. In fact, most prototyping platforms for physical computing (Arduino [3], mbed [20] as well as tangible construction kits for teaching programming concepts (e.g., Lego Mindstorms [26]) do not tackle these issues [27] since their philosophy brings a separation between the control/programming layer and the physical arrangement of the devices.

So, the question is: how to design a simple enough physical activity that accounts simultaneously for the network deployment *and* the programming activity itself? Inspiration was found in visual programming languages (such as Max/Msp [8], Pd [24] or LabView [19]). In our proposal, network topology and function are defined through physical actions similar to *patch-cording* common to many visual programming languages; however, since our goal is to create spatially-extended distributed interactive systems, patch-cording needs to handle connections between nodes that may be hundreds of meters away (and not simultaneously visible). We propose a simple way to extend the patch-cording method: nodes are first *en-*

tangled by *preparing* them through simple physical contact before being brought apart, as shown in Figure 2. The user can for instance position (or discover) a module somewhere, touch it with another module to establish a long-range RF-based connection, then walk away and repeat the process on another place hundreds of meters away, as shown in Figure 1. In short, this paper contributes to TEI practices by considering the inherent spatial distribution of the system all the way from the earliest ideation stages to testing-in-use [35]. The proposed implementation may be one out of many, but we believe it is already capable of dealing with most long-range interactive scenarios. Through examples we make a first step to uncover the unique challenges and opportunities of the SPC paradigm that could guide the design of future tangible toolkits, home automation and urban computing systems.

Figure 2. Modules connect in a network through outlets (blue LED) and inlets (red LEDs). Connections are made by holding an outlet near an inlet; the module cycles through the inlets to let users select a specific inlet. Through short range infrared communication, modules negotiate RF connection details. The LED is then lit solid, confirming an established connection. Disconnecting modules is achieved in a similar fashion, by again holding the modules together for a brief time.

RELATED WORK

Constructions kits were conceived under the credo that in order to acquire a proper understanding of *something* one needs to be able to *build that something* from scratch [26]. For that reason, a construction kit is essentially a collection of *bricks*, each instantiating a relevant aspect or function of a given studied technology [21]. In order to understand our present technological reality, construction kits should therefore clearly expose its most salient feature: its capacity to interconnect things wirelessly and at great distances. Despite that logic, we observe that today's most popular physical computing toolkits and construction kits (such as Lego Mindstorms or the more open-ended Arduino platform) mostly target spatially constrained systems. Of course, some (already popular) physical computing kits do away with *cables* for connections and/or tablets for programming, and rely instead on the relative spatial arrangement of modules to build the interaction (e.g. VoodooIO [34], littleBits [4], Siftables [22], Cubelets or RoBlocks [28], Google Blocks [11], Topobo [25]), or for prototyping Internet Of Things (IoT) systems [16]. However, such approaches still result in spatially constrained systems by design; moreover, and spatially speaking, what is important in those approaches is the *relative* position of the modules, since these are to be deployed over a table and rarely (or never) the modules are scattered over an extended area.

On the other end of the spectrum, we find IoT and home automation systems. Sensors and actuators (both physical and virtual) are prepared without any spatial constraint in mind [5]. For instance, controlling lighting using a cellphone or actuating windows accordingly to the weather forecast. Programming is performed through IFTTT recipes, but as recent research indicates, only a minority of recipes involves physical devices [33]. One could rightly argue that prototypes such as Thingy Oriented Programming [12], commercial products such as TrackR [32] (for locating items with a tag) or Flic [18] (a multi-purpose wireless button) are examples of the proposed SPC paradigm. However, not only these instantiations have (very) basic fixed functionality -and activating it can be barely called programming- but most rely on a WiFi or Bluetooth network.

Closer to our approach are systems capable of creating adhoc networks for home automation. Sony Mesh [29] is a distributed sensor/actuator network that can be edited online, but again it relies on a tablet or computer to maintain the network, gather, process and distribute data. The price tag allows for fewer rather than more modules since the targeted market seems to be home automation and not learning and experimentation in the field of physical computing. The Reality Editor [14] is an original AR-oriented approach: passive objects and/or electronic appliances are tagged with fiducial markers, and the user can connect them using an AR interface. While this is more in line with our investigation, it still diverges considerably at the conceptual and implementation levels - from the need of a centralized server-client infrastructure to the recruiting of everyday objects as input/output interfaces with more or less arbitrary functions, thus rendering abstract programming impossible.

The ReacTable [17] is the closest example of what we see as a true SPC system: the network is created through simple gestures, and absolute positions of the modules is relevant both for the user and for the program structure. This is no coincidence since modular synthesizers were the paragon of data-flow oriented machines. ReacTable, however, is implemented over a table; modules are just Plexiglas cubes without computing power; and finally, operations include high-throughput sound streams. In our implementation, each module works more like a physical widget that can, if so desired, be permanently attached to an object to give it input/output capabilities as well as entangling it to other things far away.

DESIGN

A network is composed of several fixed-function modules or nodes. These are battery-powered sensor/actuator/processing units, exchanging data over an RF LoRa based protocol. As explained in the introduction and simply put: this is an attempt to instantiate in the physical world (and without spatial constraints) the "pipes and filter" software design pattern [7]

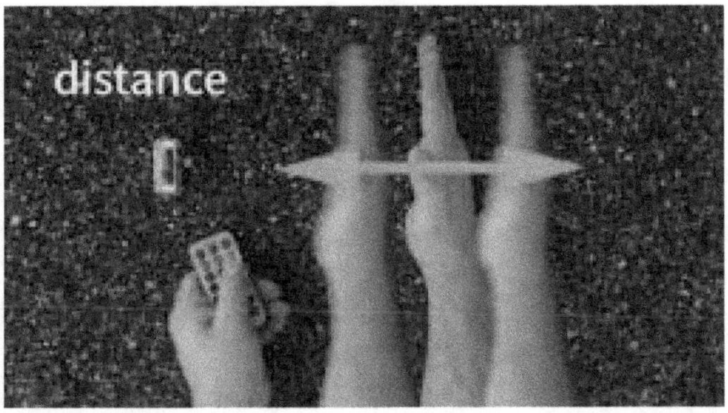

Figure 3. A teach button on the remote control activates the sensor programming mode. In this case a proximity sensor is physically trained by demonstrating a range of values.

Figure 4. A countdown alarm is made with a dial, counter, button and buzzer module. Connections are shown in green. The dial sets the top number through the 2nd inlet of the counter, the button decrements the counter through the 3rd inlet. The counter outputs a bang on zero.

and the philosophy of visual programming languages such as Max/Msp.

A typical module has three inlets and one outlet, as shown in Figure 2. The module receives data on the inlets and combine that with local sensor data (if any) to compute some function. The result is delivered through the (unique) output, and used to control a local actuator (if any). Data can be a *bang* message, forcing the module to execute its computation and deliver the result, or a *value* message such as a sensor value or a number set by a dial module. Inlets (resp. outlets) can connect to multiple sending (resp. receiving) nodes enabling arbitrarily complex network topologies and allowing for a variety of functionality. A connection between two modules is made by simply bringing the modules together, outlet near inlets. Through short range Infrared communication, modules negotiate connection details. Inlet/outlet LEDs signal each established connection. Holding the modules together makes the modules cycle the connection through its inputs, letting the user select a specific inlet. Once a connection is made, modules communicate exclusively over RF and can be deployed. Breaking particular connections is achieved in a similar fashion, by again holding the modules together.

Module Types

Conceptually, there are three types of nodes: sensors, actuators, and processing nodes. In reality, each node is a blend of these three functions. A key design constraint is to keep a manageable number of different nodes each with a simple and dedicated function, yet the set should be sufficiently rich to support a variety of scenarios.

Sensor modules work by detecting events and generating a bang at the outlet. Trigger conditions are taught by example or teach-in. As shown in Figure 3, it suffices to press a learning button and then simulate the condition limits for a few seconds. Most sensors (distance, sound-level, force, tilt, etc) can use this principle; in case teach-in is not realistic (e.g. setting a temperature range), the range can be set using values received on the second and third inlet. Note that receiving a bang on the first inlet causes the module to read and pass the sensed value through the outlet, even if this was not an "event". This is useful for data-logging and real-time sensor displays. Sensors modules include input interfaces such as dials, buttons and sliders, and automatically output their state when actuated upon (change event).

Actuator modules obey to a bang or value on the first, second or third inlet by actuating some hardware device. Typical actuator modules host a buzzer, a solenoid, an RGB LED or a display. The second and third inlet can be used to set parameters for the actuator (maximum or minimum values, type of pulse, etc).

Processing modules: Most modules contain some sort of logic, e.g. when to output and how to handle data on the inlets. However, while simple sensors and actuators may have some signal processing capacity or learning logic, processing modules are truly programmable max/msp-like objects: input parameters are given by the data on the inlets, but they also have their own internal state variables and logic. Simple examples are modules that combine inlets with logic gates, perform simple arithmetic calculations, or delay or synchronize messages.

Making Networks

The key advantage of SPC is that it integrates test analysis and design not only for physical prototyping [13] but also within the environment and in-use [35]. When studying the principle, two deployment work-flows naturally emerged. A first approach is to design and build a network on a table before deploying the modules in space. For instance, modules can be arranged on a large sheet of paper, while connections are sketched and annotated in place with pens or post-its. Alternatively, networks are programmed *in situ*. For example, counting how many people enter a building (Figure 1), is made with a few modules as follows: first, a proximity sensor module is mounted near a door, and connected to a hand-held buzzer module. Therefore, the (previously taught) activation range can be immediately tested and confirmed with a beeping sound. Then, the buzzer can be disconnected and replaced with a counter module that records the number of events. This counter module (that also works as a convenient display) can be positioned at any location within range of the RF signal.

Networks can be described as directed graphs. Figure 4, shows a simple (non-recursive) event-counter network. A dial is connected to the second inlet of the counter module, to set the top number by hand. The button module is connected to the third inlet and each button press lowers the displayed number (the first inlet of the number module increases the counter). When the counter reaches zero it outputs a bang, and the buzzer beeps. Networks can be also be cyclic. For instance the network shown in Figure 4 can be turned into a (one time) countdown sequence (i.e, a *for loop*) using a metro(nome) module. The metro function can be toggled using a bang on its first inlet. When active, if the metro is connected to the counter module, it will make it count down to zero. A buzzer will make a sound when zero is reached, but if we connect its output back to the toggle inlet of the metro, the metro would stop beating.

A popular activity in STEM (Science, Technology, Engineering, and Mathematics) education is measuring and collecting data in the environment. A simple sensor network with a metro(nome) module can be made to accomplish this as shown in Figure 5. A dial is connected to the 2nd inlet of the metronome to set the sampling frequency. The output of the metro is connected to the first inlet of a sensor module to make it output its value on a bang. A number module could then displays the sensed value in real time, a data logging module store the data on an SD card or a gateway module upload this to the Cloud.

Application Scenarios

With only a few modules a wide variety of applications can be accomplished that scale from tabletop, home, to urban computing and show the potential for the TEI community. Scenarios sketched here can be designed using traditional prototyping platforms such as Zigbee [2] mesh networks and Arduinos. However, our claim is that SPC and our initial implementation let users and designers focus on the situated design or ad-hoc solutions rather the diving into programming and debugging low-level distributed computing for custom made solutions.

Data loggers consist of one or more sensors and a metro module, to sample and log data somewhere. *Event loggers* can also count the number of particular events. More complicated networks could include number modules that show a maximum or minimum or display a timestamp. SPC logging networks could be put to use to prototype urban computing systems [23] such as sensors networks for citizen science [15], opinion gatherers [10] or in-the-wild displays [9] as it embeds computation in the real world. Because modules do not require internet, SPC could function in remote or rural areas, on the water, and possibly in balloons.

Simple communication networks such as a doorbell. Morse code signaling can be made uni or bi-directional combining a button and a buzzer. When made wearable, modules could be put to use for multi-user interaction such as games, but also as portable alarms within buildings, playgrounds or neighborhoods. Programming and deployment can be a teaching activity in itself.

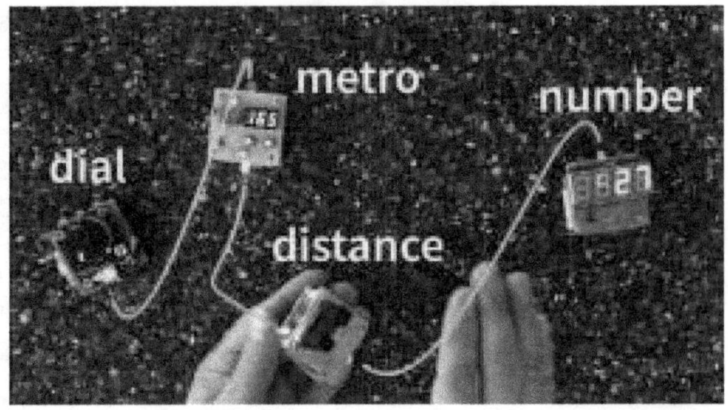

Figure 5. Measuring real time sensor values can be easily achieved using a metro(nome) module. The metro outputs a bang at a specified frequency, forcing the sensor to output its value. The number module displays it.

Sensors and alarms could be made on the spot and without requiring a smart phone network for instance to detect a flood in a basement, track temperature in an oven, etc. [31]. Baby alarms could react on sound level and could be made wearable. Other wearable applications could be found in ad-hoc reminders, for instance to support the elderly.

PROTOTYPE

A module is composed of three physical layers: (a) a reconfigurable sensing/actuation “shield”; (b) the communication layer (IR and RF transceivers) and (c) the microcontroller and power layer. The current prototype consists of hand-manufactured modules with a custom made shield housing common controls (a button, a rotary encoder), actuators (a buzzer, an RGB LED, a four digit 7-segment display), and a metronome with a start-stop button and a display for the frequency. The sensor and actuator shield does not yet use a standard physical protocol; instead, we have exposed several pins of the microcontroller (GPIO pins, I2C and SPI). We plan to standardize the connector, possibly using the Groove [30] to reuse hardware from other classic construction kits such as Phidgets or littleBits. Connecting modules manually is handled using infrared NEC IrDA protocol. Carrier detection is performed by a TSOP38238 IC. An IR beacon is generated every second by an IR LED driven at a very low current to reduce the transmission range to a few centimeters. The IR beacon broadcasts the RF node identifier. When a connection is accepted, it is stored in the EEPROM in both modules, and the modules start communicating over RF. The RF transceiver is an RFM69 module [1] , capable of transmitting at low baudrates over a distance of 300m using a license-free ISM (Industry Scientific and Medical) frequency band. Data transmission is only one way: towards the nodes connected to the outlet. Data transferred is of the simplest nature: in most of the cases, it’s a binary value (an event has taken place or not). It can also be more complex (for instance, numeric values from a sensor). The sender ID and the timing of arrival are retrieved from the header of the RF packet. A typical packet is always less than 60 bytes and it’s transmitted rarely (only when an event is detected). As this is an asynchronous data-driven network, time stamp plays an important role: the node can be set to "latch" (i.e. "compute") only when all the required data on the inlets is presented simultaneously. Alternatively, it can process the data whenever all the required data is ready on the inlets (messages sent to any inlets store the values on the objects and signal it as new data until it is used). Finally, data can be processed only when signaling this explicitly by sending a "bang" on the first (leftmost) inlet (values arriving at this inlet carry an implicit "bang" message, just as in MAX/MSP). While transmitting at maximum power (20 dB), the module needs about 100 mA. However, since transmission is infrequent, most of the time the device is in listening mode, consuming only 16mA. Therefore, we found that without any kind of power optimization (sleep modes), a 300mAh LiPo battery is sufficient to power the device for a few hours.

DISCUSSION

The goal of Spatial Physical Computing is to bridge the gap between 1) the present physical computing practices, namely programming embedded systems to be deployed later in the environment, and generally resulting in spatially constrained systems when teaching and 2) the growing reality of the Internet of Things, that nowadays rest on many different commercial APIs and diverse existing wireless infrastructures. Our approach is a basic technique for building and deploying distributed physical computing systems sharing some aspects of both worlds. No computer, tablet or smartphone is needed to configure or maintain the system. Event-driven programming is popular over mobile platforms today because it captures, in the virtual realm, the complexity of real world interactions. It is surprising then that a coherent "programming" framework has not been yet proposed in the field of physical computing nor in spatial computing [6]; we set ourselves to investigate the potential of the SPC paradigm, but for this, it is still necessary to make a number of design choices. Indeed, while developing SPC, two themes emerged related to the interaction design of such networks, detailed below.

Considerations when Making Nodes Physical

We can foresee a future in which the hardware that composes the modules will be cheap enough so that creating relatively simple Max/Msp like networks will not be more "costly" than drawing them on the computer. However, current reasons of cost and practicality make it unreasonable to break down node functionality too much. Put another way, we cannot just translate, in the physical world, the design choices made for GUI based, 2D visual programming languages. We need to find the right level of functional decomposition: on one side "thin" elements (very simple sensor or actuator modules with some functionality), and on the other side "fat" modules (or processing elements with more computer power and/or hardware interfaces). For the same reasons, we may take a hybrid approach following some design choices made on platforms such as littleBits or even Arduino. That is, instead of having a fixed function module, attaching and detaching physical parts (or "shields") to the module can reconfigure certain functional aspects - for instance inverting inputs or outputs, adding delays or setting the mode of "latching" (synchronous or asynchronous)

Finally, if one wants to realize the vision of a one dollar "coin" module that can remain functional for months or years, power remains an important handicap. We believe that given the event-driven approach (and thus extremely low average bitrate of the system), this will likely not be a problem in the next iteration of the system, at least for sensing, data processing, and LoRa RF communication. We estimate that even without new cell technology, solar charging and power optimization (periodic deep sleep), should be enough to maintain modules running for months.

Visualizing Invisible Connections

Some problems not explicitly addressed in this paper are how to simulate, analyze and debug a network before, during or after deployment. The current modules indicate a connection with a single color LED on inlets and outlet so that networks with multiple connections cannot be visually identified. Future nodes will have RGB LEDs instead so that each virtual patch-cord (i.e edge of the network) will feature a unique color. Associated with this is the problem of whole-network discovery. We are tackling this problem by using a "sniffer" module connected to the computer. It listens to all the communications in the network and represents it on a 2D interface resembling a Max/Msp patch. This software can also be used to simulate a network. In parallel, we are exploring two different Augmented Reality solutions to the problem of network monitoring. The first is similar to ReacTable and is useful when studying a system over a table, *before* deployment. It consists of projecting the invisible links between the modules and graphically represent the flow of the data. Alternatively, if we need to monitor a network already deployed in space, we may use fiducial trackers or other 3D tracking alternatives and highlight the links as virtual patch-cords or bezier curves augmenting the real space.

CONCLUSION AND FUTURE WORK

Our goal with this research is to expand the reach of physical computing and its teaching by introducing real-world, spatial (functional, aesthetic) considerations from the start. Most intriguing, and because of the expected miniaturization and cost fall of its electronic components, those modules could be shared and exchanged by all, and function as a pervasive *physical computing resource* or *currency* capable of creating and sustaining - bottom-up - the infrastructure of a smart city. Future work is to deploy the prototype modules in a STEM environment. With the help of Plan Ceibal in Uruguay [36], we are producing 50 modules for an "in-the-wild" user test, including teachers and students of various ages.

Apart from the use as a teaching platform integrating distributed system thinking, the system could become a ubiquitous sensing/actuator network covering large (rural?) areas, and if robust enough, it could even be a cheap way to prototype, tune and deploy autonomous control systems in industrial plants or farmlands. Finally, an important goal is to reduce the cost of each module under a couple of dollars, allowing for a large and truly democratic deployment as well as making it easy to repair or hack the hardware for other purposes. Low cost will render the system accessible to children of all ages (can break without fear), but also adults and creative makers.

REFERENCES

1. LoRa Alliance. 2016a. Mobile Experts White Paper for LoRa Alliance Where does LoRa Fit in the Big Picture? (2016). Retrieved Retrieved August 3, 2016 from https://www.lora-alliance.org/portals/0/documents/whitepapers/20160404JG_Mobile_Experts_Whitepaper_LoRa_Alliance.pdf.
2. ZigBee Alliance. 2016b. Zigbee. (2016). Retrieved August 3, 2016 from http://www.zigbee.org.
3. Massimo Banzi, David Cuartielles, Tom Igoe, Gianluca Martino, and David Mellis. 2016. Arduino. (2016). Retrieved August 3, 2016 from http://www.arduino.cc.
4. Ayah Bdeir. 2009. Electronics As Material: LittleBits. In *Proceedings of the 3rd International Conference on Tangible and Embedded Interaction (TEI '09)*. ACM, New York, NY, USA, 397–400. DOI: http://dx.doi.org/10.1145/1517664.1517743
5. Michael Blackstock and Rodger Lea. 2014. Toward a Distributed Data Flow Platform for the Web of Things (Distributed Node-RED). In *Proceedings of the 5th International Workshop on Web of Things (WoT '14)*. ACM, New York, NY, USA, 34–39. DOI: http://dx.doi.org/10.1145/2684432.2684439
6. C. Borcea, C. Intanagonwiwat, P. Kang, U. Kremer, and L. Iftode. 2004. Spatial programming using smart messages: design and implementation. In *24th International Conference on Distributed Computing Systems, 2004. Proceedings.* 690–699. DOI: http://dx.doi.org/10.1109/ICDCS.2004.1281637
7. Frank Buschmann, Regine Meunier, Hans Rohnert, Peter Sommerlad, and Michael Stal. 1996. *Pattern-Oriented Software Architecture, Volume 1, A System of Patterns.* Wiley, Chichester, UK.
8. Cycling74. 2016. Max connects objects with virtual patch cords to create interactive sounds, graphics, and custom effects. (2016). Retrieved August 3, 2016 from https://cycling74.com/products/max.
9. Sarah Gallacher, Jenny O'Connor, Jon Bird, Yvonne Rogers, Licia Capra, Daniel Harrison, and Paul Marshall. 2015. Mood Squeezer: Lightening Up the Workplace Through Playful and Lightweight Interactions. In *Proceedings of the 18th ACM Conference on Computer Supported Cooperative Work & Social Computing (CSCW '15)*. ACM, New York, NY, USA, 891–902. DOI: http://dx.doi.org/10.1145/2675133.2675170
10. Connie Golsteijn, Sarah Gallacher, Lisa Koeman, Lorna Wall, Sami Andberg, Yvonne Rogers, and Licia Capra. 2015. VoxBox: A Tangible Machine That Gathers Opinions from the Public at Events. In *Proceedings of the Ninth International Conference on Tangible, Embedded, and Embodied Interaction (TEI '15)*. ACM, New York, NY, USA, 201–208. DOI: http://dx.doi.org/10.1145/2677199.2680588
11. Google. 2016. Project Bloks: creating a development platform for tangible programming. (2016). Retrieved August 3, 2016 from https://projectbloks.withgoogle.com/.
12. Florian Güldenpfennig, Daniel Dudo, and Peter Purgathofer. 2016. Toward Thingy Oriented Programming: Recording Marcos With Tangibles. In *Proceedings of the TEI '16: Tenth International Conference on Tangible, Embedded, and Embodied Interaction (TEI '16)*. ACM, New York, NY, USA, 455–461. DOI: http://dx.doi.org/10.1145/2839462.2856550
13. Björn Hartmann, Scott R. Klemmer, Michael Bernstein, Leith Abdulla, Brandon Burr, Avi Robinson-Mosher, and Jennifer Gee. 2006. Reflective Physical Prototyping Through Integrated Design, Test, and Analysis. In *Proceedings of the 19th Annual ACM Symposium on User Interface Software and Technology (UIST '06)*. ACM, New York, NY, USA, 299–308. DOI: http://dx.doi.org/10.1145/1166253.1166300
14. Valentin Heun, James Hobin, and Pattie Maes. 2013. Reality Editor: Programming Smarter Objects. In *Proceedings of the 2013 ACM Conference on Pervasive and Ubiquitous Computing Adjunct Publication (UbiComp '13 Adjunct)*. ACM, New York, NY, USA, 307–310. DOI: http://dx.doi.org/10.1145/2494091.2494185
15. Steven Houben, Connie Golsteijn, Sarah Gallacher, Rose Johnson, Saskia Bakker, Nicolai Marquardt, Licia Capra, and Yvonne Rogers. 2016. Physikit: Data Engagement Through Physical Ambient Visualizations in the Home. In *Proceedings of the 2016 CHI Conference on Human Factors in Computing Systems (CHI '16)*. ACM, New York, NY, USA, 1608–1619. DOI: http://dx.doi.org/10.1145/2858036.2858059
16. Tom Jenkins. 2015. Designing the "Things" of the IoT. In *Proceedings of the Ninth International Conference on Tangible, Embedded, and Embodied Interaction (TEI '15)*. ACM, New York, NY, USA, 449–452. DOI: http://dx.doi.org/10.1145/2677199.2691608
17. Sergi Jordà, Martin Kaltenbrunner, Günter Geiger, and Marcos Alonso. 2006. The reacTable: A Tangible Tabletop Musical Instrument and Collaborative Workbench. In *ACM SIGGRAPH 2006 Sketches (SIGGRAPH '06)*. ACM, New York, NY, USA, Article 91. DOI:http://dx.doi.org/10.1145/1179849.1179963
18. Shortcut labs Sweden. 2016. Flic. the smart wireless button. (2016). Retrieved August 3, 2016 from https://www.thetrackr.com.
19. Labview. 2016. LabVIEW System Design Software. (2016). Retrieved August 3, 2016 from http://www.ni.com/labview/.
20. Mbed. 2016. Mbed. (2016). Retrieved August 3, 2016 from http://www.Mbed.com.

21. David A. Mellis and Leah Buechley. 2012. Case Studies in the Personal Fabrication of Electronic Products. In *Proceedings of the Designing Interactive Systems Conference (DIS '12)*. ACM, New York, NY, USA, 268–277. DOI: http://dx.doi.org/10.1145/2317956.2317998

22. David Merrill, Jeevan Kalanithi, and Pattie Maes. 2007. Siftables: Towards Sensor Network User Interfaces. In *Proceedings of the 1st International Conference on Tangible and Embedded Interaction (TEI '07)*. ACM, New York, NY, USA, 75–78. DOI: http://dx.doi.org/10.1145/1226969.1226984

23. Eric Paulos and Tom Jenkins. 2005. Urban Probes: Encountering Our Emerging Urban Atmospheres. In *Proceedings of the SIGCHI Conference on Human Factors in Computing Systems (CHI '05)*. ACM, New York, NY, USA, 341–350. DOI: http://dx.doi.org/10.1145/1054972.1055020

24. Miller Puckette. 2016. Pure Data. (2016). Retrieved August 3, 2016 from https://puredata.info.

25. Hayes Solos Raffle, Amanda J. Parkes, and Hiroshi Ishii. 2004. Topobo: A Constructive Assembly System with Kinetic Memory. In *Proceedings of the SIGCHI Conference on Human Factors in Computing Systems (CHI '04)*. ACM, New York, NY, USA, 647–654. DOI: http://dx.doi.org/10.1145/985692.985774

26. Mitchel Resnick. 1993. Behavior Construction Kits. *Commun. ACM* 36, 7 (July 1993), 64–71. DOI: http://dx.doi.org/10.1145/159544.159593

27. Joel Sadler, Kevin Durfee, Lauren Shluzas, and Paulo Blikstein. 2015. Bloctopus: A Novice Modular Sensor System for Playful Prototyping. In *Proceedings of the Ninth International Conference on Tangible, Embedded, and Embodied Interaction (TEI '15)*. ACM, New York, NY, USA, 347–354. DOI: http://dx.doi.org/10.1145/2677199.2680581

28. Eric Schweikardt and Mark D Gross. 2008. The Robot is the Program: Interacting with roBlocks. In *Proceedings of the 2Nd International Conference on Tangible and Embedded Interaction (TEI '08)*. ACM, New York, NY, USA, 167–168. DOI: http://dx.doi.org/10.1145/1347390.1347427

29. Sony. 2016. With MESH, anything can become a smart device! Make your very own IoT system. (2016). Retrieved August 3, 2016 from http://meshprj.com/en/.

30. Seeed Studio. 2016. groove. (2016). Retrieved August 3, 2016 from http://www.seeedstudio.com/wiki/Grove_System.

31. Supermechanical. 2016. supermechanical. (2016). Retrieved November 10, 2016 from http://supermechanical.com.

32. TrackR. 2016. Find lost Items in Seconds. (2016). Retrieved August 3, 2016 from https://www.thetrackr.com.

33. Blase Ur, Melwyn Pak Yong Ho, Stephen Brawner, Jiyun Lee, Sarah Mennicken, Noah Picard, Diane Schulze, and Michael L. Littman. 2016. Trigger-Action Programming in the Wild: An Analysis of 200,000 IFTTT Recipes. In *Proceedings of the 2016 CHI Conference on Human Factors in Computing Systems (CHI '16)*. ACM, New York, NY, USA, 3227–3231. DOI: http://dx.doi.org/10.1145/2858036.2858556

34. Nicolas Villar and Hans Gellersen. 2007. A Malleable Control Structure for Softwired User Interfaces. In *Proceedings of the 1st International Conference on Tangible and Embedded Interaction (TEI '07)*. ACM, New York, NY, USA, 49–56. DOI: http://dx.doi.org/10.1145/1226969.1226980

35. Ron Wakkary and Leah Maestri. 2007. The Resourcefulness of Everyday Design. In *Proceedings of the 6th ACM SIGCHI Conference on Creativity & Cognition (C&C '07)*. ACM, New York, NY, USA, 163–172. DOI: http://dx.doi.org/10.1145/1254960.1254984

36. Wikipedia. 2016. Ceibal project. (2016). Retrieved August 3, 2016 from https://en.wikipedia.org/wiki/Ceibal_project.

Button+: Supporting User and Context Aware Interaction Through Shape-Changing Interfaces

Jihoon Suh
Department of Human Centered Design and Engineering, University of Washington
Seattle, WA, 98195, USA
jihoons@uw.edu

Wooshik Kim
Department of Mechanical Engineering, KAIST
Daejeon, Republic of Korea
briankim13@kaist.ac.kr

Andrea Bianchi
Department of Industrial Design, KAIST
Daejeon, Republic of Korea
andrea@kaist.ac.kr

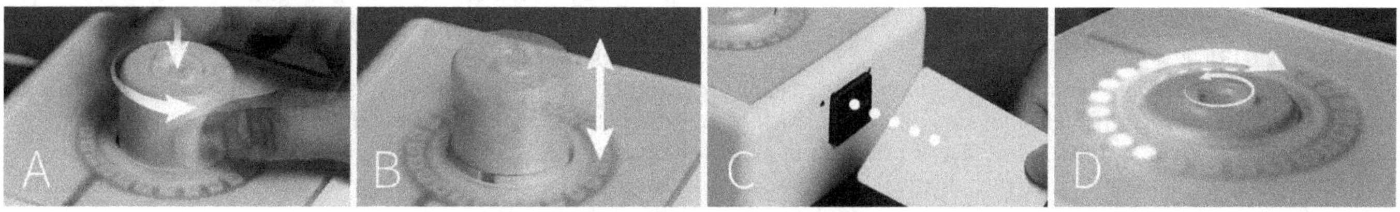

Figure 1. Components of Button+: A) rotary knob and pushbutton, B) actuated shaft with input capabilities, C) RFID reader, D) LED circular array and rotary haptic display.

ABSTRACT
Shape-changing interfaces are an emerging topic in HCI research: they merge the simplicity of tangible interfaces with the expressiveness of dynamic physical affordances. However, while prior work largely focused on technical aspects and proposed classifications of shape-changing interfaces based on the physical properties of the actuators and the user's levels of control, this work presents a classification of shape-changing interfaces based on the context and identity of the users. After introducing a new prototype for a shape-changing pushbutton, we conducted a series of workshop studies with designers and engineers to explore the design space and potential applications for this interface. We used the result of our workshops to propose a generalized taxonomy of interactions, and built two applications that reflect the proposed model. The paper concludes by highlighting future possible research directions for *context and user aware* shape-changing interfaces.

Author Keywords
Button interface; shape-changing interface; context-aware; design; personalization.

TEI '17, March 20-23, 2017, Yokohama, Japan
© 2017 ACM. ISBN 978-1-4503-4676-4/17/03…$15.00
DOI: http://dx.doi.org/10.1145/3024969.3024980

ACM Classification Keywords
H.5.2. Information interfaces and presentation (e.g., HCI): User Interfaces

INTRODUCTION
Shape-changing interfaces are becoming an increasingly interesting topic of research in HCI, mostly because they combine the intuitiveness of tangible interfaces [15] with the capability (typical of purely digital graphical interfaces) of displaying adaptive and dynamic content over time [14]. In the past, researchers have studied shape-changing interfaces with different form factors [12, 22], made from mechanical or deforming materials [7, 24, 25, 33], with both input (e.g., controllers) and output (e.g., physical displays) capabilities. Moreover, researchers have also acknowledged the advantage of shape-changing interfaces for different types of interactions through the use of dynamic affordances [32] and proposed numerous classifications [27, 29].

However, while most of prior work focused on various technological actuation methods for physical transformations and novel interaction techniques, this paper identifies a research opportunity in exploring the design space of shape-changing interfaces depending on the users and the context of use. Through a sequence of design workshops with designers and engineers, we explored in detail the benefits and design opportunities of dynamic physical affordances, and propose a novel taxonomy of interaction with shape-changing interfaces. In order to gather the most generalized results from the workshops, we designed and developed Button+, a custom-made simple shape-changing interface in the form-factor of an augmented pushbutton (arguably the most familiar and ubiquitous input interface in commercial products [1, 17]).

This paper contributes to prior work by proposing an alternative framework for classifying interactions with shape-changing interfaces, that is not based on technology [27], physical shapes [29], emotional expressiveness [20], or levels of control [28], but rather on the context of interaction (situation and users). The rest of the paper is organized as follows: we introduce prominent related work about shape-changing interfaces, and we describe the Button+ prototype. We present the workshop studies and their results, and a classification of the design space under two main dimensions. Based on this framework, we implement and present two applications that showcase the spectrum of these interactions. Finally, we discuss limitations and future avenues of research.

RELATED WORK

Shape-changing interfaces can act both as input devices and output displays, with different levels of control [28]. Therefore, it is difficult to draw a line between the input and output modalities, as changes in the physical form factor impact both on the abilities of users to manipulate the interface through affordances [5] or to understand notifications and ambient information. Though prior extensive classifications exist [29], in our review we simply present prior works categorized according to whether emphasis was on the input or output modality.

Shape-changing interfaces as output displays

Shape-changing output displays described in the literature span over a variety of physical interfaces with different mechanical properties (e.g., changes in volume, orientation, form, textures [20]), form factors (e.g., table-alike surfaces [21], robotic avatars [27], mobile devices [11]) and applications (e.g., ambient displays [e.g., 13], wearable notification systems [e.g., 10] and communication devices [26]). From the technical point of view, most shape-changing displays are made of mechanical components or special materials. For example, Surflex is a shape-change display that uses shape-memory alloys to alter its surface [4], while PneUI uses pneumatically actuating soft materials [34].

Among mechanically actuated systems, Hong et al. introduced an ambient flower-shaped avatar that changes depending on the sitting posture of the user [13], while Park et al. [26] presented Wrigglo, a peripheral smartphone avatar for interpersonal communication. More complex shape-changing displays require multiple actuators in order to render complex geometries with greater accuracy. For example, FEELEX [16] is an array of linear actuators that deforms its shape. This work influenced several similar systems which provide technical improvements and refinements, though they substantially belong to the same family of kinetic surfaces (e.g., Lumen [27], Relief [21], inFORM [7], PocoPoco [18], Dynamic bar chart [32]). A notable system in this same category, although one-dimensional, is LineFORM [24].

Shape-changing interfaces for input

Similar to output displays, shape-changing input interfaces come in a variety of forms, complexity and usages. Among the most common usages, computer assistive input controllers are a particularly popular application domain.

DO-IT is an early example of a deformable input interface [23]. Deformation was later further explored by Michelitsch et al. [22] with an interface that switches the mode of interaction depending on the way it is held or squeezed. The Inflatable Mouse [19] is a computer mouse which enables different modes of interaction through changes of volumes, while Métamorphe is a computer keyboard made of vertically actuated keys with augmented capabilities [2]. Other shape-changing input controllers have the shape of buttons or dials, such as the actuated buttons described by Snibbe et al. [31], the pneumatically actuated buttons by Harrison et al. [9], and the dynamic button-knob for mobile devices by Hemmert et al. [12]. Tiab et al. [33] recently empirically explored the affordances for various shape-changing buttons.

BUTTON+

Button+ is a shape-changing button interface with input and output capabilities (Figure 2). Because physical buttons are easy to understand, pervasive and ubiquitously found in commercially available products [1, 17], we explicitly designed Button+ with the form factor of a pushbutton so that it may be suitable for a wide range of possible interactions. Specifically, because the physicality of traditional buttons can provide implicit information to users, researchers have suggested to adopt buttons with dynamic adjustments for novel interaction techniques [1]. Button+ is our attempt to create a customizable interaction with an augmented and expressive shape-changing pushbutton interface.

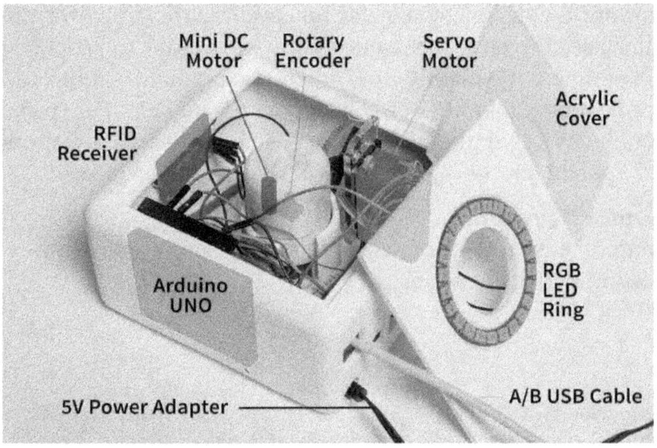

Figure 2. Button+ internal components and assembly.

PROTOTYPE

The prototype of Button+ not only mounts a regular pushdown button (Figure 1A), but it also includes a protractible/retractable knob that can be spun, pushed or pulled (Figure 1B), an RFID reader for identifying users or commands (Figure 1C), and a visual and haptic display for notifications and feedback (Figure 1D).

Button+ is shaped as a squared 132 x 132 mm 3D printed box (height: 73 mm) with rounded edges containing electro-mechanical parts, and an Arduino UNO development board wired to a controlling computer. The Button+ case hosts a cylindrical 70mm high by 38ø mm vertical shaft that can extend up to 30 mm from the top of the box. The shaft can be used as a rotary knob capable of continuous 360° spinning, sensed by a 24 step rotary encoder. The protraction of the knob was achieved by means of a custom-made rack-and-pinion geared mechanism (Figure 3). The pinion (60 teeth gear, 38ø mm) and the rack (20 teeth, height 40 mm) were laser-cut from 4mm thick acrylic sheets and are actuated by a 180° servo motor (HES-288, speed: 0.22sec/60°, torque: 2500 gf-cm at 5V) mounted on the box. Inside the box, a hollow cylinder was used to constrain the shaft to only vertical movements.

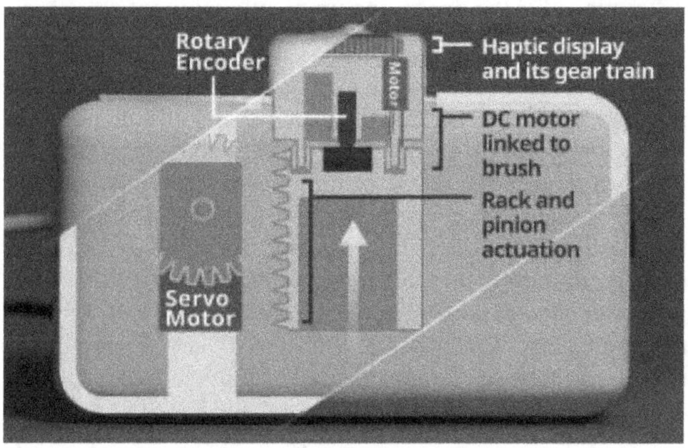

Figure 3. Rack and pinion actuation, brushing, and gearing required for the haptic display.

The servo motor was modified to be position-readable, by attaching additional wires to the internal potentiometer. This allows sensing push and pull forces applied on the knob by the user (~5.3 to ~6.3 Newtons), which results in a vertical displacement (servo motor *backdriving*). The knob is surrounded by a circular array of 24 RGB LEDs (Adafruit Neopixel ring) and it houses a custom-made rotary haptic display mounted on a small DC motor (200rpm, 0.1W at 3V). A 125 kHz RFID reader (ID-12LA) is mounted on the side of the Button+ box. The DC motor and the LED ring were powered separately by an external power supply (5V, 2A). Finally, 3D printed parts were post-processed using Tetrahydrofuran and polished with sand paper, while the top of the box was covered with a 112 x 112 mm clear sand-blasted acrylic sheet.

DESIGN WORKSHOP

To understand the design space and practical opportunities of physical shape-changing interfaces as a consumer product, we organized a series of design workshops with interaction designers and engineers. Prior studies with shape-changing interface used design workshops to collect participants' feedback and generate ideas for applications [8, 6]. Similarly, our workshop's main objective was to generate numerous applications for the Button+ interface and to describe specific input/output interactions that would take advantage of the shape-changing capabilities.

Participants

We recruited 12 volunteers (5 female) from the authors' affiliated institution (*KAIST,* South Korea*),* aged 21 to 29 (M: 25.0, SD: 2.09) of which 6 were designers and 6 engineers. All participants had a minimum of four years of study in their disciplines, with expertise in product or interaction design, mechanical or electrical engineering, and computer science. All participants were compensated with USD 10 in local currency for their time.

Method and material

We conducted a total of three design workshops. Each design workshop took approximately 90 minutes with a team composed of two designers and two engineers. It took place in a designated meeting room with a large TV screen and a table. Participants sat in a circle and were provided a pen, handouts, and paper for scribbling. A moderator (one of the authors) and a staff helper supervised the workshop sessions at all times. Workshops were also video recorded for subsequent analysis.

At the start of the workshop, after a brief welcoming session and after signing a consent form, the participants were given an introduction to the concept of shape-changing interfaces. They were then given a 5-minute demonstration of Button+, placed on the center of the table, and were encouraged to try to use it. A software with minimal GUI was used to display the numerical values from each input modality of the prototype (pushbutton state, knob rotation and vertical position). For the output modality, a computer keyboard was used to issue commands and demonstrate the visual and haptic notifications, and the protraction/retraction of the knob.

After the introduction, a 4-3-5 *brain-writing* session (a variation of the 6-3-5 brain-writing method [30]) was used to collect participant's ideas. The brain-writing method is a popular technique focused on generating a large quantity of collaborative ideas in written form. Initially, each of the four participants simultaneously drew on paper three different ideas within five minutes, then passed the sheet of paper to another participant, who further developed them. This process repeated four times, with each participant adding three ideas that refined and built upon previous ones. After 20 minutes each team produced 12 complete ideas documented on paper, each composed by four iterations (48 sketches in total). During the 4-3-5 sessions participants were allowed to ask clarifications to the moderator and to other team members.

After the 4-3-5 session, the moderator guided a discussion among the participants about the ideas that they drew on paper. Each participant was given the time to voice his/her favorite ideas, and rank them for functionality and novelty. Then, the team unanimously nominated the best four ideas and filled out the final concept sheets, with changes reflecting the team discussion. The workshop was concluded with a short debriefing, and for each team we collected the sheets containing the sketches generated during the 4-3-5 sessions and the final nominated ideas.

WORKSHOP RESULTS AND CLASSIFICATION

We reviewed all the sketches collected from the design workshops, and extracted 10 unique application ideas by merging similar concepts. Using an affinity diagram and the recordings of the discussions in the workshops, we clustered ideas according to whether emphasis was put on the identity of the users or on the context of interaction. We also considered whether the users had control over the shape-changing capabilities (e.g., customizable functions mapped to different shapes), or whether changes were system-controlled and users could simply react to them.

Following this process, we present a taxonomy of interaction with shape-changing interfaces with two orthogonal dimensions: *user-context awareness* and the *active-passive role* of the user. The resulting four areas correspond to four different interaction styles, which we named as *Situational*, *Role-based*, *"Swiss Army Knife"* and *Personalized.* The following sections describe in detail these areas and the ideas composing them.

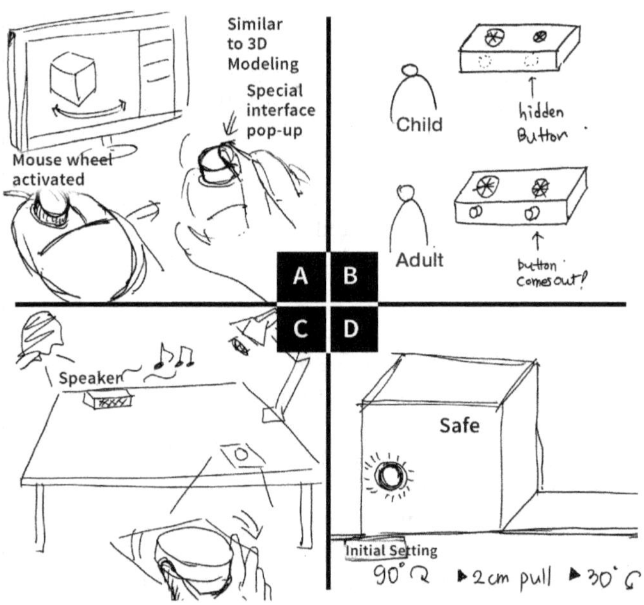

Figure 4. Sketches from the design workshops, showing possible applications of Button+: A) App Specific Mouse, B) Hidden Stove, C) Desk Universal Controller, D) Safer Safe.

Context Aware Interaction

The category *Context Aware* describes those interactions that require the interface to change shape depending on the context of use. For example, the interface could implicitly change depending on the specific types of activities that the user is performing (*Situational*), or could be explicitly changed by the user to select a specific functionality out of many (*"Swiss Army Knife"*).

Situational

Situational interaction depends on which activity the user is engaged with or the peripheral information available. For example, S1 is an idea for a game keypad that changes shape depending on the state of the game. As the game becomes more complex and the game-character evolves, the controllers available to the users dynamically change. S2 presents a computer mouse-like device that changes shape to support different types of input depending on the PC application used. Similar to previous work [19, 23], our participants described an interface that looks like a computer mouse but "acts as a more sophisticated tool when dealing with minute adjustment such as computer-aided modeling or drawings" (Figure 4A). Finally, S3 is a car navigational and audio wheel-like interface, similar to the BMW iDrive [3], that hides itself when the vehicle is in motion to minimize distractions for the driver and unintentional input.

"Swiss Army Knife"

Following the metaphor of a Swiss Army Knife, a multi-purpose knife-kit that includes multiple tools in one, our workshop participants envisioned situations in which the user can modify the shape of the interface to select specific actions among many possibilities. For example, K4 is a remote light controller that specifies the intensity or colors of different lamps located in the room. K5 is a multi-device universal remote controller for the desk (Figure 4C). Using this controller, a user can switch on/off any device in the room, as well as control other parameters of specific appliances (e.g., changing orientation and speed of a fan).

	Context Aware	User Aware
PASSIVE *REACT*	*Situational* **S1** 1Btn Game Controller **S2** App Specific Mouse **S3** Drive & Car Control	*Role-based* **R6** Hidden Stove **R7** A/C Admin Controller **R8** Biometric Safe
ACTIVE *CUSTOMIZABLE*	*"Swiss Army Knife"* **K4** Light Controller **K5** Desk Universal Controller	*Personalized* **P9** Safer Safe **P10** Instrument Effector

Figure 5. Taxonomy of Button+ interactions: *Situational*, *Role-based*, *"Swiss Army Knife"*, and *Personalized.*

User Aware Interaction

The category *User Aware* describes those interactions that depend on the identity or the role of the user. With Role-based interaction, access-privilege rules can be assigned to all users, limiting the subset of possible input that they can perform. With personalized interaction, different users can configure and customize a shared shape-changing interface to match with specific working styles or to save preferences.

Role-based

Role-based interaction means that the interface changes shape according to the current user. For example, R6 (Figure 4B) is a dial for a stove that retracts itself to hide from unauthorized users (e.g., children) and only pops out when an adult is present. R7 is a controller for a centralized air conditioning unit. The controller has minimal functionalities for most users (e.g., on/off, fan speed) but discloses the full set of input options to building managers and administrators. R8 is a dial-shaped biometric sensor embedded in a jewelry safe that is graspable and can be rotated only by authorized users.

Personalized

Different users can also choose to personalize the way they interact with a shared device by identifying themselves before usage. As an analogy, users of modern luxury cars often have the ability to save in memory their personal preferences for the settings of the seats, mirrors and other features. Similarly, our workshop users discussed ways for personalizing the settings of a shared interface and recalling these preferences upon usage. P9, for example, is a lock for a safe that allows multiple owners to create a secret combination using both the height and the rotation of a dial (Figure 4D). In this way, multiple users can make their own secret combinations for accessing private compartments of a shared safe using the same input interface. P10 is an instrument effector that can save the settings for all members of a music band (typically guitarists and bass players). One of the participants remarked that "having a dial to visually and tangibly change the controls for a guitar effector can be helpful since different members in the band usually have different preferences for their instruments."

DISCUSSION

This is not the first work that attempts to classifying the types of interaction with shape-changing interfaces: numerous interpretations have already been proposed, including the prominent work of Rasmussen et al. [28, 29]. However, while previous classifications mainly focused on the technological aspects or material properties of shape-changing interfaces [27], the emotional expressiveness of the input and output modalities [20], and the user's level of control [28], this work takes a slightly different perspective by empathizing the context of interaction.

In our framework, an interface can change shape to reflect a specific situation or the types/identities of users engaged. Examples from the workshops include those interfaces that change shape depending on *what activity* the user is performing (S1, S2, S3), and those interfaces that, through implicit affordances, prevent or grant input to *specific users* (R6, R7, R8). The common characteristic of these applications is that the shape-changing capabilities are triggered by the system and the user mostly reacts to them.

Diametrically opposite, there are interactions that still depend on the context (users or situations) but for which the user has active control over how the interface changes shapes. Examples from the workshop include interfaces that are used to *control different functionalities* or devices through shape alterations (K4, K5), or devices that are shared by multiple users and provide, by means of different shapes, a way *to specify and view custom settings and options* for each individual user (P9, P10).

Interestingly, many of the application ideas from the workshops are arguably falling into multiple groups, because, as in previous work, the categories proposed in our analysis are not mutually exclusive. It is also interesting to note that the context/user aware model proposed in this paper does not contrast with classifications from previous work, but rather complements them. For example, the concept of level of control, (system vs user control) proposed by Rasmussen et al. [28] is also described in our model in terms of passive vs active interactions (the vertical axis of Figure 5), but it is augmented by an additional dimension (user vs context awareness).

APPLICATIONS

Inspired by the results of the workshops, we developed two applications for the Button+ interface that showcase the four interactions proposed in our model. We developed a *user-aware* music player application that enables customized control for users with different access privileges, and a *context-aware* car simulation videogame that dynamically changes the input controller capabilities depending on the players' performance. For each of the two applications we considered situations in which the user is both passive (shape-changes are driven by the system and the user reacts to them) or active (the user perform input gestures by changing the interfaces shape).

Music Player

Our first application is a controller for a music player software running on a computer connected to the Button+ interface. The software was written using Java in Processing with the Minim library. The Button+ controller interface enables several functionalities, including playing/pausing music, track change, and volume control. It also provides both visual and haptic notifications. The behavior of the input interface was designed to allow interaction from multiple users who might share the control of a music player, but also have varied access privileges. By changing the shape of the controller, different physical affordances are provided to distinct users (identified by means of RFID tags) depending on their predetermined roles.

Our system acknowledges four distinct user roles (normal user, heavy user, administrator, and new user) with different abilities of controlling the system. For instance, a normal user can simply choose to play or pause a song using the pushbutton mounted on the top of Button+ knob. No other control is offered to a normal user, as the knob is completely retracted in the box. When a heavy user accesses the system, a knob controller appears from the box. The user can then change song tracks by spinning it. An administrator can, on top of these actions, also change the volume level of the music, by vertically pushing or pulling the knob. Finally, a new user has no ability to control the system: if a new user attempts to do any input, the haptic display on the of the top of the retracted knob gives feedback to signify that no input is allowed. In other words, a new user has a passive role.

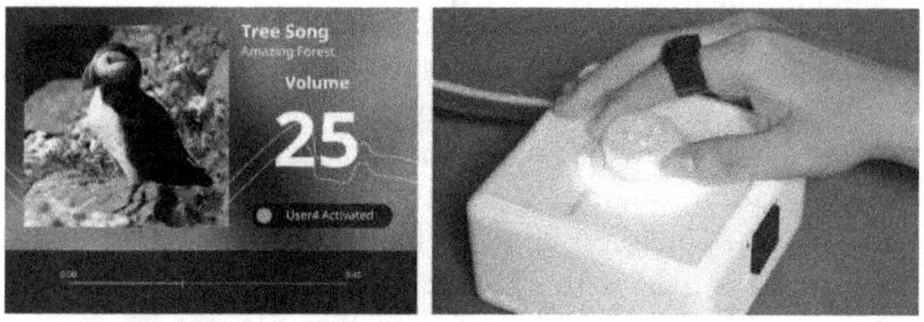

Figure 6. Demonstration of music player application.

Car Simulation Videogame

Our second application is a controller for a car simulation videogame that changes upon context. The game runs on a computer connected to the Button+ controller, and it was developed using Java in Processing with the Fisica library. The game content is displayed on a computer screen, and the interaction requires the usage of both the Button+ interface and four RFID cards disguised as one ignition key (used to start the game), and three shift gears for changing the car speed.

The goal of this game is to drive the car as far as possible avoiding obstacles until the fuel runs out. The Button+ knob is used as a steering wheel for controlling the car's left and right position. The fuel level is indicated on the screen with a graphical bar, and it is also mapped to the height of the knob: as time passes by, the knob height is gradually decreased, making steering more difficult. When the fuel tank is empty, the knob is completely retracted and the car is not controllable anymore. Finally, if the car bumps into an obstacle on the road, a haptic feedback is rendered on the top of the knob and a gas consumption penalty is assigned. Also for this application, changes of shape in the interfaces are both system and user driven.

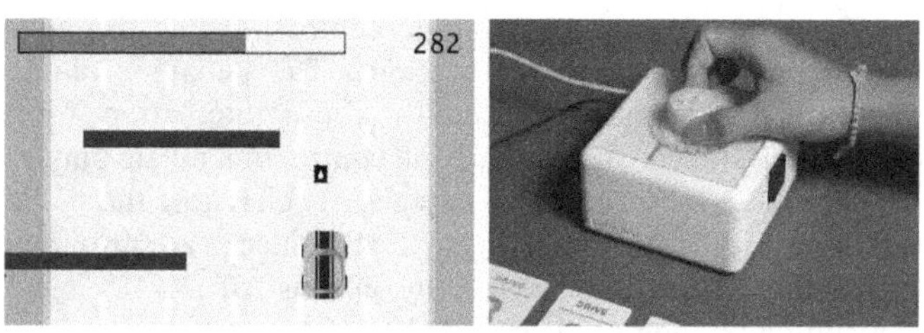

Figure 7. Demonstration of the car simulator application.

CONCLUSIONS

In this paper, we have explored the design space of a simple shape-changing button interface – the Button+ prototype. Based on this platform, we conducted a series of design workshops with the goal of generating ideas for practical products that could be enhanced by shape-changing capabilities. As a result, we collected and analyzed ideas from 12 participants and developed a taxonomy that describes user-aware and context-aware interactions. The simplicity of our prototype ensures that more complex shape-changing interfaces could still be described using the proposed model. Finally, we developed two applications that showcase the range of interactions described in our classification.

These results can be generalized for other shape-changing interfaces that do not necessarily share the same form factor of Button+. Indeed, the main motivations for choosing the current form factor is that physical buttons are among the most common and ubiquitous interfaces [17], and, as it was pointed out in previous work, they could benefit from innovative design that leverages on actuation to represent dynamic properties [1]. Button+ is only an example but we believe that the taxonomy presented in this paper can easily be applied to other shape-changing interfaces.

This work has several limitations and possibilities for future improvement. The main limitation is perhaps related to the implementation of the Button+ proof-of-concept prototype. Our prototype is bulky and could easily contain additional shape-changing input and output elements. Future work will be devoted to build better hardware with refined capabilities, following the users' feedback. For example, workshop participants commented that the haptic actuator located on the top of the knob could be more useful and effective if it were placed on the side of the knob. Also some other participants commented that the box size was larger than they expected, limiting practical application scenarios.

Another limitation is the number of participants of the workshop studies: despite that we tried our best to give voice to a variety of users by recruiting people with both engineering and design backgrounds, future iterations of this work will require more participants with a greater variety of backgrounds. Future work will be required to validate this framework and to generate practical design guidelines that support user and context aware interactions through shape-changing interfaces.

ACKNOLEDGEMENTS

This paper was supported by the MSIP, Korea, under the G-ITRC support program (IITP-2016-R6812-16-0001) supervised by the IITP.

REFERENCES

1. Jason Alexander, John Hardy, and Stephen Wattam. 2014. Characterising the Physicality of Everyday Buttons. In Proceedings of the Ninth ACM International Conference on Interactive Tabletops and Surfaces (ITS '14). ACM, New York, NY, USA, 205-208.

2. Gilles Bailly, Thomas Pietrzak, Jonathan Deber, and Daniel J. Wigdor. 2013. Métamorphe: augmenting hotkey usage with actuated keys. In Proceedings of the SIGCHI Conference on Human Factors in Computing Systems (CHI '13). ACM, New York, NY, USA, 563-572.

3. BMW iDrive: http://www.bmw.com/com/en/insights/technology/technology_guide/articles/idrive.html {Last access August 2016}
4. Marcelo Coelho, Hiroshi Ishii, and Pattie Maes. 2008. Surflex: a programmable surface for the design of tangible interfaces. In CHI '08 Extended Abstracts on Human Factors in Computing Systems (CHI EA '08). ACM, New York, NY, USA, 3429-3434.
5. Marcelo Coelho and Jamie Zigelbaum. Shape-changing interfaces. Personal Ubiquitous Computing 15, 2 (2010), 161-173.
6. Aluna Everitt, Faisal Taher, and Jason Alexander. 2016. ShapeCanvas: An Exploration of Shape-Changing Content Generation by Members of the Public. In Proceedings of the 2016 CHI Conference on Human Factors in Computing Systems (CHI '16). ACM, New York, NY, USA, 2778-2782.
7. Sean Follmer, Daniel Leithinger, Alex Olwal, Akimitsu Hogge, and Hiroshi Ishii. 2013. inFORM: dynamic physical affordances and constraints through shape and object actuation. In Proceedings of the 26th annual ACM symposium on User interface software and technology (UIST '13). ACM, New York, NY, USA, 417-426.
8. John Hardy, Christian Weichel, Faisal Taher, John Vidler, and Jason Alexander. 2015. ShapeClip: Towards Rapid Prototyping with Shape-Changing Displays for Designers. In Proceedings of the 33rd Annual ACM Conference on Human Factors in Computing Systems (CHI '15). ACM, New York, NY, USA, 19-28.
9. Chris Harrison and Scott E. Hudson. 2009. Providing dynamically changeable physical buttons on a visual display. In Proceedings of the SIGCHI Conference on Human Factors in Computing Systems (CHI '09). ACM, New York, NY, USA, 299-308.
10. Kate Hartman, Jackson McConnell, Boris Kourtoukov, Hillary Predko, and Izzie Colpitts-Campbell. 2015. Monarch: Self-Expression Through Wearable Kinetic Textiles. In Proceedings of the Ninth International Conference on Tangible, Embedded, and Embodied Interaction (TEI '15). ACM, New York, NY, USA, 413-414.
11. Fabian Hemmert, Susann Hamann, Matthias Löwe, Anne Wohlauf, and Gesche Joost. 2010. Shape-changing mobiles: tapering in one-dimensional deformational displays in mobile phones. In Proceedings of the fourth international conference on Tangible, embedded, and embodied interaction (TEI '10). ACM, New York, NY, USA, 249-252.
12. Fabian Hemmert, Gesche Joost, André Knörig, and Reto Wettach. 2008. Dynamic knobs: shape change as a means of interaction on a mobile phone. In CHI '08 Extended Abstracts on Human Factors in Computing Systems (CHI EA '08). ACM, New York, NY, USA, 2309-2314.
13. Jeong-ki Hong, Sunghyun Song, Jundong Cho, and Andrea Bianchi. 2015. Better Posture Awareness through Flower-Shaped Ambient Avatar. In Proceedings of the Ninth International Conference on Tangible, Embedded, and Embodied Interaction (TEI '15). ACM, New York, NY, USA, 337-340.
14. Hiroshi Ishii, Dávid Lakatos, Leonardo Bonanni, and Jean-Baptiste Labrune. 2012. Radical atoms: beyond tangible bits, toward transformable materials. interactions 19, 1 (January 2012), 38-51.
15. Hiroshi Ishii and Brygg Ullmer. 1997. Tangible bits: towards seamless interfaces between people, bits and atoms. In Proceedings of the ACM SIGCHI Conference on Human factors in computing systems (CHI '97). ACM, New York, NY, USA, 234-241.
16. Hiroo Iwata, Hiroaki Yano, Fumitaka Nakaizumi, and Ryo Kawamura. 2001. Project FEELEX: adding haptic surface to graphics. In Proceedings of the 28th annual conference on Computer graphics and interactive techniques (SIGGRAPH '01). ACM, New York, NY, USA, 469-476.
17. Lars-Erik Janlert. 2014. The Ubiquitous Button. interactions 21, 3: 26–33.
18. Takaharu Kanai, Yuya Kikukawa, Tatsuhiko Suzuki, Tetsuaki Baba, and Kumiko Kushiyama. 2011. PocoPoco: a tangible device that allows users to play dynamic tactile interaction. In ACM SIGGRAPH 2011 Emerging Technologies (SIGGRAPH '11). ACM, New York, NY, USA, Article 12 , 1 pages.
19. Seoktae Kim, Hyunjung Kim, Boram Lee, Tek-Jin Nam, and Woohun Lee. 2008. Inflatable mouse: volume-adjustable mouse with air-pressure-sensitive input and haptic feedback. In Proceedings of the SIGCHI Conference on Human Factors in Computing Systems (CHI '08). ACM, New York, NY, USA, 211-224.
20. Matthijs Kwak, Kasper Hornbæk, Panos Markopoulos, and Miguel Bruns Alonso. 2014. The Design Space of Shape-changing Interfaces: A Repertory Grid Study. Proceedings of the 2014 Conference on Designing Interactive Systems, ACM, 181–190.
21. Daniel Leithinger and Hiroshi Ishii. 2010. Relief: a scalable actuated shape display. In Proceedings of the fourth international conference on Tangible, embedded, and embodied interaction (TEI '10). ACM, New York, NY, USA, 221-222.
22. G. Michelitsch, J. Williams, M. Osen, B. Jimenez, and S. Rapp. 2004. Haptic chameleon: a new concept of shape-changing user interface controls with force feedback. In CHI '04 Extended Abstracts on Human

Factors in Computing Systems (CHI EA '04). ACM, New York, NY, USA, 1305-1308.

23. Tamotsu Murakami, Kazuhiko Hayashi, Kazuhiro Oikawa, and Naomasa Nakajima. 1995. DO-IT: deformable objects as input tools. In Conference Companion on Human Factors in Computing Systems (CHI '95), I. Katz, R. Mack, and L. Marks (Eds.). ACM, New York, NY, USA, 87-88.
24. Ken Nakagaki, Sean Follmer, and Hiroshi Ishii. 2015. LineFORM: Actuated Curve Interfaces for Display, Interaction, and Constraint. In Proceedings of the 28th Annual ACM Symposium on User Interface Software & Technology (UIST '15). ACM, New York, NY, USA, 333-339.
25. Ryuma Niiyama, Xu Sun, Lining Yao, Hiroshi Ishii, Daniela Rus, and Sangbae Kim. 2015. Sticky Actuator: Free-Form Planar Actuators for Animated Objects. In Proceedings of the Ninth International Conference on Tangible, Embedded, and Embodied Interaction (TEI '15). ACM, New York, NY, USA, 77-84.
26. Joohee Park, Young-Woo Park, and Tek-Jin Nam. 2014. Wrigglo: shape-changing peripheral for interpersonal mobile communication. In Proceedings of the SIGCHI Conference on Human Factors in Computing Systems (CHI '14). ACM, New York, NY, USA, 3973-3976.
27. Ivan Poupyrev, Tatsushi Nashida, and Makoto Okabe. 2007. Actuation and tangible user interfaces: the Vaucanson duck, robots, and shape displays. In Proceedings of the 1st international conference on Tangible and embedded interaction (TEI '07). ACM, New York, NY, USA, 205-212.
28. Majken K. Rasmussen, Timothy Merritt, Miguel Bruns Alonso, and Marianne Graves Petersen. 2016. Balancing User and System Control in Shape-Changing Interfaces: a Designerly Exploration. In Proceedings of the TEI '16: Tenth International Conference on Tangible, Embedded, and Embodied Interaction (TEI '16). ACM, New York, NY, USA, 202-210.
29. Majken K. Rasmussen, Esben W. Pedersen, Marianne G. Petersen, and Kasper Hornbæk. 2012. Shape-changing interfaces: a review of the design space and open research questions. In Proceedings of the SIGCHI Conference on Human Factors in Computing Systems (CHI '12). ACM, New York, NY, USA, 735-744.
30. Bernd Rohrbach. 1969. "Kreativ nach Regeln – Methode 635, eine neue Technik zum Lösen von Problemen". (Creative by rules - Method 635, a new technique for solving problems)". Absatzwirtschaft 12: 73-53.
31. Scott S. Snibbe, Karon E. MacLean, Rob Shaw, Jayne Roderick, William L. Verplank, and Mark Scheeff. 2001. Haptic techniques for media control. In Proceedings of the 14th annual ACM symposium on User interface software and technology (UIST '01). ACM, New York, NY, USA, 199-208.
32. Faisal Taher, John Hardy, Abhijit Karnik, et al. 2015. Exploring Interactions with Physically Dynamic Bar Charts. Proceedings of the 33rd Annual ACM Conference on Human Factors in Computing Systems, ACM, 3237– 3246.
33. John Tiab and Kasper Hornbæk. 2016. Understanding Affordance, System State, and Feedback in Shape-Changing Buttons. In Proceedings of the 2016 CHI Conference on Human Factors in Computing Systems (CHI '16). ACM, New York, NY, USA, 2752-2763.
34. Lining Yao, Ryuma Niiyama, Jifei Ou, Sean Follmer, Clark Della Silva, and Hiroshi Ishii. 2013. PneUI: Pneumatically Actuated Soft Composite Materials for Shape Changing Interfaces. Proceedings of the 26th Annual ACM Symposium on User Interface Software and Technology, ACM, 13–22.

LangWidgets: A Tangible Navigation System for Semantic Fields

Alisa Goikhman
Austrian Academy of Sciences
Vienna, Austria
alisagoikhman@gmail.com

ABSTRACT

English lexicography has a long and rich tradition. The digitization of the field has revolutionized it in many respects. However, from a designer point of view, this transformation is not complete. In fact, if we were to examine the layouts and arrangements of online dictionaries, we would find that they share an almost identical structure with the printed form.

Today, lexicography is again at a turning point. New research states that dictionaries should mirror the way language is organized in our brains. That is, lexicographers should partake in cognitive research and implement the findings in the process of dictionary-making.

The primary goal of *LangWidgets* is to approach this task through the user-interface perspective. Mindfully-crafted eLexicon interfaces could ease the cognitive load of users by simplifying navigation through the debris of data. In addition, they could promote a more precise mental model of the language, which, in turn, would improve the process of language acquisition.

The paper concludes with a pilot study demonstrating the future promise of the *LangWidgets* system.

ACM Classification Keywords

H.5.2 Information interfaces and presentation (e.g., HCI): User Interfaces; I.5.5 Pattern recognition: Implementation

Author Keywords

Research through Design; eLexicography; Interface Metaphor; Tangible User Interface; Conceptual Metaphor; Digital Humanities

INTRODUCTION

Dictionaries in the form we know them today were originally created in the 17th century. English lexicography has a rich and long tradition. The eLexicon, the digitalized version of the dictionary that we use today, significantly differs from its printed predecessor only in a few respects:

- Search field instead of alphabetical order
- Unlimited space instead of limited printed space
- Hyperlinks

Although these are positive developments, they do not constitute a fundamental change in the manner in which we use dictionaries.

Despite the advances brought about by the computerization of lexicography, the myriad of practices associated with disciplines such as interaction design, user interface design, and user experience design have not yet become an endemic part of the dictionary-making process.

Today, lexicography is beginning to integrate knowledge from other disciplines. It is also one of the focal points of research in Digital Humanities and many efforts are directed into making use of available technologies. However, the current attempts focus mainly on visualization tools for eLexicons. The question of how to integrate innovative interaction tools into eLexicons remains open.

LangWidgets explores alternatives to the common interactive tools in eLexicography. The suggested prototype utilizes *The Conceptual Metaphor Theory* by Lakoff and Johnson as a premise for interacting with eLexicons through tangible interfaces.

ELEXICOGRAPHY – STATE OF AFFAIRS

Lexicography is the art and craft of making dictionaries. Theoretical lexicography studies the theories of lexicons, while its practical counterpart defines their components and structure. eLexicography studies and develops computer-mediated lexicons. It is strongly influenced by computer sciences and its evolution is directly linked to innovation and progress in computation.

In the field of eLexicography, the *corpus revolution*[1] is considered to be the most significant change brought about by technology. The capacity to mechanically and automatically sort vast corpuses of text allowed for a more accurate and

[1] The corpus revolution refers to the use of large digitized and searchable collections of texts or audio recordings to study language.

TEI '17, March 20-23, 2017, Yokohama, Japan
© 2017 ACM. ISBN 978-1-4503-4676-4/17/03...$15.00
DOI: http://dx.doi.org/10.1145/3024969.3024982

dynamic representation of the modern language as well as prioritization of meanings based on frequency [6]. As a result of these additions, the amount of data available to the user for each dictionary entry has increased exponentially. This information overload presents a new difficulty for those in charge of editing and designing eLexicons. For users, it means a significantly increased cognitive load.

The layout and functionality of eLexicons have not yet adjusted to the challenges brought about by the vast amounts of available data. Thus, accepted methodologies in the field are being reevaluated. For instance, Wordnik.com, an online language resource, suggests a more democratic approach towards content: instead of the classic editorial content, Wordnik.com is compiled by means of automatic aggregation and citizen science. This initiative mirrors the modern language in its online usage and reveals fine details of our active vocabulary. However, it fails to present an intelligible overview. The interface, using only conventional elements, does not provide any tools to help navigate through the torrent of lexical data.

In summary, although specific technological developments have had a profound effect on eLexicography, there is considerable scope for future contributions to this agenda. In particular, the field of interaction design has been largely ignored and the role of *Human-Computer-Interaction* (HCI) in eLexicons is currently negligible. The usability of eLexicons and their user interfaces have rarely been evaluated [3]. eLexicons still use standard, off-the-shelf interactive elements and layouts, and the *paper paradigm*[2] prevails in the field. This is despite the fact that "the introduction of thoroughly designed interactive visual tools fully integrated with automatic data processing algorithms will help linguistic fields to take a big step forward" [11].

TOWARDS INTERDISCIPLINARY DICTIONARY-MAKING

In this section, I cite research on the benefits of implementing theories from *Cognitive Linguistics* (CL) in Lexicography. Later, I outline the role of metaphor as a central concept in CL as well as in HCI research. Subsequently, I develop and test an interface that uses the common ground of metaphor as a means to introduce CL into eLexicons.

From Cognitive Linguistics to Cognitive Lexicography

The conviction that language and cognition mutually influence one another and are both embedded in the experiences and environments of its users [2] is central to CL. This notion appeals greatly to lexicographers, who have made several attempts over the past 40 years to restructure dictionaries according to what we know about the human mental lexicon. One of these initiatives is WordNet, a lexical database for the English language that groups English words into sets of synonyms called synsets, created in the Cognitive Science Laboratory of Princeton University in 1985. WordNet's structure is consistent with research on Semantic Priming [8], which shows that words are retrieved faster if they have semantic proximity to the prime. For example, it takes a person less time to recognize the word 'novel' if it follows the word 'book' than the word 'lamp'.

[2]Two-dimensional layout of black text on a white background.

A much newer line of research named Cognitive Lexicography shows particular promise. It suggests that dictionaries should describe the language according to how humans perceive and conceptualize the world [10]. It differentiates itself from the semantic theory used in WordNet by focusing on the definitions of words and considering aspects like perception, experience, etc. when describing an entry. In a study concerning definitions of emotional terms (e.g. anger, joy, fear), Ostermann [10] demonstrates the benefits of including specifications like cause, situation or reaction, in a way that mirrors what is going on in our minds while we process these emotions.

There are many different ways in which the findings of CL could be introduced into Lexicography. For example, as mentioned above, grouping items according to semantic affiliation, or rewriting definitions to include descriptions of human behavior. However, the goal of my work is to propose an integration process that takes place within the framework of interaction design. Tangible interfaces that rely on embodied interaction can mediate the complex structure of the lexicon in a non verbal and intuitive manner.

The Metaphor as Common Ground

The process of developing tailor-made interface elements for eLexicons starts at the level of the interface metaphor.

Interface metaphors exploit knowledge of the real world that the user already has in order to provide knowledge about how to interact with the specific technology. Norman [9] explains that the interface metaphor functions in two ways. First, it is a way for designers to help users to create the correct mental model of how the product functions. Second, interface metaphors are used to signify the action that the interface allows for. Therefore, to draft effective interface metaphors for language, we should analyze the layperson's understanding of language structure and deduce what kind of references from the real world would be applicable.

A key theory in the field of CL concerning verbal communication and categorization, and the theory chosen as the basis for the current work, is Lakoff and Johnson's Conceptual Metaphor Theory [7]. These authors analyzed daily language and extracted metaphoric patterns repeatedly used in daily speech. They claimed that "the essence of metaphor is understanding and experiencing one kind of thing in terms of another" [7]. They further suggested that our day to day experiences with our body, our surroundings and our culture determine the way we conceptualize abstract ideas. In other words, a metaphor consists of two conceptual domains: the source domain from which we draw metaphorical expressions and the target domain that we try to understand; we use material concepts (e.g. a container) to explain abstract ideas (e.g. language). The metaphor on which I have based the project is: "Language is a container/physical space"[3]

- German *is full* of long words
- fluent *in* three languages

[3]This statement is consistent with the concept of "container metaphors" described in the 6th chapter of "Metaphors we live by" [7].

- *hollow* words
- *put* ideas *into* words

Conceptual metaphors about language itself are an appropriate starting point for investigation into the *Graphic-User-Interface* (GUI) and, in particular, the *Tangible-User-Interface* (TUI) as applied to eLexicons. The fact that interfaces and language are both metaphorical by nature is a great motivation to combine the two in search for intuitive interaction solutions for eLexicons.

Interface metaphors exist both in GUIs and TUIs. The latter, however, better encapsulate the physical/abstract structure of the conceptual metaphor. Fishkin [5] defines the two dimensions of the TUI as *embodiment* and *metaphor*. The concept of embodiment refers to the physical shape of the interface and describes the extent to which the digital information is perceived as related to the physical interface; in other words, the extent to which users think of the digital content as being part of the object they are manipulating [5]. The second dimension of an interface described by Fishkin, known as metaphor, deals with the expectations of the user: based on the action the user performed, does the digital content react in accordance with expectations? Does it mimic the physical experiences of the user in the real world? Because of the structural similarities between TUIs and the conceptual metaphor, the TUI is a natural vehicle for introducing CL into eLexicography.

To conclude, I have presented an argument in favor of integrating interaction design as a core practice of eLexicography. However, it is still rather unclear as to what kind of practical framework will allow for HCI to become an endemic part of eLexicography. This question is quite urgent, due to the fact that the vast majority of the world's population speaks at least one foreign language and language learners are the main users of dictionaries.

I set out to address this issue by the means of a project, following Findeli's [4] model of *Research Through Design*. The design question pursued in this project is a transformed and concretized version of its research question. The design question that this project seeks to answer is: *How might semantic relations be translated to a TUI?*

LANGWIDGETS

The project explores the potential of embodied interaction for eLexicons by means of a prototype. The prototype consists of 3 physical widgets and a microphone. The tangible, interactive widgets are connected to a GUI. The prototype is based on the general metaphor "Language is a container/physical space". Each widget is an autonomous interface metaphor that gives form to one of the following instances of the blanket metaphor:

- Synonyms are located in close proximity to one another
- Hypernyms are containers
- Different senses of the word are facets

The widgets are made of wood with conductive foam disks for the contact points. Each widget is approximately 15 by 15 by 4 cm in size, designed to fit comfortably in an adult

Figure 1. ©Alisa Goikhman. The *LangWidgets* set of physical interactive widgets and the GUI. The user can search for a specific word and browse through different types of semantic relations by interacting with each of the four widgets in turn.

user's hands. The entire tangible system communicates with the software via a single Arduino Duemilanove board. The software is built in Processing and uses the following external Libraries: rita.wordnet and Google's speech to text (STT) API. The prototype (figure1) operates as follows: to interact with the system, the user places an iron marble on the conductive foam socket located on the microphone box. The marble is used as a tangible representation of the recorded word, similar to its use in the interaction with the classic *Marble Answering Machine* [1]. The user records an English word (using the STT library) to be searched in WordNet's database, which is accessed via the Rita library. Once the word is retrieved, it is shown on the screen and the rest of the widgets are activated. The interaction with a single widget focuses on a single semantic relation. However, the output of a single widget is designed to vary in repeated interactions. In order to highlight the richness of the language, and to increase the playful element, the system displays results for a single sense of the word at a time (e.g. 'game' as either a type of activity or a type of meat). The sense is selected randomly after each call. The selection of a single item from a list of synonyms or hypernyms is also random. In the following paragraphs, I will describe each widget's technical specifications and interaction.

The Synonyms widget (figure 2.a) uses the concept of spatial distance to represent synonymous terms. It behaves like a self-retracting tape measure. By pulling one half of the widget away from the other half, the user controls the GUI animation and is shown a chain of synonyms (e.g. Game > Play > Perform > Act > Action). Consequently, the two ends of a long chain will most likely result in two seemingly unrelated words and thus reinforce the concept of distance.

The mechanism of the widget makes use of the infrared element of an optical mouse mounted on a retractable keychain reel. The rotation of the reel is then decoded using the built-in image sensor. The decoded signal is then filtered to remove noise before being used to animate the GUI. The GUI counterpart compares the received signal with predetermined thresholds corresponding to 10 cm intervals. At each successive distance step, a recursion is activated to select the next tagged synonym from the database. To allow for more than one in-

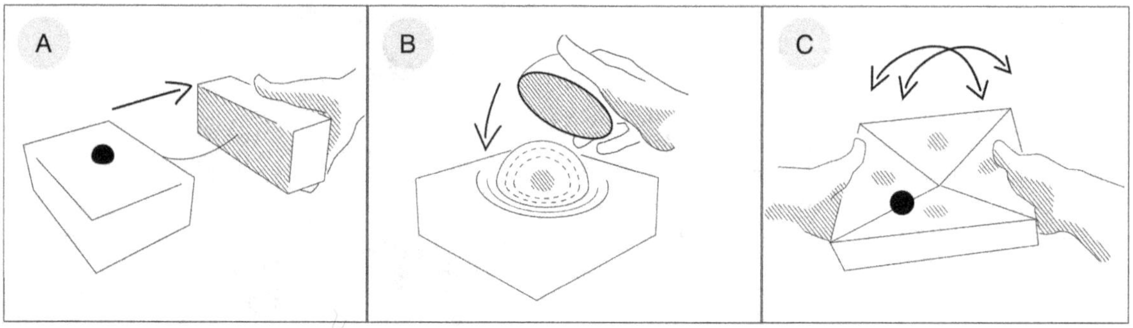

Figure 2. ©Alisa Goikhman. The three wooden widgets. a) The two halves of the Synonyms widget are connected by a retractable reel. b) The base of the Hypernyms widget has 5 circular tracks to house the half-spheres. c) The Senses widget has four tilted triangular planes on the top surface. Each plane has a nook for the marble.

teraction session per search, the foam contacts placed on the inner face of both halves of the widget annul the recursion and empty the cache each time the widget is released and snaps back together.

The Hypernyms widget (figure 2.b) explores the physical representation of the "type of" semantic relation (e.g. Bed [is a type of] Furniture [is a type of] Object [is a type of] Entity). It exploits nesting as a physical representation of the affiliation between hypernym and hyponym.

This widget is comprised of five transparent half-spheres of decreasing size that fit inside one another. With every additional layer placed on top of the wooden base, the user climbs the hypernym hierarchy to progressively more generalized terms. Each sphere has a steel rim that operates as a switch when placed on top of the conductive foam circular rail and sends a simple on/off signal. The signal then activates a recursive search for a hypernym, to a maximum of a 5-slot stack.

The Senses widget (figure 2.c) exploits inclination as a means of navigating between the different senses of a word based on the part of speech to which it refers (e.g. 'this game[n]', 'he gamed[v] the system', 'she is game[adj.]'). The widget operates like the classic marble maze game, with a nook for each part of speech. By inclining the widget, the user maneuvers the marble into one of the sockets to close the circuit. As a result, the relevant sense and use examples are displayed on the screen.

DEPLOYMENT AND TESTING

To explore the potential of the *LangWidgets* for eLexicography, the prototype was installed and tested in several international festivals in non-English speaking countries, including *Ars Electronica* in Linz (Austria) and the *New Technological Art Award* (NTAA) in Ghent (Belgium). The interface allowed the visitor to experience the entire interaction flow, either with or without guidance. Their experimentation was observed by the designer. Users were prompted to provide feedback on the prototype's potential applications, usability and needed improvements. They were asked to describe what kind of information each widget displays, rate the user experience, and give general feedback on the design.

Use cases and reception

In total, the prototype was open for public use for 37 days and approximately 750 interaction sessions took place (according to the application log files). Circa one-third of the sessions were supervised by the designer – these are the cases described below.

The interaction can be evaluated according to three core aspects:

- Technical operation of the prototype
- Users' understanding of the semantic relations presented on the screen
- Interface design and level of engagement

The prototype had several technical issues. As mentioned in the prototype description, the first interaction step is for the system to record a spoken search query. Unfortunately, this proved to be harder than during testing, as the STT algorithm had difficulty in deciphering foreign accents and the venues were too crowded to allow for a clear recording. In addition, the prototype was not sufficiently proofed against forceful handling. Specifically, the Synonyms widget was often opened too quickly, causing the mouse sensor to return out-of-scope values. This could be easily solved by setting a higher friction during the pulling-apart action, to slow the user down.

The use of a marble as the navigation element required no explanation at all and came very naturally to the majority of users, with the exception of the microphone interface where the marble should be pressed down in order to record, which was confusing for some.

In terms of content clarity, users with no linguistic background had difficulties in defining the connection between the word they searched for and the given results. At least in part, this may have been due to the fact that there were some technical barriers to content clarity in the current prototype. For example, although at the beginning of their interaction session with the Hypernyms widget, many users recognized that the output was a more general term of their query, the random factor in the recursion later impeded their understanding, as the results were not restricted to a single sense of the word (e.g. chess [is a type of] game [is a type of] meat). Similar but more overt issues occurred with the Synonyms widget, in which obscure synonyms were not filtered out from the results, which led to confusion. These issues make it clear that improvements to the system are needed, for example, limiting further iterations to a single sense of the word per interaction. Another way to address these issues is by redesigning the GUI to include an overview of the semantic map that the user browses. This way the user would be able to keep track despite the occasional deviation and/or obscure result.

The form of the widgets attracted a lot of attention. The bulkiness and simplicity of the widgets raised no apprehension on the users' side. One evident drawback of the simple box-like shape was that it lacked the signifiers that communicate the widgets' use.

The prototype succeeded beyond expectations in the engagement factor. All the users tried out each one of the controllers and circa 70% repeated their interaction with one or more of the widgets. This behavior was reinforced by the fact that the results change with each use. The majority of users' feedback was positive. The participants described the project as fun, educational and useful for language learners. The bulk of the users were not native English speakers and many of them reported discovering new senses for words with which they thought they were familiar.

When asked to comment on each widget individually, the users voted the Hypernyms widget as having the clearest connection between the semantic relations it describes and its form. However, the Synonyms widget was favored in terms of average number of repetitions (reactivation of the widget by returning the marble to it after having moved to another widget) per user, namely 2.1 times.

SUMMARY

The *LangWidgets* prototype aimed to make the following contributions:

- Proof of concept for tangible representation of lexical data
- A novel TUI designed to facilitate a playful engagement of the public in language studies
- Initial test of interface metaphors for eLexicons.

To conclude, the prototype had several technical issues, the most significant of which was the malfunctioning speech recognition. From a design perspective, with the exception of the Hypernyms widget, the form of the widgets did not communicate clearly how to interact with them, while the unconstrained output interfered with understanding. These issues have to be resolved before determining the potential contribution of interface metaphors for eLexicons.

Nevertheless, the aforementioned aims of this preliminary study were satisfied. The prototype successfully engaged the public in a prolonged interaction with "dry" lexical data, generated strong interest and received positive feedback. Users' initial response to the Hypernyms widget demonstrated that interface metaphors show promise for facilitating online language learning. In summary, the interaction sessions with the prototype provide a solid proof of concept and a motivation for future design iterations and user testing.

ACKNOWLEDGMENTS

I would like to express my gratitude to the Israel Museum, the Holon Institute of Technology and the Berlin University of the Arts for supporting this project; in particular, Shachar Geiger, Michal Rinott and Prof. Dr.-Ing. Fabian Hemmert for their comments and advice. Finally, I wish to thank Dr. Naomi Miller for language editing and proofreading.

REFERENCES

1. Durrell Bishop, Marble Answering Machine, Interaction Design, and The Mam. 1992. Durrell Bishop's Marble Answering Machine. *Design* (1992).
2. William Croft and D Alan Cruse. 2004. Cognitive Linguistics. *Cognitive Linguistics* 3, 2 (2004), XV, 356 S. DOI:http://dx.doi.org/10.1002/wcs.1163
3. Martin J Eppler, William Croft, and D. Alan Cruse. 2004. A comparison between concept maps, mind maps, conceptual diagrams, and visual metaphors as complementary tools for knowledge construction and sharing. *Information Visualization* 5, 3 (2004), 202–210. DOI:http://dx.doi.org/10.1057/palgrave.ivs.9500131
4. Alain Findeli, Denis Brouillet, Sophie Martin, Christophe Moineau, and Richard Tarrago. 2008. 04: Research Through Design and Transdisciplinarity: A Tentative Contribution to the Methodology of Design Research. *"FOCUSED" – Current Design Research Projects and Methods Swiss Design Network Symposium* (2008), 67–91.
5. Kenneth P. Fishkin. 2004. A taxonomy for and analysis of tangible interfaces. *Personal and Ubiquitous Computing* 8, 5 (2004), 347–358. DOI: http://dx.doi.org/10.1007/s00779-004-0297-4
6. Ha Hoang. 2014. Metaphor and Second Language Learning: The State of the Field. *TESL-EJ* 18, 2 (2014), 1–27. http://www.tesl-ej.org/wordpress/issues/volume18/ej70/ej70a5/http://www.tesl-ej.org/pdf/ej70/a5.pdf
7. George Lakoff and Mark Johnson. 2003. *Metaphors We Live By.* University of Chicago Press.
8. D E Meyer and R W Schvaneveldt. 1971. Facilitation in recognizing pairs of words: evidence of a dependence between retrieval operations. *Journal of experimental psychology* 90, 2 (1971), 227–234. DOI: http://dx.doi.org/10.1037/h0031564
9. Donald A Norman. 2002. *The Design of Everyday Things.* Vol. 16. 272 pages. DOI: http://dx.doi.org/10.1002/hfm.20127
10. Carolin Ostermann. 2012. Cognitive lexicography of emotion terms. *Proceedings of the 15th EURALEX International Congress* (2012), 493–501.
11. Roberto Therón and Carlos Seguín. 2014. Highly Interactive and Natural User Interfaces : Enabling visual analysis in historical lexicography. (2014), 153–158. DOI:http://dx.doi.org/10.1145/2595188.2595215

An Exploration of Mobile Shape-Changing Textures

Eve Hoggan[1,5], Yi-Ta Hsieh[2], Kalle Myllymaa[2], Vuokko Lantz[3], Johan Kildal[4], Julian Eiler[5], and Giulio Jacucci[2]

[1]Aarhus University, Denmark
firstname.lastname @ cs.au.dk

[2]University of Helsinki, Finland
firstname.lastname @ helsinki.fi

[3]Emberion Oy, Finland
firstname.lastname @ emberion.com

[4]IK4-Tekniker, Spain
firstname.lastname @ tekniker.es

[5]Aalto University, Finland
firstname.lastname @aalto.fi

ABSTRACT
This paper describes the development and evaluation of *Undulating Covers* (*UnCovers*), mobile interfaces that can change their surface texture to transmit information. The *Pin Array UnCover* incorporates sinusoidal ridges controlled by servomotors, which can change their amplitude and granularity. The *Mylar UnCover* is a more organic interface that exploits the buckling properties of Mylar, using muscle wires, to change the texture granularity. The results of two user studies show that very low frequency texture changes, using amplitude or granularity, can be distinguished with high levels of accuracy. Since small changes are perceptible, it is possible to incorporate such interfaces into mobile devices without drastically increasing their size or actuation requirements. Finally, ratings from participants indicate that UnCovers would be appropriate for attention-grabbing, or caring and supportive interpersonal messages.

Author Keywords
Shape Changing Interfaces; Haptic feedback; Mobile Communication; Mylar; Texture.

ACM Classification Keywords
H.5.2. Information interfaces and presentation (e.g., HCI): User Interfaces.

INTRODUCTION
Haptic feedback is often incorporated into interactive systems to provide information to our sense of touch [1,6]. However, this feedback is not usually static, especially in mobile devices. Existing research on mobile haptic feedback tends to make use of vibrotactile stimuli, which is transitory. The user's hand must be in contact with the device at the exact moment the feedback is provided otherwise the vibration may not be perceived. Previous research has shown that tactile perception differs depending on the body location [2]. So, even if the device is in contact with the user's skin, the detection threshold will be higher if it is in contact with less sensitive areas of the body. Research has shown that many users miss alerts from their mobile devices because of these perception issues [10].

TEI '17, March 20-23, 2017, Yokohama, Japan
© 2017 ACM. ISBN 978-1-4503-4676-4/17/03…$15.00
DOI: http://dx.doi.org/10.1145/3024969.3024983

Figure 1: Left - Pin Array UnCover, Right - Mylar UnCover.

The research reported here will demonstrate the potential of alternative forms of haptic feedback inspired by concepts from Organic User Interfaces (OUIs) and shape-changing interfaces [8] to address these perception issues. Unlike vibrotactile feedback, haptic feedback from shape-change can be static and continuous. Research in shape-change and OUIs has produced interfaces that can change their orientation, form, volume, texture, viscosity, spatiality, adding/subtracting and permeability [17]. To use shape-changing parameters [19] (size, shape, amplitude, porosity, granularity, speed, and strength) as a communication channel, it is important that users can distinguish, and identify multiple levels of these parameters. So far, these parameters have received little psychophysical attention, and, therefore, require some experimental investigation in order to understand how they are perceived.

In terms of mobile interaction, one of the most promising shape-change parameters is texture because the overall shape of the device is not affected [4], meaning that it is possible to augment an already existing rigid device, such as a mobile phone. In this paper, we evaluate the effectiveness of two techniques for dynamic and distinguishable texture displays, using shape-changing mobile interfaces, called *Undulating Covers* (*UnCovers*), shown in Figure 1. UnCovers dynamically alter the amplitude or granularity of surface control points to create different textures. Through two user studies we evaluate the distinguishability of different low frequency textures, and compare user perception, with and without visual feedback.

BACKGROUND

One of the most relevant publication for our research is Dimitriadis and Alexander's paper on shape-change notifications [3]. They developed several different types of shape-changes for mobile alerts. The most successful of which was the protrusion device. In this prototype a small arm protrudes from the display. The amplitude of this protrusion was 10mm or 15mm. The protrusion was presented either as a static stimulus or with a slow or fast pulse. The results showed that participants could detect 100% of these alerts in their pocket. Our experiment prototypes (the UnCovers) were inspired by Dimitriadis and Alexander's findings. Unlike the protrusion prototype described above, the UnCovers make use of multiple control points with much smaller amplitude changes, and include granularity control.

To fully understand the perception of shape-changes using the amplitude and granularity parameters, it is important to identify the difference threshold, also known as the Just Noticeable Difference (JND) [13]. Dimitriadis and Alexander [3] used fairly high amplitude levels of 10 and 15mm, reaching 100% detection, but did not examine the smallest perceivable changes. Since such large shape changes consume a great deal of power, as noted by Dimitriadis and Alexander, and may decrease the robustness of the technique for use in the pocket, we wanted to examine much smaller amplitude changes. According to work by Shimojo *et al.* [21] gaussian shaped ridges with amplitude levels as small as 2mm can be detected easily.

Pin arrays could be considered the first shape-changing tactile displays. For example, Lee *et al.* [12] built a 6x6 tactile shape display that uses servo-motors to control metal pins. Experiment results showed that participants could distinguish 3D vertical lines when the pins were covered with a rubber layer. However, given the large number of motors, the prototype is not suitable for mobile use.

Raffle *et al.* [16] developed an interactive membrane called Super Cilia Skin. The membrane is made up of an array of actuators, which oscillate in response to a magnetic force. This can display geometric patterns. Informal evaluations showed that users could distinguish different shapes. Somewhat similarly, the Hairlytop device [14] makes use of Shape Memory Alloy hair-like actuators to display geometric information.

Harrison and Hudson [4] proposed that texture displays could be used to provide passive tactile feedback on the surface of various different objects. User evaluations showed that participants could easily distinguish between two and four different states for different fabric prototypes. For example, there was a beaded matrix where the beads are threaded onto some elasticated material. When the material is relaxed, the beads form a set of ridges and when the material is stretched the beads become spaced out. These results are very promising but there is still work to be done to integrate the proposed texture displays with a mobile device and to determine the perceptual thresholds.

All of these findings along with related work on other types of shape-changing interfaces for mobile settings [5,18] suggest that texture-based deformations could be effective and perceivable in mobile environments, where a wide variety of applications could be developed.

THE UNCOVER PROTOTYPES

In this paper, we focus on two shape-change parameters: amplitude and granularity, both of which are key features that can help to differentiate textures. We created two prototypes, called *Undulating Covers* (*UnCovers*) [1], that can deform by altering the amplitude and granularity of surface control points on an interface. In the first prototype, the control points are based on a basic mechanical pin array. The second prototype is made from Mylar[2] and the surface buckles act as control points.

Prototype 1 – Pin Array

We selected a simple design where sinusoidal ridges, covered in a thin layer of 95% cotton 5% spandex, can be pushed and pulled through a porous surface using linear servomotors (see Figure 2). If we break the design down into the shape-changing parameters outlined by Roudaut *et al.*[19], we have:

- Area: 5.5 x 5.5cm^2;
- Granularity: 0 to 12 control points;
- Amplitude: 0.2cm;
- Porosity: 0 or 100%;
- Speed: 0.5 seconds.

The deformable section of the prototype is covered with a thin material layer because previous research has shown that such a layer acts as a spatial low pass filter [10].

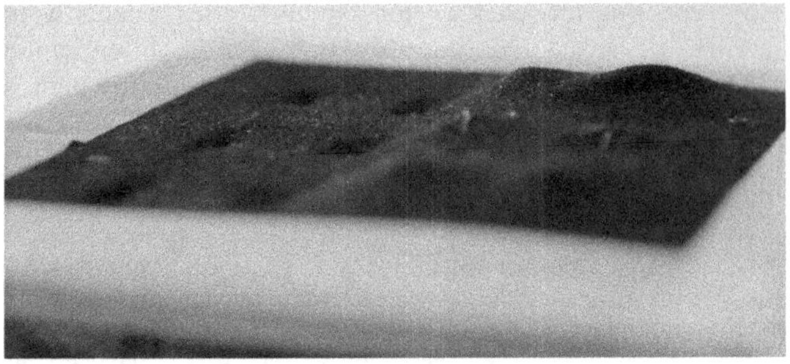

Figure 2: Pin Array UnCover, with 0 to 3mm amplitude levels.

[1] The 3D models and electronic schematics of the UnCovers are available at https://goo.gl/gVygTe

[2] http://www.dupontteijinfilms.com/filmenterprise/Datasheet.asp?ID=302&Version=US

It also prevents the mechanism from being exposed to dust or dirt that could prohibit its movement. The ridges can also be convex or concave. Previous experimental brain research has shown that detection thresholds for convex and concave stimuli are comparable [12]. This means that we can double the design space.

Prototype 2 – Mylar

The second prototype was developed specifically with granularity in mind. We wanted to be able to change the granularity of control points without requiring one motor per control point. Mylar has a great deal of potential use cases in shape-changing interfaces because it buckles in a predictable manner and only requires a single actuation location. Recent research [20] has shown that Mylar buckles into a diamond-like pattern when axial compression is applied to a cylinder. The granularity of the diamond pattern depends on the difference in circumference between the Mylar sheet and the solid mandrel underneath (see Figure 3). We used differences of 0.5mm, 1mm, and 2mm. The shape-change parameter values are as follows:

- Area: 188.5cm^2 lateral surface (radius 1.5cm, height 20cm);
- Granularity: 0 to c. 1450 control points;
- Amplitude: 0 to 3mm;
- Porosity: 0%;
- Speed: 0.5 seconds.

EXPERIMENT 1 - AMPLITUDE

As a first step, an experiment was conducted to investigate the perception of the Pin Array UnCover's amplitude changes. We used an adaptive staircase method called the One-Up Three-Down method 3IFC [13], commonly used in psychophysical research. 3IFC involves the presentation of three amplitudes per trial. The target amplitude is randomly assigned to one of the three presentations. The participant has to identify the presentation containing the target amplitude. The magnitude of the amplitude is increased after one incorrect response, and decreased after three consecutive correct responses.

The experiment participants were required to complete all 3IFC tasks and a post-study questionnaire. In each 3IFC task, the participant could touch and explore the UnCover for as long as they wished. When the participant was ready, they pressed a button to initiate the second deformation. There was a preset 3-second inter-stimulus interval for each deformation.

Participants

We recruited 18 participants (9 female, 16 right-handed, with an age range of 18 to 35) through the University and social networks. All of the participants wore headphones to mask any noise from the servomotors.

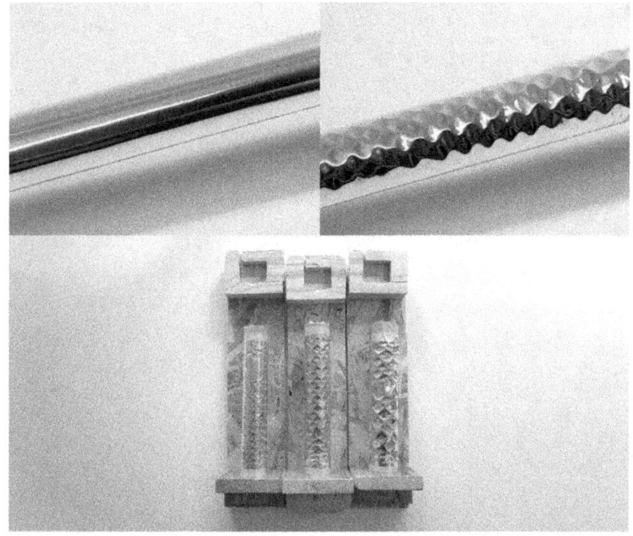

Figure 3: Mylar UnCover. Upper left: flat surface with granularity level of 0 when there is no pressure applied. Upper right: diamond-like pattern on the surface with granularity level of 1450 when Mylar is compressed. Bottom: Mylar sheets wrapped around mandrels attached to the wooden bases.

Conditions and Variables

In this experiment, the independent variable was the amplitude of the shape-change. We used seven different amplitude levels: -3mm, -2mm, -1mm, 0mm, 1mm, 2mm, 3mm. We chose our amplitude levels from within the perceivable range outlined in [11][12].

There were two modality conditions: with and without visual feedback. In the visual feedback condition, the participants were able to see the shape-change occurring. In the non-visual condition, a box covered the participants' hands so they could only feel the shape-change, not see it.

Figure 4: Experiment set-up for tactile only condition.

The experiment used a within-groups design where all participants completed tasks under all conditions. The order of the modality condition was counterbalanced. The experiment set-up is shown in Figure 4.

Results

The experiment system logged the amplitude level, modality condition, response time and accuracy. The mean accuracy rates for each amplitude level in each condition are shown in Figure 5.

A repeated measures analysis of variance (ANOVA) of amplitude accuracy rates showed a significant main effect

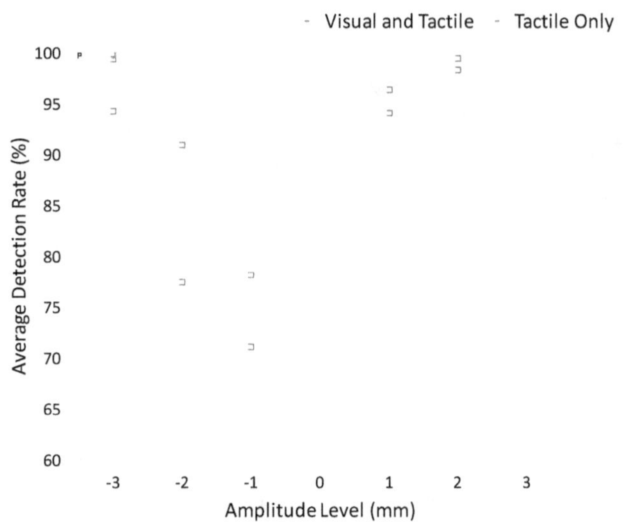

Figure 5: Mean accuracy rates for each amplitude level and modality condition.

for *Amplitude Level* (F(1.93, 108) = 44.9, p<0.05) with Greenhouse-Geisser correction. There was also a significant interaction between *Amplitude Level* and *Modality Condition* (F(1.7, 96.5) = 26, p<0.05) with Greenhouse-Geisser correction.

Bonferroni adjusted post hoc tests of *Amplitude Level* showed that the largest change of 0mm to 3mm or 0mm to -3mm (and vice versa) produced significantly higher accuracy rates than all other levels (p<0.05).

In terms of the interaction between *Amplitude Level* and *Modality Condition.*, concave levels of -3mm, -2mm, and -1mm produced higher accuracy rates in the tactile only condition than the visual and tactile condition (p<0.05). Also, for the 1mm and 2mm convex levels, the accuracy rate in the visual and tactile condition is significantly higher than the tactile only condition (p<0.05).

The lower accuracy rates for the concave amplitudes reflects findings in previous research. For example, Kappers *et al.* [9] found that concave shapes yield significantly higher standard deviations than convex ones in identification tasks. Human beings are much more often confronted with elliptic than with hyperbolic shapes in the real world and similar results are found in vision research, with hyperbolic shapes classified less accurately than elliptical shapes. That being said, the perception levels for concave ridges were still promising and indicate that they may be used to transmit information.

The reason why the concave amplitude levels tend to be detected better through the sense of touch could be because the visual feedback from such a movement is limited. Whereas, when the convex features rise out of the shell, the visual feedback is much more noticeable. We asked the participants about this issue in the post-experiment questionnaire. 83% of the participants said that they relied mainly on their sense of touch as opposed to their vision. Several participants said that, even though some of amplitude changes were very easy to detect through sight, they preferred to use touch. They also noted that smaller amplitude changes required exploration through touch.

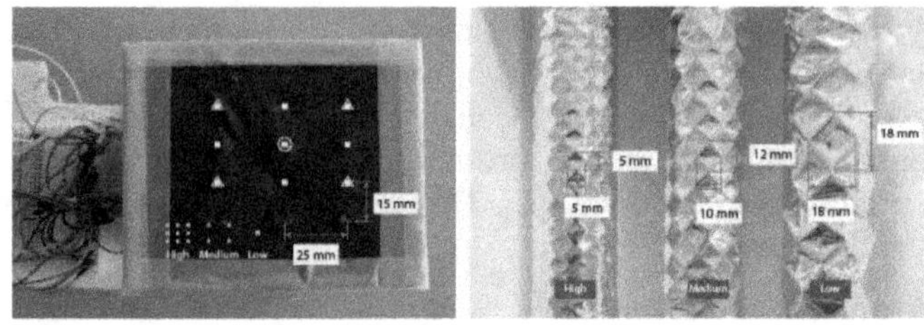

Figure 6: Granularity levels for the Pin Array (left) and Mylar (right).

EXPERIMENT 2 – GRANULARITY

A second user experiment was conducted to investigate the perception of the Pin Array and Mylar UnCovers' granularity changes (as shown in Figure 6).

We conducted a within subjects experiment to identify the distinguishability of different granularities when a user's hand is in contact with the UnCovers (with and without visual feedback).

Participants and Task

We recruited 12 participants (3 female, all right-handed, with an age range of 20 to 35) through the University and social networks. All of the participants wore headphones to mask any noise.

In each trial, two granularities were presented to the subjects in a counterbalanced order. After examining the stimuli, by touching them (with and without visual feedback), the participant was asked to identify the stimulus with the largest granularity. This comparison task was repeated for each UnCover (pin array and Mylar) four times, resulting in 24 samples for each condition.

Conditions and Variables

We used three different granularity levels for each of the UnCovers.

Pin Array:

- Small: 1 control point, raised area of $3mm^2$
- Medium: 2 x 2 control points, raised area of $15cm^2$
- Large: 3 x 3 control points, raised area of $15cm^2$.

Mylar:

- Small: 116 control points (diamonds), diamond surface area of $1.62cm^2$
- Medium: 314 control points, diamond surface area of $0.6cm^2$
- Large: 1450 control points, diamond surface area of $0.13cm^2$

The experiment was conducted under two counterbalanced conditions: tactile feedback only, and tactile plus visual feedback. In all conditions, the Uncover was placed on a table and participants were asked to touch the UnCover with their hand once the deformation was complete. In the haptic feedback only condition, a box was placed over the participants' hands and the UnCover. This was to ensure that the shape-change could not be identified visually.

Results

In this experiment, the system logged the granularity level, modality condition, response time and accuracy. The mean accuracy rates for each granularity level in each condition are shown in Figure 7.

A repeated measures analysis of variance (ANOVA) of granularity accuracy rates showed a significant main effect for *Granularity Level* ($F(1.4, 15) = 5.2$, $p=0.02$) with Greenhouse-Geisser correction. The ANOVA also showed a significant main effect for *Modality* ($F(1,11) = 22$, $p=0.001$), and for *Prototype* ($F(1,11)=14.7$, $p=0.003$). There were no significant interactions between the conditions.

Bonferroni adjusted post hoc tests of *Granularity Level* showed that the smallest granularity level produced significantly higher accuracy rates than the medium and large levels ($p<0.05$), and there was no significant difference between the medium and large levels ($p=0.61$).

As shown in Figure 8, as the difference in granularity levels increases, so do the accuracy rates. In terms of the main effects of *Modality* and *Prototype*, post hoc tests show that there are higher accuracy levels in the *Visual* and *Tactile* condition, compared to the *Tactile* condition (0.001), and that the *Pin Array* led to higher accuracy than the *Mylar* ($p=0.003$).

The results show that the detection rates with the Pin Array are generally higher than the Mylar. This may be due to the more rigid and defined structure of the Pin Array, compared to the flexible and organic structure on Mylar.

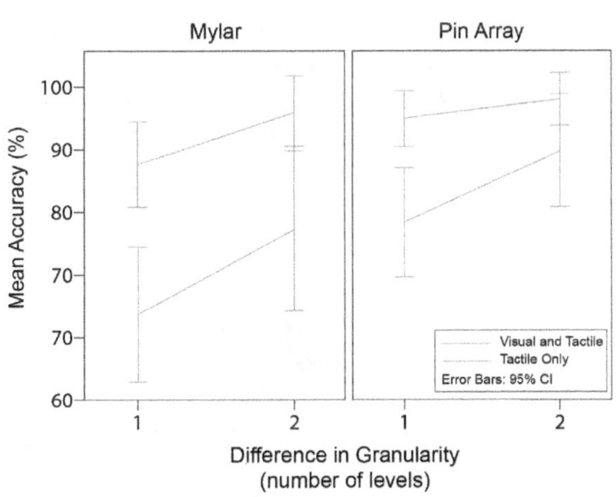

Figure 7: Mean accuracy rates for each granularity level, type of UnCover, and modality condition.

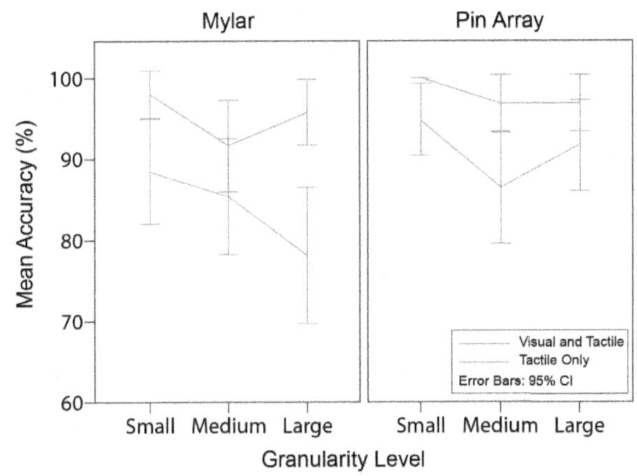

Figure 8: Mean accuracy rates for distinguishability across differences in granularity levels.

However, the Mylar detection rates increase greatly when visual feedback is provided. This is most likely because Mylar is a highly reflective material, and the enhanced contrast highlights the difference in granularities. The medium and large granularities are confused more often than the small granularity. This indicates that, even though it is theoretically possible to count the number of control points, the larger granularities may be perceived in a relative manner as it becomes more difficult to count the number of control points.

Post-Study Questionnaire

After the experiments, the participants were asked about their experiences with the UnCover amplitude and granularity changes. Several participants suggested some potential applications for this type of haptic feedback. For example, 24 of the participants said that they would use the feedback as a form of mobile alert or device state notification. Seven of the participants also said that they would like to use the Pin Array as a representation of a clock so they can check the time by touching their pocket. Lastly, another intriguing application, suggested by many of the participants, is remote interpersonal communication. Users could send textural deformations to other users' UnCovers. As stated in [8], human to human communication is a natural application of OUIs. Participants were shown all possible texture deformations, one at a time, and asked to rate how strongly [they] agree or disagree with various different interpretations of the message. The message types were based on those used in [4][7][15] and were rated on a 7-point Likert scale.

A principle components factor analysis of the 18 message types, using varimax rotations, was conducted with 3 factors explaining 78% of the variance. We chose three labels for the factors: *Caring and Supportive*, *Provocative* (negative and positive), and *Attention-Grabbing*. The factor loading matrix for this final solution is presented in Table 1. Composite scores were created for each of the three factors, based on the mean rating of the items which had their primary loadings on each factor.

	Caring & Supportive	Provocative	Attention-Grabbing
Alert	-.169	.588	.665
Anger	-.048	.887	.262
Annoyance	.437	.649	.177
Appreciation	.920	.069	.081
Attention	-.001	.419	.776
Comfort	.884	.064	-.047
Congratulations	.845	.245	.313
Emphasis	.297	.382	.657
Encouragement	.757	.290	.084
Friendship	.895	.182	.083
Frustration	.228	.883	.194
Greeting	.487	.080	.767
Intimacy	.750	.345	-.155
Joke	.385	.804	.061
Laughter	.436	.704	.211
Love	.921	.208	.091
Playful	.623	.716	-.009
Question	.491	.496	.381
Reassurance	.792	.089	.322

Extraction Method: Principal Component Analysis.
Rotation Method: Varimax with Kaiser Normalization.

Table 1: Factor loading matrix.

Attention-Grabbing was the message type that participants rated the most appropriate across all prototypes, in particular for the *Pin Array UnCover* with the highest amplitude and granularity.

Caring and Supportive messages were rated most appropriate for the highest magnitudes of shape-change for the *Pin Array UnCover*, whereas in the *Mylar UnCover*, the lower magnitudes of granularity were more appropriate.

Lastly, *Provocative* messages were associated with granularity changes in the *Pin Array* and *Mylar UnCovers*, at the highest granularity levels but were not so appropriate for the *Pin Array* amplitude changes, as shown in Figure 9.

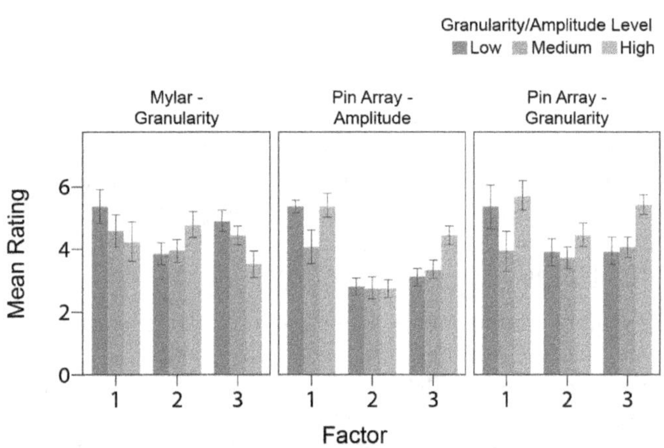

Figure 9: Mean appropriateness rating for each Factor (1: Caring & Supportive, 2: Provocative, 3: Attention-Grabbing) for each UnCover, and stimulus level. Error bars = 95% CI.

MOBILE PROTOTYPES

It is challenging to implement shape changing interfaces on mobile devices, since both the device and the interface mechanism need to share two of the device's most important resources: space and power. However, given the promising results from our experiment, it seems like mobile versions are not out of the question since very small shape-changes are perceivable, thus reducing demands on space.

We explored two types of actuators for driving the shape change. For the Pin Array Uncover we used a servomotor-based mechanism, which requires more space but can be power-efficient. In the case of Mylar Uncover, we chose to use muscle wires that are very compact in size but consume more power. Both actuators are common in shape-changing interfaces. In this section we present the practical implementation details, and discuss the compromises we made to ensure a small mobile form factor.

Mobile Pin Array Uncover

The mobile version of the Pin Array UnCover has four sinusoidal ridges that can be pushed and pulled using a single small servomotor with low power requirements (Figure 10). The ridges are 3D printed with polylactide (PLA), which means that they are robust and can withstand pressure. The shape-change mechanism makes use of a plate and lever system that is extremely compact, meaning that it can fit in a handheld device. The overall depth of the Pin Array UnCover plus mobile device is 2cm. The shape-change parameter values are:

- Area: 15.2cm^2;
- Granularity: 3x4 control points;
- Amplitude: 0.3cm;
- Porosity: 100% or 0%
- Speed: By using a servomotor, we can vary the speed of deformation (the default setting is 0.5 seconds).

Shape-Change Mechanism

A movable plate is built in to the underside of the cover. The ridges can be pushed and pulled through the cover using a servomotor, which is attached to two levers at either side of the plate (Figure 11). The servomotor is driven by an Arduino board, which also fits inside the cover.

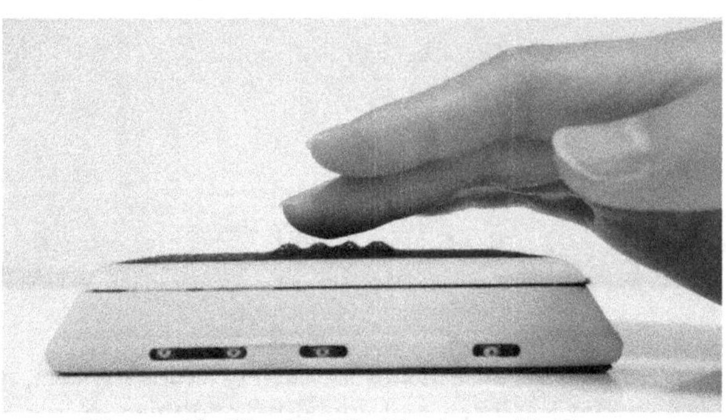

Figure 10: The Mobile Pin Array UnCover.

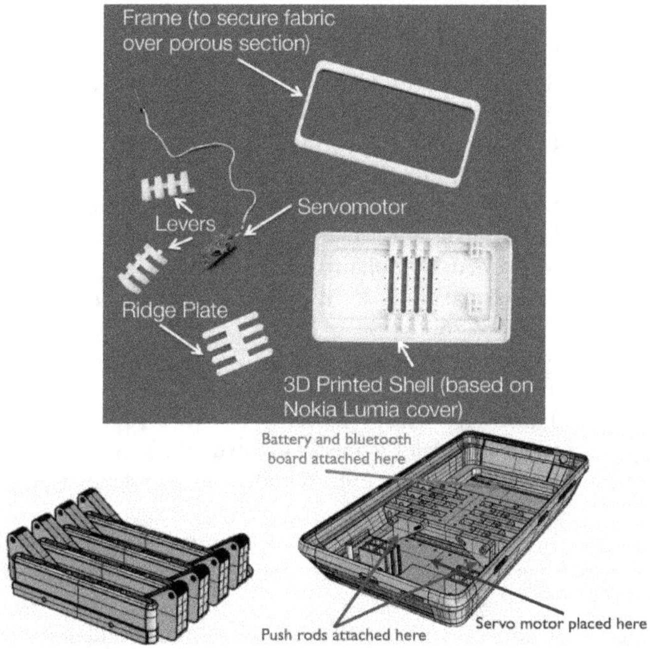

Figure 11: The mobile Pin Array UnCover components, movable plate with levers attached, and positions inside cover.

When the servo motor rotates clockwise, the plate is raised up and the ridges are pushed through the surface. When the servo motor rotates anti-clockwise, the plate is lowered so that the ridges are beneath the surface. The ridges pull the thin covering layer of material with them, creating dimples or concave features. The degree of motor rotation determines the amplitude of the texture. These shape changes are illustrated in Figure 12.

Mobile Mylar UnCover

The mobile version of *Mylar UnCover* consists of a small flexible cylinder, wrapped in a Mylar sheet, attached to the side of the phone case. Instead of implementing a movable Mylar holder at one end of the cylinder for axial compression, the compression can be triggered by bending the cylinder. The curved cylinder creates a gap in between the Mylar sheet and the cylinder, which compresses the Mylar from both ends of the cylinder. It must be noted that the diamond-like shapes are only formed on the concave side of the cylinder.

Figure 12: Illustration of potential amplitude changes in Mobile Pin Array UnCover.

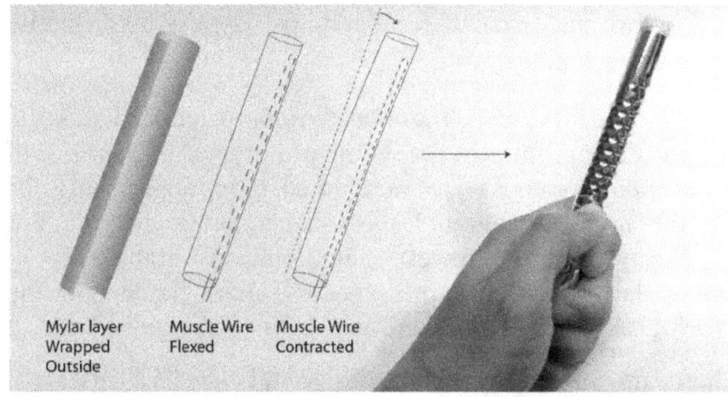

Figure 13: Mobile Mylar UnCover. A Mylar sheet is wrapped around a flexible tube with muscle wire attached inside of the tube. When the wire contracts, the tube bends toward one side and shape the Mylar.

The shape change parameter values are:

- Area: $20cm^2$ effective lateral surface (width 4cm, length 8cm);
- Granularity: 160 control points, diamond surface area of c. $0.125cm^2$;
- Amplitude: 1mm;
- Porosity: 0%;
- Speed: 2 seconds (The speed may vary according to the properties of the muscle wire and applied current).

Shape-Change Mechanism

Using muscle wires as an actuation mechanism is common in modern shape changing interfaces and robotics, such as the longitudinal tensile actuation in [18]. In our case, the muscle wire is attached to one side of the inner wall of the tube. The wire contracts when there is a current running through it, resulting in a bent tube (Figure 13). When the current stops, the flexible tube returns to its original shape.

DISCUSSION AND CONCLUSIONS

Building on previous explorations of shape-changing techniques and parameters, the experiments reported in this paper established that low frequency texture changes using amplitude and granularity can be easily distinguished. The results indicate that:

- Convex and concave amplitude changes in the Pin Array can be distinguished with 68% to 100% accuracy;
- Convex amplitude changes are distinguished more accurately when using tactile and visual feedback, whereas concave changes are distinguished more accurately through tactile feedback alone;
- Granularity changes can be distinguished with an average accuracy rate of 94% with the Pin Array and 89% with Mylar.
- The distinguishability of granularity changes in the Pin Array and Mylar UnCovers improves when using

tactile and visual feedback, as opposed to tactile feedback alone;

- Participants rated *Attention-Grabbing* messages as the most appropriate for both prototypes, *Caring and Supportive* messages were rated most appropriate for the highest magnitudes of shape-change for the Pin Array, and the lowest magnitudes of granularity in Mylar. *Provocative* messages were associated with the highest granularity levels in the Pin Array and Mylar.

There are still many challenges in this area of research. Firstly, it will be necessary to conduct longitudinal in-the-wild studies of shape-change perception to ensure that such stimuli can be successfully used as a method of information transmission regardless of the user's environment.

Furthermore, since the aim of this research is to use shape-change parameters as a form of static haptic feedback, the number of distinguishable levels of each shape-change parameter should be as high as possible. This can be difficult [10, 16], because parameters may interact with each other. If the granularity of control points decreases, it may be difficult for users to detect different amplitude levels. This is the case with the Mylar UnCover, as the granularity increases, the amplitude decreases.

It is our hope that this work will inspire other researchers to consider using texture-based shape-changing displays as a form of haptic feedback for mobile communication.

REFERENCES

1. Lorna M Brown, Stephen A Brewster, and Helen C Purchase. 2006. Multidimensional Tactons for Non-visual Information Presentation in Mobile Devices. In *Proc. MobileHCI*, 231–238.
2. Roger W Cholewiak and James C Craig. 1984. Vibrotactile pattern recognition and discrimination at several body sites. *Perception & Psychophysics* 35,6:503–514.
3. Panteleimon Dimitriadis and Jason Alexander. 2014. Evaluating the Effectiveness of Physical Shape-change for In-pocket Mobile Device Notifications. In *Proc. CHI*, 2589–2592.
4. Chris Harrison and Scott E Hudson. 2009. Texture Displays: A Passive Approach to Tactile Presentation. In *Proc. CHI*, 2261–2264.
5. Fabian Hemmert, Susann Hamann, Matthias Löwe, Josefine Zeipelt, and Gesche Joost. 2010. Shape-changing Mobiles: Tapering in Two-dimensional Deformational Displays in Mobile Phones. In *CHI '10 Extended Abstracts*, 3075–3080.
6. Eve Hoggan. 2013. Haptic Interfaces. *The SAGE Handbook of Digital Technology Research*: 342.
7. Eve Hoggan, Craig Stewart, and Laura Haverinen. 2012. Pressages: augmenting phone calls with non-verbal messages. In *Proc. UIST*, 555–562.
8. David Holman and Roel Vertegaal. 2008. Organic User Interfaces: Designing Computers in Any Way, Shape, or Form. *Commun. ACM* 51, 6: 48–55.
9. Astrid M L Kappers, Jan J Koenderink, and Inge Lichtenegger. 1994. Haptic identification of curved surfaces. *Perception & Psychophysics* 56, 1: 53–61.
10. Idin Karuei, Karon E MacLean, Zoltan Foley-Fisher, Russell MacKenzie, Sebastian Koch, and Mohamed El-Zohairy. 2011. Detecting Vibrations Across the Body in Mobile Contexts. In *Proc. CHI*, 3267–3276.
11. Roberta L Klatzky and Susan J Lederman. 2003. Touch. In *Handbook of Psychology*. Wiley & Sons.
12. Jaime M Lee, Christopher R Wagner, S J Lederman, and Robert D Howe. 2003. Spatial Low Pass Filters for Pin Actuated Tactile Displays. In *Proc. HAPTICS*, 57.
13. Marjorie R Leek. 2001. Adaptive procedures in psychophysical research. *Perception & Psychophysics* 63, 8: 1279–1292.
14. Takuya Nojima, Yoshiharu Ooide, and Hiroki Kawaguchi. 2013. Hairlytop interface: An interactive surface display comprised of hair-like soft actuators. In *Proc. World Haptics*.
15. Young-Woo Park, Chang-Young Lim, and Tek-Jin Nam. 2010. CheekTouch: An Affective Interaction Technique While Speaking on the Mobile Phone. In *CHI '10 Extended Abstracts*, 3241–3246.
16. Hayes Raffle, James Tichenor, and Hiroshi Ishii. 2004. Super Cilia Skin: A Textural Interface. *TEXTILE* 2, 3: 328–347.
17. Majken K Rasmussen, Esben W Pedersen, Marianne G Petersen, and Kasper Hornbæk. 2012. Shape-Changing Interfaces : A Review of the Design Space and Open Research Questions. In *Proc. CHI*, 735–744.
18. Simon Robinson, Céline Coutrix, Jennifer Pearson, Juan Rosso, Matheus Fernandes Torquato, Laurence Nigay, and Matt Jones. 2016. Emergeables: Deformable Displays for Continuous Eyes-Free Mobile Interaction. In *Proc. CHI*, 3793–3805.
19. Anne Roudaut, Abhijit Karnik, Markus Löchtefeld, and Sriram Subramanian. 2013. Morphees. In *Proc. CHI*, 593.
20. K A Seffen and S V Stott. 2014. Surface Texturing Through Cylinder Buckling. *Journal of Applied Mechanics* 81, 6: 61001.
21. Makoto Shimojo, Masami Shinohara, and Yukio Fukui. 1998. Shape identification performance and pin-matrix density in a three-dimensional tactile display. *Systems and Computers in Japan* 29, 2: 1–8.

3D-modeling and 3D-printing Explorations on Japanese Tea Ceremony Utensils

Pierre Lévy
Eindhoven University of Technology
Eindhoven, The Netherlands
plevy@tue.nl

Shigeru Yamada
Eindhoven University of Technology
Eindhoven, The Netherlands
shigeru_yamada@nifty.com

ABSTRACT

In this paper, we inquire aesthetical aspects of the Japanese tea ceremony, described as the aesthetics in the imperfection, based on novel fabrication technologies: 3D-modeling and 3D-printing. To do so, 3D-printed utensils (*chashaku* and *chasen*) were iteratively designed for the ceremony and were evaluated using constructivist interviews, eliciting personal construct of a tea master on the beauty of these utensils. Our findings suggest that (1) beauty in the imperfection is feasible with 3D-printers, (2) such beauty can be created at the mechanical limits of the printer and of the material, creating uncontrolled yet beautiful irregularities, (3) further research can be made on the dialogue between the designer and the machine, leaving space for beautiful mechanical uncertainty. We invite designers and design researchers (1) to look at the potential of new technologies beyond what is classically expected, (2) to consider other cultural perspectives on aesthetics and on making, leading to potential novel practices in design.

Author Keywords

3D-printing; 3D modeling, Japanese tea ceremony; utensils; personal construct

ACM Classification Keywords

H.5.m. Information interfaces and presentation (e.g., HCI): Miscellaneous;

PREAMBLE

These authors have contributed equally to this work. Yamada has designed and printed the artefacts presented in this paper, and has conducted the interviews and the analyses as part of his design master graduation project. Lévy has supervised the project, framed the project as part of a design research on everyday rituals inspired by Japanese culture, and has elaborated this paper in which have been included some parts the master graduation report of Yamada.

TEI '17, March 20-23, 2017, Yokohama, Japan
© 2017 ACM. ISBN 978-1-4503-4676-4/17/03…$15.00
DOI: http://dx.doi.org/10.1145/3024969.3024990

INTRODUCTION

This project falls within a dialogue established as a research inquiry on the potential contribution of Japanese philosophy, craft, and culture to the discipline of interaction design. It was indeed pointed out that although Japanese design is highly appreciated and considered for both everyday products and highly technical ones, very little is known about the specific qualities of designs inspired by Japanese culture and the way Japanese culture could contribute as a novel perspective on interaction design.

In past projects nurturing this dialogue, we have looked in the past on how the Japanese tea ceremony could inspire designers from many cultures to design everyday rituals based on their own context of design [5]. We pointed out a few elements that will be recalled here without being explained extensively:

(1) structural and temporal complexities – the complexity of the ceremony does not reside only in the complex relations between spaces, artefacts, and people, but also in the complex relations between gestures of different persons and between highly nested events taking place throughout the ceremony. Like cooking, it points out the importance of taking care of time at both experiential and interaction levels.
(2) designing the gesture – some gestures in the tea ceremony are formalized and associated with meaning and values. Although the interaction design community has deeply considered the value of action possibilities, this study hypothetically suggests that there is valuable space for more gestural design.
(3) aesthetics and ethics – This study has suggested again the interdependency between aesthetics and ethics [2]. Moreover, it was pointed out that the ethics transcends the World of Tea to affect ethics in the profane world (or everyday life), having itself everyday aesthetics consequences. The practice of the Way of Tea impacts everyday aesthetics and ethics.

In the current project, we intend to focus on the other way around: how current making techniques developed by interaction design can inquire, and even question some aspects of the Japanese tea culture. The aim of this project is therefore to look at how novel fabrication technologies, such as 3D-modeling and 3D-printing, which are mature enough to be involved and experimented in another framework than the one they were created for, could be accepted and support the making of new utensils for the Japanese tea ceremony. Expected output should contribute to (1) the understanding of beauty of 3D-printing artefacts from the perspective of the Japanese Way of Tea, and a reflections on (2) alternative ways of using 3D-printers considered as one tool of the new craftsmanship [3], and on (3) the synergy of the hybrid artisan [16].

Little has been found on the influence of Japanese traditional culture on novel 3D-printing techniques. Souryou Matsumura performed a Japanese tea ceremony at TEDxTokyo [10] with 3D-printed objects, but very little is known about the objects, nothing that could directly contribute to our project. The literature is richer and informative on the topic of the aesthetics of imperfection in 3D-printing techniques. Notably, Amit Zoran [15,16] argues for the hybrid artisans and the digital imperfection, presenting the Freed device and combining the artisan and the tools as a hybrid interactive system capable of creating beautiful imperfection. Although we agree and embrace the notion of hybrid interactive system between the maker and the tool, we explore here the possibly of imperfection by the tool. Whereas Zoran focuses on the imperfection in the human's gesture, we delve into the possibility of imperfection in the tool's operation. The machine limitations that Karl Willis [11] considers to be a bottleneck for interactive fabrication, we take it as an opportunity for creating beautiful imperfection.

We do not consider here the improvement of machines so they can intentionally create imperfections, but rather look into how these machines are designed and engineered in order to find ways of using them so their mechanical limitations can provoke imperfection and irregularities that are truly beautiful as suggested by Sōetsu Yanagi [14]. In this way, we find similarities with the work of the textile designer Akira Minagawa [7], who challenges the industrial embroidery machines by reaching their mechanical limits and creates beautiful irregular patterns.

JAPANESE TEA CEREMONY

A brief cultural story

The Japanese tea ceremony as mostly practiced nowadays was formalized by Sen no Rikyū in the 16th century. This formalization does not concern only the ritual aspects of the ceremony itself, but all matters related to spaces, utensils, gestural and more generally behavioral etiquette of the participants (both the host and the guests). It is a complete world, the World of Tea, that has been formalized for the tea ceremony. The World of Tea, clearly distinct from the profane world in its spiritual, social, and aesthetics dimensions, is the one of Teaism, *the cult of the beauty* [8]. Teaism, and consequently the Japanese tea ceremony, finds its cultural origins in the Japanese Zen Buddhism, and is often described based on the notions of *sabi, shibumi, and wabi.*

The term *sabi* relates to the feeling of loneliness and originates in the early Japanese poetic work. Its beauty resides in the transcendence of this loneliness, on the beauty of the evanescence of things.

In this mountain village
where I've given up
all hope of visitors,
how drab would life be
without my loneliness (Saigyō).

The term *shibumi* refers to the aesthetics of the simple and the subtle, valuing the profound beauty in what is few and expressively calm. The important aspect of this term is that it demands to value what is concrete and accessible. It is not about any abstract form of aesthetics, but rather about the beauty in the physical world, considering at the highest the imperfection of things.

The term *wabi*, often translated as rustic simplicity [9], is also and mainly used to refer to the aesthetics of this simplicity. However, it is also important to notice that *wabi* goes beyond and relates as well to the ethics related to this aesthetics.

These three notions have been extensively considered in the formalization of the utensils, which Sen no Rikyū has established in collaboration of craftsmen of the time. A famous example of such collaboration is the request of Sen no Rikyū to the tile maker Chōjirō to create tea bowl following *wabi* principles. Chōjirō is the first potter of a still-existing line of potters known as the *raku* family. However, the work of Sen no Rikyū, that Akasegawa [1] described as avant-gardist of its time, has continuously evolved throughout generations of craftsmen.

Therefore, we dare to believe that our exploration of crafting tea ceremony utensils with 3D-printers, although very humble in comparison to the quality of craft embedded in beautiful utensils usually used in tea ceremonies, can be considered in line with explorative attempts of making tea utensils with the tools and techniques of the time.

The aesthetics of the imperfection

As mentioned previously, the Japanese tea ceremony relates to an aesthetics and ethics that consider to its highest the profound beauty of transience and imperfection. A famous anecdote illustrates well this aspect of *wabi*:

"Rikyū was watching his son Shoan as he swept and watered the garden path. "Not clean enough," said Rikyū, when Shoan had finished his task, and bade him try again. After a weary hour the son turned to Rikyū: "Father, there is nothing more to be done. The steps have been washed for the third time, the stone lanterns and the trees are well sprinkled with water, moss and lichens are shining with a fresh verdure; not a twig, not a leaf have I left on the ground." "Young fool," chided the tea-master, "that is not the way a garden path should be swept." Saying this, Rikyū stepped into the garden, shook a tree and scattered over the garden

gold and crimson leaves, scraps of the brocade of autumn! What Rikyū demanded was not cleanliness alone, but the beautiful and the natural also. [8]"

In regard to this perspective, in this project, looking at how novel fabrication technologies could be used for the making of Japanese tea ceremony utensils, we do not aim at a 'perfect' result with a complete control of the technology. Rather, we aim at leaving space for an aesthetics of the imperfection to occur. This leads to two major considerations. First, in the way Sen no Rikyū shook the tree for the imperfection to come from the leaves, we aim at 'inviting' the tool to create the imperfection. This requires that we aim to control the 3D-printer in a way that the results are not fully predictable ahead. This can be done by either exploring at the limits of what the 3D-printer can mechanically do, or playing with modifiable parameters of the machine and its 3D-modeler. Moreover, this requires an explorative attitude, iteratively making and evaluating outcomes. Second, the evaluation of each printed utensils is not about how the outcome fits our expectation, but rather how the result fits the aesthetics of the imperfection. Expert evaluation is therefore necessary, to step out of the making expectation and to evaluate how the result fits the Way of Tea.

EXPERIMENT

Objectives

As a consequence of the two aforementioned considerations, a successful 3D-printed design is one recognized by the experts as having intrinsic qualities fitting with the aesthetics of the imperfection and fitting within the tea ceremony (we call this appropriateness).

It is important to notice here that users and experts are the same: the tea master serves the tea. Evaluation is therefore done with experts, who are also the users of the utensils. Moreover, the design researchers involved in the making of the utensils and authors of this paper have also experience with the tea ceremony.

Process

All evaluations of utensil were done by an expert of such aesthetics: a tea master of the *urasenke* school of tea. In order to understand not only which sample of utensils he appreciates, but also and mostly based on which qualities and values (either inherent to the utensils or in relation with another aspect the tea ceremony), we based our evaluation on constructivist interviews. Directly derived from the George A. Kelly's Personal Construct Theory [4], these are designed as an instrument for the qualitative elicitation of personal constructs. Their purpose is to let the interviewee use her/his own terms to express her/his own experience. This way, the interviewer can describe the interviewee's mental model without any significant influence from her/his own mental model.

The results of the interviews are used to either initiate a new iteration on the making of a similar utensil, or as a means to establish a general reflection on (1) establishing the qualities found in the series of 3D-printed utensils that fit with the aesthetics of the imperfection, (2) how the 3D-printing techniques can support the making of utensils for the Japanese tea ceremony, and (3) what aspects of this exploration can be used to explore another utensils of the ceremony.

In this paper, we present our inquiry based on two utensils of the Japanese tea ceremony: the *chashaku* and the *chasen*. Both were made using 3D printers using Fused Deposition Modeling (FDM) technology. For the *chashaku*, we explored how inquired some *beautiful* 3D-printed and evaluated characteristics. The aim is to address the making of beautifully imperfect utensils through 3D-printing. For the *chasen*, following the *chashaku* experiment, a unique series of samples were 3D-printed. The aim was to investigate the level of imperfection to be perceived as beautiful.

Although made for another study, a Japanese tea ceremony using the 3D-printed *chashaku* mentioned in this paper has been performed and recorded. A video submitted together with this paper (cf. [6] for a longer version) shows an excerpt of the ceremony. This ceremony is a *yobanashi*, that is done in the evening. Usually performed by candlelight, this one is performed using an intelligent light installation which behaves according to the progress of the ceremony and the actions of the host and the guests. Here as well, the perceived beauty of the light and of its movements were the main challenge of this installation.

chashaku

The *chashaku* is a little tea scoop used to take the tea powder out of its caddy. It is traditionally crafted through cutting bamboo, dried for material stability, bended with heat to create the head part of the scoop, waiting for months with string for tensioning until the material remember the bend, and then curved on the entire body.

Figure 1. traditional *chashaku* (front) and ***chasen***The *chashaku* were designed using Autodesk Fusion 360. A first iteration consisted in a variation of dealing with various filaments, smoothness of the surface, orientation of the printing (impacting the patterns due the moving head of the 3D-printer), etc. The aim of this iteration was to provide enough variety to engage the expert into a comparison and a discussion on where the beauty resides.

During the making of the *chashaku*, switching between the 3D modeler, the 3D printer and printed objects, we noticed the already known challenge of crafting with digital means. On one side, hand-craft allows for a direct, immediate and tangible contact with the material and with the object as it is being crafted, creating a seemingly continuous aligning flow between what is intended, what is actually being made, and what is discovered along the way. On the other side, the digital approach prevents the direct and immediate access to the object and the material as the model is being digitally created, which imposes a much less smooth flow in the work.

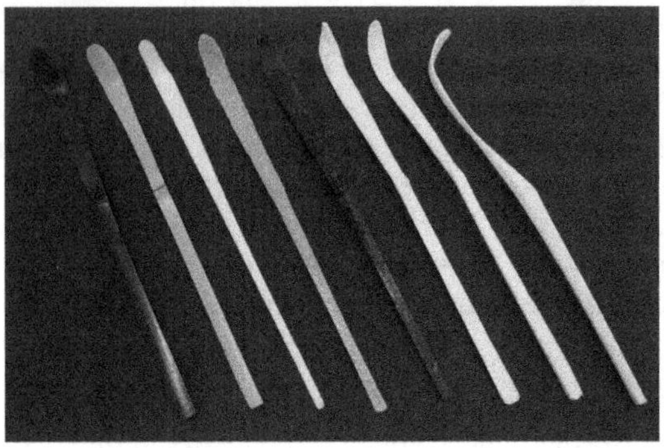

Figure 2. samples of the first iterations of *chashaku* (the first two from the left are traditional bamboo *chashaku* shown as reference)

Seven *chashaku* were evaluated, one of which being a traditional bamboo one. The evaluation took place in the 4.5 tatami tea room of a tea master who was the expert. Other utensils used for the tea ceremony were kept at hand. The reasons for this is to keep the situation as close as possible to the normal context of use, and to allow the expert to manipulate the objects in expected ways for the ceremony, i.e., together with other utensils.

Figure 3. *chashaku* evaluation

The expert could examine each *chashaku* and order them by order of preference and appropriateness. Then a Socratic interview was conducted, which lasted for nearly 1.5 hours. The entire session was recorded for further analysis. The interview was first transcript and then analyzed to render the personal construct (cf. Figure **4**). The construct itself was then discussed among the researchers (cf. Figure 5), which led to four propositions of expectedly improved *chashaku* (cf. Figure 6).

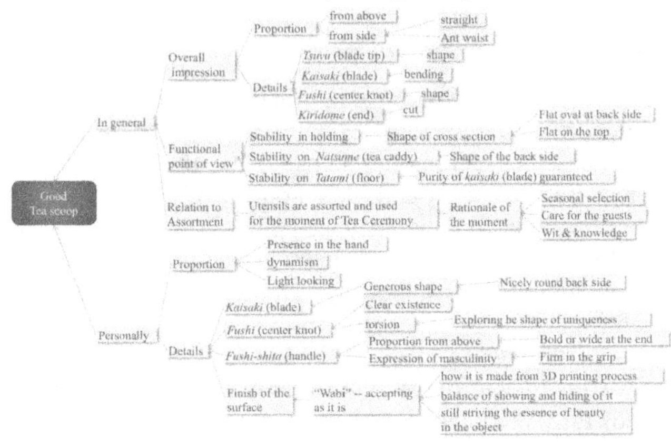

Figure **4**. expert construct on the evaluation of *chashaku*

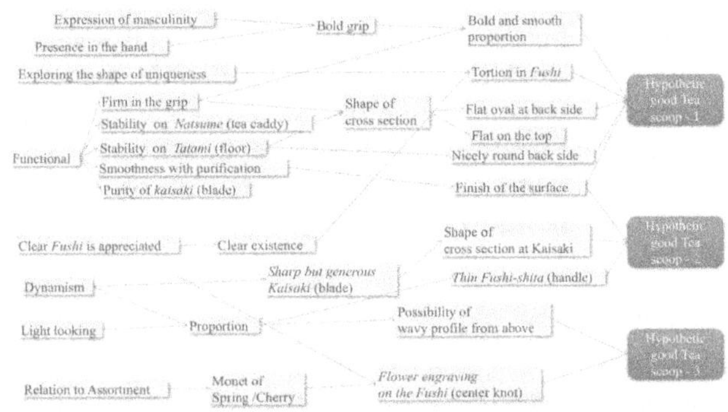

Figure **5. Synthesis for a new series of 3D-printed *chashaku***

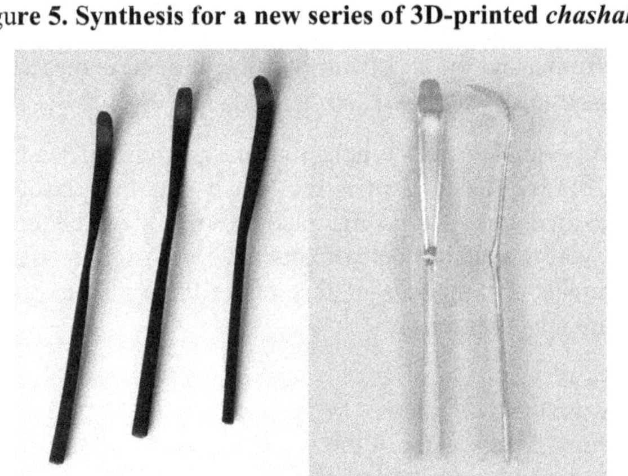

Figure 6. 'Improved' 3D-printed *chashaku* (numbered from left to right $c1_a$, $c1_b$, c2, and c3 respectively. c3 is shown both from the top and the side. Numbers refer to the hypothetic good tea scoop described in Figure **5.)**

Each of the four propositions was based on the results of the previous analysis/synthesis, as shown in Figure 5. In Figure 6, the *chashaku* $c1_b$ ('c' stands for *chashaku*) is from the similar 3D-model as $c1_a$ (and answers to the same evaluation points), but the finishing is smoother than $c1_a$.

$c1_a$ and $c1_b$ are '*to be bold yet smooth'* proportion. Also the shape '*provides stability when handled'*. Most importantly, these tea scoops are printed in a certain direction and then polished so that the layers of the FDM 3D-printing can give a feeling of wood-like texture on the surface.

c2 was designed to have especially the '*full figured back side in the tip of the tea scoop*'. The printing direction was also made such as it can provide a touch feel of bamboo or plant like texture on the surface.

c3 was designed with '*clear waist*' and '*lightness*' of the proportion. Moreover, it refers to cherry blossom so that the tea scoop could be used for an expected ceremony planned in spring following the current experiment. The model data file of this *chashaku* is accessible at [12].

In the same conditions as previously, the three 'improved' *chashaku* were evaluated by the expert. He acknowledged the improvement in comparison to the first ones. $c1_b$ was preferred and well appreciated, although more improvement was required due to the instability of the *chashaku* once put on the tatami: it would flip on its side each time, which appears not to be a beautiful imperfection.

chasen

The *chasen* is a tea whisk made from a unique piece of bamboo used to stir and to foam the tea powder with a small amount of hot water. The lower part is the handle and the upper part the actual whisk.

Despite many valuable trials to 3D-print the upper part, we have not reached a quality that would be satisfactory enough to properly evaluate it by the expert (cf. Figure 7).

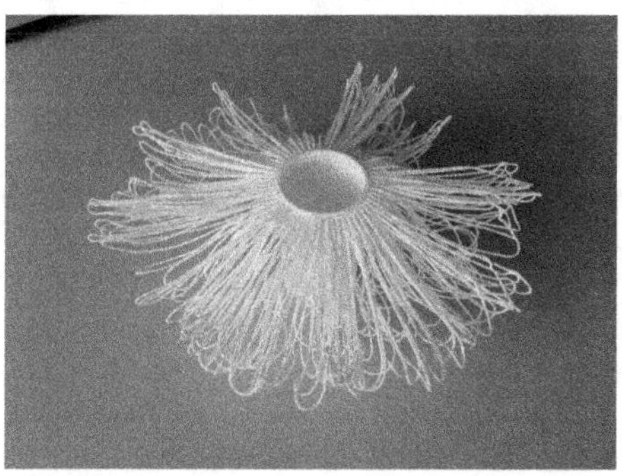

Figure 7. ***chasen*** **upper part trial**

However, the lower part of the *chasen* was sufficient for our experiment: despite the fact that the main function of the *chasen* was not feasible, the expert could still manipulate the printed object and evaluate its quality in term of aesthetics of the imperfection and appropriateness. Five samples were created, all with a similar diameter (diameters varying between 28mm and 32mm) and height (50mm), the same material (black PolyLactic Acid – PLA). Only the movement speed of the printer head was different for each sample, keeping the head temperature was fixed at 220 °C. The feeding amount of the material was controlled on the assumption to be proportional to the speed of the head. The head speeds were default speed, and then two, three, four, and six times faster (from left to right on Figure 8, respectively). The G-code file and its generator algorithm (processing file) can be found at [13].

From the perspective of an aesthetics of perfection, it is assumed that the slower the speed of the printer head the more beautiful. However, from the perspective of an aesthetics of imperfection, speeding up the head might lead to beautiful and valuable imperfections.

Figure 8. Sample of 3D-printed ***chasen*** **handles**

In the same conditions as for the *chashaku*, the expert was asked to evaluate the five samples. The sample at the center in Figure 8 was preferred, which was described by the expert as having a nice balance between regularities and irregularities. The personal construct can be seen in Fig. 9.

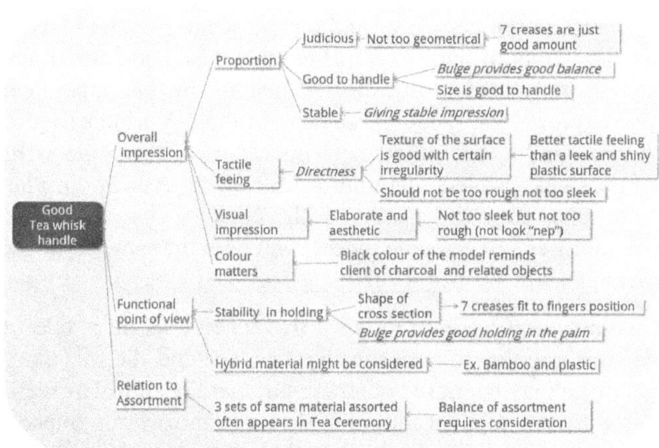

Figure 9. Personal construct on the ***chasen*** **handles evaluation**

The main conclusion of this evaluation pointed out that irregular pattern made with higher printing speed gives better tactile feeling than the one with regular pattern. Moreover, the ones with slight irregularities (samples 2 and 3) were preferred in the visual impression. Therefore, we suggest that the beauty in the imperfection is perceived both at the visual and tactile level at the same time, and that the relation between both modalities matters.

We suggest here that pushing the 3D-printer head to a faster speed than recommended led to a sort of mechanical uncertainty, which is at the origin of imperfections perceived as beautiful. It is because the machine could not act 'perfectly' that uncertainty in its process occurred, leading to beauty in the imperfection. ***The beauty was made without really trying: the maker should let the machine do.*** It is also to notice that a balance needs to be found: beyond a certain speed of the 3D-printer head, aesthetics degenerates badly.

CONCLUSION

These two experiments, making and evaluating 3D-modelled and 3D-printed utensils for the Japanese tea ceremony, pointed out the potential acceptability of 3D-printed objects within the Japanese Way of Tea. However, this is done following a few aspects discussed here.

An implied aspect of these two experiments, which strengthens the need of an expert evaluation, is the necessary effort to appreciate the artefacts not in regards to the existing and well-accepted (i.e., traditional) ones, but rather as they are. In other words, the 3D-printing designer should not attempt to imitate traditional artefacts, but rather should find beauty with the making techniques and the used materials. This notion, which is important in Zen, invites to look for beauty of things 'as it is', i.e., in their thusness.

Another valuable aspect pointed out in this paper is that, according to the aesthetics in the imperfection, the value of the 3D-printed artefacts is made by what is usually considered as weakness of the 3D-printer. It is because the 3D-printer cannot print perfectly smooth out surfaces at higher speed that beautiful patterns and irregularities appeared on the *chashaku* and on the surface of the *chasen* handle. Going to the limits of the machines, and sometimes beyond, may lead to unexpected beauty. In this paper, we have explored the speed of the head of the 3D-printer for the *chasen* handle, but other experiments could be done with temperature, printed material… Moreover, even in similar conditions there is a very little chance that the same irregularities can be made twice, even with the same settings, opening space for beautiful uncertainty.

This last point leads to the idea that when making is taking place in a dialogue between the designer and the machine, outcomes may be more uncertain, but more beautiful as well. It is a matter of trust and confidence both towards oneself and towards the machine. This, however, raises again the issue of digital fabrication, in which the dialogue is discontinued: the beautiful imperfection brought by the machine is accessible to the designer long after the digital model was created, which prevents the qualitatively good dialogue.

Last, but not least, we hope to have clearly evoked and strengthen the idea that considering other cultural perspectives on aesthetics and ethics, on making and on assessing can lead to novel perspectives and practices in interaction design, and to open the discipline to a richer and larger design space yet to be explored.

ACKNOWLEDGEMENT

The two authors would like to thank dr. Michel Sougi Decré for his expertise on Japanese Way of Tea, as well as dhr. Chet Bangaru, dr.ir. Carl Megens and ir. Roy van den Heuvel for their expertise on the 3D-modelers and the 3D-printers.

REFERENCES

1. Genpei Akasegawa. 1990. *Sen no Rikyu: Mugon no zenei [Sen no Rikyu, Silent avant-guarde]*. Iwanami Shoten.
2. Alain Findeli. 1994. Ethics, Aesthetics, and Design. *Design Issues* 10, 2: 49–68. http://doi.org/10.2307/1511628
3. Joep Frens and Bart Hengeveld. 2013. To make is to grasp. In *Proceedings of the International Association of Societies of Design Research 2013* (IASDR2013).
4. George Kelly. 1991. *The Psychology of Personal Constructs*. Routledge.
5. Pierre Lévy. 2015. Exploring the challenge of designing rituals. In *6th International Congress of International Association of Societies of Design Research* (IASDR 2015).
6. Pierre Lévy. 3D-modeling and 3D-printing explorations on Japanese tea ceremony utensils. Retrieved November 16, 2016 from http://plevy.fr/tei17
7. Perhonen Minä. 2005. *minä perhonen 2 embroidery*. Bunka Publishing Bureau, Tokyo.
8. Kakuzo Okakura. 1906. *The Book of Tea*. La Alameda Press.
9. Sen Sōshitsu. 2014. *Vie du Thé, Esprit du Thé*. Arléa Editions.
10. TEDx Talks. 2014. *Traditional tea ceremony: Souryou Matsumura at TEDxTokyo 2014*. Retrieved August 9, 2016 from https://www.youtube.com/watch?v=LcFtwWlIT5I&index=6
11. Karl D.D. Willis, Cheng Xu, Kuan-Ju Wu, Golan Levin, and Mark D. Gross. 2011. Interactive Fabrication: New Interfaces for Digital Fabrication. In *Proceedings of the Fifth International Conference on Tangible, Embedded, and Embodied Interaction* (TEI '11), 69–72. https://doi.org/10.1145/1935701.1935716
12. Shigeru Yamada. Tea Scoop (Cherry blossom) by suppomi. *Shapeways*. Retrieved November 16, 2016 from http://www.shapeways.com/product/MQ4DJURNU/tea-scoop-cherry-blossom
13. Shigeru Yamada. GitHub - suppomi/ChasenHandle_3DSpiralTrochoid: G-Code generator for 3D printing with simple model viewer. Retrieved November 16, 2016 from https://github.com/suppomi/ChasenHandle_3DSpiralTrochoid
14. Soetsu Yanagi. 1989. *The Unknown Craftsman: A Japanese Insight into Beauty*. Kodansha International, Tokyo.
15. Amit Zoran. 2016. A Manifest for Digital Imperfection. *XRDS* 22, 3: 22–27. https://doi.org/10.1145/2893491
16. Amit Zoran, Roy Shilkrot, Suranga Nanyakkara, and Joseph Paradiso. 2014. The Hybrid Artisans: A Case Study in Smart Tools. *ACM Trans. Comput.-Hum. Interact.* 21, 3: 15:1–15:29. https://doi.org/10.1145/2617570

Expected Behavior and Desired Appearance of Insect-Like Desk Companions

Diana Löffler
Würzburg University
Würzburg, Germany
diana.loeffler@uni-wuerzburg.de

Alexandra Kaul
Würzburg University
Würzburg, Germany
alexandra.kaul@stud-mail.uni-wuerzburg.de

Jörn Hurtienne
Würzburg University
Würzburg, Germany
joern.hurtienne@uni-wuerzburg.de

ABSTRACT
Prior work on zoomorphic desktop companions has shown that these can fulfill a wide range of functionality and convey emotional value. When mimicking familiar animals or pets, however, users may develop unrealistic expectations about the available functionality and behavior of the companion. To amend this limitation, we propose insect-inspired concepts as a way to utilize our intuitive understanding of insects without raising unrealistic expectations of the companions. We built 11 tangible insect prototypes with varying forms and levels of abstraction and illustrated their potential behavior in video vignettes. The prototypes and vignettes were shown to 22 participants to elicit desired functionalities of insect-inspired companions, possible ways of conveying these and the meaning insect companions could have for the user. The results open up a realistic design space for the appearance and behavior of insect-inspired robots as desktop companions.

Author Keywords
Autonomy; robotic assistants; intuitive use; interactive devices; notification systems; zoomorphic interfaces.

ACM Classification Keywords
H.5.m. Information interfaces and presentation (e.g., HCI): Miscellaneous.

INTRODUCTION – AUTONOMOUS NOTIFIERS
When objects around us start to move autonomously, we tend to interpret their behavior as intentional, feel a sense of agency, and treat them as our peers [27]. Consequently, autonomously moving objects engender social behavior towards technology, and elicit complex emotions like solicitude and empathy [17]. Moreover, users tend to personify autonomous objects and establish a relationship with them, which leads to a high product valuation and an increased forgiveness towards unreliability. For example, the vacuum cleaning home robot Roomba might have gained its huge commercial success because people see it as a social entity in their homes, interpreting its unpredictable movements as personality traits and intentional acts [33]. Therefore, autonomous devices might deliver their functionality in ways that are entertaining and engaging for the users, creating an overall positive user experience [9, 17, 31].

TEI '17, March 20-23, 2017, Yokohama, Japan
© 2017 ACM. ISBN 978-1-4503-4676-4/17/03…$15.00
DOI: http://dx.doi.org/10.1145/3024969.3024992

The advantages that come along with autonomy have been already discovered for the design of notification tools. In our increasingly stimulating digital environments, researchers have been seeking for years less obtrusive ways to convey information of varying importance to the user [37]. Among strategies like the use of meta-information [34], appropriate notification timing [7], taking into account different levels of user awareness [23], exploiting the phenomenon of change blindness [14], or displaying information in the peripheral visual field through ambient displays [10], autonomy proposes a new way of delivering information and suggestions through companions with which users bond. This experience-driven approach provides emotional interaction capabilities beyond efficiency and performance, like intimacy, sympathy, and delightedness [29]. As a consequence, users might enjoy receiving information more and be more likely to follow suggestions [25] compared to traditional channels like push notifications on the smartphone or calendar alerts.

One common approach to design autonomous companions that convey information to the user is by mimicking the real world through adopting lifelike, zoomorphic forms and behaviors. This design strategy allows users to rely on prior embodied knowledge and eases interaction by building on positive attitudes towards animals and pets in particular. Since it is important that notifiers are designed in a way that potentially disruptive information can be perceived with minimal cognitive effort [22], allowing the user to build on prior knowledge is a key for intuitive interaction [13]. Such systems let users disseminate information very quickly without having to spend much cognitive effort or time to learn an arbitrary mapping between content and notification cue [23]. Despite the advantages of life-like actuated devices, there are also pitfalls. For example, zoomorphic companions bear the risk that expectations are raised that cannot be met by the device and result in disappointment

[9]. For example, most robotic devices cannot be fed, put into water (e.g., replicas of marine creatures), cannot follow the user or jump on its lap like a pet dog. Hence, instead of borrowing from very familiar companion animals like dogs or cats, we instead investigate adopting biomimicry patterns of insects. People possess profound knowledge of different insect species [20], yet they are less familiar than pets and therefore harbor a smaller risk to raise wrong expectations. Moreover, insects are the most diverse animal species [32] and open a wide design space for visual, acoustic and haptic information channels.

In this paper we investigate how well insect forms and behaviors can be used to intuitively convey various messages and suggestions to the user, as well as the impact of this on user experience. We present an empirical study in which 22 participants were shown different insect companions, designed to vary in parameters like insect type, size, biomorphic vs. abstract shape, sound and light features, movement patterns, color, visual features like antennae or wings. The participants' task was to come up with suitable actions for different tasks/notifications and to assign suitable tasks to different forms of insect behavior. In addition, we confronted them with 11 videos of insect prototypes in a desktop-setup and captured their responses and comments. The results allow identifying the most acceptable and appropriate insect forms and behaviors for notification purposes, as well as a vocabulary for intuitive cue-content mappings. The empirical findings extend our knowledge about advantages when drawing on prior embodied experience with animals for the design of robotic devices and expand the design space for zoomorphic autonomous desktop companions.

RELATED WORK – LIFE-LIKE DESKTOP COMPANIONS

From Leonardo da Vinci's flying machine sketches 500 years ago to the invention of Velcro, nature has been always an important inspiration when designing new technology. In the field of human-computer interaction (HCI), researchers took inspiration from various sources. To mention a few examples, Jung et al. drew ideas from adaptive movements of living creatures for designing objects with surface-changing properties [16]; the field of socially interactive robotics frequently draws upon anthropomorphic and zoomorphic features and gestures (e.g. [8]); and, most famous, a two-dimensional pointing device was named 'computer mouse'. In all cases, bio metaphors guide design decisions and provide meaningful analogies for users when interacting with artificial entities.

Recently, bio-inspired robot companions are investigated in a variety of fields, including nursing, home care, smart homes, entertainment, and office contexts. Of particular interest are the psychosocial effects of companions, as they are able to (partly) fulfill the human need to build social relationships [28]. Affiliation is in turn linked to many cognitive processes, emotions, positive health outcomes and overall well-being [4]. But users do not automatically bond with any companion. Instead, propinquity, similarity, attractiveness, and reciprocal liking have been identified as facilitating factors [18].

The office serves as a particularly interesting field of investigation, as workers spend a significant part of their daily time sitting at their desks, and are prone to interruptions by alerts and notifications, causing inefficiency as well as symptoms of inattention and hyperactivity [19]. Hardware companions in the office context (called 'desktop companions' from now on) promise to support the user's information management by combining multiple notification channels and functioning as a gatekeeper for important and user-defined alerts. In addition, desktop companions offer opportunities for persuasion by presenting behavior-relevant information that is not readily explicit for the user, e.g. prolonged sitting times [21]. Beyond informing the user, they maintain an empathic relationship with the user that offers capabilities for emotional interaction. Some notable examples in the development and design of desktop companions are introduced in the following.

Actuated Everyday Objects – Actuated Desktop items

Due to recent advances in computing, sensing and actuation technology, researchers, designers and manufacturers attempt to augment everyday objects in order to provide functions and services beyond the object's original purpose [30]. For example, DeVito & Ramani investigated how an office lamp, capable of movement in three-dimensional space, could be controlled by user gestures [6]. In a gesture eliciting study, participants were asked to come up with gestures for different tasks like turning the light on and off or moving the spotlight to a specific location. A depth camera tracked the users' hands and allowed their low-cost prototypical Tabletop Assistive Droid to recognize gesture input. Overall, the aim of this research was to find a more natural way to interact with moving, and thus life-like, physical objects in an augmented workspace. In another recent work, Bailly et al. explored the potential benefits of 'alive' objects in an augmented desktop workstation [2]. A formative user study revealed that a desktop workplace is not a fixed environment because users change the location and orientation of their computer monitor, mouse or keyboard up to several times a day. The authors therefore prototyped a setting in which these devices were actuated, along with possible application scenarios. However, the focus of this work was on ergonomic and functional aspects, neglecting the affective dimension of autonomy.

Anthropomorphic Companions – Sitting Posture

Jafarinaimi and colleagues introduced a small shape-changing office companion called 'Breakaway' to remind people to get out of their office chair and stand up to interrupt prolonged sitting times [15]. Designed as an ambient sensor-driven display in the form of a sculpture inspired by the human body and posture, Breakaway slouches when the user sits continuously for hours in the office chair without standing up. After the office worker took a break, Breakaway changes its shape into an upright position. The design was initially evaluated with a single person over the course of two weeks and the results showed that the movement of the sculpture indeed encouraged the user to take more breaks. The authors conclude that the outcome of this small study is promising for nudging the user towards positive changes in behavior.

Zoomorphic Companions – Pet Dogs and Insects

'Camy' is a half-digital, half-tangible desktop assistant resembling a dog [29]. The electronic companion is equipped with a webcam covered in furry fabric and resides in the user's workspace as PC peripheral. In a study in which Camy was introduced to users, the authors aimed at exploring the effects of the pet dog analogy on users' emotional experiences. Use cases covered Camy delivering system information, assisting or playing with the user, acting as personal security keeper and supporting video chatting or photo shooting. Due to its social presence and it being perceived as low-intelligence product, users acted forgiving towards dysfunctionality or distracting functions. In addition, fidgeting with Camy served as a brief pause for users, helping them to better concentrate on a subsequent main task afterwards. This is in line with recent research showing that cute pets not only promote caring behavior, but also have positive effects for focusing on tasks, which increases task efficiency and creativity [24].

Despite these advantages of life-like interactive objects, there are also some drawbacks. Applying anthropomorphism or zoomorphism changes how users understand and interact with technical devices by drawing on prior knowledge and experiences with human and animalistic life [30]. This raises expectations regarding functionality or behavior that cannot be fully met, leading to confusion or frustration [3]. This holds especially true for experiences in pet ownership, as users might compare devices with certain personality traits and behaviors of their familiar companion animals at home like dogs, cats and rabbits. In addition, in most of the cases, zoomorphic features are only used to communicate a system state or status changes to the user by mapping it to associated animalistic expressions. For example, a system can contract after getting touched by the user in order to 'protect' itself. Conveying information, notifications and suggestions to the user beyond mere system states and emotion display have rarely been examined.

Against this backdrop of prior work, we find it worthwhile exploring the zoomorphic potential another biological class has to offer for designing life-like objects and companion robots: insects. Insects are less familiar to users compared to typical pet animals, but nevertheless offer a great variety in forms and behaviors humans are aware of [20]. As they are the most diverse biological class on earth [32], representing more than half of the known species of living organisms, they offer a wide inspiration with possibilities for audio, visual and haptic feedback, and supposedly gesture interaction. Also, in their dominant role in all environments that support human life, insects have been thoroughly shaping human civilizations and have helped cultural and scientific evolution (e.g., through genetic studies, the production of shellac, or natural and biological control of pests). Insects attract our attention in various ways, because insects can be harmful to humans (e.g., insect-borne diseases, damage to stored products and vegetation) and also beneficial (e.g., producing silk or beeswax, aesthetical values). In any case, as a result of our genetic makeup and learning history, many insects automatically elicit strong emotional responses, an effect that can be leveraged for the affective design of robot companions that are intuitive to understand.

To inform the design process of autonomous desktop companions, one has to unveil desirable functions of desktop companions (the what-level of interaction), the way the functions should be accomplished making use of insect forms and behaviors (the how-level) and the way the participants as potential future users experience these functions (the why-level) [12]. Therefore, in a two-part user study, we gathered user feedback on 11 tangible insect prototypes shown in video vignettes and elicited user-defined actions and interpretations of various notification types.

USER STUDY: METHOD

Participants

Twenty-two student volunteers with a background in Human-Computer Interaction were recruited at a German university campus (16 male) to participate in this study. The participants' ages ranged from 19 to 28 years (M_{age}=22.1, SD_{age}=2.98) and their backgrounds were in human-computer interaction, media communication and law. Each participant was reimbursed for his or her time in form of course credit or 10 Euro.

Design and Material

To find out how insect-like companions should be designed to be acceptable and appropriate, the first author created 11 different prototypes following the framework of tangible autonomous interfaces introduced by Nowacka and Kick [26] and considering results of previous own work [20]. We varied the prototypes on the dimensions of physical form (similarity to the real world, visible technology and amount of physical modalities) and the complexity and ambiguity of the behavior (see Table 1 for an overview). Regarding physical form, four levels of abstract vs. biomorphic form were possible. In the abstract – high condition, the shape of the insect model was significantly changed, including altered proportions and the omission of legs, wings and antennae, and a change of colors. Companions in the abstract – low condition had no legs and the colors were slightly changed compared to the insect that served as their model, but this level included typical insect elements like wings and antennae. In the biomorphic – low group, prototypes were abstracted through artificial colors like white plastic or metal, by showing a mechanical inside or by adding a display. Finally, the biomorphic – high condition included companions with clearly visible tripartite body, a natural color scheme, realistic proportions as well as antennae and wings. We created video prototypes as design probes for each of the 11 prototypes. Sound and light effects were randomly assigned. These videos served to find out how users perceive the different prototypes when displaying notifications related to a desktop-work scenario through various motions, light and sound. In each video, the motion pattern of each companion was shown first, followed by a close-up and one or two notification behaviors (notifying the user of a smartphone push notification, reminding the user to drink water), see Figure 1. Each video lasted between 30 to 40 seconds.

Two lists to be presented to the participants were created through a brainstorming session with subsequent voting for the best items. List (A) contained 25 tasks and notifications a companion could communicate to the user. We made sure

Prototype Photo	Insect Model	Abstract vs. Biomorphic Form	Length in cm	Movement (Video)	Material & Color	Antennae & Wings	Sound, Light & Display (Video)
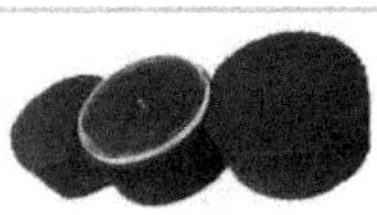	ant	abstract (high)	7.6	slow, straight, steady, crawling	black rubber	-	artificial chirping, display
	beetle	abstract (high)	3	slow, rounded paths, steady, rolling	green rubber	-	artificial bee, top light
	bee	abstract (low)	4	rather fast, round paths	wood, gold, paper	antennae, wings	artificial mosquito
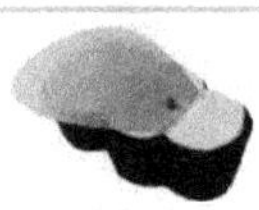	fly	abstract (low)	7	fast, circling, round, some rests	beige and black cloth, blue paper	wing	zoomorphic mosquito
	moth	abstract (low)	5.2	fast, light-approaching, rather straight	wood	wings	front lighting
	beetle	biomorphic (low)	4.8	slow, straight, steady, moving legs	white plastic	-	zoomorphic bee
	beetle	biomorphic (low)	5.7	fast, rounded paths, crawling legs	pink transparent plastic	antennae	-
	cater-pillar	biomorphic (low)	8	slow, straight, body movement	silver metal	antennae	underside lighting
	locust	biomorphic (low)	4.2	fast, jumping, long rests, stiff legs	green plastic	antennae	zoomorphic chirping, display
	butter-fly	biomorphic (high)	5.5	slow, round paths, long rests, flying	plastic, colorful wings	antennae, proboscis, wings	-
	cock-roach	biomorphic (high)	9	fast, jagged, hectic, moving legs	dark plastic	antennae, wings	rear part lighting

Table 1. Specifications of the 11 pre-designed zoomorphic prototypes, with photos.

that the tasks and notifications covered the following topics: drawing the users' attention to a specific location (4x), messages with social content like greeting (2), notifications about certain events (5x), suggestions to the user like a reminder to stand up (7x) and information about the system status, e.g. communicating that a task is executed (5x). The aim of this elicitation part of the study was to find out which insect characteristics prove to be the most suitable in communicating information in a human-readable way by observing patterns created by the users themselves. List (B) comprised 16 items with insect-behavior that should be interpreted by the user. For example, hiding because of loud noise, circling an object of interest or chirping. This interpretation phase aimed at helping us to identify plausible mappings between insect behavior and HCI-related information, a pre-condition that the understanding of the zoomorphic feedback will happen intuitively [30].

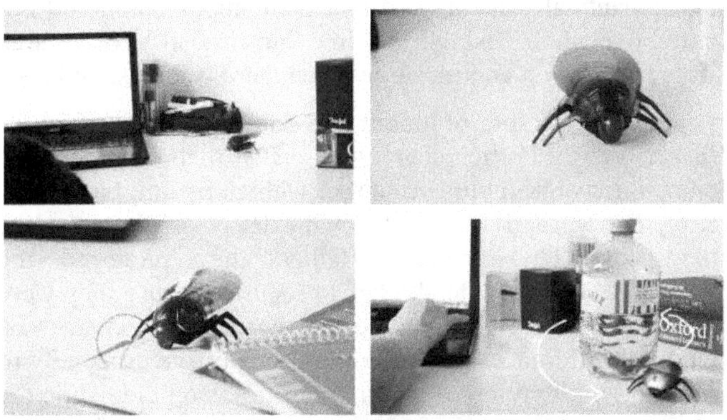

Figure 1. Upper left: The companion and its motion pattern is introduced in a desktop setting. Upper right: close up. Lower left: Companion notifies of an incoming smartphone push notification. Lower right: companion suggests to drink water.

Procedure

Participants provided written consent that they approve audio and video recording throughout the whole study. The study consisted of two parts, and their order was counterbalanced across participants. In one part, participants watched video prototypes of 11 different insect companions in infinite loop and gave feedback via 'thinking aloud' on how they perceived the pre-designed characteristics and behaviors. In these video vignettes, the otherwise passive prototypes demonstrated a movement pattern and partly made use of sound output, light and displays, for details see Table 1. In order to avoid biasing the participants, we did not give the prototypes names or name the insect type that was the model for design. In the other part of the study, participants had time to familiarize with the 11 passive prototypes via visual and haptic inspection. Next, they were provided with the two task lists (A) and (B). Whether a participant worked through list (A) or (B) first was counterbalanced across participants. List (A) of 25 tasks and notifications, e.g., indicating a missed phone call, and were asked to demonstrate the most suitable action using an assigned insect prototype as a puppet. In order to keep the time required for the experiment as well as repetition low, each participant worked through the list items using three of 11 prototypes. When working on the first third of the items on the list, they used one randomly selected prototype out of 11; when working on the second and last third of the list, another. List (B) required the participants to think of information that could be communicated by 16 insect-specific behaviors, for example, being attracted by light, see Figure 2. The participants were always invited to explain their thoughts and ideas, and their responses were captured with a video camera. Every session lasted between 45 and 60 minutes.

USER STUDY: RESULTS

In the following, we present the qualitative data gathered in the elicitation/interpretation part as well as the reactions of the participants on the video probes. Due to page restrictions, we refrain from reporting individual data points for all 41 shown tasks/ behaviors and comments on each of the 11 prototypes. Instead, we provide a condensed version of our participants' feedback in form of design recommendations. To achieve this, the second author of this work, who conducted the user study, wrote down all statements and comments made by the participants and grouped them according to similarity. We report the most frequent answers.

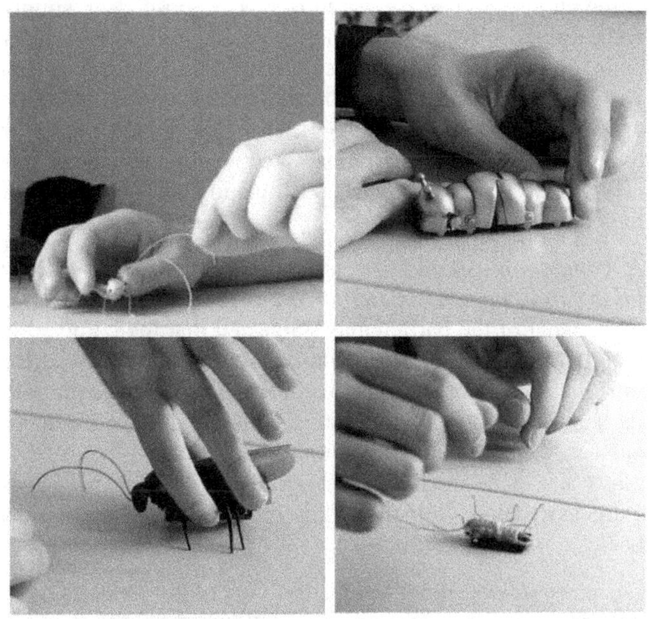

Figure 2. Upper left: antenna movement as greeting. Upper right: touching the user to attract attention. Lower left: Crawling in a square to notify about a meeting in a meeting room. Lower right: companion is turning itself on its back to say goodbye.

Desired functions of desktop companions

A companion needs to be able to capture the users' attention and draw it to a specific location. The most common user-defined gestures for this task included various forms of motion (either of the companion itself or only parts of it like the wings, antennae or head). The companion can increase the urgency of the notification by increasing its speed of movement (crawling, moving the wings, jumping), poking the user, or making use of additional features like sound or light. If the companion wants to draw the users' attention to a specific object located on the desk, it can crawl or even fly to the object, circle it, touch it with its antennae or guide the users' attention by illuminating or pointing at it with a laser. If the object/event/person of interest is located outside of the room, the participants agreed that the companion has to make use of symbols (e.g. walking in the shape of a "P" for printer, shaping an arrow with its antennae, leaving a luminous trace) or use other means like a display, projection or even speech output.

Perceived as part of a caring relationship, a companion should convey suggestions to the user that promote the users' wellbeing. Users suggested that the companion could keep track of working hours, nutrition and water intake, heartbeat, as well as sitting times, and provide recommendations accordingly. For example, if the user did not stand up for a long time, the companion could recommend to take a break and engage in physical activity by jumping from the table, or performing intensified movement itself, like running in a circle or fluttering with its wings. To nudge the user to drink more water, the companion could move or unroll its proboscis, or simply walk around a water bottle on the table. To make the user calm down, a slow movement of its wings synchronized with the breathing rhythm of the user was seen as most appropriate. In order to suggest the user to quit work for today and go home, participants came up with ideas like orbiting the key of the car and touching the off-button of the computer.

A companion should be able to notify the user about information the user missed or wants to deal with at a later time. Most of the participants suggested that the companion simply crawls to the device on which the user received the information (computer, phone, smartphone), touches it with its sensors, or rests next to it. The second most common answer was that the companion displays a text or color or plays a user-defined sound as an alert. Warning messages were associated with the black-yellow stripe pattern of a bee.

The companion has to inform the user about its status and progress when performing a task. When the companion is working on a task, e.g., performing a search, it can demonstrate its state as 'busy' through rhythmic activities, like moving the wings or antennae, glowing, or walking from A to B or in an infinity symbol. On the other hand, if the companion is waiting for a new task from the user, it can indicate waiting through a cleaning movement, walk to a marked spot on the desk, form a question mark with its antennae or display a microphone symbol on a display. To indicate that the companions' battery has to be charged, it can turn itself to the back, although participants clearly preferred that the companion takes care of recharging itself.

A companion should recognize the user and follow social practices. Like a pet, users would like to be recognized by their robot companion. When coming to the office for the first time of the day, the companion should 'look' at the user with its 'head' and greet, for example by performing a lively movement, making noise, or waving with its antennae. In turn, crawling to a charging station, playing sound or turning off lights were associated as goodbye gestures. When the user does not want to be disturbed by the companion or perceives its presence as annoying, making a loud noise by clapping the hands or waving the hands to chase away the companion were considered appropriate. In order to summon the companion when it is not visible, one possibility would be to turn on a desktop lamp, so the companion would approach the light beam. Such interaction possibilities increase the chance that the robotic device is seen as a partner instead of a tool [5]. Participants also mentioned that the companion should not crawl over their desk all the time, but instead have an area where it can rest and recharge when there is no task at hand.

Features desirable of insect-like companions

Insect type. Participants mentioned that they dislike companions resembling an insect with an overall bad image (e.g., one strongly associated with decay or disease), like the cockroach or moth. Rather, they preferred the prototypes of the butterfly, bee or locust, because they were considered as beautiful, cute and entertaining characters. Cultural differences might play a stronger role especially in the context of preferred insect types. For example, while the locust was a popular animal for the German participants in this study, a locust might have a very bad reputation in areas where locust plagues are common.

Biomorphic vs. abstract appearance. The 11 companion prototypes resembled four levels of abstraction (biomorphic – high, biomorphic – low, abstract – low, abstract – high). Overall, participants clearly opted for the designs in the low biomorphic condition. While they rejected too abstract and technical appearances, they also mentioned that a too realistic look was scary. Rather, the insect type, which was the model for the design of the companion, should be visible but slightly alienated. Most interestingly, the finding that an insect replica that appears almost, but not exactly, like a real insect elicits feelings of revulsion among some participants reminds of the uncanny valley effect found for replicas high in human likeness.

Movement. Too many, thin or natural looking legs were perceived as 'ugly'. Participants preferred a medium and steady speed. Slow motions were perceived as boring and tiresome, whereas hectic motions as too distracting (except when the notification was extremely urgent). Participants wished that the companion rests when there is no task at hand.

Material and color. Colorful prototypes (e.g. butterfly, locust) were clearly preferred over monochrome (e.g. white plastic beetle, metallic caterpillar). Rubber and cloth were perceived as less suitable for a technical device. Three participants did not like seeing the mechanical inside of the companion, and a few mentioned that their companion should be fabricated out of high quality material.

Antennae and wings. Participants liked antennae very much as well as the companion using them to touch and point to objects. However, too thin and natural looking antennae were rated as disgusting. The proboscis of the butterfly and associated gestures received positive feedback, but was described as too unobtrusive to notice it. Movable wings represent an attractive way to communicate information, and two wings were preferred over only one.

Sound, light and display. 95% of the participants were in favor of the use of sounds. However, sound should be treated as a means for more urgent alerts and only used from time to time. The type of sound was very important, whereas the natural sounds of the mosquito, fly and bee were least preferred, because they reminded the subjects of real insects which created a conflict with the robotic appearance. Again, this suggests a kind of uncanny valley effect for insect replicas. Instead, participants opted for unobtrusive, more artificial, 'squeaky' sounds and vibration. When conveying very specific content, speech output is a valid option, as well as the use of displays. A simple color changing LED light was preferred over a screen, since the companion was not seen as an alternative to the smartphone, but rather an extension. Lighting was seen as a pleasant and important notification channel.

Experiences with insect-like companions
Although insects are certainly less fancied than typical pet animals like cats and dogs, overall, 77% of the participants in the user study would like to see their desk enlivened with an insect-like companion. With regard to the video probes they found insect companions 'funny', 'cute', 'cool' and 'fascinating'. They also mentioned that even if the companion would have less functionality, they still value its entertaining and caring character. One participant even mentioned that a robotic friend would increase her anticipation to go to work. Getting suggestions and notifications delivered by a robotic companion was welcomed as an alternative to monitoring the screen of the smartphone or having to check a calendar app. The participants wished that they could rely on the companion as a gatekeeper for relevant information, letting them concentrate on their work but still knowing that they will not miss out on something important. Five participants would like to use such a companion only at their working desk, three subjects saw its potential only in their free time rather than at work, and seven subjects would like to use it in both their free time and in a working context. The concerns of those participants who did not want to use a companion at all were that they did not like animals (1x), found movements at their desk too disturbing (2x) or were only interested in using gadgets that offer a clear functionality (2x).

DISCUSSION

Acceptance and benefits of zoomorphic desktop companions
Belonging to the field of calm technology [36], desktop companions are not primarily designed for function, which is why usability criteria like low error rate or ease of use are not the primary criteria to evaluate their success [22]. As suggested by Hallnäs and Redström, whether people are accepting the presence of an artifact that expresses something as part of their environment is a more suitable criterion of success [11]. While two of the participants in our user study indeed mentioned the lack of a clear functionality from which they would benefit and therefore had no use of a companion device, overall, the majority would welcome the presence of a zoomorphic companion on their desktops. One participant actually said that the device could increase her motivation to go to work. This shows that even the simple zoomorphic prototypes used in our study offered the users capabilities for social encounters and allowed for a pleasant interaction, building on established human skills. More general, zoomorphic desktop companions might be capable of harvesting some of the manifold gains the interaction with companion animals and pet ownership has on humans' health and well-being, e.g. cardiovascular benefits, decreased stress and loneliness [1]. Moreover, research in different domains including nursing care showed that similar benefits of animal assisted activities could be observed through physical interactions with robots [35]. Therefore, zoomorphic desktop companions offer a possibility to investigate psychological, physiological, and social effects of robots in an office context. For this purpose, taking inspiration from different animal species and balancing the design between naturalistic and artificial seems a good way to reap benefits of human-animal interaction and avoiding pitfalls like disappointment resulting from unmet expectations with familiar pets.

Insect-inspired concepts for life-like interactive objects
Zoomorphism changes the way in which users make sense of a computing device by projecting expectations of animalistic life onto it [30]. We conducted the user study in order to identify desirable zoomorphic forms and behaviors leaned from insects as a way of conveying information to the user in an intuitive way. We derived a vocabulary of mapping notification content to insect behaviors from our participants' output in the study, and identified design implications for insect-like desktop companions in office environments. The results demonstrated that some gestures can be directly borrowed from human-insect interaction and function as a communication vocabulary with the robotic companion. For example, summoning the companion with a light beam and chasing it away with noise, making use of disturbing insect features to increase the urgency of an alert, inspecting an object with antennae to draw attention to it or displaying black-yellow stripes as a warning. However, since the range of insect-inspired notifications is limited

when it comes to very specific notification content (e.g. the meeting at 10 AM takes place in room 120), the additional use of display, light, sound and/or speech output was considered adequate.

In addition to pursuing zoomorphism as a metaphor for design, the literature suggests keeping some other higher-level goals in mind as well. For example, Jafarinaimi et al. propose abstractness, non-intrusiveness, publicity and aesthetics as desirable objectives in the office context [15]. The insect companions designed for the user study did make use of data abstraction. Instead of displaying raw sensor data of sitting times, water intake etc. or conveying information through displays and speech, the companion mapped the to-be-communicated content to certain behaviors. The companion presented information in a non-obtrusive way, making it available without interrupting work; the user can easily ignore it when she is too busy or does not want to access the information. In addition, the publicity of the information display has to be considered. Since the office is a public environment, the companion should present personal information in an appropriate way. Data abstraction is one means to increase the willingness to display data in the office. Finally, as the companions are designed as personal objects, they need to be inquisitive and sustain interest over time. Although autonomous interfaces are usually perceived as entertaining, individualization might play an important role.

SUMMARY AND OUTLOOK

Autonomous desktop companions are viewed in social settings, balancing issues of privacy while presenting information or suggestions to the user in non-obtrusive fashion. By gathering initial feedback about insect-like prototypes, we collected ideas that help designing potential interactions for zoomorphic companion devices. The overall goal of this research is to exploit psychosocial advantages of biomorphism in an office context, as well as benefits regarding intuitive use. We propose insects as source for inspiration, as they open up an interesting design space, potentially avoiding pitfalls of animalistic designs that borrow from pets that are too familiar. However, insect-like companions have to be carefully designed in order to not elicit aversion in users, dislike or even fear. Drawing on insect types with a positive image, aesthetic and cute designs and making use of the stylistic means of abstraction increase acceptance. As future work, we aim to derive a high fidelity prototype from our study results and test the gestures suggested by the users in a real world setting. Overall, this research contributes to our understanding of the effects of autonomous behavior of technical devices in order to facilitate the design of joyful yet functional companion robots that provide users with capabilities for emotional and social interaction.

REFERENCES

1. Sandra B. Barker, and Aaron R. Wolen. 2008. The benefits of human-companion animal interaction: a review. *Journal of veterinary medical education* 35.4: 487-495.
2. Gilles Bailly, Sidharth Sahdev, Sylvain Malacria, and Thomas Pietrzak. 2016. LivingDesktop: Augmenting Desktop Workstation with Actuated Devices. In: *Proceedings of the 2016 CHI Conference on Human Factors in Computing Systems*. ACM, 2016. S. 5298-5310.
3. Christoph Bartneck, Elizabeth Croft, and Dana Kulic. 2008. Measuring the anthropomorphism, animacy, likeability, perceived intelligence and perceived safety of robots. In *Metrics for HRI Workshop, Technical Report*, volume 471, pages 37–44. Citeseer.
4. Roy F. Baumeister, and Mark R. Leary. 1995. The need to belong: Desire for interpersonal attachments as a fundamental human motivation. *Psychological Bulletin*, 117, 497-529.
5. Beaudouin-Lafon, Michel. Instrumental interaction: an interaction model for designing post-WIMP user interfaces. In: *Proceedings of the SIGCHI conference on Human Factors in Computing Systems*. ACM, 2000. S. 446-453.
6. Matthew P. DeVito, and Karthik Ramani. 2014. Talking to TAD: Animating an Everyday Object for Use in Augmented Workspaces. In *ASME '14 International Design Engineering Technical Conferences and Computers and Information in Engineering Conference*. American Society of Mechanical Engineers.
7. James Fogarty, Scott E. Hudson, and Jennifer Lai. 2004. Examining the robustness of sensor-based statistical models of human interruptibility. *CHI14*, ACM, 207-214.
8. Terrence Fong, Illah Nourbakhsh, and Kerstin Dautenhahn. 2003. A survey of socially interactive robots. *Robotics and autonomous systems*, 42.3, 143-166.
9. Maartje M. A. Graaf, and Somaya B. Allouch. 2016. The Influence of Prior Expectations of a Robot's Lifelikeness on Users' Intentions to Treat a Zoomorphic Robot as a Companion. *International Journal of Social Robotics*, 1-16.
10. Edward S. De Guzman, et al. 2004. Exploring the design and use of peripheral displays of awareness information. *CHI'04 extended abstracts on Human factors in computing systems*. ACM, 2004.
11. Lars Hallnäs, and Johan Redström. 2002. From use to presence: on the expressions and aesthetics of everyday computational things. *ACM Transactions on Computer-Human Interaction*, 9.2 (2002): 106-124.
12. Marc Hassenzahl. 2010. *Experience Design: Technology for All the Right Reasons*.

13. Jörn Hurtienne, and Luciënne Blessing. 2007. Design for Intuitive Use-Testing image schema theory for user interface design. *16th International Conference on Engineering Design.*
14. Stephen S. Intille. 2002. Change blind information display for ubiquitous computing environments. *UbiComp 2002*, Springer Berlin Heidelberg, 91-106.
15. Nassim Jafarinaimi, Jodi Forlizzi, Amy Hurst, and John Zimmerman. 2005. Breakaway: an ambient display designed to change human behavior. *CHI'05 extended abstracts on Human factors in computing systems*. ACM, 2005.
16. Heekyoung Jung, Youngsuk L. Altieri, and Jeffrey Bardzell. 2010. SKIN: designing aesthetic interactive surfaces. In: *Proceedings of the fourth international conference on Tangible, embedded, and embodied interaction*. ACM, 2010. 85-92.
17. Jinyung Jung, Bae Seok-Hyung, and Kim Myung-Suk. 2013. Three case studies of UX with moving products. *Proceedings of the 2013 ACM international joint conference on Pervasive and ubiquitous computing*. ACM.
18. Nicole Krämer, Sabrina Eimler, Astrid von der Pütten, and Sabine Payr. 2011. Theory of companions: What can theoretical models contribute to applications and understanding of human-robot interaction? *Applied Artificial Intelligence*, 25(6), 474-502.
19. Kostadin Kushlev, Jason Proulx, and Elizabeth W. Dunn. 2016. Silence Your Phones: Smartphone Notifications Increase Inattention and Hyperactivity Symptoms. In: *Proceedings of the 2016 CHI Conference on Human Factors in Computing Systems*. 1011-1020. ACM.
20. Diana Löffler, Birgit Wallmann-Sperlich, Juri Wan, Jennifer Knött, Anna Vogel, and Jörn Hurtienne. 2015. Office ergonomics driven by contextual design. *Ergonomics in Design: The Quarterly of Human Factors Applications*, 2015, 23. Jg., Nr. 3, S. 31-35.
21. Diana Löffler, Takashi Toriizuka, Yuki Sakakibara, Philipp Schaper, and Jörn Hurtienne. 2015. Examining the design space of insect inspired notifications. In *Proceedings of the 2015 ACM International Joint Conference on Pervasive and Ubiquitous Computing and Proceedings of the 2015 ACM International Symposium on Wearable Computers*. 145-148. ACM.
22. Jennifer Mankoff, Anind K. Dey, Gary Hsieh, Julie Kientz, Scott Lederer, and Morgan Ames. 2003. Heuristic evaluation of ambient displays. In *Proceedings of the SIGCHI conference on Human factors in computing systems*. ACM. 169-176.
23. Tara Matthews, Anind K. Dey, Jennifer Mankoff, Scott Carter, and Tye Rattenbury. 2004. A toolkit for managing user attention in peripheral displays. *UIST04*, ACM. 247-256.
24. Hiroshi Nittono, Michiko Fukushima, Akihiro Yano, and Hiroki Moriya. 2012. The power of kawaii: Viewing cute images promotes a careful behavior and narrows attentional focus. *PloS one* 7(9). e46362.
25. Don Norman. 2002. Emotion & design: attractive things work better. *interactions* 9 , 36–42.
26. Diana Nowacka, David Kirk. 2014. Tangible autonomous interfaces (tais): Exploring autonomous behaviours in tuis. In *Proceedings of the 8th International Conference on Tangible, Embedded and Embodied Interaction.* 1-8.ACM.
27. Byron Reeves, and Clifford Nass. 1996. *The Media Equation: How People Treat Computers, Television, and New Media Like Real People and Places*. Cambridge University Press.
28. Hayley Robinson, Bruce MacDonald, Ngaire Kerse, and Elizabeth Broadbent. 2013. The psychosocial effects of a companion robot: A randomized controlled trial. *Journal of the American Medical Directors Association*, *14*(9), 661-667.
29. Yea-Kyung Row, and Tek-Jin Nam. 2014. Camy: Applying a pet dog analogy to everyday ubicomp products. In *Proceedings of the 2014 ACM International Joint Conference on Pervasive and Ubiquitous Computing, UbiComp '14*, 63–74, New York, NY, USA. ACM.
30. Michael Schmitz. 2011. Concepts for life-like interactive objects. In *Proc. of TEI 2011*, 157–164. ACM.
31. Sowmya Somanath, Ehud Sharlin, and Mario Costa Sousa. 2013. Beyond Actuated Tangibles: Introducing Robots to Interactive Tabletops. In *Proc. TEI 2013*.
32. Nigel E. Stork. 1993. How many species are there? *Biodiversity & Conservation*, 2(3), 215-232.
33. Ja-Young Sung, Lan Guo, Rebecca. E. Grinter, and Henrik I. Christensen. 2007. “My roomba is rambo": intimate home appliances. In *Proc. of UbiComp 2007*, 145–162. Springer-Verlag.
34. Peter Tarasewich, Tashfeen Bhimdi, and Myra Dideles. *Increasing the effectiveness of notification cues in mobile environments*. AMCIS04, 402.
35. Kazuyoshi Wada, Takanori Shibata, Tomoko Saito, and Kazuo Tanie. 2004. Effects of robot-assisted activity for elderly people and nurses at a day service center. *Proceedings of the IEEE*, *92*(11), 1780-1788.
36. Mark Weiser, and John Seely Brown. 1997. The coming age of calm technology. Beyond calculation. *Springer New York*. 75-85.
37. David D. Woods, Emily S. Patterson, and Emilie M. Roth. 2002. Can we ever escape from data overload? A cognitive systems diagnosis. *Cognition, Technology & Work*, 4(1), 22-36.

Needle as Input: Exploring Practice and Materiality When Crafting Becomes Computing

Sarah Schoemann
Georgia Institute of Technology
Atlanta, GA 30308
sschoemann3@gatech.edu

Michael Nitsche
Georgia Institute of Technology
Atlanta, GA 30308
michael.nitsche@gatech.edu

ABSTRACT
A growing body of research combines craft and interaction design. The "Stitch Sampler" project, a sew-able musical instrument and craft platform, stands in this context. In particular, the project serves to underline the importance of two conceptual themes that have emerged in HCI over the last decade, specifically the "material turn" of research on computing and the "practice" or "action-centric" turn in HCI. We present that our prototype and its evolution process as an example of a third trend in HCI research that has developed closely along-side these shifts, with relation to research specifically on craft practice. We discuss the Stitch Sampler and related work that couple electronics and smart materials with craft practices. In that way the act of crafting has in some cases *become* a form of computation.

Author Keywords
Craft; Materiality; Practice; Design; Tangible Computing.

ACM Classification
H.5.m. Information interfaces and presentation Miscellaneous

INTRODUCTION
This paper chronicles the research and design process behind the creation of a series of iterative prototypes designed to connect computing with fine crafting. The prototypes, created as part of an artist-informed research project are sewable, soft circuit interfaces that function as instruments for digital music performance, while simultaneously acting as surfaces to practice the traditional handicraft work of decorative hand-sewing (Figure 1). This series of interactive objects were created as part of a five months long collaboration with artisan clothing designer Karen Glass, the creator of a sustainable fashion brand Zerowaste and a small staff of part-time studio assistants who principally manufacture the company's unique garments. Our iterative design process which included multiple meetings with the designer and two sessions of informal user testing with staff members, lead to a series of prototypes which were influenced by both the mission and studio technique used in the creation of these handcrafted clothes. In a series Glass contributed to the prototyping process by discussing and demonstrating various garment construction techniques on site in Zerowaste's studio and provided feedback at several key points in the design process, directly informing the iterative design of our multiple prototypes.

TEI '17, March 20 - 23, 2017, Yokohama, Japan

ACM 978-1-4503-4676-4/17/03...$15.00
DOI: http://dx.doi.org/10.1145/3024969.3024999

The potential for the material practices of fine artists and crafters to inform and contribute to the design research process is a promising topic within the field of human computer interaction [28, 31, 34, 35]. But it remains critical for tangible interface development and much in need of conceptual approaches to structure this cross-domain collaboration. In sharing our experience, learning from Glass, and prototyping interactive technology in response to the fine craft practice of her and her studio staff, we seek to demonstrate the potential of craftsperson-researcher collaborations for generating new knowledge in the form of designed artifacts [16]. We emphasize the material and situated qualities of this collaboration and how they affected the evolution of these artifacts over time.

Through our work with Glass and her staff, we explored new possibilities for integrating computing into traditional handiwork crafts – and vice versa. The project builds on the rich discourse within HCI on practice-based and material exploration as well as hybrid computational and craft objects. The development of hybrid objects like the Stitch Sampler combine computational resources with traditional modes of craft. They serve an important role in developing conversations about both situated practice and materiality in computing. Zoran and Buechley use the hybrid nature of their project to "restore" a ceramic object by means of 3D printing. They "subvert" digital fabrication [46] as the material and functionality of 3D printed components conceptually clash with that of the handcrafted materials. Rosner et al. use hybrid approaches towards "new understandings of expressivity, skill and value" [34]. Our case adapts their critical use of the hybrid object to develop an educational project.

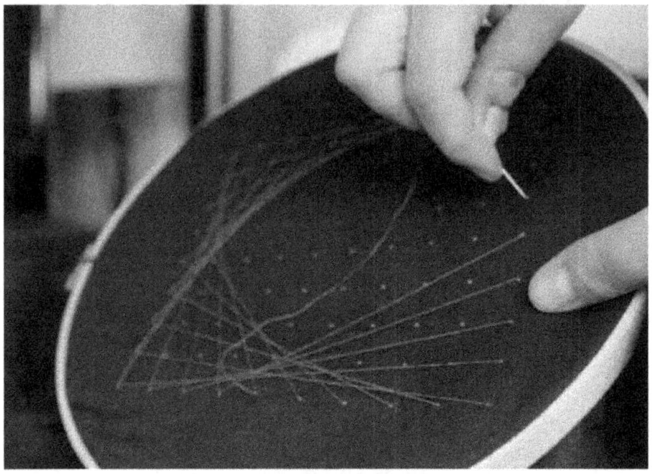

Figure 1. The fourth and final iteration of our prototype, a decorative sewing instrument which generates tones when the needle enters the fabric.

Through our collaboration with Glass, we had to adjust our thinking about the process of creating this novel interface itself. The result, an amalgam of computing input, performance object and fine-craft tool, exemplifies the generative and explorative possibilities best realized through a research through design approach, in which one is "renegotiating reality rather than hypothesizing about it." It connects to the concept of *craft research* defined as "research into, for and through craft practice" [13, 22].

Following a research through design methodology, Stitch Sampler operated through iterative prototyping in response to particular situated context, in our case a studio employing artisan hand-crafters. In this method, Stitch Sampler is tied to recent shifts towards action and practice based design research as well as the turn towards materiality. Both have become integral dimension of human computer interaction research.

These two "turns" concern an erosion of previously-held binaries, the first the between the individual and the social context of computing and the second between the digital and tangible interaction experiences that ultimately push an interface's material qualities. Our prototype can be viewed as one example of an emerging conversation around these collapsing boundaries between the practice of interfacing with a device and the practice of traditional creative practices, such as fine-craft techniques. In the context of our prototype the act of crafting itself (in this case hand-sewing) is transformed into a form of input that not only generates output in the form of traditional needlework, but also acts as a computational input, controlling the output of digital audio and adding a performative dimension to the activity of crafting.

The paper will first discuss the underlying two shifts in HCI discussion and will briefly contextualize the work in relation to other craft-based interface development. The main focus will be on the design and development process as an example for a new hybridity where the craft materials become part of the computational thinking and the interactive functionality relates to (and interrogates) the cultural framework of the crafter. We close with a claim to re-envision craft practices as practices of computing and a novel perspective to the integration of craft and interaction design.

BACKGROUND

Practice and Action Centric Turns in HCI

Research approaches that are similar to the so-called "practice turn" in HCI, have long been a feature of community based research in the social sciences and relate to theoretical frameworks developed by figures such as Vygotsky, Lave and Wegner.[42]. Existing frameworks contextualize individual actions and shared practices within the larger sociocultural conditions in which individuals exist and participate. Only in recent years however, have these themes become a prominent focus of research in the context of computing. In a call for a more unified research agenda Kuutti and Bannon note that the primacy of the "interaction" model of computing (i.e. computing construed as occurring between user and interface) has been supplanted by methods more attendant to the situated nature of technological practices [20, 39] Because of its regard for both the physical and social context of computing, the 'practice turn' has been advanced particularly by researchers focused on computer supported collaborative work (CSCW) [24].

Within interaction design research the rise of ubiquitous computing, particularly in the last decade, has led to an increased awareness of the importance of context [6]. Innovations in novel methods of input, as part of the larger shift from the desktop to mobile devices have lead design researchers to focus on the role of embodiment within computing practices. Tangible interactions in particular have signaled a shift towards more situated forms of computing as they are designed for more diverse and more specific physical and social contexts. As Fernaeus, Tholander and Jonsson note, the use of tangible objects in computing has gone hand in hand with this turn towards action-oriented methods and ontologies [10, 11]. As new technologies allow manipulation to become more central to the work of computing the purpose of these devices has shifted from one of simply mediating the manipulation of information, to tangibles becoming what Fernaeus et al. call "resources for action" in which tangibles objects themselves are capable of generating knowledge through their ability to reflect changes in state mediated by the human hand [10]. They are not only a combination of representation and control – as outlined in early frameworks of TEIs, but they are also in conversation with the material practices such as craft that operate within them [41].

Consequently, in the context of working with craft materials that also double as computing tools, "state changes" might come to mean more than changes registered computationally but also the creative act of mark-making by drawing, sewing, or any other means.

The Material Turn

The transition from the desktop paradigm towards ubiquitous computing via increasingly varied forms of input has also led researchers in HCI to extend questions once reserved for the interaction between user and machine to the role that the materiality of technology itself plays in computing practices [17]. This so called "material turn" in interaction design has animated discussions about the need for new methods and vocabulary with which to better analyze and understand 'material interactions' as well as the need to develop new methods for designing towards material considerations [45]. Asresearch focused on this interstice between computation and crafting have noted, craft materials create new stress points and limitations that designers may not experience when working with more traditional computing "hardware," while at the same time, introducing novel uses and unique affordances that are a direct result of the unusual character of the material [8, 25].

Crafting with Electronics

Scholarship on both the "practice-turn" and "material-turn" cite the entrée of traditional craft, art and industrial design techniques into computing contexts (often through the development and increased availability of "smart" materials and hobbyist electronics development platforms) as an important dimension of the turn towards materiality within computing and an important addition to design research more broadly [17, 10, 23].

Hybrid practices can cut both ways between traditional forms of making and contemporary technologies. Fine craft practitioners may make use of digital fabrication techniques like computer aided design to augment traditional production methods for non-computational objects, while digital technologies are easily embedded in clothing designs, architecture or other designed objects using traditional fabrication techniques [37]. Given this slippage between high and low tech materials and practices and between technical and non-technical domains it stands to reason that the categorization of practices of design, whether on the scale of buildings or handmade objects as fundamentally separate from practices of computing is perhaps already a false binary.

Vallgårda traces this idea of conceptualizing computational technology as simply another "material" of the built environment back to the research of educational technology pioneer Seymour Papert [43]. Papert, when asking students to construct devices to solve open ended problems by developing their own tools, promoted the idea of the computer as just another of the suite of materials available with which his students could work, alongside basics like string, plastic containers, or weights. "Just as pendulums, paints, clay, and so forth, can be "messed around with," he proposed "so can computers." [24]. With the turn to and ongoing rise of physical computing, the "messiness" goes both ways as those artifacts also work through what Polanyi termed "tacit" knowledge and remain part of a cultural practice and frame[28].

Contemporary research into alternative forms of electronics tinkering that eschew the pre-made ecosystem of commercially manufactured components also argue for a view of computing as materially integrated with everyday forms of creativity. For example, Mellis et al. advocate for the idea of an "un-tool-kit" in which flexible sensors and circuits are crafted with paper and conductive ink [21].

Following this call, Perner-Wilson suggests what she calls a "kit of no parts" approach to computing, which positions the act of constructing interactive objects with textiles and paper-crafts in a framework of handcrafting. Perner-Wilson advocates the use of a creative method in which crafts and electronics are fully integrated and which "emphasizes the expressive qualities of diverse materials as well as the skill and creativity of the builder" [25]. Our sewable prototype, in marrying the act of stitching with digital music-making, also seeks to leverage these combined material affordances and creative possibilities through an explicitly hybrid craft/computing practice.

THE PROJECT

Soft circuitry as an intervention into a fine-art/fashion context aligns with existing explorations of digital craft practice for wearable and other non traditional devices by academic researchers, designers and hobbyists [4, 14].

This series of prototypes, created by our team of student designers and titled the "Stitch Sampler" are tangible interfaces that allow multiple users to perform music by interacting with traditional needlework materials. Because the design process was informed by the working process of a specific designer and a team of studio-based practitioners the inspiration for our prototype was (in part) an early request from Glass for a tool to teach newer studio assistants the rhythmic and methodical practice of decorative hand-sewing technique. Although our research team declined the invitation to create a design intervention that would be potentially more oriented towards increasing manufacturing productivity than supporting the agency or creativity of users, we were nonetheless inspired to attempt to augment the process of hand sewing with interactive technology.

By applying the technology of soft-circuitry to a craft-based production, our prototype draws on the work of digital craft innovators such as Buechley and Perner-Wilson, Tan and Peppler and others [21, 25, 26, 27, 29, 40] who have pioneered the integration of electronics into traditional craft, utilizing materials such as conductive fabric and thread as intermediaries between off the shelf parts and hand fabricated objects.

As with many pre-existing projects that incorporate soft circuitry, our design transplants a straightforward input mechanism (a handmade switch) into an unexpected material context (a traditional embroidery stitch sampler) which interfaces with manufactured components (in our case the Lilypad MP3 microcontroller and Bluefruit Keyboard HID). The prototypes appear, at first glance, indistinguishable from decorative needlework projects where fabric is stretched across a wooden embroidery hoop that one interacts with using a sewing needle and thread. The unobtrusiveness of the computing hardware is one of the more unique aesthetic qualities of the device of our prototypes awhich arose naturally from our design research process working directly with the Zerowaste studio assistants. While our prototype was a playful interface rather than a direct answer to [Anon]'s request for a teaching tool for workers. It retained a commitment to faithfully representing the hand making process and respecting the skillset of the Zerowaste staff by incorporating their existing practice into the interaction. We hoped the craftspeople at Zerowaste would be able to interact with the piece without the burden of navigating an unfamiliar interface or needing to learn any unnecessary techniques. Thus, we modeled our prototype's use on their existing practice without alteration of the key tools or handling.

THE DESIGN PROCESS

Working with Craft Practitioners

Much of the research on craft practitioners in the field of HCI has investigated the use of technology to "mediate" existing craft practices, such as those of recreational crafters [32, 33, 35, 36, 37]. They provide a rich background of existing technologies an approaches but Stitch Sampler also leans on work of artist-practitioners such as Becky Stern in the design of our collaboration with Atlanta-based fashion designer and social entrepreneur Karen Glass. Stern, a developer of tutorials for hobbyist tinkerers on the consumer electronics website Adafruit.com, focuses on creative uses of computing technology as integrated subtly into store-bought clothes. Input methods often play off the garments natural affordances and features, with for example, a zipper doubling as a covert on/off switches [38]. In designing an appropriate form of interaction with computing elements, we also looked to the material affordances of a pre-existing object (the embroidery hoop) employing a research through design process approach to investigate the practice of our collaborator and to understand the material encounters associated with her work process.

The Philosophy and Material Practices of *Zerowaste*

Zerowaste apparel is created locally in Atlanta, Georgia and is described not as a company but an artistic "life-work" project of Glass' the brand's founder and a former fashion industry veteran. Zerowaste operates out of a studio space at the Goat Farm, a twelve acre mixed use development and arts venue in the converted buildings of a former cotton gin factory adjacent to downtown Atlanta [18]. In addition to hosting regular public arts programming, The Goat Farm is home to the city's largest community of both individual fine artists and small companies belonging to local creative professionals. The context of this community speaks to Glass' positioning of her work both within the world of fine craft as well as embracing the ethos of a small business owner. An answer to the wasteful excesses of "fast-fashion" manufacturing practices common to contemporary ready-to-wear brands, the title Zerowaste represents Glass' commitment to creating ethically sourced and manufactured clothing [1]. It emphasizes a holistic and environmentally aware approach to fashion that defines the "spirit" of Zerowaste's operation.

Zerowaste's line of clothes is characterized by a distinctive deconstructed aesthetic, in which one-of-a-kind pieces are assembled from existing used and vintage garments through a studio-based practice of hand-sewing and embellishment, Even the fabric scraps left from her work are later donated to other creatives, such as assemblage artists and papermakers within the Atlanta community, and Glass emphasizes this, displaying images of the mixed media artwork that has been created with her textile remainders on the company's website as a testament to her commitment to sustainable entrepreneurship [15].

Designing an Object for *Zerowaste's* Hand-Making Context

Student designers underwent an initial period of getting acquainted with Glass and the story of the *Zerowaste* project. This involved a series of meetings including hands on presentations by Glass about her studio's working methods, close examinations of her garments and explanations about her process of sourcing materials and training staff.

As part of *Zerowaste*'s commitment to sustainability, Glass works primarily with local residents on her upcycled creations. In the interest of seeing Atlanta's own fashion and creative economy grow, Zerowaste employs women who lack previous experience as seamstresses through a local non-profit organization that provides job placement to women dealing with trauma or life disruptions that have impacted their careers. [anonymized] offers on the job training to support their development as "freelance entrepreneurs build[ing] their businesses as independent contractors" [15].

Through the process of becoming familiar with Glass' methods it became clear that the place she was most interested in facilitating a technology-based intervention was within the company's local manufacturing practice. Describing the process of cultivating new talent in her shop, Glass showed examples of samples which illustrated the range of quality possible in hand-stitching, which she defines in terms of consistency and accuracy. Even, uniform stitching is one of the skills most difficult to master as a novice. Yet it is precisely this attention to detail which she sees as crucial to the production of her garments.

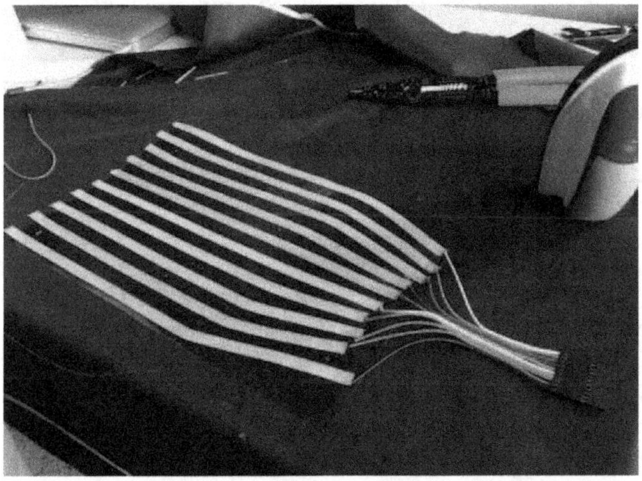

Figure 2. Using iron-on fusible interfacing to connect the conductive fabric to wire jumper cables.

Initial Design

Responding to this request for a digital intervention that could enhance the experience of apprenticing seamstresses in-situ by helping them to develop steadier and more consistent hand-stitching, our team sketched ideas with pens and paper as well as through experimentation with conductive and conventional textiles for preliminary prototypes. This prototyping process, of "sketching in hardware" as a method of discovering through the process of design was particularly important to our project, given the unique design context. Prototyping allowed us to experiment with the affordances of both the traditional crafting context of hand sewing and more unusual conductive textile materials to discover the design possibilities and affordances offered by integrating these conductive materials and manufactured components to the context of fine hand-stitching [45] (Figure 2).

In a context in which fine motor skill and attention to visual detail was key we aimed for an interaction that would provide the most physically unobtrusive augmentation possible. Like existing design artifacts that are integrated into traditional craft practices such as Pschetz et al.'s augmented knitting interface known as the "movement crafter" we wanted to design a technology that could be introduced into the process of crafting without inhibiting the crafters actions or interrupting their pattern of movement [30].

Our prototyping experiments lead us to investigate the material affordances of the sewing needle, itself already a conductive material, by augmenting the core interaction of stitching with a normal needle and thread. Sandwiching two layers of conductive fabric, one powered, the other grounded on either side of an insulating layer of non-conductive fabric, we settled on a design in which the act of plunging the needle through the fabric layers acted as the closing of a switch. This turned the practice of stitching through the fabric into a novel form of input. It, thus, inherently included crafting in the tangible design and used the "logic" and experience of sewing as its starting point. However, it did not touch on the cultural or aesthetic themes of Zerowaste nor its holistic production philosophy.

First Prototype: Adding Sound

Although an LED was initially used to test the material interaction between power source, fabric and needle, we decided on sound-feedback for our prototype, so as to allow users to focus on the stitching itself as a form of self-generated visual feedback, rather than complicating it with a digital intervention. Adding a visual element (LED) to the already visual practice of perfecting the stitch was superfluous and did not connect to the cultural production philosophy of Zerowaste.

Glass maintained, in discussions with the researchers, that when it comes to sewing, rhythm and pacing are skills developed as part of an advanced seamstress' practice. This feedback led to a turn to acoustic "signaling." Audio, in the form of sampled musical notes, triggered by the needle's closure of the circuit was chosen by our team as a way to inject the practice of rhythmic sewing with a temporal element. To match Zerowaste's "handmade" and "organic" aesthetic we initially chose recording samples of analog instruments such as guitar string plucks, brass bells and chimes.

Initially the sounds were imagined as sort of user-activated metronome or time-keeping device, but based on knowing Glass aesthetic, we erred towards sound samples that included a long audio decay, lasting two to four seconds from their start to their fading to silence. Users, could time their stitches by the ebbing volume or, when sewing more quickly, create a layering effect of the sample over time. Instead of a metronome, the tool organically turned into an instrument to respond to the crafter's personality.

As a musical instrument or performance object, the prototype fell within a rich tradition of experimentation by researchers and artists in the NIME (New Interfaces for Musical Expression) community, who have innovated the use of novel forms of computation for creative and performance-based practices. But it arrived in that context through the lens of crafting. Stitch Sampler combines musical interaction with craft-based activity, not as sonification but in response to the given limitations, and specific cultural context of the material practice [4, 5].

Second Prototype: Adjusting Materials, Going Wireless

We started by testing our initial prototype on a normal Arduino Uno board communicating via USB to a laptop. While testing our conductive circuit, being wired to a laptop via Arduino proved useful as we found that not all fabrics performed equally at insulating our conductive materials. A swatch of recycled cotton Oxford shirt (we adhered to the Zerowaste's methods of using recycled materials for all non-conductive textiles used in the prototypes) but the thin cotton of the shirt lead our switch to register as indefinitely closed, for example, which forced us to switch to using the Arduino's analog pins and adjusting the values needed to trigger a sound file according to the computer's serial read. Notably, this change of hardware and code was purely called for by the materials in use.

Once we had swapped our cotton fabric for some considerably thicker boiled-wool (sourced from a felted waistcoat) we moved to using a micro controller with portable power and on board sound (the Lilypad MP3 board) which would allow us to de-tether from the laptop. Unfortunately, this hardware solution was also quickly discarded when we realized that the board would not allow for polyphonic sound, meaning that overlapping sound feedback would be unmanageable.

Material Trade-offs and Moving Towards a Multi-Tonal, Multi-User Experience

The next phase of physical "sketching" or prototyping included two builds of a second iteration of our interface design, each of which featured multiple sewable "inputs" (parallel strips of fabric adhered with fusible interfacing to a non-conductive panel with embedded jumper wires for leads). As Buechley has noted in extensive research on E-Crafts, it is often in interfacing between the flexible conductive materials of crafters and the rigid off-the-shelf parts from traditional electronics, that projects tend to break down [2]. Such was the case with our initial prototypes. The conductive panels and fusible interfacing were too tough and thick to sew through, and as a result this second version of the Stitch Sampler was visually compelling but lost much of its appeal as a sewing practice aid. Feedback from a visit to Glass' studio where we conducted the first of two testing sessions with the studio assistants (they were invited to try out the prototypes without any more specific prompt) confirmed our suspicion that it was not a faithful representation of their sewing practice, they noted the stiff fabric, in particular. However, the integration of multiple musical inputs was well received. Notes were faint because of the board's low-powered audio output, but Zerowaste testers enjoyed triggering different tones, even while struggling to sew through the overly thick material.

Momentarily setting aside the question of the thick conductive panels, we decided to switch technology platforms, from the Lilypad Mp3 with its on-board but weak audio, to a simple low-power keyboard-emulator board, the Bluefruit EZ-Key HID, which would allow further develop the potential for playing multiple notes simultaneously by triggering sounds samples wirelessly from a nearby laptop.

Switching to this hardware had several advantages for the Stitch Sampler project, beginning with the board's relatively low cost of approximately $20, which allowed us to develop and test multiple prototypes in parallel. Two boards were wired up with rechargeable li-poly batteries and header-pins which allowed them to be transferred between different iterations of our design. Because the board came pre-loaded with WASD and arrow key inputs among its twelve pins, we were able to integrate it directly with our prototype.

We also found that when pairing the board with a laptop it was possible to connect multiple Bluetooth devices at once, allowing two users to collaboratively play notes from their respective Stitch Samplers through the same computer. Such shareable "at hand" quality is noted as a particular affordance of tangible interfaces which distinguishes them from traditional one to one desktop computing [10]. It also exemplifies one of the many overlaps of material condition, interaction design, and hybrid functionality which are exposed by the process of conducting design research in situ.

Capacitive Sensing and Emergent Interactions

As users tested the second iteration of the device, pricking the fabric panels to activate sounds, we became aware of another affordance of the Bluefruit board, it has enabled the Stitch Sampler to accept capacitive input. A user's hand would make contact with the grounded fabric backing when gripping the embroidery hoop during use. This meant that fully piercing both layers of fabric with the needle was no longer necessary to register a key press. While this pushed our design further from its original intent as a training device (it was now only necessary to lightly touch the surface of the fabric with the needle to create sounds and a stitch did not need to be completed) it supported the musical control of the prototype. As one participant noted: the interaction had become so intuitive and engaging that "it was hard to put down" When asked to give feedback about the Stitch Sampler, users would continue poking out notes while answering questions. The interaction design proved to be engaging on an almost tacit, unconscious level in these cases. While the original functionality had been compromised, the tangible nature of sewing and touching materials had shifted into the foreground through the ongoing exploration.

Third Prototype: Adjusting the Design of the Interface

In order to compromise between the affordances of a fully-sew-able teaching tool with easily pierced layers and a playful performance object with multiple musical inputs, a third prototype was created in which a decorative pattern of eyelets was cut into the black fabric in circles that corresponded to rings of conductive fabric which we ironed into place creating six concentric connectors. Those activated six different notes that a user could activate by sewing into or between the rings.

Unfortunately, even though the conductive fabric (no longer coated with fusible interfacing) was easier to penetrate in this third version, users were still uninterested in stitching through the hand-cut eyelets. Rather than inviting sewing

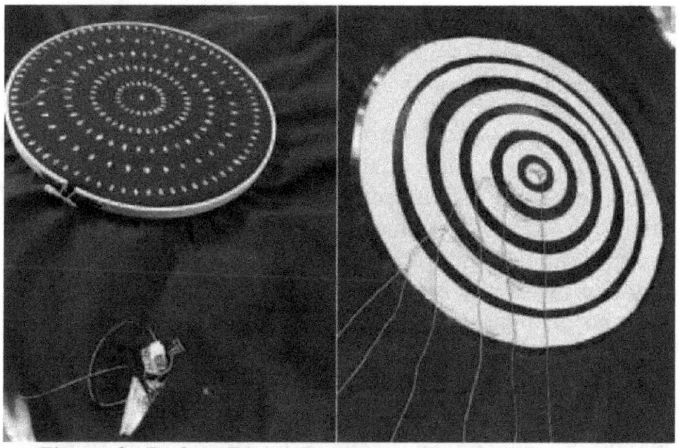

Figure 3. (Left to Right) Prototype three and the exposed fabric circuitry during the building process.

between them to create melodies, this new version simply made for a more appealing surface to lightly pluck at with the sewing needle. The act of *stitching*, ie. plunging the needle completely through all layers of the fabric, was not necessary to produce sound. When the project was presented back to the seamstresses at the Zerowaste studio during the second user testing session, it became clear that this iteration of the Stitch Sampler was not a more inviting sewing surface (the staff was still not inclined to sew through the fabric) but had become a more interesting musical interface to playfully interact and perform with.

Through this emerging use, the Stitch Sampler had turned into a kind of speculative design object on sewing itself [7]. It might interrogate notions of materiality and practice but it no longer leaned on the craft as productive action itself in the actual interaction method. While this prototype was a success in the sense that it captured the imagination of users and inspired playful, performative interactions, it was not successful at merging a platform for craft production with computing (in the form of digital music-making) because the design did not encourage users to produce actual stitches (figure 3).

Figure 4. Our third prototype being tested by *Zerowaste* staff.

Fourth and Final Prototype: Stitching Sounds

The emerging use of the third prototype at Zerowaste made it clear that the staff of Zerowaste was not experiencing the Stitch Sampler as a sew-able object. Building on the ongoing material-computational evolution, the final task had to be to encourage a more robust connection between the act of sewing and music-making. Our final version of the prototype was created using the same techniques as version three, however the sewable eyelets through which the conductive fabric traces were visible were made considerably smaller (around 2mm diameter) and organized into a grid (see Figure 1). Ten conductive fabric contacts, each assigned to a different note, run horizontally across the grid (see Figure 2). In this final version, the conductive ground fabric on the back of the prototype is covered, preventing capacitive touch and encouraging users to stitch fully through much smaller, laser-cut holes, encouraging users to sew between them and create decorative geometric designs while generating digital music. The act of sewing was not only referenced but re-integrated as a necessity of the piece (Figure 5).

This design no longer addresses Glass' initial request for a teaching aid as stitching is constrained to the holes in the fabric and thus it can no longer emulate stitching practices of a professional seamstress. The final artifact instead represents the material and conceptual compromises' that were negotiated while trying to merge a craft practice with a form of digital interface, embodying our findings and subsequent considerations and compromises in both its limitations and affordances.

CONCLUSION

The development of Stitch Sampler traces a narrative of how craft and interaction design intertwine. The detailed description of the process illustrates the moments when crafting and computing merge, diverge, and form hybrids. This can happen on the technological level of the artifact (e.g. the thickness of the cloth might demand analog contact detection, as outlined in the second prototype), on the level of practice (e.g. in the returning to the act of sewing as interaction method in the fourth prototype), or on the level of personal and cultural framing of the craft (e.g. in the move to sound as digital output in response to Zerowaste's "spirit" in the first prototype). Notably, the design did not only respond to the craft but allowed the craft to emerge as the interaction "logic."

By beginning the process of material and situated exploration early, and iterating often, we avoided a possible pitfall of interaction design with novel materials and technologies: namely the issue of trying to force materials and practices to conform to the designer's concept rather than letting them guide the exploration. Ultimately, our prototypes did not succeed as a digital tool for practicing a fine craft technique as we had intended to. But this initial projected usage adjusted itself along the way as the bare utility was replaced by a more holistic inclusion of craft as practice in the design.

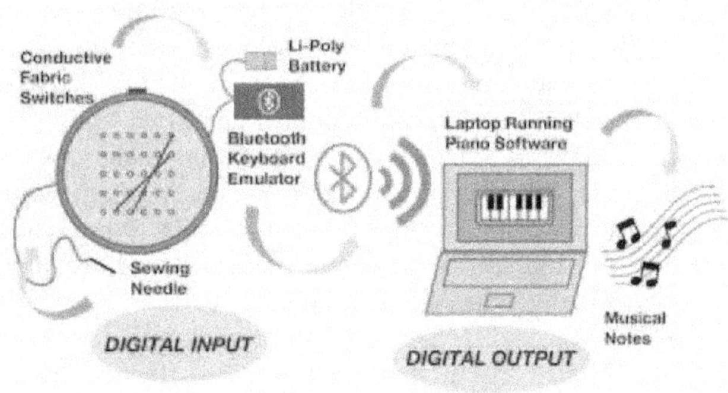

Figure 5. Diagram of digital input and output in prototype 4

The resulting prototypes of the Stitch Sampler simultaneously fall short and exceed our expectations in terms of their practical application and expressive possibilities, respectively. Because of the way it constrains use towards a deliberately recreational and expressive end, our final prototype of the technology signifies the biggest departure of our project from Glass' original request for a tool that would increase the efficiency and uniformity of a craft production technique. At the same time, it demonstrates the clearest integration of craft practice into the tangible interaction design as a result of the evolutionary process.

If research through design is valued for how it allows the possibility of objects "creating a design space around themselves" [14], then this project succeeded and the expressive, and performative aspects of the tool were ultimately crucial to this success. Through its evolution it created a context in which material qualities, craft practices and notions of utility could be explored and held in tension.

No matter how well-intentioned the desire to increase the efficiency of Zerowaste's production might be for a socially conscious entrepreneur like Glass, the playful and ultimately somewhat disruptive quality of the tool that emerged through our design-research process functioned as a safeguard of sorts. It prevented the TEI from becoming simply a functionalist tool for disciplining the hands of workers or, vice versa, the craft becoming reduced to a fashionable reference cleared of its own multi-layered messy practice.

Through collaboration, ongoing discussion and feedback sessions with Glass and informal tests with the staff of her studio we discovered that there may not be a seamless way to digitally augment the craft of professional hand sewers without introducing other material challenges and complications to the craft process that interfere with a users ability to produce conventional results. And that, in order to integrate craft to tangible interaction design, the process has to step beyond utilitarian perspectives. In the here presented case study, this was achieved through a gradual conversation between design and craft practice and materials. It settled on a playful expressive output coupled with a productive practice.

Following the natural through-line from HCI research on craft and technology that posits historic manufacturing technologies as the predecessors to modern computing and analysis suggests, that the contemporary act of programming might itself be likened to a form of craft practice [8, 19]. We suggest that more research should be focused on hybrid forms of computation and crafting. Not just through explorations of how we can utilize the combined material elements of crafts and computing to create new hybrid objects, but rather to explore the ways in which the *context* and *actions* involved in crafting and computing can be brought into synch so as to create new kinds of hybrid activities and practices.

REFERENCES

1. Allie Bashuk. 2016. zerøwaste: use everything until it's non-usable. *Creative Loafing Atlanta* (April 2016).
2. Leah Buechley and Michael Eisenberg. 2009. Fabric PCBs, Electronic Sequins, and Socket Buttons: Techniques for e-Textile Craft. *Personal Ubiquitous Comput.* 13, 2 (February 2009), 133–150. DOI:http://dx.doi.org/10.1007/s00779-007-0181-0
3. Leah Buechley and Hannah Perner-Wilson. 2012. Crafting Technology: Reimagining the Processes, Materials, and Cultures of Electronics. *ACM Trans. Comput.-Hum. Interact.* 19, 3 (October 2012), 21:1–21:21. DOI:http://dx.doi.org/10.1145/2362364.2362369
4. Angela Chang and Hiroshi Ishii. 2007. Zstretch: A Stretchy Fabric Music Controller. In *Proceedings of the 7th International Conference on New Interfaces for Musical Expression*. NIME '07. New York, NY, USA: ACM, 46–49. DOI:http://dx.doi.org/10.1145/1279740.1279746
5. Perry Cook. 2001. Principles for Designing Computer Music Controllers. In *Proceedings of the 2001 Conference on New Interfaces for Musical Expression*. NIME '01. Singapore, Singapore: National University of Singapore, 1–4.
6. Paul Dourish. 2004. What We Talk About when We Talk About Context. *Personal Ubiquitous Comput.* 8, 1 (February 2004), 19–30. DOI:http://dx.doi.org/10.1007/s00779-003-0253-8
7. Anthony Dunne. 2008. Hertzian Tales: Electronic Products, Aesthetic Experience, and Critical Design, MIT Press.
8. Ylva Fernaeus, Martin Jonsson, and Jakob Tholander. 2012. Revisiting the Jacquard Loom: Threads of History and Current Patterns in HCI. In *Proceedings of the SIGCHI Conference on Human Factors in Computing Systems*. CHI '12. New York, NY, USA:

ACM, 1593–1602. DOI:http://dx.doi.org/10.1145/2207676.2208280

9. Ylva Fernaeus and Petra Sundström. 2012. The Material Move How Materials Matter in Interaction Design Research. In *Proceedings of the Designing Interactive Systems Conference*. DIS '12. New York, NY, USA: ACM, 486–495. DOI:http://dx.doi.org/10.1145/2317956.2318029
10. Ylva Fernaeus, Jakob Tholander, and Martin Jonsson. 2008a. Beyond representations: towards an action-centric perspective on tangible interaction. *International Journal of Arts and Technology* 1, 3-4 (January 2008), 249–267. DOI:http://dx.doi.org/10.1504/IJART.2008.022362
11. Ylva Fernaeus, Jakob Tholander, and Martin Jonsson. 2008b. Towards a New Set of Ideals: Consequences of the Practice Turn in Tangible Interaction. In *Proceedings of the 2Nd International Conference on Tangible and Embedded Interaction*. TEI '08. New York, NY, USA: ACM, 223–230. DOI:http://dx.doi.org/10.1145/1347390.1347441
12. Ylva Fernaeus, Anna Vallgårda, Mili John Tharakan, and Anders Lundström. 2012. Touch and Feel Soft Hardware. In *Proceedings of the Sixth International Conference on Tangible, Embedded and Embodied Interaction*. TEI '12. New York, NY, USA: ACM, 359–362. DOI:http://dx.doi.org/10.1145/2148131.2148217
13. C. Frayling. 1993. *Research in art and design*, Royal Coll. of Art, London (United Kingdom).
14. William Gaver. 2012. What Should We Expect from Research Through Design? In *Proceedings of the SIGCHI Conference on Human Factors in Computing Systems*. CHI '12. New York, NY, USA: ACM, 937–946. DOI:http://dx.doi.org/10.1145/2207676.2208538
15. Karen Glass. zerøwaste. Retrieved July 24, 2016 from http://www.zerowastekarenglass.com/
16. Connie Golsteijn, Elise Hoven, David Frohlich, and Abigail Sellen. 2014. Hybrid Crafting: Towards an Integrated Practice of Crafting with Physical and Digital Components. *Personal Ubiquitous Comput.* 18, 3 (March 2014), 593–611. DOI:http://dx.doi.org/10.1007/s00779-013-0684-9
17. Shad Gross, Jeffrey Bardzell, and Shaowen Bardzell. 2014. Structures, Forms, and Stuff: The Materiality and Medium of Interaction. *Personal Ubiquitous Comput.* 18, 3 (March 2014), 637–649. DOI:http://dx.doi.org/10.1007/s00779-013-0689-4
18. Lynne Guey. 2013. A 12-Acre "Goat Farm" Is Transforming The Arts Scene In Atlanta. (June 2013). Retrieved July 27, 2016 from http://www.businessinsider.com/goat-farm-leads-atlantas-arts-scene-2013-6
19. Nicolai Brodersen Hansen, Rikke Toft Nørg\a ard, and Kim Halskov. 2014. Crafting Code at the Demo-scene. In *Proceedings of the 2014 Conference on Designing Interactive Systems*. DIS '14. New York, NY, USA: ACM, 35–38. DOI:http://dx.doi.org/10.1145/2598510.2598526
20. Kari Kuutti and Liam J. Bannon. 2014b. The Turn to Practice in HCI: Towards a Research Agenda. In *Proceedings of the 32Nd Annual ACM Conference on Human Factors in Computing Systems*. CHI '14. New York, NY, USA: ACM, 3543–3552. DOI:http://dx.doi.org/10.1145/2556288.2557111
21. David A. Mellis, Sam Jacoby, Leah Buechley, Hannah Perner-Wilson, and Jie Qi. 2013. Microcontrollers As Material: Crafting Circuits with Paper, Conductive Ink, Electronic Components, and an "Untoolkit." In *Proceedings of the 7th International Conference on Tangible, Embedded and Embodied Interaction*. TEI '13. New York, NY, USA: ACM, 83–90. DOI:http://dx.doi.org/10.1145/2460625.2460638
22. Kristina Niedderer and Katherine Townsend. 2014. Designing Craft Research: Joining Emotion and Knowledge. *The Design Journal* 17, 4 (December 2014), 624–647. DOI:https://doi.org/10.2752/175630614X14056185480221
23. Nithikul Nimkulrat. 2012. Hands-on Intellect: Integrating Craft Practice into Design Research. *International Journal of Dsign* 6, 3 (2012), 1–14.
24. Seymour Papert. 1988. Computer as Material: Messing About with Time. Retrieved July 27, 2016 from http://www.papert.org/articles/ComputerAsMaterial.html
25. Hannah Perner-Wilson. Kit-of-No-Parts. Retrieved July 27, 2016 from http://kit-of-no-parts.at/
26. Hannah Perner-Wilson and Leah Buechley. 2010. Handcrafting Textile Mice. In *Proceedings of the 8th ACM Conference on Designing Interactive Systems*. DIS '10. New York, NY, USA: ACM, 434–435. DOI:http://dx.doi.org/10.1145/1858171.1858257
27. Alan Poole and Anne Poole. 2016. Functional Interactive Tatting: Bringing Together a Traditional Handicraft and Electronics. In *Proceedings of the TEI '16: Tenth International Conference on Tangible, Embedded, and Embodied Interaction*. TEI '16. New York, NY, USA: ACM, 551–555. DOI:http://dx.doi.org/10.1145/2839462.2856529
28. Michael Polanyi. 1967. *The Tacit Dimension*, Anchor Books.
29. Ernest Rehmi Post, Margaret Orth, P.R. Russo, and Neil Gershenfeld. 2000. E-broidery: Design and Fabrication of Textile-based Computing. *IBM Syst. J.*

39, 3-4 (July 2000), 840–860. DOI:http://dx.doi.org/10.1147/sj.393.0840

30. Larissa Pschetz, Richard Banks, and Mike Molloy. 2013. Movement Crafter. In *Proceedings of the 7th International Conference on Tangible, Embedded and Embodied Interaction*. TEI '13. New York, NY, USA: ACM, 393–394. DOI:http://dx.doi.org/10.1145/2460625.2460709
31. Gabriela T. Richard and Yasmin B. Kafai. 2015. Making Physical and Digital Games with e-Textiles: A Workshop for Youth Making Responsive Wearable Games and Controllers. In *Proceedings of the 14th International Conference on Interaction Design and Children*. IDC '15. New York, NY, USA: ACM, 399–402. DOI:http://dx.doi.org/10.1145/2771839.2771926
32. Daniela Rosner, Jean-François Blanchette, Leah Buechley, Paul Dourish, and Melissa Mazmanian. 2012. From Materials to Materiality: Connecting Practice and Theory in Hc. In *CHI '12 Extended Abstracts on Human Factors in Computing Systems*. CHI EA '12. New York, NY, USA: ACM, 2787–2790. DOI:http://dx.doi.org/10.1145/2212776.2212721
33. Daniela K. Rosner. 2010. Mediated Crafts: Digital Practices Around Creative Handwork. In *CHI '10 Extended Abstracts on Human Factors in Computing Systems*. CHI EA '10. New York, NY, USA: ACM, 2955–2958. DOI:http://dx.doi.org/10.1145/1753846.1753894
34. Daniela K. Rosner, Miwa Ikemiya, and Tim Regan. 2015. Resisting Alignment: Code and Clay. In *Proceedings of the Ninth International Conference on Tangible, Embedded, and Embodied Interaction*. TEI '15. New York, NY, USA: ACM, 181–188. DOI:http://dx.doi.org/10.1145/2677199.2680587
35. Daniela K. Rosner and Kimiko Ryokai. 2009. Reflections on Craft: Probing the Creative Process of Everyday Knitters. In *Proceedings of the Seventh ACM Conference on Creativity and Cognition*. C&C '09. New York, NY, USA: ACM, 195–204. DOI:http://dx.doi.org/10.1145/1640233.1640264
36. Daniela K. Rosner and Kimiko Ryokai. 2010. Spyn: Augmenting the Creative and Communicative Potential of Craft. In *Proceedings of the SIGCHI Conference on Human Factors in Computing Systems*. CHI '10. New York, NY, USA: ACM, 2407–2416. DOI:http://dx.doi.org/10.1145/1753326.1753691
37. Daniela Rosner, Marco Roccetti, and Gustavo Marfia. 2014a. The Digitization of Cultural Practices. *Commun. ACM* 57, 6 (June 2014), 82–87. DOI:http://dx.doi.org/10.1145/2602695.2602701
38. Becky Stern. 2013. Smart Textiles Talk (slides) #WearableWednesday. (May 2013). Retrieved July 25, 2016 from https://blog.adafruit.com/2013/05/29/smart-textiles-talk-slides-wearablewednesday/
39. Lucy A. Suchman. 1987. *Plans and Situated Actions: The Problem of Human-Machine Communication*, Cambridge University Press.
40. Verily Tan and Kylie Peppler. 2015. Creative Design Process in Making Electronic Textiles. In *Proceedings of the 14th International Conference on Interaction Design and Children*. IDC '15. New York, NY, USA: ACM, 327–330. DOI:http://dx.doi.org/10.1145/2771839.2771908
41. B. Ullmer, and H. Ishii Emerging frameworks for tangible user interfaces. *IBM Syst. J.*, 39, 3-4 (2001), 915-931.
42. Anna Vallgårda. 2014. Giving Form to Computational Things: Developing a Practice of Interaction Design. *Personal Ubiquitous Comput.* 18, 3 (March 2014), 577–592. DOI:http://dx.doi.org/10.1007/s00779-013-0685-8
43. Anna Vallgårda and Johan Redström. 2007. Computational Composites. In *Proceedings of the SIGCHI Conference on Human Factors in Computing Systems*. CHI '07. New York, NY, USA: ACM, 513–522. DOI:http://dx.doi.org/10.1145/1240624.1240706
44. Mikael Wiberg et al. 2012. "Material Interactions": From Atoms & Bits to Entangled Practices. In *CHI '12 Extended Abstracts on Human Factors in Computing Systems*. CHI EA '12. New York, NY, USA: ACM, 1147–1150. DOI:http://dx.doi.org/10.1145/2212776.2212408
45. Mikael Wiberg. 2014. Methodology for Materiality: Interaction Design Research Through a Material Lens. *Personal Ubiquitous Comput.* 18, 3 (March 2014), 625–636. DOI:http://dx.doi.org/10.1007/s00779-013-0686-7
46. Amit Zoran and Leah Buechley. 2012. Hybrid Reassemblage: An Exploration of Craft, Digital Fabrication and Artifact Uniqueness. *Leonardo* 46, 1 (October 2012), 4–10. DOI:https://doi.org/10.1162/LEON_a_00477

Sketching-in-Light: Enabling Hybrid Prototyping of Low-Resolution Lighting Displays

Marius Hoggenmueller[1,2], Alexander Wiethoff[1], Martin Tomitsch[2]
[1] Department for Informatics, University of Munich, Germany
[2] Design Lab, Faculty of Architecture, Design and Planning, The University of Sydney, Australia
marius.hoggenmueller@campus.lmu.de, alexander.wiethoff@ifi.lmu.de,
martin.tomitsch@sydney.edu.au

ABSTRACT
Low-resolution lighting displays are commonplace in internet-of-things devices, wearable products and embedded interfaces. However, prototyping such displays is challenging and cumbersome as methods, specific domain knowledge and skills are only available to experts. In this paper we present a novel toolkit to assist with designing and evaluating the characteristics of low-resolution lighting displays as well as content variations using different materials. We describe the components of the toolkit, which include a tablet, a custom-built app and low-cost prototyping materials, and its use within the context of a design study. The toolkit can easily be replicated and adopted by others working in this domain to prototype low-resolution lighting displays without requiring any previous expertise in hardware prototyping.

Author Keywords
Tangible Lighting-Design; Embedded Low-resolution displays; Toolkit; Hybrid Prototyping.

ACM Classification Keywords
H.5.m. Information interfaces and presentation (e.g., HCI): Design;

INTRODUCTION
Innovations in light-emitting diode (LED) technology enables the creation of new visual displays that are unique in size, shape, material, pixel arrangement and resolution. Due to the great flexibility, designers from various domains are using digital media as a design material: applications range from wearable LED displays that fit into clothing and lifestyle accessories, wayfinding displays and digital signage, to large-scale architectural structures created of individual pixel elements. These displays are characterized by their low resolutions, in some cases featuring a complex pixel or three dimensional shape (3D) pattern, and their lighting quality, which distinguishes them from conventional 2D rectangular screens [6]. Depending on the display's resolution and the context in which they are deployed, content can be explicit text-based or abstract (see Figure 1).

TEI '17, March 20-23, 2017, Yokohama, Japan
© 2017 ACM. ISBN 978-1-4503-4676-4/17/03…$15.00
DOI: http://dx.doi.org/10.1145/3024969.3025001

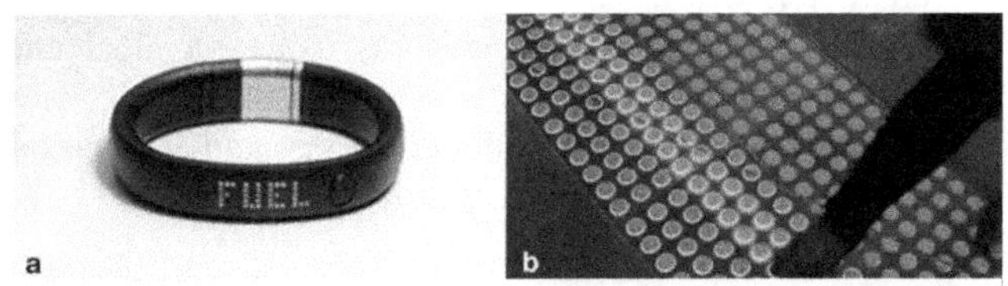

Figure 1. Examples of low-resolution lighting displays in different contexts: (a) Nike+ FuelBand to track and display physicial activities, (b) Ground-embedded traffic light display. Photo credits: (a) © Peter Parkes (licensed under https://creativecommons.org/licenses/by/2.0/) (b) © Büro North.

As with any design, sketching and creating early prototypes is crucial for "getting the right design and getting the design right" [3]. According to Buxton, sketches should be plentiful and quick to make, while prototypes are important for the iterative refinement of an idea. However, this is still a challenge when it comes to the **creation and representation of content** in the design process of low-resolution (low-res) lighting displays. Due to the characteristics of low-res lighting displays, prototyping visual content via conventional digital media displays is not always sufficient. An often underestimated parameter when working with lighting includes **designing lighting as material:** transparency as a material's property can be used to filter or conceal light aimed at influencing the visual experience of low-res lighting displays [5]. To achieve an overall aesthetic result, the material's choice should be included already in early prototyping stages to perform more design iterations along with content explorations. Therefore, appropriate tools are needed to support designers without having an expert knowledge in materials and engineering.

The toolkit presented in this paper, *Sketching-in-Light*, addresses the following limitations of current prototyping approaches: (1) Low-fidelity (low-fi) prototyping methods and tools from related fields (i.e., graphical user interface design) cannot be adopted easily due to specific properties, including low resolution and lighting quality. (2) Designers working in this domain therefore have to employ high-fidelity prototyping already early in the design process (i.e., using the *real* components of an eventual design) before having concepts evaluated on a lower level. (3) Doing so results in increased time and cost spent on prototyping, especially if experts from other domains, e.g. electrical engineering, have to be included due to a lack of knowledge in engineering and programming by the design team.

Our toolkit enables:

- Sketching with light on the same level as sketching with paper and pen taking into account a display's specific characteristics.
- *Hybrid* crafting of early designs using physical and digital materials.
- Performing more design iterations fast and at low-cost before the actual implementation.

RELATED WORK

Creating prototypes as early design instantiations for future products is a widely used practice in various design disciplines. For graphical user interfaces (GUIs), designers can choose from a wide range of prototyping methods and tools during different *fidelity* stages of the design process [8]. For example, paper prototyping as a low-fidelity technique is often used in early phases to communicate ideas in collaborative design teams or to evaluate various concepts with users in a time and cost-effective manner [1].

However, since the prototypes' *material* influences the design aspects that can be manifested by a prototype [8], conventional paper prototyping techniques cannot be simply applied to any context. Researchers and designers have therefore begun to develop methods to adapt low-fi prototyping techniques for novel interface domains: Wiethoff et al. created Sketch-a-TUI for prototyping tangible user interfaces (TUIs) using physical objects made of cardboard on a capacitive touchscreen [12]. Broy et al. developed a prototyping toolkit for stereoscopic 3D displays using different depth layers illuminated via a tablet computer as a backlight source [2]. Ullmer et. al presented a physical overlay onto digital pads to create tangible UIs fast and at low cost [11]. In the domain of dynamic, interactive lighting design, Wiethoff et al. presented LightBox [13], a miniature lighting lab to explore content proposals for low-res lighting displays, however, they did not include lighting variations affected by the choice of materiality aspects, as highlighted in our work. In this context, Griffiths stresses the importance of traditional materials in lighting design since "texture, color and patina of materials add to a product's character something that technology is unable to replicate [5]". Within the broader field of interaction design, Robles and Wiberg argue to focus on the materiality of both, the digital and physical, referring to a "material turn" in interaction design [10]. In this vein, we argue that the choice of material should be more carefully considered for low-res lighting displays and reflected in prototypes, which is not feasible when working solely with digital artifacts as a simulation source. Further, we propose hands-on crafting techniques in this domain, incorporating the idea of *"hybrid crafting"*, defined by Goldsteijn et al. as "everyday creative practice of using combinations of physical and digital materials, techniques or tools [4]".

SKETCHING-IN-LIGHT

Our toolkit *Sketching-in-Light* is intended for building mock-ups of low-res lighting displays. It allows designers to create visual content using a large variety of physical and digital materials we refer to as tangible lighting design (TLD). The prototyping steps include (a) **Physical Sketching**, which involves painting and crafting with translucent materials on tracing paper, (b) **Configuring the Display Mock-up** using various physical overlays, including the inserted sketch, (c) **Hybrid Prototyping** by attaching the display mock-up onto a digital tablet serving as a light source and animating the sketch with configurable light patterns. For overview purposes, the prototyping steps are described in the above-mentioned order, however, the actual prototyping activities reinforce each other and can be carried out iteratively.

a. Physical Sketching

Drawing and sketching by hand is a powerful technique that is widely used by interaction designers to express and discuss

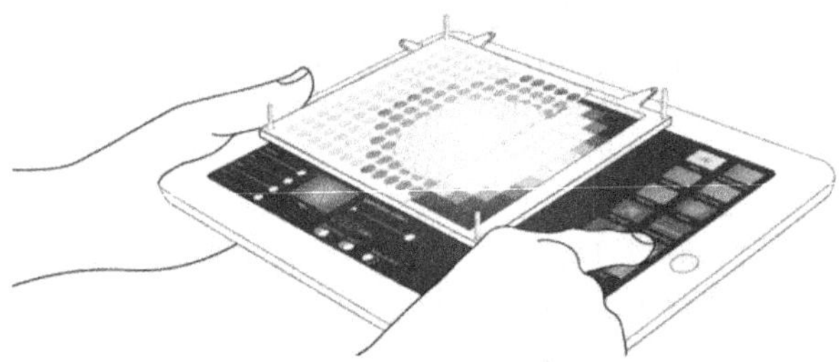

Figure 2. Hybrid prototyping environment including a digital tablet augmenting a display mock-up with dynamic lighting patterns.

early ideas [1]. However, digital painting applications provide only a limited number of input devices, such as mouse or stylus. In comparison, there is a large variety of materials and tools that can be used for making things in the physical world [7]. For *Sketching-in-Light*, we therefore augment the digital sketching canvas with physical materials, creating a *hybrid* prototyping environment. The use of physical materials allows designers to experiment with various tangible materials that offer transparent or translucent qualities, such as watercolor paints, water based ink, colored silk paper and cellophane foil which have not yet been included in lighting design. These tangible materials further enable a wide range of crafting activities, such as painting with a brush, drawing and sketching with a pen, as well as creating a collage by cutting out and assembling shapes. As *support material* we used DINA4 Canson Tracing Paper Pads with 90gsm paper weight. Due to the non-opaque

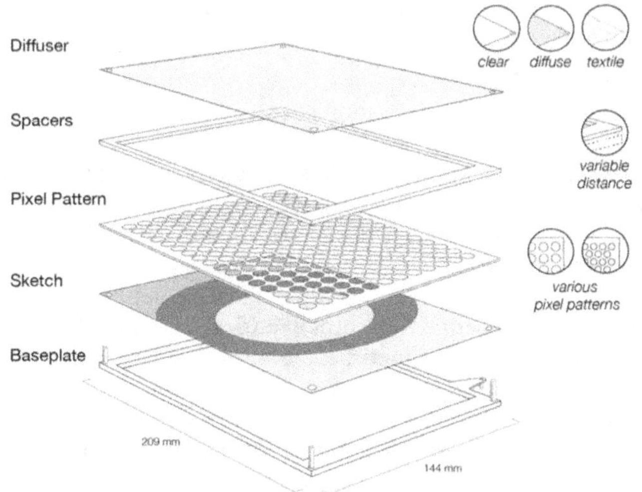

Figure 3. Example configuration of the display mock-up.

properties of all materials used, the sketch can be illuminated and animated through a digital tablet as a backlight source (described in step c). To see the final effect of the illuminated display, the sketch can be directly designed on top of a digital tablet[1], similar to commercially available tracing boards.

b. Configuring the Display Mock-up

As any low-res lighting display comes with unique features in terms of resolution, pixel configurations and materials, we created physical overlays to simulate different *pixel patterns* and *lighting qualities*. The laser-cut overlays are all freely-available as templates[2] consisting of a baseplate, pixel pattern sheets, spacers and diffuser sheets (see Figure 3). All templates measure 209x144 millimeters, adjusted for the use with an Apple iPad Pro (12.9 inches). For the baseplate (3mm black acrylic), nylon screws (M2 x 16mm) are bolted onto the plate to stack up the perforated sketch and overlays. For a better alignment with the top-left corner of the iPad (see Figure 2), the baseplate has three tabs with nylon screws facing down. To simulate various pixel configurations and shapes, we designed pixel pattern templates that can be easily modified. For our initial use case, prototyping an ambient lighting display, we laser-cut a grid system with 17x12 circular holes from 0.8mm white opaque polypropylene. Cutting the pixel sheets from other materials (e.g. black opaque, etc.) can be used to increase the lighting contrast. Further, our toolkit allows to experiment with *diffusion* which is a critical parameter influencing the lighting quality [5]: we therefore assembled sheets from polypropylene (clear and translucent) as well as *spacers* to easily change the lighting diffusion. The physical overlays aim to stimulate designers to experiment with materials (e.g. translucent textiles for wearables) along with content, while keeping in mind that they do not necessarily represent the actual light quality of the finished product.

c. Hybrid Prototyping

In the final prototyping step, designers can use our toolkit to illuminate the physical display mock-up (see Figure 2). Similar to [2], we use an iPad as a background light, however, with additional user interface (UI) control elements (see Figure 4) to augment the display mock-up with lighting effects and other digital media (e.g. images). Therefore, the toolkit app[2] is divided into a background lighting area on top of which the display mock-up is placed (see Figure 4a) and control elements below and on the right hand site. The virtual pixel grid is aligned with the pixel pattern sheet described in section b. For other display configurations the grid must be edited within the code. With the controls on the right-hand side (see Figure 4b), users can choose from a list of i) predefined lighting patterns and ii) options for customizable content. With the controls in the lower left-hand section (see Figure 4c), users can adjust hue and brightness as well as playback settings (e.g. speed, forward/backward, fading, etc.). In the lower right-hand section (see Figure 4d), users can find context-sensitive controls when a customizable content option is selected.

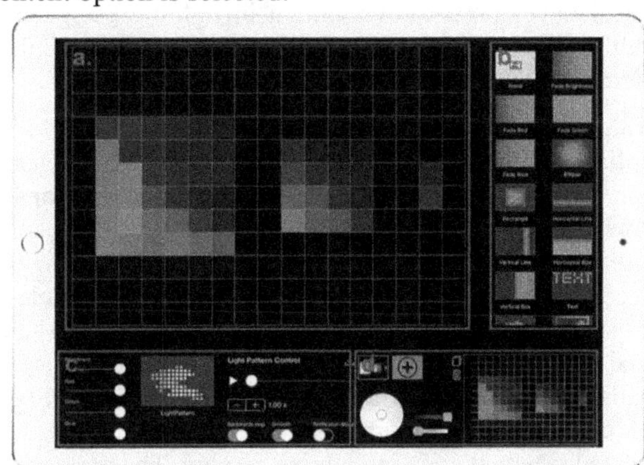

Figure 4. Sketching-in-Light toolkit application: (a) area for placing the display mock-up, (b) list to select from lighting patterns and content options, (c) playback settings, (d) controls for the customizable content (here the drawing tool selected).

In total, we implemented eight predefined lighting patterns that are defined by changes in *color*, *brightness* and *pixel position*. These variables were chosen based on previous research evaluating lighting patterns for low-res lighting systems [9]. Further, the set is supplemented by a drawing tool to create customized lighting patterns through simple key frame animations. The drawing tool (selected in Figure 4) can be used by two means: either animating the hand-crafted sketch drawing directly onto the tracing paper which does not impair the functionality of the touch screen, or creating "digital only" animations onto a small-scale preview screen while the display mock-up is placed on the iPad. For prototyping text-based content, we implemented a 4x5 pixel

[1] To protect the screen we used glass screen protector foil with 9H hardness (mohs scale of mineral hardness).

[2] https://hoggenmari.github.io/Sketching-in-Light/

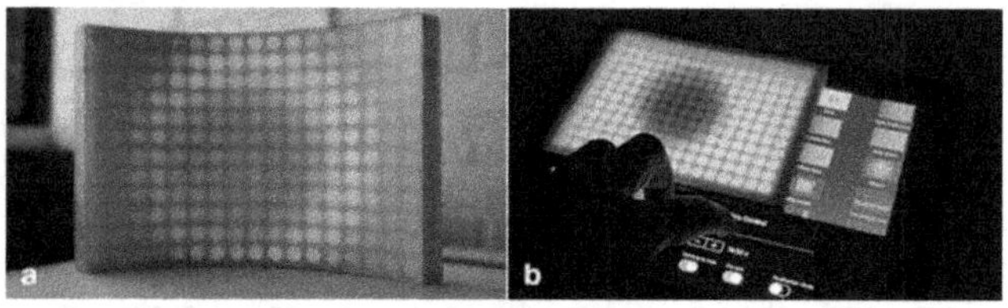

Figure 5. (a) Hi-fi prototype of the ambient light display (b) Low-fi prototype using *Sketching-in-Light.*

font including alphabetic and numeric characters; text messages and scrolling options that can be edited by the user. Furthermore, users can pick images from a photo library that are subsequently mapped onto the pixel grid. This enables the use of the internal camera or previously saved online content as a source.

Finally, we developed a Java-based library to allow for the development of visualizations in Processing[3]. Using this library, the visual output from the Processing sketch can be directly displayed on the toolkit app, thus using the physical display mock-up as an output medium. Providing such a physical development environment in lighting design, our toolkit enables users to move from initial sketches to initial implementations without requiring the final hardware.

USING SKETCHING-IN-LIGHT IN CONTEXT

In collaboration with a small company in the smart home sector, we used *Sketching-in-Light* in an industrial context for the conceptual design of an ambient lighting display visualizing the performance of residential solar panels. The project used an existing pre-production prototype made of high-power RGB LEDs, round reflectors, diffusor film and a curved shape (see Figure 5a). To design the display visualizations we created a display mock-up using a 17x12 pixel pattern and a diffusor sheet with 3mm spacers to simulate the actual ambient lighting display. The scale of the display mock-up was approximately 1:2.5. Although the mock-up did not have the curved shape of the high-fidelity prototype, the augmented display mock-up (see Figure 5b) provided a realistic impression of the actual display in terms of resolution and smoothness of colors.

During a workshop session, we made our toolkit available to the company's product team to create design proposals for the visualization of solar and electricity performance data. Workshop participants were able to easily move between the three prototyping stages, using physical and digital materials. They also adopted the toolkit in unintended ways, such as expressing dynamic content through physical materials by manually moving silk paper cutouts back and forth behind the display frame. The workshop participants found our toolkit to be a valuable design tool as it enabled them to create and explore content variations for a new medium. Following on from the workshop, we were then able to implement and evaluate some of the proposed visualizations using our custom-developed Processing library.

DISCUSSION

The *Sketching-in-Light* toolkit extends previous work by integrating crafting and combining physical and digital materials. This approach offers designers to fluently move between sketching and prototyping [3] across various levels of fidelity. Working with physical materials allows the iterative exploration of conceptual ideas in a time and cost-effective manner. Through the digital tablet application, designers can refine their prototype and fine-tune its visual appearance and dynamic behavior. Going back and forth between the stages of physical sketches and hybrid prototyping, we consider our toolkit as a *supportive enabler* for creating and exploring early ideas in the design process of low-res lighting displays.

Limitations. Simulating low-res lighting displays without actual hardware comes with several limitations: using a digital tablet as a backlight source does not provide the same brightness levels as high-power LEDs and the evenly illuminated tablet surface differs from the punctual lighting sources produced by single LEDs. Further, the flat, rectangular shape of the tablet restricts prototyping of 3D display shapes, such as the curved ambient lighting display used in our design workshop. Some design decisions (e.g. display format, pixel pattern) were based on this existing ambient lighting display used in the workshop. In its current version, the toolkit requires programming to adapt the toolkit to other dimensions and pixel grids. To remove this limitation, we are planning to further develop the toolkit application to support customized pixel configurations based on the created template.

Benefits of Sketching-in-Light. We consider the following advantages that stimulate the design process by having a toolkit for fast and low cost exploration of visual experiences of lighting displays along with content:

- Our approach is easy to replicate for others.
- There are no additional lighting components required.
- It provides the ability to simulate specific characteristics of displays such as pixel configurations and lighting qualities.
- Fluid use of physical and digital materials.

CONCLUSION

Designing with low-resolution lighting displays comes with several challenges, one being that prototyping still demands a high level of technical expertise and low-fi prototyping methods are hardly available in this domain. We therefore presented a prototyping toolkit to create content for low-res lighting displays proposing the use of various materials. The toolkit can be used by designers without requiring any skills in hardware prototyping. It can also be used in co-design sessions with prospective users or other stakeholders,

[3] https://processing.org

facilitated by designers. We described the use of our toolkit in a real-life context with a potential user group that could benefit from such low-cost and easy-to-use tools. We hope that our toolkit will enable designers of low-res displays to test out multiple display configurations and content variations early in the design process, leading to more aesthetic and enjoyable products.

ACKNOWLEDGEMENTS

This work was supported by a fellowship within the FITweltweit programme of the German Academic Exchange Service (DAAD) and partly funded by the Lehre@LMU programme at Ludwig-Maximilian University of Munich (LMU). We would like to thank the participants from our design workshop.

REFERENCES

1. Mark Baskinger, M. Cover story: Pencils before pixels: a primer in hand-generated sketching. *Interactions 15,2* (Mar. 2008), 28-36. http://doi.acm.org/10.1145/1340961.1340969
2. Nora Broy, Stefan Schneegass, Florian Alt and Albrecht Schmidt. Framebox and mirrorbox: Tools and guidelines to support designers in prototyping interfaces for 3D displays. In *Proc. CHI 2014.* http://doi.acm.org/10.1145/2556288.2557183
3. Bill Buxton. Sketching User Experiences: Getting the Design Right and the Right Design. *Morgan Kaufmann,* 2007.
4. Connie Golsteijn, Elise van den Hoven, David Frohlich and Abigail Sellen. Hybrid crafting: towards an integrated practice of crafting with physical and digital components. *Personal and Ubiquitous Computing 18, 3 (2014), 593-611.* http://dx.doi.org/10.1007/s00779-013-0684-9
5. Alyn Griffiths. 21st Century Lighting Design. Bloomsbury Visual Arts.
6. Kim Halskov and Tobias Ebsen. 2013. A framework for designing complex media facades. *Design studies 34(5).* http://dx.doi.org/10.1016/j.destud.2013.04.001
7. Mami Kosaka and Kaori Fujinami. UnicrePaint: Digital Painting through Physical Objects for Unique Creative Experiences. In *Proc. TEI 2016.* http://doi.acm.org/10.1145/2839462.2856553
8. Youn-Kyung Lim, Erik Stolterman and Josh Tenenberg. The anatomy of prototypes: Prototypes as filters, prototypes as manifestations of design ideas. In *Proc. TOCHI 2008.* http://doi.acm.org/10.1145/1375761.1375762
9. Andrii Matviienko, Vanessa Cobus, Heiko Müller, Jutta Fortmann, Andreas Löcken, Susanne Boll, Maria Rauschenberger, Janko Timmermann, Christoph Trappe, Wilko Heuten. Deriving Design Guidelines for Ambient Light Systems. In *Proc.* MUM 2015. http://doi.acm.org/10.1145/2836041.2836069
10. Erica Robles and Mikael Wiberg. Texturing the "Material Turn" in Interaction Design. In *Proc. TEI 2010.* http://doi.acm.org/10.1145/1709886.1709911
11. Brygg Ullmer, Christian Dell, Claudia Gill et al. (2011). Casier: Structures for Composing Tangibles and Complementary Interactors for User Across Diverse Systems. In *Proc. TEI 2011.* http://doi.acm.org/10.1145/1935701.1935746
12. Alexander Wiethoff, Hanna Schneider, Michael Rohs, Andreas Butz and Saul Greenberg. (2012). Sketch-a-TUI: low cost prototyping of tangible interactions using cardboard and conductive ink. In *Proc. TEI 2012.* http://doi.acm.org/10.1145/2148131.2148196
13. Alexander Wiethoff and Magdalena Blöckner. Lightbox: exploring interaction modalities with colored light. In *Proc. TEI 2011.* http://doi.acm.org/10.1145/1935701.1935799

AWElectric: That Gave Me Goosebumps, Did You Feel It Too?

Kristin Neidlinger
Therapeutic Biomedia,
Sensoree Design Lab
San Francisco, CA, USA
kristin@sensoree.com

Khiet P. Truong
Human Media Interaction,
University of Twente
Enschede, NL
k.p.truong@utwente.nl

Caty Telfair
Art History, University of
California Berkeley
Berkeley, CA, USA
catytelfair@berkeley.edu

Loe Feijs
Designed Intelligence, TU
Eindhoven
Eindhoven, NL
l.m.g.feijs@tue.nl

Edwin Dertien
Creative Technology,
University of Twente
Enschede, NL
e.dertien@utwente.nl

Vanessa Evers
Human Media Interaction,
University of Twente
Enschede, NL
v.evers@utwente.nl

ABSTRACT
Awe is a powerful, visceral sensation described as a sudden chill or shudder accompanied by goosebumps. People feel awe in the face of extraordinary experiences: the sublimity of nature, the beauty of art and music, the adrenaline rush of fear. Awe is healthy, both physically and mentally. It can be shared by people who are witnessing the same phenomenon, but traditionally it cannot be communicated remotely across time or distance: to feel awe involves real time experience, and explaining the experience that gave rise to it does not always induce the feeling of awe itself. We want to make this sensation something that can be transmitted, and therefore present AWElectric, a wearable interface that can detect awe, enhance it, and create it in another person. Our shared goosebump design embeds inflatable biometric displays in 3D print fabric. The AudioTactile fabric transmits an awe-inducing sound frequency to the partner that physically manifests the tingles, chills, and goosebumps that awe provokes.

ACM Classification Keywords
H.5.m. Information Interfaces and Presentation (e.g. HCI): Miscellaneous

Author Keywords
bio-sensing; tactile interface; haptic; remote communication; affective computing; awe; goosebumps; wearable technology; inflatable; 3d print; AudioTactile; embedded fabric; extimacy

INTRODUCTION
The emotion that you feel when you have reached the top of a mountain and are overwhelmed with amazement by the vast views of nature. The one you feel when you hear a beautiful piece of music that gives you goosebumps up your spine. The one that makes you shudder and tingle with the thrill of discovering a new idea. That is the sublime, visceral emotion of awe.

TEI '17, March 20 - 23, 2017, Yokohama, Japan

ISBN 978-1-4503-4676-4/17/03...$15.00
DOI: http://dx.doi.org/10.1145/3024969.3025004

Experiencing awe is good for people. Many studies have reported its positive effects on mental as well as physical well-being [36, 32, 29]. The healthiest people experience the most awe. Some report feeling the goosebump sensation simultaneously. However, awe is an individual sensation that cannot be shared remotely across time and distance.

Hence, inspired by the phrase "That gave me goosebumps, did you feel it too?" we have developed AWElectric (see Fig. 1). AWElectric is a wearable tactile interface that, by animating the physical experience of piloerection caused by awe and inducing it in another person, amplifies the wearer's sensation as well as making it possible to share it.

We define awe as a complex emotion, a mix of fear and wonder that invokes physical sensations. We sought to exhibit this sensation in a tangible way with the quality 'extimacy'. Extimacy is a term Sensoree[1] defines as externalized intimacy, showing how one feels on the inside to the outside world. By employing biosensors to read body systems, we translate the emotional state to visual, audio, or tactile displays. This gives the body a voice with real-time tangible interactions that offers biofeedback for the wearer as well as acts as a form of communication with others. AWElectric's engagement of multiple senses aims to intensify the experience of awe, create heightened awareness, and structure new memories. This design also enables sharing of the experience with the other person that has potential to create a learned behavior for those completely unfamiliar with it. It is reported that up to 40% of the population does not experience the phenomenon of awe [7, 11]. With the neuroplasticity of our brain, we are able to learn and re-pattern behaviors and these sensations.

This paper presents the design of AWElectric. We focus particularly on describing how we aimed to make the awe sensation

[1] Sensoree, http://www.sensoree.com

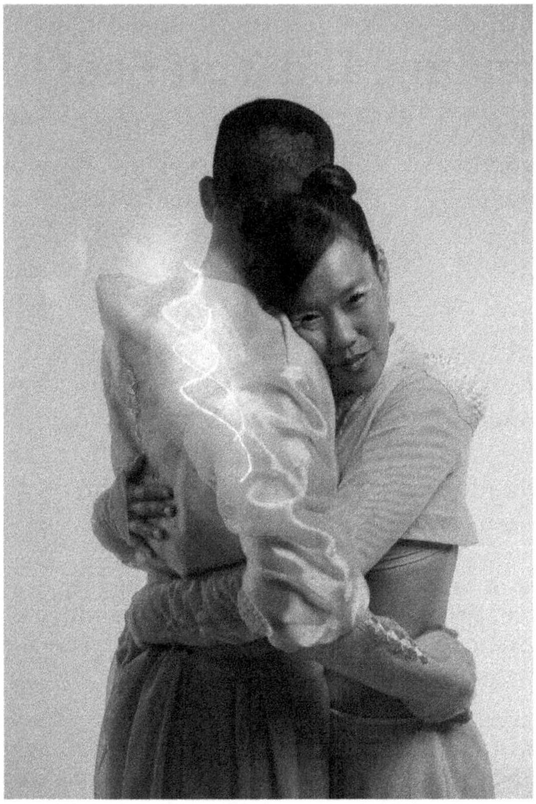

Figure 1: The AWElectric is a duet design (photo by Elena Kulikova). ©sensoree

tangible and share-able. We introduce our newly developed inflatable biometric displays in 3D print fabric. Also, we describe how our design employs an awe-inducing sound frequency that is transmitted to embroidered speakers to evoke the feeling of awe in another person.

BACKGROUND

Feeling of awe

Keltner & Haidt [19] define awe as an emotion that arises as a response to a stimulus that is vast and that transcends current frames of reference (vastness), such that a new mental scheme is needed to accommodate what is being perceived (accommodation). The experience of awe is often associated with descriptive terms such as chills, thrills, goosebumps, frisson, and shivers ([7, 8, 11, 35]) that describe the feeling of amazement that goes beyond the emotions of happiness or joy and manifests in physical sensations. In one of the first studies on thrills, Goldstein (1980) [11] describes this experience as: *"a chill, shudder, tingling, or tickling. It may be accompanied by a feeling of "hair standing on end" or "goosebumps" on the arms. Thrills are invariably associated with sudden changes in mood or emotion. They may be accompanied by sighing, palpitation, tension of the jaw and facial muscles, a feeling of "lump in the throat", or incipient weeping."* Subsequent studies have shown that among other displays (correlates) of awe is the display of goosebumps [34, 5].

Goosebumps and other correlates of awe

Piloerection, also referred to as goosebumps, is the visible erection of body hair in humans (or animals) [6]. Piloerection is known to occur as a reaction to cold or to fearful situations, but it also occurs as a reaction to strong emotional experiences WITH awe [18, 16]. In a study by Schurtz et al. (2012) [34], participants kept a four-week journal and added a detailed entry each time they experienced goose bumps. Goosebumps resulting from the experience of awe were found to be the second most frequently occurring type after reactions to cold. Emotional piloerection appears to cause physiological changes in the autonomic nervous system (ANS). By elicting piloerection through exposing participants to moving film audio tracks and music, Benedek et al. (2010) [6] found that piloerection is primarily accompanied by an increase of phasic electrodermal activity (EDA) and respiration depth. Similar findings were obtained in an earlier study by Craig (2005) [8] where sections of music were used to elicit chills. Results suggested that the experience of chills corresponded to significant changes in electrodermal activity but not in skin temperature. In summary, these studies show that goosebumps and changes in electrodermal activity are important physiological correlates of the experience of awe.

Positive effects of feeling awe

Experiencing awe not only feels good, it is also good for your health and can serve a social function. Studies have reported positive effects of awe on mental as well as physical and social well-being.

The healthiest people feel awe more often. Biologically this was tested in a study investigating the relation between experiencing positive emotions and the level of proinflammatory cytokines. It was found that awe was the strongest predictor of lower levels of proinflammatory cytokines [36]. Elevated levels of proinflammatory cytokines have been related to chronic diseases such as diabetes. Hence, experiencing awe can help keep these levels low and thereby contribute to better physical health.

The feeling of awe has also been found to enhance mental well-being in that it expands people's perception of time [32]. In three experiments, Rudd et al. (2012) [32] found that participants who felt awe (as compared to other emotions) felt they had more time available, were less impatient and were more willing to volunteer their time to help other people. Participants who felt awe strongly preferred experiences over material products and experienced greater life satisfaction.

Finally, a study by Piff & Dietze (2015) [29] shows that awe can serve a social function. In several experiments, induced awe led to increased ethical decision-making, generosity and prosocial behaviors. Awe can help shift people's views away from the individual to the broader social context and thereby enhance prosocial values.

Feeling awe is good for people. The studies presented underscore the importance and positive effects of awe. Hence, with our design AWElectric, we aim to communicate the feeling of awe from one individual to the other, and to create a community of heightened awareness instigating better health and togetherness.

RELATED WORK

In this digital era, maintaining social relationships over a distance has been made much easier by the invention of the telephone, video conferencing and internet. Many of our social interactions with our friends, family and loved ones are mediated, for example, through phone and video calls, short text messages, and email. However, these communication devices focus on text, audio-only and audiovisual communication. The ability to communicate things experienced through our other senses, such as smell, taste, and touch, has not been developed until recent years. In addition, the form-factor of sensors has greatly improved such that these can easily be embedded in wearables such as clothing.

Remote communication through tactile interfaces

Since touch is one of the main nonverbal communication channels for conveying intimate emotions in a way that text, audio, and video cannot, researchers have been developing haptic feedback technology for remote communication in order to increase feelings of intimacy, social presence and togetherness. Systems have been developed for specific affective touch events such as hugging [23, 12, 37]. Gooch & Watts (2010) [12] tested the concept of social presence (i.e., the sense of 'being there') through a 'thermal hug belt' that people can wear and that produces thermal stimuli as a proxy for the body warmth that one would feel from the other during hugging. Their study showed that people who received thermal hugs perceived a higher level of social presence than people who did not receive the hugs. Huggy Pajama is another wearable system that aims to communicate hugs remotely [37], in this case, between parents and children. The system consists of a small mobile doll with several pressure sensors. When the doll is hugged by the sender, the device sends hug signals to a haptic jacket that the receiver is wearing and that simulates the feeling of being hugged.

A haptic device for remote communication of a more intimate affective event, kissing, was developed by Saadatian et al. (2014) [33]. This physical interface is able to transmit a kiss between two remotely connected people. The amount of force and shape of the sender's kiss is sensed and transmitted to the receiver's device who experiences the replicated kiss through the actuators.

Other examples of systems that have been developed for mediated touch events include systems for communicating handholding [13], pokes [25] and handshakes [4] (for a more extended review of devices for mediated social touch, the reader is referred to [38, 14]). With recent advancements in digital taste and smell technology [31], remote multisensory communication will become even more of a reality in the near future. The examples described show promising results and confirm that communicating emotions through tactile interfaces is indeed possible [17].

Affective communication through wearable technology and smart clothing

Emotions can be measured in multiple modalities such as speech, facial expressions, body movements and postures, gestures, as well as physiological signals. For affective wearables [27], physiological measurements, measurements in the autonomic nervous system (ANS), seem to be more suitable and effective [15, 21]. With the growing trend of 'quantified self' and the development of wearable bio-sensors, the continuous measurement and monitoring of affect through biosignals such as heart rate variability (e.g., [21]), galvanic skin response (e.g., [21]), and brain activity (e.g., [22]) becomes more and more feasible.

The form factor of these sensors also makes embedding in garments possible as shown by several works that aim to measure and react to human emotions through clothing. Examples include the Galvanicator [28], a glove that maps galvanic skin response measurements to LED displays to show the wearer's arousal, and the Philips Bubelle skin dress [1] that displays the wearer's emotions through colors based on biometrics. In a similar vein, the Ger Mood Sweater™ [2] reveals the wearer's inner state by measuring galvanic skin response and displaying colors in the sweater. This design also has a therapeutic motive as it can help people who have difficulties recognizing other people's emotions and/or conveying their own emotions. Helping people with mood disorders has also been the main motivation for the designs of Lightwear [30], a scarf that can administer light therapy for on-the-go treatment of seasonal affective disorder, and SWARM [39], another scarf that reacts to the wearer's own emotions as well to the emotions of the people in their surroundings.

Our design AWElectric contributes to the research of remote multisensory affective communication, and wearable technology. In creating AWElectric, we are amplifying and communicating the feeling of awe to another person, fostering behavioral affective mimicry at a distance and creating new awareness and memory. To the best of our knowledge, AWElectric is the first design that addresses the remote communication of awe through wearables.

DESIGN CONCEPT

Concept

In developing AWElectric, we were inspired by the question, "That gave me goosebumps, did you feel it too?" This question, often asked, implies that we want to share with others this intense sensation that comes from the body's emotional base, a sensation best summed up in the French term 'frisson,' which is defined as aesthetic chills or emotion-centered shudders from music, art, and ideas. This sensation on the skin signifies an emotional rush and clarity. We sought to create a goosebump prosthetic to illustrate this latent sense in a tangible interaction that enhances the phenomenon and shares it.

In 2015, we designed AWE Goosebumps, our first wearable in the awe series [3]. Here we carried out preliminary research and conducted the interviews outlined below. We explored the

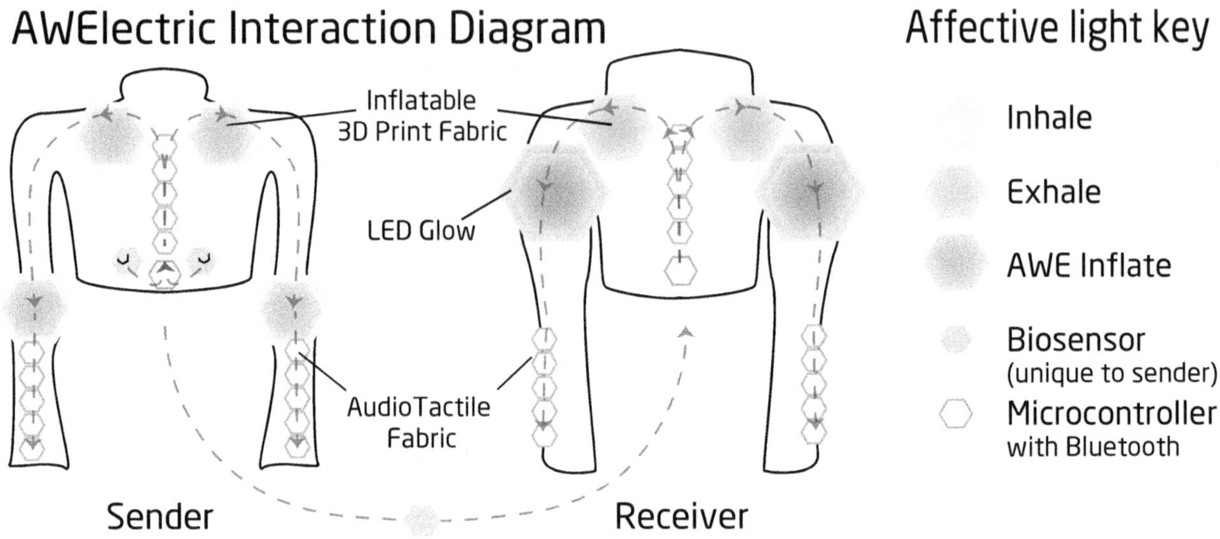

Figure 2: Overview of AWElectric interaction. ©sensoree

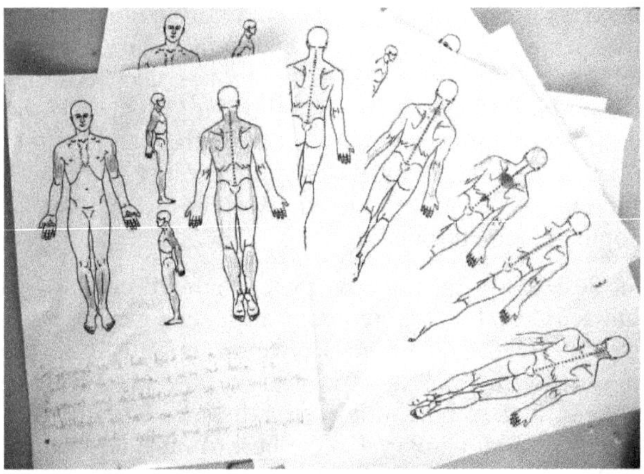

Figure 3: Body outline chart where participants drew to indicate where they feel different types of goosebumps and the impetus. ©sensoree

concepts and form factors that inform the remote design of AWElectric.

The AWElectric is a pas de deux - a dance for two - as the design works as a duet; see Fig. 1 and Fig. 2. The sender design has a series of biosensors that reads the emotional peak of awe, that subtle mix of wonder and fear. Then, bio-responsive designs of inflatable 3D printed Goosebump Fractals animate and amplify the sensation. Once detected, this sensation is sent to the receiver design via AudioTactile fabric that plays a frequency that induces the rush of goosebumps.

In designing new skin, we were inspired by the single cell that is networked to affect the whole organism. This influenced a modular and generative approach and led to the design motif of geodesic domes by Buckminster Fuller. We sought to follow the triangular building base that is the structure of the five and six sided polygons which form geodesic architecture as the parameters for the wearable components.

Method

We focused on the human-centered design approach. First we pre-screened with verbal interviews to find out how awe was experienced. From the initial responses, we focused on the reported body-centered sensations as they were psychical tangible reactions to the emotion of wonder. Narrowing the focus led to further research of noted aesthetic goosebumps and the question arose of how to separate those from the most commonly reported variety, goosebumps as a response to cold.

From the initial responses, some people reported not feeling goosebumps at all, some only from cold, some also from awe, or fear, and some had multiple impetuses. They expressed different locations for the various triggers. This made us more curious to further a location study and presented a design opportunity to not only re-pattern the sensation in the wearer but also share it from one person to another as a training tool.

For the study, we asked the randomly selected "feelers" to draw the various types of goosebumps they felt represented by different colors on the body outline chart; see Fig. 3. This is a common chart used to represent pain and alignment in the medical field. We re-purposed the chart to see if we could collect data to define emotional patterns of the body. Perhaps in the future these ideas could be used to re-pattern healthy counterparts to pain.

Results

In order to do a qualitative study, we worked with the twelve feeler interviewees, ages 19-55, that reported heightened sensations. We noted that it was common for them to show the feelings with gestures, extending 10-20 cm from their own body. We asked them to document location and impetus on the body outline chart. They were to list as many different types they felt and choose colors to illustrate. Some had up to five varieties of goosebumps or skin sensations; 10/12 noted goosebumps from cold, 7/12 aesthetic frisson, 6/12 reports were from physical contact like caressing, 4/12 from fear, and 2/12 reports of sensing paranormal activity.

The twelve felt the goosebumps on different parts of their bodies. The majority of 11/12 felt goosebumps on the outside of their lower arms. 10/12 felt goosebumps on their back, 9/12 of them on the upper back and 7/12 of them on the lower back. 2/12 felt goosebumps all over their body. The cold sensation was primarily on the outside of the arms. Fear was located behind the neck. The frisson feeling traveled up medially, from mid-back to shoulders, up the spine, then down distally to the outside of the forearms.

The colors interviewees chose to assign to different impetuses varied, but locations were similar. Half chose blue for cold. Five used the same color for all types, but with various shading. Orange was the most common color chosen by 4/12 for emotional goosebumps, and then red and purple.

These color choices and locations informed the final design of the wearable. Since the sensations were patches, the design became modular. Colors translated to fabric choices and LED lights. The goosebumps were 3D modeled in fabric and became pneumatic to amplify the sensation. The fabric was embedded with speaker actuators to trigger and send the feeling. This design process will be explained in detail in the next sections.

SENSING

Although it is not the main focus of the current paper, for this conceptual design a measurement of awe is necessary. How we intend to infer awe from physiological measurements is ongoing.

To the best of our knowledge, there is currently one sensor for accurate goosebump detection, the flexible skin piloerection monitoring sensor by Kim et al. (2014) [20] that measures the physical rise of the hair on the skin.

With our work, we were seeking to infer the sensation of awe from aggregation of measurements of other physiological inputs. Our goal was to understand how this aesthetic feeling physically manifests thus giving insight into how to prompt and reproduce the sensation in a tangible format.

In order to find physiological inputs useful to infer the sensation or effect of awe, we consulted a medical doctor whose focus is on mindfulness and stress reduction. Based on his advice and previous literature, we decided to look at heart rate variability (HRV) first to find the peak of excitement before the moment of wonder. As reported in previous work, changes in electro-dermal activity (EDA), HRV, and respiration are correlated with the feeling of goosebumps. We assume as argued before that the moment of goosebumps coincides with the feeling of awe. A combination of a peak in heart rate, a gap in respiration rate and an increase in electro-dermal activity

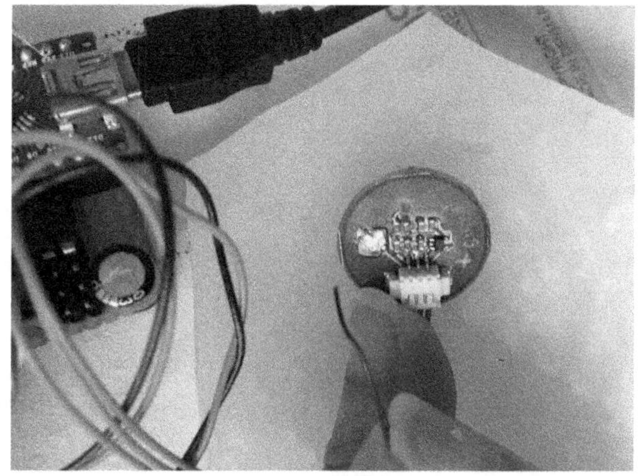

Figure 4: The EDA sensor for the AWE Goosebumps. ©sensoree

Figure 5: First version of laser cut fabric of AWE Goosebumps to contain the inflatable pockets. ©sensoree

(reduction of skin resistance) is likely to work as indicator. In future work, we will investigate how to correctly fuse this combination of EDA, respiration, and HRV data to improve awe inference and we will develop and more formally evaluate awe detection.

For the AWE Goosebumps, we designed an EDA circuit Fig. 4 and sought to add HRV and breath. Initially we chose an optical heart rate sensor[2] to detect the HRV and used small microcontroller boards (Arduino nano) connected through Bluetooth. To trigger the design on demand for testing purposes, we also added a separate control in a cell phone using the Bluetooth connection. In the next incarnation we used EDA measurements taken with a Bitalino bio sensing board[3] and a conventional commercially available chest strap for HRV measurement. As an experimental breath rate sensor, we added a body sensor made with conductive fabric. Variations in body circumference resulted in periodically stretching the fabric amounting to a small change in resistance. Seeking to find a quick peak of excitement that was lower than the peak of fear or surprise, we started testing with validated videos to

[2] Pulsesensor, http://pulsesensor.com/

[3] Bitalino, http://bitalino.com

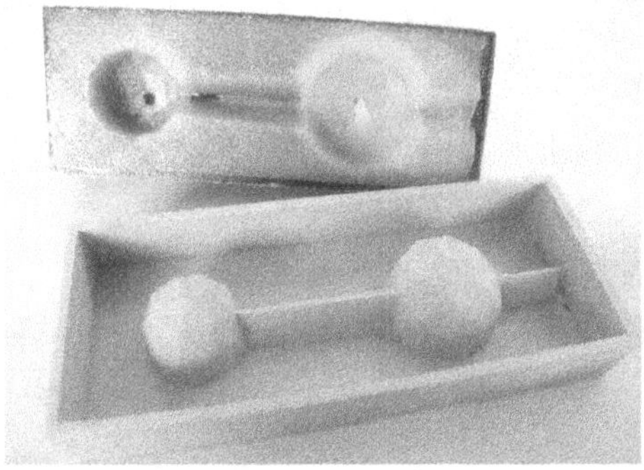

Figure 6: An iteration of the two pocket inflatable actuator. ©sensoree

Figure 7: The final actuator hexagon design. ©sensoree

define the moment of awe. This portion of research is being continued as we feel more data is needed to create a suitable algorithm for aggregation of this sensor data.

ACTUATION

Tactile interface

The skin is like a flexible touch screen that covers the entire human body. As the largest organ, this external casing is covered with nerve receptors that sense touch. The skin acts as an interface that communicates information from environmental factors in the external world and between people. It offers a way to create bonds both to the world and to other people. It even elicits extimacy on a basic level.

The tactile sense is the first sense to develop in the fetus; it creates our first responses and dialogues. In 2016, most current technologies rely on vision, screens, and sound. With the advent of touch screens, we see design opportunities to enhance the tactile experience by creating new ways to communicate through the sensation of touch. But haptic technology used in cell phones today uses the same vibration motors from pagers in the 1980s. What we are doing is instead very new: our inflatable 3D print fabric mimics the ripple of skin and the AudioTactile fabric creates a subtle, oscillating tickle to evoke the shutter and manifestation of awe.

Pneumatics

The use of pneumatics for shape-changing interfaces is currently gaining a lot of interest in the HCI community, e.g. [24, 26, 40]. In AWElectric, we continue pursuing our idea of amplifying emotions using inflatables that we have been investigating during a series of workshops and experiments [24].

To mimic the shimmer of excited skin, we chose silicone inflatables for the skin-like texture. Initially, we experimented with templates from Soft Robotics Toolkit[4]. For materials, we found Silicone Ecoflex 0030 by Smooth-on[5] to be the most skin-like and quickly switched to fabric to replace paper backing. The Soft Robots Toolkit mold design curls like an inchworm and we desired more of a bump sensation, so we designed a round pock-like pattern with two inflatable chambers, see Fig. 6. The mold was 3d printed; the inflatable pocket then cast, and after retrieval placed on a silicone encased fabric. This first model had inconsistency with the inflation of the series of inflatables. One of the two pockets would always inflate before the other due to small variances in wall thickness and distance. One way to resolve this was to have an external fabric shell to restrain the quick raising bump and force the air to distribute to other cells, see Fig. 5. This informed the idea for a casing with a fixed structure like laser cut stiff fabrics in the first version to the rigid 3D prints in the fabric of this version. The final resolved inflatable pocket was a hexagon shape with internal branched (snow flake) pattern inside to add the required stiffness, see Fig. 7. A number of these pockets were used as modular design with the 3D print fabric on top.

The air flow necessary to inflate the pockets is relatively small although the pressure is substantial (in the order of magnitude of 20 psi / 1.5 bar). Since the system has to be wearable and battery powered, the pumps and valves have to operate at a low (i.e. 5V) voltage. A miniature air pump normally used for blood pressure monitors could both generate the required pressure and airflow, while (at the same time) operate at low voltages (3–6V). For controlling the airflow, releasing the pressure and emptying the pockets, besides the pumps also valves were necessary. We eventually chose small SMC 070 series pneumatic valves which operate at 5.0V. In order to keep inflation consistent every pocket has its own individual pump and valve. Since the current consumption of both valves and pumps is substantial, an amplifier circuit (a ULN2803 Darlington array) was added to the control system (consisting of the previously described Arduino Nano microcontrollers with Bluetooth modules). The complete system can be powered by a 5V mobile charger power bank consisting of a 3.7V LiPo cell and 5V boost converter.

To accentuate the theme of extimacy, as a final step, we added LED lights to articulate the interaction of the sensors reading the body. With bio-sensors as the source, we intend to also express the biorhythms and sensation with emotional qualities of light. Based on the interviews, we chose colors for breathing rate reflected with a pulsing orange glow. When the goosebumps are detected the inflation is highlighted with a violet tremor, see Fig. 2.

[4]Soft Robotics Toolkit http://softroboticstoolkit.com

[5]Ecoflex 0030 https://www.smooth-on.com/product-line/ecoflex/

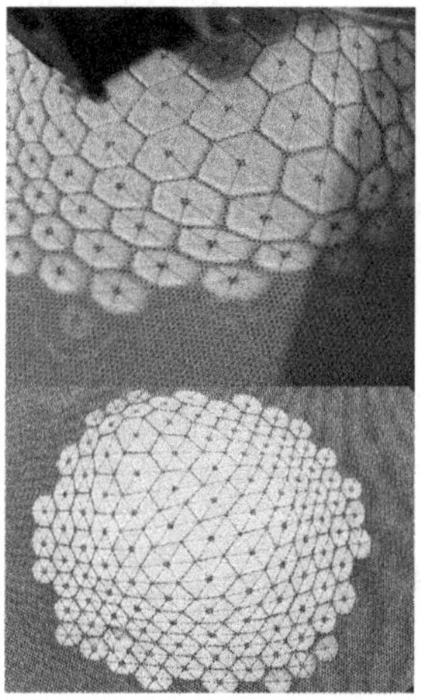

(a) 3D print fabric

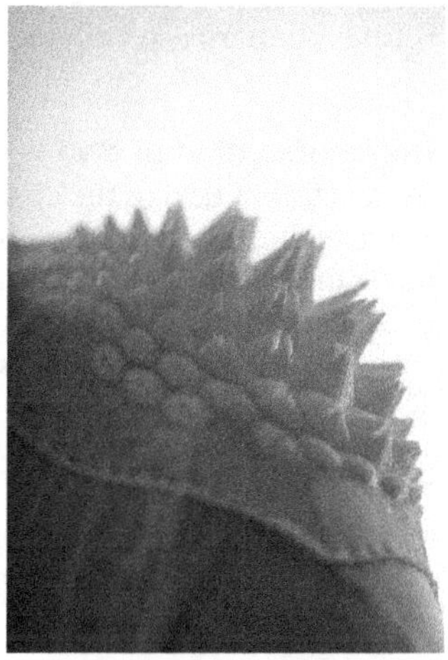

(b) Hexagon spikes

(c) Inflated Goosebump Fractals

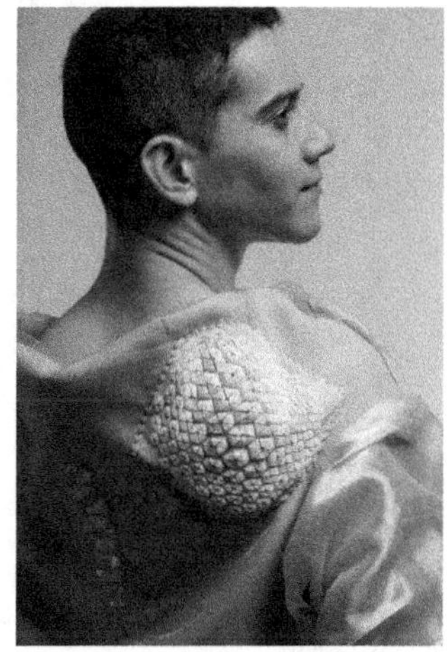

(d) Inflated Goosebump Fractals

Figure 8: The 3D printed inflatable Goosebump Fractals (photos by Elena Kulikova). ©sensoree

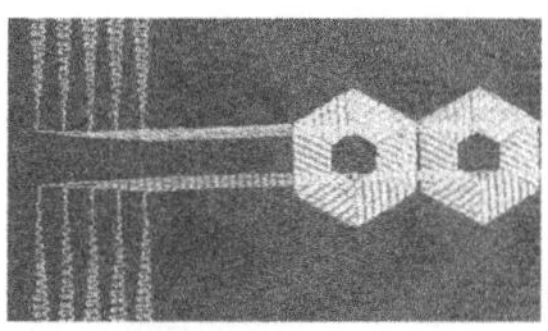

(a) Stitching through increased resistance

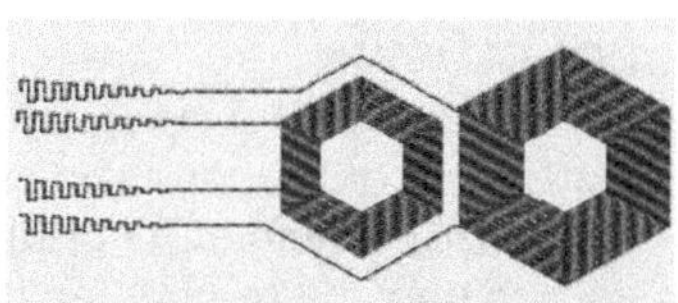

(b) Stitching around

Figure 9: Embroidered stitching design. ©sensoree

Goosebump Fractal 3D print fabric

We have developed a new technique of 3D print fabric showcased by the AWElectric design. Inspired by the human body that requires connective tissue between the bones, we have created this fabric with flexible joint material between the 3D prints. For materials, we found a study yet elastic, power mesh fabric and a rigid printing filament like polylactide (PLA) cooperated well. This dynamic juxtaposition of substrates mimics the body's articulations, movements, and expressions.

The design of the Goosebump Fractals are a digital representation of skin cells and the machine gesture of polygons, where we highlight digital architecture. The 3D print generative design follows the theme of geodesic architecture. The Goosebump Fractals are a series of hexagonal spikes designed to house a larger hexagon shaped silicone inflatable which expands when the emotional peak is elicited. The inflation opens the hexagon spikes into six sub-triangles to animate the raising of the hair follicles. Fig. 8 shows the 3D printed inflatable Goosebump Fractals.

AudioTactile fabric

Most interviewees reported frisson from listening to powerful music, but specific songs were unique to the person and often supported by a memory of a time and/or location. These insights inspired further investigation of auditory fundamentals. Infrasonic frequencies that are inaudible to human hearing but which animals hear and communicate with influenced the design. For example, the fact that elephants hear with their feet. Listening to the vibrations of the earth, they can detect the presence of other herds nearby, and the cadence communicates signals of community or potential danger. Also, the fact that many animals listen to the vibrations of the earth and can detect natural phenomenon like earthquakes. We believed that these nonverbal connections might give us insight into the human experience of awe as a subtle resonance. We therefore tested low frequencies on skin and found around 40 Hertz to tickle skin and simulate the feeling of frisson. The novelty of this design lies in the use of low frequencies to invoke aesthetic sensations.

To incorporate this interaction into a wearable, we embedded 'speakers' in fabric. Common music speakers are composed of three parts: electromagnetic coil on flexible surface, a cone, and a fixed magnet. For this wearable form factor, we embroidered the coil from conductive thread onto fabric substrate which forms a lateral hexagon replacing the cone shape. The magnet is then embedded in the center of the coil in the fabric. This shape changes the speaker into a haptic actuator and the low frequencies are expressed in reverberation like a vibration motor. The frequency is software generated offering more authority over the oscillation.

This new form factor creates AudioTactile fabric which is different from a loudspeaker. The hexagon stitching of the fabric speaker is also unique and a delightful invention. The initial construction was inspired by the Pied-de-pulse project [10] but Sensoree expanded the concept using a Litze-type wire and this new multi-triangular shape. We found that the hexagonal coils are easier to embroider than circle loops since less adjacency-hits occur. Also, we found that stitching through the coils increased their resistance (Ohms) most likely because of cutting inner wires inside the Litze, so the supply lines were embroidered around the hexagons, see Fig. 9

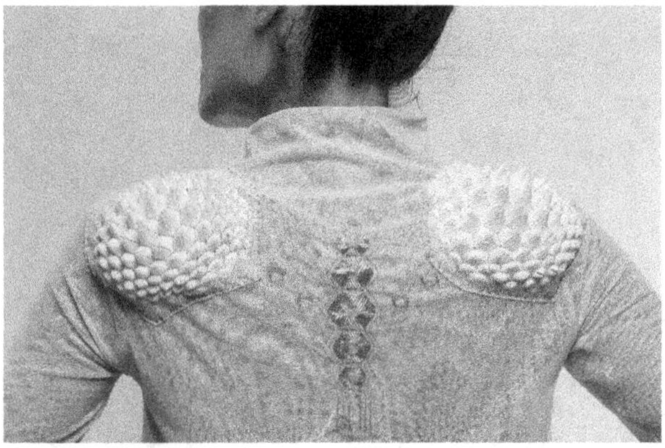

Figure 10: The embroidered speakers with the inflatable 3D printed Goosebump Fractals (photo by Elena Kulikova). ©sensoree

For the design of the coil pattern we worked with the Oogway turtle graphics library described in Feijs and Hu (2013) [9], to which a special Tajima format extension was added. To generate the low frequency pulse pattern, we found that an H-bridge circuit works best: unlike a single transistor Arduino driver, the H-bridge produces no DC offset (less heat). In the final design, the vibration sense of thrill was successful, but we found there was still some heat issues if activated continuously. More research of the form factor is planned for future iterations.

In the theme of the geodesic dome that is comprised of five and six sided polygons, the design has five hexagons in series according to the direction and position where people reported the highest sensations, see Fig. 10: starting from the kidney level or mid back, up the spine, and down the outer forearms. The embroidered speakers vibrate in this sequence initiating from medial to distal. The tickle produced amplifies the feeling in the sender and induces the shutter of piloerection in the receiver; see Fig. 8.

The AudioTactile fabric was well received by users. We saw potential to create many patterns of pulsation in the future. Like a haptic Morse code, there is opportunity to create a nuanced language.

INTERACTION

Control

The AWElectric duet has a microcontroller board (Arduino Nano) which interfaces the necessary biosensors, manages the drivers for pneumatics and AudioTactile fabric and makes the remote connection. For short range wireless communication conventional Bluetooth modules (HC-06 Bluetooth - serial module) have been added which make the connection between the two designs. Since Bluetooth cannot make point-to-point connections easily, a host system is necessary. For short-range experiments and exhibitions a host / hub system has been designed using a RaspberryPi single board computer with a standard (linux compatible) Bluetooth dongle. This host / hub function next installed on a smartphone, thus allowing the two pieces to be connected over any geographical distance (provided there is a cellular network present).

Communication of awe

In the current design the communication of awe is half-duplex. The sensing part is located in the female "sender" design and reads the emotional peak. This triggers the actuation of the air pumps to inflate the 3D print fabric modules and vibrates the embroidered speakers up the back and down to the forearms. Then, the male "receiver" design AudioTactile fabric remotely plays the goosebump frequency and inflates his 3d print fabric modules, see Fig. 2.

This interaction of awe sensing and amplification creates a feedback loop that both increases the awe-experiencing wearer's awareness and can help re-pattern the sensation for those lacking the ability. With the neuroplasticity of our brain, these sensations can be learned. The AWElectric interaction offers learned behaviors of aesthetic appreciation for both wearers.

CONCLUSION

AWElectric is a novel wearable tactile interface that enhances the feeling of awe and shares the feeling with another. The biometric inflatable 3D print fabric amplifies the feeling of goosebumps by mimicking the ripple of skin, as well as the AudioTactile fabric that creates a tickle to invoke the feeling of goosebumps.

We are inspired to create future research. Since awe is often found from a combination of factors, in the future we would like to find the emotional peaks between a combination of sensors and events to understand more subtly how this aesthetic feeling physically manifests, and then work to reproduce the sensation. We would then like to further develop and validate our awe sensing algorithm. Finally, we plan to carry out more extensive user studies into the remote communication of awe with our design. We aim to investigate how we can instigate health and wonder into life by means of a shared human connection with the amplification of awe.

ACKNOWLEDGMENTS

Thank you to Vanessa Evers, Angelika Mader and the University of Twente for support of initial research of the AWE Goosebumps and studies. Creative technology students; Fabienne Heijne, Artur Shkribliak, and Szandra Iván. Special thank yous to Andrea Minuto, Thomas Beelen, Eugénie Lacombe, and Isa Pfab. We would like to extend our gratitude to the MU Foundation, Eindhoven, NL, (http://www.mu.nl) for the grant to continue research for the remote design Body Elektrische. This grant was paired with the Designed Intelligence team at TU Eindhoven consisting of Loe Feijs, Frank Delbressine, and Bin Yu (AudioTactile fabric). Extended technical development of AWElectric came from the University of Twente Creative Technology team David Goedicke (sound), and Emiel Harmsen (lighting). Furthermore, gratitude to Elena Mitro (Goosebump Fractal 3D modeling) and Colin Willson (3D print technician).

REFERENCES

1. 2007. Philips Bubelle Skin Dress Design Probes. https://www.90yearsofdesign.philips.com/article/67. (2007). Accessed: 2016-07-30.
2. 2010. Ger Mood Sweater. http://sensoree.com/moodsweater. (2010). Accessed: 2016-07-29.
3. 2015. AWE Goosebumps. http://sensoree.com/artifacts/awe-goosebumps. (2015). Accessed: 2016-11-15.
4. J. N. Bailenson, N. Yee, S. Brave, D. Merget, and D. Koslow. 2007. Virtual interpersonal touch: expressing and recognizing emotions through haptic devices. *Human Computer Interaction* 22 (2007), 325–353.
5. M. Benedek and C. Kaernbach. 2011. Physiological correlates and emotional specificity of human piloerection. *Biological Psychology* 86 (2011), 320–329. Issue 3.
6. M. Benedek, B. Wilfling, R. Lukas-Wolfbauer, B. H. Katzur, and C. Kaernbach. 2010. Objective and continuous measurement of piloerection. *Psychophysiology* 47 (2010), 989–993.
7. M. C. Colver and A. El-Alayli. 2016. Getting aesthetic chills from music: The connection between openness to experience and frisson. *Psychology of Music* 44, 3 (2016), 413–427.
8. D. G. Craig. 2005. An exploratory study of physiological changes during "chills" induced by music. *Musicae Scientiae* 9, 2 (2005), 273–287.
9. L. M. G. Feijs and J. Hu. 2013. Turtles for tessellations. In *Proceedings of Bridges 2013 : Mathematics, Music, Art, Architecture, Culture*. 241–248.
10. L. M. G. Feijs and M. Toeters. 2016. Pied de pulse: packing embroidered circles and coil actuators in pied de poule (houndstooth). In *Proceedings of Bridges 2016 : Mathematics, Music, Art, Architecture, Culture*. 415–418.
11. A. Goldstein. 1980. Thrills in response to music and other stimuli. *Physiological Psychology* 8, 1 (1980), 126–129.
12. D. Gooch and L. Watts. 2010. Communicating social presence through thermal hugs. In *Proceedings of First Workshop on Social Interaction in Spatially Separated Environments (SISSI2010)*. 11–19.
13. D. Gooch and L. Watts. 2012. Yourgloves, hothands and hotmits: devices to hold hands at a distance. In *Proceedings of the 25th Annual ACM Symposium on User Interface Software and Technology UIST '12*. 157–166.
14. A. Haans and W. A. IJsselsteijn. 2006. Mediated social touch: a review of current research and future directions. *Virtual Reality* 9 (2006), 149–159.
15. J. Healey. 2015. Physiological Sensing of Emotion. In *Oxford Handbook of Affective Computing*, R. A. Calvo, S. K. D'Mello, J. Gratch, and A. Kappas (Eds.). Oxford University Press, Oxford.
16. Konečni V. J. 2005. The aesthetic trinity: awe, being moved, thrills. *Bulletin of Psychology and the Arts* 5 (2005), 27–44. Issue 2.
17. Smith J. and K. MacLean. 2007. Communicating emotion through a haptic link: Design space and methodology. *International Journal of Human-Computer Studies* 65 (2007), 376–387.
18. W. Jänig. 2006. *The integrative action of the autonomic nervous system*. Cambridge University Press, Cambridge.
19. D. Keltner and J. Haidt. 2003. Approaching awe, a moral, spiritual, and aesthetic emotion. *Cognition and Emotion* 17, 2 (2003), 297–314.
20. J. Kim, D. G. Seo, and Y.-H. Cho. 2014. A flexible skin piloerection monitoring sensor. *Applied Physics Letters* 104 (2014), 253502.
21. K. H. Kim, S. W. Bang, and S. R. Kim. 2004. Emotion recognition system using short-term monitoring of physiological signals. *Medical & Biological Engineering & Computing* 42 (2004), 419–427.
22. Y.-P. Lin, C.-H. Wang, T.-P. Jung, T.-L. Wu, S.-K. Jeng, J.-R. Duann, and J.-H. Chen. 2010. EEG-based emotion recognition in music listening. *IEEE Transactions on Biomedical Engineering* 57, 7 (2010), 1798–1806.
23. F. F. Mueller, F. Vetere, M. R. Gibbs, J. Kjeldskov, S. Pedell, and S. Howard. 2005. Hug over a distance. In *Extended Abstracts CHI'05*. 1673–1676.
24. K. Neidlinger and E. Dertien. 2015. Interactive inflatables: amplifying human behaviors. In *Proceedings of the 9th International Conference on Tangible, Embedded, and Embodied Interaction (TEI'15)*. 489–491.
25. Y. W. Park, S. Hwang, and T. J Nam. 2011. Poke: emotional touch delivery through an inflatable surface over interpersonal mobile communications. In *Proceedings of the 24th Annual ACM Symposium on User Interface Software and Technology UIST '11*. 61–62.
26. L. Perovich, P. Mothersill, and J. B. Farah. 2014. Awakened Apparel: Embedded Soft Actuators for Expressive Fashion and Functional Garments. In *Proceedings of the 8th International Conference on Tangible, Embedded, and Embodied Interaction (TEI'14)*. 77–80.
27. R. W. Picard and J. Healey. 1997. Affective wearables. *Personal Technologies* 1, 4 (1997), 231–240.
28. R. W Picard and J. Scheirer. 2001. The galvactivator: A glove that senses and communicates skin conductivity. In *Proceedings of the 9th International Conference on HCI*. 1538–1542.
29. P. K. Piff, P. Dietze, M. Feinberg, D. M. Stancato, and D. Keltner. 2015. Awe, the small self, and prosocial behavior. *Journal of Personality and Social Psychology* 108 (2015), 883–899. Issue 6.

30. H. P. Profita, A. Roseway, and M. Czerwinski. 2015. Lightwear: an exploration in wearable light therapy. In *Proceedings of the 9th International Conference on Tangible, Embedded, and Embodied Interaction (TEI'15)*. 321–328.
31. N. Ranasinghe, K. Karunanayaka, A. D. Cheok, O. N. N. Fernando, H. Nii, and P. Gopalakrishnakone. 2011. Digital taste and smell communication. In *Proceedings of the 6th International Conference on Body Area Networks*. 78–84.
32. M. Rudd, K. D. Vohs, and J. Aaker. 2012. Awe expands people's perception of time, alters decision making, and enhances well-being. *Psychological Science* 23 (2012), 1130–1136. Issue 10.
33. E. Saadatian, H. Samani, R. Parsani, A. V. Pandey, J. Li, L. Tejada, A. D. Cheok, and R. Nakatsu. 2014. Mediating intimacy in long-distance relationships using kiss messaging. *International Journal of Human-Computer Studies* 72 (2014), 736–746. Issue 10.
34. D. R. Schurtz, S. Blincoe, R. H. Smith, C. A. J. Powell, D. J. Y. Combs, and S. H. Kim. 2012. Exploring the social aspects of goose bumps and their role in awe and envy. *Motivation and Emotion* 36 (2012), 205–217.
35. J. A. Sloboda. 1991. Music structure and emotional response: Some empirical findings. *Psychology of Music* 19 (1991), 110–120.
36. J. E. Stellar, N. John-Henderson, C. L. Anderson, A. M. Gordon, G. D. McNeil, and D. Keltner. 2015. Positive affect and markers of inflammation: discrete positive emotions predict lower levels of inflammatory cytokines. *Emotion* 15 (2015), 129–133. Issue 2.
37. J. K. S. Teh, A. D. Cheok, R. L. Peiris, Y. Choi, V. Thuong, and S. Lai. 2008. Huggy pajama: a mobile parent and child hugging communication system. In *Proceedings of the 7th International Conference on Interaction Design and Children (IDC '08)*. 250–257.
38. J. B. F. Van Erp and A. Toet. 2015. Social touch in human-computer interaction. *Frontiers in Digital Humanities* 2 (2015), 14. Issue 2.
39. M. A. Williams, A. Roseway, C. O'Dowd, M. Czerwinski, and M. R. Morris. 2015. SWARM: An actuated wearable for mediating affect. In *Proceedings of the 9th International Conference on Tangible, Embedded, and Embodied Interaction (TEI'15)*. 293–300.
40. L. Yao, R. Niiyama, J. Ou, S. Follmer, S. Della, and H. Ishii. 2013. PneUI: pneumatically actuated soft composite materials for shape changing interfaces. In *Proceedings of the 26th annual ACM symposium on User interface software and technology (UIST'13)*. 13–22.

Popfab: A Case for Portable Digital Fabrication

Nadya Peek
MIT Center for Bits and Atoms
peek@mit.edu

Ilan Moyer
Shaper Tools Inc.
ilan@shapertools.com

ABSTRACT

We present a case study of Popfab, a portable multi-purpose digital fabrication tool. It is uses interchangeable heads (3D printer, CNC mill, and CNC knife) on a general-purpose motion platform that folds into a briefcase. Popfab contributed to the discussion of the future of digital fabrication tools by demonstrating the feasibility of both portability and both additive and subtractive manufacturing on a single platform. Portability is not yet a widely considered option for digital fabrication tools, but with Popfab we demonstrate that general site-specific personal fabrication is possible.

ACM Classification Keywords

J.6.b Computer-aided manufacturing (CAM): Computer-Aided Engineering; H.5.2.j Prototyping: User Interfaces; H.5.2.o User-centered Design: User Interfaces

Author Keywords

Digital fabrication; Machine Building; CNC; CAD/CAM; Portability; Prototyping; 3D printing

INTRODUCTION

Digital fabrication tools are increasingly of interest to interaction researchers [4]. Digital fabrication enables the production of unique parts with changes only in digital instructions. Therefore, the learning curve for digital fabrication is more similar to that of a computer program than the mastering of a manual skill, improving the accessibility of precision fabrication.

However, most digital fabrication tools are made either as large machine-shop tools or tabletop devices. To fabricate things with these machines users therefore have to travel to where the machine is. Computers also used to be large—even room-sized. But introducing portability to computer designs in the form of desktop computers, laptops, and later smartphones has allowed computation to be employed in many diverse contexts for many unanticipated applications. Can portability make a similar difference in digital fabrication?

Portability in digital fabrication tools could allow for site-specific fabrication using local materials. Jacobs and Zoran for example transported digital fabrication tools to collaborate with traditional ostrich eggshell jewelry craft in a hunter-gatherer community [1], introducing a new hybrid practice. Quitmeyer and Perner-Wilson developed a fully wearable studio practice for digital crafting in harsh hike-to environments, but the studio does not yet include digital fabrication tools [8]. As fab-in-the-wild efforts increase, portable tools become more relevant.

Figure 1. Popfab, a portable multi-purpose digital fabrication tool. Here it is configured with a 3D printing head for fused deposition modelling.

Portability could also introduce more flexibility in use of space. If a school for example did not have a room to allocate to a makerspace, portable digital fabrication tools could provide the functionality of makerspace tools without dedicated space. Portable tools could also be used in temporary locations, such as outdoors when weather permits, or at events such as hackathons, or as part of disaster relief efforts.

To explore the possibilities of portability in digital fabrication, we produced a portable and multi-purpose digital fabrication machine tool, Popfab, shown printing outdoors in Figure 1. Popfab provides a functional demonstration of portable additive and subtractive fabrication.

TEI '17, March 20 - 23, 2017, Yokohama, Japan

ISBN 978-1-4503-4676-4/17/03. . . $15.00

DOI: http://dx.doi.org/10.1145/3024969.3025009

RELATED WORK

Hand tools such as a drill, router, jigsaw, or belt sander are categorically portable. However, they lack the precision of computer numerical control (CNC), and require mastery of craft in their use. Schoop et al. augment hand tools with user feedback [10], but the user still must operate the tool and could make mistakes. CNC tools introduce autonomous precision, but also a work-envelope. The bed size of these tools becomes a crucial specification—it determines the size of the parts that can be fabricated.

The Shopbot Tools *Handibot* gets around the work envelope limitation by having end mill stick out of the machine tool [13]. The *Handibot* can be placed on any surface to mill into it. The *FreeD* and the *Shaper Origin* both avoid work envelope limitations by pairing local computer-controlled precision with less precise, global, hand-held motion [18, 9]. These examples are all subtractive machine tools, whereas Popfab also has other heads, including additive.

Weichel et al. and Teibrich et al. demonstrate milling and 3d printer combination machines [16, 12], but their machines do not easily accommodate other end effectors.

Site-specific production also includes measurement and design phases. Weichel et al. demonstrate tools that make the transfer of dimensions more fluid [15]. Lau et al. demonstrate a tool that helps users design context-specifically [2]. Willis et al. demonstrate a series of fabrication tools which use real-time input as their designs [17]. Popfab is only portable at the fabrication stage, but does not address in-context or portable design.

WALK-THROUGH

We present Popfab, a portable, multi-purpose digital fabrication tool that fits in a briefcase. How might someone use this tool, and how does this differ from how digital fabrication tools are currently used?

Imagine being confronted with a problem for which a technical solution could be rapidly prototyped. As an example, imagine a simple part breaking for which a replacement could be 3D printed. Popfab has a 3D printing 'head', a milling head, and a spring-loaded holder that can fit a blade or pen. The user who wishes to 3D print a replacement part opens the Popfab briefcase and pops up the z-axis, fixing it into its popped-up position with two thumbscrews. The user selects the 3D printing head and attaches it to the z-axis via its kinematic mount. The mount is preloaded with another single thumbscrew. The machine is powered through wall power and controlled through USB. The user connects the machine to a laptop and starts the machine's control software. After zeroing the 3D printing head on machine's bed[1], Popfab is ready to used as a regular 3D printer. The pop-up and zeroing procedure takes a few minutes.

Imagine if instead a user would like to rapidly prototype a circuit board. Popfab's Z-axis is popped up in a similar fashion,

Figure 2. The different Popfab end effectors (or 'heads') are attached after the machine is popped up. Without a head attached the z-axis can fold down into the rest of the suitcase.

Figure 3. A three-groove kinematic coupling allows for repeatable repositioning of the heads with a single thumbscrew for preload.

but now the user instead selects the milling head, attaching it through the kinematic mount. After zeroing the head Popfab is ready to be used as a milling machine subtractively removing copper from a circuit board blank.

IMPLEMENTATION

The mechanical architecture of Popfab represents a compromise aimed at optimizing both support for multiple fabrication methods and ease of setup, under the constraint of portability. The portability of Popfab is mostly achieved by folding the machine, but also by reducing the available work envelope. The first Popfab machine was made in 2012, at the time its work envelope was not dissimilar to popular consumer 3D printers or mini-mills with a work volume of $10\times10\times20$ cm.

Our approach is a XY stage built into the base of a briefcase, with a folding Z axis supporting a cantilevered arm on which the toolhead is mounted. This configuration minimizes the complexity of the folding mechanism by limiting it to one axis. We anticipated that attempting to cantilever a two-axis stage as stiffly and repeatably would be significantly more

[1] The zeroing operation is the same for all heads and entails the user moving the head down until it is physically touching the bed, and marking this as the zero position. This process is the same for commercial (non-portable) CNC tools.

Figure 4. A swivel knife head, a spindle head, and an FDM 3D printing head.

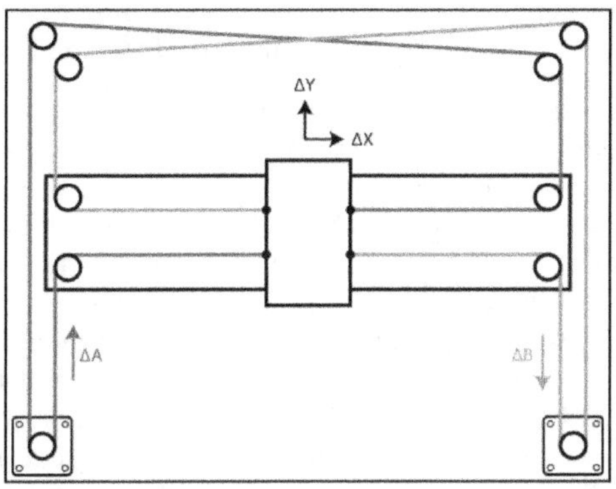

Figure 5. CoreXY reference mechanism used with permission from [5]. To move the center stage in X **and** Y**, the motors move the belts in directions** A **(red) and** B **(blue). The equations of motion are** $\Delta X = \frac{1}{2}(\Delta A + \Delta B)$, $\Delta Y = \frac{1}{2}(\Delta A - \Delta B)$, $\Delta A = \Delta X + \Delta Y$, $\Delta B = \Delta X - \Delta Y$.

difficult. Furthermore, setting up a two-axis folding stage would add to the users' setup time and introduce opportunities for inconsistent mechanical alignment after each setup.

For the XY stage we chose to use a parallel kinematic stage so that we could avoid the extra moving mass required when stacking the X stage on top of the Y serially [14]. Specifically, we chose *CoreXY* [5], a variation on H-bot kinematics with and additional crossing of the timing belt (see Figure 5). CoreXY offers high spatial efficiency (the ratio of work envelope to mechanism envelope), low inertia (well suited to 3D printing), and sufficient stiffness for low-force machining.

With this overall architecture the folded Z tower nests into the XY stage (see Figures 2 and 6), and the build surface is moving rather than the head. Most 3D printers avoid moving the print in XY because it can cause tall prints to shake under their own mass during rapid accelerations, and also because the inertia of the moving stage changes throughout the print. However, we decided this trade-off was acceptable because the limited height travel on the machine precludes printing very tall parts, and this is not a concern when milling. CoreXY uses a timing belt for XY, which is good for high-speed motion in 3D printing, but not as good for high-force applications such as milling metal. Because our spindle is intended for milling circuit boards, it does not encounter cutting forces high enough to make this a concern.

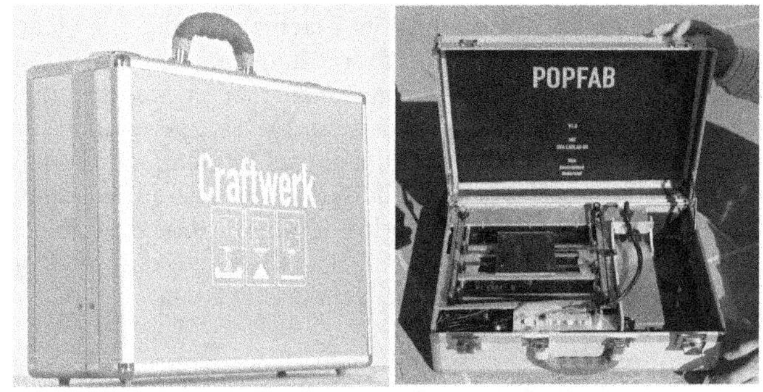

Figure 6. Popfab's z-axis folds down to fit into a briefcase.

Toolheads are easily interchangeable due to the use of a ball-and-groove kinematic mount (see Figure 3 for the coupling and Figure 4 for the different tool heads). These interfaces are typically found in precision machine design because of their extremely good positioning repeatability [11]. For Popfab though their key attribute is high stiffness with a single source of preload—in our case provided by an easy-to-use thumb knob. This makes changing toolheads simple and tool-less. New toolheads can easily be added.

For Popfab, we have created a 3D print head, a spindle head, a swivel knife head, and a plotter head. We also have an experimental microscope head (for gigapan), and a pipetting head. Creating heads requires the 3-groove pattern for mounting, and integration into the electronics and controls.

For the control electronics and power, we used an off-the-shelf 3D printer board *Printrboard Rev C* from Printrbot with 4 stepper motor controllers, running *Marlin* firmware to interpret G-code, and a 200W power supply [6, 3]. For streaming the G-code from the control computer, we used *Pronterface* [7]. At the time of design, this combination was an affordable off-the-shelf solution for G-code running 3D printers. For our specific implementation, we contributed parallel kinematics code to the open-source Marlin codebase. However, this electronics and software combination was limited in its usability for different processes such as milling, gigapan, or pipetting. We for example used the same controller component for the spindle motor as for the heating element of the 3d print head. Issues that arose with this approach are further discussed in the limitations section.

Alongside the briefcase machine, we have a auxiliary case that contains the heads, power supply, end mills, and knives. We attempted to make Popfab as self-contained as possible, but decided on an accessories bag for weight distribution and ease of carrying. We also used the auxiliary case to store some materials including vinyl, copper-clad boards, and PLA filament, as well as a portable soldering iron and a supply of surface-mount electronic components.

USAGE

Popfab is meant to be a portable alternative to a digital fabrication workshop such as a makerspace. As far as we know, Popfab is the only 3D printer that can qualify as a 'personal item such as a laptop or briefcase' for airplane carry-on, and it also happens to be a milling machine. It has traveled to 3 different continents as carry on luggage[2]. Its small form factor and high production value have made it well suited for exhibitions and demonstrations, and it has spent much time working as a demonstration of digital fabrication. We have also used Popfab to mill circuit boards for last-minute demos while travelling, or to 3D print hooks we thought could be useful in the cafe we were in. However, we only had one Popfab, and most of its usage remains anecdotal.

Limitations

The size of objects produced with Popfab is limited by what material can be placed into the machine's work envelope. Popfab can be used to fabricate on-site, but can only make things smaller than itself.

Popfab is not battery powered, which limits its portability. Popfab runs on 12-24V DC, and we estimate Popfab could use up to 80W during operation, making it possible to run on e.g. a car battery. However, with a redesign of the electronics for low-power, these numbers could be significantly improved.

A less obvious limitation stems from multi-head control. Making new heads for Popfab such as a laser diode for laser cutting is mechanically trivial. However, for the electronics and control software we used tools originally designed for 3D printers. The hardware expected a certain flavor of G-code that could be generated by some .stl slicers typical of 3D printing, but not e.g. by off-the-shelf toolpath planners for CNC mills. We produced the appropriate G-codes for milling by writing custom post-processors for milling instructions, and wrote other custom G-code translators to be able to use e.g. the plunger on the pipetter. However this G-code hacking was a usability limitation that prevented other users from easily using Popfab for general fabrication besides 3D printing. A more flexible electronic control and software solution would be better for this kind of multi-process tool.

DISCUSSION

We developed Popfab to explore portability for digital fabrication—what is the laptop of digital fabrication and how is it useful? In practice, we predominantly used Popfab to demonstrate digital fabrication. But Popfab did served as as a discussion tool for what the future of digital fabrication could look like— a functioning machine (albeit with usability kinks) as a prop with which to imagine a future where people can carry personal digital fabrication tools around with them.

In the near future, there are clear wins for portability with digital fabrication such as site-specific or temporary location fabrication and flexible use of space (e.g. classroom). Portability entails ease of transport, but crucially also ease of set up. If these kinds of tools were to exist, digital fabrication could be employed more flexibly both in new places, but also at unusual times or on-the-go. Materials that might be difficult to remove from a site can still be used with digital fabrication tools if the tools are brought there.

[2]Surprisingly, although it has been on more than 20 flights, airport security only asked to open the Popfab briefcase once—for most airports apparently a pop-up digital fabrication machine does not look suspicious in X-ray at all.

One of the challenges of portability in digital fabrication is that today's digital fabrication tools are not entirely self-sufficient. A host of secondary hand tools and materials are necessary to produce finished objects. For Popfab, we started accumulating these accessories in an ever-growing side case. 3D printed parts for example need their support materials removed, CNC milled parts need their last attachment tabs to be filed off. Digital fabrication needing a context of tools dovetails into Quitmeyer and Perner-Wilson's portable studio practice. Another consideration is the availability of raw materials such as thermoplastic and UV cure resins for 3D printing, cardboard and polymers for laser cutting, copper-clad boards for PCB fabrication, etc. Portable and widely available digital fabrication machines would mean that demand for auxiliary tools and feedstock would go up. Perhaps this is a future where corner stores sell materials and tools instead of finished products.

In the long term, we hope that portable digital fabrication tools change not only how we currently use digital fabrication tools, but how people interact with objects and products more generally. Digital fabrication tools might become part of a point-of-sale at stores and markets, producing parts on demand. Where coffeeshops now offer wifi and electricity for laptop wielding patrons, perhaps later they will offer fabrication space and feedstock. Portable personal fabrication tools could greatly change how we currently deal with supply chains and inventory. We think that this has great opportunity for enabling a future where personal fabrication plays a more pervasive role in our lives.

CONCLUSION

We introduced Popfab, a multi-purpose machine tool. One of its key features is portability—it fits the functionality of a 3D printer, CNC mill, CNC knife, and other heads into a single briefcase by using a pop-up machine platform. Its portability enabled quick-start on-site digital fabrication. Popfab's portability did not come at the expense of its precision or utility as a machine tool. Popfab contributes to a discussion of the future of digital fabrication machines by demonstrating the feasibility of portability. It also demonstrates versatility by using multiple heads.

In the future, we hope that the benefits of portability (including site-specific fabrication and flexible workspace) are included in many more digital fabrication systems. We also hope that lessons learned about versatility and extensibility of these tools' control systems are incorporated into future implementations.

ACKNOWLEDGMENTS

The authors would like to thank Erik de Bruijn and others at Ultimaker, David Wallace of MIT Cadlab, and Neil Gershenfeld of the MIT Center for Bits and Atoms.

REFERENCES

1. Jennifer Jacobs and Amit Zoran. 2015. Hybrid Practice in the Kalahari: Design Collaboration through Digital Tools and Hunter-Gatherer Craft. In *Proceedings of the 33rd Annual ACM Conference on Human Factors in Computing Systems*. ACM, 619–628.

2. Manfred Lau, Greg Saul, Jun Mitani, and Takeo Igarashi. 2010. Modeling-in-context: User Design of Complementary Objects with a Single Photo. In *Proceedings of the Seventh Sketch-Based Interfaces and Modeling Symposium (SBIM '10)*. Eurographics Association, Aire-la-Ville, Switzerland, Switzerland, 17–24. http://dl.acm.org/citation.cfm?id=1923363.1923367

3. Marlin. 2016. Marlin Firmware. http://www.marlinfw.org/. (2016). accessed 2016-08-09.

4. David Mellis, Sean Follmer, Björn Hartmann, Leah Buechley, and Mark D. Gross. 2013. FAB at CHI: Digital Fabrication Tools, Design, and Community. In *CHI '13 Extended Abstracts on Human Factors in Computing Systems (CHI EA '13)*. ACM, New York, NY, USA, 3307–3310. DOI: http://dx.doi.org/10.1145/2468356.2479673

5. Ilan Moyer. 2012. Core XY. http://corexy.com/. (2012). accessed 2016-01-09.

6. Printrbot. 2016. Printrboard Rev. F6. https://printrbot.com/shop/printrboard-rev-f6. (2016). accessed 2016-08-03.

7. Pronterface. 2016. Printrun. http://www.pronterface.com/. (2016). accessed 2016-08-03.

8. Andrew Quitmeyer and Hannah Perner-Wilson. 2015. Wearable studio practice: design considerations for digital crafting in harsh environments. In *Adjunct Proceedings of the 2015 ACM International Joint Conference on Pervasive and Ubiquitous Computing and Proceedings of the 2015 ACM International Symposium on Wearable Computers*. ACM, 1285–1293.

9. Alec Rivers, Ilan E. Moyer, and Frédo Durand. 2012. Position-correcting Tools for 2D Digital Fabrication. *ACM Trans. Graph.* 31, 4, Article 88 (July 2012), 7 pages. DOI:http://dx.doi.org/10.1145/2185520.2185584

10. Eldon Schoop, Michelle Nguyen, Daniel Lim, Valkyrie Savage, Sean Follmer, and Björn Hartmann. 2016. Drill Sergeant: Supporting Physical Construction Projects through an Ecosystem of Augmented Tools. In *Proceedings of the 2016 CHI Conference Extended Abstracts on Human Factors in Computing Systems*. ACM, 1607–1614.

11. Alexander H. Slocum. 1992. Design of three-groove kinematic couplings. *Precision Engineering* 14, 2 (1992), 67 – 76. DOI: http://dx.doi.org/10.1016/0141-6359(92)90051-W

12. Alexander Teibrich, Stefanie Mueller, François Guimbretière, Robert Kovacs, Stefan Neubert, and Patrick Baudisch. 2015. Patching Physical Objects. In *Proceedings of the 28th Annual ACM Symposium on User Interface Software & Technology*. ACM, 83–91.

13. Shopbot Tools. 2014. Handibot Kickstarter Page. https://www.kickstarter.com/projects/1320575205/handibottm-a-smart-digital-power-tool. (2014). accessed 2016-07-09.

14. Lung-Wen Tsai. 1999. *Robot analysis: the mechanics of serial and parallel manipulators*. John Wiley & Sons.

15. Christian Weichel, Jason Alexander, Abhijit Karnik, and Hans Gellersen. 2015a. SPATA: Spatio-Tangible Tools for Fabrication-Aware Design. In *Proceedings of the Ninth International Conference on Tangible, Embedded, and Embodied Interaction (TEI '15)*. ACM, New York, NY, USA, 189–196. DOI: http://dx.doi.org/10.1145/2677199.2680576

16. Christian Weichel, John Hardy, Jason Alexander, and Hans Gellersen. 2015b. ReForm: Integrating Physical and Digital Design Through Bidirectional Fabrication. In *Proceedings of the 28th Annual ACM Symposium on User Interface Software & Technology (UIST '15)*. ACM, New York, NY, USA, 93–102. DOI: http://dx.doi.org/10.1145/2807442.2807451

17. Karl D.D. Willis, Cheng Xu, Kuan-Ju Wu, Golan Levin, and Mark D. Gross. 2011. Interactive Fabrication: New Interfaces for Digital Fabrication. In *Proceedings of the Fifth International Conference on Tangible, Embedded, and Embodied Interaction (TEI '11)*. ACM, New York, NY, USA, 69–72. DOI: http://dx.doi.org/10.1145/1935701.1935716

18. Amit Zoran and Joseph A. Paradiso. 2013. FreeD: A Freehand Digital Sculpting Tool. In *Proceedings of the SIGCHI Conference on Human Factors in Computing Systems (CHI '13)*. ACM, New York, NY, USA, 2613–2616. DOI: http://dx.doi.org/10.1145/2470654.2481361

Combining Practices in Craft and Design

Clement Zheng
Georgia Institute of Technology
& National University of Singapore
clement.zheng@gatech.edu

Michael Nitsche
Georgia Institute of Technology
Atlanta, GA
michael.nitsche@gatech.edu

ABSTRACT
Combining practices of craft and tangible interaction design opens up new opportunities for both domains. But structuring cross-domain collaboration between the two poses challenges. How can we set up a crafter-designer collaboration to utilize the different fields of expertise and include separate practices? We address this question through a co-design research approach that stands in context with existing work discussed. We propose a design perspective that builds on an initial distinction between the collaborators, repositions the construction of the brief, and culminates into a collaboration through the shared object. This perspective is described in a collaboration between an interaction designer and a ceramic artist. The resulting collaboration model is presented through this co-design driven collaborative case study in pottery and interaction design that exemplifies collaborative practices to improve tangible designs.

AUTHOR KEYWORDS
Craft; physical computing; design collaboration.

ACM Classification Keywords
H.5.2. [Information Interfaces]: User Interfaces—input devices and strategies; interaction styles; user-centered design.

INTRODUCTION
Craft theory and craft practices have always been a component of tangible interface construction but increasingly have become important reference points for interaction design at large. New technologies allow the inclusion of physical making practices in digital prototyping and the socio-technological history of craft offers a rich context for interaction design. It emphasizes phenomenological approaches in the social-material context of hybrid making. This is reflected in many exemplary projects that either reference craft practices [36] or present digital interventions on existing crafts [29]. Yet, the challenge remains to balance this meeting of craft and design practices in a productive way. As successful as many of the craft-related projects are, they largely present unique case studies that do not offer a model for structuring this domain encounter on a larger scale. A critical structure is needed to support a balanced practical approach. An overbearing of new technology that merely utilizes craft is as flawed an approach as a romanticized revivalist perception of craft practices to set a new agenda for interaction design. How can we structure a collaboration of interaction design and craft in the most successful and equally balanced way?

TEI '17, March 20-23, 2017, Yokohama, Japan
 ISBN 978-1-4503-4676-4/17/03 $15.00
DOI: http://dx.doi.org/10.1145/3024969.3024973

To answer this question, this paper applies an action research methodology to tangible interface design starting from a critical review, to practical exploration, to a case study example for the development of a TEI device. This paper suggests a structured collaborative practice that ultimately emphasizes the shared object in a new way.

BACKGROUND

Craft as Reference in Interaction Design
Craft theory and craft practices have become important reference points that integrate physical making practices in digital prototyping. At that same time, the socio-technological history of craft offers a rich context for interaction design that emphasizes phenomenological approaches. Numerous tangible interaction projects either reference craft practices or present digital interventions on existing crafts.

Related Work
There are various approaches that relate craft to interaction design. For the purposes of this argument, we can divide them into three main approaches.

Technological/artistic approaches target novel combinations of crafting and digital interaction to either lead to new technological combinations or an individual project that exemplifies a certain approach through its unique expression. Projects often combine craft practices such as fiber arts or paper craft with novel materials such as conductive thread and/or ink and can lead to new technologies like the Lilypad [7] or hybrid forms such as ePaper [16]. Here, craft and prototyping techniques are combined to explore a richer technological vocabulary for designers and practitioners. They present a blended practice that combines traditional craft methods with novel materials and tools [6]. Initial frameworks are emerging – set within the frame of such a technological perspective (e.g. [37] for paper circuits, [4] for soft circuits). But the area is dominated by a plethora of individual projects that combine craft and digital components to explore individual forms of expression. Many of these examples can be found in the demo and art showcases of conferences such as CHI, TEI, or UIST.

Ethnographic/educational approaches build on the social context of craft to explore novel practices. Scholarly work in this category looks at creative practices to inform educational and design approaches. For example, Buechley and Perner-Wilson observed 40 crafters to learn from them and inform their designs for a hybrid craft [6]. Goodman and Rosner build on their ethnographic work with gardeners and knitters to develop information technology [13]. Peppler investigates the overlap of crafting and digital media to inform novel educational approaches [24]. These works are valuable explorations of how to contextualize interaction design in existing craft traditions and practices. They probe the context of craft practices for new interaction design approaches. However, at the same time, craft itself had to adjust to new digital production techniques and this complicates such a positioning.

Craft-based approaches consist of modifications to existing crafting practices. They are often transformative but focus less on the development of new technologies and more on the application of existing ones to traditional practices and the resulting changes. Traditions of craft are challenged by personal fabrication and digital tools that often simplify and speed up processes [12], or existing trades such as jewelry making are enriched through a critical digital design dialogue toward "interactive jewellery" [36]. These tools—3D printers, laser cutters, programmable sewing machines, to name a few—are not new but their role in craft practices is still emerging which leads to a collision "and through this collision a new value for craft thinking, processes, and knowledge is beginning to emerge" [27]. In craft-based approaches, this emergence originates in the workshop not the lab [3]. It realizes in the adoption of digital technologies into existing craft practice by crafters.

Depending on the constellation of the participants, these three perspectives often overlap and allow for the development of novel hybrid approaches by individual crafter/designers (e.g. [38]). The success of such hybrid work often depends on the dual-identity of a crafter-designer or a close collaboration that is noted but its nature and structure remain largely unclear. It is this overlap that we aim to support with our own work and it is here, that we see the biggest need for a structured co-design approach: to lay out a collaborative critical practice. This notion of "critical making" [28] meets the concept of "thinking through craft." [1]. Where the practical engagement with and the individual as well as shared critical reflection on the material and the object form a collaborative practice that inherently combines craft and interaction design without conflating them.

Approach and Principles

Our approach to develop a structure for craft-design collaboration on tangibles puts emphasis on a material and critical process (like Ratto and Adamson) and it aims at inclusion of specific craft practices (like Rosner and Buechley). However, it differs in the layout of its process through a co-design informed approach. Co-design grew out of related design approaches such as participatory design and user-centered design and sees different partners "working together in the design development process" [31]. It focuses on creative collaboration processes between different practitioners and is seen as an instance of co-creation. Our approach combines this co-design focus with the "reflective practitioner" model introduced by Schön [32]. As a result, it supports a differently weighed approach to structure individual collaborations between crafters and designers.

The procedural perspective of our approach was one from the design side approaching the craft but aiming for the construction of a shared dialogue through the structure of the collaboration over time. Three key elements shaped our approach to a structured combination of craft and interaction design: creativity, practice and experience, and the role of the object itself. The creativity of the TEI designer and crafter needed support, namely through the effective combination of their practices. This led us to a new role of the object as partner in the emerging dialogue.

Approach through Creativity

Creativity is a key element not only in design but also in craft and personal creative practices of the craftsperson. It cannot be excluded from the development of a general approach in the combination of craft and interaction design [21]. Particular creative practices of crafters often define their specific engagement and the quality of the resulting work. Thus, we aimed at clear inclusion of any such personal practices and concerns.

Definitions of creativity itself vary depending on the context they are applied in [33]. Amabile's micro level looks at how immediate surroundings and social context might affect creativity and proposes a "Consensual Assessment Technique" [2] that looks at a shared assessment of creativity based on subjective criteria. We did not apply this tool as an analytical assessment instrument upfront but the consensual method is reflected in the later stages of the here-proposed collaboration. Like Amabile, Csikszentmihalyi rejects the idea of the "genius" as the single source of all creativity and explores creativity in a three layered system model of *domain*, *field*, and *individual* [9]. These provide working areas not only for an approach of the designer toward the crafter but also means to locate a possible intervention within the creative practice itself. It allows different locales where the collaborators in the craft-design arrangement enter each other's domains, where they evolve into alternating gatekeepers of their fields, and manage cross-selections of each other's ideas into a new creation.

Separate Practice

Design evolved as an own discipline from the distinction between material production and the planning and preparation processes for that production. Design thinking, the "concrete integrations of knowledge that will combine theory with practice for new productive purposes" [5] differs from the material practices of craft that are themselves production-based. However, the relationship between the three key practices "design, craft and art can be seen to occupy an unstable territory of permanently shifting allegiances." [18] These allegiances adjust to particular practices. There is, for example, ample work on analyses of workplace practices in design research. Because we focus on experiential practice and encounter with the material, the Science, Technology, and Society (STS) informed activity system by Keller & Keller served as a useful approach to structure the analysis of different practices and their emergent relations. As a pair that includes craft practice (a blacksmith) and analytical observation, the Kellers' work mirrors the set up proposed by our model. They trace an umbrella plan from an initial brief to an experientially informed encounter with the material and emergent object design [17]. This approach informed the analytical first stage of our approach but our resulting structure ultimately differs from the Kellers'. Because we remained interested in the encounter with the material, a second key concept was that of a "surprise" encounter with these material qualities during the production process. Herein we relate to Ingold and Hallam, who outline creative practice with materials as generative, relational, temporal, and ultimately improvisational [14]. Their forward-looking concept of practice as a constant process of bringing-into-being that is shaped by in-the-moment encounters with others and with the material influenced our own design of the collaborative process between crafter, designer, and material.

Active Objects

Largely building on Heidegger and Deleuze & Guattari, Ingold further proposes to look at "real" objects as constantly coming into being through relational networks wherein all participants collaborate and the human ones "follow the materials" [15] (a concept also used by Schön). He emphasizes objects not as finished constructs but as dynamic unfoldings of forces constantly at work. A thing, here, is not a proof or even a trace but an active ingredient of a larger dialogue contextualized far beyond a single manipulation. Ingold's particular focus on materials suits our approach for a material- and practice-based collaboration. It establishes the thing as an active part of a never-ending dialogue between all partners involved in the process. As the agency of the objects increases we see them becoming ever more important collaborants in a participatory design process.

That is, why this paper follows a research through design approach [11] that has found increasing traction in design research, including the combination of craft and design [19, 20]. Our approach differs from the ideal of a holistically educated crafter-interaction designer. It builds on a model that involves a designated designer and a crafter, wherein the two do not directly collaborate from the beginning to deliver a defined product, nor do they try to blend their fields of expertise into one. The emerging space for a dialogue is not a shared single practice but a dialogue and the object is a material artifact engaged in the unfolding discourse. The following will outline an example implementation of this approach as well as a discussion of results.

CERAMIC INTERFACE

The sample project started in spring 2015, in the production labs at Georgia Institute of Technology on the one hand and the ceramic workshop of the crafter on the other. It consists of a collaboration between Clement Zheng, as a designer in the field of Industrial Design, and Amy Roberson, a ceramic craftsperson. Its goal was to structure their collaborative process in a way that would harness the creative input and individual practice of both partners without diluting either one's expertise in the process. The transactions with the craftsperson evolved over the course of this collaboration, from an initial *investigative* phase to understand craft and craftsperson, to an *exploratory* phase of discussing possible collaboration opportunities, to an *implementation* phase to prototype the interactive artifact. As we will elaborate in the following, these phases manifested from the focus on creativity, different practices, and active objects outlined above.

Investigation: Mapping Craft and Crafter

The designer is trained in the fields of industrial design and interaction design, specializing in designing tangible interactive products. His practice typically involves designing, building, and programming tangible interactions. These prototypes often employ digital fabrication techniques such as 3D printing and laser cutting. Zheng had no prior experience with ceramics in his work. The first phase of the research involved an approach of the designer to the craft and crafter. No fixed product goal was set apart from the explorative encounter, which comprised of a series of informal interviews and observations of the crafter at her workplace, as well as personal encounters with the craft itself.

The Systems Model of Creativity

Csikszentmihalyi's system model [9] of creativity provides a useful approach to frame Roberson's practice as a crafter: Roberson produces craft objects within the *domain* of ceramic arts and has been a practicing artist in residence at the Mudfire Gallery in Atlanta since graduating in 2012 from a Fine Arts program in ceramics. She is personally drawn towards the three dimensional canvas of expression which ceramics offer, and is particularly interested in pottery for its tradition of producing not only beautiful objects but also objects of utility—"I love that people can use my pieces daily, rather than having them on a wall to be looked at only". This balance of form and function remains important to her practice and evident in the work that she produces. This would later emerge as an opportunity for collaboration between interaction design and her ceramic craft.

Roberson is an active contributor to the local craft scene in Atlanta, which can be seen as a *field*. As an artist in residence in a city gallery, she teaches and assists amateur and professional ceramic artists in the community. In addition, she participates in art festivals around the city. Her work is sold through those art festivals as well as through the online craft marketplace Etsy. Within this field, Roberson has established an identity for herself, especially for her use of simple, functional forms coupled with playful and vibrant glazes.

Roberson's work is influenced by her *individual* interests and passion. In particular, she is attracted to the Electronic Dance Music culture, and she tries to imbue her work with the same fun and playfulness that she enjoys through her use of glaze and color. This establishes a unique signature in her work, even as she claims a much wider overarching influence of the Mid Century Modern movement in her work. In line with her attraction to playful and vibrant visuals, Roberson is also attentive to color trends. In her repertoire of tools is a set of Pantone color swatches which she refers to in choosing glazes for her pieces.

Figure 1. Left: Glazed mugs by Amy Roberson. Right: Colorful base detail at the bottom of a cup.

Exploring Process and Materials

Roberson's craft processes could be divided into two distinct methods that either fall into a relatively structured "umbrella plan" [17] that allows for more precise planning and effective performance, or into a more "improvisational" [14] crafting that specifically embraces elements of surprise as part of its production. This second method is employed for experimentation and allows a large amount of improvisation in the making process itself; "when experimenting with a new form, I like to have the clay in my hands to be able to make slight adjustments and see them from all sides." Roberson deploys this method typically when exploring a new form on the wheel or with new glazes and color combinations. The "umbrella plan" method described by the Kellers is more a top-down, linear, funneling approach. This method is typically employed by Roberson during the production of a series for a collection. It features a strong initial brief and set procedure with few improvisations or surprises allowed in the process.

Encountering the Craft

A separate vein of exploration involved a first-hand experience of the craft itself by the designer, who had no experience of working with ceramics. This was an intimate process wherein the designer experienced the basics of working with clay and pottery tools over multiple sessions working on own (mostly flawed) ceramics. This experiential approach stands in contrast to the analytical transactions with the craftsperson but was carried out in tandem with the interviews and discussions with the craftsperson.

Limited as such a preliminary encounter with the craft was, it allowed the designer to discuss basic materials and processes with the same language as the craftsperson. This experience was helpful in generating 'action' knowledge, or what Polanyi calls "tacit knowledge" [26], which heavily depends on embodiment and the ability to "interiorize" knowledge to re-apply it in practice." Even though the tacit knowledge of the crafter far outweighs that of the designer, this encounter allowed the conversation to emerge over a shared experience, albeit between an expert and an amateur. In addition, this first-hand experience increased the sensitivity and empathy one had towards the craft and process. It supported a feedback loop between the conversation with the craftsperson, and the personal encounters with the craft, and influenced the generation of ideas for potential collaborations between digital media and craft. Experiencing the practice was not meant to turn the designer into an expert potter but to encounter the material and the practices as active components to prompt questions about them. As the collaboration continued and a deeper engagement with the craftsperson was established, the flow of ideas shifted and begin to gain specificity towards Roberson's crafting practice and identity as a craftsperson. These included the insights described in the previous section, such as her use of colors and glazes, and the tensions between form and function in her work, which connected to the tacit exploration of these components at the hand of the designer.

Tensions and Opportunity

The tension between form and function is a recurring dilemma that occurs throughout Roberson's work. As a craftsperson, she creates her pieces with the intent that customers will use and interact with the pieces. This is evident in the colorful detail that she creates at the base of her vessels, a detail that is only revealed through interacting with the object (see figure. 1 right). However, many of her pieces end up not as functional objects but as display ornaments. During an interview, Roberson recounts her personal encounter of this dilemma with her grandmother, who would not use her granddaughter's pieces as she deemed them "too pretty". Roberson intends others to see and "use" her objects, pick them up, uncover hidden specifics, and manipulate them. This specific dilemma faced by the crafter stood out as a unique opportunity for collaboration; one that the brief was eventually developed around.

Exploration: Developing the Brief

If the first stage of an investigation into craft and crafter is a phase of research into craft, then the brief is the hinge which turns the collaboration to a research through craft and design [11]. As with most design briefs, it consists of a goal, constraints to work within, and is formulated between "motivation" and "creation" phases [8]. However, some important aspects of the brief stood out from our case, which we highlight below.

Role of the Brief

Up to this point, the perspective was that of the designer approaching the craft practice and practitioner. The brief is developed by the designer as a response, and thus as a turning point. We observed in our case that the designer stands on fertile middle ground; as an approaching amateur to craft, the designer has gained insights on the craft practice and understands the motivations which drive the crafter in her work, and simultaneously, as a professional in the design domain, the designer is conscious of his strengths and capabilities. Practically, designers are trained to integrate often diverse fields into their process (such as business, engineering, sciences) [8]. All of them shape the development of tangible interfaces in experimental as well as industrial settings. Crafters are trained on a specific material manipulation process and the set of skills that are relevant to that process. This difference of breadth versus depth training of design and craft practitioners was observed not only in our case, but also in other collaborations [34].

The brief aimed to not only bank on the opportunities identified in the previous phase, but also exploit the strengths and motivations of both designer and crafter to drive a successful collaboration. This focus on process differs from the more uni-directional client-to-designer problem statement that defines a typical design brief [8]. Our brief aimed not at a product but a shared object: a "thing coming into being," able to connect both practices and to create opportunities for craft and design in the collaborative object-making process. Besides anchoring the collaboration to a type of object, the brief also divided the work between crafter and designer on the shared tangible interface object. Neither crafter nor designer were experts in the other collaborator's domain. Consequently, the goal was to provide sufficient constraints to ensure the gradual assembly of craft and design outcomes, yet leave enough room for both, crafter and designer, to explore within their own domains.

Lastly, the brief follows Amabile's consensual assessment - evaluating the outcome based on the judgments and expectations of both crafter and designer. This differs from a more formal, criteria-driven evaluation approach found in a typical design brief [8]. The brief serves as a catalyst, and sets a new trajectory for craft and design to collaborate. Building on Ingold and Hallam's emphasis on improvisation in craft practice, we propose that the brief should afford a process, which is malleable to the "surprises" that might emerge [14]. The presentation to and acceptance of the brief marked the start of the task-driven and object-focused collaboration between crafter and designer.

Brief: Building an Interactive Lamp

In our case, the brief called for the creation of an interactive lamp. Notably, we were less concerned about the novelty of the object as a product (commercial lamps responding to touch exist) and more about the appropriate framing of the next steps in the collaboration. The nature of the lamp object relates to Roberson's personal interest in electronic dance music and her practice involving vibrant glazes as well as the playful trademark details within her ceramics. It specifies a tangible user interaction with the lamp, where physical interactions with the lamp affect the hue and color of the light produced by the ceramic lamp. It also sought to address an important personal dilemma to the crafter—the detachment of her functional pieces from any actual use. Embedding physical interactions in the object ultimately require the audience to pick up the object to engage with it. Through the brief, the interaction design answered to the crafter's personal experience and concerns regarding function.

The brief's targeted outcome (the lamp object) was not seen as a product but instead as a shared common ground for continuous critical engagement. Practically, the lamp was broken down into its various components, with the crafter responsible for the ceramic lamp body, and the designer responsible for the electronics and programming.

Implementation: Sharing Lamp Making

The third stage covered the implementation of the hybrid lamp and combined specifics of craft and design practices as well as shared and differing techniques. It is nearly impossible to embed electronics in clay that will be fired at temperatures between 1000–2400 Fahrenheit. This meant that the electronic sensing component had to be assembled onto the finished ceramic. It also meant that the ceramic needed to be constructed with this later assembly in mind. This material condition shaped collaboration and object design. The lighting component of the lamp was based on readily available RGB LEDs but the sensing system proved to be more challenging. There is a huge body of applicable work on embedding sensors to create tangible interfaces. In the implementation, this led to the choice of accelerometers to sense the interactions, as they can be connected to the ceramics without disrupting the craft process. The accelerometers in turn informed the first interaction model of the lamps—the hue, saturation and value of the emitted light are affected by the lamp's different movements. The technical benefit of using an accelerometer was that as it senses general Cartesian acceleration but allows for flexible use of that information. Different physical interactions and behaviors can be incorporated through reprogramming. This enabled the same basic electronics to be packaged in future versions of the lamp and to respond to different ceramic bodies, making room for improvisation during the implementation process. The craft-based benefit was that this interaction design addressed a key concern of Roberson with her existing objects. She had complained about the non-use of her objects as they had been deemed "too pretty" to be touched and used. The tangible interaction design using accelerometers actively addressed this problem.

The implementation went through iterations of divergent and convergent phases. During the divergent phases, the crafter and designer engaged in individual exploration, developing their respective components. During the convergent phases, the prototypes were assembled and evaluated for areas of improvement and new insights in the development of the tangible interface. The end of each divergent-convergent cycle culminated in an assembled object which bears the traces of the process, and functions as a point for reflection and discussion for the next iteration.

Divergent Phases

Guided by the brief as well as insights that emerged during the course of implementation, both crafter and designer individually explored and exercised their expertise within their responsibilities during divergent phases. The housing and assembly of the electronics to the ceramic lamp body was the main focus of the tangible interface designer. Adafruit's 5V Pro Trinket was used for the micro-controller, while WS2812b LEDs were used as the light source. Prototypes iterated through initial breadboard models, to more robust packages encapsulated with a custom-made platform. Different clamping methods had to be devised to secure the electronics in response to each ceramic body. This often required work from the crafter, such as the addition of holes in the ceramic, a standard procedure in ceramic craft. A variety of digital fabrication methods were employed as fitting electronics to the ceramic lamp body became more complex. These range from laser cut plastic assemblies to 3D printed cases. A custom circuit board was eventually designed and fabricated for a more stable electronics board. The designer's iterative exploration on packaging the electronics components resulted in smaller, more robust fixtures. In addition, later fixtures were also more flexible in adapting to different ceramic body forms.

Figure 2. Electronics revision from breadboard model to custom circuit board with digital fabricated platforms.

The form, size and texture of the ceramic body was the crafter's focus during the divergent phases. The exploration began with paper sketches of possible forms the lamp might take, as a reflector of light and as a form for users to hold and interact with, but also as an object in itself with its presence in a room. A few forms were eventually shortlisted and turned in clay. These pieces were then fired with different color glazes. Different glaze and textures were tested with the tangible interactions in mind. While the crafter's past concerns with glaze and color were typically aesthetic in nature, now they had to consider the tangible user interactions (e.g. touch) and light reflecting qualities of the ceramic surface. The crafter also experimented with a variety of techniques to produce different forms which could afford different kinds of tangible interactions. A roly-poly form required the crafter to merge two turned clay parts along a narrow seam, while a faceted body was also made entirely via hand sculpting; a process significantly different from the crafter's usual process of turning clay on a wheel.

Figure 3. Different ceramic forms produced by the crafter.

Convergent Phases

The different elements from both crafter and interaction designer were assembled together and evaluated during the convergent phases. The first assembled prototype met the initial expectations of both collaborators but it also led to new considerations that emerged while the collaborators interacted with the object. The glossy and smooth texture of the glaze—which the crafter typically applied to her other pieces—raised the issue of the user's hands slipping during interaction. In addition, the LEDs were too bright to look at while interacting with the lamp. At this stage, the crafter's own preferences and the tangible interaction designer's approaches did not yet conflate but their differences became visible and critiqued by both. This critique of the prototype involved both crafter and designer and often reversed their roles. The designer would argue about the glaze and the crafter critique the light fixture. The object involved both participants in a shared reflection of the decisions made in the divergent phase and enabled both parties to engage in a better understanding of the collaboration process.

Figure 4. Assembled prototypes; first prototype (up left) to more current (bottom right).

Surprises sometimes emerged during the convergent phase, prompting improvisation on the collaborators' part. For example, the crafter produced a larger ceramic body for the second prototype (see fig. 4 upper right). The weight of the second form made it difficult for a user to interact with the lamp in the same way as the first (see fig. 4 upper left). Instead, the second prototype encouraged the user to pivot the lamp on the edge of its base, which then enables it to roll along its circumference. This new affordance required an improvisation of code optimization, which was quickly adapted to support the new interaction model.

This emergent interconnection—the "surprise"—that emerged during the second assembly, and the improvisation that followed, gave rise to a different interaction concept. Instead of a single expert changing the material and the digital construction, the new insights were part of the literally productive dialogue between two experts on the grounds of the emerging objects. At this point designer and crafter were also more familiar with each other's process and domain. With the first two prototypes as reference, the discussion went beyond improvements of the existing models. New approaches to develop interactive ceramic lamps, as well as innovative ideas for the different lamp components were raised. The collaboration between crafter and designer continued and at this point of writing they are at the fourth iteration of the interactive ceramic lamps. Since the second prototype, more ceramic forms and interactions were explored, including the 'roly-poly' and faceted forms as well as new methods of organizing the cables and electronics with the ceramic lamp body. Both crafter and designer are now more confident of their individual roles and what they can achieve through this collaboration. In contrast to the first prototypes which was developed close to the initial brief, subsequent prototypes deviated from the initially prescribed tangible interaction. The tangible interface emerged over time in this dialogue of objects and co-designers. The crafter pushed the physical characteristics of the ceramic bodies to afford different physical interactions, while the tangible interaction design of the lamps emerged from the designer responding to these new shapes and forms. The dialogue between both crafter and designer occurred not only person-to-person but increasingly over the object as well. In our case, we read these gradual steps toward the development and optimization of a range of possible products as signs for a successfully initiated collaboration that never conflated expertise but remained active through the differences of all partners involved.

Consensual Assessment

No external assessment was conducted throughout the implementation process, rather the outcomes of each iteration were evaluated against the expectations of the crafter and designer collaborators. This follows Amabile's consensual assessment technique, where "a product is creative to the extent that expert raters independently agree upon this judgment" [2]. Such a dynamic and emerging assessment method serves our goal of establishing a collaborative practice, in contrast to developing an optimized product. The *personal* and *domain* impact of this collaboration both provided evidence in support of such an assessment technique. Roberson varied her *personal* crafting and glazing techniques in reaction to the outcomes of each iteration. As she reflected: "This rounded form is good to hold, but I want to see how an open form will change the quality of light", and "I want to try a more neutral glaze to see its effect on the different color hues." These were direct responses to the operation and design of the electronics and LEDs. They exemplify her response to and engagement with the collaboration through its objects.

Furthermore, the outcomes of each iteration catalyzed discussion and idea generation among Roberson and her peers at Mudfire gallery (her *field*) as well. Roberson reported on an impromptu discussion with her peers about "incorporating electronics into ceramics" while she was working on her part at the studio, resulting in several new ideas, one of which was a "faceted lamp body that changes the lighting effect as it rests on different faces" (The fourth prototype, see figure 4). Here, the shape of the lamp, the means of its construction, even its ideation would have been impossible for either collaborator alone but emerged from the social environment of the crafter. They were developed in absence of the designer and indicate possible extensions of the model to reach wider collaborating partners within the targeted craft *domain*. Given that crafters often have highly individualized skillsets, this would allow for a larger range of expertise and indicate a wider reach. It also responds to our initial interest to build a model that supports further collaboration and participation across domains as these contributions are indicators for a discussion that reaches not only the single collaborating crafter but her peers as well.

The collaboration's impact on the crafter's practice motivated her to continue the partnership months after the original project had ended. Even prompting discussions on pushing the collaborative outcomes beyond experimentation and refining them for the marketplace. A critical and/or financial success of such a new product would indicate that the *field* acknowledges the success of the collaboration.

DISCUSSION

This sample project describes a long term collaboration between crafter and designer (one and a half years at this time of writing). It stands in contrast to shorter term "workshop"-style collaborations between crafters and designers that start off as product-oriented, such as the research carried out by Tung et al. [34], as well as other educational approaches [24]. We observed numerous challenges emerging from this long term collaboration and reflected on the process to meet them. The focus was on the role of shared object, as well as the involvement of differing yet connecting practices.

Iterative diverging-converging process

Compared to the co-prototyping process employed in the workshop conducted by Tung et al. which tightly coupled designer and crafter for short term engagement, our practice-based co-design study revealed a need for periods of individual exploration leading to subsequent assembly and evaluation. As the designer noted in reflection: "I am accustomed to specifying every aspect of a 'product', from measurements to materials to color and texture. For this collaboration however, I felt like I was designing a system to work with the craft"—speaking about an adjustment of his work to the practice as such instead of to the resulting object. Such an approach leverages the separate fields of expertise of both crafter and designer as distinct and often asynchronous practices; both crafter and designer had to schedule this collaboration around their separate practices. This cyclical process of co-investigation, individual exploration and assembly may prove to facilitate a longer term craft-design collaboration beyond a single project. The assembled object in our case study serves not as an answer to the brief, but rather as "a method of collecting and preserving information and understanding" [19] as Mäkelä argues; a trace in the shared process that assembles both practices over the evolution of the object.

Objects to think with

Seymour Papert describes "objects-to-think-with" as artifacts in which there is "an intersection of cultural presence, embedded knowledge, and the possibility for personal identification" [23]. He referred to such objects in an educational context but we observe that our ceramic lamps took on the same role. They provided a platform to connect the asymmetrical expertise and practices of crafter and designer. Through the process of co-design, we observe crafter and designer working less on following a strict product goal, but instead responding to the prototypes built.

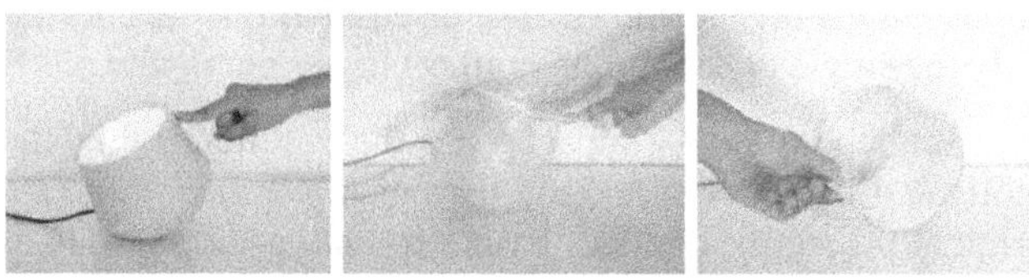

Figure 5. Left, Middle: nudging the lamp to increase light intensity. Right: resting the lamp to dim it.

The crafter adjusted crafting process and techniques to respond to new understanding of the sensors and electronics. Most notably, the third 'roly-poly' form marked a significant leap from the initial plan for the crafter, as she sought to imbue the ceramic bodies with more playful affordances for tangible interaction capable to be sensed by the accelerometer. On the other hand, the designer began to develop new tangible interactions responding to the physical characteristics of each new ceramic body. The designer describes his approach to later ceramic pieces as a case of asking the piece "how would I want to interact with you?" allowing the tangible interaction design to emerge from physically handling and exploring the potential of each form. Interactions for the 'roly-poly' body were developed from such an object-led approach: forcefully nudging the roly-poly will increase the intensity of the lamp's light, while resting it gently on its side dims the lamp (see fig. 5). Such a reflection and implementation process would be difficult for an interaction designer, or even a designer-crafter hybrid practitioner. It is a process facilitated by the dialogue fueled by the difference between practitioners of craft and design collaborating over the making of an object. It continuously leverages the role of the object as object-to-think with. In our case, the reflection continues to inform the tangible interaction design.

Digital fabrication's supportive role

Digital fabrication has been applied to craft-technology research from many different angles. In their work *hybrid reassemblage* and *hybrid basketry*, Zoran et al. employed digital fabrication to explore the tensions between hand-crafted and digital manufacturing [38, 39]. In another collaboration, 3D printing was used as a rapid prototyping tool to conceptually explore craft possibilities [30]. Digital fabrication processes have also been imagined as embodied craft in which humans replace machines [10]. From our case study, we observe that digital fabrication is employed as a pragmatic means of interfacing the craft outcome with the sensing system for tangible interaction design. In many ways, this use of digital fabrication resonates with Gershenfeld's prediction of the technology fulfilling a "market of one" [12]. It was employed in unique production runs to support the tangible interaction design in response to unique ceramic forms produced by the crafter. At no point of our project did we ever consider to replace the crafted component with a personal fabrication-based one as this would have intruded into the dialogue we had established between designer and crafter through separate practice.

OUTLOOK

Combining craft and design remains an ambitious goal with much promise. "Design intervention is an interface between tradition and modernity, and calls for matching craft production to the needs of modern living. It can, and has been shown to, play a role in empowering the disenfranchised and the marginalized." [35] We cannot claim such an impact but present an emerging practice for a constructive collaboration between the two domains that does not attempt a direct merger but a critical dialogue. Thus, it proposes an inherently inclusive and additive approach for emerging participatory and collaborative practices. Through our case study, we observe enabling mechanisms that support craft-design collaborations. Our collaboration leveraged the role of "objects to think with" to inspire improvisations in individual practice where collaborators respond to each other's work. Evaluating each outcome through consensual assessment also created space for critical reflection that catalyzes and steers subsequent making efforts. We observe the importance of the experiential and investigative initial approach from design to craft and craftsperson in establishing empathy and uncovering opportunities for collaboration. This paper presents a process-based and co-design inspired 3-step approach that allows the objects to become active components in the critical development. In our model, the collaboration ultimately does not center on a single component, but it uses the divergence and convergence between experts, materials, and objects over time to structure a dialogue that, we hope, helps to informs future TEI design processes that combine craft and interaction design.

ACKNOWLEDGEMENTS

We thank our collaborator Amy Roberson and the crafters at Mudfire gallery for their patience and support.

REFERENCES

1. Adamson, G. Thinking Through Craft. Berg Publishers, New York, 2007.
2. Amabile, T. M. Creativity in Context. Westview, Oxford, UK, 1996.
3. Bell, N. R. Craft Futures. A Generation at Hand. Renwick Gallery of the Smithsonian American Art Museum, Washington, DC, 2012.
4. Berzowska, J. and Bromley, M. Soft Computing through Conductive Textiles. In Proceedings of the International Foundation of Fashion Technology Institutes Conference (Toronto, CAN, April 12-14, 2007).
5. Buchanan, R. Wicked Problems in Design Thinking. Design Issues, 8, 2 (1992), 5-21.
6. Buechley, L. and Perner-Wilson, H. Crafting technology: Reimagining the processes, materials, and cultures of electronics. ACM Trans. Comput.-Hum. Interact., 19, 3 2012), 1-21.
7. Buechley, L. and Qiu, K. Sew Electric. HTL Press, Cambridge, MA, 2014.
8. Cross, N. Engineering Design Methods: Strategies for Product Design. John Wiley & Sons., Chichester, 2008.
9. Csikszentmihalyi, M. Creativity. The Psychology of Discovery and Invention. Harper Collins, New York, London, Toronto, New Delhi, Auckland, 1996.
10. Devendorf, L. and Ryokai, K. 2015. Being the Machine: Reconfiguring Agency and Control in Hybrid Fabrication. In Proceedings of the 33rd Annual ACM Conference on Human Factors in Computing Systems (CHI '15). ACM, New York, NY, USA, 2477-2486.
11. Frayling, C. Research in Art and Design. Royal College of Art Research Papers, 1, 1 (1993), 1-5.
12. Gershenfeld, N. Fab. The Coming Revolution on your Desktop. Basic Books, New York, Cambridge, MA, 2005.
13. Goodman, E. and Rosner, D. From garments to gardens: negotiating material relationships online and 'by hand'. In Proceedings of the SIGCHI Conference (Vancouver, BC, 2011). ACM, New York, 2011.
14. Ingold, T. and Hallam, E. Creativity and Cultural Improvisation: An Introduction. Berg, City, 2007.
15. Ingold, T. The Textility of Making. Cambridge Journal of Economics, 34 (2009), 91-102.
16. Karagozler, M. E., Poupyrev, I., Fedder, G. K. and Suzuki, Y. Paper generators: harvesting energy from touching, rubbing and sliding. In Proceedings of the 26th annual ACM symposium on User Interface Software and Technology (St. Andrews, UK, 2013). ACM, New York, 2013..
17. Keller, C. and Keller, J. D. Thinking and Acting with Iron. In Understanding Practice. (eds S. Chaiklin/ J. Lave) Cambridge University Press, Cambridge, UK, 1994. 125-144.
18. Lees-Maffei, G. and Sandino, L. Dangerous Liaisons: Relationships between Design, Craft and Art. Journal of Design History, 17, 3 (2004), 207-219.
19. Mäkelä, M. Knowing Through Making: The Role of the Artefact in Practice-led Research. Knowledge, Technology & Policy, 20, 3 (2007), 157-163.
20. Nimkulrat, N. Hands-On Intellect: Integrating Craft Practice into Design Research. International Journal of Design, 6, 3 (2012), 1-14.
21. Nitsche, M., Quitmeyer, A., Farina, K., Nam, H. Y. and Zwaan, S. Teaching Digital Craft. In Proceedings of CHI '14 EA (April 26-May 1 2014, Toronto, CAN) ACM, New York, 2014. 719-730.
22. Owen, C. L. Design education and research for the 21st century. Design Studies, 11, 4 (1990), 202-206.
23. Papert, S. Mindstorms: Children, Computers, and Powerful Ideas. Basic Books, New York, 1980.
24. Peppler, K. New Opportunities for Interest-driven Arts Learning in a Digital Age. The Wallace Foundation, Bloomington, IN, 2013.
25. Peppler, K. and Glosson, D. Stitching Circuits: Learning About Circuitry Through E-textile Materials. Journal of Science Education and Technology, 22, 5 (2013), 751-763.
26. Polanyi, M. The Tacit Dimension. Doubleday & Co. Inc., Garden City, NY, 1966.
27. Press, M. Handmade Futures: The Emerging Role of Craft Knowledge in Our Digital Culture. The Press of the Nova Scotia College of Art and Design, Halifax, CAN, 2007.
28. Ratto, M. Critical Making: conceptual and material studies in technology and social life. The Information Society: An International Journal, 27, 4 (2011), 252-260.
29. Rosner, D. and Ryokai, K. 2010. Spyn: augmenting the creative and communicative potential of craft. In Proceedings of the SIGCHI Conference on Human Factors in Computing Systems (CHI '10). ACM, New York, NY, USA, 2407-2416.
30. Rosner, D., Ikemiya, M., and Regan, T. 2015. Resisting Alignment: Code and Clay. In Proceedings of the Ninth International Conference on Tangible, Embedded, and Embodied Interaction (TEI '15). ACM, New York, NY, USA, 181-188.
31. Sanders, E. B.-N. and Stappers, P. J. Co-creation and the new landscapes of design. CoDesign, 4, 1 2008), 5-18.

32. Schön, D. A. Educating the Reflective Practitioner. Toward a Design for Teaching and Learning in the Professions. Jossey-Bass, San Francisco, 1987.
33. Sawyer, R. K. Explaining Creativity. The Science of Human Innovation. Oxford University Press, Oxford; 2012.
34. Tung, F.-W. and Chen, I.-C. Collaboration of Designers and Craft Artists on Innovative Design Praxis. In Proceedings of the 5th International Congress of International Association of Societies of Design Research (IASDR) (Tokyo, JP, Aug 26-30, 2013) 2013,.
35. UNESCO. Designers meet Artisans. A Practical Guide. UNESCO, Craft Revival Trust, New Delhi, India, 2005.
36. Versteeg, M., van den Hoven, E. and Hummels C. 2016. Interactive Jewellery: a design exploration. In Proceedings of the TEI '16: Tenth International Conference on Tangible, Embedded, and Embodied Interaction (TEI '16). ACM, New York, NY, USA, 44-52.
37. Zhu, K. A framework for interactive paper-craft system. In Proceedings of the CHI '12 Extended Abstracts on Human Factors in Computing Systems (Austin, Texas, USA, 2012). ACM, New York, 2012.
38. Zoran, A. and Buechley, L. Hybrid Reassemblage: An Exploration of Craft, Digital Fabrication and Artifact Uniqueness. Leonardo, 46, 1 (2010), 4-10.
39. Zoran, A. 2013. Hybrid basketry: interweaving digital practice within contemporary craft. In ACM SIGGRAPH 2013 Art Gallery (SIGGRAPH '13). ACM, New York, NY, USA, 324-331.

SqueezaPulse: Adding Interactive Input to Fabricated Objects Using Corrugated Tubes and Air Pulses

Liang He* **Gierad Laput†** **Eric Brockmeyer†** **Jon E. Froehlich***

* University of Maryland, College Park, Maryland, United States

† Carnegie Mellon University, Pittsburgh, Pennsylvania, United States

* {lianghe, jonf}@cs.umd.edu, † gierad.laput@cs.cmu.edu, † ebrockme@andrew.cmu.edu

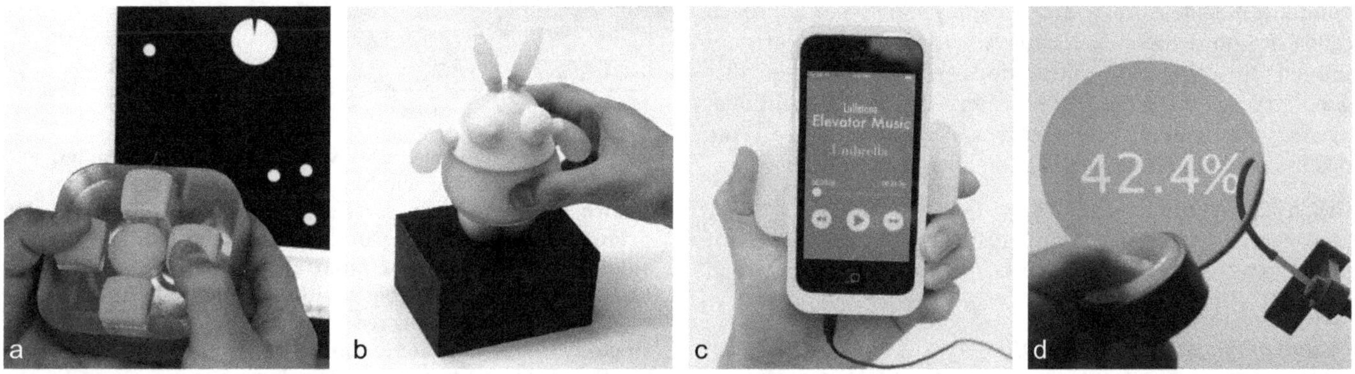

Figure 1. We introduce *SqueezaPulse*, a technique for creating interactive fabricated objects using acoustic sensing without external circuitry or power but one single microphone. Above, four example applications show the flexibility and value of our approach: (a) a gamepad controller; (b) a soft and interactive bunny; (c) a squeezable phone case; and (d) a force sensor.

ABSTRACT

We present *SqueezaPulse*, a technique for embedding interactivity into fabricated objects using soft, passive, low-cost bellow-like structures. When a soft cavity is squeezed, air pulses travel along a flexible pipe and into a uniquely designed corrugated tube that shapes the airflow into predictable sound signatures. A microphone captures and identifies these air pulses enabling interactivity. We describe the underlying acoustic theory used to inform our design, an informal examination of the effect of different 3D-printed corrugations on air signatures, and our resulting SqueezaPulse implementation. To demonstrate and evaluate the potential of SqueezaPulse, we present four prototype applications and a small, lab-based user study (*N*=9). Our evaluations show that our approach is accurate across users and robust to external noise. We conclude with a discussion of limitations and future work.

Author Keywords

Fabricated objects; passive acoustic sensing; soft cavity; pipe; squeeze interactions; corrugated tube; air pulse.

ACM Classification Keywords

H.5.2. Information interfaces and presentation (*e.g.,* HCI): Input devices and strategies.

 ISBN 978-1-4503-4676-4/17/03…$15.00

DOI: http://dx.doi.org/10.1145/3024969.3024976

INTRODUCTION

Fabrication techniques such as 3D printing, laser cutting, and casting have been increasingly used to build physical prototypes in HCI. Incorporating interactive functions into fabricated objects, however, is still a cumbersome and highly decoupled process. In response, an emerging body of work aims to imbue fabricated objects with interactive capabilities throughout the rapid prototyping cycle, including via custom-designed optics [36], touch sensitive electronics [29], active acoustic-enabled structures [11], and precision sensors [35]. Building on this growing literature, we introduce *SqueezaPulse*, a technique for creating interactive fabricated objects using acoustic sensing without embedded circuitry, wiring, or power (Figure 1). Our novel approach shapes small puffs of air into identifiable but inaudible sound signatures via custom fabricated structures.

We were inspired by passive airflow mechanisms in bellows and accordions, which were designed to furnish strong blasts of air without requiring external power. We synthesize similar principles for constructing simple *squeezable units* that can be used for input control. SqueezaPulse is comprised of three core parts: (i) a soft and squeezable cavity to generate airflow; (ii) a tube designed with specific inner-wall corrugations to shape the airflow into unique acoustic signatures, effectively acting as a physical filter [2]; and (iii) a microphone connected to a computer that classifies these signatures for interactive inputs. Figure 2 provides an illustrative example of creating an interactive 3D-printed bunny. Because each tube produces a unique signature, only a single embedded microphone is necessary to sense multiple inputs. To verify the feasibility and the accuracy of our approach, we built four prototype applications and present results from a lab-based study with nine participants.

In summary, our work contributes: (i) a passive acoustic sensing and machine learning-based approach for recognizing distinct puffs of air; (ii) a distillation of design implications for fabricating corrugated tubes for robust and accurate sensing; (iii) and a wide range of illustrative applications across different prototyping platforms, demonstrating feasibility and accuracy. Since our approach relies on the detection of passive puffs of air, we are not limited to "squeeze" interactions. Any technique that generates air puffs (*e.g.,* blowing) offers an additional avenue for making fabricated objects interactive. We discuss these and other application areas in the Discussion.

RELATED WORK

Our work builds on prior research in the areas of prototyping interactive objects, acoustic sensing, and squeezable interfaces.

Prototyping and Fabrication of Interactive Objects. Making things interactive is an essential part of physical prototyping in HCI. As noted in the Introduction, a large body of emerging work has begun to explore how to embed interactivity into the ever-growing repertoire of fabricated objects (*e.g.,* 3D prints). For example, 3D-printed, optically clear pipes have been used for sensing, displaying, and embedding interactive elements [1,36]. Broader approaches have also been explored, including linear arrays of strain gauges[13], computer vision techniques [26] and generic tubular pathways [28], all of which offer the potential to transform plastic or photopolymer-based 3D prints into interactive objects. Beyond rigid outputs, additive manufacturing-based fabrication of soft materials have also been investigated, including techniques for embedding tightly-coupled electronics into layers of felt or fabric [8,23]. Although these efforts require designers to embed particular structures in the model (*e.g.,* optically clear tubes or print voids), they nonetheless offer the unique ability to reduce the need for traditional electronic circuitry. Likewise, our approach offers similar tradeoffs. Further, our approach aims at providing a robust and reusable mechanism (*i.e.,* corrugated tubes) that could be attached on different fabricated objects for interactive controls.

Acoustic Sensing as Input. A large body of work in HCI has explored acoustic-based sensing across multiple interactive applications. Approaches can be categorized as active [5,11,16,19], which recognize user input by relying on a sustained source of sound such as from a sweep frequency generator, or passive [6,7,8,10,18,22,24,27], which do not require electronically generated sounds. Our work builds on the growing area of using passive acoustics for interaction—in particular, interactive acoustic sensing with custom-designed, 3D-printed structures. For example, *Tickers* [31] is a labeling toolkit that uses printed percussion instruments to label different 3D-printed objects. *Acoustic*

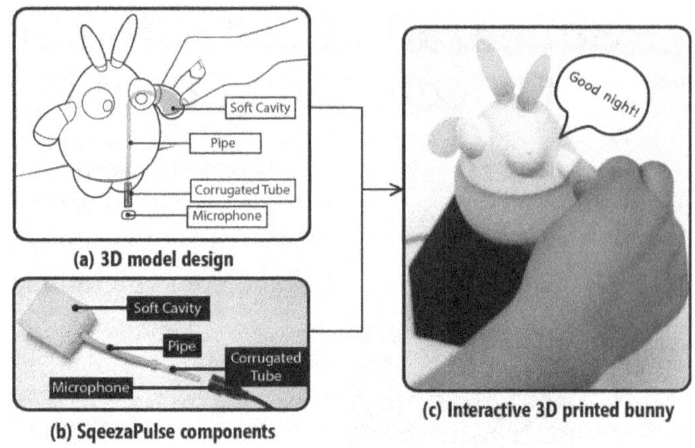

Figure 2. SqueezaPulse uses soft cavities, flexible pipes, and corrugated tubes to enable interactive fabricated objects. Shown above, a user squeezes a soft hand embedded into a 3D-printed bunny, which generates an identifiable air pulse. While we depict only one input above, the interactive bunny actually has six squeezable cavities—each cavity is connected to its own uniquely designed corrugated tube which leads to a single shared microphone, which is the basis of our approach. See the supplementary video for a demo.

Voxels [12] builds a wide range of acoustic filter applications by embedding a matrix of primitives inside 3D-printed objects. Additionally, *Cilllia* [20] senses acoustic input based on printed fur on the arbitrary surface of 3D-printed objects. Closest to our work is *Lamello* [27], an acoustic model-based approach using comb-like structures for real-time processing of computational events. While Lamello enables new interactive input on 3D-printed objects, the approach is limited to strikes generated by the movement of physical components as input. Together, the above techniques highlight the breadth, scalability, and practicality of passive acoustic sensing techniques.

Soft Interfaces for Squeeze Interactions. Prior work has investigated squeeze interactions with soft primitives or objects, which can enable new, playful and innovative interfaces [3,4]. For instance, *Skweezee* [34] explored design implications for squeeze interactions based on hand gesture training and testing on large squeezable primitives. In practice, integrating deformable structures and material could add rich interactions to daily objects. For example, *Squeeze Me* [14] mounts a squeezable cover on a tablet providing expressive human robot interactions. *FuwaFuwa* [10] is a sensor module that can be embedded and used for measuring the deformation of soft objects such as cushions and plush toys. Likewise, soft sensors, which are made of soft and elastic material (*e.g.,* silicone, flexible 3D printing filament), could also support interactive controls by using pneumatics [15,18,32,37], or using special-purpose pressure sensors, as in the work by *Slyper* and colleagues [33]. Our approach allows designers to prototype squeezable interactions with the deformable and soft parts embedded in general fabricated objects.

In summary, our work introduces a novel passive sensing approach for prototyping interactive objects, solely relying on pulses of air, without additional sensors, circuitry, or complex mechanisms, except for a single microphone. Previous approaches require either an active source of sound (*e.g.,* [11] uses speakers and ultrasound) or individual sensor pairs (*e.g.,* in [32], each block requires individual pressure sensors). Unlike prior work, our approach does not require an active sound or pressure source, which is cumbersome and noisy. Further, our corrugated tubes are easy to fabricate and are reusable.

THEORY OF OPERATION

Our approach is based on corrugated acoustic theory [2]. Air flow through corrugated pipes can be manipulated and shaped by different corrugation designs [24]. To dampen or alter sound in airflow systems, corrugated pipes are found in a range of industrial and domestic applications such as air conditioning systems, vacuum cleaners, musical toys (*e.g.,* [24]), and flexible risers in the oil industry.

Corrugated acoustic theory is based on two fundamental concepts: *standing waves* and the *Cummings acoustic model* [24]. Standing waves are common in wind and brass instruments which are tube shaped (*e.g.,* flute). The sound frequency, amplitude, harmonics, and timbre of the standing wave are affected by the properties of the tube. Interestingly, whether the tube is straight or bent (*e.g.,* into circles) has minimal impact on the generated sound, although a very sharp bend does have some effect [30]. Thus, we use flexible tubes as channels for transmitting air flow from the soft cavity to corrugated tubes.

Based on the principles of standing waves, the Cummings acoustic model [24] is widely used to inform the design of large corrugated pipes. In this model, air flow, and therefore the resulting sound, is shaped by the velocity of sound c_0, the tube's length L, tube's inner radius R, the volume of the cavity between two consecutive corrugations, the area presented by the cavity to the tube, and the spatial period of corrugations (pitch) P_c. More precisely, the diagram of corrugated tube is illustrated in Figure 3, where d is the height of the corrugation. The relationship between these factors is shown in (1), where wave number $n = 1, 2, 3...$, representing a group of generated frequencies.

In our work, we parameterized and explored the corrugated tubes based on the aforementioned theories (Figure 3). While these theories may be directly codified into a rule-based classifier, in our preliminary experiments we found that a machine learning-based empirical approach performed better, perhaps accounting for small deformities in tube design due to fabrication limitations.

DESIGN SPACE OF CORRUGATED TUBES

As noted above, corrugated tube length, gaps between corrugations, corrugation shapes, and corrugation distributions play key roles in characteristically altering airflow. While exhaustively exploring each permutation and combination is intractable, we opted instead to select 12 corrugated tubes that contained exemplar parameters (through trial and error). Once selected, we then conducted one-to-one comparisons to help us fully understand how these form factors characteristically alter transient puffs of air. This work extends the explorations conducted in *Acoustruments* [11], with a particular novel focus on investigating the interior texture of the tubes and its impact on spectral signatures.

$$f_n = \frac{nc_0}{2L\sqrt{1+\frac{d}{P_c}(1+\frac{d}{2R})}} \qquad (1)$$

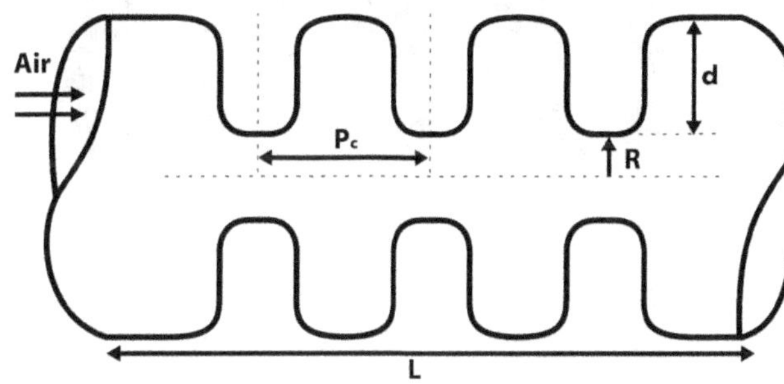

Figure 3. A corrugated tube diagram and equation.

Before we began our design space explorations, we tested the "strength" of the air pulse on 3D-printed pipes with different interior diameters. In general, thin pipes are better at preserving air energy and diameters between 1.6-3.2 mm produced superior performance. Bigger diameters resulted in weaker pulses while thinner ones blocked air flow. Additionally, as expected [24], we found that the outputted signal is proportional to the strength of the input air puff and that it attenuates as the tube becomes longer. In our trials, most air pulses were detectable using tubes that were 25 cm or shorter. We observed that air puffs passing through corrugated tubes had a significant effect on uniquely shaping acoustic signatures (qualitatively verified through visual inspection of the spectrogram). Because we rely on air pulses, our technique makes slightly audible but faint sound bursts.

To investigate how tube design directly affects the eventual output signal, we used the model in corrugated acoustics for guidance and performed side-by-side comparisons of two representative tubes that differed in one controlled parameter (*e.g.,* tube length). As shown in Figure 4, we experimented with: different lengths (*e.g.,* Tube A *vs.* Tube D), inner tube diameters (*e.g.,* Tube D *vs.* Tube F), the distance between two consecutive corrugates (*e.g.,* Tube E *vs.* Tube F), corrugate shapes (*e.g.,* Tube E *vs.* Tube J), and corrugation distributions (*e.g.,* only Tube L has an asymmetric corrugation distribution). We studied discrete parameters of corrugated tubes for the purpose of exploring how physical factors affect the production of air puffs, since there is a lack of evidence in theory showing if it works with small fabricated parts having imprecise corrugations (*e.g.,* 3D-printed tubes). In the next section, we describe the results of these informal experiments.

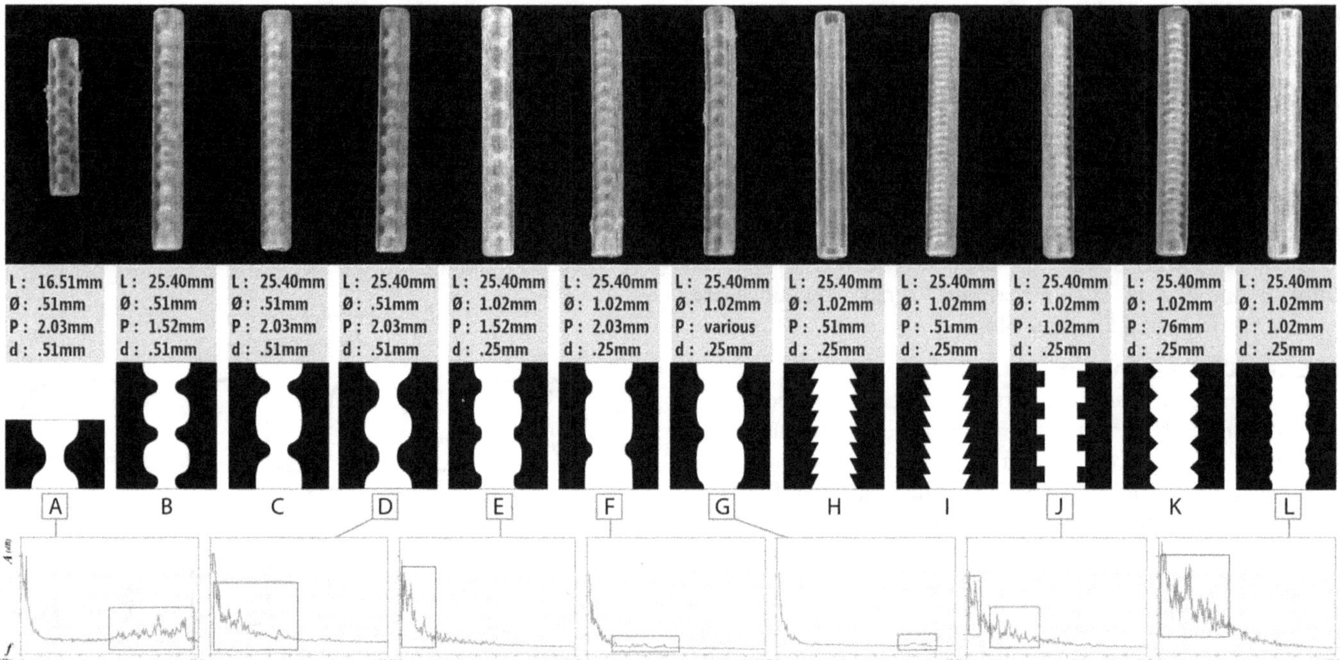

Figure 4. We conducted an informal exploration of corrugation variables that affect airflow, including: L: length, Ø: inner diameter, P: distance between corrugations, d: corrugation height. (Top row) actual 3D-printed tubes. (Middle row) corresponding diagrammatic views with parameters. (Bottom row) magnitude spectrums of signal generated through the representative corrugated tubes. The red rectangles in the plots highlight characteristically different energies across spectral signatures.

Corrugated Tube Length

To experiment with the effect of tube length on sound, we designed two tubes with similar corrugations but different lengths (Tube A and Tube D). As Figure 4 shows, air flow through a longer corrugated tube produces sound with energy at lower frequency bands, which is aligned with the Cummings model. As the length decreases, the energy of the spectrum shifts toward higher bands.

Corrugated Tube Inner Diameter

We also altered the tube's inner diameter. Again, our experiments confirmed theoretical predictions. The signal generated by a smaller diameter has more power at higher frequency bands while the output caused by a bigger diameter has more power at lower bands (*i.e.,* a smaller diameter tube produces higher pitch sounds). As Tube D and Tube F demonstrate, a mere 0.5mm disparity is sufficient to produce characteristic changes in the spectral signal.

Corrugation Distribution

The overall distribution of corrugations within a tube's interior wall also influences airflow, although it is not predictable by the learned model. With a symmetrical distribution, the output spectrum (Tube E) looks smoother than that out of an asymmetrical distribution (Tube L). Nonetheless, both variations show energy levels centered around lower frequency bands.

Space between Corrugations

The distance between successive corrugations can also impact airflow. In Figure 4, the group of Tube E and Tube F shows that only a small increase in interval distance between two corrugations can result in dramatic changes in air pulse generation. In the output of Tube F, the spectrum looks more flat than that of Tube E. In addition to uniformly distributed corrugations, incremental gaps also lead to slight differences in frequency output. As seen in Tube G, increasing gaps between corrugations generates tiny peaks among higher frequency bands and is sufficient for characteristically altering the spectral signal, which can eventually be used for input detection.

Corrugation Shape

Internally, corrugations can have uniquely varying shapes (*e.g.,* cubic, sawtooth ridges, sinusoidal contours, *etc.*). The corrugation surface can alter the reflection path of the passing sound waves, which results in the variation of frequency in the output. Tube E and Tube J illustrates a comparison of curved and cubic corrugations. Although the profiles of both output frequencies are similar, cubic corrugation causes more peaks among the middle frequency bands, which is highly differentiable.

Exploring Simultaneous Inputs

While not a physical property of the corrugated tubes themselves, we also wanted to explore whether our approach could be used to detect *simultaneous* inputs using a *single* microphone. From our experiments, we observed that the spectral results produced by individual air structures can be simply "summed up," forming a new combined output that is distinct enough to be identified by the microphone. Similar to single inputs, all combinations of simultaneous inputs require training for recognition. Additionally, we observed that our approach could support the detection of multiple types of squeezing on a single soft cavity (as long as the squeeze creates an observable signal, see Bunny and deformable pressure sensor examples).

IMPLEMENTATION

SqueezaPulse is comprised of three core parts: (i) a soft and squeezable *cavity,* (ii) a *corrugated tube* and (iii) a *microphone*. The cavity and the corrugated tube are hidden inside the body of an object and connected to a flexible latex pipe. When a soft cavity is squished, it produces a blast of air that tunnels through the corrugated tube, characteristically altering the sound wave, and then through the latex pipe to an awaiting microphone. Using supervised learning, we can identify these unique pulses of air and use them to build interactive fabricated objects.

To build a SqueezaPulse object, one must first convert a portion of their fabricated design into a soft and squeezable cavity, then connect a 3D-printed corrugated tube using a latex pipe, and finally position an electret condenser microphone next to the outlet of the corrugated tube. Multiple soft cavities and corrugated tubes can exist in the fabricated object if unique corrugations are used for each embedded tube. Below, we describe the fabrication of the soft cavities and corrugated tubes as well as our passive sensing approach.

Fabrication

Our soft cavities are made of silicone rubber compounds, but other approaches are likely possible (*e.g.,* elastic printing filament such as TangoPlus [1]). To simplify our process, we 3D-printed molds for silicone casting (analogous to that in [37]) with a regular desktop 3D printer (*e.g.,* MakerBot) and PLA or ABS filament. Further, we used Sil-Poxy glue to bond silicone with other plastic 3D-printed parts. We found that silicone casting works well at a low cost. For example, for a 2.6 cc model, it only costs ~\$0.20, a win compared to traditional methods for 3D printing soft cavities (*e.g.,* \$4.50 via Objet Connex, which is a constant print cost). For precision purposes, we printed our corrugated tubes from bottom to top along with the axes of the tube in an Objet Eden260V printer with a resolution of 600 dpi (42 microns) and clear UV-cured photopolymer. Theoretically, 3D printers with a resolution of at least 0.2mm should work.

Passive Acoustic Sensing

We use an off-the-shelf microphone for capturing air pulses (*Audio-technica ATR3350*). The incoming audio data is recorded as a linear Pulse-Code Modulation (PCM) (sampling rate: 44kHz), and stored in a circular buffer (buffer size: 5×1024). Before any further processing, we compute the Root Mean Square (RMS) of the captured audio to detect steady state (inactive) *vs.* squeezed state (active). If the onset is met, the data in the buffer is transformed into frequency domain using a Fast Fourier Transformation (FFT). Next, we downsample the raw FFT data into 128 bins and use it to derive more features: band ratios, mean, standard deviation, min index, max index, center of mass, and spectral kurtosis. These features are fed into a machine learning algorithm, where we utilize a Support Vector Machine model (SVM) for either classification or regression (the latter is used for estimating squeeze strength). For classification, we trained a Sequential Minimal Optimization (SMO)-based SVM using default optimization parameters (kernel=polynomial, C=100, e=1.0). For regression, we optimized a SMOreg using the polykernal with default optimization parameters. Both models are provided by the library of Weka [2], and they work for all computation executed on a *MacBook Pro (Core 2 Duo, SD-Mid 2009)* with a ~50ms latency.

EXAMPLE APPLICATIONS

To demonstrate the viability of our approach, how it integrates with existing fabrication techniques (*e.g.,* 3D printing), and to touch on different points in our design space, we prototyped four example SqueezaPulse applications. To view working demonstrations, see the supplementary video uploaded with the paper.

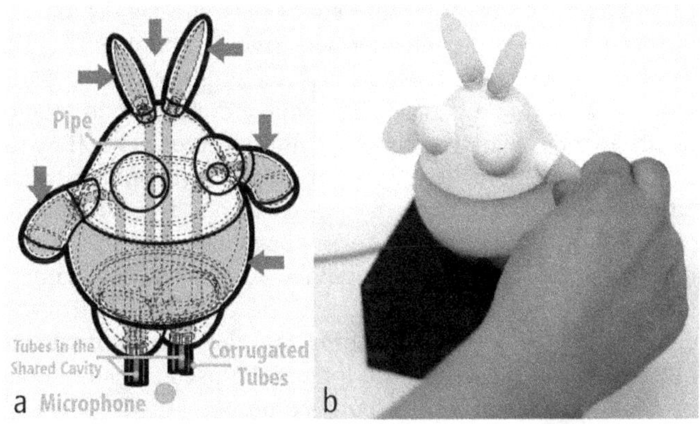

Figure 5. The interactive bunny: (a) interact with the bunny by squeezing soft parts (gray areas); (b) squeezing the bunny in real world. Blue arrows point to squeezable, interactive areas.

Interactive Toy. We created an interactive 3D-printed bunny doll with soft ears, hands, and body built on a base box, which encloses the microphone (Figure 5). We replaced both ears, hands, and the belly with soft cavities (gray areas in Figure 5). All soft parts are connected to the bottom microphone through pipes inside the bunny's body. Six different corrugated tubes (two were attached to the large cavity of the belly) were used with one shared microphone to distinguish inputs. Besides pressing each cavity, our prototype also supports simultaneous squeeze inputs, (*e.g.,* multiple combinations of squeezing both ears and hands). Interestingly, poking and pressing the belly could be differentiated by our approach, because they cause different deformations on the soft belly and therefore affect the air flows through two different corrugated tubes (the two

[1] http://www.stratasys.com/materials/polyjet/rubber-like

[2] http://www.cs.waikato.ac.nz/ml/weka/

corrugated tubes in the belly cavity). These inputs were programmed to support interactive storytelling, such as playing a character-driven sound or animation.

Deformable Force Sensor. To demonstrate how our approach can estimate squeeze strength, we made a simple force sensor using a regression-based model. In this example, squeezing is performed on a large soft pad, embedded within in a rigid 3D-printed case (Figure 6a). When the pad is pressed, the ratio between the estimated force and the maximum pressure value is shown on screen (Figure 6b). We trained a regression-based model using data samples collected at three equally spaced pressure levels (no pressure, half pressure, and full pressure).

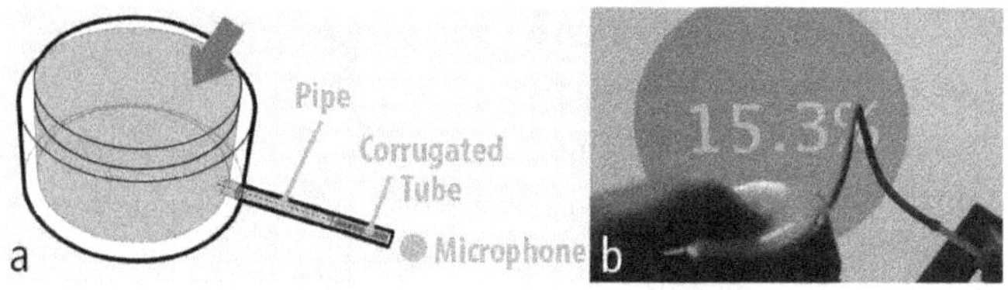

Figure 6. The force sensor: (a) pressing the soft pad generates an air flow; (b) detecting different pressure force.

Gamepad. Instead of a game controller with rigid buttons, we built a gamepad controller with five soft buttons (Figure 7), which provides a more natural feeling. Four cubic pads serve as directional buttons that receive touch-up and touch-down events, while a circular button (center) offers a selection-type input (*e.g.,* a click event). All buttons were embedded in a clear case fabricated using laser-cut acrylic pieces, bonded layer by layer. Together, this prototype offers a multi-input passive device for controlling games. For example, in a Pac-man game, the user can control the character's movements by pressing the four directional buttons, while the central button can be used to change the character's properties *(e.g.,* body color).

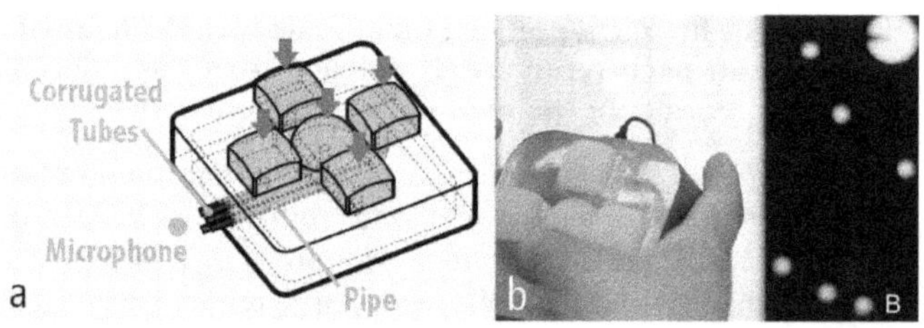

Figure 7. The gamepad: (a) pressing each soft button on the game controller generates a puff of air; (b) playing a Pac-Man game using our gamepad.

Smart Case. We also built a 3D-printed case for a handheld device with two soft buttons on the side to encourage eyes-free, tangible interaction while also limiting screen occlusion (Figure 8). These buttons can be used to power interactive applications on the phone. For example, for controlling a music player without waking up the screen, for snoozing or turning off an alarm clock without looking at the phone screen, and for capturing a photo with one hand when the other hand is occupied.

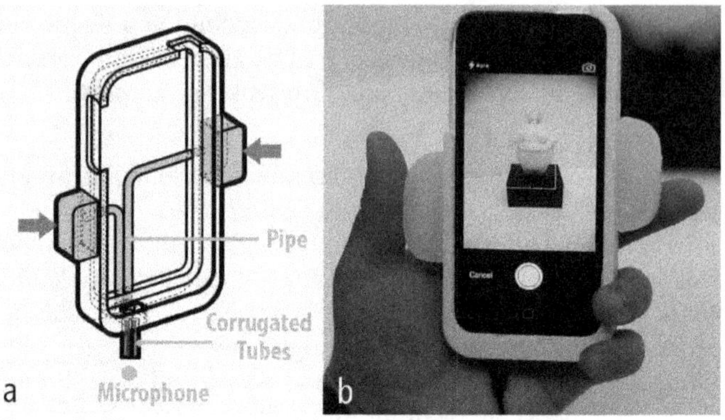

Figure 8. The smart case: (a) squeezing soft buttons generates air flows; (b) squeezing both buttons to take a photo.

EVALUATION

Our evaluations sought to answer the following questions: (i) How accurately can we classify unique air puffs? (ii) How robust are our classifiers when trained per-user *vs.* cross-user? (iii) How robust is our approach to noise? To address these questions, we conducted a user study with nine participants (aged 23-29, five female). We focused on evaluating our three classification-based applications: the gamepad, the interactive bunny, and the smart case. We also describe a follow-up noise robustness experiment.

Procedure

The study was conducted in our lab and included a 30-minute data collection session. Before the start of each session, an experimenter briefed participants and showed them how to use the prototypes. Participants were encouraged to interact with the prototypes in whichever way they wanted during data collection to improve ecological validity. All participants followed the same sequence of directed interactions starting with the gamepad controller, the bunny, and then the smart case. Participants performed specific interactions after hearing a beep sound. We collected two rounds of data for each prototype and recorded 30 samples of each interaction per round. We also collected 60 samples per prototype of 'noisy' data. For this, participants were asked to make noise on and around the device by tapping, repositioning, knocking, talking, *etc.* but to not actually press a soft button or cavity. These samples were used to evaluate *false positives* and *true negatives*.

In total, we collected 12,420 interactions—1,380 per participant (see Table 1). For the gamepad controller, we recorded press-down and press-up events on each directional button (four buttons; eight events total) and a click event on the central button. For the interactive bunny, we recorded individual cavity squeezes (four total), simultaneous squeeze inputs (both ears and both hands; two events total) and multiple inputs on one single cavity (press down on head to compress belly and poke belly; two events total). For the smart case, individual and simultaneous squeezing on soft buttons were trained (two buttons; three events total).

Prototype	Soft Button/Cavity	Interaction	# of Samples/Person
Gamepad	Left, right, top, down buttons	Press down	60 of each (240 total)
	Left, right, top, down buttons	Press up	60 of each (240 total)
	Center button	Click	60
	N/A	Noise	60
Bunny	Left & right ear; left & right hand	Squeeze	60 of each (240 total)
	Both ears, both hands	Simultaneous squeeze	60 of each (120 total)
	Body press	Press down	60
	Body poke	Poke	60
	N/A	Noise	60
Smart Case	Left & right buttons	Press down	60 of each (120 total)
	Both buttons	Simultaneous press	60
	N/A	Noise	60
Total			1,380

Table 1: The data collected during our in-lab sessions.

A laptop was used for recording acoustic data. Likewise, the laptop also received data from a connected camera feed, which served as our visual baseline for inferring user's squeeze strength and behavior.

Results

We ran a post-hoc analysis to simulate the real-time accuracy assessment with a per-user classifier, which was trained on an individual's own training data samples. We separated each participant's data into nine sets and applied 10-fold cross validation to train the classifier. The mean accuracy for the gamepad, the interactive bunny, and the smart case was: 99.4% (*SD*=0.7%), 98.2% (*SD*=1.3%), and 100% (*SD*=0%) (Figure 9). This demonstrates high robustness for per-user training. Particularly, the smart case is favorably perfect in this case.

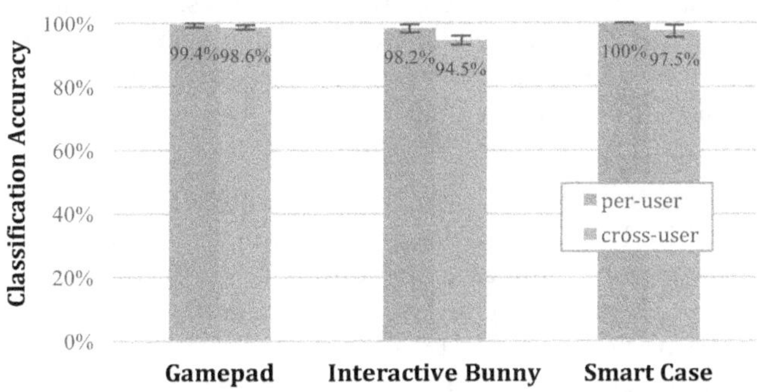

Figure 9. Classification Accuracy of per-user classifier (blue) *vs.* cross-user classifier (orange) for three applications: gamepad, interactive toy, and smart case.

We also conducted a second post-hoc analysis to examine if our approach worked across users. We estimated the performance by using a general classifier excluding that user's data for training. We trained the classifier using data from eight participants and tested using data from ninth participant with all combinations (*i.e.*, 9-fold cross validation). Figure 11 shows the results: the mean accuracy for the gamepad, the interactive bunny and the smart case were 98.6% (*SD*=0.8%), 94.5% (*SD*=1.4%), and 97.5% (*SD*=1.9%). Overall, cross-user classification accuracy is, as expected, lower than per-user classification; however, accuracy is still well above 90% demonstrating the generalizability of our approach.

The confusion matrices from our cross-user classification experiments shown in Figure 10 help uncover sources of error. For the gamepad, a major source of error was 4.4% of *Other* (*i.e.*, illegal input) events were classified as *Bottom Button Up* events. In the interactive bunny, 16.1% of *Press* input was incorrectly classified as *Poke* input. This is likely because both interactions compress the belly cavity and the resulting air flow through the two corrugated tubes creates a similar signature. Furthermore, another error happened between the category of *Right ear* and *Both Ears,* contributing 33.7% of the misclassified instances. Among the two soft buttons on the smart case, most of the error was caused between *Right Button* squeezing and *Both Buttons* squeezing, which had 66.7% of the misclassifications.

Supplementary Study: Noise Robustness

To further investigate the robustness of our approach to sound noise in various environments, we tested the gamepad controller in both a quiet office (~51dB) and a noisy coffee shop (~80dB) separately with 5 participants from the previous study. In both situations, we ran 20 trials, and each trial had 27 random inputs (*e.g.*, press down on top button, click center button, *etc.*) on the gamepad's soft buttons. In total, we collected 540 inputs. We then counted the number of correctly detected events to compute the accuracy. In this experiment, the accuracy of correctly detected button squeezing was 98.1% (*SD*=1.0%) in the quiet place and 96.8% (*SD*=1.5%) in the noisy environments. While slightly lower in the coffee shop, these results demonstrate our approach's general robustness to noise.

DISCUSSION

Although our user studies show promising results, some limitations exist. First, as with other acoustic-based sensing techniques, ambient noise has a small but undesirable impact on accuracy. One possible solution is to add sound damping material (*e.g.*, sponge) around the microphone for noise reduction. Additionally, sensing is not possible for very slow presses since airflow is weak and barely detectable by the microphone. Our corrugated tube designs offer capabilities for tracking noticeable changes in air energy at the moment of pressing buttons or exerting discrete force. Thus, our force sensing example can detect the magnitude of discrete presses, but not continuous pressure trajectories.

Further, the act of squeezing exacts physical wear and tear to prototyped objects. We suspect that this could alter the object's acoustic response over time. We did not perform any long-term evaluations, but generally, holes in pipes or cavities will ultimately affect the air pressure flowing across the corrugated channel. Future studies should stress test the system by manually poking holes and monitoring accuracy degradation. We suggest follow-up investigations that examine whether the machine learning model will still work *e.g.*, six weeks after it was trained.

Nonetheless, our approach can be easily extended to support

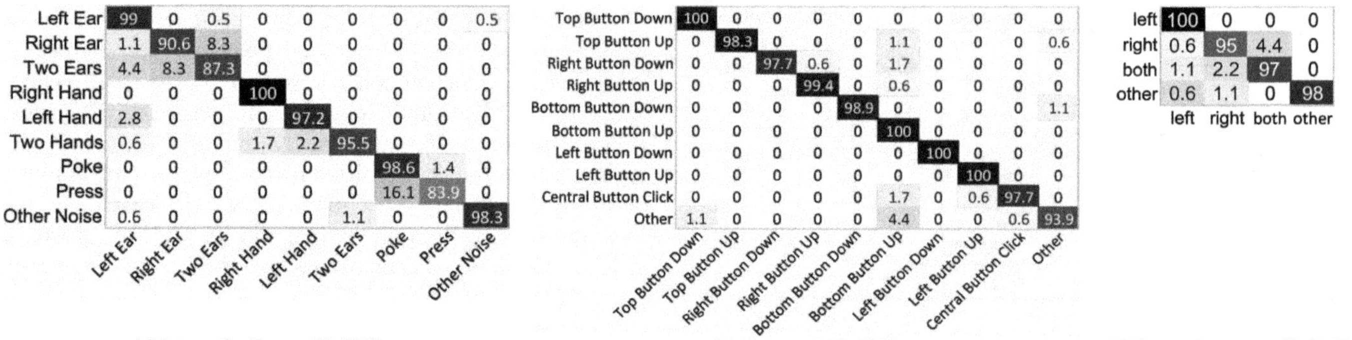

	Left Ear	Right Ear	Two Ears	Right Hand	Left Hand	Two Ears	Poke	Press	Other Noise
Left Ear	99	0	0.5	0	0	0	0	0	0.5
Right Ear	1.1	90.6	8.3	0	0	0	0	0	0
Two Ears	4.4	8.3	87.3	0	0	0	0	0	0
Right Hand	0	0	0	100	0	0	0	0	0
Left Hand	2.8	0	0	0	97.2	0	0	0	0
Two Hands	0.6	0	0	1.7	2.2	95.5	0	0	0
Poke	0	0	0	0	0	0	98.6	1.4	0
Press	0	0	0	0	0	0	16.1	83.9	0
Other Noise	0.6	0	0	0	0	1.1	0	0	98.3

(a) Interactive Bunny (N=4860)

	Top Button Down	Top Button Up	Right Button Down	Right Button Up	Bottom Button Down	Bottom Button Up	Left Button Down	Left Button Up	Central Button Click	Other
Top Button Down	100	0	0	0	0	0	0	0	0	0
Top Button Up	0	98.3	0	0	0	1.1	0	0	0	0.6
Right Button Down	0	0	97.7	0.6	0	1.7	0	0	0	0
Right Button Up	0	0	0	99.4	0	0.6	0	0	0	0
Bottom Button Down	0	0	0	0	98.9	0	0	0	0	1.1
Bottom Button Up	0	0	0	0	0	100	0	0	0	0
Left Button Down	0	0	0	0	0	0	100	0	0	0
Left Button Up	0	0	0	0	0	0	0	100	0	0
Central Button Click	0	0	0	0	0	1.7	0	0.6	97.7	0
Other	1.1	0	0	0	0	4.4	0	0	0.6	93.9

(b) Gamepad (N=5400)

	left	right	both	other
left	100	0	0	0
right	0.6	95	4.4	0
both	1.1	2.2	97	0
other	0.6	1.1	0	98

(c) Smartphone case (N=2160)

Figure 10. Confusion matrix of classification accuracies from our cross-user studies. Each cell indicates the percentage of squeeze trials assigned to a predicted class (row) for each actual class (column). N=number of total squeeze trials.

any interaction that can generate puffs of air as input. Specifically, we can integrate blowable, hands-free interaction to wearables or fabricated objects by implanting them with corrugated tubes. For instance, by 3D printing a porous air plane and channeling those holes on the surface to the corrugated tubes and the microphone, we are able to interact with the plane by blowing interactions (Figure 11). Here, we eliminate the need for squeezable cavities altogether. Unlike BLUI [22], interaction is not limited to flat surfaces (screens); single channel, linear arrays, and non-planar localization can be achieved with a single microphone. Overall, this extends to any interaction that integrates pulses or streams of air.

Figure 11. The blowable air plane: blowing toward the holes on the surface to interact with this 3D-printed plane.

Finally, our corrugated tubes are easy to fabricate and re-usable. However, fabricating corrugated tubes using traditional 3D printing techniques requires a specific operating range. Notably, a 3D printer should be able to print tube-like structures with diameters between 1.6-3.2 mm. Our corrugated tubes were printed on clear UV-cured photopolymer (Objet Connex). More recently, we have experimented with common FDM materials (*i.e.,* PLA, ABS) on consumer-grade printers (*e.g.,* MakerBot), which worked but with modifications to the corrugated structures (*e.g.,* we smoothed the corrugations to avoid support materials) to account for lower-resolution prints. While our soft cavities were created with silicon molds, we believe future 3D printers, which can combine multiple filament materials (*e.g.,* with flexible and standard filament), could create SqueezaPulse designs in a single print.

CONCLUSION

In this paper, we introduced SqueezaPulse, a technique to embed soft, low-cost, passive air structures for prototyping and fabrication of interactive objects. The air pulses generated by squeezing the soft cavity embedded in fabricated objects are detected as interactive input through a reusable and uniquely designed corrugated tube. Multiple inputs can be detected by a shared and attachable microphone, without an external sustained sound source or circuitry. We described a machine learning-based acoustic sensing approach for recognizing air pulses, experimented with a set of corrugated tube designs, and demonstrated the feasibility and accuracy of our approach with four example applications and a user study.

REFERENCES

1. Eric Brockmeyer, Ivan Poupyrev, and Scott Hudson. 2013. PAPILLON: designing curved display surfaces with printed optics. Proceedings of the 26th annual ACM symposium on User interface software and technology - UIST '13: 457–462. http://doi.org/10.1145/2501988.2502027
2. W. Burstyn. 1922. Eine neue Pfeife (a new pipe). Tech. Phys 3: 179–180.
3. Luc Geurts, Vero Vanden Abeele, Karen Vanderloock, Jolien Deville, and Jelle Saldien. 2014. Skweezee Studio: Turn your own plush toys into interactive squeezable objects. Proceedings of the 8th International Conference on Tangible, Embedded and Embodied Interaction -TEI'14: 377–380. http://doi.org/10.1145/2540930.2567896
4. Luc Geurts. 2013. Skweezees : Soft Objects that Sense their Shape Shifting.
5. Sidhant Gupta, Daniel Morris, Shwetak Patel, and Desney Tan. 2012. SoundWave: Using the Doppler Effect to Sense Gestures. Proceedings of the 2012 ACM annual conference on Human Factors in Computing Systems - CHI '12: 1911–1914. http://doi.org/10.1145/2207676.2208331

6. Chris Harrison and SE Scott E Hudson. 2008. Scratch Input: Creating Large, Inexpensive, Unpowered and Mobile Finger Input Surfaces. Proceedings of the 21st Annual ACM Symposium on User Interface Software and Technology: 205–208. http://doi.org/10.1145/1449715.1449747

7. Chris Harrison, Robert Xiao, and Scott Hudson. 2012. Acoustic barcodes: passive, durable and inexpensive notched identification tags. 1–5. http://doi.org/10.1145/2380116.2380187

8. Scott E Hudson. 2014. Printing Teddy Bears : A Technique for 3D Printing of Soft Interactive Objects. Proceedings of the SIGCHI Conference on Human Factors in Computing Systems: 459–468. http://doi.org/10.1145/2556288.2557338

9. Sungjae Hwang, Andrea Bianchi, and Kwang-yun Wohn. 2012. MicPen : Pressure-Sensitive Pen Interaction Using Microphone with Standard Touchscreen. 1847–1852.

10. Gota Kakehi, Yuta Sugiura, Anusha Withana, et al. 2011. FuwaFuwa: Detecting Shape Deformation of Soft Objects Using Directional Photoreflectivity Measurement. ACM SIGGRAPH 2011 Emerging Technologies: 5:1–5:1. http://doi.org/10.1145/2048259.2048264

11. Gierad Laput, Eric Brockmeyer, Scott E. Hudson, and Chris Harrison. 2015. Acoustruments: Passive, Acoustically-Driven, Interactive Controls for Handheld Devices. Proc. CHI: 2161–2170. http://doi.org/10.1145/2702123.2702414

12. Dingzeyu Li and David I W Levin. Acoustic Voxels : Computational Optimization of Modular Acoustic Filters.

13. Chin-yu Chien Rong-hao Liang, Long-fei Lin Liwei, and Chan Bing-yu Chen. FlexiBend : Enabling Interactivity of Multi-Part , Deformable Fabrications Using Single Shape-Sensing Strip. Figure 1: 3–7.

14. Patrizia Marti. 2015. Evaluating the Experience of Use of a Squeezable Interface. SEPTEMBER 2015: 42–49. http://doi.org/10.1145/2808435.2808461

15. V Marynel, Eric Brockmeyer, and Ruta Desai. 2015. 3D Printing Pneumatic Device Controls with Variable Activation Force Capabilities.

16. Adiyan Mujibiya, Xiang Cao, Desney S Tan, Dan Morris, Shwetak N Patel, and Jun Rekimoto. 2013. The Sound of Touch : On - body Touch and Gesture Sensing Based on Transdermal Ultraso und Propagation. 189–198. http://doi.org/10.1145/2512349.2512821

17. Roderick Murray-Smith, John Williamson, Stephen Hughes, and Torben Quaade. 2008. Stane: Synthesized Surfaces for Tactile Input. Proceedings of the SIGCHI Conference on Human Factors in Computing Systems: 1299–1302. http://doi.org/10.1145/1357054.1357257

18. Ryuma Niiyama, Xu Sun, Lining Yao, Hiroshi Ishii, Daniela Rus, and Sangbae Kim. 2015. Sticky Actuator: Free-Form Planar Actuators for Animated Objects. Proceedings of the Ninth International Conference on Tangible, Embedded, and Embodied Interaction - TEI '14: 77–84. http://doi.org/10.1145/2677199.2680600

19. Makoto Ono, Buntarou Shizuki, and Jiro Tanaka. 2013. Touch & activate: adding interactivity to existing objects using active acoustic sensing. Proceedings of the 26th annual ACM symposium on User interface software and technology: 31–40. http://doi.org/10.1145/2501988.2501989

20. Jifei Ou, Gershon Dublon, Chin-yi Cheng, Felix Heibeck, Karl Willis, and Hiroshi Ishii. 2016. Cilllia - 3D Printed Micro-Pillar Structures for Surface Texture , Actuation and Sensing. c.

21. Joseph A Paradiso, Che King Leo, Nisha Checka, and Kaijen Hsiao. 2002. Passive Acoustic Sensing for Tracking Knocks Atop Large Interactive Displays. Proceedings of the 2002 IEEE International Conference on Sensors 1: 521–527. http://doi.org/10.1109/ICSENS.2002.1037150

22. Shwetak N Patel and Gregory D Abowd. 2007. Blui. Proceedings of the 20th annual ACM symposium on User interface software and technology - UIST '07: 217. http://doi.org/10.1145/1294211.1294250

23. Huaishu Peng, Jennifer Mankoff, Scott E. Hudson, and James McCann. 2015. A Layered Fabric 3D Printer for Soft Interactive Objects. Proceedings of the 33rd Annual ACM Conference on Human Factors in Computing Systems - CHI '15: 1789–1798. http://doi.org/10.1145/2702123.2702327

24. B. Rajavel and M. G. Prasad. 2013. Acoustics of Corrugated Pipes: A Review. Applied Mechanics Reviews 65, 5: 050000. http://doi.org/10.1115/1.4025302

25. Matthew Reynolds, Alexandra Mazalek, and Glorianna Davenport. 2007. An acoustic position sensing system for large scale interactive displays. 2007 IEEE Sensors: 1193–1196. http://doi.org/10.1109/ICSENS.2007.4388622

26. Valkyrie Savage, Colin Chang, and B Hartmann. 2013. Sauron: embedded single-camera sensing of printed physical user interfaces. Proceedings of the 26th annual ACM symposium on User interface software and technology: 447–456. http://doi.org/10.1145/2501988.2501992

27. Valkyrie Savage, Andrew Head, Björn Hartmann, Dan B. Goldman, Gautham Mysore, and Wilmot Li. 2015. Lamello: Passive Acoustic Sensing for Tangible Input Components. Proceedings of the 33rd Annual ACM

Conference on Human Factors in Computing Systems - CHI '15: 1277–1280. http://doi.org/10.1145/2702123.2702207

28. Valkyrie Savage, Ryan Schmidt, Tovi Grossman, George Fitzmaurice, and Björn Hartmann. 2014. A Series of Tubes: Adding Interactivity to 3D Prints Using Internal Pipes. Proceedings of the 27th annual ACM symposium on User interface software and technology - UIST '14: 3–12. http://doi.org/10.1145/2642918.2647374
29. Valkyrie Savage, Xiaohan Zhang, and Björn Hartmann. 2012. Midas: Fabricating Custom Capacitive Touch Sensors to Prototype Interactive Objects. Proceedings of the 25th annual ACM symposium on User interface software and technology - UIST '12: 579–588. http://doi.org/10.1145/2380116.2380189
30. Catherine Schmidt-jones. 2011. Standing Waves and Wind Instruments 2 What Makes the Standing Waves in a Tube. Most: 1–10.
31. Lei Shi, Idan Zelzer, Catherine Feng, and Shiri Azenkot. 2016. Tickers and Talker: An Accessible Labeling Toolkit for 3D Printed Models. Proceedings of the 2016 CHI Conference on Human Factors in Computing Systems: 4896–4907. http://doi.org/10.1145/2858036.2858507
32. Ronit Slyper and Jessica Hodgins. 2012. Prototyping Robot Appearance, Movement, and Interactions Using Flexible 3D Printing and Air Pressure Sensors. Proceedings of the 21st IEEE International Symposium on Robot and Human Interactive Communication - RO-MAN'12 1: 6–11. http://doi.org/10.1109/ROMAN.2012.6343723
33. Ronit Slyper, Ivan Poupyrev, and Jessica Hodgins. 2011. Sensing Through Structure: Designing Soft Silicone Sensors. Proceedings of the fifth international conference on Tangible, embedded, and embodied interaction - TEI '11: 213–220. http://doi.org/10.1145/1935701.1935744
34. Karen Vanderloock, Vero Vanden Abeele, Johan A.K. Suykens, and Luc Geurts. 2013. The skweezee system: enabling the design and the programming of squeeze interactions. Proceedings of the 26th Annual ACM Symposium on User Interface Software and Technology: 521–530. http://doi.org/10.1145/2501988.2502033
35. Martin Weigel, Tong Lu, Gilles Bailly, Antti Oulasvirta, Carmel Majidi, and Jürgen Steimle. 2015. iSkin: Flexible, Stretchable and Visually Customizable On-Body Touch Sensors for Mobile Computing. Proceedings of the 33rd Annual ACM Conference on Human Factors in Computing Systems - CHI '15: 2991–3000. http://doi.org/10.1145/2702123.2702391
36. Karl Willis, Eric Brockmeyer, Scott Hudson, and Ivan Poupyrev. 2012. Printed optics: 3D printing of embedded optical elements for interactive devices. Proceedings of the 25th annual ACM symposium on User interface software and technology - UIST '12: 589–598. http://doi.org/10.1145/2380116.2380190
37. Lining Yao, Ryuma Niiyama, Jifei Ou, Sean Follmer, Clark Della Silva, and Hiroshi Ishii. 2013. PneUI: Pneumatically Actuated Soft Composite Material s for Shape Changing Interfaces. Proceedings of the 26th annual ACM symposium on User interface software and technology - UIST '13: 13–22. http://doi.org/10.1145/2501988.2502037

Experience and Ownership with a Tangible Computational Music Installation for Informal Learning

Anna Xambó
Georgia Tech
Atlanta, GA, United States
anna.xambo@gatech.edu

Brigid Drozda
Museum of Design Atlanta
Atlanta, GA, United States
bdrozda@museumofdesign.org

Anna Weisling
Georgia Tech
Atlanta, GA, United States
aweisling3@gatech.edu

Brian Magerko
Georgia Tech
Atlanta, GA, United States
magerko@gatech.edu

Marc Huet
Georgia Tech
Atlanta, GA, United States
mbhuet@gmail.com

Travis Gasque
Georgia Tech
Atlanta, GA, United States
tgasque@gmail.com

Jason Freeman
Georgia Tech
Atlanta, GA, United States
jason.freeman@gatech.edu

ABSTRACT

In this paper we present a preliminary design and initial assessment of a computational musical tabletop exhibit for children and teenagers at the Museum of Design Atlanta (MODA). We explore how participatory workshops can promote hands-on learning of computational concepts through making music. We also use a hands-on approach to assess informal learning based on *maker interviews*. Maker interviews serve to subjectively capture impromptu reflections of the visitors' achievements from casual interactions with the exhibit. Findings from our workshops and preliminary assessment indicate that experiencing and taking ownership of tangible programming on a musical tabletop is related to: *ownership of failure*, *ownership through collaboration*, *ownership of the design*, and *ownership of code*. Overall, this work suggests how to better support ownership of computational concepts in tangible programming, which can inform how to design self-learning experiences at the museum, and future trajectories between the museum and the school or home.

ACM Classification Keywords

H.5.5. Information Interfaces and Presentation (e.g., HCI): Sound and Music Computing: Systems; K.3.2. Computers and Education: Computer and Information Science Education: Computer science education

TEI '17, March 20-23, 2017, Yokohama, Japan

© 2017 ACM. ISBN 978-1-4503-4676-4/17/03...$15.00

DOI: http://dx.doi.org/10.1145/3024969.3024988

Author Keywords

Tangible User Interfaces; Hands-on Learning; Informal Learning; Computer Science Education; Algorithmic Composition; Music Performance; Field Study.

INTRODUCTION

During the last decade there has been a flurry of research on tabletop tangible user interfaces (TUIs). However, much of this research has been conducted in laboratory settings, creating a call for an increase in real-world or "in the wild" studies that tackle real-world problems [8]. Tabletop environments have been researched as a suitable platform for supporting collaboration and informal learning in education [12], with examples in the classroom [3, 4, 48] and in museum settings [9, 23, 36]. Abstract and complex concepts have been implemented and studied in museums within short-term and casual interactions, as discussed in [9] on environmental sustainability, in [23] on animal species or in [36] on cultural heritage. Computing is an important 21st century skill that has struggled to engage a diverse student population. It is an open question whether or not computational concepts can be learned on tabletops in a way which raises curiosity and maintains participant engagement even beyond the collaborative or casual experience.

Our research explores the informal learning of computational concepts using the TuneTable, a tangible tabletop interface for easily making music through code. The interest remains on whether or not, and how, children and teenagers can informally gain content knowledge in and positive attitudes towards computing in public settings by means of making music. Informal learning in museums is related to *experience* and *ownership* from interacting with exhibits or environments. Experience relates to learning from hands-on explorations, and ownership relates to the motivation for self-learning after being exposed to a learning activity. This research focuses on the nature of experience and ownership in tangible interaction. This approach is in alignment with Dewey's vision [10] of emphasizing the learner's experience, which has inspired hands-on museums and science centers, such as the Exploratorium in San Francisco, and hands-on learning with tangible user interfaces (TUIs). This work is a follow-up of [50] and the open question on how to assess informal learning through casual interactions with a tangible music interface. It is also informed by the work around the National Science Foundation-funded project EarSketch [16] and their educational perspective of teaching coding concepts by making music with a low entry level using music samples. This approach aligns with Science, Technology, Engineering, Art and Math (STEAM) [29] education by incorporating the arts when learning STEM fields. Drawing from our experiences with TuneTable at MODA, we aim to contribute to the current discourse surrounding methodologies within the arts and maker culture. Of particular interest to us is the use of participatory workshops and interviews. Here we present our preliminary findings of the hands-on, informal learning process undertaken by young visitors when engaging with tangible music coding.

BACKGROUND

Learning Computer Science and Music

There is a tradition of teaching programming by means of music. An early example is the generation of music programs written in the LOGO programming language [5]. More recent examples span a wide range, from teaching computational concepts through musical live coding practices using Scratch [44]; teaching computing concepts through Sonic Pi, a specific musical live coding environment that runs on the Raspberry Pi [1]; teaching both computer science (CS) and computer music concepts using Processing [33]; teaching how to program with Python by manipulating media content, such as sound [19]; to teaching computer programming concepts for building computer music applications and algorithmic compositions using JythonMusic [31]. Our research is mainly inspired by EarSketch [16], which promotes teaching computer science concepts by making music via writing code in either JavaScript or Python or by dragging and editing blocks in Blockly language [30]; and through the use of music samples from an extensive collection.

Tangible Play and Learning in Museums

Hands-on education was first explored by Montessori [35] and Fröbel [17] and later in the CS domain by Papert [38]. Play is an important component of learning [11]. A range of science centers promote playful experiences for learning STEM concepts, such as the Exploratorium [2]. There is a small but growing body of research that assesses and accounts for visitor learning during short-term, informal interactions (e.g., [21]), but we know little about how visitors learn computational thinking concepts through such experiences.

Tangible user interfaces (TUIs) is a broad term that refers to the design of physical artifacts that represent and control digital information. TUIs include a wide range of interfaces [15, 39]. The benefits of learning with tangible technologies have been presented by [37]. For example, Zuckerman et al. [51] explored digital Montessori-inspired Manipulatives, also known as MiMs, and endorsed their suitability for hands-on learning and group work. As a subgroup of TUIs, interactive tabletops have been reported as suitable environments for collaborative learning [20]. There are a number of systems and studies based on TUIs for music performance in public settings of which some are tabletop-based (e.g., Composition of the Table [24], the Jam'O Drum [7] or the Reactable [26]). Computational thinking practices are less explicit in these TUIs because they focus on facilitating music creation. We argue the need to make computational concepts more explicit in alignment with tangible programming [15, 18, 22]. Tangible programming for children has been investigated in public settings [15], in particular, a TUI for children was used to promote learning to code at the Boston Museum of Science [22]. There is little research to our knowledge on tabletop TUIs for music and STEAM education in informal settings, an area in which this paper contributes.

TUNETABLE: LEARNING TO CODE BY MAKING MUSIC

TuneTable[1] is an ongoing tabletop prototype that expanded EarSketch concepts onto a multi-touch tabletop with tangible programming blocks. It has been developed using open source technologies. Inspired by Reactable's [26] tabletop design, there is a lower infrared camera dedicated to the identification of tangible objects placed on the table using the computer vision software reacTIVision [27], which recognizes a set of symbols known as fiducials. There is also a projector in the base of the table, designed to provide real-time visual feedback to interactors via Processing [40]. The TuneTable project started in 2014 as a group graduate design project in co-author Magerko's Digital Media studio course at Georgia Tech and has been developed over three subsequent semesters.

Programming Language for TuneTable

The programming language syntax went through several iterations, informed by both informal observations of users and weekly project team discussions. The music performance software of Reactable [26] influenced this work, as well as the graphical representations of sound compositions in [43]. TuneTable was also inspired by the tangible programming language developed in [22] and the tangible representations of the musical instrument Tangible Sequencer.[2] Both TUIs keep a balance between simplicity in language and, respectively, computationally or musically interesting results. The overall aim of TuneTable was to develop a simple language that should make visible programming concepts by means of making music. It differentiates from the previous two examples in that it uses a standalone tabletop interface, which affords collaboration; and that it explores computational concepts applied to music making.

Users compose algorithmically using hand-sized acrylic blocks that can be placed on the table. There are 7 types of building blocks, including 1 controller, 2 sound generators,

[1]The code is publicly available at `https://github.com/mbhuet/TuneTable` (accessed July 25, 2016).

[2]`http://www.tangiblesequencer.com` (accessed July 25, 2016).

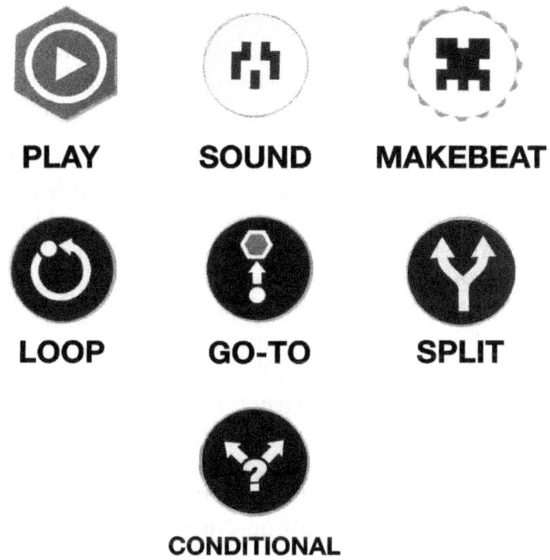

Figure 1. An example for each of the 7 types of tangible programming blocks.

and 4 functions, which are shown in Figure 1. There is a collection of 29 blocks in the version used for this study. It is possible to create both parallel and sequential connections between them. A visual flow path is projected in real time for each of the existing sequences of interconnected blocks, building a colored trail through each connected sequence. The data flow of the sounds that are playing is also indicated in real time, in alignment with Bret Victor's recommendations on learnable programming [47]. Paths that are inactive are colored in grey. For each new object placed on the table, a dashed footprint for a new object is projected, guiding and encouraging users to expand their compositions. See Figure 2 for an example of a musical sequence. Next, we describe each of the types of blocks.

- `play()` block (red, green, blue): This object is a controller and defines the start of a sequence of at least one sound. It has a hexagonal shape. The color of the flow path is defined by the color of the *play()* block. A projected play button next to the block can be touched to start the sequence. If touched, the sequence starts and a stop button replaces the play button so that the sequence can be stopped at any time. When the sequence reaches the end (the last block in the signal chain), the play button is projected again so that the sequence can be started again. There are 3 *play()* blocks.
- `sound()` block: This object is a sound generator that contains three different music samples. The sample can be switched by tapping on one of three buttons generated around the block, numbered 1–3. It has a circular shape. The current selection of sounds is drawn from the chiptune sample bank developed for EarSketch by the electronic musician Richard Devine. This particular style of music was chosen after several rounds of feedback from users, the majority of whom enjoyed the "gaming" quality of the 8-bit sounds over more traditional rock samples and ambient tracks. All sounds are in sync. There are 14 sound blocks.

Figure 2. A sequence of tangible blocks with, from top to bottom, and following the order of the sequence, a *play()* block, a *sound()* block, a *conditional()* block and two *sound()* blocks.

- `makeBeat()` block: This object is a sound generator of sample rhythm patterns similar to the *makeBeat()* function in EarSketch. It has a gear shape to be distinguished from sound blocks. There are 3 different *makeBeat()* blocks for a 4-, 8- and 16-beat patterns, respectively. This is the only block that can produce sound independent from the *play()* block and encourage users to tap inside the indented areas to build their own custom rhythmic sequences.
- `loop()` block: This block is a function that spawns a projected, self-contained looping path, inside which additional sound blocks can be added. It has a circular shape. The more sound blocks are added, the bigger the looping path becomes. A projected number next to the block with plus and minus buttons can set the number of loops, which works by counting down to zero. There are 2 *loop()* blocks.
- `go-to()` block (red, green, blue): This block represents a function, pointing the flow path to the play button associated with its own color (a red *go-to()* block points to the red *play()* block, and so on). It has a circular shape. This block allows users to "jump" between sequences, building more complex compositions and enabling collaborations between individuals and groups working on the table at the same time. There are 3 *go-to()* blocks.
- `split()` block: This block splits the signal into two paths running in parallel. It has a circular shape. There are 2 *split()* blocks.
- `conditional()` block: This block creates a binary path that allows the user to switch between two possible branches on a sequence chain. It has a circular shape. There are 2 *conditional()* blocks.

Physical Design

The physical design of the table has been adapted to a museum setting and to the activity of casual making music in collaboration. This table was originally developed by [49] and used in [32]. We decided to incorporate a set of transparent orange acrylic panels allowing visitors to see what is behind the scenes of the table. We replaced small wheels attached to the table with larger, more robust wheels for easy mobility. We implemented a storage system for the blocks to avoid stacking

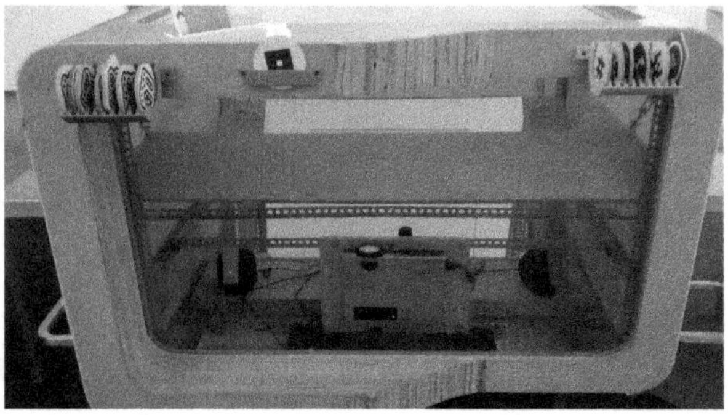

Figure 3. Close-up of the TuneTable.

them on the edges of the table. These mountable block holders, designed and printed through 3D modeling, are placed in a trough-like style at the corners of the table, providing space for users and evoking the experience of selecting vinyl at a jukebox. We also added custom mounting brackets to hold separately preferred blocks. We wanted to ensure that blocks were easy to access from multiple sides of the table, were easy to see, did not interfere with visitors' interactions, and saved space in an organized way. Figure 3 shows a close-up of these elements.

As for the icons representing the sounds, we drew inspiration from the video game *Space Invaders*, which aligns with the chiptune sounds. We developed a black and white customized block icon generator with Processing. We selected the set of icons by making sure that the images were distinct enough from one another, and that they could be individually identified. As for the icons representing the functions, we chose metaphors that were simple and clear, mostly using arrows, basic symbols and colors for the *go-to()* and *play()* blocks.

STUDY DESIGN

Research Questions

Our overarching research question is whether or not, and how, children and teenagers can informally gain content knowledge in and positive attitudes towards computing through experience and ownership in public settings. The focus remains on how to facilitate informal learning through casual interactions and how to assess to what extent children and teenagers learn from them. In particular, we are interested in a preliminary insight on: (1) how can we assess informal and hands-on learning of music and code in an open form; (2) to what extent teaching the technology behind the scenes of the artifact can help to learn music and coding concepts; (3) to what extent a participatory and experiential design approach in informal learning can help users feel ownership; and (4) to what extent an interactive tabletop is useful to promote this educational approach.

Setting

The Museum of Design Atlanta[3] (MODA) is a museum located in Atlanta, Georgia, devoted exclusively to design. MODA's mission is to advance the understanding and appreciation of design as the convergence of creativity and functionality through exhibitions, education, and programming for visitors of all ages.

[3] `http://www.museumofdesign.org` (accessed July 25, 2016).

As a precursor to the study, a collaboration between MODA and the TuneTable team informally started in Spring 2016. We observed two of their in-house workshops of 1.5 hours duration each to get a sense of their teaching approach: a hands-on workshop on Arduino with 4 children and a hands-on workshop on littleBits [6] and LEGO with 2 children aged 6–7 years old. This provided us with valuable knowledge not only regarding the demographics of current MODA patrons, but an inside look into how they structure, prepare for, and run kid-centric technology-based workshops. Workshops at MODA are carefully prepared by co-author Drozda, a design thinking and innovation educator who develops interdisciplinary programs that combine cutting-edge STEAM tools with the design process. Her emphasis on exploratory learning serves to emphasize the learning process rather than an end result, encouraging self-motivation and confidence in the kids themselves. Beyond the classroom, she also works to incentivize kids to continue work at home, and on occasion she conducts informal "mini-interviews" through social media.

Teaching practices at MODA are inspired by hands-on and experiential education. They resonate with project based learning [28], and a minimal intervention in education, such as the experiment of the Hole-in-the-Wall in India [34]. The TuneTable is located in the lobby area at MODA, with the aim at inviting patrons to freely interact with and learn from the table, similar to the Hole-in-the-Wall experiment. In MODA, ownership is a key term that refers to the mastery of the material, a desire to continue to self-learn and build upon that, and the desire to teach others. Thus, it represents a successful interaction with an exhibit, and by extension a fruitful visit to the museum. Here we investigate the nature of ownership and experience within a tangible and tabletop environment.

Participants

We conducted observations of two school field trips. In the first school field trip, there were about 20 campers, who ranged in age from 11–16 years old and came with 2 adult chaperones/teachers. Some of the students and chaperones participated in the workshop. There was a fairly even balance of girls and boys. In the second school field trip, there were 24 campers divided into 4 groups who came with 10 adult chaperones/teachers. The ages ranged 8–14 years old. From here on, F1-G1 refers to the group of the first field trip, whilst F2-G1 up to F2-G4 refer to the four groups of the second field trip.

Procedure

The two field trips were 1.5 hours divided into two parts of forty-five minutes: an interactive, guided tour of the current exhibition and a hands-on design activity in the lobby/design bar area of MODA that promotes comprehension and practice of the design process. The difference between school field trips and in-house workshops is that in the former there is less time for the hands-on activity and the number of patrons is larger. Moreover, in field trips there are chaperones who can engage with the activity. In the in-house workshops, instead, parents are invited to engage with the activity at the end so that children celebrate their achievements with them. The hands-on design activity was on the TuneTable. The activity was a challenge: creating an audiovisual piece for a music album.

During the TuneTable activity, the artifact was introduced as a collaborative work between Georgia Institute of Technology (Georgia Tech) and MODA. In F1-G1, campers were invited to learn about both the TuneTable and EarSketch. Tutorials were kept informal and campers were encouraged to jump in to the two activities as they wanted. In the second field trip, the 4 groups were introduced to the TuneTable with more detail, including hardware, software, and the blocks. Campers were exposed to the topic of design process by discussing that the TuneTable is a musical instrument with an open-ended design. Moreover, it was discussed as a prototype to teach coding and computational music in an innovative way, establishing connections with the current exhibit on wearable technology. For example, the reacTIVision software was explained as how it sees and reacts to the fiducials on the blocks. Fiducials were compared with barcodes and with the QR codes that the Oculus Rift in the wearable technology exhibition uses for augmented reality. Processing was also introduced more briefly, which was run in front of the students. Students were familiar with Blockly and Scratch with regard to programming experience. The TuneTable blocks were also introduced, e.g., the 3 *makeBeat()* blocks, the 3 *play()* blocks and the 3 *go-to()* blocks. Often the *loop()* block was introduced as similar to block coding. Computer science aspects of the table and its functions were also explained by comparing it to different Scratch blocks. Then students were encouraged to explore themselves the different blocks. Finally, the groups created a piece together.

Data Collection

We collected data in the wild [42], as opposed to lab studies. The facilitator of the activity recorded video snippets of the group's interactions using a handheld mobile phone. The role of the facilitator is a trade-off between adapting an action research approach of intervening in the scene [41] and minimal intervention. This approach is suitable for such an early stage of research to help visitors think aloud during their casual interactions. The videos were captured focusing on patrons' hands interacting with the blocks. This approach excludes the observations of eye-contact and face-to-face behavior, which can be useful in later stages of this research. In the case of EarSketch, only the screens of the computers were recorded. After fifteen to twenty minutes, students tended to show to chaperones/teachers their piece and ease back from the table. If they did so sooner, the facilitator walked over and asked questions to provoke them to inquiry about their composition. The enquiries were video recorded, as well as the piece playing and a final reflection about it. This recording approach is termed *maker interviews* and has been used extensively by co-author Drozda for teaching LEGOs, littleBits, or Minecraft [46], among others. The video is used as a way to making reflection fun and to show that designing with this technology is worth a video. It also aligns with the use of social media, which is commonly experienced by patrons in their everyday life. The questions are open-ended and try to support complex imaginative play.

Data Analysis

We had informal discussions between the first four authors before, during, and after data collection. Our discussions were about visitors' behaviors around the table with a focus on the videos from the field trips. We identified and iterated over 4 emerging themes related to the research questions and workshop experiences:

1. *Ownership of failure*: It refers to how failure is faced during the learning process of computational concepts on a tabletop interface, and whether self-learners can maintain motivation to seek solutions and continue self-education through failure.
2. *Ownership through collaboration*: It refers to the impact of tabletop collaboration to the sense of ownership of computational concepts. It also embraces a sense of shared ownership, a term that refers to the group acquiring mastery of the material.
3. *Ownership of the design*: It refers to the satisfaction in the music composition as the first step in participating in the design process of the tabletop interface. It indicates the ability to transfer knowledge to other uses of design and the design thinking process coming from multiple exposures of creating.
4. *Ownership of code*: It refers to the understanding of computational concepts on a tabletop interface.

FINDINGS

The MODA educators recorded 13 video snippets of the first field trip, and 14 video snippets of the second field trip. The videos captured different moments of the activity, from initial exploration of the table, to the creation of the audiovisual piece, to the reflection on it with maker interviews. The group F1-G1 was late. Thus, a single huge group was asked to create an audiovisual piece together due to the time constraints. In F2, campers were divided into 4 groups and each created an audiovisual piece. G4 was formed as a mixture of girls from previous groups. Each group spent about twenty minutes with the table for experiential play and learning.

EarSketch vs. TuneTable

In F1-G1, the EarSketch group consisted of one girl and four boys, whilst TuneTable was used by a larger group of 6 to 8 campers. There were five laptops open to EarSketch (see Fig. 4) and an additional computer with a projection of the web application, which was controlled by the educator. The two teams worked for about 20 minutes. Most of the EarSketch team had prior coding experience. The difference between the EarSketch and the TuneTable's experience is that in the former, campers had a larger sound palette to explore (e.g., dubstep samples). For example, a boy sat down at EarSketch and spent a long time exploring the dubstep samples, whilst another boy was experimenting with rhythm and beats. In

Figure 4. A laptop with EarSketch at MODA.

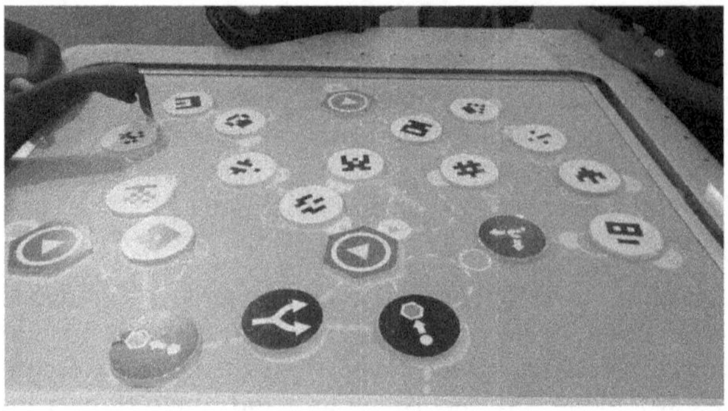

Figure 5. A group creating an audiovisual piece with the TuneTable using 3 *play()* blocks, 2 *go-to()* blocks, a *conditional()* block, a *split()* block, and 14 *sound()* blocks.

the TuneTable, instead, campers worked with the given subset of sounds provided by the tangible objects. Another prominent difference was the way of coding: in EarSketch campers typed the code (they worked with the scripted version of EarSketch), whereas coding in the TuneTable was through the use of physical blocks. This more individualized experience with EarSketch was visible when, for example, a girl who was working with a computer had the opportunity to collaborate with a MODA intern who has some Javascript experience. This one-to-one interaction helped her to get further in coding during the short amount of time. TuneTable was found to be easier to operate, and the tangible blocks were introduced to the groups by comparing them to Blockly, which they already had exposure to. Our future intent is to support transfer knowledge from TuneTable in the museum to EarSketch at the school or at home, however the duration of the study did not allow us to do that yet. This comparison between the two platforms helped us to start exploring the different affordances of each platform and the potential challenges we might face when transferring from one platform to the other.

Coding Errors in TuneTable

It was difficult to tell whether campers were understanding the error messages with the table. In a number of occasions, there were many blocks on the table, of which a number of them were unused. Based on how campers moved the blocks on the table, it seemed that they often thought that the blocks were being used. For example, a common error was to combine the play button with the *makeBeat()*, not realizing that this combination was not working. Sometimes the sound blocks were having difficulty in staying connected due to momentarily recognition issues with the computer vision engine. However, we noticed that the campers did not try rearranging them to straighten their connected visual flow path.

Even though campers were introduced to the different types of tangible blocks, it is unclear from the videos whether groups were understanding the computational concepts, such as *loop()*, *conditional()*, *split()*, or *go-to()*'s, because they were either not used or they were disconnected from other blocks on the table. For example, F2-G1 did not investigate why the loop was not working and shifted to exploring other blocks.

Designing and Listening to the Audiovisual Pieces

Teaching what technologies are behind the scenes of the table proved to be useful for campers to be more critical with their achievements. In particular, campers were critical with the sounds produced. For F2-G1, the sounds were like "an annoying video game", or "just really glitchy". However, the criticism was on the sound design and sound outcome, as opposed to the design of the tangible representations of computational concepts or the visual feedback.

Each audiovisual piece varied in complexity. The configurations ranged from basic configurations, such as not using functions (F2-G2); to using a few functions, such as *makebeat()* and *loop()* in case of F2-G1; to using a range of functions, such as *conditional()*, *split()*, and *go-to()*'s in case of F2-G3 (see Fig. 5).

There was a clear distinction between the design process of the piece vs. the performance of the piece, between building and listening. Both were quite collaborative in nature. In the presentation of the piece, there were a number of synchronized actions. For example, often campers coordinated on hitting play buttons and synchronizing other activations during the piece, such as F2-G3, in which they coordinated to touch the *play()* block in sync for a synchronized start; or F2-G2, in which three different people worked to make the play button run. However, at the same time, the interaction was little once the configuration of the piece was defined. This was closer to a listening activity, as opposed to a performance activity. Group members were staring at the table, listening to the music composition. "Don't touch it!" said a camper from F2-G2. In F2-G4, some of the campers were even dancing when listening to their piece.

The facilitator celebrated perseverance with the compositions, as MODA generally does with the different aspects of the design process. From the maker interviews, it is hard to tell whether campers were learning computational concepts, which informs us about what we need to consider in future research. The facilitator challenged the groups if they looked stuck. For example, in F2-G1, she challenged the campers to try more than one *play()* block.

Collaboration in TuneTable

Collaboration happened in many ways. The groups worked in collaboration during the design process of the piece. For example, F1-G1 decided in team what sounds worked best. The groups also collaborated when performing the piece, as discussed in the previous section. Groups also collaborated on composing and solving problems. For example, F2-G2 had two blocks that were glitching because they were placed very closed together. As a team, they decided to line the sounds up so they linked the blocks again and solved the glitching. We also identified different group dynamics. For example, F2-G2 was mostly run by older girls who were telling another girl not to place blocks in a certain way.

In the museum, ownership happens if patrons retain any interest on the topic. It is related to persistence of work, to when people come back and want to work more on a topic. Field trips were mostly rushed so it is difficult to tell whether visitors took long-term ownership. However, we observed that some of them did take short-term ownership of certain aspects, e.g., when sharing what they learned between them.

DISCUSSION

Next, we discuss four preliminary levels of ownership that we observed in the field trips and that inform our future work: *ownership of failure*, *ownership through collaboration*, *ownership of the design*, and *ownership of code*.

Ownership of Failure

Failing is part of the learning process. Solving errors in the code is part of learning to program, yet it is less obvious how to tackle error handling on a tabletop interface. Moreover, in informal learning there is little time for working on errors or 'debugging'. An open question is how to strengthen the relationship between error handling and failure in a tabletop environment in informal learning; in particular, how to embrace error handling processes in short-term tabletop interaction, so that students are able to identify programming errors, are motivated to solve them, and solve them within a short time scale. Another open question is how to promote ownership of failure and successes built on persisting through mistakes within a tabletop environment. Making the errors visible as part of the TUI contrasts with the tangible programming language proposed by [22], a physical jigsaw puzzle in which it is very difficult to produce a syntax error.

When campers were asked about their understanding of errors that they created or learned from, the focus often turned to the functionality of the TuneTable itself. Students usually pointed out sounds they liked or disliked and potential table glitches. Even with more leading questions from the facilitator, ownership of trial and error learning did not seem readily embraced. A potential approach is to be more explicit about the errors in code as part of the learning process and their manifestation in the table. For example, letting the students know that errors in the tangible programming language will inhibit a program from running properly, and asking them awareness questions about whether, for example, every block on the table is connected. In the next design iteration of the table we will consider how to make more visible the error messages for unused blocks in a standalone format, as opposed to use the help of a facilitator.

Ownership through Collaboration

Discovery and knowledge transfer happened in collaboration, in alignment with project based learning [28]. For example, understanding how the blocks work or creating a piece together. This indicates the suitability of a tabletop interface for informal learning in museum settings, as already pointed out by [12, 50]. Even though collaboration was generally egalitarian between campers, there were also less egalitarian situations. It is unclear to what extent the facilitator should intervene in unequal group dynamics. The effect of an intervention is that it can inhibit the creative flow of the group. In addition, facilitators often have to consider chaperone/teacher involvement in teaching, which can affect the facilitator's intervention. MODA facilitators may find themselves collaborating with the chaperones, similar to the second field trip, or teaching alone as in the first field trip. Collaboration in informal learning is essential, which includes both peer-to-peer learning and learning from chaperones/facilitators. A little level of intervention from the facilitator promotes peer-to-peer learning, yet it is an open question how to best intervene when students are stuck or seem to not understand the computational concepts. A potential approach to addressing these collaboration challenges is discussed in [13] as a longer-term peer-to-peer collaboration, which should be adapted to shorter-term and in-the-wild collaborations. Future work should address how the table can support multiple perspectives of collaboration, both with and without a facilitator's intervention.

Ownership of the Design

Presenting the table as an iterative prototype design, and learning how the table works, promoted critical thinking among campers about the design process. Yet, the design of the table is still fixed. For example, a useful feature would be the ability to customize the sounds from the large EarSketch database, so that students can work with sounds of their choice. We noticed more interest on critiquing the table in the second field trip, in which there was a better understanding of how the eye of the table, i.e., camera and computer vision engine, works. The ownership of the design process as a tool aligns with participatory design [45], STEAM education [29] and project based learning [28] applied to informal learning in a museum setting.

During the creation of the final piece, compositions of the groups went through iterations, and a reflection process was raised by facilitator's questions to students about their design decisions. The maker interviews proved to be useful as an open form of inquiry and reflection, similar to the research methods used in the digital arts [25] and the maker culture. It seems that one of the key roles of a facilitator is precisely to help students to learn about critical thinking, and that a tabletop can be a suitable platform to learn about it. This knowledge can in turn be transferred to other design fields and media. At this stage, however, it is an open question how to make patrons reflect critically on their artistic work from tabletop interactions, with no intervention from a facilitator.

Ownership of Code

As previously discussed, there is a tension between the level of intervention of the facilitator and the group dynamics with their own pace of learning. Ownership is related to the understanding of the concepts, and time can be a factor. It is thus still an open question how to effectively deliver computational concepts within a 20-minute session in a self-contained and modular style. Students who have come back to the TuneTable are visibly more consistent with their interactions and take clearer ownership than students who do not come back. This became apparent through the videos and arguably it can be solved with a more explicit intentionality from the facilitator and signage. For example, showing a display describing the seven building blocks of the tangible programming language, and adding teasers with questions such as "Do you know that you are coding?" or "TuneTable is designed to teach coding" can be helpful. The silence of the table when nobody plays and from people who stored the blocks in the storage area and left, could be also a preventing factor.

It is important to think about how to raise motivation and increase intention to persist in computing beyond learning small snippets of code within short-term interactions. Both the educator and the interactive system should promote this approach. In the case of MODA, with a variety of design activities available to visitors, educators often encourage students to follow their interests. This style is influenced from multi-sensory learning centers, as well as the Reggio Emilia approach [14]. Design provocations are intended to be positive introductions to the subject matter. Educators are mindful that a negative experience with EarSketch, for instance, might lead to a distaste for coding. A pedagogical challenge is how to teach coding in alignment with educational principles of informal learning in public settings. For example, clearer connections could be made more visible between TuneTable and EarSketch by comparing Blockly code (as opposed to the script code) and tangible programming. However, arguably, using Blockly with older campers than fifth graders can be less inspiring as they perhaps prefer to work with scripting programming languages that they already know.

In order to support and motivate self-learning and ownership among students in informal learning, technologies need to be known, accessible and free. A successful example of ownership of code are the MODA Minecraft workshops led by co-author Drozda, in which students are passionate about Minecraft and start circuitry and learn syntax that is similar to Python or Java. Another successful example is the story of the challenge with the 3D printer Tinkercad. Drozda led numerous field trip tutorials that introduced the open-source, browser-based CAD program, Tinkercad, and gave a challenge that any student who created an original 3D model in Tinkercad could have the model printed by MODA. Although this challenge was presented to numerous groups, only one student completed it. The student learned it first through MODA, but it was then re-enforced in school, which was probably a key factor to the student's progress. This example indicates that trajectories from school to museums can promote self-learning and ownership in informal learning contexts. However, an emerging challenge is to motivate students with new, less popular educational platforms operated with code that are accessible within short-term interactions, and to support longer-term interactions from these experiences.

CONCLUSION AND FUTURE WORK

In this paper we introduced the design of the TuneTable system, a musical tabletop for learning tangible programming through music, and presented its initial assessment at MODA. We explored whether informal learning can occur through experience and ownership, and identified four related themes: *ownership of failure*, *ownership through collaboration*, *ownership of the design*, and *ownership of code*. Although in-the-wild research can be more risky, we discovered that short video snippets, and in particular, maker interviews led by the facilitator of the activity, are a helpful tool for scanning informal learning of music and code adapted to each group dynamics. At this stage, it was useful that the programming activities were open and flexible. Future work includes comparing this methodological approach with other reflective techniques, e.g., concurrent or retrospective, in terms of noisiness.

We investigated the benefits of teaching how the table works to students by participatory and experiential design, and found that they can become more critical. However, some computing processes need to be more visible from a pedagogical design perspective, such as error messages and error processes. Future research points to exploring how to deal with error messages in a tangible programming language. Also, we discovered that the tabletop promoted hands-on collaboration. However, computational concepts were hardly explicitly discussed. Future work includes developing best practices on how to teach and inquire students about computational concepts. Also next steps include exploring how to incentive patrons to come by themselves with no intervention of the museum's facilitators. This would include visible signage and teasers. In addition, the assessment of participatory workshops and maker interviews should be adapted to more open self-learning.

Finally, we pointed directions on how to better support ownership of computational concepts in tangible programming. This aims at promoting not only self-learning experiences at the museum, but also trajectories between the museum and the school or home. We should think technologies and props to support self-learning beyond the museum experience, so that it can have impact at a longer term. In particular, a better link between the TuneTable and EarSketch could be designed for supporting trajectories between the museum and the school or home. This could foster connections between groups online.

Overall, this paper showed a successful interdisciplinary collaboration between the museum and academia.

ACKNOWLEDGMENTS

We are thankful to Jessica Anderson who has collaborated in the first version of the TuneTable. We are grateful to Paul Clifton for advice on tabletop building and to Ali Mazalek for generous table donation. Thanks to Laura Flusche, Blair Banks, Neil Miller and the MODA staff for their constant help and enthusiasm during this study. Our thanks also to the participants of this study. The TuneTable project receives funding from the National Science Foundation (DRL #1612644).

REFERENCES

1. Samuel Aaron and Alan F. Blackwell. 2013. From Sonic Pi to Overtone: Creative Musical Experiences with Domain-Specific and Functional Languages. In *Proceedings of the First ACM SIGPLAN Workshop on Functional Art, Music, Modeling & Design (FARM '13)*. 35–46.
2. Sue Allen. 2004. Designs for Learning: Studying Science Museum Exhibits that Do More than Entertain. *Science Education* 88, Suppl. 1 (2004), S17–S33.
3. Alissa N. Antle. 2015. Scratching the Surface: Opportunities and Challenges from Designing Interactive Tabletops for Learning. In *Learning Technologies and the Body: Integration and Implementation*, Victor R. Lee (Ed.). Routledge (Taylor & Francis), 55–73.
4. Alissa N. Antle, Jillian L. Warren, Aaron May, Min Fan, and Alyssa F. Wise. 2014. Emergent Dialogue: Eliciting Values During Children's Collaboration with a Tabletop Game for Change. In *Proceedings of the 2014 Conference on Interaction Design and Children (IDC '14)*. 37–46.
5. Jeanne Bamberger. 1979. *Logo Music Projects: Experiments in Musical Perception and Design*. Massachusetts Institute of Technology.
6. Ayah Bdeir. 2009. Electronics as Material: littleBits. In *Proceedings of the 3rd International Conference on Tangible and Embedded Interaction (TEI '09)*. 397–400.
7. Tina Blaine and Tim Perkis. 2000. The Jam-O-Drum Interactive Music System: A Study in Interaction Design. In *Proceedings of the 3rd Conference on Designing Interactive Systems (DIS '00)*. 165–173.
8. Anders Bruun, Kenneth Eberhardt Jensen, Dianna Hjorth Kristensen, and Jesper Kjeldskov. 2016. Escaping the Trough: Towards Real-World Impact of Tabletop Research. *International Journal of Human-Computer Interaction* (2016), 1–17.
9. Sarah D'Angelo, D. Harmon Pollock, and Michael Horn. 2015. Fishing with Friends: Using Tabletop Games to Raise Environmental Awareness in Aquariums. In *Proceedings of the 14th International Conference on Interaction Design and Children (IDC '15)*. 29–38.
10. John Dewey. 1938/1997. *Experience and Education*. Kappa Delta Pi.
11. Beverlie Dietze and Diane Kashin. 2012. *Playing and Learning in Early Childhood Education*. Pearson Canada.
12. Pierre Dillenbourg and Michael Evans. 2011. Interactive Tabletops in Education. *International Journal of Computer-Supported Collaborative Learning* 6, 4 (2011), 491–514.
13. Elizabeth Dobson and Karen Littleton. 2016. Digital Technologies and the Mediation of Undergraduate Students' Collaborative Music Compositional Practices. *Learning, Media and Technology* 41, 2 (2016), 330–350.
14. Carolyn Edwards, Lella Gandini, and George Forman (Eds.). 1993. *The Hundred Languages of Children: The Reggio Emilia Approach to Early Childhood Education*. ERIC.
15. Ylva Fernaeus and Jakob Tholander. 2006. Finding Design Qualities in a Tangible Programming Space. In *Proceedings of the SIGCHI Conference on Human Factors in Computing Systems (CHI '06)*. 447–456.
16. Jason Freeman, Brian Magerko, Tom McKlin, Mike Reilly, Justin Permar, Cameron Summers, and Eric Fruchter. 2014. Engaging Underrepresented Groups in High School Introductory Computing through Computational Remixing with EarSketch. In *Proceedings of the 45th ACM Technical Symposium on Computer Science Education (SIGCSE '14)*. 85–90.
17. Friedrich Fröbel. 1885. *The Education of Man*. A. Lovell & Company, New York.
18. Daniel Gallardo, Carles Fernández Julià, and Sergi Jordà. 2008. TurTan: A Tangible Programming Language for Creative Exploration. In *3rd IEEE International Workshop on Horizontal Interactive Human-Computer Systems (TABLETOP 2008)*. IEEE Computer Society, Los Alamitos, CA, 89–92.
19. Mark Guzdial. 2003. A Media Computation Course for Non-Majors. In *ACM SIGCSE Bulletin*, Vol. 35. 104–108.
20. Amanda Harris, Jochen Rick, Victoria Bonnett, Nicola Yuill, Rowanne Fleck, Paul Marshall, and Yvonne Rogers. 2009. Around the Table: Are Multiple-Touch Surfaces Better than Single-Touch for Children's Collaborative Interactions?. In *Proceedings of the 9th International Conference on Computer Supported Collaborative Learning (CSCL '09)*. 335–344.
21. Michael S. Horn, Brenda C. Phillips, Evelyn Margaret Evans, Florian Block, Judy Diamond, and Chia Shen. 2016. Visualizing Biological Data in Museums: Visitor Learning With an Interactive Tree of Life Exhibit. *Journal of Research in Science Teaching* 53, 6 (2016), 895–918.
22. Michael S. Horn, Erin Treacy Solovey, and Robert J.K. Jacob. 2008. Tangible Programming and Informal Science Learning: Making TUIs Work for Museums. In *Proceedings of the 7th international Conference on Interaction Design and Children (IDC '08)*. 194–201.
23. Eva Hornecker. 2008. "I don't Understand it Either, but it is Cool" – Visitor Interactions with a Multi-Touch Table in a Museum. In *3rd IEEE International Workshop on Horizontal Interactive Human-Computer Systems (TABLETOP 2008)*. 113–120.
24. Toshio Iwai. 1999. Composition on the Table. In *Proceedings of the 26th International Conference on Computer Graphics and Interactive Techniques (SIGGRAPH '99)*. 10.
25. Carey Jewitt, Anna Xambó, and Sara Price. 2016. Exploring Methodological Innovation in the Social Sciences: The Body in Digital Environments and the Arts. *International Journal of Social Research Methodology* (2016), 1–16.

26. Sergi Jordà. 2008. On Stage: The Reactable and Other Musical Tangibles Go Real. *International Journal of Arts and Technology* 1, 3/4 (2008), 268–287.

27. Martin Kaltenbrunner and Ross Bencina. 2007. reacTIVision: A Computer-Vision Framework for Table-Based Tangible Interaction. In *Proceedings of the 1st International Conference on Tangible and Embedded Interaction (TEI '07)*. 69–74.

28. John Larmer, John Mergendoller, and Suzie Boss. 2015. *Setting the Standard for Project Based Learning*. ASCD.

29. John Maeda. 2013. STEM + Art = STEAM. *The STEAM Journal* 1, 1 (2013), 34.

30. Anand Mahadevan, Jason Freeman, and Brian Magerko. 2016. An Interactive, Graphical Coding Environment for EarSketch Online using Blockly and Web Audio API. In *Proceedings of the 2nd Web Audio Conference (WAC '16)*.

31. Bill Manaris and Andrew R. Brown. 2015. *Making Music with Computers: Creative Programming in Python*. CRC Press.

32. Ali Mazalek, Claudia Winegarden, Tristan Al-Haddad, Susan J. Robinson, and Chih-Sung Wu. 2009. Architales: Physical/Digital Co-design of an Interactive Story Table. In *Proceedings of the 3rd International Conference on Tangible and Embedded Interaction (TEI '09)*. 241–248.

33. Adam L. Meyers, Marilyn C. Cole, Evan Korth, and Sam Pluta. 2009. Musicomputation: Teaching Computer Science to Teenage Musicians. In *Proceedings of the Seventh ACM Conference on Creativity and Cognition (CC '09)*. 29–38.

34. Sugata Mitra and Vivek Rana. 2001. Children and the Internet: Experiments with Minimally Invasive Education in India. *British Journal of Educational Technology* 32, 2 (2001), 221–232.

35. Maria Montessori. 1912. *The Montessori Method*. Frederick A. Stokes, New York.

36. Reese Muntean, Kate Hennessy, Alyssa F. Wise, Susan Rowley, Jordan Wilson, Brendan Matkin, Rachael Eckersley, Perry Tan, and Ron Wakkary. 2015. Belongings: A Tangible Interface for Intangible Cultural Heritage. In *Proceedings of the Electronic Visualisation and the Arts (EVA 2015)*.

37. Claire O'Malley and Danae Stanton Fraser. 2004. Literature Review in Learning with Tangible Technologies.

38. Seymour Papert. 1980. *Mindstorms: Children, Computers, and Powerful Ideas*. Basic Books, New York.

39. Hayes Solos Raffle, Amanda J. Parkes, and Hiroshi Ishii. 2004. Topobo: A Constructive Assembly System with Kinetic Memory. In *Proceedings of the SIGCHI Conference on Human Factors in Computing Systems (CHI '04)*. 647–654.

40. Casey Reas and Ben Fry. 2007. *Processing: A Programming Handbook for Visual Designers and Artists*. MIT Press.

41. Peter Reason and Hilary Bradbury-Huang. 2015. *The SAGE Handbook of Action Research*. SAGE.

42. Yvonne Rogers. 2011. Interaction Design Gone Wild: Striving for Wild Theory. *Interactions* 18, 4 (2011), 58–62.

43. Gerard Roma and Perfecto Herrera. 2010. Graph Grammar Representation for Collaborative Sample-Based Music Creation. In *Proceedings of the 5th Audio Mostly Conference: A Conference on Interaction with Sound (AM '10)*.

44. Alex Ruthmann, Jesse M. Heines, Gena R. Greher, Paul Laidler, and Charles Saulters II. 2010. Teaching Computational Thinking Through Musical Live Coding in Scratch. In *Proceedings of the 41st ACM Technical Symposium on Computer Science Education (SIGCSE '10)*. 351–355.

45. Douglas Schuler and Aki Namioka. 1993. *Participatory Design: Principles and Practices*. CRC Press.

46. Daniel Short. 2012. Teaching Scientific Concepts using a Virtual World–Minecraft. *Teaching Science* 58, 3 (2012), 55–58.

47. Bret Victor. 2012. Learnable Programming. `http://worrydream.com/LearnableProgramming/`.

48. Alyssa F. Wise, Alissa N. Antle, Jillian Warren, Aaron May, Min Fan, and Anna Macaranas. 2015. What Kind of World Do You Want to Live In? Positive Interdependence and Collaborative Processes in the Tangible Tabletop Land-Use Planning Game Youtopia. In *Proceedings of the Conference on Computer Supported Collaborative Learning (CSCL '15)*. ISLS Press.

49. Chih-Sung Wu and Ali Mazalek. 2008. Tangible Tracking Table: An Interactive Tabletop Display. In *IEEE Workshop on Tabletops and Interactive Surfaces (ITS '06)*, Vol. 8. 1–3.

50. Anna Xambó, Eva Hornecker, Paul Marshall, Sergi Jordà, Chris Dobbyn, and Robin Laney. 2016. Exploring Social Interaction With a Tangible Music Interface. *Interacting with Computers* (2016).

51. Oren Zuckerman, Saeed Arida, and Mitchel Resnick. 2005. Extending Tangible Interfaces for Education: Digital Montessori-Inspired Manipulatives. In *Proceedings of the SIGCHI Conference on Human Factors in Computing Systems (CHI '05)*. 859–868.

Kinetic Pelvic Limb Model to Support Students' Understanding of Spatial Visualization in Gross Anatomy

Erica Malone, MS
Texas A&M University
Dept. of Veterinary
Integrative Biosciences
College Station, TX
emalone@cvm.tamu.edu

Jinsil Hwaryoung Seo, MFA, Ph.D.
Texas A&M
University
Dept. of Visualizations
College Station, TX
hwaryoung@tamu.edu

Michelle Pine, DVM, Ph.D.
Texas A&M University
Dept. of Veterinary
Integrative Biosciences
College Station, TX
mpine@cvm.tamu.edu

Brian Smith, MFA
Texas A&M
University
Dept. of Visualizations
College Station, TX
brimism@gmail.com

ABSTRACT
Visual aids currently being used for anatomy education are often only designed to help identify structures and, in some cases, to facilitate understanding of the spatial relationships amongst structures. However, a knowledge of the basic functions of structures is crucial to understanding anatomy and is vastly neglected in the design of instructional tools. One major concept which current tools lack the ability to demonstrate is basic biomechanics. A possible solution to address this oversight is the creation of a kinetic, interactive model that demonstrates movement. Creation of this type of model should incorporate aspects of many different disciplines and should facilitate learning by providing engaging and intuitive interaction. To test this hypothesis, a physically based interactive kinetic simulation model of the canine pelvic limb was constructed. From the user studies, positive student feedback as well as improved quiz scores show that the interactive simulation model had a positive effect on student comprehension in anatomy education.

Author Keywords
Anatomy education; kinetic model; physical simulation; interaction; movement;

ACM Classification Keywords
H.5.m. Information interfaces and presentation (e.g., HCI): Miscellaneous.

INTRODUCTION
Obstacles in education in many traditional disciplines are rarely approached with solutions from new areas of study. This lack of outreach can be detrimental to growth and the innovative process. Illustrating highly visual concepts related to movement in gross anatomy is one such obstacle. Gross anatomy courses are most often taught using diagrams and cadavers as well as the occasional static model [2]. These illustrations, however useful for identification and rote memorization, are rarely able to accurately or clearly demonstrate movement [8]. Incorporating aspects of visualization sciences such as design, kinetic sculpture, and physical computing to the task of demonstrating movement could provide more valuable tools for teaching and learning gross anatomy [8].

Tools currently available for teaching gross anatomy are either limited in their ability to demonstrate movement or are lacking a physical and tactile element. A long relied upon example that clearly illustrates these limitations is a diagram. Using diagrams, which are both two-dimensional and static, to illustrate functional anatomy, which is three-dimensional and in constant motion, may only allow for a limited amount of understanding. To address this, virtual tools and static models for improving identification and spatial reasoning skills have been implemented in classrooms in recent years with seemingly positive results [7]. Unfortunately, even with the move toward three-dimensional interactive tools, the issue of visualizing movement remains to be addressed.

In this paper, we investigate how our interactive kinetic simulation model affects students' understanding of movement in 3D space utilizing surveys and observations.

BACKGROUND

The Current State of Anatomy Education
With the time, cost and ethical issues that these cadavers pose combined with the decreasing time and curriculum dedicated to gross anatomy, the development of innovative tools to scaffold learning in the anatomy classroom has skyrocketed [8]. Technology has played a crucial role in this development as many of these new tools rely on the unique perspectives and opportunities that new technologies continue to present. From simple use of dissection videos [13] and videos including renderings of 3D models [1], to web-based virtual reality programs [11] and augmented reality interfaces [5, 12], the incorporation of technology in anatomy education has proven beneficial.

TEI '17, *March 20-23, 2017, Yokohama, Japan*
© 2017 ACM. ISBN 978-1-4503-4676-4/17/03…$15.00
DOI: http://dx.doi.org/10.1145/3024969.3024994

Although cadaver dissection continues to be the preferred method of understanding and interpreting anatomical knowledge, the incorporation of supplemental aids which utilize the latest technological advances is of increasing importance to accelerate and enhance anatomy education [14]. However, to gain the most from the application and inclusion of these tools, we must insure that they facilitate a complete understanding of anatomy. To do this, tools must address both the recognition of structure and application of terminology as well as the understanding of functional anatomy. Further, while addressing these criteria, tools should be careful not to demand a higher degree of spatial understanding than is already implicit in the content presented.

While 2D images, videos and computer programs may aid student learning, they lack the elements which allow students to explore spatial reasoning [7]. 3D simulation models address this issue in part, but are limited in that they can only be viewed on 2D screens. This creates an additional obstacle for students to overcome as they must have enough initial understanding of spatial reasoning to be able to explore a space in which they are not physically present. Recent development in virtual and augmented reality has shown promise for 3D anatomical visualization for enhanced spatial reasoning but are difficult to present in a lab or classroom setting, and also lack tangible learning experiences. It is clear that the most effective methods for enhancing anatomy education incorporate both physical and virtual technological tools. This combination best facilitates the true objective of learning anatomy which includes both the understanding of function as well as recognition of structure [8].

The Importance of Interactive Engagement in Education

Educational psychologists are constantly searching for the best way to facilitate learning. Studies on the most effective methods for learning and teaching were being conducted as early as 1937. Generally, these studies have shown that the more engaged the student is in learning the material, the better they will understand and retain the knowledge [4]. Further, these studies have been useful in classifying such methods and helping us to understand the cognitive processes involved in certain activities [9]. Particularly, learning models developed by educational psychologists such as Edgar Dale [4], Charles Hoban [4], Samuel Zisman [4], and Benjamin S. Bloom [3] bring light to the benefit students gain from interaction and engagement while learning anatomy.

"The Learning Pyramid," classifies learning methods as either passive or active and ranks them in a pyramid according to the amount of retention each facilitates. Active methods involving interaction such as "doing" and "simulating" are ranked at the bottom of the pyramid, corresponding to the greatest amount of retention, while passive methods such as "reading" and "hearing" are at the top of the pyramid. This educational model indicates that moving anatomy education away from textbooks and lectures, (passive methods resulting in as little as 10% retention), to the use interactive simulations models, (active method resulting in 90% retention), could improve retention of this foundational medical knowledge by as much as 80% [4].

"Bloom's Taxonomy" further supports the use of interactive models. The revised taxonomy reveals that remembering factual knowledge, (such as memorizing structure names and functions), requires the lowest possible level of understanding and demands only the most basic cognitive processes. According to the model, a complete understanding requires far more advanced knowledge levels such as contextual and conditional knowledge and should be accomplished using high-level cognitive processes such as applying, analyzing, evaluating, and creating [3, 9]. A versatile instructional tool such as an interactive simulation model engages students in these higher-level cognitive processes and enables the development of a more complete knowledge of functional anatomy.

MODEL DESIGN

The pelvic limb model is based on the skeletal structure of a canine pelvic limb. Bones in the pelvic limb were cast using Alumilite Super Plastic Casting resin. Material choice for the pelvic kinetic model was based on construction of a previous thoracic limb kinetic model as well as experimentation [10]. Components such as structural support, muscle function simulation, simulated muscle structure, and simulated skeletal structure all had to be considered during model construction.

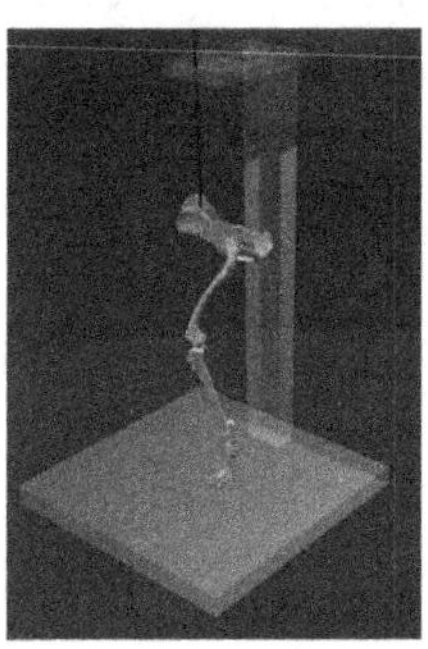

Figure 2. Model design with Plexiglas stand created with 3D animation software.

MATERIALS AND METHODS

Implementation of a servo motor system for simulating muscle function included the addition of the following materials to the model stand and simulated bones:

- Four Standard Size Generic High Torque Servo Motors (FS5106B):
- Four Lynxmotion Aluminum Multi-Purpose Servo Brackets:
- One Arduino board, one computer equipped with Arduino software and at least one USB port and a breadboard.
- Miscellaneous items including strings, nuts and bolts.

Servo-Motor Muscle Simulation

Four standard size generic high torque servo motors (FS5106B) were mounted onto the model. Two of these motors were mounted directly to the femur of the model using Lynxmotion aluminum multi-purpose servo brackets, while the remaining two were mounted on the top of the Plexiglas stand using the same mounts. Each of the four servo motors included a large vertical motor arm which extended approximately an inch and a half on either side of the center of rotation of each motor. An assortment of small, medium and large zinc-plated screw eyes was put on the model and the stand at major origin and insertion points as well as along the cranial and caudal aspects of the long bones. White nylon string was attached at one end to the furthest point from the center of rotation on the servo motor arm. The other end of the string was fixed onto a screw eye representing a point of insertion or origin common to a muscle group. When an action could not be created by direct connection of the motor arm and attachment site on the bone, the string used to create the action of one muscle would first run through the screw eye representing an origin or insertion of a different muscle, and then run back to its appropriate location on the model, creating a pulley system. Strings also ran through screw eyes in the middle of long bones when crossing multiple joints to guide it and prevent unwanted rotation, abduction or adduction of the limb.

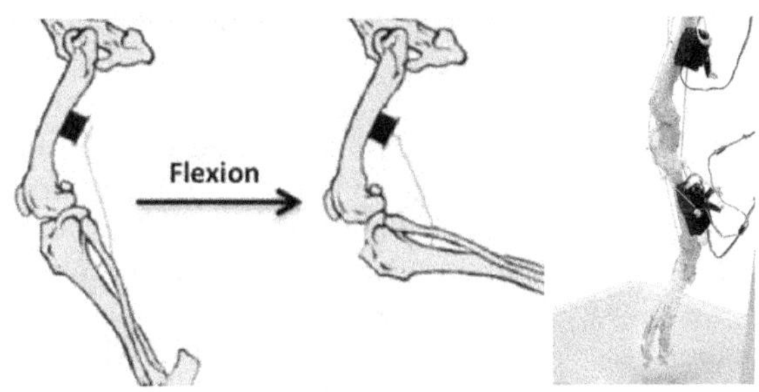

Figure 3. Example of implementation of servo motor system to simulate muscle function.

A single two-foot long threaded rod was run through the middle of the specialized armature at the top of the model stand and through the midline of the sacrum. Washers and nuts were used to adjust the height of the limb on the rod as well as for support. In addition to hardware, epoxy and epoxy putty fixed the rod to the sacrum and accounted for uneven surfaces allowing for proper alignment of the pelvic girdle. An Arduino MEGA 2560 microcontroller and one full-sized bread board were placed at the top, back of the armature at the top of the model stand, opposite the threaded rod. Various lengths and colors of extension wires allowed the Arduino microcontroller to connect to the servo motors which were mounted on the femur. A Macintosh laptop, equipped with Arduino software and a USB port, was attached to the Arduino microcontroller with a USB cord.

Creating Interaction

A computer was connected to the Arduino microcontroller via a USB port and a serial monitor, or text-input window was displayed on the computer screen. The user would type the name of a muscle into the serial monitor and hit the return button on the computer. Motors that represent that muscle's action would then be activated, turning the motor arm 90 to 180 degrees, thus creating the action of the muscle that was typed.

For muscles which have different actions based on whether or not the limb is bearing weight users had the option of typing only the name of the muscle, which would demonstrate the action of the muscle on a limb that was not bearing weight, or add the word "Weight" to the end of the muscle name to see the action of the muscle while the limb was bearing weight. In order to accommodate the software used, a "camel-case" text input method was employed. The camel-case input method allows the user to exclude spaces between words while practicing the spelling structure names.

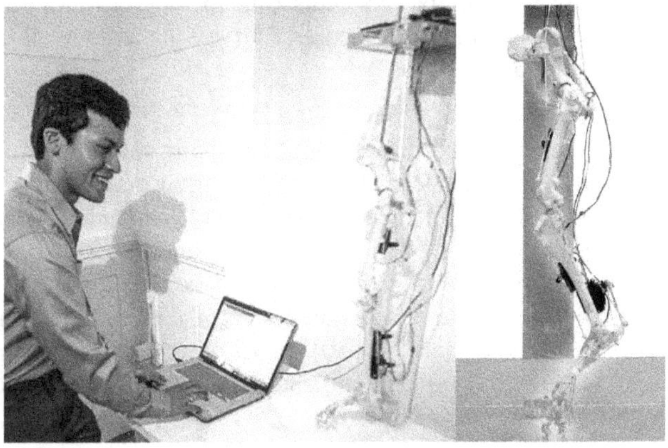

Figure 4. Model on display at "The Creative Anatomy Art Showcase" (left). Side view of our kinetic pelvic model (right).

USER STUDIES

User studies included a class of undergraduate students enrolled in the Biomedical Anatomy course at Texas A&M University. Generally, students enrolled in this course are preparing for a professional career in human or veterinary medicine.

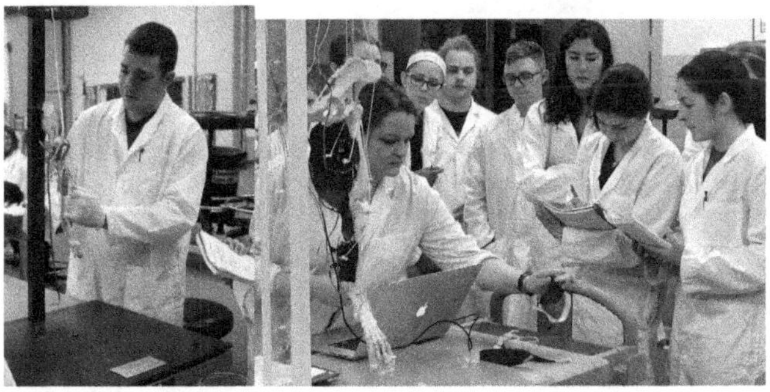

Figure 5. Undergraduate student interacting with previous thoracic limb kinetic model (left). Undergraduate students studying gross anatomy using the interactive simulation model (right).

Students in the course were separated into two different sections based on their lab period – section 500 (N=58) and section 501 (N=50). One section of students, section 501 (control group), was allowed only the materials normally provided to them during the course. The other section, section 500 (experimental group), also had access to these materials, but were allowed access to the interactive simulation model for individual and group study as well. Students from both groups spent same amount of time (two hours) during the studies. Both at the introduction and at the conclusion of the study, all students were given a pop-quiz. The quiz focused on evaluating the students' understanding of concepts which the model was capable of demonstrating. The experimental group was asked to complete a questionnaire which evaluated their perceived effect of the model on their ability to understand related concepts using a 5-point Likert Scale Survey.

RESULTS

The impact of the interactive simulation model on the ability of students to visualize concepts related to gross anatomy was analyzed using quiz scores, survey data as well as observation data.

Quiz Scores

User studies revealed that the students using the interactive simulation model performed better than their peers who did not use the model. The average quiz score for students who used the model (N = 58) improved significantly ($p < 0.05$) from mean: 49.83% (SD: 21.50%) to mean: 65.26 % (SD: 18.76%), while the average quiz score of the students who did not use the model (N = 50) only improved from mean: 49.50% (SD: 18.77%) to mean: 58.60% (SD = 18.87%) – not a significant difference.

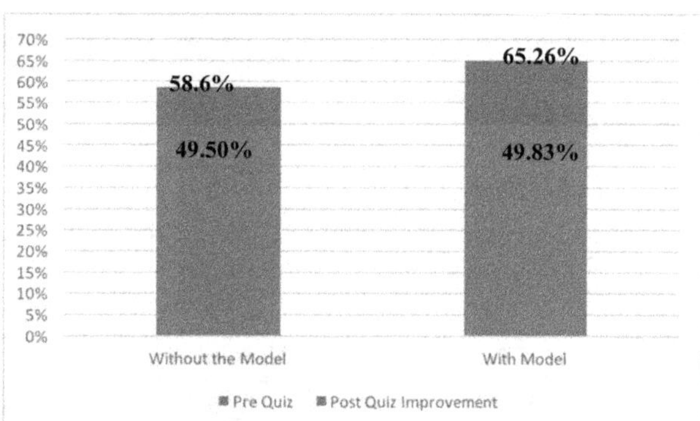

Figure 6. Bar graph comparing mean quiz scores.

Scores on the pre-quiz between the two groups were not significantly different (p= 0.47). However, scores on the post-quiz revealed that the students who used the model performed significantly better (p = 0.03) than students who did not use the model.

Student Feedback

Evaluation of student feedback on surveys showed that the model helped 68.4% of students with at least one concept related to movement. 60.41% of students agreed that the model was specifically helpful in understanding the concept of fixator muscles. 67.31% of students who used the model agreed that it was helpful in understanding contraction and relaxation of muscles and 57.12% agreed that the model helped them to understand the action of muscle groups. When asked whether the model improved their understanding of a concept which they struggled with before interacting with the model, a majority of students, (51.64%), agreed that it had. Students attributed the benefit of the model first to the ability to watch flexion and extension, then to being able to see joints move and finally to the overall simulation of muscle movement. Results from student surveys on questions regarding the model construction revealed that 75.55% of the students found it easy to use.

CONCLUSION AND FUTURE WORK

While kinetic, interactive models for learning gross anatomy are a vastly under researched area, evidence collected from studies on current tools being used in anatomy education reveal that an obvious gap in anatomy education exists that can be bridged with these types of tools. Implementation of a physically based interactive kinetic simulation model in an undergraduate biomedical anatomy has revealed an improvement in student ability to visualize and understand concepts related to movement. The fact that the model helped a large majority of them to understand at least one concept related to movement is further evidence of the necessity and vast potential benefit of these types of teaching and learning tools in anatomy education.

Some students reported that the model might have benefited them more if the movements had not been as sudden. They described a few of the actions as "jerky" which caused the entire limb to sway. This swaying confused some students as they were unable to distinguish purposeful movement from movement that occurred unintentionally. This may be attributed to the limitations caused by the weights of the cast bones and low torque of the servo motors that we used. Changing the speed of the servos still resulted in "jerky" movement regardless, as the servos were likely approaching their maximum load by moving the weight of the limb and would twitch when fully extended, indicating strain on the motor. Overcoming this limitation might involve the use of better motor placement, use of pulleys and gears for smoother movement, or using stronger, smoother, and more precise motors. The range of motion which the model is capable of demonstrating can also be improved by assuring a smooth surface for bones to articulate with one another and employing motors that are able to pull string farther than a few inches at a time.

Future work with this model includes the development of a companion application for students to use alongside the model. A mobile application will provide a more intuitive interaction method for students as well as eliminate the need for wires, freeing the student from the necessity to view movement based on the position of the computer. The application will utilize wireless Bluetooth communication with the model which will allow the student to choose from a variety of muscle functions or actions. A student will choose which muscle function or action they would like to see and the physical model will simulate that function for them.

As an extension to this application a virtual 3D representation of the model for students to reference when the physical model is not available will be available within the application. Any action or function that the physical model is capable of will also be available with the virtual model.

REFERENCES

1. Al-Khalili, S. M., and Coppoc, G. L. (2014). 2D and 3D Stereoscopic Videos Used as Pre-Anatomy Lab Tools Improve Students' Examination Performance in a Veterinary Gross Anatomy Course. Journal of Veterinary Medical Education, 41(1), 68-76. doi:10.3138/jvme.0613-082r
2. Albanese, M. (2010). The gross anatomy laboratory: A prototype for simulation-based medical education. Medical Education, 44(1), 7-9. doi:10.1111/j.1365-2923.2009.03536.x
3. Anderson, L. W., and Krathwohl, D. R. (2001). A taxonomy for learning, teaching, and assessing: A revision of Bloom's taxonomy of educational objectives. New York: Longman.
4. Benjes-Small, C., and Archer, A. (n.d.). Tales of the Undead... Learning Theories: The Learning Pyramid. Retrieved March 01, 2014, from http://acrlog.org/2014/01/13/tales-of-the-undead-learning-theories-the-learning-pyramid/
5. Blum, T., Kleeberger, V., Bichlmeier, C., and Navab, N. (2012). Mirracle: An augmented reality magic mirror system for anatomy education. 2012 IEEE Virtual Reality (VR). doi:10.1109/vr.2012.6180909
6. Brueckner, J. K., and Macpherson, B. R. (2004). Benefits from peer teaching in the dental gross anatomy laboratory. European Journal of Dental Education Eur J Dent Educ, 8(2), 72-77. doi:10.1111/j.1600-0579.2003.00333.x
7. Chatterjee, A. K. (2011). The Importance of Spatial Ability and Mental Models in Learning Anatomy (Doctoral dissertation, Purdue University, 2011). Ann Arbor, MI: ProQuest LLC. Retrieved from http://www.purdue.edu/policies/pages/teach_res_outreach/c_22.html
8. Collins, J. P. (2008, September 09). Modern approachs to teaching and learning anatomy.BMJ: British Medical Journal, 337(Sep09 1), 665-667. doi:10.1136/bmj.a1310
9. Krathwohl, D. R. (2002). A Revision of Bloom's Taxonoy: An Overview.Theory Into Practice, 41(4), 212-218. doi:10.1207/s15430421tip4104_2
10. Malone, E. R., and Pine, M. D. (2014). Creation of KineticModel for Learning Gross Anatomy.Explorations, 6, 63-65.
11. Petersson, H., Sinkvist, D., Wang, C., and Smedby, Ö. (2009). Web-based interactive 3D visualization as a tool for improved anatomy learning. Anatomical Sciences Education Anat Sci Ed, 2(2), 61-68. doi:10.1002/ase.76
12. Seo, J., Storey,J ., Chavez, J., Reyna, D., Suh, J., and Pine, M., 2014. ARnatomy: tangible AR app for learning gross anatomy. In *ACM SIGGRAPH 2014 Posters* (SIGGRAPH '14). ACM, New York, NY, USA, Article 25,
13. Theoret, C. L., Carmel, É, and Bernier, S. (2007). Why Dissection Videos Should Not Replace Cadaver Prosections in the Gross Veterinary Anatomy Curriculum: Results from a Comparative Study. Journal of Veterinary Medical Education, 34(2), 151-156. doi:10.3138/jvme.34.2.151
14. Wilhelmsson, N., Dehlgren, L. O., Hult, H., Scheja, M., Lonka, K., and Josephson, A. (2010). The Anatomy of Learning Anatomy. Advancement in Health Science Education, 15, 153-165.

The Haptic Body Scale: Designing Imprecision in Times of the Quantified Self

Anne Wohlauf
Universität der Künste Berlin
Berlin, Germany
anne.wohlauf@udk-berlin.de

Fabian Hemmert
Bergische Universität Wuppertal
Wuppertal, Germany
hemmert@uni-wuppertal.de

Reto Wettach
Fachhochschule Potsdam
Potsdam, Germany
reto.wettach@fh-potsdam.de

ABSTRACT
Followers of the *Quantified Self* movement track, analyze and compare vital and environmental data to optimize themselves. It can be stressful to keep all the measured values under control when pursuing this ambitious way of life. Body weight can be an especially emotional issue for many people and slight differences can be perceived as lack of discipline, although little fluctuations are natural. In this paper, we present a tangible display for body weight, based on floor rigidity. It displays body weight without numbers, which makes it less suitable for comparisons, while still giving the user an idea about their weight. We describe the metaphorical foundations of the concept, as well as the development of two prototypes, which implement the envisioned full-body weighing experience. We demonstrate how the design of a display can influence the users' connotation of data.

Author Keywords
Haptic display; tactile feedback; floor; tangible interaction; user experience

ACM Classification Keywords
H.5.2. User Interfaces: Haptic I/O; Prototyping

INTRODUCTION
On the one hand, there are positive consequences of the *Quantified Self* movement. Followers log various inputs, states and performances to gain "self-knowledge through numbers" and choose which need to be adjusted to achieve well-being [34]. Tracking devices, mobile applications and websites can be used as motivational tools and to support, or substitute, a personal trainer.

Body weight is logged by the majority of current self-tracking applications. In most cases, it is displayed as numbers in standardized terms (such as kilograms, pounds, etc.), often with a high accuracy and at short intervals, in order to improve data resolution and give precise results. However, this accuracy may also have disadvantages. Changes in the body weight of an average healthy individual are caused by various factors, many of which are not related to exercising, eating or other behavior [5]. Most of the current body-weight tracking applications do not account for these fluctuations. Therefore, users with a good constitution who are dieting, practicing sports or exercising, can be at risk of becoming frustrated by insignificant weight changes.

The current custom of precision enhancement in self-tracking may have psychological side-effects, from obsession to frustration. Therefore, this work seeks to critically review the current state of self-quantification, and advocate imprecision.

An analysis of the current weight visualization and an analysis of peoples' current weighing experience revealed several design opportunities to improve the weighing experience. Above all we submit the approach to make use of an embodied metaphor in order to encourage users to reflect on data. Although data is supposed to be neutral, it depends a lot on how we display and perceive it. In order to demonstrate this, we want to present the Haptic Body Scale that aims to improve users' experience of weighing themselves or rather receiving the measurements (see Figure 1).

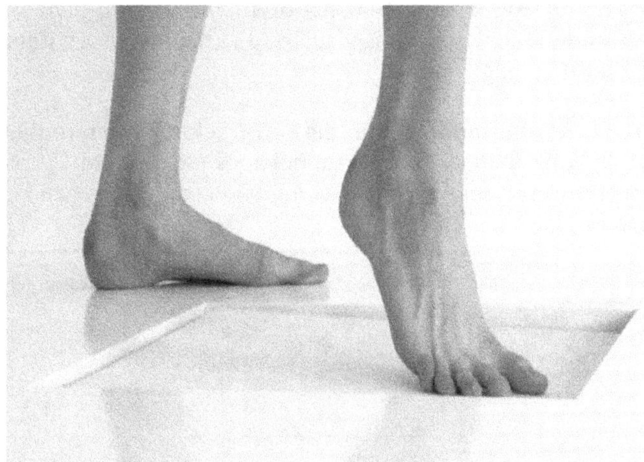

Figure 1. The Haptic Body Scale prototype, displaying weight tendencies through rigidity when stepped upon.

TEI '17, March 20-23, 2017, Yokohama, Japan
© 2017 ACM. ISBN 978-1-4503-4676-4/17/03...$15.00
DOI: http://dx.doi.org/10.1145/3024969.3025003

Metaphorical mappings are an active field of Human-Computer-Interaction (HCI) research [14,15,28]. Interaction models based on embodied knowledge (through embodied metaphors) can support users' experience [2]. This research also follows this path: the Haptic Body Scale is based on an initial survey conducted with a group of weight-conscious students.

RELATED WORK

This project is located at the intersection of different areas of research: critical design, floor-based haptic displays and rigidity-based displays. But first of all, we want to give an overview of how weight is visualized at the moment within the self-tracking community.

Weight visualization within the self-tracking community

By looking at smart phone applications (see Figure 2) for general fitness and weight tracking two conclusions can be drawn.

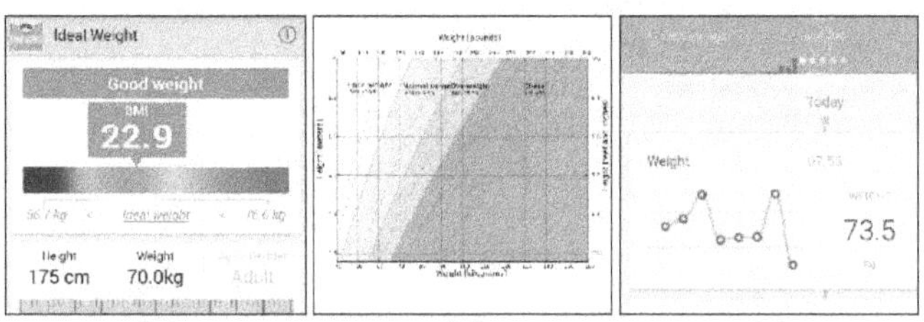

(a) (b) (c)

Figure 2. (a) The Application "Ideal Weight" [10] visualizes underweight in blue (b) A Body mass index chart [33] by the World Health Organization (WHO) visualizes underweight in white and seems to be a reference for many applications (c) The Application "Withing's Health Mate" [11], accompanying the Withing's smart scale, visualizes weight development in a way that temporary fluctuations of two kilograms seem to be significant.

First, body weight and its development is usually visualized with a precision that is not in the very nature of body weight. Body weight is often displayed with an accuracy of one or two digits after the decimal point [11]. Furthermore some applications suggest to measure the users' weight multiple times a day. As a healthy adult, variations in body weight are normal and can be as large as 2 kg (4.4 pounds) due to measurement error, clothing, food consumption and fluid balance or for women due to the menstruation cycle [5,17,23,26]. We did not take applications in consideration that are particularly assigned for people with explicit weight problems or chronic diseases. In that case, a high accuracy of measurements may be useful.

And second, underweight is usually visualized in a less alarming way than overweight. In many visualizations, a colored visualization of the body mass index (BMI) is used. The BMI is a value derived from the weight and height of a person [22]. Usually, higher weight is presented in the color red and lower weight in green, blue or white [10,33]. Conventionally in the western world, red in user interfaces is used for alarms and emergencies, green for normal activities and blue and white for neutral states [7]. While overweight is visualized consistently negative, underweight is often visualized in neutral connoted colors which could cause users to underestimate the potential health dangers of being underweight.

Critical Design

Several projects in the field of interaction design research scrutinize and critically reflect self-quantification. Vos investigates the 'quantified brunch' [31], while Broomfield proposes objects for 'data obsessives' [4], which include a tool for the introduction of micro time zones. Dauner's 'disciplinary machine' [6] that converts the step counter data into an overly precise analogue print-out on paper, underlining the potential of compulsiveness in self-tracking. Wang [32] analyzes existing domestic objects in regard to "Asimov's First Law" [1], which postulates that a robot may not harm a human being. Wang claims that weighing scales do harm human beings, albeit psychologically. She proposes different weighing scales, which allow for lying to oneself about the weight and for outsourcing the task of telling the weight to another person, thereby obeying Asimov's law.

We aim to add to this body of research by approaching the topic from a 'haptic display' point of view.

Floor-based haptic displays

Haptic displays often focus on haptic feedback via users' fingers, but also using the floor as a haptic display is being actively researched, often presenting sound feedback for cross-modal effects. Some projects in this area simulate surfaces, e.g. in virtual reality, mixed reality or locomotion interfaces. ALF [27] and EcoTile [30] use shape changing floors, Active Shoes [3] and Frozen Pond [24] use methods of sonification. Another area of floor-based haptic feedback is non-visual navigation. Projects in this area include vibro-tactile [29] and shape changing shoes [8]. A third area of floor-based haptic feedback utilizes simulated floor materials as an awareness tool, as in Fu and Li's "Haptic Shoes" [9] which communicate stock market information through vibration. This work provides insights into how the floor can be used as a display, demonstrating a beneficial approach to displaying 'quantified self' data. As this project is concerned primarily with body weight, actuating the floor's rigidity is proposed as a fitting approach.

Rigidity-based displays

Several HCI projects investigate rigidity as a display. Jansen's Mudpad [16] is a multi-touch input device that uses magnetic liquid to create a surface of variable viscosity. MimicTile [19] is an interface for mobile devices that recognizes gestures and reacts to squeezing. The flexibility can vary through actuation of the shape-memory materials embedded inside. A control device to manipulate objects in virtual environments simulates softness [25]. JamSheets by Ou et al. actuates the deformability of a structure by adding and removing liquids inside [21]. One of several scenarios of the mobile device called SqueezeBlock [12] is to feel the

amount of unread e-mails by increasing the rigidity of its case.
These three last areas of research provide valuable insights into critical reflection of societal developments through design, using the floor as a haptic display. Rigidity of the floor material is used as a style of actuation. In this work, we propose to combine the three.

DESIGN OPPORTUNITIES

By taking the related work of weight visualization and weighing procedure into account, we phrased three design opportunities to conceptualize an alternate, less frustrating body scale that encourages body intuition rather than an external valuation:

- The scale may compensate for natural fluctuations as large as two kilograms (which are normal for healthy adults)
- The scale may communicate increasing distance to the users' ideal weight in the same way, no matter if the weight is increasing or decreasing. It should convey the fact that neither extremity carries a risk and requires action. The ideal weight (range) of the user would be set preferably, in consultation with a doctor.
- The scale may make use of an embodied interaction in order to enhance the users' reflection on their body intuition. The implementation of a playful enjoyable interaction metaphor may encourage a less negative perception of measurements away from the ideal weight (range). Therefore, current language can be a source of inspiration.

CONCEPT

The Haptic Body Scale displays changes in the user's weight, by changing the rigidity of an actuated floor surface that they step on. The larger the discrepancy (in either direction) to their subjective ideal weight, the more flexible the floor becomes. If the user is in the range of their ideal weight, they stand on a firm floor. The further away to their supposed ideal weight, the more the floor moves. Comparable to a springboard, they sink in as they step on the scale, but bounce up as they move.
This interaction metaphor originates from the fact, that people are said to be feeling "up" or "low" when they experience positive or negative affects [18]. In fact, one of the definitions for depression indicates, that it is "a depressed or sunken place or part; an area lower than the surrounding surface" [13]. We hope to "uplift" and comfort the users, by connecting undesirable measurements with bouncing interactions.

USER TESTING

For this experimental prototypes we decided to conduct qualitative individual interviews (see table 1) of 30 to 40 minutes, each accompanied by an informal user test of the prototype. We gathered feedback about the user experience of both of the Haptic Body Scale prototypes and their connotations, rather than the technical performance or accuracy of the display. We recorded the users' answers, but also observed their behavior as they tried out the prototypes.

Goal of the interview part	Questions asked
In the first part, we talked about the motivation of the Haptic Body Scale to give an introduction.	• Do you have a personal ideal weight (range)? • Have you ever experienced frustration concerning your weight? • How do you feel about fluctuations in your weight?
In the second part, the participants tried out and described their experience of the three different states of the Haptic Body Scale after they got an explanation of the functionality.	How does it feel… • to be in the range of the ideal weight = rigid ground? • to be slightly out of the range of the ideal weight (2-5 kilograms above or under) = moderately flexible? • to be out of the range of the ideal weight (5-8 kilograms above or under = very flexible? They were asked to describe their experience and how they like the approach and the prototype's implementation of • the replacement of the numerical display by a haptic display • the compensation of fluctuations • communicating underweight and overweight in the same way
In the third part, the participants were asked to compare the experience of the Haptic Body Scale with a regular scale, especially in regards to frustration potential.	• Do you think there are differences in the frustration potential? • What else is different? • What does the Haptic Body Scale do better/worse than a regular scale?

Table 1. Structure of the qualitative user test

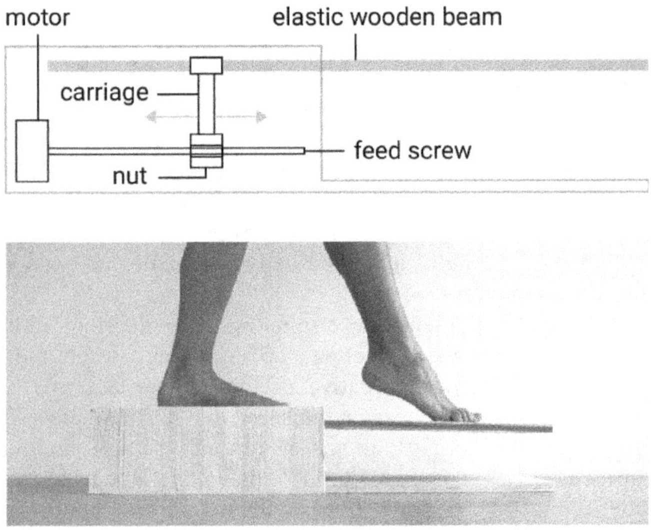

Figure 3. The flexibility of the beam (side view)

Target group

Since we took the self-tracking community as a starting point, we aimed at people without overweight, underweight or chronic disease but technology enthusiasts who are interested in aspects of self-improvement. As the majority of wearables users (which include tracking devices) are between 18 and 34 years old [20] we invited participants of that age group.

PROTOTYPES

An iterative prototyping process allowed us to explore a haptic display that users can step on. Through informal user tests, we wanted to learn about the users' experience of feeling weight through various degrees of floor flexibility. Implementing a numerical and standardized weighing function, or setting an ideal weight was not part of our prototype requirements. Two full-size prototypes and tested with users.

Prototype I: construction

Our first prototype is based on CDLEE (control of deformable length of an elastic element) softness display's construction [25], which we adapted from being small-scale to large-scale so it could be used by users as a full-body scale. The prototype is illustrated in Figure 3. It consists of an elastic wooden beam, a feed screw, a carriage with a nut, and a motor. As shown in Figure 3, the flexibility of the beam corresponds to the position of the carriage and can thus be changed continuously.

Prototype I: user responses

In preparation for an informal user test, we informed seven users (four female, three male, aged 22-34) about the concept of the Haptic Body Scale. They were then asked to try the three states of the system, ranging from rigid over moderately flexible to very flexible. During the accompanying interviews, we asked them about how it felt, what connotations they had and how the haptic display of their

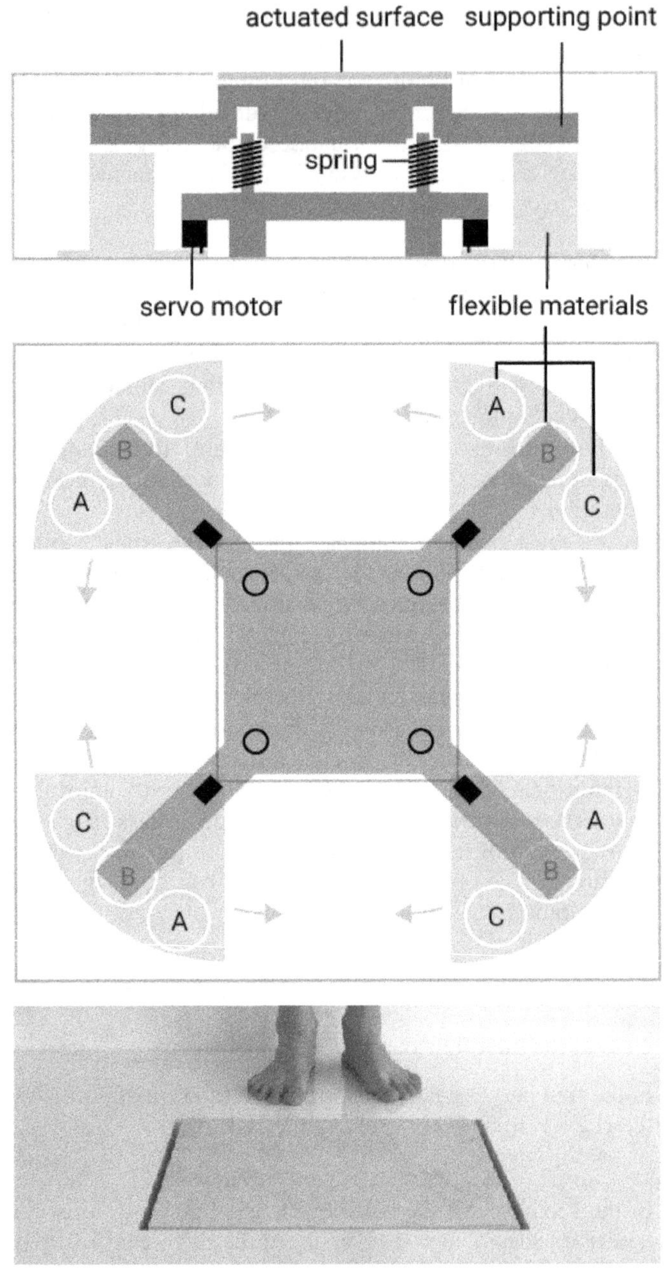

Figure 4. The supporting points of the upper frame can be set to different materials and therefore users can explore three degrees of rigidity

relative weight could influence them emotionally.

All users indicated that they were not in need of a precise number display. Additionally, they also did not always want to know the minor fluctuations of their weight. The users were able to distinguish easily between the three states. Five users mentioned negative connotations when stepping on the prototype.

Key quotes:

- "I feel really heavy because the floor bends as I step on it."

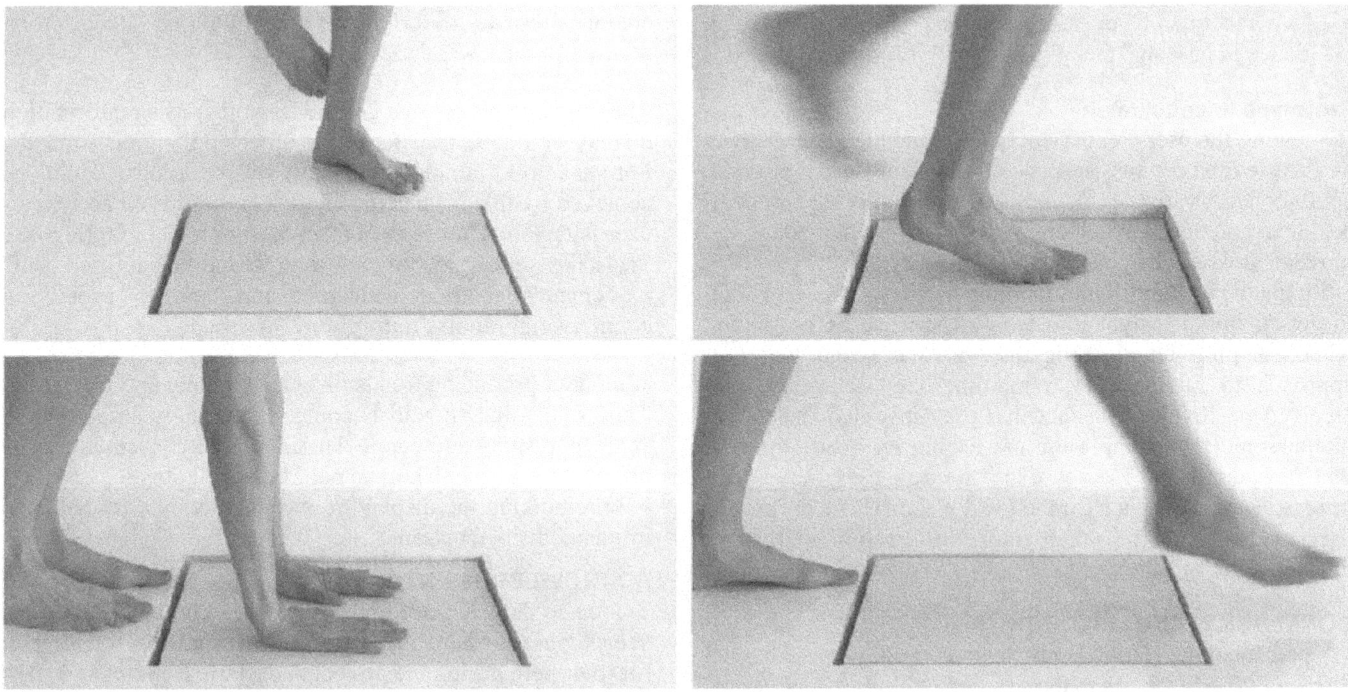

Figure 5. A user enacts different interactions with the Haptic Body Scale (Prototype II)

- "I like the wooden surface, it's different to a regular scale."
- "It is a good feeling to step barefoot on it."
- "It doesn't feel like I expected it to."

Key observations:

- Five of the participants stepped very timidly on the scale
- Two tried to move as little as possible when trying out the flexible state of the prototype
- Six users preferred the most rigid state of the prototype

Prototype I: conclusion

After building and testing the first prototype, we concluded that the general idea of a haptic, and therefore imprecise, scale was received positively, but that the haptic experience needed adjustment. States of yielding seemed to be easy to distinguish for the users, so the next iteration should not just yield, but implement a more flexible and "bouncing" character, in order to provide a more positive connotation and a more pleasurable, playful experience.

Prototype II: construction

We built the prototype which is shown in Figure 4 based on the system of a turret head. The lower frame of the construction is floor-mounted and connected to four discs that can be rotated simultaneously using servo motors. On top of every disc, three feet with different material properties are mounted. Depending on the angle, the supporting points of the upper frame that the users are stepping on are laying on top of the feet A, B or C. All feet provide different degrees of rigidity. Setting mode A results in a firm stand since the feet are made out of non-flexible material. For feet B and C, we chose air filled membranes of different volume to achieve more flexible stands. In between the lower and upper frame, the positioning of metal springs as spacers allow free movement of the discs, ensuring that the actuated surface is flush with the scale's casing.

Prototype II: user responses

In the second informal user test, we presented the prototype to eight users (five female, three male, aged 22-36). Six of the participants tested the first prototype and were asked to compare their experience with the first prototype. Seven out of eight users expressed that they enjoyed the bouncing states.

Key quotes:

- "It feels nice."
- "If the movement was smoother, it could be really meditative."
- "It's actually much more fun to be out of the ideal weight range"
- "I don't know if I could renounce a traditional numerical scale. There might be situations when I want to know my exact weight."
- "This one [prototype I] fits better to the concept."
- "On the other scale [prototype I] I felt heavier, here I feel lighter."

Key observations:

- As we interviewed the participants, they were acting out situations they could imagine if they were using the scale at their home
- Three users "dipped their toe" (see Figure 1) to check the scale's result, two used their hands before they stepped on it to test the haptic display's flexibility

- Two ran quickly over the actuated surface to "take a glance in passing" (see Figure 5)

Prototype II: conclusion

Reviewing the users' experience, we concluded that the use of an evolved air suspension system can provide continuously variable flexibility. By involving product designer and mechanical engineers, a smoother bouncing movement would be possible.

Utilizing the two prototypes in initial user tests, we were able to get an initial insight into their experience of weighing, when stepping on a haptic display. We found that our approach to facilitate a "trampoline-like" sensation was received positively. The fact that they invented their own interactions (for example the pre-testing by hand) showed that they adopted the metaphor that the scale uses: movement or backlash for distance (to the ideal weight). The proposals they made should be taken into consideration in further development.

CONCLUSION AND OUTLOOK

We presented the Haptic Body Scale, a rigidity-based haptic display for body weight that users step on. Initial, qualitative user tests indicated that users appreciated a display for their body weight that omits numbers, and rather provides a rather imperfect, and therefore less comparable, type of display.

What we learned from our project is, that using a haptic floor-based display with a playful approach can influence the connotation of data. Data that is generally perceived negatively is reframed in a positive way. Numerous users stated that the use of the Haptic Body Scale is "fun", but only a long-term in-situ study with actual weight data could show how it changes body awareness and self-perception. The approach of translating quantitative data into a haptic experience might be suitable for other areas of application. This may be particularly the case for potentially frustrating data, as is the case of body weight. Here, a playful presentation could help users to keep their motivation if they struggle to keep or reach their ideal weight.

In a lot of cases, precise values are not required, and can be replaced by knowing of whether they are within a certain range. In these cases, haptic ground-based displays could be applied, especially when a close metaphorical connection is implied. The observation that some of the users enacted the checking of their weight in passing, demonstrated, how haptic floor-based actuation could work as an ambient display in other contexts. The actuated surfaces can be integrated in floors, steps of a staircase and doorsteps.

The Haptic Body Scale is not just a tangible display but a visual display too: By standing on it, users can see how much the actuated surface is sinking in. This is another advantage of showing the relative weight instead of the absolute: it leaves room for interpretation. The fact that neither numbers nor other quantifications are used to display the measurement result brings up the question of if and how users would communicate the results. This way users would possibly create alternate descriptions that might influence their relation to their weight.

The principle of actuated ground flexibility as an information display could be transferred to other application contexts. For example, ambient displays in buildings could be achieved by this means, e.g. by displaying inside activity as users step into a house or in front of a door. The Haptic Body Scale has set out to critically review the "Quantified Self" movement's fixation with precision, and to provide a counterweight to its "unforgiving" accuracy.

With data-producing trends like self-tracking and Internet of Things in mind, it will become increasingly important to analyze, display and curate data in a more conscious way in order to comply with human nature. The Haptic Scale shows, how rethinking the display of and interaction with data can influence its perception.

ACKNOWLEDGMENTS

Thanks to the team of the Design Research Lab Berlin, Lisa Weiss, Susann Hamann, Matthias Löwe and Josefine Zeipelt for their help during the project and Marie Beuthel and Berit Greinke for proofreading.

REFERENCES

1. Isaac Asimov. 1968. *I, Robot*. Grafton Books, London.
2. Saskia Bakker, Alissa N. Antle, and Elise Van Den Hoven. 2012. Embodied metaphors in tangible interaction design. *Personal and Ubiquitous Computing* 16, 4: 433–449. http://doi.org/10.1007/s00779-011-0410-4
3. Roberto Bresin, Anna de Witt, Stefano Papetti, Marco Civolani, and Federico Fontana. 2010. Expressive sonification of footstep sounds. *the Interaction Sonification workshop (ISon) 2010, Stockholm, April 7, 2010*, 51–54.
4. Andy Broomfield. Objects for Data Obsessives. Retrieved July 28, 2016 from http://datarelationships.newmediathinking.com/
5. Zafra Cooper, Christopher G Fairburn, and Deborah M Hawker. 2013. *Cognitive-behavioral treatment of obesity: a clinician's guide*. Guilford Publications.
6. Joanna Dauner. 2012. Disziplinarapparat. Retrieved July 28, 2016 from http://joannadauner.de/wordpress/portfolio/disziplinarapparat/
7. Alan Dix, Janet Finlay, Gregory Abowd, and Russell Beale. 2004. Human-Computer Interaction. *Human-Computer Interaction* Third, January: 834. http://doi.org/10.1207/S15327051HCI16234
8. Martin Frey. 2007. CabBoots: shoes with integrated guidance system. *Proceedings of the 1st international conference on Tangible and embedded interaction*, 245–246.

9. Xiaoyan Fu and Dahai Li. 2005. Haptic shoes: representing information by vibration. *proceedings of the 2005 Asia-Pacific symposium on Information visualisation-Volume 45*, 47–50.
10. Google Play. Ideal Weight. Retrieved July 28, 2016 from https://play.google.com/store/apps/details?id=mmapps.bmi.calculator
11. Google Play. Health Mate. Retrieved July 28, 2016 from https://play.google.com/store/apps/details?id=com.withings.wiscale2
12. Sidhant Gupta and Tim Campbell. 2010. Squeezeblock: Using virtual springs in mobile devices for eyes-free interaction. *Proceedings of the 23nd ...*: 101–104. http://doi.org/10.1145/1866029.1866046
13. Random House. 1986. *Webster's new universal unabridged dictionary*. Barnes & Noble Books, New York, New York, USA.
14. Jörn Hurtienne and Johann Habakuk Israel. 2007. Image Schemas and Their Metaphorical Extensions – Intuitive Patterns for Tangible Interaction. *Proceedings of the 1st international conference on Tangible and embedded interaction*: 127–134. http://doi.org/http://doi.acm.org/10.1145/1226969.1226996
15. Hiroshi Ishii. 2008. Tangible bits: beyond pixels. *Proceedings of the 2nd international conference on Tangible and Embedded Intreaction (TEI '08)*: xv–xxv. http://doi.org/10.1145/1347390.1347392
16. Yvonne Jansen. 2010. Mudpad: fluid haptics for multitouch surfaces. *CHI'10 Extended Abstracts on Human Factors in Computing Systems*, 4351–4356.
17. Timothy G. Lohman, Alex F. Roche, and Reynaldo Martorell. 1988. Anthropometric standardization reference manual. *Human Kinetics Books*: 177. http://doi.org/10.1002/ajhb.1310040323
18. Brian P Meier and Michael D Robinson. 2006. Does "feeling down" mean seeing down? Depressive symptoms and vertical selective attention. *Journal of Research in Personality* 40, 4: 451–461.
19. Yusuke Nakagawa, Akiya Kamimura, and Yoichiro Kawaguchi. 2012. MimicTile: a variable stiffness deformable user interface for mobile devices. *Proceedings of the SIGCHI Conference on Human Factors in Computing Systems*, 745–748.
20. Nielsen. Tech-Styles: Are Consumers Really Interested in Wearing Tech on their Sleeves? Retrieved July 28, 2016 from http://www.nielsen.com/us/en/insights/news/2014/tech-styles-are-consumers-really-interested-in-wearing-tech-on-their-sleeves.html
21. Jifei Ou, Lining Yao, Daniel Tauber, Jürgen Steimle, Ryuma Niiyama, and Hiroshi Ishii. 2014. jamSheets: thin interfaces with tunable stiffness enabled by layer jamming. *Proceedings of the 8th International Conference on Tangible, Embedded and Embodied Interaction*, 65–72.
22. M. P. Pai and F. P. Paloucek. 2000. The origin of the "ideal" body weight equations. *Annals of Pharmacotherapy* 34, 9: 1066–1069. http://doi.org/10.1345/aph.19381
23. Patrica Pliner and Alison S. Fleming. 1983. Food intake, body weight, and sweetness preferences over the menstrual cycle in humans. *Physiology and Behavior* 30, 4: 663–666. http://doi.org/10.1016/0031-9384(83)90240-8
24. Antonio De Sena, Carlo Drioli, Federico Fontana, et al. 2009. Auditory and haptic augmentation of floor surfaces.
25. Aiguo Song, Jia Liu, and Juan Wu. 2008. *Softness haptic display device for human-computer interaction*. INTECH Open Access Publisher.
26. June Stevens, Kimberly Parker Truesdale, Jill Elisabeth McClain, and Jianwen Cai. 2006. The definition of weight maintenance. *International journal of obesity (2005)* 30, 3: 391–399. http://doi.org/10.1038/sj.ijo.0803175
27. Toshiaki Sugihara and Tsutomu Miyasato. 1998. The terrain surface simulator ALF (Alive! Floor). *Proc. of VRSJ ICAT'98*: 170–174.
28. Dag Svanaes and William Verplank. 2000. In search of metaphors for tangible user intefaces. *Proceedings of DARE 2000 on Designing augmented reality environments*, 121–129.
29. Yuichiro Takeuchi. 2010. Gilded gait: reshaping the urban experience with augmented footsteps. *Proceedings of the 23nd annual ACM symposium on User interface software and technology*, 185–188.
30. Yon Visell, Jeremy R Cooperstock, Bruno L Giordano, et al. 2008. A vibrotactile device for display of virtual ground materials in walking. *International Conference on Human Haptic Sensing and Touch Enabled Computer Applications*, 420–426.
31. Ivo Vos. The Brunch. *2008*. Retrieved July 28, 2016 from http://www.ivovos.com/brunch.php
32. Alice Wang. 2009. Asimov's first law/alarm clocks. *Proceedings of the 3rd International Conference on Tangible and Embedded Interaction*, 31–34.
33. Wikimedia. Graph of body mass index showing the various divisions. *2006*. Retrieved July 28, 2016 from https://commons.wikimedia.org/wiki/File:Body_mass_index_chart.svg
34. Gary Wolf. Quantified Self. Retrieved July 28, 2016 from http://antephase.com/quantifiedself

WireMolding: 3D Modeling Approach Involving Molding with Wire

Kazumi Yoshimura
Meiji University
Nakano, Tokyo, Japan
ev30587@meiji.ac.jp

Keita Watanabe
Meiji University
Nakano, Tokyo, Japan
watanabe@fms.meiji.ac.jp

TEI '17, March 20-23, 2017, Yokohama, Japan
ACM 978-1-4503-4676-4/17/03.
http://dx.doi.org/10.1145/3024969.3025059

Abstract
Due to the popularization of personal 3D printing, individuals without a technical background have opportunities to manipulate 3D data. However, creating 3D data needs technical knowledge and it is difficult for beginners. Especially when we make practical tools for personal belongings or furniture with a 3D printer, it is difficult because of being necessary to design such tools to fit in with objects. In this paper, we propose WireMolding, a 3D modeling approach for practical personal 3D printing with which sketches can be created to construct a 3D model from the bi-dimensional shape of a physical wire mold. We developed a prototype system and demonstrated the usefulness of this concept at the example of use cases.

Author Keywords
Personal fabrication; 3D printing; 3D modeling; fitting in with physical objects.

ACM Classification Keywords
H.5.2. Information Interfaces and Presentation: User Inter- faces - Input devices and strategies

Introduction
Due to the popularization of economically priced personal 3D printers, individuals without a technical background have opportunities to manipulate 3D data. In this trend, it is assumed that more non-technical

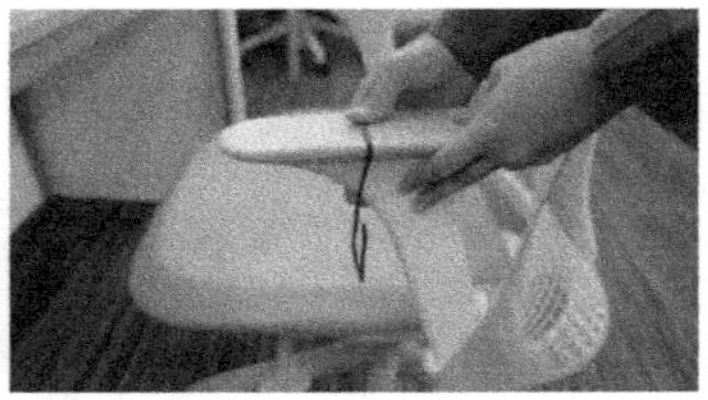

Figure 1: Molding with wire

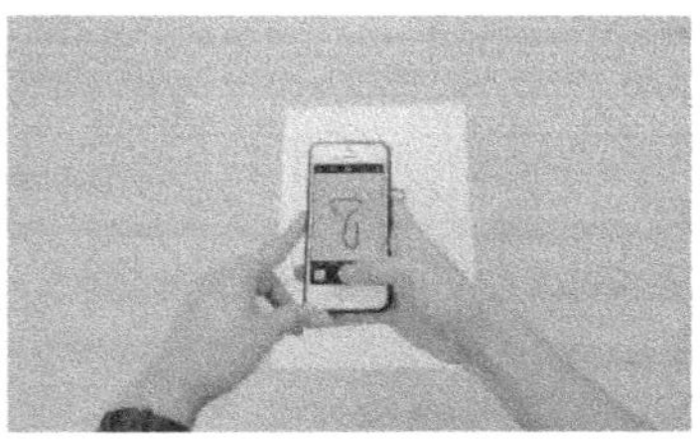

Figure 2: Taking photo of mold

Figure 3: Importing the sketch into 3D modeling software and creating a 3D model

users become to design and fabricate personalized products based on personal desires [1]. However, 3D modeling is difficult for beginners because it is a method of manipulating immaterial objects on computer screens and needs to plan thoroughly by using some techniques before beginning the modeling. Especially when we create 3D data of practical tools for personal belongings or furniture, we need to use professional measurement instruments and have technical knowledge to transform physical objects into 3D models. According to Hudson et al., casual makers, who are users without technical skills jumped into creating their 3D models with only minimal planning [2]. For beginners, it is also necessary that 3D modeling software is easy to operate even if they have minimal plan.

Some methods and devices have been proposed to solve this problem. They simplify measuring and modeling by eliminating the need for technical skills and reducing the process flow of 3D modeling. In this paper, we propose WireMolding, which is an approach of molding objects with a wire and scanning the molds for 3D modeling.

Related Work

Weichel et al. proposed SPATA [3], which is a system that automatically reflects the dimensions and angles of physical objects measured by a device, such as vernier caliper, on 3D model data. This system enables simplify 3D modeling workflows by skipping the process of measuring process and inputting the object size. Weichel et al. proposed MixFab [4], and Gannon et al. proposed Tactum [5], which are systems for shaping 3D models by capturing the size and shapes of real objects or human body parts in virtual reality (VR) space. These are systems, which make 3D modeling less complex by displaying real objects or part of the body together with a 3D model in the VR space and being able to create 3D models with gesture input. Akiyama et al. proposed Fitter [6], which enables a 3D printer to print objects that fit in with real objects by capturing figures of real objects using a tablet and printing models along the captured image. However, these methods can be applied only to objects whose size can be manipulated in VR space or on a tablet. As systems that simplify to fabricate some attachments or stand type tools, Chen et al. proposed Reprise [7] and Igarashi et al. proposed AutoConnect [8]. These systems are displaying a 3D object that has the same shape and size of a real object in software and fabricate 3D models with the operation to select a model type and parameters. In such systems, however, since users need to set parameters in order to modify the detailed shape, it seems that they are still complicated in operation for beginners and need to be improved more on the degree of freedom of modeling. Moreover, although MakerBot Industries, LLC created a tablet application called PrintShop for this problem, the app goes no further than enabling the creation of 3D shapes from drawings on paper. On the contrary, our method can simplify the creation of 3D models by molding physical objects.

WireMolding

Because wire is malleable, we can mold parts of physical objects by pressing wire firmly against them. By scanning or taking photos of the molds bi-dimensionally, we can obtain bi-dimensional data, convert them into Scalable Vector Graphics (SVG) format, and create 3D model data by importing the SVG images into 3D modeling software. Since images are

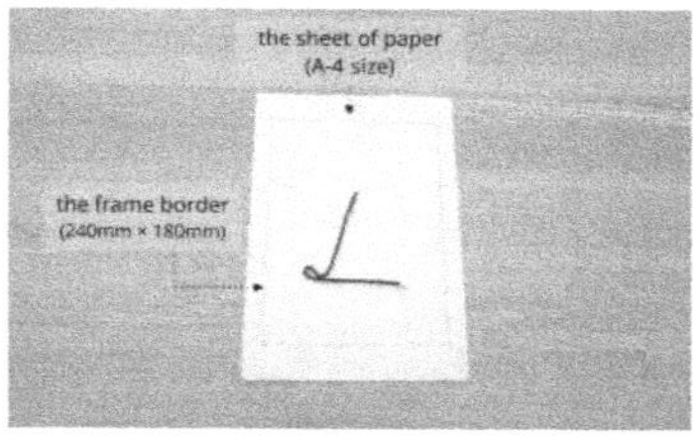

Figure 4: Sheet of paper used in the system

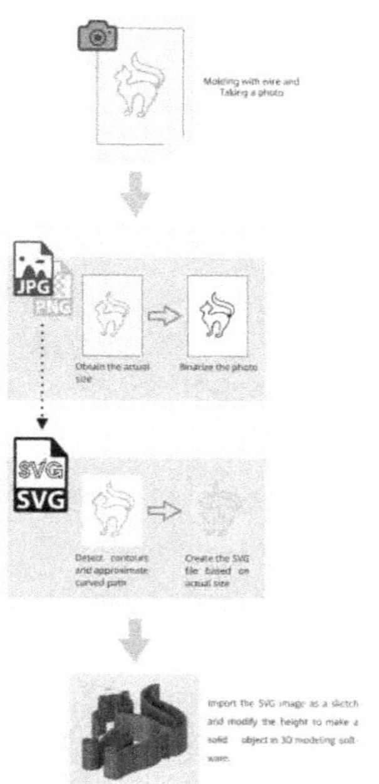

Figure 5: System configuration of first prototype

imported, it is not necessary to measure the physical objects to obtain plain scales of them.

It is also possible to form arbitrary shapes with a wire by just simply bending it along them. Therefore, our approach enables to create curved surface more instinctively and more reversibly than only by using a general 3D modeling software.

Procedure of WireMolding

The first step of using WireMolding is to mold wire along the desired shape (Figure 1). The next step is to place the molded wire within the black frame of a rectangle drawn on a piece of paper, and take a picture with a smartphone so that the edges of the picture fit in the frame (Figure 2). Then, by dragging and dropping the picture onto our system, it will be converted into an SVG image and a sketch of a 3D model will be obtained. Finally, by importing the sketch into modeling software, a 3D model, whose shape is the same as the molded wire, can be created (Figure 3).

First Prototype

WireMolding uses NIPPOLY Jiyujizai wire COLOR 3.2$\phi \times$3m Karasu wire made by Nihonkasen Co., Ltd. The wire is soft and easy to bend, so even complex shapes can be easily formed with it. The wire can also maintain the shape onece it is formed. To detect the contour of the wire from photos, the wire should be black and thick. If more detailed molding is required, thinner wire, e.g., 0.9 or 2.0 mm in diameter, can be used. Moreover, an A-4 size sheet of paper with a rectangle (H 240mm × W 180mm) used as a frame border is used when a picture of the molded wire is taken (Figure 4).

We developed a prototype system, which processes to output a sketch of a 3D model (Figure 5). First, the system obtains the actual size of a wire mold based on the frame border of an imported photo.. Then, it binarizes the photo. After that, it detects the outline of the wire mold and finds curved path approximated to the contours. Finally, it generates an SVG file based on the curved path. At the same time, it converts the pixel units into metric units using the obtained size. From this process, it generates an actual size sketch data for 3D modeling software.

Use Cases and Discussion

There are three use cases that apply to WireMolding:

1. Modeling by only molding physical objects
2. Modeling by a combination of molding and free manipulation with wire
3. Modeling by a combination of multiple 3D models made using WireMolding

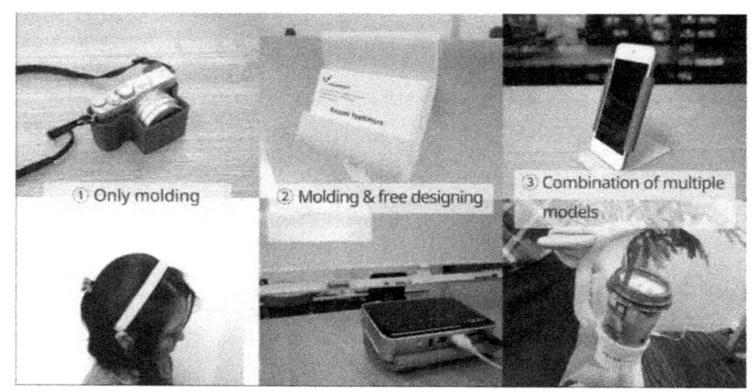

Figure 6: Examples of 3D printed items made by using WireMolding

Use case 1 is effective when making some cases or some fixing tools for personal belongings. We wind the wire around the physical object to obtain the mold of wire in the direction you want to cover the object or the direction you want to fasten it. As examples of fabrication, we create a case of camera and a headband fitting in with the maker's head (Figure 6-1). Moreover, when making parts to attach to personal belongings such as your desk, your smartphone, a pair of your glasses and so on with a 3D printer, designing 3D models that accurately depict the physical objects is easy with the use case 2. We fabricate a business card holder that can be attached to a laptop computer and a projector stand as examples of use case 2 (Figure 6-2). When we made the business card holder, we finished modeling in about 3 minutes: it took 1–2 minutes to mold the shape with a wire and 1–2 minutes to take a photo, output a sketch, and modify the height to make the object three-dimentional, and the modeling was very easy. The connecting part of the printed business card holder successfully fit in the curve of the display of the laptop computer. However, because wire molds were formed by hand, the models necessarily included some warping, even if they were carefully fixed before taking a picture. This problem can be resolved by applying correction to the curve of the sketches when they are outputted.

When we create a 3D model from one sketch, we can normally modify only one axial length against one sketch. For this reason, when fabricating multiple solid objects that have several axial lengths, we cannot make 3D models with only one sketch. Therefore, we need to make several sketches, as with use case 3. In this study, we took an approach to print every part of a 3D model against each sketch and fabricate assemblies later. We fabricated an iPod stand and a drink holder that can be attached the armrest of chair we previously fabricated as prototypes of use case 3 (Figure 6-3). The drink holder is made up of two parts: a hook for a chair and a basket for a cup. As this example shows, we can deal with various patterns of this use case by standardizing joints that connect 3D printed objects to each other.

Conclusions and Future Work

We proposed WireMolding, which is an approach to simplify 3D modeling by using automatically created full-scale sketches of 3D models from physical molds made of wire. By determining the physical input of modeling, we could easily create complicated curved surfaces with this approach. Moreover, by automatically converting sketches of 3D models to actual size, this approach reduced the number of processes and enabled efficient modeling.

In the future, we aim to improve the quality of 3D models can be created using WireMolding and to make it unnecessary to do modeling when 3D printing, by developing an application for using this approach with tablets and implementing functions such as fixing the shapes of sketches, creating solid objects from sketches and making standardized joint.

References

1. Neil Gershenfeld. *Fab: The Coming Revolution on Your Desktop--from Personal Computers to Personal Fabrication.* Basic Books, New York, 2005.
2. Nathaniel Hudson, Celena Alcock, and Parmit K. Chilana. Understanding Newcomers to 3D Printing: Motivations, Workflows, and Barriers of Casual Makers. In Proc. of CHI '16, pp. 384-396, 2016.

3. Christian Weichel, Jason Alexander, Abhijit Karnik, Hans Gellersen. SPATA: Spatio-Tangible Tools for Fabrication-Aware Design. In Proc. of TEI '15, pp. 189-196, 2015.
4. Christian Weichel, Manfred Lau, David Kim, Nicolas Villar, Hans W. Gellersen. MixFab: a mixed-reality environment for personal fabrication. In Proc. of CHI '14, pp. 3855-3864, 2014.
5. Madeline Gannon, Tovi Grossman, George Fitzmaurice. Tactum: A Skin-Centric Approach to Digital Design and Fabrication. In Proc. of CHI '15, pp. 1779-1788, 2015.
6. Yoh Akiyama, Homei Miyashita. Fitter: A System for Easily Printing Objects that Fit Real Objects. In Proc. of UIST '16 Adjunct, pp. 129-131, 2016.
7. Xiang 'Anthony' Chen, Jeeeun Kim, Jennifer Mankoff, Tovi Grossman, Stelian Coros, Scott E. Hudson. Reprise: A Design Tool for Specifying, Generating, and Customizing 3D Printable Adaptations on Everyday Objects. In Proc. of UIST '16, pp. 29-39, 2016.
8. Yuki Koyama, Shinjiro Sueda, Emma Steinhardt, Takeo Igarashi, Ariel Shamir, Wojciech Matusik. AutoConnect: computational design of 3D-printable connectors, In Proc. of ACM SIGGRAPH Asia 2015, Article 231, 11 pages, 2015.

A Thermal Pattern Design for Providing Dynamic Thermal Feedback on the Face with Head Mounted Displays

Zikun Chen
Graduate School of Media Design, Keio University
Japan
zkzk.chen@kmd.keio.ac.jp

Roshan Lalintha Peiris
Graduate School of Media Design, Keio University
Japan
roshan@kmd.keio.ac.jp

Kouta Minamizawa
Graduate School of Media Design, Keio University
Japan
kouta@kmd.keio.ac.jp

TEI '17, March 20-23, 2017, Yokohama, Japan
ACM 978-1-4503-4676-4/17/03.
http://dx.doi.org/10.1145/3024969.3025060

Abstract
This paper presents our preliminary exploration of providing dynamic thermal haptic feedback on the face. We have designed a thermal feedback prototype that integrates Peltier modules directly with a head mounted display which is able to provide thermal output directly on users' faces. We explored the possibility of providing dynamic thermal feedback which could present information and enhance user experience through designing four initial dynamic thermal patterns of our prototype. We also conducted a preliminary user experiment and analysis of the design of different patterns ("dynamic information") to evaluate the design on three aspects, the accuracy of recognition of dynamic stimuli, smoothness of the movement and comfort level. Our results indicate that the accuracy of recognition of dynamic stimuli was approximately 71.84%.

ACM Classification Keywords
H.5.2. [Information Interfaces and Presentation (e.g. HCI)]: User Interfaces

Author Keywords
thermal display; thermal haptics; dynamic thermal; head mounted display

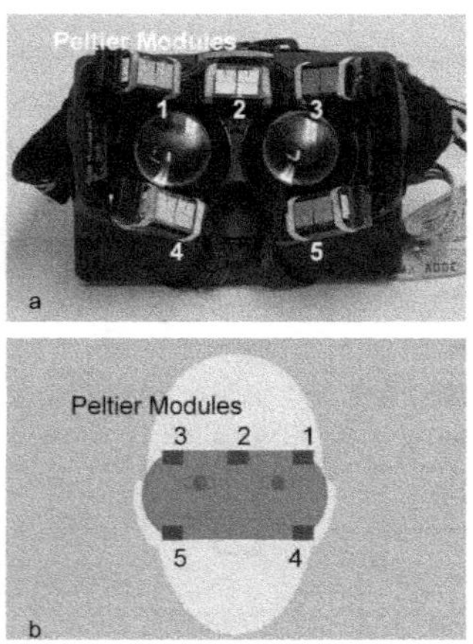

Figure 1: a. Distribution of Peltier Modules on the VR HMD. b. Locations of thermal modules when the user wearing the HMD (Main View)

Introduction

In the current VR experience design, providing haptic feedback, has been widely explored to enhance the user's presence in the virtual reality (VR) environments. Vibrotactile feedback to simulate attacks in the game, etc. [19] and directional cueing in virtual reality [4], a flywheel on the headset to provide mechanical simulation [6], and muscle stimulation for enhanced haptic feedback [14] are some of the recent works that have demonstrated enhancement of user experience with haptic feedback in virtual reality.

In our recent works, we present our exploration of providing thermal haptic feedback as a part of the VR experience [17, 16]. Past researches have discussed effects of thermal feedback on human perception, in areas such as interpersonal communication and human-computer interaction [5, 15] and on body locations such as the hands [8], arms [13, 12] and forehead [16]. Our work on integrating thermal feedback modules (Peltier modules) with an Oculus Rift Head Mounted Display (HMD) for exploring giving thermal stimuli directly on the user's face, which is relatively the most sensitive part on the body to temperature change [9, 7], has provided a new approach to combine thermal feedback with VR experience [17, 16]. And we have explored some basic functions of thermal feedback, such as enhancing immersive feeling, and providing directional cue in a virtual space.

In most of previous researches, a common feature is that thermal feedback is provided as a static thermal sensation to the users [2, 13, 12, 16], hence what users receive are stimuli at fixed points. Therefore in this work, we focus on whether we can create a *flow of thermal feedback* effect, i.e., a "dynamic thermal sensation" by providing sequentially timed thermal feedback on the face, for presenting more complex information or simulating material or movement.

As a preliminary exploration, we evaluated our design of dynamic thermal sensation pattern which consists of two consecutive static thermal feedback stimuli.

System Description

Hardware

As shown in Figure 1a, the device consists of five 2 x 1.5 cm Peltier modules mounted on the HMD face side (inside), which are in direct contact with the user's face and are distributed to the left, center and right parts of the forehead, and left and right cheeks respectively(Figure 1b). Each Peltier module is controlled by a full bridge motor and through the Arduino Nano board. The rate of temperature change (ROC) is set at 3°C/s, at which the user is able to detect a temperature change on the skin almost immediately[10].

Pattern Design

In this research, we aim to explore the effect of providing dynamic thermal feedback by designing patterns for operating Peltier modules. According to the distribution of Peltier modules we have shown, we intend to use different combinations of sequential actuation of these Peltier modules to provide the dynamic thermal feedback. As the initial step of this work, we implemented four basic patterns, Up, Down, Left, Right as shown in Figure 2. In this design, each dynamic stimulus was provided in combination of two static stimuli. These first and second static stimuli were provided consecutively in order to provide the dynamic pattern of thermal feedback. For example, as shown in Figure 2, when operating Element 1 and 3, and then the Element 4 and 5 consecutively, users would be able to feel the thermal feedback moves from top to bottom, etc.

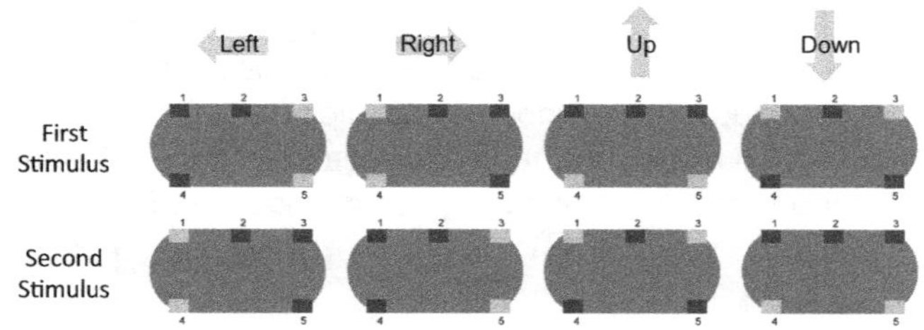

Figure 2: Design of operation patterns of Peltier modules on HMD for simulating movement in four basic directions (User View)

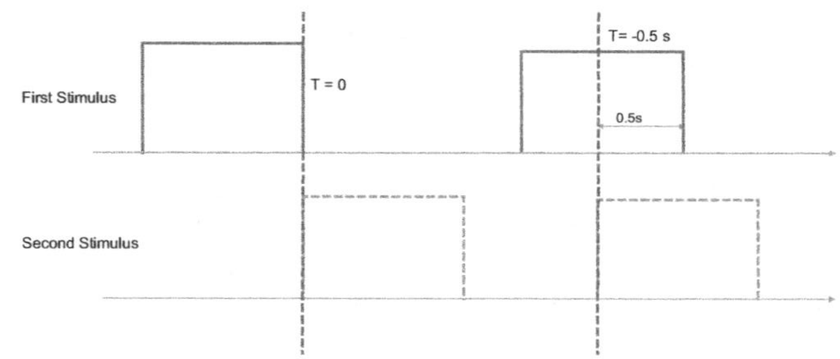

Figure 3: Inter-Stimulus Interval T = 0 and T = -0.5 illustrated

Parameters
According to studies by D. R. Kenshalo, Dirian-Smith et al., the ability to perceive temperature changes depends on a number of factors [11, 3]. Hence in this study, for evaluating this design, we set parameters to compare the perception of the dynamic thermal feedback with different scenarios while using this setup. According to our main purpose, the most important factors we need to discuss are those that represent the relationship between first and second static stimuli in the operation patterns. As such, one of the key parameters is the Inter-stimulus interval (T, unit: second) between two static thermal stimuli (Figure 3). This parameter T is calculated from the end of the first static thermal stimulus till the beginning of the second static thermal stimulus. So when $T = 0$, it means the second static stimulus starts as long as the first stimulus ends. We also took into account the situations when $T \neq 0$, as $T < 0$ (the latter stimulus starts before the previous one ends) and $T > 0$ (there is interval between two stimulus). Since when $T > 0$, the interval will cause discontinuous sensation, which is not our main goal in this study, so in this study, we only discussed $T = 0$ and $T < 0$, and respectively set dynamic stimulus into two types as $T = 0$ and $T = -0.5$.

For other factors mentioned in studies by Kenshalo, Dirian-Smith et al., such as duration of every static stimulus, as Banks and Stevens suggested in their researches, at thermally sensitive site on bodies, 1 second was the critical duration; at shorter duration, intensity and duration traded but not proportionally, and at duration longer than 1 second, there was no further influence of duration on the threshold, hence when considering about the duration setting in this study, we decided to set the duration for every static stimulus as 1 second [1, 18]. At the same time, we do not need to compare the effects of different temperatures. In general, human's thermal sensors are relatively more sensitive to cold stimuli than to warm stimuli [7, 16], and as one main direction of our future work with thermal feedback is to simulate fluid like water flow or wind, which are usually cooler than the average temperature of human skin, so at this stage we set amplitude of temperature change as -3°C from skin temperature within 1 second using the temperature change rate at 3°C/s.

Therefore for dynamic stimulus on each direction, we set two types of stimulus: the first, stimulus consists of two static stimuli with zero inter-stimulus interval ($T = 0$); and the second stimulus consists of two static stimuli with

$T = -0.5s$ inter-stimulus interval. These two types of dynamic stimulus were used in our user experiment.

While evaluating our design, we aimed to discuss the potential of providing dynamic thermal feedback. As such, one important aspect was whether users could perceive the movement direction of dynamic thermal stimuli provided by our setup. Since the movements were simulated by Peltier modules at different location on HMD, another important aspect to identify was whether users feel the dynamic stimuli more like "moving" or "jumping" on their faces. We also took into account users' comfort feelings when they used our setup. Therefore, we set the following dependent variables for data collecting and analysis.

- The accuracy of perception of the movement direction of the dynamic thermal feedback (the percentage of correct answers of the direction that the user perceived when received the dynamic stimuli).
- The smoothness of the movement that the user felt in the experiment (using the Likert scale).
- Users' comfort feeling to different sets of tests (using the Likert Scale).

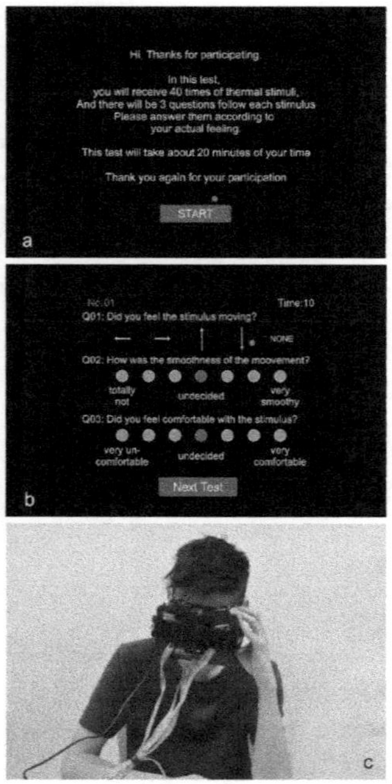

Figure 4: a. Start scene b. Test scene of user experiment application where the users reported their answers. c. A participant doing the user experiment.

User Experiment

According to our purposes of comparison, at the current stage we conducted an experiment. As mentioned before, we chose four basic directions (Figure2), and for each direction, we set two types of dynamic stimulus (When $T = 0$ and $T = -0.5s$). For each task in the experiment, we gave one dynamic stimulus on the subject's face. We repeated a same dynamic stimulus five times, and all stimuli were provided in random order. Hence for each subject, in one experiment they received in total 40 times of the dynamic stimuli (4 directions, 2 inter-stimulus interval, 5 times for each type of dynamic stimulus). According to the study by Jones et al.[7], in experimental studies of thermal perception, stimuli are usually presented every 10 seconds, so we set 10 seconds as the minimal interval between every two task to let subjects' skin adjust to the same temperature with Peltier modules which attached to their faces. Each experiment lasted approximately 20 minutes per participant.

The application depicted in Figure 4a and 4b was used to generate stimuli and collect the user responses. As shown in Figure 4, the application consists of two scenes, the start scene (Figure 4a) provided introduction of the experiment, and the test scene (Figure 4b) contained the number of stimuli at top-left and a countdown timer at top-right of the screen, and below were questions subjects had to answer to. Subjects used a mouse to select their answers and the application automatically collected data of their operation during the experiment.

Procedure

At the beginning, each participant was explained on the system and the concept. Next, during the training phase, the subjects were allowed to familiarize with the user interface, and the procedure operation method (filling out the questionnaire), and to experienced all types of temperature stimuli. All procedures were conducted in VR environment where subjects wore our HMD with Peltier modules during the training and experiment. After the training, the experiment was commenced.

In the experiment phase, after receiving a dynamic stimulus, the timer on the top-left started counting down from 10s to 0, and the subjects were asked to answer three questions about the stimulus(Figure 4). When answering the first question, subjects were allowed to choose NONE when they didn't detect the dynamic stimuli. When subjects

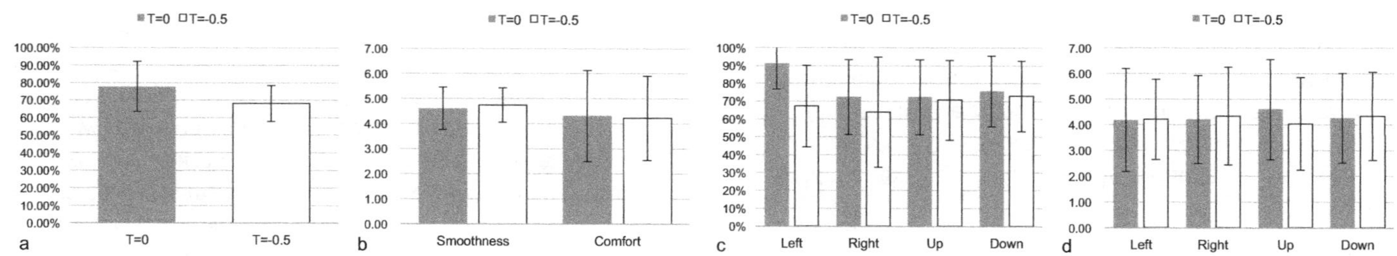

Figure 5: a. Overall accuracy and b. smoothnes/comfort levels c. Average accuracy of subjects' perception of dynamic thermal stimuli in different directions. d. Average smoothness of movements of stimuli in different direction.

clicked the option buttons, their answers were automatically collected and saved in file. After finishing the questions, and if the timer already became 0, subjects could press the Next Test button to start next task when they were ready.

Results

Ten healthy participants were involved in the experiment, 7 males and 3 females with an average age of 26. Taking into account the sample size, we first carried out a preliminary analysis to compare the results under different conditions.

Overall, 95.83% of all stimuli were perceived during the experiment. Accuracy of the perception of dynamic feedback direction was 71.84%(Figure 5a). Meanwhile, the averages of smoothness and comfort were 4.67 (SD = 0.75) and 4.26 (SD = 1.75) respectively (Figure 5b). In direction left, right, up, and down, when $T = 0$, the average accuracy of subjects' perception of dynamic stimuli respectively was 91.11%, 72.22%, 72.22%, 75.56%, and the average smoothness was 4.18, 4.20, 4.60, 4.26 respectively. When $T = -0.5s$, the average accuracy was 67.22%, 63.89%, 70.56%, 72.78% and average smoothness was 4.21, 4.34, 4.03, 4.33 respectively.

Discussions and Future Work

Result Discussions

According to the results, the overall accuracy for the perception of movement of dynamic stimuli in this study was (71.84%). Thus, this preliminary result shows promise that by arranging the operation patterns of the Peltier modules on the HMD, it is possible to provide the dynamic thermal feedback which was not previously available.

We compared the perception of two types of dynamic stimuli in different directions. As observed in Figure 5c, in each direction, when $T = 0$ the result was higher than when $T = -0.5s$. However, further analysis revealed that there was no significant difference between the results of each direction with different inter-stimulus intervals. This could mainly be caused by the current sample size which was not large enough for reaching a more reliable conclusion. Therefore in our next step, we plan to continue the user experiment to collect results from more participants and conducted further discussion for assessing our setup.

The average smoothness was higher than 4(the uncertain option on the Likert Scale). Only one subject rated the smoothness below 4, which was 3.18 (SD = 1.77). Although there was no obvious difference between $T = 0$ and $T = -0.5s$ according to (Figure 5d), one subject gave comment that he felt the speed of the stimuli were different sometimes which might be caused by the interval between two static stimuli.

The average comfort level was higher than 4 as well, but the result showed a very high standard deviation. This was because the comfort feeling varied among individuals in the experiment. Two subjects who gave very positive comments on this setup after the experiment, rated the comfort at an average of 5.98 (SD = 0.73) and 7.00(SD = 0.00) respectively, while some participants gave relatively negative comments. The subject who had the lowest average comfort level, which was 1.85 (SD = 0.84), said he didn't like the stimuli, and mentioned that his comfort reduced because the Peltier modules were a bit too hard. Another subject whose average comfort level was 2.98 (SD = 0.66), told us that the sensitivity of his skin was relatively high, so he felt the thermal stimuli were a bit too intense during the experiment, he also said that he didn't like temperature change at small area on skin. Participants who were not used to HMDs also felt it was not very comfortable during the experiment.

Limitations and Future Work

In this study, as the initial step of our exploration in providing dynamic thermal feedback on the face in VR experience, we designed four basic operation patterns for Peltier modules integrated on an HMD to simulate dynamic movement of thermal feedback. With more results, we would conduct further discussions on this design.

For future work, there are more parameters worth exploring, such as more values of inter-stimulus interval, various temperature intensities corresponding to different contexts, number of Peltier modules and distance between them, etc.

We plan to redesign the contact surface of the HMD as well. Constrained by the shape of the HMD we used, we could integrate limited Peltier modules to it in this study, thus in future work, we intend to explore better distribution with more Peltier modules to provide dynamic thermal feedback with higher smoothness and accuracy of users' perception. Besides, as the subject participated in our user experiment has mentioned, the Peltier modules might cause discomfort. Therefore we intend to reduce the discomfort caused by the hardness of Peltier element for enhancing users' comfort.

Based on this design, We intend to make new contents such as interactive applications for simulating water flow or wind flow on the user's face. With combination with thermal feedback, we believe the thermal contents could provide enriched experience for users and enhance users' experience in virtual environment.

Acknowledgment

This research was conducted as part of the JST-ACCEL "Embodied Media" project.

REFERENCES

1. WP Banks. 1976. Areal and temporal summation in the thermal reaction time. *Sensory processes* 1, 1 (1976), 2–13.
2. Mohamed Benali-Khoudja, Moustapha Hafez, Jean-Marc Alexandre, Jamil Benachour, and Abderrahmane Kheddar. 2003. Thermal feedback model for virtual reality. In *International Symposium on Micromechatronics and Human Science*, Vol. 1. 153–158.
3. Ian Darian-Smith and Kenneth O Johnson. 1977. Thermal sensibility and thermoreceptors. *Journal of Investigative Dermatology* 69, 1 (1977), 146–153.

4. Victor Adriel de Jesus Oliveira, Luciana Nedel, Anderson Maciel, and Luca Brayda. 2016. Localized Magnification in Vibrotactile HMDs for Accurate Spatial Awareness. In *EuroHaptics 2016*. 55–64.

5. D Gooch. 2009. *An Investigation into Communicating Social Presence With Thermal Devices*. Ph.D. Dissertation. MSc Dissertation.

6. Jan Gugenheimer, Dennis Wolf, Eythor R Eiriksson, Pattie Maes, and Enrico Rukzio. 2016. Gyrovr: Simulating inertia in virtual reality using head worn flywheels. In *Proceedings of the 29th Annual Symposium on User Interface Software and Technology*. ACM, 227–232.

7. Hsin-Ni Ho and Lynette A Jones. 2006. Contribution of thermal cues to material discrimination and localization. *Perception & Psychophysics* 68, 1 (2006), 118–128.

8. Dhruv Jain, Misha Sra, Jingru Guo, Rodrigo Marques, Raymond Wu, Justin Chiu, and Chris Schmandt. 2016. Immersive Scuba Diving Simulator Using Virtual Reality. In *Proceedings of the 29th Annual Symposium on User Interface Software and Technology (UIST '16)*. ACM, New York, NY, USA, 729–739. DOI: http://dx.doi.org/10.1145/2984511.2984519

9. Kenneth O Johnson, Ian Darian-Smith, and Carole LaMotte. 1973. Peripheral neural determinants of temperature discrimination in man: a correlative study of responses to cooling skin. *Journal of Neurophysiology* 36, 2 (1973), 347–370.

10. L. A. Jones and H. N. Ho. 2008. Warm or Cool, Large or Small? The Challenge of Thermal Displays. *IEEE Transactions on Haptics* 1, 1 (2008), 53–70.

11. DR Kenshalo. 1976. Correlations of temperature sensitivity in man and monkey, a first approximation. *Sensory functions of the skin with special reference to man* (1976), 305–330.

12. Sven Kratz and Anthony Dunnigan. 2016. ThermoTouch: Design of a High Dynamic Temperature Range Thermal Haptic Display. In *Proceedings of the 2016 CHI Conference Extended Abstracts on Human Factors in Computing Systems*. ACM, 1577–1582.

13. Wonjun Lee and Youn-kyung Lim. 2010. Thermo-message: exploring the potential of heat as a modality of peripheral expression. In *CHI'10 Extended Abstracts on Human Factors in Computing Systems*. ACM, 4231–4236.

14. Pedro Lopes, Alexandra Ion, and Patrick Baudisch. 2015. Impacto: Simulating Physical Impact by Combining Tactile Stimulation with Electrical Muscle Stimulation. In *Proceedings of the 28th Annual ACM Symposium on User Interface Software & Technology (UIST '15)*. ACM, New York, NY, USA, 11–19. DOI: http://dx.doi.org/10.1145/2807442.2807443

15. Mutsuhiro Nakashige, Minoru Kobayashi, Yuriko Suzuki, Hidekazu Tamaki, and Suguru Higashino. 2009. Hiya-Atsu media: augmenting digital media with temperature. In *CHI'09 Extended Abstracts on Human Factors in Computing Systems*. ACM, 3181–3186.

16. Roshan Lalintha Peiris, Liwei Chan, and Kouta Minamizawa. 2016. Thermocons: Evaluating the Thermal Haptic Perception of the Forehead. In *Proceedings of the 29th Annual Symposium on User Interface Software and Technology*. ACM, 187–188.

17. Roshan Lalintha Peiris, Wei Peng, Zikun Chen, Liwei Chan, and Kouta Minamizawa. ThermoVR: Exploring Integrated Thermal Haptic Feedback with Head Mounted Displays. In *In Proc of CHI '17*. (Accepted for publication).
18. Joseph C Stevens, William C Okulicz, and Lawrence E Marks. 1973. Temporal summation at the warmth threshold. *Perception & Psychophysics* 14, 2 (1973), 307–312.
19. Shafiq ur Rehman, Jiong Sun, Li Liu, and Haibo Li. 2008. Turn your mobile into the ball: rendering live football game using vibration. *IEEE Transactions on Multimedia* 10, 6 (2008), 1022–1033.

Quantifying Children's Engagement with Educational Tangible Blocks

Jaewon Cho
Dept. of Human ICT
Sungkyunkwan University
Suwon, Republic of Korea
choinae0914@gmail.com

Junwoo Yoo
Dept. of Human ICT
Sungkyunkwan University
Suwon, Republic of Korea
grochi@gmail.com

Ju-young Shin
Dept. of Human ICT
Sungkyunkwan University
Suwon, Republic of Korea
shinjuyoung1120@gmail.com

Jun-dong Cho
Dept. of Human ICT
Sungkyunkwan University
Distinguished Visiting Professor
North University of China
jdcho07@gmail.com

Andrea Bianchi
Dept. of Industrial Design
KAIST
Daejeon, Republic of Korea
andrea.whites@gmail.com

TEI '17, March 20-23, 2017, Yokohama, Japan
ACM 978-1-4503-4676-4/17/03.
http://dx.doi.org/10.1145/3024969.3025062

Abstract
Playful learning is a powerful method to enhance children's engagement with teaching material, often resulting in better learning. Several prior works demonstrated the existence of a relation between tangibles and engagement, but they did not characterize it with specific measures. Therefore, this paper aims to describe the degree of engagement with tangible blocks by quantifying children's proactive and passive actions during a learning session. Based on a user study with 36 kindergarten children, our findings show that tangibles support a higher degree of engagement, fosters attention and collaboration, and possibly lead to more active learning.

Author Keywords
Tangible interaction; Engagement; Learning; Collaboration.

ACM Classification Keywords
H.5.3. Information interfaces and presentation (e.g., HCI): Collaborative computing.

Introduction
Educators and researchers argue that students who are actively involved in tasks, such as analyzing, synthetizing and evaluating, gain a better understanding of teaching material than those who are

passively receiving information [6]. This process is called *active learning* and is linked with cognitive engagement activities that can be detected while students are learning, such as active manipulations (e.g., highlighting), constructive generations (e.g., notes, drawing) and interactions (e.g., discussing with peers, playing) [2]. Based on this framework, researchers claim that tangible interfaces – which blend digital and physical elements – are more engaging than traditional teaching methods because they promote interactive and constructive ways of learning, explorations supported by real-time feedback [10, 15] and self-expression through ideation [12]. However, while many researchers argue that tangible interfaces naturally support an engaging and fun experience that results in active learning (an activity known as *playful learning* [11]), and offer examples of interfaces that support this theory [10], few papers have attempted to describe and quantify the active engagement level of children using tangible interfaces for learning [3, 4, 8].

This paper contributes to the literature in the field by further exploring the relation between tangible interaction and active learning with a study specifically designed to analyze the level of engagement of 36 kindergarten children interacting with tangible blocks in three different pedagogical settings (traditional, tangible and collaborative). Our results provide additional empirical evidence supporting the use of tangible interfaces as a tool for boosting engagement and potentially increase the active learning of children.

Related Work

The seminal theoretical works promoting the usage of tangible interfaces for playful leaning [8, 11] are supported by a vast literature of empirical research. Researchers agree that the differences in learning when using physical, tangible settings (e.g., books, toys) or their digital counterparts (e.g., video, games) are not a direct product of the different interfaces, but rather the result of the level of engagement and enjoyment that these technologies provide [7, 13]. For example, Yannier et al. [15] demonstrate that simply adding tangible elements to a game interface does not directly enhance children's learning of basic physics principles. Instead, children's engagement and understanding are correlated with how immersive, interactive and physical the learning environment is. Analogous results have been reported for other augmented learning technologies, such as the FeelSleeve haptic interface for reading [14], the FingAR puppet system for promoting reasoning on emotional states [1], the Hunting of the Snark physical exploration game [10, 11] and the ActiveCubes by Jacoby et al. [5].

The common finding of these works is that physical environments provide higher engagement and enjoyment for children, and consequently more active learning [4, 13]. A second factor in support of tangible interfaces for boosting active learning is that they naturally lead to better collaborations and reduce conflicts, by promoting cooperation and discussion among children when faced with problem-solving tasks [16]. Tangibles also help to solve conflicts between team members, as children naturally learn to take turns and share control of physical interfaces more readily than when they use digital tools [9].

User Study

We designed a comparative study with kindergarten children to assess different levels of engagement – defined as "children's verbal expressions, consistent

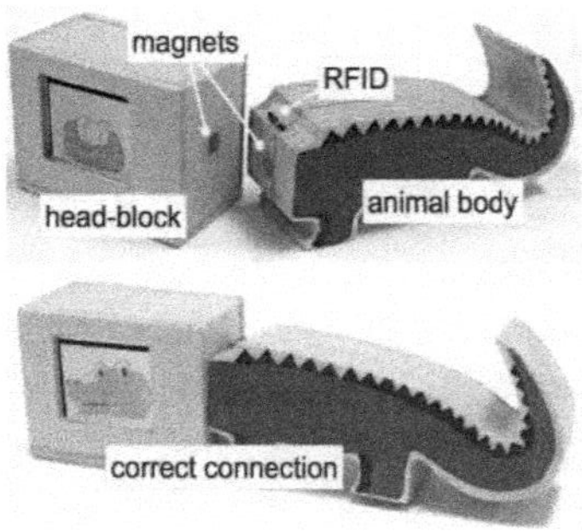

Figure 1. *Head* and *body* blocks.

Figure 2. Examples of connected blocks and a game challenge. In the background, a page from the digital book used in the study.

involvement and desire to continue interacting and playing" [11] - in three common pedagogical scenarios: 1) a digital illustrated book read aloud by an adult (e.g., [7]), 2) a tangible block interface supervised by an adult used by a single child (a situation that resembles how children could use the system at home with a parent), or 3) the same tangible block interface used by two children simultaneously (a situation resembling a learning activity in a kindergarten with a supervising teacher).

Book learning content

We designed a digital pictorial book with custom learning material for the experiment and displayed it on a touch-screen device as an interactive slideshow with sound (digital book). The material we designed is an illustrated description of six different animals living in Africa: a lion, a zebra, a giraffe, a leopard, a hippo and a crocodile. Each animal features five knowledge units: 1) the written name of the animal in the local language and 2) in English (the second language); 3) the color/textures of the animal's skin; 4) the animal's living habits, such as where/how the animal lives (e.g., ground vs. water/alone vs. in group) or what it eats (e.g., meat vs. plants); and 5) unique characteristics (e.g., lions are predators, zebras live with giraffes, giraffes are the tallest, leopards climb trees, hippos have webbed toes, crocodiles lay eggs). All of the material in the book is presented using simplified native language for children in 24 illustrated pages.

Tangible learning platform and interaction

In our tangible system, 2 types of blocks representing different animal parts (bodies and heads) can be connected (similarly to the ActiveCubes [5]). They provide feedback to users about the correctness of the match (Figure 1). Using several layers of machine-carved wood-sheets glued together, we built unpowered blocks representing the bodies of the six animals described in the illustrated book. On the neck is a magnet for supporting connections with a head-block and a tiny RFID tag for unique identification. The bodies are painted, and their maximum dimensions are 16.5 x 8 x 3.6 cm thick. The head-blocks, on the other hand, are powered components and consist of a micro-controller (Arduino Mini Pro), a 1.8" color TFT LCD display, an RFID reader (ID-12LA), a magnet and a Li-Po battery, all encased in a wood box measuring 33 x 70 x 47 mm. When a head-block is connected to an animal's body-block, the RFID reader detects and deciphers the RFID tag to determine if both body parts belong to the same animal. Graphical feedback on the screen notifies about the correctness of the match.

The blocks are meant to support playful learning through a simple puzzle-like interaction. At the beginning of the game, the blocks are not connected. Once started, the display located in the head-block shows a *challenge,* by means of an image picturing one of the animals' properties described in the illustrated book (Figure 2). To solve this challenge, children have to find and connect the head-block with the animal body that best matches the question. If the question is answered correctly, the head of the animal appears on the LCD screen, completing the figure. If the match is not correct, then negative feedback is displayed on the screen and the children are encouraged to try a different head–body combination. Finally, using a special RFID card, it is possible to pass on to the next question. In total, the game comprises 30 challenge questions presented in random order (6 animals x 5 properties).

Participants
We recruited 36 kindergarten children (19 females) aged 5 to 6 (M: 5.4, SD: 0.5). On a scale from 0 to 3, children reported (with the help of their parent) a level of native language reading ability of 1.4 (SD: 0.9). 32 children had previously learned some English (second language) but the average reported reading-ability was 0.3 (SD: 0.6). On a scale from 1 to 5, children reported familiarity with touchscreen devices of 3 (SD: 1.2).

Evaluation method and measures
Following a between-subjects design, 12 children were assigned to each of the 3 conditions: *book*, *tangible* and *tangible team*. In the *tangible team* condition, the teams were generated by pairing children who already knew each other. Each condition consisted of a prologue, a learning session – in which children were asked to memorize the information in the book – and an epilogue. Each session was video-taped for later analysis and supervised by a trained and nationally certified school teacher in "electronic information and communication" with experience teaching children.

The prologue and epilogue were the same across the conditions. In the prologue, the children – accompanied by a parent – were introduced to the experiment. We provided a refreshment for the child along with an ice-breaking session. Meanwhile, the parent signed a consent form and provided basic demographic information about the child. In the epilogue, the children filled out two pictorial paper questionnaires to assess their level of self-reported interest and the accuracy of learning the material.

The learning sessions of the experiment were consistent across the conditions, with the role of the teacher being that of a mere facilitator and supervisor rather than a knowledge provider, as in more traditional settings [7]. The teacher ensured that the child remained focused on the topic by asking and answering questions, using the child native language. In the *book* condition, after displaying the content for each animal (five knowledge units), the screen displayed an interactive quiz with five randomized challenges, which the children had to solve independently. Each challenge consisted of an image representing an animal property on one side and the icons of the six animals on the other. A correct match resulted in prompting the next challenge, while a mistake required the children to try again. A button on the screen allowed children to review the material related to the challenge, and the teacher read aloud the content displayed.

In the *tangible* and *team* conditions, for each of the 30 challenges provided by system, the children were allowed to freely connect the blocks and attempt to match them correctly, or to navigate through the book content using the touchscreen. Also in these conditions the children were encouraged to ask questions and explore block combinations.

We collected 2 types of measure for engagement: the first was a short self-assessment questionnaire that asked children to evaluate their level of interest on an iconic 3-point Likert scale (similar to [15]) for both the content and the tools used in the experiment. Moreover, we analyzed and transcribed the video recorded during the study and extracted the results of the challenges, as well as the occurrences of passive and proactive behaviors. We classified the children's actions into five groups: engagement with questions (e.g., children answering questions only when directly asked vs. children asking questions or speaking without solicitation), focus (e.g., losing attention vs. making eye contact with the teacher), content engagement (e.g., reviewing the book material upon the teacher's suggestion vs. spontaneously), body feedback (e.g., leaning one's head on the table vs. maintaining an engaged posture) and language feedback (e.g., sighing or complaining vs. verbal expressions of interest).

In the tangible *team* condition, similarly to [9], we extracted actions indicating conflicts (e.g., blocking, complaining), collaborations, and request for control. Learning performance was measured using a paper quiz with 30 pictorial questions (the same as the practice challenges), in randomized order. Each question was an image describing a unique animal feature that had to be matched with one of the six animals' icons. No written text was used, as most children in the study could not read.

Results

The numbers of occurrences of proactive and passive actions from the video analysis were classified into five groups (Figure 3). Since the assumption of homogeneity of variance-covariance matrices was violated, we did not run a MANOVA. Instead we considered the average normalized percentages and analyzed them using a single one-way ANOVA followed by post-hoc analysis using Bonferroni CI adjustments, with $\alpha=0.05$.

The average normalized percentages revealed differences for learning environment ($F_{(2,33)}=13.3$, $p<0.01$, $\eta_p^2=0.44$), with the tangible and team conditions having significantly more proactive actions (i.e., fewer passive actions) than the book condition ($p<0.01$). In the self-assessment questionnaires, the interest in the teaching method received an average score of 2.8 of 3 (0.42), and the material received a score of 2.9 (0.36), with an interclass correlation coefficient of 0.78 (95% confidence interval 0.54-0.89). A Kruskal–Wallis non-parametric test revealed no differences in the scores across conditions. In terms of learning performance, we found no differences in the quiz scores (M: 23.8/30, SD: 3.5), but in the practice quiz we recorded significant changes in the total number of wrong matches ($F_{(2,33)}=7.3$, $p<0.01$, $\eta_p^2=0.3$) and failed challenges ($F_{(2,33)}=8.9$, $p<0.01$,

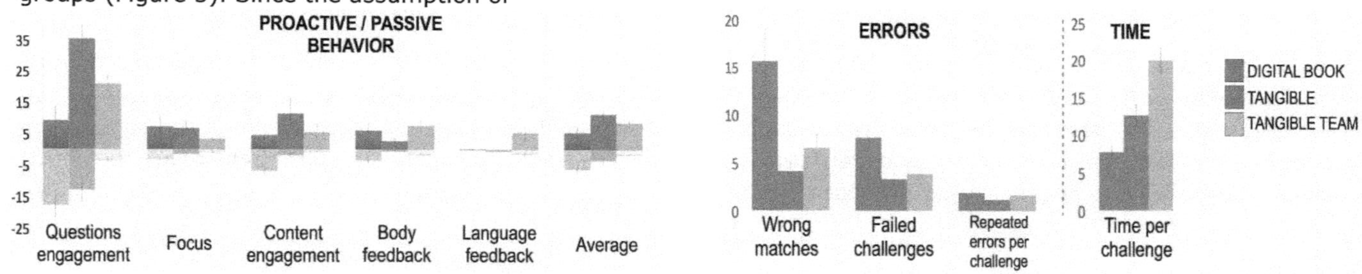

Figure 3. Passive (light tint) and proactive (dark) action groups for each learning environment (book, tangible, team) in five categories and on average (left). Average number of errors and time for the practice challenges (right).

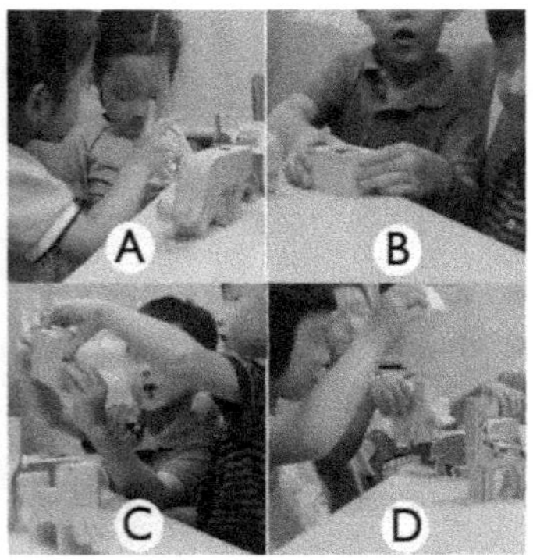

Figures 4. Children using tangibles together. Establishing rules for turns (A) and sharing of control (B). Two children perform an action together on one (C) or two (D) blocks.

$\eta_p^2 = 0.35$), with the book condition performing worse ($p<0.01$). The average time per challenge was also different across the conditions ($F_{(2,33)}=21.6$, $p<0.01$, $\eta_p^2 = 0.56$) with all pairwise comparisons significant at $p<0.05$ (see Figure 3 – right).

Discussion

Based on this study, we report 3 main findings. Firstly, the children were clearly more actively engaged when using the tangible blocks than not the digital book alone. The high values for *questions* and *content* engagement show that the children were more interested in asking and answering questions or autonomously reviewing the material when using tangibles. Moreover, the high number of errors, in conjunction with the fastest response time for solving a question in the book condition, indicates that the children working on a challenge did not take enough time to think carefully and opted for a trial-and-error approach. These combined results suggest that the higher level of engagement provided by tangibles is a powerful tool, not only for critical thinking and problem solving [e.g., 8, 10, 15] but more generally for supporting active learning.

A second result stems from the different usage patterns with blocks in the solo versus collaborative modes. Collaborative learning does not increase the overall amount of proactive actions performed by children, but it reduces the number of passive actions. These results can be explained by examining the collaboration patterns among the children: most of the teams adopted a turn-taking approach to solve the challenges, so that each child worked on only roughly half the total challenges. It is therefore not surprising that the individual number of proactive actions per child decreased, as only one child at a time was engaged with the blocks. However, the fact that the number of passive actions also decreased showcases that the children, as in previous work [4], remained attentive outside their turn: *"I enjoy studying with friends using blocks,"* said a child.

Finally, the last result concerns collaborative learning and conflict resolution. In the *team* condition, few conflicts arose and the children were capable of autonomously dealing with them. Most of the teams came up with rules and turn-taking strategies for using tangibles on their own. In Figure 4A, for example, a child indicates a *two-turns-each* policy using fingers. Otherwise, the children spontaneously gave up control (4B) or asked the teacher to mediate. In case of conflicts, they children resolved them by collaborating together. For example, they grabbed and moved a single block together (4C) or a block each to form a single match (4D).

Limitations and Conclusions

This paper presents a study that quantitatively characterizes children's level of engagement when learning with a digital book vs. tangible blocks. We found that the high degree of engagement provided by tangibles fosters attention and proactive attitudes among the children, resulting in more active learning, and reduced conflicts. The limitations of this work are related to the generalization of the results to other tangible interfaces and the possible novelty effects of the tangible blocks during the study. Future works will attempt to investigate alternative physical form factors and collaborations with larger teams.

Acknowledgements

This research was supported by the Ministry of Trade, Industry and Energy(MOTIE), KOREA, through the Education Support program for Creative and Industrial Convergence (S-2016-0117-000). Andrea Bianchi was supported by the MSIP, Korea, under the G-ITRC support program (IITP-2016-R6812-16-0001) supervised by the IITP.

References

1. Bai, Z., Blackwell, A. F., and Coulouris, G. Exploring Expressive Augmented Reality: The FingAR Puppet System for Social Pretend Play. In *Proc.* of CHI '15, 1035-1044.
2. Chi, M. T. H., and Wylie, R. 2014. The ICAP framework: linking cognitive engagement to active learning outcomes. In Educational Psychologist, 49(4), 219-243.
3. Horn, M.S., Crouser, R. J., and Bers, M. U. 2012. Tangible interaction and learning: the case for a hybrid approach. Personal Ubiquitous Comp. 16, 4.
4. Inkpen, K. M., Ho-Ching, W.L., Kuederle, O., Scott, S. D., and Shoemaker, G. B. D. (1999) This is fun! We're all best friends and we're all playing: supporting children's synchronous collaboration. In *Proc.* of CSCL '99.
5. Jacoby, S., Josman, N., Jacoby, D., Koike, M., Itoh, Y., Kawai, N., Kitamura, Y., Sharlin, E., Weiss, P. L. T. (2007) Tangible User Interfaces: Tools to examine assess and treat dynamic constructional processes in children with Developmental Coordination Disorders. International Journal on Disability and Human Development, 5, 257-263.
6. Alison King. (1993) From sage on the stage to guide on the side. In College Teaching, 42, 30-35.
7. Lauricella, A. R., Barr, R., Calvert, S. L. (2014) Parent-child interaction during traditional and computer storybook reading for children's comprehension: Implications for electronic storybook design, International Journal of Child-Computer Interaction, 2(1), 2014, 17-25.
8. Paul Marshall. 2007. Do tangible interfaces enhance learning? In *Proc.* of TEI'07. ACM (2007), 163-170.
9. Olson, I. C., Leong, Z. A., Wilensky, U., and Horn, M.S. It's just a toolbar!: using tangibles to help children manage conflict around a multi-touch tabletop. In *Proc.* of TEI'11. ACM (2011), 29-36.
10. Price, S. and Rogers, Y. V. 2004. Let's get physical: the learning benefits of interacting in digitally augmented physical spaces. Comput. Educ. 43, 1-2 (August 2004), 137-151.
11. Price, S. and Rogers, Y. V., Scaife, M., Stanton, D., Neale, H. (2003) Using 'tangibles' to promote novel forms of playful learning. Interacting with Computers, 15 (2), pp. 169-185.
12. Raffle, H. S., Parkes, A. J., and Ishii, H. Topobo: a constructive assembly system with kinetic memory. In *Proc.* of CHI '04. ACM (2004) 647-654.
13. Xie, L., Antle, A.N., and Motamedi, N. Are tangibles more fun?: comparing children's enjoyment and tangible user interfaces. In *Proc.* of TEI '08, 191-8.
14. Yannier, N., Israr, A., Lehman, J. F., and Klatzky, R. L. FeelSleeve: Haptic Feedback to Enhance Early Reading. In *Proc.* of CHI '15, 1015-1024.
15. Yannier, N., Koedinger, K.R., and Hudson, S. E. Learning from Mixed-Reality Games: Is Shaking a Tablet as Effective as Physical Observation? In *Proc.* of CHI '15, 1045-1054.
16. Zuckerman, O., Arida, S., and Resnick, M. Extending tangible interfaces for education: digital mon al montessori-inspired manipulatives. In *Proc.* of CHI '05, 859-868.

HapticAid: Haptic Experiences System Using Mobile Platform

Tomosuke Maeda
KMD Embodied Media Project
4-1-1 Hiyoshi, Kohoku-ku,
Yokohama, Kanagawa, Japan
t.maeda@kmd.keio.ac.jp

Keitaro Tsuchiya
KMD Embodied Media Project
4-1-1 Hiyoshi, Kohoku-ku,
Yokohama, Kanagawa, Japan
Tsuchiya.Keitaro@gmail.com

Roshan Peiris
KMD Embodied Media Project
4-1-1 Hiyoshi, Kohoku-ku,
Yokohama, Kanagawa, Japan
roshan@kmd.keio.ac.jp

Yoshihiro Tanaka
Nagoya Institute of Technology
JST PRESTO
Gokiso-cho, Showa-ku, Nagoya,
Aichi, Japan
tanaka.yoshihiro@nitech.ac.jp

Kouta Minamizawa
KMD Embodied Media Project
4-1-1 Hiyoshi, Kohoku-ku,
Yokohama, Kanagawa, Japan
kouta@kmd.keio.ac.jp

TEI '17, March 20-23, 2017, Yokohama, Japan
ACM 978-1-4503-4676-4/17/03.
http://dx.doi.org/10.1145/3024969.3025063

Abstract
We developed HapticAid, which is a wearable haptic augmentation system. This system enhances the skin vibrations that occur during touch and provide them as haptic feedback on the wrist. We revised HapticAid to be wearable and mobile by using a mobile platform and installed a digital signal processing to control haptic feedback for haptic experiences. This paper describes the implementation of our system, design of digital signal processing the method of wearing our system for haptic experiences.

Author Keywords
Haptic Augmentation; Haptic Feedback; Wearable Device; Embodied Media

ACM Classification Keywords
H.5.2. [User Interfaces]: Haptic I/O

Introduction
Many advancement devices augment human ability. In this study, we define the elements of augmentation as enhancement, enchantment, and empathy. We define these about three elements as follows.

Enhancement: The users' sensations intensify.

Enchantment: The users can alter each sensation and enchant things using each sensation.

Empathy: The user can share and communicate each sensation with others.

In visual sensation, eyeglasses enhance seeing capabilities, a fisheye lens can transmute like fish eye image captured on camera, and Parallel Eyes [1] exchanges one user's visual sensation with another's. Similar to auditory sensation, hearing aids can support or partially fix hearing deficits; a voice changer alters the user's voice, and a telephone call enables sharing and communicating of voice signals.

Therefore, we focus on the haptic augmentation. We proposed HapticAid, which obtains the haptic feedback signal from a fingertip and subsequently processes it to the [2]. We have revised HapticAid using a mobile platform that uses a haptic control engine, as shown in Figure 1. This system can control haptic signal and frequency filters. In this study, we describe the implementation of revised the HapticAid, haptic control engine and frequency filters for enchantment. Enchantment is like haptic design for entertainment. The devices around us install haptics and they will increase in the future.

Related Works

In this section, we review conventional approaches on haptic enhancement, enchantment and empathy. In the haptic enhancement, Tactile Contact Lens [3] uses principle of the leverage, thereby enabling the determination perception of irregularities on surfaces.

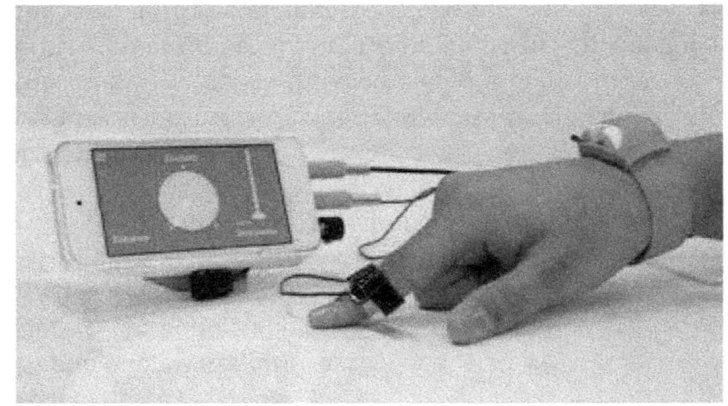

Figure 1: HapticAid system overview.

Lump detection [4] for performing a laparoscopic surgery can detect a lump, and provide real-time feedback using a tactile display. Stochastic resonance [5][6] can enhance the haptic perception, which provides white noise on the wrist. In the haptic enchantment, diminished haptics [7] displayed altered haptics that used a projector and transducer. In the haptic empathy, SMASH [8] can provide remote spectators with an enhanced experience while watching based on haptic. TECHTILE toolkit [9] utilizes audio signal to produce tactile vibration that enables to record and playback. TWECH [10] can research a haptic signal based on a neural network and share it.

These approaches are difficult to use with a bare finger, and wearable devices simplify use. We combine the

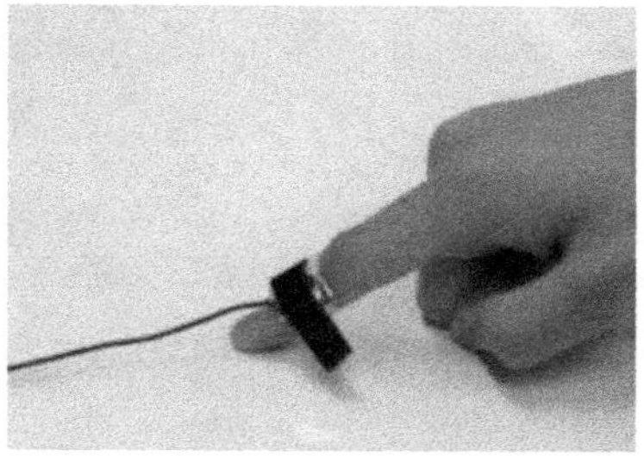

Figure 3: Haptic Sensor.

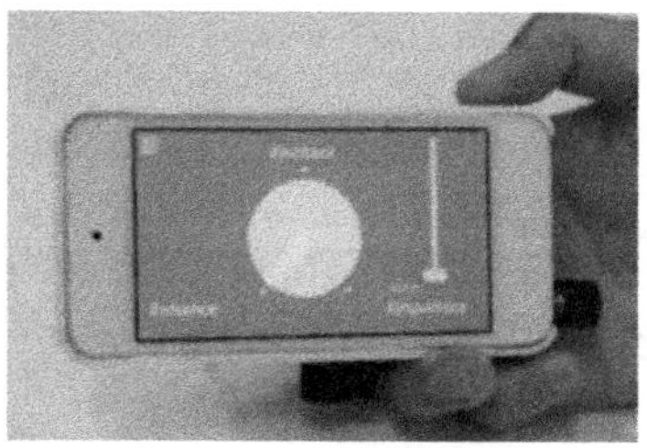

Figure 4: Haptic Control Engine.

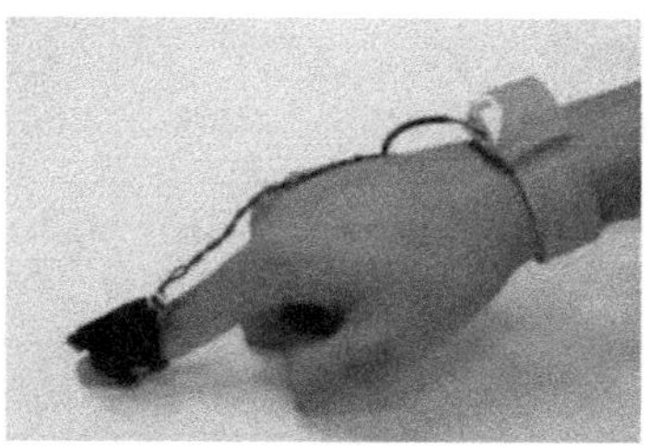

Figure 5: Wearable Haptic Actuators.

haptic enhancement, enchantment and empathy to wearable, mobile, and simple devices.

Implementation

To achieve haptic augmentation, we developed a haptic feedback system based on skin vibration. This system provides haptic feedback on the wrist. We explain the reason for the feedback location being the wrist. Every feedback system has the echo and audio howling. We determined the location least affected by this problem to be the wrist. This system sends vibration, which can reach on a finger [11]. Our current system makes use of three components: a sensor that can directly acquire the signal of haptic sensation from the fingertip with pre-amplification (Haptic Sensor), frequency filter for haptic experiences, which includes enhancement, enchantment, and empathy (Haptic Control Engine), and wrist-worn haptic actuator (Wearable Haptic Actuators) to apply for augmented haptic sensation. Our system diagram shows Figure 2.

Figure 2: System diagram.

Haptic Sensor: We use the wearable haptic vibration sensor using a polyvinylidene fluoride (PVDF) film worn on the middle phalanx instead of the fingertip. This has been made to avoid any interference between the finger and object touched by the user. The sensor can detect the haptic signal through skin vibrations, which propagates from the fingertip. This sensor cannot acquire signal sufficient for digital signal processing. Therefore, we developed a preamplifier for this sensor. The preamplifier is a precision instrumentation amplifier (INA126).

Haptic Control Engine: The measured signal can be output as the change in electric voltage, which is similar to a sound signal. We use an iPod touch, which can process the digital signal processing and be installed on our iOS application. Our application can control haptic signal. We can create the frequency filter, envelope, delay, amplitude, etc. In addition, we developed the power amplifier for haptic signals, which are amplified through it, as shown in Figure 4, to drive the haptic actuator on the wrist. This system can use wireless technology such as WiFi and Bluetooth to communicate and share haptic experiences.

Wearable Haptic Actuators:
Haptic Wristband: To assemble the wearable system, voice coil vibrator (ALPS ELECTRIC CO., LTD. Forcereactor Tough Type) is installed in a wristband, crafted with a 3D Printer. "Haptic Wristband" can deliver the modulated haptic sensations on the wrist.
Haptic Ring: This actuator, which the voice coil actuator (iPhone 6S Taptic Engine) has installed can provide haptic feedback on a finger.

Haptic Effect Design

Our system can create filters for haptic experiences like sound effect. We developed two haptic effect designs, which are reverberation and distortion.

Reverberation:
We developed the reverberation filter, which provide the delay haptic feedback. The users can feel to soften when they touch an object. Figure 6 shows the graph of reverberation.

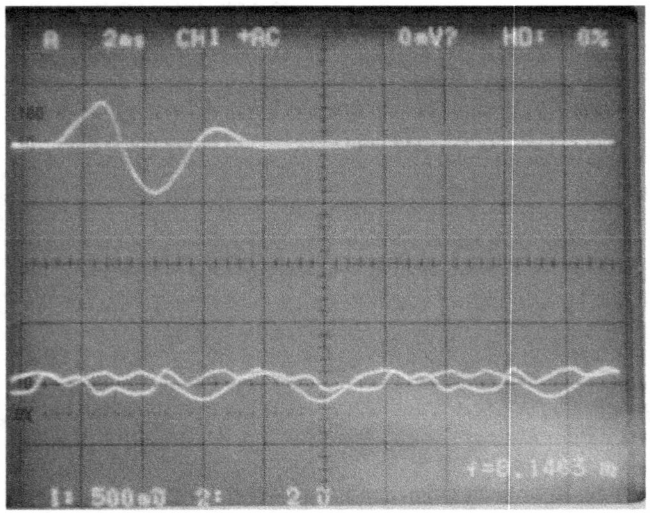

Figure 6: Graph of reverberation Above: Input signal. Below: Output signal.

Distortion:
A distortion filter can provide rough texture when the users touch the objects because the distortion filter clips signal wave, as shown in Figure 7.

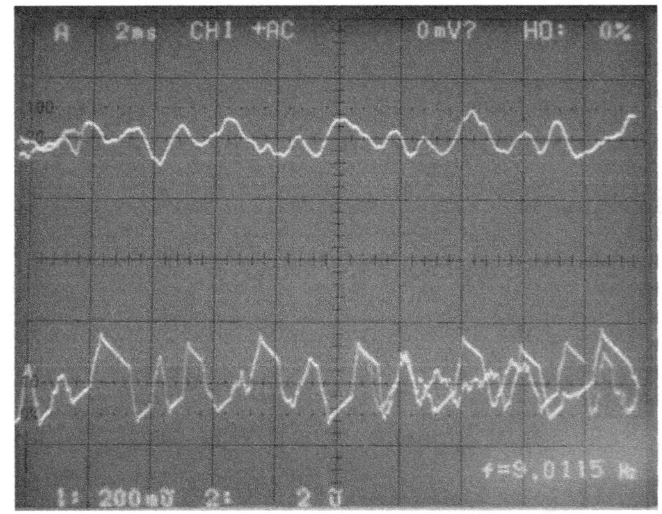

Figure 7: Graph of distortion. Above: Input signal. Below: Output signal.

Applications

HapticAid system focuses on three key areas: Haptic Enhancement, Haptic Enchantment, and Haptic Empathy. This section describes the method of wearing the system for experiencing haptic sensations through enhancement, enchantment, and empathy.

Enhancement
The user wears the system to provide haptic feedback based on his/her own skin vibration, as shown in Figure 8. In the enhancement, the user uses his/her own skin vibration on the wrist. that which provides own the wrist. Haptic Control Engine uses the frequency filter, which is based on the skin vibration propagation [12].

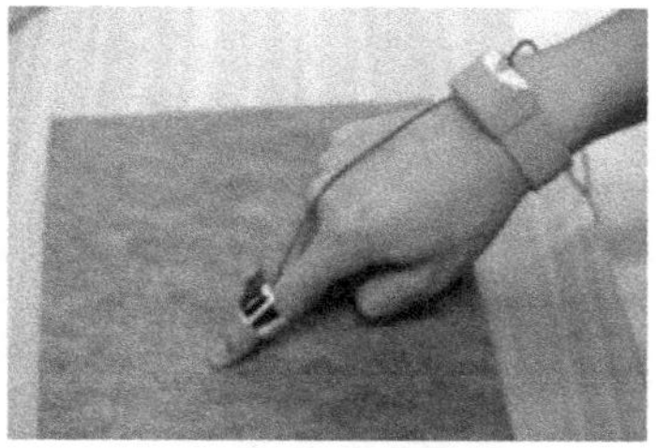

Figure 8: Enhancement

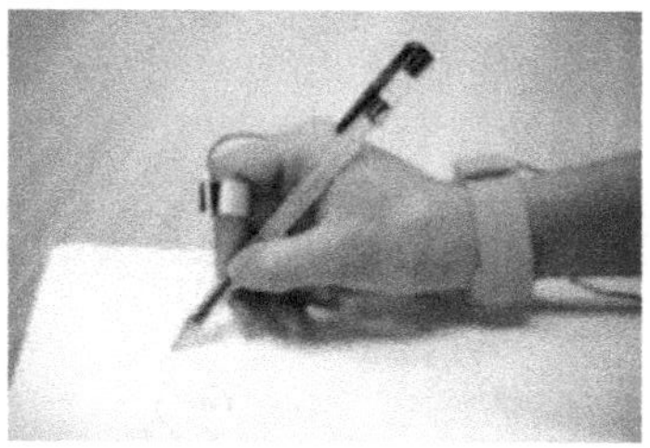

Figure 9: Enchantment

Figure 10: Empathy

Enchantment

The user wears a system similar to enhancement, as shown in Figure 9. We use envelope, delay for enchantment. The user can feel different haptic sensation from that felt without uses of the system. For example, the users can feel haptic feedback like jumping when the character jumps in the smartphone game. The users can enchant objects such as pen, paddle, rackets when they touch them.

Empathy

In empathy, the user can share the haptic sensations with other people. One user wears the haptic sensor on a finger and another wears the haptic ring on the same finger their hand. Our system can send haptic information from the haptic sensor to our other system, as shown in Figure 10.

Discussion

We created two haptic effect filters. We used haptic signal like sound signal, which is simple to use for enchanting objects. Therefore, we can create the haptic effect similar to the sound effect with system.

A limitation of our system is that we can only use one input sensor and one output sensor. We cannot use multi-haptic feedback with our system. The maximum value of power amplification is approximately 5 W, sufficient to actuate the small haptic transducers.

Conclusion and Future works

In this paper, we described a wearable haptic experiences system using a mobile platform with installed haptic effect filters. Our system can input the analog signal and provide haptic feedback based on haptic signals, e.g. like sound signal. Therefore, the Haptic Control Engine can be installed with haptic effect filters.

We envision that mobile devices can embed such haptic sensors and actuators for augmentation haptics in daily life.

Acknowledgements

This work is supported by a JST ACCEL Embodied Media Project and JSPS KAKENHI Grant Number 26700018. The authors are grateful to S. Arima who created project movie, T. Sasaki who developed 3D model of Haptic Control Engine, and H.Fushimi who offered music in project movie.

References

1. Kasahara, S., Ando, M., Suganuma, K., & Rekimoto, J. (2016, May). Parallel Eyes: Exploring Human Capability and Behaviors with Paralleled First Person View Sharing. In *Proceedings of the 2016 CHI Conference on Human Factors in Computing Systems* (pp. 1561-1572). ACM.
2. Maeda, T., Peiris, R., Masashi, N., Tanaka, Y., & Minamizawa, K. (2016). HapticAid: Wearable Haptic Augmentation System based on Skin Vibration Sensing *EuroHaptic 2016 Work in progress.*
3. Kikuuwe, R., Sano, A., Mochiyama, H., Takesue, N., Tsunekawa, K., Suzuki, S., & Fujimoto, H. (2004, October). The tactile contact lens. In *Sensors, 2004. Proceedings of IEEE* (pp. 535-538). IEEE.
4. Tanaka, Y., Fukuda, T., Fujiwara, M., & Sano, A. (2015). Tactile sensor using acoustic reflection for lump detection in laparoscopic surgery. *International journal of computer assisted radiology and surgery*, *10*(2), 183-193.
5. Lakshminarayanan, K., Lauer, A. W., Ramakrishnan, V., Webster, J. G., & Seo, N. J. (2015). Application of vibration to wrist and hand skin affects fingertip

tactile sensation. *Physiological reports*, *3*(7), e12465.

6. Seo, N. J., Kosmopoulos, M. L., Enders, L. R., & Hur, P. (2014). Effect of remote sensory noise on hand function post stroke. *Frontiers in human neuroscience*,*8*, 934.
7. Ochiai, Y., Hoshi, T., Rekimoto, J., & Takasaki, M. (2014, June). Diminished haptics: towards digital transformation of real world textures. In *International Conference on Human Haptic Sensing and Touch Enabled Computer Applications* (pp. 409-417). Springer Berlin Heidelberg.
8. Iekura, M. S., Hayakawa, H., Onoda, K., Kamiyama, Y., Minamizawa, K., & Inami, M. (2015, November). SMASH: synchronization media of athletes and spectator through haptic. In *SIGGRAPH Asia 2015 Mobile Graphics and Interactive Applications* (p. 20). ACM.
9. Minamizawa, K., Kakehi, Y., Nakatani, M., Mihara, S., & Tachi, S. (2012, March). TECHTILE toolkit: a prototyping tool for design and education of haptic media. In *Proceedings of the 2012 Virtual Reality International Conference* (p. 26). ACM.
10. Hanamitsu, N., Nakamura, H., Nakatani, M., & Minamizawa, K. (2015, November). Twech: a mobile platform to search and share visuo-tactile experiences. In *SIGGRAPH Asia 2015 Mobile Graphics and Interactive Applications* (p. 10). ACM.
11. Chartier, M., Thomas, N., Shao, Y., & Visell, Y. (2016) Toward a Wearable Tactile Sensory Amplification Device: Transfer Characteristics and Optimization. *Work in Progress of the 2016 Haptic Symposium Conference.* IEEE.
12. Tanaka, Yoshihiro, et al. "Wearable skin vibration sensor using a PVDF film."*World Haptics Conference (WHC), 2015 IEEE*. IEEE, 2015.

Escaping Chair: Furniture-Shaped Device Art

Takeshi Oozu
Empowerment Informatics
Tsukuba University, Tsukuba,
Ibaraki, Japan
t_ozu@vrlab.esys.tsukuba.ac.jp

Aki Yamada
Empowerment Informatics
Tsukuba University, Tsukuba,
Ibaraki, Japan
yamada@emp.tsukuba.ac.jp

Yuki Enzaki
Empowerment Informatics
Tsukuba University, Tsukuba,
Ibaraki, Japan
enzaki@emp.tsukuba.ac.jp

Hiroo Iwata
Empowerment Informatics
Tsukuba University, Tsukuba,
Ibaraki, Japan
iwata@kz.tsukuba.ac.jp

TEI '17, March 20-23, 2017, Yokohama, Japan
ACM 978-1-4503-4676-4/17/03.
http://dx.doi.org/10.1145/3024969.3025064

Abstract
A furniture-device is a device having the furniture appearance and physical input and output functions. The Escaping Chair is a furniture-device capable of having physical and dynamic interaction with a subject to create self-awareness toward the intent of their actions and personification of the furniture-device. The chair interacts with bystanders by trying to move away from nearby people. By fleeing this, the device tries to make a person unable to sit on it, stimulating their perception toward their sitting action, while also making the person consider the Chair's "personality." We exhibited the chair and collected feedback via conversation and observation. During exhibition the exhibit, the chair succeeded in making subjects perceive their own movements and to feel a semblance of will in the chair during their interactions, as we planned, and even making them sympathize with it. Exhibition also raised further challenges to explore in user interaction.

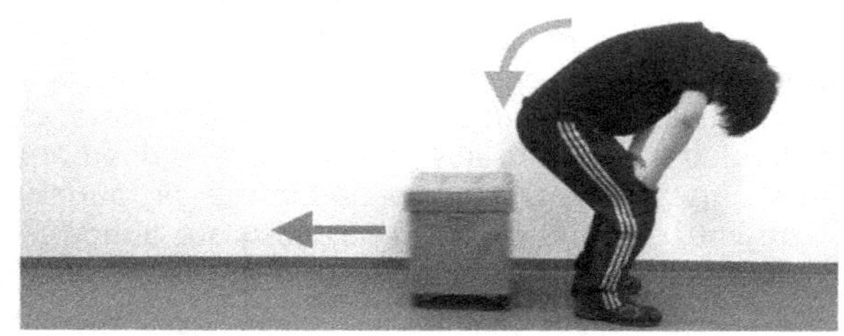

Figure 1: The chair trying to escape from a person sitting down.

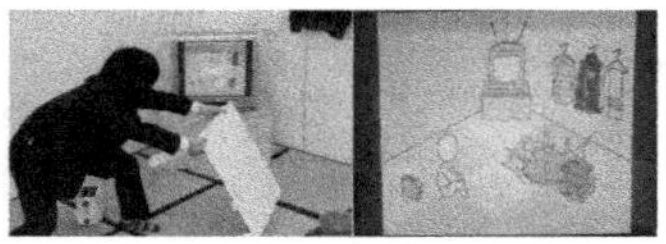

Figure 2: "Hako-sekai Ojisan." Here is an example of real world input triggering a reaction in the virtual world shown in the monitor.

Author Keywords
device art; furniture device; personification; interaction; perception;

ACM Classification Keywords
H.5.2. Information interfaces and presentation (e.g., HCI): User Interfaces-Interaction styles; Prototyping.

Introduction and Motivation
A furniture-device is the device having furniture appearance and added physical input and output functions. The Escaping Chair is a furniture-device that tries to escape from nearby people. When it detects a person approaching, the chair moves away to in order to prevent the subject from sitting down. Having this characteristic, this furniture-shaped device proposes a new method for stimulating a person's perceptions, such as what the act of "sitting" means. In other words, The chair remind them the meaning of sitting action, which is usually ignored, by betraying our expectation to the chairs and other sitting surfaces such as "stable" or "not moving themselves around." At the same time, although this device is a machine with a simple function, and of course without will, we expect that the user feels a semblance of will in the device through their interaction with it, and treats it as another "person."

Related work
As a different form of device-art that moves itself in response to a person's action, the CirculaFloor can be cited. The CirculaFloor device supports a person's locomotion by moving to where the person will walk to convey them [2]. In a different manner, the Escaping Chair tries to betray a person's sitting motion by escaping from the person when it detects their approach, emphasizing its existence as a communicative subject with the person. Other Artworks using furniture with internal mechanical structures, include The Table[8], Robotic Chair[7] and Balance From Within[3]. Of these three, however, only The Table interacts with human body and its motion. Although the Escaping Chair resembles The Table in the manner of interaction where it moves itself based on the people nearby, The Table requires a particular external environment(e.g. computers, camera system, and a room set up for The Table) which make it difficult to put The Table in various environments. In this regard, The Escaping Chair has ability to do operate independently from its environment and can be exhibited in a variety of ways. In the same manner, It can be said that the Escaping chair's autonomous system will enable its solo-operation without anybody to control, whereas other interactive furniture such as the trash barrel robot [10], robotic foot stool "Ottoman" [1], robot drawers [6] and sofa-bot [5] are remote controlled

Motivation
The idea of a furniture-device arose from my previous artwork, "Hako-Sekai Ojisan," which used furniture in a room (e.g. table and cooking stove) as input mechanisms to a virtual world containing the same placement of the furniture. As input mechanisms, each furniture piece had one function to affect the virtual world [9]. When we displayed this work, many visitors demonstrated interest in the furniture pieces, trying many different ways of interacting with them. Visitors would move and tilt the furniture and beat the table in order to obtain various reactions. Seeing these interactions, we decided to focus on a single object to create richer interaction between the person and the artwork by giving it various means of operation and response, and thus created The Escaping Chair, which has both input/output functions. The function of the Chair was inspired from the mischievous prank of pulling a chair away as another person tries to sit on it.

Implementation
Basic configuration
The basic configuration of the chair is as follows; 1 Arduino Uno as the processor, 4 Ultra sonic range

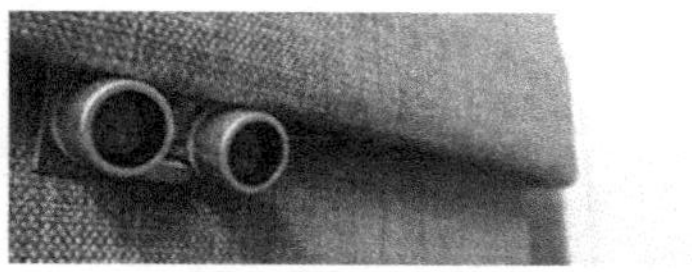

Figure 3: Sensor-unit close up.

Figure 4: Motor unit mounted on the bottom.

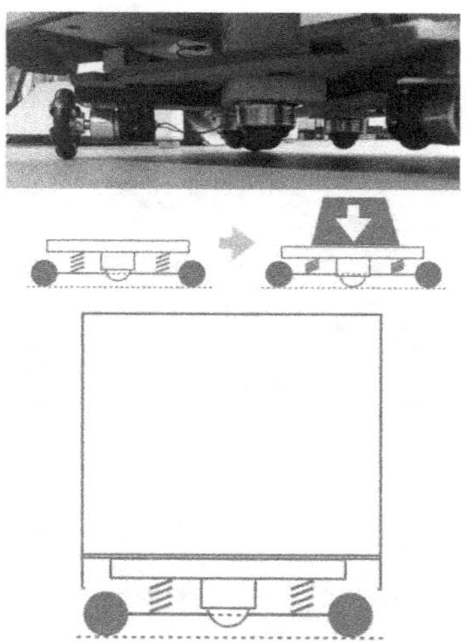

Figure 6: Top, load distribution system installed on the Escaping chair V1. Middle, depiction of its performance. Below, depiction of installation to the chair.

finders (USRF) as sensor inputs, 4 omni wheels connected with the motors as the drive system, and an actual box chair for the casing material and container for electrical components. HC-SR04 was used as USRF, which has 2cm to 400cm non-contact measurement function with a ranging accuracy of 3mm, minimum. While deciding the configuration, The Chair's accessibility from all directions was considered in order to make it possible to react to a person from any direction and allow a flexible exhibition style. Thus, we chose a box chair without backrest, giving no specific front and rear to the Chair. The same applies for the locomotion units. They are made of omni wheels which enable omni-direction movement [4] and motors that are mounted on each corner of the chair-bottom and placed along the wheel direction parallel to the diagonal of the chair-bottom so that it is able to in any direction without rotating. In order to react to input from every side, the sensors are mounted on each edge of the top cover. They detect objects approaching from each direction and when they detect any object within 40 cm, the pre-set threshold that is slightly farther than the distance where a person is able to sit on it, they send a signal to the processor. The processor then activates the motor-units to move in the opposite direction from where the signal came from.
In addition, the actual box chair appearance is expected to create a familiar look that makes users initially perceive the device as a plain piece of furniture.

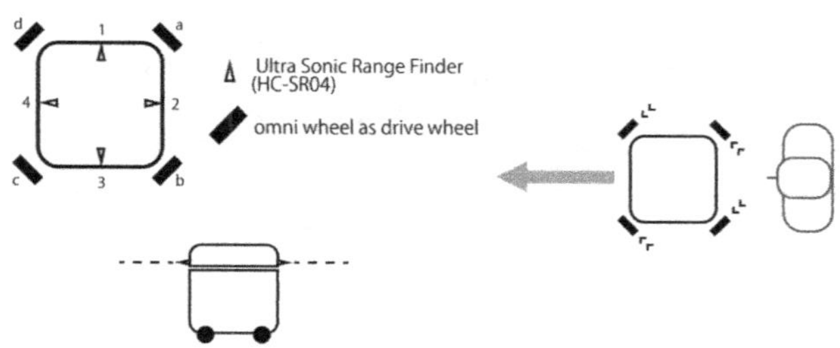

Figure 5: Left, configuration of the chair. Right, depiction of the chair interaction with the person nearby.

Prototyping process

Through the prototyping process, The Escaping chair was developed in stages, so there are 3 distinct prototypes of the chair that have different configurations of driving/load distributing systems, although all these share the same sensor system described above. All the parts were selected based on their accessibility in the case of more were required during development.

Escaping Chair V0

Chair V0 was the first developed Escaping Chair with no load distribution system, which leads a motor shaft to brake. For the drive system, RA250015-58Y91 geared motor (gear ratio= 15:1) and #4571398310089 omni wheel. Chair V0 and V1 sense the outer environment only when not in motion.

Escaping Chair V1

Installing a load distribution system which uses 4 springs and 4 ball casters, Chair V1 solves the braking problem which Chair V0 had. The ball casters are floating above 10mm in their neutral state and when a load of more than 8kg is applied to the chair, the springs will shrink and the casters reach to the ground and distribute the load. The allowable load of each caster is up to 30 kg and 120kg for 4 casters, which is sufficient support for the 80kg body weight of a typical adult male, even if one caster fails to reach the ground. In order to hide the system for the Chair's preference and transfer the load, a fabric membrane was installed inside the chair at 50mm deep from the bottom. However, with this system, the Chair's weight is 1.5 times heavier than Chair V0, which leads to slower motion of the Chair and affects interactions. In this configuration, a person who tries to sit with a quick motion will actually succeed in sitting on the Chair, even if it has tried to move away.

Figure 7: An example of visitors' interaction with the chair. Here, they are trying to surround it.

Major comments	Number of groups mentioned
feel pity	2
feel it's will	2
machine-like	2
cute/ funny	2
creepy	1
irrational	2

Table 1: Major comments mentioned by the visitors during conversation. The numbers are counted by groups (6 groups in total).

Escaping Chair V1.5

Chair V1.5 has a more powerful drive system than the previous versions, using a TAMIYA 540K75 geared motor (gear ratio=75:1) and TD-80 omni wheel (allowable load=30kg). With this system, Chair V1.5 has the potential to move much faster than previous versions, and has the ability to successfully move away from anyone who tries to sit on it. However, there are some problems in this system; if it works on a full duty ratio, it may cause wheel derailment and motor displacement in a very short time. So at Chair V1.5, this system run at 40% of the peak duty ratio with gradual increment and decrement adjustments of the duty ratio. Also, this drive system requires a larger space than the previous system, so the load distribution system has changed to take the load directly from chair's body with 4 hooks. Chair V1.5 has the capability to sense its external environment at any time, so it can change its direction even while moving.

Exhibition and Feedback

The Chair V1.5 was exhibited at the Empowerment Studio, at Tsukuba University on October 12th, 2016 and received feedback via observation and conversation during/after subject interaction with the Chair. We didn't use any questionnaire forms in order to get their immediate reactions to the chair and receive more dynamic and personal feedback. At the exhibition, all visitors had announced via poster that the Chair moves away from the nearby persons. During the exhibition, we collected feedback from 6 groups/ 10 people in total. Feedback acquired during that process and will be used to guide the future direction of development for this project.

Conversational feedback

We asked exhibition visitors general questions like "Playing with the chair, what do you think and feel about this moving furniture?." To summarize the comments obtained, some individuals who already knew about chair's mechanical and electronic details, said that they felt the chair appeared more machine-like, rather than human-like. Conversely, those who did not know about internal systems generally commented that they felt more personified intentions in the chair. Among those comments, one observer noted, "I felt it's will since the chair discarded its duty and function as the chair to let people sit on it." Also, there were some people who showed sympathy toward the chair, saying "It's pitiful," when the chair was surrounded by people from all directions and tried to move away. In addition, there was a person who patted the top of the chair after interacting with it. From the comments and reactions obtained, we believe that during interactions with the chair subjects actually feel a semblance of its will, and sympathy to the chair, despite its mechanical nature.

Observational feedback

From the observations of the visitor's behavior , many were interested in the chair's motion. Since the chair moves in response to an object within a certain distance, there were people who would walk in front of the chair and observe its response motion with interest. Also, we observed a relationship between the magnitude of the reaction and visitors' posture and direction when the chair moved. When visitors interacted with the chair while facing toward it, they simply followed the chair's movement with their eyes. On the other hand, when visitors actually attempted to sit down, they showed not only a larger reaction in an attempt to see the direction where the chair went, and an emotional reaction such as laughing at the chair's response. Based on these observations, visitors did in fact perceive their own sitting movement while the interaction with the chair.

Results and future applications

From the feedback above, it can be said that the visitors personified the chair and became aware of their sitting motion. However, as a number of experienced visitors pointed out, the chair can only detect the presence of an object from its distance, and not the targets' pose. Adding extra range sensors on the top of the chair would enable better analysis of human movement. Also, the instability of the chair's drive system needs to be improved upon. For the "machine-like" label given by those who already knew the chair's system in detail, we propose the installation of more variable movement patterns in addition to the current straight-line escape motion of the chair. For Future development, we are planning to make multiple copies of this device, continuing to develop aspects of interaction and communication with nearby people, and to develop its application in the living space.

References

1. David Sirkin, Brian Mok, Stephen Yang, and Wendy Ju. 2015. Mechanical Ottoman: How Robotic Furniture Offers and Withdraws Support. In Proceedings of the Tenth Annual ACM/IEEE International Conference on Human-Robot Interaction (HRI '15). ACM, New York, NY, USA, 11-18.
2. Hiroo Iwata, Hiroaki Yano, Hiroyuki Fukushima and Haruo Noma. 2005. CirculaFloor. *IEEE Computer Graphics and Applications, January-February*, 64-67.
3. Jacob Tonski. 2012. Balance From Within. Retrieved October 20, 2016 from: http://jacobtonski.com/balance-from-within/
4. Kenjiro Tadakuma. 2011. Omnidirectional Mobile and Driving Mechanism. *Journal of the Robotics Society of Japan,* Vol.29 No.6, 516-519[in Japanese].
5. Marco Spadafora, Victor Chahuneau, Nikolas Martelaro, David Sirkin, and Wendy Ju. 2016. Designing the Behavior of Interactive Objects. In Proceedings of the TEI '16: Tenth International Conference on Tangible, Embedded, and Embodied Interaction (TEI '16). ACM, New York, NY, USA, 70-77.
6. Mok, B., Yang, S., Sirkin, D., Ju, W. 2015. A Place for Every Tool and Every Tool in Its Place: Performing Collaborative Tasks with Interactive Robotic Drawers. Proceedings of Robot and Human Interactive Communication (RO-MAN 2015). August 31-September 3, 2015. Kobe, Japan.
7. Max Dean and Matt Donovan. 2006. Robotic Chair. Retrieved October 20, 2016 from: http://raffaello.name/projects/robotic-chair/
8. Max Dean and Raffaello D'Andrea. 2001. Table. Retrieved October 20, 2016 from: http://raffaello.name/projects/table/
9. Takeshi Oozu. 2015. Hako Sekai Ojisan. *School of Art and Design University of Tsukuba Graduation studies and practice work*, 66.
10. Yang, S., Mok, B., Sirkin, D., Ive, H., Maheshwari, R., Fischer, K., Ju, W. 2015. Experiences Developing Socially Acceptable Interactions for a Robotic Trash Barrel. In Proceedings of Robot and Human Interactive Communication (RO-MAN 2015). August 31-September 3, 2015. Kobe, Japan.

devEyes: Tangible Devices on Augmented Passive Surfaces

Liviu Coconu
Independent Researcher
Vienna, AT-1030, Austria
liviuc@live.com

Hans-Christian Hege
Zuse Institut Berlin (ZIB)
Berlin, DE-14169, Germany
hege@zib.de

Abstract
We present a novel approach to turn smartphones/tablets into tangible near-surface devices with augmented reality (AR) capability on virtually any passive surface, like desks, tables and wallboards. A low-cost optoelectronic add-on for the device back camera enables position tracking on an almost-invisible printable fiducial marker grid. This approach is promising in terms of adoption potential because it can be used anywhere with existing devices, requires no dedicated hardware installations and is applicable to a broad range of real-world applications.

Author Keywords
Passive surface device integration; ubiquitous computing; augmented reality.

ACM Classification Keywords
H.5.2. User interfaces: Input devices and strategies (e.g., mouse, touchscreen): Miscellaneous;

TEI '17, March 20-23, 2017, Yokohama, Japan
ACM 978-1-4503-4676-4/17/03.
http://dx.doi.org/10.1145/3024969.3025065.

Introduction
Mobile devices have become mainstream for most people. With increasing processing power and various on-board sensors, they make an excellent choice as tangibles as well as for augmented reality (AR) applications such as PokemonGo [1]. However, their

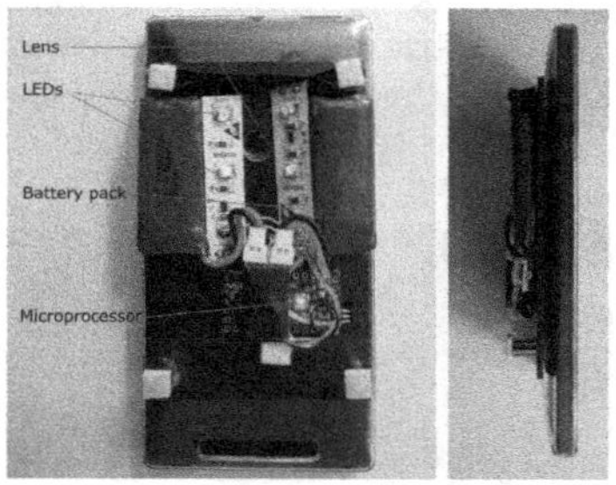

Figure 1: devEyes add-on prototype.

The primary goals for the device add-on have been low cost and reasonably small size. It has to maintain a distance of ~10 mm to the underlying surface. Given its simplicity, the current prototype can be further miniaturized or integrated in the device itself.

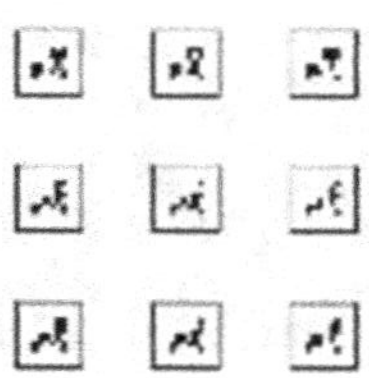

Figure 2: Fiducial marker grid for position tracking

Figure 3: The devEyes system in action. From top to bottom: multi-device AR interaction with additional projection; Battleship game in AR + projection; AR-only surfing in a domestic environment.

prevalent use is still on-device interaction, which confines the user in a small screen space.

Conducted studies have revealed benefits of integrating devices with interactive surfaces, for example for co-located collaboration [6] and the tangible community has been long advocating bridging the gap between computing and the physical world. The idea of using smartphones as tangible devices in an AR context has been explored by [2] in the context of an interactive multi-touch display using an IR camera for estimating an initial device position and a color dot pattern to retrieve position and orientation. The THAW system [4] is similar in approach, but places the device against a computer screen. Other related systems are [3] and [7]. We propose a system that eliminates the need for an underlying active surface to track the device position and orientation and enables near-surface tangible interaction on virtually any printable passive surface.

Design and Implementation

The presented system, called devEyes, is an early prototype consists of the several components.

Device Add-on (hardware, Figure 1) enables the device camera to track features on a very close surface (~1cm). More precisely, a small and inexpensive macro lens allows camera focus on very close objects while an array of 4 LEDs around the camera ensures adequate lighting. An on-board microprocessor (Arduino) is generating short stroboscopic LED light pulses to significantly reduce motion blur control due to the standard 30fps frame rate. This works well up to a reasonable movement speed and also saves battery power.

Fiducial markers. In order to track position and orientation the system uses fiducial markers printed on the surface. These have been designed for real-time tracking. We use square markers with an empty quarter so their orientation can be quickly detected (Figure 2). 2D coordinates are encoded in 2 x 9 bits plus a simple 3 CRC sum. This works well in achieving a detection rate of 20+ fps. To achieve almost-invisibility, which is important for the ability to optionally augment the surface with projection as well as due to aesthetic considerations, the fiducial markers are printed on white paper in pure yellow and we use UV LEDs for illumination (yellow appears black in UV).

Software infrastructure

The prototype software system is implemented on Nokia Lumia 830 (Windows Phone 8.1) with the OpenCV library. The device add-on uses an Arduino Nano chip to control the LEDs in pulse-width modulation (PWM), on/off, etc. Devices communicate with desktop server application over a custom UDP protocol.

Applications

We have envisioned and are working on quite a few possible applications for the system: co-located collaboration, magic lens applications, table games, smart mouse and generally extending computing environments onto passive surfaces. *Tiles* is an app that simulates an "immersive desktop" environment in which the device is used as a smart mouse/magic lens. Either in AR-only (Figure 3 bottom) or with projection (top), the user can explore a virtual workspace and hover/manipulate/displayed/edit content on the device. *Battleship* is a variant of the popular ship sinking table game in which each player uses a device and fires at the opponent's ships until it destroys them.

Discussion and Future Work

Compared to previous systems, we consider that our system is adding value in a few key points. It is usable anywhere, only a passive surface is needed (but easily augmented with projection whenever it makes sense). It integrates seamlessly with the existing functionality of devices while adding rich tangible interactions. No glasses or other wearables are needed.

On the limitations side, it requires additional hardware, although low-cost. This could be mitigated by incorporating it in the device itself. The position tracking algorithms is currently running at ~25fps. A higher frame rate or frame interpolation should be beneficial for the perceived user experience. Better usage of other device sensors like accelerometer, gyroscope, NFC etc. should enrich user experience. For instance, tilting/3D orientation can be derived from the device sensors. Further real-world applications are necessary for demonstrating the usability of the technology, including the usage on vertical surfaces.

References

1. Alexander M. Clark, Matthew T. G. Clark, Pokémon Go and Research: Qualitative, Mixed Methods Research, and the Supercomplexity of Interventions International Journal of Qualitative Methods January-December 2016, doi:10.1177/1609406916667765
2. T. Cuypers, Y. Francken, C. Vanaken, F. V. Reeth, and P. Bekaert. Smartphone localization on interactive surfaces using the built-in camera. In Proc. Procams, pages 61--68, 2009.
3. Mayank Goel , Brendan Lee , Md. Tanvir Islam Aumi , Shwetak Patel , Gaetano Borriello , Stacie Hibino , Bo Begole, SurfaceLink: using inertial and acoustic sensing to enable multi-device interaction on a surface, Proceedings of the SIGCHI Conference on Human Factors in Computing Systems, April 26-May 01, 2014, Toronto, Ontario, Canada, doi:10.1145/2556288.2557120
4. Sang-won Leigh , Philipp Schoessler , Felix Heibeck , Pattie Maes , Hiroshi Ishii, THAW: tangible interaction with see-through augmentation for smartphones on computer screens, Proceedings of the adjunct publication of the 27th annual ACM symposium on User interface software and technology, October 05-08, 2014, Honolulu, Hawaii, USA
5. Johan Sanneblad , Lars Erik Holmquist, Ubiquitous graphics: combining hand-held and wall-size displays to interact with large images, Proceedings of the working conference on Advanced visual interfaces, May 23-26, 2006, Venezia, Italy
6. Julian Seifert , Adalberto Simeone , Dominik Schmidt , Paul Holleis , Christian Reinartz , Matthias Wagner , Hans Gellersen , Enrico Rukzio, MobiSurf: improving co-located collaboration through integrating mobile devices and interactive surfaces, Proceedings of the 2012 ACM international conference on Interactive tabletops and surfaces, November 11-14, 2012, Cambridge, Massachusetts, USA
7. A. D. Wilson and R. Sarin, 2007. BlueTable: connecting wireless mobile devices on interactive surfaces using vision-based handshaking. In Proceedings of Graphics interface 2007 (Montreal, Canada, May 28 - 30, 2007). GI '07, vol. 234. ACM, New York, NY, 119-125.

Grassffiti: Drawing Method to Produce Large-scale Pictures on Conventional Grass Fields

Yuta Sugiura
Keio University, 4-1-1 Hiyoshi, Kohoku, Yokohama, 223-8526 Japan
sugiura@keio.jp

Koki Toda
The University of Tokyo, 7-3-1 Hongo, Bunkyo, Tokyo, 113-0033 Japan
koki.t.kmd@gmail.com

Takashi Kikuchi
Keio University, 4-1-1 Hiyoshi, Kohoku, Yokohama, 223-8526 Japan
tkiku393760@gmail.com

Takayuki Hoshi
The University of Tokyo, 7-3-1 Hongo, Bunkyo, Tokyo, 113-0033 Japan
takayuki_hoshi@ipc.i.u-tokyo.ac.jp

Youichi Kamiyama
Keio University, 4-1-1 Hiyoshi, Kohoku, Yokohama, 223-8526 Japan
beta.kamiyama@gmail.com

Takeo Igarashi
Masahiko Inami
The University of Tokyo, 7-3-1 Hongo, Bunkyo, Tokyo, 113-0033 Japan
takeo@acm.org
inami@inami.info

TEI '17, March 20-23, 2017, Yokohama, Japan
ACM 978-1-4503-4676-4/17/03.
http://dx.doi.org/10.1145/3024969.3025067

Abstract
We propose a drawing method to create large-scale pictures in public space. We use a property of anisotropic reflection to show images on the grass field. We created a prototype of roller type device which can control the angle of grass. We observed that our system entertains people in public exhibition.

Author Keywords
Grass field; BRDF; Interactive Surface.

ACM Classification Keywords
H.5.m. Information interfaces and presentation (e.g., HCI): Miscellaneous.

Introduction
Public displays are very important to show information for many people at the same time. One of the common displaying method is LCDs display but it consumes electric power. On the other hand, projection-type displays are suitable for public purpose. Accordingly, the environment does not require large-scale modifications. In addition, it is possible to switch the projection rapidly and project colorful images. However, projectors have disadvantages. For example, the projected images are hard to see in a bright room.

Moreover, the electricity costs due to the continuous projection are quite high.

We propose a display technology that utilizes the phenomenon whereby the shading properties of grass change as the fibers are raised or flattened (Figure 1). There are many places where a grass has been laid such as soccer field, golf field, park and so on. The property is in accordance with Bidirectional Reflectance Distribution Function (BRDF). In our pervious study, we have proposed display technology that utilizes these material properties in fur objects such as carpets [7]. In this work, we apply these techniques to show largescale images on grass fields.

Our method doesn't require to use any ink and electric power to keep patterns. In addition, our technology can turn these ordinary objects into computer displays without requiring or creating any non-reversible modifications to the objects.

Figure 1: GraffitiGrass can converts grass fields into large canvas.

Related Work

We are not the first to display information by manipulating the shape of "existing" physical materials or controlling their reflectance. Rice paddy art is an attempt to create large-scale drawings in a farm space over a long period of time, by planting seeds that have buds of various colors[1]. Karesansui is a Japanese traditional culture method of drawing patterns in a garden with stones[2]. A modern version of this art form, Lazy man Zen garden, is able to draw a pattern automatically in sand [4]. Large patterns can also be drawn by walking on the snow[3]. Hanna's Water Calligraphy device is attached to a bicycle and dispenses water from a hose array to draw Chinese characters on the streets over [1]. A lawn mower can be used to draw striped and circular patterns on grass fields.

The BRDF displays have been proposed in computer graphics and art fields [3][5]. Hullin et al. proposed a method to change the reflection of an object on a water surface by creating and controlling waves on the surface at a high speed [2]. Ochiai et al. proposed a method to project images on the back of a vibrating soap bubble to create a membrane screen [6]. Wooden Mirror is an artwork that is drawn from reflected light by controlling an array of wooden blocks [8]. Our method is advantageous because it is possible to use existing objects in the environment (e.g. standard carpet) as BRDF displays without making any permanent modifications to them.

---

1 http://www.cbc.ca/strombo/news/living-artworks-in-japans-rice-paddys.htm

2 http://en.wikipedia.org/wiki/Japanese_rock_garden

3 http://www.viralnova.com/simon-beck-snow-art/

Roller Type Device

We leverage the phenomenon that raised fur looks different from flattened fur. Fur fibers have a natural growth direction, and one can flatten the fur by sweeping the surface in that direction and raise it by sweeping the surface in the opposite direction. Since raised and flattened regions of fur have different reflectance properties, one can visually distinguish them. In general, flattened fur reflects more light and looks brighter than raised fur.

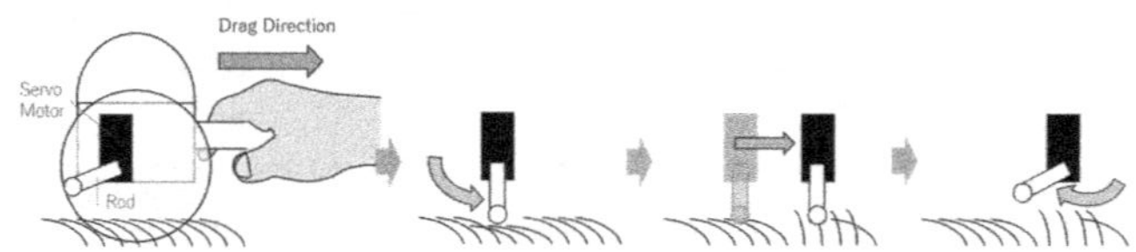

Figure 2: Principle of drawing method.

The hardware consists of 16 fur-raising components attached to the bottom of the roller as shown in Figure 2. Each component consists of a rod and a servomotor that lowers and lifts the rod. When the rod is lowered, it raises the fiber as the user moves the roller (Figure 3). In addition, a rotary encoder is mounted on the wheel shaft to measure the horizontal movement of the roller. The rotary encoder and servomotors are controlled by an Arduino Mega ADK microcontroller. The system lowers and raises the rods according to the measurements of the rotary encoder to leave patterns on the grass.

Drawing process with the device is as follows. The user first measures the size of the canvas and prepares a binary dot matrix of appropriate size using an application program. Our current application program provides four methods to prepare the dot matrix.

Figure 3: Overview of roller type device.

Figure 4: Patterns can be erased by grand roller.

Second, the user transmits the dot matrix data to the device and starts drawing the pattern on the fur surface by moving the device over its surface in the direction opposite to the fur growth direction. The surface needs to be fully flattened by hand before drawing. The user presses the red button on the device to initiate drawing. If the dot matrix consists of a single row, the drawing finishes after a single sweep. If the user continues the sweep, the pattern will be repeated. When the dot matrix consists of multiple rows, the user needs to repeat sweeps multiple times. The system indicates the end of a sweep with an LED mounted on it, and the user starts the next sweep by pressing the red button. To assist the user in aligning the starting point of the sweeps, the system leaves a tick mark at the beginning of each sweep. The user aligns the starting point by pressing the red button and placing the roller so that the mark on the roller aligns with the tick mark. Pressing the yellow button lets the user repeat the same row. The user can move the roller backwards to erase the pattern already drawn. In this case, all the rods are lowered automatically. The blue button clears the drawing data.

The horizontal and vertical extents of a dot are 25 mm and 31 mm, respectively, assuming that the roller moves horizontally. The main limiting factor is the size of the servo motors and capability of the rotary encoder. The drawing speed is constrained by the speed of the servomotors. In our current implementation, the maximum speed of the roller sweep is 15 cm/sec, and the device fails to generate an appropriate pattern if the user sweeps the device faster than this limit. Erasing a pattern can be done by a ground roller (Figure 4).

Result and Demonstration

As a result, we were able to draw not only images but also words. Figure 5 shows a welcome message drawn on the grass which can be used as a message at the entrance of facilities such as parks. Figure 6 shows an image that is drawn with multiple sweeps.

We exhibit our prototype system in a public demonstration space. Grass has been laid in the public space.

Figure 5: Displaying welcome message.

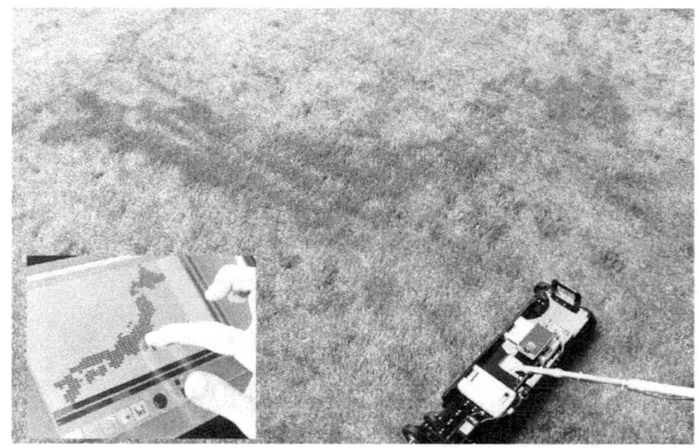

Figure 6: Large-scale can be drawn by divided into multiple segments.

Limitation and Future Work

Compared to the other displays, our method takes time to display an image. Therefore, our system intends to display still image rather than animations. Also, with our system, full color images cannot be displayed.

However, by controlling the angle of the fur, the darkness of the image can be changed so for the future work we plan to draw grayscale image with our method.

Concussion

We proposed a method to draw large-scaled images on the grass field. We use a property of anisotropic reflection to show images on the grass field which require neither ink nor electricity. We created a prototype and observed that our system could draw large-scale images on the grass field to entertain people in public exhibition.

Acknowledgements

This work was supported by JSPJ KAKENHI Grant Number 26700017.

References

1. Hanna, N. Water Calligraphy Device. http://www.nicholashanna.net/.
2. Hullin, M.B., Lensch, H, Raskar, R., Seidel, H., and Ihrke, I. Dynamic display of BRDFs. In Computer Graphics Forum (Proc. EG), pp. 475-483.
3. Malzbender, T., Samadani, R., Scher, S., Crume, A., Dunn, D., and Davis, J. Printing reflectance functions. ACM Trans. Graph. 31, 3, Article 20 (June 2012), 11 pages.
4. Master, B. Lazy man Zen garden, http://youtu.be/rNGPErdIqZA.
5. Matusik, W., Ajdin, B., Gu, J., Lawrence, J., Lensch, H. P. A, Pellacini, F., and Rusinkiewicz, S. Printing spatially-varying reflectance. ACM Trans. Graph. 28, 5, Article 128 (December 2009), 9 pages.
6. Ochiai, Y., Oyama, A., Hoshi, T., and Rekimoto, J. Theory and Application of the Colloidal Display: Programmable Bubble Screen for Computer Entertainment. In Proc. ACE '13, Springer, pp. 198-214.
7. Yuta Sugiura, Koki Toda, Takayuki Hoshi, Youichi Kamiyama, Takeo Igarashi, and Masahiko Inami. 2014. Graffiti fur: turning your carpet into a computer display. In Proceedings of the 27th annual ACM symposium on User interface software and technology (UIST '14). ACM, New York, NY, USA, 149-156. DOI=10.1145/2642918.2647370
8. Rozin, D. Wooden Mirror. http://www.smoothware.com/danny/woodenmirror.html

Sprite Catcher: A Handheld Self Reflection and Mindfulness Tool for Mental Healthcare

Matthew Barker
Department of Computing and Communications, Open University, Walton Hall, Milton Keynes, MK7 6AA
Matthew.barker@open.ac.uk

Janet Van der Linden
Department of Computing and Communications, Open University, Walton Hall, Milton Keynes, MK7 6AA
Janet.VanDerLinden@open.ac.uk

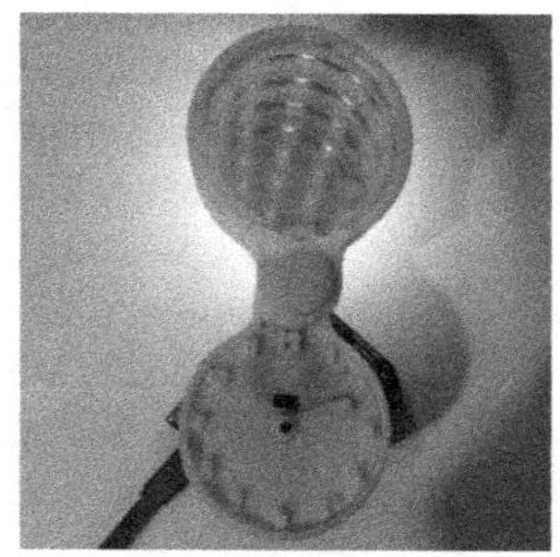

Fig.1 - The Sprite Catcher

TEI '17, March 20-23, 2017, Yokohama, Japan
ACM 978-1-4503-4676-4/17/03.
http://dx.doi.org/10.1145/3024969.3025068

Abstract

This paper describes the rationale behind the ongoing development of Sprite Catcher – a handheld, tangible interactive tool for treating depression and anxiety. The current design, which is intended to encourage the user to practice self-reflection and mindfulness, is the product of participatory design conducted with counsellors from a local mental health charity and with a university psychology researcher. Through a review of previous work in this area, a description of a use scenario and an overview of the design's functions and concepts, we illustrate where the project is heading and which research questions we aim to respond to.

Author Keywords

Tangible, Reflection, Mindfulness, Depression, Mental Healthcare, Wellbeing, Embodied Interaction

ACM Classification Keywords

J.3.m. Life and Medical Sciences: Health

Introduction

This ongoing interaction design study has been initiated in response to a healthcare problem whose gravity is becoming increasingly apparent for healthcare professionals and HCI researchers. The most recent mental healthcare demographic study by the NHS[1] calculated that 16.6%% of all men and 24.9% of all women in England have been diagnosed with depression at some point in their life. The outcomes of previous tangible technology design research have indicated that it might be feasible to design tangible interactive devices that help in the treatment of this mental condition. Drawing on this work and on the input of an expert participatory design team, we have developed *Sprite Catcher*: a mobile, tangible device that encourages self-reflection and mindfulness in-clinic and at home.

The participatory design team for this project has been composed of ourselves, a university mental healthcare researcher and a team of counsellors from a mental healthcare charity. We have been the designers and researchers and the other parties have been our consultants, helping us to shape design around the needs of the target users'. To establish the criteria for the design we organised a number of meetings between the stakeholders at various stages in the design and prototyping process. These discussions gave us the primary focus that our interaction design should encourage self-reflection and mindfulness. We start with a review of these elements in the paper. The more intricate outcomes of our discussions will be dealt with later on.

Literature Review

The following excerpt from a psychology research paper on cognitive behaviour therapy helps to convey something of the role that self-reflection can play in therapy for depression: "When you find your interpretation of a situation is erroneous and you correct it, you probably discover that your mood improves, you behave in a more functional way and/ or your physiological arousal decreases." (p. 32) [3]. The notion that technologically aided self-reflection can enhance a person's life has received plenty of attention in HCI research in recent years but not necessarily as described above. Baumer's [2] review of self-reflection research in HCI defines *education, design processes* and/or *self-knowledge* as the three areas of focus that have been covered. Amongst those that target *self-knowledge* there are only a handful of studies that have covered tangible interaction modalities - *Emoti-meter* [14], *MyInnerLife* [6] *InternetOfSoftThings*[8], and *TOBE* [7]. Amongst these we could only find two examples of projects - *Emoti-meter* and *InternetOfSoftThings*, where the goal has been to design for mental health issues specifically.

Mindfulness has received less attention relatively to reflection in HCI research. Akama and Light [1] have claimed that where mindfulness in the past has been discussed, it has been misconceived. There has, they argue, been a certain level of ignorance about what mindfulness means and how valuable it can be. Drawing on discussions with our mental healthcare participatory design team, we have an understanding of mindfulness that is shaped by its meaning in the healthcare context. We conceive it as a state of mind, in which a person is brought to an awareness of their own thought stream. As described by psychology researchers Bishop et al. [4] mindfulness is "bringing awareness to current experience – observing and attending to the changing field of thoughts, feelings

[1] National Statistics Adult Psychiatric Morbidity Survey: Common mental disorders 2014, p. 52

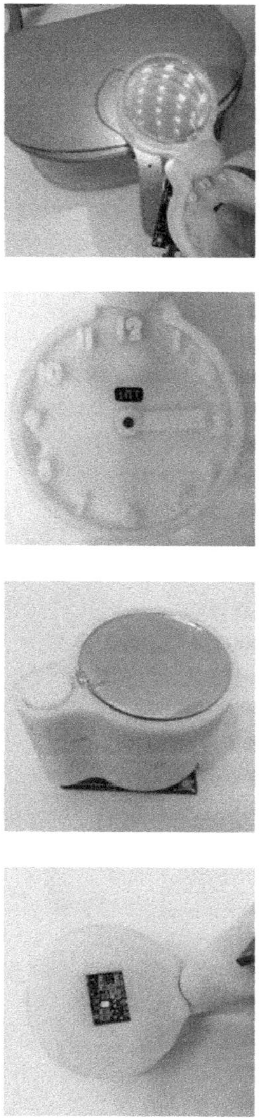

Fig. 2. Images of the latest sprite catcher prototype

and sensations from moment to moment...Rather than getting caught up in ruminative, elaborative thought streams about one's experiences and its origins, implications and associations, mindfulness involves a direct experience of events in the mind and body" (p. 235).

We have been able to find a small body of tangible interaction research that relates to this interpretation – *The Mindfulness Sphere* [13], *Mind Spheres* [10] and *Inner Garden* [12] all draw on mindfulness as an important health benefit. Only one of these, the mindfulness sphere [13], was appropriated for use in the mental healthcare context especially though.

Use Scenario

To convey how the final sprite catcher design (Fig. 2) manifests these two concepts – self-reflection and mindfulness, we now describe a use case:

Laura suffers from depression. She receives counselling for her illness and attends peer group classes. One day the counsellor gives her a sprite catcher device and instructs her in how to use it. Laura tucks it away in her handbag. The following day (Saturday) while she is at home, Laura begins to feel anxious. She finds that she is ruminating about something that she heard one of her colleagues at work say. She cannot seem to stop the cycle of negative thoughts tumbling over and over in her head and a feeling of hopelessness and self-dislike is starting to build. She remembers that she was given the sprite catcher device the previous day. She doubts it can help her but decides to dig it out of her handbag anyway. Laura opens it by sliding the display around and away from the clock face and then changes the time on the clock to reflect that on her watch. Next, she looks around the room to find something that might reflect her current emotions. She sees an old, forgotten, purple shoe in the corner of the room under a pile of clothes and decides to make that her target. Laura walks over to the shoe, holds the sprite catcher up to it and then presses the button in the centre of the clock face. Suddenly, purple light begins to rush into the display and whizz around, like sprites dancing. She finds that the longer she holds the button down, the more the light rushes in. The feeling of sucking sprites from the shoe into the catcher is unusual but pleasant and it's starting to take Laura's attention away from her ruminations. She lets go of the button when she feels that she has enough. Now, holding the device back in front of her Laura begins to rock it gently backwards and forwards. As she does so, the wild sprites are soothed and begin to slow down into a more organised, more rhythmical dance. The more smoothly she rocks, the more relaxed they become, as if she is taming them – and her thoughts, rocking them to sleep. Laura finds her ruminations beginning to recede further as she focuses on the calming light display. When she is satisfied with this she closes the device and pops it back into her bag.

At various moments over the next few days, Laura does the same thing – capturing sprites in the device to reflect her experiences. As she does so she starts to notice more of the objects and items that are around her at home, on the bus, at work etc. She becomes curious about what kind of sprites they may produce. This sense of wonder about the world is positive and productive for Laura, it helps her to reactivate the dormant, creative part of her mind and stop focusing on her internal worries.

At the end of the week it's time for another counselling session. During the session, Laura takes the device out of her bag and begins to use it as a stimulus. She uses the clock hand to cycle back in time to the beginning of the week and then slowly scrolls back through to the present. As she cycles forwards, the sprites she has captured appear on the display. She talks about each one with her counsellor in turn, reflecting upon the experiences they represent.

Design Implementation

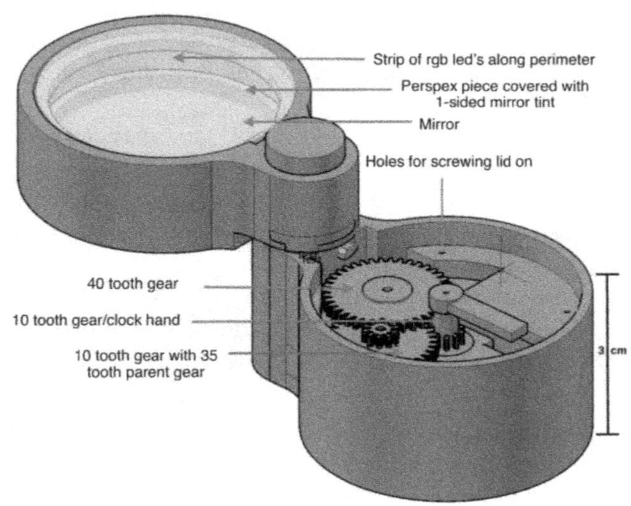

Fig. 3 - Internal workings of the display barrel (left) and clock barrel (right) seen from above

The design is composed of two main barrels which are connected by a hinge. Inside the clock barrel there are a series of gears (fig. 3) that connect the clock hand to a rotary encoder (this component has a built-in button). The gears ensure that the day corresponds with the time. There is also an accelerometer, vibrating disc motor, battery and a microcontroller. Inside the display barrel (fig. 3) there is a mirror at the bottom and a piece of Perspex with a sheet of one-way mirror tint stuck to it at the top. The two mirrors face each other. A strip of LED's runs around the perimeter of the barrel (fig. 3) and a colour sensor (fig. 4) sits at the bottom of the barrel facing outwards.

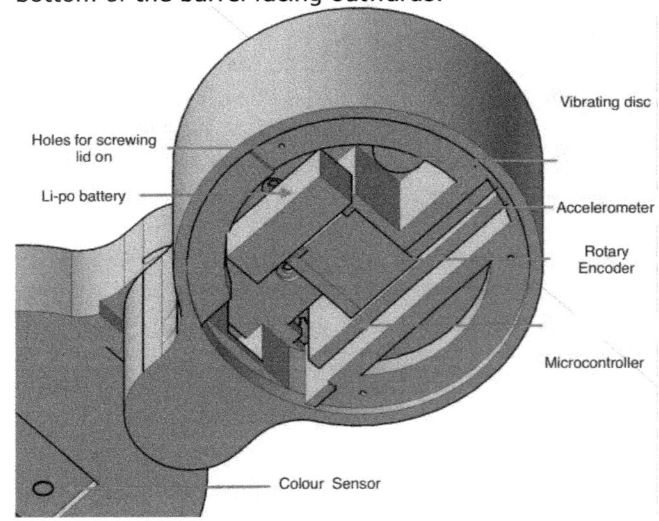

Fig. 4 - Internal workings of the display barrel (left) and clock barrel (right) seen from below

Functionality: To use the device, the user must select the time by moving the clock hands manually, hold the device up to a colourful object and press the clock face - i.e. the rotary encoder button. When the button is pressed down, the colour sensor detects a colour, the LED's in the display barrel light up with the registered colour and the vibrating motor whirrs. The longer the button is held down, the brighter the lights become. In the display barrel, the two mirrors reflect the light from the LED's backwards and forwards between themselves repeatedly. This gives the mesmerising impression that there is infinite depth in the barrel (fig. 2).

When the user depresses the button, the microcontroller records a *time stamp* (rotary encoder position) and associates it with a colour (colour sensor) and brightness (length of time for which the button was pressed). The device has been programmed to log as many of these events as the user likes – disc space permitting. Subsequently, whenever the user moves the clock hand to a time for which a colour has been registered, the colour is played back on the LED's. The amount of brightness entered by the user is also played back.

Discussion and Future Work

The sprite catcher captures and then plays back memory cues to the user to encourage them to self-reflect. Discussions with the co-design team informed us that we should try to minimise the amount of information in these memory cues and make them abstract. Firstly, it was felt that photographs and other forms of rich media contain too much provocative information for people suffering with depression. Recent research [9], has shown that in some cases self-reflection can actually increase rather than nullify a person's ruminations. Our approach is an attempt to marginalise these negative effects. Secondly, we felt that abstract representations might lead to more meaningful recollections as the ambiguity would force users to *search out* and *make sense of* the memory themselves rather than relying on the media to represent it.

Another notable aspect of the design is the fact that it has a tangible rather than digital form. The motivation for this partly comes from previous experimental HCI research by Whittaker et al. [11], who found that people are likely to create stronger emotional relationships with physical memento's than they are with digital ones. It is also, however, derived from psychology research around embodied cognition, which has had a strong influence on tangibles design research [5] and features as a fundamental part of the cognitive behaviour therapy model that is used in treatment of depression and anxiety by the NHS [16].

The aesthetic look and visual effects of the device are a third important factor to mention. Like other devices designed for mindfulness e.g. *Mind Spheres* [10], the sprite catcher uses visceral sensory stimulus to capture the attention of the user, jolt them out of their ruminations and stem their internal dialogue. Discussions with our participatory design team led us to the conclusion that it would not be enough to simply catch and hold their attention and suspend them in a state of flow. For in the process of absorbing their attention, we would shut out the external world. This could mean that the device becomes a tool for hiding from difficult life situations rather than confronting them.

We decided, consequently, that we should aim to design a handheld device that extends the user's focus beyond the bounds of their relationship with it alone. So, rather than shutting out the external world, the device should include the external world in the interactive scheme, making the user engage with objects in their local environment mindfully and reflectively.

One final design requirement of note was that it should be enjoyable, intuitive and easy to use. Our co-design team made us aware that depressed users are likely to become frustrated with technology very quickly and are often less resilient than others. For this reason, the sprite catcher has been given a single button for control and instilled with an element of fun in its interaction design.

Future work is both about further technological improvements and user studies. The next stage of the technological development is to programme the microcontroller so the user can change the pattern of the LED's by shaking the device rhythmically. The microcontroller will detect movement through its accelerometer. This will add another layer to the amount of information that the user can record and play back. We will also be fitting the device with a smaller microcontroller that can be slotted inside the clock barrel with the other components.

Following this we will be running some user studies. An important part of this will be finding out how well the device performs as a tool for memory recall. It captures very little information about the life events – only the time that it happened and the colour of an object in the local environment. Other memory cues collected by the device – brightness and movement of the lights – are more abstract, relating to emotions and feelings rather than tangible features of the environment. We will explore how effectively this abstract representation of an event can aid recall. *Pix - a* ring that can be used to take a picture and then display it in low resolution [15], has recently played with the idea that blurry images can hold emotionally meaningful information. We would like to take the opportunity to further explore this concept. The majority of the user studies, however, will focus on exploring the impact that our design approach can have on mental wellbeing. We will be undertaking a qualitative analysis of the user-experience and a quantitative analysis of the colour sensor and accelerometer data registered by users. We will be looking to see if there are any emergent patterns in how the device is used and what impact they have. These studies will be carried out with the service users of the local community mental health charity.

References

1. Yoko Akama and Ann Light. 2015. Towards mindfulness: between a detour and a portal. *Proceedings of the 33rd Annual ACM Conference Extended Abstracts on Human Factors in Computing Systems*, ACM, 625–637.
2. Eric P S Baumer, Vera Khovanskaya, Mark Matthews, Lindsay Reynolds, Victoria Schwanda Sosik, and Geri Gay. 2014. Reviewing reflection: on the use of reflection in interactive system design. *Proceedings of the 2014 conference on Designing interactive systems*, ACM, 93–102.
3. Judith S. Beck. 2011. *Cognitive Behavior Therapy: Basics and Beyond*. http://doi.org/10.1017/CBO9781107415324.004
4. Scott R. Bishop, Mark Lau, Shauna Shapiro, et al. 2004. Mindfulness: A proposed operational definition. *Clinical Psychology: Science and Practice* 11, 3: 230–241. http://doi.org/10.1093/clipsy/bph077
5. Paul Dourish. 2004. *Where The Action Is*. http://doi.org/papers2://publication/uuid/79F86CF1-BEE4-4A62-8D53-3A9B63AD34EB
6. Elisabeth Eichhorn. 2010. Recording inner life.

Proceedings of the fourth international conference on Tangible, embedded, and embodied interaction, ACM, 313–314.

7. Renaud Gervais, Alexis Gay, Fabien Lotte, and Martin Hachet. 2016. TOBE : Tangible Out-of-Body Experience. *Proceedings of the TEI '16: Tenth International Conference on Tangible, Embedded, and Embodied Interaction*: 227–235. http://doi.org/10.1145/2839462.2839486
8. Martha Glazzard, Richard Kettley, Sarah Kettley, Sarah Walker, Rachel Lucas, and Matthew Bates. 2015. Facilitating a "non-judgmental"skills-based co-design environment. *Design4Health Conference, July*, 13–16.
9. Berry Eggen Ine Mols, Elise Van den Hoven. 2016. Informing Design for Reflection: an Overview of Current Everyday Practices. *In Proceedings of the 8th Nordic Conference on Human-Computer Interaction*.
10. Bob Young Loe Feijs, Martina Hessler, Steven Kyf n. 2008. Design and semantics of form and movement.
11. Daniela Petrelli and Steve Whittaker. 2010. Family memories in the home: Contrasting physical and digital mementos. *Personal and Ubiquitous Computing* 14, 2: 153–169. http://doi.org/10.1007/s00779-009-0279-7
12. Joan Sol Roo, Renaud Gervais, and Martin Hachet. 2016. Inner Garden: an Augmented Sandbox Designed for Self-Reflection. *Proceedings of the TEI'16: Tenth International Conference on Tangible, Embedded, and Embodied Interaction*, ACM, 570–576.
13. Anja Thieme, Jayne Wallace, Paula Johnson, et al. 2013. Design to Promote Mindfulness Practice and Sense of Self for Vulnerable Women in Secure Hospital Services. *Proceedings of the SIGCHI Conference on Human Factors in Computing Systems*, 2647–2656. http://doi.org/10.1145/2470654.2481366
14. Helen Thomas, Morag McDermont, Penny Hall, Dorothy Baker, and Roz Hall. 2014. *Girls Making History*. Retrieved from http://kwmc.org.uk/wp-content/uploads/2013/04/GMHFinalreportFINAL.pdf
15. Maarten Versteeg, Elise van den Hoven, and Caroline Hummels. 2016. Interactive Jewellery: a design exploration. *Proceedings of the TEI'16: Tenth International Conference on Tangible, Embedded, and Embodied Interaction*, ACM, 44–52.
16. NHS - A Cognitive Behavioural Therapy Approach. Retrieved October 24, 2016 from http://www.hpft.nhs.uk/_uploads/documents/help-for-adults/cbt2-cbt-approach.pdf

Balance, Cogito and Dott: Exploring Media Modalities for Everyday-life Reflection

Ine Mols[1,2]
i.mols@tue.nl

Elise van den Hoven[2,1,3,4]
elise.vandenhoven@uts.edu.au

Berry Eggen[1, 2]
j.h.eggen@tue.nl

[1]Eindhoven University of Technology
Eindhoven, the Netherlands

[2]University of Technology Sydney,
Sydney, Australia

[3]ARC Centre of Excellence in Cognition and its Disorders
Macquarie University
Sydney, Australia

[4]Duncan of Jordanstone College of Art and Design, University of Dundee, UK

TEI '17, March 20-23, 2017, Yokohama, Japan
ACM 978-1-4503-4676-4/17/03.
http://dx.doi.org/10.1145/3024969.3025069

Abstract
Reflection in and on everyday life can provide self-insight, increase gratitude and have a positive effect on well-being. To integrate reflection in everyday life, media technologies can provide support. In this paper, we explore how both media creation & use in different modalities can support reflection. We present the ongoing work of designing and building Balance, Cogito, and Dott, focusing on media in audible, textual and visual form. We discuss our research-through-design process and address the differences between modalities in terms of interaction, tangibility, and the integration in everyday life.

Author Keywords
Reflection; Media Technology; Design for Remembering

ACM Classification Keywords
H.5.m. Information interfaces and presentation (e.g., HCI): Miscellaneous

Introduction
We all accumulate vast amounts of media (photos, souvenirs, e-mails etc.), often focused on special events such as holidays. Capturing more mundane aspects of life is far less common, even though our

experiences of everyday can become valuable memories [9,16]. Reflection *in* and *on* everyday life can help to appreciate our mundane experiences and can provide self-insight, support behavior change and improve wellbeing [10]. We explore the potential of media technology to support such reflective remembering [12]. With the design of three concepts we explore the use of different media to support reflection in both the creation and retrieval of media. The three concepts are complementary by exploring audio; visual media and text, each integrated into everyday life practices.

Reflection & Media

Design for reflection has increasingly become a topic of interest within HCI [1, 4, 10]. With everyday life reflection, we aim to support a broad type of reflection that incorporates multiple aspects of life [10]. Although most people engage with reflection throughout their lives, it can be very challenging and systems could take a supporting role in this process [4, 10]. Elaborate overviews of design for reflection are given elsewhere by domain [2], level of reflection [4] or adopted strategy [10]. Here, we focus on how *media* can be used to support reflection.

Media and reflection relate in two main ways. First, during media *retrieval*, media can serve as an external trigger for reflection. Photos or other media can bring things to mind otherwise forgotten [15], provide new information or support comparison. However, media as a trigger is not a singular interaction, the way people engage with their media or data often involves an iterative process of preparation, collection, integration and reflection [7].

Secondly, the process of media *creation* can be reflective as well. For example, when capturing experiences people reflect on what is 'photoworthy' and 'reframe' the situation [8]. Choosing how to represent a thought, feeling or experience in media can be reflective. Such expression-driven reflection [10] is for example seen in diary writing and leveraged in creative therapies, but also applied in technologies such as the design of a color picker in Affective Diary [14]. Both reflection in creation (or expression) and reflection in retrieval can become connected when media is created with the intention to trigger reflection in the future.

Design Research Process

We adopt a research-through-design process [5, 17] to explore the potential of media supported reflection. Rather than exploring a single design we have chosen to develop three concepts in parallel, to focus on the design space emerging between these instances [5]. Rather than focusing on either reflection in creation or reflection in retrieval we designed all concepts to facilitate both. To further differentiate from existing technology for reflection we designed the concepts with the following qualities. The concepts are *open-ended* in terms of what is reflection upon. The threshold to create media is lowered by being *small* and *light-hearted*. The created media is small; a brief text, short audio fragment or single visual, which can be quickly created or retrieved. The interactions are quick and lighthearted, rather than emotionally heavy (which for example diaries can be). Finally, all concepts have a *tangible presence* in the home environment and are *integrated* in everyday life practices.

With the design and evaluation of the concepts we address the following aims: explore the differences

Exploration for Balance

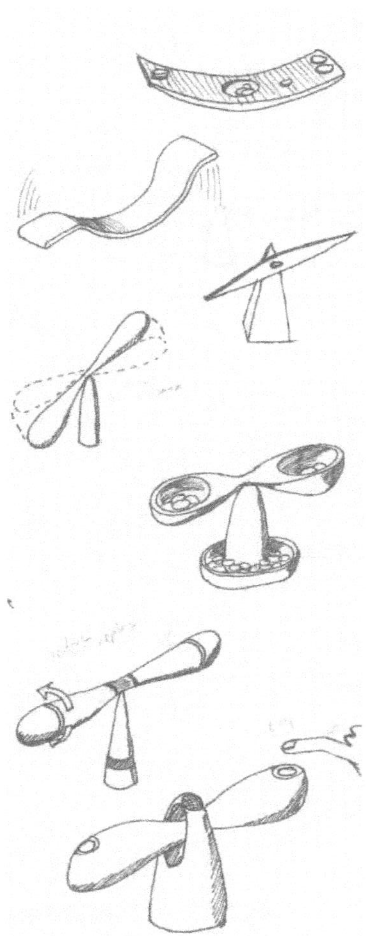

Fig. 1 Sketches of the development of balance

between different media modalities and their effect on capturing and reflecting, explore differences between reflection driven by expression (media creation) and retrieval (media use), explore how aspects of system openness, initiate and interaction support integrating reflection in everyday life [10].

Below, we will describe each concept, illustrated with explorations from the design process and a photo of the current prototype. As the work is ongoing, the different concepts are in varying states of implementation.

Audio Concept: Balance

We explore the audio modality in the Balance concept. An abstract object (inspired by a traditional measuring scale) is used as a personal voice-recorder to collect daily reflections. The concept is intended to be used when coming home after a day of work. This transition is suitable for reflection and often evaluative in nature: how was my day? This evaluation is stimulated by recording voice memos on two sides, representing opposite aspects of life, e.g. positive and negative, or work and home. The concept stimulates reflection in media creation by requiring to put thoughts into words. Additionally, each entry adds weight to the balance, depending on the force used when tapping to record. As such, the object becomes an abstract representation of the balance in everyday life and stimulates adding thoughts on the opposite site.

For retrieval, we propose three different scenarios, two focused on short triggers and one for more elaborate exploration. One can tap the center of the device to replay one of yesterday's recordings to continue these thoughts (for instance during morning commute). Secondly, one can turn either side of the Balance to get a random trigger from that side: for example requesting a positive trigger for mood regulation [3] or a negative trigger to revalue past reflections [6]. For more elaborate reflection, the past recordings can be browsed in a personal online database.

Design & Implementation

Different shapes have been explored using dials, weights or internal weight shifting (see Figure 1). Figure 2 shows the current mock-up prototype. Balance is implemented using a Raspberry Pi, connected to power and the internet. Through a USB soundcard, a microphone and speakers are connected, integrated into the central 'foot' unit. Both sides are equipped with a pressure sensor to measure the "weight" added to a recording. The different positions could be prototyped using a servo that moves the arm. However, this results in a more mechanical feel. For a more natural interaction that 'wobbles' when tapping or changing position, we aim to implement an internal weight shifting. We are currently in the process of prototyping this. We aim to implement these aspects in a wooden exterior with a warm rather than technical feel.

Figure 2: *Left*: Balance mock-up. *Right*: Implementing recording and replaying in the prototype in progress.

Sketches of Cogito

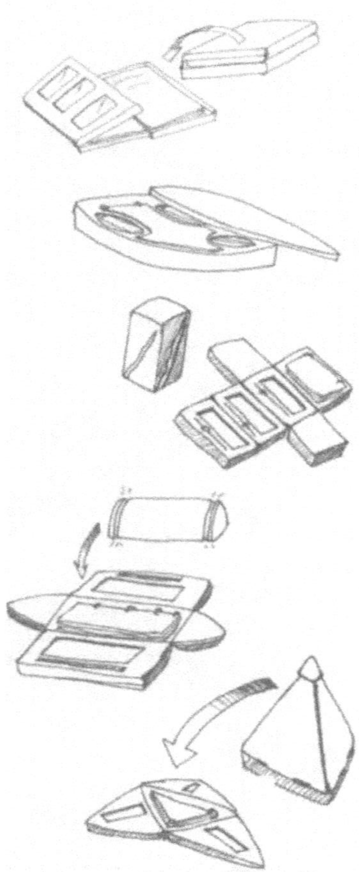

Fig. 3 Exploring how to combine multiple small screens and room for writing in an unfolding object.

Text Concept: Cogito

Writing is considered the oldest medium for reflection, especially in private diaries but increasingly in social digital practices such as online fora and blogs [11]. Inspired by these developments we have designed Cogito to send 'messages to the self'. The system combines the low threshold of mobile messages with the potential of manual writing, combining the benefits of both. Short text messages can be sent throughout the day during brief moments of realization, experienced emotions or short breaks. These are mainly intended as notes for future elaborations, rather than expressive reflection in themselves. The main reflection with Cogito is intended during media retrieval. The Cogito object stores the messages and gets 'filled'. To stimulate frequent reflection, Cogito attracts attention when 'empty' or when 'full'. When no messages are sent for a while, the object slowly and faintly glows to stimulate more messages to be sent. The object becomes 'full' when a certain amount of messages are sent but have not been further explored or reflected on, which results in a more active, restless blinking of the object.

The object can be opened up to explore the content, showing several messages together to allow for comparing and abstracting [13]. The user can change the message on each segment to find inspiring combinations. The center holds a paper note block to support further drawing connections, doodling or writing for additional reflection. By combining digital and hand-written text we aim to leverage the benefits of both. Digital message can easily be created on the go, easily stored, combined and browsed. Manual writing could stimulate further expression or a 'slow' reflection.

Figure 4: Cogito mock-up. Left: closed state, wooden exterior where lights will be implemented in the edges. Right: opening the segments reveals multiple screens and a paper notepad.

Implementation

This concept is currently in an initial state of implementation. After deciding on how to combine digital and hand-written text, we are now focusing on exploring the form factors of the Cogito object. For the mobile text, we aim to use a frequently used mobile messaging platform (for example Whatsapp) to integrate into current everyday practices. These messages will be retrieved by a Raspberry Pi and processed to be displayed on one of several LCD displays in the Cogito object. Figure 4 shows a mock-up, both in open and closed state. We use light in the edges of each segment to communicate the state of the device when closed.

Visual Concept: Dott

The concept Dott will stimulate users to create abstract visual art based on everyday life experiences. The system includes a mobile application and custom display in the home. A selection of photos can be chosen to transform into an abstract representation, generated through automatic image processing. To stimulate reflection in creation, several parameters of the visualization can be tweaked. We are mainly

Visual Exploration Dott

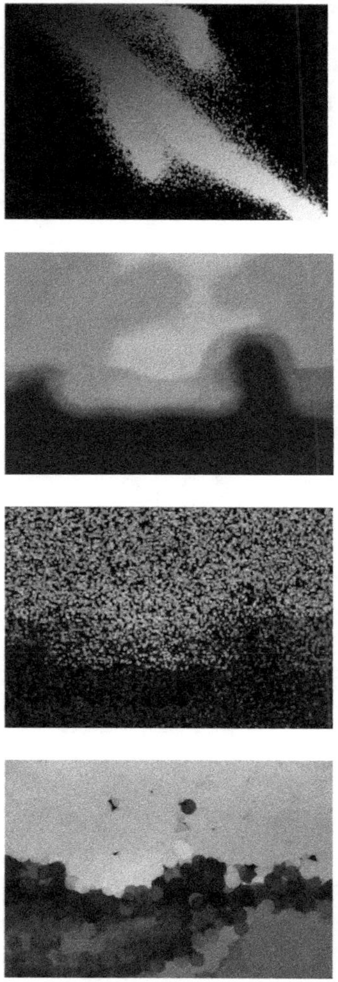

Figure 5: Exploration of generated visualizations based on photos.

interested in using the colors of the photos, by choosing different sources and tweaking parameters visualizations become brighter, darker, more calm or chaotic. Reflection is stimulated by considering how to represent experiences or emotions in such an abstract form. In the home, reflection is triggered by the artwork as a peripheral display, either when noticed by the primary user or by others. To stimulate frequent change, the artwork will slowly fade after 24 hours. In addition to adding new work, past visualizations can be browsed in the app and displayed again.

Implementation

A first version of the Dott system is implemented, with the application prototyped on the Android system. The current application can create one visual style, but we aim to develop more in the future. Currently, the visual consists of colored circles of which the size, number, and transparency can be tweaked (see the bottom two images of Figure 5). From the phone, the created artwork is uploaded to a dedicated Dropbox folder. The artwork-display is created using an Android tablet covered with thin canvas and lined with a frame to replicate an artwork, which retrieves the uploaded images from Dropbox and displays them (see Figure 6).

Figure 6: Dott running on Android phone and custom display.

Discussion & Conclusions

Balance, Cogito and Dott have been developed in parallel. By reflecting on the similarities and differences between these concepts, the following topics raised interesting discussion and questions for future work.

Modalities & Tangibility

All the forms of digital media used to support reflection are intangible in and of themselves. In the designs, they are manifested on displays (textual or visual) or exist only in space and time when played (audible). The media is given a presence by being embodied in tangible objects. Especially in Balance and Cogito, the tangible interaction plays an important role. The movement and configuration in Balance provide an extra layer of information and allow for interaction with the audio. The challenge of browsing through an intangible modality as audio has also influenced the retrieval scenarios in which randomness plays an important role. In Cogito, opening the object opens up its content: one can dive into the thoughts and memories. Different messages are positioned separate from each other, providing more room for comparison. We included a possibility for handwriting in this concept as we perceive the slowness and directness of this to be very suitable for reflection; more so than digital text. One question that arises is whether reflection will mainly focus on the content of the media, or if the object itself becomes the subject of reflection?

Modalities & Interaction

The different media, by their nature, are interacted with in different ways. The textual media requires full attention because only when read the content reveals itself. Visual media can be directly looked at but can blend into the periphery as well. In contrast, the presence of audio binary: either the audio is not perceived ('hidden in the object') or is being played, and therefore present throughout the space, even when physically turning away from it. All types of media are intended to trigger reflection through interaction. However, the media that can not be perceived without interaction (textual or audible), does not provide such a reflective trigger directly. Rather, the object by its movement (Balance) or light (Cogito) provides this trigger to *use*. How will the separation between trigger-to-use and trigger-to-reflect influence the reflection of people? Does it make triggering easier or does it add an additional threshold?

Visibility and Disclosure

The home is a semi-public space, but reflection can be very personal. During the design process, it became clear that personal content should not be directly "on display". The different modalities required different strategies to fulfill this requirement. The visual media of Dott remains private through a high level of abstraction. For both Balance and Cogito, the private content is hidden within the object, while the triggers to use (light and movement) do not disclose personal information. Will people perceive the different concepts to be equally private? Or will they disclose different levels of personal information in the different concepts?

In the future, we will use these concepts in a semi-comparative home study. By comparing between and generalizing across these concepts we aim to gain more insight in how to support reflection with personal media in everyday life.

Acknowledgements

This research was supported by STW VIDI grant number 016.128.303 of The Netherlands Organization for Scientific Research (NWO), awarded to Elise van den Hoven.

References

1. Eric P.S. Baumer. 2015. Reflective Informatics: Conceptual Dimensions for Designing Technologies of Reflection. In *Proceedings of the 33rd Annual ACM Conference on Human Factors in Computing Systems* (CHI '15). 585-594. DOI: http://dx.doi.org/10.1145/2702123.2702234
2. Eric P.S. Baumer, Vera Khovanskaya, Mark Matthews, Lindsay Reynolds, Victoria Schwanda Sosik, and Geri Gay. 2014. Reviewing reflection: on the use of reflection in interactive system design. In *Proceedings of the 2014 conference on Designing interactive systems* (DIS '14). ACM, New York, NY, USA, 93-102. DOI: http://dx.doi.org/10.1145/2598510.2598598
3. Susan Bluck. 2003. Autobiographical memory: Exploring its functions in everyday life. *Memory 11*, 2, 113–123. http://dx.doi.org/10.1080/741938206
4. Rowanne Fleck and Geraldine Fitzpatrick. 2010. Reflecting on reflection: framing a design landscape. In *Proceedings of the 22nd Conference of the Computer-Human Interaction Special Interest Group of Australia on Computer-Human Interaction* (OZCHI '10). ACM, New York, NY, USA, 216-223. http://dx.doi.org/10.1145/1952222.195226
5. William Gaver. 2012. What should we expect from research through design?. In *Proceedings of the SIGCHI Conference on Human Factors in Computing Systems* (CHI '12). ACM, New York, NY, USA, 937-946. http://dx.doi.org/10.1145/2207676.2208538

6. Ellen Isaacs, Artie Konrad, Alan Walendowski, Thomas Lennig, Victoria Hollis, and Steve Whittaker. 2013. Echoes from the past: how technology mediated reflection improves well-being. In *Proceedings of the SIGCHI Conference on Human Factors in Computing Systems* (CHI '13). ACM, New York, NY, USA, 1071-1080. DOI: http://dx.doi.org/10.1145/2470654.2466137
7. Ian Li, Anind Dey, and Jodi Forlizzi. 2010. A stage-based model of personal informatics systems. In *Proceedings of the SIGCHI Conference on Human Factors in Computing Systems* (CHI '10). ACM, New York, NY, USA, 557-566. DOI=http://dx.doi.org/10.1145/1753326.1753409
8. Siân E. Lindley, Abigail C. Durrant, David S. Kirk, and Alex S. Taylor. 2008. Collocated social practices surrounding photos. In *CHI '08 Extended Abstracts on Human Factors in Computing Systems* (CHI EA '08). ACM, New York, NY, USA, 3921-3924. http://dx.doi.org/10.1145/1358628.1358957
9. Ine Mols, Elise van den Hoven, and Berry Eggen. 2014. Making memories: a cultural probe study into the remembering of everyday life. In *Proceedings of the 8th Nordic Conference on Human-Computer Interaction:* (NordiCHI '14). ACM. 256-265. http://dx.doi.org/10.1145/2639189.2639209
10. Ine Mols, Elise van den Hoven, and Berry Eggen. 2016. Technologies for Everyday Life Reflection: Illustrating a Design Space. In *Proceedings of the TEI '16: Tenth International Conference on Tangible, Embedded, and Embodied Interaction* (TEI '16). ACM, 53-61. http://dx.doi.org/10.1145/2839462.2839466
11. Catharine O'Sullivan. 2005. Diaries On-line Diaries, and the Future Loss to Archives; or, Blogs and the Blogging Bloggers Who Blog Them. *The American Archivist 68*, Spring/Summer 2005, 53–73.
12. Abigail J. Sellen and Steve Whittaker. 2010. Beyond total capture: a constructive critique of lifelogging. *Commun. ACM* 53, 5 (May 2010), 70-77. http://dx.doi.org/10.1145/1735223.1735243
13. Ursula M. Staudinger, U.M. Life reflection: A social-cognitive analysis of life review. *Review of General Psychology 5*, 2 (2001), 148–160.
14. Anna Ståhl and Kristina Höök. 2008. Reflecting on the design process of the Affective Diary. In *Proceedings of the 5th Nordic conference on Human-computer interaction: building bridges* (NordiCHI '08). ACM, New York, NY, USA, 559-564. http://dx.doi.org/10.1145/1463160.1463245
15. Elise van den Hoven, and Berry Eggen, The cue is key: Design for real-life remembering. *Zeitschrift für Psychologie 222*, 2 (2014), 110.
16. Ting Zhang, Tami Kim, Alison Wood Brooks, Francesca Gino, and Michaell I. Norton. 2014. A "Present" for the Future: The Unexpected Value of Rediscovery. *Psychological Science 25*, 10. 1851–1860.
17. John Zimmerman, Jodi Forlizzi, and Shelley Evenson. 2007. Research through design as a method for interaction design research in HCI. In *Proceedings of the SIGCHI Conference on Human Factors in Computing Systems* (CHI '07). ACM, 493-502. http://dx.doi.org/10.1145/1240624.1240704

Designing Swing Compass with Liveliness: From Personal to Public Interactions

Kenny K. N. Chow
School of Design
The Hong Kong Polytechnic University, Hong Kong
sdknchow@polyu.edu.hk

TEI '17, March 20-23, 2017, Yokohama, Japan
ACM 978-1-4503-4676-4/17/03.
http://dx.doi.org/10.1145/3024969.3025070

Abstract
This paper describes the ongoing project Swing Compass, a configurable recommendation system whose framework is built upon the notion of embodied interaction and blending theory in pursuit of meaning making in users from the operational to the reflective levels. The framework, named "liveliness", is summarized as a protocol of cognitive processes and the methodology includes interpretive analyses, experience prototyping, and user participation. The first instance of Swing Compass is a handheld personal device, which analogically maps recommended items based on intrinsic properties to directions on the compass rose. The second instance is a table-sized public installation, which explores to map out recommendations with their physical locations. Swing Compass is lively in that the recommendations change over time to avoid selection bias. The design challenges span from human scales, perceived affordances, to perception and interpretation of changes. The empirical findings provide real and particular samples for the protocol and inform specific design guidelines for future development.

Author Keywords
Embodied cognition; blending; embodied interaction; imagination; reflection; selection; liveliness.

Figure 1: Swing Compass arranges items in a compass-like fashion for user selection.

ACM Classification Keywords
H.5.m. Information interfaces and presentation (e.g., HCI): Miscellaneous

Introduction
Swing Compass is a configurable recommendation system allowing users to select from a set of items that are spatially arranged on its interface like a compass rose. Together with a designed physical case, a user's tablet computer or mobile phone is turned into a "compass of choices" (see Figure 1 for an instance of Swing Compass). Icons of items are displayed at different directions (e.g., N, E, W, S) on the compass rose according to either intrinsic properties (in a conceptual space) or actual geographical positions (in a physical space). Selecting an icon is like targeting along the corresponding direction. Built upon the metaphor: choices "swing from one side to another", the system tracks users' selections and sometimes prompts one to turn the compass with the body for under-explored or unaware options, eliciting reflection on one's selection pattern. Examples of everyday selection include deciding which items to shop at a supermarket, which dishes to order at a restaurant, or which songs to put in the playlist for a day.

Related Concepts
Based on embodied interaction [1], embodied schema [2], conceptual metaphor [3], and blending theory [4], people's familiarity with the mundane world, bodily basis and emergent nature of meaning making, are integral to the design framework of Swing Compass, named "liveliness".

"Metaphor" originally from Greek means, "to transfer". People understand something through metaphor by "transferring" or mapping from the qualities of another thing. George Lakoff and Mark Johnson points out numerous examples of metaphors from everyday life, which shape basic, entrenched concepts in our minds (e.g., we say and see something good as "high quality", because GOOD is UP). These conceptual metaphors arise from structures or patterns recurring in our bodily experiences (e.g., things up above are usually more difficult for one to access and so more precious), what Johnson calls image or embodied schemata.

Gilles Fauconnier and Mark Turner's blending theory (in which metaphor is regarded as a kind of asymmetric static blend) extends to explicate emergent thoughts. The notion is built upon ideas including mental spaces [5] and frames [6, 7]. Mental spaces are "small conceptual packets" [4] (p. 40) that an individual constructs for representing particular scenarios as perceived, imagined, or remembered. A mental space typically contains elements of the scenario and relations between them, which are structured by a frame from long-term memory [8] (p. 21). By integrating two or more mental spaces with mappings between corresponding elements and relations, new "blended" meaning is made. Blending is emergent that the output of one blend can become input to another new blend, forming a conceptual integration network. Frames, mental spaces, and blends can be built on bodily experiences (e.g., turning away from something bad), in other words, embodied.

Paul Dourish's embodied interaction argues that designing interactive systems should incorporate people's familiarity with the everyday world, in terms of physical habits or social practices. In fact, everyday experience also entails perception of liveliness, including reaction, adaptation, autonomous transformation, and contingent changes [9] (pp. 10-12). These characters of liveliness match the bodily basis and emergent nature of blending. We propose that blending people's mundane experiences (e.g., turning away from something) with contingent changes over time is a promising way to articulate meaning from the operational to the reflective levels.

The Liveliness Framework

The liveliness framework has two principles: immediate blends of people's mundane experiences and then further elaboration of the blends prompted by contingent, curious changes over time. It can be summarized in two stages of interaction, each of which involves four cognitive processes. At the initial stage: 1.1 Perceiving affordances; 1.2 Receiving quick feedback; 1.3 Triggering immediate blends; 1.4 Becoming second nature. At later stages of use: 2.1 Noticing changes; 2.2 Invoking interpretive frames; 2.3 Elaborating metaphorical blends; 2.4 Reflecting on the situation. While Donald Norman's seven stages of action [10] (pp. 45-48) is goal-oriented, the liveliness framework centers on multiple levels of interpretation via blends triggered by contingent, enduring changes. The protocol will be illustrated through the Swing Compass project in the next section.

The Handheld Swing Compass

The first instance of Swing Compass is a handheld personal selection device with options displayed at different directions on the compass rose according to a preset topology (e.g., in case of music playlists creation, going east for more intense music, going west for softer pieces) based on intrinsic properties. In addition, each option (e.g., Radiohead or Beethoven) is annotated with categorization attributes (e.g., Rock or Classical) through which the system can compare the similarity between a user's consecutive choices. Based on configurable moderation, the system recommends options for the user at every stop. By default the recommendations are of similar kinds (e.g., intense Rock at the east, soft Rock at the west, etc.), compared with the user's last choice. If the user turns with the compass, options of contrasting kinds (e.g., Classical) show up. At this initial stage:

1.1 Perceiving affordances – From the physical case and the compass-rose interface, the user may see it like a handheld compass or Chinese fengshui compass. One knows he or she can turn with it. The subtle rotation of the compass rose on the interface in accordance with little change in orientation additionally invites the user to turn.

1.2 Receiving quick feedback – The user sees icons (options) showing up when one orients at a certain angle, and then fading out when one turns. One can also turn back to bring the fading icons back. If the user turns further away, a different set of icons fades in. The coupling of turning the compass and seeing icons fading forms a motor-sensory feedback loop.

1.3 Triggering immediate blends – The act of turning, the fading-in and fading-out, look familiar to the user, who forms a blend with the mundane experience of turning around to look for something. The fading icons on the compass rose are comparable to the physical targets coming in and out the field of view when one looks around. The gap is that one keeps the head down looking at the icons, in contrast to looking ahead to the physical targets. The immediate blend is a new operation of turning to look for something different or interesting.

1.4 Becoming second nature – Just after a few turns, one becomes accustomed to the turning and unaware of the gap between looking down and looking ahead. The operation becomes automatic in following uses.

If the user sticks with similar kinds of options (e.g., Rock) for consecutive selections, the system hides those kinds for next selection in order to prompt the user to turn. After a turn, it reveals the contrasting kinds (e.g., Classical). Through this intervention, the user has to physically swing to open up other possibilities or alternatives. At this later stage:

2.1 Noticing changes – The user notices that many options are cut and becomes curious. After a turn, one uncovers other options.

2.2 Invoking interpretive frames – The user tries to make sense of the curious changes by invoking a frame, such as advice or intervention due to biased behavior.

2.3 Elaborating metaphorical blends – The frame structures a remembered or imagined scenario, for example, parents controlling choices available to their kids. This constructed scenario and the current curious scenario developed from the earlier blend (1.3) become inputs to the next blend. The output is an imaginary narrative that the compass "notices" the user's biased behavior and "advises" the user to turn to other under-explored choices.

2.4 Reflecting on the situation – The compass challenges the user's selection pattern and suggests alternatives. The user may feel annoyed by the choice limitation or thankful for the suggestions.

Experience Prototyping and Results

Laboratory experiments with seventeen participants are conducted. Detailed results and discussion are published elsewhere [11]. The experiments involve one participant at a time in a set of activities, followed by a semi-structured interview. The activities are designed to let participants experience the prototype for the two stages suggested by the framework. Comparing the above interpretive analyses with empirical findings informs a set of design guidelines.

#1 Animating feedback to embody meaning
Animated feedback helps users make crucial meaning. The displayed icons fade in and out continuously in accordance with user orientation. This animated feedback simulates and foregrounds how the shooting target moves across the surrounding when one looks around, which is the major mapping in the immediate blend (1.3).

#2 Physical dimensions matter
The turning action in Swing Compass entails the variable of weight, which is commonly overlooked in designing interactive systems. The empirical findings inform the power of physical variables on embodied meaning. Physical dimensions of bodily action, such as size, weight, softness, or surface texture in object manipulation, should be considered.

#3 Changes can take intuitive, interactive forms
Changes over time may take different forms. The changing number of available options in Swing

Compass may not be well noticed. To make the changes easy to notice and interpret, we might consider more intuitive, interactive forms. For example, some icons in Swing Compass might become "reluctant" and show up slowly.

The Table-sized Swing Compass

The second instance of Swing Compass is a table-sized interactive public installation, which resembles the kind of compass used in a ship for sea navigation. Multiple tablet computers will be put inside the flat, circular top compartment of a designed bar-table-like stand, with openings on the top for the displays (see Figure 2 for the first prototype). The top compartment can be turned, and the tablets display differently according to different orientations. In the handheld version, items are displayed at different directions according to a topology based on intrinsic properties. As the table version is placed at a fixed location, the topology can be geographical (e.g., different restaurants, retailers, etc. nearby at different directions). If one turns the table, unexpected items (e.g., non-governmental organizations with their services related to the meal or the shopping items, such as those running schools compared with toys shops) will be shown, as a provocative call to shift from shopping to giving. Meanwhile, if music playlists creation is to be applied, the installation will be a jukebox supporting selections. For dinning at a restaurant, it can be an ordering kiosk.

Major challenges of this extension include changes from a personal context of use to a public setting, and from the mobile situation to the fixed location.

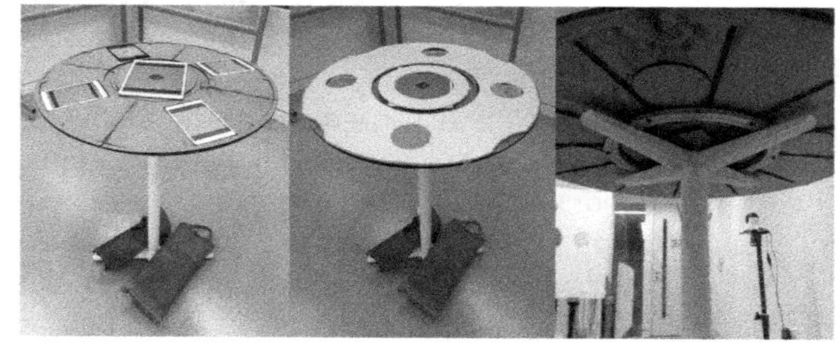

Figure 2: The prototype has multiple tablets in the top compartment, which can be turned.

The following is design considerations based on the liveliness framework and guidelines.

Perceivable affordances and animated feedback
The table compass should have perceivable physical features and/or digital effects inviting users to turn the tabletop without explicit instructions. Users typically do not assume the top of a bar table can be turned. Meanwhile, some of them may casually tap the screens without any intention to select. Hence, the touch-screen feature may need to be disabled and other means for user selection may be required. The fading effects of icons based on the turning action should be followed from the handheld version to the table one.

Physical dimensions of motor action
Turning the table compass subtly differs from turning the handheld counterpart. One may move around the table or just stand still, rather than turning the body. The consequence of changing forms and scales of both the motor action and the compass should be scrutinized. When turning the table, one may not feel like turning the body to see around. Meanwhile, the difference between the mobile situation and the fixed location needs to be considered too. Using the

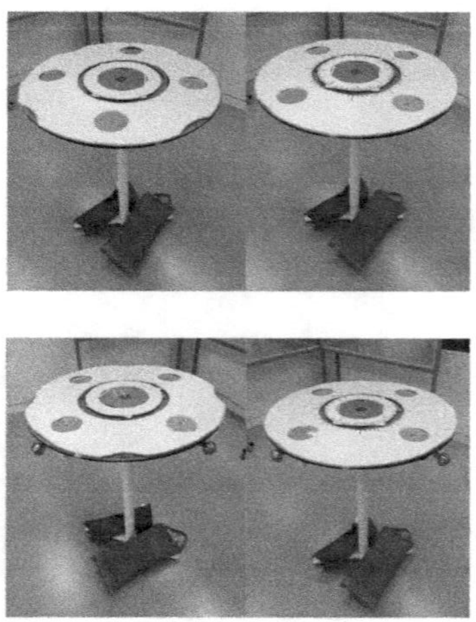

Figure 3: Four types of physical features, namely just a groove between the inner disc and outer ring, with instrument-like markings, with door handle-like knobs, and with both markings and knobs.

handheld compass, one may think of navigation in the field. Yet, interacting with the table compass standing at a fixed spot may limit their imagination.

Changes in intuitive forms

Users coming to the table compass may not intend to spend much time on it. They probably just make one or two selections before they go. The later stage of use may not even exist, not to mention incorporating changes at those moments to make them curious. More intuitive forms of changes should be considered, rather than reducing the number of available icons. For example, initially all icons are of the same kind, and suddenly replaced by those of the other kind.

Experience Prototyping and Findings

The first set of experiments is designed to investigate people's exploration with the table compass and possible imagination elicited by it, including four different physical features on the table compass in search of perceivable affordances (see Figure 3). Four participants (2 females and 2 males) are invited to experience it. Major findings include: (1) the marking and groove is the more important feature than the handles to invite one to turn; (2) the change of icons from shopping to giving is unexpected, curious, but can be confusing too.

The second set of experiments engages seventeen participants with the second prototype (Figure 4). Major changes in this prototype include physical buttons added for user selection, changing icon design, and the display orientation. Major findings from the experiments include: (1) the icons are displayed upright relative to the table center rather than to the user, making participants to look at other side of the table like following the pointing direction of the compass; (2) a few participants find the shift from shopping to giving sensible, yet the connection still needs to be strengthened.

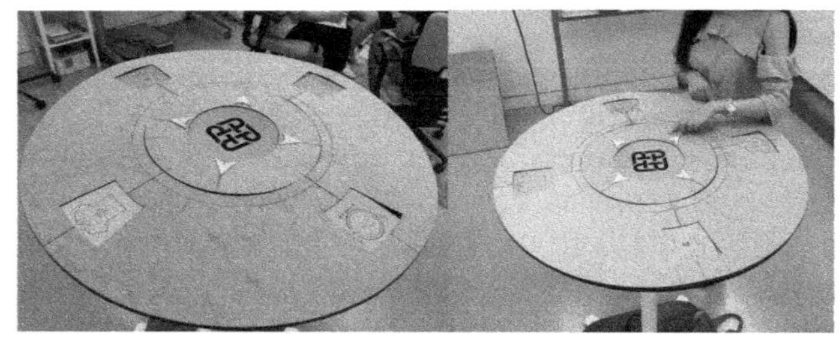

Figure 4: The second prototype of the table-sized compass.

Conclusion and Future Work

This paper articulates the meaning construction processes via embodied and emergent blends from operation to reflection. It suggests a methodology, starting with interpretive analyses, followed by user participation. To illustrate, the ongoing Swing Compass project is discussed. The development of Swing Compass from the personal context to the public setting poses new challenges, yet also demonstrates the transferability of the framework across different contexts of use. The construction and deployment of the installation in the real context will follow, and situated data and feedback will be collected with a view to generate real and particular substances for the design narratives.

Acknowledgements

We thank all the participants. We gratefully acknowledge the grant from The Hong Kong Polytechnic University.

References

[1] P. Dourish, *Where the Action Is: The Foundations of Embedded Interaction*, Cambridge, Mass.: MIT Press, 2001.

[2] M. Johnson, *The body in the mind : the bodily basis of meaning, imagination, and reason*, Chicago: University of Chicago Press, 1987.

[3] G. Lakoff, and M. Johnson, *Metaphors we live by*, Chicago: University of Chicago Press, 2003.

[4] G. Fauconnier, and M. Turner, *The way we think : conceptual blending and the mind's hidden complexities*, New York: Basic Books, 2002.

[5] G. Fauconnier, *Mental spaces : aspects of meaning construction in natural language*, Cambridge ; New York, N.Y.: Cambridge University Press, 1994.

[6] M. Minsky, *A Framework for Representing Knowledge*, Cambridge, Mass., 1974.

[7] C. J. Fillmore, "Frames and the Semantics of Understanding," *Quaderni di Semantica,* vol. VI, no. 2, pp. 222-254, 1985.

[8] S. Coulson, *Semantic leaps : frame-shifting and conceptual blending in meaning construction*, Cambridge: Cambridge University Press, 2001.

[9] K. K. N. Chow, *Animation, embodiment, and digital media human experience of technological liveliness*, Basingstoke: Palgrave Macmillan, 2013.

[10] D. A. Norman, *The Design of Everyday Things*, New York: Basic Books Inc., 2002.

[11] K. K. N. Chow, "Swing Compass: A Metaphorical and Embodied Approach to Structuring Choices for User Reflection," *Information Design Journal,* vol. 22, no. 3 (forthcoming), 2016.

Felted Paper Circuits Using Joomchi

Nicholas A. Knouf
Cinema and Media Studies
Program
Wellesley College
Wellesley, MA, 02481, USA
nknouf@wellesley.edu

TEI '17, March 20–23, 2017, Yokohama, Japan
ACM 978-1-4503-4676-4/17/03.
http://dx.doi.org/10.1145/3024969.3025071

Abstract
The integration of electronics and paper is a burgeoning topic for tangible interaction. Here we show how to use the Korean technique of hand-felting paper known as *joomchi* to embed electronics in paper after the sheet forming process. This method requires the use of specialized papers that are amenable to joomchi. We present embedded LEDs, multi-layer circuit "sheets", and speakers. While labor-intensive, joomchi both enables one to completely integrate paper and electronics, while also making tangible connections between ancient and modern craft.

Author Keywords
paper circuits; hanji; joomchi; craft

ACM Classification Keywords
J.5 [Arts and Humanities]: Arts, fine and performing

Introduction
The deep integration of paper and electronics is a growing area of interest for human-computer interaction researchers [7]. Given thousands of years of experience with different forms of paper around the world, paper provides a versatile material for new forms of tangible interaction due to its affordances of ubiquity, familiarity, and ease of modification.

Recent work surrounding the integration of paper and electronics has followed a number of different trajectories. Researchers have shown how to embed electronic components during the forming of individual sheets of paper, developing what they call "pulp-based computing" [3]. The combination of thermochromic inks and layers of paper have enabled artists and designers to create works that change color in response to touch and heat [6, 23, 24]. New developments in inexpensive conductive ink and paint have allowed for the printing and/or drawing of circuits on the surface of paper [9, 20, 21]. Shape-memory alloys have provided for novel movement mechanisms [14, 22, 19]. Copper tape has enabled the construction of "circuit stickers" that can be used to teach the basics of electronics [15, 16]. Various forms of cutting and depositing copper traces on the surface of paper have allowed for new kinds of flexible speakers [10, 18, 17]. Combinations of some or all of these techniques have suggested new ways to think about the intersection of electronics and books [4, 13, 12]. In sum, there is now a vibrant community of researchers tracing out various potentialities for paper computing.

We contribute to this body of work by showing how to use the Korean method of hand-felting paper called *joomchi* to embed electronic components into the paper after the sheets have been formed. Joomchi requires specialized papers with particular material qualities such as the Korean paper called *hanji*, a long-fibered paper made from parts of the paper mulberry tree [8]. Hanji has recently become more well-known in the West through the dedicated advocacy of the artist and researcher Aimee Lee. Joomchi enables one to take a stack of multiple sheets of paper and, through repeated hand agitation with water, felt the individual sheets into a single sheet, with the electronic components embedded *within* the paper itself. This creates a seamless integration of paper and electronics without the complication and difficulty of processing fibers and forming paper by hand.

Paper Characteristics

While there is a large amount of research into the integration of paper and electronics, few of these projects have addressed the specific *materiality* of particular kinds of paper, although the pulp-based computing research of Coelho *et al.* is a notable exception [3]. We think this is a significant oversight, as different types of paper have unique characteristics depending on the choice of fiber, method of separating fibers, and sheet-forming process, amongst other considerations. Here we give a brief overview of why we are working with hanji and why such paper is necessary for joomchi, illustrating how long-fibered papers like hanji could be of interest to the TEI community.

Papermaking is an ancient craft, and all manner of plant fibers have been used to make paper, such as cotton, wood pulp, or the leaves of invasive weeds [5]. Here we are interested in the particular qualities of the inner bark or "bast" of paper mulberry trees, known as *dak* in Korea or *kozo* in Japan (hanji is almost exclusively made of *dak*, while Japanese paper, known as washi, can be made from *kozo* or other plant fibers) [1, 8]. *Dak* fibers are rather long in comparison to other plant fibers (on the order of 12mm, in comparison with 4mm for Western-style pulp), and the process of hand-beating *dak* in order to make pulp does not chop up these fibers but allows them to retain their length [1, 8]. The particularities of the hanji sheet-forming process also allows for an incredibly strong sheet, so much so that hanji has been used for windows, floors, shoes, teapots, umbrellas, and armor, amongst many other objects [8].

No matter the source fiber, "pulp" generally refers to these processed plant fibers suspended in water. This pulp becomes *paper* through hydrogen bonding of cellulose between the fibers themselves as the water evaporates from the pulp after a sheet has been formed [1, pg. 290]. Hanji's strength comes primarily from this hydrogen bonding of its long fibers. Because of this strength, the fibers between two or more sheets of hanji can be "felted" together through joomchi, a craft that has existed for hundreds of years and has recently become well-known amongst papermakers due to the teaching of workshops by artists such as Jiyoung Chung and Aimee Lee [2, 8]. Joomchi involves wetting sheets of hanji (or washi made of kozo) and, through various forms of hand agitation and manipulation, melding multiple sheets into one through the formation of new hydrogen bonds between fibers of the original sheets.

Because of the merging of multiple layers of hanji into a single sheet through joomchi, any inclusions (for example, electronic components) that we place on interior sheets become a part of the new single sheet of hanji. This allows us to take advantage of the characteristics of hanji without having to embed the electronics as inclusions at the time of sheet formation, an option unavailable to most given the specialized equipment and training necessary to make hanji or other types of specialized paper. We are also able to draw upon the wide variety of dyed papers available on the market. While labor intensive, joomchi therefore enables anyone to embed electronics into paper (rather than placing them on the surface, as in many other paper electronics projects), while at the same time extending an ancient craft into new directions.

Example Joomchi Procedure

We use a slightly modified form of joomchi from that described by Jiyoung Chung in her book *Joomchi & Beyond* [2]. Credit goes to Chung for creating easy-to-follow recipes for different types of joomchi; we nevertheless outline the most basic steps here, as well as provide visual documentation in Figure 1. Joomchi has many variations that could be of use to the paper computing designer, and we encourage those interested to examine Chung's book.

1. On a single sheet of hanji (Japanese washi made from kozo can also be used), sew the electrical circuit desired (Figure 1a).
2. Place additional sheets of hanji above and below the sewn sheet(s) from Step 1 (Figure 1b).
3. Thoroughly wet with a spray bottle all sheets of hanji. It is helpful to wet each sheet individually, building up the stack sheet by sheet, and ensuring that there are few to no air bubbles between the sheets (Figure 1c).
4. For the first "round" of joomchi, accordion fold along the horizontal edge, then roll into a cylinder. Agitate the cylinder by compressing it evenly in your hand, ensuring that all parts of the cylinder receive equal agitation. The cylinder needs to remain wet throughout this process, so spray with additional water as needed. Agitate for ten minutes (Figures 1d and 1e).
5. Unroll the cylinder, and roll it up in the opposite direction. Agitate for 10 minutes.
6. Unroll and unfold the sheet, then accordion fold in the vertical direction. Repeat steps 4 and 5.

Unroll and unfold the sheet. At this point you will have agitated for around 40 minutes (Figure 1f). The next step can be repeated *ad infinitum*, but should be done at least four to five times.

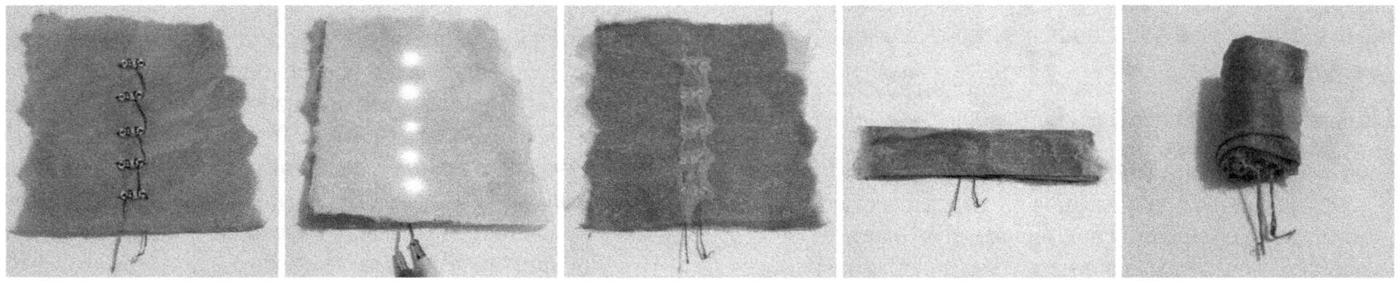

(a) LED sequins sewn with conductive thread

(b) Stack of hanji sheets, before wetting: light blue bottom layer, dark blue sewn layer, light blue top layer

(c) Thoroughly wetted hanji stack

(d) Accordion folded hanji stack

(e) Accordion folded stack rolled into a cylinder

(f) Unrolled and unfolded hanji stack after four 10 minute "rounds" of joomchi

(g) Crumpled and wetted hanji ball

(h) Uncrumpled hanji ball

(i) Dried sheet of hanji after a total of around 110 minutes of joomchi

(j) Dried sheet of hanji, powered

Figure 1: Illustration of joomchi steps

(a) Hanji sheet from Figure 1 that has been re-wetted, draped over an object, and left to dry.

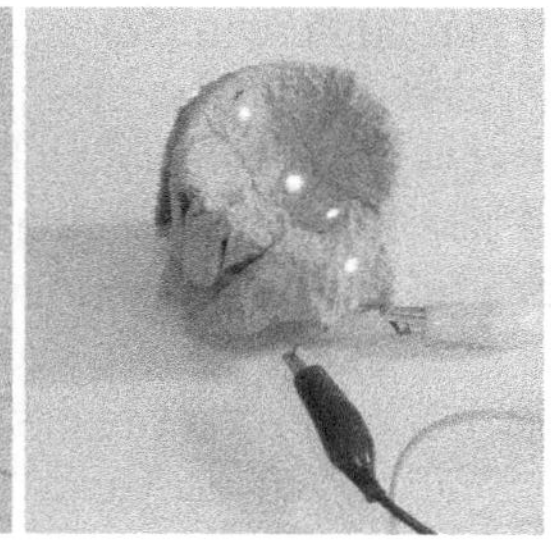

(b) Draped circuit without underlying object, showing how the sheet retains its form.

Figure 2: Draping circuits made of hanji after joomchi.

7. Re-wet the sheet and crumple it into a ball. Agitate by squeezing the ball evenly for 10 minutes (Figures 1g and 1h).

A properly felted sheet of hanji will take at least 80 minutes of hand agitation, and likely upwards of 120 minutes (Figures 1i and 1j). The amount of agitation needed is dependent on the original size of the sheet (in this example the sheet was around 5" on a side) as well as the number of sheets in the stack[1]. As is clear from the figures and the list of steps, joomchi is likely not amenable to the embedding of large, inflexible components, although new techniques might make this possible. For now, inclusions need to be small and/or malleable, such as small LED sequins and conductive thread. As well, inclusions need to be able to withstand being soaked in water, at least for the duration of the joomchi and drying processes. So far standard LED sequins have continued to work even after being continually soaked in water during joomchi, but their long-term viability is an open question. Conductive threads will likely move around somewhat during joomchi, thus threads carrying differing signals need to be separated by a reasonable distance at the time of sewing.

Following joomchi, the sheet is by default relatively stiff, with the feeling of leathery skin. This can be modified by gently rubbing the sheet in one's hands to soften the paper [2]. With enough time, the paper takes on the characteristics of cloth, with all of the draping possibilities that implies.

Further examples

The example shown in Figure 1 involved sewing five LilyPad LED sequins[2] to a sheet of hanji using conductive thread. We show here other examples of felted paper electronics made through joomchi.

- It is possible to take a sheet of hanji after joomchi and, by re-wetting it, allow it to drape and take the form of an underlying object. We took the sheet shown in Figure 1 and draped it over an egg cup and let it dry. The resulting sheet retains its shape even without the underlying object (see Figure 2).
- Because of hanji's strength, we can have electronic inclusions that can be seen from the front and back of the sheet, creating what we could call a "sheet circuit". By using layers of hanji as insulators *between* two individual layers that have electronic inclusions, we can replicate the insulating material of printed circuit boards (see Figure 3).

[1] There is often some shrinkage in both horizontal and vertical dimensions after joomchi.

[2] https://www.sparkfun.com/products/10081

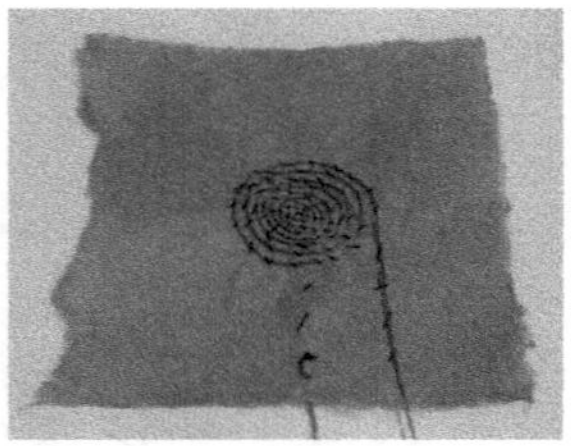

(a) Embroidered speaker made from conductive thread, front.

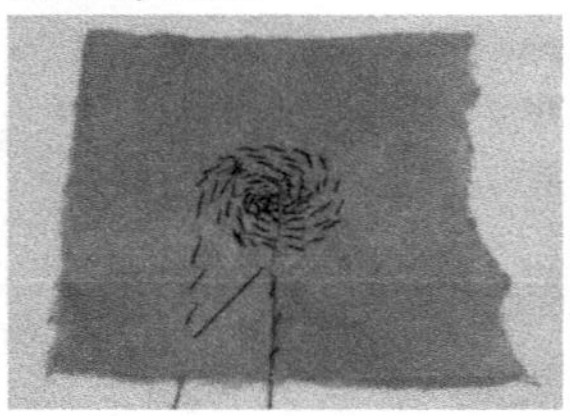

(b) Embroidered speaker made from conductive thread, back.

(c) Embroidered speaker after joomchi, showing placement of neodymium magnet.

Figure 4: Creating a paper speaker through joomchi.

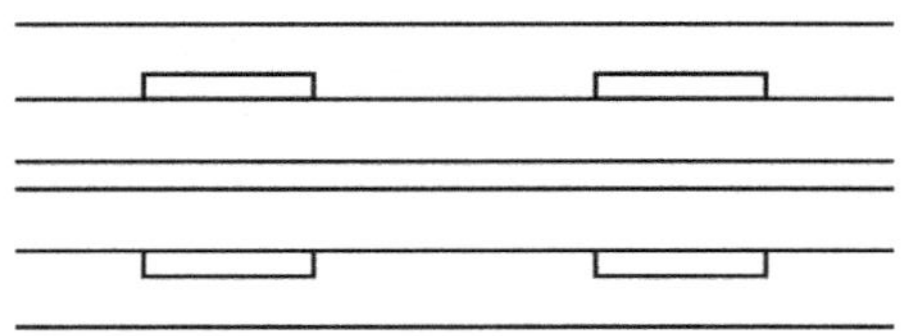

(a) Diagram of a hanji stack forming a "sheet circuit", shown end-on before the individual sheets have been felted together through joomchi.

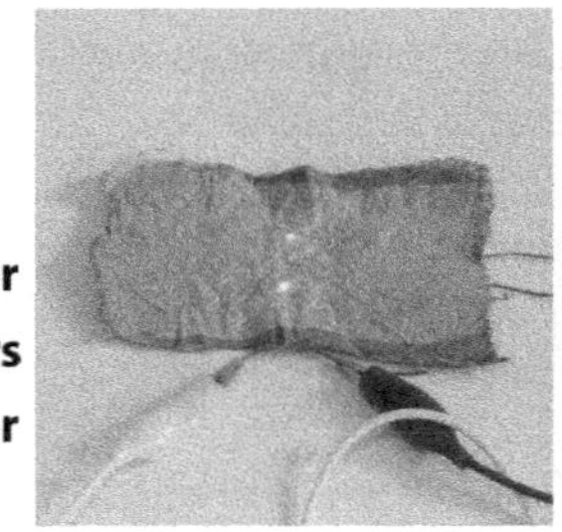

(b) Front side of a hanji "sheet circuit" after joomchi.

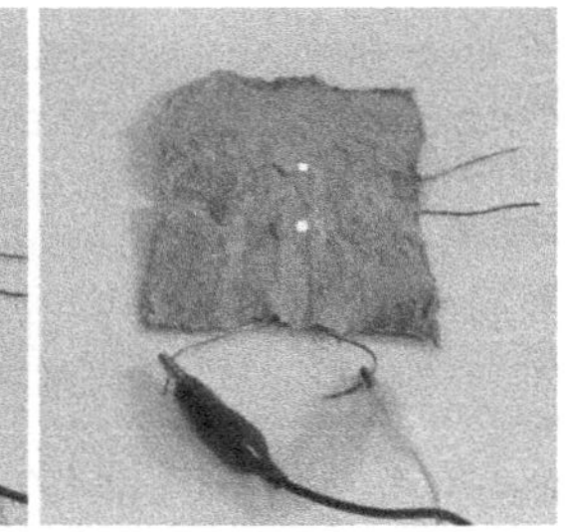

(c) Back side of a hanji "sheet circuit" after joomchi.

Figure 3: Creating a "sheet circuit".

- We can also create paper speakers by sewing conductive thread in a spiral pattern and attaching a powerful neodymium magnet, drawing upon the work of Hannah Perner-Wilson (see Figure 4) [10, 11].

These examples act as proofs of concept that show some of the potential for the embedding of electronics in paper through joomchi.

Future Work

The examples of paper circuits in this paper are the beginning of our research into the intersection of hanji, electronics, and joomchi. We intend to further refine our procedure to make the sewing more resilient to joomchi, as well as considering other methods of joomchi besides the basic one used in this paper. We will also explore the possibility of using conductive inks or paints to create bend and capacitive sensors, as well as the embedding of NFC tags for the storage of small amounts of data *within* the paper itself. The purpose of our investigations is to weave together the most appropriate affordances of paper and electronics. In sum, we hope that others consider how the specific material qualities of different types of paper could be useful in creating novel paper circuits, while at the same time enabling one to extend old forms of craft into new directions.

Acknowledgements

This project was funded in part through a Wellesley College faculty award. Thanks to the two anonymous reviewers for their comments. Many thanks to Lisa Cirando for teaching me all I know about papermaking, hanji, and joomchi. I would also like to thank Jeff Stout for insightful conversations about paper circuits.

REFERENCES

1. Timothy Barrett. 2005 [1983]. *Japanese Papermaking: Traditions, Tools, and Techniques.* Floating World Editions, Easthampton, Massachussetts.
2. Jiyoung Chung. 2011. *Joomchi & Beyond.* Beyond & Above, Providence.
3. Marcelo Coelho, Lyndl Hall, Joanna Berzowska, and Pattie Maes. 2009. Pulp-based Computing: A

Framework for Building Computers out of Paper. In *CHI '09 Extended Abstracts on Human Factors in Computing Systems (CHI EA '09)*. ACM, New York, NY, USA, 3527–3528. DOI: http://dx.doi.org/10.1145/1520340.1520525

4. Natalie Freed, Jie Qi, Cristina Sylla, and Pedro Branco. 2011. Beyond the Binding: Exploring the Future Book. In *Proceedings of the 8th ACM Conference on Creativity and Cognition (C&C '11)*. ACM, New York, NY, USA, 445–446. DOI: http://dx.doi.org/10.1145/2069618.2069742
5. Dard Hunter. 1978 [1947]. *Papermaking: The History and Technique of an Ancient Craft.* Dover Publications, New York.
6. Tatsuya Kaihou and Akira Wakita. 2013. Electronic Origami with the Color-changing Function. In *Proceedings of the Second International Workshop on Smart Material Interfaces: Another Step to a Material Future (SMI '13)*. ACM, New York, NY, USA, 7–12. DOI:http://dx.doi.org/10.1145/2534688.2534690
7. Fredéric Kaplan and Patrick Jermann. 2010. PaperComp 2010: First International Workshop on Paper Computing. In *Proceedings of the 12th ACM International Conference Adjunct Papers on Ubiquitous Computing - Adjunct (UbiComp '10 Adjunct)*. ACM, New York, NY, USA, 507–510. DOI: http://dx.doi.org/10.1145/1864431.1864500
8. Aimee Lee. 2012. *Hanji Unfurled: One Journey into Korean Papermaking.* The Legacy Press, Ann Arbor.
9. David A. Mellis, Sam Jacoby, Leah Buechley, Hannah Perner-Wilson, and Jie Qi. 2013. Microcontrollers As Material: Crafting Circuits with Paper, Conductive Ink, Electronic Components, and an "Untoolkit". In *Proceedings of the 7th International Conference on Tangible, Embedded and Embodied Interaction (TEI '13)*. ACM, New York, NY, USA, 83–90. DOI: http://dx.doi.org/10.1145/2460625.2460638
10. Hannah Perner-Wilson. 2011. *A Kit-of-No-Parts.* Master's thesis. Massachusetts Institute of Technology.
11. Plusea. 2012. Embroidered Fabric Speaker. (2012). Retrieved January 5, 2017 from http://www.instructables.com/id/Embroidered-Fabric-Speaker/.
12. Jie Qi. 2012. *The Fine Art of Electronics: Paper-Based Circuits for Creative Expression.* Master's thesis. Massachusetts Institute of Technology.
13. Jie Qi and Leah Buechley. 2010. Electronic Popables: Exploring Paper-based Computing Through an Interactive Pop-up Book. In *Proceedings of the Fourth International Conference on Tangible, Embedded, and Embodied Interaction (TEI '10)*. ACM, New York, NY, USA, 121–128. DOI: http://dx.doi.org/10.1145/1709886.1709909
14. Jie Qi and Leah Buechley. 2012. Animating Paper Using Shape Memory Alloys. In *Proceedings of the SIGCHI Conference on Human Factors in Computing Systems (CHI '12)*. ACM, New York, NY, USA, 749–752. DOI: http://dx.doi.org/10.1145/2207676.2207783
15. Jie Qi and Leah Buechley. 2014. Sketching in Circuits: Designing and Building Electronics on Paper. In *Proceedings of the SIGCHI Conference on Human Factors in Computing Systems (CHI '14)*. ACM, New York, NY, USA, 1713–1722. DOI: http://dx.doi.org/10.1145/2556288.2557391

16. Jie Qi, Andrew "bunnie" Huang, and Joseph Paradiso. 2015. Crafting Technology with Circuit Stickers. In *Proceedings of the 14th International Conference on Interaction Design and Children (IDC '15)*. ACM, New York, NY, USA, 438–441. DOI: http://dx.doi.org/10.1145/2771839.2771873

17. Jess Rowland. 2013. Flexible Audio Speakers for Composition and Art Practice. *Leonardo Music Journal* 23 (2013), 33–36.

18. Jess Rowland and Adrian Freed. 2012. Flexible Surfaces for Interactive Audio. In *Proceedings of the 2012 ACM International Conference on Interactive Tabletops and Surfaces (ITS '12)*. ACM, New York, NY, USA, 315–318. DOI: http://dx.doi.org/10.1145/2396636.2396688

19. Greg Saul, Cheng Xu, and Mark D. Gross. 2010. Interactive Paper Devices: End-user Design & Fabrication. In *Proceedings of the Fourth International Conference on Tangible, Embedded, and Embodied Interaction (TEI '10)*. ACM, New York, NY, USA, 205–212. DOI: http://dx.doi.org/10.1145/1709886.1709924

20. Michael Shorter, Jon Rogers, and John McGhee. 2014a. Enhancing Everyday Paper Interactions with Paper Circuits. In *Proceedings of the 2014 Conference on Designing Interactive Systems (DIS '14)*. ACM, New York, NY, USA, 39–42. DOI: http://dx.doi.org/10.1145/2598510.2598584

21. Michael Shorter, Jon Rogers, and John McGhee. 2014b. Practical Notes on Paper Circuits. In *Proceedings of the 2014 Conference on Designing Interactive Systems (DIS '14)*. ACM, New York, NY, USA, 483–492. DOI: http://dx.doi.org/10.1145/2598510.2602965

22. Paul Strohmeier, Kaja Vembe Swensen, Cameron Lapp, Audrey Girouard, and Roel Vertegaal. 2012. A Flock of Birds: Bringing Paper to Life. In *Proceedings of the Sixth International Conference on Tangible, Embedded and Embodied Interaction (TEI '12)*. ACM, New York, NY, USA, 333–334. DOI: http://dx.doi.org/10.1145/2148131.2148208

23. Kohei Tsuji and Akira Wakita. 2013. Transience: Aesthetics of Dynamic Colors Inside Japanese Calligraphy. In *Proceedings of the 7th International Conference on Tangible, Embedded and Embodied Interaction (TEI '13)*. ACM, New York, NY, USA, 387–388. DOI: http://dx.doi.org/10.1145/2460625.2460706

24. Takahiro Tsujii, Naoya Koizumi, and Takeshi Naemura. 2014. Inkantatory Paper: Dynamically Color-changing Prints with Multiple Functional Inks. In *Proceedings of the Adjunct Publication of the 27th Annual ACM Symposium on User Interface Software and Technology (UIST'14 Adjunct)*. ACM, New York, NY, USA, 39–40. DOI: http://dx.doi.org/10.1145/2658779.2659103

Field Computing: Wearable Devices for Citizen Science

Jen Liu
Carnegie Mellon University
Pittsburgh, PA 15219, USA
jenliu@cmu.edu

TEI '17, March 20-23, 2017, Yokohama, Japan
ACM 978-1-4503-4676-4/17/03.
http://dx.doi.org/10.1145/3024969.3025072

Abstract
"Field Computing", is an ongoing interdisciplinary research project to design and build wearable devices for use in citizen science applications. The works from this project is derived from the fields of wearable electronics, citizen science and environmental biomonitoring through a critical design perspective. Background and prior research is shared that discusses considerations for technology and design, along with documentation and description of *Portable Workspace*, an initial project for "Field Computing". *Portable Workspace* is a wearable that unfolds into a physical computing studio for building hardware in outdoor environments. The current work in progress, *Data HarVest*, is a wearable tool that collects physical artifacts and contextual data about fungi for scientific surveys. Early prototypes for this tool are then discussed along with design considerations.

Author Keywords
Wearable electronics; citizen science; environmental biomonitoring; outdoor; critical design; hci; textiles.

ACM Classification Keywords
H.5.m. Information interfaces and presentation (e.g., HCI): Miscellaneous.

Introduction
This research focuses an interdisciplinary investigation across the fields of wearable electronics, citizen science and environmental biomonitoring. Under the conceptual framing of "Field Computing", a series of projects are currently in progress and are discussed as part of this paper. This work researches and creates digital interactions and technologies that can be used to explore, facilitate and intervene in relationships between human users, non-human users (which include plants, animals and other organisms) and their environments.

With "Field Computing", a critical design practice is leveraged to build wearable devices that draw attention outside of the user's body and actions to connect them to how they interact with the environment around them. As environmental concerns are growing every day, these devices can play a critical role in sensing the changes around us to solve these problems.

Background and Context
Taking its name from fieldwork and field research in scientific contexts, "Field Computing" is studying how technology can be developed and used outside of a studio, lab or makerspace to collect data about the environment. Because of the proposed open-source nature and shifting of contextual sites of practice for this research, the tools and techniques that will come out of this work is suitable for the use in citizen science as a means to collect environmental data by laypeople.

By utilizing a critical design approach, the tools and technology that come out of this project will provoke dialogue surrounding how we currently engage with the environment and what potential interactions we could have, especially as non-scientists working in data collection for citizen science. This idea of citizen science is especially provoking in the context of critical design because it allows us to speculate how nonscientists and "non-experts" can contribute to scientific study [4].

In working with wearable electronics, I am interested in researching new ways in how computing technology can be embedded into fabrics and garments by utilizing traditional textile techniques. By incorporating affordances of wearable electronics such as portability, wearability and mobility with established textile craft, new designs and interactions can be fashioned for how data can be collected regarding the surrounding environment. This follows the line of work of e-textile practitioners like Kate Hartman, Maggie Orth, and Kobakant who have done extensive research and experimentation in integrating digital technology into garments [1, 2, 7].

The textile techniques that I focus on researching and developing are directed towards creating tools that can be used for environmental biomonitoring. Through the design process, materials and techniques are selected and utilized which can endure the nature of outdoor environments. I also incorporate technologies and designs that have been previously developed for environmental biomonitoring and citizen science work such as weather sensors and data logging systems [3, 8,9,11].

Portable Workspace
This past summer an initial project for "Field Computing" was completed during an artist residency at the Iowa Lakeside Laboratory, a biological field station located in northwest Iowa. The outcome,

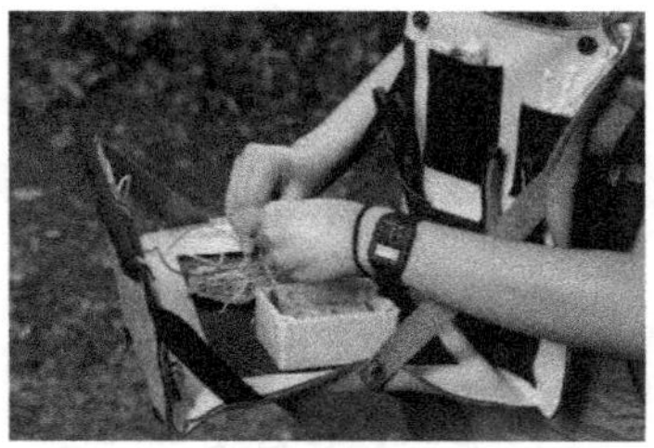

Figure 1: *Portable Workspace* in use as a surface for building an environmental sensor system.

Portable Workspace, is designed to be a wearable device that unfolds into a physical computing studio (see Figures 1 and 2). The device contains the tools and work area for a user to build a project when they are outside of a regular lab or maker space.

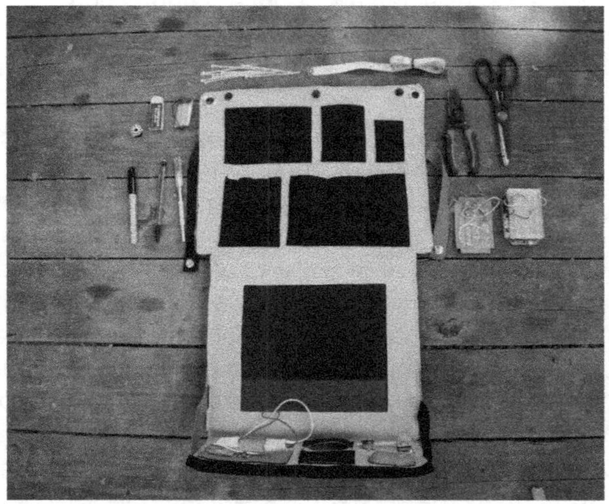

Figure 2: *Portable Workspace* shown spread out with tools and materials that can be carried in the device.

This project builds upon Wearable Studio Practice, a collaboration between Hannah Perner-Wilson and Andy Quitmeyer in building portable studios during a research expedition to the Panamanian jungle [10]. The inspiration and design of the *Portable Workspace* was based off hikes into the surrounding prairie land with research scientists and observing their practices in wearing backpacks on the front of their body in order to easily access notebooks, field guides or writing devices. This tool was designed to consider how a computing practice can be brought out into the field to build electronics that monitor natural environments.

A prototype was first constructed out of cardboard and paper to model size and functionality. From there, a more refined version was built using neoprene fabric, nylon webbing and hardware. The workspace portion is attached to a harness worn on the body so that it sits across the chest of the user. There are several pockets of varying sizes on the panels closest and furthest to the body to allow for storage of different tools and equipment while the center panel has a rigid plastic material built in so it can function as a table. By building this prototype as a portable structure, it explores changing sites of production for technology. This change can allow practitioners to respond more readily to the context in which they are creating in.

Work in Progress: Data HarVest

The current project in development for "Field Computing" is *Data HarVest*, a wearable device that can be used to collect physical artifacts and digital data from the environment. Specifically for this iteration, this device is focused on collecting information regarding fungi samples during a foray. A foray is an informal scientific survey which can be conducted by amateurs or scientists in which a species, in this case mushrooms, are collected and catalogued [6].

Mushrooms, the fruiting bodies of fungi, are the targeted specimen for this iteration of this device due to their sensitivities to the environment. Depending on varying temperature and moisture conditions, mycelium, the vegetative part of a fungus that resides underground will grow and develop to produce the spore-releasing mushrooms above ground [5]. Mycelia also absorb nutrients through their environments, in such that they can be used as a marker to track and reflect upon the overall health of the local climate [6].

Figure 2: Fungi samples collected from a mushroom foray with the Western Pennsylvania Mushroom Club.

Figure 4: Sample of fly fishing vests used in consideration for design of Data HarVest.
From top-left clockwise: Char Bloom Vest, Allen Gallatin Ultra Light Fishing vest, Filson Fly Fishing Guide Vest, Filson Foul Weather Fly Fishing Vest

Through measuring and recording the conditions that various mushrooms are found during a particular foray, the information can be used to help understand not just the various conditions for particular fungal growth but also how an environment may change over time. Although this project is currently focused on mycology, there is potential for this device to be used in various fields of research for data collection.

Using design research methods, conversations and interviews with members of the Western Pennsylvania Mushroom Club, were conducted to gain insights to the necessary design and technology functions this device would require. The device is designed to support the foray through a wearable intervention modeled after vests used in fly-fishing, a garment that can hold multiple tools and gears for this sport. Since *Data HarVest* is a wearable device that needs to be able to store specimens, along with hardware components for data collection and function in outdoor environments, design references from fly-fishing vests serve as a useful and informative guideline.

In addition to helping citizen scientists collect specimen, *Data HarVest* supports logging of contextual information during the foray. Wearable sensor inputs includes GPS, temperature, soil moisture and voice recordings. The collected data is documented so that information from subsequent walks, whether at a later point in time or by other people wearing the device, can be cross-referenced and compared. By collecting a combination of physical artifacts and contextual digital data, this device allows its users to create a synoptic view of their environment.

Data HarVest is currently in the initial prototyping phase. The general functions have been established and now work has progressed to the refinement of technology and design of the device. This process is discussed in the following section. Additionally, although this project is currently focused in mycology, there is potential for this device to be used in various fields of research for data collection.

Design Considerations
In assessing multiple designs for fly-fishing vests, several design features can be identified including wearability, tool storage and materials used for construction (see Figure 4). With wearability, several vests feature adjustable straps and buckles to allow for quick adjustments, whether the vest is being worn by multiple users or if the vest needs to be worn over clothing of varying thicknesses. These vests also tend to be designed to fit over the shoulders and end at the waistline to prevent any movement constriction such as bending over. One vest even has the function to "detach at top and bottom so that it can be worn on pack fronts" (Patagonia vest). For tool storage, pockets of multiple sizes are built in with different closures in these vests, usually placed near the bottom of the vest or closer to the chest area for easier access. In terms of materials used in the vest, many vests use a combination of rip stop nylon, mesh and other quick-drying lightweight polyester fabrics. Hardware includes snaps, zippers, buckles and utility keepers that allow for additional tools to be hung off the vest. This analysis of design considerations in fly fishing vests will serve as an important framework for *Data HarVest* as the project moves forward.

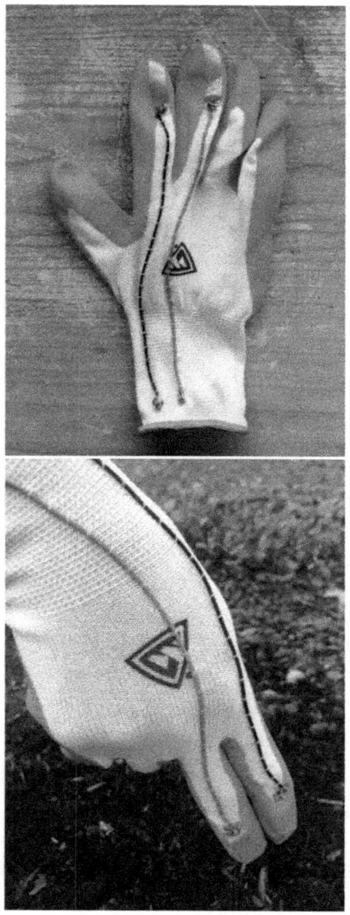

Figure 5: Soil sensor glove prototype that is used to detect moisture levels of the ground.

Prototyping of Sensors
The sensors inputs are currently being tested separately and modified so that it can be included as a sewable component into the overall design. Considerations are also being made into the placements of these sensors on the user's body from a design and technical perspective.

One sensor that is under development is a glove that is worn in addition to the vest which can be used to detect soil moisture. A soil moisture sensor typically consists of two probes that function as a variable resistor. These probes are placed into the ground to measure the conductivity between the two points. The more moisture or water that is in the earth, the higher the conductivity will be between the probes, resulting in lower resistance.

The sensor is built into a glove by embedding conductive materials so that the index and middle fingers of the glove becomes the probes. When the two fingers are inserted perpendicularly into the ground, a reading can be taken of the current moisture levels. As a wearable, the sensor becomes a more portable and readily accessible to be used, while the gesture required for taking a reading allows the user to interact with the physical environment in an intimate manner. Since only two fingers of the gloves are currently being utilized for the soil moisture sensor, there is potential to add additional sensing capabilities to the other fingers.

When this sensor is paired with other components that compiles digital and physical data about the environment, *Data HarVest* will be able to formulate a summarized representation of a location.

Future Work
Data HarVest will be refined and deployed within the context of local forays for mushroom exploration. The concept will be used to engender and study conversations with experts and non-experts on the role of wearability and technology in field work. Iterations will be made according to the usability and needs of these users out in the field. In addition, this device could potentially be used to collect, study and survey a large range of specimen in various contexts.

Conclusion
"Field Computing" is an ongoing series of interdisciplinary work that speculates upon the tools and devices necessary to compute and sense to aid citizen scientists in the wild. *Portable Workspace* and *Data HarVest* are two initial projects based on this concept that explores the relationship between the body and the surroundings using wearable devices. Along with researching new methods of physical and wearable computing possibilities, future iterations and work will continue to take on a critical perspective of how technology and tools can be used in field research by citizen scientists to monitor the natural environment.

References
1. Hartman, Kate. *Prosthetics Technologies of Being.* 2012. Retrieved October 15, 2016 from http://research.ocadu.ca/socialbody/project/prosthetic-technologies-of-being.

2. Kobakant. *How to Get What you Want,* 2009. Retrieved October 17, 2016 from www.kobakant.at/DIY/.

3. Kuznetsov, Stacey and Eric Paulos. 2010. Participatory Sensing in Public Spaces: Activating Urban Surfaces with Sensor Probes. In *Proceedings of the 8th ACM Conference on Designing Interactive Systems.* (DIS '10), 21-30. http://doi.acm.org/10.1145/1858171.1858175.

4. Kuznetsov, Stacey. 2013. Expanding our visions of citizen science. *Interactions.* Vol. 20, Issue 4, July + August 2013, 26-31. http://doi.acm.org/10.1145/2486227.2486234.

5. Lincoff, Gary A. 1981. *National Audubon Society Field Guide to North American Mushrooms.* Knopf, New York.

6. Money, Nicholas P. 2011. *Mushroom.* Oxford University Press, New York.

7. Orth, Maggie. *Touch,* 2007. Retrieved October 15, 2016 from www.maggieorth.com/art_Touch.html.

8. Paxton, Mark and Steve Benford. 2009. Experiences of participatory sensing in the wild. In *Proceedings of the 11th international conference on Ubiquitous computing.* (UbiComp '09), 265-274. http://doi.acm.org/10.1145/1620545.1620584.

9. Pierce, James and Eric Paulos. 2012. Designing everyday technologies with human-power and interactive microgeneration. In *Proceedings of the Designing Interactive Systems Conference*. (DIS '12), 602-611. http://doi.acm.org/10.1145/2317956.2318047.

10. Quitmeyer, Andy and Hannah Perner-Wilson. 2015. Wearable studio practice: design considerations for digital crafting in harsh environments. In *Adjunct Proceedings of the 2015 ACM International Joint Conference on Pervasive and Ubiquitous Computing and Proceedings of the 2015 ACM International Symposium on Wearable Computers.* (UbiComp/ISWC'15 Adjunct), 1285-1293. http://doi.acm.org/10.1145/2800835.2807926.

11. Tse, Rita and Giovanni Pau. 2016. Enabling street-level pollution and exposure measures: a human-centric approach. In *Proceedings of the 6th ACM International Workshop on Pervasive Wireless Healthcare.* (MobiHealth '16), 1-4. http://doi.acm.org/10.1145/2944921.2944925.

Demulti Display: A Multiplayer Gaming Environment for Mitigating the Skills Gap

Shogo Yamashita
The University of Tokyo
Tokyo, Japan
shogo-yamashita@g.ecc.u-tokyo.ac.jp

Akira Mastuda
The University of Tokyo
Tokyo, Japan
akira.matsuda.ut@gmail.com

Natsuki Hamanishi
The University of Tokyo
Tokyo, Japan
hamanishinatsukilab@gmail.com

Shunichi Suwa
Sony Computer Science Laboratories
Tokyo, Japan
Shunichi.Suwa@sony.com

Jun Rekimoto
The University of Tokyo
Sony Computer Science Laboratories
Tokyo, Japan
rekimoto@acm.org

TEI'17, March 20-23, 2017, Yokohama, Japan.
Copyright © 2017 ACM 978-1-4503-4676-4/17/03.
http://dx.doi.org/10.1145/3024969.3025074

Abstract
Although doing sports and games together is effective to create good social connections, a large skill gap among players reduces the enjoyment in such activities. In this research, we technologically enhance sports and gaming activities in the real world. The gaming environment is aimed at mitigating the differences in ability without reducing the enjoyment. For the initial approach of the research, we implemented a setup for enhancing table games by using a liquid crystals display. The system shows different images to each player using a polarization-based technique. As the application, we implemented an augmented PONG game. The game has a function to support players depending on their scores in the match. This setup can apply to a projector for a wider gaming field for enhancing game activities requiring body movements such as Table Tennis and Air Hockey.

Author Keywords
Augmented Sports; Skills Gap; Multiplex Imagery

ACM Classification Keywords
H.5.m [Information interfaces and presentation (e.g., HCI)]: Miscellaneous

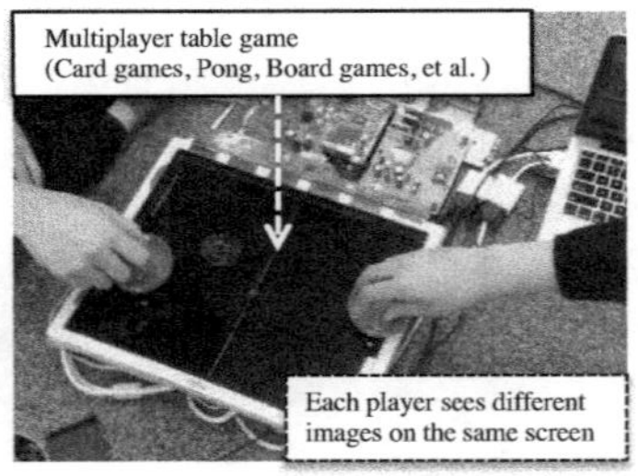

Figure 1: A multiplayer gaming environment configured by Demulti Display. The environment shows different images to each player looking at the same screen.

Figure 2: Demulti Display: A liquid crystal panel changing the polarization angles of lights from a video display device (Display, projector, et at.) on each pixel. Demulti Display is on a liquid crystal display in this picture.

Introduction

Doing game activities together is good for creating social connections with others. However, significant differences in ability among players might reduce the enjoyment and create a sense of discomfort during the activity. In general, players with more experience make allowances for the opponents to avoid this situation. Nevertheless, this effort eventually reduces the total enjoyment of the event since other players sometimes feel the effort of the skill modification.

In the case of playing video games, players can fill the gap in ability among players without reducing the enjoyment. The reason is that players can use a stronger player character and/or useful items to modify their abilities. On the other hand, in the real world, acquiring abilities for a game consumes considerable amounts of time and efforts. Therefore, filling the gap during the activity is not feasible in most cases.

In this research, we technologically enhance games using tangibles in the real world to mitigate the skills gap among players. The installation improves their abilities in real-time depending on the scores in the game. For instance, in the case of an air-hockey game using paddles, the losing player can have skills of vanishing shots and/or curve shots. For the initial approach of the research, we implemented a setup for enhancing table-game experiences such as a board game and a card game (Figure 1). The system is a liquid crystal panel that can change polarization angles from a video display device such as a display and a projector. We named the panel Demulti Display. The gaming environment with Demulti Display can show different images to each player looking at the same environment, and change the difficulty of the game in accordance with their ability.

Related Work

There are several types of research on technologically augmented sports and games. The Bouncing Star project [3], and HoverBall [7] aim to enhance sports using balls. The balls implemented by the projects fly and move in the gaming field by actuators such as a jet spraying device and propellers. The systems can moderate the skill difference among players in the activity. However, the applications are still limited due to the restriction of the machines such as battery life and robustness. Lumisight Table [4] and Ex-Field [1] can provide different images to users surrounding a screen by using a parallax-barrier-based technology. The system shows some images simultaneously, but users can only see one of the images from the same direction. Therefore, the system cannot provide different images to users sitting or standing on the same side, which some board games require. ExPixel [8] can also provide different images to users by using a polarization-based technology. However, this setup requires two projectors with circular polarization filters, while our system can use an LCD or a projector for household use. In existing research on displays capable of presenting personalized information to different users, there are no investigations on skill-deference moderation in games [6, 5]. Augmented Reality glasses can provide the augmented gaming environment. However, the limited size of the field of view may reduce the experience.

Demulti Display

Demulti Display can be configured for a multiplayer gaming environment for table games. The environment can show different images to each player by a polarization-based technique. This technology enables the game to provide appropriate difficulty to each player looking at the same gaming field in accordance with the ability of the player. This should mitigate the skills gap among players without reducing the enjoyment.

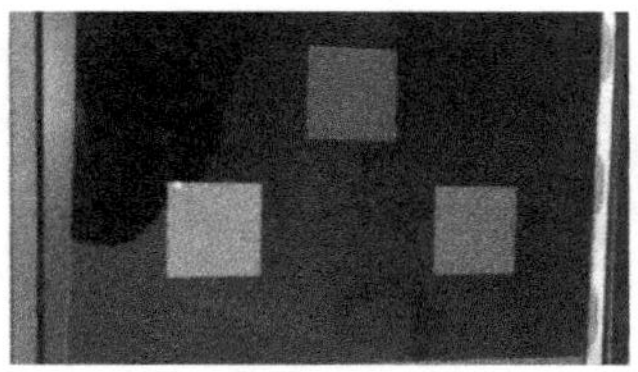

(a) Three square-shaped graphics displayed on a liquid crystal display

(b) View from player 1 wearing glasses with polarizing sheets (polarizing angle 45°)

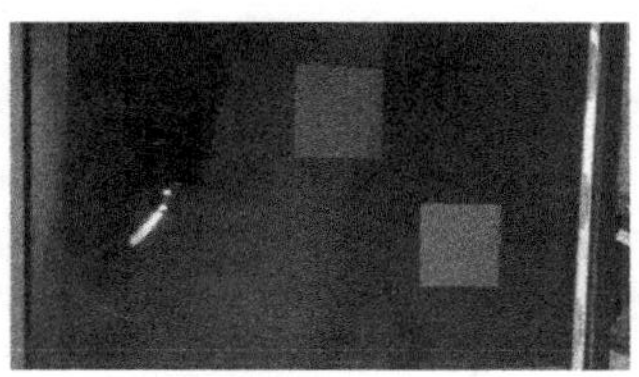

(c) View from player 2 wearing glasses with polarizing sheets (polarizing angle -45°)

Figure 3: A table gaming environment configured with Demulti Display. The environment can show different images to each player by a polarization-based technique. Two players wear glasses coated with polarizing sheets.

Implementation

System configuration

Demulti Display is a liquid crystals panel, which can be mounted on a video display device such as a display and a projector. Figure 2 shows the configuration of a gaming environment using a display (LCD) with Demulti Display. Both of the panel and the display are connected to a computer. In the game, two players wear glasses made of polarizing sheets, and they can sit face-to-face or on the same side of the setup. The polarization angle of glasses for one of the players makes a right angle with the other glasses of players.

Providing different images to each player

The LCD under the Demulti Display emits polarized light from the screen. Each pixel on the panel has the ability to change the angle of polarized light. Therefore, the Demulti Display can create images, which have different polarization angles on a pixel-by-pixel basis. Figure 3 (a) shows the view of the display. (b) is the view of player 1 wearing glasses with polarizing sheets (polarizing angle $45°$), and (c) is the view of player 2 (polarizing angle $-45°$). As shown in Figure 3 (b), the red square on the right is invisible from player 1, and the green square on the left is hidden from player 2. The reason is that light shielding occurs when the polarization angles of light from the screen are at a right angle to the angle of polarizing sheets on the glasses.

Liquid crystal panel

We took the liquid crystal panel apart from a color TN-type LCD (VL-178SSL). We removed the liquid crystal layer coated with two polarizing sheets in the LCD. The number of pixels is 1280×1080. Each pixel consists of three sections to control the polarization angles for three colors (RGB). The rotation angles through each section are

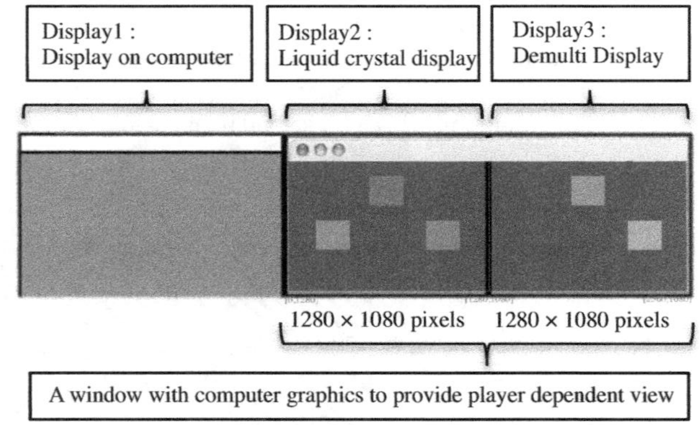

Figure 4: The multi-display configuration of the computer. A window with computer graphics to provide the player-dependent views is placed at the left edge of the display 2, and the right edge of the window matches with the right side of display 3.

changeable via a D-sub port in the same way as a sub-display connected to a computer. For instance, displaying whole white screen on the panel means rotating the polarizing angles by around $90°$ to $120°$ on all pixels. Displaying gray screen changes the polarizing angles by around $45°$ to $60°$. The rotation angle depends on the liquid crystal panel.

Example Program

We shows a example for showing a blue square to each player, a green square to one of the players only and a red square to the other player as shown in Figure 3 in this section.

Display setting

The multi-display configuration of the computer is shown in Figure 4. Figure 5 shows the window to change the polarization angles for providing different images to players. The display on the computer, LCD, and Demulti Display are

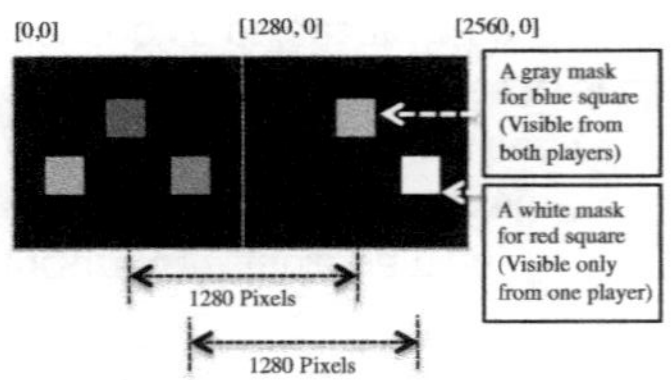

Figure 5: A window to show the red square only to one of the players, and green to the other player, and blue square to both of the players.

recognized as display 1, display 2, and display 3 respectively. Display 2 is placed at the right side of the display 1, and display 3 is set just right side of the display 2 in the multi-display setting. In Figure 4, we generate a window of 2560×1080, and place the left edge of the window to the left edge of display 2. The right side of the window matches with the right edge of display 3.

Software setting

The computer graphics to provide the player-dependent views is as follows. The setup shows the red square only to one of the players, and green to the other player. Both of the players can see the blue square.

We create three 200 pixels squares on display 2 for the LCD in the window between [0,0] and [1280,0] as shown in Figure 5. In addition, we create two 200 pixels squares on display 3 in the windows between [1280,0] and [2560,0]. The X value of the gray square is 1280 pixels right of the blue square, and the X value of the white square is 1280 pixels right of the red square. Both squares' Y values are the same as them. This setting matches the physical size and position of the white and gray square with the red square and blue square respectively as shown in Figure 6.

The mechanism to provide different images to players is shown in Figure 7. The pixels on the red square rotate the polarization angle by around $90°$ counterclockwise from the original angle. The pixels on the blue square rotate the polarization angle by around $45°$. By the rotation, the polarization angles on the red square become $-45°$, and those on the blue square become $0°$. For this reason, player 1 (polarizing angle $45°$) cannot see the red square, and player 2 (polarizing angle $-45°$) cannot see the green square.

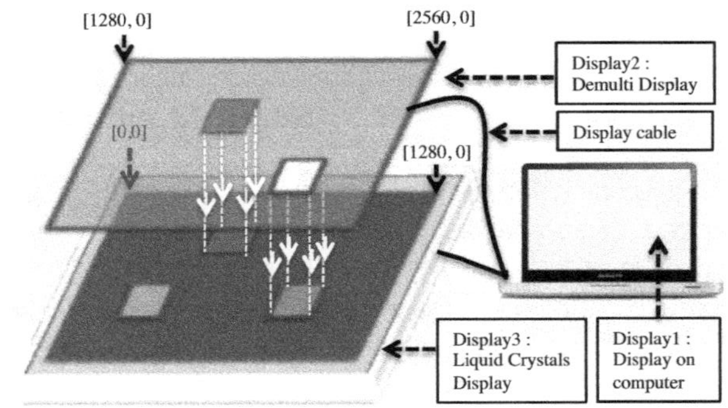

Figure 6: The resolution and size of the LCD are the same as the Demulti Display. The size and position of the white and gray squares physically match with the red square and blue square respectively.

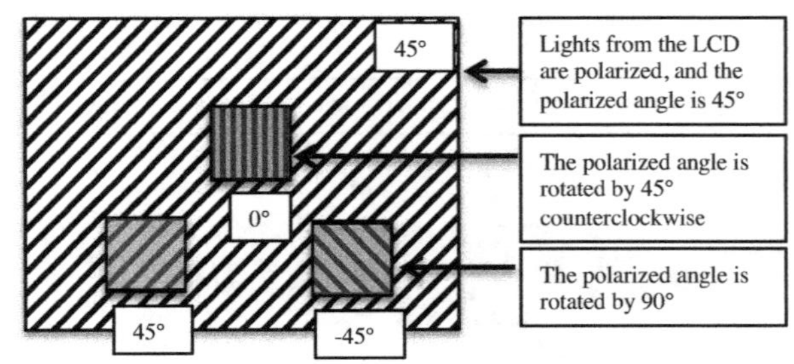

Figure 7: Polarization angles on the environment. The masks on Demulti Display rotate polarization angles. By the rotation, the polarization angles on the red square become $-45°$, and those on the blue square become $0°$.

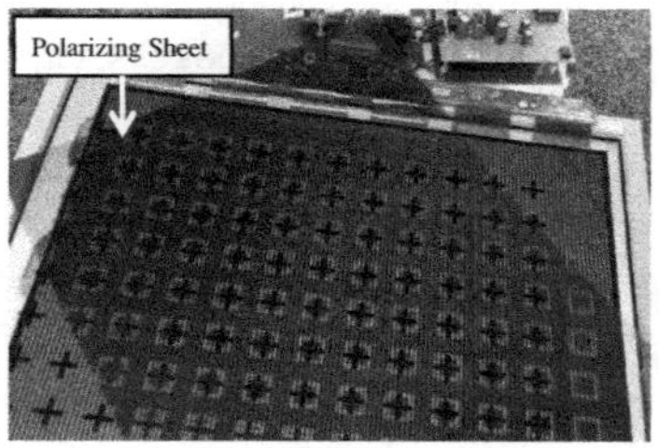

Figure 8: A calibration method for physically matching the sizes and intervals of masks on Demulti Display with the graphics on the LCD.

Calibration

The size of the computer graphics on the LCD must physically match with the masks on the Demulti Display. For calibration, the LCD displays fixed size crosses on the screen in the same intervals, and Demulti Display shows squares on the screen in the same way. By mounting a polarizing sheet, we can see both of the graphics on the LCD and the panel as shown in Figure 8. For matching the physical sizes of the graphics on the display and Demulti Display, users can expand and/or scale down the graphics by a simple GUI.

Application: Augmented Pong Game

We implemented an augmented pong game using the function to provide different images to each player. In the game, players control bars to bounce a ball to other side using paddles in the real world. A USB camera takes images of the fields around each paddle, and the system tracks the paddles using an image processing technology known as optical flow. In the gaming area, a box titled "Item" appears at a random place at random intervals. If the ball hits the box, the player gets one supporting item giving them an advantage in the game. We implemented two items from the "item" box as follows.

Small ghosts bouncing the ball: A number of ghosts appear in the gaming field. They are invisible for one of the players. They bounce the ball to the other direction when they hit the ball.

Big ghosts hiding the ball: A few ghosts appear in the filed. One of the players cannot see the ball while it is under one of the ghosts.

Since one of the players cannot see the ghost, he/she cannot predict the direction change of the ball in the game.

This function enhances the difficulty in the pong game only for one player. Moreover, the losing player gets stronger support than the winning player, such as bigger and more ghosts. Therefore, players would be able to enjoy the game independent of their skill even if there is a large skill gap between players. For a pilot study to validate the function, two players played the game. During the game, one of the players commented, "The bounce of the ball by a hidden goat is unexpected and difficult to receive." However, the other player mentioned, "I can slightly see the ghost, and can predict the bounce indeed." This contradiction is caused because the system still has a limitation that it can not completely hide the image for one of the players. We found the system can increase the difficulty only for a player, but more quantitative analyses are required to validate the concept [9, 2].

Limitations and Solution

The system uses linear polarization to separate images to each player. Because of this, the function is only available when players view the gaming field from fixed angles. For example, if player1 moves the head position or orientation, he/she can somewhat see the graphics for player 2 in the gaming field. Therefore, players cannot change their head positions. Another issue is that players can slightly see the graphics hidden even if the panel rotates the polarized angles by 90° counterclockwise from the original angle from a player.

Circular polarization instead of the linear polarization solves the first issue as follows: If we put a quarter-wave plate on the Demulti Display, the panel emits circular polarization. In this case, the players can wear 3D glasses using circular polarization, which are widely used for 3D movies. To let player 1 only see right or left handed circularly polarized lights, we can put a half-wave plate on one side of the

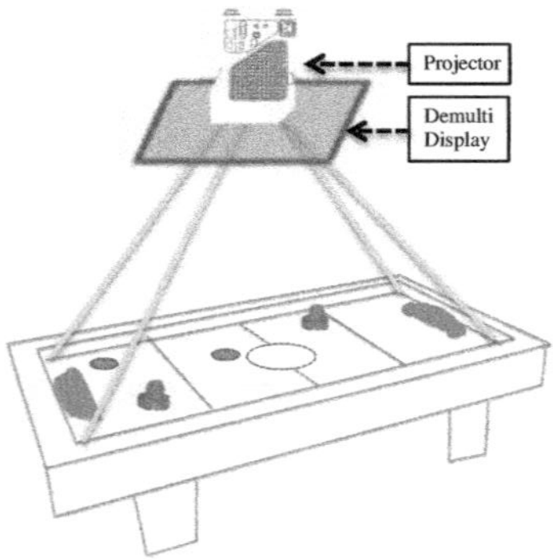

Figure 9: Augmented Air hockey using a projector with Demulti Display. The setup can hide the puck from one of the players by projecting exactly same color as the puck or by showing fake pucks in the field.

Figure 10: Board games enhancement. In the game, an experienced third person can help the less experienced player by showing secret messages or diagrams only visible from him/her in the gaming field.

glasses. To let player 2 only see the opposite rotation direction of circularly polarized lights, we can put a half-wave plate on the other side of the glasses. This plate reverses the rotation direction of the circular polarization. Therefore, the 3D glasses with a half-wave plate carry only left or right circularly polarized lights to player 1 or player 2 respectively. A characteristic of TN-type LCD causes the second issue. Using an IPS-type LCD as Demulti Display can solve the problem. Using a DLP-Link type of 3D projector is also an alternative; however, this requires customized active shutter glasses where each side can down the shutters at the same time. We can also use the projector for providing the augmented games for more than 2 players by combining it with our polarization-based technology.

Future Work

As the initial phase of the research, we used an LCD under the panel. Thus, the gaming field is quite small. However, the setup can use a projector for a larger gaming field. In this case, we can use the function works with tangibles such as Air Hockey and Table tennis. To make the setup general, we can make gaming API that directly controls the two monitors for game developers.

Air hockey

Figure 9 shows a future application on Air hockey using a projector with Demulti Display. For skill-gap mitigation, the environment can hide the puck from one of the players by projecting exactly same color as the puck to the gaming field, or projecting fake pucks which have the same color and the size randomly in the field. The system uses polarization. Since polarized lights become natural lights when reflected, we have to put a silver screen on the gaming field which can sustain the polarization property even after the reflection. We can also paint the gaming filed by a silver spray instead of having the screen.

Board games

The system can apply to board games. Figure 10 shows an example of a board game with Demulti Display. In the game, an experienced third person can help less experienced player in the game by writing a secret message only visible for him/her in the field. This function is useful when one of the players is new to the game, and he/she needs an experienced supporter. Previously, in this situation, the assistant needs to tell the advice aloud, but sometimes the other player can hear the message. This reduces the enjoyment in the game. However, Dumlti Display can avoid the situation since the adviser can just write messages and/or diagrams in the environment.

Conclusion

We have introduced the Demulti Display, a panel to configure a multiplayer table gaming environment. The game can provide appropriate difficulty to each player following the ability and/or the score of the player. Therefore, the environment would make games enjoyable even if there is a significant skill gap. We took a polarization-based approach to providing different images to each player. For the first trial of the research, we used a liquid crystal display to configure a table gaming field with the Demulti Display. We also implemented an augmented pong game to adjust the gaming difficulty for each player depending on the score. The setup can use a projector to provide a larger gaming space. Therefore, the system can be applied to sports and games using a 3D space such as Air Hockey and Table Tennis.

Acknowledgements

We thank all authors, and HongoTechGarage in the University of Tokyo for providing me the opportunity to work on this project.

REFERENCES

1. Kazuhisa uanaka Hisataka suziki, Akihiko shirai. 2016. Glassless Augmented Display for Public Signage. In *Proceedings of the 2016 Virtual Reality International Conference*. ACM, 23–25.
2. Robin Hunicke. 2005. The case for dynamic difficulty adjustment in games. In *Proceedings of the 2005 ACM SIGCHI International Conference on Advances in computer entertainment technology*. ACM, 429–433.
3. Osamu Izuta, Toshiki Sato, Sachiko Kodama, and Hideki Koike. 2010. Bouncing Star project: design and development of augmented sports application using a ball including electronic and wireless modules. In *Proceedings of the 1st Augmented Human International Conference*. ACM, 22.
4. Yasuaki Kakehi, Makoto Iida, Takeshi Naemura, Yoshinari Shirai, Mitsunori Matsushita, and Takeshi Ohguro. 2005. Lumisight table: An interactive view-dependent tabletop display. *IEEE Computer Graphics and Applications* 25, 1 (2005), 48–53.
5. Abhijit Karnik, Diego Martinez Plasencia, Walterio Mayol-Cuevas, and Sriram Subramanian. 2012. PiVOT: personalized view-overlays for tabletops. In *Proceedings of the 25th annual ACM symposium on User interface software and technology*. ACM, 271–280.
6. Diego Martinez Plasencia, Jarrod Knibbe, Andy D Haslam, Eddie James Latimer, Barnaby Dennis, Gareth J Lewis, Matthew Whiteley, and David Coyle. 2014. ReflectoSlates: personal overlays for tabletops combining camera-projector systems and retroreflective materials. In *CHI'14 Extended Abstracts on Human Factors in Computing Systems*. ACM, 2071–2076.
7. Kei Nitta, Keita Higuchi, and Jun Rekimoto. 2014. HoverBall: augmented sports with a flying ball. In *Proceedings of the 5th Augmented Human International Conference*. ACM, 13.
8. Hisataka Suzuki, Rex Hsieh, Ryotaro Tsuda, and Akihiko Shirai. 2015. ExPixel FPGA: multiplex hidden imagery for HDMI video sources. In *ACM SIGGRAPH 2015 Posters*. ACM, 71.
9. Penelope Sweetser and Peta Wyeth. 2005. GameFlow: a model for evaluating player enjoyment in games. *Computers in Entertainment (CIE)* 3, 3 (2005), 3–3.

Exploring a Modular Approach to Redesigning Interfaces for Physical Interactive Devices

Michael D. Jones
Casey Walker
Zann Anderson
Candice Lusk
Andrew Bryce
Brigham Young University
Provo, UT 84602 USA
mike.jones@byu.edu

Abstract

Tools for creating graphical user interfaces (GUIs) hide implementation details associated with changing the position, size or shape of a widget. For example, a GUI designer can change the position of a button without explicitly reimplementing the code that determines if the button has been clicked. We seek to provide a similar experience for moving tangible widgets on physical interactive devices (PIDs). One reason that GUI design tools can hide implementation details is that widgets are modules. In this work in progress, we describe a system for leveraging modularity to hide implementation details associated with changing the position, size and shape of widgets in PID interfaces. We have used the system to design, redesign and fabricate 10 interfaces for 3 example applications. Fundamentaly, working with atoms to make PID interfaces is different than working with pixels to make GUI interfaces–but modularity in PID widgets appears to be a promising way to hide implementation details in PID interface redesign and fabrication.

Author Keywords

tangible interaction; interface redesign; 3D printing

TEI 2017, March 20–23, 2017, Yokohama, Japan.
ACM ISBN 978-1-4503-4676-4/17/03.
http://dx.doi.org/10.1145/3024969.3025075

ACM Classification Keywords
H.5.2. [Information Interfaces and Presentation (e.g. HCI)]: Miscellaneous

Introduction
We address the problem of simplifying the redesign and fabrication of tangible widget positions, sizes and shapes for PIDs. This problem is important to designers who create functional prototypes of PIDs because simplifying the physical interface redesign process allows a designer to explore more interface variations in less time.

Other widget sets for PIDs have been proposed [10, 8, 6] but none of them simplify redesign. Prototyping methods for quickly iterating PID interface designs have also been proposed [3, 1] but lack fidelity in functionality, shape, and placement. Previous work utilizing modular GUI elements in PID design [2] utilized modularity in electronics design but did not explore modularity in widget repositining. We seek a process that has higher fidelity in physical interaction while retaining fluidity. Our work also diverges from previous work by focusing only on the placement of interactive elements into PIDs, rather than programming or coupling of sensors with custom hardware.

Designers of 2D GUIs have long had interface design tools that support rapid interface redesign. Widgets used in these tools are software objects that can be automatically re-instantiated with a new position, size or shape without rebuilding the entire interface.

The question that drives this work is: what is possible if one utilizes aspects of GUI design in PID design? Or, what can one learn from tools for redesigning GUIs to create better tools for redesigning PID interfaces?

In this work in progress, we consider modularity in widgets for PIDs. A key aspect of GUI widgets is that they are modular. Modularity simplifies design changes by reducing the impact of each individual change on the widget itself and on the interface as a whole. Changing one part of a widget, such as the color, does not change other parts, such as the code needed to handle an input event. Moreover, changes to one widget do not affect other widgets. In the context of PIDs, modularity might similarly contain changes to only those parts directly impacted by the change.

We have built a tool called Morphi for exploring modularity in the context of redesigning and re-fabricating PID interfaces. We asked 2 students to craft several interfaces for 3 devices with Morphi. In this small study, users were able to create and fabricate new interfaces without re-fabricating the entire device. Algorithms that support re-instantiating widgets correctly managed implementation details associated with the changes.

We will bring a total of 10 variations on interfaces to 3 different functional PIDs to the conference. These objects and interfaces are shown in Figures 2-7. Participants will be able to interact with the devices. We will switch interfaces to demonstrate the process.

Morphi
Morphi is a tool for iterating through tangible UI designs in a PID when the PID housing is a hollow shell that contains sensors on a prototyping board. Morphi contains three parts: reconfigurable widgets, automatic instantiation and removable panels.

Widgets are buttons, sliders and knobs that transfer motion from interactive surface elements to embedded sensors along an internal mechanism. The interactive surface element is the piece that the user sees, touches and moves to create input. Inside the PID, an embedded sensor converts that motion into an electrical signal. The internal mechanism transfers motion from the interactive surface element to the internal sensor. Internal mechanisms contain several moving parts. The geometry of these parts depends on relative positions of the surface elements and the embedded sensor.

A widget instantiation algorithm computes the geometry of the internal mechanism from the placement of the interactive surface element and the internal sensor. Generating the geometry of the internal mechanisms is tedious when done manually and needs to be precisely correct but the geometry is easy to compute algorithmically.

Removable panels are pieces of the PID housing that contain interactive surface elements. When the position, size, type or shape of an interactive surface element changes, the panels contain those changes to just a part of the housing so that only a few panels, rather than the entire housing, need to be re-printed.

To use Morphi, a designer marks interactive surface element locations on a 3D CAD model of the PID housing. Morphi places the interactive surface elements as marked and computes the internal mechanisms. The parts are 3D printed for assembly.

From the designer's perspective, the significance of this process is that Morphi abstracts the internal mechanisms allowing the designer to focus on form and aesthetic. This simplifies placement and re-positioning of widgets–making it more like placement and repositioning of widgets in GUIs.

The novelty of Morphi is that it decouples interactive surface elements from the embedded electronics. This means that the UI can be modified without modifying the embedded electronics. The contribution of Morphi is that it is a step toward a tangible UI design process that has the flexibility of a graphical UI design process.

Widgets

Each widget in Morphi is split into three modules. This allows the widgets to be customized such that two of the modules can be easily changed.

The modules in a widget are tangible interactive surfaces, internal mechanisms, and embedded electronics. The tangible interactive surface element is the part the user sees, touches, and interacts with. The internal mechanism transfers user generated motion from the tangible interactive surface element to the embedded electronics. The embedded electronics are off-the-shelf components that convert motion into a signal which is processed by a computer program. Embedded electronics are connected and placed on a breadboard inside the device housing.

The designer changes the position, size and shape of the tangible interactive surface elements and Morphi's instantiation algorithm computes the internal mechanisms needed to connect the surface elements to the electronics. This is similar to hiding implementation details in GUI interface redesign.

Figure 1 shows the modular button, knob, and slider widget designs(starting from left to right). The

Figure 1: Modular button, knob and slider widgets for use in PIDs. Widgets are shown in blue connected black hexagon-shaped housing panels and silver electronic components. Widgets can be automatically instantiated to fit different placements on the housing surface.

elements of widgets are each rendered in shades of blue with the housing panel shown in black. The electronic components are silver or gray. The interactive surface element for the button, shown on the left, is the blue hemisphere above the black housing panel. Interactive surface elements for the knob and slider are obscured by the housing panel. The long blue vertical shafts in each widget are the internal mechanisms and the silver components (mostly obscured for the button, but visible) at the bottom of each widget are the electronic components.

A button consists of a detachable cap, a friction-fit collar, a rod with a ball joint on one end, and a bracket. The user creates motion by pressing on the detachable cap. The motion is transferred through the rod to the ball joint. The bracket attaches the ball joint to an electronic button, on which the ball sits. The electronic button is pressed when the ball moves.

The detachable cap is the interactive surface element for the button widget. Morphi generates the collar, rod and ball joint, and bracket based on the position of the cap.

The knob consists of a detachable dial and a flexible rod with rigid ends as shown in the center of Figure 1. The user twists the dial and the flexible rod transfers that rotation to a potentiometer knob. Morphi determines the length and curvature of the rod based on the positions of the dial and the electronics.

The rod transfers torque while remaining flexible. The rod consists of a flexible inner core surrounded by two helices. The helices are made from rigid material and are joined by small rigid rods that pass straight through the center of the core. The flexible core, helices, and connecting rods are printed as a single unit.

The slider consists of a detachable handle and three joints: a ball joint near the handle, a prismatic joint along the shaft, and a knuckle joint as shown on the right side of Figure 1. The user moves the handle to create linear motion on the housing surface. The joints translate the linear motion of the handle into rotational motion of the potentiometer knob. Software translates knob rotation back into linear motion to match the motion of the slider.

Given the position of the handle on the surface and the length and orientation of the track, Morphi computes the length range of the prismatic joint and adds the joints necessary to connect the prismatic joint to the handle and the knob.

As the handle moves along the surface, the distance and angle between the handle and the knob change. A

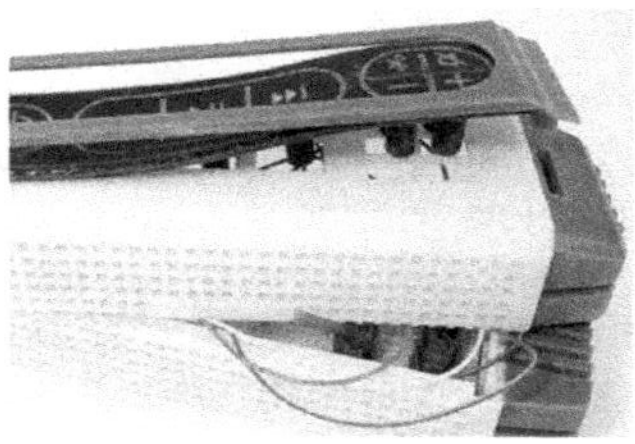

Figure 2: Partially disassembled speaker (see also Figure 4) which contains a faceplate printed in a flexibible black material.

Figure 3: An alarm clock (see Figure 5) design showing internal mechanisms, printed in blue and black, that connect interactive surface elements to electronics. The removed facet contains a knob that was connected to the flexible blue rod right of center.

ball joint under the housing panel allows a member of the prismatic joint to pivot relative to the slider handle. At the other end, a knuckle joint attaches the lower end of the prismatic joint to a shackle.

Instantiating Widgets

Given the locations of widget interactive surface elements on the housing surface, the instantiation algorithm computes the internal mechanisms needed to connect the interactive surface elements to the electronics, and cuts holes in the housing to allow mechanisms to pass through the housing.

If the mechanisms for two or more widgets collide inside the housing, the algorithm detects and reports, but does not resolve, the collision. Collisions between internal mechanisms are an example of how building PID interfaces with atoms is different than building GUI interfaces with pixels.

Connecting mechanisms are not printed in place and require assembly. To aid in assembly, the algorithm adds raised 3D printed labels to the different mechanisms and then generates a text document pairing each widget with the right labeled mechanisms.

Panels

Unlike moving GUI widgets on a 2D screen, which requires only recoloring pixels, moving widgets on a PID involves moving atoms. Placing widgets in panels contains the widgets in different modules, which reduces the amount of housing that needs to be reprinted when a widget is changed.

It is up to the designer to split the housing into panels based on their plans for the interface. As a starting

Figure 4: Three versions of an interface for a Bluetooth speaker realized using the faceplate panel strategy.

Figure 5: An alarm clock with a sports ball theme. The designer placed interactive surface elements in interchangeable panels which facilities rapid exploration of interface layouts.

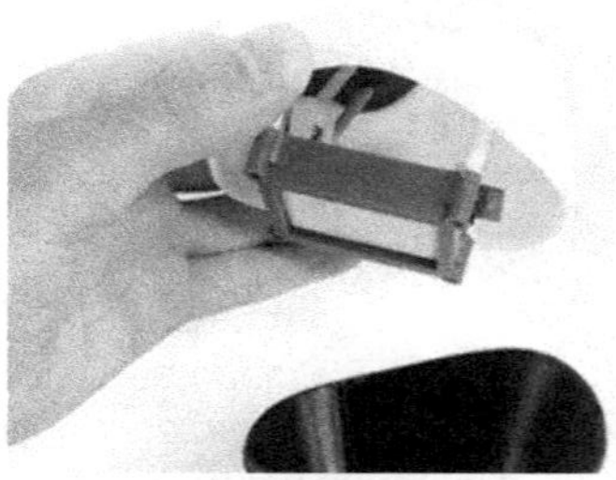

Figure 6: The self-contained interface panel used in the shifter (see Figure 7). The blue frame holds the circuitry and the grey rods left of center are part of the mechanism that connects the interactive surface elements to the electronics.

point, we explored three strategies for creating these panels: face-plates, facets, and self-contained.

A faceplate panel contains all of the widgets for the interface in one piece. Facet panels partition the interface surface area into different panels that can be replaced individually. The self-contained approach places the interface and the electronics into a single removable component which is replaced when the interface changes. Each kind of panel is represented in one of the three example applications described next.

Example Applications

Two undergraduate design students used Morphi to construct three iterations of interfaces for each of two PIDs and four interfaces for a third device. In some cases, electronics had to be moved in order to avoid internal mechanism collisions. The example applications were a bluetooth speaker, an alarm clock, and a volume controller mounted on a car gear shifter.

Parts for the examples were printed using a Stratasys Objet260 Connex3 multi-material 3D printer and programmed using a RedBearLab Blend Micro Arduino processor connected via Bluetooth to a desktop PC. Morphi was implemented using the Rhinoceros 5 C# developer tools.

The Bluetooth radio, shown in Figures 4 and 2, is an example of the faceplate panel strategy. The alarm clock uses the facet panel strategy and is shown in Figures 3 and 5. Finally, the volume controller for a car radio uses the self-contained approach to modularizing components and is shown in Figures 7 and 6.

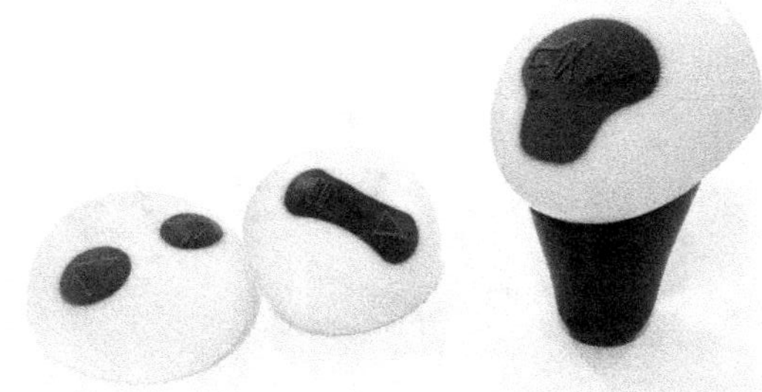

Figure 7: A music controller intended to be mounted on a gear shifter in a car with a manual transmission with two variations on the inteface included on the left.

Discussion

We have built Morphi to explore modularity for reducing the effort needed to change the position, size or shape of a PID widget. Much work remains to make moving a widget in a PID as easy as moving a button in a GUI.

We have assumed that a 3D printed object can be modified only by printing and using new pieces. Recent work in reshaping 3D printed objects by removing and adding material [5, 9] may eventually support reshaping interactive surface elements and PID housings.

Also, we have not explored how the modular process in Morphi can be integrated with a physically-based sculpting process. For example, it may make sense to sculpt the PID housing as in [4, 7] but to place the widgets in Morphi. In this process, a designer can explore functional versions of several interface layouts defined in software.

Acknowledgements

This work is funded by NSF Grant IIS-1406578.

References

[1] Avrahami, D., and Hudson, S. E. Forming interactivity: A tool for rapid prototyping of physical interactive products. In *Proceedings of the 4th Conference on Designing Interactive Systems: Processes, Practices, Methods, and Techniques*, DIS '02, ACM (New York, NY, USA, 2002), 141–146.

[2] Greenberg, S., and Fitchett, C. Phidgets: Easy development of physical interfaces through physical widgets. In *Proceedings of the 14th Annual ACM Symposium on User Interface Software and Technology*, UIST '01, ACM (New York, NY, USA, 2001), 209–218.

[3] Hudson, S. E., and Mankoff, J. Rapid construction of functioning physical interfaces from cardboard, thumbtacks, tin foil and masking tape. In *Proceedings of the 19th Annual ACM Symposium on User Interface Software and Technology*, UIST '06, ACM (New York, NY, USA, 2006), 289–298.

[4] Jones, M. D., Seppi, K., and Olsen, D. R. What you sculpt is what you get: Modeling physical interactive devices with clay and 3d printed widgets. In *Proceedings of the 2016 CHI Conference on Human Factors in Computing Systems*, CHI '16, ACM (New York, NY, USA, 2016), 876–886.

[5] Peng, H., Wu, R., Marschner, S., and Guimbretière, F. On-the-fly print: Incremental printing while modelling. In *Proceedings of the 2016 CHI Conference on Human Factors in Computing Systems*, CHI '16, ACM (New York, NY, USA, 2016), 887–896.

[6] Savage, V., Chang, C., and Hartmann, B. Sauron: Embedded single-camera sensing of printed physical user interfaces. In *Proceedings of the 26th Annual ACM Symposium on User Interface Software and Technology*, UIST '13, ACM (New York, NY, USA, 2013), 447–456.

[7] Savage, V., Follmer, S., Li, J., and Hartmann, B. Makers' marks: Physical markup for designing and fabricating functional objects. In *Proceedings of the 28th Annual ACM Symposium on User Interface Software & Technology*, ACM (2015), 103–108.

[8] Savage, V., Head, A., Hartmann, B., Goldman, D. B., Mysore, G., and Li, W. Lamello: Passive acoustic sensing for tangible input components. In *Proceedings of the 33rd Annual ACM Conference on Human Factors in Computing Systems*, CHI '15, ACM (New York, NY, USA, 2015), 1277–1280.

[9] Teibrich, A., Mueller, S., Guimbretière, F., Kovacs, R., Neubert, S., and Baudisch, P. Patching physical objects. In *Proceedings of the 28th Annual ACM Symposium on User Interface Software & Technology*, UIST '15, ACM (New York, NY, USA, 2015), 83–91.

[10] Vázquez, M., Brockmeyer, E., Desai, R., Harrison, C., and Hudson, S. E. 3d printing pneumatic device controls with variable activation force capabilities. In *Proceedings of the 33rd Annual ACM Conference on Human Factors in Computing Systems*, CHI '15, ACM (New York, NY, USA, 2015), 1295–1304.

Tangible Audio Game Development Kit: Prototyping Audio Games with a Tangible Editor

Michael Urbanek
TU Wien
Institute for Design &
Assessment of Technology
Vienna, A-1040, Austria
michael.urbanek@tuwien.ac.at

Florian Güldenpfennig
TU Wien
Institute for Design &
Assessment of Technology
Vienna, A-1040, Austria
florian.gueldenpfennig@tuwien.ac.at

TEI 2017, March 20–23, 2017, Yokohama, Japan.
ACM ISBN 978-1-4503-4676-4/17/03.
http://dx.doi.org/10.1145/3024969.3025077

Abstract
Audio games are a genre of computer games that waive visual output and solely rely on audio. The majority of audio games (as well as video games) lack publicly available editors that allow the creation of new games or maps within the framework of the respective game. Additionally, no existing game or map editors make use of tangible interaction to facilitate embodied interaction during the creation of games. However, many elements in audio games can be mapped in a profitable way to a tangible editor. We therefore propose the Tangible Audio Game Development Kit that allows fast, iterative and collaborative audio game prototyping by combining physical objects. In this paper, we introduce a first prototype of this concept and present a user study featuring three game design experts. We discuss the results and explain the next steps in advancing the audio game editor based on the feedback.

Author Keywords
Audio Games; Tangible User Interface; Game Editor; Prototyping.

ACM Classification Keywords
H.5.2 [Information interfaces and presentation (e.g., HCI)]: User Interfaces.

For a video demo please visit https://youtu.be/FoKslGo32xo, last accessed on Dec. 22, 2016.

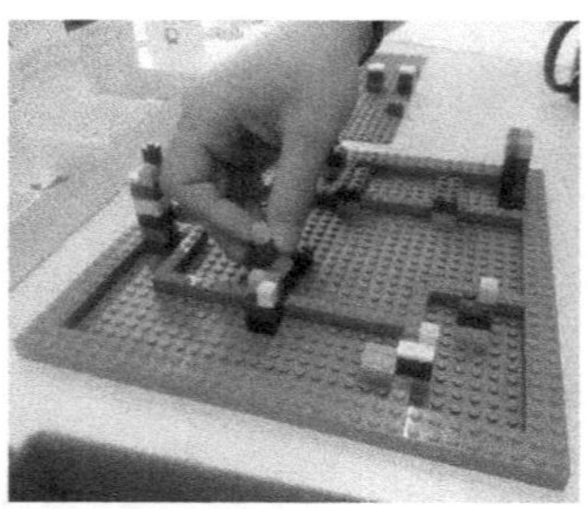

Figure 1: One of the experts (participant 2) playing the pre-built game. The expert explained the game while he played through it by moving his avatar. In this picture, he removed a destroyed obstacle.

Introduction & Related Work

Over the last decades, the video games industry has turned into a multi-billion Dollar business. While many of the current games rely on bespoke computer graphics, other productions achieved major successes by focusing on excellent game play or game narrative (e.g., Minecraft, which implemented few graphical features as a deliberate design decision). Besides the mainstream video games, there is a small but active niche-community, which waives visual output completely: audio games. The audio gamer does not want or is not able to rely on visual feedback (e.g. visually impaired people) and therefore solely relies on audio. Generally, such games are developed by people without visual impairments for people without (full) vision. However, as the positive response to the commercial iOS audio game series Papa Sangre [1] shows, a great number of people with normal vision enjoys audio games as well. Such audio games can be played in front of a computer [7], on a mobile phone [1], employing in- or out-door user tracking [5, 10] or with an extra utility (controller) [3]. Usually, these games are first person-centered experiences using spatialized 3D sound that allows sound localization, creating a space that can be explored through audio. For better localization and immersion, headphones are recommended. In audio games, every object that does not emit or reflect sound is "inaudible and not perceivable" [6]. In analogy to video games, such inaudible objects would be invisible.

Creating games: Few video games (e.g. Warcraft III, 2002) provide a map editor in addition to the base game that enable game designers, prosumers (e.g. modders) or casual players to extend the original game. The arrangement of objects (by dragging/dropping of, e.g., characters, walls or trees) with the editor specifies the look and setup of the resulting new level. Hence, the editor including objects can be considered an editable representation of the game itself.

In addition to placing objects, some editors support the users in scripting for introducing logic to the game and therefore in creating their own game mechanics. Usually, game editors run on a computer and are operated by classic I/O interfaces only (e.g. keyboard, mouse). This year, a tangible video game creation kit named Boxels (http://www.bloxelsbuilder.com/, last accessed on December 22, 2016) was introduced to the market, which makes use of a tablet app to take pictures of physical blocks in different colors. These images are then translated into game levels to create 2D video games. Hence, Bloxels constitutes a commercial tangible editor for designing, for example, 2D Jump'n'Run games.

We argue that the concept of a tangible editor is also very appropriate for audio games for two reasons. Firstly, due to the nature of audio games (no graphics, less complexity, focus on strong narrative) they constitute a promising candidate for being shaped by tangibles rather than by a software editor. Secondly, using a tangible editor, audio games can be (co-)designed by people with impaired vision by grasping the different objects.

The use of tangibles as well as the combination of them was utilized before in the area of sound design. AudioCubes [8] is a tangible user interface that consists of several cubes that produce and modify sound depending on the spatial relation of the cubes. Another example is the tabletop user interface Reactable [2] that also uses physical artifacts to generate and modify sound. Here, every artifact (cube) also has its own function. The tangible sequencer presented in [4] also enables sound manipulation by incorporating the combination of physical artifacts. The mapping of physical artifacts as utilized in AudioCubes, Reactable or Block Jam has not been employed yet to create a tangible editor for audio games and will act as the primary concept of the Tangible Audio Game Development Kit (TAGDK). TAGDK as proposed in this paper is a mixed spatial relational system that draws on well established tangible interaction principles as proposed by Ullmer and Iishi [9] (physical representation at this prototyping stage: Lego; digital representation: Unity3D).

We therefore propose the concept and first prototype implementation of the TAGDK that allows audio game prototyping by placing and combining tangible artifacts that provide a physical representation of game objects. We introduce TAGDK and test a first implementation with three game design experts (Figure 1 shows one expert interacting with it). Our primary motivation in this paper is to find out if the concept is feasible and to gain further inspiration. We report this feedback and explain how we will use it to advance the TAGDK. In future design iterations we will refine the concept as well as implement a tracking device to remove the *Wizard-of-Oz* component (see User Study section) in this paper (e.g., see Figure 6).

Figure 2: The TAGDK elements represented by respective LEGO bricks. Currently, the editor supports 13 different elements from three different categories (*Objects*, *Properties*, *Links*). From back to front: The TAGDK Objects (Avatar, Obstacle, Soundsource, Item, Character, Portal), the TAGDK Properties (Message, Direction, Destructible, Harmful, Move, Win Condition) and TAGDK Links.

TAGDK: Tangible Audio Game Development Kit

The TAGDK allows audio game prototyping by placing and combining haptic artifacts. The motivation of this framework is that even people with little training can intuitively pick TAGDK artifacts, place them on a table, hence, prototype the audio game, "sit back", and play the game immediately without knowledge of software programming. Due to this agility, the TAGDK can be used to iteratively prototype audio game concepts including rapid revisions (see Figure 4 for an illustration). It can also be used to build audio games collaboratively (e.g. by sharing one kit on one table). The main target group is people who are interested in audio game design (beginners and experts) with or without normal vision.

Element	Description
Avatar (O)	First-person avatar controlled by the player.
Obstacle (O)	Insurmountable object.
Soundsource (O)	Continuous source of sound within the game scene.
Item (O)	Item a player can interact with.
Character (O)	In-game character that is not controlled by the player.
Portal (O)	Player is teleported to associated other Portal element (logically connected with Link element).
Message (P)	Text-to-speech message.
Move (P)	Makes an object movable.
Direction (P)	Determines the direction of an element (e.g. move-axis).
Destructible (P)	Property of an object that flags it as destroyable.
Harmful (P)	Property of an object that flags it as emitting damage.
Win Condition (P)	Property of an object that ends the game if reached.
Link (L)	Logically links two or more objects together.

Table 1: Elements of the TAGDK editor represented by LEGO bricks. Currently 13 elements in three categories (O...*Object*, P...*Property*, L...*Link*) are supported. Elements can be combined to accomplish different responses or outcomes. Note Table 2 for further explanations regarding the combinations of the elements.

In TAGDK, every artifact has a defined function that can be combined with other artifacts. In the following, we will call them the TAGDK elements. In a combination of multiple el-

Figure 3: Representation of an "enemy" using LEGO bricks. From bottom to top: A Character object (green) that is also an Obstacle (red, so the enemy is not a "ghost") with a Soundsource (blue) that has an Item (yellow) and is Movable (brown). The enemy is Destructible (orange) and Harmful (red), logically Linked (black) with something else and moves in the given Direction (white arrow).

ements, the order is without relevance. In the TAGDK prototype as proposed and tested in this paper (Figure 2), three different categories of elements are introduced: *Objects*, *Properties* and *Links* (see Table 1 for a detailed description). *Objects* include game elements like Avatars, Obstacles, Soundsources, Items, Characters and Portals, which are typically found across different game genres. They also define the main actors or characters of the prospective audio game prototype, similar to the interactable objects (obstacles, portals, interactables) as proposed by Röber and Masuch [6]. *Properties* modify (combined) objects without adding additional complexity. Properties are Message, Move, Direction, Destructible, Harmful and Win Condition. *Links* are used to logically link two or more objects together. The combination space of the TAGDK elements is defined in a 2-dimensional matrix (see Table 2 for an excerpt).

User Study

The aim of the initial study in this paper is to get feedback from game design experts about the TAGDK. This information will be used to define the design of a tracking device (currently implemented by a *Wizard-of-Oz* component as described below), and to make sure that the proposed game elements are useful, powerful whilst not too complex (are the functions "atomic"?), and clear (are the virtual functions understandable?).

Experimental prototype: In the current prototype, we opted for using LEGO bricks as they can be combined and disassembled easily, and more importantly, they were suitable for mapping the required functions of the TAGDK. LEGO bricks are stackable and distinguishable in terms of form, size and color. Every LEGO brick used in this game-expert study constitutes a physical representation of one of the TAGDK elements (cf. also description above): *Objects* are represented by 2x2 sized LEGO bricks, *Properties* by 1x1

Figure 4: The concept of the TAGDK framework illustrated. An audio game designer playing their prototype immediately after placing the artifacts on the table. Every combination of artifacts results in a game object (enemies, items, ...). User input is entered with a wireless controller. User or game feedback is audio only through headphones.

sized blocks (except, the direction element is represented as 3D-printed 1x2 LEGO compatible arrow) and *Links* as 1x1 blocks (see Figure 2). In combination, these LEGO bricks form game objects in an audio game built with the TAGDK. One of the exemplary game objects could be an "enemy" as shown in Figure 3. Note, in the current prototype, the LEGO game map is rendered into a playable audio game by a *Wizard-of-Oz* or researcher, who observes the participant and then uses a Unity3D application that we have created as a tool for editing the respective audio game.

Study setup: We tested our TAGDK concept with three game design experts (more than a decade of professional experience each; recruited through the university network) using individual semi-structured interviews and hands-on

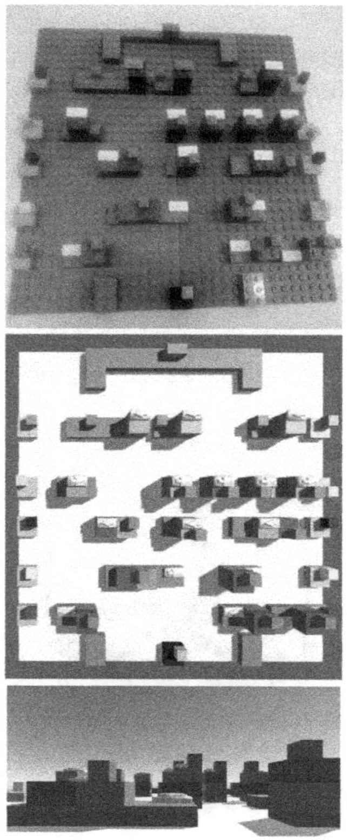

Figure 5: A Frogger game built with the TAGDK framework. The first image illustrates the Frogger game built with LEGO bricks by the expert (participant 3). The second image shows the top view of the game, rendered in Unity3D. In the third image, the first-person view of the avatar is shown. This visual output is for debug purposes only and not for the end-user, because audio games waive visuals completely.

	(A)vatar	(O)bstacle	(S)oundsource	(I)tem	(C)haracter	(P)ortal
(A)vatar			Sound while moving	Items to start with		
(O)bstacle			Sound when colliding	Drops when destructed (D)	Character perceptible	
(S)oundsource	Sound while moving	Sound when colliding		Item audible	Character audible	Portal audible
(I)tem	Items to start with	Drops when destructed (D)	Item audible		Drops when destructed (D) or at collision (M)	
(C)haracter		Character perceptible	Character audible	Drops when destructed (D) or at collision (M)		
(P)ortal			Portal audible			

Table 2: An excerpt of the combination possibilities of *Object* elements in the TAGDK framework. A combination of an object with the same object is not supported. The order of combination is without relevance. LEGO brick images taken from https://shop.lego.com/en-US/Pick-a-Brick, last accessed on December 22, 2016.

sessions with the TAGDK prototype. All sessions (lasting 60-90 minutes) were video-recorded for later qualitative thematic analysis (exploratory and inductive coding). During each semi-structured interview, the experts were asked for their critical opinion about the TAGDK and its applicability as an (audio) game editor. The subsequent hands-on sessions were split into two parts. Firstly, the experts were invited to build their own audio game using the TAGDK LEGO prototype. Secondly, a pre-built TAGDK audio game was shown to the experts. The experts then explored this third-party game and explained how they played it. Figure 1 shows one expert while playing the pre-built game.

First Results & Outlook

The expert interviews provided encouraging feedback on the concept of the TAGDK. All experts understood it with little training time (5-10 minutes) and thought that tangibility might be a promising concept for (audio) game editors due to the extended embodied experience it introduced to the conventionally *flat* software design activity of editing.

"It's a nice tool to test game elements physically. It's much better than describing ideas verbally," participant 1 said. All participants were able to build audio games and explain the pre-built level. Two of the three experts created a Frogger game in which a player had to cross a street without getting hit by an obstacle. The expert's LEGO prototype, the rebuilt Unity3D prototype and the avatar's first person view in Unity3D is shown in Figure 5. Besides approval, the experts also provided valuable feedback for improving the next iteration of the TAGDK.

First of all, the experts commented on the delay between LEGO prototyping and having the playable prototype available due to the *Wizard-of-Oz* component (rendering the game by hand in Unity3D). This critique was anticipated by the authors and the next major effort will be to develop the tracking device as outlined in Figure 6. In this paper, however, we omitted this implementation effort for a hi-fi prototype, as we wanted to obtain the experts' opinion before this

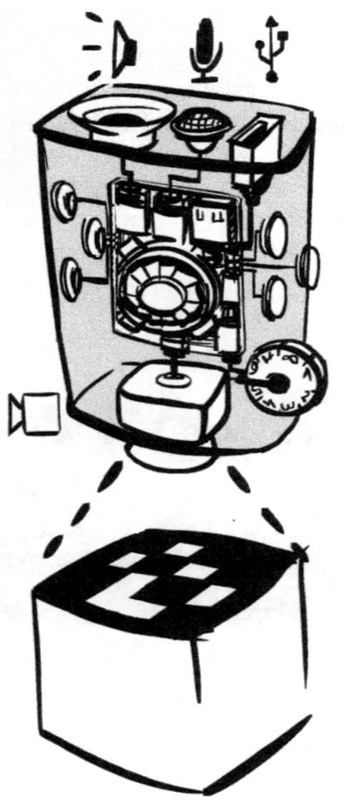

Figure 6: Draft of a tangible programmer element for TAGDK (a handheld device with tactile buttons; standalone with no extra PC, etc.). A camera at the bottom identifies game objects with markers. Photographed TAGDK elements then get labeled as different game elements using buttons (instead of different LEGO bricks, it employs different buttons on the device). An integrated speaker provides auditive feedback, a microphone can be used for sound recording (e.g., audio messages for the later game). Additional game sound files can be uploaded through USB.

investment. Their feedback will be considered in the design of this device/hi-fi prototype.

The game design experts thought it might be useful that in a future implementation, individual TAGDK elements should be linkable on an individual basis (i.e., they demanded some extensions of the combination matrix in Table 2). As a specific example, participant 1 wanted to create an object that had to be destroyed to win the game by combining the Win Condition with the Destructible property.

One issue raised by participant 1 and 3 was a missing option for creating templates. In the example of Frogger given above, templates could have been used for the cars without building every car from scratch again. Therefore, the option to create templates will be considered in the next iteration.

In addition, the experts requested more scripting support similar to conventional computer programming (e.g. conditions, or randomization). Still, it was advised to create this function without adding too much complexity.

We also identified issues with using LEGO bricks. The combination of elements led to larger chunks that were not instantly clear with regard to the resulting behavior. The preliminary results showed that the "mental mapping" of the color to its respective function demanded too much time from the designers. Most importantly, we do not want to constrain the concept and its accessibility by relying on color coded bricks, since one important target group of our tangible audio games editor might be visually impaired people. Thus, for the final tangible prototype, LEGO will not be used.

Outlook: The next design iteration of this framework will include a tangible prototype, drawing on the expert's feedback about the concept prototype in this paper. We have started experimenting with embedded ODROID computers to build a tangible editor in the shape of a handheld device with tactile buttons (see Figure 6 for description). Game objects will be represented by physical cubes (or other shapes that clearly tell the designer about the respective function) with optical markers. Their properties will be specified by the TAGDK programmer (handheld device) using buttons and other tactile controls. A picture of the whole game area through the built-in camera sets the game objects in relation, providing information about the objects in virtual space. Hence, the handheld and its built-in camera is used to label individual objects (assign functions) as well as to capture the whole map (relations of the objects to each other). With this device we will then conduct further studies with game designers, and we will also use it to evaluate if tangible editors are appropriate for blind designers to create audio games.

We hope that the TAGDK framework raises additional awareness about audio games and encourages more researchers to include non-visual games into their studies.

Acknowledgments

We would like to thank *Peter Fikar* for creating the illustrations in Figure 4 and Figure 6. His efforts are highly appreciated.

REFERENCES

1. Somethin' else. 2010. Papa Sangre. (2010). Retrieved October 24, 2016 from *https://itunes.apple.com/en/app/papa-sangre/id407536885?mt=8*.
2. Martin Kaltenbrunner, Sergi Jorda, Gunter Geiger, and Marcos Alonso. 2006. The reacTable*: A Collaborative Musical Instrument. In *15th IEEE International*

Workshops on Enabling Technologies: Infrastructure for Collaborative Enterprises. IEEE, 406–411.

3. Philip Mendels and Joep Frens. 2008. The Audio Adventurer: Design of a Portable Audio Adventure Game. In *Fun and Games*. Springer, 46–58.
4. Henry Newton-Dunn, Hiroaki Nakano, and James Gibson. 2003. Block Jam: A Tangible Interface for Interactive Music. In *Proceedings of the 2003 Conference on New Interfaces for Musical Expression*. National University of Singapore, 170–177.
5. Iana Podkosova, Michael Urbanek, and Hannes Kaufmann. 2016. A Hybrid Sound Model for 3D Audio Games with Real Walking. In *Proceedings of the 29th International Conference on Computer Animation and Social Agents*. ACM, 189–192.
6. Niklas Röber and Maic Masuch. 2004. Interacting With Sound: An Interaction Paradigm for Virtual Auditory Worlds. In *Proceedings of the 10th International Conference on Auditory Display*.
7. Jaime Sánchez and Mauricio Lumbreras. 1999. Virtual Environment Interaction Through 3D Audio by Blind Children. *CyberPsychology & Behavior* 2, 2 (1999), 101–111.
8. Bert Schiettecatte and Jean Vanderdonckt. 2008. AudioCubes: a Distributed Cube Tangible Interface based on Interaction Range for Sound Design. In *Proceedings of the 2nd International Conference on Tangible and Embedded Interaction*. ACM, 3–10.
9. Brygg Ullmer and Hiroshi Ishii. 2000. Emerging Frameworks for Tangible User Interfaces. *IBM systems journal* 39, 3.4 (2000), 915–931.
10. Eric Velleman, Richard van Tol, Sander Huiberts, and Hugo Verwey. 2004. 3D Shooting Games, Multimodal Games, Sound Games and More Working Examples of the Future of Games for the Blind. In *International Conference on Computers for Handicapped Persons*. Springer, 257–263.

Extending the Design Space of Tangible Objects via Low-Resolution Edge Displays

Ahmed Sabbir Arif[1], **Brien East**[1], **Sean DeLong**[1], **Roozbeh Manshaei**[1], **Apurva Gupta**[2], **Manasvi Lalwani**[2], **Ali Mazalek**[1,2]

Synaesthetic Media Laboratory
[1]Ryerson University
Toronto, Ontario, Canada
a.s.arif@gmail.com, {beast, sean.delong, roozbeh.manshaei}@ryerson.ca

[2]Georgia Institute of Technology
Atlanta, Georgia, USA
{apurva.gupta, manasvi.lalwani, mazalek}@gatech.edu

TEI '17, March 20-23, 2017, Yokohama, Japan
ACM 978-1-4503-4676-4/17/03.
http://dx.doi.org/10.1145/3024969.3025078

Abstract
We developed a custom tangible that uses LED arrays around the edges as a low-resolution display to provide real-time visual feedback on the current state of the system. We developed a guideline for mapping different types of edge feedback to different tangible interactions. We evaluated its effectiveness in an informal user study where users interacted with a tabletop and tangible system with the edge feedback enabled. Results suggest that edge feedback provides a better understanding of the system.

Author Keywords
LEDs; point lights; active/passive tangibles; feedback.

ACM Classification Keywords
H.5.m. Information interfaces and presentation (e.g., HCI): Miscellaneous.

Introduction
Brygg et al. [26] defined tangibles, also known as tokens, as *"discrete, spatially reconfigurable physical objects that typically represent digital information"*. A tangible could be either passive or active. Passive tangibles employ a one-way communication model, typically from the tangibles to other interactive devices, hence cannot reflect changes in the digital model. Active tangibles, on the other hand, maintain a two-

Figure 1. An active tangible augmented with low-resolution edge display (i.e., LED array).

way communication between the tangibles and other devices, therefore can reflect changes in the digital model. Passive or active tangibles, together with other interactive devices, form a tangible user interface [26].

Feedback is an important part of interactive systems. It communicates the results of an interaction, making it visible and understandable. Feedback answers questions across four categories, specifically the user's *location* on a chain of tasks, *current state* of the system, *future state* of the system, and the *outcome* of an action [19]. Feedback not only informs users of whether they are moving closer to accomplishing a task or not but also when errors occur and how to address them.

Prior studies showed that feedback can provide users with a better understanding of the system, facilitating a swift transition from novice to expert [14]. Yet most current tangibles are passive and do not provide any feedback on tangible interactions [22]. They usually rely on an additional device to provide feedback (i.e., an interactive tabletop), confining the interaction space within the proximity of that device. Some tangibles provide visual feedback on the display, when available, i.e., notification window, but this feedback often occludes the information on the screen. It also typically requires a user action upon receipt (i.e., a tap to discard a notification window) affecting the natural flow of the task at hand [2]. In this paper, we propose augmenting tangibles with a low-resolution edge display (Figure 1) to provide real-time visual feedback on user interactions and the current state of the system.

The remainder of the paper is organized as follows. We start with a literature review of existing work exploring non-graphical displays for visual feedback. We then discuss the motivation of the work, and propose a guideline for mapping different types of edge feedback to different tangible interactions. We then apply it to an existing tabletop and tangible system to demonstrate its effectiveness. We evaluate the system in an informal investigation. Finally, we conclude with speculation on future extensions to the work.

Related Work

Harrison et al. [10] explored the types of information conveyed by a single-color point light in current devices, and investigated whether their design space could be enriched by using varying light intensity over time. They identified twenty-four different light behaviors, and based on an evaluation, recommended eight of them to use in a mobile device domain (e.g., different beacon, flash, brightness, pulse, and blinking behaviors). Xu and Lyons [30] developed two smartwatch prototypes to demonstrate that low-resolution edge feedback could offer smart capabilities. The first prototype was augmented with four LEDs in the four directions and the second was augmented with twelve LEDs arranged corresponding to the hours on a watch face. Both used different colors, brightness, and blinking patterns to provide users with feedback on different smartwatch apps and their respective parameters.

Kanis et al. [12] augmented a bracelet with a 5×5 LED array that automatically exchanged information between users when they shook hands. It created a cycling animation on each successful data transfer episode. Similarly, Williams et al. [28] designed a digital bracelet for remote text messaging. It included six studs in a row, each containing four LEDs in red, blue, green, and white. Five of the studs represented individuals and one represented whole-group activity. It used a pulsing white LED to indicate that a message is waiting from the corresponding individual. The colored LEDs glowed to convey a specific type of message (i.e., availability of a user), preset by the members of the group.

In a different study, Tarasewich et al. [25] investigated how much information could be encoded and understood by users in visual displays ranging in size from two to nine LEDs and using different display characteristics, such as colors and blinking patterns. Similarly, Campbell and Tarasewich [5] studied how much information could be realistically presented on a pixel-based micro-sized display. Both investigations revealed that users can quickly learn a relatively large number of feedback with a few LEDs and their performance and preference increase with multiple LEDs and effective display designs.

Visual feedback on tangible objects is not as well explored. Almost all current tangibles provide visual feedback on an integrated display screen when available [3,13,15,16] or on an external display, such as an interactive wall [8,24] and interactive tabletops [23,29]. Some have also explored lights [11] and other forms of feedback, such as haptic [20–22] and auditory [4]. Several tangibles provide visual feedback through a small number of LEDs [6,17,27]. However, no prior work has explored the full potential of low-resolution edge display in the context of tangibles.

Motivation

Apart from increasing the user's awareness of the current state of the system, the following potentials of a low-resolution edge display have motivated the work.

Low mental and perceptual demand. In theory, edge feedback should require fewer mental and perceptual activities than other feedback types. Particularly, textual and graphical feedback require users to move their foci from one part of the visual field to another and usually require a user-action upon receipt (i.e., a tap on the screen to remove the notification window). These restrict the possibility of task parallelism and reduce user performance both in terms of speed and accuracy [2]. Auditory feedback, on the other hand, is unreliable in noisy places and relies on an additional sensory organ (i.e., our ears), which increases perceptual demand. Edge feedback is free from most of these limitations.

Swift conversion and transition. Low-resolution edge displays could be added to most active tangibles, allowing designers to incorporate edge feedback in their system. Since the display need not compromise or alter physical design of the tangibles, existing users do not have to learn an entirely new interaction, accommodating a swift transition from old to new tangibles.

Extensibility. Although, we explore edge feedback in the context of active tangibles, low-resolution edge displays could be added to other interactive systems as well, i.e., wearable devices and computer accessories.

Independent interactions. Edge feedback could also extend the support for independent interactions with active tangibles. In a tabletop and tangible system, it could aid users in performing actions off-the-table since they could confirm and verify the actions through the feedback provided on the tangibles, without being reliant on the tabletop display. Some existing tangibles (e.g., Siftables [16]) support independent interactions by providing visual feedback on an integrated display screen. However, this often occludes the information on the screen. Edge feedback is free from this limitation.

Group interactions. Edge feedback could extend group interactions with tangibles, where users use multiple tangibles to interact with the system. Many systems provide visual feedback on an external display for group interactions (e.g., stacking), which force users to work in a proximity to the display. This also limits independent interactions with the tangibles. Some active tangibles provide visual feedback on integrated display screens. However, when stacked, users could only see the display of the top tangible. Some active tangibles (e.g., Stackables [13]) attach the display on the side to address this, but are not intended for tabletop interaction since the side-screen is difficult to see when on the table. Low-resolution edge display augmented tangibles address this by providing feedback directly on the tangibles that is visible even when tangibles are stacked.

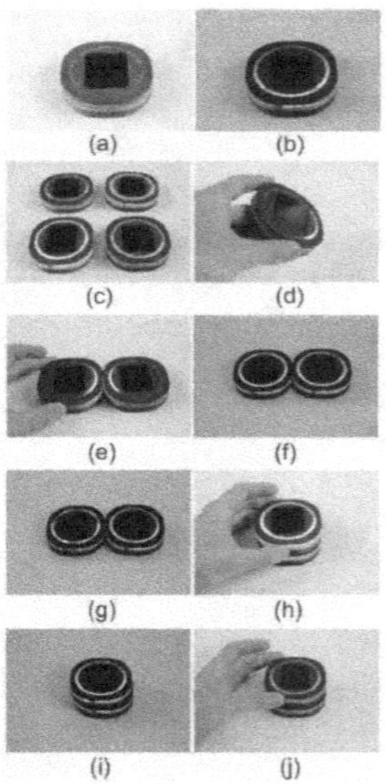

Figure 2. Edge feedback on different tangible interactions: (a) inactive tangible, (b) turned on tangible, (c) tangibles representing different items, (d) tilt notification, (e) neighboring notification, (f) valid neighboring, (g) invalid neighboring, (h) stacking notification, (i) valid stacking, and (j) invalid stacking.

Feedback Mapping

Table 1 proposes a guideline for mapping different types of edge feedback to different tangible interactions. This guideline is inspired by Harrison et al. [10] and Xu and Lyons's [30] findings and current practices in consumer products, e.g., [1,9], and has been evaluated through a series of informal lab tests. Apart from notifications on direct interactions though tap, touch, tilt, shake, flip,

#	Manipulation	Interaction	Action	Edge Feedback
Single Tangible	Direct *On/off-the-table*	Changes via tap, touch, tilt, shake, flip/rotate, or tactile buttons	Turn on a tangible	*Pulse/blink[1] in multiple colors & change color to white[3]*
			Detection confirmation	*Blink[1] along the edge corresponding to tilt/rotate angle[2]*
			Change an item	*Change color to represent the new item*
			Change a value	*Change illumination[4]*
			Remove an item	*Change color to white[3]*
			Turn off a tangible	*Turn off display*
	Indirect	Changes via another device or system actions	Change an item	*Change color to represent the new item & pulse/blink[1]*
			Change a value	*Change illumination & pulse/blink[1]*
			Remove an item	*Pulse/blink[1] & change color to white[3]*
Multiple Tangibles	Direct *On/off-the-table*	Neighboring	Detection confirmation	*Blink[1] along the edges that have been neighbored[2]*
			Valid combination	*Change all tangibles to alternating colors[5]*
			Invalid combination	*Pulse/blink[1] the invalid tangible in color red[6]*
		Stacking	Detection confirmation	*Flash along all edges*
			Valid combination	*Change all tangibles to alternating colors[5]*
			Invalid combination	*Pulse/blink[1] the invalid tangible in color red[6]*

[1]Pulse or flash rates may differ for different tangibles and systems [30], but must occur for a limited number of times, preferably once or twice
[2]Or the full array if the angle or direction cannot be determined or is irrelevant
[3]Or any other color representing a neutral state
[4]Illumination represent values, that is brighter or dimmer for higher or lower values, respectively
[5]For instance, if three tangibles are nearby/stacked, represented by color x, y, and z, then all tangibles will use alternating colors x-y-z
[6]If an invalid tangible/s cannot be determined then all tangibles blink in red (or a color picked to represent error)

Table 1. Edge feedback on direct/indirect tangible interactions.

rotate, and tactile buttons on the tangibles, and indirect interactions thorough another device or system, Table 1 also provides guidelines on how to notify the users of a valid or an invalid group interaction, such as stacking and neighboring. Figure 2 illustrates several types of edge feedback from the table.

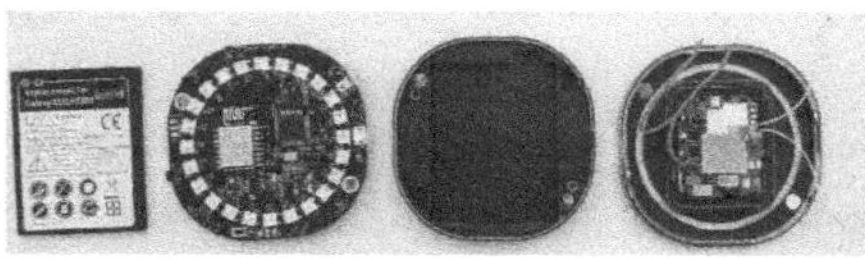

Figure 3. Components of the custom active tangibles from left to right: battery, custom printed circuit board with 24-LED ring, bottom of case, top of case including smartwatch.

Figure 4. A user exploring gene networks with low-resolution edge display augmented active tangibles using the Sparse Tangibles [3] system.

Demonstration

We demonstrate how augmenting a low-resolution edge display to an existing system increases its functionality, usability, and provide users with a better understanding of the system.

Custom active tangibles. We designed and developed custom active tangibles, called Actibles [7], using different components of an LG G Watch, a custom circuit board, and a 3D printed case. Actibles include a 41.91 mm IPS LCD displays (37.9×46.5×9.95 mm), 4 GB internal storage, 512 MB RAM, and a 9-axis sensor. They run on the Android Wear OS. The custom circuit board contains 8 omnidirectional hall effect sensors for neighboring and stacking detection, an ESP8266 Wi-Fi chip, and an array of 24 LEDs in a circular pattern (Figure 3). They control all inertial sensors using an 8-bit microcontroller. Any device, such as a tabletop, can communicate with Actibles using a simple TCP/IP server.

Interactive tabletop. A MultiTaction [18], 1397 mm, 1209.6×680.4 mm touchscreen area at 1920×1080-pixel resolution, placed horizontally on a custom stand was used as an interactive tabletop. It detected the tangibles using its default 2D fiducial marker tracker.

Sparse Tangibles. We picked Sparse Tangibles [3], an existing tabletop and tangible system to demonstrate the proposed feedback mapping. Sparse Tangibles enables collaborative exploration of gene and protein networks on an interactive tabletop using active tangibles (Figure 4). Originally, it used smartwatches with a custom case as active tangibles. Its custom tangibles were also augmented with LED arrays, but did not use it to provide feedback. We picked this system for our demonstration because it utilizes a wide range of on/off-the-table tangible interactions, including tap, multi-touch, shake, and stacking, which makes it ideal for demonstrating different types of edge feedback.

Tangible interactions. The system enables users to select an organism or a gene network and construct expressive queries using active tangibles. To load a network on the tabletop, the user first navigates to the intended organism/gene by performing vertical swipes on the tangible touchscreen, selects the item by tapping, and then places the tangible on the tabletop. To perform a query on the loaded network, the user picks up another tangible, selects a query parameter, such as hub density, and stacks it on the other tangible/s. This updates the network to display only hubs that meet the selected criteria. The user can remove an item from a tangible by shaking it.

Feedback mapping. We assigned different feedback types to all supported tangible interactions and state changes based on Table 1. We used the colors *green* and *blue* to represent organisms and genes, respectively, since they are commonly used in biological network visualization tools. Similarly, we used *red* and *white* to represent errors and neutral states.

An Informal Evaluation

We invited five experienced computational biologists to our lab to interact with the customized Sparse Tangibles

Figure 5. A researcher demonstrating the active tangibles augmented with LED arrays to the participants before the informal evaluation.

Question	Disagree	Neutral	Agree
Q1) *User Experience*	0%	60%	40%
Q2) *Understandability*	0%	40%	60%
Q3) *Off-the-table*	20%	60%	20%
Q4) *Extensibility*	0%	20%	80%

Table 2. Results of the informal evaluation.

system (Figure 5). They were all employees of a biomedical research center. Their age ranged from 20 to 39 years, on average 29.6 (SD = 6.8). Three of them were male, and two were female. They all had experience working with biological networks. Three of them responded that they frequently work with biological networks, while two responded that they occasionally do.

All participants arrived together. Upon arrival, we demonstrated the system and allowed them to interact with it. Then, they were asked to fill out a short questionnaire involving the following questions: (Q1) edge feedback enhances tabletop and tangible interaction experience, (Q2) provides a better understanding of the system and system events, (Q3) facilitates off-the-table interactions, and (Q4) will be useful in other interactive systems. Table 2 illustrates the results.

Results were mostly neutral or positive. Most participants responded that edge feedback provided a better understanding of the system and system events. Interestingly, most participants responded that edge display did not enhance or reduce their on/off-the-table tangible interaction experience. This is most likely because they were unfamiliar with the system prior to the study. Although we demonstrated the system and allowed them to interact with it, such brief exposure to the system was most probably not enough to fully grasp the functionality of the system, making it difficult for them to compare the experience with and without the edge display. Interestingly, in response to Q4, most participants commented that edge display could be useful in other interactive systems. They most probably responded to this question envisioning edge display in a system they are more familiar with. One participant (female, 31 years), for example, commented that edge display could be useful in a tabletop system that allows tracking filters in clustering alignments. Also, noteworthy that in the demonstration and interactive session, participants used active tangibles augmented with a display screen. They, therefore, responded to the questions in comparison to tangibles that can display visual feedback on the integrated display screens. Nevertheless, participants perceived edge display to be helpful in making the system and events more understandable (Q2). Their responses may have been more optimistic if they used tangibles that do not include a display screen as a baseline.

Conclusion

We proposed augmenting tangible objects with a low-resolution edge display to provide real-time visual feedback on the current state of the system. We presented a guideline for mapping different types of edge feedback to different tangible interactions. We demonstrate its effectiveness in an informal evaluation that revealed that visual feedback on edge display provides a better understanding of the system.

Future Work

The informal evaluation did not investigate all potential benefits of the edge display. In the future, we will fully evaluate it in a formal study. We will also extend our guideline to support more actions and explore edge display in the context of smaller tangibles that cannot incorporate 24 LEDs.

Acknowledgements

This work has been supported in part by NSF-IIS grant 1320350, the Canada Research Chairs program, NSERC, the Canada Foundation for Innovation, and the Ontario Ministry of Research and Innovation.

References

1. Amazon. Amazon Echo. Retrieved January 21, 2017 from https://www.amazon.com/dp/B00X4WHP5E
2. Ahmed Sabbir Arif, Benedikt Iltisberger, and Wolfgang Stuerzlinger. 2011. Extending mobile user ambient awareness for nomadic text entry. In *Proceedings of the 23rd Australian Computer-Human Interaction - OZCHI '11*, 21–30. https://doi.org/10.1145/2071536.2071539
3. Ahmed Sabbir Arif, Roozbeh Manshaei, Sean Delong, Brien East, Matthew Kyan, and Ali Mazalek. 2016. Sparse Tangibles: collaborative exploration of gene networks using active tangibles and interactive tabletops. In *Proceedings of the TEI '16: Tenth International Conference on Tangible, Embedded, and Embodied Interaction - TEI '16*, 287–295. https://doi.org/10.1145/2839462.2839500
4. Saskia Bakker, Debby Vorstenbosch, Elise van den Hoven, Gerard Hollemans, and Tom Bergman. 2007. Weathergods: tangible interaction in a digital tabletop game. In *Proceedings of the 1st international conference on Tangible and embedded interaction - TEI '07*, 151. https://doi.org/10.1145/1226969.1227000
5. Christopher Campbell and Peter Tarasewich. 2004. What can you say with only three pixels? *Proceedings of the 6th International Symposium on Mobile Human-Computer Interaction - MobileHCI '04*: 1–12. https://doi.org/10.1007/978-3-540-28637-0_1
6. Lee Chia-Hsun, Ma Yu-Pin, and Jeng Taysheng. 2003. A spatially-aware tangible interface for computer-aided design. In *CHI '03 extended abstracts on Human factors in computing systems - CHI '03*, 960. https://doi.org/10.1145/765891.766094
7. Brien East, Sean DeLong, Roozbeh Manshaei, Ahmed Sabbir Arif, and Ali Mazalek. 2016. Actibles: open source active tangibles. In *Proceedings of the 2016 ACM on Interactive Surfaces and Spaces - ISS '16*, 469–472. https://doi.org/10.1145/2992154.2996874
8. Mathieu Le Goc, Pierre Dragicevic, Samuel Huron, Jeremy Boy, and Jean-Daniel Fekete. 2015. SmartTokens: embedding motion and grip sensing in small tangible objects. In *Proceedings of the 28th Annual ACM Symposium on User Interface Software & Technology - UIST '15*, 357–362. https://doi.org/10.1145/2807442.2807488
9. Google. Google Home. Retrieved January 21, 2017 from https://madeby.google.com/home
10. Chris Harrison, John Horstman, Gary Hsieh, and Scott Hudson. 2012. Unlocking the expressivity of point lights. In *Proceedings of the 2012 ACM annual conference on Human Factors in Computing Systems - CHI '12*, 1683. https://doi.org/10.1145/2207676.2208296
11. Doris Hausen, Sebastian Boring, Clara Lueling, Simone Rodestock, and Andreas Butz. 2012. StaTube: facilitating state management in instant messaging systems. In *Proceedings of the Sixth International Conference on Tangible, Embedded and Embodied Interaction - TEI '12*, 283. https://doi.org/10.1145/2148131.2148191
12. Marije Kanis, Niall Winters, Stefan Agamanolis, Anna Gavin, and Cian Cullinan. 2005. Toward wearable social networking with iBand. *Extended Abstracts Proceedings of the 2005 Conference on Human Factors in Computing Systems*: 1521–1524. https://doi.org/10.1145/1056808.1056956
13. Stefanie Klum, Petra Isenberg, Ricardo Langner, Jean-Daniel Fekete, and Raimund Dachselt. 2012. Stackables: combining tangibles for faceted browsing. In *Proceedings of the International Working Conference on Advanced Visual Interfaces - AVI '12*, 241. https://doi.org/10.1145/2254556.2254600
14. Gordon Kurtenbach and William Buxton. 1994. User learning and performance with marking menus. In *Proceedings of the SIGCHI conference on Human factors in computing systems celebrating interdependence - CHI '94*, 258–264. https://doi.org/10.1145/191666.191759
15. Ali Mazalek and Ahmed Sabbir Arif. 2014. Mobile-based tangible interaction techniques for shared displays. In *Proceedings of the 16th international conference on Human-computer interaction with*

mobile devices & services - MobileHCI '14, 561–562. https://doi.org/10.1145/2628363.2645668

16. David Merrill, Jeevan Kalanithi, and Pattie Maes. 2007. Siftables: towards sensor network user interfaces. *Proceedings of the 1st international conference on Tangible and embedded interaction - TEI '07*: 75. https://doi.org/10.1145/1226969.1226984
17. Jane Meyers, Jeffrey LaMarche, and Michael Eisenberg. 2010. Craftopolis: blending tangible, informal construction into virtual multiuser communities. In *Proceedings of the 9th International Conference on Interaction Design and Children - IDC '10*, 242. https://doi.org/10.1145/1810543.1810581
18. MultiTaction. MultiTaction. Retrieved January 21, 2017 from https://www.multitaction.com/
19. Joe Natoli. 2014. Feedback: 5 Principles of Interaction Design To Supercharge Your UI (5 of 5) | Give Good UX | Joe Natoli. Retrieved January 17, 2017 from http://www.givegoodux.com/feedback-5-principles-interaction-design-supercharge-ui-5-5
20. Donghan Park and Hyunseung Choo. 2016. Vibration based tangible tokens for intuitive pairing among smart devices. In *Human Aspects of Information Security, Privacy, and Trust*, Theo Tryfonas (ed.). Springer International Publishing, 48–56. https://doi.org/10.1007/978-3-319-39381-0_5
21. James Patten and Hiroshi Ishii. 2007. Mechanical constraints as computational constraints in tabletop tangible interfaces. In *Proceedings of the SIGCHI conference on Human factors in computing systems - CHI '07*, 809. https://doi.org/10.1145/1240624.1240746
22. Esben Warming Pedersen and Kasper Hornbæk. 2011. Tangible bots: interaction with active tangibles in tabletop interfaces. In *Proceedings of the 2011 annual conference on Human factors in computing systems - CHI '11*, 2975. https://doi.org/10.1145/1978942.1979384
23. Jun Rekimoto, Brygg Ullmer, and Haruo Oba. 2001. DataTiles: a modular platform for mixed physical and graphical interactions. In *Proceedings of the SIGCHI conference on Human factors in computing systems - CHI '01*, 269–276. https://doi.org/10.1145/365024.365115
24. Jan Richter, Bruce H. Thomas, Maki Sugimoto, and Masahiko Inami. 2007. Remote active tangible interactions. In *Proceedings of the 1st international conference on Tangible and embedded interaction - TEI '07*, 39. https://doi.org/10.1145/1226969.1226977
25. Peter Tarasewich, Christopher S.Campbell, Tian Xia, and Myra Dideles. 2003. Evaluation of visual notification cues for ubiquitous computing. *Proceedings of 5th International Conference on Ubiquitous Computing(Ubicomp2003)*: 349–366.
26. Brygg Ullmer, Hiroshi Ishii, and Robert J. K. Jacob. 2005. Token+constraint systems for tangible interaction with digital information. *ACM Transactions on Computer-Human Interaction* 12, 1: 81–118. https://doi.org/10.1145/1057237.1057242
27. Danli Wang, Yunfeng Qi, Yang Zhang, and Tingting Wang. 2013. TanPro-kit: a tangible programming tool for children. In *Proceedings of the 12th International Conference on Interaction Design and Children - IDC '13*, 344–347. https://doi.org/10.1145/2485760.2485841
28. Amanda Williams, Shelly Farnham, and Scott Counts. 2006. Exploring wearable ambient displays for social awareness. *Extended Abstracts on Human Factors in Computing Systems (CHI'06)*: 1529–1534. https://doi.org/10.1145/1125451.1125731
29. Andy Wu, Jung-bin Yim, Eric Caspary, Ali Mazalek, Sanjay Chandrasekharan, and Nancy J Nersessian. 2011. Kinesthetic Pathways: a tabletop visualization to support discovery in systems biology. In *Proceedings of the 8th ACM conference on Creativity and cognition - C&C '11*, 21. https://doi.org/10.1145/2069618.2069624
30. Cheng Xu and Kent Lyons. 2015. Shimmering smartwatches: exploring the smartwatch design space. *Proceedings of the 9th International Conference on Tangible, Embedded, and Embodied Interaction - TEI '15*: 69–76. https://doi.org/10.1145/2677199.2680599

ForceClicks: Enabling Efficient Button Interaction with Single Finger Touch

Sangeon Yong
GSCT, KAIST
Daejeon, South Korea
koragon2@kaist.ac.kr

Liwei Chan
Dept. of Computer Science
National Chiao Tung University
Hsinchu, Taiwan
liweichan@cs.nctu.edu.tw

Edward Jangwon Lee
GSCT, KAIST
Daejeon, South Korea
noshel@kaist.ac.kr

Juhan Nam
GSCT, KAIST
Daejeon, South Korea
juhannam@kaist.ac.kr

Roshan Peiris
Keio Media Design
Yokohama, Japan
roshan@kmd.keio.ac.jp

TEI '17, March 20-23, 2017, Yokohama, Japan
ACM 978-1-4503-4676-4/17/03.
http://dx.doi.org/10.1145/3024969.3025081

Abstract
ForceClicks is a novel touch button input technique for consecutive clicking which incorporates touch force sensors. From force data of a single continuous touch over time, ForceClicks detects peaks and generates discrete clicks. Compared to typical button interaction, this is effective in a sense that consecutive clicks do not require finger positional movements. Additionally, stable force over a certain time threshold can trigger an alternate state, *long press*, and can be mapped to other actions. The usability of ForceClicks has been evaluated in terms of a) scattering level and b) efficiency. Results suggest higher stability than typical touch, especially when the task requires visual engagement on remote content. The relatively scatter-free characteristic of ForceClicks allows it to be applied on rapid clicking while gaming, and reduce of visual dedication allows easier control of external devices, and two applications, a shooting game and a number picker, are presented for demonstration.

Author Keywords
force touch; 3D touch; touch screen; gestures

ACM Classification Keywords
H.5.2 [User Interfaces]: Input devices and strategies (e.g., mouse, touchscreen)

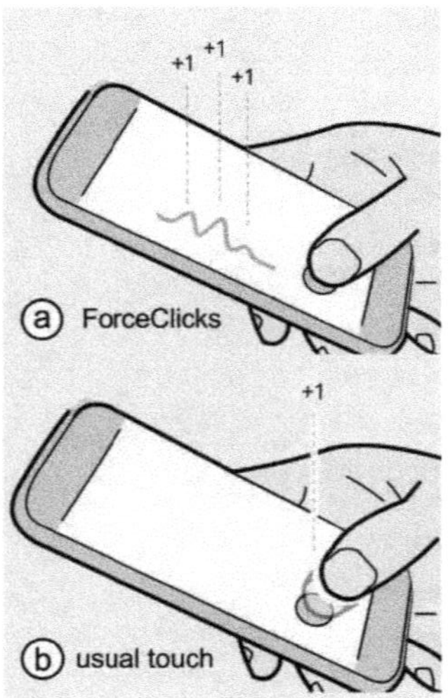

Figure 1: ForceClicks

You can access the video of ForceClicks through the link below.
https://youtu.be/im5fEsX6yHE

Introduction

Touch-activating button is generally considered efficient, but repeating the actions on the same button may cause misses. These misses occur due to increase in touch point scattering over multiple landings. Unlike physical buttons, which provide tangible interfaces and the user is able to haptically ensure every interaction, it is difficult to reduce this scattering as touch-activated buttons do not provide tactile feedback. Missing a button while consecutive tapping often happens when the task requires users' visual dedication at remote content, such as pressing onscreen buttons while concentrating on the entire game screen.

To reduce such scattering and missing problems, in this research we propose *ForceClicks*, a novel button input technique that incorporates force of touch.

ForceClicks

By analyzing force change of a single touch over time, ForceClicks detects peaks of the force curve and recognizes those as discrete clicks. Figure 1 illustrates the difference between ForceClicks and ordinary click. While ordinary clicks require the user to initiate a new touch for every click, ForceClicks can receive consecutive inputs without requiring further finger movement. Additionally, ForceClicks also features *long press*, a mode that is triggered by maintaining constant touch force over a certain amount of time.

Zero physical movement of fingertip brings several benefits compared to ordinary touch buttons. First, scattering of the position of each consecutive touch is reduced. This suggests that users are able to consecutively click on a button without missing even when they are not able to pay visual attention on the button. Second, it reduces the fatigue of finger as less physical movement is required than ordinary clicking.

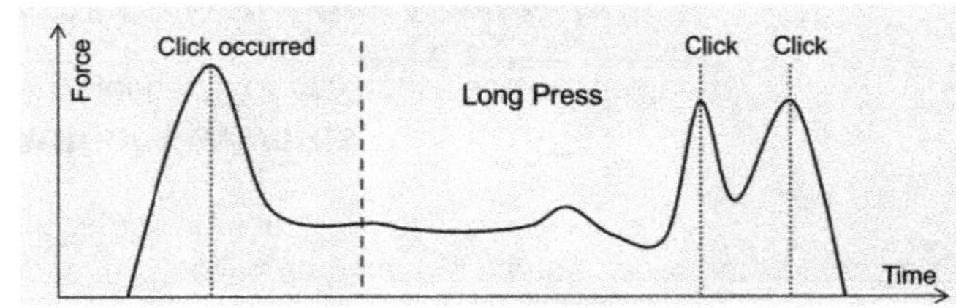

Figure 2: basic mechanism of ForceClicks

Approach

Typical touch force input, such as iPhone's peek-and-pop, sets an absolute force threshold for feature activation and requires the user to practice and adapt their finger force levels to the system. Regarding to setting absolute force thresholds as activation triggers, previous research indicates that proper force of touch control can be done when users are given visual feedback of currently applied force and extended input time. With both conditions provided, users were able to properly home into several intervals without any problems [1, 3]. However, when the input time was reduced to an instant, users showed only 58.5% success rate with six force intervals, compared to 99.9% with two [2]. This suggests that without visual feedback and sufficient input time, users are not able to precisely control the absolute magnitude of touch force. Therefore, in ForceClicks, rather than setting absolute force thresholds we focus on relative force change over time and extract data, rather than absolute force intensity.

The force profile that occurs during a force click is shown in Figure 2. Here, the ForceClicks algorithm observes the rising and falling slopes on the profile and identifies the peak at which a "click" is triggered.

To find peaks in the force values, we define three states

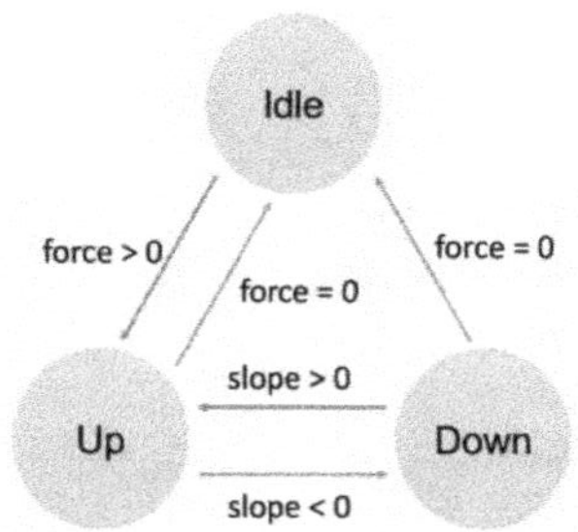

Figure 3: state diagram of ForceClicks

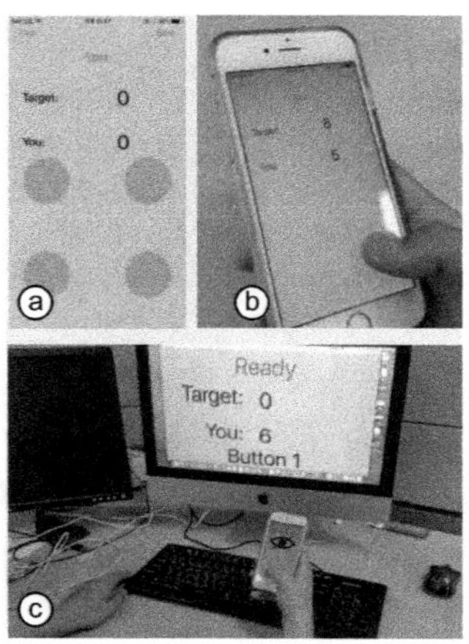

Figure 4: experimental design

of touch: *idle, up,* and *down*. Each state corresponds to the current force change direction. *Idle* state occurs when the button is untouched, that is, zero force. *Up* and *down* states occur when the first time derivative of force changes sign: the system enters up state when the force begins to increase and down state upon decrease. Releasing the button causes the force value to hit zero and the state returns to idle. Counting discrete clicks can be done at either *up to down* or *down to up* transitions, and conducting simple user tests on both settings suggest that counting down to up (or idle to up) transitions produce more accurate clicks.

Although this simple three-state approach with down to up (positive edge) triggering can be used for consecutive discrete clicking without difficulties, incorporating *long press* feature – maintaining a level of force over a certain time – into the system for additional functions requires a more complex input model. For most users, maintaining equal force over time is impossible and unintended peaks of force tend to appear when they try to apply constant force. Therefore, in order to properly parse discrete clicks alongside with long presses from touch force data, distinguishing between intended and unintended peaks is essential.

Long press state is entered when force is held in an even level over a certain amount of time – no intended clicks, or peaks, occur over a time threshold. In order to rule out unintended peaks, two criteria are set based on user observations and force peaks are considered as intended only when both are sufficed. First, intended clicks must have a short up state. User observations suggest that most clicks are done in a swift manner, therefore up slopes longer than 30 frames (0.5 seconds) are set to be regarded as unintended clicks. Second, the second time derivatives of force during an intended click must have a wide range: difference between the maximum and minimum value must be larger than a certain threshold. The lifespan of a click is defined as follows: a click starts at the beginning of an up state and ends when down state begins and a) continues more than 5 frames, b) another up state starts before 5 frames, and c) user removes touch and enters idle state within 5 frames. A wider range of second derivatives in an up slope implies that an intended click should start and end with higher acceleration, and 0.2 has been set as the minimum range threshold of an intended click.

User Study

This study explores the performance of ForceClicks in terms of scattering level and efficiency regarding existing touch-activating buttons (e.g., TouchClicks).

Experimental Design

The study was a within-subject design with two variables, operation and vision. The operation variable includes ForceClicks or TouchClicks conditions. The vision variable describes whether the participants' vision is engaged with the input control or with the remote content, i.e., vision-on-control or vision-off-control conditions. All tests were implemented on Apple's iPhone 6s. For each trial, the participant was instructed to reach a randomly assigned number of clicks (between 8-12) on 1 of 4 buttons displayed on the phone screen with the assigned interface conditions, as shown in Figure 4a. The number of clicks being performed was displayed on the phone screen in vision-on-control condition (Figure 4b), and on the remote screen in vision-off-control condition (Figure 4c). In vision-off-control condition, the phone screen turned black after the participants performed the first click. Button positions were randomized, and both interface conditions were counter-balanced. The Clicks were repeated for 10 times for each button position. In total, each participant performed 2x2x4x10 = 160 trials.

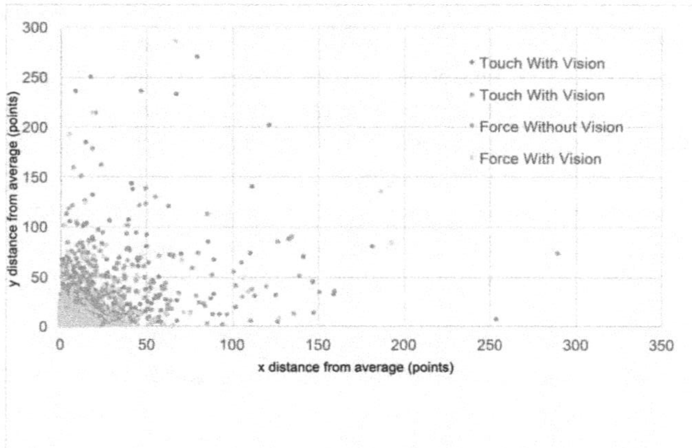

Figure 5: Variance distribution of four test conditions.

Ten participants (8 males and 2 females, all right-handed, with average age 27) were recruited. All participants used smart phones. After being introducted to the study, they received a 5-min training session, going through all conditions.

Result Discussion

Figure 5 shows the position accuracy results of four conditions. The scattered colors manifest that the variance of position decreases When using ForceClicks. On average, the position variance is doubled when participants use the touch-activating buttons (23.117 to 55.228), and the vision does not affect the position accuracy (40.315 to 38.030). On the other hand, the time consumption of both conditions are similar (0.189 to 0.173). This result can show the scatter-free property of ForceClicks. Also, most participants mentioned that ForceClicks is easy to learn, and less fatiguing to the finger.

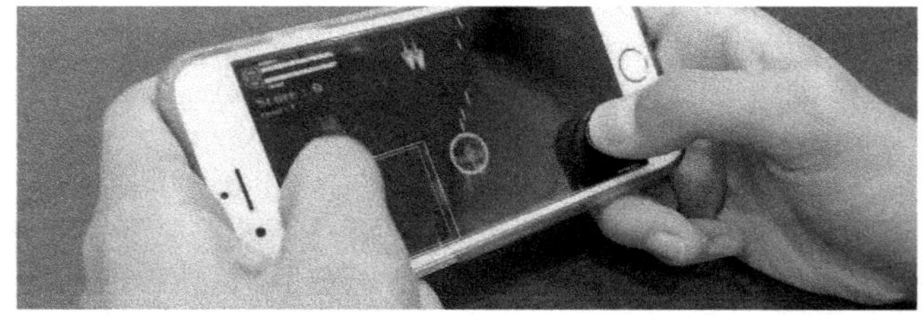

Figure 6: Space shooting game implemented with ForceClicks.

Example Applications

Two example applications have been implemented to demonstrate how ForceClicks can be used in real-world applications. The first application is a simple shooting game, and the second is a number picker. We implemented them by utilizing both discrete clicks and long press in ForceClicks.

Space Shooting Game

Figure 6 shows the simple space shooting game to demonstrate the advantage of ForceClicks. On the left part of screen, users can control the spaceship's location. On the right, a ForceClicks button is placed instead of ordinary touch buttons for gunfire. Discrete clicks fire individual missiles, and long press mode fires a continuous laser weapon. Due to the less-scattering characteristic of ForceClicks, users can fire weapons more easily while visually paying attention to targets such as enemy vessels and obstacles.

Number Picker

To test the usability of the long press mode, we implemented a number picker using ForceClicks. Discrete clicks on the button increase the number by one. Entering the long press mode increases the number continuously, and the increasing speed can be dynamically changed by controlling touch force: greater force speeds up the increase. This number

Figure 7: Number Picker implemented with ForceClicks.

picking can be efficient in a sense that the finger can stay on the button until it reaches the target number while controlling the speed of number change.

Conclusion

ForceClicks is a novel button interface for pressure-sensitive touch screens that do not require releasing the finger, fixed force threshold, or haptic feedback for consecutive clicks. While ForceClicks buttons look and feel identical to ordinary buttons, enabling the touching fingertip to rest on the button during consecutive cliks offer two benefits: a) less scattering and b) less fatigue. We performed an experiment to compare ForceClicks and ordinary touch buttons and received positive feedbacks in efficiency and usability. Additionally, two sample applications were implemented:a) space shooting game and b) number picker, to demonstrate the practical usage of ForceClicks.

Future Work

ForceClicks is an on-going project and we are actively seeking and working on further potential improvements. First, although a single ForceClick button may be placed anywhere on the screen, under multitouch situations iPhone force sensors have a problem that the force readings of nearby touches interfere with each other. This acts as a design restriction: ForceClick buttons should be placed far enough. We are seeking for a software workaround to overcome this. Second, our force thresholds for filtering out unintended clicks rely on user observations and parameter tunings. We plan to fine-tune the parameters by employing more statistical data into our model. Finally, long press also requires improvement. Currently, long press mode triggers upon a constant level of force over a fixed time threshold, and this disables interaction with the button for a certain amount of time. For example, in the space shooter game, continuous lasers can be fired only after a pause in shooting discrete missiles. Ideas that can reduce this threshold will surely improve ForceClicks.

REFERENCES

1. Sachi Mizobuchi, Shinya Terasaki, Turo Keski-Jaskari, Jari Nousiainen, Matti Ryynanen, and Miika Silfverberg. 2005. Making an impression: force-controlled pen input for handheld devices. In *CHI'05 extended abstracts on Human factors in computing systems.* ACM, 1661–1664.
2. Esben Warming Pedersen and Kasper Hornbæk. 2014. Expressive touch: studying tapping force on tabletops. In *Proceedings of the SIGCHI Conference on Human Factors in Computing Systems.* ACM, 421–430.
3. Graham Wilson, Craig Stewart, and Stephen A. Brewster. 2010. Pressure-based Menu Selection for Mobile Devices. In *Proceedings of the 12th International Conference on Human Computer Interaction with Mobile Devices and Services (MobileHCI '10).* ACM, New York, NY, USA, 181–190. DOI:http://dx.doi.org/10.1145/1851600.1851631

My Tablet Is Moving Around, Can I Touch It?

Alejandro Catala
Human Media Interaction
University of Twente, The Netherlands
a.catala@utwente.nl

Mariët Theune
Human Media Interaction
University of Twente, The Netherlands
m.theune@utwente.nl

Dirk Heylen
Human Media Interaction
University of Twente, The Netherlands
d.k.j.heylen@utwente.nl

TEI '17, March 20-23, 2017, Yokohama, Japan
ACM 978-1-4503-4676-4/17/03.
http://dx.doi.org/10.1145/3024969.3025082

Abstract
Touch displays moving autonomously, i.e., being *self-actuated*, are starting to be part of system prototypes reported in the literature. In the future, user interactions with such prototypes may take place while the display is moving. However, since current prototypes do not yet require this type of interaction, there is a lack of empirical evidence reporting issues related to touch input in such conditions. This leads us to propose two basic questions: Can we request users to deliver touch gestures during the actuation? Which aspects should we take into account when having touch input in these moving devices? In order to start to answer these questions, we report in this paper a first study to get an insight into how people perform and feel it when they have to carry out touch input on a self-actuated tablet. The preliminary results show that the self-actuated tablet does not necessarily need to be still during touch interaction, and that single-touch gestures based on drag or tap are preferable over others. Furthermore, the results also revealed an issue with tap gestures because of the movement of the tablet.

Author Keywords
Self-actuated tablet; Touch input; Gesture; Movement.

ACM Classification Keywords
H.5.2 User Interfaces: Input devices and strategies, Interaction styles, Evaluation/methodology; H.1.2 User/Machine Systems: Human factors.

Introduction
Some emergent research is starting to incorporate touch-enabled displays which can move autonomously. For example, there are tangible devices to enable layered visual interaction by varying the elevation of the tablet display [12], a tangible game with a tablet that moves between landmarks on a regular tabletop [3], self-actuated vertical displays to draw formulas on a whiteboard [1], or even quadcopters with flexible displays to bring videoconferencing functions to the space surrounding the users [4]. In all these samples of technological contributions, users may need to deliver touch commands or select targets on the screen while the display could be moving. However, although the authors do show possible uses of self-actuated displays, they do not consider touch interaction to be carried out while the display is moving. Consequently, they do not discuss the touch input issues that can arise by having such actuation.

In our own ongoing research we are developing artificial agents embodied in self-actuated tablets, to be used in tabletop games, which can require input while the agents are moving around to deliver more engaging and appealing interactive experiences to the users. To support this type of interaction, we need to find out more about the limitations of touch input in self-actuated tablets. Beyond the well-known issues in touch input, such as the fat finger problem [7], exit errors [13], occlusion or the positioning of the interactive widget and device [2], or biomechanical constraints [5][1615], there is a lack of evidence on the difficulties related to touch input specifically affected by the movement of the displays. Hence, we present an exploratory study that is the first of this kind to provide empirical results on which interaction issues users have to face if requested to deliver touch input in self-actuated tablets. It will help to characterize this sort of interactions, and will therefore support the future design of interactive systems involving such devices by allowing us to take more informed design decisions. With this paper, we want to provoke discussion on to which extent touch input can be considered during actuation and, hopefully, our observations will open new opportunities by inspiring the research community to bring new scenarios and use case prototypes that include touch input in moving tablets.

Related Work
The concept of actuation on tabletops is broad and diverse in purpose (e.g. [11], [6], [15]). When considering related work on user interaction with self-actuated tangible objects, we must distinguish self-actuation of tangibles that do not have touch displays from those that do. For example, Vonach et al. implemented modular actuated tangible objects [14], whose position and rotation can be controlled but without any capability to receive touch input yet. Pedersen and Hornbæk presented a set of interactions using their *tangible bots*, motorized tangibles capable of moving on an interactive tabletop [9]. Visualization and touch input happen around the device, on the tabletop interface. The previous examples cannot render advanced visual content in the device itself, or receive more integrated and direct touch input, which would expand the possibilities of tangible interfaces. An

Figure 1. Self-actuated tablet moving sideways

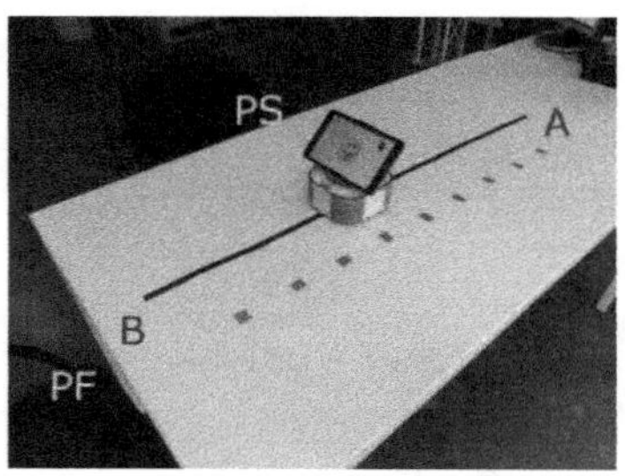

Figure 2. Overview of the experimental setting

example of a more advanced graphics integration is the case of the Sifteo Cubes [8][10]. Its creators included a small graphical interface as part of the tangible, although without any kind of actuation.

Some works consider self-actuated displays to provide advanced visual feedback and touch input capabilities. The work by Sim et al. on G-raffe presents a tangible block supporting the elevation of a display to enable 2.5d visual interaction [12], so that the tangible can show different information depending on both the location and the height of the display. Bader et al. [1] discuss some use cases for self-actuated displays, such as guiding a person in using a coffee machine, or guiding a user through an exhibition. It also reports a system for a self-actuated vertical surface capable of drawing formulas on the whiteboard. The work presented in [3] reports the design of a tangible game that uses an actuated tablet to augment digitally a regular tabletop. Gomes et al. [4] presents a toolbox for exploring interaction with tangible and displays in the mid-air, based on quadcopters in the space surrounding the user. Among the interactions and potential scenarios, it presents DisplayDrones, in the form of quadcopter with a touchscreen display to bring picture and video capabilities.

Despite the effort to develop new technology and explore use case scenarios with self-actuated displays, as shown in related work, touch input is being relegated to interactions in which the device remains still. We consider that touch input in moving displays may open new possibilities for interaction and new scenarios. As a first step forward to better understand the issues of touch input when the tablet is moving around, we carried out the following exploratory study.

Study Design

In this exploratory study we focused on some of the typical touch gestures (tap, drag, rotate, scale) that can be carried out in a regular tablet, and looked for issues that may arise if people are requested to interact while the surface is moving.

Apparatus

We prepared a tabletop (150x75cm) setting with a self-actuated tablet: a Samsung Tab A 7" (model T280) with a screen size of 150x94mm. It was mounted with a 45° angle on top of a plywood case of 13.6x13.6x5.7cm, containing a Zumo Robot by Pololu[1] (see Figure 1 and Figure 2). We chose this configuration because we are interested in applications in which the user is seated and the tablet is partially angled to facilitate the visualization. To facilitate the implementation and reproducibility of interactions between trials, we restricted the movement of the robot to follow a 1-meter-long line as shown in Figure 2 by implementing a line-follower program.

Gestures

Touch gestures had to be performed on a smiley representing a virtual character on screen (see Figure 1). The smiley was 4.3 cm in diameter and located in the center of the display. It was able to recognize all gestures (tap, drag, rotate, zoom) at all times, giving immediate visual feedback by applying the corresponding translation, rotation and scale transforms and showing a thumb up icon when the expected gesture was completed. Any touch event outside of the smiley was ignored. For a trial to be

[1] Zumo Robot: https://www.pololu.com/product/2510

successful, the user had to carry out the intended gesture and achieve the required completion conditions. In particular, **Tap** was implemented with the facility class *GestureDetector. SimpleOnGestureListener* provided by the Android SDK, and therefore the tap gesture succeeded as soon as it was notified by the corresponding listener. For the **Drag**, the user had to drag the smiley at least 6 cm. The **Rotate** gesture required users to rotate the smiley at least 90 degrees in any direction. The **Scale** gesture required users to pinch until the smiley was half size, or zoom until it was at least double size. With this range of gestures, we covered instant stationary gestures as well as different dynamic touch input with one or two fingers.

Method and Procedure

Sixteen healthy adults ranging from 23 to 41 years old (m=29.8, sd=4.5) participated in the study (4 women). They were all users of smartphones with multi-touch capacitive screen. Before starting the test, each participant performed the gestures without actuation to get acquainted with the task and to ensure he/she was able to carry out the gestures. Then, each participant proceeded with 24 trials, which corresponded to a single combination of trajectory, speed and gesture (as explained below). Before each trial, the graphical interface displayed an icon representing the gesture to be carried out. The user had to respond by saying aloud the expected gesture, to confirm he/she was ready. The experimenter could then activate the trial remotely to allow the robot to go from point A to B (see Figure 2). The user had to complete the requested gesture before the robot reached the end of the line. If the trial was completed successfully, the robot made a beep, and stopped, and the thumb up icon was displayed. The trials were grouped in blocks of the four gestures, being administered randomly. The blocks were controlled by Trajectory first, and then by Speed, which were also administered randomly. Repetitions were not considered because gestures were basic well-known touch gestures and users were adults, and, therefore, we wanted to observe the interaction issues rather than learnability of gestures. After each single block, participants were requested to answer the question: *To carry out the touch gestures, the robot speed was: __ (0=Too slow...10=Too fast)*. After testing the three different speeds for each trajectory, the participants were asked to express their preferences regarding the speeds and gestures.

In this study, we considered two different relative movements of the self-actuated tablet. The Trajectory could be either *Forward*, with the user seated at place PF, or *Sideways*, when seated at place PS (see Figure 2). We decided to limit the trajectory to these two relative movements in order to keep the number of trials manageable, and because they account for two main situations of the robot crossing an interactive space defined by the tabletop: when the tablet is approaching the user and when the tablet is crossing the interactive space in front of the user. Other trajectories such as moving away or any complex combination of trajectories were not explored in this study.

The speed at which the tablet moved varied at three different levels of *Speed.* The related work involving touch displays does not report speeds. Hence, we considered speeds similar to the ones reported in related works involving actuated tangibles. In particular, we established *Speed 3* (S3), the highest

Table 1. Error counts

	Forward			Sideways			
	S1	**S2**	**S3**	**S1**	**S2**	**S3**	All
TAP	0	2	3	0	0	5	10
DRAG	0	0	1	0	0	0	1
ROTATE	1	2	4	0	3	5	15
SCALE	0	2	3	0	0	1	6
All	1	6	11	0	3	11	32

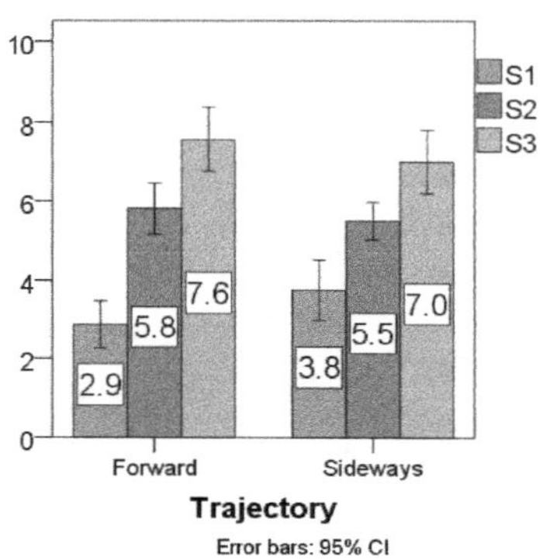

Figure 3. Perceived speed appropriateness

speed, to be 36 cm/s, which is just a few centimeters per second below the speed reported in [9], and *Speed 2* (S2) to be 26 cm/s, which is close to the one reported in [14]. With these two speeds, we can get a deeper insight on what would happen if we embedded a touch display on a self-actuated tangible moving at similar speeds to those in two different tangible settings. Finally, the slower speed tested, *Speed 1* (S1), was set at 13 cm/s. In this way, with a range of speeds, we can observe to which extent delivering touch input is affected by the motion.

Results and Discussion

Table 1 shows the error counts. Overall, 91.6% of the trials were successful (=(384-32)/384, where 384 = 16 users x 24 trials). The results suggest that it would be feasible to consider users delivering simple touch gestures on a tablet while being actuated. The trajectory of the tablet with respect to the user does not seem to be an important factor, of course, provided that the user is facing the tablet in a similar way to the configurations tested. However, the speed matters when touch input is involved. The results reveal some important aspects that must be taken into account if interactions really need to include touch input during actuation. The main observations and remarks are summarized as follows:

Touch input requires slower speed than with tangibles

We have tested a range of speeds, where S2 and S3 were selected to be similar to the speeds reported related work. As suggested by the counts in Table 1, in order to avoid interaction errors, slower speeds are recommended. S1 is more suitable for touch input. Figure 3 shows the perceived appropriateness of the speeds tested. Thus, we should avoid disproportionate speed when touch input is involved. Some users expressed in their comments that Speed 1 "is fine and convenient even for more complex gestures as *Rotate*", and that Speed 2 would still be "a bit too fast as to carry out the interactions with comfort".

Multi-point or stationary gestures can be problematic

Rotate and Scale are typical gestures requiring, in the implementation used in the study, two fingers. They involved participants doing turning or pinching/zooming trajectories with their fingers, and therefore when the tablet is moving, it is expected that interaction issues are more frequent than in simpler gestures. Indeed, most of the failures were concentrated on those multi-touch gestures, in particular the Rotate gesture at speed S3. Sometimes, *Tap* also resulted in a problematic gesture at speeds S2 and S3. The point is that above a certain speed, the users experienced issues to perform a single tap because tablet motion caused the finger to drag slightly, preventing the tap from being correctly detected. Moreover, in 13 tap trials, the users needed to tap several times until the gesture was recognized. This issue would require to implement a suitable tap detector for self-actuated tablets, different from the one provided by the Android SDK. For instance, by considering single Down or Up events when the target does not really expect dragging, or by increasing the thresholds to filter accidental or unintended Move events that are triggering the drag instead of a tap gesture.

Single-point gestures are preferred and better performed

Figure 4 and Figure 5 depict the user preferences for speeds and gestures respectively. Participants showed their preference for S1 and S2 in similar proportion.

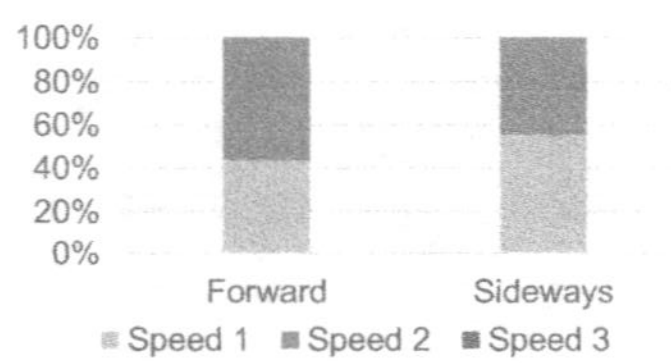

Figure 4. Speed preference

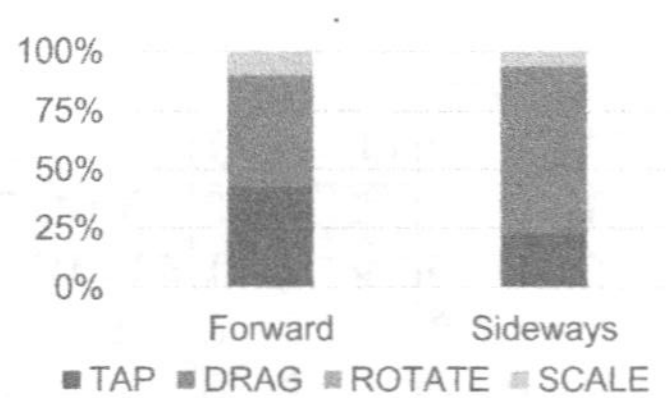

Figure 5. Gesture preference

However, in their comments they pointed out that a suitable speed would be between S1 and S2, which would explain the mixed preference. Single-touch gestures like *Tap* and *Drag* are the most preferred ones. The top gesture is Drag, in terms of both success and preference. Despite having to drag a long distance to traverse (at least 6 cm), it seems to be more convenient than *Tap* as it does not have the detection issue. Although all gestures can be performed at low speeds, issuing taps or drags would be recommended.

Limitations and Future Work

Among all the different issues that could be interesting to explore when interacting with self-actuated tablets, we started investigating only a subset of operational characteristics and touch gestures to better understand the most basic and likely issues present. Regarding gestures, we chose a diverse subset of typical gestures so that single-touch, multi-touch, dynamic and stationary were represented. Even in this case, the results and conclusions on trajectory and speed must be interpreted in terms of the four gestures considered and the related experimental conditions.

Taking into account the lack of previous reports about touch input issues on self-actuated tablets, we focused the study on basic interactions to better understand and determine potential issues. We chose quite demanding completion conditions for the gestures (i.e. rotation angles, dragging distances and scale factors) so that users were actually challenged. However, future work should focus on studying the target size and/or the precision to carry out gestures, as well as exploring more interactions involving movement in games and specific real applications.

In some applications, touch input may be less intensive, or other input modalities can be more relevant in a given context. We could need to combine gesture input, for example, with grasping and pushing, or fiduciary cards in the mid-air, etc. This means that the higher speeds tested could be re-enabled when combining several modalities. Exploring other more complex interactions, not only touch, would also be interesting. Nevertheless, we believe that we must first contribute with empirical evidence on which issues touch input introduces on self-actuated tablets. After that, we can explore the combination of different input modalities as part of our future work, with the aim of providing a comprehensive framework to support interactions on self-actuated tablets.

We aim to develop playful artificial agents embodied in self-actuated tablets, or surface-bots, with similar hardware to the one implemented for this study. For this kind of application, we need to allow users to provide commands and select targets on the screen while agents are moving. Our future work will focus on the design of menus and other widgets with appropriate target selection techniques for these devices. In this context, we will explore alternative implementations to tap detectors to overcome the identified issues and we will study drag based gestures in depth to be both effective and accurate. In this way, we will complete the study of issues with self-actuated tablets by testing possible widget solutions.

Acknowledgements

This project has received funding from the European Union's Horizon 2020 research and innovation programme under the Marie Sklodowska-Curie grant agreement No 701991.

References

1. Patrick Bader, Valentin Schwind, Norman Pohl, Niels Henze, Katrin Wolf, Stefan Schneegass, Albrecht Schmidt. 2015. Self-Actuated Displays for Vertical Surfaces. Human-Computer Interaction – INTERACT 2015 Volume 9299 of the series Lecture Notes in Computer Science pp 282-299.
2. Peter Brandl, Jakob Leitner, Thomas Seifried, Michael Haller, Bernard Doray, and Paul To. 2009. Occlusion-aware menu design for digital tabletops. In CHI '09 Extended Abstracts on Human Factors in Computing Systems (CHI EA '09). ACM, New York, NY, USA, 3223-3228.
3. Fernando Garcia-Sanjuan, Javier Jaen, Alejandro Catala. 2015. Augmented Tangible Surfaces to Support Cognitive Games for Ageing People. In Ambient Intelligence - Software and Applications, Volume 376 of the series Advances in Intelligent Systems and Computing pp 263-271.
4. Antonio Gomes, Calvin Rubens, Sean Braley, and Roel Vertegaal. 2016. BitDrones: Towards Using 3D Nanocopter Displays as Interactive Self-Levitating Programmable Matter. In Proceedings of the 2016 CHI Conference on Human Factors in Computing Systems (CHI '16). ACM, New York, NY, USA, 770-780.
5. Eve Hoggan, John Williamson, Antti Oulasvirta, Miguel Nacenta, Per Ola Kristensson, and Anu Lehtiö. 2013. Multi-touch rotation gestures: performance and ergonomics. In Proceedings of the SIGCHI Conference on Human Factors in Computing Systems (CHI '13). ACM, New York, NY, USA, 3047-3050.
6. Masahiko Inami, Maki Sugimoto, Bruce H. Thomas, and Jan Richter. 2010. Active Tangible Interactions. Tabletops-Horizontal Interactive Displays, 171-187
7. Aurélien Lucchi, Patrick Jermann, Guillaume Zufferey, and Pierre Dillenbourg. 2010. An empirical evaluation of touch and tangible interfaces for tabletop displays. In Proceedings of the fourth international conference on Tangible, embedded, and embodied interaction (TEI '10). ACM, New York, NY, USA, 177-184.
8. David Merrill, Emily Sun, and Jeevan Kalanithi. 2012. Sifteo cubes. In CHI '12 Extended Abstracts on Human Factors in Computing Systems (CHI EA '12). ACM, New York, NY, USA, 1015-1018.
9. Esben W. Pedersen and Kasper Hornbæk. 2011. Tangible bots: interaction with active tangibles in tabletop interfaces. In Proceedings of the SIGCHI Conference on Human Factors in Computing Systems (CHI '11). ACM, New York, NY, USA, 2975-2984.
10. Clément Pillias, Raphaël Robert-Bouchard, and Guillaume Levieux. 2014. Designing tangible video games: lessons learned from the sifteo cubes. In Proceedings of the SIGCHI Conference on Human Factors in Computing Systems (CHI '14). ACM, New York, NY, USA, 3163-3166.
11. Eckard Riedenklau, Thomas Hermann, and Helge Ritter. 2012. An integrated multi-modal actuated tangible user interface for distributed collaborative planning. In Proceedings of the Sixth International Conference on Tangible, Embedded and Embodied Interaction (TEI '12), Stephen N. Spencer (Ed.). ACM, New York, NY, USA, 169-174
12. Jungu Sim, Chang-Min Kim, Seung-Woo Nam, and Tek-Jin Nam. 2014. G-raffe: an elevating tangible block supporting 2.5D interaction in a tabletop computing environment. In Proceedings of the adjunct publication of the 27th annual ACM symposium on User interface software and technology (UIST'14 Adjunct). ACM, New York, NY, USA, 87-88.
13. Philip Tuddenham, David Kirk, and Shahram Izadi. 2010. Graspables revisited: multi-touch vs. tangible input for tabletop displays in acquisition and manipulation tasks. In Proceedings of the

SIGCHI Conference on Human Factors in Computing Systems (CHI '10). ACM, New York, NY, USA, 2223-2232.

14. Emanuel Vonach, Georg Gerstweiler, and Hannes Kaufmann. 2014. ACTO: A Modular Actuated Tangible User Interface Object. In Proceedings of the Ninth ACM International Conference on Interactive Tabletops and Surfaces (ITS '14). ACM, New York, NY, USA, 259-268.

15. Malte Weiss, Florian Schwarz, Simon Jakubowski, and Jan Borchers. 2010. Madgets: actuating widgets on interactive tabletops. In Proceedings of the 23nd annual ACM symposium on User interface software and technology (UIST '10). ACM, New York, NY, USA, 293-302.

16. Katrin Wolf, Christian Müller-Tomfelde, Kelvin Cheng, and Ina Wechsung. 2012. PinchPad: performance of touch-based gestures while grasping devices. In Proceedings of the Sixth International Conference on Tangible, Embedded and Embodied Interaction (TEI '12), Stephen N. Spencer (Ed.). ACM, New York, NY, USA, 103-110.

Vital+Morph: A Shape-changing Interface for Remote Biometric Monitoring

Alberto Boem
Integrative and Global Majors
Empowerment Informatics
University of Tsukuba, Japan
alberto@vrlab.esys.tsukuba.ac.jp

Kai Sasaki
Integrative and Global Majors
Empowerment Informatics
University of Tsukuba, Japan
kai@ai.iit.tsukuba.ac.jp

Shori Kano
Integrative and Global Majors
Empowerment Informatics
University of Tsukuba, Japan
kano@golem.kz.tsukuba.ac.jp

TEI'17, March 20–23, 2017, Yokohama, Japan.

http://dx.doi.org/10.1145/3024969.3025083

Abstract

In this paper we introduce Vital+Morph, a prototype of a shape-changing interface intended to be used as a media for remote biometric monitoring. Signals measured by a Vital Signs Monitoring Station are *physicalized* into a series of reactive tangible objects with a life-like behavior. Through this interface a person can feel the internal state of an hospitalized patient, as a new form of communication and awareness over distance. We propose a perceptual equivalent of an imaginative material capable of displaying digital information through shape-changing, and start to explore the social impact in complex contexts such as health care. Ultimately, Vital+Morph proposes an unusual viewpoint of the relations between bodies, clinical data and future materials.

Author Keywords

Shape-changing; alternative display; information visualization; presence; health care.

ACM Classification Keywords

H.5.2 [Information interfaces and presentation (e.g., HCI)]: Input devices and strategies.

Introduction

Today large amount of data are being collected about our bodies, environment and social relationships. The increas-

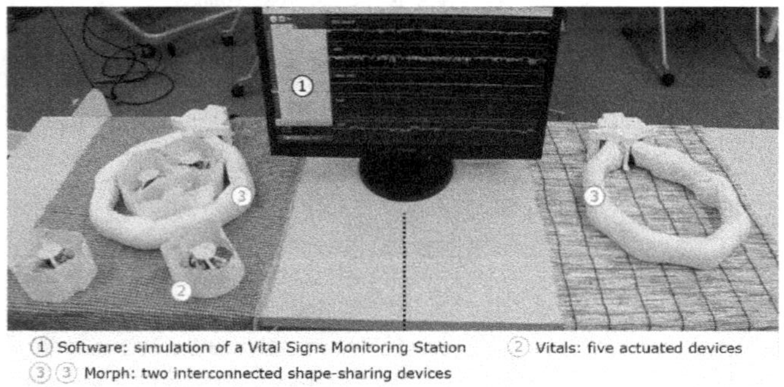

Figure 1: The three main elements that compose Vital+Morph: 1) a software, 2) a series of five *vitals*, 3) two interconnected and synchronized *morphs*

ing availability of Internet of Things devices will enable novel ways to get engaged with digital data in our daily environment. In this paper we introduce Vital+Morph (Fig.1), a prototype of a shape-changing interface designed as a media for remote physical connection and awareness. Data coming from a Vital Signs Monitoring Station (placed in an hospital) are *physicalized* in real-time into a series of five physical devices. These elements are surrounded by an input-output device that helps remote people to share their physical presence by actively deforming it.

We propose Vital+Morph as an interface for remote biometric monitoring. The project is still under development and has gone through a limited series of tests. In this paper we focus the attention on the design process and implementation of the prototype. The interactions and different functions will be briefly presented. Finally, we summarize and discuss the results of a series of preliminary informal evaluations. Through this prototype we aim to contribute to the exploration of novel relations between bodies, clinical data,

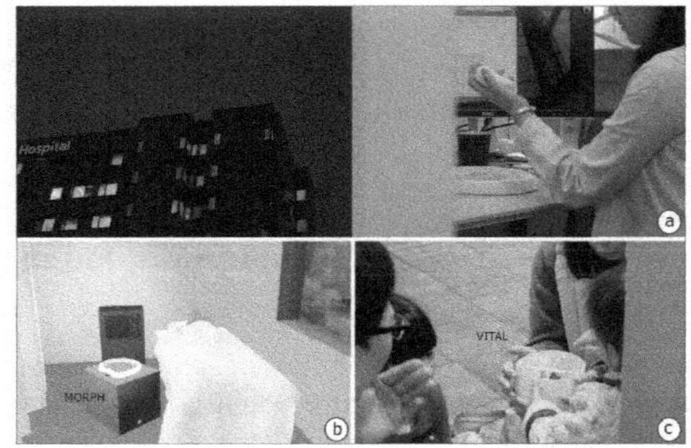

Figure 2: An illustration of the possible application of Vital+Morph: (a) an illustration of the main concept; (b) a rendering of an Intensive Care Unit; (c) a *vital* element carried by one of the patient's relatives.

and future 'computational materials': *how to get physically engaged with clinical data* ? *How they can be integrated in our daily life* ? In addition we would like to provoke a discussion on the impact of shape-changing interfaces, their possibilities and limitations in complex contexts such as health care (Fig.2).

Related work

Vital+Morph can be framed into the emerging research area of *data physicalization*, which includes a series of practices and attempts for helping people explore, understand and communicate digital data using computer-supported physical representations [4]. This emerged from recent and anticipated technological advances in digital fabrication, tangible user interfaces and shape-changing displays that will radically change the way how digital data can be made physical. In addition, since the introduction of visions such

Figure 3: A cluster of bubbles. Photo: ⓒⓑ author

Figure 4: A paper mock-up of the Vital+Morph bi-directional communication. Photo: ⓒⓑ author

as the one of Radical Atoms [3], several researchers have started a systematic reflection on how future *computational materials* can impact and develop novel forms of human-machine interaction.

Several studies have been conducted in the HCI field in order to investigate the usage of bio-signals as a means of communication. Heartbeat, respiration and body heat are the most studied among others because of their symbolic meaning and the availability of reliable and affordable sensors. Most of these systems represent and share bio-signals between distant users through tactile and thermal feedback, in order to promote a more intimate connection and emotional awareness. Some prominent examples are 'Mobile Feelings' [7] and 'Breathing Frame' [5]. Vital+Morph tries to explore a novel territory of communication and awareness, between the hospital and the outside. It is important to mention that a project developed by Kerridge [1] represents an important precursor of "Vital+Morph", even though it employs a more speculative design approach.

Design process

Materials and information

The continuous production of data is usually expressed through the use of verbs such as "flow"and "stream". They mark a strong analogy between information technologies, natural elements (such as water and air), and physiological process like blood circulation or respiration. Ultimately, streams are associated with the idea of life, representing a living entity. In order to design a novel shape-changing interface we started to think about a material that can embody the idea of flow and stream, but can also be directly touched, and carried around without using any sort of containers. This led us to imagine a novel material capable of displaying digital information by shifting from a stable shape

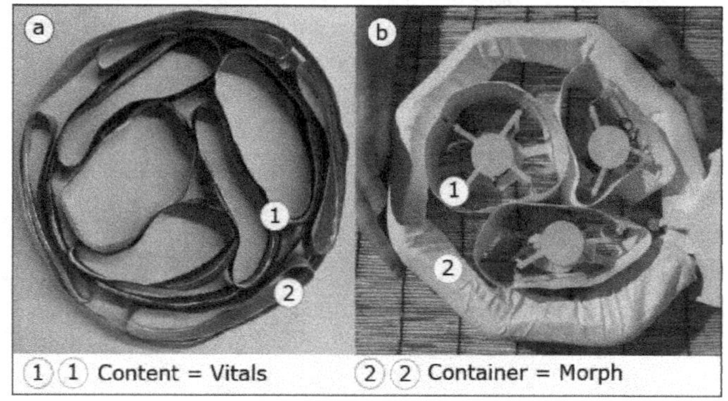

Figure 5: The paper mock-up (a) and the final prototype (b).

into an unstable shape, like from a "solid"to 'liquid' state and vice versa. Since this kind of material does not exist, we have designed a perceptually equivalent one. The following section summarizes the design process of such imaginative material.

Paper prototype

In order to prototype our new material we looked at existing natural elements such as soap bubbles (Fig.3). By observing the process of formation and aggregation of bubbles we derived our design (Fig.5). We started to explore these forms by transferring them to a tangible realm through some stylized paper models. These have been used as probes for discussing and refining the overall shape and the functions of the display. We have identified two important elements : 1) five elements that act as display for the data, 2) a container. We named the former as *vitals* and the latter as *morph.* Each stream of data is displayed through a single surface that changes shape accordingly. We have decided to use five elements because there are five fundamental vital signs. The configuration presented in Fig.5 enables dif-

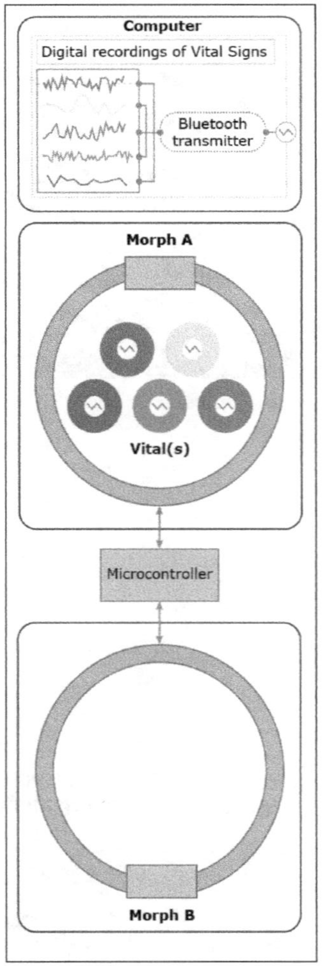

Figure 6: A schematic representation of the system. Photo: author

ferent interactions between a user, the material and data. In this way each data stream can be perceived individually and taken to an intimate level. Being independent, the *vitals* can be moved in different places. Distributing them to different users can lead to a novel form of "co-monitoring"of data: each user can shares the responsibility of monitoring a piece of information. In addition, by placing the *vitals* inside the circular contour (the *morphs*), differences between data streams can be detected easily by comparing the deformations of their surfaces. If the *vitals* are used for displaying the vital signs coming from the hospital, the *morph* is conceived as a shape-sharing interface. Through this system, distant located users can communicate and interact with each other by exchanging the shape and motion of the physical element (Fig.4).

Technical implementation

The basic framework of Vital+Morph is presented in Figure 6. In this section we introduce the implementation of the prototype by describing its main components: the software, the *vitals* and the *morph*.

Software

A software written in Processing reads a text file containing the recordings of five different physiological signals, and plot them on a monitor. Each signal is transmitted to its corresponding vital using via Bluetooth.

Data selection

Instead of measuring vital signs from a real patient we have used a set of data obtained through Physio Data Bank[1], a public database of physiologic data. For this prototype we choose 24 hours recordings of a 80 years old woman hospitalized after a surgery. We select five signals: heart rate (pulse), arterial pressure, respiratory rate, pulmonary arterial pressure, and central venous pressure. At this stage we implemented a simple direct mapping between each signal and actuators.

[1] https://physionet.org/physiobank/

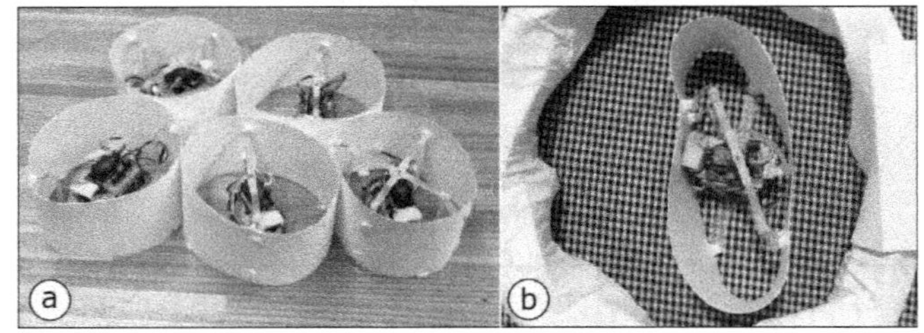

Figure 7: *Vitals*: the five different elements (a). When actuated a *vital* element will present the received signal through physical deformation (b).

Vitals

In order to implement the shape-changing material described above, we have designed the surface of the *vitals* to be deformed by a single internal actuator. Already some work has been done in the area of soft robotics to explore similar solutions for design deformable robots. Sugiyama and Hirai [8] proposed a circular robot modeled as a rheological object, which consists of a series of SMA actuators attached to the inside of a rubber shell. When voltage is applied to a wire, it causes a contraction resulting in a deformation of the shell. We started from this example, but with a single actuator only. As shown in Figure 7 each *vital* is composed of a paper cylindrical surface that surrounds the actuated mechanism, an Arduino Pro Mini 328, a Bluetooth receiver module, and a lythium-ion polymer battery hosted in a custom made container (Fig.8). In order to increase the deformation effect the paper surface is coated with few layers of latex paint. The actuation is provided by a mechanism driven by a micro servo motor (Tower Pro SG90)

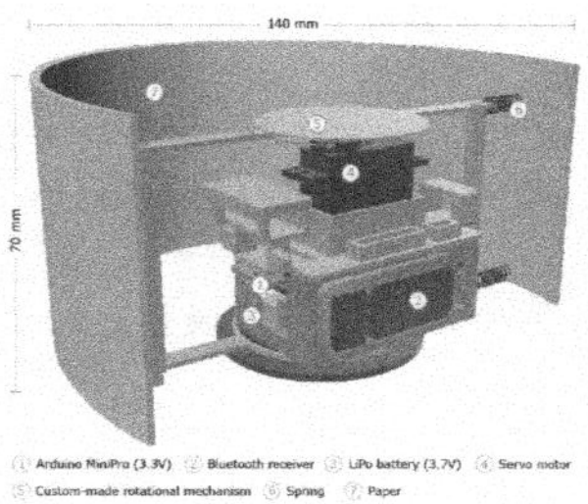

Figure 8: The different parts of a *vital* element. Photo: ⓒⓘ author

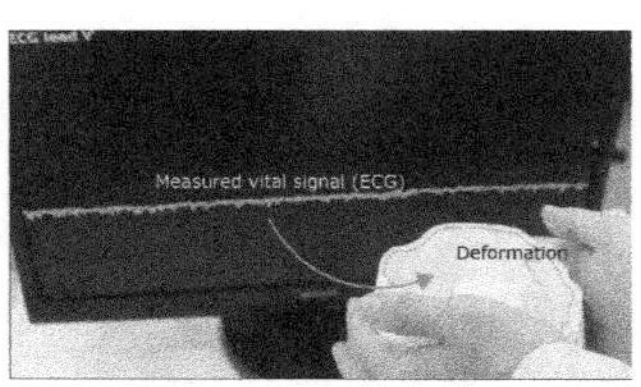

Figure 9: The relation between the signal measured by the VSMS and a *vital* element. Photo: ⓒⓘ author

that actuates at a speed of 0.1 sec/60 deg. The servo is connected to the paper surface with small springs (radius: 2mm, length: 100mm). When the shaft of the servo motor rotates the spring pulls the paper, which causes a deformation of the surface. Such solution helps to smooth the effect of the motor rotation and provides a simple form of indirect haptic feedback. Since the deformation is caused by a single motor, a series of customized horns for the servo have been developed. Each configuration gives a different deformation. The horns on the top of the motor are then vertically linked to a passive rotational element on the bottom of the structure. Then the paper surface is connected with the bottom of the module through a plastic stand. This prevents the cylinder from moving freely and at the same time improves the quality of the shape-changing effect.

Morph

The concept of shape-sharing using paired remote robotic systems was previously introduced by Sekiguchi et al. [6]. We employed this idea for implementing the *morph* elements. The current version is composed of two synchronized elements composed of a group of eight actuators (for each *morph*) linked together and enclosed in a soft cover (Fig. 10). In order to provide an input-output mechanism we have used an analog feedback type of servo motors (Adafruit LLC 1450), where position sensing and actuation are provided in a single element. The motors are then connected with a custom made linear type of linkage (Fig. 11). The two devices are then connected and synchronized through an Arduino Mega board, which implements a direct mapping between the position sensor of a motor to the opposite one, and backwards. Finally the motor chain was covered with a handmade soft cover composed of an elastic surface, and reinforced internally with a sponge-like material. This helps to enrich the tactile qualities of the device by making it more soft.

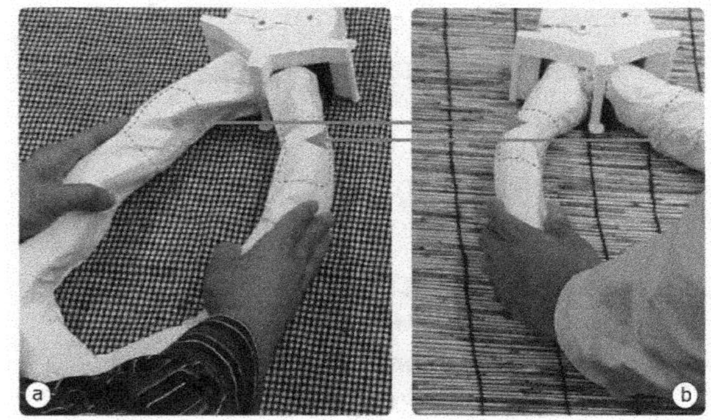

Figure 10: *Morphs*: the two synchronized devices.

Preliminary evaluation: issues and limitations

In order to understand the limitations and potential of this prototype we have organized a series of informal meetings and presentations with colleagues, students and the general public. We recorded a general appreciation of the aesthetics and feel of the interface. Many users said that the global interface "*looks like a living organism*", and "*feels good in my hands*". These comments support the idea that designing shape-changing interfaces with a life-like behavior can help people to relate more strongly with the digital content displayed through them. In addition, many users expressed an interest regarding the applications scenario of Vital+Morph: "*I never thought about this possibility*", others said that "*it will be useful for the aging society*". However some of them pointed out some personal concerns: "*it is a creepy perspective* [...] *I don't want to have such kind of device in my house*". Even if informal evaluations underline the power of *physicalizations*, as a very effective but also intrusive way for displaying data in daily environments. In spite of this a critical point many participants noted the diffi-

Figure 11: One *Morph* element opened to reveal its content. Photo: 🅭🅯 author

culty of clearly understanding the correlation between data and deformations.

Future work

Future development will focus both on improving the technical properties of the current prototype, and enhancing the capability of displaying data through shape-changing, such as:

- improving the *vitals* : testing different materials (silicone, gels) in order to give better durability and appearance in combination with a faster and precise actuation.
- Developing a novel vocabulary for the *morph*: establishing a lexicon of shape-sharing for remote physical presence.
- Investigating more appropriate and expressive mapping strategies for representing data through shape-changing. The methodology proposed by Houben et al. [2] represents a promising starting point.
- Exploring potential interactions between the *morphs* and the *vitals*, since at the moment there are no explicit relations.

The implementation of all these features requires, however, a consistent evaluation on how effectively the relation between data and shape-changing can be actually communicated and recognized by the users, and more specifically an understanding of how people would relate and interact with such system. There are many important questions to answer in order to improve the design and the use in real life scenarios. Regarding the design, they imply the investigation on more general open questions shared within the research field of *data physicalization* and shape-changing interfaces. Therefore testing this interface in a real scenario (the hospital and outside) represent a very critical step for our research.

Conclusion

In this paper we presented a work in progress of a system that allows clinical data to be *physicalized* in real-time through a novel shape-changing display. We described the design process, the possible interactions, and the implementation of each single element. A preliminary evaluation was also reported, but more structured user testing will help us refine the current prototype and proving its effectiveness in real-life scenario.

REFERENCES

1. Jacob Beaver, Sarah Pennington, and Tobie Kerridge. 1995. *Material Beliefs*. London: Goldsmiths, University of London / Interaction Research Studio.
2. Steven Houben, Connie Golsteijn, Sarah Gallacher, Rose Johnson, Saskia Bakker, Nicolai Marquardt, Licia Capra, and Yvonne Rogers. 2016. Physikit: Data Engagement Through Physical Ambient Visualizations in the Home. In *Proceedings of the 2016 CHI Conference on Human Factors in Computing Systems (CHI '16)*. ACM, New York, NY, USA, 1608–1619. DOI: http://dx.doi.org/10.1145/2858036.2858059
3. Hiroshi Ishii, Dávid Lakatos, Leonardo Bonanni, and Jean-Baptiste Labrune. 2012. Radical Atoms: Beyond Tangible Bits, Toward Transformable Materials. *interactions* 19, 1 (Jan. 2012), 38–51. DOI: http://dx.doi.org/10.1145/2065327.2065337
4. Yvonne Jansen, Pierre Dragicevic, Petra Isenberg, Jason Alexander, Abhijit Karnik, Johan Kildal, Sriram Subramanian, and Kasper Hornbæk. 2015. Opportunities and Challenges for Data Physicalization. In *Proceedings of the 33rd Annual ACM Conference on*

Human Factors in Computing Systems (CHI '15). ACM, New York, NY, USA, 3227–3236. DOI: http://dx.doi.org/10.1145/2702123.2702180

5. Jina Kim, Young-Woo Park, and Tek-Jin Nam. 2015. BreathingFrame: An Inflatable Frame for Remote Breath Signal Sharing. In *Proceedings of the Ninth International Conference on Tangible, Embedded, and Embodied Interaction (TEI '15)*. ACM, New York, NY, USA, 109–112. DOI: http://dx.doi.org/10.1145/2677199.2680606
6. Dairoku Sekiguchi, Masahiko Inami, and Susumu Tachi. 2001. RobotPHONE: RUI for Interpersonal Communication. In *CHI '01 Extended Abstracts on Human Factors in Computing Systems (CHI EA '01)*. ACM, New York, NY, USA, 277–278. DOI: http://dx.doi.org/10.1145/634067.634231
7. Christa Sommerer and Laurent Mignonneau. 2004. Mobile Feelings: wireless communication of heartbeat and breath for mobile art. In *Proceedings of the 14th International Conference on Artificial Reality and Telexistance (ICAT2004)*. 346–349.
8. Yuuta Sugiyama and Shinichi Hirai. 2006. Crawling and jumping by a deformable robot. *The International journal of robotics research* 25, 5-6 (2006), 603–620.

Designing Interactive Systems for Balance Rehabilitation after Stroke

Héctor A. Caltenco
Anna Olsson
Afshin Aliyari
Charlotte Magnusson
Lund University
221 00 Lund, Sweden
hector@certec.lth.se
mte11aol@student.lu.se
afshin.aliyari@certec.lth.se
charlotte@certec.lth.se

Ingibjörg Hjaltadóttir
Thóra B. Hafsteinsdóttir
Helga Jónsdóttir
Ingibjörg Bjartmarz
University of Iceland
101 Reykjavík, Iceland
ingihj@hi.is
t.hafsteinsdottir@umcutrecht.nl
helgaj@hi.is
ingibjar@landspitali.is

David McGookin
Mikko Kytö
Aalto University
02150 Espoo, Finland
david.mcgookin@aalto.fi
mikko.kyto@aalto.fi

TEI '17, March 20-23, 2017, Yokohama, Japan
ACM 978-1-4503-4676-4/17/03.
http://dx.doi.org/10.1145/3024969.3025084

Abstract
This paper presents four different tangible interactive prototypes designed to support the continuation of balance rehabilitation at home. The interactive prototypes are designed to provide a more enjoyable and experience when performing balance rehabilitation exercises. Early results from preliminary tests with stroke survivors and rehabilitation professionals are promising. The aim of the designs is to allow people at different levels of rehabilitation to engage into balance training and perform the exercises according to their current skills.

Author Keywords
User studies; stroke; activity; tangible interaction; co-design; participatory design.

ACM Classification Keywords
H.5.m. Information interfaces and presentation (e.g., HCI): Miscellaneous

Introduction
Stroke is the leading cause of long-term disability in western countries [10] resulting in life-altering changes for both the stoke survivor and their closest family. Loss of balance is common among stroke-survivors. Difficulties with posture and balance make it difficult for persons to walk, and thus to leave the home to

socialize or perform other outdoor tasks. After intensive rehabilitation in a dedicated rehabilitation setting, the majority of stroke survivors with residual impairments are discharged and then rely on informal caregivers (frequently close family members) [5].

Effective rehabilitation of stroke survivors is required to help them accomplish daily activities (cooking, washing, etc.) and lead an independent life. After discharge, much of this rehabilitation occurs at home, through performing different types of exercises and activities. Such as training in activities of daily living, strength training, cardio-vascular training, balance training, gait training and postural control [4]. However, training exercises can be difficult to integrate into the existing lives of stroke survivors. Exercises can be repetitive and difficult to perform correctly. Which leads to stroke survivors losing confidence and giving up on rehabilitation, losing the benefits it could provide. Thus, it is important to investigate how to better support the continuation of rehabilitation at home.

Donker et. al. [1] used interactive tiles for balance training during stroke rehabilitation sessions. They showed that providing real time visual feedback improved motivation and was helpful for balance rehablitation. Auditory feedback via sonification is also helpful for improving motoric skills [2]. Stienstra et. al. [8] studied how movement sonification improves proprioception during speedskating, if it is latency-free, and the richness of data details generated by the movement are preserved in the richness of sound parameters, such as dynamics, loudness, tempo, pitch and timbre. Other relevant work has proven the benefits of movement sonification on proprioception and awareness [3,7].

Moreover, music and rhythm therapy are proven to help stroke survivors to increase the feeling of being connected to their own body. A study by Thornberg et. al. [9] shows that music and rhythm exercises were considered positively challenging for stroke survivors, while facilitating motor planning and coordination. Music is also a significant motivation factor while training which can give emotional pleasure [9]. Pleasant sounds tend to persuade the user into behavioural change [8].

The *ActivABLES* research project is aimed at investigating the role interactive technologies can play for stroke survivors and support activities and training at home, in between formal therapy sessions or after discharge. Even though the *ActivABLES* project focuses on a range of different aspects of physical rehabilitation, the present paper presents different interactive prototypes designed to support the continuation of balance rehabilitation at home. The goal is to provide a more enjoyable and experience when performing balance rehabilitation exercises. We present early results from the initial testing of our prototypes.

Interactive Tangible Prototypes

Balance training and postural control can be performed in different ways. Active balance training happens when one must constantly move to maintain equilibrium. Passive balance training is where one will stay in balance if one doesn't move. Balance can be performed in static surfaces or dynamic surfaces. Static surfaces are firm, uneven or compliant surfaces which do not move regardless of the location or amount of force applied to them. Dynamic surfaces will move or tilt if any external force is applied, disturbing its center of gravity.

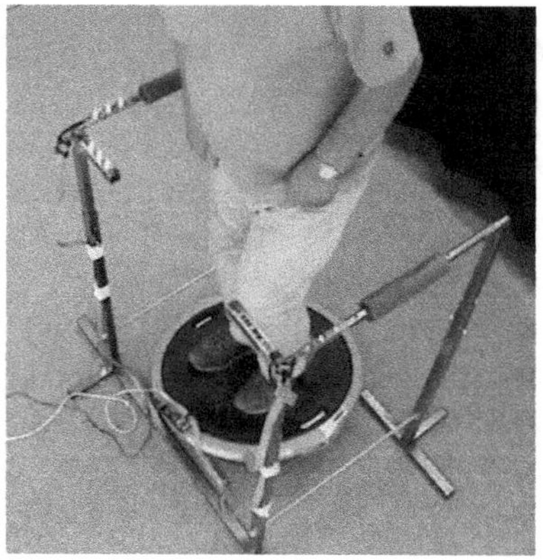

Figure 1. Stroke survivor using ActivBOSU, leaning slightly towards the right. Therefore the front-right and back-right indicators are lighted green.

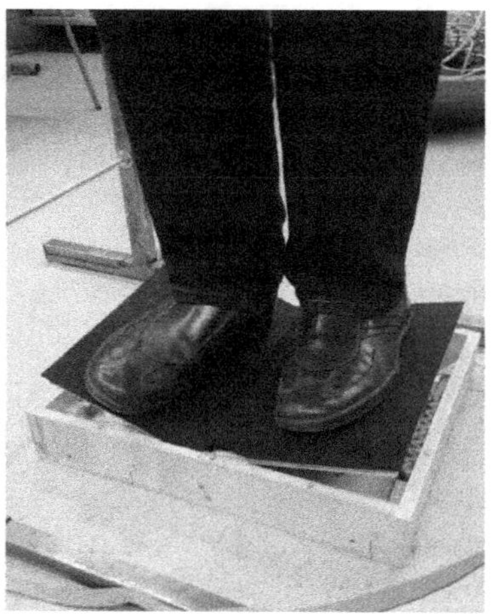

Figure 2. ActivPEDALS linked together by a rubber sheet. The same safety handle bars are used as in ActivBOSU.

In this section we present three different interactive prototypes designed to train passive and active balance while sitting or standing using static and dynamic surfaces. Performing exercises with these interactive objects could be done in different ways, depending on the preferences and motivation of the individuals. Due the benefits of music and rhythm therapy as well as the added motivation factor, the designed interactive balance-training devices are used to play/create music while performing rehabilitation exercises.

ActivBOSU

The ActivBOSU is a dynamic surface that can be used to train active or passive balance while standing. It consists of a BOSU balance board instrumented with an Arduino microcontroller, a 3-axis accelerometer which detects the tilt angle and direction. The safety support handle bars are equipped with RGB LED strips that provide visual feedback on the amount and direction of the tilt. All LED indicators are placed in the frontal half of the support handle bars so the user can see them without having to turn the head around (Figure 1). The Arduino UNO microcontroller sends the accelerometer signals to a computer running Ableton Live which produces different sound effects depending on the amount and direction of the tilt. Tilting the device affects both music and light simultaneously.

Two training programs were developed. In the active balance training program, if the user is standing still in a vertical position no light or sound are on. If the user is moving or standing still in tilted positions different sound landscapes and LEDs are activated, depending on the direction. The intensity of music and colour of light depends on how much the balance board is tilted. The light in the direction where the board is tilted is lighted up. In the "safe zone" when the balance board is just slightly tilted, the colour of the light is green, then yellow and when the light turns red the person shall be careful not to lose his/her balance.

In the passive balance training program, when the person is standing still and centred, soft classical music can be heard and no lights on. If the user tilts the platform, the music gradually gets distorted and the colour of the led-lights goes from green, to yellow, to red depending on how much the ActivBOSU tilts. The constructed prototype has only one degree of difficulty, but it is possible to inflate or deflate the BOSU ball to make it less or more stable, one can also change how sensitive the light/music feedback is with a new calibration.

During the development of the prototype the ergonomic aspects were considered. The plate where the feet are placed is suitable for all sizes and shapes of feet. The user is free to place his/her feet in an angle that feels comfortable and can easily change it without changing any settings. Stroke-survivors need to be able to hold on to the safety handles in order to minimize the risk of falling. The handles are designed so that they should be stable, comfortable to hold on to, fit into a normal home or local for rehabilitation, be movable and not leaving permanent marks in the floor. The handles are adjustable in height and distance from each other.

ActivPEDALS

ActivPEDALS is a variation of ActivBOSU. It is designed as two independent dynamic surfaces that can be used to train active or passive balance while standing, in addition of being able to train ankle flexion, extension, pronation and supination while standing or sitting.

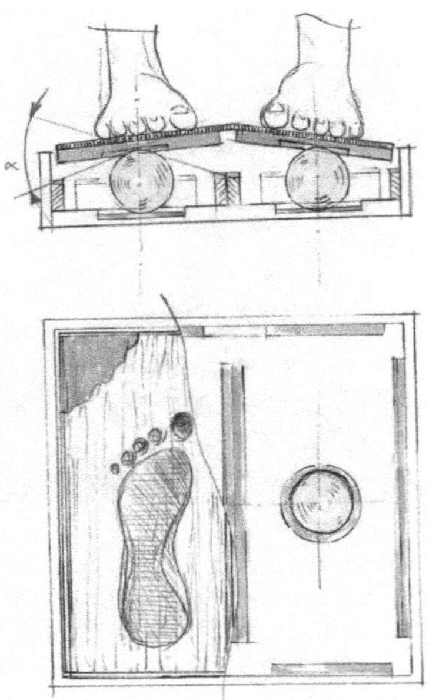

Figure 3. ActivPEDALS illustration. Two independent platforms (blue) standing over rubber balls (yellow) and eight pressure sensors (pink) that detect contact between platforms and the box. Two pressure sensors under the rubber balls detect the weight distribution of the person standing on the prototype.

ActivPEDALS consists of a wooden box with two independent platforms standing over rubber balls fixed at the bottom of the box, which allow the platforms to tilt towards the edges of the box. The platforms can be link-together to act as a single large platform instead (Figure 2). Each platform is instrumented with an accelerometer that detects the amount and direction of tilt. Eight Pressure sensors detect if there is contact between the platform edges and the box (Figure 3).

An Arduino UNO microcontroller sends the signals from both accelerometers and the eight multiplexed pressure sensors to a computer running Ableton Live which produces different sound effects depending on the amount and direction of the tilt of each platform and the amount of pressure on the sensors. The tilt and contact signals affects different sound parameters and lights at the same time. One can increase or decrease the stability of the platforms by easily exchanging the balls inside the box for ones with larger or smaller diameter. One can also change how sensitive the light/music feedback is with a new calibration.

ActivPEDALS can be used to train balance standing with one foot over each platform, in which case it has the same training programs for training while aiming to stand still and aiming to keep balance while actively leaning towards different sides. It provides extra sound layers and effects linked to the accelerometer signal of the second platform and different drum sounds for each of the pressure sensors. Lights are off if the platforms are centred and balanced. If a platform is slightly tilted the corresponding LEDs will light up green, or red if a platform activates a pressure sensor. The intensity of the light is mapped to the amount of tilt or pressure.

ActivCUSHION and ActivFOAM

ActivCUSHION and ActivFOAM are a static compliant-surfaces that can be used to train active balance while sitting or standing. These kinds of surface and training are used at the beginning of rehabilitation, when is difficult to keep balance when training in dynamic surfaces. They are designed to challenge balance and provide postural training.

ActivFOAM consists of a soft-compliant foam board for standing on, while ActivCUSHION consists of an inflatable cushion for seating on. Both of them are covered with a sandwich design of pressure-sensing fabric material (FlexTiles [6]). Which consists of two electrode layers of zebra fabric and a force sensitive layer of piezo resistive fabric in between (Figure 4).

The two layers of fabric are oriented orthogonal to each-other to form a matrix of pressure sensors with a resolution of 16 x 16 and 16 x 24 sensors for ActivCUSHION and ActivFOAM respectively. All rows and columns in the sensor matrix are connected to two 8-channel analog multiplexers (74HC4051) with pull-down 20Kohm resistors. The multiplexed rows go to the analog inputs of an Arduino microcontroller. The multiplexed columns are connected to the digital output pins, which sends 5V signals to one column at a time.

The working principle of ActivFOAM and ActivCUSHION is different from that one of ActivBOSU and ActivPEDALS, but the applications are similar. Instead of visual feedback using LED strips, the visual feedback is given to the user via a computer display. The corresponding pressure matrix is displayed on the screen as an array of black squares that change gradually towards white depending on how much

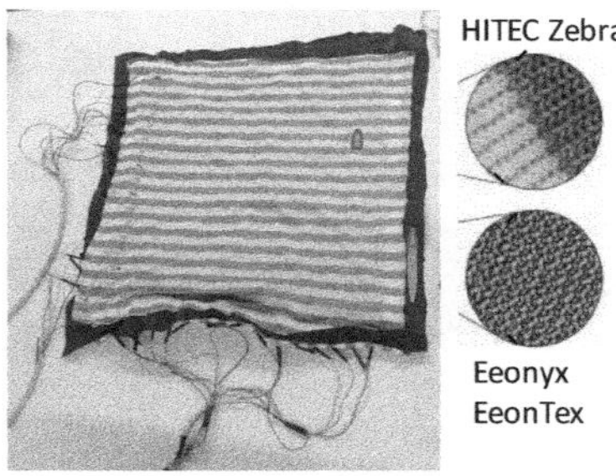

Figure 4. Pressure sensor matrix cover for ActivFOAM and ActivCUSHION. Sandwich design of two electrode layers of zebra fabric and a force sensitive layer of EeonTex piezo resistive fabric in between.

Figure 5. Testing visual feedback of the pressure sensor matrix cover for ActivFOAM and ActivCUSHION.

pressure is registered in each sensor (Figure 5). The sound feedback is the same as in the other prototypes, but instead of using the tilting of the platforms, the center of gravity of the shape(s) registered by the pressure sensor matrix is used. If more pressure is registered in e.g., the left foot, then the sound effect will play as if the user was tilting towards the left. ActivCUSHION follows the same principle, but for practicing balance while sitting.

Preliminary Evaluations

A preliminary evaluation of the prototypes was performed by three stroke survivors and by a group of rehabilitators and physical therapists. The preliminary tests started with a short interview to gather background information about their lives before and after the stroke, their rehabilitation, what has worked well and what can be improved, goals, interests, and motivation to perform exercises. After the interviews, participants tested the interactive tangibles using the passive balance and active balance training programs. Afterwards, a short discussion about the test was done.

ActivBOSU

The results from the preliminary tests of ActivBOSU with stroke-survivors were promising. The prototype was described as uncomplicated, flexible, motivating and stimulating by one stroke survivor. This person said it was more fun to train the balance when music was included, which lead to higher motivation to train. It was a general agreement by stroke survivors and rehabilitators that ActivBOSU needs to have more music or sound options and different training-programs to make the training fun and motivating over time. Led-lights was included in the support handle bars to give feedback on how the user tilted the balance-board and it helped the user to find a straighter body-position. However, it was hard for one of the stroke survivors to look down to see the lights. Whenever he tried to look at them, he felt he lost his balance. Visual feedback should be provided at eye-level to avoid this problem. The third stroke survivor felt the feedback was overwhelming, and would have preferred to be able to use it without any additional feedback – at least initially. This reflects the well-known fact that stroke survivors are a very diverse population.

ActivPEDALS

One of the design ideas of ActivePEDALS was to make the active balance training safer and easier, since the range of motion is lower than the one of ActivBOSU. But in fact, both stroke survivors and rehabilitators found it harder to keep balance with ActivePEDALS. We believe, this is mostly due to the independent plates. However, the rehabilitators found it potentially very useful to rehabilitate ankle flexion/extension and pronation/supination while sitting. Moreover, it has good potential for more complex musicalization, due to the independent plates and the added pressure sensors. And it could be a more challenging option for rehabilitees with better balance.

ActivFOAM and ActivCUSHION

During these tests, auditive feedback was not available and only visual feedback was demonstrated. ActivFOAM was seen by the rehabilitators as promising, since balance rehabilitation of all stroke survivors starts with similar foam-mats and having one that could provide visual and musical feedback for balance and posture while standing and sitting was something they looked forward to.

Conclussions

In general, continuing to train balance at home, after discharge, is important for stroke survivors to keep their functional level. Incorporating music into interactive tangibles for balance rehabilitation can potentially help the motivation and make the training more enjoyable and fun. Moreover, having a set of different interactive tangibles to train passive and active balance, and having static and dynamic surfaces will allow people at different levels of rehabilitation to engage into balance training and perform the exercises.

Acknowledgements

We would like to extend our gratitude to all the stroke survivors in Sweden and health care professionals in Finland taking part in the research. The authors also gratefully acknowledge NordForsk for the support given to the project ActivABLES, as well as the EU for the support of the related project 689947 STARR.

References

1. V Donker, P Markopoulos, and B Bongers. 2015. REHAP Balance Tiles: A modular system supporting balance rehabilitation. *Pervasive Computing Technologies for Healthcare (PervasiveHealth), 2015 9th International Conference on*, 201–208. http://doi.org/10.4108/icst.pervasivehealth.2015.259278
2. Alfred O Effenberg. 2007. Movement Sonification : Motion perception , behavioral effects and functional data. *Proceedings of the 2nd International Workshop on Interactive Sonification (ISon 2007)*, 1–4.
3. Frank Feltham and Lian Loke. 2014. The slow floor: increasing creative agency while walking on an interactive surface. *Proceedings of the 8th International Conference on Tangible, Embedded and Embodied Interaction*: 105–112. http://doi.org/10.1145/2540930.2540934
4. Hanne Kaae Kristensen, Charlotte Ytterberg, Dorrie Lee Jones, and Hans Lund. 2016. Research-based evidence in stroke rehabilitation: an investigation of its implementation by physiotherapists and occupational therapists. *Disability and rehabilitation*: 1–11. http://doi.org/10.3109/09638288.2016.1138550
5. B J Lutz, M E Young, K J Cox, C Martz, and K R Creasy. 2011. The crisis of stroke: experiences of patients and their family caregivers. *Topics in stroke rehabilitation* 18, 6: 786–797. http://doi.org/10.1310/tsr1806-786; 10.1310/tsr1806-786
6. Patrick Parzer, Kathrin Probst, Teo Babic, et al. 2016. FlexTiles: A Flexible, Stretchable, Formable, Pressure-Sensitive, Tactile Input Sensor. *Proceedings of the 2016 CHI Conference Extended Abstracts on Human Factors in Computing Systems*, ACM, 3754–3757. http://doi.org/10.1145/2851581.2890253
7. Prashant Srinivasan, David Birchfield, Gang Qian, and Assegid Kidané. 2005. A pressure sensing floor for interactive media applications. *ACE '05: Proceedings of the 2005 ACM SIGCHI International Conference on Advances in computer entertainment technology*, 278–281. http://doi.org/http://doi.acm.org/10.1145/1178477.1178526
8. Jelle Stienstra, C.J. Overbeeke, and Stephan Wensveen. 2011. Embodying Complexity Through Movement Sonification : Case Study on Empowering the Speed-skater. *Proceedings of the 9th ACM SIGCHI Italian Chapter International Conference on Computer-Human Interaction: Facing Complexity*: 39–44. http://doi.org/10.1145/2037296.2037310
9. Kerstin Thornberg, Staffan Josephsson, and Ingrid Lindquist. 2014. Experiences of participation in rhythm and movement therapy after stroke. *Disability and rehabilitation* 36, 22: 1869–74. http://doi.org/10.3109/09638288.2013.876107
10. C D Wolfe. 2000. The impact of stroke. *British Medical Bulletin* 56, 2: 275–286. http://doi.org/10.1258/0007142001903120

Nellodee 1.0: A Living Book to Enhance Intimacy with Head Gestures and Kinetic Typography

Sanghyun Yoo
School of Arts Media and Engineering
Arizona State University
Tempe, Arizona, USA
cooperyoo@asu.edu

Chandana Lakshminarayana
University of California, San Diego
San Diego, California, USA
clakshmi@eng.ucsd.edu

Avinandan Basu
Indian Institute of Technology
Guwahati, Assam, India
avinandanbose@gmail.com

TEI '17, March 20-23, 2017, Yokohama, Japan
ACM 978-1-4503-4676-4/17/03.
http://dx.doi.org/10.1145/3024969.3025086

Abstract
We advance the notion of a "living book" to explore how digital texts can enhance the potential for emotional relationships between readers and books. Our prototype of a living book, called Nellodee, is a user interface system to help readers to be companion with books. In this paper, we present two key concepts of Nellodee: head gesture recognition for expressions of opinion, and kinetic typography as emotional feedback.

Author Keywords
Living book; head gesture interface; kinetic typography; interaction design; enhancing intimacy; computer-mediated communication

ACM Classification Keywords
K.3.1 [Computers and Education]: Computer Uses in Education -- computer-assisted instruction (CAI); H.5.2 [Information Interfaces and Presentation]: User Interfaces – user-centered design.

Introduction
In the digital era, there are boundless possibilities for using technology to enhance electronic books (e-books). Computational interfaces and ubiquitous computing allow us to create new forms of liveliness,

Figure 1. A reader interacting with Nellodee while reading the novel "Frankenstein"

interaction, and emotional contact. Many current researches exploring interaction techniques for e-book focus on mimicking natural behavior of reading paper books. For example, Yoon et al. [10] studied the use of multi-touch navigation technique enabling users to bookmark a page in a casual manner. Tajika et al. [9] applied flexible plastic sheet with bend sensors, to reproduce the natural page-turning actions as used in reading a book. There is a general lack of imagination on display with current e-books, often called "books under glass" for their limited efforts to reproduce the affordances of print text on a screen.

In our work, we embrace the unique relationships we already have with books and ask how interface design can enhance e-books for learning and engagement. We leverage emerging technologies to exploring a concept we call a "living book." Our design goals are to enhance the social relationship between the user and the book while embracing the user's expectations of what a book should be, and avoiding overcomplicating the reading experience.

A Living Book

Designs that incorporate ambient awareness of user presence have been widely used to enhance intimacy between objects and users. In a recent book dealing with these objects responding to our needs and come to know us, David Rose examines six human desires that influence designing: omniscience, telepathy, safekeeping, immortality, teleportation, and expression. [6] In the context of e-books, telepathy and expression capture important aspects of our relationship with text. Telepathy is a desire to connect to the thoughts and feelings of others with ease and transparency. Expression represents people's desire to fully express themselves in many forms and media.

Emotional Book Design: Kinetic Typography

Our living book goes beyond the ambient awareness of user presence to engage in an emotional dialog with reader. In order to explore other modes of emotional engagement, we propose to use the text in the book itself to emote through the subtle employment of kinetic typography. Kinetic typography is the typography associated with text that moves or changes over time. There are several techniques to express emotions through text. Varying typographic parameters like font, size, color, and contrast is one way of expressing emotions through text. [5] We explicitly chose to focus on kinetic typography rather than follow the ongoing efforts in the book design space to incorporate images, videos, sounds, and other multimedia. Multimedia can induce cognitive confusion by focusing attention away from the core task of reading comprehension [1], and thus we found it incongruent with our goals.

In our conceptual prototype we used a class of kinetic typography techniques called analogous motion, which uses movements reminiscent of human actions to convey emotional content. [4] For example, a "jumping" motion can convey feelings of happiness and excitement, and applying that motion to individual words of the text might do the same. As a second example, mirroring the motion of the input interaction gestures can engender rapport and a feeling of connectedness. [2]

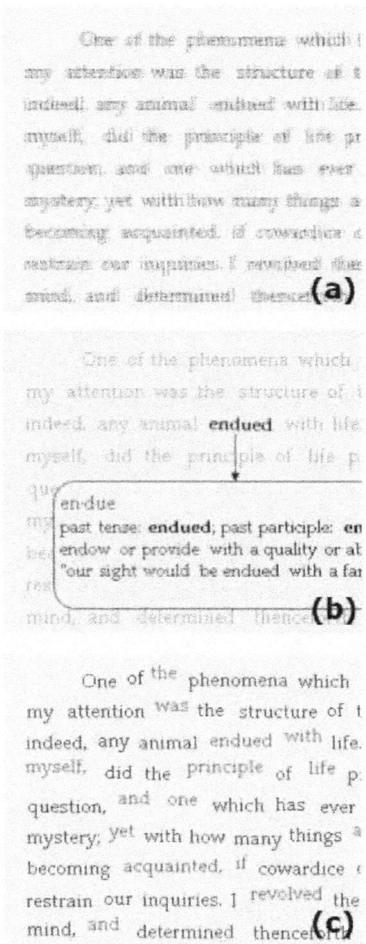

Figure 2. Screenshot of Nellodee: (a) Text shakes left and right when 'No gesture' is recognized, (b) Provides definition of academic vocabulary, (c) Text shakes up and down when 'Yes gesture' is activated

Silent Conversations: Head Gesture

In the living book, kinetic typography is a response to relevant user actions. Forms of non-verbal communication may indicate acknowledgement, agreement/disagreement or interest/disinterest. Head gestures play an important role in human-human interactions. Simple yet powerful gestures like nodding the head to say 'yes' and shaking it to say 'no' can enhance communication by increasing trust, clarity and support. Recent advances in the field of computer science have resulted in efficient head and gaze tracking systems that return reliable data about users' position and orientation in space. [3] Morency et al. [5] studied the use of gestures in user interfaces using vision based gesture recognition techniques. The detected head gestures were used for dialog box confirmation and browsing of documents. Ruiz et al. [8] performed a study in which given a task to perform on the device, end-users were to guess the gesture that would execute the task. In our approach, inputs from the readers to digital textbooks are provided through head gestures to increase the level of social engagement between the user and the textbook.

Nellodee

Nellodee, named after a character in Neal Stephenson's sci-fi novel "The Diamond Age", is a conceptual prototype that tries to make reading more engaging by building a friendly rapport with the reader. This prototype is a standalone application that takes head nod/shake gestures and the proximity of the user from the screen as inputs to deliver emotional feedback using kinetic typography. (Figure 1) It aims at providing a unique reading experience to anyone who is enthusiastic about reading. Hence it targets audience of all age groups.

Interactions with Nellodee

Input interactions are composed of few head gestures, which are common in natural human-human communication namely, nodding, shaking, and sneaking. The detection of inputs was done using FaceAPI; a library implemented by Seeing Machines, which returns the x, y, z co-ordinates of the location of the head with respect to webcam as the origin and the angles that the head makes with x, y and z-axes respectively. When user's intentional head gestures are recognized, Nellodee provides emotional feedback using kinetic typography.

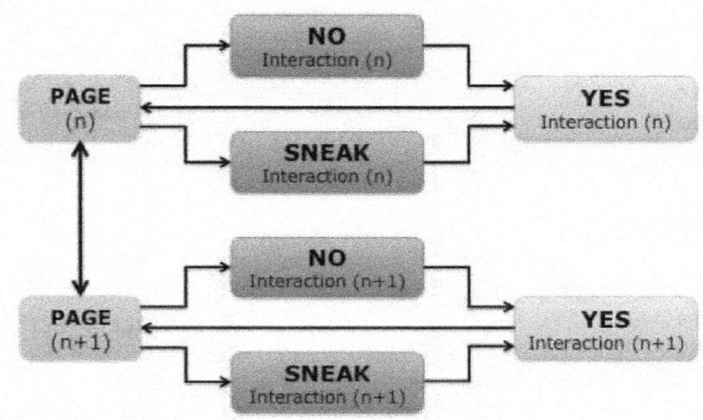

Figure 3. User flow of Nellodee

Interaction 1. No gesture

Shake gesture of the head is used to express "no" or "I did not understand". In Nellodee, these shake gestures are used to express that the user did not understand the meaning of the words. Vocabulary hints are provided after the text mirrors user's gesture by trembling left and right. (Figure 2a, 2b)

Interaction 2. Sneak gesture
It is natural to go closer and have a look to explore more about an object of interest. When the user comes closer to the book, Nellodee provides interesting hidden text related to the page. The response is the text flipping around to reveal the additional information behind the page. This interaction gives the user a sense of discovery of supplementary information to learn something new and exciting about the book.

Interaction 3: Yes gesture
The gesture of nodding is used as an input interaction to express "yes" or "I understand". When the reader is finished with learning from previous response, he can nod his head to convey that he would like to go back to the page he was currently reading. (Figure 3) Nellodee expresses the emotion of joy and happiness by making the words jump up and down, which is also mirroring the up-down head motion of the user. (Figure 2c)

Discussion and Conclusion

This prototype advances the idea of the "living book" as a design framework with potential impact in everyday reading and education. Developing a set of interface cues that enhance the historical relationship between user and text and the emotional resonance of that relationship has the potential to support the metacognition and beneficial emotional aspects of reading. Reading is a process, which is characterized by a flow. Creating a set of unobtrusive but supportive gestures through ambient awareness, head and gesture tracking and other methods could reinforce the flow state that typifies our best interactions with books.

References

[1] Downing, J. *Reading and Reasoning*. Oxford: Chambers, 1979.

[2] Gratch, J., Wang, N., Gerten, J., Fast, E. and Duffy, R. "Creating Rapport with Virtual Agents", *International Conference on Intelligent Virtual Agents*, 2007.

[3] Kapoor, Ashish, and Rosalind W. Picard. "A real-time head nod and shake detector." In *Proceedings of the 2001 workshop on Perceptive user interfaces*, pp. 1-5. ACM, 2001.

[4] Lee, J., Forlizzi, J., and Hudson, S. E. "The Kinetic Typography Engine: An Extensible System for Animating Expressive Text". In *UIST'02.*, pp. 81-90, ACM, 2002.

[5] Morency, Louis-Philippe, and Trevor Darrell. "Head gesture recognition in intelligent interfaces: the role of context in improving recognition." In *Proceedings of the 11th international conference on Intelligent user interfaces*, pp. 32-38. ACM, 2006.

[6] Rose, D. *Enchanted Objects: Design, Human Desire, and the Internet of Things.* Scribner, 2014.

[7] Radway, Janice A. *A Feeling for Books: The Book-Of-The-Month Club, Literary Taste, and Middle-Class Desire.* Chapel Hill: Univ. of North Carolina Press, 1997.

[8] Ruiz, Jaime, Yang Li, and Edward Lank. "User-defined motion gestures for mobile interaction." In *Proc. of the SIGCHI Conference on Human Factors in Computing Systems*, pp. 197-206. ACM, 2011.

[9] Tajika, Taichi, Tomoko Yonezawa, and Noriaki Mitsunaga. "Intuitive page-turning interface of e-books on flexible e-paper based on user studies." In *Proceedings of the 16th ACM international conference on Multimedia*. ACM, 2008.

[10] Yoon, D., Cho, Y., Yeom, K., and Park, J. H. "Touch-Bookmark: A lightweight navigation and bookmarking technique for e-books." In *CHI'11 Extended Abstracts on Human Factors in Computing Systems,* pp. 1189-1194. ACM, 2011.

Exploring Eyes-free Interaction with Wrist-Worn Deformable Materials

Victor Cheung
Carleton University
Ottawa, ON, Canada
victor.cheung@carleton.ca

Alexander Keith Eady
Carleton University
Ottawa, ON, Canada
alex.eady@carleton.ca

Audrey Girouard
Carleton University
Ottawa, ON, Canada
audrey.girouard@carleton.ca

TEI '17, March 20-23, 2017, Yokohama, Japan
ACM 978-1-4503-4676-4/17/03.
http://dx.doi.org/10.1145/3024969.3025087

Abstract
Recent work has explored how on-the-wrist devices can be augmented with displays, sensors, and aesthetics to produce a new genre of wearable, digital jewelry. Most often, these devices are augmented with hardware (e.g., touch-screens, gyroscopes) to receive wearer input. Breakthroughs in sensing materials allow novel inputs such as squeeze, bend, and stretch, which may be more suited to interaction with a discreet wearable.

We explore interactions with a flexible bracelet that can be manipulated through bend, stretch, and touch. We discuss the process involved in fabricating materials that convert these actions into measurable parameters. We particularly focus on eyes-free interactions with bracelets that take advantage of the tactile feedback from the act of deformation, and demonstrate some early, low-fidelity prototype concepts.

Author Keywords
Wearables; Deformation User Interaction; Bracelets; Digital Jewelry.

ACM Classification Keywords
H.5.2. Information interfaces and presentation: User Interfaces – Interaction styles, prototyping.

Introduction

Wearables are digital devices that can be worn on the body. They are typically equipped with sensors (e.g., pedometer, heart-rate monitor) and displays (e.g., LCD screen, LED light), and are often used for tasks like tracking personal biometrics in real-time or recording and analyzing daily activity. Besides being a popular research area in HCI, wearables are also receiving tremendous attention from sectors such as personal behaviour monitoring and healthcare [12].

One popular category of wearables is on-the-wrist devices (OWDs), which resemble watches or bracelets. OWDs benefit from the wrist being an easily accessible and socially acceptable site of interaction [20]. As a personal device, OWDs can also be regarded as fashion objects, and designers can explore their aesthetics in addition to interactions [19]. Emerging sensing materials and fabrication techniques allow new methods of interacting with wearable devices, which are different from most existing approaches to interactive wearables (e.g., [16,21]) in that actions applied to the structural materials (e.g., band of a smartwatch) can be sensed as user inputs; bringing robust, eyes-free interactions to OWDs. This area has not been well explored and may offer other advantages such as reducing power use, fabrication costs, and the bulkiness of devices.

In this paper we turn our attention to the current state of on-the-wrist devices, and to new materials and fabrication processes available. We contribute by presenting our early, low-fidelity deformable on-the-wrist prototypes, and an interaction language applicable to these devices. We also discuss the implications, and propose a testing plan for the utility of eyes-free deformable on-the-wrist wearables.

Related Work and Design Choices

We begin with the current state of on-the-wrist devices in academia and industry, and how they inspire our exploration in deformable OWDs. Next we examine examples of potential materials and sensors in fabricating deformable OWDs. We then discuss the considerations that informed our design of interactions for OWDs, such as eyes-free interaction and the involvement of both the wearing and activating hands.

Wearables and On-the-Wrist Devices

Researchers have used OWDs to gather data and communicate with the wearer. For example, Lyons et al. [16] created Facet, a bracelet comprising multiple segments featuring touch-screen displays, allowing its wearer to manage different levels of information detail from several applications. Fortmann et al. [6] proposed integrating LEDs for information display, along with sensors for data capture and buttons for user interaction into charms and gems on a bracelet, and recommended that device aesthetics and personal customization should be considered in OWD design.

Commercial "smart bracelets" are information focused but handle information display in diverse ways. For example, FitBit Flex2 [5] features notification lights, rather than the full displays found on smart watches like the Apple Watch [1]. In between are OWDs like the Under Armor Band [28], which have embedded, specialized displays. The use of different sensing and display components in OWDs must balance the ability to gather and convey information while maintaining a form appropriate to a wrist-worn device; increased size or bulky additions can lead to usability issues [21]. This is especially true for devices in the form of bracelets, which should not hinder common hand movements [6].

Besides what and how data are presented on an OWD, how people interact with OWDs is another area of research interest, especially regarding the novel interaction techniques enabled by their form and functionality. Pakanen et al. [21] designed Squeezy Bracelet as a communication device, where wearers squeezed pipets to create, read, and send messages. Tarun et al. [27] proposed Snaplet, which used bends on a bracelet display to determine context of use and user input. Perrault et al. [24] created WatchIt using resistive potentiometers on the wristband of a smartwatch for finger control, to support eyes-free interaction. These three works have inspired our initial design, where we propose to create a deformable on-the-wrist device for eyes-free interaction.

Materials and Fabrication Methods

Researchers have investigated the use of deformable materials as user interfaces (e.g., [3,14,23]), and have suggested that these novel materials could generate intuitive and adaptive interaction techniques. We have identified several materials and fabrication techniques applicable to the context of on-the-wrist devices.

Stretch/Pressure sensors made from conductive polymers offer simple interaction through deformation. The resistance of the sensor changes as it is stretched/pressed, giving a measurement of the magnitude of deformation (e.g., tension and stretch [17], pressure [18]). Similarly, carbon black pigment can be used with silicone rubber or other polymers to create custom conductive elements suitable for detecting touch [9] or strain [13]. Other methods of making stretch/touch sensors include printing conductive ink onto flexible substrates [29], and embedding optical sensors to detect transmissivity changes in elastic fabric [26]. Stretch and pressure are two interesting inputs that have not been explored in the context of interacting with the structural materials of an OWD.

Bend sensors have been used in wearables focusing on the hand and wrist [11]. These sensors, both uni- and bi-directional, can be used to detect deformations along one axis in specific parts of a deformable device. In the context of OWDs, they could be used to create discrete interaction areas within the device.

Breakthroughs in **deformable circuits** have facilitated robust fabrication of deformable OWDs. Researchers have used flexible circuits [15] and flexible displays [7] to create deformable mobile devices. The combination between these technologies and stretchable circuit technology [22] offers the potential for deformable OWDs being both bendable and stretchable.

Interacting with Deformables

An interesting characteristic uniquely afforded by deformable user interfaces is the provision of non-visual and tactile feedback through force/tension and people's understanding of the spatial positioning of their hands. For example, stretching a band creates tension that the user can feel. Once learned, we often rely on this spatial knowledge and tactile feedback to perform complex tasks without looking, like tying a shoelace. This drives the concept of eyes-free interaction, where the user *"can interact confidently in the absence of graphical feedback"* [20:126]. We focus on the input modalities of eyes-free interaction supported by the deformable materials used to create OWDs, as discussed in the next section.

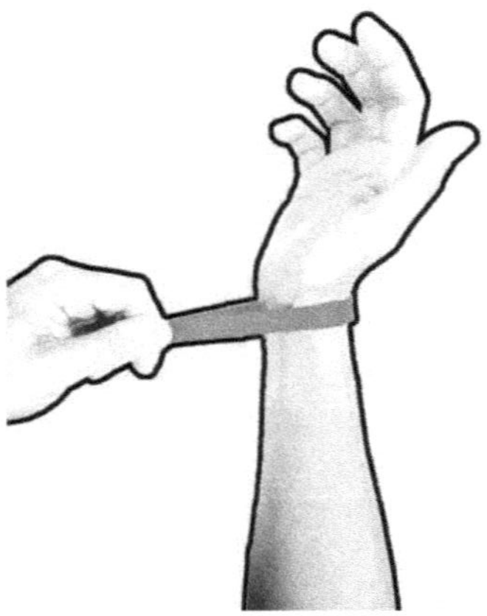

Figure 1. Interacting with a deformable on the wrist device: Pinching-along and pulling.

Figure 2. Exploratory prototype with embedded bend sensor.

Designing Eyes-Free Interactions for OWDs

In the context of deformable OWDs (e.g., bracelets), the wearing hand serves as an anchor to provide a fixed point or counter force to the actions of the activating hand. In designing interactions for OWDs, the style of interaction is often no longer purely one-handed, as it is with the Squeezy Bracelet [21] or most non-deformable wearables [16,24]. For example, the force of the tension created in stretching or pulling the device necessitates the wearing hand to perform a counter, or balancing force, typically from the opposite wrist, to support successful deformation. This may offer opportunities similar to the structural holds that have been identified in flexible display interactions [4].

Interestingly, deformable devices designed for use on the hand and wrist typically assume forms that designate the wearing hand also as the activating hand (e.g., [8,10,25]). This would not be possible for a deformable OWD, as locating the device fully on the wrist makes its accessibility to the wearing hand uncomfortable or impossible more most people.

For intentional interaction, we believe that the material properties of deformable devices are best utilized when both hands are involved (Figure 1). This is different from sensor augmentation which does not require bimanual interaction, as we see with wearable devices in the existing literature (e.g., [16,21]). Yet, to our knowledge, none have looked at interaction languages for deformable wearables.

In view of such discrepancy, we developed an interaction language that captures the fundamental actions available for bimanual eyes-free interactions for OWDs. We began with informal brainstorming sessions within our research group with various expertise in interaction design and fabrication by putting elastic bands (flat, slightly loose) on our wrists, and freely manipulated the bands. This method was similar to that used by Lee et al. [14], where participants were provided with deformable materials (paper, plastic, cloth), to elicit deformation-based gestures. However, we did not target any specific tasks to gain a better understanding of what actions an OWD afforded. The basic motion types we found were consistent with those identified by Lee et al. using an elastic cloth (except crumpling), and with a few additional interactions more specific to bands (e.g., pinching). We then adapted and summarized these gestures into our interaction language for OWDs, as illustrated in Figure 3.

This language highlights the partial bimanual nature of the actions using separate descriptions of the activating hand (AH) and wearing hand (WH). We use this notion instead of "dominant" and "non-dominant" hands, as these actions can be performed by either, and are dependent on which hand is wearing the device. To provide more context, this language includes measurable parameters for implementation, such as magnitude and direction of bend and stretch, as well as force of pressure. Using these parameters, designers can choose between discrete inputs (e.g., binary through a threshold value) and continuous inputs (e.g., mapping of magnitude of bend to a range of values).

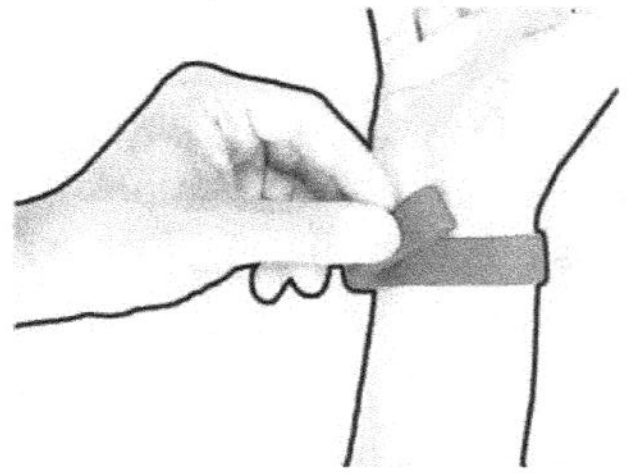

Bending/Folding

AH's fingers apply force at two ends, device forms an arc, or a loop when the ends touch. Measurable as magnitude of bend.

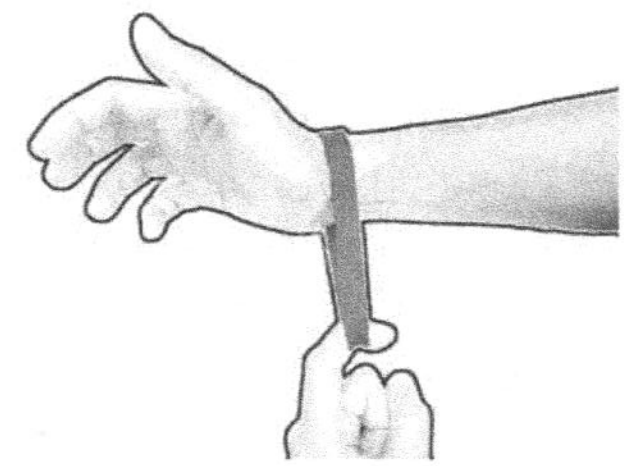

Stretching

AH's finger(s) forms a hook and pulls part of the device away from the WH, which functions as an anchor to maintain the tension. Measurable as magnitude of stretch.

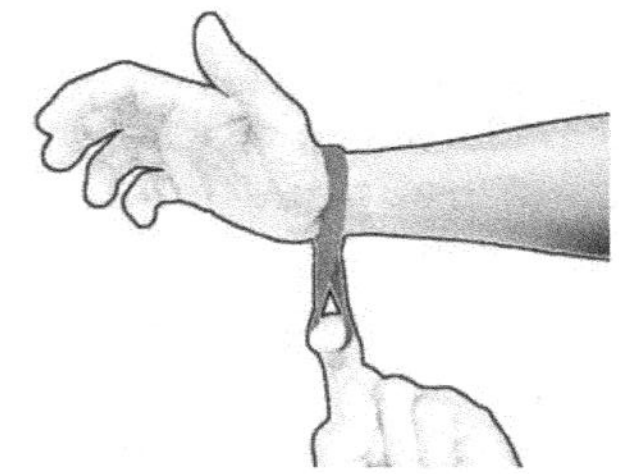

Twisting

AH's finger(s) forms a hook under the device and turn. WH functions as an anchor to provide a counter force in the twist. Measurable as angle of rotation.

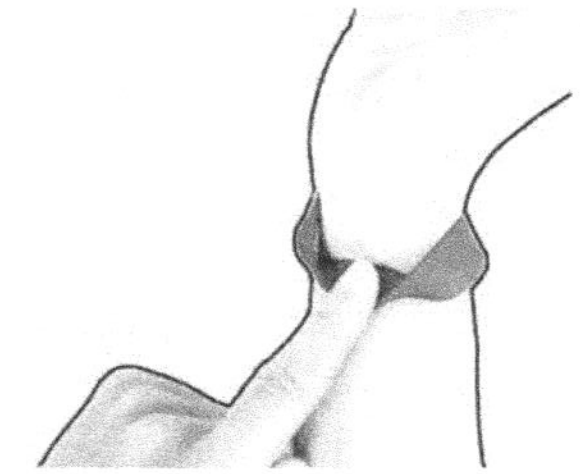

Rolling

AH's finger(s) presses on the device against WH, and rubs in a direction. WH functions as a surface to provide friction and support to the motion. Measurable as angle and location of rotation.

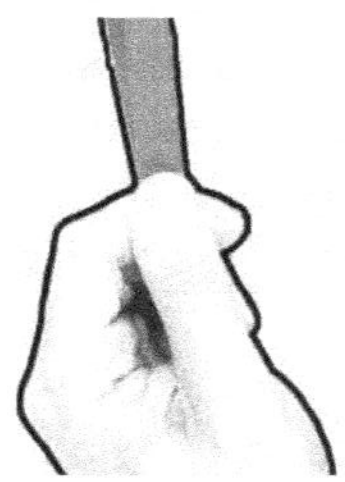

Pinching-along

AH's fingers pinch part of the device and press together. It is different from Bending/Folding where the ends of the action are further apart. Measurable as force of pressure.

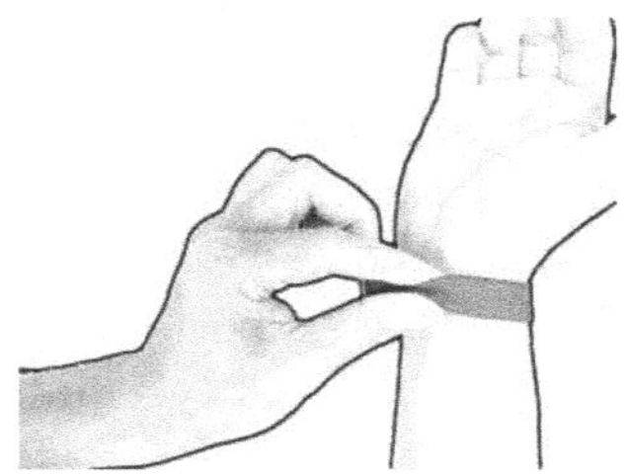

Pinching-across

AH's fingers pinch part of the device and press together. It is similar to Pinching-along but in a different direction. Measurable as force of pressure.

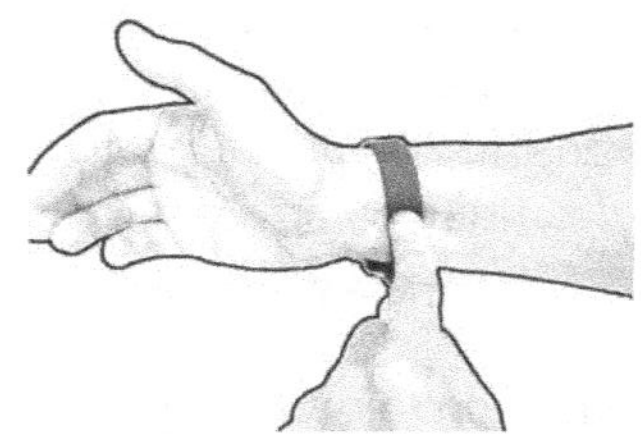

Squeezing

AH's finger(s) apply pressure on to a part of the device. WH functions as a surface to provide a normal force against the motion. Measurable as force of pressure.

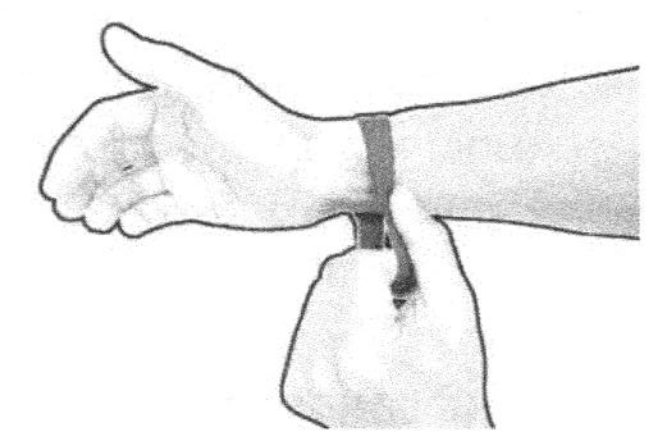

Touching

Both AH and WH work in tandem to create a rigid surface for the AH's thumb to touch/slide on. Measurable as magnitude of stretch and force of pressure.

Figure 3. Illustration of eyes-free interactions for an on-the-wrist device (OWD). We highlight the roles of the Activating Hand (AH) and Wearing Hand (WH) in the partial bi-manual interaction commonly found in the actions: AH serves as the hand performing the named action, and in some actions the WH is the necessary anchor to complete the action. These actions do not distinguish dominant and non-dominant hands.

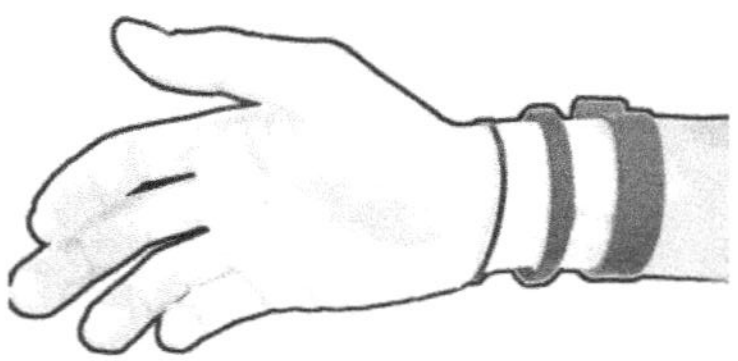

Band shapes: round and thin, flat and narrow, flat and wide.

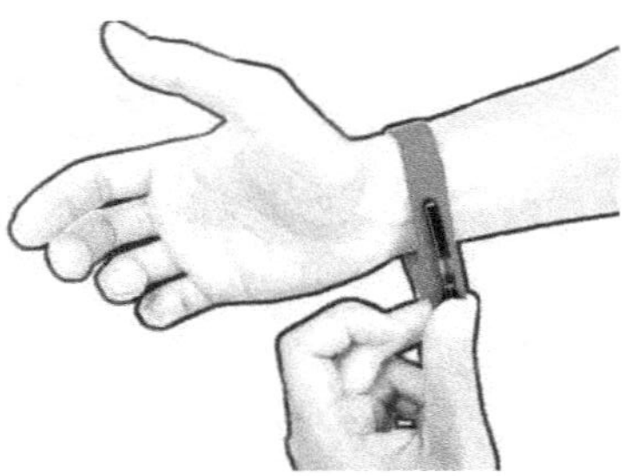

Band with bend sensor.

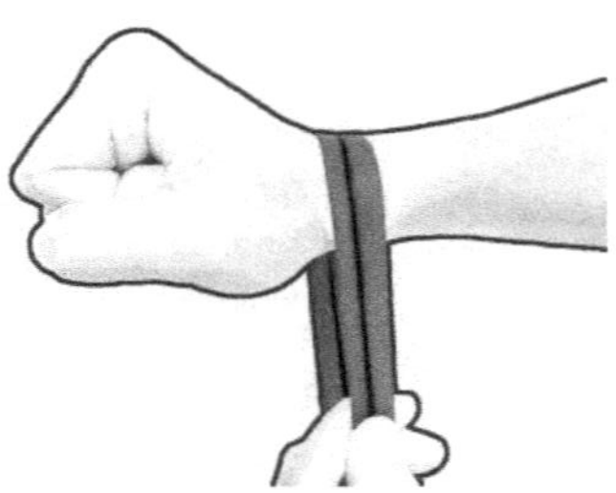

Band with stretch sensor.

Figure 4: Forms and sensor augmentation for low-fidelity, deformable OWDs.

We also note the possibility to combine some of the deformation actions, as well as additional actions when the device is worn differently. For example, a person can pinch-along and stretch the device at the same time, forming a pull action (Figure 1), or shift a loosely worn device along one's arm. For simplicity, we limit our current vocabulary to those that involve bending and/or stretching, and leave the combinations and other wearing styles for future iterations of the interaction language.

In summary, the actions in the language are applicable to a wide range of OWDs, from bands of different widths to different tightnesses, as long as they afford bending and stretching deformations. Yet, some actions might be easier to perform if the device has some width and is worn loosely on the wrist: similar to the setup we used during the informal brainstorming sessions when developing the interaction language.

Prototyping and Exploration

We have identified two areas of exploration to begin describing the potential of deformable on-the-wrist devices: fabrication and interaction. As a technical challenge, we will apply the materials and methods used in deformable device prototyping and fabrication to create devices capable of detecting and capturing an array of deformation-based interactions. Along with this, we will use the experience prototyping technique described by Buchenau and Suri [2] to identify the interactions best suited to deformable OWDs, drawing from the preliminary interaction set that we have identified here. We believe this technique is more appropriate for initial exploration on informing research and discovery; rather than the observational technique used by Lee et al. [14], which is more suitable for designing gestures and interfaces with a given set of commands. We will then identify and explore possible applications for these devices.

We will employ low-fidelity prototypes; silicon rubber bands of various shapes, fitted with bend and stretch sensors; to explore possible interactions that will inform both the design of higher fidelity, sensing prototypes and the interactions that we will test with users.

Demonstration

During the conference, we will present low- and medium-fidelity prototypes (e.g., Figure 2, Figure 4) demonstrating a selection of materials, fabrication techniques, and embedded sensors. It is our intention to provoke discussion, exchange ideas, and foster collaboration opportunities at the conference.

Conclusion

Wearables, and particularly on-the-wrist devices, are gaining attention in areas like personal behaviour monitoring and healthcare [12]. We believe that deformation-based interactions and materials are suited to OWDs. We propose to explore the fabrication of deformable OWDs, and to use these prototypes to build on and validate a deformation-based eyes-free interaction language for on-the-wrist devices.

Acknowledgements

This work was supported and funded by the National Sciences and Engineering Research Council of Canada (NSERC) through a Discovery grant (402494/2011), a Create grant (465639-2015), and by the Ministry of Ontario through an Early Researcher Award (ER15-11-101). The views expressed in the publication are the views of the Institution and do not necessarily reflect those of the Province.

References

[1] Apple Inc. Watch. 2016. http://www.apple.com/watch/.

[2] Buchenau, M. and Suri, J. Experience prototyping. *Designing Interactive Systems*, (2000), 424–433.

[3] Chien, C., Liang, R.-H., Lin, L.-F., Chan, L., and Chen, B.-Y. FlexiBend: Enabling Interactivity of Multi-Part, Deformable Fabrications Using Single Shape-Sensing Strip. *ACM Symposium on User Interface Software & Technology*, (2015), 659–663.

[4] Dijkstra, R., Perez, C., and Vertegaal, R. Evaluating effects of structural holds on pointing and dragging performance with flexible displays. *SIGCHI Conference on Human Factors in Computing Systems*, ACM Press (2011), 1293–1302.

[5] Fitbit Inc. Fitbit Flex 2™ Fitness Wristband. 2016. https://www.fitbit.com/ca/flex2.

[6] Fortmann, J., Root, E., Boll, S., and Heuten, W. Tangible Apps Bracelet: Designing Modular Wrist-Worn Digital Jewellery for Multiple Purposes. *ACM Conference on Designing Interactive Systems*, (2016), 841–852.

[7] Gotsch, D. HoloFlex : A Flexible Holographic Smartphone with Bend Input. *CHI Extended Abstracts on Human Factors in Computing Systems*, (2016), 3675–3678.

[8] Hoang, T.N., Smith, R.T., and Thomas, B.H. Passive Deformable Haptic glove to support 3D interactions in mobile augmented reality environments. *2013 IEEE International Symposium on Mixed and Augmented Reality, ISMAR 2013*, (2013), 257–258.

[9] Holman, D., Fellion, N., and Vertegaal, R. Sensing Touch Using Resistive Graphs. *Proceedings of the 2014 conference on Designing interactive systems - DIS '14*, (2014), 195–198.

[10] Kang, B.B., Lee, H., In, H., Jeong, U., Chung, J., and Cho, K.J. Development of a polymer-based tendon-driven wearable robotic hand. *Proceedings - IEEE International Conference on Robotics and Automation 2016–June*, (2016), 3750–3755.

[11] Kim, D.H. and Park, H.S. Thumb joint angle estimation for soft wearable hand robotic devices. *IEEE International Conference on Rehabilitation Robotics 2015–Septe*, (2015), 91–94.

[12] Kinnaird, P. and Talgam-Cohen, I., eds. Wearable Computing: Getting Dressed in Tech. *XRDS 20*, 2 (2013).

[13] Kumbay Yildiz, S., Mutlu, R., and Alici, G. Fabrication and characterisation of highly stretchable elastomeric strain sensors for prosthetic hand applications. *Sensors and Actuators A 247*, (2016), 514–521.

[14] Lee, S.-S., Kim, S., Jin, B., et al. How users manipulate deformable displays as input devices. *SIGCHI Conference on Human Factors in Computing Systems*, (2010), 1647–1656.

[15] Lo, J. and Girouard, A. Fabricating Bendy: Design and Development of Deformable Prototypes. *IEEE Pervasive Computing Special Issue on Fabrication and Printing 13*, 3 (2014), 40–46.

[16] Lyons, K., Nguyen, D., Ashbrook, D., and White, S. Facet: A Multi-Segment Wrist Worn System. *ACM Symposium on User Interface Software & Technology*, (2012), 123–130.

[17] Mattmann, C., Clemens, F., and Tröster, G. Sensor for measuring strain in textile. *Sensors 8*, 6 (2008), 3719–3732.

[18] Mei, H., Wang, R., Wang, Z., Feng, J., Xia, Y., and Zhang, T. A flexible pressure-sensitive array based on soft substrate. *Sensors & Actuators: A. Physical 222*, (2015), 80–86.

[19] Miner, C., Chan, D., and Campbell, C. Digital jewelry: wearable technology for everyday life. *Extended Abstracts on Human Factors in Computing Systems*, (2001), 45–46.

[20] Oakley, I. and Park, J.-S. Designing Eyes-Free Interaction. In *Haptic and Audio Interaction Design*. 2007, 121–132.

[21] Pakanen, M., Colley, A., Häkkilä, J., Kildal, J., and Lantz, V. Squeezy Bracelet -Designing a Wearable Communication Device for Tactile Interaction. *Nordic Conference on Human-Computer Interaction*, (2014), 305–314.

[22] Panasonic Corporation. Panasonic Develops a Stretchable Resin Film and Its Application Materials For Stretchable Electronics | Headquarters News | Panasonic Newsroom Global. *Press Release*, 2015, 1. http://news.panasonic.com/global/press/data/2015/12/en151224-3/en151224-3.html.

[23] Panëels, S. and Strachan, S. Exploring Interactions with a Flexible Tactile Device for Multi-Context Interaction. *Extended Abstracts on Human Factors in Computing Systems*, (2016), 2632–2639.

[24] Perrault, S.T., Lecolinet, Eagan, J., and Guiard, Y. Watchit: simple gestures and eyes-free interaction for wristwatches and bracelets. *SIGCHI Conference on Human Factors in Computing Systems*, (2013), 1451–1460.

[25] Strohmeier, P., Vertegaal, R., and Girouard, A. With a flick of the wrist: Stretch Sensors as Lightweight Input for Mobile Devices. *Proceedings of the Sixth International Conference on Tangible, Embedded and Embodied Interaction - TEI '12*, (2012), 307.

[26] Sugiura, Y., Inami, M., and Igarashi, T. A thin stretchable interface for tangential force measurement. *User Interface Software and Technology*, (2012), 529–536.

[27] Tarun, A.P., Burleson, W., Environments, M., Lahey, B., Girouard, A., and Vertegaal, R. Snaplet : Using Body Shape to Inform Function in Mobile Flexible Display Devices. (2011), 329–334.

[28] Under Armor Inc. Under Armour UA Band | Sleep Fitness Tracker | US. 2016. https://www.underarmour.com/en-us/ua-band.

[29] Wessely, M., Tsandilas, T., and Mackay, W.E. Stretchis : Fabricating Highly Stretchable User Interfaces. *User Interface Software and Technology*, (2016), 697–704.

Human and Dog : An Experimental Game using Unequal Communication Mechanic

Hsincheng Hou
Department of Computer Science and Information Engineering
National Taiwan University,
Taipei, Taiwan
dihimono@gmail.com
Kuan-Ting Chou
Graduate Institute of Networking and Multimedia
National Taiwan University,
Taipei, Taiwan
gary9716@gmail.com
Mike Y. Chen
Department of Computer Science and Information Engineering
National Taiwan University,
Taipei, Taiwan
mikechen@csie.ntu.edu.tw

TEI '17, March 20-23, 2017, Yokohama, Japan
ACM 978-1-4503-4676-4/17/03.
http://dx.doi.org/10.1145/3024969.3025089

Abstract
Inequality of communication capabilities may cause an awkward experience in real life. However, in terms of gaming, this can be a challenging and interesting mechanic. *Charades*[1], where one player tries to express a word via body language while others try to guess it, is a good example of such cases. Different from most digital co-op games, which equal communication mechanics have been widely used, we experiment with this unequal communication mechanic. Thus, we have designed a digital co-op game called Human and Dog, in which 2 avatars, a human and a dog, communicate to solve a series of puzzles with unequal communication capabilities. Ultimately, we conducted an experiment to evaluate our game. Several interesting patterns were discovered from our observation. We then concluded some design suggestions from our collected data for future reference.

Author Keywords
Game Design; Cooperative Game; Puzzle Solving; Unequal Communication Capabilities

ACM Classification Keywords
K.8.0 [Personal Computing]: General *Games*.

Introduction

Cooperative design has been an integral part of many digital games, and one of the core mechanics is communication. Digital games with equal communication patterns can be widely seen, most of which adopt voice or text chat. Others employ body language like *Mute Robot*[8] and *Way*[4] or pre-defined symbols like *Portal 2*[3]. On the contrary, cases with unequal communications happen seldom appear in the scenes of digital game design, while such situation does occur in reality when people trying to communicate with deaf or mute people but knowing little about sign language, or even trying to communicate with pets. Inspired by these real-world situations, we designed Human and Dog, featuring two protagonists: a human, and a dog. Each of them has asymmetric advantages that can be utilized to solve certain tasks and communicates with each other through unequal communication capabilities. In order to explore the game design, each puzzle contains different types of information and mechanic for players to communicate. This paper is structured as follows: we first summarize the related works on communication patterns, mechanics, and how challenges affect players. Next, we introduce the game design, including the game mechanics, the game design patterns and the brief sketch of each level. Finally, we describe the experiment used to evaluate our game, present the results, and discuss the findings.

Related Work

Challenge is considered to be one of the key components of game-play and has been an important research topic. Cox et al. studied how the level of physical and cognitive challenge can affect a player's experience of immersion and concluded that cognitive challenge may have greater effect on immersion [5]. Iacovides et al. investigated how players solve challenges and identified some player strategies [9]. Although Knowledge Exchange was considered a co-op strategy in this work, it has become a challenge in our game. Thus, we will discuss how misunderstanding is tackled in the game. Both Cox and Iacovides quoted the Flow theory [6], which suggests that flow is achieved because of a balance between the perceived level of challenges and the person's skills.

Prior works have explored and analyzed co-op game design patterns. Cases of board games have been studied by Hsi et al., where they yielded some interesting findings that may be useful for game designers [11]. This also presented an ontology with a view to analyzing game play [14]. Bjork and Holopainen presented a large quantity of game design patterns [12], including cooperative and social interaction patterns. Rocha et al. presented a framework of several co-op game design patterns and analyzed the actual impact of using these game mechanics to design a cooperative video game [10], which is later extended by El-Nasr et al. who proposed Cooperative Performance Metrics (CPMs) to evaluate game experiences [7]. Also, Toups et al. analyzed the communication mechanics of 40 co-op games using grounded theory [13], Some of the which also emerged in our game: environment modifying mechanic appeared in the form of players using auxiliary items to represent their message in the last puzzle. Emergent mechanic means players extend certain mechanic for communication usage. Jumping is an example and we will discuss how it was used in the later section. Express/emotional means that some mechanics contain the emotional meaning such as gesture and body language.

Game Design

Our game is a two-player co-op puzzle-solving game built with Unity3D [2]. The game involves two players with tow consoles connected via Internet. To enhance the interaction, we adopted two cooperative game design patterns, *Complementarity* and *Information Asymmetry*. *Complementarity*, defined by Rocha et al. [10], implies that players play different roles to complement each others' activities in the game. *Information Asymmetry* indicates that different players would acquire and perceive different information during gameplay. Furthermore, the most important mechanic of our game is unequal communication. We experiment this mechanic with two characters, a human and a dog character described below:

- **Human Character**
  The human is able to operate intricate moves like typing. Human can aosl use verbal language to communicate with the other player.
- **Dog Character**
  The dog has a different range of sensing capabilities regarding olfaction and vision, so certain clues can only be detected by this character. Also, its smaller figure allows it to pass through narrow areas. In the setting of our game, the dog was transformed from a human. Although it can understand what the human is saying, its response are limited to 4 different kinds of vocal patterns (whine, howl, bark, and anger.)

Level Design

Our goal for the levels is to explore the game design with different information and mechanics and examine how players communicat. Below are the sketches of the levels:

1. **Symbolic information problem:**
   Players have to get the password of a door and tap in on the numpad on the wall. The dog can get the digits of the code by sniffing around, and the human needs to figure out the permutation with a clue on a desk. (Figure 1 **(a)** and **(b)**)
2. **Discrete spatial information problem**
   This problem consists of two parts. The first is to look for a narrow secret passage way that only the dog can get through. After the dog passes through the passage, both players have to communicate in different rooms to solve the second part of the puzzle. (Figure 2 **(c)**) The second part is a modified 8-puzzle where the back side faces the human and the normal side faces the dog. Therefore, the dog should instruct the human to move the tiles. (Figure 2 **(a)** and **(b)**)
3. **Continuous spatial information problem**
   The part is a first person shooting game for the human to destroy 3 invisible mushrooms. These mushrooms are invisible to the human, but visible to the dog. (Figure 3 **(b)** and **(c)**) The dog must show the locations of the mushrooms for the human to shoot at to complete the level.
4. **Auxiliary items represented information problem**
   In the last level, players are provided with a set of poker cards and a periodic table.(Figure 3 **(a)**) A name written on the floor can only be discovered by the dog, (Figure 1 **(c)**) and it is the password for a computer which can only be operated by the human.

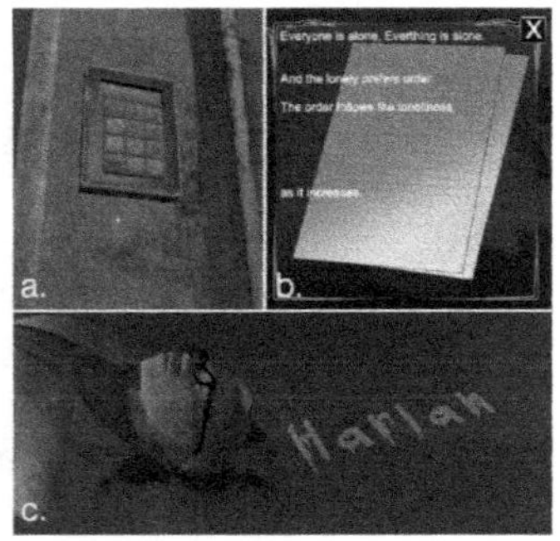

Figure 1: (a): The keypad from dog's view. **(b)**: The clue on the nearby desk. **(c)**: The name that can only be seen by dog.

Figure 2: (a) & **(b)**: The modified 8-puzzle seen on the side of human and dog, respectively. **(c)**: The passage that only the dog can pass through.

Figure 3: (a) The auxiliary items: poker cards and periodic table. **(b)** & **(c)**: The mushroom in the dog's and the human's view respectively.

Study Design

In order to understand user behaviors and the gaming experience, 16 participants were recruited (F=5;M=11;Age=20 to 27). Before the game, game rules and operations for both players were introduced. The avatars were randomly assigned and the duration of game-play was around 40 to 50 minutes. After the game, participants filled up a questionnaire about their gaming habits and a 5-point Likert-scale questionnaire for their gameplay experience of Human and Dog such as difficulty and enjoyment. A short semi-structured interview is also conducted to understand their strategies, communication protocols, and behaviors in certain situations.

Result

We received overall positive feedbacks from the participants. Average enjoyment of each puzzles is all rated high (above 3.75 out of 5.0). (Figure 4) Although there is no significant difference between puzzles within subject comparison among all metrics, some explanation can still be made based on the consistent proportion of the collected data. As for overall difficulty, six out of eight human players rate puzzle two as the most difficult. They thought the puzzle design is a little too hard for them to figure out even they with the hint saying "Maybe there is a similar sliding mechanism behind this wall." These human players thought the most confusing part is the mirroring design, as the space is at the upper-left position in figure 2(a) while at the upper-right position in figure 2(b) (Figure 2 **(a)** and **(b)**). Four out of eight human players considered puzzle three as the most easiest one because it contains the lowest level of cognitive challenge. In terms of enjoyment, six out of eight dog players rated puzzle 4 the most interesting one. This is because they had the most expressing capabilities and interactive mechanics among all puzzles, which made them feel more

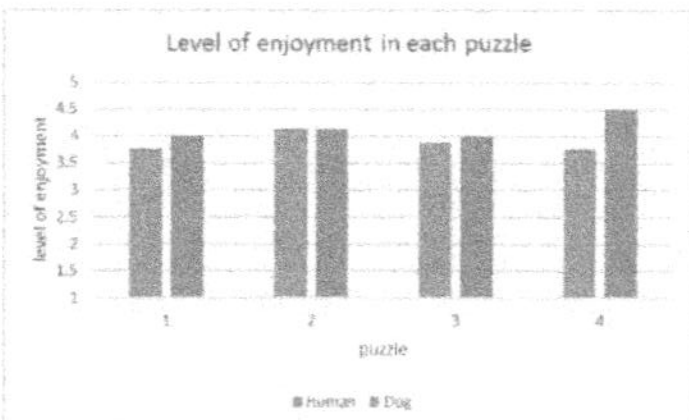

Figure 4: The level of enjoyment in each puzzle.

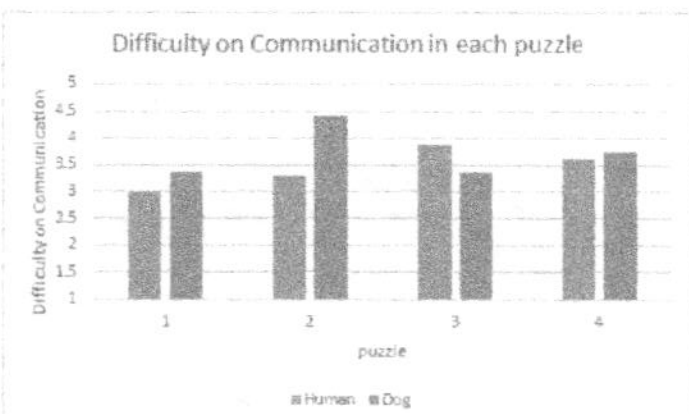

Figure 5: The level of difficulty on communication in each puzzle.

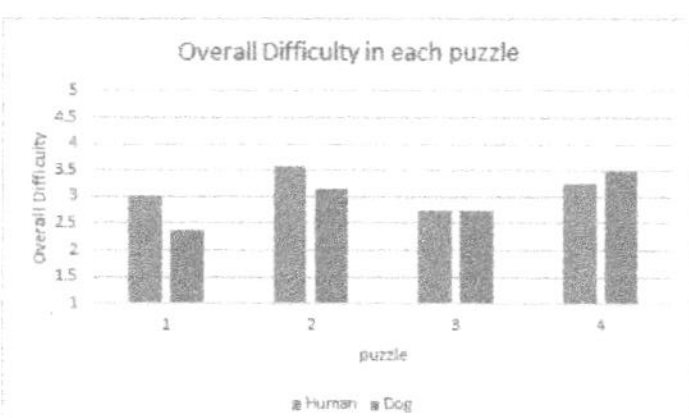

Figure 6: The level of overall difficulty in each puzzle.

active. In terms of difficulty on communication, five out of eight dog players thought puzzle 2 was the most difficult one. One of the reasons was that the human players could only imagine what the puzzle may look like behind the wall and the mirroring design would make the human players think there is a complex mapping of it. The other reason was that some human players would play around the puzzle before they realize they need to communicate with the dog players, at which point the 8-puzzle is already scrambled too complex for the dog players to solve.

Communication Patterns

After the experiments, various communication patterns are identified as listed below:

1. **Mapping dog vocal patterns to certain meanings**
   At the beginning of the game, most players would settle down the mapping of positive and negative. Some distinguish positive and negative by the number of voice or by the 4 vocal patterns of the dog. For example, "If the answer is yes, bark once; otherwise, bark twice." For another example, "If it's yes, bark; otherwise, whine or use the angry voice." In the first puzzle, some of the human players would map the digits by the times of barking to represent a digit or ask a yes-no question about whether the next digit is a certain number. In the second puzzle, most of the human players would map the next direction to the number of dog voice or a kind of voice. A few would map the position of a tile to the number of barks. In the third puzzle, the human players may iteratively correct their aiming direction by asking "Should I aim upward,downward,leftward or rightward" and shoot until they have shot a target.

2. **Narrowing Down**
   We also saw that some of the human players would perform queries to narrow down possibilities. For example, in puzzle three, the human players would ask "Is the mushroom on the ground?". In the last puzzle, the human players would ask how long the name is first and when they were communicating via the periodic table, some of the human players would ask "Is the element in the first group?".

3. **Taking turns in the lead**
   Most of the time, the human players would take the lead. However, the dog may discover key informations of the puzzle first, and it would try to draw attention from the human with its sound. For instance, in the third puzzle, the human did not know the locations of the mushrooms so they would let the dog lead the way. In the last puzzle, some of the dog players would actively pick the cards and the human players would guess what the dog managed to convey.

4. **Body Language Expression**
   Except the dog would express the information with its sound, it may also use certain kinds of body language. For example, in the third puzzle, the human players would guess the location of a mushroom based on the direction the dog faced. Some of the dog players would use jumping to indicate there is something around its current location or something on the wall with higher position. For example, in the last puzzle, the dog player would use jumping to express that the

element with smaller atomic number is in the group aligned with the dog's location.

5. **Communicating with auxiliary items**
   In the last puzzle, poker cards and a periodic table were provided to help communicate. Players would use poker cards to represent a number. Two kinds of behavior were found. One is the representation of seperate digit, while the other is that id the total value. In addition, the number would be the order of an alphabet in the name or the atomic value of an element, which further represent some alphabets in the name. Other interesting mappings were also discovered like using a suits of cards to represent the group number of elements and another one to represent the period of elements.

Discussion
After observing the game-play and the interviews, we have found some game issues under the unequal communication mechanic.

1. **Narrowing the information gap**
   Although Information Asymmetry is pretty common in many cooperative games, there is a challenge in our communication mechanicm which requires the human player iteratively ask questions to shape his own understanding of the information the dog player has. If the human players is not good at this kind of communication or the information is beyond his understanding, they would feel frustrated. To address this issue, there are two approaches. The first is to place a hint to help human players shape their understanding. The other one is enhancing the communication capability of dog players under the no-direct-voice constraint, such as visualizing where the dog is looking at while it is barking.

2. **Avoiding making a over-complex puzzle**
   In the second level, some human players have pretty diverse imagination of what the dog saw at the other side of the room. The information gap seemed to be too large. Hence, a hint was provided to the human for addressing this issue.

3. **Avoiding repetitive tasks for players**
   After the quantitative analysis, we found that there is a positive correlation between the enjoyment of the dog and the overall difficulty of that in each puzzle, but a drop between the enjoyment of the human and the overall difficulty of the human in the last one. A possible reason may be that repetitive tasks are needed to solve this puzzle (i.e. asking for the alphabet), which lowers the enjoyment. This can also explain why the second puzzle has the highest enjoyment within the four, where the answer is the shortest (4 steps to solve the puzzle), and requires the least queries.

Conclusion
In this paper, we present a game experimenting about unequal communication mechanics, which few games have explored before. We explored the game design with the information type and conducted an experiment to evaluate our game and understand players' behavior and experience. Finally, we identified various communication patterns and addressed some game issues for future reference. We hope to see more future work experimenting with this mechanic.

References

[1] Charades. Wikipedia. Retrieved January 2, 2016 from https://en.wikipedia.org/wiki/Charades.

[2] Unity. unity3d. http://unity3d.com/, 2005.

[3] Portal 2. http://www.thinkwithportals.com/, 2011.

[4] Way. http://www.makeourway.com/, 2011.

[5] Cox, A., Cairns, P., Shah, P., and Carroll, M. Not doing but thinking: The role of challenge in the gaming experience. In *Proceedings of the SIGCHI Conference on Human Factors in Computing Systems*, CHI '12, ACM (New York, NY, USA, 2012), 79–88.

[6] Csikszentmihalyi, M. *Flow: the psychology of optimal experience*. HarperPerennial, New York, 1991.

[7] El-Nasr, A., Milam, E., Lameman, M., and Mah, S. Understanding and evaluating cooperative games. In *Proc. CHI 2010*, ACM SIGCHI (2010).

[8] Hsu, C.-Y., Tung, Y.-C., Wang, W.-H., and Wang, H.-Y. Mute robot: Cooperative gameplay through body language communication. In *CHI '14 Extended Abstracts on Human Factors in Computing Systems*, CHI EA '14, ACM (New York, NY, USA, 2014), 281–284.

[9] Iacovides, I., Cox, A. L., Avakian, A., and Knoll, T. Player strategies: Achieving breakthroughs and progressing in single-player and cooperative games. In *Proceedings of the First ACM SIGCHI Annual Symposium on Computer-human Interaction in Play*, CHI PLAY '14, ACM (New York, NY, USA, 2014), 131–140.

[10] J. B. Rocha, S. Mascarenhas, R. P. Game mechanics for cooperative games. In *ZDN Digital Game* (2008).

[11] J. P. Zagal, J. Rick, I. H. Collaborative games: Lessons learned from board games. In *Simulation and Gaming, vol.37* (2006), 24–40.

[12] S. Björk, J. H. Patterns in game design. California, USA: Charles River Media (2004).

[13] Toups, Z. O., Hammer, J., Hamilton, W. A., Jarrah, A., Graves, W., and Garretson, O. A framework for cooperative communication game mechanics from grounded theory. In *Proceedings of the First ACM SIGCHI Annual Symposium on Computer-human Interaction in Play*, CHI PLAY '14, ACM (New York, NY, USA, 2014), 257–266.

[14] Zagal, Mateas, F.-V., and Hochhalter, L. Towards an ontological language for game analysis. In *Digital Interactive Games Research Association Conference (DiGRA 2005)* (2005).

Vibrette: Aiding Smoke Cessation with Tangible Game Devices

Michael Urbanek
TU Wien
Institute for Design &
Assessment of Technology
Vienna, A-1040, Austria
michael.urbanek@tuwien.ac.at

Peter Fikar
TU Wien
Institute for Design &
Assessment of Technology
Vienna, A-1040, Austria
peter.fikar@tuwien.ac.at

Roman Ganhör
TU Wien
Institute for Design &
Assessment of Technology
Vienna, A-1040, Austria
roman.ganhoer@tuwien.ac.at

Michael Habiger
TU Wien
Institute for Design &
Assessment of Technology
Vienna, A-1040, Austria
michael.habiger@tuwien.ac.at

Hilda Tellioğlu
TU Wien
Institute for Design &
Assessment of Technology
Vienna, A-1040, Austria
hilda.tellioglu@tuwien.ac.at

TEI 2017, March 20–23, 2017, Yokohama, Japan.
ACM ISBN 978-1-4503-4676-4/17/03.
http://dx.doi.org/10.1145/3024969.3025090

Abstract
Smoking is a serious health problem and there exists a number of different aids to quit this habit. However, nicotine dependency is a complex addiction and not all means of cessation suit every smoker. In this work we present *Vibrette*, a mobile tangible device designed to ease the smoking craving by offering a distractive game. We illustrate the design process, show different design alternatives and discuss the decisions made. Furthermore, we give an overview about an ongoing user study and reflect on the insights we gathered during the field-test. Finally, we show our conclusions and how these will influence the future work and next design iterations of the prototype.

Author Keywords
Tangible; Distraction; Vibrotactile; Smoking Cessation; Game.

ACM Classification Keywords
H.5.2 [Information interfaces and presentation (e.g., HCI)]: User Interfaces.

Figure 1: The first three design cycles of the prototype. Step I: An Arduino Mega prototype with visual feedback; Step II: a prototype made of a cardboard roll; Step III: the first 3D printed model.

Introduction & Related Work

The World Health Organization defines in its International Classification of Diseases Nicotine dependence (ICD-10, F17.2) as "[a] cluster of behavioral [...] phenomena [...] that typically include a strong desire to take the drug" [6]. Consequently a variety of tools and medication exist supporting people to quit smoking. While all of these tools target to reduce nicotine cravings and withdrawal symptoms the specific approaches differ.

Nicotine replacement medicine contains small amounts of nicotine, however, these can come with undesired side effects or unexpected difficulties [3]. E.g., nicotine patch can irritate and harm the skin, nicotine chewing gum is different to regular chewing gum as chewing must be done according to the patient information leaflet to unfold its full effect.

Other approaches target the habit and the process of smoking by imitating it with different and less harmful means. The group of electronic nicotine delivery systems, such as electronic cigarettes (e-cigarettes), is commonly believed to be such an example [7]. However, so far there is too little data to affirm the often claimed effectiveness and health promises of such substitutes [2].

Mobile apps in turn try to go without any nicotine and build solely on the people's will to quit smoking. Edwards et al. [5] presented *CigBreak*, a gamified tool to support smoke cessation. The goal of *CigBreak* is to cut as many cigarettes as possible by swiping over the display. Participants reported that the app provided distraction among other effects in a playful way. *Crush the Crave* is another mobile application that draws on distraction from craving [1]. While these applications rely on a mobile phone other approaches utilize dedicated tangible objects trying to increase awareness of personal smoking habits and to influence one's smoking behavior such as *UbiLighter* [8].

To the best of the authors' knowledge there is no approach so far that aims to distract smokers by means of an embodied tangible object, even though this could have some rewarding benefits. First, a cigarette is often something special within the daily routine of a smoker, therefore a purpose built device seems a sensible approach to fit a cigarettes exceptional stance especially when designed to mimic a cigarettes shape in its broadest sense. Second, tangible devices can be designed to be operational without any preparation time just as cigarettes. Third, tangible devices principally allow user interaction without visual contact which gives designers unique possibilities for novel and maybe unusual interaction mechanics. Thus, tangible objects can potentially not only raise awareness of one's own smoking process, it can also distract a smoker from the craving by offering an alternative interaction in the respective situation.

Vibrette - Design & Development

In order to support people to quit smoking we designed a tangible mobile device that pursues following ideas: it is entertaining and diverts smokers from smoking cigarettes and, it is be instantly operational without any additional devices such as smartphones and the like. Furthermore, it holds up an entertaining mood by continuously increasing its difficulty as this can help to distract smokers from acute cravings [4].

The presented prototype, *Vibrette*, is a tangible mobile device in the size and shape of a bigger cigar that allows a user to play a memory game based on vibrations and tactile feedback. The gameplay is based on the popular electronic game *Simon* where four different colored buttons light up in a sequence that has to be repeated by a player. Whenever a player succeeds to repeat the sequence without an error the sequence lengthens by one. A round of game is

Figure 2: The last three design cycles of the prototype. Step IV & V: Adjustments on the 3D model to improve stability of the components; Step VI: Three different forms in different sizes.

over when a player fails to repeat a sequence correctly. The motivation is to play sequences as long as possible.

Vibrette uses a similar game mechanic, however, instead of a visual sequence (consisting of four different colors) *Vibrette* provides tactile sequences (consisting of two different vibration lengths) via a vibration motor that has to be repeated by a player by pressing a button accordingly. During the first design iteration a sequence could have more than two vibration lengths. Initial studies showed that these were too hard to distinguish which in turn lead to frustrated participants as they were not able to replay a given sequence. Aiding players in memorizing and replaying a sequence, the vibration motor is active as long as a player presses the button. Hence tactile feedback about the input-sequence is given simultaneously.

In the following a game cycle is described:

A player presses the button on top of the device and starts a game (*start*).

A sequence of vibrations of different length is played (*demonstrate*). Additionally a LED on the device lights blue.

The player tries to repeat the pattern (*repeat*).

If the player can repeat the whole vibrating sequence without a single error (*success*), the device adds a vibration to the pattern and goes to status (*demonstrate*). Additionally a LED on the device lights green.

If the player cannot repeat the whole vibrating sequence without a single error (fail), the game stops with a unique vibration pattern (*end*). Additionally a LED on the device lights red.

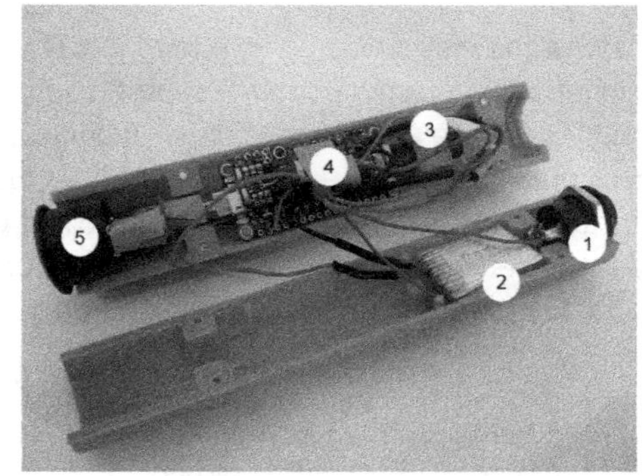

Figure 3: The interior of *Vibrette* prototype. (1) The push button for providing feedback to the system; (2) the battery; (3) the vibration motor for providing tactile feedback to the user; (4) Arduino; (5) power on/off.

The prototype's design is intended to be portable, therefore size and mobile runtime are crucial factors. In an initial design meeting the participants decided on the basic design requirements for the prototype: it should be fit in one hand and should be completely usable within one hand; the minimum runtime should exceed at least three hours constant playing without recharging. To achieve the given requirements the prototype went through various design versions with different materials, sizes, shapes and colors in order to find the most suitable combination of those.

The first stage of the prototype was based on an Arduino Mega, a button and a LED (Figure 1). The purpose of the first prototype was to get a basic understanding of the game play. The second prototype consisted of an Adafruit Bluetooth LE processor, a button, a vibration motor and a power switch. In this design stage we were able to discuss the final product's look (size, shape) and feel (material, handling). During this phase fundamentally different shapes were 3D printed following a rapid prototyping approach, however, the initially intended cigar shape turned out to be the most promising. (Figure 2). Figure 3 shows the interior of the final *Vibrette* prototype.

Ongoing User Study

To better understand the potential and limitations of our prototype we conducted a first preliminary field study. In this evaluation five participants were given the *Vibrette* for one to three weeks and asked to use it in their daily lives. During the evaluation we collected quantitative log data. The *Vibrette* logged when a participant played with the *Vibrette* prototype, how long a game session lasted, the vibration pattern and the participant's responses. These data gave insights about how often and how long the *Vibrette* prototype was used and if this corresponded with the difficulty of the vibration patterns. Additionally, qualitative data were acquired either in form of a physical diary or semi-structured interview. These complemented the quantitative data by adding information to the survey that could not be gathered automatically by the device's algorithms, such as cigarette consumption or overall wellbeing. Five persons attended the preliminary user study.

The users described the shape, size and color of the *Vibrette* prototype as being appropriate. Especially the color was highlighted as "easy to find in my handbag", while shape and size were referred to as "fits well in the palm of the hand". There was also a tendency among the participants to associate shape, color and vibrotactile modality of the signals with a sex toy. One participant stated that the prototype reminded her on a Dead Man's Switch. The game mechanics were rated as being fun and distractive, however, there was also critic about the game being too rigorous when evaluating a user's input, especially when a participant misinterpreted a signal (long for a short or vice versa). Participants also sometimes had problems to distinguish a playing sequence from a feedback sequence and to identify the color of the built-in multicolor LED. There was neither negative nor positive feedback according to the remaining parts of the user interface. One participant said that she can imagine the *Vibrette* having an impact on her smoking behavior. Another user criticized technical aspects of the prototype regarding the missing feedback of the battery status, quick discharge and technical problems during the charging process. However, we were not able to reproduce these issues using the same device in our lab.

Discussion & Future Work

Even though the prototype is in its early stage it is able to fulfill its main purpose, distraction. While most of the participants understood the idea and used *Vibrette* instead of smoking, some simply liked to play the game and smoked while playing (Figure 4). While this is clearly against the intention of the proposed device it indicates the playful and entertaining character of our approach. However, *Vibrette* is meant to be a complementary tool to other intervention techniques and can only support a smoker's decision to quit smoking.

The shape and color were assessed as sufficient, however, participants expressed their wish for a smaller or better integrated device. This matches with the comment of one user that the "game can be played without other people around noticing it." This statement is especially interesting as smoking cigarettes is becoming widely illegal in public places and the *Vibrette* could serve as a substitute comfortable with the law.

The participants found the gameplay compelling, however, relying solely on vibrotactile feedback was challenging for

Figure 4: A user testing *Vibrette* while smoking her cigarette.

most users. Based on this feedback we tried to fine tune the timing and the vibration lengths and pauses in between and conducted a small study. Regardless of the finding that people's perception can vary heavily we assume that vibration timing will play a key factor in ensuring user satisfaction. It was mentioned repeatedly that the provided visual feedback through LED was basically welcomed, however, the brightness of the LED was too low. This issue can be solved easily using different LED and adjusting them to shine brighter. We suppose that with better timing and more distinguishable signals the importance of the visual feedback will decline.

Despite the simple gameplay participants said that the game can be mesmerizing. However, when closer integration with smartphones via Bluetooth is implemented the possibilities for more features will increase. This includes high score lists that can be shared with friends or fine tuning the vibration lengths according to a user's preferences. Figure 5 depicts a scribble for a possible *Vibrette* app where users are able to select different levels, gather badges or share their high scores.

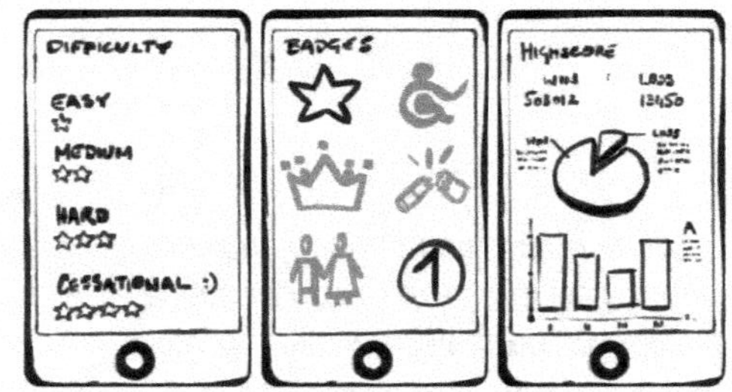

Figure 5: A scribble of the upcoming app for the *Vibrette* prototype. User's are then able to select different levels, gather badges and look at their highscores.

As the preliminary results of our ongoing user study show such interventions can have an impact on a user's daily routine. Interviews with participants and discussions with experts indicate that such interventions targeting concentration exercises could be of relevance for other therapies, e.g., as supplement in an ADHD (Attention Deficit Hyperactivity Disorder) therapy or stress relief. However, this needs further investigations and respective user studies. Another issue that has to be addressed is the long term motivation of such persuasive and awareness raising tool.

Acknowledgements
We would like to thank all participants for offering their time and efforts. This work is funded by "Gemeinsame Gesundheitsziele aus dem Rahmen-Pharmavertrag, eine Kooperation von österreichischer Pharmawirtschaft und Sozialversicherung".

REFERENCES

1. Neill Bruce Baskerville, Laura Louise Struik, David Hammond, G Emmanuel Guindon, Cameron D Norman, Robyn Whittaker, Catherine M Burns, Kelly A Grindrod, and K Stephen Brown. 2015. Effect of a Mobile Phone Intervention on Quitting Smoking in a Young Adult Population of Smokers: Randomized Controlled Trial Study Protocol. *JMIR Research Protocols* 4, 1 (2015), e10.
2. Priscilla Callahan-Lyon. 2014. Electronic cigarettes: human health effects. *Tobacco control* 23, suppl 2 (2014), ii36–ii40.
3. Mayo Clinic. 2014. Quit-smoking medicines: Boost your chance of success. (2014). Retrieved December 29, 2016 from http://www.mayoclinic.org/healthy-lifestyle/quit-smoking/in-depth/quit-smoking-products/art-20045599?pg=1.
4. Kathryn L DeLaughter, Rajani S Sadasivam, Ariana Kamberi, Thomas M English, Greg L Seward, S Wayne Chan, Julie E Volkman, Daniel J Amante, and Thomas K Houston. 2016. Crave-Out: A Distraction/Motivation Mobile Game to Assist in Smoking Cessation. *JMIR serious games* 4, 1 (2016), e3.
5. EA Edwards, J Lumsden, C Rivas, L Steed, LA Edwards, A Thiyagarajan, R Sohanpal, H Caton, CJ Griffiths, MR Munafò, and others. 2016. Gamification for health promotion: systematic review of behaviour change techniques in smartphone apps. *BMJ open* 6, 10 (2016).
6. World Health Organization and others. 2016. International Statistical Classification of Diseases and Health Related Problems, 10th Revision. ICD-10 Version: 2016. (2016). Retrieved December 29, 2016 from http://apps.who.int/classifications/icd10/browse/2016/en.
7. Jessica K Pepper, Sherry L Emery, Kurt M Ribisl, Christine M Rini, and Noel T Brewer. 2015. How risky is it to use e-cigarettes? Smokers' beliefs about their health risks from using novel and traditional tobacco products. *Journal of Behavioral Medicine* 38, 2 (2015), 318–326.
8. Philipp M Scholl, Nagihan Kücükyildiz, and Kristof Van Laerhoven. 2013. When Do You Light a Fire? Capturing Tobacco Use with Situated, Wearable Sensors. In *Proceedings of the 2013 ACM conference on Pervasive and ubiquitous computing adjunct publication.* ACM, 1295–1304.

EchoSnap and PlayableAle: Exploring Audible Resonant Interaction

Peter Bennett
University of Bristol
Bristol, UK, USA
pete@peteinfo.com

Gascia Ouzounian
University of Oxford
Oxford, UK
gascia@gmail.com

Christopher Haworth
University of Leeds
Leeds, UK
c.p.haworth@leeds.ac.uk

James Wheale
Pervasive Media Studio
Bristol, UK
james.wheale@gmail.com

TEI '17, March 20-23, 2017, Yokohama, Japan
ACM 978-1-4503-4676-4/17/03.
http://dx.doi.org/10.1145/3024969.3025091

Abstract
This paper presents two projects that use the audible resonance of hollow objects as the basis of novel tangible interaction. EchoSnap explores how an audio feedback loop created between a mobile device's microphone and speaker can be used to playfully explore and probe the resonant characteristics of hollow objects, using the resulting sounds to control a mobile device. With PlayableAle, the tone made by blowing across the top of a bottle is used as a method of controlling a game. The work presented in this paper builds upon our previous work exploring the concept of *resonant bits*, where digital information is given resonant properties that can be explored through physical interaction. In particular, this paper expands upon the concept by looking at resonance in the physical as opposed to digital domain. Using EchoSnap and PlayableAle to illustrate we present a preliminary design space for structuring the continuing development of audible resonant interaction.

Author Keywords
Tangible User Interface; Resonant Bits; Mobile Interaction.

ACM Classification Keywords
H.5.2. User Interfaces: *Interaction Styles.*

Introduction
Prior work on *resonant bits* [3, 2, 4] explored human-computer interaction based on the resonance between a mobile device's movement and digital information contained inside. Deliberate movement of a device in synchrony with a chosen resonant bit imparts more energy into that particular bit over the others allowing it to be singled out and activated. EchoSnap and PlayableAle build upon this technique by investigating how making the resonating system both physical and audible leads to new nuanced, playful and subtle resonant interaction techniques.

We explore two distinct ways of harnessing the resonance of hollow bodied objects: first, we look at how mobile devices can produce and control feedback propagating inside a physical object; second, we examine how the user can manually create the resonance through actions such as blowing or rubbing. EchoSnap explores the former by investigating how mobile devices can be used to create resonance through the use of audio feedback. PlayableAle investigates the latter by exploring how the resonant properties of drinks glasses and bottles can be used to produce tones that can be used to control digital applications.

Resonance and Feedback in the Arts
Our exploration of resonant interaction with hollow objects has been inspired by numerous artworks, music, and installations that exploit resonance and feedback as mediums and concepts for musical composition and interaction. One such example is the composer Alvin Lucier's *'I am sitting in a room'* (1969), which consists of a spoken text that is recorded and then played back into the room it was recorded in. The recording is then played back in the same room, where it is rerecorded, and played back again. The process is continuously repeated. The recording quickly builds up into rich tones that match the room's natural resonant frequencies. Another work by Lucier, *Empty Vessels* (1981), uses the resonant feedback of glass bottles as the basis of an installation, where audiences interact with the feedback as they move around the gallery. *Pea Soup* (1974; revised 2001-14) by Nicolas Collins uses a self-stabilising network of oscillators in creating a feedback-based installation whereby the pitch of the feedback is continuously shifted to a different frequency whenever the feedback reaches a certain amplitude threshold. This results in what Collins describes as *'architectural melodies'... 'a site-specific raga reflecting the acoustical personality of the room'*.

Another sound installation that exploits the phenomena of audio feedback, *Microphone* (1970) by David Tudor, which was commissioned as part of the Pepsi Pavilion at the Osaka World's Fair in 1970, explores the feedback created between two shotgun microphones and a large array of speakers in a spherical auditorium. A subsequent recording of *Microphone* for Cramps Records from 1978 reveals feedback as a rich source of compositional material, with lush and varied lines and layers of howling, shrieking, humming, whirring, and whining sounds that are always in the process of growing louder or becoming quieter, often suddenly, as the input and output of an audio signal meet and recede. Harnessing the chaotic power of resonance has also been explored in 'Hybrid Resonant Assemblages' [15], whereby audio feedback loops are introduced into structures or piles of materials and found objects.

Figure 1. Sonically probing objects with EchoSnap. Different tones are produced from the different vessels; the app uses the frequency of the tone to control digital functions.

Figure 2. Using EchoSnap to 'pick up' and mix colour. Each jar is identified by its particular resonant tone. Creating a feedback tone in a jar adds more of that colour.

Resonance and Feedback in HCI

Several projects have explored the use of resonance and feedback as a method of human-computer interaction. Touch & Activate [14] uses the response from a swept frequency acoustic signal passing through an object to determine how it is being touched or held. This is achievable as the resonant characteristics of the object change as it is held in different ways. The use of a phone's microphone and speakers as a means of tangible control has been explored in Acoustruments [9], where multiple pathways are created between a phones microphone and speaker. The speaker sends out a tone, which changes as the shape of the pathway changes, allowing the phone to detect a variety of different deformations. The use of a physical object's resonant properties has been explored with work into acoustic identification [1], whereby an object can be constructed so that when struck an identifying set of frequencies will be produced.

There are also a class of project that link tangible interaction with resonance, feedback and sound. Tangible Acoustic Interfaces [1] explore how the rich acoustic signals that propagate through solid objects can be used to control sound production in a digital synthesiser. The Sound of Touch [7] provides a spatula-like device which can be used to firstly record a sound and then subtly play it back via digital convolution while the interface is then being scraped, hit and stroked on another texture, allowing for the nuanced physical interactions to control the digital recording. Bottles [7] highlight the simplicity of how audio interaction can be mapped to tangible interaction. Simply lifting the lid of a bottle uncorks the sound contained within. The Smule Ocarina app [13] shows how when a mobile phone's microphone is used in an unconventional way (blowing into the microphone) and is coupled with physical modelling synthesis, the phone can be used for expressive performance.

Using feedback loops as part of an instruments control scheme has been explored with the D-Box [11], where digital signals are converted into control voltages before being fed back into the digital signal chain. This work indicates the possibility of creating resonance linked to digital processes so that the noise and nuance of feedback in the physical domain is added back into the digital domain.

Overall, our investigations differ from these prior projects in two ways. First, we are interested in resonant feedback as a 'felt' medium, exposing the process to the user and making it audible, as opposed to hiding the process. Second, we aim to investigate the how resonant interaction can become a skilful and engaging activity, as opposed to simply using it as method of replicating conventional interactions (button, sliders etc.). By combining these two aims, of skilful manipulation of resonant bits through an exposed feedback loop, we aim to put the user in control of a novel nuanced form of physical-digital interaction.

EchoSnap

The EchoSnap project explores the possibilities of probing the natural resonance of everyday objects and using the resulting tones to control digital interactions. The EchoSnap app operates a simple signal processing routine: when activated, the smartphone's microphone is routed to its loudspeaker, which creates feedback when set to a sufficient volume. The dominant frequenc(ies) of the feedback are determined by the resonant characteristics of the loudspeaker, microphone and acoustic environment in which the feedback propagates. If one of these has a resonant peak then that frequency will be continually reinforced as sound passes from loudspeaker to microphone. The size of the phone allows one to manipulate these resonant peaks and shape the frequency and timbre of the feedback. By placing the smartphone inside a resonant chamber, different acoustic properties can be sounded and explored (Figure 1). The qualities of this tone (pitch, duration, volume) can in turn be detected by the app, which then controls the digital processing; creating a system that performs as well as listens. For instance, the pitch of the tone detected may be used to modulate the amplitude of the feedback path, resulting in fast vibrato in smaller objects, and a slowly undulating vibrato in objects with a larger cavity. Current prototypes that will be demonstrated at TEI include:

Feedback instrument. In its purest form of interaction, the feedback created can be used to play notes with found objects (Figure 1). Developing from this a slightly more technologically advanced version detects the tone produced by the feedback and introduces harmonics of the fundamental pitch into the feedback path, creating a richer feedback sound.

ColourPicker. Three pots sit on your desk, each containing liquid of cyan, magenta and yellow hues (Figure 2). 'Dipping' your phone to the top of the pot generates a feedback tone that adds the colour to the digital colour palette on the phone. This demonstrates how the acoustics of an object can be used as a unique identifier.

ResoHarp. By placing the phone near your mouth it is possible to shape the feedback by changing the shape of your mouth, controlling the sound in a similar manner to a 'mouth harp'. This allows the user to silently mouth words and have the EchoSnap app create the sounds by resonating with your open mouth. This opens up the possibility of fine control of the feedback loop using your body whilst also exploring the possibility of turning audible resonant interaction into a very performative form of interaction.

Echosnap concept designs for future implementation include the following two applications.

ResoCache. This app allows you to drop information into hollow objects to be retrieved later. The hollow object is identified by it's signature resonant frequencies, which when detected allows the user to write or read information out of that location.

Networked 'musical trigger'. In the same manner in which actuators (such as solenoid 'beaters') can be placed on everyday objects and coordinated to play rhythmic patterns, multiple phones running the EchoSnap app, connected over a network and placed in resonant chambers can be used to realise musical works based on resonant feedback nodes.

PlayableAle

In contrast to EchoSnap, where the phone generates the resonance in the object, PlayableAle explores the possibility of using physical resonance to control a digital device. Developing the project in the context of creating interactive drinks, we first explored the possibility of using wine glasses and their ability to 'sing' as the basis of interaction, but instead settled on blowing across the top of a bottle to create a pitched tone, using the phenomenon of Helmholtz resonance.

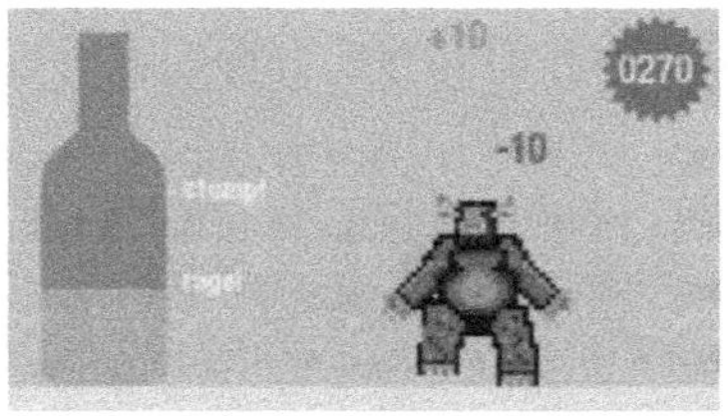

Figure 3. PlayableAle dance game. Players can either increase points by making the yeti dance (stomp) or lose points by making the yeti rage.

The PlayableAle system consists of both an app and a custom bottle that has level markers printed down the side, each one labelled with a function associated with that level. When the player consumes the drink, the level of the beer decreases and when the top of the bottle is blown across, the resulting pitch can be used to accurately determine the level of drink in the bottle and hence the function selected (Figure 3).

The PlayableAle project explores issues around skill and resonant interaction, as users need to learn and master the skilled action of sounding a tone by blowing across a bottle top before they can progress on to playing the game. Different bottle shapes can be more difficult to achieve a clear tone with, thus providing tangible increases in level. The quality of the tone produced (duration, clarity) can be used as additional input to the game adding an additional level of skill. Multi-user experiences are achieved by detecting multiple tones. This results in the equivalent of a 'digital jug band' where the bottle playing takes on a performative aspect as well as being the method of interaction with the app.

Controlling content using a bottle provides ample opportunity for novel interactions that otherwise would be difficult to achieve. For instance, unlocking a secret VIP door in a bar using PlayableAle may feel more natural than texting a door to unlock. Three users, for example, drinking down to different points, to create a chord across the three bottles, would be an example of shared interaction being necessary to unlock a door. Linking a tangible controller to drinking allows the possibility of exploring multisensory cross talk. For instance sound affects the way we perceive flavor [6]. The higher the frequency the sweeter we taste something, the lower the frequency the more bitter flavours are perceived. PlayableAle poses some interesting avenues for exploring frequency and flavour with feedback through a digital device.

Audible Resonant Interaction Design Space

From our experience of designing and informally testing EchoSnap and PlayableAle we propose parameters that outline a design space of resonant interaction with hollow bodies also building on prior work classifying interactive feedback techniques [12]. The design space consists of antagonistic design choices which when considered as a multi-dimensional system creates a framework within which to discuss new designs.

Digital vs. Analogue Resonance. Does the resonant system lie in the physical or digital realm? We have found that by making the resonance physical a greater degree of nuance and skill may be required to interact with the system. Further work is required in finding out how to successfully create systems that contain interlinked digital and physical resonators.

Relative vs Absolute Pitch. Are the tones used to trigger content fixed or relative to other tones? PlayableAle currently uses predetermined frequencices; however using relative pitches may lead to greater flexibility in for instance using different bottles.

Input vs Output Resonance. Is the resonance used as an input controller into the computer as in PlayableAle, or as an output to the user as in EchoSnap? Due to the feedback being within the audible range there may often also be the case of unintended output.

Single vs. Multiple Users. If multiple resonances are used, how do they interact? Are they harmonically related? Are the users working to resonate a single system (such as multiple people pushing a swing) or are they resonating with different systems?

Discussion and Future Work

The simple question of asking how feedback and the resonance of hollow objects can be used as a method of human-computer interaction has opened up a wide design space full of novel possibilities. Areas for further discussion and exploration include the following:

Skilful interaction. Putting the user firmly in the loop between the physical and digital worlds encourages the development of rich and skilful bodily interaction. The analogue nature of creating resonant feedback allows for skill to be developed in harnessing the technique.

Responsive Resonance. With the addition of actuation objects can be designed that can change their shape and resonance in response to how they are used. Could be seen as a subset of shape changing interfaces.

Specifically designed resonant objects. By designing new objects for their resonant properties the affordances surrounding resonant interaction can be explored. A first step for will be the development of a range of resonant chambers tuned to musical scales and pairing these with digital operations.

Interlinked resonance. What happens when multiple feedback systems are interconnected? This may be achieved through combining physical resonance and digital resonance. Can physical resonance such as blowing and rocking be used as input to a digital resonant bit?

We propose that in addition to being a novel method of tangible interaction, the use of audible resonance offers insight into existing areas of tangible interface exploration:

Exposed sensing. Given that the audio feedback used by EchoSnap is readily apparent to the user, the method in which the computer is sensing its environment is exposed, potentially giving the user more insight into the computer's actions, a key tenet of 'seamful computing' [5].

Explorative interaction. The resonant properties of hollow objects vary greatly, encouraging the exploration of different resonances and leading to playful and inquisitive interaction possibilities, particularly in the appropriation of existing objects as impromptu containers of information.

Conclusion

This paper has presented EchoSnap and PlayableAle, two applications of using the acoustic resonance of hollow objects as a method of human-computer interaction. We have presented our initial findings in a design space and indicated directions for further work on the concept. The technique allows for the identification, within limitations, of individual objects without the use of embedded electronics and paves the way for a new variety of novel tangible interaction based on the skilful manipulation of resonance.

Acknowledgements

Thanks to Kai Oliver for work developing PlayableAle and everyone who has taken part in game testing. This project was funded by AHRC grant no AH/M010163/1.

References

1. Alain Crevoisier and Pietro Polotti. 2005. Tangible acoustic interfaces and their applications for the design of new musical instruments. In *Proceedings of the international conference on New Interfaces for Musical Expression* (NIME '05).
2. Peter Bennett, Kirsten Cater, Stuart Nolan, Jarrod Knibbe, and Mike Fraser. 2015 Tangible Gestural Interaction with Resonant Bits. In *Proceedings of the Tangible Gesture Interaction workshop,* (TEI'15)
3. Peter Bennett, Jarrod Knibbe, Florent Berthaut, and Kirsten Cater. 2015 Resonant Bits: Controlling Digital Musical Instruments with Resonance and the Ideomotor Effect. In *Proceedings of the international conference on New Interfaces for Musical Expression* (NIME'15)
4. Peter Bennett, Stuart Nolan, Ved Uttamchandani, Michael Pages, Kirsten Cater, and Mike Fraser. 2015. Resonant Bits: Harmonic Interaction with Virtual Pendulums. In *Proceedings of the Ninth International Conference on Tangible, Embedded, and Embodied Interaction* (TEI '15)
5. Matthew Chalmers and Ian Maccoll. Seamful and seamless design in ubiquitous computing. In *Proceedings of Workshop At the Crossroads: The Interaction of HCI and Systems Issues,* UbiComp'03
6. Anne-Sylvie Crisinel, Stefan Cosser, Scott King, Russ Jones, James Petrie, and Charles Spence. 2012. A bittersweet symphony: Systematically modulating the taste of food by changing the sonic properties of the soundtrack playing in the background, Food Quality and Preference, Volume 24, Issue 1, April 2012, Pages 201-204
7. David Merrill, Hayes Raffle and Roberto Aimi. 2008. The sound of touch: physical manipulation of digital sound. In *Proceedings of the SIGCHI Conference on Human Factors in Computing Systems* (CHI '08).
8. Hiroshi Ishii. 2004. Bottles: A Transparent Interface as a tribute to Mark Weiser. *IEICE Trans. Inf. & Syst.*
9. Gierad Laput, Eric Brockmeyer, Moshe Mahler, Scott E. Hudson, and Chris Harrison. 2015. Acoustruments: passive, acoustically-driven, interactive controls for handheld devices. In *ACM SIGGRAPH 2015 Emerging Technologies*
10. Dingzeyu Li, David I. W. Levin, Wojciech Matusik, and Changxi Zheng. 2016. Acoustic voxels: computational optimization of modular acoustic filters. *ACM Trans. Graph.* 35, 4, Article 88 (July 2016)
11. Andrew McPherson and Victor Zappi. 2015. Exposing the Scaffolding of Digital Instruments with Hardware-Software Feedback Loops. In *Proceedings of the international conference on New Interfaces for Musical Expression* (NIME'15). Baton Rouge, Louisiana, USA, 162-167
12. Dario Sanfilippo and Andrea Valle. Towards a typology of feedback systems. 2012. In *Proceedings of the International Computer Music Conference* (ICMC'12)
13. Ge Wang. 2009. Designing Smule's iPhone ocarina. In In *Proceedings of the international conference on New Interfaces for Musical Expression* (NIME'09)
14. Makoto Ono, Buntarou Shizuki, and Jiro Tanaka. 2013. Touch & activate: adding interactivity to existing objects using active acoustic sensing. In *Proceedings of the 26th annual ACM symposium on User interface software and technology* (UIST '13)
15. John Bowers and Annika Haas. 2014. Hybrid Resonant Assemblages: Rethinking Instruments, Touch and Performance.In In *Proceedings of the international conference on New Interfaces for Musical Expression* (NIME '14).

InstructiBlocks: Designing with Ambiguous Physical-Digital Models

Peter Bennett
University of Bristol
Bristol, UK
pete@peteinfo.com

Duncan Boa
University of Bristol
Bristol, UK
duncan.boa@bristol.ac.uk

Mike Fraser
University of Bristol
Bristol, UK
mike.fraser@bristol.ac.uk

Ben Hicks
University of Bristol
Bristol, UK
ben.hicks@bristol.ac.uk

TEI '17, March 20-23, 2017, Yokohama, Japan
ACM 978-1-4503-4676-4/17/03.
http://dx.doi.org/10.1145/3024969.3025092

Abstract
In this paper we present InstructiBlocks, a system for constructing ambiguously defined physical-digital models, with the role of supporting the task of early stage ideation and design space exploration. Construction blocks tagged with RFID chips allow digital labelling with the build instructions. As each label only gives partial information on how to build the model it is possible for the designer to create a wide variety of models around the particular constraints that are present in both the physical blocks available and the digital instructions contained within them. In this context ambiguity is enabled by the digital instructions and there is no master copy, rather the state of the physical-digital model is determined by the interplay between the user, the physical blocks and digital instructions. In this paper we ask: Can an ambiguously defined model lead to greater design ideation and design space exploration? Are there benefits to 'human-actuated' interfaces, where a physical-digital model is constructed manually?

Author Keywords
Tangible User Interface; Computer Aided Design.

ACM Classification Keywords
H.5.2. Information interfaces and presentation: Interaction Styles; User-centred Design.

Figure 1. Spaceship building task. All models are built from the same instructions.

Introduction

Physical models play a variety of important roles in the process of design, from the initial stages of form finding and prototyping, through to high fidelity representations and fully functioning prototypes. Recent progress in 3D printing has enabled an ever-tighter link between creating a digital model and the production of a physical prototype. However, the transfer from digital model to physical model is often limited to a direct one to one mapping, with the physical model being as direct a copy of the digital 'master copy' as possible given the prototyping process. A variety of tangible user interfaces have addressed this through tightly coupled bidirectional interaction, where a change in the digital model updates the physical model and likewise a change in the physical model updates the digital model. We propose that the approach of tightly coupled bidirectional physical-digital models favours accuracy and computer readability over the human skills of imagination, interpretation and play. In this paper we explore whether the physical and digital forms can be coupled ambiguously in a manner so as to combine the affordances of digital modelling with the hands-on benefits of physical modelling, a concept that is termed herein as 'human-actuated' interaction and builds upon previous research into 'hybrid physical-digital fabrication' [3]. To explore this we have developed the InstructiBlocks system with the aim of bringing the digital model out of the computer and embedding assembly instructions within the physical blocks.

The InstructiBlocks system introduces two novelties to the process of physical-digital modelling. First, and unlike 3D printing, the users are 'in the loop', allowing on the fly interpretation, reflection, decision-making and remodelling, allowing a single ambiguous digital model to be the generator of numerous similar but different designs (Figure 1). Second, the approach allows distributed embedded instructions of a variety of forms.

Ambiguity in Design

Ambiguity is a powerful resource for designers. It provides the space for imagination and encourages reinterpretation of existing models: *'By impelling people to interpret situations for themselves, it encourages them to start grappling conceptually with systems and their contexts, and thus to establish deeper and more personal relations with the meanings offered by those systems'* [7]. We propose that the attempt to eliminate ambiguity from physical-digital tangible interfaces and the unquestioned ideal of a 'one to one' mapping between physical and digital, although well intentioned may be misguided, or at the very least limiting. We instead propose a less directly coupled approach that embodies a level of ambiguity that encourages play and reinterpretation. The central tenet of the approach is to link digital models to physical models in a manner that accentuates the positive benefits of the physical (immediate, playful interaction) and the digital (generative, reconfigurable processing). We contend that fluid reinterpretation of a block's relation to other blocks may help to prevent problem-solving issues such as design fixation, or the 'blind adherence to a set of ideas or concepts limiting the output of conceptual design' [12]. Our approach it that of 'ambiguity through human-actuation', where in being made to manually assemble a model, the user has to make decisions based upon impartial knowledge, resulting in the questioning of the principles behind each block's placement. As a tool, InstructiBlocks aims

Figure 2. Models designed by study participants (on left) and then rebuilt from the instructions by the following participant (on right).

to not only allow the use of ambiguous assembly instruction, but also allow for reinterpretation and ambiguous reuse in different scenarios. This raises the question of how to design the system in a manner that supports multiple interpretations and also leads to potential difficulties in evaluating the system, especially with the aim of creating a system that acts as a blank canvas for user interpretation. An approach that has been suggested for blank canvas systems is '*...to have clear interpretation at low levels of interpretation, but open a space for interpretation at higher levels*' [17].

Lego User Interfaces

InstructiBlocks relates in form to previous projects exploring the use of Lego blocks as a form of tangible input to a computer. The motivation behind many of these projects can be summed up in that '*few people know how to use graphics modelling packages, but everyone can build things out of blocks*' [1]. The possibility of combining the hands-on playability of Lego with the processing power of digital computation is also the motivation behind the InstructiBlocks system. Examples of Lego based tangibles include: LegoWall [4] which uses a variety of Lego bricks fitted with a microprocessor, allowing the brick to both be identified and also have its position tracked when placed on a baseplate on the wall. An example application of LegoWall is the tracking and display of ships moving between ports, with digital projection adding information such as the type of cargo carried. CityScope [11] uses Lego as a building tool and then augments the Lego cityscape models with digitally projected information such as wind or solar radiation around the city. Dr LegoHead [2] uses Lego as a tool for narrative construction, where adding or removing elements from the model opens up new narrative paths. In terms of rapid prototyping, Lego has been explored as a method of quickly sketching new tangible user interfaces [14], where the blocks are tracked with computer vision allowing the quick iteration and prototyping of new tangible interface concepts. Lego has also been explored as a lo-fi but fast method of 3D printing. Fabrickation [16] aids the user by converting a 3D model into a 'brickified' version that can be assembled by hand. The emphasis in this case is firmly on speeding up the process of printing and does not address changes that the user may make when assembling the model manually. Legolization [18] takes a similar approach, but is focused on the structural integrity of the resulting Lego models.

Tangible User Interfaces for Design

InstructiBlocks builds upon previous work into 'constructive tangible user interfaces' [19], and follows both in the lineage of the 'Computational Construction Kit' (CCK) explored first in architectural form finding projects [19] and also tangible programming languages [10]. In systems such as ActiveCube [13], electrical connections between each block combined with microprocessors within each block allow the overall topology of the resulting form to be sensed through the block network. A benefit of this method being that occlusion as is the case with vision systems is not a problem. A subset of constructive tangible user interfaces that is particularly relevant to this project is the class of tangible interfaces that use Lego, and is introduced in the following section. InstructiBlocks also relates to Tangible Interfaces for Computer-Aided Design (CAD). Examples of tangible CAD systems that do not use a one-to-one mapping between physical and virtual structures include SPATA [20], digitally augmented callipers and bevel measurement tools that

Figure 4. RFID chips attached to the inside of Lego bricks are used to link instructions to each block.

connect directly to CAD software, and Cubik [15], a bi-directional modelling interface, that maps common CAD operations such as extrude to a tangible controller that can be assigned to different modelling surfaces on the digital model. The Triangles system, rather than mapping physical structure, uses the triangular tokens to create 'a physical embodiment of digital information topography' [9]. An example of a high fidelity shape-changing tangible interface is InFORM [1] that uses a 30x30 grid of linear actuators to create a surface that can very rapidly transform shape.

InstructiBlocks

The InstructiBlocks system allows an instruction to be attached to each block of a construction kit, as a designer is building a model with the kit, each block can be placed on a 'block reader' and interrogated (Figure 3).This is achieved through the placement of a small radio frequency identification tag inside each block (glass capsule 125kHz RFID chips measuring 12mm x 2.12mm) which are detected by the base unit containing an RFID module (ID-12LA) and an Arduino connected to a laptop running a Processing sketch. This approach was chosen as it allows for scalability and the ability to use any number of blocks given that each RFID chip has a unique identifying address. In addition to being able to read instructions from the blocks, users are able to use a keyboard to type new instructions into each block. The choice of using text instructions over graphical was made as text instructions are simple to input and even a single word can provide a descriptive yet ambiguous instruction. Investigation into graphical means of displaying ambiguous instructions, such as sketches, photos or videos will be undertaken in future work.

Scoping Study

To evaluate InstructiBlocks we conducted a scoping study with fifteen participants to gather qualitative feedback. The evaluation involved three tasks. First the participants were asked to build a model spaceship out of one set of blocks where the instructions had been preloaded and were the same for all participants (Figure 1). The second task was to build a 'mystery model' that had been left in another set of blocks by the previous participant. The aim was to see how users interpreted an unknown model from a variety of instruction formats. The third and final task was to encode the blocks with a new model for the next participant to assemble. The aim was to explore the language used to pass on instructions and also the methods people used in encoding the blocks.

Eight of the fifteen participants were recruited from the computer science department and seven from the Pervasive Media Studio, where people's backgrounds are predominantly in the arts, in order to obtain a variety of feedback. Enquiring as to the participants' familiarity with Lego, two of the fifteen participants had not played with Lego as a child and three currently own Lego. Eleven of the participants currently work with or regularly use some form of 3D computer modelling or CAD.

The first task used the same instructions for every participant, using simple descriptive instructions (Users are free to question the blocks in any order they choose and use these digital instructions to inform how they build their physical model. The results (Figure 1) show both a consistent recognisability between the models whilst exhibiting a wide variety of interpretation. Constructing the spaceship was a popular task, and was

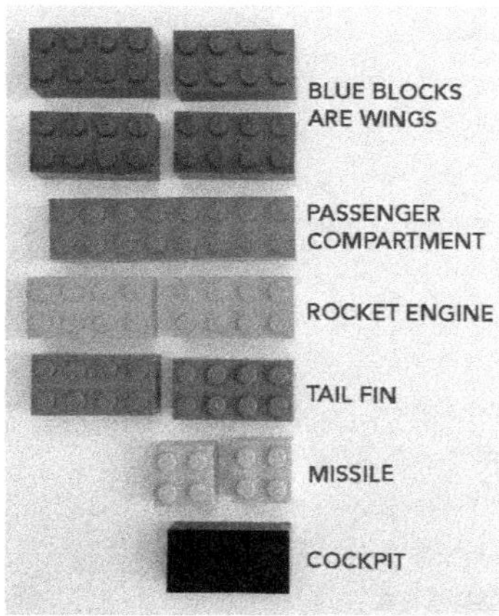

Figure 5 Spaceship instruction set. Instructions are revealed on the laptop screen when brick is placed on the RFID reader.

Figure 6 Placing an InstructiBlock on the green cross displays its instructions. Instructions can be also overwritten.

deemed to be *"quite easy, but I was intrigued of all the different possibilities so I wanted to try out lots of different things"*.

The second task of constructing the 'mystery model' left encoded in the blocks by the previous participant was found to be somewhat more challenging due to the variety in the format and detail of instruction and the importance different users gave to aspects such as block colour *"...the last person didn't care about the colours in the way I did"*. The mystery model was often guessed correctly by the next participant, sometimes from the final form and sometimes from clues within the instructions *"...the instructions gave away what it was before... it used boat specific words such as stern and starboard"*, however some instructions required work to understand before they could be applied *"I didn't know what I was building, until I looked at everything and sort of decoded what Y1 and Y2 and everything was."* Some of the user-generated instructions were too unambiguous leaving little room for creativity *"...it was more difficult to be open with... it felt like there was a set way it should look, it felt like it could of only gone into sort of one setting"*.

The third task of creating a new model from scratch and encoding the blocks with the instructions took on average longer to complete. Opinions on this ranged from being much more fun than recreating an existing model to less fun. *"I thought it was more fun to build someone else's... because you are given something and then it's totally up to your imagination what you do. Though I totally enjoy making my own thing, I think it's really cool to see how people respond to the same thing."* One noticeable difference is that during the third part of the evaluation people appeared to enter a deeper state of concentration, which was not always enjoyable for the participant *"I think it was more fun to build the existing one... as much as I did like the [third task]... but I think I was overthinking it"*. Throughout the tasks, the actual interface of placing blocks on the RFID reader remained mostly transparent to the users and only a few comments were made about the ease of use of the interface *"The system was very responsive and fast. Could be confusing (or perhaps fun) for bigger models"*.

Future Work

InstructiBlocks has laid the basis of an ambiguity-mediated physical-digital modelling system. Both the construction system (Lego) and the digital instructions (plain text) have been chosen to be as simple as possible. From this foundation there are numerous areas for future investigation into ambiguity-mediated physical-digital models.

Digital operations. Currently there are no digital manipulations carried out by InstructiBlocks. Examples would include the generation, sorting or ordering of digital instructions. An example being tracking which blocks are most used and assigning them a 'hotter' colour than less used blocks. An example of a generative digital feature would be the parametric assignment of parts to each block, for instance changing the ratio in an architectural model between different groups of component, such as window bricks to wall bricks.

Language, encoding and fidelity. The spaceship-building task used a total of 12 instruction words and 12 blocks to describe a design space that produced recognisably similar model spacecraft and encouraged in depth discussion around design choices. One possibility is to investigate creating instructions that are progressively refined or revealed over subsequent design iterations (e.g. Blue blocks are wings -> Blue blocks form a single long wing -> Blue blocks form a single long wing bisecting the fuselage half way along). Using this method InstructiBlocks could be used as a method of capturing and interrogating design rationale.

Block reader. Support for specific forms of information encoding may be achieved with dedicated physical forms for the block reader. For instance, relational encoding may be achieved through the use of two indents, so that two blocks can be selected simultaneously and a relationship chosen between them. Likewise, group selection may be achieved by having a funnel into which a large number of blocks can be placed, each being individually read by RFID as it passes through. A potential issue with the current InstructiBlocks system is the inability to probe a block whilst it is in-situ. Further iterations of the InstructiBlocks hardware will address this by investigating how a hand-held RFID reader could be used to interrogate the blocks whilst in the model so as to avoid disassembly.

Human-Actuated Interfaces

In the wider research context we view InstructiBlocks as forming preliminary work into the exploration of 'Human-Actuated Interfaces, where motion and shape-changing abilities in tangible interfaces may be achieved through human involvement as opposed to motors or other mechanical means. This hands-on approach aligns closely with the tangible user interface inspiration of board games, where the physical tokens act as both input and representation and are kept updated and in order by the players. We propose that this process of 'manual updating' may bring closer engagement between the person and the tangible user interface. In this regard, InstructiBlocks can be seen as a non-automatic relation to projects such as 'smart sand' [8], where assembly instructions are distributed throughout a material.

Conclusion

In this paper we have presented InstructiBlocks, a system for creating ambiguously defined physical-digital models. In this paper we have used InstructiBlocks to explore how ambiguous digital instructions combined with low fidelity construction kits (e.g. Lego) can encourage ideation and design space exploration. Here *"...ambiguity provides a frame of reference that allows the use of inaccurate sensors, inexact mappings, and low-resolution displays because it encourages users to supplement them with their own interpretations and beliefs."* [7]. The scoping study suggests that the InstructiBlocks system allows for the creative generation and exploration of multiple designs around a theme, however further work is required to gauge the level of ambiguity in the instruction language that best promotes creative reinterpretation. The system also indicates that manual construction (human-actuated) of physical-digital models may allow hands-on time for reflection and become a novel method of capturing design rationale.

Acknowledgements

Thanks to all of the participants who took part in the user study. This project was funded by EPSRC grant no EP/N009568/1.

References

1. David Anderson, James L. Frankel, Joe Marks, Darren Leigh, Eddie Sullivan, Jonathan Yedidia, and Kathy Ryall. 1999. Building virtual structures with physical blocks. In *Proceedings of the 12th annual ACM symposium on User interface software and technology* (UIST '99)
2. Richard Borovoy. 1996. Dr. LEGOHead, Ph.D.: a real-world story construction environment. In *Proceedings of the 1996 international conference on Learning sciences* (ICLS '96)
3. Laura Devendorf and Kimiko Ryokai. 2015. Being the Machine: Reconfiguring Agency and Control in Hybrid Fabrication. In *Proceedings of the 33rd Annual ACM Conference on Human Factors in Computing Systems* (CHI '15)
4. George W. Fitzmaurice. 1996. PhD. Graspable User Interfaces. *University of Toronto, University of Toronto.*
5. Sean Follmer, Daniel Leithinger, Alex Olwal, Akimitsu Hogge, and Hiroshi Ishii. 2013. inFORM: dynamic physical affordances and constraints through shape and object actuation. In *Proceedings of the 26th annual ACM symposium on User interface software and technology* (UIST '13)
6. John Frazer. 1995 *An evolutionary architecture*, Architectural Association, London.
7. William W. Gaver, Jacob Beaver, and Steve Benford. 2003. Ambiguity as a resource for design. In *Proceedings of the SIGCHI Conference on Human Factors in Computing Systems* (CHI '03)
8. Kyle W. Gilpin, and Daniela Rus. 2013. What's in the bag: A distributed approach to 3d shape duplication with modular robots. *Robotics: Science and Systems VIII* (2013)
9. Matthew G. Gorbet, Maggie Orth, and Hiroshi Ishii. 1998. Triangles: tangible interface for manipulation and exploration of digital information topography. In *Proceedings of the SIGCHI Conference on Human Factors in Computing Systems* (CHI '98)
10. Hideyuki Suzuki and Hiroshi Kato. 1995. Interaction-level support for collaborative learning: AlgoBlock—an open programming language. In *The first international conference on Computer support for collaborative learning* (CSCL '95)
11. Mohammad Hadhrawi and Kent Larson. 2016. Illuminating LEGOs with Digital Information to Create Urban Data Observatory and Intervention Simulator. In *Proceedings of the 2016 ACM Conference Companion Publication on Designing Interactive Systems* (DIS '16 Companion)
12. David G. Jansson, and Steven M. Smith. 1991 Design fixation. *Design studies, Elsevier, 12*, 3-11
13. Yoshifumi Kitamura, Yuichi Itoh, and Fumio Kishino. 2001. Real-time 3D interaction with ActiveCube. In *CHI '01 Extended Abstracts on Human Factors in Computing Systems* (CHI EA '01)
14. Kristian Gohlke, Michael Hlatky, and Bram de Jong. 2015. Physical Construction Toys for Rapid Sketching of Tangible User Interfaces. In *Proc. of TEI,* ACM, New York, NY, USA, 643-648.
15. Surapong Lertsithichai and Matthew Seegmiller. 2002. CUBIK: a bi-directional tangible modeling interface. In *CHI '02 Extended Abstracts on Human Factors in Computing Systems* (CHI EA '02)
16. Stefanie Mueller, Tobias Mohr, Kerstin Guenther, Johannes Frohnhofen, and Patrick Baudisch. 2014. faBrickation: fast 3D printing of functional objects by integrating construction kit building blocks. In *Proceedings of the SIGCHI Conference on Human Factors in Computing Systems* (CHI '14)
17. Phoebe Sengers and Bill Gaver. 2006. Staying open to interpretation: engaging multiple meanings in design and evaluation. In *Proceedings of the 6th conference on Designing Interactive systems* (DIS '06)

18. Sheng-Jie Luo, Yonghao Yue, Chun-Kai Huang, Yu-Huan Chung, Sei Imai, Tomoyuki Nishita, and Bing-Yu Chen. 2015. Legolization: optimizing LEGO designs. *ACM Trans. Graph.* 34, 6, Article 222 (October 2015)

19. Brygg Ullmer, and Hiroshi Ishii. 2000 Emerging frameworks for tangible user interfaces" *IBM Syst. J., IBM Corp, 39*, 915-931

20. Christian Weichel, Jason Alexander, Abhijit Karnik, and Hans Gellersen. 2015. SPATA: Spatio-Tangible Tools for Fabrication-Aware Design. In *Proceedings of the Ninth International Conference on Tangible, Embedded, and Embodied Interaction* (TEI '15)

Elsa: Temporary Ice Jet 3D printing

Hiroki Fujita
School of Media Science,
Tokyo University of technology
Katakura-machi 1404-1,
Hachioji,Tokyo, Japan
m01123652c@edu.teu.ac.jp

Akito Nakano
Graduate School of Media and
Governance, Keio University
Endo 5322, Fujisawa,
Kanagawa,Japan
akito@sfc.keio.ac.jp

Hisakazu Hada
School of Media Science,
Tokyo University of technology
Katakura-machi 1404-1,
Hachioji,Tokyo, Japan
hadahskz@stf.teu.ac.jp

TEI 2017, March 20–23, 2017, Yokohama, Japan.
ACM ISBN 978-1-4503-4676-4/17/03.
http://dx.doi.org/10.1145/3024969.3025093

Abstract
In this paper, we propose a method to instantly create and insert 3D printing by using ice spray, which vanishes completely and does not produce any waste. Ice-spray printing provides a handy and speedy object molding capability, which allows individuals to freely print their ideas. We present a system that creates ice pillars almost identical in lengths by using image-processing technology and Arduino to control the movement of ice sprays.

Author Keywords
fabrication; rapid prototyping;

ACM Classification Keywords
H.5.2 [User Interfaces]: Prototyping

introduction
The introduction of various three-dimensional (3D) printers by using fused deposition modeling (FDM) technology and stereolithography technology has given artists the freedom to easily create what they model on computers. The size of 3D printers keeps decreasing, and the time for shaping an object is shortening.

The problem about conventional 3D printers is that they produce mass waste material. In this paper, the authors propose a method to create an object instantly by using ice spray, which will vanish completely and does not produce any waste. Benefits of using ice spray as a 3D printing material are threefold. The first is to allow mass-production of accurate objects and rapid prototyping. The second is that no solid waste are formed; therefore, an individual can freely create objects. Lastly, this type of printing requires less energy and space for sculpturing than FDM. With such benefits, ice spray modeling allows handy and speedy object printing capability, which could be used by individuals to freely create their ideas anytime and anywhere.

However, if a creator uses plastic to develop what they need temporarily, considerable waste material is produced. In rapid prototyping, which creates objects through trial and error in a short period, it is not necessary for the product to remain for a long time. We considered fabricating a temporary existence of a model, which completely disappears so as not be produce waste material or garbage. Therefore, we propose to use ice as a printing material. Ice vaporizes, thus disappearing completely, and garbage is not produced even after printing. We attempted to control and use of ice spray to rapidly fabricate an object by using ice. Ice spray can create ice objects rapidly.

Related Works

Examples of existing related works regarding rapid prototyping are provided as follows. Research about rapid prototyping is growing along with widespread use of 3D printers. However, rapid prototyping, which repeats trial and error many times, creates not only an object but also considerable amounts of garbage, such as support materials and incorrect objects. Furthermore, products fabricated through rapid prototyping will become garbage in a short period.

3Doodler[1] has a pen-type device, which a user can hold with one hand and shape by using a free-hand technique. This device allows users to intuitively shape an object as if they are drawing it, without requiring to model it, and still allows the possible creation of complex shapes in a short amount of time. For 3Doodler, which allows users to create free-hand shapes, the shaping process is not assisted by a system; therefore, even if rapid shaping is possible, the output lacks in measurement accuracy.

Protopiper[2] creates pipe-shaped object of the intended size and shape by processing tape into a pipe-shaped form. The user creates a rough shape of target objects as wire-frame models by using these pipes in the actual size. Further, there is an advantage to allow natural shaping that does not require modeling on CAD. However, the tape used for modeling would accumulate into a large amount of trash in the future.

LaserOrigami[5] is used to solve the problem of joining a 3D object ’ s parts for composition when creating it by using a laser cutter. Although there is a limit to the possible complexity of the outcome, this system can produce seamless 3D objects. The system also has the advantage of eliminating the process of assembling for the hands of artists.

WirePrint[4] creates very high-speed rapid prototyping by using a conventional FDM 3D printer. Unlike conventional FDM 3D printing method, this system shapes an object by tracing a wire frame in one stroke and makes printing faster.

There are some studies, which used tape measure[3] or calipers[6] to create a 3D model of an actual size object. By using these, it is possible to measure the actual object and output accurate model data on the CAD through minimal operation.
One of the problems of rapid prototyping is the creation of a large amount of garbage. This garbage does not only comprise support materials but also incorrect prototypes that do not fit the objective or that is finished use.

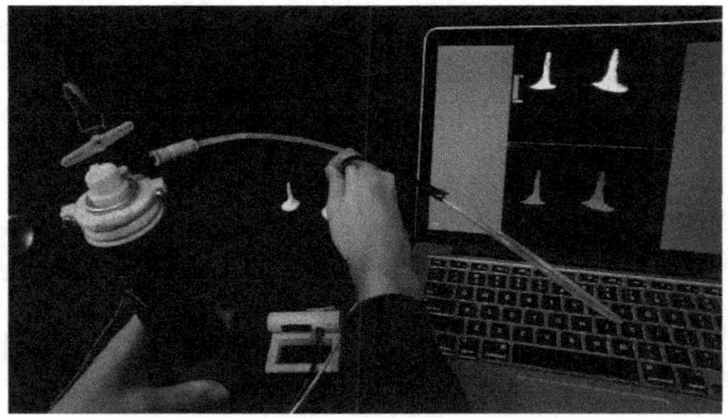

Figure 1: Appearance of a system

Products molded through rapid prototyping will be disposed off as garbage. You can prototype with temporarily existing objects.
Therefore, we propose a new rapid prototyping method that uses ice as a printing material. A product formed by ice melts and vaporizes after certain hours. Our proposed system ensures that nothing remains after creating prototypes.

Proposal

Current 3D printers create several amounts of garbage when printing objects. In this research, we used materials that will vanish in the air after certain hours to build ideas and needs rapidly without concerning about waste disposal. We propose to build objects by using ice through spraying and controlling the movement through a tablet PC and Arduino. The ice will disappear in few hours, thus preventing wastage. Therefore, we choose ice to realize an object that can be shaped quickly without thinking of wastes. Moreover, artists creating ice art can leave their work on the street, without contemplating about any garbage. We used a spray of ice that is sold at a drugstore for avoiding heat stroke. The main purpose of this spray is to rapidly create

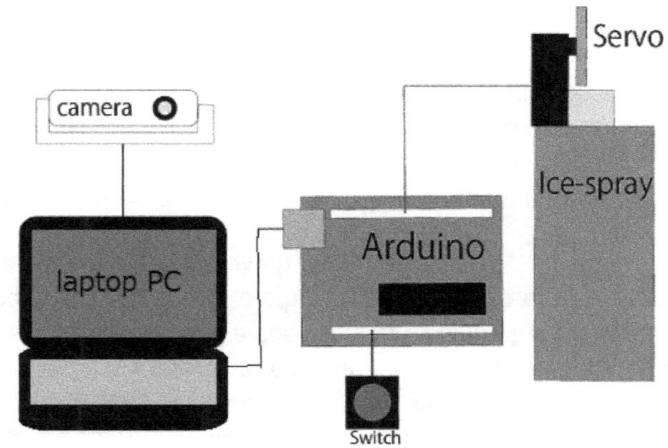

Figure 2: System Overview

cold towels to cool down a heated body. We propose a new rapid prototyping method that uses ice spray to create pillars. To support rapid prototyping of ice, we developed a system that controls the shape of ice to create the same size of ice pillars by using computer vision.

Implementation

Figure. 2 shows an overview of our implemented system. A user pushes a switch to control a servomotor attached on a spray to create an ice pillar of any shape. A camera of a tablet is used to perform the “background subtraction” method to create same sized pillars. A user pushes a switch or double-clicks to automatically create same sized ice pillars.

Operation

Arduino controls the servomotor and switch. In addition, it is connected to a PC to receive a set of commands. When a switch is pushed, Arduino begins injecting ice through a servomotor spewing spray. Figure. 3 shows the move-

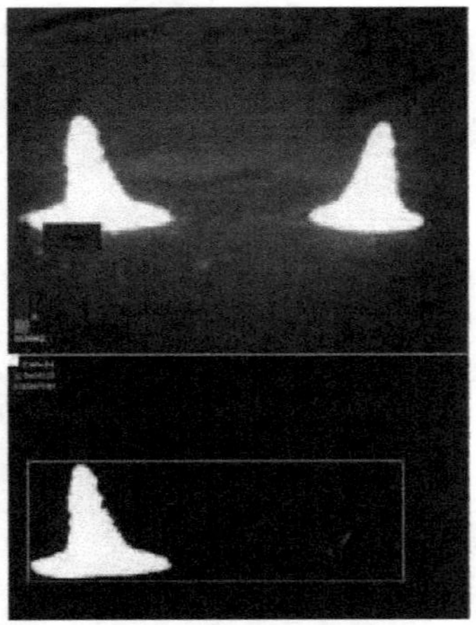

Figure 4: Background Subtraction of an Ice Image.

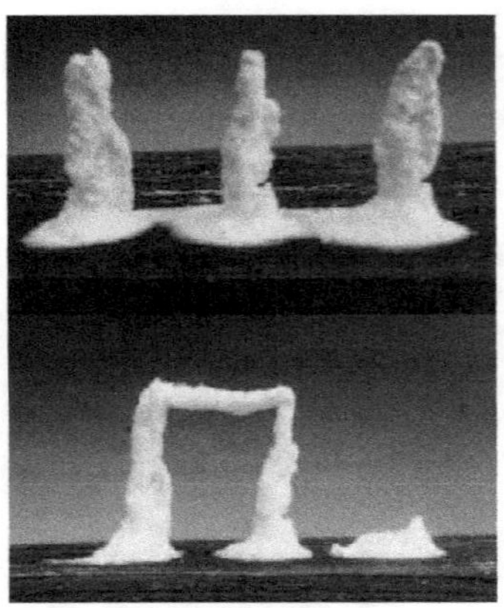

Figure 5: Rectangular shape is formed with three same sized pillars.

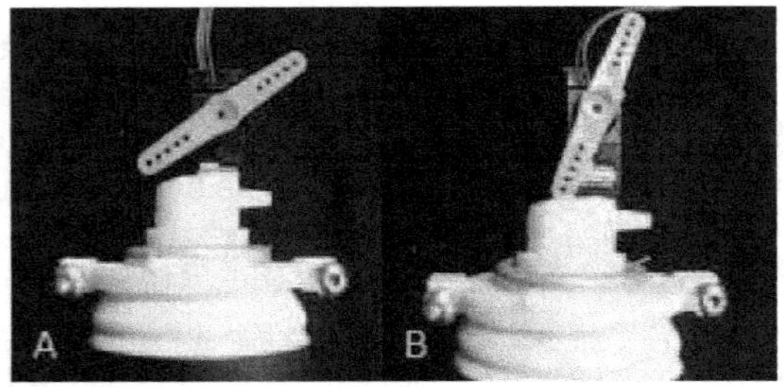

Figure 3: Movement of servomotor to push a spray

ment of servomotor pushing spray. A webcam and OpenCV are used to create pillars of the same height. This system recognizes the height and color of an ice pillar to use as a reference. As the injection of spray is only controlled by a switch attached to the Arduino, a user could easily control the location of creating pillars through this mechanism.

Background Subtraction
To calculate the height of pillars, the user first selects a pillar that is used as a benchmark. Next, he/she confirms that a selected pillar is covered by a rectangular frame on display. After choosing a pillar, the software calculates the pillar height and determines the amount of ice to inject. After selecting the "background subtraction" mode, the user pushes the switch to begin injection of ice. The injection is automatically stopped when the length of the pillar reaches the desired height (same as the reference).

Determining a Threshold
Our software allows the determination of a threshold by using a slider installed in the UI. It eases the selection of an object used as the benchmark. To select a target, a user can select an object on display and the software creates a rectangle that covers an object by using the same color as that of the object. When a threshold is determined, the rectangle will stop its movement. This implies that the threshold is good enough to determine a single object. The threshold can be changed directly from the slider on the UI, therefore easing the selection of a desired object.

Discussion
One limitation of rapid prototyping by hand is the difficulty in creating same sized objects. Therefore, we attempted to employ simple computer vision technologies to easily create same size objects. Our system uses the "background subtraction" method to compare the original and created objects. Figure.4 presents the photograph of the creation of the almost same size object through background subtraction by using a camera.

Figure.5 shows a result of creating a rectangle by using the ice pillars. We created a rectangle of the same size by using three ice pillars. It is difficult to create the same size objects by hand; therefore, we employed a computer vision to control the spray and create the same sized object similar to the copy-and-paste method. This allows a user to create a prototype much easily because the user must only move a nozzle slowly to create the same sized objects. Moreover, this feature is useful in reducing the user's mistakes. Figure. 6 shows a handle of a cup created by using the ice spray. Ice is easy to attach to other objects; therefore, we can create attached objects such as handles.

As ice is used as the material of this system, maintaining a particular shape for a long time is difficult. In addition, the ice easily breaks with the application of a slight force, and thus cannot be used for supporting a heavy object. This is not a limitation of our system that aims at very rapid prototyping.

Figure 6: Handle of a Cup

Future Work
In this research, we implemented a system to create multiple ice pillars of the same size. The next step of this research is to combine the present system with a measurement device, such as a tape measure[3] or a vernier, for tangible design[**?**] of existing objects.

At present, only simple shapes, such as those of pillars and arches can be molded. To solve this problem, we are considering shaping at CNC. By shaping with the use of a machine, it becomes possible to stack ice accurately and surely, so the range of modeling increases.

Conclusion
Conventional rapid prototyping has the problem of producing waste material in large quantities. To solve this problem, the authors propose ice as a printing material, which allows instant prototyping, and will vanish completely with time. This paper presents a system, which creates ice pillars almost identical in lengths by using image-processing technology and Arduino to control the movement of ice sprays. Ice objects can use any surface for printing unlike FDM; hence, ice printing can be considered as a new printing method that never existed before.

REFERENCES
1. 2015. 3Doodler. (2015). http://3doodlerstart.com/
2. Harshit Agrawal, Udayan Umapathi, Robert Kovacs, Johannes Frohnhofen, Hsiang-Ting Chen, Stefanie Mueller, and Patrick Baudisch. 2015. Protopiper. *Proceedings of the 28th Annual ACM Symposium on User Interface Software & Technology - UIST '15* (2015), 427–436. DOI: http://dx.doi.org/10.1145/2807442.2807505
3. Jay Lee, Victor Su, Sandia Ren, and Hiroshi Ishii. 2000. HandSCAPE: a vectorizing tape measure for on-site measuring applications. *Proceedings of the SIGCHI conference on . . .* 2, 1 (2000), 137–144. DOI: http://dx.doi.org/10.1145/332040.332417
4. Stefanie Mueller, Sangha Im, Serafima Gurevich, Alexander Teibrich, Lisa Pfisterer, François Guimbretière, and Patrick Baudisch. 2014. WirePrint: 3D printed previews for fast prototyping. *UIST '14: Proceedings of the 27th annual ACM symposium on User interface software and technology* Figure 2 (2014), 273–280. DOI: http://dx.doi.org/10.1145/2642918.2647359
5. Stefanie Mueller, Bastian Kruck, and Patrick Baudisch. 2013. LaserOrigami. *Proceedings of the SIGCHI Conference on Human Factors in Computing Systems - CHI '13* (2013), 2585. DOI: http://dx.doi.org/10.1145/2470654.2481358
6. Christian Weichel, Jason Alexander, Abhijit Karnik, and Hans Gellersen. 2015. Spata. *Proceedings of the Ninth International Conference on Tangible, Embedded, and Embodied Interaction - TEI '14* (2015), 189–196. DOI: http://dx.doi.org/10.1145/2677199.2680576

HoloMuse: Enhancing Engagement with Archaeological Artifacts through Gesture-Based Interaction with Holograms

Christina Pollalis
Wellesley College
Wellesley, MA 02148, USA
cpollali@wellesley.edu

Whitney Fahnbulleh
Wellesley College
Wellesley, MA 02148, USA
wfahnbul@wellesley.edu

Jordan Tynes
Wellesley College
Wellesley, MA 02148, USA
jtynes@wellesley.edu

Orit Shaer
Wellesley College
Wellesley, MA 02148, USA
oshaer@wellesley.edu

TEI '17, March 20-23, 2017, Yokohama, Japan
ACM 978-1-4503-4676-4/17/03.
http://dx.doi.org/10.1145/3024969.3025094

Abstract
We present HoloMuse, an AR application for the HoloLens wearable device, which allows users to actively engage with archaeological artifacts from a museum collection in ways that are otherwise not possible. We designed HoloLens to facilitate learning and engagement with museum collections without taking away from the experience of viewing an original artifact within the context of an exhibit. HoloMuse can be used inside the gallery or in the classroom. It enables users to pick up, rotate, scale, and alter a hologram of an original archeological artifact using in-air gestures. Users can also curate their own exhibit or customize an existing one by selecting artifacts from a virtual gallery and placing them within the physical world so that they are viewable only using the device. We intend to study the impact of HoloMuse on learning and engagement with college-level art history and archeology students.

Author Keywords
Augmented Reality; museums; gesture-based interaction; education.

ACM Classification Keywords
H.5.m. Information interfaces and presentation (e.g., HCI): Miscellaneous;

Figure 1: A user rotating an artifact.

Figure 2: A user customizing an exhibit by placing an artifact in the physical world.

Introduction
Augmented reality (AR) technology poses unique opportunities for museums to bring exhibits "to life" and to allow visitors to experience and engage with original artifacts in new ways. Indeed, many museums are experimenting with the use of AR for increasing visitor engagement. Examples of AR applications for museums include the "Skin and Bones" application in the National Museum of Natural History, the "Ultimate Dinosaurs" exhibit at the Cincinnati Museum Center, and the "ROM Ultimate Dinosaurs" at the Royal Ontario Museum.

However, current AR applications, which utilize tablets and phones, often divert visitor attention from the original artifact and from the context within which it is presented to the screen. Such applications provide only limited interactions with the original artifact, which typically include viewing a virtual layer superimposed on the artifact or manipulating a superimposed object using on-screen touch gestures. Therefore, an important open question is how can AR enhance a visitor's engagement and understanding of authentic artifacts without taking away from viewing them within an exhibit context?

The increasing availability of wearable AR devices, such as the Microsoft Hololens [11], provides opportunities to develop AR experiences in which users can see the world and other people around them without holding an additional mediating device (e.g. phone) but also interact through mid-air gestures and movement with 3D holograms that are superimposed on the physical world. Users can add, remove, and place holograms within their physical environment and interact with them in ways similar to interacting with physical objects in the real non-digital world – e.g. walking around an artifact to view it from different perspectives, rotating an object, picking it up, and placing it within the physical space. In addition, users can engage with holograms in ways not always possible in the real physical world such as scaling and altering (e.g. by removing a layer of paint).

In this abstract, we present our first prototype of HoloMuse, an AR application for engaging with archaeological artifacts using the HoloLens device. HoloMuse allows users to actively engage with holograms of archeological artifacts presented in the Anonymous Museum – an academic fine-arts museum on the Anonymous College campus. These holograms are constructed from 3D scans of artifacts from Ancient Greece ranging from the 500 B.C.E period to the late 6th century B.C.E period.

Using HoloMuse, users can interact with these artifacts in ways otherwise not possible, including picking up, rotating, scaling, and removing a paint layer (see Figure 1). Users can also curate their own exhibit, or add artifacts to an existing exhibit, by selecting artifacts from a virtual gallery and placing them within the physical world (see Figure 2). HoloMuse can be used inside the gallery or in the classroom. Through active interaction and careful examination of the properties of an individual artifact and of the relations between artifacts, we expect to enhance the learning and understanding of archeological artifacts. We believe that allowing people to actively interact with original

Figure 3: A user using an air gesture to select an artifact.

artifacts will lead to new pedagogical approaches to archaeology and art history. This paper also includes photos taken with the HoloLens camera that demonstrate what the user sees through the device.

Related Work

Studies have found that engagement with objects is vital for enhancing visitor understanding and overall enjoyment in a museum space [1]. Actively engaging with artifacts has been proven to enhance visitor experience as it allows them to expand their visual and verbal vocabulary and makes them feel more comfortable around the art [9, 13]. Advances in mobile technology and augmented reality have been extensively incorporated into museum applications and guides [12]. Here we discuss applications that were designed with the goal of increasing user engagement with objects in museums. For example, ArteMuse [14] is a mobile application that enhances the experience of beginner users when engaging with works of art. Its evaluation indicated that when using the application visitors spent more time viewing works of art, were more engaged when interacting with them, and had a subjectively better experience in the museum. Participatory mobile applications, such as ArtLinks [4, 5], and Imprints [2], allow for personalization of exhibits and interaction with other visitors by sharing personalized tags created for objects in the museum. Repentir [8], is an AR application that allows a user to digitally explore under an oil painting's surface by removing a layer of paint. Another example of a novel interface for engaging with artifacts and self-curating is the Pen in the Cooper Hewitt Smithsonian Design Museum. The Pen is given to visitors with their admission ticket and allows visitors to "collect" and "save" objects from the museum exhibits [3]. These objects can be explored further by transferring them to large interactive tables or can be used in the Immersion Room, where visitors can use their pens to select wallpapers from the permanent museum collection, see them projected on the walls, and manipulate them. The pen also allows for extended interaction since a visitor can view or share the collected artifacts through a web browser and more objects can be added during a later visit to the museum.

Several AR guides have been developed for museums. For example, GuidiGo [10], ARCO [15], The AR Guide [7], and ARtSense [6] have been developed for research purposes. Museums also offer AR apps as supplementary gadget to their exhibits, such as the "ARTours" application at the Stedelijk Museum in Amsterdam that uses AR to place artifacts in a public park, and the "Get Surreal" application at the San Francisco Exploratorium that turned its After Dark event at the museum into an AR experience. However, to date there is a lack of substantial research on how AR applications impact users' engagement, understanding and enjoyment in an art exhibit. There is also little work about how AR applications can be used for customizing and curating.

HoloMuse

HoloMuse is an AR application that utilizes the HoloLens device to allow users to directly interact with holograms of archaeological artifacts from the Anonymous Museum's collection.

In the current prototype, users can select a hologram from a virtual gallery, by focusing their gaze on a particular hologram and selecting it using a voice

Figure 4: A user placed multiple holograms to curate their own exhibit space.

Figure 5: The directional arrow that allows other users to locate the exhibit space.

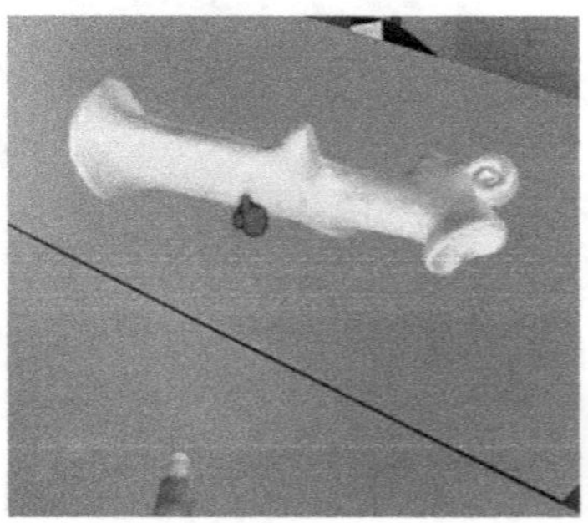

Figure 8: A user removed the material of an artifact.

command or an in-air gesture (see Figure 3). Users can rotate and scale the hologram using in-air gestures, and then place it within their field of view with an air-gesture tap so that the hologram remains on the selected position unless moved again. Users can place multiple holograms in various positions, thereby customizing the exhibit space and curating their own collection (see Figure 4).

Users can invite others to visit the customized space they created by sharing their exhibit (currently by handing the HoloLens to another person), we are currently implementing a visiting mode – where virtual arrows will appear when the user turn their head in the general direction of a hologram to help the user locate the added holograms in the space (see Figure 5).

To encourage users to learn more about an individual artifact and to study it carefully, as well as to consider the relations between artifacts, we are currently implementing features that will allow users to request and present additional information (text and voice) about an artifact (see Figure 7), and to select an artifact from an inventory (see Figure 6).

Figure 6: A user opening a virtual gallery to select an object to place in the space.

Figure 7: A user requested more information about an artifact.

Design Process

Our design process follows a human-centered approach. We work closely with users – on-campus museum visitors and students, as well as museum curators and faculty with expertise in art history and archaeology, to explore the potential of wearable AR in promoting meaningful engagement and learning with archeological artifacts in and outside the museum. We are planning to employ both qualitative and quantitative research methods to refine and validate our design, and then to evaluate the impact of the system on learning and engagement.

Preliminary Evaluation

We conducted a preliminary evaluation of HoloMuse, presenting it as an interactive demo in the library where about 20 users interacted with the application (see Figure 9). Most users enjoyed the application and were able to select and manipulate a hologram using gestures without significant problems. However, some had difficulties making HoloLens specific gestures and required practice. This issue could be resolved through a brief tutorial on the use of the HoloLens platform.

Figure 9: A user interacting with the HoloMuse demo in the library.

Implementation
HoloMuse is implemented using HoloLens for Unity 5.4.0f3-HTP (Unity HoloLens Technical Preview), Visual Studio 2015 (Update 3) with Tools (1.4), and Windows 10 SDK (10.0.10586) installed. Archeological artifacts were scanned using Artec Spider and modeled using Artec Studio 10 and 11.

Conclusion and Future Work
We present HoloMuse, an AR application that utilizes the HoloLens device to allow users to actively engage with archaeological artifacts from a museum collection using gaze, in-air gestures, and whole body interaction (e.g. walking). We designed HoloMuse to facilitate learning and engagement with museum collections without taking away from the experience of viewing an original artifact within the context of an exhibit. HoloMuse can be used inside the gallery or in the classroom. It enables users to manipulate and relate archaeological artifacts in ways otherwise not possible.

We are currently iterating on the design and implementation of HoloMuse, focusing on the development of sharing a curated exhibit through a 'visiting mode'. We are also planning to create an interface for museum curators and faculty to upload content to the application. We plan to study the impact of HoloMuse on learning and engagement by deploying it in the on-campus Anonymous Museum, making it available for college-level art history and archeology students.

References
1. Bell, C. The Museum as 'Cultural Econology.' 2002. Retrieved October 25, 2016 from http://echo.iat.sfu.ca/library/bell_02_museum_ecology.pdf.
2. Boehner, K., J. Thom-Santelli, A. Zoss, G. Gay, J.S. Hall, and T. Barrett. Imprints of place: creative expressions of the museum experience. 2005. Retrieved on November 3, 2016. CHI '05 Extended abstracts on Human factors in computing systems.
3. Cooper Hewitt. The New Cooper Hewitt Experience. 2016. Retrieved November 3, 2016 from http://www.cooperhewitt.org/new-experience/.

4. Cosley, D., J. Baxter, S. Lee, B. Alson, S. Nomura, P. Adams, C. Sarabu, and G. Gay. A tag in the hand: supporting semantic, social, and spatial navigation in museums. 2009. Retrieved on November 3, 2016. In Proceedings of the 27th international conference on Human factors in computing systems.

5. Cosley, D., J. Lewenstein, A. Herman, J. Holloway, J.Baxter, S. Nomura, K. Boehner, G. Gay. ArtLinks: Fostering social awareness and reflection in museums. 2008. Retrieved on November 3, 2016. In Proceeding of the 26th annual SIGCHI conference on Human factors in computing systems.

6. Damala, A. and P. Cuband. Bridging the Gap between the Digital and the Physical: Design and Evaluation of a Mobile Augmented Reality Guide for the Museum Visit. 2008. Retrieved November 1, 2016 from http://dl.acm.org/citation.cfm?id=1413660.

7. Damala, A., N. Stojanovic, T. Schuchert, J. Moragues, A. Cabrera, and K. Gilleade. Adaptive Augmented Reality for Cultural Heritage: ARtSENSE Project. 2012. Retrieved November 3, 2016 from http://www.academia.edu/2296517/Adaptive_Augmented_Reality_for_Cultural_Heritage_The_ARtSENSE_project.

8. Hook, J., J. Briggs, M. Blythe, N. Walsh, P. Olivier. Repentir: a digital exploration beneath the surface of an oil painting. 2013. Retrieved on January 1 2017. CHI '13 Extended abstracts on Human factors in computing systems.

9. Leder, H., B. Belke, A. Oeberst, and D. Augustin. A model of aesthetic appreciation and aesthetic judgments. British Journal of Psychology95, 4, 489-508. 2004. Retrieved November 2, 2016 from http://echo.iat.sfu.ca/library/bell_02_museum_ecology.pdf.

10. Mason, M. The MIT Museum Glassware Prototype: Visitor Experience Exploration for Designing Smart Glasses. 2016. Retrieved November 3, 2016 from http://dl.acm.org/citation.cfm?id=2872278.

11. Microsoft. Microsoft HoloLens. 2016. Retrieved November 1, 2016 from https://www.microsoft.com/microsoft-hololens/en-us.

12. Museum ID. British Museum – Augmented Reality: Beyond the Hype. Retrieved November 2, 2016 from http://www.museum-id.com/idea-detail.asp?id=336.

13. Rothstein, E. From Picassos to Sarcophagi, Guided by Phone Apps. 2010. Retrieved November 1, 2016 from http://www.nytimes.com/2010/10/02/arts/design/02apps.html.

14. Shaer O., J. Olsen, M. Edwards, C. Valdes. Art App-rectiation: Fostering Engagement and Reflection in Museums through a Social-Mobile Application. 2011. Retrieved November 1, 2016 from http://www.museumsandtheweb.com/mw2011/papers/art_app_reciation_fostering_engagement_and_ref.html.

15. Wojciechnowski, R., K. Walczak, M. White, and W. Cellary. Building Virtual and Augmented Reality Museum Exhibitions. 2004. Retrieved November 1, 2016 from http://dl.acm.org/citation.cfm?id=985060.

Corus: A Holographic Candle System with Intuitive Gestural Interaction and Ambient Feedback to Promote Co-Sleeping

Meric Dagli
School of Design
Carnegie Mellon University
Pittsburgh, PA 15213, USA
mdagli@andrew.cmu.edu

Julia Petrich
School of Design
Carnegie Mellon University
Pittsburgh, PA 15213, USA
jpetrich@cmu.edu

Rossa Kim
Nehal Vora
School of Design
Carnegie Mellon University
Pittsburgh, PA 15213, USA
rossak@andrew.cmu.edu
nehalv@andrew.cmu.edu

Austin S. Lee
School of Design
Carnegie Mellon University
Pittsburgh, PA 15213, USA
austinlee@cmu.edu

TEI '17, March 20-23, 2017, Yokohama, Japan
ACM 978-1-4503-4676-4/17/03.
http://dx.doi.org/10.1145/3024969.3025095

Abstract
Corus is a concept for a holographic candle system that helps cohabitating couples become more synchronized in their sleep routines. The components of our proposed system design are a main candle in the bedroom and other "satellite" candles around the home. In our proposed design, holographic candles will offer calming notification and ambient feedback. Users will also be able to interact with the candles through natural, intuitive, and form-specific gestural inputs, as well as through a mobile app. These proposed inputs and ambient feedbacks are integral to Corus. Moving forward, we would like to explore how our proposed interactions work in real home environments, further prototyping the inputs and feedbacks using Leap Motion and more sophisticated hologram projection.

Motivation
With Corus, we were motivated to create a sleep solution in a family context. Most sleep and health solutions on the market today consider individuals, not groups, which is inherent in the technologies and the design of their systems. This is where we saw an open space for prototyping new designs while using newer, developing technologies. Specifically, we were interested in cohabitating couples and how a sleep

solution might offer benefits for a couple, both individually and together.

We found cohabitation a rich and interesting field for intervention as it is an important moment of transition in which two adult individuals with potentially divergent lifestyles start living with each other in a new environment. Sometimes, this transition is smooth, often when couples have similar sleep schedules already. But it can become more difficult when one or both partners have to adjust to a new routine. We reframed the problem of couple sleep consistency and quality as one related to both physical health and relationship health. This was something we carried throughout our design process.

Related Work

Corus is related to various research topics, bridging sleep studies with HCI research and more. Since it primarily intends to promote dyadic sleep in cohabitating couples, one of Corus' roots is in current co-sleeping studies, which examine couples' sleep health on the whole rather than focusing on merely on individuals. Since we present Corus as a system which will use holographic candle projections that are controlled by gestural inputs (which we intend to prototype using Leap Motion) and a smart mobile application, our proposed design also relates to past and current research on augmented reality (AR) interfaces, and more specifically, to those that use candles as a metaphor in HCI design. Corus is prototyped with a 15th century inspired technique, Pepper's ghost illusion [15]; therefore, its 3D prototype is also an example of how AR interfaces can be prototyped by using universally-accessible materials.

Below, we will give some of the key examples from these fields to position our work.

Sleeping

In one of the co-sleeping studies [8], dyadic sleep's effect on both a couple's physical and mental health is investigated. The authors discuss that even when sleeping together, in the same bed, affects the objective measurements of sleep negatively, couples self-reported that they prefer to sleep with their partners. The authors conclude that although going bed and sleeping together may have objective costs, "the subjective sleep experience of partners are increased, probably due to the sense of safety and security with being with a close other."

Candle as a Control Input in HCI Design

Since the candle is a universal everyday object, which is powered by fire (and a flame), interactions around candle as a physical object are considered intuitive in many cultures. Other than being a light source, the candle has also varying meanings and associations in different cultures [2]. Although the metaphor of the candle and using a candle as a control input is not new to the field of interaction design, we see the space to provide a more holistic experience by combining 'systems thinking' with 'designing for interactions' via a candle metaphor. In some of the related research, candles (the physical object) are used directly. For example, several works use candles as a part of a meditative interface system by leveraging the affordances of a physical candle and the known ways of interacting with a candle such as lighting or blowing it out, e.g. [3], [9], [13]. Another example of using physical candles as a part of a system is "the candle recorder" [7]. The authors envisioned a tealight candle as a power switch in their recorder and speaker system which users can turn on or turn off by lighting or blowing out a candle. On the other hand, other sensorial feedbacks of operating candles such as shadows are proposed to be used as an interface, or more specifically, a "display for ambient communication delivery"[4].

Candle Metaphor in HCI Design

The candle, as a metaphor, has also appeared in the fields of human-computer interaction and interaction design, both conceptually and in real-life scenarios. In both conceptual and on-market products (e.g. [5], [6]) universal visual representation of candles are used as signifiers. Often the three-dimensional shape of candles are mimicked by using physical computing components such as LED lights with "white shaded enclosures" as well as sensors such as motion sensors, microphones to mimic the behavior of "natural" candle light, e.g. [11].

Holographic Projection Prototyping: Pepper's Ghost to Hologram Pyramid

A hologram can be defined as a virtual three dimensional recreation of an image, created using light imagery (e.g. projection) floating in space, giving the image, a perspective and depth [1]. The different angles of a hologram can be viewed by changing the angle of observation [12]. Holographic projection systems are the setups that attempt to mimic the behavior of a holograph in real-life, mostly with visual seams. One of the ancestors of these holographic display systems is Pepper's ghost configuration [14], which has been used in sub-sectors of entertainment industry (such as theaters or amusement parks) since 19th century. The Pepper's ghost configuration, which is named after chemistry professor John Henry Pepper [10], is a common illusion used in theaters in the 19th century. As Bimber and Raskar [1] put, a Pepper's ghost configuration is a technique in which a large sheet of glass is mounted in front of a theatre stage (with a 45° angle toward the audience). Due to the self-reflection of the mounted glass, the audience can see the mirrored image of an off-stage area. This way, theater producers can create an early "augmented reality" by overlapping "reality" with another image, which is invisible to viewers' eyes. One of the drawbacks of Pepper's ghost illusion is that it is limited to only one side of view. Although Pepper's ghost technique still used in entertainment industry, improved versions of it have been developed. One of these versions is called a hologram pyramid, which usually is in the form of a three-sided pyramid, mainly made of transparent acrylic sheets using a large display, sized between 30" and 50". It works by reflecting three-sided visuals from the display to the transparent acrylic (Plexiglass) sheets that reflect the visuals to the center of the pyramid that gives the illusion of a three-dimensional holograph. Although a hologram pyramid can be viewed from its three or more sides, it does not enable viewer to freely view the "hologram" since the illusion interrupts at the seams (or the edges of the transparent pyramid). Therefore, the projected content is not truly a hologram but a holographic projection. Although hologram pyramids have some drawbacks, we have used a four-sided holograph inspired a votive-style candle enclosure for the live demo of our concept. Here, we have used Pepper's Ghost technique as a way to demonstrate our concept. In actuality, we propose the sensors for gestural inputs be embedded in the base of the holographic votive unit.

Figure 2: Each of users has a different accent color on their app. The color of candle changes based on how balanced the compromises being made around sleep are and visualized on their smart device.

Design

Our concept is currently in video prototype of interactions (see: concept video) and non-functioning prototype of physical form phase (see: live demo video).

We propose the implementation of the proof of concept prototype as followed by the conceptual system map. (Fig. 1)

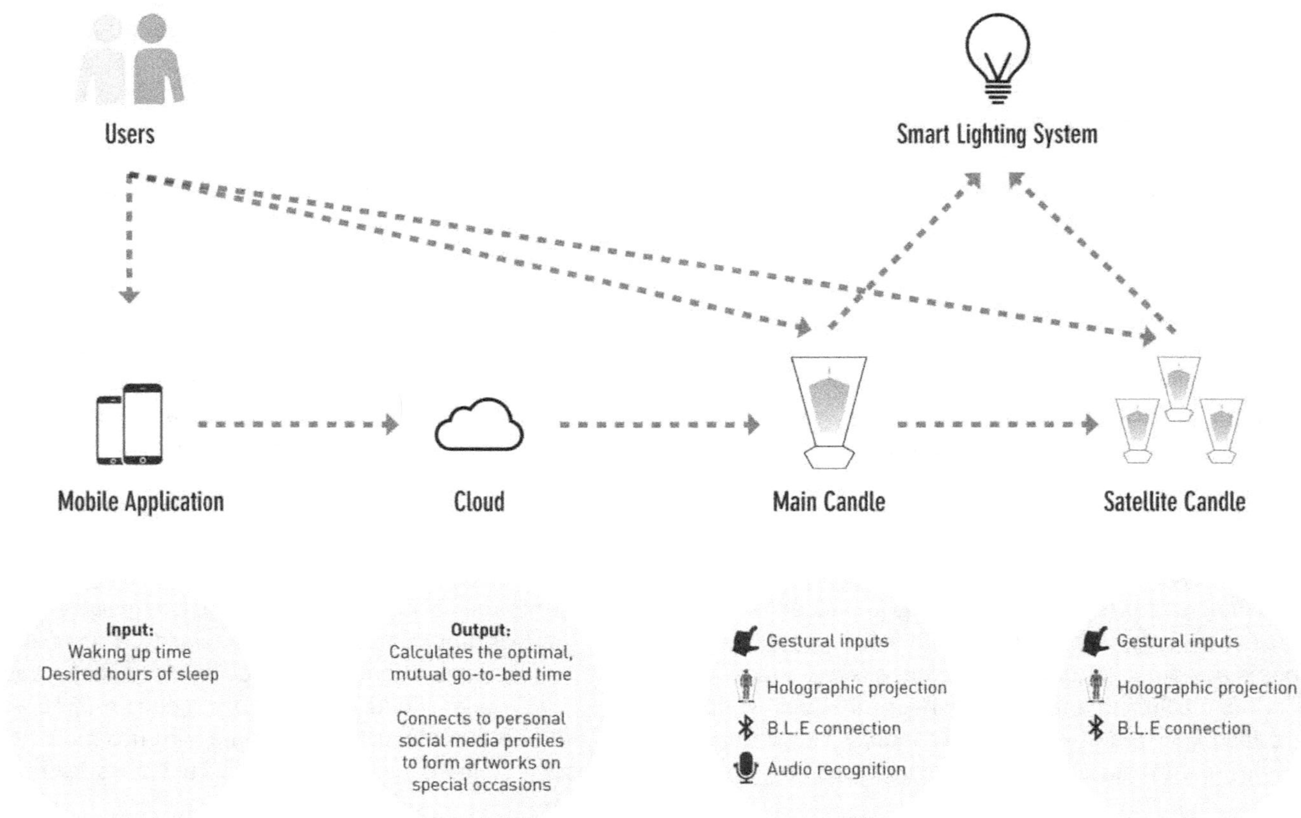

Figure 1: Corus Conceptual System map

Figure 3: Different snapshots from live demo done by using Pepper's Ghost Technique

The hardware components of Corus are a main candle in the bedroom and other "satellite" candles around the home. The candles themselves are projected inside the holographic projection votive. We propose motion sensors within the votive to allow the flames to respond to body movements of users such as walking past or hand gestures. These sensors will understand through passive infrared motion detectors and will perceive emitted infrared energy when users are nearby. We also propose an embedded microphone within the main votive unit which will recognize the level of audio signals. (Fig. 1) We chose a holographic system over other more physical interfaces to allow for a more dynamic form in the candle. This way, the projection can display different information based on the time of the day. The candle would appear sometime after sunset, creating the ambient, candlelit environment for evening decompression before bedtime. During the day, however, we propose that the wax of the candle take on a different form, which can be customized to display information as per user's preference; e.g. birthdays, weather, travel plans, gathered from the user's e-mail account or social media. This division of the two main forms by time of day may help users to visually associate the form of the system more readily to the time and what activities may be most appropriate, knowing when and how soon bedtime is approaching.

Software component

We propose that Corus connects to a smart home system for the lights in the home. The candles are connected to and can control the lighting system through Bluetooth. Corus will be able to control the lights in two ways: through the app that connects through private Web-based cloud services and through gestural inputs on the candles themselves. The cloud services will be linked to the users' social media from which we propose Corus pulls relevant information to display in the form of art. This will remind and delight the users each morning. The candles themselves will offer feedback to the users in their color. Each of the two users will have a different accent color on their app that will be visualized in the candle's color by collecting data from the users' behavior to help the couple see how balanced their compromises being made around sleep are. (Figure 2)

The app will be used foremost to set goals and initial preferences, but it also will function as a secondary notification of approaching bedtime and a dashboard of analytics of evening conversation energy, dynamics, and volume.

Affordances

Corus combines physical and virtual elements.

Physical characteristics

As a guiding and training tool, Corus will afford its users the gentle reminder of the late-growing hour in an ambient and non-prescriptive way. It will also function as a fixture, in how it will connect to and control the smart lighting system throughout the house. The device itself will have two holographic projection forms: in the evening and night, it will be a candle, and in the day, it will become an artifact of the couple's upcoming day, pulling from the couple's social media or calendar or defaulting to weather.

Virtual characteristics

The form of Corus itself (as a candle) signifies the possible interactions with the object. Since Corus

Figure 4: (1) Fanning the Flame to Snooze or Delay the Bedtime, (2) Snapping Fingers to Spark the Flame and Turn on the Lights, (3) Pinching the Flame to Put out the Flame and Turn Off the Lights

involves holographic projections, these visual features should be created to encourage physical interactions with the device. These projections are subject to change as per validity of the intended use.

Prototype

We created a three-dimensional model to demonstrate Corus' holographic projection votive using a volumetric display to understand the effect of holographic technology. (Figure 3) Corus is currently in video prototype stage which showcases four parts of our user
1. Virtual inputs + intuitive output

First, we demonstrate the way the onboarding of our mobile application will be used to set user preferences. We propose that these inputs will be optimized by the Corus system to generate clear and intuitive outputs that will guide the user towards the bedroom in the evening.

2. Gestural inputs + virtual output
Second, we show how gestural inputs to a hologram in Corus can be used to guide the system in an interactive manner. We demonstrate our proposed intuitive gestures: fanning the flame to snooze or delay the bedtime, snapping fingers to spark the flame and turn on the lights, and pinching the flame to put out the flame and turn off the lights. (Figure 4)

3. Smart lighting system
Third, we propose that Corus connects both the holographic and the screen-based controls to a smart lighting system that nudges the couple to go to bed at the optimal time calculated with the user preference inputs. We demonstrate how the lights may dim, to provide a further signifier of the approaching bedtime.

4. Sensor input + virtual output
Lastly, we show how Corus may sense the audio intensities in the bedroom and how the smart lighting system may respond to these inputs. Corus will sense the lowering intensities of the night time conversations and starts dimming the lights and slowly turning off towards the end.

Discussion and Future Work

We see Corus as a possible solution that not only assists in the physical health of each partner but also as a product that can assist in promoting a couple's relationship health. Corus will primarily tackle sleep as a pillar of relationship health, but it also points toward some other metrics of relationship health, most notably, communication and closeness. There are many pillars of relationship health, and those merely scratch the surface. Although Corus offers a potential design intervention to help couples sleep more dyadically, we wonder how solutions like Corus that offer ambient feedback and gentle prodding could help in these other areas that are key to a successful relationship. As we look to our next steps, we plan to create a more functioning prototype and do further research with cohabitating couples to examine Corus' validity as both a tool for sleep and health and a fixture for the home.

References

1. Oliver Bimber and Ramesh. Raskar. 2005. *Spatial augmented reality : merging real and virtual worlds*. A K Peters.
2. Paul Coulton, Jonny Huck, Andrew Hudson-Smith, et al. 2014. Designing interactive systems to encourage empathy between users. *Proceedings of the 2014 companion publication on Designing interactive systems - DIS Companion '14*, ACM Press, 13–16. http://doi.org/10.1145/2598784.2602770
3. Michelle Hlubinka, Jennifer Beaudin, Emmanuel Munguia Tapia, and John S An. 2002. AltarNation: interface design for meditative communities. *CHI'02 extended abstracts on Human factors in computing systems*, Figure 1: 612–613. http://doi.org/10.1145/506443.506509
4. Tuomas Lappalainen, Ashley Colley, Jenine Beekhuyzen, and Jonna Häkkilä. 2016. Candle Shadow Display for Ambient Communication Delivery. *Proceedings of the 2016 ACM Conference Companion Publication on Designing Interactive Systems - DIS '16 Companion*, ACM Press, 13–16. http://doi.org/10.1145/2908805.2908809
5. LuDela. LuDela. Retrieved October 4, 2016 from https://ludela.com/
6. MIPOW USA. 2014. PLAYBULB candle - Color LED Flameless Candle with Mobile App by MIPOW USA — Kickstarter. Retrieved October 4, 2016 from https://www.kickstarter.com/projects/mipowusa/playbulb-candle-color-led-flameless-candle-with-mo
7. Tek-Jin Nam, Sunyoung Park, and Jouke Verlinden. 2009. A model to conceptualize interactivity. *International Journal on Interactive Design and Manufacturing (IJIDeM)* 3, 3: 147–156. http://doi.org/10.1007/s12008-009-0069-5
8. F P Pankhurst and J A Horne. 1994. The influence of bed partners on movement during sleep. *Sleep* 17, 4: 308–15.
9. J R Parker. 2008. Buttons, simplicity, and natural interfaces.
10. John H. Pepper. 1879. Improvement in apparatus for producing optical illusions.
11. Philips. 2016. Philips Hue | Meet Hue. Retrieved October 4, 2016 from http://www2.meethue.com/en-us/
12. Dragi Tiro, Admira Poturiovic, and Nevzudin Buzadjija. 2015. The possibility of the hologram pyramid applying in the rapid prototyping. *2015 4th Mediterranean Conference on Embedded Computing (MECO)*, IEEE, 25–30. http://doi.org/10.1109/MECO.2015.7181907
13. Daisuke Uriu and Naohito Okude. 2010. ThanatoFenestra. *Proceedings of the 8th ACM Conference on Designing Interactive Systems - DIS '10*, ACM Press, 422. http://doi.org/10.1145/1858171.1858253
14. M Walker. 1994. *Ghostmasters: A Look Back at America's Midnight Spook Shows.*
15. 2009. Pepper's ghost could bring videoconferences to life. *New Scientist 204*. http://doi.org/10.1016/S0262-4079(09)63056-6

Eyewear to Make Me Smile – Can Electric Muscle Stimulation increase Happiness?

Lai Yen-Chin
Keio Media Design
Keio University
Yokohama, Japan
laiyen@kmd.keio.ac.jp

Junichi Shimizu
Keio Media Design
Keio University
Yokohama, Japan
jun.shimi@kmd.keio.ac.jp

YuanLing Feng
Keio Media Design
Keio University
Yokohama, Japan
yfeng@kmd.keio.ac.jp

Takuro Nakao
Keio Media Design
Keio University
Yokohama, Japan
a8111140@kmd.keio.ac.jp

Kai Kunze
Keio Media Design
Keio University
Yokohama, Japan
kai@kmd.keio.ac.jp

TEI '17, March 20-23, 2017, Yokohama, Japan
ACM 978-1-4503-4676-4/17/03.
http://dx.doi.org/10.1145/3024969.3025097

Abstract
This paper suggests a prototype system making users smile using electrical muscle stimulation (EMS). We present design considerations, our approach, and the current system setup. We continue to describe our first insights into using an unobtrusive EMS setup to stimulate smiles and show first findings from our entry in this year's UIST student innovation competition. We also outline our approach and follow-up experiments to potentially use this technology to improve user's mood.

Author Keywords
Electric Muscle Stimulation; Smile; Smart Glasses

ACM Classification Keywords
H.5.m [Information interfaces and presentation (e.g., HCI)]: Miscellaneous

Introduction
With the increases in mental issues and disorders on the rise, we want to explore if we can change or better enhance our mood using technology [3, 6]. Given James-Lange Theory of Emotion that suggests that physiological reactions can induce feelings and emotions, people can feel happier just by smiling more throughout the day [2]. We want to create technologies to manage better our affect. This paper presents an initial small step towards that direction.

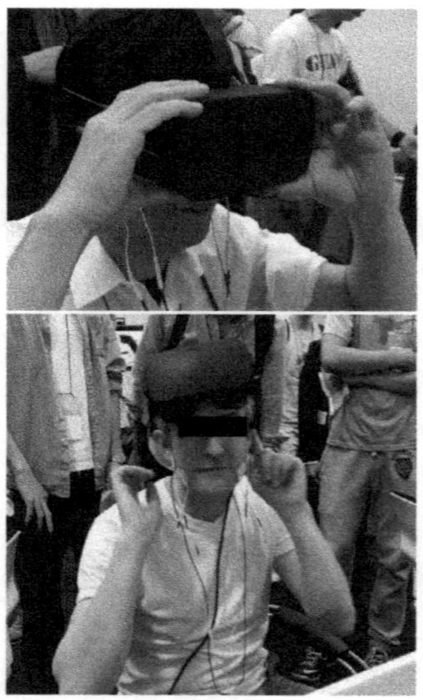

Figure 1: Setup and pictures from the student competition

Our contributions are as follows: (1) we evaluate if it's possible to induce smiles using a relative unobtrusive Electric Muscle Stimulation (EMS) setup, (2) we discuss a electrode placements and other issues suitable for inducing smiles with the potential to integrate them in a smart glasses design, (3) we show insights learned from participating in the UIST student innovation competition with our prototype system, (4) we present an initial experimental design to evaluate if induces smiles from EMS can actually change the user's emotion.

Overall, we believe it's an important first step to investigate EMS for emotion control.Given we will get clearance from the ethics board of our institution, participants at TEI can try an excellent demonstration of our technology at TEI (after signing a consent form).

Approach

There are already technologies utilizing James-Lange Theory of emotion; most prominently, the Smile-encouraging digital appliances by Tsujita and Rekimoto [9]. However, their approach is to "force" the user to smile for interactions with digital devices. For example, to turn your alarm clock off in the morning you have to smile to your alarm clock.

Our approach is different. We are following embodiment theory and some indication of psychology that it might be possible to induce emotions by physically changing your appearance using external stimuli. In our case by making you smile using electric muscle stimulation. Of course, the movement is very different from a voluntary or "forced" smile (like in Tusjita's work): only a few muscles can be activated etc. Yet, there is interesting work from Barrett et al. in constrained psychology lab studies that it might be feasible [1].

In this paper, we are introducing our first step to induce smiles with unobtrusive hardware. In a next step, in future work, we wil evaluate the mental effects of EMS.

Student Competition Entry: FaceCook

We participated in a Student Innovation Competition at UIST a large international HCI conference with an application to induce smiles using EMS. The basic idea for our competition entry was to create a game between 2 users. One user is in a virtual environment and gets different smile intensities (smirk, smile, stronger smile). See Figure 1 for pictures from the competition. A user outside of the virtual environment has to guess which smile intensity the other user sees. Our entry won the "Innovative UI Award" in the competition. In the following we will go over the system setup as well as the initial trials during the competition.

Experimental Setup

We use a modification[1] to the EMS toolkit prototype by Peiffer et al. [7].

To generates a smiling facial expression by actuating the usersâĂŹ facial muscles with an electrical muscle stimulation (EMS) unit. This unit provides 2 independent channels with an intensity of up to 70 mA. Each channel has 2 round electrode pads sized 32mm in diameter.

Electrode Placement

The electrodes were placed on specific locations of the cheek to maximize the cheek muscle stimulation. These locations were selected due to the nerve position on the human face, as shown in figure. In order to generate a smiling facial expression, we put electrode pads around zygomatic branches and buccal branches.

[1] http://plopes.org/ems

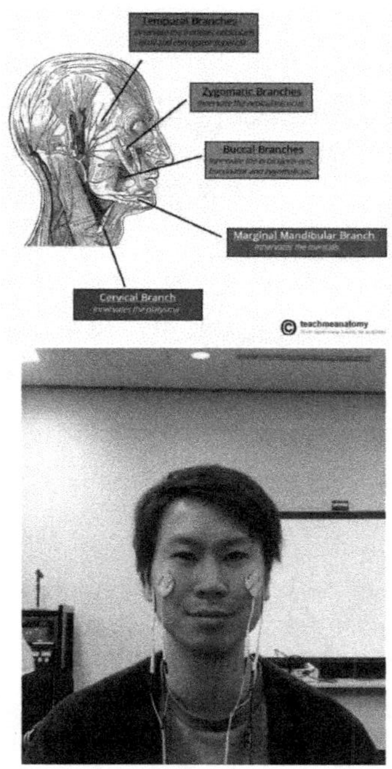

Figure 2: The top schematic shows the facial nerve. The second picture shows the electrode placement used in our trials: we put electrode pads at the zygomatic branches and buccal branches to induce the smile

We conducted an experiment on 23 participants in the Student Innovation Contest held at the large international HCI conference.

Initial Experiments
As inducing smiles is highly dependent on the right electrode placement and time for the placement was limited (to 1-2 minutes per participant), it was unfortunately unpractical to play the game as introduced above. Therefore, in each trial, we set up a virtual environment using the Oculus Rift head mount display(HMD) with 3 videos presenting different levels of smiling/laughing faces. Each video triggers a different intensity of electrical stimulation which generated different facial muscles movements on the participants.

Initial Results
8 participants had their cheek muscles stimulated accurately to create a smiling expression of three levels. For 14 participants we could see a "smiling effect" (twitching) for the correct facial muscles, however the 3 stages for smiling were not distinguishable. For one participant we could not induce an effect at all. This seems at the first glance not so encouraging, however given the short setup phase (1-2 minutes) to find the right muscles. We believe that this can be improved. After the competition we found also another electrode placement (placing the second electrode on the lower cheek underneath the mouth) that seems to work more reliable for a quick setup (and for some application field). Yet, we will continue to use the previous setup as it is better integratabtle in a smart glasses design.

In the following we give a couple of qualitative statements from the participants. The participants stated that "With this system, I feel it is easier for me to smile." And one of the participants also described the feeling as "It is tricky because I did feel that I was smiling more when my facial muscles moved but the stimulation also made me feel uneasy." For the content in our experiment design, some participants thought "It is good that the stimulation and the content were showing the same level of smiling/laughing. It made the system easier to understand." However, one of the participants commented that it was difficult to differentiate between the effectiveness of the system, or the general idea of the proposed work that was amusing, that caused him or her to smile.

Next Steps
The major next steps are for us to make the smile stimulation over EMS more reliable. Here we made already a couple of improvements, as it's easier for us to find the right positions for the electrodes. Also just increasing the time for electrode adjustments to around 5 minutes already helps (not possible during the contest).

The most interesting follow up research is of course if changing a user's face using EMS actually can influence their perceived happiness over a short or longer time. Here we will follow the controlled experimental setups from psychology first and assessing the effects for shorter durations [1].

If these experiments go well, we will integrate the technology in a smart eyewear design and will explore long term, more unconstrained mood effects using an EMS glasses design (as shown in the sketches in Figure 3).

Related Work
As mentioned before the closest to our work is Tsujita et al.'s research using smiles as an interaction modality and "happiness counter" [9].

Regarding EMS, there is also exiting research using it for interactive systems as an output modality from pedestrian cruise control to guiding drawings [8, 5].

Figure 3: Concept: from electrodes to a smart eyewear device to induce smiles

There are a couple of psychologists, most prominently Barrett and Ekman, assessing the effects of inducing smiles over EMS [1, 4]. We see these studies as complimentary as they strengthen our hypothesis about the emotional influence of smiling, however they are conducted in highly constrained lab environments with more obtrusive setups (more electrodes etc.).

We are unaware of any work that uses EMS in the face as a interaction technology.

Conclusion

We have presented our first insights in how to use EMS to stimulate smiles and showed first findings from the student innovation competition at a large international HCI conference.

We believe that EMS is an interesting technology to evaluate in terms of embodiment and would like to show our findings and spark discussions demonstrating our system for the TEI community.

Acknowledgements

This work is partly supported by the JST CREST Project on Experience Supplements.

REFERENCES

1. Lisa Feldman Barrett. 2012. Emotions are real. *Emotion* 12, 3 (2012), 413.
2. Walter B Cannon. 1927. The James-Lange theory of emotions: A critical examination and an alternative theory. *The American journal of psychology* 39, 1/4 (1927), 106–124.
3. Alain Ehrenberg. 2016. *The weariness of the self: Diagnosing the history of depression in the contemporary age.* McGill-Queen's Press-MQUP.
4. Paul Ekman, Richard J Davidson, and Wallace V Friesen. 1990. The Duchenne smile: Emotional expression and brain physiology: II. *Journal of personality and social psychology* 58, 2 (1990), 342.
5. Pedro Lopes, Doăa Yüksel, François Guimbretière, and Patrick Baudisch. 2016. Muscle-plotter: An Interactive System based on Electrical Muscle Stimulation that Produces Spatial Output. In *Proceedings of the 29th Annual Symposium on User Interface Software and Technology.* ACM, 207–217.
6. Mark Olfson, Benjamin G Druss, and Steven C Marcus. 2015. Trends in mental health care among children and adolescents. *New England Journal of Medicine* 372, 21 (2015), 2029–2038.
7. Max Pfeiffer, Tim Duente, and Michael Rohs. 2016. Let your body move: a prototyping toolkit for wearable force feedback with electrical muscle stimulation. In *Proceedings of the 18th International Conference on Human-Computer Interaction with Mobile Devices and Services.* ACM, 418–427.
8. Max Pfeiffer, Tim Dünte, Stefan Schneegass, Florian Alt, and Michael Rohs. 2015. Cruise Control for Pedestrians: Controlling Walking Direction using Electrical Muscle Stimulation. In *Proceedings of the 33rd Annual ACM Conference on Human Factors in Computing Systems.* ACM, 2505–2514.
9. Hitomi Tsujita and Jun Rekimoto. 2013. Smile-encouraging digital appliances. *IEEE Pervasive Computing* 4, 12 (2013), 5–7.

Spatial Calibration of Airborne Ultrasound Tactile Display and Projector-Camera System Using Fur Material

Shigo Ko
Keio University.
Yokohama, Hiyoshi 3-14-1, Japan
shigo_ko@imlab.ics.keio.ac.jp

Yuta Itoh
Keio University.
Yokohama, Hiyoshi 3-14-1, Japan
itoh@imlab.ics.keio.ac.jp

Yuta Sugiura
Keio University.
Yokohama, Hiyoshi 3-14-1, Japan
sugiura@imlab.ics.keio.ac.jp

Takayuki Hoshi
The University of Tokyo.
Tokyo, Hongo 7-3-1, Japan
takayuki_hoshi@ipc.i.u-tokyo.ac.jp

Maki Sugimoto
Keio University.
Yokohama, Hiyoshi 3-14-1, Japan
sugimoto@imlab.ics.keio.ac.jp

TEI '17, March 20-23, 2017, Yokohama, Japan
ACM 978-1-4503-4676-4/17/03.
http://dx.doi.org/10.1145/3024969.3025061

Abstract
Airborne Ultrasound Tactile Displays (AUTD) are tactile displays that can generate vibrotactile sensation on human skin. Combining an AUTD with a projector-camera system, it is possible to present synchronous visual and haptic stimuli that is physically aligned in the 3D space. To maintain the synchronous sensation as realistic as possible, an accurate crucial to spatial calibration between the AUTD and the projector-camera system is required. This paper thereby proposes a calibration method for the AUTD system by utilizing fur material to recognize the output focal points of an AUTD in the camera coordinate system. Our method simplifies the calibration procedure with calibration error of 2.63 mm.

Author Keywords
Device Calibration, Airborne Ultrasound Tactile Display, Projector-Camera System

ACM Classification Keywords
H.5.m. Information interfaces and presentation.

Introduction
Airborne ultrasound tactile displays (AUTD) are tactile displays that generate vibrotactile sensations on human

skin[1]. These displays are different from other tactile sensation devices because it can create midair haptic sensation without touching the display devices. By combining an AUTD with a projector-camera system to project images, it is able to produce synchronized visual and tactile stimuli without contact[2]. To combine the AUTD and projector-camera system requires special calibration. There is a remarkable prior calibration method uses a microphone and three-dimensional(3D) stages[3], that requires designated devices, and data collection is time consuming. This research proposes a way to simplify the calibration procedure by using a fur material and recognizing fur fluffing changes to obtain correspondence points between the AUTD and camera image coordinate.

Related Work

There are many haptic devices to produce tactile sensation, such as devices placed on fingertips [8] and a vibration belt on user's waist[9] to produce virtual contents by contact. Also, non-contact devices produce tactile sensation such as air jets[10]. In such research, users must wear or hold devices to perceive the tactile sensation.

AUTD[1] is an ultrasound speaker array that can create an ultrasound focal point in midair. A 3D stage, microphone, and multiple AUTD are used to project an ultrasound to human skin to measure tactile sensation resolution[4]. A user touches a projected image in midair which presents haptic feedback by the AUTD and creates a tactile sensation for the user[5].

Other than producing tactile sensation, AUTD sound pressure distribution was visualized by viscosity fluid visualization[3]. An AUTD was used to draw 2 dimensional pictures by sound pressure stimulus on a fur material [6]. Also, a set of AUTDs controlled floating particles in 3 dimensional space by phased ultrasound waves[7].

Theory

Each device used in this study has an individual coordinate system, including a camera image coordinate P, camera position coordinate C, and AUTD coordinate system W. Corresponding points between each coordinate system are used to calculate transformation matrices corresponding to each device.

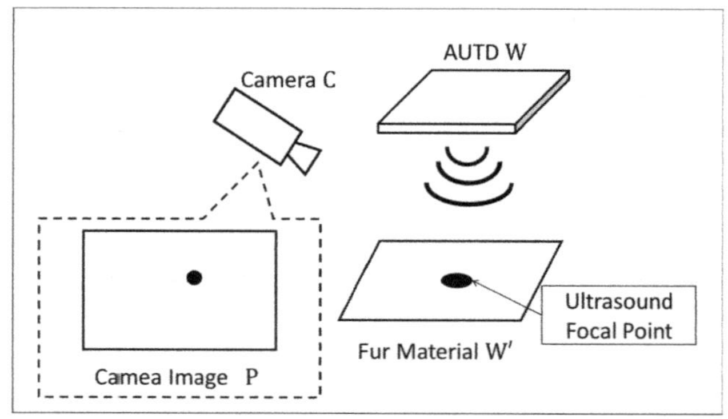

Figure 1: Devices and coordinate systems.

Plane Projective Transformation

Plane projective transformation matrices are calculated to correspond with the planes of the camera coordinate system and AUTD coordinate system. In this study, the transformation of the AUTD coordinate system is obtained as a relative coordinate system from the camera coordinate system. To convert a point in the camera image coordinate system $\boldsymbol{p} = (u, v)$ and plane in the AUTD coordinate system $\boldsymbol{w} = (x'_w, y'_w)$, we use homogeneous coordinates (which is represented as ~ in

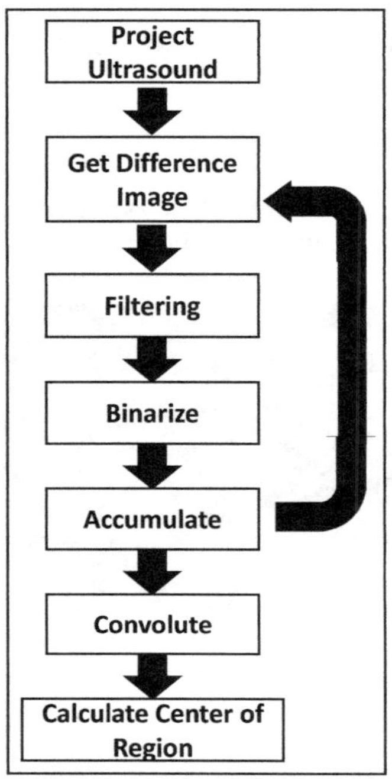

Figure 2: Work flow to recognize the ultrasound focal point.

formulas) and plane projective transformation matrix, $\boldsymbol{H}$ as shown below.

$$\tilde{\boldsymbol{p}} \approx \boldsymbol{H}\tilde{\boldsymbol{w}} \tag{1}$$

$$\Leftrightarrow \begin{bmatrix} u \\ v \\ 1 \end{bmatrix} \approx \begin{bmatrix} h_{11} & h_{12} & h_{13} \\ h_{21} & h_{22} & h_{23} \\ h_{31} & h_{32} & 1 \end{bmatrix} \begin{bmatrix} x_w{}' \\ y_w{}' \\ 1 \end{bmatrix} \tag{2}$$

At least four corresponding point pairs are required to estimate the coefficients of the plane projective transformation matrix. To reduce error more than four pairs of projections point can be used.

Perspective Projection Transformation

The projection matrix is calculated to correspond to the camera 3D coordinate system and AUTD 3D coordinate system and convert points between the AUTD coordinate system $\boldsymbol{W} = (x_w, y_w, z_w)$ and the image coordinate system $\boldsymbol{p} = (u, v)$, which is represented in the following formula.

$$\tilde{\boldsymbol{p}} \approx \boldsymbol{P}\widetilde{\boldsymbol{W}} \tag{3}$$

$$\tilde{\boldsymbol{p}} \approx \boldsymbol{K}[\boldsymbol{R}|\boldsymbol{t}]\widetilde{\boldsymbol{W}} \tag{4}$$

$$\Leftrightarrow d\begin{bmatrix} u \\ v \\ 1 \end{bmatrix} \approx \begin{bmatrix} f_x & 0 & c_x \\ 0 & f_y & c_y \\ 0 & 0 & 1 \end{bmatrix} [\boldsymbol{R}|\boldsymbol{t}] \begin{bmatrix} x_w \\ y_w \\ z_w \\ 1 \end{bmatrix} \tag{5}$$

$$\Leftrightarrow \begin{bmatrix} x_w \\ y_w \\ z_w \end{bmatrix} \approx \boldsymbol{R}^{-1}\left(\boldsymbol{K}^{-1}\left(d\begin{bmatrix} u \\ v \\ 1 \end{bmatrix}\right) - \boldsymbol{t}\right) \tag{6}$$

$\boldsymbol{K}$	*Matrix of Camera Intrinsic Parameters*
$\boldsymbol{R}$	*Matrix of Rotation*
$\boldsymbol{t}$	*Vector of Translation*
f_x, f_y	*Focal Length*
c_x, c_y	*Center of Image*

Table 1: Parameters of Formulas 4, 5, and 6.

At least six corresponding point pairs of convert points in the image coordinate system to the AUTD coordinate system are required to estimate the coefficients of the perspective projection transformation matrix: the rotation matrix $\boldsymbol{R}$ and translation vector $\boldsymbol{t}$.

Implementation

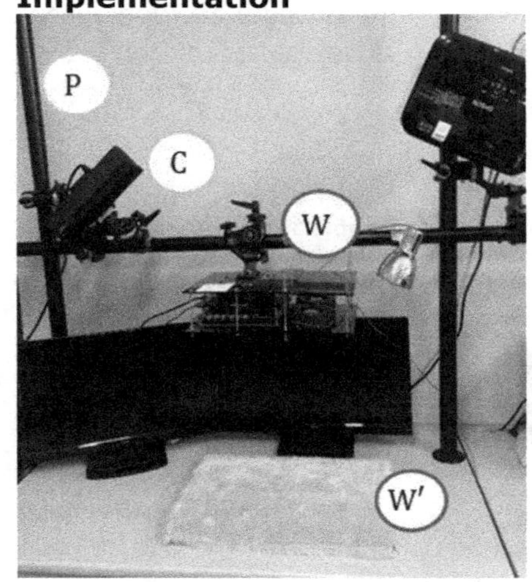

Figure 3: Appearance of the hardware system

The system was consists of an AUTD, camera, projector, and fur material. After placing the fur material under the AUTD, the ultrasound focal point was recognized by changing the fluffing of the fur

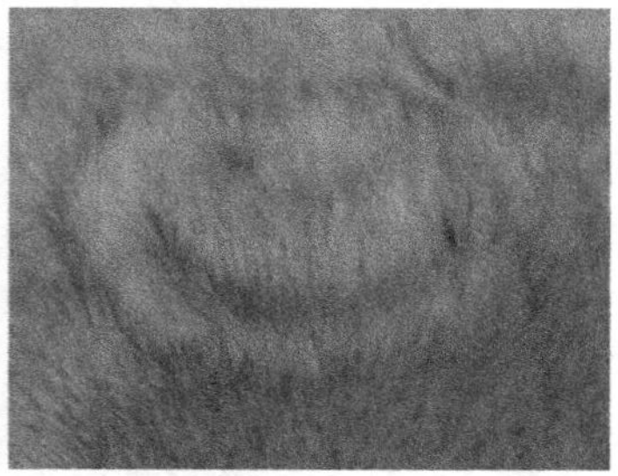

Figure 6: An image drawn on fur material using ultrasound projection.

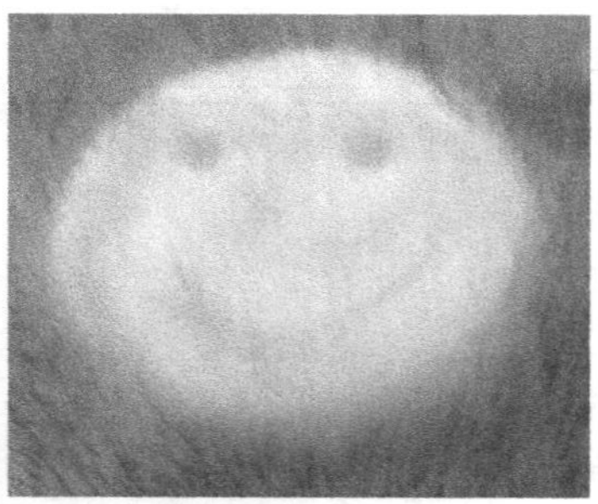

Figure 7: Convolution of the image on the fur material and the image projected from the projector.

material by the ultrasound projected from the AUTD. Figure 2 shows the system flow to recognize the ultrasound focal point. At first, the ultrasound was projected to the fur material to obtain an amplified differential image between the current and previous camera frames(Figure 4). Next, a median filter applied to the differential image to reduce white spike noise in the difference image (Figure 4) then the image was binalized by Otsu's method (Figure 4).

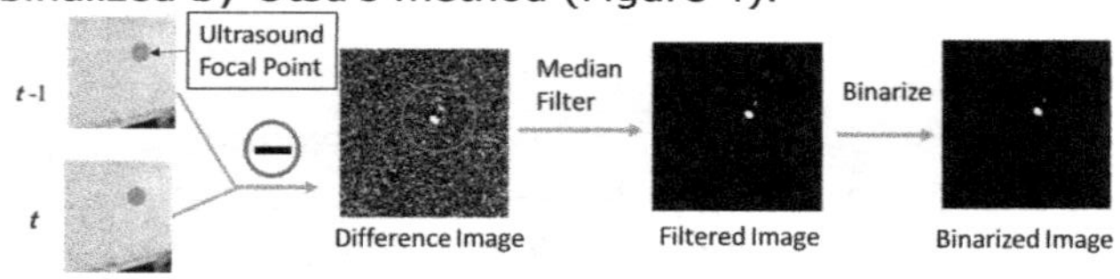

Figure 4: Method to Make Binarized Image

This operation was repeated several times to accumulate output images (Figure 5). To reduce environmental noise, the differential images was convoluted with Non-ultrasound Image using the formula below.

$$\mathrm{P} = \sum_{i}^{n_t} \frac{\mathrm{P}_{ti}}{n_t + n_f} - \sum_{j}^{n_f} \frac{\mathrm{P}_{fj}}{n_t + n_f} \quad (7)$$

$\boldsymbol{P}$	*Accumulated Image*
$\boldsymbol{P_t}$	*Projected Ultrasound Image*
$\boldsymbol{P_f}$	*Non-ultrasound Image*
$\boldsymbol{n_t}$	*Number of* $\boldsymbol{P_t}$
$\boldsymbol{n_f}$	*Number of* $\boldsymbol{P_f}$

Table 2: Parameters of Formula 7.

The weighted center of the region was calculated from the results of the convoluted image (Figure 5) and used as one of correspondence points to estimate the transformation matrices.

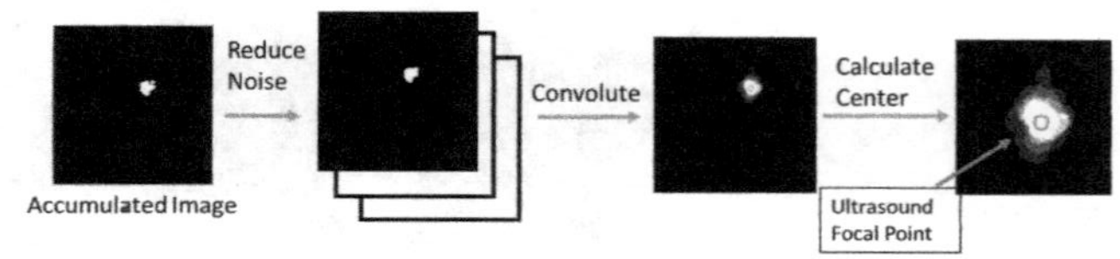

Figure 5: Method to Recognize Ultrasound Focal Point from

Experiment

To evaluate the precision of the ultrasound focal point recognition, we measured the re-projection error of the ultrasound focal points. The distance from the AUTD to the fur material was 450 mm and assumed to be parallel. After calculating the plane projective transformation matrix, the same projection points were converted to points in the image coordinate system by the plane projective transformation matrix from the AUTD coordinate system. The errors between the true point and calculated point were evaluated. Each calculation of the plane projective transformation matrix included nine points and for sets. These results are shown in Table 3. In addition, each point error is shown in Figure 8 and each show error and standard deviation is shown in Figure 9.

Average of error	*2.63mm*
Standard deviation	*1.39mm*

Table 3: Re-projection error of the ultrasound focal point when the plane projective was used.

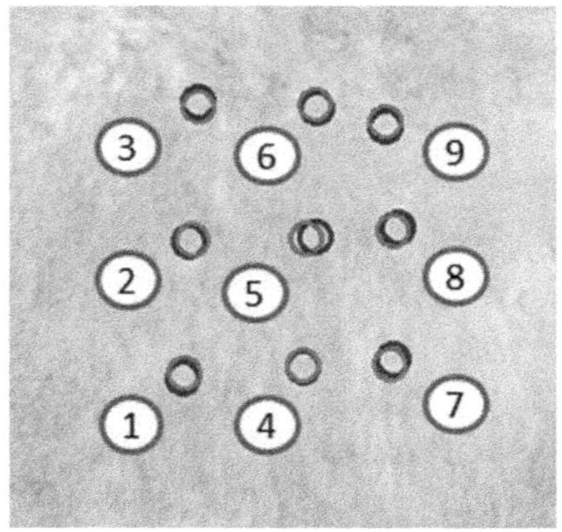

Figure 8: Error of each projection point.

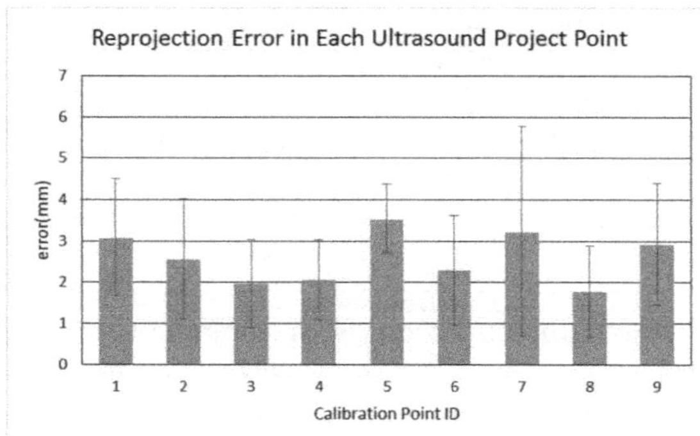

Figure 9: Re-projection error for each ultrasound projection point

Integrate AUTD and Projector-Camera System

By using the transformation matrices between the AUTD-camera and camera-projector coordinate systems, we can convert the AUTD coordinate system to the projector coordinate system (Figure 10). This provides synchronized projected ultrasounds and images by the AUTD-projector conversion model. The calibration result was demonstrated by drawing a static picture on the fur material using ultrasound projection as (Figure 6) and a project image to the static picture (Figure 7).

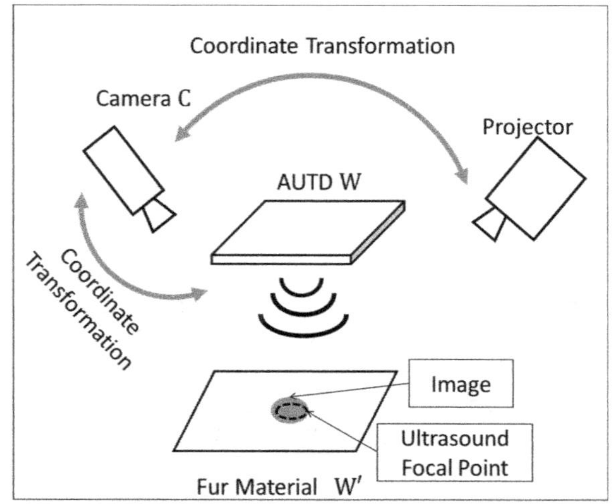

Figure 10: Calibration of the AUTD and projector-camera systems.

Conclusion

In this study, we proposed a method to simplify spatial calibration between the AUTD and projector-camera system. We recognized the ultrasound focal points by obtaining differential images of fluffing changes on the fur material during the ultrasound projection. We combined the AUTD and projector-camera systems using a calibration model for both AUTD-camera and camera-projector systems. In the experiment, the plane projective transformation matrix showed an averaged re-projection error: 2.63 mm as the result of the calibration between AUTD and camera coordinate systems.

Acknowledgements
This work was supported by JSPJ KAKENHI Grant Number 15H01701.

References
1. Takayuki Hoshi et al., Noncontact Tactile Display Based on Radiation Pressure of Airborne Ultrasound, IEEE Transactions on Haptics, pp.155–165, 2010.
2. Kazuma Yoshino et al., Measuring Visio-Tactile threshold for Visio-Tactile Projector, SICE Annual Conference 2012, pp.1996–2000, 2012.
3. Takayuki Hoshi, Visualization of Pressure Distribution of Airborne Ultrasound Tactile Display Utilizing Viscous Fluid, 2013 JSME Conference on Robotics and Mechatronics, 2A2–B04(1–3), 2013.
4. Keisuke Hasegawa et al., Aerial Display of Vibrotactile Sensation with High Spatial-temporal Resolution Using Large-aperture Airborne Ultrasound Phased Array, IEEE World Haptics Conference 2013, pp.31-36, 2013.
5. Yasuaki Monnai et al., Haptomime: Mid-air Haptic Interaction with A Floating Virtual Screen, UIST '14, pp.663–667, 2014.
6. Yuta Sugiura et al., Graffiti Fur: Turning Your Carpet into a Computer Display, UIST'14, pp.149–156, 2014.
7. Yoichi Ochiai et al., Pixie Dust: Graphics Generated by Levitated and Animated Objects in Computational Acoustic-potential Field, SIGGRAPH 2014, Article No. 85, pp.1–13, 2014.
8. Kouta Minamizawa et al., Gravity Grabber: Wearable Haptic Display to Present Virtualmass Sensation, ACM SIGGRAPH 2007 Emerging Technologies, Article No. 8, 2007.
9. Robert W. Lindeman et al., Wearable Vibrotactile Systems for Virtual Contact and Information Display, VirtualReality, pp.203-213, 2006.
10. James C. Gwilliam et al., Design and Control of an Air-Jet Lump Display, IEEE haptics Symposium 2012, pp.45-49, 2012.

DOK: Enhancing Child Patient Empowerment

Marleen van Bergeijk &
Bart Hengeveld
TU Eindhoven
Industrial Design.
De Zaale, 5612 AZ,
Eindhoven, Netherlands.
mvm.vanbergeijk@gmail.com
b.j.hengeveld@tue.nl

Selma Otto
Wilhelmina Kinderziekenhuis
UMC Utrecht, PO Box 85090
3508 AB, Utrecht, Netherlands
s.otto@umcutrecht.nl

TEI '17, March 20-23, 2017, Yokohama, Japan
ACM 978-1-4503-4676-4/17/03.
http://dx.doi.org/10.1145/3024969.3025066

Abstract
In this paper we present DOK, a tangible conversation tool aimed at empowering child patients during medical triads. Current medical triads tend to exclude child patients, making them bystanders of their own illness: triads are highly wordy, cognition-heavy and mostly take place between doctor and parent. In this ongoing research we aim to develop a tool that empowers child patients by allowing them more input and initiative in the conversation. We present our theoretical backbone, point out opportunities for tangibles, and describe the current version of DOK.

Author Keywords
Empowerment; patient-centered care; pediatric care; communication; medical triads; tangible interaction.

ACM Classification Keywords
H.5.2. [Information Interfaces and Presentation]: User Interfaces — Theory and Methods, User-Centered Design.

Introduction
Hospitals are dominated by protocols and procedures. This is especially detrimental for young children, who cannot fully grasp the concept of being ill nor oversee the necessary steps for their recovery. Furthermore, young children are inherently dependent on adults in

terms of communication, projection and coping. Currently, more and more hospitals are trying to shift towards Patient Centered Care (PCC), which means "treating the patient as a unique individual" [13, 15] rather than as "a cluster of diseases". In pediatric care the terms Family Centered Care (FCC) or Patient and Family Centered Care (P&FCC) are the more frequently used terms, understood as "The professional care and guidance to the child and the family by means of involvement, participation and cooperation supported by empowerment and treatment" [11, translated]. Central to PCC and FCC is that medical staff works towards (1) understanding the patient's point of view, (2) responding to their needs [7] and (3) shared decision-making [17]. However, often FCC focuses on communication between parents and the medical staff, isolating the child itself [4, 9].

We aim to empower child patients in their personal health situation, empowerment being the "social process of recognizing, promoting and enhancing peoples' abilities to meet their own needs, solve their own problems and mobilize the necessary resources in order to feel in control of their lives." One way to do so follows from research by Coyne (2006), who revealed that child patients need to be informed to understand their illness, want to be more actively involved in their care, and want to prepare themselves for procedures and 'getting better' again [4].

In this research we describe the development of DOK, a tangible conversation tool that enables children to take on a more active role during medical triads. We developed DOK in a close collaboration with Wilhelmina pediatric hospital Utrecht, the Netherlands (WKZ).

Medical triads

Medical triads are organized moments in which doctor, child patient and parent sit together to discuss the medical status quo of the child.

Asymmetry in medical triads

Most literature describes the interaction between doctor and parent while little attention is paid to the child's participation [20, 4]. This same review also suggests that child contribution in medical consultations is very low [20, 21]. As such, medical triads involving (young) children are highly asymmetrical and seem more like dyads [20]. Moreover, there is also asymmetry between parent and child as they differ in status, knowledge and communicative skills [19].

Turn-taking

In medical triads a child's input is highly dependent on the doctor's approval: children are asked for input mostly when looking for symptoms during medical-history-taking. Often however, the child's input is taken over by a parent who wants to reassure that information is being communicated properly. From the doctor, the conclusive part of the conversation about actions, advice and treatments are mostly directed at the parent [20].

Contribution of the child

The child is often not valued as being a competent decision maker. Especially when protesting, a child is seen as incompetent, whereas incompetence is hardly discussed when the child agrees [3]. However, a developmental cognitive study has indicated that children can play a more active roll in taking initiative during discussions in their interaction with adults, than has been assumed [20]. Also, a good doctor-child interaction leads to a good relationship, which in turn leads to more satisfaction, more compliance and an improved health experience. The recognition and personal contribution positively affect the child's self-determination and self-esteem [10, 14].

Conversation Skills

Children in these settings have (1) "the cognitive need to be informed (the need to know and understand)" and (2) "the emotional need to be taken seriously (the need to feel known and understood)" [6]. This means the doctor needs to bring instrumental skills to the table as asking questions and providing information as well as affective skills such as reflecting feelings and showing empathy [21].

Opportunities for tangibles

We see great potential for tangibles in the context described above:

- As Shaer and Hornecker [18] point out, tangibles create a medium for shared discussion and collaborative learning, and can stimulate a dialogue between different parties. By interacting with tangibles, actions (through which meaning is expressed) become visible, creating group awareness. Also the discussion can be shared by handing over objects, showing or sharing something, etcetera, making initiative taking more accessible for the child (e.g. [9]). Tangibles provide 'the space and affordances' to interact with multiple users [1].
- Another benefit of tangibles is that they allow for cognitive deloading through tangible thinking: by coupling a motor action to a meaning we externalize our thinking; physical and spatial information can be put into speech [8]; our cognition is formed by the mind, body and also the environment [5].
- The current set-up of medical triads only speaks to our cognitive conversational skills. We sit still and the meaning that is created is verbal and thus intangible. This is hard to grasp and follow for a child as he lacks experience, cognitive skills and knowledge. We believe tangibles can improve this situation significantly, based on the vast body of tangibles for children dating back from Froebel's 'physical manipulatives', and later digital manipulates [16] to the myriad of tangibles for play and learning we have seen over the past decade of TEI conferences.

Design brief

Based on (1) our literature study as well as; (2) the perspective of the medical staff on Patient Centered Care captured through interviews involving an expert panel eight staff members (nurses, doctors, managers); (3) a discussion panel with 80 employees of the hospital; and (4) our observations in 8 medical triads, involving children between 4 and 16 years old, we defined the following design brief:

"To design for an improved experience for children between 7 - 9 years old during the doctor's conversation, that empowers the child during in the health process?"

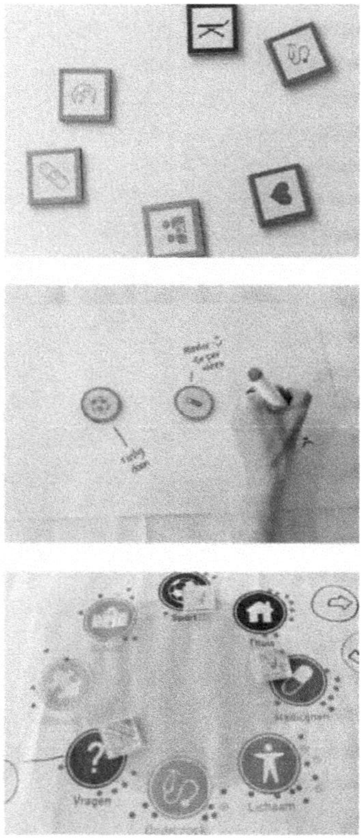

Figure 1, top and middle: Explorations of (annotated) token-based systems from the first iteration; Bottom: exploration of a conversation structuring table-mat.

Our choice for this specific age group was based on discussions with WKZ's principle investigator on FCC: children younger than 7 will likely have difficulty understanding the health situation, whereas teen-aged children are more skillful on a cognitive, emotional and social level in expressing their opinion. The group of 7 to 9-year-olds was seen as a fitting target group as these children can have an opinion on things yet might lack skills and confidence to express these. We used the Developmentally Situated Design card set [2] to gather more insights in designing for this age group.

Research through design approach

First iteration: exploring the solution domain

We approached our design brief following a research-through-design approach [23]. For the first, explorative, iteration we started off with investigating three topics: (1) How to turn children into active participants and contributors during the doctor's conversation; (2) How to make the conversation more understandable for the child; and (3) How to stimulate a more symmetrical conversation. We explored these directions using brainstorms and bodystorms and clustered the results.

Based on the results we decided to pursue the direction of *physicalizing the conversation* itself using tangibles, i.e., creating a set of tangible tools that could both represent a conversation as well as steer it, comparable to how Ullmer and Ishii's modeled interaction with TUIs [22]. We created lo-fi prototypes, eventually settling on token-based approaches (see Figure 1). We informally tried several out in actual doctor's conversations within the WKZ. Just to explore the potential of our designs. The try-out involved one doctor and four children with their parents. All freely consented to participate. Our preliminary insights from this first iteration were:

- Using iconic, associative tokens helped triggering children to think about relevant topics, whereas open, customizable tokens provided too little structure;
- Having topics physically on the table seemed to encourage children to talk about their topics of choice, even when they were shy;
- Handing the tokens to the child and parent(s) in the waiting room provided a shared moment of preparation;
- Parents reported that their child had been more vocal during the doctor's conversation than usual;
- Equal access to the topic tokens for all participants seemed to create a shared space for communication and negotiation;
- The participating medical staff reported having enjoyed working with the tokens and perceived it as a positive doctor-patient interaction form. They appreciated that it improved the situation of the child as its input could not be ignored

DOK

Based on these preliminary design insights we developed DOK, a more product-like, interactive research product [12]. DOK consists of several components, which we describe here (see Figures 2 and 3). After describing DOK's components we give a short scenario of use.

Topic Tokens

DOK includes a set of acrylic topic tokens (see Figure 2, item 1), in three colors (one for each participant in the

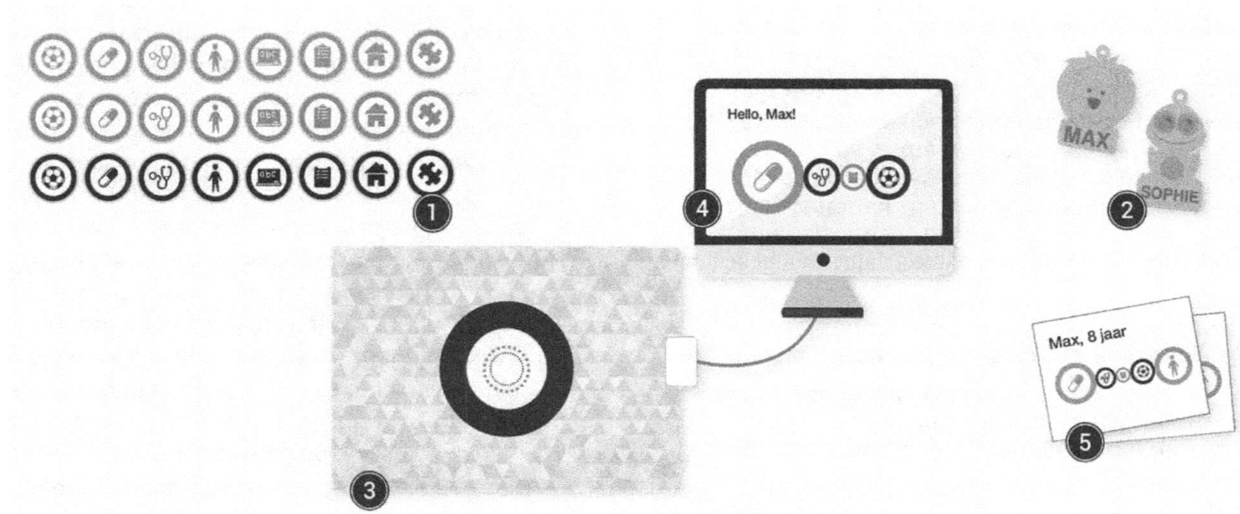

Figure 2. Overview of our final design DOK. The system consists of (1) topic tokens for all participants, (2) personal key chain tokens for individual children, (3) an interactive table-mat with embedded RFID reader and LED pixel ring, (4) visualization software for generating conversation time line visualizations, and (5) personal printouts of the conversation visualizations.

triad). Pictograms on the tokens indicate conversation topics. Each token is RFID.

Interactive desk mat

DOK includes an interactive tablemat (item 3), which contains an embedded RFID reader and LED pixel ring. When a token is placed in the center the mat recognizes the token, making the LED pixel ring light up in the token's color, thus providing visual feedback: 'the token has been detected and is 'officially' the topic of conversation.'

Conversation visualization

When a topic token is placed it is also added to an on-screen conversation timeline (item 4), which is visualized as a row of circles. The sizes of the circles indicate the time spent on the topic (larger is longer), the color matches the discussed token's color, as such recording who initiated the topic; the pictogram indicates the conversation topic. At the end of the conversation the generated time line visual is printed (item 5) and handed to the child, along with the instruction to make annotations and keep it in an accompanying conversation diary. As such the child leaves with a physical reminder of the conversation, generated by his own actions. The prints represent an informal health dossier from a child's perspective.

Figure 3: The actual DOK prototype. In this picture: the interactive tablemat and tokens, with in the background the conversation visualization.

Personal key chain
In order to keep track of all conversations per child, the children receive a personalized RFID tagged token (item 2) that can be scanned at the beginning of the conversation.

Scenario of use
When arriving at the waiting room desk, child and parent receive a full set of tokens each so they can prepare for the doctor's conversation while waiting. They can select the topics they wish to address. This increases the child's feeling of empowerment and self-esteem, as it helps being aware of what you want to say is a statement that you are going to actively and autonomously contribute.

When child and parent enter the conversation room they present their topic tokens and briefly explain why they chose them. The doctor adds his own tokens, as such laying out the agenda. The child can start by placing his most important token in the middle. After this the conversation can flow naturally, placing a new token for each change of topic or perspective. To the child, the tokens serve as a motivation and a physical reminder to actually express what was on his mind before entering the context of the conversation. At the end of the conversation the visualization of the conversation time line is shown to child and parent, and printed. This creates a moment for summarizing and reflecting. The child can take the opportunity to write or draw notes on the print. At home the print is kept in the child's personal folder. The print can be shown to and discussed with family members or friends. It can support the child in explaining what the doctor said, recalling things or asking for additional explanations afterwards.

Evaluation

We are currently informally evaluating DOK in medical triads, after asking (and getting) the formal consent of parents and child patients. A longitudinal trial has been set up; we currently wait for the formal approval of the WKZ's medical ethical committee.

References

1. Antle, Alissa N. 2007. The CTI framework: informing the design of tangible systems for children. In *Proceedings of the 1st international conference on Tangible and embedded interaction*, 195-202.
2. Tilde Bekker, Alissa Antle. 2011. Developmentally Situated Design (DSD): A design tool for child-computer interaction. In *Proceedings of the SIGCHI Conference on Human Factors in Computing Systems,* 2531-2540.
3. Gillian Bricher. 2000. Children in the hospital: issues of power and vulnerability. *Pediatric Nursing 26*, 3 (2000): 277-282.
4. Imelda Coyne. 2006. Children's experiences of hospitalization. *Journal of Child Health Care 10*, 4, 326-336.
5. Jelle van Dijk, Remko van der Lugt, Caroline Hummels. 2014. Beyond distributed representation: embodied cognition design supporting socio-sensorimotor couplings. In *Proceedings of the 8th International Conference on Tangible, Embedded and Embodied Interaction*, 181-188.
6. George L. Engel. 1992. How much longer must medicine's science be bound by a seventeenth century world view? *Family Systems Medicine* 10, 3, 333.
7. Ronald M. Epstein. 2000. The science of patient-centered care. *Journal of Family Practice* 49, 9, 805-810.

8. Susan Goldin-Meadow. 2005. *Hearing gesture: How our hands help us think*. Harvard University Press.
9. Bart Hengeveld. 2011. *Designing LinguaBytes: a tangible language learning system for non- or hardly speaking toddlers.* Doctoral thesis. Eindhoven University of Technology, the Netherlands
10. Margaret Kelly, Susan Jones, Val Wilson, and Peter Lewis. 2012. How children's rights are constructed in family-centred care A review of the literature. *Journal of Child Health Care 16*, 2, 190-205.
11. Jos M. Latour, Monique van Dijk. Patiëntveiligheid vanuit de patiënt. *Tijdschrift voor Kindergeneeskunde 82*, 5, 184-188
12. William Odom, Ron Wakkary, Youn-Kyung Lim, Audrey Desjardins, Bart Hengeveld, Richard Banks. 2016. From Research Prototype to Research Product. *In Proceedings of the 2016 CHI Conference on Human Factors in Computing Systems, CHI '16*. pp. 2549–2561.
13. Rinchen Pelzang. 2010. Time to learn: understanding patient-centred care. *British journal of nursing 19*, 14.
14. Isaac Prilleltensky, Geoffrey Nelson, Leslea Peirson. 2001. The role of power and control in children's lives: An ecological analysis of pathways toward wellness, resilience and problems. *Journal of Community & Applied Social Psychology 11*, 2, 143-158.
15. Richard W. Redman. 2004. Patient-centered care: an unattainable ideal? *Research and theory for nursing practice 18*, 1, 11-14.
16. Mitchel Resnick, Fred Martin, Robert Berg, Rick Borovoy, Vanessa Colella, Kwin Kramer, Brian Silverman. 1998. Digital manipulatives: new toys to think with. In *Proceedings of the SIGCHI conference on Human factors in computing systems*, 281-287.
17. Anne Rogers, Anne Kennedy, Elizabeth Nelson, Andrew Robinson. 2005. Uncovering the limits of patient-centeredness: implementing a self-management trial for chronic illness. *Qualitative Health Research 15*, 2, 224-39.
18. Orit Shaer, Eva Hornecker. 2010. Tangible user interfaces: past, present, and future directions. *Foundations and Trends in Human-Computer Interaction* 3, 1–2: 1-137.
19. Michael Siegal. 2013. *Knowing children: Experiments in conversation and cognition*. Psychology Press.
20. Kiek Tates, Ludwien Meeuwesen. 2000. 'Let Mum have her say': turntaking in doctor–parent–child communication. *Patient education and counseling 40*, 2, 151-162.
21. Kiek Tates, Ludwien Meeuwesen. 2001. Doctor–parent–child communication. A (re)view of the literature. *Social Science and Medicine 52*, 839–851.
22. Brygg Ullmer, Hiroshi Ishii. 2001. Emerging Frameworks for Tangible User Interfaces. *Human-Computer Interaction in the New Millenium*. 579-601.
23. John Zimmerman, Jodi Forlizzi, Shelley Evenson. 2007. Research through design as a method for interaction design research in HCI. In *Proceedings of the SIGCHI conference on Human factors in computing systems*, 493-502.

Tangible Interaction for Stroke Survivors: Design Recommendations

Charlotte Magnusson
Héctor A. Caltenco
Lund University
221 00 Lund, Sweden
charlotte@certec.lth.se
hector@certec.lth.se

David McGookin
Mikko Kytö
Aalto University
02150 Espoo, Finland
david.mcgookin@aalto.fi
mikko.kyto@aalto.fi

Ingibjörg Hjaltadóttir
Thóra B. Hafsteinsdóttir
Helga Jónsdóttir
Ingibjörg Bjartmarz
University of Iceland
101 Reykjavík, Iceland
ingihj@hi.is
t.hafsteinsdottir@umcutrecht.nl
helgaj@hi.is
ingibjar@landspitali.is

TEI '17, March 20-23, 2017, Yokohama, Japan
ACM 978-1-4503-4676-4/17/03.
http://dx.doi.org/10.1145/3024969.3025073

Abstract
In this paper we outline the initial stages of a human centered design process aimed at the design of novel technology (tangible interactive objects) for stroke survivors. We found it useful to support standard methods, such as interviews and focus groups, with a video prototype in order to make the concept of tangible interaction, which was novel to our users, more clear. In addition we carried out a co-design workshop together with stroke survivors. Based on these activities, we present a set of preliminary design guidelines for tangible interaction for stroke survivors.

Author Keywords
User studies; stroke; activity; tangible interaction; co-design; participatory design.

ACM Classification Keywords
H.5.m. Information interfaces and presentation (e.g., HCI): Miscellaneous.

Introduction
Stroke is a significant societal and public health challenge, and the third highest factor of morbidity and mortality worldwide. Much of the rehabilitation occurs at home, through performing different types of exercises and activities. It is the goal of the project ActivABLES to investigate how tangible interaction can

Video sketch

Figure 1. Snapshots of the video illustrating the project

be used to better support the continuation of rehabilitation at home.

Technology for Stroke Rehabilitation

Existing techniques to support rehabilitation, although shown to improve patient independence, suffer from problems that degrade their effectiveness. Uzor and Baillie [14] found exergames to be successful in overcoming lack of interest and commitment to fall rehabilitation. A similar approach has been proposed, but not evaluated, for Stroke rehabilitation [6]. Whilst exergaming can provide improved adherence to rehabilitation programmes it is not without issue. Axelrod et al. [1] looked at the practices around home rehabilitation. They identified that areas that would be most suitable for home rehabilitation were often kept for relaxation. This is in contrast to [14] and other work that uses interactive visualization for training [10], which need to interface to a television to present visual feedback to the user. But items such as televisions are often used by several persons in a household, reducing the opportunities for exercising. Bagalkot, Sokoler and Shaikh [2] extends on this, by arguing that rehabilitation must also consider the wider social context of the rehabilitee life. Fitzpatrick et al. [7] also note that is it is important to remember the context of rehabilitation, in particular the emotional and physical support network of friends, and that caregivers must also be considered. A balance should be struck between rehabilitation practice and what the individual stroke survivor wants, finds fun and motivating.

Tangible interaction offers significant potential benefits, creating interfaces that are easy to handle for persons with cognitive or motor impairments [11], can be small and portable, to overcome the issues raised by Axelrod et al [1] and Fitzpatrick, Balaam, & Egglestone [7] of exergames and TV visualizations, and naturally supporting ADL exercises through their physical design. There is still little study of their use with stroke survivors. Vandermaesen et al. [15] developed a tangible table top game to support lifting and left/right movement skills. However, they evaluated only with stroke rehabilitation nurses and not with stroke survivors themselves.

Co-design with stroke survivors

Current work on co-design has largely involved able-bodied people. Björkquist, Ramsdal et al. [4] found that it can be difficult to involve older senior users in focus groups due to lack of information about different services. There is also the challenge of adapting activities to suit the prospective users. The physical and cognitive ailments of ageing can add several challenges to a co-design process [9]. Technology to be tested needs to be either very robust – or the activity well supported by persons able to cover up technology prototype imperfections [12]. Hendriks et. al. [8] identified seven challenges for doing co-design with people with dementia. These challenges seem to come down to 3 fundamental concerns that can apply also to co-design with stroke survivors: 1) the lack of approach for co-designing with these users 2) the over appreciation of the visual and the verbal and 3) the perception of participatory design/co-design – which normally assumes that partners of (relatively) equal cognitive and physical abilities participate in the design process. An example from [16] showed comic like strips useful in focus groups with persons who had had a stroke, and physical objects and props have been found to be a useful tool when involving persons with speech impairments in a design process [16].

Tangible lo-fi prototypes

1 2 3

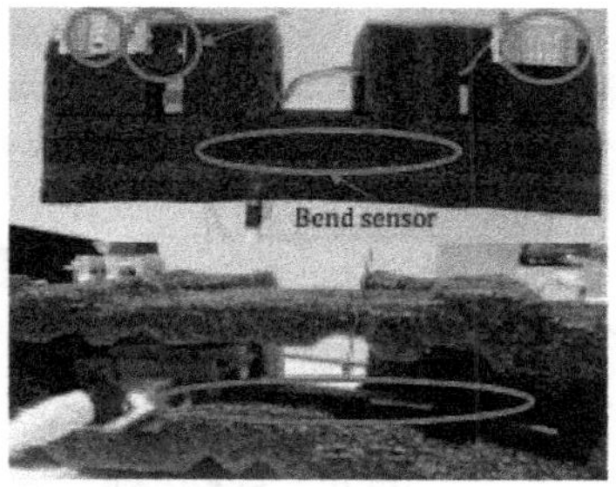

Figure 2. Flex charging massager prototype (1 active indicator, 2 vibrator, 3 charge indicator)

1 2 3

pressure sensors

Figure 3. Balance board prototype (1 buzzers, 2 balance indicator, 3 bar-graphs)

Project ActivABLES – Initial User Studies

The initial user studies in ActivABLES consisted of interviews and focus groups involving 2 specialist physicians, 5 speech/language therapists, 6 occupational therapists, 8 physical therapists, 1 neuropsychologist and 3 nurses were carried out in Sweden, Finland and Iceland. We carried out three focus groups with in total 16 stroke survivors (4 women, 12 men) in Sweden and Iceland, and one focus group with 5 family members (4 women, one man). To support the discussions, a video sketch/video prototype was developed (Figure 1). Tangible interaction may be well known within the research community, but is not a concept known to the general public. Thus, it was deemed necessary to have an initial illustration of what the kind of technology to be developed within the project might be like.

In addition we carried out a co-design workshop at a Rehabilitation Center in Reykjavik, Iceland. 5 researchers of the ActivABLES project, 5 stroke survivors, 2 of their relatives, and one health care professional participated in the workshop. The participating stroke survivors were affected by a range of different and very individual challenges like motion, balance, verbal communication, etc., but all of them were active in the workshop. To introduce some possible designs, the video prototype (Figure 1) was shown. Two different demonstration Lo-Fi interactive prototypes created with littleBits® (http://littlebits.cc) were also demonstrated. The first prototype symbolized a "Flex-charging massager" (Figure 2). It contains a bend-sensor, which detects how much the prototype is being bent around the middle. By flexing down the object using both hands repeatedly, the charging indicator started to fill-up. Once the "charge-indicator" is full, the "active- indicator" turns on and the prototype starts to vibrate. The massager discharges slowly over time, to keep it working one has to repeatedly flex it from time to time. If the "charge-indicator" gets empty, the "active-indicator" turns off and the vibrator stops. The second prototype was a balance board (Figure 3). It contained two pressure sensors one could step on. The pressure difference between the sensors is monitored and indicated visually and audibly. Indication is made on the side that had more weight on, via a bar-graph and a buzzer (speaker). If the pressure difference between the sensors is small enough, the "balanced-indicator" is turned on and a small DC-motor starts rotating. After the prototypes were demoed, participants were divided into 3 mixed groups in separate rooms. Each group started with a brainstorming session of around 30 minutes. After the brainstorming session, each group was instructed to spend about 20 minutes to choose one or two ideas and prepare a presentation of these the whole group. Then, participants were brought into the same room and each group was instructed to explain and demonstrate their chosen idea(s) to the rest of the participants. Each group had 5 minutes for the demonstration. The workshop concluded with a short discussion of the ideas and on the project.

The above activities were recorded and later transcribed, and analyzed qualitatively in order to identify common themes.

Discussion

Participants in our activities have been stroke survivors, but also family members and health care professionals. The mix has been important, since different stakeholders have different perspectives. This became

Design principles 1

Support the user in keeping a good balance between activity and rest.

Exercises need to have a purpose/meaning, and should be embedded in activities.

Safety & security needs to be considered

The system should provide reminders, and support the user remembering and getting started.

Activity goals should preferably be broken down into subgoals, to allow the stroke survivor to "win many small victories".

Feedback and awareness on activity and progress should be provided.

Provide a sense of accomplishment and empowerment.

Designs should be easy to use, but not childish.

particularly apparent when one compared the comments from stroke survivors with the comments made by family members. It is quite clear that anyone designing for stroke survivors need to involve persons at least from both these groups. If the technology is intended to be used also in a health care setting, health care professionals should also be involved in the design process.

Even though there is a risk of restricting the design potential of the workshop by presenting design alternatives on video and demonstration prototypes, we believe that both the video (Figure 1), and the physical examples (Figure 2) and (Figure 3) were very useful. Tangible technology may be standard fare for interaction designers, but for people in general it is something unfamiliar and unknown. The video served as a way to familiarize users with the technology, as well as a way to provide concrete examples that could be commented on. The prototypes developed as examples for the workshop had a similar function, but had the added advantage of being concrete and possible to test hands-on. Thus the video prototypes worked as expected [18] also in the present context. An advantage of the video prototype was that it was possible to reasonably quickly generate a fairly wide range of ideas. As for the workshop example, although fast prototyping tools like littleBits® were used, it still takes some time and effort to produce working physical prototypes. By using both approaches we were able to get the benefits of both a wide range of visualized ideas, and a few more concrete examples - something that can be particularly important when also involving users who are unfamiliar with the technology and may have cognitive difficulties [4,5].

For the co-design workshop it turned out to be important both that several of the participants had been "primed" [13] by taking part in earlier focus groups, and that persons who were used to design work (two design researchers) were present. Coming up with design ideas is not trivial, and by having experienced persons around we were able to support the participants in the process. A potential risk with this approach is that the experts might influence the designs too much, and we tried to deal with this by having two groups that were only monitored by a design researcher. In the groups where a design researcher participated the researcher helped elaborate ideas from the stroke survivors, and tried to avoid making new suggestions. While bodystorming together with stroke survivors during the co-design workshop, "empathy" has been a defining characteristic of the relationship between the design researchers, stroke survivors and healthcare professionals [17].

We found that activities involving balancing, standing up/sitting down, walking and activating the less good side of the body would allow us to reach a wide range of stroke survivors. Training of cognitive skills such as concentration, memory, planning, coordination and language/speech may be useful to add into the design. Analyzing the different user activities we arrived at a set of design principles for the technology to be developed - see Design principles 1 and 2.

Inspired by Balaam et al [3] we have designed materials and activities (video, prototypes, discussions and design activities) intended to help persons articulate what motivates them, and what they feel is important. Compared to [3] we have taken a more generic, toolkit oriented approach as the starting point

Design principles 2

Social use and the social context should be considered.

The technology should support patient – family - professional communication

Motivation is key; designs need to be either useful and/or fun

Indoor and outdoor use should be considered.

Designs need to support different speeds and should be adjustable, personalizable and multimodal to allow use by persons with different sensory abilities.

Avoid excluding users with aphasia.

Designs should be flexible, easy to move and allow users to reappropriate the technology.

To support different skill levels, it needs to be possible to adjust a suitable level of challenge.

for our design. We have involved not only stroke survivors and their families, but also health care professionals. Although our results with regards motivation generally agree with the lessons presented by Balaam et al [3], we also find a subtle difference: Not only is balance between work, duty and fun important, but also balance between activity and rest. Additionally, we present concrete guidelines for the interaction design of tangible interactive objects intended to support activity after a stroke.

Although we state that the system should provide reminders, it is important to note that a tangible object can be said to be a reminder in itself [19], which is yet another argument for the development of these kinds of devices.

In the interviews with health care professionals, it was pointed out that co-location of interaction and feedback can be important, since it can put additional strain on both attention and cognition to focus on the interaction while monitoring what is happening elsewhere. This recommendation is in line with what was found in [5], that co-location of interaction and feedback can be quite crucial when designing for persons with cognitive disabilities.

Future work will include further co-design activities and prototype development making use of the identified design principles. We also plan an extended analysis of the materials gathered from our initial activities.

ACKNOWLEDGMENTS

We would like to extend our gratitude to all the stroke survivors, partners and spouses, health care professionals taking part in the focus groups and interviews as well as the the Stroke organizations in Iceland, Sweden and Finland. The authors also gratefully acknowledge NordForsk for the support given to the project ActivABLES, as well as the EU for the support of the related project 689947 STARR.

References

1. Lesley Axelrod, Geraldine Fitzpatrick, Jane Burridge, et al. 2009. The reality of homes fit for heroes: design challenges for rehabilitation technology at home. *Journal of Assistive Technologies* 3, 2: 35–43. http://doi.org/10.1108/17549450200900014
2. Naveen Bagalkot, Tomas Sokoler, and R Shaikh. 2012. Integrating physiotherapy with everyday life: exploring the space of possibilities through ReHandles. *Proceedings of the Sixth International Conference on Tangible, Embedded and Embodied Interaction*, 91–98. http://doi.org/10.1145/2148131.2148152
3. Madeline Balaam, Stefan Rennick Egglestone, Geraldine Fitzpatrick, et al. 2011. Motivating mobility: designing for lived motivation in stroke rehabilitation. *Proceedings of the SIGCHI Conference on Human Factors in Computing Systems*: 3073–3082. http://doi.org/10.1145/1978942.1979397
4. Catharina Bjørkquist, Helge Ramsdal, and Kjetil Ramsdal. 2015. User participation and stakeholder involvement in health care innovation – does it matter? *European Journal of Innovation Management* 18, 1: 2–18. http://doi.org/10.1108/EL-01-2014-0022
5. Héctor A. Caltenco and Henrik Svarrer Larsen. 2014. Designing for Engagement: Tangible Interaction in Multisensory Environments. *NordiCHI '14 Proceedings of the 8th Nordic Conference on Human-Computer Interaction: Fun, Fast, Foundational*, 1055–1058. http://doi.org/10.1145/2639189.2670274
6. Frank Delbressine, Annick Timmermans, Luuk

Beursgens, et al. 2012. Motivating arm-hand use for stroke patients by serious games. *34th Annual International Conference of the IEEE Engineering in Medicine and Biology Society*.

7. Geraldine Fitzpatrick, Madeline Balaam, and Stefan Rennick Egglestone. 2010. Involving stroke survivors in designing for rehabilitation at home. *Proceedings of the NordiCHI'10 Nordic Conference on Human-Computer Interaction*: 13–15.
8. Niels Hendriks, Liesbeth Huybrechts, Andrea Wilkinson, and Karin Slegers. 2014. Challenges in doing participatory design with people with dementia. *Proceedings of the 13th Participatory Design Conference on Short Papers, Industry Cases, Workshop Descriptions, Doctoral Consortium papers, and Keynote abstracts - PDC '14 - volume 2*: 33–36. http://doi.org/10.1145/2662155.2662196
9. Niels Hendriks, Frederik Truyen, and Erik Duval. 2013. Designing with dementia: Guidelines for participatory design together with persons with dementia. *Lecture Notes in Computer Science (including subseries Lecture Notes in Artificial Intelligence and Lecture Notes in Bioinformatics)*, 649–666. http://doi.org/10.1007/978-3-642-40483-2_46
10. A. S. Macdonald, D. Loudon, P. J. Rowe, et al. 2007. Towards a design tool for visualizing the functional demand placed on older adults by everyday living tasks. *Universal Access in the Information Society* 6, 2: 137–144. http://doi.org/10.1007/s10209-007-0078-8
11. David McGookin, Euan Robertson, and S.a. Brewster. 2010. Clutching at Straws: Using Tangible Interaction to Provide Non-Visual Access to Graphs. *Proceedings of the 28th international conference on Human factors in computing systems - CHI '10*: 1715. http://doi.org/10.1145/1753326.1753583
12. Kirsten Rassmus-Gröhn and Charlotte Magnusson. 2014. Finding the way home. *Proceedings of the 8th Nordic Conference on Human-Computer Interaction Fun, Fast, Foundational - NordiCHI '14*, ACM Press, 247–255. http://doi.org/10.1145/2639189.2639233
13. Elizabeth B.-N. Sanders, Eva Brandt, and Thomas Binder. 2010. A framework for organizing the tools and techniques of participatory design. *Proceedings of the 11th Biennial Participatory Design Conference on - PDC '10*: 195. http://doi.org/10.1145/1900441.1900476
14. Stephen Uzor and Lynne Baillie. 2014. Investigating the Long-term Use of Exergames in the Home with Elderly Fallers. *Proceedings of the 32nd Annual ACM Conference on Human Factors in Computing Systems - CHI '14*, 2813–2822. http://doi.org/10.1145/2556288.2557160
15. Marijke Vandermaesen, Tom De Weyer, Kris Luyten, and Karin Coninx. 2014. PhysiCube : providing tangible interaction in a pervasive upper - limb rehabilitation system. *Tei'14*, c: 1–8. http://doi.org/10.1145/2540930.2540936
16. Stephanie Wilson, Abi Roper, Jane Marshall, et al. 2015. Codesign for people with aphasia through tangible design languages. *CoDesign* 11, February: 37–41. http://doi.org/10.1080/15710882.2014.997744
17. Peter Wright and John McCarthy. 2008. Empathy and experience in HCI. *Proceeding of the twenty-sixth annual CHI conference on Human factors in computing systems - CHI '08*: 637–647. http://doi.org/10.1145/1357054.1357156
18. Emilie Young and Russell Greenlee. 1992. Participatory video prototyping. *Posters and short talks of the 1992 SIGCHI conference on Human factors in computing systems*: 28. http://doi.org/10.1145/1125021.1125047
19. Oren Zuckerman. 2015. Objects for change: A case study of a tangible user interface for behavior change. *Tei 2015*: 649–654. http://doi.org/10.1145/2677199.2687906

Iyagi: An immersive storytelling tool for healthy bedtime routine

Manya Krishnaswamy
School of Design
Carnegie Mellon university
Pittsburgh, PA 15213, USA
manyak@andrew.cmu.edu

Bori Lee
School of Design
Carnegie Mellon university
Pittsburgh, PA 15213, USA
boril@andrew.cmu.edu

Chirag Murthy
School of Design
Carnegie Mellon university
Pittsburgh, PA 15213, USA
cmurthy@andrew.cmu.edu

Hannah Rosenfeld
School of Design
Carnegie Mellon university
Pittsburgh, PA 15213, USA
hannahr@andrew.cmu.edu

Austin S. Lee
School of Design
Carnegie Mellon university
Pittsburgh, PA 15213, USA
austinlee@cmu.edu

TEI '17, March 20-23, 2017, Yokohama, Japan
ACM 978-1-4503-4676-4/17/03.
http://dx.doi.org/10.1145/3024969.3025076.

Abstract
This paper documents an attempt to support parents and children in co-creating dynamic, fun and consistent bedtime routines through immersive and interactive storytelling. The proposed system, Iyagi, would be designed to ease the friction experienced by parents and children as they transition from evening activities into the bedtime routine as well as move between different stages and spaces within the bedtime routine. The key features of Iyagi would include: (1) Unfolding of a story across multiple rooms in which key bedtime activities take place; (2) Incorporating the physical space, projection of stories, objects, and the parent and child into the story; (3) Unique interactions with tangible objects, tied to the immersive story; (4) Natural interactions through voice, motion and tangible interactions; (5) Progressively calming activities and environments to ease children to sleep. The work presented follows a non-linear process that moved back and forth between user-centered research, idea generation, prototyping and evaluation. Outlined in this paper are learnings and insights from research that evolved into a proof-of-concept prototype. We've also included preliminary thoughts on opportunities for future development of the concept.

Author Keywords
Immersive storytelling; Projection based environments; Smart objects and environments; Internet of Things; Tangible interaction; Voice interaction; Motion sensing; Environmental storytelling.

ACM Classification Keywords
H.5.2 User Interfaces [Interaction styles]; H.5.2 User Interfaces [User-centered design]; H.5.2 User Interfaces [Voice I/O]; D.2.2 Design Tools and techniques [User Interfaces]; I.3.6 Methodology and techniques [Interaction techniques]

Introduction
From our research into family sleep, we found that consistent bedtime and routines are important to keeping families healthy, happy and emotionally sound. Hectic schedules and friction around bedtime, however, can get in the way. It can lead to nagging and yelling, leaving children upset and parents frustrated.
Iyagi would address bedtime struggles through immersive storytelling, moving parents and children through a healthy, consistent, and engaging bedtime routine. Parents and children can interact with the story through touch, movement and voice.

Though not a sleep solution in its most literal sense, by reducing the stress and anxiety associated with bedtime - making children look forward to sleep and parents feel successful in their parenting skills - Iyagi helps everyone in the family sleep easier.

In this paper we present our concept for Iyagi alongside existing design work in the realm of children's bedtime routine and storytelling. We describe our process in brief, followed by an overview of the Iyagi system and how it works.

Related Work
In order to situate our project within the larger design community, we provide an overview of work looks similarly at bedtime routines and storytelling.

Bedtime / Wakeup Routine
We were inspired by a range of interesting projects addressing bedtime and wakeup routines. The reverse alarm clock, a design research project from Carnegie Mellon University, is designed to keep young children from interrupting their parents' sleep in the middle of the night [4]. Mobero is a smartphone application that assists children in building independence and easing parental frustration at bedtime [7]. There have been a number of commercial applications of bedtime related tools by companies like Johnson and Johnson (Bedtime app) and Philips (Sonicare). These solutions concentrate on particular habits or activities within the routine. Some of them take the form of a to-do lists for parents, but they do not adapt over time.

Storytelling
Because of its significance at bedtime, storytelling is the focus of many interesting sleep-related interventions. Some of the early work in this area includes the MIT Media lab's SAGE and The University of Maryland's PETS [2]. Zenbo, by Asus and Jibo are both home service robots that are capable of telling stories. While we agree that smart products are an important aspect of storytelling, they can be limiting. Expecting a child to interact with the same product every day seems somewhat unrealistic as well as unnecessary given the number of other apps and tools designed to facilitate stories.

Spaces and Interactions
Interactive spaces allow for rich interactions. This approach can be seen in spaces like the Exploratorium in San Francisco, CA where children explore complex concepts physically [6]. In addition, theme parks like Disneyland and Universal Studios have also displayed creative uses of interactions in physical space. StoryRooms [1] attempted to design room-sized immersive storytelling experiences for children. However, this solution is too complicated and expensive for daily use in homes.

Within the commercial landscape, there are several products that embrace immersive storytelling experiences. The Samsung Electronics website is marketing a live VR storytelling app called Bedtime VR

Figure 1: The Iyagi system consists of a smart projector, motion-sensing object tags and a smartphone application.

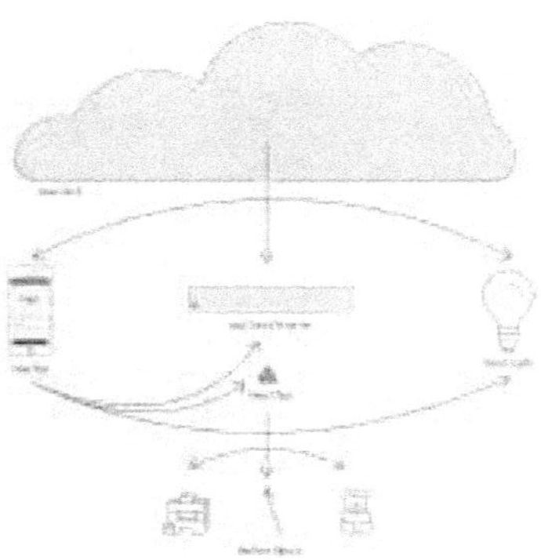

Figure 2: System map

Stories, which brings parent and child together inside a VR world when they can't be physically together However, this solution requires VR headsets, which is unnatural and renders the user blind to the surrounding reality.

Research Process

We conducted user interviews, both at the exploratory and evaluative stages of our design process. We spoke to an expert in the field of human-computer interaction, and four parents (a parent with a four-year-old son, a parent with a four-year-old son and three-year-old daughter, a parent with one-year-old twin sons and a four-year-old daughter and a parent with a four-year-old son and two daughters aged six and eight). Each of these conversations helped us to identify key needs of parents and children around bedtime as well as identify opportunities to appropriately intervene in this important part of a family's day. From this research, we unearthed several key insights that informed the rest of our design process. These insights were later translated into actionable principles which guided our final design solution.

- Bedtime is a microcosm of parenting - When parents are successful at getting their children to sleep without friction - yelling and crying - they feel like good parents. When bedtime is a struggle, they feel like they have failed.
- Independence is important, but so are meaningful bedtime moments - Parents want their children to grow up to be responsible and independent, and bedtime can provide a platform for giving children increasing amounts of responsibility. However, bedtime is also a special time for parents and children, and parents love to be a part of it.
- Transitional moments are points of intense friction - Transitions are hard, and most of the friction that associated with bedtime occurs during transitional moments, when children have to move from one activity to the next or one space to the next.

Interspersed within our research, we conducted several rounds of brainstorming and generated a range of concepts from feasible to impossible. A digital art and play board concentrated on the transition from playtime into the bedtime routine. An augmented path guided children through the bedtime routine with a series of projections. Finally, a companion object would help children understand and manage time, as well as participate in bedtime activities along with the child. Showing these concepts to parents generated a lot of reactions, and the feedback proved valuable in pushing our process forward. Parents favored concepts that supported, not replaced them. Tools that facilitated collaborative play also proved desirable as opportunities to support moments for emotional parent-child bonding. Natural interactions and immersive environments emerged as some of the most successful elements of our concepts. These elements are reflected in our final design of Iyagi.

Design Principles

Having gathered a plethora of insights from research, we distilled key learnings into actionable principles to guide the direction of our designs, help us prioritize features, and keep the needs of our users in mind. The following three design principles form the basis of our concepts and serve as metrics against which to evaluate our design.

1. Support moments of transition - A seamless transition to bedtime can mean the difference between a restless sleep for both parent and child and a peaceful night of healthy sleep. Transitional moments offer a unique opportunity for meaningful intervention.
2. Let parents parent - While parents are excited about tools and technology that help them build independence in their children, some things should remain human. Any intervention

Figure 3: Tooth brushing as an interaction with the story

Voice Interactions With System	
Action	Input
Invoke system	"Iyagi…"
Start story	"Iyagi, start"
Stop story	"Iyagi, stop"
Start another story	"Iyagi, another"
Voice Interactions With Story	
Action	Input
Follow prompt on projection	e.g. "Jack lived with his…" e.g. count stars

Figure 4: Voice interaction taxonomy

into a bedtime routine should simply support what parents already do best, parent.

3. Grow with the child - Much more than bedtime changes as a child grows. A technological solution should consider these many changes, adapting both content and interaction to meet the changing needs of a growing child.

In addition to these guiding principles, each of our design decisions focused on maintaining natural interactions, creating interactive spaces and choreographing environments.

Iyagi

Iyagi is a concept for an interactive, immersive storytelling system aiming to support parents and children through a fun and consistent bedtime routine. Iyagi would reduce the stress associated with transitional moments around bedtime by moving parents and children through space, alongside a dynamic storytelling adventure.

System Map

The Iyagi smart system would consist of several connected devices, the primary of which would be a modular projector with embedded speakers, voice recognition and motion detection sensors. To supplement Iyagi's virtual storyscapes, Internet-of-Things (IoT) enabled smart tags would transform normal bedtime items, like toys and toothbrushes, into smart objects that could be incorporated into Iyagi's virtual world. Children would engage with the adventure by completing bedtime tasks to help their favorite characters and progress the story. A mobile app would support the system's operational backend as well as offer an additional way to control the bedtime story. Iyagi would also connect to smart lighting systems, to make the storyscapes even more immersive as well as create progressively calming environments to prepare children for sleep. The Iyagi would seamlessly connects these unique devices into one cohesive system.

Interaction Taxonomy

While considering the Iyagi system, it was important to consider how parents and children might move through their normal bedtime routine, largely uninterrupted. Voice interaction, and incorporation of normal bedtime objects would allow Iyagi to be integrated into a range of bedtime routines, while immersive stories and engaging activities would support parents in facilitating successful bedtime routines.

User Journey

Iyagi would support friction free transitions by moving parents and children from room to room and task to task, following friendly characters in an adventure. Iyagi could be started in any enabled room through voice activation or with the app. When it's time to move, Iyagi would indicate this with visual cues, sending the parent and child into the next room where the interactive story would continue. Lights in the house would progressively dim, calming the child before sleep. Finally, in the bedroom, Iyagi's projection would scale down to the size of a night-light, leaving the characters to fall asleep alongside the child.

Scenario of Use

Sam is a 4-year-old boy with a big imagination. Like most children his age, Sam loves bedtime stories, and Iyagi's immersive storyscapes make bedtime an even greater adventure. When it is time for bedtime to start, Sam's dad initiates the Iyagi the system in an enabled room. A notification will be sent to Sam's dad if they are late getting started to encourage consistency and reduce anxiety. Once started, Sam's dad reads the story aloud as Iyagi's projectors bring the story to life. The system listens, and advances the story as Sam's dad recites key words. Iyagi leaves space for natural conversation between Sam and his dad, only advancing as the story is read aloud. Iyagi invites Sam into the interactive story as he engages with tagged objects to complete bedtime related tasks. Brushing his teeth, cleaning up his toys, or putting on his pajamas allow Sam to help his favorite characters through the Iyagi adventure and progress the immersive story. Lights dim as the two move from room to room, relaxing Sam for bed. Once in the bedroom, Sam and his dad finish the story before Iyagi's projection shrinks down to become a nightlight to guide Sam to sleep.

Proof-of-concept prototype

Concept video: https://vimeo.com/188435350
Interactions demonstration video:
https://vimeo.com/188435916
Smartphone app walkthrough video:
https://vimeo.com/188453407

With a sound proof-of-concept prototype, we have begun considering the design of a working prototype to test the smart projector and smart tags. This prototype will allow us to test our envisioned interactions with potential users, and gather feedback to help us enhance the design of Iyagi.

Smart Projector

The prototype for the smart projector will use the Intel Edison board along with the Intel RealSense 3D Camera, microphone and speakers to be IoT, voice, motion and gesture enabled [5]. Amazon's Alexa Voice Service (AVS) API will allow us to integrate voice capabilities into our system.

Object Tags

The smart object tags will be injection molded and will contain a Z-Wave chip and accelerometer sensor. Z-Wave is the industry standard for smart home devices and would provide us with the coverage needed to operate reliably [3].

Future Work

While the initial response to our concept was positive, much work is still needed to test, refine and develop this concept. Once we have a working prototype, we would like to conduct contextual interviews to observe the effects of our system on families. While the scenario of use outlined here considers a single child, we would also need to conduct additional research to understand how our system might work within other family contexts.

We would also like to explore potential partnerships to support a service ecosystem around Iyagi. This might include the incorporation of smart home technologies to maximize Iyagi's potential to immersive experience. Partners might include Philips Hue or Google Nest. Finally, we anticipate opportunities for an e-commerce partnership with someone like Amazon, to enable in-app purchase of content for the Iyagi system.

Acknowledgements

We would like to thank Mark Choi, Peter Weeks, Tom Visser and Jeroen Raijmakers of the Philips Design team for taking the time out of their busy lives to review our work and offer their professional expertise to our work. Thank you to our generous interview participants, who shared their amazing stories that helped bring our vision to life. Finally, we would like to thank the Carnegie Mellon University School of Design for making this project possible.

References

1. Alborzi, Houman, Joe Hammer, Alex Kruskal, Abby Lal, Thomas Plaisant Schwenn, Lauren Sumida, Rebecca Wagner, Jim Hendler, Allison Druin, Jaime Montemayor, Michele Platner, Jessica Porteous, Lisa Sherman, Angela Boltman, Gustav Taxén, and Jack Best. "Designing StoryRooms: Interactive Storytelling Spaces for Children." *Proceedings of the Conference on Designing Interactive Systems Processes, Practices, Methods, and Techniques - DIS '00*, August 2000. Accessed September 23, 2016. doi:10.1145/347642.347673.

2. Druin, Allison, Isabella Revett, Thomas Plaisant Schwenn, Lauren Sumida, Rebecca Wagner, Jamie Montemayor, Jim Hendler, Britt Mcalister, Angela Boltman, Eric Fiterman, Aurelie Plaisant, Alex Kruskal, and Hanne Olsen. "Designing PETS." *Proceedings of the SIGCHI conference on Human factors in computing systems the CHI is the limit - CHI '99*, May 1999. Accessed September 15, 2016. doi:10.1145/302979.303103.

3. Gomez, Carles, and Josep Paradells. "Wireless Home Automation Networks: A Survey of Architectures and Technologies." *IEEE Communications Magazine* 48, no. 6 (June 2010): 92-101. Accessed September 09, 2016. doi:10.1109/mcom.2010.5473869.

4. Ozenc, Kursat F., James P. Brommer, Bong-Keum Jeong, Nina Shih, Karen Au, and John Zimmerman. "Reverse Alarm Clock: A Research through Design Example of Designing for the Self." *Proceedings of the 2007 Conference on Designing Pleasurable Products and Interfaces - DPPI '07*, August 2007. Accessed September 10, 2016. doi:10.1145/1314161.1314196.

5. Peter, Ma. "Using an Intel® RealSense™ 3D Camera with the Intel® Edison Development Platform." Intel Software Developer Zone. May 20, 2015. Accessed September 28, 2015. https://software.intel.com/en-us/articles/using-intel-realsense-technology-in-combination-with-the-intel-edison-development-platform.

6. Robert J., Semper. "Science Museums as Environments for Learning." *Physics Today* 43, no. 11 (November 1990). Accessed October 01, 2016. doi:10.1063/1.881216.

7. Sonne, Tobias, Jörg Müller, Paul Marshall, Carsten Obel, and Kaj Grønbæk. "Changing Family Practices with Assistive Technology: MOBERO Improves Morning and Bedtime Routines for Children with ADHD." *Proceedings of the 2016 CHI Conference on Human Factors in Computing Systems - CHI '16*, May 2016. doi:10.1145/2858036.2858157.

TurnTable: Towards More Equivalent Turn-Taking

Carolyn Fu
MIT System Design and Management
1 Amherst St.
Cambridge, MA 02142, USA
cjfu@mit.edu

Kritika Dhanda
Harvard GSD
48 Quincy St.
Cambridge, MA 02138, USA
kdhanda@gsd.harvard.edu

Marc Exposito
MIT Media Lab
75 Amherst St.
Cambridge, MA 02142 USA
exposito@mit.edu

Haeyoung Kim
Harvard GSD
48 Quincy St.
Cambridge, MA 02138, USA
hkim1@gsd.harvard.edu

Yan Zhang
MIT Media Lab
75 Amherst St.
Cambridge, MA 02142 USA
ryanz@mit.edu

TEI '17, March 20-23, 2017, Yokohama, Japan
ACM 978-1-4503-4676-4/17/03.
http://dx.doi.org/10.1145/3024969.3025079

Abstract
In this paper, we introduce a prototype for a tangible interface to encourage turn-taking in group discussions. Teams with better distribution of turn-taking have been found to outperform those with poorly distributed turn-taking. Making teams aware of their turn-taking dynamics thus has the potential to improve their performance. This paper explores the use of a tangible interface as a means to both increase team members' awareness of their turn taking dynamics, while actively driving the conversation towards more equivalent turn-taking. The construction of a prototype called a TurnTable is detailed, as well as potential enhancements to the design to improve group performance.

Author Keywords
Turn-taking; Inflation; Tangible Interfaces.

ACM Classification Keywords
H.5.2. Information interfaces and presentation: Prototyping

Introduction
Turn-taking refers to how individuals take turns to speak in a group conversation. Teams that have poorly distributed turn-taking (i.e. where the conversation is dominated by a few individuals) have been found to perform worse on a general battery of tasks (such as brainstorming and puzzle solving), compared to those in which turn-taking is better distributed [1]. Turn-taking allows for more group members to contribute to

Figure 1: Group discussion around the TurnTable prototype. (pg. 4)

Figure 2: Inflation of the TurnTable, which drives turn-taking dynamics. (pg. 4)

the discussion, enabling a greater diversity of opinion on any given task, thus better leveraging the group's collective intelligence. In particular, turn-taking can prevent against "groupthink", where individual members with dominant personalities eclipse conversation so as to cause other members to "conform his or her opinion to what s/he believes to be the consensus of the group" [2]. More details about this research are given in the subsequent related work section.

The aim of this project is to develop a prototype that can encourage better turn-taking in group discussions, so as to improve group performance. A tangible interface, known as the TurnTable, is developed so as to increase a group's awareness of their turn-taking dynamics, and drive alternative dynamics. Tangible Interfaces show interesting potential in this area because of their ability to increase "embodied facilitation", using structure to "(shape) emerging social configurations", by "determining trajectories of action or providing implicit suggestions" [3].

Related Work

Given the benefits of turn-taking, various studies have attempted to (1) measure it in team discussions, (2) provide feedback to team members, as well as (3) actively intervene on teams' turn-taking performance.

(1) Measuring turn-taking: Effective turn-taking has traditionally been represented by various factors. The most common is speaking duration, to measure the equivalence in length of turns. However, studies have also considered the frequency of turns, quality of turns, as well as factors which can influence the transition of turns. Morris et al., Sturm et al. and Kim et al. measured the quantity of conversation contributed by each person in terms of speaking time [4][5][6], however Kim et al. also included the frequency of turn-taking, i.e. the "interactivity level" between participants.

(2) Providing turn-taking feedback: In prior work, these metrics have been provided to team members through different types of feedback, with the intention of encouraging members to self-calibrate towards more equitable turn-taking. Primarily, the type of feedback given is real-time, public, visual feedback. Sturm et al. provided feedback in the form of a "histogram presented on a public display" [5], while Morris et al. provided "visualizations reflecting speech contributions" on a tabletop display [4]. Kim et al. provided private visual feedback, where participants were each given a mobile phone, which displayed a graphic depicting "interactivity level", "balance in participation" and "speaking time" at their visual periphery [6].

In general, all types of feedback were found to enable self-mediation of turn-taking dynamics. Morris et al. found that their visual feedback "increased participation equity… in terms of amount of conversation contributed by each person" [4]. Sturm et al. likewise found "more equal participation of all meeting members" [5], and Kim et al. found a "dramatic reduction in overlapping conversation", a reduction in the "difference between dominant and non-dominant people" such that it was no longer significant, and an increased likelihood to "collaborate with their teammates as one group" [6].

However, the actual benefit of such feedback on group performance was unclear, as the method of providing feedback often appeared to confound the benefits of

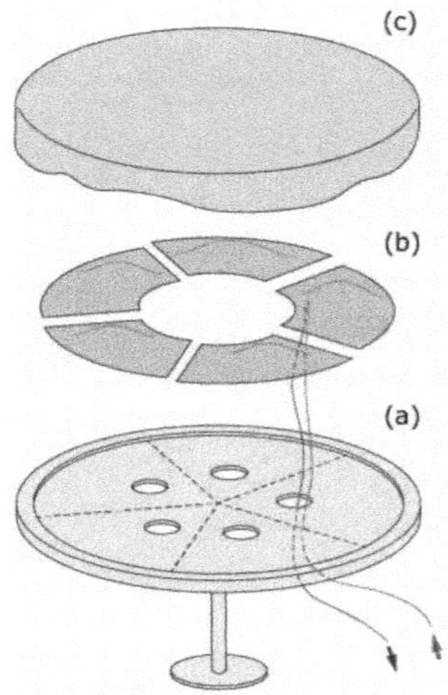

Figure 3: Schematic of the TurnTable layers. (pg. 4)

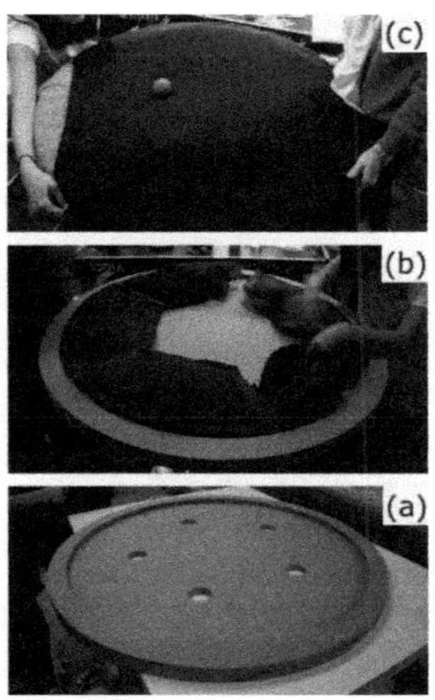

Figure 4: Actual layers of the TurnTable. (pg. 4)

turn-taking itself. Buisine et al. postulated that a more attractive device would "increase users' motivation" to participate [8] – however this does not necessarily increase the quality of group discussion.

Despite increasing their speaking equity, participants in Morris et al.'s study were found to do this by engaging in "filler speech", such as "asking other group members for their opinions", but did not actually "(suggest) an answer or (offer) information" [4]. Participants in Sturm et al.s' study also "indicated that they were distracted" by the visual feedback, as "thinking about what to do with the information would distract them too much from the actual discussion going on" [5]. Kim et al. factored for this in their experiment, designing their mobile phone-based display to only "(update) gradually so that it does not require constant attention from the user", and avoid text and small details "so that a mere glimpse would be sufficient for information retrieval". Its aim was to only draw attention during an "extreme change in the group dynamics" [6].

(3) Active turn-taking intervention: The studies primarily utilized passive feedback, hoping that awareness of turn-taking dynamics would drive a change in behavior. Some of these were more active, such as Buisine et al., who found that the act of forcing a group to interact over a table versus at a flip chart resulted in significantly more equitable verbal contributions [9]. However, more active interventions were only hypothesized, and not developed.

Sturm et al. suggested that if "distributions of speaking time and visual attention (fell) beyond certain standards of acceptability", a tabletop display might change so as to force participants to discuss the displayed information [4]. Morris et al. further suggested that the group discussion could be designed to require "cooperative gesturing… the active involvement of all group members to execute certain actions", such as "all (holding) hands to end discussion" [4]. Basu et al. also installed lights into their "facilitation lab", the aim of which was to focus lights of certain colors and intensities on each team member, depending on their level of participation [7].

The Concept

The objective of this TurnTable project is to develop a tangible means of effecting more equitable turn-taking. Prior work has focused on visual displays of turn-taking feedback. With this project, we seek to enrich the quality of turn-taking feedback through use of a tangible display, while leveraging the tangibility to also interweave active intervention of turn-taking dynamics. The TurnTable has two main objectives: (1) make turn-taking feedback a more organic element of group discussion, and (2) drive conversational dynamics.

As demonstrated by the literature, making turn-taking dynamics attractive is useful both to increase the level of engagement, and also to improve equivalence of turns. However this must be done organically, without requiring excessive attention from team members such that it detracts from conversation. Prior work has also shown that considering how to change the conversation dynamics may be a significant cognitive burden on team members – which the implementation of *active* intervention may serve to mitigate. The TurnTable aims to use tangibility to develop an interface which both passively provides awareness of turn-taking dynamics, but actively drives discussion at the same time – interweaving both feedback and discussion and skipping the need for interpretation. Fundamentally, it also aims to be a beautiful and playful interface that can encourage engagement around it.

The physical form of the TurnTable, described in the next section, evolved out of the following considerations: (1) to enable a productive and equal discussion to sit around a table as mentioned before in the related work section; (2) to provide a voice driven pointer which would have an element of randomness associated with the turn taking – the red ball driven by the inflating table; and (3) to include a playful design aspect to the randomness so that the speaker would not be hassled with the distraction – the inflating table.

Prototype

The primary components of the table are a set of microphones underneath the table, and an inflatable top which can change its topography (fig 2). As the level of conversation at one side of the table increases (currently measured by volume), inflatable airbags within the table cause that side of the table to inflate relative to the rest of the table. This drives the motion of a red ball. Thus, when an individual begins to speak excessively, the table topography changes, making the red ball roll away from him, towards others who have been speaking less (fig 1). A summary of the TurnTable's objectives, functionality and construction can be found in the following video: https://www.youtube.com/watch?v=GY47MVJesVE

Construction: The table comprises three main sections. The first (fig 3a, fig 4a) is the base, which houses the air pumps and microcontrollers which control air flow. We have used the Pneuduino toolkit[1], which comprise air pumps and control boards developed at the MIT Media Lab. These allow us to control the airflow from an air pump to the second layer of the table, which is a set of inflatable bags [9] (fig 3b, fig 4b). In the current version, there are five such air bags, each corresponding to five microphones placed at their location around the table. Depending on the volume detected by the microphone, the amount of air driven to these inflatable bags changes. The final layer is a flexible fabric top, which provides a smooth, continuous surface topography for the table (fig 3c, fig 4c).

Inflation algorithm: Inflation is triggered when an individual has spoken significantly *more* than other members at the table. As such, the bags do not inflate as a function of total volume spoken – rather, they inflate as a function of the amount spoken over and above the *average* that the group has spoken. The bags are actively deflated as an individual's contributions regress to the group's average (fig 5). Hence, one individual may begin to speak a lot, but as long as other individuals match his quantity of speaking, the table levels out again and loses its contours. If all but one individual has been speaking, then all of the other bags but his will inflate, creating a valley that the ball will then roll into.

1 http://pneuduino.org

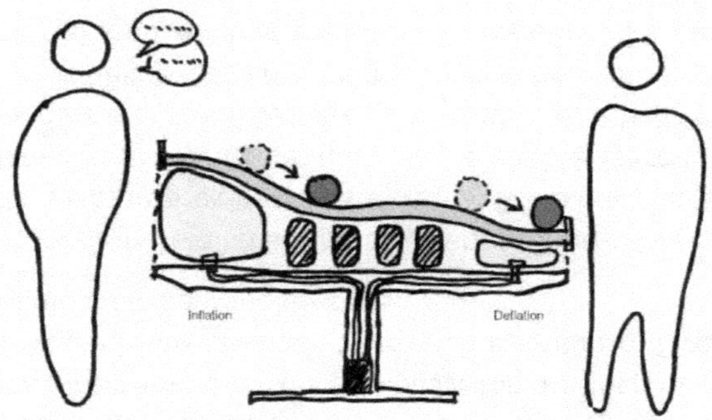

Figure 5: The TurnTable inflates the respective airbag of the individual who is speaking more than average, and deflates that of the individual speaking less than average.

At the moment, inflation is driven by speaking volume. However, alternative measures of turn-taking can be used, as have been explored in the literature – such as quantity of speech, quality of speech, or physical biometrics.

Ball: In this version, a single red ball has been used simply as an indicator to the group as to whose turn it is to speak next. A ball is used fundamentally because it can roll over the contoured surface – however its roundness also contributes to a randomness as to who should speak next. If one individual has been dominating the conversation and his airbag is inflated, the ball can randomly roll to any one of the other non-contributing team members.

The ball can also be used as more than a symbol, but as a means of actively determining the center of conversation. This can be done by replacing the ball with a spherical microphone -- where the ball serves to amplify the voice of whomever it has rolled towards, thereby wresting attention from whomever it rolled away from.

Discussion

As aforementioned, the goal of this tangible interface is to interweave feedback and intervention in an organic manner so as to enhance group discussion performance. The TurnTable is unique in that feedback does not require interpretation for conversational dynamics to change – both because metrics are provided in tangible form (allowing actual quantities to be ambiguous and therefore "sensed", as opposed to a chart where group differences are more precise and must be read), and because dynamics are modified by the table automatically. Because it inflates as a function of the group average as opposed to individual contribution, feedback is also provided as a representation of cumulative rather than instantaneous contribution.

Despite its advantages, we note that the risks of distraction are high with the current iteration of the TurnTable. Most significantly, it may incur a level of urgency or panic about the ball rolling to or away from members (or even off the table), stilting the quality of discussion. In the problem-solving exercises conducted in prior work, such distraction proved to be harmful to the overall discussion quality. It is also very likely that in some cases, non-equitable discussion is essential, such as when hearing from experts, and in those cases, individuals should be allowed to choose to dominate the conversation in a way that the TurnTable does not currently allow. Active intervention on turn-taking may also be much more acceptable in some cultures than others.

Figure 6: Use of many small balls instead of a single ball, to affect conversation less drastically.

Overall, it is worth considering that forced dynamics may be beneficial in some types of group discussions and not others – for example, brainstorming may in fact benefit from this type of forced turn-taking frequency, so as to increase the overall amount of ideas produced.

Future Work

Firstly, studies must be done where the TurnTable is used in actual experiments of group discussion, to determine its impact on turn-taking, group and individual performance. The value of a tangible interface for turn-taking can thus be compared against other existing feedback and intervention devices.

It would also be interesting to incorporate how the table affects different personalities which tend to have a strong impact on respective social encounters of the group members – Varying degrees of talkative to quiet, or from dominant to rather non-dominant members, or aggressive to shy members. The table could be geared to each individual personality by taking in passive voice measurements over time to allow for the response of the table to be calculated for each member differently to suit their personality type.

Future work is also aimed at attenuating the type of intervention provided by the table. For example, a milder form of intervention can be enabled through the use of many small balls, as opposed to one ball (fig 6). This will allow the change of conversation to be more gradual, and remove the sense of urgency of a single ball racing to or away from you. Additionally, factors such as the speed of inflation, level of friction of the surface, or even shape of the ball can all be modified so as to change the pace of discussion, or the probability of conversation distribution. The table could also take into account other social parameters like the volume and pitch of the speaker which are other ways of measuring the personality traits of the speakers, encouraging the quiet or less dominant members of the group to speak up thus reinforcing equivalent participation in the group discussion.

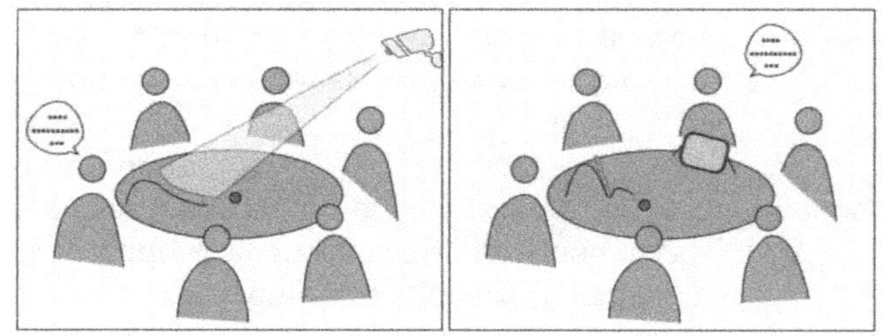

Figure 7: Modification of the TurnTable design to support other discussion needs.

To enable greater productivity, the shape of the table can also be changed so as to allow for a flat, non-inflatable peripheral ring on which work can be done. The shape of the table may even be used for other presentation needs, such as forming a cove that can aid in sound amplification for a device, or which can serve as a projection surface (fig 7). The table can also be used in distributed settings, as a means of giving distance members a tangible local presence.

References

1. Woolley, A. W., Chabris, C. F., Pentland, A., Hashmi, N., & Malone, T. W. (2010). Evidence for a collective intelligence factor in the performance of human groups. Science 330:686–688. (pg. 2)
2. Kulyk, O., Wang, J., & Terken, J. (2006). Real-Time Feedback on Nonverbal Behaviour to Enhance Social

Dynamics in Small Group Meetings. Machine Learning for Multimodal Interaction Lecture Notes in Computer Science, 150-161. doi:10.1007/11677482_13. (pg. 2)

3. Hornecker, E., Buur, J. (2006). Getting a Grip on Tangible Interaction: A Framework on Physical Space and Social Interaction. Proc. CHI'06, ACM, 437-446. (pg. 2)
4. Morris, M., Cassanego, A., Paepcke, A., Winograd, T., Piper, A., & Huang, A. (2006). Mediating Group Dynamics through Tabletop Interface Design. IEEE Computer Graphics and Applications, 26(5), 65-73. doi:10.1109/mcg.2006.114 (pg. 2,3)
5. Sturm, J., Herwijnen, O. H., Eyck, A., & Terken, J. (2007). Influencing social dynamics in meetings through a peripheral display. Proceedings of the Ninth International Conference on Multimodal Interfaces - ICMI '07. doi:10.1145/1322192.1322238 (pg. 2,3)
6. Kim, T., Chang, A., Holland, L., & Pentland, A. (2008). Meeting mediator. Proceeding of the Twenty-sixth Annual CHI Conference Extended Abstracts on Human Factors in Computing Systems - CHI '08. doi:10.1145/1358628.1358828 (pg. 2,3)
7. Basu, S., Choudhury, T., Clarkson, B., Pentland, A. (2001). Towards Measuring Human Interactions in Conversational Settings. Proceedings of the IEEE Int'l Workshop on Cues in Communication at CVPR 2001. (pg. 3)
8. Kulyk, O., Wang, J., & Terken, J. (2006). Real-Time Feedback on Nonverbal Behaviour to Enhance Social Dynamics in Small Group Meetings. Machine Learning for Multimodal Interaction Lecture Notes in Computer Science, 150-161. doi:10.1007/11677482_13 (pg. 3)
9. Buisine, S., Besacier, G., Aoussat, A., & Vernier, F. (2012). How do interactive tabletop systems influence collaboration? Computers in Human Behavior, 28(1), 49-59. doi:10.1016/j.chb.2011.08.010 (pg. 3)
10. L. Yao, R. Niiyama, J. Ou, S. Follmer, C. Della Silva, and H. Ishii, "PneUI: pneumatically actuated soft composite materials for shape changing interfaces," 2013, pp. 13–22. (pg. 4)

Developing a Tangible Gaming Board for Post-Stroke Upper Limb Functional Training

Pan Wang
Division of Industrial Design
National University of Singapore
4 Architecture Drive, Singapore
wang.pan@u.nus.edu

Tian Ma Xu
Health & Social Science
Singapore Institute of Technology
10 Dover Drive, Singapore
Tim.Xu@singaporetech.edu.sg

Gerald Choon Huat Koh
School of Public Health
National University of Singapore
12 Science Drive 2, Singapore
gerald_koh@nuhs.edu.sg

Hamasaki
HIKARISOFT Co. Ltd, Japan
Kami-Amakusa Kumamoto
hamasaki@hikarisoft.com

Christian Gilles Boucharenc
Division of Industrial Design
National University of Singapore
4 Architecture Drive, Singapore
didcgb@nus.edu.sg

Ching Chiuan Yen
Division of Industrial Design
Keio-NUS CUTE Center
National University of Singapore
4 Architecture Drive, Singapore
didyc@nus.edu.sg

TEI '17, March 20-23, 2017, Yokohama, Japan
ACM 978-1-4503-4676-4/17/03.
http://dx.doi.org/10.1145/3024969.3025080

Abstract

Low patient motivation and compliance has been reported as a main barrier to effective rehabilitation. This study aims to provide an engaging and intuitive tool to increase the motivation of elderly stroke survivors in rehabilitation program. We present a tangible gaming board for the training of upper limb gross motor and fine motor skills. 64 RGB LED rotary encoders are evenly distributed on the board into eight rows. A modular design allows for training of various hand functions with interchangeable sizes of knobs attached on the rotary encoders. Preliminary usability testing of the game "Lights Invader" with eight elderly stroke survivors suggested that the gaming board has a high acceptance rate among all the participants, the game interface is easy to understand and the game is fun to play with. User feedback on the features that need to be improved are discussed in this paper.

Author Keywords

Tangible user interaction; interactive game; stroke; upper limb training; elderly.

ACM Classification Keywords

H.5.m. Information interfaces and presentation (e.g., HCI): Miscellaneous;

Introduction

Stroke ranks as the second leading cause of serious and long-term physical disability in the world, fifteen million people suffer a stroke per year [30]. Stroke risks increases with age, an estimation of 75% of stroke survivors are elderly (age>65) [14]. Over 80% percent of stroke survivors suffer from different level of upper limb impairment (e.g. loss of sensation, limited range-of-motion or paralysis) [28]. Arm reaching and various hand functions are the fundamentals to almost all the activities in daily living (ADL). Stroke survivors can have difficulties to perform daily tasks with their affected arm (e.g. open a water bottle, turn a knob). To regain lost function, such a survivor often needs to go through long-term and intensive rehabilitation trainings. Evidence shows that an active participation in rehabilitation yields faster and better function recovery [19], and the recovery of arm-hand function is often associated with improved ability to perform daily activities and with a higher quality of life [20]. However, low patient motivation and compliance have been identified as common issues which can decrease the effectiveness of rehabilitative training [10; 18]. Patients often find the highly repetitive exercises monotonous and thus lead to decreased interest [18]. Rehabilitation is often long-term and the effect is not immediately visible, and patients may lose confidence in their recovery and dropout in the process [8].

Game-based rehabilitation is a relative new approach to stroke rehabilitation to increase patient motivation by integrating entertainment elements in the training tasks and providing feedback to allow the patients to see their progress [26]. However, most of the games are designed to train only one type of function - either arm movements or hand movements [5; 7]. Game systems focusing on the functional training of the hand, such as multi-touch screens and robotic devices, often are expensive and difficult to be widely implemented. Despite a great number of elderly patients, most of the games are not specifically designed to cater the needs of the elderly stroke survivors. To make gaming technology for functional training more accessible and appropriate for the elderly stroke survivors, we aim to further investigate the design of tangible interface to enhance the training of arm-hand functions. In this paper, we present a tangible gaming board for the training of upper limb gross motor and fine motor skills. We also present the design and initial usability testing of the game "Lights Invader".

Related Studies

Games for upper limb training were commonly integrated with robotic devices and motion sensors (e.g. webcam sensor, wearable sensor). Robot-aided rehabilitation can provide intensive repetitive movements training and objective measures of patient motor functions [16]. Colombo et al. [9] developed a simple game task which requires patients to grasp and controlling a robotic handle with transducer to detect the exerted force/torque in different directions, the system can provide precise measure of patient performance. Popović et al. [23] compared the differences of two training systems with/without feedback. Both studies indicated that feedback is an essential element to be included to increase patient motivation and training effectiveness. Joshi and Bråthen [17] presented a non-game robotic interface with different sizes of haptic knobs to train various movements of wrist and hand. Robot-assisted rehabilitation typically focuses on improving level of motor functions (range-of-motion, strength) by providing simple tasks for articular movements [9], instead of ADL-based functional training. A few studies explored the design of games to train real-life tasks by using daily objects such as a fork and knife [5] or cup/tennis [15] to play games on a multi-touched tabletop screen. However, both of robotic devices and multi-touch tabletop are usually expensive and therefore difficult to be widely implemented. Games developed utilizing motion sensors (e.g. Kinect, Wii Remote) are often low-cost [2; 7]. Yet, the drawbacks are that: (1) it is difficult to capture both gross motor and fine motor movements, (2) it is difficult to accurately detect small movements, therefore may not cater to the training needs for severely affected patients [22], and (3) lack of familiarity and steep learning curve may reduce the confidence level and training efficiency among elderly users [1; 12].

Evidence suggests that utilizing tangible objects that the elderly are familiar with and providing a simple tangible interface with simplified elements help to reduce the learning curve among elderly [3; 13; 24]. In addition, a tangible user interface (TUI) can support post-stroke training through the integration of physical representations with digital representations [27], which allows for the tracking of the training performance and progress objectively. One study introduced a tangible interactive board with LED cubes for the training of shoulder reaching through simple LED games. The preliminary interface testing with four patients suggested the game interface is simple and understandable for elderly stroke survivors [29]. However, the board did not support the training of fine motor skills. Therefore, we propose a system for elderly patients which investigates the integration of tangible objects with digital controllers to train both arm and hand functions.

Design Requirements

The establishment of our game design requirements was based on the interview with three experienced occupational therapists in Singapore and literature review [6; 11; 22]. Therapist input was integrated along the iteration design process to ensure the game satisfied therapy requirements. Evidence related to elderly motivation requirements was reviewed and summarized. The needs of elderly players and stroke rehabilitation can be summarized as follows: (1) meaningful game tasks to guide useful and appropriate upper limb functional training, (2) demonstration and recording of the performance and progress feedback, (3) intuitive game interface with simplified elements, (4) supportive social game play such as competition and cooperation, (5) game difficulty levels should be appropriately designed (not too easy or too difficult), and (6) game rules should be easy for the elderly to master and to understand.

Game Design

Targeted Motions

The training of upper limb functions mainly aims to improve or to regain the physical functions related to ADL. Common upper limb movements usually include (1) flexion and extension of shoulder, elbow, wrist and thumb, (2) internal and external rotation of shoulder, (3) abduction and adduction of shoulder, finger and thumb, (4) pronation and supination of forearm, (5) ulna and radial deviation of wrist, and (6) opposition and reposition of finger [4; 25]. We aim to focus on the training of reaching function, hand grasping, pinching and turning functions as these functions are very commonly used in daily life. For example, patients often have difficulties with daily life-related tasks such as opening a jar/bottle, turning knobs on electronic

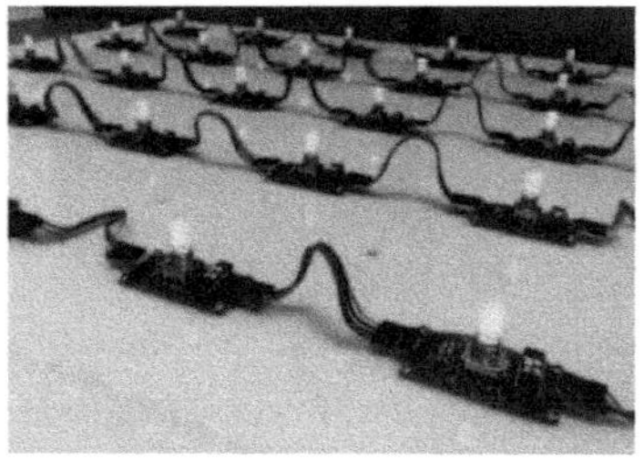

Figure 1: 64 units linked up in eight rows

Figure 2: Prototype with 5cm and 0.7cm rotary encoders (full lit)

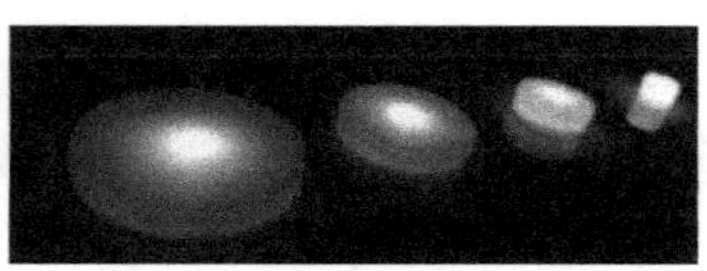

Figure 3: Rotary encoders with four different sizes

devices (e.g. microwave, washing machine) and doors, or turning keys.

Hardware and Software

The design for our game board was inspired by the traditional 8*8 analog rehabilitation checkerboard (which elderly patients are familiar with). We augmented game elements through 64 tactile RGB rotary encoders that were equally distributed across an 8 x 8 grid structure of customized white acrylic board. An Arduino Mega 2560 R3 was used as the master to control 64 I2C slave devices (ATTiny84). Each slave device was programmed an "address" and linked together with a RGB rotary encoder on each unit. Color and encoder position data was transmitted between Arduino Master board and I2C slave devices. I2C slave devices are linked up in sets of eight, and all the eight sets share four lines in a parallel configuration (5V, GND, SDA, SCL) (Figure 1). Game logic was programmed using Arduino IDE. Player scoring was indicated on a connected 16x32 RGB LED matrix panel.

A modular design allows interchangeable sizes of the caps of the rotary encoders to cater to the various types of trainings for fine motor skills. Traditional training methods often include multiple devices to train these separate functions. Our system sought to cater to the different types of trainings using this interchangeable structure. Rotary encoder with full rotation, which supports two ways of input-pushing and turning, was used as the main controller for our game. By referring to the standard dimensions of assessment tools in Action Arm Research Test (ARAT) [21], additional knobs with four different diameters (2.5cm, 5cm, 7.5cm, 10cm) can be attached on the rotary encoder (diameter: 0.7cm) to train various hand functions such as gasping and pinching that are commonly used in daily life (Figure 2, Figure 3). The targeted motions and examples of the relevant daily activities are illustrated in Table 1.

Tasks	Illustration	Controller Size	Daily activities (examples)
Reaching & Pushing		0.6cm, 2.5 cm, 5cm, 7.5cm, 10cm	Reaching a direction/ an object
Grasping & Turning		5cm, 7.5cm, 10cm	Opening bottles or jars, turning door knobs, holding a cup
Pinching & Turning		0.6cm, 2.5 cm	Turning a key, picking up a coin

Table 1 Targeted motions and examples of relevant activities

Based on the suggestion from therapists, and also by referring to the dimensions of a currently commonly used upper limb training checkerboard, the playable area of the board was set as 96cm by 96cm to provide sufficient spatial affordance for shoulder training. Therapist can select appropriate work areas (i.e. rows of LEDs) and size of controllers, depending on each patient's range-of-motion and training needs.

Game Design: Lights Invader

Different mini games can be created on the interactive board by defining game rules and controlling certain features of the LEDs, such as colors, patterns or speed. For example, our first game "Lights Invader" was designed in the way that player needs to protect four blue LEDs in the central of the board by defeating the red invaders getting closer to it. Red LEDs randomly light up from four sides of the board and move towards

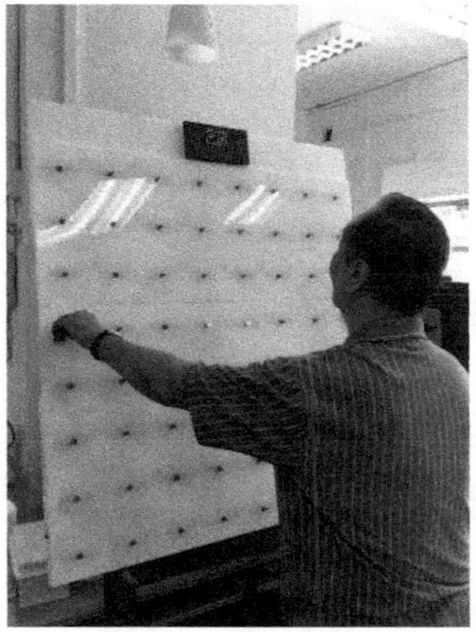

Figure 4: User testing (single-player)

Figure 5: Collaborative gameplay

the blue area in the center. The invader moves at the speed of 5 seconds in level one, 3 seconds in level two, and 2 seconds in level three. Player needs to turn/press the red LED off before they reach the blue area to score one point. The player will lose one point once the blue area is attacked by the red invader. In two-player collaborative gameplay, two players are required to eliminate the red LED invaders together by using one gaming board. The invader moves at the speed of 3 seconds in level one, 2 seconds in level two, 1 second in level three. The player(s) will need to score 50 points to complete level one, 100 points to complete level two and 150 points in level three. The goal/dosage is set for testing purpose for now, and it can be modified by therapist in the future.

Preliminary User Testing

The purpose of usability testing was mainly to help us to understand whether: (1) the game is fun to play with, (2) the interface is appropriate, (3) the game challenge level is appropriate (not too easy or too difficult), (4) the game tasks can guide appropriate rehabilitation movements, (5) the game board can support two players to play together. System Usability Scale (SUS), a ten-item 5-point Likert scale (from 1 "disagree" to 5 "agree") was used in the testing to obtain subjective assessments of usability. A few questions to understand user suggestions regarding the game design were also asked.

Eight stroke patients (6 males, 2 females) from Adventist Nursing and Rehabilitation Center (ANRC) with a mean age at 62.87 (SD=14.64) were invited to play the game. Five of them have full active range of motion on both arms and three have partial range of motion with the affected arm. One participant had the problem of left neglect following stroke. Two of them have Mild Cognitive Impairment (MCI). Participants were invited to play the game one-by-one after a brief introduction and demonstration on how to play the game. They were asked to play all the three levels of "Lights Invader" in standing position first by pressing the button, and then by turning the knobs with their affected arm (Figure 4). After the testing session, participants were asked to fill up the usability questionnaire, followed with a short interview. Participants were randomly paired into groups to play the collaborative game (Figure 5); the gameplay was observed by our researcher and two therapists.

Results and Discussion

1. Game Interface: all the participants reported that the game interface is easy to understand, the prototype was easy to use, and they would like to play the game frequently in the future. None of them thought they need the support of a technical person to play the game. All of them agree that the various functions in the game were well integrated without inconsistency. Five out of eight of them believed that most of people can easily learn how to play the game without learning a lot of things. Three selected the option "agree somewhat" as to whether they thought it may not be easy for people with severe dementia to learn. One therapist noted that two participants who refused to play the Kinect games (center activity) with the reason that "I don't know how to play" when asked to try out our prototype, agreed to play without hesitation. We assume it was because the tangible element made the game technology look more accessible and less intimidating.

2. Gameplay: all the patients agreed the game was fun to play with. Participants stated the game required high

concentration and hand-eye coordination, and the game was also considered helpful to train cognitive skills, visual attention and response speed.

3. Feedback: participants thought the color indication and score display was clear and easy to understand. However, visual and sound feedback was recommended for further improvement: (1) showing indication when being attacked by the invaders, (2) adding music to make the experience more engaging, and (3) adding "beep" sound to help patient (especially for those who have partial neglect) to be more alert when the invaders are getting closer.

4. Challenges: seven of them agreed that "the game is fun to play with". The only participant who selected "agree somewhat" thought the game was too easy for him to play. He suggested that the "invaders" should move faster and we could include more "invaders" to make the game more challenging. Six patients agreed that they felt very confident playing the game, while another two participants selected "agree somewhat" and one participant chose "neutral". The main reason was "speed is too fast" in the last level. Therapists suggested that we should allow them to select the level of difficulty by simply modifying some parameter (e.g. speed) so that they can prescribe game tasks that suits patient capacities.

5. Social Interaction: Verbal collaboration was observed at the beginning of the gameplay; more physical collaborations were observed after playing together for a while. Players were observed helping their partners to "kill" the invader at the other side. Two therapists who observed the game session suggested that the board can be used in two-player collaborative play as patient can stretch out to help with each other so that the reaching training still can be achieved. Yet, two players with different stroke severity may have different level of performance was better played to help their partner more often, so that they may end up exercising more than the "weaker one". Designers may want to carefully design the game rules to encourage the weaker player to perform more exercises.

6. Other Features: three participants suggested that the height of the prototype should be adjustable to allow for patient to play in sitting position as well, so it can cater to the needs of wheelchair-bounded patients. One therapist suggested a stand for the gaming board which can adjust height and angle to cater the training needs for patients with different severity levels/at different recovery stages.

Conclusion

The preliminary user testing suggested that the tangible game interface is simple and intuitive enough for the elderly patients to understand. Feedback needs to be enhanced to make the game experience more engaging. In the future, we will develop two-player games by combining two of the interactive boards together to support both competitive and cooperative gameplay. A study will be conducted to compare the effects of the two-player competitive game, two-player cooperative game, single-player game, and traditional checkerboard on patient motivation, participation, and function recovery among stroke survivors.

Acknowledgements

This research is supported by the National Research Foundation, Prime Minister's Office, Singapore under its International Research Centres in Singapore Funding Initiative. We highly appreciate the support from ANRC, Singapore and Hikarisoft Co. Ltd in this study.

References

1. Rikke Aarhus, Erik Grönvall, Simon B. Larsen, Susanne Wollsen. 2011. Turning training into play: Embodied gaming, seniors, physical training and motivation. *Gerontechnology 10*, 2, 110-120.
2. Gazihan Alankus, Amanda Lazar, Matt May, and Caitlin Kelleher. 2010. Towards customizable games for stroke rehabilitation. In *Proceedings of the SIGCHI Conference on Human Factors in Computing Systems* (CHI '10). ACM, New York, NY, USA, 2113-2122. DOI=http://dx.doi.org/10.1145/1753326.1753649
3. Trent Apted, Judy Kay, and Aaron Quigley. 2006. Tabletop sharing of digital photographs for the elderly. In *Proceedings of the SIGCHI Conference on Human Factors in Computing Systems* (CHI '06)., 781-790. DOI=http://dx.doi.org/10.1145/1124772.1124887
4. William D Band and Barbara Sanders. 2007. Therapeutic exercise for physical therapist assistants (2nd. ed), Baltimore, MD : Lippincott Williams & Wilkins, 28-54.
5. Luuk Beursgens, Annick Timmermans, and Panos Markopoulos. 2012. Playful ARM hand training after stroke. In *CHI '12 Extended Abstracts on Human Factors in Computing Systems* (CHI EA '12), 2399-2404. DOI: http://dx.doi.org/10.1145/2212776.2223809
6. Burke, J., McNeill, M., Charles, D., Morrow, P., Crosbie, J., and McDonough, S., 2010. Designing engaging, playable games for rehabilitation. In *Proceedings of the 8th International Conference on Disability, Virtual Reality & Associated Technologies*, 195-201.
7. Burke, J.W., McNeill, M., Charles, D.K., Morrow, P.J., Crosbie, J.H., and McDonough, S.M., 2009. Optimising engagement for stroke rehabilitation using serious games. *The Visual Computer 25*, 12, 1085-1099.
8. Abel WL Chen, Yan Tong Koh, Sean WM Leong, Louisa WY Ng, Patricia SY Lee, and Gerald CH Koh. 2014. Post Community Hospital Discharge Rehabilitation Attendance: Self-Perceived Barriers and Participation over Time. *Annals of the Academy of Medicine, Singapore 43*, 3, 136-144.
9. Roberto Colombo, Fabrizio Pisano, Alessandra Mazzone, Carmen Delconte, Silvestro Micera, M Chiara Carrozza, Paolo Dario, and Giuseppe Minuco. 2007. Design strategies to improve patient motivation during robot-aided rehabilitation. *Journal of NeuroEngineering and Rehabilitation*, 4, 3.
10. Teresa M. Damush , Laurie Plue, Tamilyn Bakas, Arlene Schmid,and Linda S. Williams. 2007. Barriers and facilitators to exercise among stroke survivors. *Rehabilitation Nursing 32*, 6, 253-262.
11. Eletha Flores, Gabriel Tobon, Ettore Cavallaro, Francesca I. Cavallaro, Joel C. Perry, and Thierry Keller. 2008. Improving patient motivation in game development for motor deficit rehabilitation. In *Proceedings of the 2008 International Conference on Advances in Computer Entertainment Technology* (ACE '08), 381-384. DOI=http://dx.doi.org/10.1145/1501750.1501839
12. Kathrin M. Gerling, Frank P. Schulte, and Maic Masuch. 2011. Designing and evaluating digital games for frail elderly persons. In *Proceedings of the 8th International Conference on Advances in Computer Entertainment Technology* (ACE '11), Article 62 , 8 pages. DOI=http://dx.doi.org/10.1145/2071423.2071501
13. Ya-Xuan Hung, Pei-Chen Huang, Kuan-Ta Chen, and Woei-Chyn Chu.2016. What do stroke patients look for in game-based rehabilitation: a survey study. *Medicine 95*, 11.
14. Internet Stroke Center,2016,Stroke Statistics,Retrieved November 2, 2016 from http://www.strokecenter.org/patients/about-stroke/stroke-statistics/
15. Ard Jacobs, Annick Timmermans, Marc Michielsen, Maaiken Vander Plaetse, and Panos Markopoulos. 2013.

CONTRAST: gamification of arm-hand training for stroke survivors. In *CHI '13 Extended Abstracts on Human Factors in Computing Systems* (CHI EA '13), 415-420.DOI:http://dx.doi.org/10.1145/2468356.2468430

16. Michelle J Johnson. 2006. Recent trends in robot-assisted therapy environments to improve real-life functional performance after stroke. *Journal of Neuroengineering and Rehabilitation 3*, 1, 1.
17. Suhas Govind Joshi and Heidi Bråthen. 2016. Lowering the Threshold: Reconnecting Elderly Users with Assistive Technology Through Tangible Interfaces. In *International Conference on Human Aspects of IT for the Aged Population* Springer, 52-63.
18. Michael T. Jurkiewicz, Susan Marzolini and Paul Oh. 2011. Adherence to a home-based exercise program for individuals after stroke. *Topics in stroke rehabilitation 18*, 3, 277-284.
19. Gerald Choon-Huat Koh, Sanjiv K. Saxena, Tze-Pin Ng, David Yong, Ngan-Phoon Fong. 2012. Effect of duration, participation rate, and supervision during community rehabilitation on functional outcomes in the first poststroke year in Singapore. *Archives of physical medicine and rehabilitation 93*, 2, 279-286.
20. Nancy G. Kutner, Rebecca Zhang, Andrew J. Butler, Steven L. Wolf, and Jay L. Alberts. 2010. Quality-of-life change associated with robotic-assisted therapy to improve hand motor function in patients with subacute stroke: a randomized clinical trial. *Physical Therapy 90*, 4, 493-504.
21. Michelle McDonnell. 2008. Action research arm test. *Australian Journal of Physiotherapy 54*, 3, 220.
22. Joel C. Perry, Julien Andureu, Francesca Irene Cavallaro, Jan Veneman , Stefan Carmien and Thierry Keller. 2010. Effective game use in neurorehabilitation: user-centered perspectives. *Handbook of Research on Improving Learning and Motivation through Educational Games, IGI Global*.
23. Maša D. Popović, Miloš D. Kostić, Sindi Z. Rodić, and Ljubica M. Konstantinović. 2014. Feedback-Mediated Upper Extremities Exercise: Increasing Patient Motivation in Poststroke Rehabilitation. *Biomed Research International 2014*.
24. Kyuye Song, Sekwang Lee, Sung-Bom Pyun, and Laehyun Kim. 2016. Comparative Study of Tangible Tabletop and Computer-Based Training Interfaces for Cognitive Rehabilitation. In *International Conference on Universal Access in Human-Computer Interaction* Springer, 414-424.
25. Gary Kielhofner. 2009. Conceptual foundations of occupational therapy practice. FA Davis.67-86.
26. Katie Thomson, Alex Pollock, Carol Bugge, and Marian Brady. 2014. Commercial gaming devices for stroke upper limb rehabilitation: A systematic review. *International Journal of Stroke 9*, 4 (Jun), 479-488.
27. Brygg Ullmer and Hiroshi Ishii. Emerging frameworks for tangible user interfaces. *IBM systems journal 39*, 3.4, 915-931.
28. Derick T Wade, Fiona M Collen, Gillian F Robb, and Charles P Warlow. 1992. Physiotherapy intervention late after stroke and mobility. *British Medical Journal 304*, 6827 (Mar), 609-613.
29. Pan Wang, Raymond K.C. Koh, Christian Gilles Boucharenc, and Ching-Chiuan Yen. 2016. Lights Out: An Interactive Tangible Game for Training of Post-Stroke Reaching. In *Proceedings of the 2016 CHI Conference Extended Abstracts on Human Factors in Computing Systems* (CHI EA '16), USA, 1937-1944. DOI: http://dx.doi.org/10.1145/2851581.2892422
30. World Heart Federation,2016,The global burden of stroke,Retrieved November 2, 2016 from http://www.world-heart-federation.org/cardiovascular-health/stroke/

BalanSAR - Using Spatial Augmented Reality to Train Children's Balancing Skills in Physical Education

Danica Mast [1,2] d.mast@hhs.nl
Michel Bosman [1,3] m.h.bosman@hhs.nl
Sylvia Schipper [1,4] s.j.schipper@hhs.nl
Sanne de Vries [1] s.i.devries@hhs.nl

The Hague University of Applied Sciences
The Netherlands

1) *Research Group Healthy Lifestyle in a Supporting Environment*
2) *Communication & Multimedia Design,*
User Experience Design - Faculty IT & Design
3) *Physical Education & Motor Learning* - Faculty Health, Nutrition & Sport
4) Industrial Design Engineering - Faculty Technology, Innovation & Society

TEI '17, March 20-23, 2017, Yokohama, Japan
ACM 978-1-4503-4676-4/17/03.
http://dx.doi.org/10.1145/3024969.3025085

Abstract
Balancing is one of the essential motor skills to adopt and maintain an active lifestyle in child- and adulthood. Visual perception plays an important role in learning balancing skills. Current balancing exercises, however, offer few opportunities for practicing visual perception.

A technology we consider promising for Physical Education (PE) is Spatial Augmented Reality (SAR), the projection of (interactive) animations onto three-dimensional surfaces. We present BalanSAR, a novel combination of SAR, existing PE balancing exercises and traditional PE gym equipment. By projecting animations onto the gym floor and existing equipment, visual perception in balancing exercises can be practiced more effectively.

We propose a study to investigate the feasibility and the effect of using SAR on the efficiency and effectiveness of PE in terms of children's motor skills and their motivation in PE and physical activity in general.

Author Keywords
Physical education; balancing; motor skills; spatial augmented reality; projection mapping; exertion; motivation

ACM Classification Keywords
H.5.2 Information Interfaces and Presentation: User Interfaces - Miscellaneous.

H.5.2 Information Interfaces and Presentation: User Interfaces—evaluation/methodology; interaction styles

H.5.1 Multimedia Information Systems: Artificial, augmented and virtual realities

Introduction
In this project, existing knowledge about motor skills learning, visual perception, spatial augmented reality, exertion interfaces and gym equipment are linked to the wishes, needs and experiences of the current generation of children. Spatial Augmented Reality (SAR) is applied to existing balancing exercises using traditional equipment, transforming it into a novel application: BalanSAR.

By projecting (interactive) video images onto the gym floor and equipment in these exercises we can improve experience and stimulate visual perception and implicit learning. This technology offers the opportunity to stimulate the visual perception of children while balancing and hereby improving the motor skills learning process. For example, by projecting bubbles and fish swimming at various speeds along with the child during the exercise, the visual perception can be stimulated during the exercise, making the exercise more challenging and allows for different levels of difficulty. Applying (interactive) SAR, balancing exercises can automatically adapt to a child's particular motor skill level and stimulate their imagination and preferred learning style.

BalanSAR capitalizes on the needs of both PE teachers and children. Through interactive video projection and sensor technology it will become possible to:

- Improve balancing skills of children
- Positively influence the motor learning process of children
- Better differentiate and connect to the motor skill level of individual children
- Address the self-regulation learning process of children
- Letting children have control over their own learning process
- Appeal to the experiences and imagination of children

The purpose of our study is to investigate the feasibility and the effect of using spatial augmented reality on the efficiency and effectiveness of PE in terms of children's balancing skills and their motivation in PE and physical activity in general.

Related Work
Several related research areas were examined to gain necessary insight to develop and design BalanSAR.

Healthy Lifestyle & Motor Skills
The majority of children in the Netherlands don't meet the 60-minute physical activity guideline [9] [22]. Children are also significantly less fit, have poorer motor skills and are heavier than 30 years ago [21]. The control of fundamental motor skills is associated with children's physical activity level [2] [11] [15] [28]. There are also strong indications that there is a longitudinal relationship between mastery of fundamental motor skills at age six and physical activity at age 26 [1] [5] [10]. Children with good motor skills often have an active lifestyle, perform better cognitively and are less likely to be overweight and have falling accidents than children with poorer motor skills, both on the short and long term [1] [5] [10]. Practicing motor skills could lead to a healthier lifestyle on the long term.

Balancing

Fundamental motor skills can be divided into balancing, locomotive and manipulation skills. Balancing skills are conditional for the other two categories and the acquisition of more complex and context-specific motor skills [3]. Visual perception plays a crucial role in learning balancing skills. When a child balances, he will look at a fixed point (central observation), but from the corners of his eyes he will unconsciously register the moving environment (peripheral observation). Both sight and balancing affect each other in a cycle called the perception-action cycle [16].

PE teachers attempt to stimulate an active lifestyle. They do this (among other things) by focusing on motor skills development of children, a key objective of PE. During current PE lessons children often perform traditional balancing exercises; walking or doing exercises on floor lines, the bench (positioned normally, inverted or tilted against the wall rack) or on the beam. Fundamental balancing motor skills are practiced in this manner, but implicit ways to influence the visual perception are hardly taken into account.

Technology & PE

A national survey in 2013 shows PE teachers would like to gain more insight into children's motor skills and methods that can help develop those skills [19]. Co-creation sessions conducted with children (part of the NRO-NWO project 'Co-design with kids') show that children think of technological solutions when given design assignments to improve PE. Nevertheless, the gym space has hardly changed over the last decades., Even though technology has made its way into our daily lives and into the professional sports setting over the last few decades, within PE the use of technology is still very limited.

Exergames provide an interesting addition to PE that can motivate children into exercising. When taught within a learning framework, exergaming can help children to understand the effects of exercise and may motivate them to exercise and adopt a healthy lifestyle on the long term [8]. Furthermore, exergaming can improve balancing skills and exergames can be a practical tool in PE to improve postural stability of 9 and 10 year old children [24] [25].

Nintendo's Balance Board introduced balancing as a form of input for playing games. In WiiFit players can play multiple balancing games such as Hula Hoop, Snowboard Slalom, Tightrope Walk, Soccer Heading, etc. These games are nevertheless aimed at entertainment; motor learning is not a key objective.

A technology that seems promising for enhancing physical education is Spatial Augmented Reality (SAR, also known as projection mapping) [12]. SAR can provide an extra motivation when applied to traditional exercises. Hanging off a bar [13] shows that a projected animation of a river and a raft on the floor can motivate people to hold on to the bar above the projection longer than without the animation.

Prototype

BalanSAR consists of three balancing exercises that are frequently used in PE. A video of our prototypes can be found at: https://youtu.be/2bduhPHjWX4

Hardware

A video projector projects (interactive) animations on various undergrounds (gym floor, bench, equipment). The video projector is placed at an angle in front of the setup to make sure as much floor space as possible can be projected upon with a minimum amount of shadowing.

Figure 1: Bench-Balancing

Figure 2: Balancing Stones

Figure 3: Rope Swinging

BENCH-BALANCING
(Figure 1) A traditional exercise where the bench is either put normally, upside down, at a vertical angle, partially or fully on a moving surface, to vary the difficulty of the exercise.

BALANCING STONES
(Figure 2) A similar exercise to the previous one, but with balancing stones instead of a bench. This allows for different balancing skills.

ROPE-SWINGING
(Figure 3) An exercise where two benches are used with swinging ropes in between. The goal of this exercise is to swing from one bench to the other.

Software
We developed software in Processing that generates an animation of fishes and bubbles. This corresponds with the theme that is already being used in PE classes for these exercises (PE teachers tell the story that the bench is a bridge in a pond, surrounded by sea creatures).
Variables that can be adjusted are the quantity, speed, size, direction and background color of the animated objects. The generated animation is streamed via Syphon so that it can be received by projection mapping software (MadMapper).

Proposed Study
We will study usability, user experience, the short and long-term effects (on user experience, motivation, motor and balancing skills) by testing the exercises over a period with multiple classes in primary education with children aged 4 to 8 years old. These tests will result in iterations to refine BalanSAR and gain ideas for further application of SAR in PE.

Usability
We will conduct usability tests to make BalanSAR fast and easy for PE teachers to use and intuitive for children to play. By conducting play tests, observation and interviews we will determine possible improvements

User Experience
User experience tests will give insight in the effect of SAR on the experience of children, making BalanSAR better targeted at their imagination and more motivating. By observing, video analysis and user experience testing methods such as the Smileyometer [18] [17] and FunSorter [20] [26] we will test both long and short-term user experience:

- How do children experience BalanSAR when first encountered?
- How do children experience BalanSAR on the long term?

Measuring Balancing Skills
By testing the prototype with children, we aim to gain insight into the impact of SAR on the motor skills learning process. We will measure how well the children can balance by performing measurements pre and post intervention. Balancing as a skill can be divided in static (standing) and active (moving) balancing [24].
Functional assessment of balancing skills can be done with tests such as the timed Up & Go test (TUG) [14] [27], Functional Reach Test [7] [6] and the Balance Error Scoring System (BESS) [23]. For Quantitative (computerized) assessment, the Wii Balance Board has proven to be a valid inexpensive device [4]. We will have to examine the validity for using these instruments to measure children's balancing skills.

Further Work

Software

Variables we consider adding to the software are:

- Various thematizations
  - Canyons to address vertigo and possible fearful-emotions
  - Adding scary animals (crocodiles, sharks) to make the exercise more exciting for older children
- Adding helping 'friends' or animals for emotional support and feedback
- Giving children control of thematizations and level of difficulty

Based on the results of user tests we will decide which additions will be made to the current software.

Interaction

By adding interaction to our prototype, we can make the exercises more challenging and improve the user experience. An interactive feature we are considering is to have the animation react to the user movements to adjust the level to the child's skills, for example touching physical or projected objects while balancing like adding interactive fishing rods to catch fish.

Gamification

By turning some of the mentioned interactive features into games, having a goal and possibly keeping track of progress, we expect we can motivate children to keep practicing longer. We are planning to research the effects of gamification on user experience, motivation and learning effects in a future study.

Realization

We are working together with a gym equipment manufacturer/supplier and a company that provides technical projection solutions to work towards a production model that can be used in PE practice. When realizing BalanSAR as a product we have to take into account the needs of PE teachers, schools and children.

A technological product that can be used in a PE setting by PE teachers needs to be:

- Easy to use (No complicated interface, no programming, no time-consuming setup)
- Versatile (Usable for various age categories and various exercises)
- Affordable (Schools have limited budgets, no expensive computers or hardware, preferable using equipment already owned by schools or available in the gym space)

These needs were collected during a brainstorm session at the 2016 'from playing tag to tagging'-event (van tikken naar taggen) where we demonstrated our early prototypes to PE teachers.

Conclusion

Balancing is an essential motor skill for a child's ability to adopt an active lifestyle. Balancing is frequently practiced during PE, but the role of visual perception on this skill is rarely taken into account. BalanSAR creates an environment that interacts with the child, supporting the (motor skills) learning process. The current prototypes give us the opportunity to test if Spatial Augmented Reality is a useful addition to PE.

References

1 Bernard, K. Long-Term Importance of Fundamental Motor Skills: A 20-Year Follow-Up Study. *Apaq, 31(1)* (2014), 31-67.

2 Bouffard, M., Watkinson, E. J., Thompson, L. P., Causgrove Dunn, J. L., and Romanow, S. K. A test of the activity deficit hypothesis with children with movement difficulties. *Adapted Physical Activity Quarterly, 13* (1996), 61-73.

3 Clark, J. E., Metcalfe, J. S. The mountain of motor development: A metaphor.. *Motor development: Research and reviews, 2* (2002), 163-190.

4 Clark, R. A., Bryant, A. L., Pua, Y., McCrory, P., Bennell, K., and Hunt, M. Validity and reliability of the Nintendo Wii balance board for assessment of standing balance. *Gait & Posture. 31 (3)* (2010), 307–310.

5 D'Hondt, E., Deforche, B., Gentier, I., Verstuyf, J., Vaeyens, R., Bourdeaudhuij, I., and Lenoir, M. A longitudinal study of gross motor coordination and weight status in children.. *Obesity, 22(6)* (2014), 1505-15-11.

6 Donahoe, B., Turner, D, and Worrell, T. The Use of Functional Reach as a Measurement of Balance in Boys and Girls Without Disabilities Ages 5 to 15 Years. *Pediatric Physical Therapy 6.4* (1994), 189-193.

7 Duncan, P. W., Weiner, D. K., Chandler, J., and Studenski, S. Functional reach: a new clinical measure of balance. *Journal of gerontology 45.6* (1990), M192-M197.

8 Ennis, C. D. Implications of exergaming for the physical education curriculum in the 21st century. *Journal of Sport and Health Science, 2(3)* (2013), 152-157.

9 Hildebrandt, V. H., Bernaards, C. M., and Stubbe, J. H. *Trendrapport Bewegen en Gezondheid 2010/2011 (TNO)*. Leiden, 2013.

10 Lloyd, M., Saunders, T. J., Bremer, E., and Tremblay, M. S. Long-term importance of fundamental motor skills: a 20-year follow-up study. *Adapted physical activity quarterly, 31(1)* (2014), 67-78.

11 Lubans, D. R., Morgan, P. J., Cliff, D. P., Barnett, L. M., and Okely, A. D. Fundamental movement skills in children and adolescents. *Sports medicine, 40(12)* (2010), 1019-4035.

12 Mast, D., de Krom, J., and de Vries, S. Exploring the Application of Interactive Video Projection in Physical Education. *In Proceedings of the Ninth International Conference on Tangible, Embedded, and Embodied Interaction* (2015), 551-555.

13 Mueller, F., Toprak, C., Graether, E., Walmink, W., Bongers, B., & van den Hoven, E. Hanging off a bar. *In CHI'12 Extended Abstracts on Human Factors in Computing Systems* (2012), 1055-1058.

14 Nitz , J. C, Kuys, S., Isles , R., and Fu, S. Is the Wii Fit™ a new-generation tool for improving balance, health and well-being? A pilot study. *Climacteric,13(5)* (2010), 487-491.

15 Okely, A. D., Booth, M. L., and Patterson, J. W. Relationship of physical activity to fundamental movement skills among adolescents. *Medicine and science in sports and exercise, 33(11)* (2001), 1899-1904.

16 Pijpers, R., Savelsbergh, G.J.P., Bakker, F. De koppeling tussen relevante informatie en bewegingen (1). *Lichamelijke Opvoeding 80 (4)* (1992), 152-155.

17 Read, J.C., MacFarlane, S. Casey, C. Endurability, engagement and expectations: Measuring children's fun. *Interaction Design and Children*, 2 (2008), 1-23.

18 Read, J. C. Validatin the fun toolkit: An instrument for measuring children's opinions of technology. *Cognition, Technology & Work*, 10, 2 (2008), 119-128.

19 Reijgersberg, N., Werff, H. v.d., & Lucassen, J. *Nulmeting bewegingsonderwijs: onderzoek naar de organisatie van het bewegingsonderwijs in het primair onderwijs.* Mulier Instituut, Utrecht, 2013.

20 Risdwn, K., Hanna, E., Kanerva, A. Dimensions of intrinsic motivation in children's favorite computer activities. *Society for Research in Child Development*, 7 (1997).

21 Runhaar, J., Collard, D. C. M., Singh, A. S, A. S., Kemper, H. C. G., Mechelen, W. van, and Chinapaw, M. Motor fitness in Dutch youth: differences over a 26-year period (1980–2006). *Journal of Science and Medicine in Sport, 13(3)* (2010), 323-328.

22 Schonbeck, Y., Talma, H., van Dommelen, P., Bakker, B., Buitendijk, S. E., Hirasing, R. A., and van Buuren, S. Increase in prevalence of overweight in Dutch children and adolescents: a comparison of nationwide growth studies in 1980, 1997 and 2009.. *PLoS One, 6(11)* (2011), e27608. doi: 10.1371/journal.pone.0027608.

23 Sheehan, D.P., Lafave, M. R., Katz, L. Intra-rater and inter-rater reliability of the balance error scoring system in pre-adolescent school children. *Measurement in Physical Education and Exercise Science*, 15, 3 (2011), 234-243.

24 Sheehan, D. P. and Katz, L. The effects of a daily, 6-week exergaming curriculum on balance in fourth grade children. *Journal of Sport and Health Science 2(3)* (2013), 131-137.

25 Sheehan, D. P. and Katz, L. The impact of a six week exergaming curriculum on balance with grade three school children using the Wii Fit+.. *International Journal of Computer Science in Sport, 11(3)* (2012), 5-22.

26 Sim, G., MacFarlane, S., Read, J. All work an no play: Measuring fun, usability and learning in software for children. *Computers & education*, 46, 3 (2006), 235-248.

27 Williams, E. N., Carroll, S. G., Reddihough, D. S., Phillips, B. A., and Galea, M. P. Investigation of the timed 'up & go'test in children. *Developmental Medicine & Child Neurology 47(8)* (2005), 518-524.

28 Wrotniak, B. H., Epstein, L. H., Dorn, J. M., Jones, K. E., and Kondilis, V. A. he relationship between motor proficiency and physical activity in children.. *Pediatrics, 118(6)* (2006), e1758-e1765.

ShapeShift: Mediating User Interaction Through Augmented Shading and Shadow

Dixon Lo
Carnegie Mellon University
5000 Forbes Ave.
Pittsburgh, PA 15213, USA
dlo1@andrew.cmu.edu

Austin Lee
Carnegie Mellon University
5000 Forbes Ave.
Pittsburgh, PA 15213, USA
austinslee@cmu.edu

Jiyoung Ko
Carnegie Mellon University
5000 Forbes Ave.
Pittsburgh, PA 15213, USA
jko1@andrew.cmu.edu

TEI '17, March 20-23, 2017, Yokohama, Japan
ACM 978-1-4503-4676-4/17/03.
http://dx.doi.org/10.1145/3024969.3025088

Abstract
In this paper, we describe ShapeShift, our initial exploration into creating a holistic object augmentation by extending physical properties of objects with augmented reality. As a first step, we choose manipulations of shading and shadow for exploration. Shading and shadow are form-giving properties of an object. These attributes play two main roles in perceiving the object: (1) they delineate physical properties of the object (form and texture) and (2) contextualize the object's relation to its environment. This project aims to give shadow and shading the ability to change the perception of an object, allowing for new affordances and interactions to emerge.

Author Keywords
Shadow; Shading; Augmented Reality

ACM Classification Keywords
H.5.1. Multimedia Information Systems [Artificial, augmented, and virtual realities]; H.5.2 User Interfaces [Theory and methods]

Introduction
Consumer augmented reality (AR) is bringing a world of mixed reality into our everyday lives through various

display techniques that are screen/camera based, see-through based, and projection based. These technologies are changing the way we interact with our environment. However, future visions of AR are replete with overlaid textual and symbolic representations of information.

Pitfalls of using AR to augment objects

Criticisms of overlaid textual and symbolic visions of AR such as Keiichi Matsuda's "Hyper Reality" video [8] show a dystopian future where such methods result in a cognitively oversaturated world. To avoid this, we advocate AR to be used in a way that is perceived as integrated with the object it is augmenting.

Potentials of using AR to augment future interfaces

Applications of AR are not limited to existing technology; research into new types of interfaces, such as Radical Atoms [3], foresees our interaction with objects that no longer have static form. These objects are no longer able to rely on traditional modes of static form-based affordance. Here, we see an opportunity for AR to introduce more malleable and situation-based-affordances into these objects.

Augmenting physical properties

To address the pitfalls of the current approach in using AR on objects, and to illustrate the possibilities of AR with future interfaces, we have chosen to explore the augmentation of shadows and shading, which are physical qualities that all objects already have, as a way to integrate digital and physical into a holistic object.

Manipulations of shading and shadow utilize the user's existing schema of the physical attributes to create an intuitive understanding of the augmented layer instead of relying on textual or symbolic layers, which require cognitive interpretation. Furthermore, the form-giving qualities of shading and shadow can be used to create an illusion of shape change, allowing previously static forms to exhibit on-demand affordances to guide user interactions. Given the aforementioned qualities of shading and shadow, we also envision this new approach of AR to guide interactions with future shape-changing interfaces.

Related Work

Augmented forms on physical objects

Leithinger [1] demonstrates the usage of AR to complete forms, which have their structure defined by a physical actuated pin array. Similar to this project, we create objects that are a combination of physical and digital. In contrast to Leithinger's approach of using AR to augment incomplete forms, we aim to modify the completed form of physical objects, enabling those objects to convey more information beyond their static form.

Augmented shadow

Underkoffer [5] demonstrated the use of simulated shadows to visualize the casted shadow of buildings at different times of day. In this research, a solid shadow is generated from a building model without walls; Underkoffer allows an incomplete form to generate a complete shadow. Another project, Remnants of Form [10], allows an object to show emotion through its shadow, an indicator to the viewer that a certain type of interaction is expected (e.g. for the viewer to seem less aggressive when the shadow displays fear). As a final example, Pne-UI [6] uses a digital shadow as an interface to manipulate soft body interfaces.

By utilizing a similar interplay between form and shadow/shading as the above examples, we aim to give illusions of form change within the object via shadow and shading manipulation.

Using attributes of objects to display digital information/affordances
In "The coming age of calm technology", Mark Weiser [7] describes a string that shows the transfer of digital information, where the physical behavior of the string is used to visualize the abstract transfer of information. In "Switch! Energy Ecologies in Everyday Life" Maze and Redstrom [9] describe a piece of furniture that visualizes energy habits through the fading, flaking, cracking and wrinkling of its surface. Timo Arnall's [11] work uses light and long exposure photography to construct light based structures of wireless signals.

These projects are examples of the physical properties of objects being used to communicate previously unseen attributes of those objects. We have found that shadow and shading can also be used to visualize invisible information contained in objects. For example, data can be given weight by having an object appear to sink into the table because of the quantity of data it contains.

Shape changing interfaces & affordances
The fictional material Perfect Red [3] demonstrates the vision of radical atoms, that objects and interfaces no longer have static physical forms.

Because of the lack of consistent forms, it is difficult for these objects to communicate what they are able to do through the traditional concept of static affordance. Here, shadow and shading manipulations can be used with form changing interfaces to foreshadow and communicate possible future states of the objects.

Exploring Shading / Shadow
Shading and shadow are form-giving qualities of an object. These attributes play two main roles in perceiving the object: (1) they delineate physical properties of the object (form and texture) and (2) contextualize the object's relation to its environment. In this paper, our aim is to extend the ability of the two form giving qualities to cause changes in the perception of an object, allowing for new affordances and interactions to emerge. By doing so, we can enable hardware interfaces to be perceived as malleable as software interfaces. At the same time, we aim to create virtual layers integrated with the object, such that after augmentation, the combination of object and augmented information is viewed as a single holistic object. Shadow and shading present an excellent area to apply this concept, as they cannot exist independently of the object.

We envision the usage of form giving attributes of shadow and shading to extend existing physical properties of static objects. This paper introduces four examples of shadow and shading manipulation to illustrate its potential for shaping interaction: (1) Localized shading change, (2) full object shading change, (3) object shadow change, and (4) environmental shading change. We further hypothesize that the illusion of form change can be used to indicate interaction possibilities for future shape changing interfaces.

(1) Localized Shading Change

Figure 1: Example of localized shading manipulation.

Description
Localized shading changes give the illusion of shape change to targeted areas of an object (Figure 1).

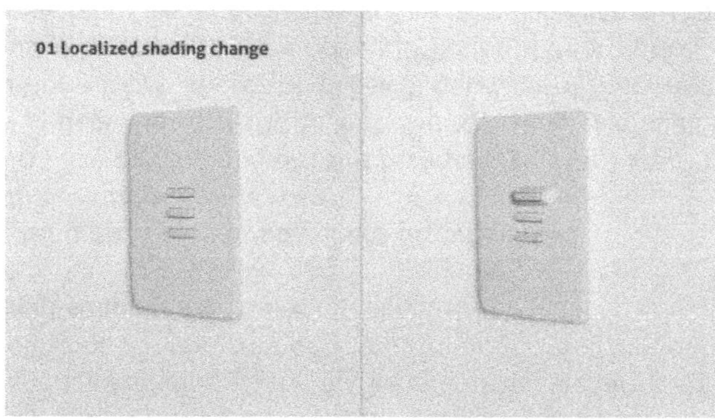

Figure 2: On the right, localized shading manipulations add more elevation to emphasize the top button.

Applications in current devices
In traditional digital interfaces, designers are able to highlight or de-emphasize on screen controls through manipulation of digital properties such as color and opacity. This creates a clear hierarchy guiding users to the correct interactions. By creating the illusion of elevation change through manipulation of shading in AR, we can create previously nonexistent hierarchy in hardware interfaces as well (Figure 2). This is especially useful for devices with no screen-based interface.

Applications in future shape changing interfaces
Localized shape change can be used to indicate the possibilities of manipulation of a shape changing form. The illusion of shape change can be used to simulate the actual change that will occur if an interaction is performed, allowing the user to anticipate possible shape change options.

(2) Full Object Shading Change

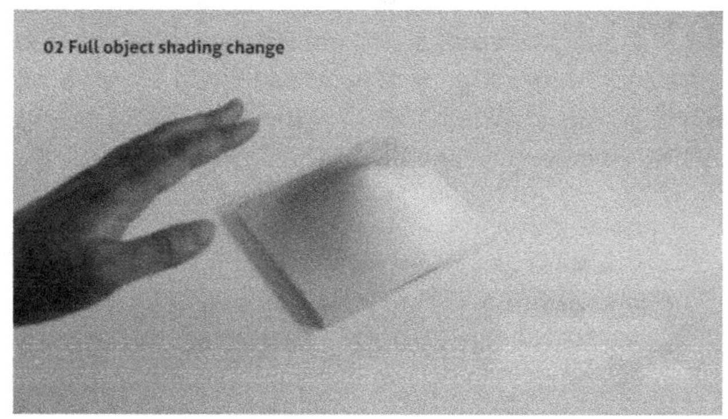

Figure 3: Example of full object shading manipulation.

Description
Use of shading changes to manipulate overall form of a full object (Figure 3).

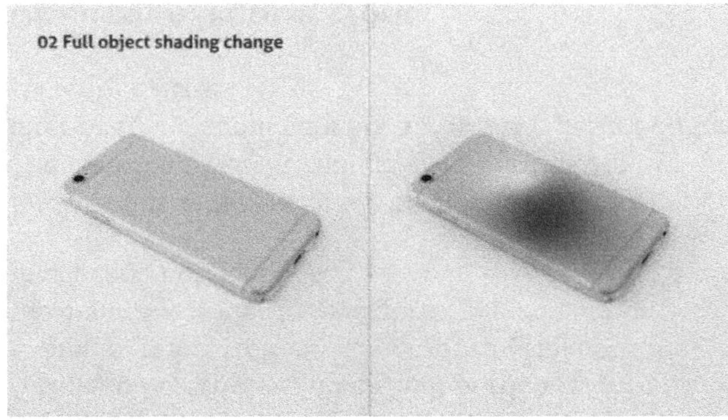

Figure 4: Phone on right bends upward to signal "Pick me up".

Applications in current devices
Our example shows an object expanding upward, drawn toward the user's hand (Figure 4). This is similar to the hover or mouse over state in the graphical user interfaces (GUI). Additionally, an object operating as part of a group is able to signal priority over surrounding objects.

Applications in future shape changing interfaces
Future shape changing objects will also need to operate as a system of artifacts. Here, flexibility of form allows objects to differentiate themselves from their neighbors.

(3) Object Shadow Change

Description
Manipulation of the shadow casted by objects to give them a feeling of weightlessness (Figure 5).

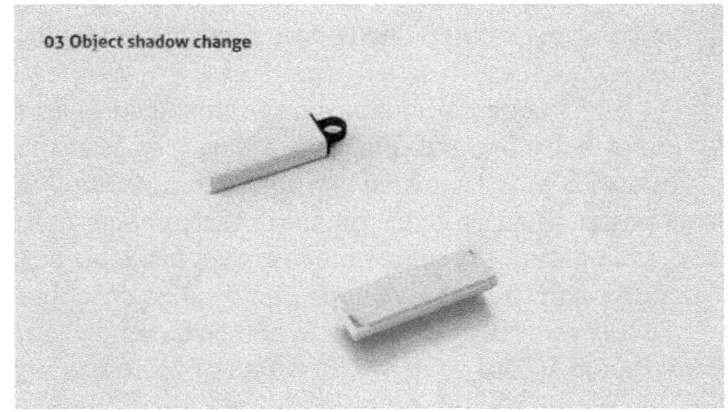

Figure 5: An empty USB drive floats, while the drive weighted down by data sits on tabletop.

Applications in current devices
The illusion of variable weight can be used for a variety of purposes. It can be used to visualize state changes within the object. For example, when files are deleted from an external hard disk, the disk can begin to float to indicate that it is unburdened (Figure 5). This illusion can also be used to signal priority; a higher priority document can float higher on a desk for example. Variable weight can also be used to imbue objects with animalistic qualities or emotion; a floating object can be seen as happier, or less formal.

Applications in future shape changing interfaces
Projects such as ZeroN [4] introduce interfaces that defy gravity. Through the manipulation of shadow, we are able to simulate a floating effect to hint that such interactions are possible with the interface.

(4) Environmental Shading Change

Description

Manipulation of shading of an object's immediate surrounding to give the object an illusion of weight by sinking it into the surface it rests on (Figure 6).

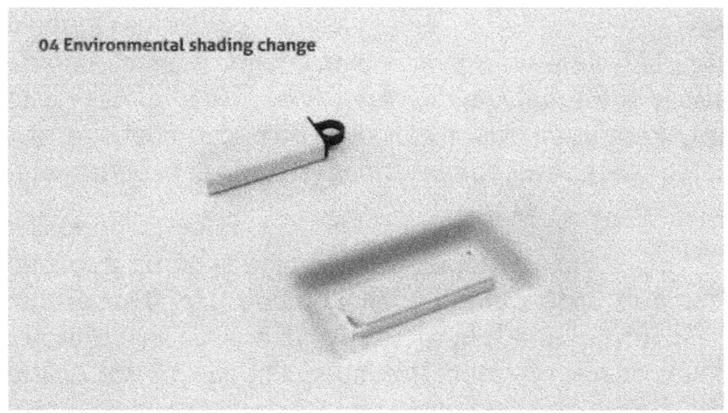

Figure 6: USB drive filled with data sinks into table, while the empty drive sits on top.

Applications in current devices

A sinking object gives a sense of burden (Figure 6). For example, a smartphone can gradually sink into the table surface under the weight of accumulating unchecked notifications.

Applications in future shape changing interfaces

The illusion of weight change will afford future interfaces the same benefits as we have described for current devices.

Discussion/Future Work

We have found that that changes in shading are able to create an illusion of shape change within a physical form for holistic object augmentation. Shadow manipulation and local area shading manipulation were both successful in creating the illusion of an object with variable weight. However, the extent of the illusion is contingent on the shape of the object; for example, it is easier to create the illusion of shape change on flat, non-textured surfaces.

We have received a range of feedback on our early prototypes. With current day objects in mind, respondents thought that our concept of ShapeShift may be useful in the medical training. Objects on a surgeon's tray are laid out in specific arrangements, and it is important that there is nothing blocking their view of instruments and their patient. Assuming a world of pervasive AR, using shadow for full body form change and weight change to indicate the correct instrument to use could be less intrusive than a disconnected textual overlay.

Our next step is to implement shading and shadow change on both screen/camera based and see-through based AR platforms.

On see through platforms, such as the Hololens, we realize the challenge of displaying shadows when rendered pixels blend additively with the background. The Hololens uses a combination of a tinted visor that naturally darkens areas not covered by rendered pixels, and perceptual brightness illusions [2] to create the effect of dark colors in Holograms. We will explore similar techniques in our implementation.

Finally, having explored shading and shadow as an example of holistic object augmentation, we aim to expand to other physical attributes of objects for similar experimentation; color, sound, and texture are examples of such attributes.

References

1. Daniel Leithinger, Sean Follmer, Alex Olwal, Samuel Luescher, Akimitsu Hogge, Jinha Lee, and Hiroshi Ishii. 2013. Sublimate: state-changing virtual and physical rendering to augment interaction with shape displays. In *Proceedings of the SIGCHI Conference on Human Factors in Computing Systems* (CHI '13). ACM, New York, NY, USA, 1441-1450. DOI: http://dx.doi.org/10.1145/2470654.2466191

2. Edward H Adelson. 1993. Perceptual Organization and the Judgement of Brightness. *Science 262, no. 5142* (1993): 2042-044. Doi:10.1126/science.8266102.

3. Hiroshi Ishii, Dávid Lakatos, Leonardo Bonanni, and Jean-Baptiste Labrune. 2012. Radical atoms: beyond tangible bits, toward transformable materials. *interactions* 19.1:38-51.

4. Jinha Lee, Rehmi Post, and Hiroshi Ishii. 2011. ZeroN: mid-air tangible interaction enabled by computer controlled magnetic levitation. In *Proceedings of the 24th annual ACM symposium on User interface software and technology* (UIST '11). ACM, New York, NY, USA, 327-336. DOI=http://dx.doi.org/10.1145/2047196.2047239

5. John Underkoffler and Hiroshi Ishii. 1999. Urp: a luminous-tangible workbench for urban planning and design. In *Proceedings of the SIGCHI conference on Human Factors in Computing Systems*(CHI '99). ACM, New York, NY, USA, 386-393. DOI=http://dx.doi.org/10.1145/302979.303114

6. Lining Yao, Ryuma Niiyama, Jifei Ou, Sean Follmer, Clark Della Silva, and Hiroshi Ishii. 2013. PneUI: pneumatically actuated soft composite materials for shape changing interfaces. In *Proceedings of the 26th annual ACM symposium on User interface software and technology* (UIST '13). ACM, New York, NY, USA, 13-22. DOI: http://dx.doi.org/10.1145/2501988.2502037

7. Mark Weiser, John Seely Brown. 1997. The coming age of calm technology. *Beyond calculation*. 75-85.

8. Matsuda Keiichi. 2016. HYPER-REALITY. Video. Retrieved October 25, 2016 from https://vimeo.com/166807261

9. Ramia Mazé, Johan Redström. 2008. Switch! Energy ecologies in everyday life. *International Journal of Design* 2.3.

10. Sang-won Leigh, Asta Roseway, and Ann Paradiso. 2015. Remnance of Form: Altered Reflection of Physical Reality. In *Proceedings of the Ninth International Conference on Tangible, Embedded, and Embodied Interaction* (TEI '15). ACM, New York, NY, USA, 411-412. DOI=http://dx.doi.org/10.1145/2677199.2690874

11. Timo Arnall. 2013. Making Visible: Mediating the material of emerging technology. Ph.D Dissertation.

Seamless Multithread Films in Virtual Reality

Oneris Daniel Rico Garcia
Keio University
Yokohama, Japan
garciaoneris@kmd.keio.ac.jp

Benjamin Tag
Keio University
Yokohama, Japan
tagbenja@kmd.keio.ac.jp

Naohisa Ohta
Keio University
Yokohama, Japan
naohisa@kmd.keio.ac.jp

Kazunori Sugiura
Keio University
Yokohama, Japan
uhyo@kmd.keio.ac.jp

TEI '17, March 20-23, 2017, Yokohama, Japan
ACM 978-1-4503-4676-4/17/03.
http://dx.doi.org/10.1145/3024969.3025096

Abstract
In this paper we are proposing a new system for the production of VR stories that allow users seamless interaction with the content. Our system plays real life footage rather than animation allowing for interactive live-action experiences. The unaware empowered users take subliminal decisions by focusing their attention at predefined ROIs. The moment a decision is taken is always placed seconds before the actual video branching happens to allow the system to preload only the chosen storyline in order to keep the computational workload as low as possible. We believe that this unique system will not only change the way we experience VR contents, but will rather lead to a paradigm shift in film production.

ACM Classification Keywords
H.5.1 [Information interfaces and presentation (e.g., HCI)]: Artificial, augmented, and virtual realities

Author Keywords
Virtual Reality, Seamless, Filmmaking, Multithread Stories

Introduction and Motivation
If we put a cat into a box with a device that has a 50% chance of killing the cat within a minute, the cat is dead and alive at the same time, when we open said box after one minute. Erwin Schrödinger's theory of the multiverse says

that when we decide between options, all of the options are happening, but in different parallel universes [8]. When a scriptwriter lets film characters take one or another decision, the other option is therefore happening simultaneously, we could just not get to see it. The goal of this project is to give audiences a seamless opportunity to choose the path of the story they are currently engaged with.

"Heavy Rain" was released in 2010 [1]. This video game let players choose what they wanted to do, changing the story as they played along. Therefore, different people playing the same game experience different courses of action as they take different choices. The concept of interaction with content used in games has often been the foundation for interactive video contents. However, having to have an obvious click in form of an artifact to select an option on the screen takes users out of the story and back to the artifact. Therefore, with every choice the users can make, the immersion is interrupted.

The development of Virtual Reality (hereafter: VR) is a breakthrough in screening options. As Harmon from SCEA argues, visual media has always been shown through a window, i.e. audiences only see a portion of what is around. [6] In the consumer market for mass audiences, Imax[1] and Surround Sound[2] were attempts to break out of these constraints that define traditional film. Nevertheless, so far only VR has had the power to eliminate that window and allow users to dive into the actual scene. The created sense of remote presence is accomplished by using a set of motion tracking sensors attached to a screen fixed with optics that replicate the human field of view [4].

The possibilities our interface opens to content producers and users span from film characters responding to the viewer, changes in dialogue, to completely new branches in the storyline opening up. Interaction between the audience and characters will be made possible, and therefore directors will gain tools to create a whole new world of interactive stories. Since the control users are given over the experience is proportional to the level of immersion, viewers will receive unknown powers enabling them to create their own evil hero, kind villain or even brand new stories by simply following their points of interest in the presented story [9].

Related Works

Even though storytelling in VR has recently become a hot-topic, our strategy appears to be unique to the field. In 2014 Google's ATAP created the animated short film "Duet", in which VR was used to show two stories simultaneously to the viewer [3]. By turning around users could follow either one of the two storylines. The fundamental difference between ATAP's concept and our approach is that even if the viewer has multiple possibilities to seamlessly chose from, there will only be one story at a time. This can be described in logical terms as "If "A" then "B" or if "C" then "D"; but "B" or "D" will never convey". The number of possible stories that split into branches and then reunite again is given by the formula:

$$X = (2^F)/2$$

"F" is defining the number of division points where the story splits up and the user makes a seamless choice, and "X" is defining the number of thereout deriving possible storylines. In a hypothetical story with five decision points, the viewer has a chance to watch 32 possible experiences.

Another strategy on attacking storytelling in VR has been

[1] http://www.imax.com/content/imax-difference
[2] http://www.dolby.com/us/en/technologies/surround-sound.html

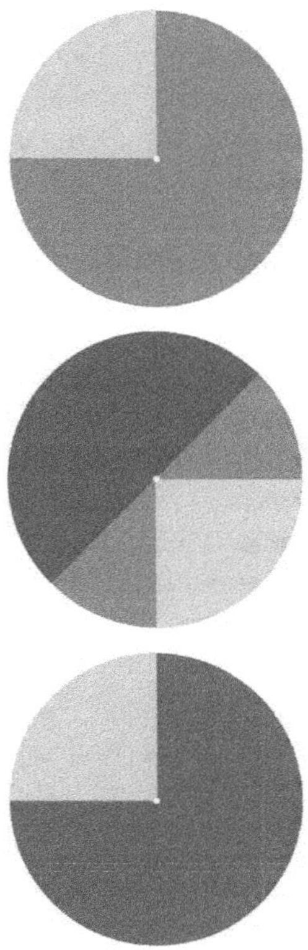

Figure 1: As the user is changing the POV (yellow), invisible parts of the original story (blue) can be altered (red).

Motorola's Spotlight Stories project that resulted in the VR shortfilm "Windy Day" (2013) [2]. This short film had the particularity of using the screen of any Motorola phone to show the animation which would happen as the user wanders around the virtual space. This is a fine example of an orientation based triggered experience. The actions will only happen when the user is looking at the precise spot the system needs the user to look at. Therefore, the length of the short film varies from user to user, but in the end every user will still have experienced the same story. The main advantage of this kind of production is that users are able to take as long as they want to appreciate their surroundings, since the story will wait until they follow the action. Our approach takes the available experience time available to the user a step further by driving the story based on the interest of the user. If a user wants to enjoy, for example, a landscape, the film does not have to wait for the user to carry on to where the action is happening. We instead propose to adapt the film and take the action to the places the user is looking at, i.e. the action will come to the user. (Figure 1)

The most recent example is the 2016 short film "Injustice" created by Kalpana. In the same fashion as Heavy Rain the film lets users witness the action until an option pops up that gives the opportunity to select a choice or chose a line of preset dialogue [5]. As the users do this a stop and frisk situation develops in front of them. Injustice can be understood as a hybrid between Heavy Rain and our approach.

The differences between these projects and our strategy are that we are making the experience indeed seamless. We believe that the pause to click and chose an option causes an interruption of the immersive experience. Furthermore, instead of making the user manipulate objects in front of him, we believe it is more effective to give this power to the film director and allow him to manipulate elements outside the user's point of view. (Figure 1) In products like Injustice the user is susceptible to notice the changes in the actors and props as one option is chosen over the other. As can be seen in the next section, this kind of interaction can affect the transparency of the whole system.

Our Approach

For the here presented project the VR headset will not only be used for enhancing the video projection experience, but is rather enabling the usage of the metadata which is being retrieved by the motion tracking sensors. Interpreting that data allows the software to know what points of interest the users are paying attention to. It is therefore enabling us to avoid the "obvious click" since the region of interest (ROI) is evident. The interface can then use that ROI and present the viewers with the storyline matching their subliminal choice without the need of any conscious interaction from the user and without stopping at any point the film. In other words, we are creating a transparent VR system, i.e. we do not present the user as a privileged viewer, but an unaware and empowered spectator. [7] The user does not know what is happening in his back and where he decides the progress of the story, therefore we can achieve a new level of immersion.

We are currently producing a prototype short film in which we implement our concept method of interactive VR.[3] It will start as a regular VR film, but at certain points in the timeline of the film we place triggers which, depending if the user looks at them or not, will or will not activate an alternative storyline. All these processes will happen without the user being aware of them. There will be neither

[3] Animated Prototype: Exemplary trigger point and story branching can be viewed here: https://sendvid.com/krzpghg9

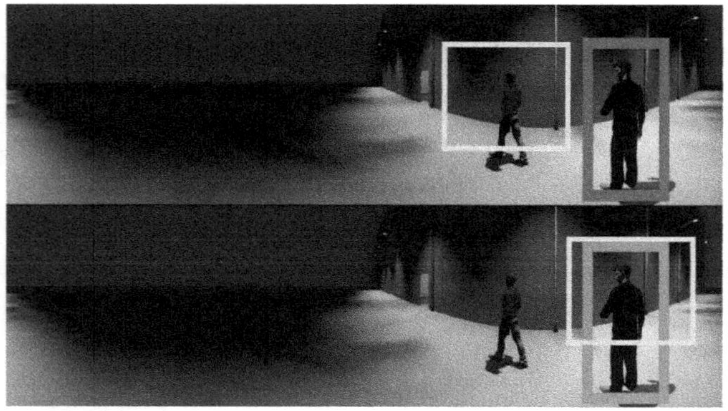

Figure 2: Yellow Rectangle: User POV; Trigger for alternative storyline not activated by perspective (red rectangle) or activated trigger by user (green rectangle)

any cues indicating that a decision is made, nor will there be any noticeable signs for users to know that their story is being changed. (Figure 2)

In terms of academics and filmmaking, our approach has some unique implications. Because of the fact that users are in control of the framing, the craft of the cinematographer and it's traditional language of lighting and camera position will be challenged. Due to users' new ability to chose where the story is going, montage and directing will be affected. Actor's will not be limited to the frame size, also the frame will not guide user's eyes, therefore a full body language performance is necessary. This can be exploited to add subtexts to the stories since there will no longer be a "fourth wall"[4] at any given moment. By using a wearable device, such as an HMD, we are building a bridge between the user and the filmmaking process itself.

[4]The fourth wall is a performance convention in which an invisible, imaginary wall separates actors from the audience.

Technical Aspects

Besides using the Unity Engine as our production platform, the device to enjoy the film will be Sony's console based VR solution PlayStation Virtual Reality (PSVR). Due to it being the same hardware for every user, product compatibility is guaranteed for developers. In terms of technical requisites, our main efforts will be to combine developments already done into an intuitive open platform so that all filmmakers can employ it for their own projects.

One of the major hurdles for our production is to create cuts between storyline branches that do not happen via editing in post production. This is necessary for the experience to become absolutely seamless when users take decisions that further our story. This means the script has to be written with the shooting plan in mind and an anticipation for the head motion required by the user to trigger one branch or another. This without a doubt adds a burden to scriptwriters and film-crew in general, but as already mentioned this kind of storytelling has been done before, it is the screening method what we propose to innovate. It is fundamental to pre-visualise the shooting plan (in our case we created a 3D animation precisely staging the actors' actions), because the position of the triggers and the actors can not be within the same frame when they change. This way we can reposition actors without fearing a jump-cut[5], because the viewer is not looking at them. (Figure 3)

For this kind of film production and presentation computational power and necessary hardware are of crucial importance. In order to transition from one video to another

[5]A jump cut is a cut in film editing in which two sequential shots of the same subject are taken from camera positions that vary only slightly if at all. This type of edit gives the effect of jumping forward in time.

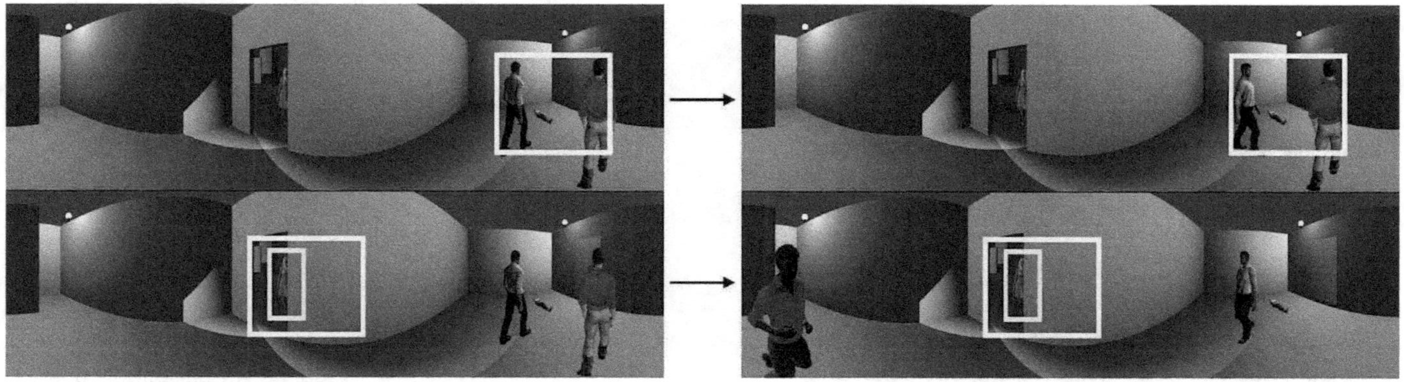

Figure 3: Example of how actors can be repositioned outside user's ROI. Top: User follows characters; no change in position. Bottom: User watches door; characters out of frame can be repositioned.

at a single frame accuracy, the video about to be played next should be preloaded into the system memory. To avoid having two videos loaded while the current one is being played (which would be extremely demanding on the hardware), the trigger point in which we choose the branch that is going to be shown next should be located at a time before the branching happens. Therefore, the decision (A or B) has already been made when the system has to show the next branch of the story. This way the system has time to load only the next branch to be played, making it more efficient and avoiding any jarring, because the transition will take only one frame to replace the scene outside the user's point of view. In cases where the decision points and the actual change in the video occur with a load cushion time, if the user look back to the area to be replaced, this will act as a cancel feature. Meaning, a change will only happen when the user is not looking at it (Figures 4,5).

Future Developments

Social VR and Live Editing: Most VR HMDs are connected to a bigger system which also serves separate displays. In most cases those are used as mirror displays for the content being shown in the HMD, so that audiences can see what is happening inside the VR experience. We intend to make use of those displays by showing a version of the film shot with regular film cameras of the same actions the user is watching on the HMD. These images outside the headset will also be showing what the HMD user is looking at, hence the HMD user will be live editing an interactive film for audiences.

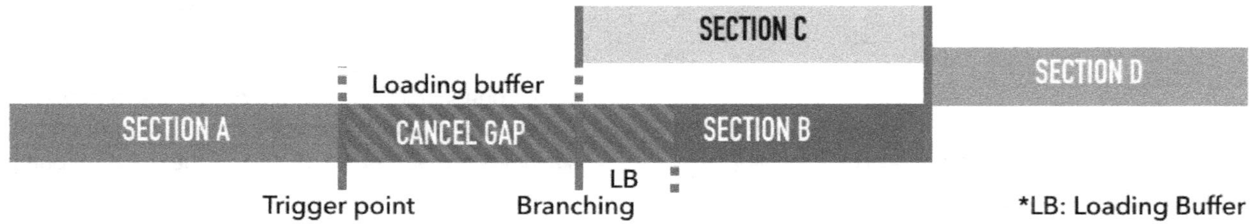

Figure 4: Overview of the system with a branching and joining moment.

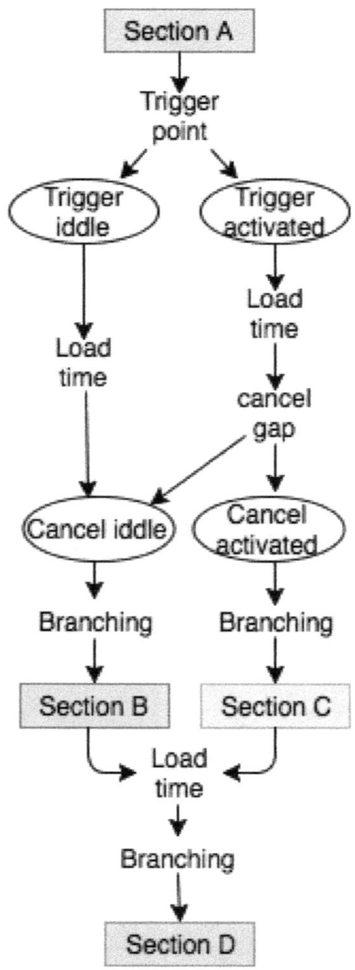

Figure 5: Software execution flow chart based on figure 4 hypothetical example.

Light Field: By being able to record and play back VR video while retaining the capacity of changing the vantage point will enable the user to move their head in VR and look behind objects. In combination with eye tracking technology we could accurately emulate human depth of field as well as it has been demonstrated by HMD headsets like the FOVE. These new dimensions of interaction can also add another layer to storytelling VR project.

REFERENCES

1. 2010. Heavy Rain. PlayStation CD-ROM. (2010).
2. 2013. Windy Day. (2013).
3. 2014. Duet. (2014).
4. Devesh Kumar Bhatnagar. 1993. *Position Trackers for Head Mounted Display Systems: A Survey*. Technical Report.
5. Jaehee Cho, Atit Kothari, Zixu Ding, Yeongmin Won, Stephanie Fawaz, and Xu Cheng. 2016. Injustice: Interactive Live Action Virtual Reality Experience. In *ACM SIGGRAPH 2016 VR Village (SIGGRAPH '16)*. ACM, New York, NY, USA, Article 9, 2 pages. DOI: http://dx.doi.org/10.1145/2929490.2929493
6. Vernon Harmon. 2015. Embrace Virtual Reality With Sony. (2015.). https://www.youtube.com/watch?v=_Su45ND3pDc
7. Marie-Laure Ryan. 2001. *Narrative As Virtual Reality: Immersion and Interactivity in Literature and Electronic Media*. Johns Hopkins University Press, Baltimore, MD, USA.
8. E. Schrödinger. 1935. *Die gegenwärtige Situation in der Quantenmechanik*. Die Naturwissenschaften, Volume 23, Issue 48, pp.807-812.
9. Bob G. Witmer and Michael J. Singer. 1998. Measuring Presence in Virtual Environments: A Presence Questionnaire. *Presence: Teleoper. Virtual Environ.* 7, 3 (June 1998), 225–240. DOI: http://dx.doi.org/10.1162/105474698565686

Sparklry: Designing "Sparkle" of Interactive Jewelry

Maho Oki
Future University Hakodate
116-2 Kamedanakano-cho,
Hakodate, Hokkaido, Japan
okimaho@acm.org

Koji Tsukada
Future University Hakodate
116-2 Kamedanakano-cho,
Hakodate, Hokkaido, Japan
tsuka@acm.org

TEI '17, March 20-23, 2017, Yokohama, Japan
ACM 978-1-4503-4676-4/17/03.
http://dx.doi.org/10.1145/3024969.3025053

Abstract
At present, many projects embed smart LEDs –multiple LEDs dynamically controlled by computers – into clothes or accessories to support novel expressions or daily activities. However, most of them do not consider the "sparkle" of traditional jewelry. We propose a presentation technique for interactive jewelry called "Sparklry", which can present "sparkles" on a jewel stone using internal LEDs. These sparkles are designed by integrating (1) a traditional jewel, (2) a light shielding sheet with small slits, and (3) an LED array. We developed a prototype and several examples of jewelry to explore appropriate designs of slits and LED patterns. Moreover, we developed two prototypes.

Author Keywords
Interactive Jewelry; sparkle; LED; augmented Jewelry.

ACM Classification Keywords
H.5.m. Information interfaces and presentation (e.g., HCI): Miscellaneous; See

Introduction
Many projects these days embed smart LEDs –multiple LEDs dynamically controlled by computers – into clothes or accessories to support novel expressions or daily activities. For example, Fujimoto[3] developed an LED body suit that can enhance dance performances by

Figure 1: Examples of a same jewelry (crystal Swarovski) with/without our system.

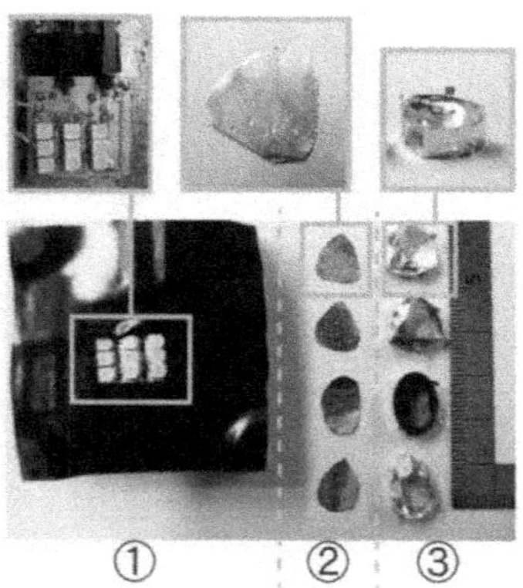

Figure 3: First prototype of the Sparklry. 1: a LED matrix, 2: slit sheets, 3: Swarovski stones.

combining body expression and lighting effects. Ringly [9] is a commercial interactive jewelry capable of representing the status of a smartphone using an LED, a vibrator, and Bluetooth communication. There are also some toolkits that support the creation of wearable systems, like LilyPad [1] or Sparkle [6]. Thus, there are many wearable accessories and support technologies; however, most of them did not care about the "sparkle" of traditional jewelry. There are various cutting / polishing techniques that add attractive "sparkles" to traditional jewels (e.g., diamond). In this paper, we focus on a new technique to add "sparkle" to jewelry, "Sparklry", by integrating conventional jewelry and computer technologies.

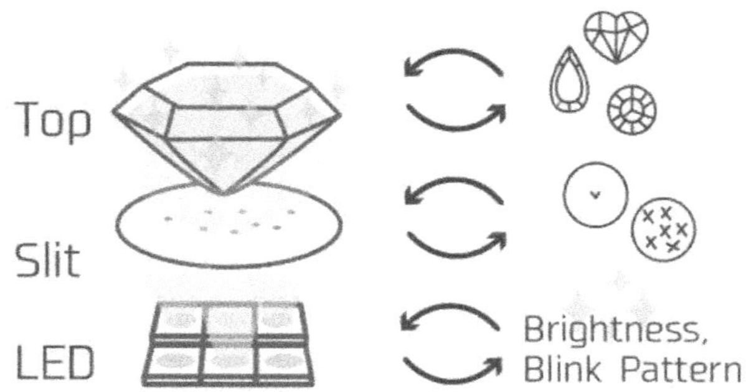

Figure 1: Basic concept.

Sparklry

The key idea of our system is to design the "sparkle" of jewelry by combining (1) a traditional jewel, (2) a light all directions. We set one of the stones on the system using a stone setting. The slit sheets are created from silver Origami papers. We prepared many slit designs and cut the papers using a CNC paper cutter (Roland iDecora). The LEDs are designed as a 3 × 3 LED matrix.

We soldered 9 white chip LEDs (UW1143B, 400 mcd, 2.7 × 3.5 mm) on our original board. The LEDs are controlled by Arduino. We developed software to generate various light patterns. Figure 2 shows the two blinking examples of the same jewelry with/without our system. Without our system, the jewel projects flat light and looks like a cheap toy. On the other hand, many small sparkles appear on a jewel using our system, which makes it look like traditional jewelry under great lighting. Figure 4 shows additional examples using our system.

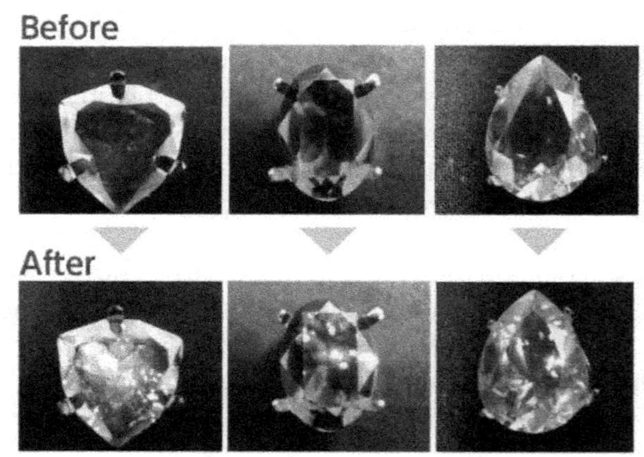

Figure 4: Examples of jewelry augmented by our system.

First Prototype

The first prototype is designed to explore appropriate designs of a slit sheet and LED patterns (Figure 3). We prepared Swarovski stones that are beautifully cut from all directions. We set one of the stones on the system using a stone setting. The slit sheets are created from silver Origami papers. We prepared many slit designs and cut the papers using a CNC paper cutter (Roland iDecora). The LEDs are designed as a 3 × 3 LED matrix. We soldered 9 white chip LEDs (UW1143B, 400 mcd, 2.7 × 3.5 mm) on our original board. The LEDs are controlled by Arduino. We developed software to generate various light patterns. Figure 2 shows the two blinking examples of the same jewelry with/without our system. Without our system, the jewel projects flat light and looks like a cheap toy. On the other hand, many small sparkles appear on a jewel using our system, which makes it look like traditional jewelry under great lighting. Figure 4 shows additional examples using our system.

Applications

Next, we developed two prototype applications: an earring-type and a showcase-type.

Earring-type prototype

The earring type prototype is designed to be as small as possible to make it easier to wear. The device structure is shown in Figure 5. The controller part is separated from the earring (LED) part and connected by thin wires. It is hidden behind the ear when the earring is worn (Figure 6 bottom). The controller part has a micro-controller (ATMega328P-AU, Atmel), an acceleration sensor (KXR94-2050), and a small battery (SparkFun). These are housed in the case printed by a 3D printer, which is attached to the ear hook.

The earring part consists of the main Swarovski stone, three LEDs, a slit sheet, and eight small Swarovski stones for decoration. The LEDs (NFSW036CT, 9.2 cd, 3.5 × 3.5 mm) and slit sheet are arranged to fit under the main Swarovski stone (crystal color, 12 × 12 mm). We attached eight small Swarovski stones (8 × 4 mm) for decoration around the main Swarovski (Figure 5 and 6) to hide the LEDs completely. We bonded the metal clip to the back of the LED board. We made slits (size: 0.2 mm, number: about 20) on the slit sheet in the same way as in the first prototype. The prototype detects the wearer's movement using the acceleration sensor and blinks at random for a certain period of time.

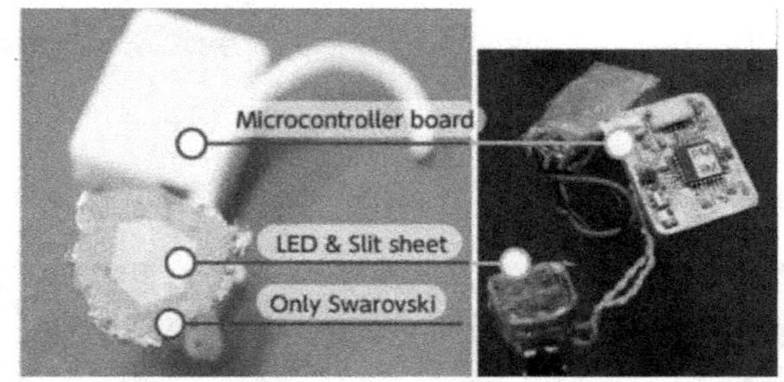

Figure 5: Earring-type prototype.

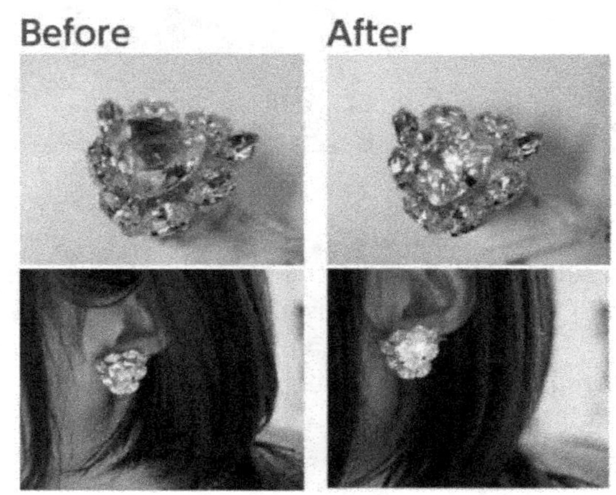

Figure 6: Examples of the earring type prototype. Left: turn off LEDs, right: turn on LEDs.

Showcase type prototype

The showcase type prototype is designed such that people can see sparkles with various Swarovski stones using our system. It is a small box on top of which the Swarovski stone is set (Figure 7). People can change the kind of Swarovski and the slit sheet. The user can watch the effect of the sparkles using our system in his/her hand from various angles. The device consists of a micro-controller (Arduino Pro mini), an acceleration sensor (KXR94-2050), a small battery, and an LED board. We thought that more LEDs could increase the expression of the sparkle of the Swarovski. Therefore, we selected small but low-brightness LED (OSWT1608, 74 mcd), and arranged nine LEDs on the LED board. These are housed in a case (about 7 cm × 7 cm ×5 cm), and the LED board is attached to the cover of the box. We designed the cover such that it has a hole to set the slit sheet and Swarovski unit just above the LEDs and printed it using the 3D printer. We bonded velour fabric on top of the cover to adjust the appearance of the jewelry case. The LEDs basically alternate between on and off for a certain period. Moreover, people can change the lighting pattern by tilting the device.

Discussion

Slit design

We found that the number of slits was also important while experimenting using the first prototype. Fewer slits (e.g., 1 slit per LED) produced less and weak sparkles on the Swarovski. Many slits (e.g., 30 slits per LED) made it too bright and lit the whole Swarovski stone. It is expected that the amount of the light incident on the Swarovski depends on the slit's size/shape/number. The position of the slit also influences the reflection of light on the Swarovski stone. Therefore, we will explore suitable parameters of the slit's size/shape/number and derive the relationship between the surface of the Swarovski and slits to make sparkles effectively.

Figure 7: Showcase-type prototype.

Related works

Many research projects embed smart LEDs into clothing or accessories for both aesthetic and performance purposes. For example, there are LED body suits that enhance dance performance[3], wearable lighting devices that explore lighting effects around a person's face [8], and a wearable display device that uses the afterimage effect created by a user's movements[5]. The "Beauty Technology"[4] uses the body's surface as an interactive platform by way of LEDs or sensors attached to the skin or fingernails.

Other art projects[10,11] that have been developed include beautiful fashion accessories that light up by using LEDs and the original case. Some commercial, interactive accessories are capable of representing the status of a smartphone using LEDs[2,7,9].

Although there are many wearable devices that use LED lighting, most of them do not augment traditional accessories, and they are especially lacking in "sparkle." Various cutting and polishing techniques exist to add attractive "sparkles" to traditional jewels (e.g., diamond). We think that integrating these techniques with computer technology can make jewelry more impressive and more expressive while maintaining a natural appearance; therefore, we proposed and prototyped a new technique for adding "sparkle" to jewelry by integrating conventional jewelry and multiple LEDs that are dynamically controlled by computers.

Acknowledgements
This project is supported by JSPS 25700019.

Video URL
https://youtu.be/VyQlLyRWm_M

References
[1] Buechley, L., Eisenberg, M., Catchen, J., and Crockett, A. The LilyPad Arduino: Using Computational Textiles to Investigate Engagement, Aesthetics, and Diversity in Computer Science Education. *Proceedings of the SIGCHI Conference on Human Factors in Computing Systems*, ACM (2008), 423–432.

[2] CuteCircuit. Mirror Handbag. http://shop.cutecircuit.com/products/mirror-handbag.

[3] Fujimoto, M., Naotaka, F., Terada, T., and Tsukamoto, M. Lighting Choreographer: An LED Control System for Dance Performances. *Proceedings of the 13th International Conference on Ubiquitous Computing*, ACM (2011), 613–614.

[4] Katia Vega and Fuks, H. *Beauty Technology*. Springer International Publishing, Cham, 2016.

[5] LIU, X., Vega, K., Qian, J., Paradiso, J., and Maes, P. Fluxa: Body Movements As a Social Display. *Proceedings of the 29th Annual Symposium on User Interface Software and Technology*, ACM (2016), 155–157.

[6] SparkFun Electronics. Sparkle Kit - Diamond. https://www.sparkfun.com/products/retired/12729 .

[7] Swarovski. Swarovski Activity Tracking Jewelry. http://www.swarovski.com/Web_US/en/91215/promotion/Swarovski_Activity_Tracking_Jewelry.html.

[8] Zhao, N. and Paradiso, J.A. HALO: Wearable Lighting. *Adjunct Proceedings of the 2015 ACM International Joint Conference on Pervasive and Ubiquitous Computing and Proceedings of the 2015 ACM International Symposium on Wearable Computers*, ACM (2015), 601–606.

[9] RINGLY: Smart Jewelry and Accessories. https://ringly.com/.

[10] KYEOK KIM. http://www.kyeokkim.com/.

[11] Dian Luo. http://showtime.arts.ac.uk/dianluo.

Second Skin: An Exploration of eTextile Stretch Circuits on the Body

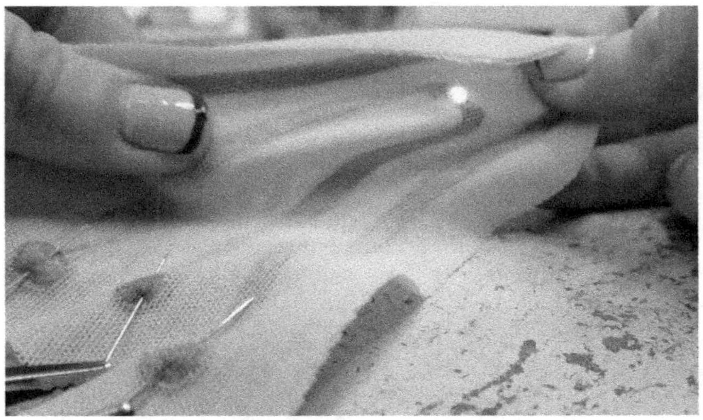

Figure 1: Testing the elasticity of a stretch circuit panel. The LED and button are inserted into tiny unbonded pockets, through tiny slits the back of the fabric, and secured with conductive thread. Please refer to our video figure to see the sample being stretched.

Rachel Freire
Rachel Freire Studio
London, United Kingdom
rachel@rachelfreire.com

Cedric Honnet
DataPaulette
Paris, France
cedric@datapaulette.org

Paul Strohmeier
Human Centered Computing
University of Copenhagen
Copenhagen, Denmark
p.strohmeier@di.ku.dk

TEI '17, March 20-23, 2017, Yokohama, Japan
ACM 978-1-4503-4676-4/17/03.
http://dx.doi.org/10.1145/3024969.3025054

Abstract
Second Skin is a stretch electronic textile (eTextile) garment that adapts to the shape of the body. It is designed as both a provocative outer shell and a functioning undergarment, or foundation garment. Using elastic materials and building on techniques from cutting edge sportswear manufacturing, it facilitates wearable electronics which can recede from the users attention. We consider Second Skin as a platform that other researchers can use to add functionality of their own. In our exhibit, people can interact with a prototype version of Second Skin as well as with material samples to gain a better understanding of its look, feel and material capabilities.

Author Keywords
Wearable electronics; prototyping; electronic textiles; materials development; manufacturing; soft circuits

ACM Classification Keywords
H5.m. Information interfaces and presentation (e.g., HCI): Miscellaneous. J.5 Arts and humanities: Arts, fine and performing.

Video Figure
https://youtu.be/vd2GedFZLIs

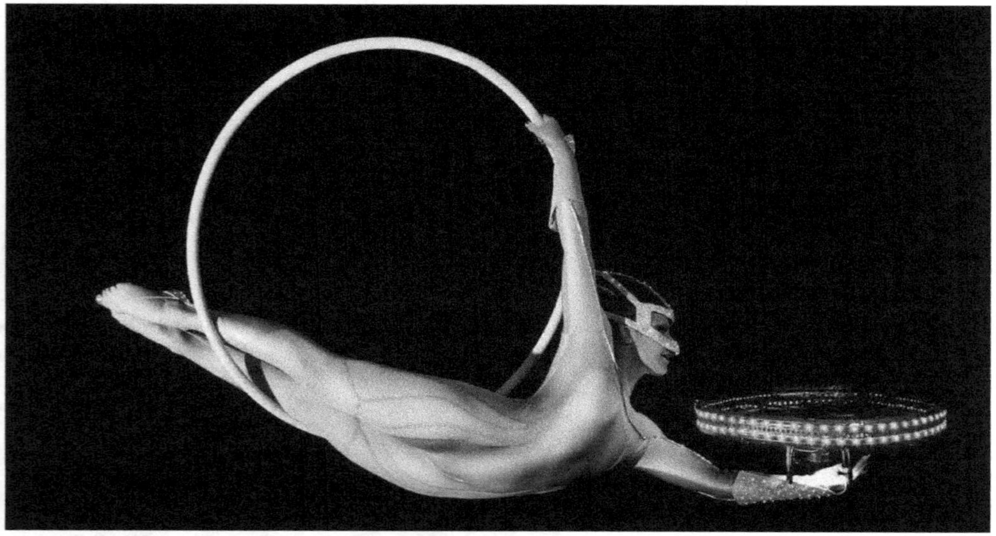

Figure 2 - Empress Stah performs a show choreographed with a drone. She is wearing a prototype Second Skin suit, testing seam lines on the body for placement and strain relief. Headpiece and cuffs incorporate eTextiles. The intent is to have a fully addressable eTextile suit which can be synced with the drone. Photo © Empress Stah www.zerocentral.london

Introduction

The growing field of wearable garments is theatrical in the sense that electronics often require heightened physical awareness. Second Skin seeks to address the issue of how electronic fragility may compromise functionality in the context of a garment. Hard surfaces and brittle materials mean we must adapt our behaviour to be sensitive to devices which are supposedly designed to serve us. Elastic eTextiles (Figure 1) have the potential to minimise such limitations: allowing electronic elements to disappear from tactile perception, giving more freedom to the wearer.

We present Second Skin, an evolving eTextile prototyping suit designed as a platform for experimentation of electronics on the body. Using conductive and resistive materials, special bonding adhesives and films, it is a practical solution to integrate stretch circuitry into garment technology.

Second Skin is designed with physical performers in mind. It is currently in development with an aerialist (Figure 2) and a sonic artist who uses dancers and acrobatic performers in her installation work. Wearables for physical performance should not constrain the performers' freedom of movement in any way. To support full body movement, the eTextile garments and electronics must be able to stretch and deform with the body. The project addresses issues such as strain relief and circuitry on joints, offering ways to bridge gaps where cables and wires would make electrical connections impractical. They must be able to withstand pressure and high velocity movement while having an absolutely flat profile so as to allow the performer to freely glide over silks, ropes and hoops.

This provides Second Skin with the ultimate durability test. Once Second Skin can support demanding physical performances, it will be more than capable to overcome the theatrical nature of our current generation of wearables and can be applied in other areas of garment technology.

Related Work

There is a long tradition of designing wearable technologies that are integrated in fashion, rather than added to the body as external devices. Joanna Berzowska designed 'Second Skins' that were used to externalize the wearers history of intimate encounters [1]. Like with our Second Skin, Berzowska decided to use the functional circuit as an ornamental element of the clothing. Explorations in wearable fashion have become commonplace in TEI, exemplified by the 2011

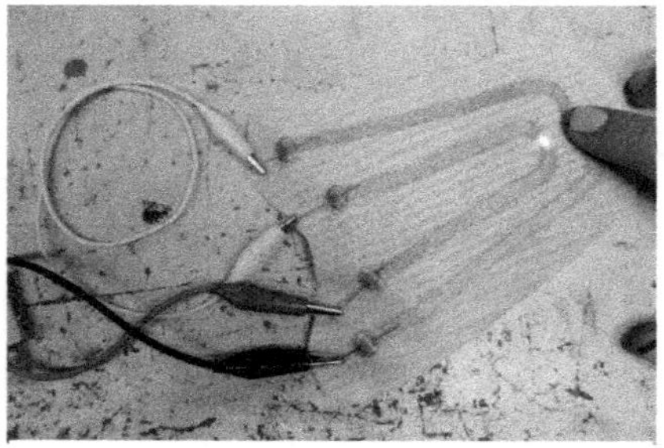

Figure 3 - Testing a stretch circuit panel. Pads of conductive lycra are left exposed to attach power. The LED and button are inserted into unbonded pockets, through tiny slits the back of the fabric, and secured with conductive thread

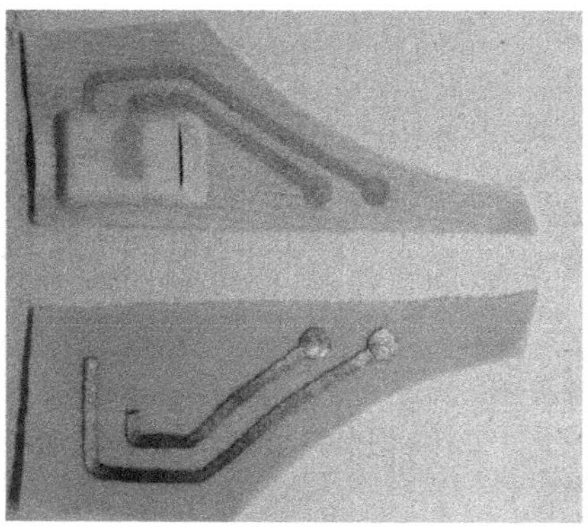

Figure 4 - eTextile battery pouch detail

design challenge in which students presented self-made superhero outfits. An exploration that not only merges electronics with clothing, but additionally blends the clothing with the body is Monarch by Kate Hartman [3]. She uses EMG signals to actuate her garments, providing users with additional expressive modalities.

The garment we present uses textiles as conductors, much like a large, soft, elastic circuit board. However, this type of textile can also be appropriated for active components. An introduction to such methods was published by Hannah Perner-Wilson and Leah Buechley [4]. Together with Mika Satomi, Perner-Wilson maintains an archive of DIY soft sensors [2].

Project Jacquard [5] presented a method of creating conductive materials that can be woven on industrial scale. Unlike Second Skin they do not focus on performance materials: the conductive circuits of project Jacquard are not elastic and therefore less robust, suited to less physically demanding applications.

Implementation

To accommodate the constraints set by designing for physical performers, Rachel opted to develop techniques established for high performance sports fabric. All textiles used in Second Skin are chosen for their low profile and their ability to stretch equally in all directions. Conductive stretch fabric (e.g. Shieldex Technik-Tex P-130 silver plated lycra – Figure 3) is used for creating electrical connections. The conductive material is sandwiched between layers of powernet (mesh) and lycra/elastine (microknit) stretch textiles to electrically insulate them (Figure 3 & 4).

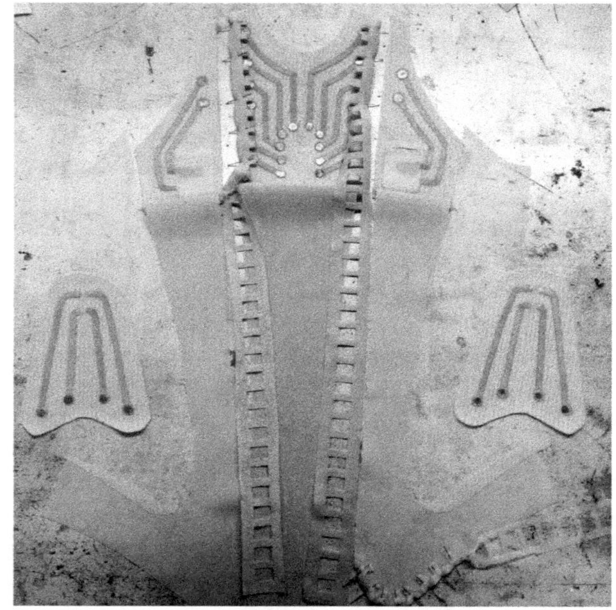

Figure 5 Toile #2:Second Skin pattern piece layout showing assembled eTextile panels and laser cut ladders to house tubing for cables

The materials are fused to each other using heat-reactive precision bonding films (Bemis Sewfree fusing) designed for stretch and recovery in sportswear and lingerie. Using bonding films as part of the circuit design selectively allows the garment to conduct or insulate. Consequently multi-layered stretch circuitry can be created.

Whilst these films must be used with extreme precision in both pressure and timing to create bonds suitable for manufacture and sale, select products exist that have a melting point low enough to be used with domestic irons, allowing for DIY and handmade sampling,

Figure 6 - Work in progress. Detail of Toile #2, sewing the eTextile panels into the garment

prototyping and garment production. Figures 4 & 5 show the process of combining individual pieces of fabric with conductive traces into a larger garment.

Motivation

This work is centred around the body, focused on intricacy, detail and craftsmanship and the power evoked by the richness of texture and the complexity of process. It is the places where the lines blur between design, craftsmanship, vocation and function.

Working in the emerging field of wearable technology means there is opportunity to shape how we attribute value to materials and technology in this newly established field. As wearables become more integrated into our lives we are entering a new era of craftsmanship and have the opportunity to devise systems which can be manufactured simultaneously on both a personal and industrial scale, while representing the values and design choices important to us.

Clothing should amplify a person, not create one. It should also come with an awareness of its environmental and sociological impact, as all design choices made directly influence the way we act and are perceived in the world. Every object has a story to tell, and these stories have a powerful impact on our lives and surroundings.

It is easy to forget that wearables exist in the real world rather than the controlled environment of the stage or a research lab. Clothing is meant to be lived in and serve a purpose, whether it is aesthetically focused to empower the wearer or exists to be completely practical and functional. The ideal garment will be both.

This project exists to serve fellow researchers as a platform to expand upon. Second Skin is designed with an eye-catching aesthetic intended for both functionality and discussion. Due to Rachel's background as a fashion and material designer, she uses the style of documentation and promotion found in fashion branding as well as high quality products suitable for sale and distribution. This helps researchers and hobbyists who wish to transfer their creations from the lab or workshop to a more public stage. The project aims to create and present a format which allows both DIY makers and large scale manufacturers to work with the same materials and a comparable toolkit, creating the potential for design which can scale according to the size of production.

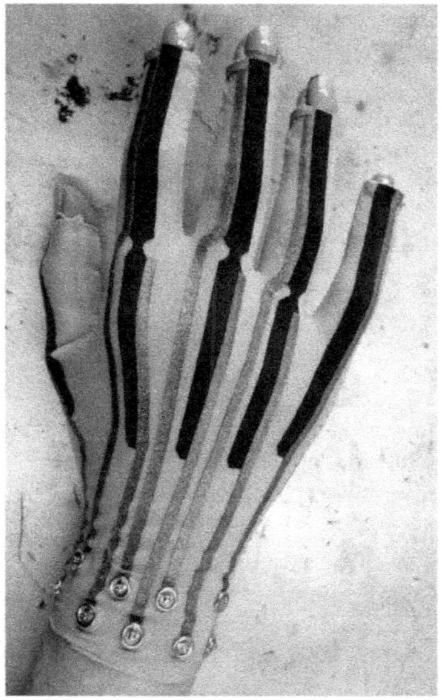

Figure 7- Fabric concept for eTextile mi.mu glove which inspired the second skin project http://mimugloves.com/

Second Skin does not have inherent uses in and of itself, but instead is looking for design functions to be added to the structure to test it's theory and application.

History

Second Skin began as a part of the mi.mu gloves project to make a super comfortable and wearable eTextile glove (Figure 7). It was created as an extension of the existing mi.mu glove which uses bend sensors and traditional electronics housed in high performance stretch textiles. The current state of the project however still requires development work in order to scale to the small size and high complexity of such a product.

Limitations & Future work

This work has an Alice in Wonderland aesthetic: it is currently constrained by scale, which gives a wonderful narrative, but limits functionality. Existing industrial machinery can be adapted to manufacture and improve the functionality of Second Skin, but currently there is no incentive for manufacturers to do so.

The next step for personal manufacturing is to experiment with laser cutting more complex shapes, exploring how much the idea can be scaled down to house more complex design ideas and how this will in turn restrict the material qualities of the garments. Finding the balance between intricacy of the electronic connections and quality of the garments will give a starting point for the direction to approach material and machine manufacturers in creating textiles and equipment to develop bonded eTextiles for multiple uses.

Presentation

The art piece will consist of an exhibit of the first prototype Second Skin (Figure 8 & 9). To facilitate interaction with the audience and exploration of the materials we will also exhibit test elements, such as a sleeve, as well as selected small samples of circuitry and garment test pieces (toiles) available for people to touch and interact with.

The full garment will be displayed on a mannequin and will have basic interactive functions to demonstrate how it conducts electricity. Viewers will be encouraged to simultaneously stretch and interact with the material to experience the extent to which it can deform and adapt to the shape of the body. To demonstrate how Second Sking can connect to existing platforms, we will enable interactivity by connecting the circuitry of Second Skin to a Twiz by Cedric Honnet [6].

Presenting the Second Skin at the Art Exhibit will allow questions and create a discussion about the chosen aesthetics of the work. This is integral to understand how people view and accept a piece of clothing. All feedback will be documented – we consider feedback to the project from an engaged audience to be a valuable addition to the project as a whole.

Conclusion

Second Skin is an exploration of eTextile stretch circuits and their implementation in a functioning full body garment as a rapid prototyping shell. Combining repurposed housing for traditional electronics and using developing materials and techniques in sportswear technology, this open source project will create and demonstrate techniques to develop stretch eTextiles. Second Skin is replicable in both a DIY and industrial

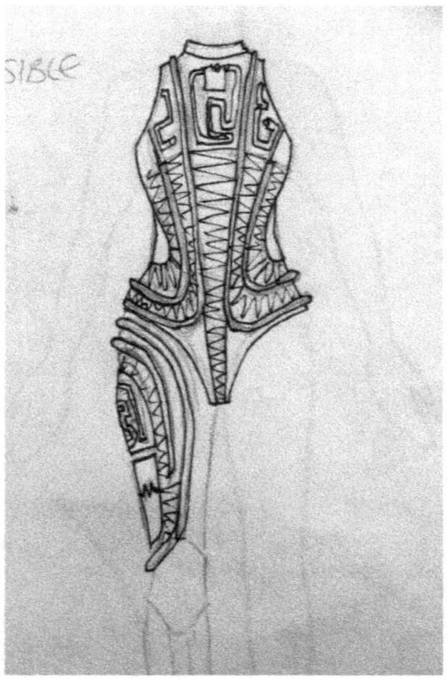

Figure 8 - Initial sketch of second skin design, imagining how to place cable housing and eTextile panels on the body. Aesthetic inspired by high altitude flight suits and pressure suits

Figure 9 - Toile #1: First toile to test shape of garment, how tubing will work in stretch fabrics, and to test strain relief. Photo © Allan Amato. Model: Logan Browning

manufacturing context. Inspiring and facilitating designers to explore new directions in bonding and stretch materials has the potential for further innovation in a new area of material development which can be scaled in an accessible way from boutique production to large scale manufacture. The aim is to bridge the often frustrating disconnect between prototyping, making and manufacture in the textile industry and create viable, provocative examples of garments on both a design and material level. Aesthetics, functionality, comfort and ubiquity play equal roles in our acceptance of technology as an extension of the self. eTextiles serve as an exciting tactile and understandable way to integrate wearables

References

1. Joanna Berzowska. 2005. Memory rich clothing: second skins that communicate physical memory. *Proceedings of the 5th conference on Creativity and Cognition*: 32–40. https://doi.org/10.1145/1056224.1056231

2. Hannah Perner-Wilson and Mika Satomi. HOW TO GET WHAT YOU WANT. Retrieved from http://www.kobakant.at/DIY/

3. Kate Hartman, Jackson McConnell, Boris Kourtoukov, Hillary Predko, and Izzie Colpitts-Campbell. 2015. Monarch: Self-Expression Through Wearable Kinetic Textiles. *Proc. TEI '16*: 413–414. https://doi.org/10.1145/2677199.2690875

4. Hannah Perner-Wilson and Leah Buechley. 2010. Making textile sensors from scratch. *Proc. TEI '10*: 349. https://doi.org/10.1145/1709886.1709972

5. Ivan Poupyrev, Nan-Wei Gong, Shiho Fukuhara, Mustafa Emre Karagozler, Carsten Schwesig, and Karen E. Robinson. 2016. Project Jacquard. In *Proc. CHI '16*, https://doi.org/10.1145/2858036.2858176

6. Andreas Schlegel and Cedric Honnet. 2016. Movement of Things: Exploring Inertial Motion Sensing When Autonomous, Tiny and Wireless. In *Proc. MOCO '16*, 1–2. https://doi.org/10.1145/2948910.2948916

Brighter than a Thousand Suns. a Uniform to Detect and Display Radiation

Susanna Hertrich
Institute of Experimental Design
and Media Cultures
Academy of Art and Design
FHNW
Basel, Switzerland
Susanna.hertrich@fhnw.ch

Akitoshi Honda
Brüsseler Str. 13
13353 Berlin, Germany
info@ahonda.org

TEI '17, March 20-23, 2017, Yokohama, Japan
ACM 978-1-4503-4676-4/17/03.
http://dx.doi.org/10.1145/3024969.3025055

Abstract
This paper describes a recent art project in which a uniform allows to detect and display nuclear radiation. Here, wearable technology is interpreted as contemporary samurai gear. The uniform comprises of a helmet with an ornament, a handheld scanning device and a box with a microcontroller. It is completed by a protective suit. The ground scanning device contains a Geiger counter kit which sends signals through the microcontroller to the ornament on the helmet which is equipped with an LED-strip. The ornament lights up in response to the measurements coming from the device. The major part of this artwork is a full HD single channel video of about 15 minutes duration that shows a young man wearing the uniform and scanning the devastated areas near the nuclear power stations in Fukushima. The video was filmed on location in May 2016.

Author Keywords
Art Project; Wearable Technology; Video; Fukushima; Radiation Measurements; Storytelling

ACM Classification Keywords
H.5.m. Information interfaces and presentation (e.g., HCI): Miscellaneous; J.5 Arts and humanities: Arts, fine and performing.

Idea
The idea behind this artwork was to find a way to use wearable technologies to engage with the invisible threat of radiation in a thought-provoking and poetic way.

Concept
After a nuclear incident, affected areas become "forbidden" grounds due to their threat for people's health. However, the physical elements of this threat cannot be perceived by our biological senses. Radiation remains invisible material for us. We are dependent on technologies that can measure the impacts of such materials. Devices that provide us with information on ambient radiation thus act as artificial sensory organs [1]. This notion of an embodied interactive technology is the fundament for this artwork where the measurement device is turned into a uniform that becomes a true extension of the body [2]. Ambient radiation is measured with an extended handheld device and then transformed into an illumination of an ornament on the helmet. Instead of being incorporated into precise numeric data, as in a commercial GM device, the information receives a symbolic meaning that is revealed over time as the short film progresses.

Uniform
The uniform comprises of three objects listed here (Figure 1).

1. A workers helmet with an ornament that is lined with an LED strip.
2. A handheld scanning device that contains a GM-kit to detect incoming particles to measure the amount of ambient radiation.
3. A box with a strap to be hung over the shoulder that contains an Arduino microcontroller and a battery.

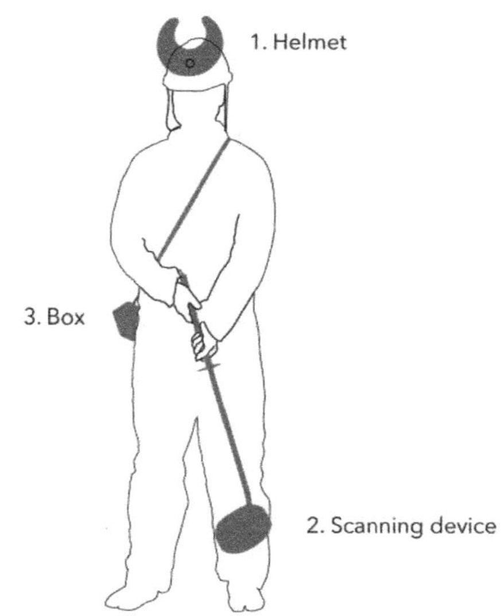

Figure 1: Sketch of the uniform showing all three objects and how they are worn and carried.

Technical description
The GM kit is embedded into the round bottom part of the scanning device. It is connected by cable to the box that contains the Arduino microcontroller. The microcontroller reads the incoming data from the GM kit and sends control signals to the ornament on the

helmet through a second cable. When a positive signal (particle detection) is received, the ornament lights up.

Figure 2: Illuminated ornament.

Aesthetics

The aesthetics of the uniform and the devices are of great importance for this work. This is at first an artwork aiming to tell a story rather than showing a refined technical solution. The design of the uniform is strongly inspired by contemporary workers gear, as well as historical samurai helmets and swords. The elements of this uniform are composed from found materials, such as a workers helmet and a conventional Tyvek[1] protective suit that are extended with custom-made forms and shapes (Figure 3). Main materials are copper and white plastics to create a unified look. The illuminated ornament on the helmet quotes ornaments from historical samurai helmets (kabuto maedate) that resemble a half-moon crescent. The form also reminds of a sun to reference the title of this work. The ornament has been carved with rays to facilitate the distribution of the LED lights that sit at its outer edge.

Figure 3: Full view of the uniform in daylight.

The shape of the scanning device resembles that of metal detector but also features some elements that hint to a Katana (long samurai sword). The title of this art project "Brighter Than A Thousand Suns" refers to the book with the same title by the German journalist and futurist Robert Jungk (first edition published in

[1] One-piece garment, usually white made from a high-density polyethylene fiber.

1956) in which he reflects on the up and coming discipline of atomic research [3].

Video

The video shows a young man wearing the uniform and scanning the devastated areas near the nuclear power stations in Fukushima. The video is shot in a neutral observing angle, mostly with a fixed camera in long shot, hinting to the wide angle landscape scenes in Hokusai's famous wood block prints [4], as well as quoting Akira Kurosawa's steady and slow camera as used in his samurai movies [5].

Inspiration

This project stands in context of number of artworks that refer to the nuclear incident in Fukushima. The following paragraph briefly introduces some works which served as a source of inspiration or share similarities with this project.

Nutopia, a collaborative project between artist Kyoko Ebata and scientist Tim Byrnes consists of several versions of mini-eco-systems that contain plants and animals kept alive by energy generated from various nuclear materials. These tiny worlds served as vehicles for a dialogue between „Ebata's fearful opposition and Byrnes's belief in the potential of (a) new energy (sources) [6]."

„Fukushima no Alice" by Daisuke Takeya stages a Japanese Lolita girl as Alice, the fictional character from Lewis Carrol's "Alice's Adventures in Wonderland" and lets her explore the landscapes of Fukushima. She adds a notion of fairytale to his photographs that show scenes of harsh reality. With that Takeya hopes to achieve that „...we are no longer certain if the current situation in Fukushima is real or just a bad dream" [7].

In „Ambient Camera: Who released the shutter?" by Kotaro Abe and Yasuaki Kakehi, the shutter of a still camera that is set up in various locations in Fukushima is driven by readings of a GM counter. The still images taken are later combined to short films following three different principles. This way, the final movies not only show the landscape but also depict information on the intensity of the radiation in the different locations [8].

Most international attention was probably achieved by a project initiated by the Japanse artist collective Chim↑Pom under the title „Don't follow the wind" [9]. In 2015, a number of Japanese and acclaimed international artists were invited to participate in a group exhibition located inside the Fukushima Exclusion Zone. As the exhibition remains inaccessible until the Japanese government waives restrictions to this area sometime in the future, the artworks left in the zone remain invisible and thus emphasize the timely dimensions of half-life in radioactive materials.

Lastly, I want to mention the photographer duo Guilleaume Bression and Carlos Ayesta who have created various photographic essays in Fukushima [10]. In their photo series „Bad dreams" they stage the invisible borders between low and heavily contaminated areas as physical borders in the form of plastic foil.

Context

This described project was created in relation to a three year research project called "Sensorium of Animals" (2016–2018) in collaboration with Dr. Shintaro Miyazaki. Situated at the Institute of Experimental Design and Media Cultures at the Academy of Art and Design in Basel (Switzerland). The project is funded by the Swiss National Science Foundation (SNF). It explores the possibilities of technology mediated systems to alter the human sensory apparatus from artistic-experimental and

media history angles. In particular, "Sensorium of Animals" focusses on the ability to "feel" man-made electromagnetic (EM) fields [11] taking inspiration from weak electric fish and their sensing abilities.
Nuclear radiation which is the concern of the described project manifest as gamma waves and x-rays at the short wavelength end of the EM spectrum. Thus, the project described in this paper directly descents from "Sensorium of Animals."

Acknowledgements
An elaborate team of people helped with this project and offered their advice and support. Connecting and programming the electronic components was taken care off by Akitoshi Honda. Advice and feedback was provided from Shintaro Miyazaki. The trip to Fukushima was guided and organized by Daisuke Takeya and Yukiko Sato. Tobias Schneider was responsible for filming and sound recording. Yuu Takahashi has been acting in the role of the "samurai". The project was realized with the help of Hessisches Landesmuseum and the Schader Foundation in Darmstadt.

For reviewing purpose an extract of the video can be seen on the platform Vimeo under the following link:

https://vimeo.com/190166481/6c2e9c4d06

References
1. Steinbuch, K. 1965. *Automat und Mensch*. Springer.
2. McLuhan, M. 1964. *Understanding media*. McGraw-Hill.
3. Robert Jungk. 1970. *Heller als tausend Sonnen*, Reinbek: Rowohlt.
4. C.a. 1830-1832. *Ejiri in Suruga Province*. The Metropolitan Museum of Art.
5. Alain Silver. 1977. *The samurai film*, South Brunswick: A.S. Barnes.
6. Nutopia 2011. Retrieved December 12, 2016 from http://nutopia2011.blogspot.ch/.
7. Fukushima no Alice. Retrieved December 12, 2016 from http://www.fukushimanoalice.com/
8. Website of Yasuaki Kakehi Laboratory, SFC, Keio University, 2016. Retrieved December 12, 2016 from http://www.xlab.sfc.keio.ac.jp/?works=ambient-camera-who-released-the-shutter.
9. Don't Follow the Wind. Frieze.com. Retrieved December 12, 2016 from https://frieze.com/article/dont-follow-wind.
10. Fukushima exclusion zone. Retrieved December 12, 2016 from http://www.fukushima-nogozone.com/.
11. Shintaro Miyzaki and Martin Howse. 2010. 16th International Symposium on Electronic Art ISEA 2010. In Detektors. Rhythms of Electromagnetic Emissions, their Psychogeophysics and Micrological Auscultation. 136–138.

Distorted Reality: Augmented 3D Photogrammetry Over HoloLens™

Denis Vlieghe*
Cube-zero
#3 11 beacon hill, London, UK
Denis@cube-zero.com

Austin S. Lee*
Carnegie Mellon University
School of Design, 5000 Forbes
Ave, Pittsburgh, PA, USA 15213
austinslee@cmu.edu

Wayne Chung
Carnegie Mellon University
School of Design, 5000 Forbes
Ave, Pittsburgh, PA, USA 15213
wcchung@andrew.cmu.edu

* These authors contributed equally to this work

TEI '17, March 20-23, 2017, Yokohama, Japan
ACM 978-1-4503-4676-4/17/03.
http://dx.doi.org/10.1145/3024969.3025056

Abstract
Our work explores the vision of integrating 3d data collected through photogrammetry into the source of the information in a physical space leveraging Mixed Reality (MR) interface platform. As a proof-of-concept prototype design, we show augmentation of the 3D data associated with the physical surrounding using HoloLens and Photogrammetry technique. Our goals are two folds: First, to introduce novel interaction design technique to duplicate and superimpose the physical world virtually in a Mixed Reality setting. Second, to understand how people will interpret and interact in this new hybrid space where artistic photogrammetry 3D renderings of the space are overlaid onto the real world as a multidimensional Mixed Reality element.

Author Keywords
Distorted Reality; Augmented Photogrammetry; Tangible Interfaces; Augmented Reality; Wearable Computing.

ACM Classification Keywords
H.5.m. Information interfaces and presentation (e.g., HCI): Miscellaneous. H.5.2 [Information Interfaces and Presentation]: User Interfaces

Introduction

Immersive media design has become increasingly pervasive in recent years as more off-the-shelf Augmented Reality (AR) and Virtual Reality (VR) devices have been introduced to the general public [3,4]. While computer technology in conceptual modeling now allows creating accurate 3D model by reading information from the real world, there haven't been many explorations in mixing real-time data from 3D scanning and reality capturing with the physical space. We explore an artwork where participants can distort spatiotemporal relation between immersive simulation and the reality of an environment. We achieve this by collecting 3D information through photogrammetry and superimposing the volumetric data onto the physical space while anchoring it onto the source. The proposed system design enables users to manipulate the 3D information and change the level of abstraction in the augmented renderings. The user should be able to zoom into the virtual structure while comparing it with the original context in the physical world.

While there have been AR applications that make wide use of graphical user interface or 3D models constructed in a CAD software, integration of reality capturing and conceptual modeling techniques in immersive platforms is an interesting space to examine. Artists and designers have been exploring the use of high definition images from real world recording as means to achieve immersive expressions (discussed in related work section). However, application of state-of-art visualization method in immersive environment leveraging Mixed Reality platform is yet to be explored to reach its full potential.

Figure 1: Distorted Reality concept: 3D data obtained from photogrammetry scanning is virtually augmented onto physical environment.

Related Work

Reality Capturing for *Immersive Expressions*

Prior artistic investigation using 2D film loop projector in an immersive film installation piece and interactive system using depth camera and stereoscopic projector to capture and visualize real world objects have demonstrated the effectiveness of applying reality capturing in both 2D and 3D AR. [3,5,6].

Reviewing Spatiotemporal Dimensions
Timescope enables participants to view a scene backwards in time at a particular location through a see-thru device by augmenting historical photos shot from the precise location where the viewer is observing [2]. Khronos projector allows people to explore movie timelines by mapping the time axis in 3D space. Viewers can push the projection surface of the art piece inwards to trip backwards in time [1].

Distorted Reality

In our system design, we integrate reality capturing via photogrammetry in an AR device to explore the impact of providing an alternate 3D view of the physical world in a Mixed Reality setting. Various visualization methods for the augmentation could include:

- Simulation of Time Manipulation – By collecting photogrammetry images in different timelines, we can archive the changes that took place in a particular location. The photogrammetry data in different timelines can be viewed in space.
- Abstraction of Space – The 3D data of the space can be rendered in realistic or abstract way to provide a poetic experience for each individual.
- Spatiotemporal Versioning – Designers and sculptors can review changes in the physical setting in immersive way by saving and importing various 3D scenes associated with the space.

Premises
Our project begins as collaboration between different disciplines – User Experience/Industrial/Architectural design - investigating the potential uses of photogrammetry in various design fields. The main reason for us to choose photogrammetry was to find quick and affordable alternatives to industrial, high fidelity 3d scanning. With a combination of current and democratized smartphones phones and apps/software we ran a series of tests in a workshop setting with product design and environment design students from CMU to measure the potential of these tools for their respective disciplines (Figure 2). The first and obvious use identified was to scan physical models and objects to be able to manipulate them digitally.

Distorted Reality
The original concept of what we refer to as "distorted reality" emerged from observing all the possible variations of outputs when capturing and creating a 3d model of a subject through photogrammetry, and the range of variation between these outputs and their real physical counterparts. Unlike IR scanning methods (e.g. lidar), which are designed to return consistent 3d point clouds regardless of light, weather, and other similar conditions, photogrammetry-generated point clouds may vary depending on these conditions, especially when reconstructing textures. Also, user-generated inaccuracies in the picture taking process will distort the final outputs.

Although inaccuracies can be seen as undesirable, the concept of distorted reality aims to harness the potential of these distortions and embrace the fact that the same subject may return different results depending on how the user viewed and photographed it, and how the capture information is processed. The scope of the project is to explore how notions of an environment can change and influence people's behaviors by introducing a system design that augments an alternative version of the environment in different level of fidelity and abstractions (figure 3).

Figure 2: Workshop material sample (left) and student project deliverable (right)

The importance of user-based experience has become more than a trend and is one of the most common foundations found across disciplines, shall it be travel, social media, interactive art, and technology. By defining the concept of Distorted Realities and by identifying the range of distortions going from high-fidelity photogrammetry to highly distorted point clouds and their corresponding application (e.g. from engineering to art), we aim to create completely new immersive venues for using AR wearable technologies.

Implementation and Future Work

We use photogrammetry software, such as ReMake, Visual SFM citation, Meshlab citation to capture 3D information from the physical world and document HoloLens integration in a concept video to demonstrate the vision of Distorted Reality. In addition, as proof-of-concept prototype, we showcase various visualization of augmenting photogrammetry data in space via video editing software. The overlay of 3D data could act like

Figure 3: Interface design concept for choosing various visualizations of photogrammetry augmentation

an HDR 2D photograph, creating an enhanced sense of the space. The unique aspect is that the capture of the data can come in varied resolution (dictated by the operator); and the distortion (whether on purpose or not) build on the new AR/VR environment. We envision creating an application within HoloLens that could process photogrammetry capture and enable users to import the rendered 3D data seamlessly without having to use different devices.

The vision is to enable participants to capture an environment and duplicate the surrounding structure in various timeline to achieve an immersive multidimensional experience. We envision applying the concept design in following scenarios:

Figure 5: Photogrammetry image processing to generate point cloud data using Visual SFM

Figure 4: Photogrammetry mesh data Augmented in HoloLens field of view (left), alternative point cloud rendering concept (right

Figure 6: Point clouds created from photogrammetry scan of Bedford Square in London for the Architectural Association's Aditnalta visiting school in collaboration with drone filming company SkyEdge 360 1

- Spatial versioning – By collecting photogrammetry images in different timelines, we can archive the changes that took place in a particular location. The photogrammetry data in different timelines can be viewed in space. This application would be useful for iterating designs of a physical model with temporal references. Also, the design concept would work for recording a classroom session and superimposing immersive 3D snapshots ofs highlight moments of the class asynchronously in the same location.
- Distorted landscape – The 3D data of the space can be rendered in realistic or abstract way to provide a poetic experience for each individual. This application also allows for scale manipulations where the data capture is re-rendered at a different scale than the original one. Figure 6 shows our study of using drone to achieve 3D photogrammetry of large-scale space. Scaled down representation of the space in Mixed Reality environment can instantly provide birds-eye-view reference of the architectural structure to assist navigations or help participants study the space.

Conclusion

In this paper, we introduced the vision of Distorted Reality to explore a design space where 3D photogrammetry is augmented into the real world via Mixed Reality computing platforms such as HoloLens. Such concept and interface can lead to building immersive applications that add temporal dimension in space and interactive simulation of alternate environment anchored to physical reference. It also allows for emphasizing a scene via artistic and poetic visualizations of 3D photogrammetry. Going forward, based on our preliminary concept prototype, we would like to continue our artistic investigation integrating real time capturing and rendering tools into the Mixed Reality environment.

References

1. Alvaro Cassinelli and Masatoshi Ishikawa. 2005. Khronos projector. In *ACM SIGGRAPH 2005 Emerging technologies* (SIGGRAPH '05), Donna Cox (Ed.). ACM, New York, NY, USA, , Article 10 .

2. Art+Com, Timescope. Retrieved November 1, 2016 from https://artcom.de/en/project/timescope/
3. Henry Chen, Austin S. Lee, Mark Swift, and John C. Tang. 2015. 3D Collaboration Method over HoloLens™ and Skype™ End Points. In *Proceedings of the 3rd International Workshop on Immersive Media Experiences* (ImmersiveME '15). ACM, New York, NY, USA, 27-30.
4. HoloLens at Windows 10 event. Retrieved November 1, 2016 from http://www.polygon.com/features/2016/10/27/13433658/microsoft-headsets-aim-to-democratize-mixed-reality
5. Hrvoje Benko, Ricardo Jota, and Andrew Wilson. 2012. MirageTable: freehand interaction on a projected augmented reality tabletop. In *Proceedings of the SIGCHI Conference on Human Factors in Computing Systems* (CHI '12). ACM, New York, NY, USA, 199-208.
6. Michael Naimark. 1996. Be now here (welcome to the neighborhood). In *ACM SIGGRAPH 96 Visual Proceedings: The art and interdisciplinary programs of SIGGRAPH '96* (SIGGRAPH '96), Brian Blau, Clark Dodsworth, Linda Branagan, Jean Ippolito, Ken Musgrave, and Warren Waggenspack (Eds.). ACM, New York, NY, USA, 61-.

InTouch Wearables: Exploring Ambient Remote Touch in Child-Parent Relationships

Jinsil Hwaryoung Seo
Texas A&M University
3137 TAMU, College Station, TX
hwaryoung@tamu.edu

Annie Sungkajun
Texas A&M University
3137 TAMU, College Station, TX
flora.s_secret@tamu.edu

Meghan Cook
Texas A&M University
3137 TAMU, College Station, TX
mecook20@tamu.edu

TEI '17, March 20-23, 2017, Yokohama, Japan
ACM 978-1-4503-4676-4/17/03.
http://dx.doi.org/10.1145/3024969.3025057

Abstract
InTouch Wearables is a set of wearables that consist of dresses and shoulder pieces that allow mother and child share remote touches through garments with ambient feedback. This was developed to explore how remote touches can convey emotion and help people stay connected between remote locations. This project was created based on the lead artist's personal experience with her child. In *InTouch Wearables*, a parent can increase the vividness of her conversation with a child through contextualized touch, and the loved ones may enhance the affective tone of their communication using a remote touch technology. All the electronic components of the garment for sensing human touches and actuating color-changing garment are integrated on the main fabrics. Audience will be able to touch and activate interaction between garments.

Author Keywords
Remote touch; child-parent relationship; wearables; color changing garment; creative engagement

ACM Classification Keywords
H.5.m. Information interfaces and presentation (e.g., HCI): Miscellaneous

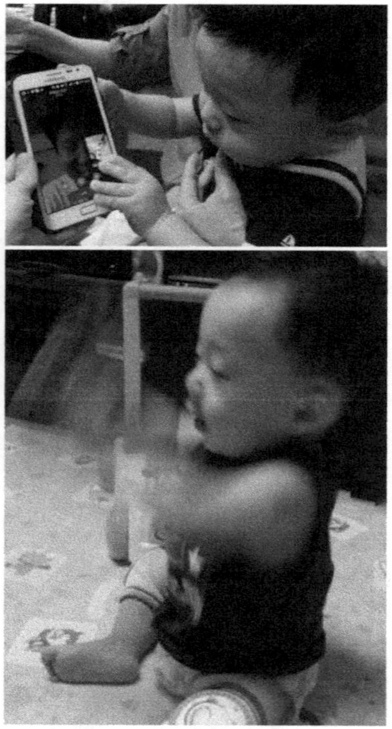

Figure 1. The artist's personal motivation: skyping with her son (top) and his active movements (bottom)

Introduction

Human interpersonal touch plays an important role in our social interaction in expressing affect and fostering intimacy. It is a special conduit through which humans convey love, comfort, care, trust, support, and appreciation. Touch is immediate in that it carries emotional meaning in ways that words cannot express. *InTouch Wearables* consists of a mother dress and a child dress. They share touch information through garments in an ambient way. The artists explore how emotion can be embodied through remote touch. This paper describes conceptual and technical details of *InTouch Wearables*.

Background

Artist's Personal Motivation

InTouch Wearables was created originally based on the lead artist's personal experience with her child. When her son was one-year-old, he stayed with his grandparents in Korea apart from the artist.

> *Even though I was able to see him everyday via Skype and watch videos of him recorded by my parents over and over, I struggled emotionally very much because I wasn't able to feel him. I felt I was missing many important moments of my son's life at that time. I wanted to touch him and wanted to be touched by him. Since he wasn't able to communicate verbally at that time, a physical touch was a very important communication between us. Apparently, I often hugged a cushion that my son used to play with and I even smelled it. That really helped me to feel the presence of him in my place."*

As an artist, she wanted to capture that moment as wearable and tangible artworks exploring the concept of remote touch. The final outcomes and the process of *InTouch Wearables* helped the artist to get immersed in the remote parent-child relationship and overcome the emotional challenge.

Importance of Touch in Child-Parent Relationship

Physical contact is important across the lifespan [1]. Touch is a very important part of developing attachment between the child and parents. It is the beginning of communication between them; the child learns to trust you and develops an emotional tie to the parents [2]. Touch is not only critical to children but it is important to parents. For many women, the period after giving birth can be an unexpected low time. An astonishing number of women - from 70 to 80 percent, according to the American Congress of Obstetricians and Gynecologists - feel depressed in the days after their babies are born. And about 10 percent experience a more serious ailment called postpartum depression (PPD). So a new relationship through touch with a child is very important to parents especially women [3].

Feeling Connected

"Remote touch" is the ability to produce physical sensations without physical interaction [4]. This concept has been experimented and created by artists and researchers. There are projects that focus on ambient communication of intimate people in remote places. BreathingFrame offers couples in long distance relationships the ability to see their partner's breath on an inflatable digital frame [5]. BodyPods is a remotely paired set of communicating chairs that facilitate a sense of presence by leveraging implicit actions such as sitting to communicate that someone you care about is home [6]. In addition, SyncDecor [7] is a pair of appliances, LumiTouch [8] is a pair of photo frames, and ComSlipper [9] is a pair of slippers, to indicate the activities of a partner who lives far away. However most of projects focus on direct communication producing physical sensations. In *InTouch Wearables*, the artists focus on creating an affective/shared moment for any parent-child relationships via ambient color changing effects on the garments. In addition, they utilize wearables as a creative interface to share messages between child and parent.

Design Explorations

Touch Interface

The first set of *InTouch Wearables* consists of a mother's dress and a child's dress. Only the child's dress has touch sensitive parts. Whenever each touch area is being touched, a capacitive sensor embedded in the garment triggers degree of touch and the touch information is sent to the mapped area of the mother's dress and changes the color of the area. The touch sensors on the child dress were distributed on the front side of the dress so that they detect non intentional movements and contacts with others. The shoulder pieces of *InTouch Wearables* have soft touch sensors that are integrated into the design. Since these are for children over 6 years and a parent, we created a soft object that they can touch or caress when they want to send touch messages each other.

Creative Engagement Through Wearables

Fabric petals on each shoulder piece of *InTouch Wearables* have unique invisible drawings and stitches. These can be only visible when the shoulder piece receives touch signals from the paired shoulder piece and UV LEDs light up. UV LEDs create a nice blue illumination on petals and the wearer can see this effect in his or her peripheral view. Each petal can be decorated by child and parent using an invisible UV marker. Through this method, family members can share messages each other or co-design their wearables.

Figure 2. (top) *InTouch* Wearables dresses, (middle) *InTouch* Wearables shoulder pieces with a soft touch sensor, (bottom) *InTouch* Wearables shoulder pieces with an embedded touch sensor

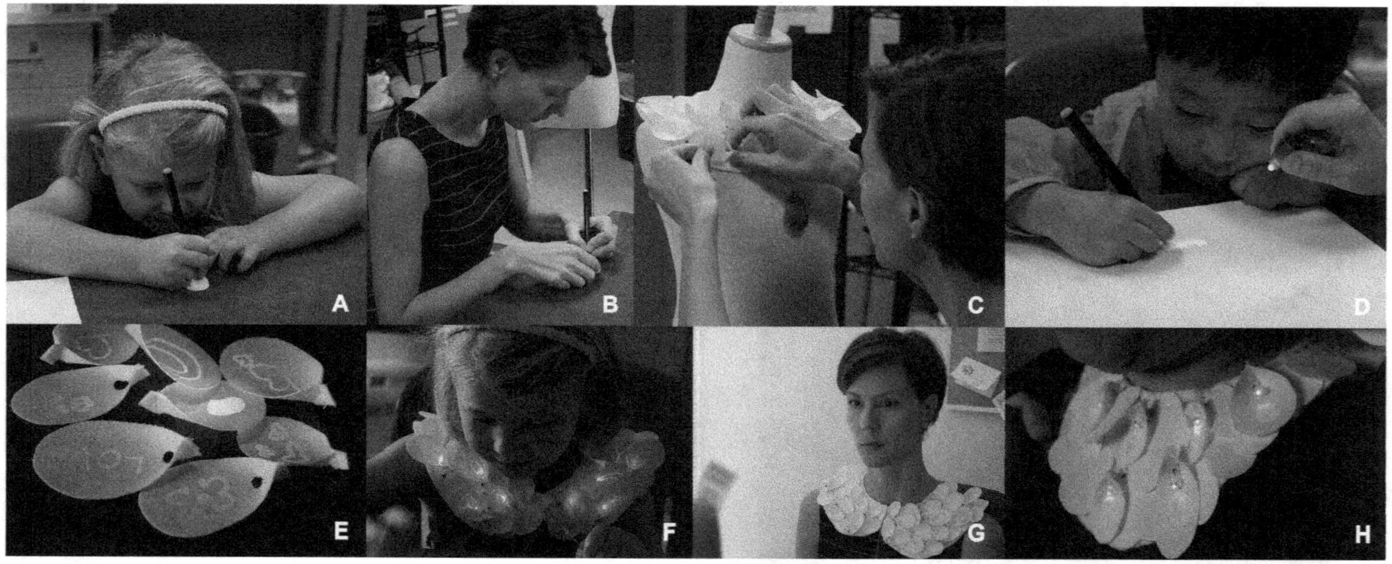

Figure 3: A. Child drawing on a petal using an invisible UV marker, B. mother drawing, C. mother putting a petal with her drawing on the InTouch shoulder piece. D. child playing with an invisible UV drawing, E. Drawn examples on fabric petals, F. child wearing a shoulder piece that reveals hidden drawing by UV LEDs, G. mother wearing a shoulder piece at work, H. close-up of UV ink drawing on petals

Implementation

InTouch Wearables has been developed in focus of three technical approaches: soft circuit, networked garments, color changing garment.

Soft Circuits

The garments are constructed from iterative explorations of soft circuits using conductive fabric, yarn and thread as well as Lilypad Arduino [10] and Light Bluebeen + [11] boards with a capacitive sensing circuit and a heat control circuit. The aesthetic and material properties are shaped equally by the needs of the electronic elements, material characteristics of the textiles and qualities of the wearer's physical movement. Placement and organization of the sensors are guided by body ergonomics, somatic expertise in 'meaning through movement' and interaction design. Together these material explorations combine to guide the design of aesthetics. Tactile interaction creates playful, intimate connections between the garment and the wearer [12].

Networked Garments

In *inTouch Wearables dresses*, the mother's garment

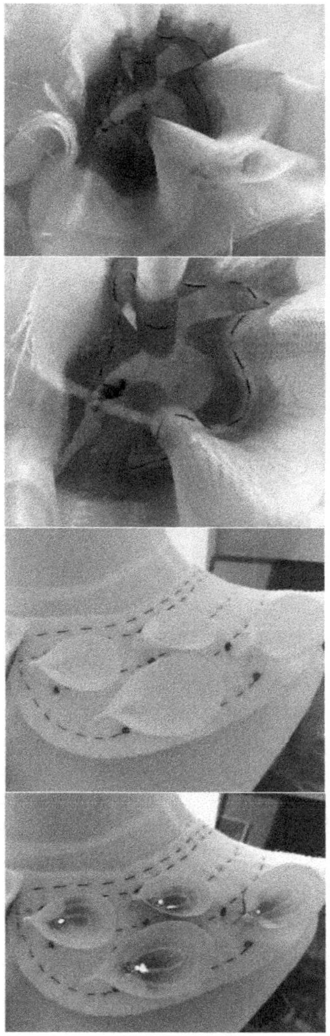

Figure 6. Color changing garment using thermochromic pigment (top) and using invisible UV ink

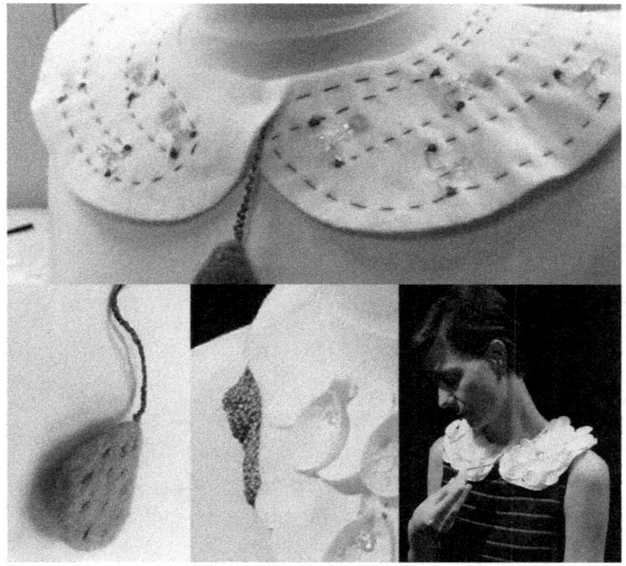

Figure 5. Soft Circuit of *InTouch Wearables*

and the child garment communicate wirelessly via an Xbee and Lilypad Arduino. The child dress has five touch sensitive spots that look like flowers. When they are triggered by human touch, the green pattern of the flower changes its color to yellow and the touch signal is sent to the mother's garment. The flower on the mother's dress mapped to the sensor on the child's dress changes its color from dark pink to white. This creates not an alert rather an ambient experience. In *InTouch Wearables* shoulder pieces, the mother's and child's garments communicate via Bluetooth on Light bluebean + board.

Color Changing Garments

The color changing aspect of the project has been utilized using thermochromic powders and invisible UV inks. Thermochromic powders are heat sensitive and the transition temperature to a different color is 86F. For the child's dress, green color powder was mixed with fabric medium and yellow acrylic paint. The mixed

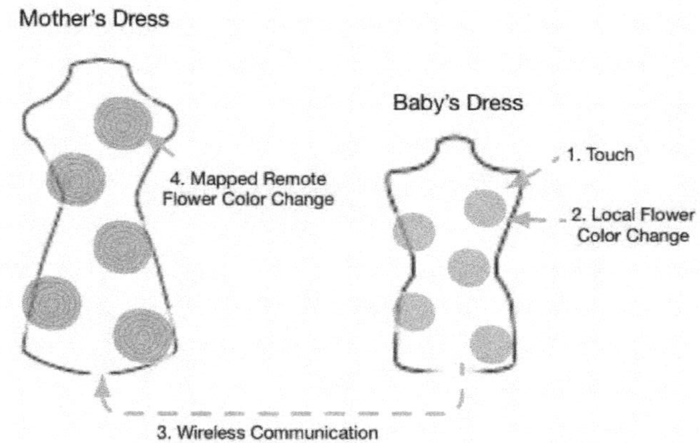

Figure 4. Network diagram of *inTouch Wearables* dresses

paint was applied to the fabric using a stencil technique (Fig. 6. top). For the mother's dress, conductive thread was stitched on the surface of pink thermochromic paint and fabricated as a flower (Fig. 6. bottom). The conductive thread was used as a heat source and connected to the heat control circuit. The color change using thermal materials tends to be slow. It creates a passive and ambient wearable interface. This supports a mother feels always so close to the child's daily life including physical movements and interaction with surroundings. Invisible UV Ink can be seen only under an ultraviolet light. The artists integrated invisible patterns on the garment.

Conclusion

InTouch Wearables explored the concept of remote touch in a parent and child relationship using color changing garments. The artists took a poetic approach rather than a practical approach and the concept was realized as tangible/wearable forms and the technology was implemented to six wearable garments. This can be expanded to different designs (i.e. cushion or toy) and applications to investigate qualities of tactile experience. Wearer-friendly designs are suggested to be worn in the daily life.

Video Link

https://youtu.be/ztErIhRWIvs

References

1. Field, T., et al., *Touch for socioemotional and physical well-being: A review.* Developmental Review, 2010. **30**(4): p. 367-383.
2. Montagu, A., *Touching: The Human Significance of the Skin*. Body, Mind & Spirit. 1986: Harper Collins.
3. Abalovich, M.e.a., *Management of Thyroid Dysfunction during Pregnancy and Postpartum: An Endocrine Society Clinical Practice Guideline.* Journal of Clinical Endocrinology and Metabolism, 2011. **92**(8).
4. Teh, J.K.S. and A.D. Cheok. *Affective Interface for Remote Non-verbal Communication*. 2008; Available from: https://yctforum.wordpress.com/2008/08/28/presentations-on-day-2/dsc05852.
5. Kim, J., Y.W. Park, and T.J. Nam. *BreathingFrame: An Inflatable Frame for Remote Breath Signal Sharing*. in *Ninth International Conference on Tangible, Embedded, and Embodied Interaction*. 2015. Stanford: ACM.
6. Papanikolaou, D., A.J.B. Brush, and A. Roseway. *BodyPods: Designing Posture Sensing Chairs for Capturing and Sharing Implicit Interactions*. in *Ninth International Conference on Tangible, Embedded, and Embodied Interaction*. 2015. Stanford: ACM.
7. Tsujita, H., K. Tsukada, and I. Siio. *SyncDecor: Appliances for Sharing Mutual Awareness between Lovers Separated by Distance*. in *CHI '07 Extended Abstracts*. 2007. ACM.
8. Chang, A., et al. *LumiTouch: An emotional communication device*. in *CHI '01 Extended Abstracts*. 2001. ACM.
9. Chen, C.Y., J. Forlizzi, and J. P. *ComSlipper: An expressive design to support awareness and availability*. in *CHI '06 Extended Abstracts*. 2006. ACM.
10. Lilypad Arduino. [cited 2015 July, 14]; Available from: https://www.arduino.cc/en/Main/ArduinoBoardLilyPad.
11. LightBlue Bean +. 2016 [cited 2016 Oct. 15]; Available from: https://punchthrough.com/bean.
12. Schiphorst, T., *Soft(n): Towards a Somaesthetics of Tactile Interaction*, in *CHI09*. 2009, ACM. p. 2427-2438.

Tea with Crows: Experiencing Proactive Ubiquitous Technology by Interactive Art

Young Suk Lee
Indiana University, South Bend
South Bend, IN 46615, USA
yslnm@umail.iu.edu

Figure1. Tea with Crows
Motion Interactive Sculpture

TEI '17, March 20-23, 2017, Yokohama, Japan
ACM 978-1-4503-4676-4/17/03.
http://dx.doi.org/10.1145/3024969.3025058

Abstract
"Tea with Crows" is an interactive sculptural installation seeking to enable a poetic use of technology that offers stimulation and provocation. It does so by embedding aesthetic elements, experimental ideas and practical usage into ubiquitous computing. This multi-modal interactive piece connects people to each other, and constructs social conversation while engaging in innovative ambient design and technology. "Tea with Crows" explores experiential aesthetic by embedding playful kinetic motion and shape changing interfaces into everyday objects. The transformable form, function, and action of the sculpture are synchronized between the tea table and chandelier enriching the human experience. Ultimately, "Tea with Crows" aims to bring an expressive digital object with ubiquitous computing into the foreground of our everyday life by creating proactive interaction beyond the calm display.

Author Keywords
Art; Interactive sculpture; Aesthetic Interaction; Pro Active Technology

ACM Classification Keywords
H.5.m. Information interfaces and presentation (e.g., HCI): Miscellaneous

Figure2. Before Interaction

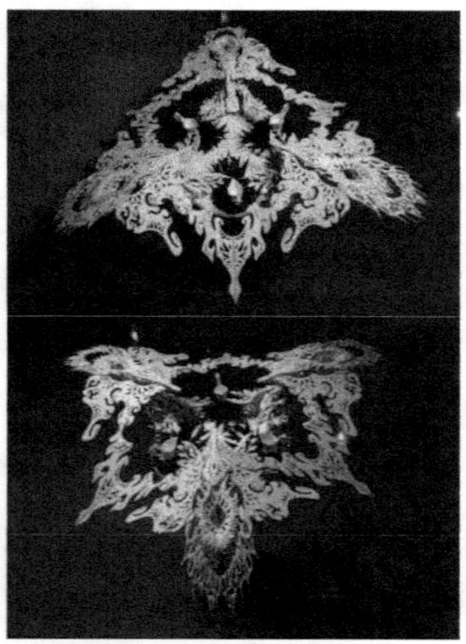

Figure3. After Interaction

Tea with Crows

Motion Interactive tea table

Introduction

Ultimately, I intend to create a novel Design that integrates art, technology and human need that cares user experience goals such as fun, emotionally fulfilling, all while being supportive of creativity and aesthetics. [9] I suggest an expressive tangible artifact to enlarge the creative vision of how 'Proactive Ubiquitous Computing' [7] is diffused between innovative art and aesthetic interaction. "Tea with Crows", will be reviewed on how "the experience driven design" is embedded in our everyday life. I intend to create the intricate aesthetic interaction through an interactive shape-changing interface that transforms into two variable roles between everyday furniture and sculpture. The dual transformation of form and function that is activated by audience participation will enrich experience through Art and Technology. The other aspect of this experience aims to bring playful interaction from the kinetic motion of a living organism.

Work Description

"Tea with Crows" is a motion interactive shape changing sculpture that consists of two design components: a stand-alone sculpture that transforms into a tea table for three people, and a kinetic chandelier which hangs from the ceiling. Using a 3D modeling process, I printed assemblages of over 223 plastic and metal pieces, connected the delicate segments of the table and the chandelier, tested the sensors and lastly embedded servo motors. It took 6 months to construct both of the pieces. The table is expressed as a big white swan sculpture. When audiences are nearby, the table opens its wings in three directions like the blooming of a flower. Once the table is opened, the table reveals three cups and dishes, inviting the audience to "tea time." The upper sculpture is then activated, drawing the audiences' attention upward. Three black birds that are latched onto the chandelier begin playful dancing motions. When the audience interacts with all three cups at the same time, they hear happy laughing sounds from the birds. When the audience leaves 'Tea with Crows' after tea time ends, the table transforms back into it's original swan shape. This video demonstrates how the real time interaction works between the table, chandelier, and the audience member. https://vimeo.com/184890191

Motivation

Our life has been made so convenient by using personal devices such as smartphones, laptops, tables etc. Technology offers so much information and entertainment via internet browsing, social networking, and games that create exciting virtual reality. Ironically however, these activities often prevent us from connecting to people nearby us. When people get together for a cup of coffee, concert or a meeting, the common experience now is that people pay half attention to the real world while the other hand is holding and interacting with their personal device. But "Tea with Crows" creates an engaging interaction that opens a shared experience between people by encouraging active participation into the ubiquitous computing. The interactivity aims to connect people's emotion to each other with the technology in a social setting, rather than being distracted by an individual interaction with technology. As McCarthy and Wright claimed:" we don't just simply use or admire technology but we *live* with it." "The interaction with technology can involve emotions, value, ideals, intentions, and strong feelings." [2] In the similar vein, "Tea with Crows" explores ubiquitous technology which has increasingly become embedded in our life through

Figure5. Tea with Crows
Motion Interactive Chandelier

Figure6. Tea with Crows
Interactive cups and dishes

everyday objects in order to support the complex human needs. It also strongly encourages us to explore an opportunity that technology lives and co-evolves alongside us.

Figure 4. Tea with Crows
Motion Interactive Chandelier

Aesthetic Interaction

While aesthetics and interaction are tightly interwoven, I intend to create an intricate appearance, rich interaction, and diverse functions that enable the creation of aesthetic interaction. This is accomplished by considering both sensory and conceptual quality [3]. The aesthetic interaction from "Tea with Crows" is not only speaking to the shape or structure of sculpture; it also suggests the "experiential aesthetics" in order to reach to a holistic quality such as excitement, curiosity, attraction from the interaction [5]. The emotional fluctuation and variable inspiration can be gained through a contingency of the intrinsic experience with interactivities. Also, "Tea with Crows" intends to combine the multisensory elements that people can touch, see the kinetic movements and hear the sound elements. This expressive interactivity allows people to have a bodily interaction with a digital artifact that address physical, cognitive, sensual, and aesthetic modes of human experience [4].

The main shift from the task-oriented design to the present designs expands the research focus as well; it not only focuses on ease of use but also *how to look and feel. [7]* I intend to create an interactive piece that enriches the audience's experience from unique aesthetics and playful interaction that simulates a living organism. I embedded four unique characters that inspired me by animal's movement in "Tea with Crows" as various interactive kinetic motions: The first white sculpture gracefully opens up folded wings like an elegant swan, while the second black sculpture's motion from the ceiling has 3 more dynamic movements. Very fast and repeatable crow's flapping that looks like a bird is hysterically picking the metal chandelier, awkwardly rotates back and forth, and slowly fold the segments of the wing in a very quiet and creepy way, "human beings possess a deeply rooted response to motion, recognizing innately in it a quality of "being alive" provoking a significantly deeper and emotional response from users." [1] I observed that the kinetic motion has not only increased the audience's engagement, but has inspired a wide range of emotional responses.

Calm to Active Ubiquitous Computing

The vision of Ambient Intelligence promises a seamless integration of computational technology woven into everyday life regardless of our attention [8]. Furthermore, ubiquitous Computing has been perpetually enmeshed into the background of our life more so than active interaction with a user. Particularly, raising a great attention that there is a significant shifting from proactive computing to proactive people, underlying the interaction design direction was the goal to attempt to enlarge ambient experience.

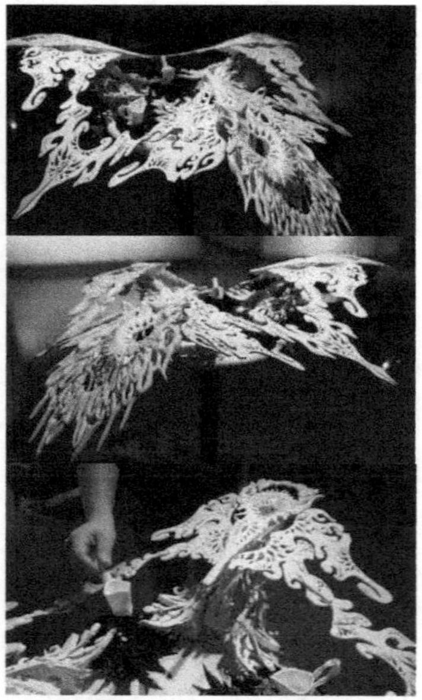

Figure8. Tea with Crows
Interactive tea table

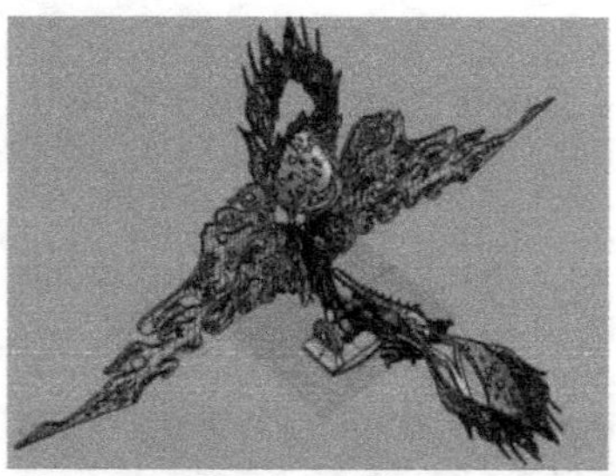

Figure9. 3D modeling process

Materials: plastic, wood, metal, feather, Arduino, motion sensor, magnetic sensors, light bulbs etc.

The object which is no longer solely designed just for passive usage; instead, the design is capable of fulfilling human desire through an act of engagement of the world. This claim advocates that pervasive computing needs to be oriented towards engaging approach by excitement of interaction. [7] The interaction focuses on playfulness and creativity by endorsing the movements towards experience driven design from task-oriented design. [6] Active Ubicomp can be achieved by intermingling the consensus elements of aesthetic artifacts, and participating with the aesthetic activity, making users position shift from spectators to participant. "Tea with Crows" allows users to initiate to active and variable form and use in the functions through everyday furniture that could engage with the ambient system. This interactivity aims to bring the ambient objects and ubiquitous computing to the foreground instead of as a backdrop; otherwise, it exists as a sculptural element for display or remains as mundane objects.

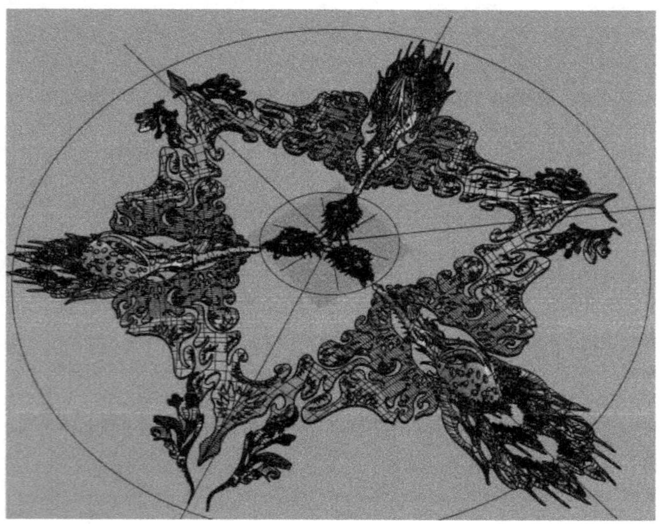

Figure7. Tea with Crows
3D Render Image

References

1. Hiroshi Ishii, Brygg Ullmer. 1997. Tangible Bits: Toward seamless interfaces between people, bits, and atoms. In Proceedings of CHI 1997, ACM Press
2. John McCarthy, Peter Wright. 2007. Technology as Experience, The MIT Press.
3. J.P. Djajadiningrat, W.W. Gaver, J.W. Frens. 2000. Interaction Relabelling and Extreme Characters:Methods for Exploring Aesthetic Interactions, In the proceedings of the 3rd conference on Designing interactive, 66-71
4. Mark Weiser. 1999. The computer for the 21st century, Special issue on ACM SIGMOBILE Mobile Computing and Communications Review, 3-11, 1999, New York, USA
5. Maiken Hillerup Fogtmann, Jonas Fritsch, Karen Johanne Kortbek.2008. Kinesthetic Interaction:Revealing the Bodily Potential in Interaction Design. In proceedings of the 20th Australasian Conference on Computer-Human Interaction, 89-96
6. Philip Ross, David V. Keyson. 2007. The case of sculpting atmospheres: towards design principles for expressive tangible interaction in control of ambient systems. Journal Personal and Ubiquitous Computing, 69-79
7. Yvonne Rogers. 2006. Moving on from Weiser's Vision of Calm Computing: Engaging Ubicomp Experiences. In proceedings of the 8th international conference on Ubiquitous Computing, 404-421
8. Youn-kyung Lim. 2013. Discovery-Driven Prototyping for user-Driven Creativity, PERVASIVE computing, Published by the IEEE CS 1536-1268/13, IEEE
9. Yvonne Rogers, Helen Sharp, Jenny Preece. 2002. *Interaction Design: beyond human-computer interaction*, New York: John Wiley & Sons, Inc. ISBN 0-471-49278-7.

The Design and Evaluation of Embodied Interfaces for Supporting Spatial Ability

Jack Shen-Kuen Chang
Polytechnic Institute, Purdue University
Synaesthetic Media Lab (SynLab), Ryerson University
JackSKChang@gmail.com

ABSTRACT
Shown in many longitudinal studies, spatial ability is important to learning and career success. This paper, inspired by [2,14], presents the new generation of TASC (Tangibles for Augmenting Spatial Cognition) to illustrate how (re)design lessons can be learned, how existing evaluation methods can be applied, and how new evaluations may be generated or envisioned, when a TEI (tangible and embodied interaction) system is built to study spatial ability.

Author Keywords
Embodied cognition; tangible interaction; virtual environment; spatial cognition; spatial ability; game; STEM

ACM Classification Keywords
H.5.m. Information interfaces and presentation (e.g., HCI): Miscellaneous.

INTRODUCTION
Spatial cognition is about how we retrieve, organize, and use spatial information in relation to the environments. The ability to process and apply spatial information is vital to our daily lives. Such ability is characterized or defined as spatial ability. In many professions, spatial ability has been shown as an important cognitive factor. For example, the United States' 2012 Report to the President [15] asked for one million additional STEM (science, technology, engineering, and mathematics) graduates to meet the increasing demand from the workforce. This reinforced the importance of spatial ability, as many longitudinal studies showed that spatial ability is highly associated with STEM learning and career success. Selected longitudinal studies are: 1) Study of Mathematically Precocious Youth (SMPY) [13], which followed more than 5,000 academically performant students for 35 years starting from 1971. This study showed that spatial ability strongly links to success in STEM fields; 2) In 2009, Wai et al. [16] examined 50 years of research, with samples extracted from 400,000 participants who were tracked for at least 11 years. Wai's results were coherent with those from SMPY's, and indicated that spatial ability can be a strong predictor of STEM performance.

TEI '17, March 20-23, 2017, Yokohama, Japan
© 2017 ACM. ISBN 978-1-4503-4676-4/17/03...$15.00
DOI: http://dx.doi.org/10.1145/3024969.3025033

Understanding and manipulating spatial information is also important for interaction design. Many TEI/HCI (human-computer interaction) systems are unified together with seminal design frameworks, which contain spatial-related themes. For instance, the RBI (Reality-Based Interaction) framework [10] analyses and consolidates interaction styles with the themes of *Environment Awareness and Skills* (for spatial information related to objects and environments), Naïve Physics, Body Awareness and Skills, and Social Awareness and Skills. Hornecker's framework [9] also enumerates the elements for tangible interaction: *Spatial Interaction*, Tangible Manipulation, Embodied Facilitation, and Expressive Representation.

While spatial ability is important, and the use of the ability is common in TEI systems, these following observations are the motivations (M1 to M3) that drive this research.

M1. Need to "get to the bottom" of it more: Not many studies focus on how TEI systems can directly influence spatial ability even though spatial manipulation is a common theme in TEI/HCI. Of the few TEI-related we find and include here are BDC (emBodied Digital Creativity [14]) and TASC's prototypical/conceptual 1st generation (Gen1) [2]. Meanwhile, spatial ability studied in cognitive science has involved the role of the body (egocentric vs. allocentric [12]; figural, vista, or environmental [6]), while TEI often includes the body and its movements in the interactions. Therefore, with those 2 sub-observations (few TEI systems directly study spatial ability; the body does play a role in spatial ability), we believe there are potentials to understand *more* about the effects of TEI on spatial ability.

M2. Spatial ability-specific TEI system: Findings from cognitive science have shown that spatial abilities are independent from one another. For example, perspective taking ability (spatial orientation) is not directly correlated to mental rotation [7]. Therefore, extending M1, a TEI system designed for supporting spatial ability research should target a particular spatial ability. This is also something mentioned/inspired by the design framework proposed by Clifton et al. [2].

M3. Where is the "space" in "spatial"?: Many spatial ability tests or training materials are surface-based: administered with paper, or digitized then provided with computer monitors. We are not questioning the validity of those tests or training materials because they are indeed well-developed and widely-used in many fields. But with the rising availability of VR which affords 3D perception, it is certainly worth exploring the notion of "putting space (3D perception) back to spatial (spatial tests or training materials)". Extending from this idea, new design and evaluations that put emphasis on the body (movements in physical 3D space; engaging visuo-motor skills with tangible objects) should promise research potentials.

With those motivations, we envision this work to contribute to the (re)design and evaluation for embodied interfaces built to support and improve spatial ability.

RELATED WORK

In this section, selected projects in the literature are analyzed, along with certain aspects of their application and limitation to this research.

Common Coding Theory & Spatial Ability

BDC [14] is among the few studies that investigate the effect of TEI on spatial ability (mental rotation), which is also one of the inspirations to this study. It is based on a branch of embodied cognition, "common coding theory" (ideomotor theory) [8], which claims that there are mental common codes that link perception, cognition, and action. Such links can be activated by multiple modalities of input, as well as when self-movement is recognized. BDC built a wearable exoskeleton (the puppet) which captures and displays the user's full-body movements onto a 3D avatar. A user performs rotation-based spatial tasks with the avatar by controlling the puppet. With spatial pre/post-tests, the result showed that users with the TEI condition (the puppet) had more improvement in mental rotation ability than other conditions that had less embodiment and tangibility (e.g., keyboard, XBox gamepad). BDC is about designing a TEI system to immerse users and engage their spatial ability. TASC Gen1 started with the question "how can another spatial ability (perspective taking) be studied through the lens of TEI?".

Design Framework

Very recently Clifton published his design framework [2], which is arguably the first one to systematically connect TEI design and spatial cognition. This framework analyses TEI systems in a design space populated by three dimensions with subcategories of: Aspects of Spatial Cognition, Embodiment, and Intervention. Throughout the course of this research, we will generate design lessons learned then compare them with this framework. The goal is to see if/how new design opportunities emerge by comparing the framework with the iterative (re)design process, and how generation(s) of TASC differ in design and evaluation.

Evaluation Methods

In terms of evaluation, we are not very concerned about evaluating a novel TEI system's usability or aesthetics with common approaches such as usability heuristics or interface criticism methods. We are interested in the power and limitation of 2D spatial ability tests for 3D based TEI system, and how to develop new spatial ability evaluations from a TEI (re)design experience.

While there are many (2D, paper-based) spatial ability tests, and they can be found on the NSF (of the US)-supported SILC website (Spatial Intelligence and Learning Center), it is worth noting that there is very little work that considers how to code, analyze, and classify spatial activities and strategies when TEI is involved. Among the few found, the most relevant are: Antle and Wang [1] compared spatial strategies using motor-cognitive skills between tangible and multi-touch interface users. Esteves et al. [3] provided a video coding method with 20 epistemic actions (actions that are not made directly for the goal, but are trial and errors that can reduce work complexity). They later expanded the method as the ATB Framework (Artifact, Tool, and Body) to analyze TEI-related spatial strategies, and conducted "the evaluation of the evaluation" on the framework's reliability, validity, and predictive power. ATB has certain limitations. For example, its coding method relies much on each rater's subjective interpretation; high level of action granularity; and it's originated from hand movement analysis, so its applicability to full-body movement is yet to be validated. Also, ATB does not directly study spatial ability. However, the evaluation framework, including how it was developed and further evaluated, has inspired us to study TEI-related spatial strategies when a certain spatial ability is engaged.

RESEARCH QUESTIONS

These research questions are relevant to this work. **R1.1:** What is the iterative (re)design process for a TEI interface built to support spatial ability (TASC Gen1 to Gen2)? **R1.2:** How can that (re)design be compared to the design framework proposed in [2]? **R2.1:** What are the effects of TEI interfaces on perspective taking spatial ability? **R2.2:** How is such spatial effect different from other low- or non-TEI interfaces? **R3.1:** How to use existing evaluations for a spatial ability-based TEI system? **R3.2:** What are the new evaluation methods we can generate or envision from the said (re)design process and spatial effects?

METHOD (AN ONGOING PROJECT)

We have several ongoing projects to address those research questions. Here we briefly describe one of the projects: TASC Gen2, a newer significant version as a result from our participatory and iterative design process. TASC Gen2 establishes embodiment using virtual and tangible interactions to engage perspective taking ability, allowing the user to solve a series of virtual spatial puzzles with increasing difficulty.

Overview

TASC is a VR-TEI system designed to study perspective taking ability, a kind of spatial ability that involves imaging looking at objects or environments form different points of view. This ability is important in STEM education, or trainings for pilots and drivers.

Establishing Embodiment with VR-TEI

Based on common coding theory [8] and inspired by Malazek's BDC project [14], TASC engages spatial ability by establishing embodiment, which is achieved in three ways (Figure 1): 1) The user wears an Oculus Rift head mounted display (HMD), which tracks her head movements and provides a 3D, immersive view of the virtual environment (VE); 2) Leap Motion is attached on the HMD so that the user's hand movements can be captured and rendered as virtual hands in the VE; 3) A table with two long tangible blocks is placed in front of the user. Each block can only be moved linearly as it is constrained on a rail. A block's movement is captured with a corresponding ultrasonic distance sensor. The blocks (designed and made of wood) add sensory coherence to the virtual fences (described more below).

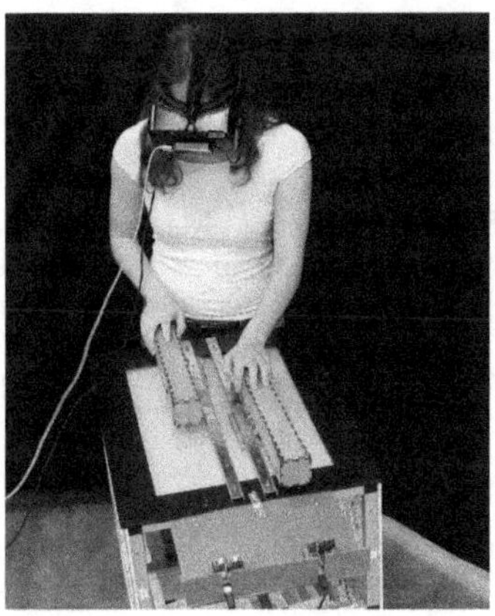

Figure 1. The physical setup of the TASC system

The VE, a game made in Unity, situates the user in a farm with structures such as a cabin, windmills, bushes, and a stack of logs. There is a standing horse whose initial position is always separated by 2 long fences from the user's ground character position. In each level, the goal is to move the physical blocks to align the virtual fences' openings, revealing a pathway for the horse to run toward to the user's ground position in the farm.

Switching Perspectives for Spatial Tasks

The user switches between two perspectives to solve a series of spatial puzzles. In GV (ground view), see Figure 2, the user sees things from on the ground. As mentioned, she is separated from the horse with two fences. With the fence design (one is taller than the other), she can see the positions of fences' openings, surrounding objects (bushes, windmill) as landmarks. However, in this view, moving the physical blocks does not reposition the virtual fences. In AV (aerial view), see Fig 3, the user looks down from above the farm as a bird's eye view. With AV, the user gets to have a holistic overlook about the spatial relationships of farm's objects (including where her GV location is). She also gets to move the virtual fences by moving the physical blocks. However, the fences' openings are hidden to her in AV. Therefore, she needs to keep switching so the incremental spatial information gained from one perspective can be applied to the other. Levels have increasing spatial difficulty, engaging and challenging them to keep using perspective ability to solve the puzzle in each level.

Figure 2: Ground View (the openings are aligned, the puzzle is solved, the horse runs toward the user.)

Figure 3: Aerial View (the short orange cylinder is the user's GV location)

Evaluation

The evaluation is conducted with multiple conditions of the system, each with different levels of tangibility or embodiment. For example, one condition is that the user plays the same horse-finding game on a computer with keyboard and mouse, without the HMD, Leap Motion, and tangible blocks.

The evaluation aims to answer these two main questions: 1) How does a user involve her body to solve the spatial tasks? This can be expanded to sub-questions like: What are the commonality and uniqueness of their spatial strategies? What are their problem-solving aids? How does one's perspective switching behavior change over the course of the gameplay? How can those observations be compared between interface conditions? This first question is studied with video recording, observation, note-taking, post-interaction interview, and data logging.

The second evaluation question is: 2) Does the interface engage and improve the user's perspective taking spatial ability? This is assessed form a pre/post-test intervention method: the user takes a perspective taking ability test before and after playing the game. Hegarty's team's PTSOT (Perspective Taking and Spatial Orientation Test)

[5,11] is chosen for this intervention procedure. PTSOT is not designed for children like Frick's perspective taking test is [4], so it guarantees more validity for TASC's convenience sampling with college students (mostly older than 18 years of age). The perspective taking ability change is compared among different conditions of the interface.

CONCLUSION & FUTURE WORK

In this paper, I present the study's motivations based on observations from related literature. I also list inspirational theories, projects, and design framework, along with what their application and limitation may be to the research. I describe the TASC Gen2 system, a VR-TEI interface that aims to utilize embodiment to support and improve perspective taking ability. Levels of tangibility and embodiment may yield different spatial ability performances, therefore, conditions of TASC will be used in the evaluation. The next steps include incorporating cognitive factors and VR interaction design for more levels, followed by designing and conducting the qualitative and quantitative evaluations. The findings I gather from this re-design and evaluation process, along with other ongoing projects, will help achieve the study's overarching goals of: to summarize design lessons learned, to examine/use existing evaluations, and to generate/envision new evaluations for tangible and embodied interfaces designed for supporting spatial ability.

ACKNOWLEDGMENTS

I would like to thank these professors for their academic and logistical support (in the order of when I started collaborating with each): David Whittinghill, James Mohler, Patrick Connolly, Ali Mazalek, Tim Welsh, and Michael Nitsche. I especially thank Ali for inviting me to work with her SynLab Ryerson. I also thank these past and current "SynLabbers" for the teamwork, particularly: Paul Clifton, Georgina Yeboah, and Alison Doucette. The research is supported by Canada's SSHRC #1-51-52341.

REFERENCES

1. Alissa N. Antle and Sijie Wang. 2013. Comparing Motor-cognitive Strategies for Spatial Problem Solving with Tangible and Multi-touch Interfaces. In *Proceedings of the 7th International Conference on Tangible, Embedded and Embodied Interaction* (TEI '13), 65–72. https://doi.org/10.1145/2460625.2460635
2. Paul G. Clifton, Jack Shen-Kuen Chang, Georgina Yeboah, Alison Doucette, Sanjay Chandrasekharan, Michael Nitsche, Timothy Welsh, and Ali Mazalek. 2016. Design of embodied interfaces for engaging spatial cognition. *Cognitive Research: Principles and Implications* 1, 1: 24. https://doi.org/10.1186/s41235-016-0032-5
3. Augusto Esteves, Saskia Bakker, Alissa N. Antle, Aaron May, Jillian Warren, and Ian Oakley. 2014. Classifying Physical Strategies in Tangible Tasks: A Video-coding Framework for Epistemic Actions. In *Proceedings of the Extended Abstracts of the 32Nd Annual ACM Conference on Human Factors in Computing Systems* (CHI EA '14), 1843–1848. https://doi.org/10.1145/2559206.2581185
4. Andrea Frick, Wenke Möhring, and Nora S. Newcombe. 2014. Picturing perspectives: development of perspective-taking abilities in 4- to 8-year-olds. *Frontiers in Psychology* 5. https://doi.org/10.3389/fpsyg.2014.00386
5. M Hegarty, M Kozhevnikov, and D Waller. 2008. Perspective taking/spatial orientation test. *University California Santa Barbara. Retreived from: http://spatiallearning.org/resource-info/Spatial_Ability_Tests/PTSOT.pdf.*
6. Mary Hegarty, Daniel R. Montello, Anthony E. Richardson, Toru Ishikawa, and Kristin Lovelace. 2006. Spatial abilities at different scales: Individual differences in aptitude-test performance and spatial-layout learning. *Intelligence* 34, 2: 151–176. https://doi.org/10.1016/j.intell.2005.09.005
7. Mary Hegarty and David Waller. 2004. A dissociation between mental rotation and perspective-taking spatial abilities. *Intelligence* 32, 2: 175–191. https://doi.org/10.1016/j.intell.2003.12.001
8. Bernhard Hommel, Jochen Müsseler, Gisa Aschersleben, and Wolfgang Prinz. 2001. Codes and their vicissitudes. *Behavioral and Brain Sciences* 24, 5: 910–926. https://doi.org/10.1017/S0140525X01520105
9. Eva Hornecker and Jacob Buur. 2006. Getting a Grip on Tangible Interaction: A Framework on Physical Space and Social Interaction. In *Proceedings of the SIGCHI Conference on Human Factors in Computing Systems* (CHI '06), 437–446. https://doi.org/10.1145/1124772.1124838
10. Robert J.K. Jacob, Audrey Girouard, Leanne M. Hirshfield, Michael S. Horn, Orit Shaer, Erin Treacy Solovey, and Jamie Zigelbaum. 2008. Reality-based Interaction: A Framework for post-WIMP Interfaces. In *Proceedings of the SIGCHI Conference on Human Factors in Computing Systems* (CHI '08), 201–210. https://doi.org/10.1145/1357054.1357089
11. Maria Kozhevnikov and Mary Hegarty. A dissociation between object manipulation spatial ability and spatial orientation ability. *Memory & Cognition* 29, 5: 745–756. https://doi.org/10.3758/BF03200477
12. Sandra C. Lozano, Bridgette Martin Hard, and Barbara Tversky. 2007. Putting action in perspective. *Cognition* 103, 3: 480–490. https://doi.org/10.1016/j.cognition.2006.04.010
13. David Lubinski and Camilla Persson Benbow. 2006. Study of Mathematically Precocious Youth After 35 Years: Uncovering Antecedents for the Development of Math-Science Expertise. *Perspectives on Psychological Science* 1, 4: 316–345. https://doi.org/10.1111/j.1745-6916.2006.00019.x
14. Ali Mazalek, Sanjay Chandrasekharan, Michael Nitsche, Tim Welsh, Paul Clifton, Andrew Quitmeyer, Firaz Peer, Friedrich Kirschner, and Dilip Athreya. 2011. I'M in the Game: Embodied Puppet Interface Improves Avatar Control. In *Proceedings of the Fifth International Conference on Tangible, Embedded, and Embodied Interaction* (TEI '11), 129–136. https://doi.org/10.1145/1935701.1935727
15. Steve Olson and Donna Gerardi Riordan. 2012. *Engage to Excel: Producing One Million Additional College Graduates with Degrees in Science, Technology, Engineering, and Mathematics. Report to the President.* Executive Office of the President. Retrieved September 20, 2016 from http://eric.ed.gov/?id=ED541511
16. Jonathan Wai, David Lubinski, and Camilla P. Benbow. 2009. Spatial ability for STEM domains: Aligning over 50 years of cumulative psychological knowledge solidifies its importance. *Journal of Educational Psychology* 101, 4: 817–835. https://doi.org/10.1037/a0016127

Designing Gaze Simulation for People with Visual Disability

Shi Qiu
Eindhoven University of Technology
Eindhoven, Netherlands
sqiu@tue.nl

ABSTRACT
In face-to-face communication, eye gaze is integral to a conversation to supplement verbal language. The sighted often uses eye gaze to convey nonverbal information in social interactions, which a blind conversation partner cannot access and react. My doctoral research is to design gaze simulation for the blind person, to improve the conversation quality between sighted and blind people in face-to-face communication. Designing gaze simulation will consist of two primary parts: to help the blind person feel the gaze from the sighted and to simulate the natural gaze for the blind person as a visual reaction. This paper outlines the motivation, context, research methods, and completed and future steps of my research.

Author Keywords
Social interaction; eye tracking; engagement, visual impairments

ACM Classification Keywords
H.5.2. [Information Interfaces and Presentation]: User Interfaces, K.4.2 [Computers and Security]: Social Issues – Assistive technologies for persons with disabilities.

INTRODUCTION
Gaze and mutual gaze are important in the development of trust and deeper relationships [1]. McNeill emphasizes that nonverbal cues such as gazes are integral to a conversation and that ignoring them means ignoring part of the conversation [2]. Gaze signals, frequently used by the sighted in social interactions, are visual cues, which are normally inaccessible to blind and low-vision people. They can hardly feel gaze signals from others during a face-to-face conversation, and they miss out on the large amount of incidental information that the sighted takes for granted [3]. In addition, sighted people often feel uncomfortable in interpersonal interactions with blind people who lack appropriate eye contact. Sighted people may make negative judgements about those with patterns of eye contact noticeably different from the norm [4]. In my doctoral research, I will focus designing natural gaze simulation for the blind person, to improve the conversation quality between sighted and blind people in face-to-face communication through the following three iterations:

TEI '17, March 20-23, 2017, Yokohama, Japan
© 2017 ACM. ISBN 978-1-4503-4676-4/17/03…$15.00
DOI: http://dx.doi.org/10.1145/3024969.3025034

1. I explore nonverbal signals between sighted and blind people in face-to-face communication and focus on gaze signals. Relevant design concepts are developed, which aims to let the blind person feel and react gaze signals from the sighted.

2. A Tactile Band system is implemented to let the blind person feel the eye gaze from the sighted. A user experiment tests and envisions the use of the Tactile Band system.

2. Through E-Gaze glasses (E-Gaze) system, I propose a gaze model that simulates natural gaze for the blind person as a visual reaction to the sighted. A user experiment will use the E-Gaze system as a test bed to find out how the conversation quality would be influenced in face-to-face communication between sighted and blind people.

CURRENT STAGE OF RESEARCH
This paper provides an overview of the first two and a half years of work on this doctoral research. Early in my PhD program, a qualitative study was conducted on nonverbal signals (gaze, facial expressions, body gestures etc.) for blind people in face-to-face communication and problems they had due to the lack of visual signals [5]. Further, the research scope was narrowed down and focused on gaze signals. A conceptual design of E-Gaze glasses was proposed, aiming at creating gaze communication between blind and sighted people in face-to-face conversations. Twenty totally blind and low vision participants were interviewed to evaluate and envision four design features of the E-Gaze [6].

In order to make gaze signals accessible to the blind person, we developed a prototype, namely Tactile Band. The tactile feedback enabled the blind person to feel attention (gaze signals) from the sighted and tried to enhance the level of engagement in face-to-face communication [7]. To simulate natural gaze for blind people, we implemented a working prototype, E-Gaze glasses, an assistive device based on eye tracking. E-Gaze established the "eye contact" between blind and sighted people in face-to-face conversations [8]. We refined gaze behaviors of the E-Gaze and designed a gaze model that combined eye-contact mechanism with turn-taking strategy, which linked the eye gaze animation with the conversation flow (Figure 1). We further proposed an experimental design to test the E-Gaze and hypothesize that the model-driven gaze simulation can enhance the conversation quality between sighted and blind people in the face-to-face communication [9].

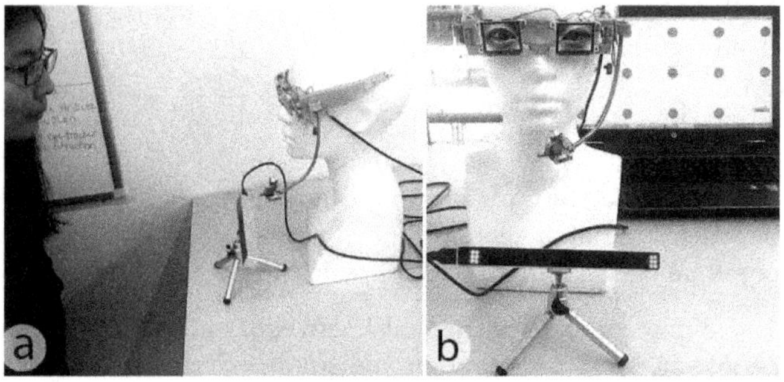

Figure 1.(a) The sighted is fixating at the E-Gaze; (b) E-Gaze system.

MOTIVATION AND CONTEXT

In many instances, the eyes of the blind people are conspicuously unattractive, and/or deformities might be present which made the person less appealing to others [10]. We had an investigation of twenty blind people [5]. They were interviewed about the nonverbal signals for face-to-face communication with the sighted people. Some blind people in the investigation tended to wear the black glasses to hide their eyes in face-to-face communication. One of them said she was not able to express the appropriate eye gestures. She had an illness of nystagmus and she could not control the movement of the eyeball. It could easily mislead the sighted towards her eye gaze gestures. As a blind person, she often felt difficulties in meeting people, because she could not see and establish eye contacts with the sighted people. She felt socially isolated. Lack of eye contact might cause the sighted to feel that the blind person was not fully in communication [10].

In communication or activities between the sighted and the blind people, the impatience, discomfort, or intolerance of the sighted is an important factor in determining the possible extent of the involvement for the blind person. Social skills training were developed for the blind people. For example, training the blind person to simply "look" in the direction of a sighted person who is talking to her. However, the meaning of the gaze signals among the sighted people is more than that simple and unnatural intimation. In face-to-face communication, a sighted speaker consciously or unconsciously uses gaze or eye contact to communicate with the conversation partner. Through the conversation partner's eyes, she can sense interest, engagement, happiness etc.

RELATED WORK

Designing gaze simulation for the blind person draws on theories of gaze behavior and related research on simulating gaze behavior of agents or avatars.

A number of studies have investigated gaze behaviors of sighted people in social occasions. Argyle studied that in dyadic (two-person) conversations, about 75% of the time people are listening, which coincides with gazing at the speaker [11]. Goodwin explained the role of gaze in turn-taking by considering the gaze interaction between hearers and speakers. He claimed that the speaker's look away at the beginning of turns occurs to avoid overloading information in the planning of an utterance [12]. Kendon suggested that seeking or avoiding looking at the face of the conversation partner has important function to regulate the flow of conversation in dyadic conversations and to ensure smooth turn-taking [13].

Simulating gaze behavior applied in agents or avatar systems indicate noticeable effects on human-agent or human-avatar communication. Garau et al. described an experiment to investigate the importance of eye gaze between humans in four mediated conditions: video, audio-only, random-gaze avatars and inferred-gaze avatars. In inferred-gaze, gaze was tied to turn taking in the conversation. The result showed that the inferred-gaze avatar significantly outperformed the random-gaze model and also outperformed audio-only on several response measures [15]. Such research on gaze behaviors concentrated on its relationship with turn-taking phenomena that linked gaze behaviors with speaking and listening modes in conversations. Most current avatar systems display gaze behaviors based on turn-taking strategies rather than being reactive. In reactive systems, the sighted user's gaze behaviors should trigger an instant response from the avatar side which in turn influences the user, resulting in a tightly coupled feedback loop [16]. These reactive responses can be triggered by tracking eye gaze from the user.

RESEARCH QUESTIONS

My doctoral research is concerned with designing gaze simulation for the blind person, to improve the conversation quality between sighted and blind people in face-to-face communication. In more detail, the following research questions are relevant:

1. Which kind of nonverbal signals is important to let the blind person perceive in face-to-face communication?

2. How to let the blind person feel gaze signals from the sighted in face-to-face communication?

3. How to design and simulate the natural gaze for the blind person as a visual reaction?

4. Does "eye contact" simulation improve the conversation quality between sighted and blind people in face-to-face communication and how?

DESIGN AND RESEARCH APPROACH

Three primary studies are proposed as follows: to explore nonverbal signals for the blind person in face-to-face communication, to let the blind person perceive the eye gaze and to simulate the natural gaze to enhance the conversation quality between sighted and blind people in face-to-face communication.

Exploring nonverbal signals

Nonverbal communication plays an important role in social interactions. Most nonverbal communication relies on visual signals such as eye contact, head nods, facial expressions and body gestures. Visual nonverbal signals are inaccessible for the blind and hardly accessible for low vision individuals. A qualitative study was conducted on nonverbal signals for the blind people in face-to-face communication and problems they met due to the lack of visual signals. We interviewed 20 blind and low-vision participants and collected qualitative data for the further analysis. Our results indicated that blind participants seldom sensed positive feelings from visual signals in a conversation and they tended to have an indirect and fuzzy understanding of eyes and eye gestures.

We discussed how our findings could be relevant for design: the sighted conversation partner's visual signals with meanings (e.g. eye contact and smile) needed to be detected to help the blind person perceive the signal and feel more engaged in face-to-face communication.

A conceptual design of E-Gaze glasses was proposed, assistive to create gaze communication between blind and sighted people in face-to-face conversations. We also interviewed 20 totally blind and low-vision participants to envision the use of the E-Gaze. We explained four features of E-Gaze to participants using persona and use scenarios. Participants discussed the features on their usefulness, efficiency and interest. The results helped us clarify the design direction and the further research.

Perceiving the eye gaze

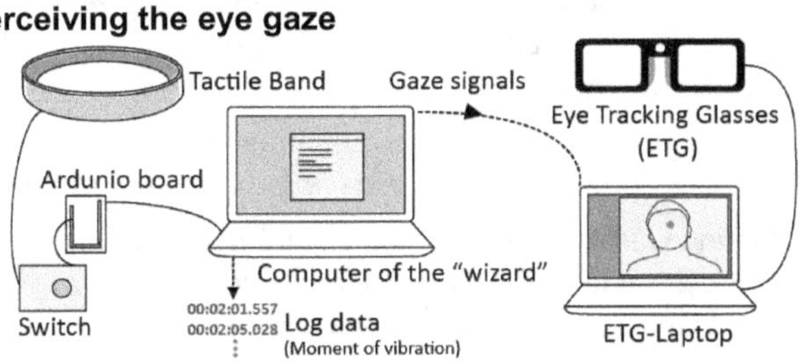

Figure 2.Overview of the Tactile Band system.

We presented a prototype, namely Tactile Band, to aim at testing the hypothesis that tactile feedback can enable the blind person to feel attention (gaze signals) from the sighted and enhance the conversation quality in face-to-face communication. We tested our hypothesis with 30 participants with a face-to-face conversation scenario, in which the blindfolded and the sighted participants talked about a given daily topic. A Wizard-of-Oz method was used to map gaze signals to vibration signals. The SMI Eye Tracking Glasses (ETG) is connected to an ETG-Laptop, detecting gaze signals of the sighted participant in real-time (Figure 2). The "wizard" observed the real-time gaze video from iView ETG 2.0 (the controller and eye tracking software) installed on the ETG-Laptop. If the gaze hit the facial region of the blindfolded participant, a slight vibration was triggered by the wizard.

Results and design improvements were discussed from three perspectives: 1) *scenario*, improving the scenario so that it relies more on gaze communication; 2) *prototype*, improving the wearability of the Tactile Band (e.g. on the wrist, less visible than around the forehead) with fine-tuned intensity of the tactile feedback. Other types of tactile feedback can also be explored besides vibration, such as a sense of pressure caused by shape changing of the material; 3) *experiment*, a short training session is necessary for better understanding of the relation between tactile feedbacks and gaze signals.

After improving and completing the system, real blind participants will be involved in the experiment. A comparative study of the effect of the Tactile Band will be conducted between the real blind participants and the blindfolded participants.

Simulating the natural gaze

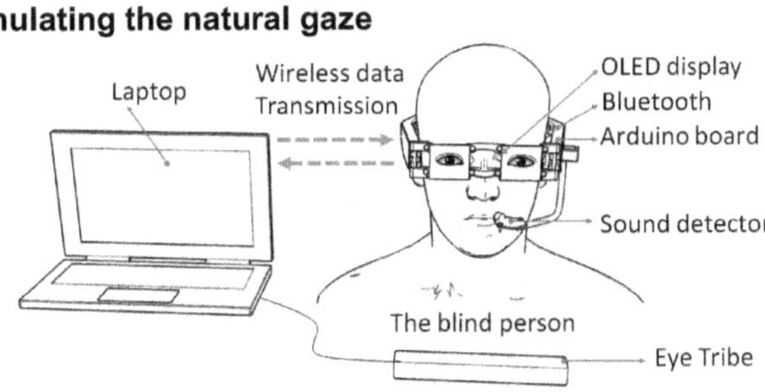

Figure 3.Overview of the E-Gaze system.

We implemented a working prototype, E-Gaze glasses (Figure 3), an assistive device based on an eye tracking system. E-Gaze simulated natural gaze for blind people, especially establishing the "eye contact" between blind and sighted people to enhance their engagement in face-to-face conversations. The gaze behavior was designed based on a model that combined eye-contact mechanism and turn-taking strategy. This model interpreted the corresponding relationship between the conclusive gaze behavior and the interlocutors' conversation flow[9]. The gaze animation of the E-Gaze was driven by two sensors: the gaze signal from the Eye Tribe Tracker and the audio signal from the sound detector. The Eye Tribe Tracker was used to detect the gaze signal from the sighted to provide input for eye contact mechanism, while the sound detector was used to detect the blind person's speaking for turn-taking strategy.

We propose an experimental design to test the E-Gaze and hypothesize that the model-driven gaze simulation can enhance the conversation quality between sighted and blind people in the face-to-face communication. In the experiment, we will compare responses of the sighted to the blindfolded participant with E-Gaze in a dyadic-conversation scenario. E-Gaze will display gazes with four conditions: E-Gaze without gaze simulation, E-Gaze with constant gaze, E-Gaze with random gaze and E-Gaze with the model-driven gaze simulation. The level of conversation quality will be measured using questionnaires with four subjective measures: relatedness, partner closeness, engagement and partner evaluation.

In our future work, we will let the blind person to wear both tactile device and E-Gaze in the experiment, not only to enable the blind person to feel the gaze from the sighted, but also to send the "e-gaze" to the sighted in a dyadic conversation.

EXPECTED CONTRIBUTIONS

Through the user study, prototypes and user experiments I have described above, I will continue to focus on and contribute to the following in my doctoral research:

1. Understanding nonverbal signals of the blind people in face-to-face communication, especially the meaning of gaze signals. This will guide the design for gaze simulation for the blind person.

2. Functional interactive prototype for gaze simulation will be produced for experiments, enabling the blind person to feel the eye gaze and to send "e-gaze" to the sighted as a visual reaction.

3. Two hypothesizes will be examined:

   Tactile feedback can enable the blind person to feel attention (gaze signals) from the sighted and enhance the conversation quality in face-to-face communication;

   Simulating natural gaze can enhance the conversation quality between sighted and blind people in face-to-face communication.

4. A model-driven gaze for the blind person will be created to test whether it improves the conversation quality, comparing to other gaze patterns.

ACKNOWLEDGEMENTS

I would like to thank my supervisors, Matthias Rauterberg and Jun Hu, and my colleague, Siti Aisyah Anas in Eindhoven University of Technology and collaborator, Hirotaka Osawa in University of Tsukuba.

REFERENCES

1. Michael Argyle and Mark Cook. 1976. *Gaze and mutual gaze*. Cambridge University Press.
2. David McNeill.1992. *Hand and mind: What gestures reveal about thought*. University of Chicago Press J.
3. Jolanta Sak-Wernicka.2014. The effect of nonverbal cues on the interpretation of utterances by people with visual impairments. *Journal of Visual Impairment & Blindness (Online)*, 108(2), 133.
4. Phoebe C. Ellsworth and Linda M. Ludwig. 1972. Visual behavior in social interaction. *Journal of Communication*, 22(4), 375-403.
5. Shi Qiu, Jun Hu, and Matthias Rauterberg.2015. Nonverbal Signals for Face-to-Face Communication between the Blind and the Sighted. In *Proceedings of International Conference on Enabling Access for Persons with Visual Impairment*, 157–165.
6. Shi Qiu, Hirotaka Osawa, Jun Hu, and Matthias Rauterberg. 2015. E-Gaze: Create Gaze Communication for People with Visual Disability. In *Proceedings of the 3rd International Conference on Human-Agent Interaction*, 199–202.
7. Shi Qiu, Matthias Rauterberg, and Jun Hu.2016. Designing and Evaluating a Wearable Device for Accessing Gaze Signals from the Sighted. In *Proceedings of the 18th International Conference on Human-Computer Interaction*, 454–464.
8. Shi Qiu, Siti Aisyah Anas, Hirotaka Osawa, Matthias Rauterberg, and Jun Hu. 2016. E-Gaze Glasses: Simulating Natural Gazes for Blind People. In *Proceedings of the 10th International Conference on Tangible, Embedded, and Embodied Interaction*, 563–569.
9. Shi Qiu, Siti Aisyah Anas, Hirotaka Osawa, Matthias Rauterberg, and Jun Hu. 2016. Model-Driven Gaze Simulation for the Blind Person in Face-to-Face Communication. In *Proceedings of the 4th International Conference on Human-Agent Interaction*, Accepted.
10. Vincent B. Van Hasselt.1983. Social Adaptation in the Blind. *Clinical Psychology Review*, 3(1), pp.87-102.
11. Michael Argyle.1994. *The psychology of interpersonal behaviour*. Penguin UK.
12. Charles Goodwin. 1981. *Conversational Organization: Interaction between hearers and speakers*. New York: Academic Press.
13. Adam Kendon.1967. Some functions of gaze-direction in social interaction. *Acta psychologica,* 26, pp.22-63.
14. Justine Cassell, Torres Obed E, and Scott Prevost. 1999. Turn taking versus discourse structure. In *Machine conversations*, 143-153, Springer US.
15. Maia Garau, Mel Slater, Simon Bee, and Martina Angela Sasse. 2001. The impact of eye gaze on communication using humanoid avatars. In *Proceedings of the SIGCHI conference on Human factors in computing systems*, 309–316.
16. Michael Kipp and Patrick Gebhard.2008. Igaze: Studying reactive gaze behavior in semi-immersive human-avatar interactions. In *Intelligent Virtual Agents*, 191–199.

Communicating Built Heritage Information Using Tangible Interaction Approach

Eslam Nofal [a,b] **Rabee M. Reffat** [b] **Andrew Vande Moere** [a]

[a] Research[x]Design, Department of Architecture, KU Leuven, Belgium
{eslam.nofal, andrew.vandemoere}@kuleuven.be
[b] Department of Architecture, Assiut University, Egypt
rabee@aun.edu.eg

ABSTRACT
Built heritage objects possess multiple types of information, varying from simple, factual aspects to more complex qualitative information and values, such as the architectural qualities, the construction techniques, or symbolic meanings of monuments. This qualitative information is relatively difficult to communicate using the conventional ways like museum labels or audio guides. Nonetheless, tangible interaction is a promising paradigm for communicating tacit information, its qualities have been demonstrated in a wide range of applications in different realms. Therefore, this study investigates how tangible interaction can enable the communication of qualitative information of built heritage to lay visitors. The main objectives of this study are communicating tacit and architectural qualities of built heritage in a physical form, investigating the effect of tangible interaction on social interaction among heritage visitors, and enhancing visitors' in-situ experience of built heritage or 1:1 replicas. Our early findings indicate the capability of tangible interaction for engaging museum visitors to accomplish additional endeavors, and facilitating their understanding of cultural values and architectural qualities of built heritage.

Author Keywords
Tangible interaction; qualitative information; built heritage; cultural learning; museum visitors; architectural qualities.

ACM Classification Keywords
H.1.2 User/Machine Systems; H.2.2 Physical Design; H.4.3 Communications Applications; H.5.2 User Interfaces; J.5 Arts and Humanities.

INTRODUCTION
Heritage sites and monuments are not just physical objects, but they also communicate multiple types of information and values over time. Built heritage information types tend to vary from factual or quantitative information (e.g. monument functions or building date), which are relatively easy to represent, to more tacit qualities and values (e.g. architectural qualities, cultural values, symbolic meaning of a monument) that due to their abstract and subjective character are typically more challenging to transfer to visitors by the conventional means (e.g. museum labels, audio-guide, etc.). Recent digital technology advancements have enabled various innovative opportunities for more informative, engaging and potentially enjoyable way of communicating heritage information. As a result, built heritage information has already been represented via a variety of paradigms, such as virtual reality (VR) for visualizing the virtual reconstruction of built heritage, or augmented reality (AR) for immersing users in historical stories. We believe that tangible interaction offers a promising paradigm for communicating heritage information, which has the added quality to be relatively affordable, collaborative and intuitive. For instance, particular qualities of tangible interaction have been demonstrated in a wide range of applications in different realms, such as its effectiveness for collaborative and participative processes in public spaces in comparison to touch interfaces [1], and its touch and manipulation affordance in interactive exhibits, which attracts more visitors and prompts them for further exploration [7].

In comparison to graphical user interfaces (GUIs), tangible user interfaces (TUIs) are relatively intuitive and they do not only afford objects in an abstract physical form, but also can incorporate particular material attributes (e.g. size, shape, texture, color, weight) to convey information in addition to the digital representation [8]. Furthermore, tangible interfaces are capable of making use of people's experience of interacting with real world objects [4]. As such, evidence from educational psychology shows the manipulation of physical representations of information and utilization of TUIs to facilitate understanding [6]. The physical properties of heritage artefacts may thus invoke visitors' pre-existing knowledge to discover their meaning, functionality or use, and consequently lead to more intuitive or memorable forms of communication. Accordingly, users might be allowed to touch heritage artefacts (or their replicas), providing not only the subjective experience of its

TEI '17, March 20–23, 2017, Yokohama, Japan.
© 2017 ACM ISBN 978-1-4503-4676-4/17/03...$15.00.
DOI: http://dx.doi.org/10.1145/3024969.3025035

shape, materiality or weight, but also for a tactile exploration of its potential use and for more understanding of the architectural qualities.

It is not a surprise that heritage communication has already benefited from recent TUI advances. For instance, tangible smart replicas have been used in museum exhibitions to provide an additional layer (narrative content) of story-telling on top of presented factual information [9]. Furthermore, anecdotal evidence shows that the touch and manipulation affordances of TUIs in interactive exhibits tend to attract more visitors and even persuade them to explore further and deeper [7]. Tangible installations can also be deployed in outdoor heritage environments wherein lack of power supplies or digital networks can exist. For example, the 'interactive belt' [11] supports the visit of archaeological sites by enabling visitors to select the story they want to listen to and to be part of it, triggered by specific points of interests. Moreover, a monument of urban space per se 'City Mouse' is utilized as a tangible user interface [2], a landmark of a large stone sphere representing the globe, which people could push to a rolling motion in order to rotate a 3D image of the Earth that is visualized on a screen next to the landmark.

These examples, among others, demonstrate how the combination of physical and digital is still relatively unexplored, but potentially particularly valuable for the field of built heritage communication, such as when the digitally augmented experience makes some sort of meaningful connection to the actual heritage context, for instance the social, cultural and physical characteristics of the physical reality. Apart of the engagement level, the focus of this study extends to include the level of understanding and knowledge gain that leads to informal cultural learning; a setting that stimulates users for envisaging the exploration and realization of cultural value [5]. This setting accommodates users who seek knowledge for pleasure or those who seek knowledge based on genuine motivation; such as a general visitor.

Consequently, this PhD study explores an effective communication approach that conforms to the context of built heritage, copes with the limitations of the conventional ways in conveying the qualitative information of built heritage, and finds the missing interrelations of information. Therefore, we aim to investigate the causal effect of tangible interaction on the sense-making of heritage visitors by providing them with a meaningful and interactive experience that stimulates people to think, discover and make meaningful connections with built heritage without any external help. In particular, we are working towards the following three inter-connected research objectives:

1. ***First objective:*** to facilitate the communication of tacit and architectural qualities of built heritage to lay visitors. How does the physical affordance of tangible interaction affect the communication of built heritage information?
2. ***Second objective:*** to investigate the effect of tangible interaction on the social interaction among heritage visitors. How does a multi-user tangible interaction influence the sociability among heritage visitors? and how does this lead to informal cultural learning?
3. ***Third objective:*** to enhance the visitors' in-situ experience of built heritage, moving from a museum context to a real heritage environment, such as a monument, a historic site or a 1:1 replica. What is the most appropriate tangible interaction approach for a real heritage environment to communicate its information, and how does it enhance visitors' experience?

RESEARCH APPROACH AND METHODOLOGY

Our approach extracts knowledge from the field of human-computer interaction (HCI) by developing experimental designs and carrying out field studies. Each study is assigned to accomplish one of the abovementioned research objectives.

Museum Experiment

We conducted our first study at the Royal Museums of Art and History in Brussels. We chose a context of *Djoser Pyramid Complex*, one of the world's oldest large-scale stone structure. The chosen story to be communicated was related to the translation of the pharaoh's journey along the Nile to visit each of the *Nomes* (the territorial divisions of ancient Egypt) and their local Gods, into the physical architecture of the entrance colonnade of this complex: it has been suggested that each *niche* (the space created between adjacent columns) in the entrance colonnade represents a shrine where the *Nome Gods* of ancient Egypt were accommodated during an annual festival [3]. The architectural layout of the colonnade might have been designed to portray the Nile river; the end chamber could represent the delta; and the processing of the pharaoh along the corridor and passing by each Nome shrine may evoke a ritualized version of the pharaoh's journey along the Nile to visit each of the Nomes and their local Gods.

For the aim of the first study, we developed three different interactive installations (and experimental conditions) in order to compare the causal influence of the tangible interaction on the sense-making of the visitors, as shown in Figure 1. Each condition consisted of an interactive navigation (input) and a passive representation (output) element. For the navigation, a map of ancient Egypt with its territorial divisions of 42 Nomes was used as the main interaction method, either via touch screen (*Touch-Dix*) or via a tangible interactive surface featuring a movable 3D-printed statue of pharaoh Djoser on the map (*Tang-Dix* and *Tang-Phys*). Each condition contained a representation view of the entrance colonnade that dynamically changed according to the user interaction. This view varied from a digital display showing a walk-through in a rendered 3D model of the colonnade (*Touch-Dix* and *Tang-Dix*) to a 3D, physical rendition of the colonnade that was semi-attached to the installation (*Tang-Phys*).

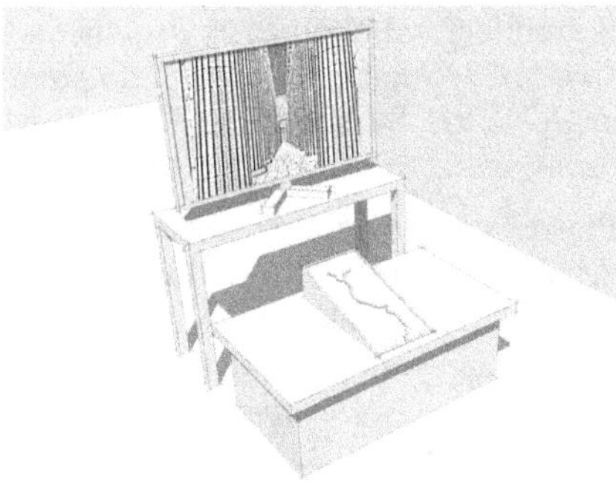

Fig. 2a. *Touch-Dix* setup

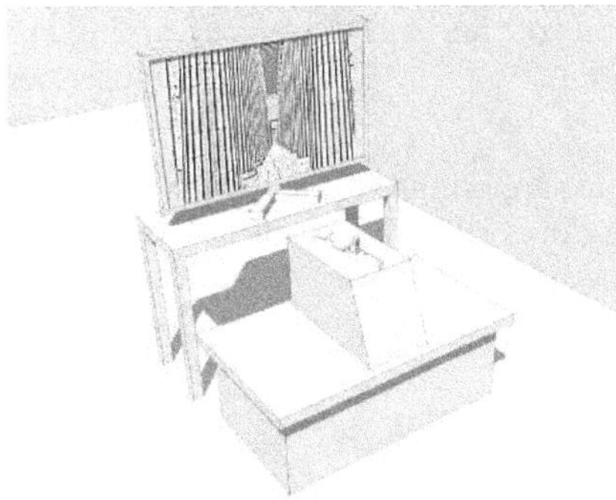

Fig. 2b. *Tang-Dix* setup

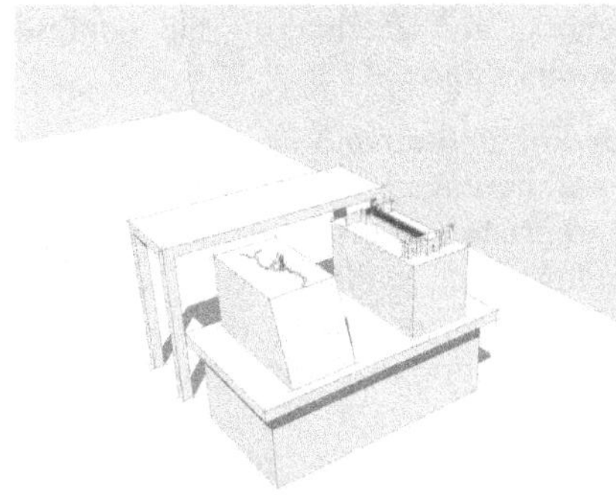

Fig. 2c. *Tang-Phys* setup

Fig. 2d. *Touch-Dix* study

Fig. 2e. *Tang-Dix* study

Fig. 2f. *Tang-Phys* study

Figure 1. Different conditions for communicating the architectural story of the entrance colonnade of Djoser Pyramid Complex: a) and d) touch navigation and digital representation; b) and e) tangible navigation and digital representation; and c) and f) tangible navigation and physical representation.

In order to test the feasibility, reliability and validity of the proposed conditions and methods, we conducted a lab study and two-day pilot study [10] before we carried out the large-scale study at the Antiquity Department of the aforementioned museum, which comprises the largest collection of Egyptian antiquities in Belgium. During the study, each condition was introduced with a brief explanation about the general context of the building (i.e. location and historical period) and about their purpose of interaction (i.e. exploring the architectural symbolism of the entrance colonnade). Visitors were allowed to participate individually or in groups, and as such included couples and dozens of children on a museum school trip. All the interactions were observed, logged and video recorded. The experiment wrapped up with a semi-structured interview that was audio-taped, and which focused on the comprehension of the meaningful relationship between the map and the colonnade. The interview also included questions about how the colonnade looked like, in order to capture how people perceived the architectural characteristics of the space (e.g. height, fluting of the columns) that were not explicitly relevant to understand the story, yet still are valuable heritage and architectural qualities to be appreciated or remembered. Participants also filled in a user experience questionnaire (ueq-online.org), covering both classical usability aspects (i.e. efficiency, perspicuity, dependability) and user experience aspects (i.e. originality, stimulation).

The findings of this study indicate how the tangible characteristics of an interactive prototype museum installation influence the engagement of museum visitors to accomplish additional efforts, facilitating their understanding of cultural values and architectural qualities of built heritage.

FUTURE WORK

Future directions will focus on applying different tangible interaction approaches on different types of qualitative information of built heritage. By then we can establish a base for the communalities and differences between these different approaches to identify what can be generalized and specialized. Therefore, a model for tangible interaction will be developed for communicating the qualitative information of built heritage. Referring to the aforementioned research objectives, we already accomplished the first one through the previous museum study. Future work extends to cover the remaining objectives.

Towards Objective 2

We are currently preparing for the next study by developing the concept of *PaperPulse* [12] to apply it on the *Masataba of Neferirtenef* at the same museum in Brussels. This study aims to investigate the effect of tangible interaction on the social interaction among heritage visitors. Therefore, it is dedicated to multi-users (e.g. school visits) in order to explore how this affects the sociability among heritage visitors, and facilitating the comprehension of heritage meanings and values.

Toward Objective 3

A real heritage environment will be selected for applying an appropriate tangible interaction approach in order to communicate built heritage information in-situ. For this study, more complexity is also required in terms of the type of information to be communicated.

CONCLUSION

This PhD study investigates the causal effect of tangible interaction on the sense-making of heritage visitors by providing them with a meaningful and interactive experience that stimulates people to think, discover and make meaningful connections with built heritage without any external help. We achieved our first objective through a comparative, field study in a real-world museum context. Here, we examined the influence of tangible characteristics of an interactive prototype museum installation on the visitors' perception of a particular story related to a heritage building. Future work extends to fulfill the other two objectives of investigating the effects of tangible interaction on the social interaction among heritage visitors, and enhancing the visitors' in-situ experience of built heritage.

ACKNOWLEDGMENTS

We would like to thank the Antiquity Department of the Royal Museums of Art and History in Brussels for their support and assistance during the museum experiment. We would like also to thank all the volunteers for their participation during their museum visit. The corresponding author gratefully acknowledges the PhD scholarship funded by the Egyptian Ministry of Higher Education.

REFERENCES

1. Sandy Claes and Andrew Vande Moere, 2015. The role of tangible interaction in exploring information on public visualization displays. *4th International Symposium on Pervasive Displays (PerDis'15)*, pp. 201-207. http://dl.acm.org/citation.cfm?doid=2757710.2757733
2. Jonna Häkkilä, Olli Koskenranta, Maaret Posti and Yun He. 2014. City Landmark as an interactive installation - Experiences with stone, water and public space. *8th International Conference on Tangible, Embedded and Embodied Interaction (TEI'14)*, pp. 221-224. http://dl.acm.org/citation.cfm?id=2540980
3. Alfred Hermann. 1938. Führer durch die Altertümer von Memphis und Sakkara, Berlin, p.32.
4. Jörn Hurtienne and Johann Habakuk Israel. 2007. Image schemas and their metaphorical extensions: intuitive patterns for tangible interaction. *1st International Conference on Tangible, Embedded, and Embodied Interaction (TEI'07)*, pp. 127-134. http://dl.acm.org/citation.cfm?id=1226996
5. Nazrita Ibrahim, Nazlena Mohamad Ali and Noor Faezah Mohd Yatim. 2015. Factors facilitating cultural learning in virtual architectural heritage environments: end user perspective. *ACM Journal on Computing and Cultural Heritage (JOCCH)*, 8 (2), Article 8. http://dl.acm.org/citation.cfm?id=2743013.2660776
6. Yvonne Jansen, Pierre Dragicevic, Petra Isenberg Inria, Jason Alexander, Abhijit Karnik, Johan Kildal, Sriram Subramanian and Kasper Hornbæk. 2015. Opportunities and challenges for data physicalization. *33rd Annual ACM Conference on Human Factors in Computing Systems (CHI'15)*, pp. 3227-3236. http://dl.acm.org/citation.cfm?id=2702180
7. Joyce Ma, Lisa Sindorf, Isaac Liao and Jennifer Frazier. 2015. Using a tangible versus a multi-touch graphical user interface to support data exploration at a museum exhibit. *9th International Conference on Tangible, Embedded, and Embodied Interaction (TEI'15)*, pp. 33-40. http://dl.acm.org/citation.cfm?id=2680555
8. Anna Macaranas, Alissa N. Antle, and Bernhard E. Riecke. 2012. Bridging the gap: attribute and spatial metaphors for tangible interface design. *6th International Conference on Tangible, Embedded and Embodied Interaction (TEI'12)*, pp. 161-168. http://dl.acm.org/citation.cfm?id=2148166&CFID=853679294&CFTOKEN=70617544
9. Mark T. Marshall, Nick Dulake, Luigina Ciolfi, Daniele Duranti, Huk Kockelkorn and Daniela Petrelli. 2016. Using tangible smart replicas as controls for an interactive museum exhibition. *10th International Conference on Tangible, Embedded, and Embodied Interaction (TEI'16)*, pp. 159-167. http://dl.acm.org/citation.cfm?id=2839493&CFID=853679294&CFTOKEN=70617544
10. Eslam Nofal, Vanessa Boschloos, Hendrik Hameeuw and Andrew Vande Moere. 2016. The role of tangible interaction for communicating qualitative information of built heritage. *Arqueológica 2.0: 8th International Congress on Archaeology, Computer Graphics, Cultural Heritage and Innovation*, pp. 441-444. http://ocs.editorial.upv.es/index.php/arqueologica20/arqueologica8/paper/view/4153
11. Daniela Petrelli, Luigina Ciolfi, Dick Van Dijk, Eva Hornecker, Elena Not and Albrecht Schmidt. 2013. Integrating material and digital: a new way for cultural heritage. *ACM Interactions Magazine*, Vol. 20 (4), pp. 58-63. http://dl.acm.org/citation.cfm?id=2486239
12. Raf Ramakers, Kashyap Todi and Kris Luyten. 2015. PaperPulse: An Integrated Approach for Embedding Electronics in Paper Designs. *33rd Annual ACM Conference on Human Factors in Computing Systems (CHI'15)*, pp. 2457-2466. http://dl.acm.org/citation.cfm?id=2702487&CFID=853679294&CFTOKEN=70617544

Design of Age-Inclusive Tangible User Interfaces Using Image-Schematic Metaphors

Robert Tscharn
University of Würzburg
Würzburg, Germany
robert.tscharn@uni-wuerzburg.de

ABSTRACT

Tangible user interfaces (TUIs) often employ innovative interaction technologies especially older adults are usually unfamiliar with. In most cases, this growing population has less prior knowledge of technology and fewer cognitive resources than younger adults. Consequently, inadequately designed user interfaces often constrain older adults' interactions. Image-schematic metaphors (ISM) allow a direct mapping of abstract, intangible concepts (e.g., INTEREST RATES) to physical correlates (e.g., VERTICALITY) that are grounded in humans' very basic mental representations and are expressed in discourse ("Interest rates *rose* last year."). ISM have already been explored as guidance for the design of intuitive TUIs, but whether one of their major promises–age-inclusiveness–holds true is largely an open research question. Therefore, the aim of this Ph.D. is to examine and draw on the potential of ISM theory for the design of TUIs independent of users' technological knowledge and cognitive resources.

Author Keywords

Tangible user interfaces; age-inclusive design; design theory; image-schematic metaphors.

ACM Classification Keywords

H.5.2. Information interfaces and presentation (e.g., HCI): User Interfaces – Theory and Methods.

RESEARCH CONTEXT

I am a full-time research assistant at the chair for Psychological Ergonomics at the University of Würzburg. As a lecturer and supervisor for students' projects and theses I am involved in several courses on Human-Computer Interaction (HCI) as, for example, 'Usability and Software-Ergonomics', 'Methods of User-Centered Design', and 'Accessibility and Inclusive Design'. I seek to combine my background as a psychologist with adjacent fields of HCI, focusing on older adults and intuitive interaction with innovative interfaces like TUIs. This is also the research topic of my Ph.D. which I started in March 2015.

TEI '17, March 20-23, 2017, Yokohama, Japan
© 2017 ACM. ISBN 978-1-4503-4676-4/17/03…$15.00
DOI: http://dx.doi.org/10.1145/3024969.3025036

MOTIVATION

It is estimated that 19% of the world's population will be older than 80 years by 2050 [18]. Older adults are thus a major target group for tomorrow's products leading to a steadily growing 'silver' market segment. In parallel, new technologies pave the way for advances in the field of HCI: tangible user interfaces (TUIs) and embodied interaction are examples for innovative and to most people unconventional ways of interacting with digital content. TUIs promise new and more natural interaction styles that allow for intuitive physical interaction with digital content. Here, basic procedural knowledge about object manipulation that has been accumulated over many interactions with the physical environment can easily be applied by both younger and older adults to TUIs. But to allow older adults to interact intuitively with TUIs it is highly desirable that diminished cognitive resources and a lack of prior technological knowledge do not hamper pleasant interaction. Also, it is not preferable to develop different systems for younger and older adults. Rather, efforts should be focused on age-inclusive design allowing both age groups with different resources and backgrounds to interact with the same system [14]. The underlying motivation that frames this Ph.D. is that literature promises age-inclusive TUIs without properly investigating this promise yet. Especially non-physical, abstract concepts can often be incorporated in different ways into physical, concrete TUIs. The main idea of my work is that older adults with limited cognitive resources and prior technological knowledge should profit from TUIs that are built in accordance to their mental representations of abstract concepts. My work therefore aims at applying the method of image-schematic metaphors to the design of TUIs and evaluating the outcome in terms of intuitive use and age-inclusiveness.

RELATED WORK

Intuitive Use and Image-Schematic Metaphors

Different definitions for intuitive use have been reported in the literature [4,17], but the common threads are two factors: prior knowledge and its subconscious application or transfer to a new task. This work follows the definition of Naumann et al. [17], who describe intuitive use in that '[...] the particular user is able to interact effectively, not-consciously using previous knowledge.' (p. 129). But how can intuitive use be actively designed for?

Applying image-schematic metaphors (ISM) as guidance for the design of intuitive interaction has already been tested by several researchers in the field of HCI and tangible interaction [1,2,8]. Such work is based on Johnson's landmark publication 'The body in the mind. The bodily basis of meaning, reason and imagination' [11]. He argues that through everyday experiences in the physical world all humans acquire a mental set of basic concepts, which we use to make sense of the world that surrounds us. The elemental building blocks of this set are called image schemas and help us to structure our perception and mental representation of the world. E.g., we repeatedly perceive objects as being in- or outside of containers, up in the air or down on the ground, permanently linked or having temporary contact with other objects. These perceptions form image schemas, e.g., IN-OUT, UP-DOWN, LINKAGE, and CONTACT that shape our language, cognition, and behavior. Following Johnson, image schemas are not constrained to understanding only our physical environment. Moreover, we also use image schemas when we think and speak about abstract concepts that do not have physical equivalents per se. For example, we talk about *rising inflation*, even though inflation cannot be perceived in the physical world as something moving from up to down or vice versa [8]. Thus, we seem to map abstract concepts to spatial properties from our physical scenes. This mapping is made explicit in so called ISM [11]. Here, an abstract concept is mapped to a specific image schema. We use the expression 'rising inflation', even though inflation happens in a dimensionless space. In this example, we find the ISM MORE INFLATION IS UP, where the quantity of inflation is mapped to a vertical dimension. Johnson stressed the point that metaphors like these are too omnipresent in spoken language to be regarded as only dead metaphors and automated parts of the language. Also, these ISM are similar across different cultures [12]. Besides linguistic studies, also other approaches exist for finding these metaphors (e.g., direct observation [8]) but language has proven the most feasible way for finding domain-specific ISM that are rooted in our experience in the real world [9]. Especially in TUIs, designers often lack concrete guidance on how to map abstract concepts on the world's three dimensions and physical attributes of objects. For example, the metaphor BANK TRANSACTION IS COMPULSION uses FORCE image schemas that deal with dynamic interactions between objects. This metaphor could be implemented as pushing a physical object in a TUI or even a full-body movement. Note that designing by ISM does not predetermine the type of interaction modality (e.g., GUI, TUI, or full body gestures).

Several studies indicate that interactions are intuitive to use when they follow ISM found in the users' spoken language as an indicator of their mental representation of abstract concepts [1,2]. This method has been incorporated into industrial design processes [15] and provides valuable guidance on abstract-to-physical mappings to designers while leaving room for innovative ideas [10].

Older Adults and HCI

Research shows that older adults are – contrary to public belief – not in general rejecting new technologies and want to use them as long as these are perceived as useful [6,7]. Still, they are at disadvantage when it comes to interaction with new technologies, at least partly because cognition declines as people get older [5] and interfaces are too complex. Also, older adults' previous experience with new technology is often limited, rendering intuitive use of new interaction styles difficult to achieve [4]. Studies show that the first encounter of older adults with unknown technologies and interaction styles is crucial for shaping attitudes towards these [13], emphasizing the importance of intuitive interaction – to be successful at first try. One interesting and crucial issue is older adults' high priority of avoiding errors [3]. Self-efficacy, for example, describing the trust in one's own capabilities to deal with new tasks, seems to decrease in later life [13]. In line with this, older adults seem to underestimate their capabilities to cope with new systems and act rather passive during the interaction with computing devices [7]. This is highly relevant for TUIs that often implicitly assume that users will explore new gadgets and learn the interactivity of objects and space via trial and error. But if first attempts of using an interface fail, both its perceived ease-of-use and perceived usefulness will be decreased. It will not be used again, inhibiting long-term learning of the interaction and later refinement of the users' attitude towards the product [3]. Therefore, it is essential to make unconventional interaction styles as TUIs intuitive to use especially for older adults. As a result, interaction design focusing on the elderly is receiving increased attention in HCI research and different guidelines have been proposed to facilitate the creation of age-inclusive interfaces (e.g., [3]).

For GUIs, Hurtienne et al. [10] provide an at the same time age-inclusive, intuitive and innovative radio interface based on ISM. In the work of Winkler et al. [19], younger and older adults rated new GUIs conforming to ISM as more innovative and more intuitive to use compared to market standard GUIs. The results were independent of age. Regarding TUIs, ISM have already been used to explore their benefits, but focus mostly on younger adults or children [1,8]. The insights of these studies are promising for age-inclusive TUIs, but they suffer from methodological drawbacks (e.g., extraction process of ISM prone to errors by non-experts, missing or unfair baselines, both design and evaluation carried out by the same researchers, only GUIs [2,10,19]). Also, they do not explicitly focus on older adults and assume without empirical data that age groups do not differ in their mental representation of abstract concepts and therefore will use the ISM in their spoken language. Open questions are therefore a) how to improve the methodology of an ISM supported TUI design process to be also applicable by non-experts and b) to determine if the use of ISM is really independent of age and can lead to age-inclusive TUIs that make full use of its tangible interactions.

RESEARCH GOALS AND APPROACH

The contribution of my work is twofold: First, it aims at refining the methodology of applying age-independent ISM in TUI design and provides methodological recommendations. The second aim is to test if ISM are–as predicted by literature but not investigated yet–used independently of age and that following these ISM in the design process can support the development of age-inclusive and still innovative TUIs. Figure 1 summarizes the structure of my empirical studies.

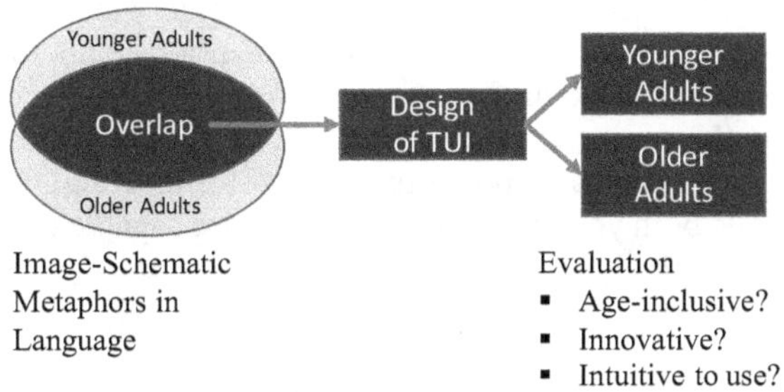

Figure 1: Macro-structure of the empirical studies.

1) *Determining the overlap of ISM between younger and older adults in spoken language*

First, a valid set of ISM must be obtained in order to base the TUI design on. Even though theory predicts and previous studies often assume implicitly that different age groups use the same ISM, to the knowledge of the author empirical data clearly indicating that younger and older adults overlap in their ISM has not been reported in literature yet. Besides supporting central claims of theories of ISM (e.g., that image schemas and ISM are based on such basic experiences that they are shared by most people), estimating the overlap between both age groups is fundamental for grounding age-inclusive TUIs on ISM. In order to tackle this research question with data from spoken language, structured and semi-structured interviews were conducted with younger (ranging from 20 to 30 years) and older adults (ranging from 60 to 85 years) in two different technological domains. The two domains were social communication between passengers of different cars (20 young; 20 old) and in-car entertainment (5 young; 5 old), because both elicit a variety of abstract concepts that are difficult to map to physical dimensions needed in TUIs. Subsequently, the recorded language material of about 13 hours was transcribed and analyzed word-by-word to extract domain-specific ISM.

ISM were extracted from all interviews by three coders, revealing a satisfactory inter-rater reliability of Kappa = 0.7 for the extraction process from spoken language. First results provide a set of shared ISM (see Figure 2). Still, only 49.8% of all ISM were shared by both age groups. Other metaphors were unique to one age group. For example, only older adults used the metaphor CONVERSATION TOPIC IS CONTAINER in their language.

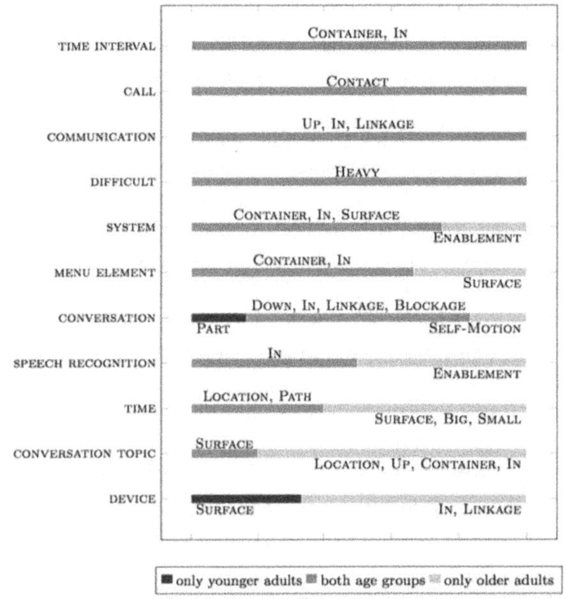

Figure 2: Preliminary examples of the comparison of age-differences in the use of ISM in spoken language (e.g., first line: TIME INTERVAL IS CONTAINER **and** TIME INTERVAL IS IN **are used both by younger and older adults).**

This finding might question the general suitability of all ISM to provide valid abstract-to-physical mappings for TUI design. For the next steps of my work, only ISM will be used that overlap between younger and older adults to provide a valid basis for age-inclusive physical-to-abstract mappings in TUIs.

2) *Evaluating ISM-based TUIs in terms of intuitive use and age-inclusiveness*

The physicality of TUIs bears many advantages for older adults like enhanced learning through concreteness and sensory directness [16]. But only few approaches and recommendations for intuitive and age-inclusive approaches exist. The basic idea of this Ph.D. is that TUIs based on ISM should provide exactly this. More specifically, the goal is to show that TUI design based on ISM reduces the impact of users' cognitive resources and prior technological knowledge on the effectivity and efficiency of the interaction. For this comparison, two types of prototypes are needed: a design based on ISM and one not explicitly based on ISM. For this, two groups of interaction designers will be provided with either a set of ISM or not (baseline). The task will be to develop a simple TUI that supports a set of specific tasks (e.g., TUI for money transfer).

To find a suitable way of presenting ISM to designers, a pre-study has been conducted, where 36 participants with a background in HCI designed GUI-based interaction concepts (that are easier to prototype). One condition, in which designers were presented with ISM to brainstorm design ideas based on ten selected ISM that were placed on the walls, was rated as a comprehensible, structuring, and creativity-supporting design method. In the main study, this approach will form the experimental condition against which the baseline will be tested. The resulting prototypes will be evaluated by younger and older adults while measuring their prior technological knowledge and cognitive resources (e.g., via neuropsychological tests). Of particular interest will be interaction performance (e.g., task times, error rates), ratings of perceived innovation (e.g., via the concept of stimulation), and intuitive use (e.g., first action is the right one, questionnaires). The hypothesis is that all prototypes will be rated as innovative and unfamiliar. Also, TUIs conforming to ISM should be more intuitive to use. Most importantly, interaction with them should be age-inclusive and show no dependency of interaction performance from prior knowledge and cognitive resources. To provide guidance in terms of an optimal integration of ISM into the design process, I will also analyze the TUI design process per se. For this, observational data and questionnaires will be used during the design phase to derive recommendations for enhancing the method of ISM for age-inclusive TUI design in future work.

CONTRIBUTION

This Ph.D. contributes by applying ISM to TUI design with the aim of creating innovative and at the same time age-inclusive TUIs. One output of this work will be methodological recommendations (e.g., finding domain-specific ISM and integrating them into the design process) as well as an estimation to which extent younger and older adults overlap in their language in terms of their use of ISM. But more importantly, if this approach reduces the impact of prior technological knowledge and cognitive resources on interaction performance, this series of studies will provide first evidence that ISM can be used as a powerful method for creating innovative TUIs both younger and older adults are capable of interacting intuitively with.

REFERENCES

1. Alissa N. Antle, Greg Corness, and Milena Droumeva. 2009. What the body knows: Exploring the benefits of embodied metaphors in hybrid physical digital environments. *Interact. Comput.* 21, 1–2: 66–75.
2. Saskia Bakker, Alissa N. Antle, and Elise Van Den Hoven. 2012. Embodied metaphors in tangible interaction design. *Personal Ubiquitous Comput.* 16, 4: 433–449.
3. Yvonne Barnard, Mike D. Bradley, Frances Hodgson, and Ashley D. Lloyd. 2013. Learning to use new technologies by older adults: Perceived difficulties, experimentation behaviour and usability. *Comput. Human Behav.* 29, 4: 1715–1724.
4. Alethea L. Blackler, Vesna Popovic, Douglas P. Mahar, Raghavendra Reddy, and Simon Lawry. 2012. Intuitive interaction and older people. In *Proc. DRS'12*, July 2011: 560–578.
5. Fergus M. Craik and Timothy A. Salthouse. 2008. *The handbook of aging and cognition*. Psychology Press.
6. Sara J. Czaja, Neil Charness, Arthur D. Fisk, Christopher Hertzog, Sankaran N. Nair, Wendy A. Rogers, and Joseph Sharit. 2006. Factors predicting the use of technology: findings from the CREATE. *Psychol. Aging* 21, 2: 333–352.
7. Arthur D. Fisk, Wendy A. Rogers, Neil Charness, Sara J. Czaja, and Joseph Sharit. 2009. *Designing for older adults: Principles and creative human factors approaches*. Boca Raton, New York: CRC Press.
8. Jörn Hurtienne. 2011. *Image Schemas and Design for Intuitive Use*. Ph.D.-thesis, TU-Berlin, Germany.
9. Jörn Hurtienne. Forthcoming 2016. How Cognitive Linguistics Inspires HCI: Image Schemas and Image-Schematic Metaphors. *Interact. Comput.*
10. Jörn Hurtienne, Kerstin Klöckner, Sarah Diefenbach, Claudia Nass, and Andreas Maier. 2015. Designing with image schemas: Resolving the tension between innovation, inclusion and intuitive use. *Interact. Comput.* 27, 3: 235–255.
11. Mark Johnson. 1987. *The Body in the mind: The bodily basis of meaning, reason and imagination*. Chicago: University of Chicago Press.
12. Zoltán Kövecses. 2006. *Metaphor in culture*. Cambridge University Press.
13. Luciana Laganá, Taylor Oliver, Andrew Ainsworth, Marc Edwards, and Luciana Lagan. 2011. Enhancing computer self-efficacy and attitudes in multi-ethnic older adults: a randomised controlled study. *Ageing Soc.* 31, 6: 911–933.
14. Patrick M. Langdon, Jonathan Lazar, Ann Heylighen, and Hua Dong (eds.). 2014. *Inclusive Designing*. Springer International Publishing, Cham.
15. Diana Loeffler, Anne Hess, and Andreas Maier. 2013. Developing intuitive user interfaces by integrating users' mental models into requirements engineering. In *Proc. Bcs-Hci'13*: 1–10.
16. Paul Marshall. 2007. Do tangible interfaces enhance learning ? In *Proc. TEI '07*, 163–170.
17. Anja Naumann and Jörn Hurtienne. 2010. Benchmarks for intuitive interaction with mobile devices. In *Proc. MobileHCI'10*: 401-402.
18. United Nations. 2013. *World Population Ageing 2013*.
19. Armin Winkler, Kristian Baumann, Stephan Huber, Robert Tscharn, and Jörn Hurtienne. 2016. Evaluation of an Application Based on Conceptual Metaphors for Social Interaction Between Vehicles. In *Proc. DIS'16*, 1148–1159.

Coupling Motion and Perception in Body Based UI

Paul Strohmeier
Human Centered Computing
University of Copenhagen
p.strohmeier@di.ku.dk

ABSTRACT
In this essay I outline my current work on motion and haptic perception. I start from my perspective on Embodied Interaction, explaining why I chose to design interfaces focusing on the body in motion. I then describe how my research has moved from creating devices that are not negatively influenced by the moving body, to devices that take advantage of the moving body. This research path has led me to investigating how vibrotactile information and proprioceptive cues are integrated and together give rise to an experience of texture. I am searching for generalizable patterns in how we process haptic information, to apply it to other modalities. I believe that this will allow us to create new embodied experiences of sensations we previously only had indirect access to.

Author Keywords
Embodied Interaction Haptic Feedback; Sensory Substitution

ACM Classification Keywords
H.5.m. Information interfaces and presentation (e.g., HCI): Miscellaneous

INTRODUCTION
Consumer interest in wearable devices is steadily increasing. Within the CHI and TEI research communities there is a trend of wanting to engage with the body in ever closer ways. This trend manifests in two slightly different streams. On the one hand projects are investigating how technologies can move ever closer to the body, for example interactive tattoos [22], makeup [5] and implantable devices [7,8]. On the other hand we are investigating the body itself: what constitutes the body, how can we design for the body, how can the body inform design, how does it mediate perception [10,12,20] etc.

I currently find myself exploring the second category of questions. For me one of the core properties of the body is that it is active agent; in my work I am exploring how the body acting in the world leads to an experience of perception. I am studying tactile perception in search of patterns generalizable to perceptual modalities that are beyond what we currently have access to.

In this essay I will outline the path that has led me to this topic, my current research, and my speculations and hopes for where this research might lead me in the future.

CONTEXT

Embodied Interaction
My interest in haptic perception was piqued by Taylor Carman's essay on the role of the body for Husserl and Merleau-Ponty [4]. Husserl suggests that tactile perception, or rather that we perceive tactile perception localized on our body, leads to bodily self-awareness. However, Husserl describes the Body as something inserted between the material world and the subjective experience of it. Carman contrasts this position with that of Merleau-Ponty, who suggests that the body is more than something inserted between the mental and physical world. Merleau-Ponty suggests that mental phenomena can only occur by the body engaging in the world; that perception is not something that happens through or to the body, but that perception is an activity of the body.

The concept of active perception was also used by Dag Svanæs to describes our perception of interactive artifacts [20]. He points out that interaction is perceived as a whole, rather than as a sum of user inputs and system outputs. For example, when operating a car with a manual clutch, we do not perceive the shifting as a composition of actions and reactions, but we perceive the whole process as one kinesthetic experience. Svanæs describes this as an *interaction gestalt*. When driving one car one day and then switching to another car the next, we perceive the differences in the clutching mechanism: the two different cars give rise to different *interaction gestalts*. Svanæs describes this as the *feel dimension*.

Technological Mediation
Rather than technology as a service that brings information to us, I would like to see technology that expands us, allows us to grasp at information far away in space and time.

TEI '17, March 20 - 23, 2017, Yokohama, Japan

ACM 978-1-4503-4676-4/17/03…$15.00
DOI: http://dx.doi.org/10.1145/3024969.3025038

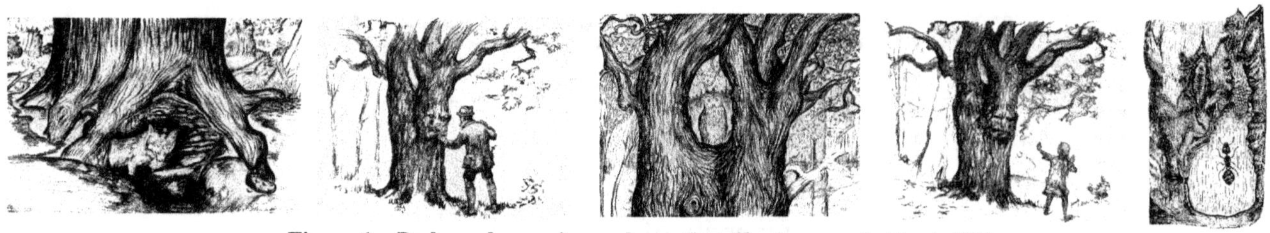

Figure 1 – Body and experience shape the affordances of objects [21]

A useful framework to discuss such design perspectives was introduced by Don Ihde. He points out different ways in which technology mediates our perception and makes a distinction between embodied mediation and hermeneutic mediation [9]: In embodied mediation, the technology itself does not become an object of perception, rather we perceive the world through the technology. The prototypical example of such a technology is the blind person's cane. Ihde contrasts this with hermeneutic mediation, which also provides information of the world, but has an additional interpretive layer. An example of this is a thermometer, which shows us numbers that we interpret to infer temperature outside. Another example is a vibrotactile notification which we interpret based on context.

Affordances and Interface Design

While we often tend to focus on the virtual aspects of digital technologies, to me, an interface is most importantly a physical thing that we interact with by physical means. Like any other object, its shape, size and appearance are not inconsequential: The shape and size of an object acquires meaning relative to our experience and bodies. Jakob von Uexküll presented the charming example of a tree, describing how a gnarly tree might look scary to an imaginative young child, while a forester might asses it for its resource value. Simultaneously the tree might act as a shelter for a fox, a place to perch on for an owl or as an entire world for an ant (Figure 1) [21].

The idea of objects acquiring meaning relative to our bodies is related to Gibson's theory of affordances [6]. Gibson suggests that we understand objects in terms of what they enable us to do with them. For example, a tea-cup has the affordance of holding a fluid, and its handle suggests to us how we can pick it up.

Objects have affordances based on their shape, and are understood relative to our bodies and experiences. If an objects shape fits the human body, like the grip of a skiing pole or an ergonomic mouse, it suggests how it might be used. By explicitly addressing the body's shape and function, well designed objects need no further instruction manual to be used.

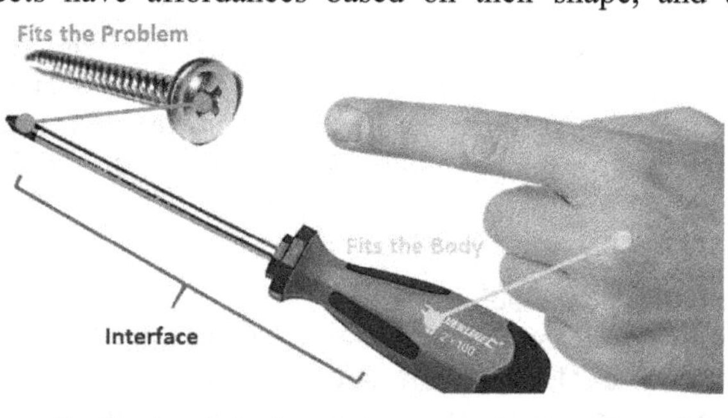

Figure 2 – Tool as interface between the body and an object poorly suited for interaction with the body

Sometimes however a device does not fit the body. For example, a screw has the affordance to hold two pieces of wood together, but its shape does not conform to our body in such a way that we can easily use it: The screw does not have the affordance to be rotated by us. That is where tools come in.

A tool (in this case a screwdriver) has two parts: one that fits the problem (the screw) and one that fits the body. The screwdriver extends the screw and the body, so that as a system we can drive the screw into the wood (Figure 2). The screwdriver can be seen as something corresponding to a computer interface: The CPUs in our everyday devices have affordances that are important to us, they conduct calculations we are not capable of. However, the CPU itself is difficult for us to interact with. Much like the screwdriver mediated between the body and the screw, we need a tool that fits both the CPU and the human body. In practice this tool consists of a chain of tools, the user facing side of this chain is what we refer to as the interface (These ideas are inspired by Bret Victor [2]).

Based on this perspective, interfaces should be designed to have the best possible fit to the human body. Based on the embodied perspective of the body discussed above, the interface must not only fit the body as one objects shape might compliment another, it must also fit the body as an active agent in the world.

PAST WORK

Respecting the body in motion

As pointed out by Marshall and Tennant, there are few interactive systems which allow and facilitate the body to move freely. Gestural input typically constrains body movement to a predefined subset, while 'mobile' systems usually assume that the user will intermittently interrupt their primary activity and stop to use them [13].

Together with Jesse Burstyn I designed DisplaySkin to address this issue [3] (Figure 3). DisplaySkin is a wrist-worn device with a cylindrical display that wraps around the wearer's arm. We designed DisplaySkin to be 'pose-aware': using a kinematic model of the user, we adjusted

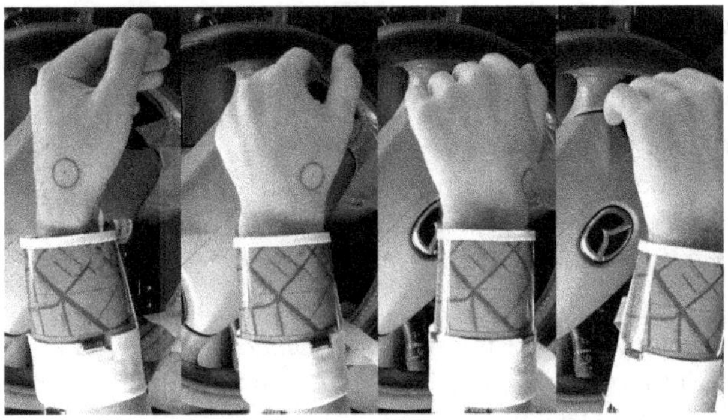

Figure 3 – DisplaySkin: Note that the image remains stable while the hand rotates [3]

content on the device to the user's perspective, so that the wearer could glance at the devices content independently of body pose.

While DisplaySkin did not constrain the user's motions, I was hoping to go beyond that. In addition to accommodating motion, I was interested in designing a device that becomes better through human motion or that takes advantage of human motion.

Working with the body in motion

We use motion and actions to understand the material world around us. We might rub fabric between index finger and thumb to feel its texture better, or sit down on a bed to feel if it is soft or hard. The next project I worked on, ReFlex [17], explored this concept: Using a strain gauge, we measured how much pressure was being exerted on a flexible smartphone prototype (Figure 4). We used this to infer the extent to which it was bent.

The smartphone prototype had an embedded recoil-style haptic actuator [23]. With this actuator we generated vibrotactile feedback based on bending of the phone. We compared generating feedback relative to the extent of the bend (High frequency when the phone is strongly bent, low frequency when it is only slightly bent) to feedback based on the actions of the user (High frequency while the shape of the phone is being changed fast, low frequency while the shape is changed slowly, and no vibration when the phone is resting in any given shape). We found that if we provided

Figure 4 – ReFlex: Flexible Smartphone Prototype [17]

pulse trains relative to the rate with which the users changed the shape of the device (so relative to the users motion), these pulse trains were not experienced as vibration, but instead changed how the material was experienced. The haptic impulses made users feel as if the material was more complex and was often described as being either less or more flexible than without feedback.

This suggests to us that the vibrotactile actuation and the motion is integrated, leading to a new sensation. Using Svanæs terminology, the interaction was not perceived in distinct action/feedback pairings, but gave rise to an *interaction gestalt*, which was experienced as a change in the *feel dimension* of the device.

CURRENT WORK

Perception Through Motion

Similar studies have also shown that if vibrotactile feedback is coupled closely with motion or pressure, these are perceived as variations in the physical properties of the vibrated material [11,16]. This is not surprising if one considers haptic perception as a closed perceptive loop [1].

I am currently exploring this closed loop of perception. Using a similar haptic actuator as used in ReFlex, I am exploring how material perception is influenced by individual parameters of haptic feedback. In an initial study, using a low friction slider augmented with the actuator, I have explored how granularity, amplitude and timbre influence how a material is experienced, if vibrated relative to how it is being moved. Results show that this method and the parameters chosen can be used to generate virtual textures. However, results also hint towards a more complex relationship between motion and actuation than initially assumed, especially the role of timbre in vibrotactile feedback should be explored further in future work [19].

FUTURE WORK

Concepts

Technology has the potential to provide us with access to sensory dimensions beyond those that we are familiar with. Moon Ribas uses technology to 'feel' earthquakes, while Neil Harbisson uses sound to perceive color [14]. We might imagine technologies that enable us to perceive ultra violet, or bat echo-location, wireless communication, or stock market activity. To perceive these in the *feel dimension,* or in what Don Ihde refers to as *embodied mediation*, rather than as symbols we need to interpret, we must design interfaces that present the information suiting the body. This means considering the active nature of perception and designing kinesthetic experiences that we can actively explore.

In my previous work I have demonstrated how the body integrates perceptive stimuli and actions, giving rise to an *interactive gestalt.* In my current work I am exploring how this resulting haptic experience can be manipulated. In future work I plan to explore applying these observations of haptic perception of materials to in air interaction: By providing the three-dimensional space around us with structured textures, different spatial directions can be given a different *feel.* This can be used to provide gestural interfaces with affordances to help users understand what gestures are possible, or how to perform them.

In an additional step, such virtual textures could provide us with sensory experience we typically do not have access to. For example, the north-south dimension could be given a different feel than the east-west dimension. Light with strong ultra-violet content might be made to feel 'harder' than light less harmful to our skin. These extra-sensory dimensions could also communicate information not typically linked to sensory experiences, for example, the space around a credit card could provide a varying haptic experience based on the current account balance. Doorways and entrances could provide the people crossing through them with a tactile experience of what to expect beyond them etc. For all these examples, the intent is to limit interpretive steps required to understand this information, designing what Don Ihde would refer to as *embodied mediation.*

Possible Implementations

Such *feel dimensions* could be presented to users with wearable haptic devices. A simple implementation might be a wristband with an IMU and a haptic actuator. This device might create a physical experience of time by generating its *feel dimension* using the motion and orientation of the hand as input and modulating it based on events and scheduled activities of the user.

An alternate approach could use an implanted device [18]. Such a device would have the benefit of being always present, which may lead to it being better integrated with the user's body-schema. Fully encapsulated devices with a haptic actuator are currently feasible, and various non-academic groups have started experimentation with implanted devices. The fidelity of such devices could further be increased with direct nerve communication, though such devices are still highly experimental [15].

CONCLUSION

In this essay I have outlined some concepts that guide my work. I have described how wanting to design devices that consider body pose eventually lead me to studying perception. In studying haptic perception I have found that we integrate vibrotactile feedback and motion: if the coupling between action and haptic feedback has a sufficiently high temporal resolution, vibrotactile feedback is no longer perceived as vibration but gives rise to a new experience, a new *feel dimension.* This provides us with a new set of tools for the design of interfaces and experiences that are explicitly based on the user's body and the active nature of perception. In the future I wish to apply what I have learned about haptic experiences to other modalities, with the intent to create embodied experiences of sensations which we usually only have symbolic access to.

Acknowledgements

This work was supported by the European Research Council, grant no. 648785

REFERENCES

1. Ehud Ahissar and Eldad Assa. 2016. Perception as a closed-loop convergence process. *eLife* 5, MAY2016. https://doi.org/10.7554/eLife.12830
2. Bret Victor. 2011. A Brief Rant on the Future of Interaction Design. *worrydream.com.* Retrieved from http://worrydream.com/ABriefRantOnTheFutureOfInteractionDesign/
3. Jesse Burstyn, Paul Strohmeier, and Roel Vertegaal. 2015. DisplaySkin: Exploring Pose-Aware Displays in a Flexible Electrophoretic Wristband. In *TEI '14*, 165–172. https://doi.org/10.1145/2677199.2680596
4. Taylor Carman. 1999. The Body in Husserl and Merleau-Ponty. *Philosophical Topics* 27, 2: 205–226. https://doi.org/10.1177/0959354399091005
5. Patricia J. Flanagan and Katia Fabiola Canepa Vega. 2013. Future fashion - At the interface. *Lecture Notes in Computer Science* 8012 LNCS, PART 1: 48–57. https://doi.org/10.1007/978-3-642-39229-0_6
6. James J Gibson. 1979. Theory of Affordances. In *The Ecological Approach to Visual Perception.* Houghton Mifflin, Boston, 127–136. https://doi.org/citeulike-article-id:3508530
7. Kayla J Heffernan, Frank Vetere, and Shanton Chang. 2016. You Put What, Where?: Hobbyist Use of Insertable Devices. *Proc. CHI '16*: 1798–1809. https://doi.org/10.1145/2858036.2858392
8. Christian Holz, Tovi Grossman, George Fitzmaurice, and Anne Agur. 2012. Implanted user interfaces. In *Proc. CHI '12*, 503. https://doi.org/10.1145/2207676.2207745
9. Don Ihde. 1990. *Technology and the life world: From garden to earth.* Indiana University Press.
10. Ozgun Eylul Iscen, Diane Gromala, and Maryam Mobini. 2014. Body image and body schema: Interaction design for and through embodied cognition. *Lecture Notes in Computer Science* 8511 LNCS, PART 2: 556–566. https://doi.org/10.1007/978-3-319-07230-2_53
11. Johan Kildal. 2010. 3D-press. In *International Conference on Multimodal Interfaces and the Workshop on Machine Learning for Multimodal Interaction on - ICMI-MLMI '10*, 1. https://doi.org/10.1145/1891903.1891931
12. David Kirsh. 2013. Embodied Cognition and the Magical Future of Interaction Design. *ACM Trans. Comput.-Hum. Interact. Article* 20, 3. https://doi.org/10.1145/2442106.2442109

13. Joe Marshall and Paul Tennent. 2013. Mobile interaction does not exist. In *Proc. CHI EA '13*, 2069. https://doi.org/10.1145/2468356.2468725

14. Noémie Jennifer. 2015. Talking to Real-Life Cyborgs About the Future of Body-Hacking | The Creators Project. *Vice*. Retrieved from http://thecreatorsproject.vice.com/blog/talking-to-real-life-cyborgs-about-the-future-of-body-hacking

15. Calogero Maria Oddo, Stanisa Raspopovic, Fiorenzo Artoni, Alberto Mazzoni, Giacomo Spigler, Francesco Petrini, Federica Giambattistelli, Fabrizio Vecchio, Francesca Miraglia, Loredana Zollo, Giovanni Di Pino, Domenico Camboni, Maria Chiara Carrozza, Eugenio Guglielmelli, Paolo Maria Rossini, Ugo Faraguna, and Silvestro Micera. 2016. Intraneural stimulation elicits discrimination of textural features by artificial fingertip in intact and amputee humans. *eLife* 5, MARCH2016: e09148. https://doi.org/10.7554/eLife.09148

16. Joseph M. Romano and Katherine J. Kuchenbecker. 2012. Creating realistic virtual textures from contact acceleration data. *IEEE Transactions on Haptics* 5, 2: 109–119. https://doi.org/10.1109/TOH.2011.38

17. Paul Strohmeier, Jesse Burstyn, Juan Pablo Carrascal, Vincent Levesque, and Roel Vertegaal. 2016. ReFlex: A Flexible Smartphone with Active Haptic Feedback for Bend Input. In *Proc. TEI '16:*, 185–192. https://doi.org/10.1145/2839462.2839494

18. Paul Strohmeier, Cedric Honnet, and Samppa Von Cyborg. 2016. Developing an Ecosystem for Interactive Electronic Implants. *Proc. Living Machines 2016*. https://doi.org/10.1007/978-3-319-42417-0

19. Paul Strohmeier and Kasper Hornbæk. 2017. Generating Haptic Textures with a Vibrotactile Actuator. *Proc. CHI '17*.

20. Dag Svanæs. 2013. Interaction Design for and with the Lived Body: Some Implications of Merleau-Ponty's Phenomenology. *Proc. CHI '13* 20, 1: 1–30. https://doi.org/10.1145/2442106.2442114

21. Jakob von Uexkull. 1934. A Stroll Through the Worlds of Animal and Men. In *Instinctive Behavior*. 319–391.

22. Martin Weigel, Tong Lu, Gilles Bailly, Antti Oulasvirta, Carmel Majidi, and Jürgen Steimle. 2015. iSkin: Flexible, Stretchable and Visually Customizable On-Body Touch Sensors for Mobile Computing. In *Proc. CHI '15*, 2991–3000. https://doi.org/10.1145/2702123.2702391

23. Hsin-Yun Yao and Vincent Hayward. 2010. Design and analysis of a recoil-type vibrotactile transducer. *The Journal of the Acoustical Society of America* 128, 2: 619–27. https://doi.org/10.1121/1.3458852

Exploring Bio-Inspired Soft Fluidic Actuators and Sensors for the Design of Shape Changing Tangible User Interfaces

Kristian Gohlke
Bauhaus-Universität Weimar
Weimar, Germany
kristian.gohlke@uni-weimar.de

ABSTRACT

This paper provides an overview of my ongoing doctoral research work and the progress made within the exploratory entry phase. The focus of my research is on the development and evaluation of bio-inspired shape changing user interfaces made from soft or malleable materials with fluidic actuation (i.e. hydraulic or pneumatic) and investigates the use, application potentials and the limitations of such systems for interaction design. The work can thereby be regarded as a subtopic of research on shape changing tangible user interfaces with a specific focus on an exploration of the capabilities of biologically inspired, flexible, fluidically pressurized membrane structures to achieve dynamic shape and volume change – based on observations that such structures are the common building blocks of most living organisms and even complex, dynamic morphologies can emerge from clusters of such *"membrane envelopes"* [1]. By contributing to a novel category of interfaces that are malleable, inherently capable of isotropic shape change and mechanically compliant, the research further intends to question the fundamental design paradigm of current technological artifacts that are commonly characterized by fixed form factors, rigid mechanisms and static enclosures. The envisioned outcome of my thesis work will include a conceptual framework of soft fluidic interfaces, augmented by case studies and design guidelines to provide researchers and design practitioners with an alternative approach to designing shape changing user interfaces by leveraging fluidic morphologies. Recent advances in research on soft robotic actuators provide an additional basis for explorations and evaluations, aimed at an adaption and evaluation of techniques and principles for tangible interaction design.

Author Keywords

Soft Interfaces; Tangible Interaction Design; Soft Robotics; Fluidic Actuation; Shape Change; TUI; Membrane; Bionics.

TEI '17, March 20 - 23, 2017, Yokohama, Japan

ACM 978-1-4503-4676-4/17/03…$15.00
DOI: http://dx.doi.org/10.1145/3024969.3025039

ACM Classification Keywords

H.5.2. User Interfaces: Haptic I/O; Input Devices and Strategies; Prototyping; Theory and Methods.

INTRODUCTION & BACKGROUND

In nature, the shape of most biological organisms emerges from a simple but essential principle: flexible membrane envelopes are (de-)formed by a pressure difference across the two sides of a membrane. The resulting shape can be further influenced by structural restrictions of membrane extension, such as local variations in softness or by tensile forces applied by adjacent structures, such as tendons (which are often also made from clustered membrane envelopes). Even complex shapes and structures can be derived from this principle by stacking and combination of individual membrane cells into larger superstructures. Thus, fluidic membrane envelopes can be regarded as the basic form-giving element of all cell-based living organisms. The shape of most natural organisms can therefore be understood as the interplay between the physical properties of a membrane (such as ductility and stiffness) and the pressure difference across it.

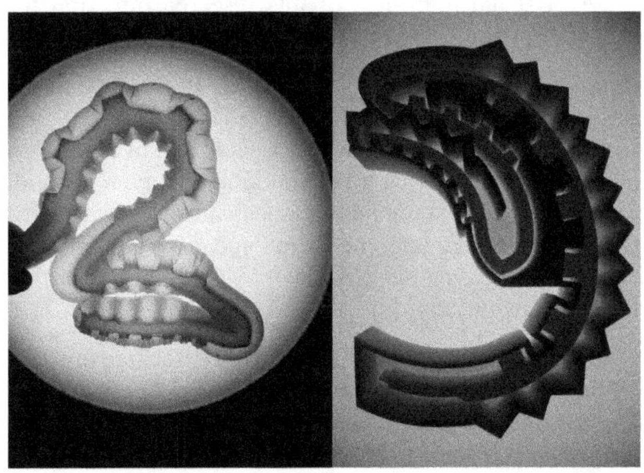

Figure 1: Pneumatic tentacle with complex deformation behavior made from soft silicone (right) / rigid 3D-printed mold used for fabrication (left). (Results from a Workshop given at Bauhaus-University Weimar / Photo: Freya Probst).

This universal principle can also be leveraged to achieve dynamic shape change by modulating the pressure inside such membrane envelopes over time. The resulting dynamic deformation behavior is embodied by the structural configuration of the cell and the material properties of the membrane envelope. Flexible membrane structures are also inherently mechanically compliant due the isotropic distribution of internal pressure across a membrane, thereby they can passively adjust to adjacent structures or external force input.

This principle has been used in architecture and bionics to derive new structures and shapes [1]. Robotics [4] and interaction design [8] have only recently begun to explore soft fluidic actuators and emphasize their potential to reduce the mechanical complexity of animated objects.

FLUIDIC SHAPE CHANGING INTERFACES

In the context of shape changing user interfaces, an approach that takes inspiration from fluidic membrane structures in nature has not been widely explored yet. Shape change as a means to provide input and output is an emerging [7] field of interest in the research on Tangible User Interfaces (TUIs). Commonly, rigid materials and mechanisms [3] have been used for this purpose. Recent developments in the area of Soft Robotics [4] leverage soft, malleable or flexible materials to achieve dynamic shape change. These soft actuators are usually connected to fluidic (i.e. air or liquid) control systems to modulate the shape change. This novel approach provides inspiration and offers a promising direction for the design and development of a new category of user interfaces where physical deformation is achieved through soft mechanisms to create dynamically controllable tangible user interfaces.

Applied in reverse, the manual deformation of physical shapes by the user's hand can also serve as an expressive means for user input when it is combined with the appropriate sensing methods. Some initial advances illustrate [6,8] the relevance of this research direction for tangible interaction design.

Potentially, bio-inspired membrane based structures and the resulting three-dimensional dynamic shapes and deformation patterns could form a basis for a novel class of technological artifacts that go beyond the commonly found, rigid and mostly static electromechanical-contraptions, characteristic to the late industrial age and complement them by a more dynamic class of physical interfaces that are based on an entirely different construction paradigm.

The proposed research work is aimed at transferring and extending techniques from the area of Soft Robotics to the field of Interaction Design and leverage their potential for creating shape changing user interfaces. Based on an initial exploration of the capabilities and limitations of existing approaches, new methods for achieving dynamically actuated shape change and dynamic structure modification will be developed and validated through this work.

Physical shape change and the manipulation of dynamic physical structures as an interaction technique can provide a means for inherently multimodal input and output, even synchronously. Therefore, an exploration of this field must include both directions. Sensing principles that appear to be particularly suited for use in soft and malleable interfaces (e.g. capacitive sensing, optical sensing approaches, magnetic field sensing, IMUs, liquid-metal filled microchannels, and others) will be investigated with the aim of developing a conceptual framework for sensing and interpreting user input through deformable interfaces and serves as a basis for contributing novel sensing methods. This could ultimately lead to the development of a sensing platform that provides opportunities for further research, design and development of soft interface applications. Initial experiments with existing fluidic actuation techniques (particularly pneumatic actuation) indicate that the proposed methods, originating from soft robotics research, are often not well suited for more fine grained or high frequency shape modulation due to latency or coarse control system tolerances and often rely on large, stationary air-compressors. Controlled shape change as a means for meaningful output in a user interface application context therefore also requires the development of new methods for actuation, particularly to improve tactile feedback or enable mobile use. Based on the capabilities of specific fluidic control systems, actuation pattern sequences for shape changing interfaces will be developed and evaluated to provide the physical and conceptual basis for achieving semantically meaningful shape change.

INITIAL WORK

In preparation for the thesis application I have conducted a series of workshops, starting in summer 2015, with a group of students from the industrial design department at the Bauhaus-Universität Weimar to explore different techniques for manufacturing fluidic membrane structures. Participants designed their own fluidically controlled actuators [see Figure 1] and interface elements, adapting and exploring fabrication methods mostly from a soft robotics background. The observations and collective hands-on experiences made during these workshops inspired follow-up research and brought up questions aimed at deriving a more systematic understanding of the effect of individual parameters (such as membrane strength, internal

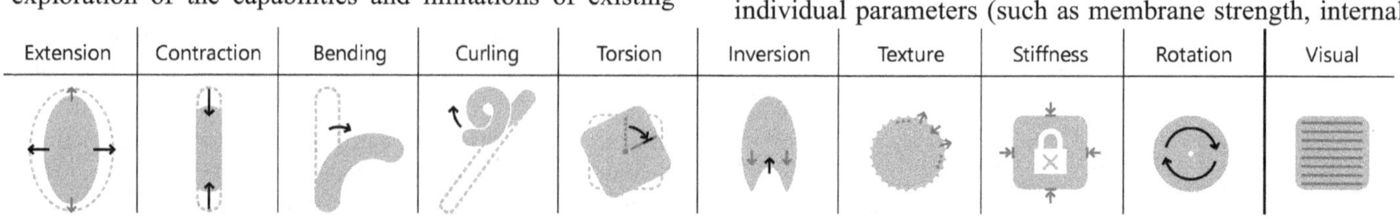

Figure 2. Schematic representation of shape change patterns that have been achieved with soft fluidic actuators. Arrows indicate major directions of force or motion. See the previous page for explanations of the deformation patterns. (Fluidic modulation of visual appearance is included for completeness but can be achieved without deformation of an actuator.)

pressure, stiffness, surface span, etc.) on the resulting shape change and its implications for interaction design.

Initial results from this line of work have already been presented at the 2016 ACM TEI Conference, based on an example of a ***Pneumatible*** [2] a novel category of *pneumatically actuated, pliable interface components, capable of generating dynamic tactile stimuli.* The paper identifies a set of parameters that influence the shape changing behavior and tactile performance of such actuators and discusses them in more detail. A complementary user study was conducted to further evaluate the potential of fluidic structures for the design of tangible interfaces with integrated *pneumotactile feedback*, based on the example of a simple button-shaped *pneumatible* [see Figure 3].

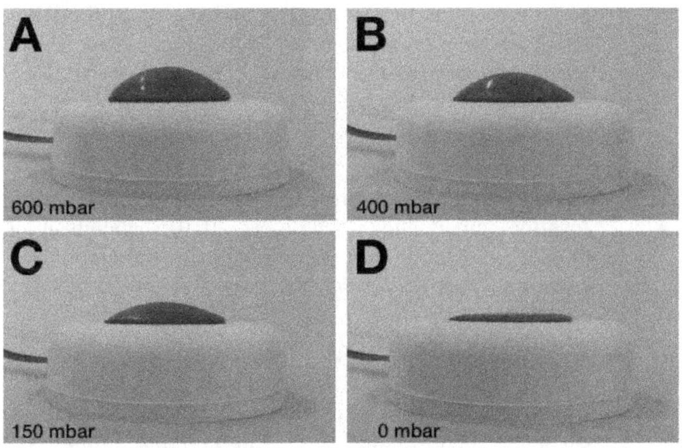

Figure 3: Case study of a simple *button-type* pneumatible at different levels of inflation. The internal pressure is modulated to provide *pneumotactile* feedback to the user.

In a smaller exploration we designed and manufactured *InflatiBits* [5], a working prototype of a modular construction kit that enables playful exploration of pneumatically actuated kinematic systems. The kit contains different building blocks such as *soft inflatable air-chambers, constraining elements, air-connectors, pressure sources,* and *sensor modules* [See Figure 4].

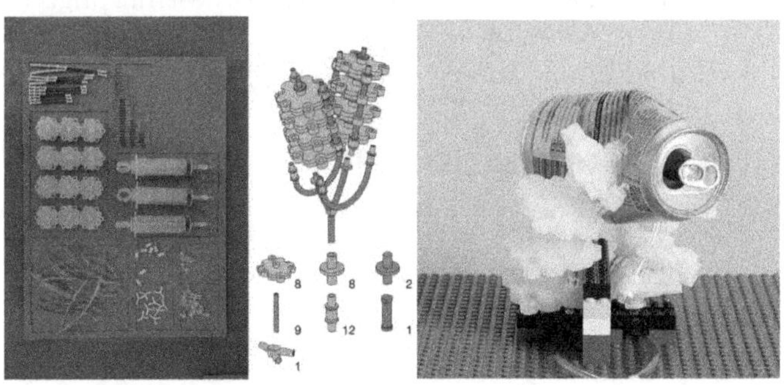

Figure 4: InflatiBits construction set (left), InflatiBits Schematic (center), example construction: soft gripper (right)

Beyond its initially intended use as a novel construction toy for children, the system also serves as a basis for rapid and playful construction with soft actuators and thereby provides a means to overcome the previously time-consuming process of exploring different fluidic actuator configurations, which usually involves some manufacturing efforts. Initial observations indicate that InflatiBits can successfully engage users in free play, as well as provide them with a tool for goal oriented prototyping with inflatable actuators. Both directions provide opportunities for more in-depth explorations.

RESEARCH QUESTIONS

Fluidic membrane structures are nature's universal element to shape and actuate (life-)forms – how can research on tangible interfaces be advanced by a biologically inspired perspective that leverages soft structures and fluidic membrane envelopes for shape change?

Which application domains can benefit from, and which interface applications can be implemented or improved with, bio-inspired fluidic shape change?

Which shape change patterns can be achieved with fluidic membrane structures and what are the challenges and current limitations to this approach?

How can soft, fluidic actuators and sensors be designed, modelled manufactured and controlled?

EXPECTED CONTRIBUTIONS AND OUTCOME

The proposed research intends to make contributions to the body of research on shape changing interfaces in the following ways:

• Extend and explore the design space for bio-inspired, shape modulated user interfaces by creating a conceptual framework and a library of actuation patterns for fluidic shape change.

• Provide tools and techniques for the design, modelling and fabrication of fluidic shape changing interfaces.

• Develop an actuation framework/platform and specific control techniques for fluidic tangible interfaces.

• Create a technical framework/platform and application examples for sensing user input through soft and malleable tangible user interfaces.

RESEARCH METHODS

The thesis follows a constructive-experimental approach to research. Technical explorations are coupled with user studies which then provide the basis for re-iterations and re-evaluation or development of experimental prototypes.

My research efforts are mainly focused on four aspects that appear central to the overall topic: (a.) development and feasibility studies of different materials and actuation techniques to generate and control fluidic shape changing interfaces, guided by an ongoing transfer of principles from fluidic shape change in nature, (b.) technical explorations of different sensing methods and (c.) ongoing evaluations of interactive prototypes and their capabilities through user studies, field observations and interviews with a focus on –

but not limited to – an analysis of qualitative aspects of such interfaces. These activities are augmented by (d.) an extensive literature review covering publications from HCI, tangible interaction design, shape changing interfaces, biology, soft robotics, architecture and adjacent domains.

CURRENT STATUS & TIMEFRAME

The work on the author's thesis project is still at an early stage and much work lies ahead. At the time of this writing, one, out of a minimum of five, envisioned technical explorations and a complementary user study have been completed. Currently the research work is conducted in part-time in parallel with a university teaching engagement and, despite being separate occupations, some overlap exists and synergies can be generated. At the current pace, the remaining timeframe until completion of the thesis work is estimated to be around three and a half years but might be reduced with a transition to a full-time research position.

OUTLOOK & NEXT STEPS

Currently, my ongoing work is focused on an extensive survey of literature mainly from research on fluidically induced shape change in soft robotics and HCI. Techniques and findings from relevant publications are analyzed and their potential for the design of tangible user interfaces is assessed. This line of work is aimed at developing a conceptual framework on fluidic membrane actuators for shape changing interfaces, thereby aimed at contributing to a better understanding of the capabilities, current limitations and challenges for soft robotics inspired work in HCI. The literature review also identified underexplored areas that provide opportunities for research. The survey further contributes a classification system of shape change patterns [see Figure 1], fluidic actuator types and control system architectures, discusses the design space of fluidic interfaces and collects resources to model and manufacture actuators that could be adapted and evaluated in future work.

CONCLUSION

In soft fluidically controlled interfaces, dynamic behavior can be embodied through shape in- and output across the whole device, even beyond the confined surfaces of display areas or dedicated hardware controls and mechanisms. Since both, the basic structural shape and the mechanical deformation behavior can be implemented by consistent mono-material structures and complex deformation behavior can be achieved, even with simple structures. The resulting design space of shapes and dynamic deformation patterns yields physical user interfaces that could challenge our current notion of a separation of hardware (rigid, solid, static, tangible) and software (dynamic, adaptive, time based, intangible) at the interface. A further outcome of this work is expected to yield a library of interaction design patterns, materials and manufacturing techniques for the design of soft, malleable and shape changing interfaces.

The broader aim of my thesis work is to investigate the potential of fluidically controlled membrane structures as a pathway towards an entirely new class of physical artifacts and interfaces that unify qualities that are currently separate characteristics of either software, hardware or even living organisms.

SUPERVISOR

Prof. Dr. Eva Hornecker has accepted the dissertation project as a supervisor and the research proposal has been accepted by the graduation committee of the Faculty of Media at the Bauhaus-Universität Weimar, Germany in May 2016.

REFERENCES

1. Klaus Bach, Hahn Bereiter, Wolfgang F. Gutman, et al. 1976. *Pneus in Natur und Technik / Pneus in Nature and Technics*. Mitteilungen des Instituts für Leichte Flächentragwerke / Frei Otto, Stuttgart.
2. Kristian Gohlke, Eva Hornecker, and Wolfgang Sattler. 2016. Pneumatibles: Exploring Soft Robotic Actuators for the Design of User Interfaces with Pneumotactile Feedback. *Proceedings of ACM TEI 2016 (TEI '16)*, ACM Press, 308–315. http://doi.org/10.1145/2839462.2839489
3. Fabian Hemmert, Susann Hamann, Matthias Löwe, Josefine Zeipelt, and Gesche Joost. 2010. Shape-changing mobiles. *Proceedings of the 28th of the international conference extended abstracts on Human factors in computing systems (CHI EA '10)*, ACM Press, 3075. http://doi.org/10.1145/1753846.1753920
4. Filip Ilievski, Aaron D Mazzeo, Robert F Shepherd, Xin Chen, and George M Whitesides. 2011. Soft Robotics for Chemists. *Angewandte Chemie International Edition* 50, 8: 1890–1895. http://doi.org/10.1002/anie.201006464
5. Christopher Kopic and Kristian Gohlke. 2016. InflatiBits - A Modular Soft Robotic Construction Kit for Children. *Proceedings of ACM TEI 2016 (TEI '16)*, ACM Press, 723–728. http://doi.org/10.1145/2839462.2872962
6. Ivan Poupyrev, Tatsushi Nashida, and Makoto Okabe. 2007. Actuation and tangible user interfaces: the Vaucanson duck, robots, and shape displays. *Proceedings of ACM TEI 2007 (TEI '07)*, 205–212. http://doi.org/10.1145/1226969.1227012
7. Majken Kirkegård Rasmussen, Timothy Merritt, Miguel Bruns Alonso, and Marianne Graves Petersen. 2016. Balancing User and System Control in Shape-Changing Interfaces. *Proceedings of ACM TEI 2016 (TEI '16)*, ACM Press, 202–210. http://doi.org/10.1145/2839462.2839499
8. Lining Yao, Ryuma Niiyama, Jifei Ou, Sean Follmer, Clark Della Silva, and Hiroshi Ishii. 2013. PneUI: Pneumatically Actuated Soft Composite Materials for Shape Changing Interfaces. *Proceedings ACM UIST 2013 (UIST '13)*: 13–22. http://doi.org/10.1145/2501988.2502037

Negotiating Ambiguity in Describing Fabrics Through Technology

Anamary Leal
Third Lab, Virginia Tech
Blacksburg, VA, 24960, USA
leal@vt.edu

ABSTRACT
Designers using tangible materials like fabric may have a limited verbal language to describe the embodied experience of feeling the material. Taxonomies exist for materials like fabric, but are not served by the population of designers we studied. How can technology be designed to better explore fabric, yet not diminish any existing ambiguities in description? We chose to study both different ways to represent the fabric and different interface designs to explore fabric. We collected many descriptors, in part by crowdsourcing, and asked how designers explored fabric, leveraging off of existing practices. We designed interfaces to evaluate a designer's understanding of fabric, with the goal to provide design guidelines on how to design interfaces with ambiguous-important domains.

ACM Classification Keywords
H.5.m. Information Interfaces and Presentation (e.g. HCI): H.5.2 User Interfaces

Author Keywords
ambiguity; design; fabric; garment design; costume design; user experience design; human-computer interaction

INTRODUCTION & MOTIVATION
In 2015, a photo of a dress went viral as it was described as black, blue, and white and gold [10]. Similarly, costume and fashion designers use different, ambiguous, and sometimes contradictory words to describe the same fabric; a single word like "soft" can describe different properties such as color, texture, or drape, or how fabric flows over objects [4]. Some might describe a fabric swatch from an expensive Chanel, or very high-quality brand, suit as "rich", while others may describe it as like a "Christmas sweater". A fabric may be "heavy" to some, but more "thick" to others. There are taxonomies for fabric [6, 1] but our designer participants did not use them.

Verbal language is no substitute for an embodied sense of understanding fabric. The rich feel of a Chanel fabric is quite different from the feel of a satin fabric. Technology presents both the opportunity and the challenge, since it enables a huge amount of information on fabrics, but does not communicate how the fabric looks, feels and drapes. The limited discourse of fabric descriptors becomes more challenging if a designer is unable to feel the fabric directly, such as online shopping.

TEI '17, March 20 - 23, 2017, Yokohama, Japan

ISBN 978-1-4503-4676-4/17/03... $15.00
DOI: http://dx.doi.org/10.1145/3024969.3025040

Additionally, taxonomies may help resolve ambiguities, but do not allow for the unclear or contradictory terms like a dress being both black, blue, white and gold. Design domains thrive on ambiguity because it allows for many people with different contexts to express multiple interpretations on a concept[5], and taxonomies may remove ambiguities.

RESEARCH OBJECTIVES & QUESTIONS
Our main objective is to study how to design technology to handle ambiguities in language and help designers explore fabric. We, my advisor, doctoral committee and I, discovered two main challenges, which evolved into research questions:

- (RQ1) what kinds of ambiguities lie in the adjectives and properties within these fabric descriptors?
- (RQ2) how can we design interactions on existing technologies that use these unstable, ambiguous descriptors as strengths to aid garment designers identify their desired fabric? We studied design interactions with respect to *representations of fabric on commonplace technology* and *designing with unstable descriptors.*

RELATED WORK
There are numerous standards and metrics currently used to describe fabric. Kawabata's work, a prominent work from fashion design, was one of the first to take physical, quantitative properties of fabric, ask experts to rate fabrics based on those properties, and generate a vocabulary of words to describe specific aspects about fabric, such as the stretchiness and drape [6]. But, from our prior studies, where we asked novice designers to describe fabric, we found a wide range of descriptors and ambiguity between the descriptors[7].

The work relies in part on information architecture, where fabric has a series of properties, descriptors and behaviors. Morville's book on information architecture posits that words are a part of the interface or how users understand a system. A word may have a large amount of context surrounding it [9]. For example, a word like "soft" may have a large amount of baggage associated with it, including properties, fabrics,

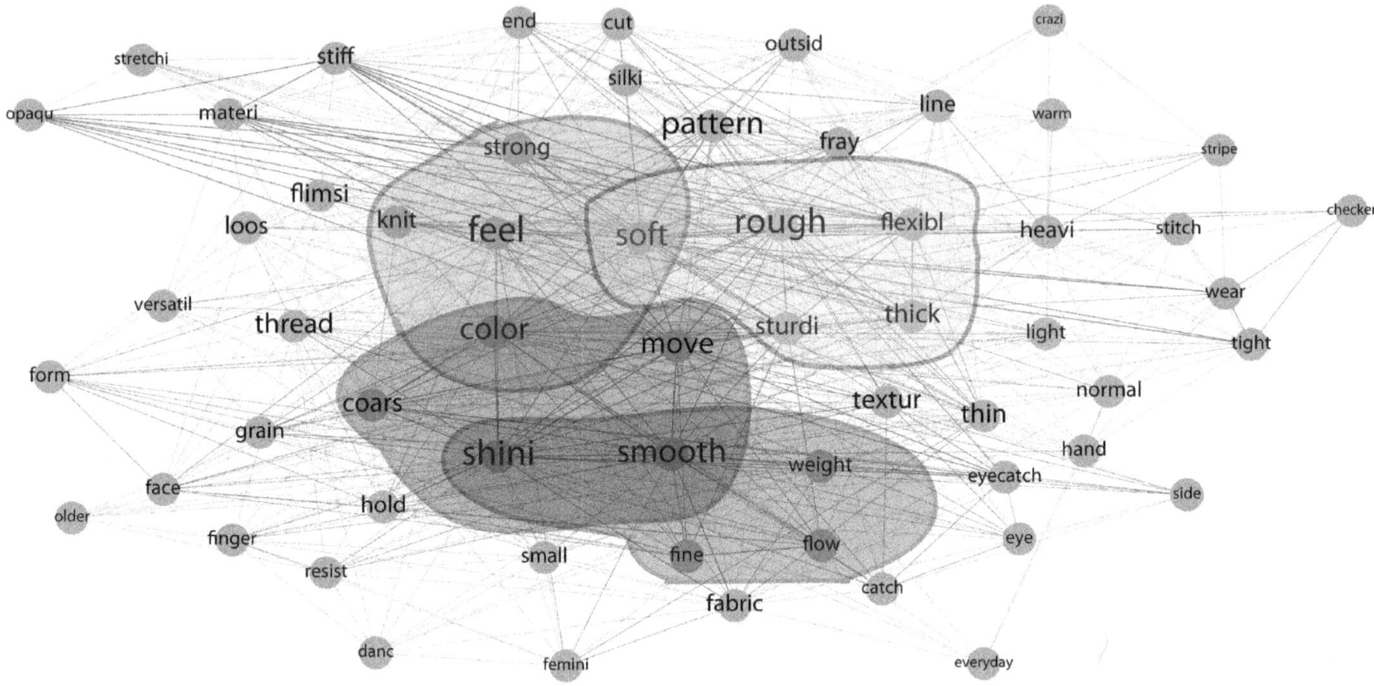

Figure 1. Network of co-occurring descriptions for fabric in our preliminary study of how designers describe fabric, in root words. Larger text represents more frequently used word, and clusters represent the top 5 words when performing topic modeling analysis.

and other words such as "fluffy", "smooth", or even "cats". However, words are not the item itself, and in our observations and in our studies, the baggage word metaphor rings true.

Methven et al. also explored how people described fabric with the goal of allowing consumers to make informed choices about fabric when shopping for clothing online. The researchers asked participants to describe fabric after feeling real fabric. Then, after filtering words, they asked participants, both live and online crowdsourced, to to group descriptor words based on their familiarity with the words and on the similarity of the words to one another. Their results group descriptors together; for example, "warm" is grouped with "cold", and "soft" with "light" [11]. We relied on these studies to give us a grounding on how to understand how designers described fabric.

Atkinson et al. collected not only descriptors but also gestures that participants used on real-world fabric while describing the fabric, extracted key features and gestures from the set, and implemented those gestures onto virtual fabric in an interactive mobile app on an iPad [2]. Our work leverages these gestures, and for more gestures, we consulted a seasoned expert designer about how designers manipulate fabric, allowing us to include additional gestures.

RESEARCH APPROACH & METHODS

My advisor and I initiated our investigation on how costume designers describe fabric, which became our first approach. A costume design expert selected a diverse collection of fabrics and asked designers to pick fabric for a task. We collected their responses in the form of video, and recorded the descriptors used.

Then, we conducted a series of text analyses on the qualitative data. Our focus was on properties, word associations, and terms associated with particular fabrics. One example of our analysis, in figure 1, is one result of using co-occurring word associations and topic modeling to generate overall topics around the words descriptors used. We found a complex network of descriptors and properties that designers used to describe fabric. Participants also shared how they explored fabric for a project. These methods, among other tools, helped us find evidence for the ambiguities in describing properties of fabric, addressing RQ1.

Relying on the success of crowdsourcing in the literature [11], our second approach for RQ1 was to use crowdsourcing to collect a large number of descriptors. To build on the literature, we chose to not make a distinction between whether the word was useful. We chose to include the more emotional terms that they eliminated, because they may present value to designers. Descriptors like "expensive" may be of value to a designer of high-end garments. Additionally, their methodology did not take into account multiple potential meanings of descriptors; for example, they found that the word "soft" was primarily associated with "light". However, a word like "soft" may also describe with a different property such as color or texture, which their groupings would not identify.

In addition to collecting descriptors and ways to explore fabric, we also wanted to study different ways to represent a tangible material individually, and how they affected a designer's understanding. Different representations of fabric include: (1) an image of fabric, (2) multiple images of the fabric in different manipulations (Draped, stretched, front and back, moving), and (3) a video of real fabric being manipulated.

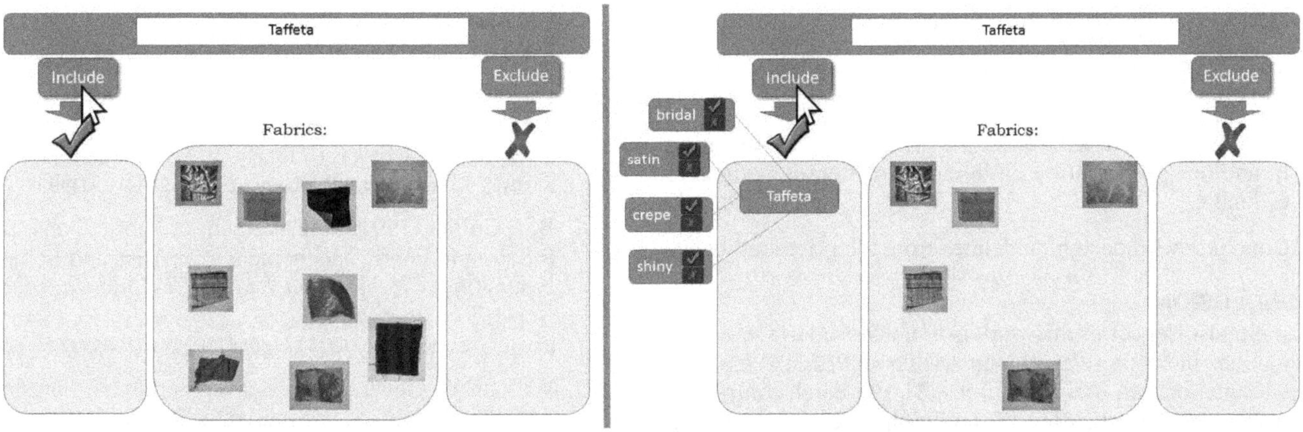

Figure 2. (a) A sketch of the fabric swatch interface, which begins with a user typing in a desired quality, like Taffeta. The user then chooses whethertaffetas should be included in the query, or excluded. Then in figure (b), right, "Taffeta" appears under the green check box, as a desired quality. Relevant qualities also pop up, and the user can include, exclude or ignore the suggested qualities. The list of fabrics change as qualities get added to either list.

To give a better idea of how representation affects a designer's understanding of fabric, we ran a separate study asking participants to describe fabric in-person, and ask crowdsource participant to describe fabric with the different representations.

From prior practices of exploring fabric, our third approach was to design interfaces that facilitate describing fabrics so that the designer will get the best understanding of the fabric. Ongoing now, we are implementing those designs for an app that will use representations and interface methods to organize and present the fabric descriptions and properties found in the prior study.

To verify both our interface designs and our representations, we will evaluate how do the different representations and interface designs affect a garment designer's perception of fabric.

In order to evolve our designs and further learn about representations with fabric, we propose iterating on designs and evaluation, based on from lessons learned in prior evaluations. The follow-up evaluation is expected to be similar to the last evaluations, differing in evolved designs. Finally, from the lessons learned in these studies, we can address RQ2 with a series of design guidelines for design domains or other domains where ambiguity is preserved.

RESULTS

Below are select high-level findings our studies, with the findings most relevant to our research questions.

Ambiguity in descriptors

Figure 1 showing how different descriptors were co-occurring with one another when describing our diverse fabrics. We also generated clusters using Latent-Dirichlet Allocation (LDA) analysis, one of the most flexible clustering topic modeling tool [3], to gain a better insight on the kinds of connections between words.

One of the biggest observations in this analysis, the first observation is ambiguity in the words themselves, such as "soft" being grouped with both "color" and "rough", implying both a visual and textural property, respectively. Thick and thin, despite being opposites, may also have other meanings beyond fabric thickness, such as yarn thickness, giving us insight on RQ1. For more details please see our upcoming submitted work here [7]. These findings reveal the importance of showing relevant, potentially contradictory words, and leave the designer to decide what interpretations make sense.

Interface Designs

Prior work discussed our various interface designs, so I highlight one of our design concepts from one of my sketches. The main inspiration for the upcoming concept was the dialogue that costume designers had when one designer delegates another to explore fabric for them. The dialogue tended to refer to specific fabrics, particular descriptors, and whether the desired fabric should match a descriptor or should not match a descriptor, such as "soft, but not thick". The dialogue also included qualities that may not matter to the designer. The resulting concept was a fabric swatch interfaces [8], with one of the resulting sketches in figure 2.

Figure 2 uses faceted search so users can specify where a quality, whether it's a particular kind of fabric, a textural property or something else entirely different, should be included or excluded from the fabrics.

In addition to this interface, we also sketched out interfaces that were focused on descriptors, or focused on the individual fabrics shown [8].

ACTIVITIES ACCOMPLISHED & REMAINING

I have accomplished the following on my dissertation:

- Collected descriptors, their co-occurrences and associated them with a variety of different kinds of fabrics.
- Evaluated how different representations of fabric affect how the fabric is described, comparing in-person participants holding real fabric with crwodsourced participants.

Remaining work for my Ph.D includes:

- Finish evaluations on different representations of fabric.

- Develop the interfaces for exploring fabrics.
- Perform the evaluation on the interfaces, representations, and how both affect a designer's understanding of fabric.
- From lessons learned, repeat the prior two steps, resulting in another full iteration on iterate on different designs to evaluate.
- Conclude with design guidelines from the prior studies.

CONCLUSION

The biggest impact of this work is to deliver interface design guidelines in for these ambiguous-rich domains, like many of the design domains in maker spaces. This research contributes in a greater understanding of the ambiguities in describing fabrics. Specifically, we deliver a network of associated words, adjectives and properties in relation to describing fabric. These representations of fabrics and ambiguous descriptors will help designers print next generation fabrics on a future 3D printer. Additionally, this work lowers the barrier of entry for newcomers to build their own custom clothing, a value found in many Do-It-Yourself (DIY), maker and Steampunk cultures.

Our research will not only help designers identify and ultimately find a desired fabric without feeling it directly, but our representations and ambiguous descriptors also help in generating next generation fabrics with technologies including additive manufacturing (3D printing). Imagine the 3D printing of fabrics, now with the opportunity to more precisely control the location and architecture of multiple layers of fabric.

REFERENCES

1. American Association of Textile Chemists and Colorists. 2011. Fabric Hand: Guidelines for the Subjective Evaluation of. In *AATCC Evaluation Procedure*.
2. Douglas Atkinson, Pawel Orzechowski, Bruna Petreca, Nadia Bianchi-Berthouze, Penelope Watkins, Sharon Baurley, Stefano Padilla, and Mike Chantler. 2013. Tactile perceptions of digital textiles. In *Proceedings of the SIGCHI Conference on Human Factors in Computing Systems - CHI '13*. ACM Press, New York, New York, USA, 1669. DOI: http://dx.doi.org/10.1145/2470654.2466221
3. David M. Blei, Andrew Y. Ng, and Michael I. Jordan. 2003. Latent dirichlet allocation. *The Journal of Machine Learning Research* 3 (mar 2003), 993–1022. http://dl.acm.org/citation.cfm?id=944919.944937
4. B. J. Collier. 1991. Measurement of Fabric Drape and Its Relation to Fabric Mechanical Properties and Subjective Evaluation. *Clothing and Textiles Research Journal* 10, 1 (sep 1991), 46–52. DOI: http://dx.doi.org/10.1177/0887302X9101000107
5. William W. Gaver, Jacob Beaver, and Steve Benford. 2003. Ambiguity as a resource for design. In *Proceedings of the conference on Human factors in computing systems - CHI '03*. ACM Press, New York, New York, USA, 233. DOI:http://dx.doi.org/10.1145/642611.642653
6. Sueo Kawabata and Nihon Sen'i Kikai Gakki. 1980. *The standardization and analysis of hand evaluation*. Textile Machinery Society of Japan. DOI: http://dx.doi.org/10.1201/9781439823767
7. Anamary Leal and Steve Harrison. Negotiating Ambiguity in Describing Fabrics Through Technology. Journal entry, submitted.
8. Anamary Leal and Steve Harrison. Practical Material Exploration of Fabric Materials in Design Domains. Submitted.
9. Peter Morville. 2014. *Intertwingled: Information Changes Everything*. Semantic Studios.
10. David Stout. 2015. This May Be Why You're Seeing the Dress as White and Gold. (Feb 2015). http://time.com/3725528/dress-explainer-white-gold-blue-black-science/
11. S Thomas, M Pawel, and J Mike. 2011. A Comparison of Crowd-Sourcing vs. Traditional Techniques for Deriving Consumer Terms. *Digital Engagement 2011* (2011).

[X]Changing Perspectives: Designing a Product Service System for Participatory Sensemaking in Multi-Stakeholder Dynamics around Public Issues

Philémonne Jaasma
PhD candidate Industrial Design
Eindhoven University of
Technology, The Netherlands
p.g.jaasma@tue.nl

Evert Wolters
PhD candidate & Consultant
Eindhoven University of
Technology, The Netherlands
evert@necker.nl

ABSTRACT
This paper outlines the background, research aims, approach and completed work as well as future plans of a co-promotion PhD project on the interface of Interaction Design and Political Administration. The aim is to design for Participatory Sensemaking in the context of multi-stakeholder participation in public issues. Through an exploratory Research through Design process we gained insight into the design context and the role that a designed Product Service System could play. We developed [X]Changing Perspectives: an interactive system, based on discussion tables, for Participatory Sensemaking in multi-stakeholder dynamics. Through interaction analysis we hope to gain insight into what aspects of this PSS can trigger Participatory Sensemaking. We aim to generalise the insights in such a way that they can be applied to other PSS's by designers and taken into account by practitioners in multi-stakeholder participation processes.

Author Keywords
Multi-stakeholder collaboration; Participatory Sensemaking

ACM Classification Keywords
H.5 Information interfaces and presentation (e.g., HCI); H.5.m Miscellaneous.

INTRODUCTION
In Western Europe, the complexity created by globalization and technological developments is increasingly being recognized in people's daily lives. The aftermath of the economic crisis of 2008 has left Western Europe with decentralisation, budget cuts and retracting welfare states (e.g. Big Society in the UK). Combined with an ageing population and the arrival of one million refugees in Europe in 2015, these are matters that concern not only government but also educational institutions, public- and private stakeholders and civilians. Today's public issues bring such different stakeholders together to rise to these challenges by multi-disciplinary collaborations [5, 10], for example in Deliberative Democracy [13].
However, the conflicting stakes, different backgrounds and shifting roles and responsibilities of the stakeholders in public issues ask for new ways of collaborating and interacting in those multi-stakeholder settings.

TEI '17, March 20-23, 2017, Yokohama, Japan
© 2017 ACM. ISBN 978-1-4503-4676-4/17/03…$15.00
DOI: http://dx.doi.org/10.1145/3024969.3025041

In our research we aim to design for Participatory Sensemaking in interactions between multi-stakeholders around public issues. To this end, we designed [X]Changing Perspectives ([X]CP): an interactive system consisting of tangible markers on round tables and a visual representation for multi-stakeholder discussions with 6 to 90 participants.

In this paper we describe the [X]CP system but we first outline the structure of the project and briefly explain Participatory Sensemaking and related theory. Then, we introduce our research question and tap into related work from different fields. We continue by describing the [X]CP system followed by brief preliminary conclusions and our plan for future work.

CONTEXT & MOTIVATION
In this PhD project the authors collaborated from their positions at a faculty of Industrial Design and at Necker van Naem, a political-administrative consultancy agency for local governance. The first author is trained as a designer, now researcher, and the second author as a political theorist, now consultant. The PhD project is aimed to comprise less than 4 years, of which, at the moment of writing, 2 years have passed.

THEORY
Our research is informed by several different theoretical concepts, which we will explain briefly as they frame our work: Habermas' distinctions of System and Lifeworld [11], Plurality [1], Phenomenology [21], Embodied Cognition [9] and Participatory Sensemaking [17].

System and Lifeworld
In his Theory of Communicative Action, Habermas [11] uses two distinctions to describe the world: he speaks of

System and Lifeworld. System refers to regulated environments such as institutions, steering media, municipalities with rigid laws or procedures. The Lifeworld encompasses everything that goes on 'between the lines' of such structures: the messy reality of everyday life, social (inter-)relations, the pluriformity of people (beyond their demographic statistics) and the complexity of their interactions and behaviour.
Habermas cautions that systemic mechanisms tend to colonise the Lifeworld, suppressing social integration. In local governance, the relevant stakeholders' roles and behaviours typically represent either System or Lifeworld, while holistically every human being is part of both. For Habermas, Communicative Action is about 'reaching understanding in the sense of a cooperative process of interpretation' [3, p. 40]. This requires stakeholders to engage in interactions that cross the boundary between System and Lifeworld.

We recognize his division of System and Life-world and use it as a context for our work. However, we differentiate in our views on *understanding*: inspired by phenomenology [21], embodied cognition [9] and social situatedness [23], we take an enactive approach [25] to the process of reaching understanding, synthesized in Participatory Sensemaking [17], which we will elaborate in the final paragraph of this Theory section.

Plurality

Habermas' view on understanding relies heavily on language and rationality. Arendt, building on political phenomenology, takes a different view: she emphasises *plurality* rather than rationality and action rather than language. Arendt [1] argues that our sense of self is constituted when we appear to other people: the subject requires the object to get to know itself. She describes action, 'handeln', as the sharing of viewpoints and opinions between people. This can be through dialogue, or for instance writing a column. Through action, people can affect other people and get to know or change their own viewpoint. The kind of action that she describes requires different people, *plurality*, and an open environment, *public space*. She characterizes human plurality by the simultaneous *distinctness* and *otherness* of people: we are connected in our diversity. She uses a table as metaphor of the public space that she envisions: people can take place around the table, which connects them while they lay out their different opinions.

We are inspired by Arendt's conviction of the importance of a public space that provides a stage for plurality, which in turn constitutes our sense of 'self' in every new action we take. Arendt's concept of action, however, is based on dialogue and thus on language. We take a more embodied approach to dialogue and action, as grounded in a phenomenological perspective on perception [21].

Phenomenology of Perception

We take a phenomenological perspective on the role of design in creating engaging interactions and experiences. We follow Merleau-Ponty's Phenomenology of Perception [21] wherein he describes that we perceive and make sense of the world by physically interacting with and in it. In other words, we explore the world through our skilful and perceptive bodies, including previous experience, skills and education. Merleau-Ponty explains that the body and the mind are interconnected and influence one another. Meaning is established only in interaction between the skillful body and the object in context. Taking a leap to the field of design, this promises that designing for tangible or spatial interactions (movements) opens up different ways to perceive and makes sense of the world- and might indeed change perspectives on the world.

Embodied Cognition

Looking at the cognitive processes behind the intertwining of the mind and the body, Embodied Cognition (EC) theory explains that our cognition does not come about by disembodied computations in the brain. Rather, EC describes how the body-in-action includes the physical and the social environment in cognition [9]. Suchman [23] explains that we do not pre-plan our actions in our minds, but rather our actions depend on the material and social circumstances: *situated action*. More specifically, Suchman [23] argues that face-to-face communication and collaboration activities are fundamental for sense-making. In line with Arendt's appreciation of plurality, she argues that people inter-subjectively construct knowledge, in the physical world as well as in social situations.

Participatory Sensemaking

Zooming in on the role of the social dynamics of multi-stakeholder interactions, De Jaegher and Di Paolo [17] propose an enactive approach to social cognition: Participatory Sensemaking. Varela et al. [25] coin the term *enactment* to stress that, as opposed to creating mental representations of the world, we enact a world of meaning through a continuous loop of perception and action, i.e. the creation of meaning or sense-*making* through the process of sensorimotor coupling [24]. De Jaegher and Di Paolo extend this concept to social environment, stating that people can engage in each other's sensemaking activities through interacting. It is in the interaction processes that meaning is created *between* different participants. The extent to which sensemaking is participatory can vary from 'guiding', that is to direct the other's attention towards an understanding, to truly participatory sensemaking, whereby the established meaning cannot be assigned to either participant alone [17].

RESEARCH QUESTION & APPROACH

The main research question of the PhD project is: 'by what aspects of *Product Service System (PSS) [X]Changing Perspectives can we achieve Participatory Sensemaking in Multi-Stakeholder Dynamics around Public Issues?'*. The term 'PSS' refers to the development of a service to implement the design intervention in context. The term 'Participatory Sensemaking' refers to our theoretical view on what kind of interactions we aim to trigger. The term 'public issues' carries in it the tension between System and Lifeworld and 'multi-stakeholder dynamics' refers to the context of participation wherein diverse or even conflicting expertise, experience and perspectives play a role.

The most important sub-question is: "How can Participatory Sensemaking be operationalised so that it can be observed, measured and attributed to PSS aspects?" This is the focus for future work.

We adopt a Research through Design approach [26]. Through several hands-on explorations and iterations 'in the wild' (with pressing public issues and real stakeholders) we reflect on the role of designed artefacts and service elements in generating Participatory Sensemaking.

RELATED WORK

We are interested in the design of participatory processes, as developed by the Participatory Design movement. We are also interested in interactive table-top systems as we build on earlier insights on designing for interactions around tables to entice collaboration.

Participatory Design

In the field of design, research in the 1970's and 1980's has been directed at democratisation of the workplace starting the Scandinavian tradition of Participatory Design. In recent years this tradition extended into, mostly consent-driven, co-design methods for horizontal collaborations [6]. Buur and Larssen [6] suggest however, that in order for innovation (the emergence of new meaning) to occur, design should allow for differences and conflict between the multi-stakeholders. Methods that bring out conflicts in participatory processes have been developed such as improvisational theatre [18] and provotypes [4]. More specifically targeted at the context of public issues, Buur and Larssen call for designers to develop "new formats of collaboration for large, complex contingents of stakeholders" [6, p137] beyond common workshops and for design-facilitators to address the role of conflict and crossing intentions.

Interactive table-top systems for collaboration

In the field of HCI and Computer-Supported Collaborative Work there has been much attention to interactive or tangible table-tops to enhance creative collaboration [e.g., 14]. There are even specific conferences on the development and application of interactive table-tops such as Horizontal Interactive Human Computer Systems (HIHCS) and Interactive Surfaces and Spaces (ISS). Earlier TEI publications have shed light on the role of tangible- [22] and multi-touch interactions [8, 12] within table-top systems, especially for application in education. Technologies used include multi-touch screens, RFID tags, projection mapping or the tracking of QR codes. Often, horizontal surfaces (used to interact on/with) were combined with vertical surfaces (displaying outcome or information): Arias respectively describes these as *action space* and *reflection space* [2]. Interactive table-tops that allow people to interact with them simultaneously (through multi-touch or tangible input) have shown to contribute to a social experience [20] meaning-making [8], shared understanding [2], cohesive storytelling [7] and equitable participation [19].

COMPLETED WORK

We started the work with a wide exploration into designing stages for interaction between multi-stakeholders ('in the wild'), from caravans in the public space, to probes, to a discussion table. Reflecting on these explorations, the discussion table seemed to provide a rich platform to iterate upon aspects that may elicit Participatory Sensemaking.

Figure 1. Overview of iterations towards [X]CP

[X]Changing Perspectives

Figure 1 visually shows, from top to bottom, how we iteratively developed [X]CP through testing low-fidelity prototypes and mock-ups of discussion tables. [X]CP [16] is an interactive system consisting of 15 tables with integrated visual tracking technology, 6 interactive tokens per table with icons, equipped with a Neopixel LED ring, a capacitive sensor and an AR marker, and one online real-time visualisation that shows all token touches, movements and their traces.

Figure 2. Implementation of [X]CP 'in the wild'

Inspired by the work of Hummels and Van Dijk [15], the focus of the design was on providing scaffolds and traces for embodied sensemaking, by enriching conversations with tangible input (scaffolds) and visible outcome (traces) of the conversations. The design was intended to bring out different perspectives and enrich deliberative conversation with embodied and social cognition and, in doing so, establish Participatory Sensemaking- in multi-stakeholder settings.

[X]CP was designed to be used in multi-stakeholders settings, e.g. in participatory decision-making sessions, such as shown in figure 2, and was tested in 12 real-life cases with 30 to 120 participants. It is part of a PSS that includes the invitation, data analysis and evaluation process before and after the [X]CP session.

[X]Changing Perspectives session

The [X]CP system allows multi-stakeholders to exchange perspectives about the central question (in the middle of the table) by associating with icons on the tokens and positioning and repositioning them on the table, the *action space* [2], as shown in figure 3.

Figure 3. Participants (re-)position tokens on the table.

Participants attribute their own meaning to the icons and the table surface. Whilst repositioning, they exchange their associations, thoughts, and anecdotes with each other while building on top of each others' stories and herewith they are co-constructing the meaning of the tokens and the relations between them (landscape). Afterwards, they create action points to realise their landscape, and attribute them to tokens. Lastly, they choose which action they will take on, or give actions to other stakeholders. This final step triggers a reflection on role taking in multi-stakeholder collaborations.

The online visualisation, the *reflection space* [2], provides the multi-stakeholders with a bird's eye overview of the history of token movements on their table in comparison to the other tables. During a session, the visualisation allows for several moments for reflection between tables: participants compare e.g. the amount of repositioning of a specific token, and the reasons for moving it that much. These explanations can obtain a role in or inspire further discussion and repositioning at other tables.

It is in the interactions around the table and the reflections on the visualisations where we look for Participatory Sensemaking to take place.

Data analysis

The conversations at each table are recorded in notes and videos [16] and coupled to the visualisation data so that, after the session, we can share a broad impression of the different perspectives and meanings that arose during the session and that ought to be taken into account in the further process of decision-making.

FUTURE WORK

The production of the fourth iteration of the PSS of [X]Changing Perspectives was recently completed. We integrated a 360° camera into the tables to improve data capturing and analysis. The upcoming and final year of the PhD is dedicated to analysing the interactions that take place during the [X]CP session, in order to consolidate which aspects of it trigger or contribute to Participatory Sensemaking. Therefore, the following actions are planned:

1. Design an 'Observation Format' for [X]CP sessions by writing an operationalisation of the theoretical principles of Participatory Sensemaking.
2. Iterate on the design of the system: redesign Action Points and fine-tune visualization
3. Test the [X] Product Service System in 3 case studies with 120 people. The aim is to acquire cases within city councils.
4. Analyse these 3 sessions according to the main research question, using the observations, video analysis, experience questionnaires, interaction and conversation analysing methods.

PRELIMINARY CONCLUSIONS

Through broad design explorations we learned that intervening in multi-stakeholder dynamics with interactive physical artefacts can result in different interactions and shifting roles in public issues. Simultaneously, we learned that the interaction process before and after the intervention should be taken into account and if possible designed for in PSS, in order to optimise the intervention's impact on the on-going interactions between the multi-stakeholders. Therefore we designed [X]Changing Perspectives: a Product Service System that includes a service for preparation and evaluation of the designed intervention: an interactive table that enriches discussion with tangibility, visibility and scalability. Further research aims to find out which aspects of such a PSS can contribute to Participatory Sensemaking.

ACKNOWLEDGMENTS

We thank our advisors Caroline Hummels and Joep Frens, students Bastiaan van Hout and Tom van Rooij for their production support, TII Umeå and Erwin Hoogerwoord for their software support, and Necker van Naem for their contribution to this PhD. We thank the municipality of Eindhoven for funding support. We thank all partners and participants of the [X]CP sessions.

REFERENCES

1. Hannah Arendt. 2013. *The human condition*. Chicago: University of Chicago Press.
2. Ernesto Arias, Hal Eden, Gerhard Fischer, Andrew Gorman, and Eric Scharff. 2000. Transcending the individual human mind—creating shared understanding through collaborative design. *Trans. Comput.-Hum. Interact.* 7, 1: 84-113. http://dx.doi.org/10.1145/344949.345015

3. Hugh Baxter. 1987. System and life-world in Habermas's theory of communicative action. *Theory and Society*, *16*, 1: 39-86.
4. Laurens Boer and Jared Donovan. 2012. Provotypes for participatory innovation. In *Proceedings of the Designing Interactive Systems Conference* (DIS '12), 388-397. http://dx.doi.org/10.1145/2317956.2318014
5. Tim Brown and Jocelyn Wyatt. 2015 (2010). Design thinking for social innovation. *Annual Review of Policy Design* 3, 1: 1-10.
6. Jacob Buur and Henry Larsen. 2010. The quality of conversations in participatory innovation. *CoDesign* 6, 3: 121-138.
7. Xiang Cao, Siân E. Lindley, John Helmes and Abigail Sellen. 2010. Telling the whole story: anticipation, inspiration and reputation in a field deployment of TellTable. In *Proceedings of the 2010 ACM conference on Computer supported cooperative work* (CSCW '10), 251-260. http://dx.doi.org/10.1145/1718918.1718967
8. Jean Ho Chu, Paul Clifton, Daniel Harley, Jordanne Pavao and Ali Mazalek. Mapping Place: Supporting Cultural Learning through a Lukasa-inspired Tangible Tabletop Museum Exhibit. In *Proceedings of the Ninth International Conference on Tangible, Embedded, and Embodied Interaction (TEI'15), 261-268.* http://dx.doi.org/10.1145/2677199.2680559
9. Andy Clark. 1996. *Being there: Putting Brain, Body, and World Together Again* (1st ed.). MIT Press, Cambridge, MA, USA.
10. Paul Gardien, Tom Djajadiningrat, Caroline Hummels, and Aarnout Brombacher. 2014. Changing your hammer: The implications of paradigmatic innovation for design practice. *International Journal of Design,* 8, 2: 119-139.
11. Jürgen Habermas. 1981. *Theorie des kommunikativen Handelns*. Frankfurt: Suhrkamp Verlag.
12. Daniel Harley, Jean Ho Chu, Jamie Kwan and Ali Mazalek. 2016. Towards a Framework for Tangible Narratives. In *Proceedings of the Tenth International Conference on Tangible, Embedded, and Embodied Interaction (TEI'16)*, 62-69. http://dx.doi.org/10.1145/2839462.2839471
13. Frank Hendriks. 2006. *Vitale democratie: Theorie van democratie in actie*. Amsterdam: Amsterdam University Press.
14. Otmar Hilliges, Lucia Terrenghi, Sebastian Boring, David Kim, Hendrik Richter and Andreas Butz. 2007. Designing for collaborative creative problem solving. In *Proceedings of the 6th ACM SIGCHI conference on Creativity & cognition* (C&C '07), 137-146. http://dx.doi.org/10.1145/1254960.1254980
15. Caroline Hummels and Jelle van Dijk. 2015. Seven principles to design for embodied sensemaking. In *Proceedings of the 9th International Conference on Tangible, Embedded and Embodied Interaction* (TEI'15), 21-28. http://dx.doi.org/10.1145/2677199.2680577
16. Philemonne Jaasma. 2016. [X]Changing Perspectives @ VNG Congres (3 July 2016). Retrieved October 22, 2016 from: https://vimeo.com/philemonne/vng2016
17. Hanne de Jaegher and Ezequiel Di Paolo. 2007. Participatory sense-making: An enactive approach to social cognition. *Phenomenology and the Cognitive Sciences*, 6, 4: 485-507.
18. Catriona Macaulay, Giulio Jacucci, Shaleph O'Neill, Tomi Kankaineen and Morna Simpson. 2006. The emerging roles of performance within HCI and interaction design. *Interact. Comput.*18, 5: 942-955. http://dx.doi.org/10.1016/j.intcom.2006.07.001
19. Paul Marshall. 2007. Do tangible interfaces enhance learning?. In *Proceedings of the 1st international conference on Tangible and embedded interaction* (TEI '07), 163-170. http://dx.doi.org/10.1145/1226969.1227004
20. Ali Mazalek, Glorianna Davenport, and Hiroshi Ishii. 2002. Tangible viewpoints: a physical approach to multimedia stories. In *Proceedings of the tenth ACM international conference on Multimedia (MULTIMEDIA '02)*, 153-160. http://dx.doi.org/10.1145/641007.641037
21. Maurice Merleau-Ponty. 1962. *Phenomenology of Perception*. Trans. Colin Smith. New York: Humanities Press.
22. Hyunjoo Oh, Anisha Deshmane, Feiran Li, Ji Yeon Han, Matt Stewart, Michael Tsai, Xing Xu and Ian Oakley. 2013. The digital dream lab: tabletop puzzle blocks for exploring programmatic concepts. In *Proceedings of the 7th International Conference on Tangible, Embedded and Embodied Interaction* (TEI '13, 51-56. http://dx.doi.org/10.1145/2460625.2460633
23. Lucy Suchman. 1987. *Plans and Situated Actions: The Problem of Human-Machine Communication.* NewYork: Cambridge University Press.
24. Jelle van Dijk, Remko van der Lugt and Caroline Hummels. 2014. Beyond distributed representation: embodied cognition design supporting socio-sensorimotor couplings. In *Proceedings of the 8th International Conference on Tangible, Embedded and Embodied Interaction* (TEI '14), 181-188. http://dx.doi.org/10.1145/2540930.2540934
25. Francisco Varela, Eleanor Thompson and Evan Rosch. 1991. *The embodied mind.* Cambridge, USA: MIT.
26. John Zimmerman, Jodi Forlizzi, and Shelley Evenson. 2007. Research through design as a method for interaction design research in HCI. In *Proceedings of the SIGCHI Conference on Human Factors in Computing Systems* (CHI '07), 493-502. http://dx.doi.org/10.1145/1240624.1240704

Maintaining and Constraining Performer Touch in the Design of Digital Musical Instruments

Robert H Jack
Centre for Digital Music
Queen Mary University of London
r.h.jack@qmul.ac.uk

Tony Stockman
Centre for Digital Music
Queen Mary University of London
t.stockman@qmul.ac.uk

Andrew McPherson
Centre for Digital Music
Queen Mary University of London
a.mcpherson@qmul.ac.uk

ABSTRACT
Expression in musical practice is inextricably tied to the touch of the performer. In digital musical instruments (DMIs) the relationship of touch to sound is indirect: the nuances and fine detail of performer control can be flattened and limited during the translation of physical gesture to physical sound. The locus of this research is in the contact made between performer and DMI: focusing on this area can grant insight on fundamental issues of human computer interaction, particularly regarding intimate and expressive control of tangible interfaces. In this paper I present my research on this topic so far, which includes empirical studies that focus on specific parameters of performance where touch plays an integral role. The first study investigates how dynamic vibrations in an instrument's body can guide the hand of a performer and assist with intonation. The second study looks at asynchrony between action and sound and the influence this latency has on the perceived quality of an instrument.

ACM Classification Keywords
H.5.5 [Information Interfaces and Presentation]: Sound and Music Computing–Methodologies and techniques

Author Keywords
Haptic interfaces; Digital musical instruments; Design framework; Tangible interaction; Multi-sensory; Touch; Physicality; Embodied cognition; Design toolkit

INTRODUCTION
This PhD research investigates the design of digital musical instruments and the role of the sense of touch in the design process. DMIs have been defined as musical instruments that consist of a gestural sensing layer that is then used to drive musical parameters of sound synthesis [17]. Unlike acoustic instruments where action and sound are tightly coupled via the physical mechanism of the instrument, DMIs lack a tight coupling between sound and tactility. *Haptic experience*, the umbrella term for perceptions pertaining to touch, is becoming increasingly important to the design of all kinds of human-computer interfaces: haptic attributes and characteristics are becoming central to our interaction with digital objects [20]. The finer detail of how haptic experience unfolds has however been under explored in comparison to research conducted on vision and audition. This research exists within a growing body of work that addresses these matters [9, 6, 15], and contributes to this discourse by shifting the focus to the design of musical instruments, a field of design where touch and 'feel' are of highest importance. This research proposes that these considerations can and should be knowingly and explicitly held into account by designers of DMIs.

Alongside audition, touch is the primary mode through which we engage with musical instruments. In fact learning a musical instrument can be understood as one of the most developed haptic cultural practices, where years of practical and theoretical training reinforce sensorimotor pathways allowing us to perform complex music. When playing an acoustic instrument we get a great deal of rich sensory information from the part of our body which makes contact with the instrument (hands, fingertips, lips, shoulders). This has been shown to contribute to temporal control [7], quality judgements [4] and expressive control [15]. For most DMIs, although touch-mediated interaction is still the primary means of control, there is no comparably rich physical experience from the instrument. By focusing on the contact that a performer makes with an instrument we gain access to an area of performer-instrument interaction that is not accessible by concentrating on hearing alone. The focus shifts to instrument physicality, that is to the physical characteristics of sound and to the action and labour of performance. This research project investigates how we can re-frame the sense of touch in the design process of a DMI. As part of this project new musical instruments have been designed specifically to investigate different aspects of touch in DMI performance.

Context and motivation
The emotional capacity of touch is central to the field of tangible computing, which calls for a rediscovery of the rich physical aesthetics of manual interaction with computers [20]. Two aspects of the idea of tangibility distinguish touch from the other senses and are of particular relevance to DMIs:'immediacy' and 'manipulation' [2]. *Immediacy* refers to the fact that the sense of touch relies on direct physical contact, and gives us an almost intimate experience of an object that the other senses can't provide. *Manipulation* refers to the bi-directional nature of touching: as both an input and an

TEI '17, March 20-23, 2017, Yokohama, Japan

DOI: http://dx.doi.org/10.1145/3024969.3025042

output act, touching is our primary means of effecting change on objects in our environment. As tangible user interfaces DMIs are important examples due to the high degree of skill required in their operation and to the expressive, culturally meaningful music they can produce.

Each of the studies presented in this paper focus on the implicit cross-modality of controlling a musical instrument: the congruencies and redundancies that exist between touch and hearing [8]. Perceptual attendance, that is the relative weighting of sensory information provided to different sensory channels, is crucial to the design of DMIs. Touch itself has a much lower bandwidth than vision or audition [6] however, the overall amount of information available to a sensory channel does not necessarily relate to its value or importance: the power of the haptic channel to transmit emotional (and at times vitally relevant) information can certainly overpower its bandwidth limitations [8]. Another way in which touch stands out from the other sensory channels is in its explicit reliance on movement: touch is never a passive sense and "movement is as indispensable to touch as light is to vision" p.8 [14].

From the perspective of embodied music cognition [15] music, too, is based on action: body movement is given prime importance in the formation of musical meaning. In the case of a DMI the relationship of action to sound does not have to be direct, and in fact the beauty of electronic music is perhaps in the shift of responsibility for sound making from the human to the machine [3]. Within the vast spectrum of approaches to DMI design, this research studies instruments that display a tight coupling of action and sound [13] due to the connection of intimate control and expressive performance [21]. A related concept is that of *ergocity* introduced by Cadoz [1], which posits that an essential property of *instrumental* interaction is the preservation of energy through both digital and physical components of a system: all signals produced by the system should correspond to the amount and shape of energy fed into the system so as to provide a more natural form of interaction. This is usually not the case with DMIs and it has been identified by many working within the field of computer music that the expressive possibilities of traditional musical instruments (such as the piano, the electric guitar or the cello) have not yet been matched by DMIs [2, 15, 17].

Haptic engagement with a DMI is guided by both static factors (material, weight, arrangement of keys, strings or frets) and dynamic factors (how it responds both physically and sonically to energy put in by the performer) [17]. Leman describes haptic feedback as "a multi-modal prerequisite for musical expressiveness" p. 163 [15] as it gives the performer a more reliable sense of how gesture translates to sound at the moment of excitation. Fostering or maintaining this kind of ergotic or familiar interaction while utilising the great sonic potential that digital technologies offer is a tough challenge for designers. This research seeks to clarify the parameters of design that can help maintain the presence of a performer's touch in their interaction with a DMI, parameters that influence the *feel* and hence the perceived quality of a DMI, and parameters that are fundamentally to do with how touch is catered for and understood in the design process. To return to perceptual attendance, if we know the important factors of touch that performers attend to, the kind of stimuli or characteristics of stimuli that naturally pop-out from the background, then we know what to simulate in high fidelity, and what we only need to give a gist of in low fidelity.

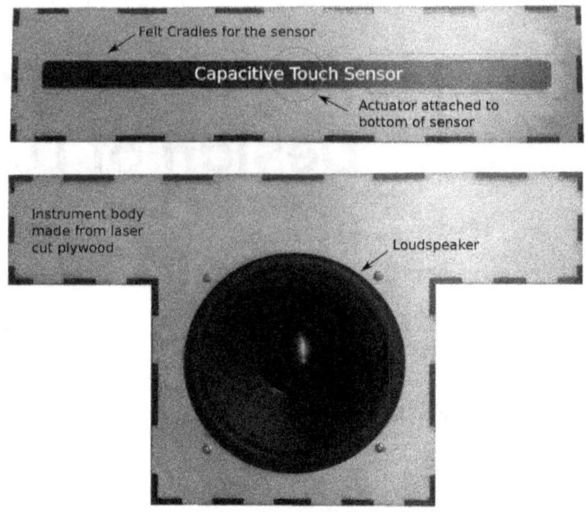

Figure 1. The top surface and front panel of the embedded instrument with vibrotactile feedback built for study 1 [12].

Research objectives and questions

The primary research objective of this project is to develop a design framework for DMIs that focuses on the sense of touch. This is achieved by looking at the parameters of design that bind touch and sound together in a DMI. The questions that this research seeks to answer can be divided into three complimentary domains: *touching and tactile orientation*; *audio-haptic immediacy and intimate control*; *excitation and note onset*. Each question has both a theoretical and technological element.

The first domain *touching and tactile orientation* aims to answer the following question: *how does the physical structure and dynamic tactile behaviour of an instrument influence a performer's control and understanding of instrument layout?* Rojas [18] proposes that learning an instrument can be understood as the development of a musical topography, one that maps out how performer-instrument relationship relates to aesthetic, ecological, and technological threads contained within the instrument's structure. This area of research looks at how such musical topographies are influenced by an instrument's physical structure.

The second domain considers the temporal relationship of audio and haptic feedback from an instrument, and aims to answer the following question: *how can the the temporal relationship between audio and haptic feedback in a DMI be designed to improve perceived controllability, perceived expressivity or perceived quality of the instrument?* This area addresses issues of perceptual attendance, studying how small changes in the perceived mechanism of a DMI can influence performance and subjective opinions about instruments.

The third domain considers how sound is excited from an instrument and aims to answer the following question: *how much of an instrument's perceived quality lies in the character of the onset of each note?* This area addresses the manner in which action translates to sound in the moment of excitation, and the specific parameters of design that influence the fluency of this translation.

Figure 2. The ceramic tile percussion instrument built for study 2 [11].

Methodology

This cross-disciplinary research builds on recent work in human-computer interaction (particularly physical and tangible computing), multi-modal perception studies, sound design and DMI research, and aims to provide both technical implementation guidelines for design and theoretical contributions on the role of touch when interacting with a musical instrument. The methodology involves a series of reduced musical instruments, that are used as a means of testing specific theoretical territory of musical interaction. Each of these prototypes are tested with musicians with varying levels of expertise and are designed to gather empirical information about their performance while provoking reflection about the dynamics of interaction with the device. The evaluation of these instruments happens through both a quantitative analysis of specific performance parameters, and through qualitative interviews with the musicians (employing amongst other evaluation techniques recognised frameworks for the evaluation of musical instruments [19]), paired with my own self-reflective assessment as the instrument designer.

COMPLETED WORK

This paper provides an overview of the first two years of this PhD project. Over this time, alongside developing a strong theoretical base, I have conducted two user studies each focused on a specific parameter of haptic interaction with DMIs.

Creating a theoretical base

The first stage of research involved the development of a preliminary design framework for the touch-led design of DMIs. Initial stages of this development were informed by working on a project with profoundly deaf people exploring their experience of music through tactile vibration [10]. Alongside this, I reviewed current research into haptics, tangible user interfaces, physical computing and DMI design. I identified the research questions that would focus the rest of this research: *navigation*, *intimacy* and *excitation*.

Study 1: intonation and tactile feedback

This first study investigated how a DMI can respond dynamically to performer control through vibrations in the body of the instrument, and how this feedback can provide the performer with additional performance information. The aim was to create vibro-tactile feedback conditions that could guide the hand of the performer whilst remaining harmonically linked to the sound output of the instrument. An embedded DMI with three vibro-tactile feedback conditions was created (see Figure 1), designed to assist intonation on an instrument with continuous pitch control. The first two conditions acted like virtual frets on the pitch continuum, vibrating or ceasing to vibrate when in tune or approaching an in tune note; the third, inspired by accounts of double bassists using haptic beating in the body of their instrument to adjust their tuning in ensemble playing [5], used beat frequency differences between the note played and the target note to guide the performer's hand. The instrument was tested with ten musicians who played the instrument while it was hidden from sight, encouraging concentration on touch and hearing alone.

I found increased tuning accuracy with each of the conditions, but noted that certain vibration patterns imposed temporal constraints that disrupted performance [12]. Although providing the most accuracy, the more temporally complex beat frequency condition was harder to integrate into performance; this was due to the time it took to unfold, whereas the simpler 'fretting' conditions made for easier integration. Musicians also reported clear preferences for a certain polarity of feedback; whether the feedback notified them of a correct or incorrect action. I also witnessed a series of emergent gestures that used the interplay of audio and haptic feedback in unexpected ways. Where previous studies used force feedback to push the performer to the right pitch, this interface required an active correction by the performer. It is interesting that both methods are successful in improving accuracy which suggests that there is great potential for integrating audio-related vibrotactile feedback for guidance tasks in interfaces although the temporal demands of performance limit the complexity of the feedback.

Study 2: immediacy, latency and intimacy

In the second study the focus shifted to the temporal behaviour of a DMI. A study was designed to test the impact of audio-haptic asynchrony (latency) on the perceived quality of a DMI (in terms of dynamic control, temporal control, quality, naturalness). The work built on a previously conducted study[16] which found that common techniques employed in DMI design exhibit action-sound latency above a threshold of 10ms set by Wessel in 2002 [21]. For the study I built a novel percussion instrument constructed of eight ceramic tiles with piezo sensors on each (see Figure 2), capable of sub-millisecond latency and negligible jitter (variation in latency).

Round one: general musicians

The first iteration of the study was conducted with general musicians who freely improvised on the instrument evaluating different latency conditions (0ms, 10ms, 20ms, 10ms$\pm$3ms) in terms of instrument quality. They also performed rhythmic tasks on the instrument which was then used to evaluate the impact of latency on their rhythmic accuracy. I found that even if the level of latency is below the degree of accuracy that can be achieved by the performer on an instrument, it can still impact on how the quality of that instrument is judged. None of the participants were able to perform with a degree of accuracy that was better than the jitter condition ($\pm$ 3ms). 20ms latency showed significantly lower ratings of quality compared to the zero or 10ms latency conditions: there were also multi-sensory by-products of some of the latency conditions, where participants put more force into their strikes as the latency increased [11].

Round two: professional percussionists

At the time of writing I have just completed a second repetition of this study with ten professional orchestral percussionists.

This study was rerun with a different sample to evaluate the impact of training on sensitivity to latency. A preliminary analysis of the data shows that percussionists were more sensitive to the latency conditions when presented side by side. The temporal accuracy with which they performed was significantly negatively impacted by the latency conditions when performing fast passages. This study illuminates how asynchrony between action and sound can have an effect on the perceived quality of an instrument. Subtle changes in the level of latency seem to demonstrate an impact on the feel of the instrument to the performer: it can temporally constrain a performer's control gestures and can create differences in how the performer judges the effort and perceived weight of strike that is needed to trigger a note.

FUTURE WORK

A focus on note onset and attack

From the studies conducted so far as part of this research it seems that a crucial aspect of DMI design is how a note comes into being; how it can be excited from the instrument. This is often seen as a trivial problem with latency being the main barrier but in fact it is a complex issue that conditions many aspects of an instrument's quality. The next study in this research project will investigate the extent to which the physical quality of an instrument, its feel, resides in its onset behaviour in combination with its physical form factor. This study will involve the creation of a series of prototype tangible instruments but this time in a more collaborative process with professional musicians. A goal of this study is to assess the impact on instrument quality of physical form factor paired with the dynamic timbral characteristics of an instrument's sound. I'm keen to discuss the evaluation technique I shall apply at the Graduate Student Consortium A final step in this research may be to conduct a survey asking both acoustic and electronic musicians to describe the feel of their favourite instruments. I then intend to build all of these findings into a wider touch-led design framework for DMIs.

CONCLUDING REMARKS

Considering musical interaction with a digital system from the perspective of touch illustrates some of the relatively simple changes to design that can improve the tangible quality of these instruments. It puts the focus on the nuance of controlling a DMI and thus also the complex choices behind the production of musical meaning, allowing us to understand what makes instruments stand apart from interfaces. This research also aims to show how, as tangible devices that are built to foster creativity and expression, DMIs serve as good places for considering our interaction with computers in general.

ACKNOWLEDGMENTS

This work was supported by EPSRC under the grant EP/G03723X/1 (Doctoral Training Centre in Media and Arts Technology).

REFERENCES

1. C. Cadoz. Supra-instrumental interactions and gestures. *Journal of New Music Research*, 38(3):215–230, 2009.
2. C. Cadoz et al. Tangibility, presence, materiality, reality in artistic creation with digital technology. In *ICMC/SMC*, pages 754–761, 2014.
3. S. Emmerson. *Living electronic music*. Ashgate Publishing, Ltd., 2013.
4. C. Fritz and J. Poitevineau. Influence of vibrotactile feedback on some perceptual features of violins. *The Journal of the Acoustical Society of America*, 136(2):910–921, 2014.
5. R. Fulford, J. Ginsborg, and J. Goldbart. Learning not to listen: the experiences of musicians with hearing impairments. *Music Education Research*, 13(4), 2011.
6. A. Gallace and C. Spence. *In touch with the future: The sense of touch from cognitive neuroscience to virtual reality*. OUP Oxford, 2014.
7. W. Goebl and C. Palmer. Tactile feedback and timing accuracy in piano performance. *Experimental Brain Research*, 186(3):471–479, 2008.
8. C. Ho and C. Spence. Affective multisensory driver interface design. *International Journal of Vehicle Noise and Vibration*, 9(1-2):61–74, 2013.
9. M. S. Horn. The role of cultural forms in tangible interaction design. In *Proc. TEI'13*, pages 117–124, 2013.
10. R. H. Jack, A. McPherson, and T. Stockman. Designing tactile musical devices with and for deaf users: a case study. In *Proc. ICMEM Sheffield*, 2015.
11. R. H. Jack, T. Stockman, and A. McPherson. Effect of latency on performer interaction and subjective quality assessment of a digital musical instrument. In *Proc. Audio Mostly*, 2016.
12. R. H. Jack, T. Stockman, and A. McPherson. Navigation of pitch space on a digital musical instrument with dynamic tactile feedback. In *Proc. TEI'16*, 2016.
13. A. R. Jensenius. Action-sound: Developing methods and tools to study music-related body movement. 2007.
14. L. E. Krueger. Tactual perception in historical perspective: David katz's world of touch. *Tactual Perception; A Sourcebook*, pages 1–55, 1982.
15. M. Leman. *Embodied music cognition and mediation technology*. Mit Press, 2008.
16. A. McPherson, R. H. Jack, and G. Moro. Action-sound latency: Are our tools fast enough? In *Proc. NIME*, 2016.
17. E. R. Miranda and M. M. Wanderley. *New digital musical instruments: control and interaction beyond the keyboard*, volume 21. AR Editions, Inc., 2006.
18. P. Rojas. To become one with the instrument: The unfolding of a musical topography. *Culture & Psychology*, 21(2):207–230, 2015.
19. C. Saitis et al. Perceptual evaluation of violins: A quantitative analysis of preference judgments by experienced players. *The Journal of the Acoustical Society of America*, 132(6):4002–4012, 2012.
20. O. Shaer and R. J. Jacob. A specification paradigm for the design and implementation of tangible user interfaces. *ACM Transactions on Computer-Human Interaction (TOCHI)*, 16(4):20, 2009.
21. D. Wessel and M. Wright. Problems and prospects for intimate musical control of computers. *Computer Music Journal*, 26(3):11–22, 2002.

Performing with Technology

Asreen Rostami
Stockholm University
Stockholm, Sweden
asreen@dsv.su.se

ABSTRACT
This research explores the use of technology in Mixed-Reality Performance, and how novel interactive technologies (VR, IoT, Bio-Data) can be used in designing such performances. Additionally, I explore the potential of these technologies to increase audience' interaction with the performance. The studies presented in this paper are still under development and mainly focus on three novel technologies within performances; Virtual Reality, Bio-Data and environmental IoT.

Author Keywords
Mixed Reality Performance; Immersion; Virtual Reality; VR; Bio-Sensing; Audience Engagement; Bodily Tracking; Biodata.

ACM Classification Keywords
H.5.m. Information interfaces and presentation (e.g., HCI): Miscellaneous;

INTRODUCTION
Designing for Mixed-Reality Performance (MRP) is challenging both in terms of technology design, and of understanding the interplay between technology, narration, and audience interactions. New technologies afford new ways for artists to engage with audiences, and for audiences to become part of the artwork. On the other hand, their deployment raises a number of issues for designers of MRP.

By taking advantage of technologies such as bio-data, participation in interactive performances can evolve from consciously deciding to send a message [3], or moving to a certain location [7], to harnessing the feedback loop of bio-processes. With this move comes a change in the agency of the audience participator. As the role of the artists can be moved more and more behind the curtain to direct audience peer-production of the content of a piece, the lines between performer, audience member, and director become blurred, and the process of designing and developing experiences changes.

TEI '17, March 20 - 23, 2017, Yokohama, Japan

ACM 978-1-4503-4676-4/17/03…$15.00
DOI: http://dx.doi.org/10.1145/3024969.3025043

OBJECTIVES
My PhD focuses on MRPs and how interactive technologies can be appropriated or designed for interactive performance, audience participation, and performers' interaction. Areas under exploration in this work include immersive performances, audience interaction in traditional and interactive settings, performers interaction, and breaking the forth wall.

In the current studies I look at technology from two perspectives; i) technology for enhancing modalities for performer, performance, or audience, and ii) technology as a tool to increase interactivity. Drawing on Brecht's method of acting [6] and his breaking the forth wall as well as relational art [2] I can formulate my research questions as:

- How novel interactive technologies (VR, IoT, Bio-Data) can be used in designing an immersive and participatory experience (performance) for an audience?
- How interacting with these technologies (as part of the performance) can change or reshape the narration of the performance?

METHODS
The first half of my PhD has focused on understanding audience's or performer's interaction with and around technology. Taking an ethnographical approach, I draw upon observation, video analysis and interviews (with both artists and audience members), to situate my understanding of the participants' (audience or performer) experience with technology. This also includes collecting data (i.e. ideas, designed artifacts) from workshops.

PROGRESS TO DATE
At TEI'17 I will be getting prepared for my 50% seminar (2.5 year of 5 year PhD program). Over the last years I have conducted a number of workshops and studies. In what follows I provide a brief description of each study.

Bio-Sensed and Embodied Participation in Interactive Performance[1]
This study [8] stems from two related workshops carried out with six months in between. The aim of the first workshop was to broadly explore the role of novel digital technologies in the context of interactive performances, including theatre and everyday public performances (i.e. commuting as a social act). The second workshop was more

[1] The results of this study is presented in a full paper, accepted at TEI 17

narrowly focused on envisioning design ideas and novel interaction modalities for an interactive movie where the main protagonist is a dancer. Both workshops provided a context to reflect on issues emerging from the participation modalities envisioned, and not merely the interactional qualities of the enabling technology. Our material for analysis was the outcome from the workshops rather than the workshop process itself.

For this study I use five design ideas and related scenarios for interactive performance systems centred on bio-sensing and bodily movement interaction modalities. The ideas were generated during two design workshops which various experts in digital technology and interactive performance participated in. These ideas provide a base for the exploration of novel opportunities for audience participation in interactive performances. We use these ideas to present three key issues concerning such interactive performances; *the temporality of input, the audience's degree of agency and control,* and *the visibility of the interaction itself.* At a time when the deployment of sensor-based devices is quickly making its way into a range of use applications (i.e. including health and medical monitoring), this paper draws attention to potential developments and issues that might emerge when designing for artistic experiences. The issues discussed constitute three paramount conceptual and interaction aspects inherent to triggering reflection on the role of the audience (i.e. from spectator to participant), and on the reconfiguration of boundaries between members of the audience, creative production teams, and performing artists.

Mixed-Reality Performance with Virtual Reality

In this work I present a case study of a commercial mixed-reality performance called *Strange Days*, designed and performed by the artist group Bombina Bombast. The performance uses 360-degree (immersive) video to virtually recreate the experience of past events, allowing audience members to visually experience them from the protagonist's point of view, using a Head Mounted Display (HMD).

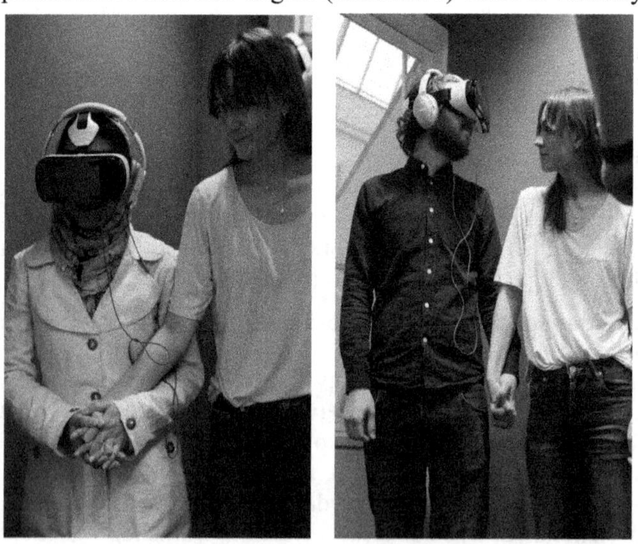

Figure 1. Embodied dialogue between performer and audience by grasping (left) and turning head (right)

Previous studies on mixed-reality performances have commonly addressed it as a hybrid structure: a combination of virtual and real worlds, different participants with multi-layered roles, and diverse layers of interaction [1]. Some of these studies have looked, for example, at the participants' experience, their interaction with technology and the extent of their resulting contribution to the performance. As a way of trying to break down the complex structure of mixed-reality performances Benford and Giannachi [1] introduced the concept of trajectories as a theoretical framework. In putting trajectories to work to analyze a collection of performances, they are able to provide a coherent understanding of the hybridity of for example, roles, time, and space in such experiences.

In this study I contribute to this discourse by bringing embodied interaction [4,5] within VR as a design strategy for MRPs that incorporate immersive video (Figure 1). This, I argue, can be used by designers or audience members to create more emotional and physical immersion with the 360-degree video or the performance itself.

This case study is grounded in two areas of research, which both influenced my approach: the understanding of the interactional characteristics of Virtual Reality as developed within HCI, and the design-related knowledge acquired through research through design-projects within the domain of interactive art using VR technology.

Performing with Smart Instrument

For this study (currently under analysis) I turn my focus from audience to performer, in order to study performers' interaction with the technology. I base my study on a fully working prototype of "smart guitar", combining acoustic guitar with different sensor technology. Data has been collected using observation, as well as interviewing 11 professional guitar players after they attended the prototype testing session.

FUTURE WORK

After my 50% seminar I plan to start at least one more ethnographic study and one final piece of work with an emphasis on design, to evaluate the results of the previous ethnographic work I have presented. These plans however are subject to change according to the status of the work.

Design Fiction for MRP

In this multidisciplinary series of workshops[2], I seek to bring together HCI scholars, designers, artists, and curators to explore the potential provided by Design Fiction [9] as a method to generate ideas for MRPs through various archetypes including scripts, programs, and posters. By

[2] The first workshop proposal has been accepted for CHI'17 and the others will be held in Stockholm

drawing attention to novel interactive technologies, such as bio-sensors and environmental IoT, I aim to explore the role of design fiction as a method for conceiving and designing MRPs through fictional scripts, programs, tickets, posters and other archetypes. By this I will try to enable a discussion with a wider community centered on the production of a number of fictional performance tropes, metaphors, and interaction modalities drawing on sensor-based interactions and IoT. The workshop themes will evolve from, but are not limited to:

- Novel ideas for technology facilitated artistic and performance experiences, and the implication of using bio-sensors, IoT, or other technologies;
- The emerging qualities of audience participation and interactions;
- The role of the artists and of various HCI practitioners in designing novel MRPs;
- The role of design fiction as a method to design for MRPs;
- the exploration of what constitutes suitable artefacts of relevant “fictions” for MRPs;
- The ethical challenges designers may face by taking advantage of these technologies (i.e. ownership of the art piece, use of private data, etc.);
- Directions and challenges for future research.

Transforming Qualities from Analysis to Design

This study will be done as the final stage of my PhD in which I will try to design a piece of performance incorporating the outcomes of previous studies.

ACKNOWLEDGMENTS

I would like to thank my supervisors, Louise Barkhuus, Chiara Rossitto and Annika Waern for their support and intellectual input. I am grateful to my friends and colleagues at Mobile Life Centre, and artist groups RATS Theatre and Bombina Bombast.

REFERENCES

1. Steve Benford and Gabriella Giannachi. 2011. *Performing Mixed Reality*. The MIT Press, Cambridge, Mass.
2. Claire Bishop (ed.). 2006. *Participation*. Whitechapel Art Gallery, London; Cambridge, Mass.
3. Teresa Cerratto-Pargman, Chiara Rossitto, and Louise Barkhuus. 2014. Understanding Audience Participation in an Interactive Theater Performance. In *Proceedings of the 8th Nordic Conference on Human-Computer Interaction: Fun, Fast, Foundational* (NordiCHI '14), 608–617. https://doi.org/10.1145/2639189.2641213
4. Paul Dourish. 2004. *Where the action is: the foundations of embodied interaction*. MIT press.
5. Elena Márquez Segura, Laia Turmo Vidal, Asreen Rostami, and Annika Waern. 2016. Embodied Sketching. In *Proceedings of the 2016 CHI Conference on Human Factors in Computing Systems* (CHI '16), 6014–6027. https://doi.org/10.1145/2858036.2858486
6. James Mcteague. 1994. *Playwrights and Acting: Acting Methodologies for Brecht, Ionesco, Pinter, and Shepard*. Praeger, Westport, Conn.
7. Omer Rashid, Ian Mullins, Paul Coulton, and Reuben Edwards. 2006. Extending Cyberspace: Location Based Games Using Cellular Phones. *Comput. Entertain.* 4, 1. https://doi.org/10.1145/1111293.1111302
8. Asreen Rostami, Donald McMillan, Elena Márquez Segura, Chiara Rossitto, and Louise Barkhuus. 2017. Bio-Sensed and Embodied Participation in Interactive Performance. In *Proceedings of the TEI '17: Tenth International Conference on Tangible, Embedded, and Embodied Interaction* (TEI '17). https://doi.org/10.1145/3024969.3024998
9. Design Fiction: A Short Essay on Design, Science, Fact and Fiction – Near Future Laboratory. Retrieved February 19, 2016 from http://blog.nearfuturelaboratory.com/2009/03/17/design-fiction-a-short-essay-on-design-science-fact-and-fiction/

Exploring Advance Interactions for Augmented Reality: From Casual Activities to In-Situ 3D Modeling

Ke Huo
Purdue University
West Lafayette, IN, US
khuo@purdue.edu

ABSTRACT

Recent emerging technologies in graphics computation, computer vision, tracking techniques, and display hardware have been accelerating transferring augmented reality (AR) applications to wider, realistic use scenarios. While AR technologies are maturing, studying appropriate interactions for AR becomes equally significant. Driven by this strong need, in this paper we focus on discussing advance interactions for creating, manipulating, and authoring virtual contents in an intuitive manner. We propose to investigate AR interactions for traditional casual applications such as visualizing contents within context, and for complex situations including In-Situ 3D modeling using AR. From our previous works, multi-modal wearable inputs, 3D interactions around mobile devices, and context aware touch inputs have been explored for different applications. Moreover, my on-going research projects and future research directions are structured in the later sections of the paper.

ACM Classification Keywords

H.5.2 Information Interfaces and Presentation: User Interfaces; I.3.6 Computer Graphics: Methodology and TechniquesInteraction techniques

Author Keywords

Tangible interaction; 3D interaction; Sketch-based 3D modeling; Mixed reality; Augmented reality

INTRODUCTION

Augmented Reality (AR) enables virtual imagery to be seamlessly combined with the real world. To achieve such experiences, AR system needs suffice three key characteristics: combining real and virtual images, registering virtual imagery with real world, and being interactive in real-time [1]. To meet these requirements, AR community has been primarily concerned with the enabling techniques such as tracking, calibration, registering, rendering, etc until recent [15]. Thanks to the vast improvement to the personal computing devices, now the AR technologies begin to become applicable to realistic scenarios. Thus, with the past accumulated enabling techniques, studying on AR interactions becomes significant for enhancing AR experiences. To this extent, my research topic is centered at exploring advance interactions for AR use scenarios which not only involves casual activities [12, 14, 13] but also sophisticated ones such as In-Situ 3D modeling [6, 5].

TEI '17, March 20-23, 2017, Yokohama, Japan

© 2017 ACM. ISBN 978-1-4503-4676-4/17/03...$15.00

DOI: http://dx.doi.org/10.1145/3024969.3025044

Various interaction techniques have been utilized for different AR applications. There have been several commercialization trials on head worn AR devices such as Google Glass [1] which uses touch input and voice input, Hololens [2] incorporates mid-air gesture and voice input, and so on. Not to mention numerous mobile devices including smart phones and tablets serve as powerful platforms for mobile AR applications. And the Pokemon Go [3] which leverages traditional touch screen is one of the representative success in mobile AR market. However, there is still a gap from being able to seamlessly experience AR due to many aspects. For example, the social acceptance of obtrusive touch input with Google Glass is debatable, the mid-air interactions could cause potential fatigue and accuracy issues, and the interactions on touch screen lacks of context awareness about the surrounding AR scene. In previous works, we attempted to address such gap via employing multimodal wearable inputs [12, 14], 3D interactions around mobile devices [13], and context aware touch inputs [6].

RELATED WORKS

Wearable Textile Inputs

With head worn AR devices, users expect to experience a hand-free operation in the augmented scene. For such AR use scenarios, the utilized interaction techniques include touch input on the side of the device, gesture recognition in front of the device, and the combinations with voice recognition. Nonetheless, they suffer from multiple disadvantages: interrupting users' hand activities, limiting interaction volume, causing fatigue for continuous mid-air interactions, and lowering social acceptance for such obtrusive movements, etc. To overcome such issues, the non-obtrusive wearable devices on hand have been explored widely as an interaction medium since it represents human intents precisely with high flexibility. FingerPad [2] provides rich interactions while maintaining a small form factor using optical and magnetic sensing. We

[1] https://www.google.com/glass/start/
[2] https://www.microsoft.com/microsoft-hololens/en-us
[3] http://pokemongo.nianticlabs.com/en/

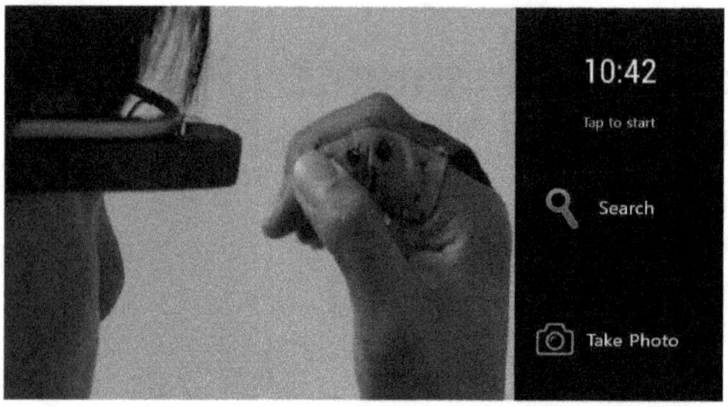

Figure 1. A finger-worn smart textile prototype provides a multimodal sensing (finger bending and pressure) to support non-obtrusive interactions.

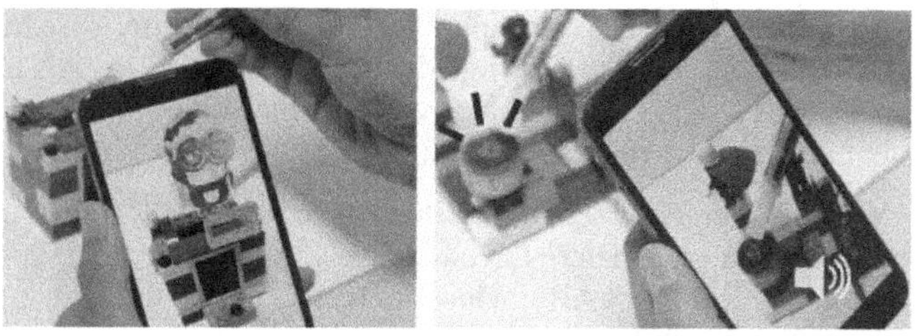

Figure 2. With 3D tracking provided from TMotion, we presents directly manipulating and authoring visual and digital contents within the augmented physical scene.

proposed utilizing somatosensory tactility based on a passive haptic feedback to enhance eyes-free interactions[12, 14] (Figure 1).

3D Interaction Around Mobiles

Modern handheld devices are commonly equipped with cameras and powerful computing units, which thus empower the mobile AR applications. Although the touch screen input seems to be a direct and efficient metaphor, it suffers from limited interaction volume, separated interaction area and the 3D contexts, etc. Several recent works explored around device interactions by embedding extra optical sensors [4], hall-effect sensors [9], or magnetometers [3] to the devices. We presented TMotion [13], a self-contained 3D input which enables spatial interactions within mobile AR setup. The passive magnetic based 3D tracking capability allows users to directly manipulate and author the virtual contents by interacting with the physical environment in a tangible manner. On contrary, early tangible AR manipulations which are based on monocular vision tracking suffers from occlusion and bulky size of the markers (Figure 2).

Interactions for 3D AR Modeling

Apart from simply visualizing virtual contents, researchers recently have shown that AR/MR can play a vital role in bridging the gap between the physical and digital worlds for designing new contents within context [10, 8, 11]. However, most of these approaches use the physical environment mainly as a dormant container of digital artifacts rather than a source of inspiration for facilitating quick digital prototyping for design ideation. In Window-Shaping [5], we leverage the touch screen and extend the touch inputs with with context

Figure 3. In Window-Shaping, users manipulate the shapes through a multi-touch interaction scheme which is mapped to the 3D context.

awareness. In our work, by utilizing Google Tango [4] which is equipped with a depth camera, any touch inputs on the screen are mapped on the physical environment to achieve 3D context aware interactions. For AR modeling scenarios, the 2D touch inputs serve well for precise control, tangible experience and novice friendly 2D sketching. On the other hand, by extending the spatial projection of the 2D inputs, the key requirements on mobility, multi-view inspections can be further sufficed (Figure 3).

Research Questions

Spatiality of the Interactions

The spatiality of the interactions are crucial for AR applications, since AR by nature is a combination of virtual contents and the physical world. In traditional UI, the traditional WIMP metaphor has been proven to be capable of supporting complex interactions. Therefore adoption of such techniques and cater them into AR applications is straightforward and helpful for the transition phase between WIMP and post-WIMP. For example, although Hololens introduces gesture recognition into the interaction scheme, the metaphor is not so different from operating on Windows OS. In our previous work, we attempts to address this question in terms of projecting interactions on subtle finger movements, direct 3D expanding of interaction volume, and mapping 2D interactions to 3D contexts.

Expressiveness of the Interactions

Most of the current AR applications remain focusing on visualizing and simply browsing the virtual contents. For such tasks, the predefined functionality usually maps with a certain input in a one-to-one manner. Thus, the richness of the interactions in these applications are determined by the variety of the discrete inputs. For instance, we manage to separate 14 different inputs using the finger worn device in [12]. Yet, in some complex AR applications involving manipulating, and authoring virtual contents, continuous inputs become essential. To this end, we explore the usages of stylus for direct 3D manipulation and interaction with physical objects (Figure 2). Finally, in some accuracy demanding AR tasks such as creating new geometry shapes in context, we introduce 2D touch inputs and interpret them in 3D contexts.

[4]https://get.google.com/tango/

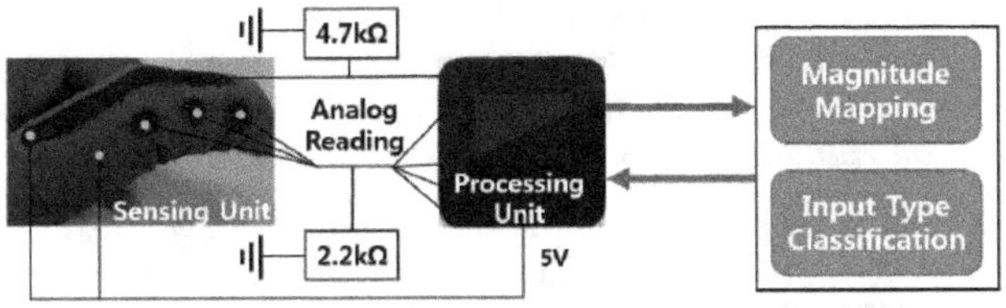

Figure 4. Schematic work-flow for finger worn textile input device.

Tangibility of the Interactions

While AR superimposes digital information onto real-world, tangible user interfaces focuses on graspable physical objects as input [7]. Thus the tangibility of the interfaces well fits the gap between purely visual augmentation and combination of ambient media. We draw inspirations of tangible user interfaces and design our interactions to better enable the users to be aware of periphery of human perception: (1) emphasizing the passive haptic feedback provided by the finger movements in [12]; (2) introducing handheld stylus for direct manipulation purpose [13]; (3) externalize users' ideation process through a handheld window and the interactive screen [5].

System Design and Implementation

Finger Worn Textile Input

The prototype (Figure 4) is fabricated on a single layer of textile where the conductive silicone rubber is painted and the conductive threads are stitched. The sensing area comprises of three equally spaced dots and a separate wide line. Strain and pressure values are extracted from the line and three dots, respectively via voltage dividers. Regression analysis is performed to model the relationship between sensing values and finger pressure and bending. A multi-level thresholding is applied to capture different levels of finger bending and pressure. A temporal position tracking algorithm is implemented to capture the swipe gesture.

Embedded Magnetic Tracking

As shown in Figure 5 embed a permanent magnet and an inertial measurement unit (IMU) in a stylus. When the stylus moves around the mobile device, we obtain a continuous magnetometer readings. By numerically solving non-linear magnetic field equations with known orientation from IMU, we achieve 3D position tracking with update rate greater than 30Hz. Our experiments evaluated the position tracking accuracy, showing an average error of 4.55mm in the space of 80mm$X$120mm$X$100mm. Furthermore, the experiments confirmed the tracking robustness against orientations and dynamic tracings.

3D Modeling in Mixed Reality

The Window-Shaping interface comprises of a hand-held Google Tango device, that serves as a local interface between the physical environment and the user. The simultaneous localization and mapping (SLAM) algorithm available with the Tango API allows for the acquisition of a point-cloud of the scene with respect to a global coordinate system. The resulting RGB-XYZ data allows users to implicitly define planes on any physical surface by simply drawing on the physical scene. Any touch input on the device screen can be unprojected on the physical environment to obtain a 3D point along with its normal in the global (world) coordinate system (Figure 6). This essentially helps users define a plane at any recognized point on a physical surface.

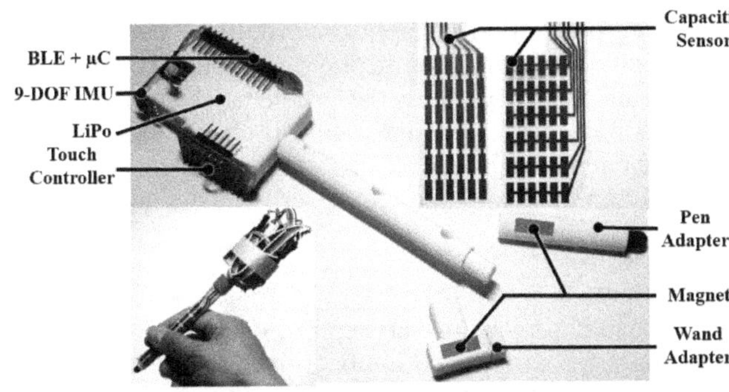

Figure 5. Working principal of magnetic tracking for TMotion.

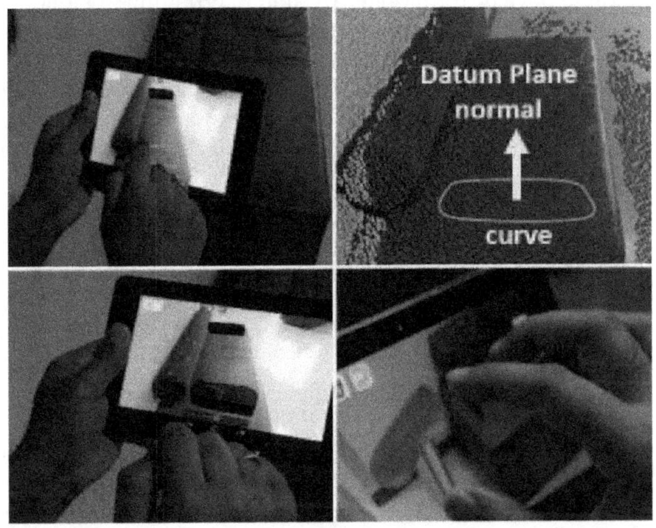

Figure 6. Window-Shaping incorporates 2D touch inputs with 3D context.

Current Work and Future Plan

Interactions for Collaborative AR

So far, in our previous works, we have been focusing on AR use scenarios for stand alone applications. For both remote and co-located collaboration tasks, managing views of the shared physical workspace to incorporate with the communication becomes valuable. However, to facilitate the communication of situational and navigational information among multiple users could be challenging for the aforementioned interaction metaphors. Besides, a common pattern through remote collaboration is mixed usages of AR scene and virtual scene. Thus, we are planning a more sophisticated view management to cater the complicated information exchanges during AR collaborations.

Interactions for Multi-Modal AR

There are three major display techniques for AR: see-through HMD, handheld devices, and projection based spatial display. For each of these moralities, researches have experimented various prototypes of interaction metaphors. Nonetheless, designing interaction metaphor for multi-modal AR setups consisting of heterogenous displays and computation devices still remain open. To address this problem, we envision two potential approaches: (1) design a uniform interaction metaphor for different modals of AR; (2) construct an abstracted layer of general communication protocols across different interaction metaphors.

Conclusion

My research topic aims at exploring advance interaction metaphors for various AR applications. Through this paper, we discussed mapping a rich set of finger inputs to discrete UI functions in AR, leveraging continuous 3D inputs around mobile devices for mobile AR, and interpreting 2D touch input with 3D context using depth sensors. For each of these projects, the enabling techniques are evaluated through preliminary user studies. As AR applications are rapidly growing in the real world, I believe the studies of appropriate interaction metaphors for different use scenarios are beneficial to the community.

ACKNOWLEDGMENTS

REFERENCES

1. Ronald T Azuma. 1997. A survey of augmented reality. *Presence: Teleoperators and virtual environments* 6, 4 (1997), 355–385.
2. Liwei Chan, Rong-Hao Liang, Ming-Chang Tsai, Kai-Yin Cheng, Chao-Huai Su, Mike Y Chen, Wen-Huang Cheng, and Bing-Yu Chen. 2013. FingerPad: private and subtle interaction using fingertips. In *Proceedings of the 26th annual ACM symposium on User interface software and technology*. ACM, 255–260.
3. Ke-Yu Chen, Kent Lyons, Sean White, and Shwetak Patel. 2013. uTrack: 3D input using two magnetic sensors. In *Proceedings of the 26th annual ACM symposium on User interface software and technology*. ACM, 237–244.
4. Xiang'Anthony' Chen, Julia Schwarz, Chris Harrison, Jennifer Mankoff, and Scott E Hudson. 2014. Air+ touch: interweaving touch & in-air gestures. In *Proceedings of the 27th annual ACM symposium on User interface software and technology*. ACM, 519–525.
5. Ke Huo, Vinayak, and Karthik Ramani. Window-Shaping: 3D Design Ideation by creating on, borrowing from, and looking at the Physical World. In *Proceedings of the 2017 International Conference on Tangible, Embedded and Embodied Interactions*. ACM, To Appear.
6. Ke Huo, Vinayak, and Karthik Ramani. 2016. Window-Shaping: 3D Design Ideation in Mixed Reality. In *Proceedings of the 2016 Symposium on Spatial User Interaction*. ACM, 189–189.
7. Hiroshi Ishii and Brygg Ullmer. 1997. Tangible bits: towards seamless interfaces between people, bits and atoms. In *Proceedings of the ACM SIGCHI Conference on Human factors in computing systems*. ACM, 234–241.
8. Manfred Lau, Masaki Hirose, Akira Ohgawara, Jun Mitani, and Takeo Igarashi. 2012. Situated modeling: a shape-stamping interface with tangible primitives. In *Proceedings of the Sixth International Conference on Tangible, Embedded and Embodied Interaction*. ACM, 275–282.
9. Rong-Hao Liang, Kai-Yin Cheng, Chao-Huai Su, Chien-Ting Weng, Bing-Yu Chen, and De-Nian Yang. 2012. GaussSense: attachable stylus sensing using magnetic sensor grid. In *Proceedings of the 25th annual ACM symposium on User interface software and technology*. ACM, 319–326.
10. Christian Weichel, Manfred Lau, David Kim, Nicolas Villar, and Hans W Gellersen. 2014. MixFab: a mixed-reality environment for personal fabrication. In *Proceedings of the 32nd annual ACM conference on Human factors in computing systems*. ACM, 3855–3864.
11. Min Xin, Ehud Sharlin, and Mario Costa Sousa. 2008. Napkin sketch: handheld mixed reality 3D sketching. In *Proceedings of the 2008 ACM symposium on Virtual reality software and technology*. ACM, 223–226.
12. Sang Ho Yoon, Ke Huo, Vinh P Nguyen, and Karthik Ramani. 2015. TIMMi: Finger-worn Textile Input Device with Multimodal Sensing in Mobile Interaction. In *Proceedings of the Ninth International Conference on Tangible, Embedded, and Embodied Interaction*. ACM, 269–272.
13. Sang Ho Yoon, Ke Huo, and Karthik Ramani. 2016a. TMotion: Embedded 3D Mobile Input using Magnetic Sensing Technique. In *Proceedings of the TEI'16: Tenth International Conference on Tangible, Embedded, and Embodied Interaction*. ACM, 21–29.
14. Sang Ho Yoon, Ke Huo, and Karthik Ramani. 2016b. Wearable textile input device with multimodal sensing for eyes-free mobile interaction during daily activities. *Pervasive and Mobile Computing* (2016).
15. Feng Zhou, Henry Been-Lirn Duh, and Mark Billinghurst. 2008. Trends in augmented reality tracking, interaction and display: A review of ten years of ISMAR. In *Proceedings of the 7th IEEE/ACM International Symposium on Mixed and Augmented Reality*. IEEE Computer Society, 193–202.

Knock Knock to Unlock: A Human centered Novel Authentication Method for Secure System Fluidity

Marisa Lu
Carnegie Mellon University
5000 Forbes Avenue
Pittsburgh, PA 15213
findme@marisa.lu

Austin Lee
Carnegie Mellon University
5000 Forbes Avenue
Pittsburgh, PA 15213
austinslee@cmu.edu

Gautam Bose
Carnegie Mellon University
5000 Forbes Avenue
Pittsburgh, PA 15213
gbose@andrew.cmu.edu

Peter Scupelli
Carnegie Mellon University
5000 Forbes Avenue
Pittsburgh, PA 15213
pgs@andrew.cmu.edu

TEI '17, March 20-23, 2017, Yokohama, Japan
ACM 978-1-4503-4676-4/17/03.
http://dx.doi.org/10.1145/3024969.3035530

DOI: 10.1145/3024969.3035530

Abstract

When a person gets to a door and wants to get in, what do they do? They knock. In our system, the user's specific knock pattern authenticates their identity, and opens the door for them. The system empowers people's intuitive actions and responses to affect the world around them in a new way. We leverage IOT, and physical computing to make more technology feel like less. From there, the system of a knock based entrance creates affordances in social interaction for shared spaces wherein ownership fluidity and accessibility needs to be balanced with security.

Author Keywords

Internet of things, automated locking, human centered design, knocking to unlock, machine learning, programmed sound and vibration threshold, rhythm, social affordance, user interface becomes environment, hybrid digital and physical

ACM Classification Keywords

Primary Classification:H. Information Systems. H.5 INFORMATION INTERFACES AND PRESENTATION (I.7)

H.5.2 User Interfaces (D.2.2, H.1.2, I.3.6)

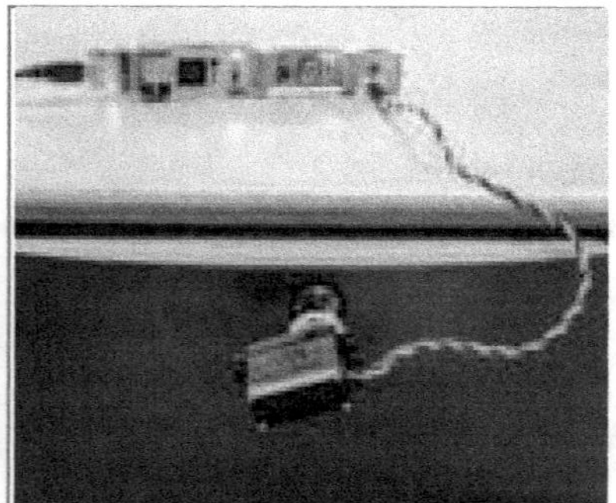

Example: Servo Motor connected to Little Bits inside a filing cabinet. The voltage of the servo motor is being measured as it locks and unlocks the drawer.

Exploration: Early prototype retrofitted to our studio door. Two sets of servo motors press the lock button and turns the handle to open the door. This one worked when user pressed an app button on their phone.

Subjects: Interaction styles (e.g., commands, menus, forms, direct manipulation) Nouns: Garnet

Introduction
Leveraging the IoT concept through deliberated and restrained design intervention, we propose a new door lock that relieves the user of extraneous cognitive burden while empowering intuitive physical reactions [6][8] — in this case the action of knocking on an entrance point or boundary is reaffirmed. The idea of knocking to unlock through a smart artifacts alludes to the ever growing design trend of redefining and blurring the edge between digital and physical environments and realities. Continued analysis of the interaction this particular design offers reveals affordances created in larger social systems that current electronic based automated security systems, and traditional keys locks do not offer.

Inspiration
The design developed first from an exploration of how to make a smarter environment out of our public studio class space. An intuitive system for smart security devices grew around removing the cognitive load and anxiety off of the user. In the studio, security is even more stressful because one is not only responsible for protecting their own possessions, but everyone else's as well as the professors. Shared spaces have an interesting dichotomy between security and the need for easy fluidity of ownership. A traditional key based system would be compromised if just one copy was lost. All keys would then have to be replaced and the lock changed. A smart locking system would be adaptable.

Hiroshi Ishii from M.I.T.'s tangible media labs spoke once that technology should feel invisible [2]. The sentiment that more technology should feel like less technology, is something this project grows from as it uses technology to bring more tangible, physical interactions to play.

Our prototyping was done within a public studio environment, wherein the space is shared by classmates, but must be locked to keep studio valuables secure. Students often forgot keys and weren't able to access their studio spaces and desks. Calling up a classmate to open the door is inconvenient, especially if one only stepped at for a second to use the restroom. We wanted a system to alleviate the cognitive burden of keeping the studio secure yet have easy, flexible accessibility that could be shared with impromptu visitors and other students. There needed to be something that created affordances for secure ownership fluidity between studios.

Envisioned Implementation and Interaction
When the user comes within range of the KnockKnocking lock (during our prototyping, identification of user was determined by their phone's location data) the knocking to unlock feature is available. Each user would have a unique knock pattern available to use across devices. This pattern would be created through a mobile platform, ideally an app. Currently we have a program written in Processing 3 that interprets mouse dicks for knocks. The user inputs their "knock" multiple times to allow the program to calculate an average pattern proportion and possible margin for error. A second program is being made to receive sound and vibration input from piezo [1] sensors attached to the door. Currently it analyzes

mouse clicks. The time between inputs is compared to each other, and if the proportional relationships are match, within a certain threshold, an authorized pattern, the system would set off a physical reaction through servo motors to open the door.

Functional Prototype

We retrofitted our studio door and cabinet drawer with servo motors that were responsive to sound and data input through the web. The idea of hacking into the existing locks is something that was inspired by Huen's work [7]. Little Bits [3], specifically the sound sensors, and the cloudBit connect servo motor movement to the internet and various APIs via IFTTT [4]. Little Bits came with a sound sensor that we attached to our cloudBit, which sent the input data it received when one knocked to IFTTT where in we wrote an applet to turn that input to voltage for the servo motor to unlock or lock the door or cabinet. First prototypes were with a single servo motor that replaced the rotating deadbolt inside a cabinet. Retrofitting allowed us to work with existing secure systems and develop the set of interactions that authenticate users. A solution based around retrofitting would have a much lower material intensity than having to rip out all existing locking mechanisms.

Limitations

Current concerns for the design center around security. The location based activation of the knock feature is dependent on the user's mobile devices location data. That being said, we found IOS location updates through IFTTT were slow to update in a timely manner. Other possible passive security measures could be achieved through various near field communications methods. The idea of semi-passive RFID tags on authorized users was brought up, but having a tag brings back the cognitive burden of having to keep a physical "key" like item to gain entrance.

Retrofitting locks, while great for working with existing systems, is time consuming customization that impedes larger scale implementation. Different environments would need different calibrations with sensors as well. Variations in the amount of passive vibration would require a robust system for ensuring accurate input analysis.

Social Affordances

For the mobile platform we hope to build, there is the possibility of having different settings to temporarily allow someone to use a certain pattern at the door while the usual authorized user has their phone in a different location. A group notification system for all authorized users — if the lock was for a shared space — would allow for a certain degree of crowd sourced control. Further aside, the action of knocking itself has social implications. Knocking to enter is like identifying yourself and asking permission to enter. Announcing one's intention to enter is completely counterintuitive for any trespasser and an implicit security measure. Other possible ramifications is negating the need for a stranger detector at your door; there's easy recognition of either identity, or identity of who gave the user permission to enter. For shared public yet private spaces, the system has opportunities for fluid ownership; after all, sharing a knocking pattern (much like one would a secret handshake) is easier than giving out and keeping track of a key.

Related Work

Huisman et al.'s "knock clock" [9] tells time completely through physical action. One would knock to receive the time in beats that the word block shaped clock would produce. The simplicity of the purely physical interaction with an otherwise fairly electronic device is appealing.

We were otherwise very inspired by the goals of the fluid interface group at MIT media labs. In our project we strove to make our design better integrated in the user's daily physical life, creating an object that's "sensitive to the intention behind physical actions" [8]

Future Work

With possible integration of various near field communication methods, knock to unlock could be used to replace of car keys. The knocking to unlock interaction could also be applied to authenticate users into secure digital systems, such as computers.

References

1. 27mm Piezoelectric Disk Elements (Contact Pickups) with 2" Leads
2. Hiroshi Ishii, "Transform: Beyond Pixels, Towards Radical Atoms" lecture at CMU https://www.youtube.com/watch?v=RtHmsFL-b-8
3. Bdeir, Ayah. 2011. LittleBits [open source library of modular electronics that snap together with magnets] http://littlebits.cc
4. Tane J.,Tibbets A., Tibet L., Tong S., 2011 IFTTT [web-based service that allows users to create chains of simple conditional statements triggered based on changes to other web services such as Gmail, Facebook, Instagram] https://www.ifttt.com
5. Donald Norman. 1992. Knowledge in the Head and World: 5-81.
6. Djajadiningrat, T., Matthews, B., and Stienstra, M. Easy doesn't do it: skill and expression in tangible aesthetics. Personal Ubiquitous Comput. 11, 8, 2007, 657-676.
7. Huen V., Office Door Hack. 2012 [automated smart door lock] http://www.valentinheun.com/portfolio/office-door-hack/
8. Fluid Interfaces Research group, 2016 MIT Media labs http://fluid.media.mit.edu
9. Huisman G., Liston M., Uboldi G., "knock clock" 2011 [clock that operated on physical interaciton] https://vimeo.com/28437345

Paranovirus: Bridging Realities Using Digital Media Simulations

Aaron Cook
Institute of Design
Illinois Institute of Technology
Chicago, IL 60661, USA
aaron.cook@id.iit.edu

TEI '17, March 20-23, 2017, Yokohama, Japan
ACM 978-1-4503-4676-4/17/03.
http://dx.doi.org/10.1145/3024969.3035531

Abstract

What is "real" can become muddled when immersive media, the imagination, and our senses overlap–as anyone who has read a scary novel on a stormy night will tell you. In the spirit of making dreams tangible, this paper reimagines how concepts from science fiction films and novels can be applied to interactions between physical reality, simulations, and the imagination. Models of presence and cognition inform a set of design principles and tactics for displaying simulations in the form of subliminal or preconscious media, which evoke the imagination to cause the simulations to appear to be physically real. Potential for abuse of such technology is illustrated through Paranovirus, a malicious software concept which infects Augmented Reality (AR) glasses and enables bad actors to covertly influence the behavior and mental states of individuals.

Author Keywords

Simulated Reality; Virtual Reality; Augmented Reality; Perception; Presence; Cognition; Design; Ethics; Digital Media.

ACM Classification Keywords

H.5.m. Information interfaces and presentation (e.g., HCI): Miscellaneous; H.5.1. [Multimedia Information Systems]: artificial, augmented, and virtual realities; H.5.2. [User Interfaces]: theory and methods.

Figure 1: An observer is unable to verify the "reality of origin" for a distant thud–was it real or imagined? Incomplete information leaves the observer to imagine possible causes based on context and shaped by their present state of mind. These could include imagining their child falling out of bed, a burglar trying to break into the house, or a ghost living in the attic.

Introduction

Hearing a bump in the night leaves us to imagine what might have caused the sound based on context and our past experiences. If we cannot determine the source of the sound after investigation, what determines whether we lay awake imagining the worst or go back to bed because it was "nothing"? [Figure 1] This paper explores how simulations, imagination, and physical reality overlap and imagines ways digital media can be used to compromise our ability to distinguish what is "real" by leveraging synergistic interactions between subtle stimulus and the human imagination. Drawing inspiration from richly depicted alternate realities in science fiction novels and film and the desire to bring those fictional worlds to life, a set design principles and tactics are proposed which exploit fundamental aspects of human perception and cognition to create the desired effects using consumer Augmented Reality glasses.

The philosophical implications of alternate realities have always raised deep questions about the nature of our existence, such as those famously explored in The Allegory of the Cave [1]. Consequences of allowing separate realities to intersect are often portrayed in science fiction: Dreams take over physical reality in *Paprika* [2], the brilliant anime masterpiece by the late Satoshi Kon, which tells the story of psychologists who use an experimental device to conduct therapy sessions within the dreams of their clients. As the story progresses, dreams begin to influence and eventually cross over and manifest themselves in physical reality, to disastrous effect. In the *Matrix* [3], a computer simulation takes over physical reality, imprisoning the whole of humanity inside and leaving them oblivious to the fact earth has become a post-apocalyptic disaster.

Powerful technologies to cross between realities are often abused, revealing the dark side of human nature: A device in the film *Inception* [4] enables individuals to break into the dreams of powerful people, extract valuable information, and influence their waking behavior. On a grand scale, the powerful Bene Gesserit sisterhood of Frank Herbert's *Dune* [5] use the "Voice" to influence individuals and manipulate the social and political landscape of entire planets. How might technologies such as these appear at their earliest phases of development? Are they feasible today?

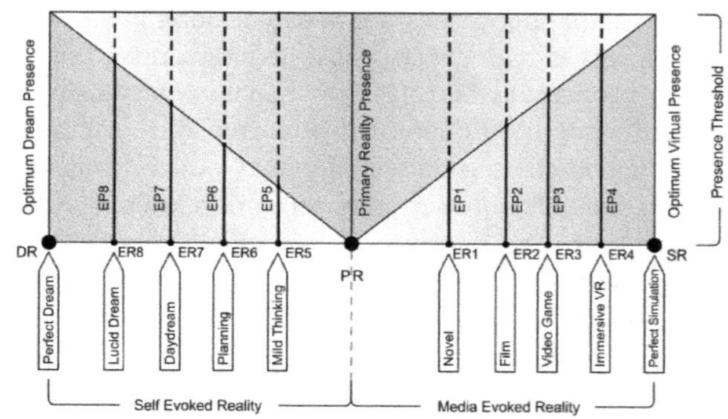

Figure 2: A sample of Media-ER and Self-ER experiences mapped on a reality-presence map which, for an individual, could occur at various moments in time. Image copyright ©2013 Pillai, Schmidt and Richir.

Speaking About Reality

Everyday reality is confusing enough, much less the overlap of multiple co-existing realities. For clarity and the author's sanity going forward, this paper adopts the Three Pole Reality Model of reality-presence [Figure 2] proposed by Pillai, Schmidt, and Richir in which objective physical reality is referred to as Primary

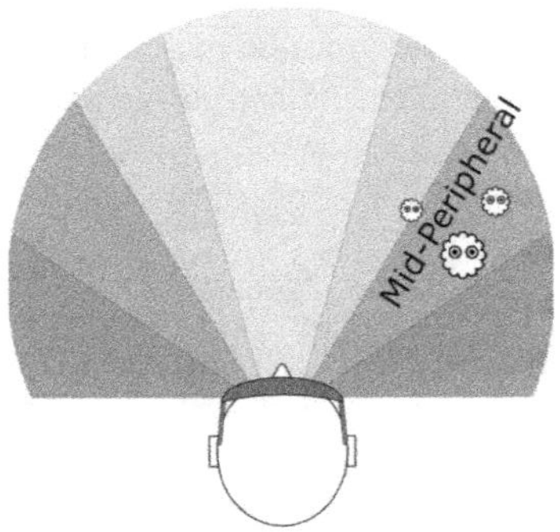

Figure 3: Indistinct shapes floating in peripheral vision demonstrate three design principles which help ensure the user does not suspect an AR device has been compromised. The shapes *stay below radar* by appearing in the peripheral field of vision, *leave room for interpretation* by lacking a clear shape, and *ensure plausible deniability* because seeing motion out of the corner of your eye is a relatively common experience.

Reality, self-evoked reality is Dream Reality and media-evoked reality is Simulated Reality. [6]

Paranovirus: Goal and Objectives

Paranovirus is an imagined software virus which gets its name from the contraction of "paranoia" and "virus". It infects Augmented Reality (AR) glasses, spreads through social exchanges in virtual space, and has one goal: to covertly influence the behavior and mental state of individuals via a remote system by instilling doubt, anxiety, and paranoia in the mind of the user. It is accomplished via these strategic objectives:

Control Host Hardware

Social networks offer a channel for gaining control of AR hardware using a Trojan horse in the form of a shared AR object or meme. AR glasses, such as Microsoft HoloLens or Magic Leap, are ideal hardware hosts because they are able to present a variety of visual and ambient auditory information to the user at the thresholds of perception [7-12]. Additionally, a user may be so accustomed to the co-existence of Simulated and Primary Reality in AR that the line between the two has blurred or disappeared.

Hack Mental Processes

Research on dreaming and consciousness suggests one neurophysiological role of sleep (Dream Reality) is to simplify and optimize Bayesian models of waking experience (Primary Reality) by using predictive coding to reincorporate sensory prediction errors into evolving generative models of waking experience and consciousness [13]. Could the introduction of a consistent set of false sensory prediction errors during waking experience cause the mind to overwrite accurate models of Primary Reality with those false errors during sleep? If so, could false errors be introduced using methods which explicitly avoid conscious awareness of the user [14] to make an individual vulnerable to manipulation in waking life?

Avoid Detection

Design principles used to introduce errors via Simulated Reality conceal the origin of media signals. [Figure 3]

1. *Stay Below Radar* to gain access to the mind using its preconscious and subliminal cognitive processing. For subliminal access, signal stimuli should be intermittent or at the low end of perceptual threshold, whereas for preconscious access, signals may be strong but only given when attention is distracted. [15] (e.g. use the periphery of the visual field or show a visual cue for only a fraction of a second)
2. *Leave Room for Interpretation* and provoke the imagination to fill in personal and contextually relevant information by transmitting signals containing intentionally ambiguous or incomplete data. (e.g. blurred shapes or muffled sounds.)
3. *Ensure Plausible Deniability*
   Signals should have content that could reasonably have originated in ordinary Physical Reality. Signals must never appear to have originated in Simulated Reality. (e.g. encountering a cockroach in daily life is plausible, encountering an angry dragon is not.)

Work Slowly

Tension and suspense can powerfully influence behavior and state of mind, particularly when experienced over

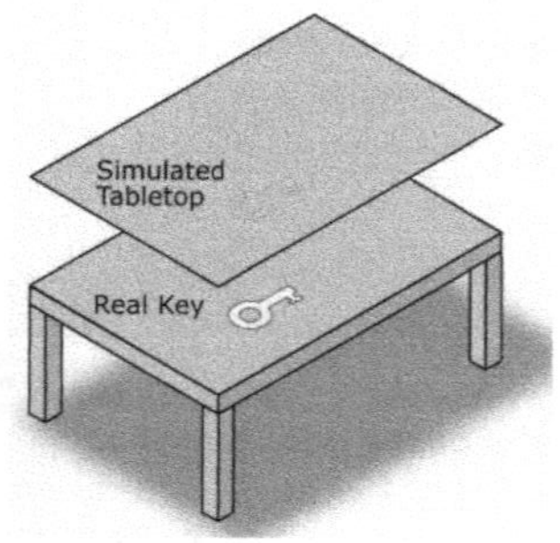

Figure 4: Misplaced or missing keys create a sense of instability that increases tension. The real keys on this table temporarily "disappear" when AR goggles overlay a simulated empty table top so that an observer cannot see the keys beneath.

Figure 5: Behavioral models and events posted on social media suggest this observer is running late–an ideal time to trigger the disappearing key from Figure 4.

prolonged periods. Key components of a theoretical framework of tension and suspense [16] were applied to compose the following tactics for influencing behavior using media signals:

Uncertainty
A blurred shape moves through simulated space at the edge of the observer's visual field, then quickly fades away when the observer's eyes or head move to take a closer look. (e.g. a group of small moving shapes near the ceiling may conjure the image of a swarm of gnats, whereas a single small shape moving along the edge of a room may appear to be a mouse.)

Instability
Object permanence is a fundamental assumption of daily life, which is why misplacing an object can be so disconcerting. Using behavior patterns from sensors and online data, important objects can be made to temporarily "disappear" using real-time masking. (e.g. an observer notices their keys are gone from the table, looks around the room, then glances back to see the keys on the table exactly where they should be.) [Figures 4 and 5]

Conflict
Micro-expressions are brief, involuntary facial movements which are crucial to social communication. Real-time masking techniques, as demonstrated in smartphone apps like *MSQRD* and *Snapchat*, could flash simulated facial expressions over real faces of peers or strangers to generate social conflict. (e.g. a slight look of disgust from a stranger in a club or brief scornful glances from a spouse)

Discussion

Our experience of the world is increasingly mediated and enhanced by digital devices which blend Primary and Simulated Reality, yet we know little of the long term impact that living between realities might have on human cognition and perception.

Paranovirus helps envision how nascent AR technology might evolve to exploit rather than assist the mind, ultimately realizing dystopian alternate realities found in science fiction. The evolution might begin with a benign app for marketing a horror film, which uses AR to simulate terrifying elements from the film in order to build anticipation, enhance viewing, or extend the narrative after viewing. (e.g. The killer's face might appear behind you in the bathroom mirror as you brush your teeth.) Mid-evolution, bad actors could release Paranovirus variants as acts of cyberterrorism, networking devices together to incite group panic or to enhance propaganda by increasing paranoia. In a highly-evolved state, Paranovirus could be weaponized by nations and used strategically to covertly influence the outcome of diplomatic negotiations, disrupt the thinking of heads of state, or manipulate public opinion of candidates during an election cycle.

Sadly, in recent times few notable misuses of media exist that could give insight into how persistent exposure to false media originating in Simulated Reality could spread through social networks to influence the behavior of individuals or populations–presumably because the conventional displays of smartphones and computers offer such clear separation between Primary and Simulated Reality. For this reason, it is urgent that we begin development of Paranovirus and conduct research on its inevitable future abuse.

Acknowledgements

Special thanks to Tom MacTavish, Anijo Matthew, Hugh Musik and Zach Pino of the Institute of Design for their guidance, support, and encouragement in this and other mind-bending endeavors.

References

1. Plato, Grube, G. M. A., and Reeve, C. D. C. 1992. *Republic*. Hackett Pub. Co., Indianapolis, IN.
2. *Paprika*. Dir. Satoshi Kon. Sony Pictures Entertainment Japan. 2006. Film.
3. *The Matrix*. Dir. The Wachowski Brothers. Warner Bros. 1999. Film..
4. *Inception*. Dir. Christopher Nolan. Warner Bros. Pictures. 2010. Film.
5. Herbert, F., and Schoenherr, J. 1965. *Dune*. Chilton Books, Philadelphia, PA.
6. Pillai, J. S., Schmidt, C., and Richir, S. 2013. Achieving presence through evoked reality. *Frontiers in psychology*, *4: 86*. DOI=10.3389/fpsyg.2013.00086
7. Kris Luyten, Donald Degraen, Gustavo Rovelo Ruiz, Sven Coppers, and Davy Vanacken. 2016. Hidden in Plain Sight: an Exploration of a Visual Language for Near-Eye Out-of-Focus Displays in the Peripheral View. In *Proceedings of the 2016 CHI Conference on Human Factors in Computing Systems* (CHI '16). ACM, New York, NY, USA, 487-497. DOI=https://doi.org/10.1145/2858036.2858339
8. Takuro Nakuo and Kai Kunze. 2016. Smart glasses with peripheral vision display. In *Proceedings of the 2016 ACM International Joint Conference on Pervasive and Ubiquitous Computing: Adjunct* (UbiComp '16). ACM, New York, NY, USA, 1769-1772. DOI=http://dx.doi.org/10.1145/2968219.2968273
9. Valentin Heun, Anette von Kapri, and Pattie Maes. 2012. Perifoveal display: combining foveal and peripheral vision in one visualization. In *Proceedings of the 2012 ACM Conference on Ubiquitous Computing* (UbiComp '12). ACM, New York, NY, USA, 1150-1155. DOI=http://dx.doi.org/10.1145/2370216.2370460
10. Alvin Raj and Ruth Rosenholtz. 2010. What your design looks like to peripheral vision. In *Proceedings of the 7th Symposium on Applied Perception in Graphics and Visualization* (APGV '10). ACM, New York, NY, USA, 89-92. DOI=http://dx.doi.org/10.1145/1836248.1836264
11. Maki Yokoyama, Yu Okano, Michi Sato, Shogo Fukushima, Masahiro Furukawa, and Hiroyuki Kajimoto. 2012. Looming silhouette: an approaching visual stimulus device for pedestrians to avoid collisions. In *Proceedings of the 3rd Augmented Human International Conference* (AH '12). ACM, New York, NY, USA, , Article 23 , 4 pages. DOI=http://dx.doi.org/10.1145/2160125.2160148
12. Tom Garner and Mark Grimshaw. 2011. A climate of fear: considerations for designing a virtual acoustic ecology of fear. In *Proceedings of the 6th Audio Mostly Conference: A Conference on Interaction with Sound* (AM '11). ACM, New York, NY, USA, 31-38. DOI=http://dx.doi.org/10.1145/2095667.2095672
13. Hobson, J. Allan, Charles C-H. Hong, and Karl J. Friston. "Virtual reality and consciousness inference in dreaming." *Frontiers in Psychology* 5 (2014): 1133. DOI=https://doi.org/10.3389/fpsyg.2014.01133
14. Alexander T. Adams, Jean Costa, Malte F. Jung, and Tanzeem Choudhury. 2015. Mindless computing: designing technologies to subtly influence behavior. In *Proceedings of the 2015 ACM International Joint Conference on Pervasive and Ubiquitous Computing* (UbiComp '15). ACM, New

York, NY, USA, 719-730. DOI=http://dx.doi.org/10.1145/2750858.2805843

15. Dehaene, Stanislas, et al. 2006. Conscious, preconscious, and subliminal processing: a testable taxonomy. *Trends in Cognitive Sciences* 10.5: 204-211. DOI=10.1016/j.tics.2006.03.007
16. Lehne, M. and Koelsch, S. 2015. Toward a general psychological model of tension and suspense. *Frontiers in Psychology 6*. p. 79. DOI=https://doi.org/10.3389/fpsyg.2015.00079

Interactive Wall: Dynamic Structure in Living Spaces

Arielle Chapin
Brown University
Providence, RI 02912 USA
arielle_chapin@brown.edu

Abstract
The Interactive Wall is a part of a dynamic living space that allows three-dimensional customization based on simple interactions. The goal is to present to users the idea of existing in a space that allows one to have a hand it forming its shape, and to understand how a user would respond to and interact with it. The project will also raise questions that should be considered when designing such dynamic systems in livable spaces. This paper will describe previous works that touch on these ideas, and will present a plan for the design, build, and interface of such an object.

TEI '17, March 20-23, 2017, Yokohama, Japan
ACM 978-1-4503-4676-4/17/03.
http://dx.doi.org/10.1145/3024969.3035532

Author Keywords
Living Spaces; Dynamic Space; Design.

ACM Classification Keywords
H.5.2. Information interfaces and presentation (e.g., HCI): User Interfaces

Introduction
People are constantly trying to customize the world around them, especially in their homes, where walls are plastered with posters or decorated with art. The short story "The Thousand Dreams of Stellavista", from J.G. Ballard's *Vermilion Sands* collection, brings the idea of home customization to a new level [1]. The homes described in the story react to the people inside of it in many ways—physically, emotionally, and behaviorally—allowing a degree of responsiveness that is unattainable with current technology. In one particular instance in the story, a man places his hand on a wall of a home, and the material of the wall extrudes itself outwards into a ledge. With one simple interaction, the shape of the home has changed.

This concept contrasts with many visions of homes of the future. Usually these visions are of "smart homes", homes imbued with some sort of digital intelligence, and often with some modicum of customization through walls and other common surfaces being made into

Figure 1: The block grid inset into a wooden "wall", with three blocks extended to create a ledge and the rest at the default position.

Figure 2: Additional blocks being extended partially on the second and bottom row.

screens. These homes provide customization on a two-dimensional level—for example, you can display any images you want—but they leave behind the possibility of three-dimensional customization.

For instance, the Future Vision design project includes walls of a classroom dynamically changing to play floor-to-ceiling video, and additional information of the person currently teaching [5]. Another example is the Openarch prototype, a design for a smart home that uses walls as displays of information that is context-dependent. Walls can too be used for video calling, video watching, and displaying dynamic wallpaper. But the home also takes advantage of the idea of flexible architecture, using movable partitions to allow the owner to decide how they want to form their space [7]. The CityOffice prototype design also makes use of such partitions, in this case to allow for the space to adapt to different forms of work; a large meeting versus many small groups of people working collaboratively, for example [4]. The prototype includes some more moving parts: tables and chairs that can move around by themselves, tables fitted with extra surface space that can fold or unfold when needed, and printers and laptop-charging spots that roll over to you when you need them. The space truly attempts to understand and adapts to the needs of those inside its walls. What's more, it does so by moving the different components of the room to where they need to go, an impossible feat when the only interaction between a person and a space is through screens or voice control.

A similar project, CityHome, is even more concerned with building such a framework into the architecture of the space [3]. The project proposes a home, most likely an apartment, where the small space is made entirely multi-purpose thanks to all the functional components being built into the walls. With simple gestures made in the air in front of a wall, one could "pull out" their bed or a dining room table. Not only does the space physically adapt, but the prototype also suggests that one could download "apps" for it that allow the space to be more personalized. Despite this, the personalization concern does seem to be lacking in the project—if the walls are built up of all the objects you theoretically need to lead an average life, how does one imprint their own style onto the space? Although the space is practical, dynamic, and adaptive to different situations, it doesn't exactly adapt to the owner's personality—and when the home does not reflect the person, it feels less like a home.

Some projects have approached the idea of dynamic three-dimensional spaces by using furniture, not a whole space, as the surface. The TRANSFORM table project explores interactivity in a similar manner, though the surface uses less direct interaction and automates much of the movement [4]. While this is an exciting prospect, the Interactive Wall project will aim to design interactions such that the user feels entirely in control of the movements—an experience that seems all the more important when the space surrounding the user is changing, as opposed to furniture inside the space.

While these designs provide templates and ideas for dynamic spaces, they don't assess any reactions to them, especially when it comes to existing in a three-dimensional space. They also don't prioritize the concern of how people imprint on the spaces they exist inside of, and make those spaces not just more expressive, but more comfortable and meaningful for

Figure 3: Basic wooden grid frame with a hole for each block.

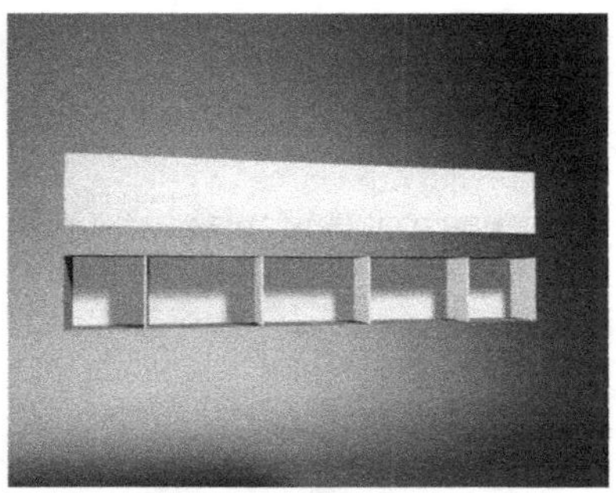

Figure 4: Torsion box revealed on the inside of a block.

users to continuously interact with. This project aims to bridge that gap by creating a prototype of a physically dynamic space and using it to explore how users would best interact with and imprint on changeable surfaces.

MIT Media Lab has, in relation to the TRANSFORM table and relevant projects, also explored the interaction with shape changing interfaces as they take on very specific types of surfaces, such as those with elastic properties. Although this project aims to have a more one-to-one relationship between block and user, future work might benefit from exploring the ability to use dynamic spaces programmed with such surface properties (and more) [6].

With the Interactive Wall emerges a new concept of a living space: one that can be molded by the inhabitant with the utmost control.

Envisioned Implementation

Instead of making a fully-moldable home, the prototype will represent a portion of a wall composed of elongated blocks that move in and out linearly to form different surface shapes. Thus, when a person interacts with the wall, they can create shelves and ledges, or basic images, by extruding blocks. (See initial 3D renderings of the Interactive Wall in Figures 1 and 2.)

This project will use simple blocks so that the user can impose their own personal taste on the wall as easily as possible. A predecessor of the TRANSFORM table, the inForm, used similar pins to display shapes. The setup of pins in the project was not a hindrance in terms of understanding the shapes being formed, which provides a stable basis of using three-dimensional manipulation of such blocks as a way to invoke basic forms [2].

Blocks were also chosen as the primary module of the wall due to their ability to act as a surface, which is extremely important in the case of shaping shelves out of the wall, as well as their basic form and ability to visually make up other shapes. Just as pixels can be used to represent pictures even in low resolution, this wall should be able to be "molded" into various forms so that is aesthetically and functionally pleasing to the user.

To make the blocks visually appealing, strong enough to act as shelves, and efficient to build, the prototype is planned to be built with a lightweight wood (and to use a torsion box design in each block to give them a reasonable amount of strength; see Figure 4).

The size of the blocks of the final prototype will be determined through testing. Blocks with smaller width and height would allow for a greater degree of control, but would be more difficult and time-consuming to work with for the user. A larger block face would be simpler, but the degree of control would diminish so much that certain use cases may become impossible or displeasing. Different contexts may indicate different size needs, and certain users may appreciate different degrees of control. Although the initial goal is to find the ideal balance of size, it would be helpful if future research examined the possibility of more modular surfaces—where larger blocks could be replaced by a matrix of smaller ones, for instance—in dynamic homes to attain the highest level of customization and control for the user.

The blocks are to move linearly, with the motion carried out by a continuous servo set up with a gear rack and pinion for each block. To provide stability, a grid will be

Figure 5: The wooden face here is pulled aside to reveal the foil underneath.

built so that each block has a supporting frame (see Figure 3). Friction will be reduced with the addition of a rolling wheel in the bottom side of each hole of the grid frame.

The ultimate goal of the design is to produce a piece that a user would feel comfortable integrating into their home environment. This means that there is an aesthetic need—just as any wall should be visually pleasing according to the owner's tastes—a functional need, and a sense of control. The Interactive Wall is meant to empower the user in their domain, and dissatisfaction in any of these areas will reduce that experience.

Interaction Overview

While building the prototype, questions about the design need to be answered through observing interactions. The current proposal is to have each block fitted with foil at its outward face, hidden with a thin piece of wood, for capacitive touch sensing. If a user touches a block lightly and holds for a small amount of time, the block will begin extending. Given more pressure, the block will begin to recede. This is an attempt to bring the interactions from J.G. Ballard's story into reality—that is, using simple strokes of the hand to produce a ledge—but it is recognized that such an interaction may not be the ideal with the adapted block design [1].

This would set up a direct haptic relationship between user and block, where through the reactions from the device the user can calibrate their pressure and find a great deal of control with relative ease. An even greater feeling of control, though, may come with a more "manual" interaction where the user can actually pull and push the blocks to the desired position.

Small prototypes will be assembled to test out different interaction modes. In each case it is likely that the interactions will be kept direct, so that the user will need to actually touch the blocks to cause movement, since motion detecting or something similar would certainly cause errors in situations where the wall is in a space with unrelated motion occurring close by.

An important aspect of the interaction will include being able to select multiple blocks to perform the same action. This will allow for easier formation of surfaces and shapes where the blocks should extend an esqual distance. When selecting blocks, a user should be able to drag their hand across one or more to select them and receive haptic feedback from vibration motors, as well as visual feedback from LEDs embedded in the blocks for a quick indication of everything that has been selected.

Conclusion

The Interactive Wall introduces an unexplored area of home interaction and control. The project will establish a base for understanding how users would interact with such a physically dynamic environment, and will seek to bring to light concerns that should be taken into account when building one. From this base further research could explore the combination of direct control and automation, more types of interactions, and different types of surfaces.

References

1. J.G. Ballard. The Thousand Dreams of Stellavista. *Amazing Stories, 36 (3)*. 48-68.

2. S. Follmer, D. Leithinger, A. Olwal, and H. Ishii. 2013. inFORM: dynamic physical affordances and constraints through shape and object actuation. In Proceedings of UIST '13, 417-426. http://dl.acm.org/citation.cfm?id=2647377&CFID=878660839&CFTOKEN=54526406.
3. Hasier Larrea, Daniel Goodman, Oier Ariño, and Phillip Ewing. CITYHOME. Retrieved December 20, 2016 from http://cp.media.mit.edu/cityhome/.
4. Hasier Larrea, Luis Alonso, and Carlos Rubio. CITYOFFICE. Retrieved December 20, 2016 from http://cp.media.mit.edu/cityoffice/.
5. Hiroshi Ishii. TRANSFORM. 2015. TRANSFORM: Beyond Tangible Bits, Towards Radical Atoms. In Proceedings of the 3rd ACM Symposium on Spatial User Interaction (SUI '15), 1-1. http://dl.acm.org/citation.cfm?id=2788958.
6. Microsoft in Business. 2015. Microsoft: Productivity Future Vision. Video. (10 March 2015). Retrieved November 11, 2016 from https://www.youtube.com/watch?v=w-tFdreZB94
7. Ken Nakagaki, et al. Materiable: Rendering Dynamic Material Properties in Response to Direct Physical Touch with Shape Changing Interfaces. In Proceedings of the 2016 CHI Conference on Human Factors in Computing Systems (CHI '16), 2764-2772. http://dl.acm.org/citation.cfm?id=2858104.
8. Openarch. What is OPENARCH? Retrieved November 1, 2016 from http://www.openarch.cc.

The Sixth Sense: Augmenting Sensory Perception through Critical Design

Awais Hameed Khan
Alyssa DiSalvo
Ki Wang Ng
Shiva Balachandran
Trevor Hunter
Peter Worthy
The University of Queensland
Brisbane, Australia
awaishameed.khan@uq.net.au
alyssa.disalvo@uq.net.au
k.ng@uq.net.au
shiva.balachandran@uq.net.au
trevor.hunter@uq.net.au
p.worthy@uq.edu.au

TEI '17, March 20-23, 2017, Yokohama, Japan
ACM 978-1-4503-4676-4/17/03.
http://dx.doi.org/10.1145/3024969.3035533.

Abstract
This paper explores the connection established between people and their surrounding environment as depicted in the popular science fiction concept "Cerebro" from Marvel's *The X-Men* series. This is done through the development of The Sixth Sense, a wearable device that augments the sensory perception of human beings by manifesting the intangible concept of poverty in one's environment into a physical experience. The concept is designed to incite awareness and reflection in the wearer through dimensions of social justice-oriented and adversarial design. The Sixth Sense, situated within critical design, proposes that social injustices should be felt by all those who inhabit a space until the systems of oppression operating within that space are subverted.

Author Keywords
Critical Design; Social Justice; Adversarial Design; Poverty; Science Fiction

ACM Classification Keywords
H.5.2. User Interfaces: Haptic I/O

Introduction
Over the past century, the science fiction ("sci-fi") genre has taken the world by storm. Its contribution to art, literature, and film has inspired a generation of

Figure 1: Cerebro

"[D]esigns and social formations are interrelated and often co-constitutive. The design of a system, then, is not so far from the design of social policy. As feminists have pointed out that the injustices of social policies are felt in the bodies of those they fail — through their incarceration, their dispossession, their injuries, their boredom, and their pain — so by implication bad designs can cause bodily hardship." [2]

technological advancements. Everything from automatic sliding doors to cellular phones has been based on depictions of imaginative future worlds in these art forms [16]. The horizon of the potential in technology that these works have unlocked is limitless; these imagined possibilities are often used as visions of alternate realities and inspiration for design directions. This paper looks to explore the establishment of a connection between a person and their surrounding environment as illustrated in sci-fi, and to conceptualize that this connection can be meaningfully embodied in a similar context using today's technology.

Sci-Fi Inspiration

One of the most interesting aspects of sci-fi characterizations in popular culture is the link between characters and their surrounding environment. The aspect of empathizing with abstract information has been depicted across a wide spectrum of data types: danger (e.g. Peter Parker's "Spider-Sense" [20]), adverse impact on the environment (e.g. Captain Planet's connection with the Earth [19]), and influence on the worlds which one exists within (e.g. "the Force" from the *Star Wars* saga [10]). Additionally, sci-fi characters are often shown to have the ability to develop deep, strong emotional connections amongst one another — to feel each other's joy and pain. This is generally exhibited in characters with telepathic abilities (e.g. Charles Xavier and Jean Grey of *The X-Men* series [21]). Such linkages also extend to the realm of being embodied in physical artifacts. This is exemplified in the *Harry Potter* franchise [15], where whenever the protagonist, Harry, comes in contact with an artefact that is linked with the antagonist, Lord Voldemort, a connection is established. Harry is able to feel how his enemy is feeling at the time. Another interesting depiction of a similar concept of connection is shown in Adam Sandler's movie, *The Cobbler* [12]. The protagonist, a cobbler, is able to take the physical form of his clients whenever he fixes their shoes with a special machine.

These themes indicate how one of the core tenets of popular sci-fi is the connection that people have with their surrounding environment, specifically in terms of the augmentation of their sensory perception. Empathy is the basic principle, but such connection may also extend to physical stimulation of the senses (e.g. the ability to feel pain, hunger, joy, elation and so much more — all from the space which one exists within). There have been various instances where senses have interplayed with one another. For instance, the phenomenon synesthesia [11] occurs when a person can visualize sound waves. Similarly, haptic feedback can be programmed into the brains of amputees, enabling them to regain the sense of touch [14].

Context

Historically, there has been a divide amongst people, values, cultures, acceptability, and thresholds of tolerance [3]. The lack of understanding, empathy, and ability to sense and experience what the others feel perpetuates systems of oppression. Some of the greatest social issues of our time can be considered derivatives of our inability to bridge these gaps.

This invites us to ask the questions: What human values could we impact by extending the palette of sensory perception in human beings through augmentation of the senses (allowing them to interpret and understand intangible, abstract data from their surrounding environment)? What aspects of the human

Figure 2: The Sixth Sense

"How heavy is this glass of water?"

"The absolute weight doesn't matter. It depends on how long I hold it. If I hold it for a minute, it's not a problem. If I hold it for an hour, I'll have an ache in my arm. If I hold it for a day, my arm will feel numb and paralyzed. In each case, the weight of the glass doesn't change, but the longer I hold it, the heavier it becomes." [17]

Narratives of Consumption:
"how objects enter people's lives and the meanings that arise from their interactions with those objects" [9]

mind could we tap into if we could enable people to physically experience walking a mile in someone else's proverbial shoes?

Concept

The premise of the proposed concept, The Sixth Sense, is to augment the sensory perception of human beings by manifesting intangible, abstract data from one's environment into a physical tangible experience. This encourages people to recognize and reflect upon in their daily lives. The idea is inspired by the artefact "Cerebro" [22] used by Charles Xavier in *The X-Men* series (see sidebar on previous page), allowing the wearer of the device to be able to physically feel the impact of the environment or people with which the connection is established. In order to demonstrate this, the intangible concept that we have built this work around is *poverty*.

The form of The Sixth Sense is a reference to the metaphor of empathizing with another by walking a mile in their shoes, and the functionality is politically inspired by dimensions of both social justice-oriented design [5] and adversarial design [4]. We designed the device as a wearable attachment, which is placed inside the citizen's shoes with its primary contact area around the ankle. The device prompts the wearer on a visceral level through real-time data inputs based on poverty levels [23] from their geographic location through GPS coordinates. Based on the magnitude of the poverty level tagged to the wearer's location, the device will tighten the grip around their ankles. The greater the magnitude, the tighter the grip becomes. The Sixth Sense attempts to symbolize the struggles of poverty through the element of sensory discomfort (pain), alluding to economic disparities that result in mental, emotional, and physical pain for impoverished people within a space. Our design decision to inflict pain is also a play on Bardzell's assertion that "bad designs can cause bodily hardship" [2] (see sidebar on previous page). The element of discomfort is predicated more so on consistent prevalence as opposed to magnitude of discomfort. The device will constantly hold its grip in place based on the location the user is in. The impact that the longevity of time in which the user is exposed to the discomfort will allow them to not just empathize, but to a degree also experience (in a small and inadequate way) the constant burden that this impoverished group endures. This is inspired by the stress management concept which highlights that it is in fact not the magnitude of stress that causes damage, but instead the prolonged duration of exposure to stress [17] (see sidebar).

The Sixth Sense as Critical Design

The Sixth Sense can be understood as a work of critical design. Dunne and Raby, the pioneers of critical design, understand it as a type of design which "uses speculative design proposals to challenge narrow assumptions, preconceptions and givens about the role products play in everyday life" [6]. While affirmative design endeavors to "[make] [consumers] buy," critical design endeavors to "[make] [citizens] think" [7]. Affirmative designs can be understood as "mute, autistic objects" which "radiate ignorance of the world around us" and are "apolitical and content free" [8]. Critical designs can be understood as "operat[ing] on a more intellectual level, bringing philosophical issues into an everyday context in a novel yet accessible way." The accessibility of critical designs in many cases relies on their status as products. Critical designs that are delivered to people within the context of their daily

"[Menstruation Machine] is equipped with a blood-dispensing system and electrodes that stimulate the lower abdomen, replicat[ing] the pain and bleeding of the average five-day menstruation period." [24]

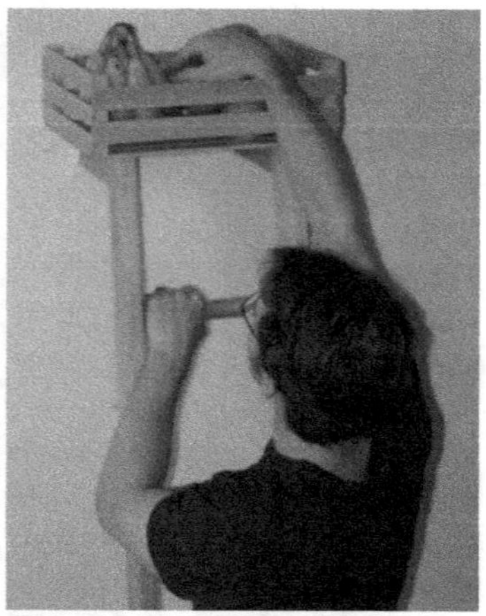

Figure 3: Marxist Fruit Bowl

"[Marxist Fruit Bowl] is a fruit bowl [which] necessitates that users climb [a] ladder, acknowledging in a small way the efforts of the often migrant- or itinerant-fieldworkers who make possible the quantity and variety of produce available for so many others' enjoyment." [18]

life (e.g. as a pair of shoes one traverses a city in) typically offer greater possibilities in terms of mediating values [8]. This does not mean that we have designed The Sixth Sense as a product to be sold, but rather that the form of the project as something that would sit within a someone's life (rather than be exhibited within a museum) gives the design, in our opinion, an added level of provocativeness. It brings the focus to the resulting "narratives of consumption" [9] (see sidebar on previous page) that people may imagine would emerge from the hypothetical use of such a product (if one were to exist).

Parallels can be drawn between The Sixth Sense and other critical designs such as Menstruation Machine [24] and Marxist Fruit Bowl [18] (see sidebar). Much like both of these examples, The Sixth Sense creates physical discomfort in order to bring greater awareness to an inaccessible experience.

Design Proposition
We suggest that The Sixth Sense should be read as a *design proposition* [1,13] that social injustices should be felt — on a physical level — by all those who inhabit a space until the systems of oppression operating within that space are subverted.

Questions that this proposition may raise include: Would the pain eventually get to even the most devoted wearers, resulting in avoidance of more impoverished areas? Would the pain cause wearers to slow down or speed up? What impact would reminders of one's own privilege have on wearers? What impact would an environment, in which everyone who could afford such shoes owned them and wore them, have on those living in poverty? And finally, inspired by the same question asked of Porcupine Dress [1]: What kind of statement would people electing to wear such shoes be making about themselves?

The Sixth Sense's Criticality
In many ways, The Sixth Sense's criticality is open to interpretation. For instance, any of the following could be inferred from the design:

- It is the responsibility of those in positions of privilege (e.g. those who can afford a pair of shoes) to work towards eliminating poverty in the spaces they inhabit. (It should be noted that the design does not suggest how such work might be carried out, or what kind of political approach such work should be grounded in.)
- Those in positions of privilege deserve pain.
- Pain resulting from intact systems of oppression should be equitably distributed amongst a local population (even if it could never fully be).

It is important to highlight that the design itself does not articulate any of these perspectives, and that the inclusion of these statements serves only to point to possible thought outcomes of experiencing the product in one's day-to-day life.

Conclusion
The Sixth Sense allows the wearers to enhance the spectrum of their sensory perception, enabling them to become more attuned to their surrounding environment. The future possibility of re-appropriation of this concept to other data types makes The Sixth Sense an interesting tool for critical design applications.

References

[1] Bardzell, J., Bardzell, S., and Stolterman, E. Reading Critical Designs: Supporting Reasoned Interpretations of Critical Design. *Proceedings of the 32Nd Annual ACM Conference on Human Factors in Computing Systems*, ACM (2014), 1951–1960.

[2] Bardzell, S. Utopias of Participation: Design, Criticality, and Emancipation. *Proceedings of the 13th Participatory Design Conference: Short Papers, Industry Cases, Workshop Descriptions, Doctoral Consortium Papers, and Keynote Abstracts - Volume 2*, ACM (2014), 189–190.

[3] Davidoff, L. Gender and the "Great Divide": Public and Private in British Gender History. *Journal of Women's History 15*, 1 (2003), 11–27.

[4] DiSalvo, C. *Adversarial Design*. MIT Press, 2012.

[5] Dombrowski, L., Harmon, E., and Fox, S. Social Justice-Oriented Interaction Design: Outlining Key Design Strategies and Commitments. *Proceedings of the 2016 ACM Conference on Designing Interactive Systems*, ACM (2016), 656–671.

[6] Dunne, A. and Raby, F. Critical Design FAQ. *Dunne & Raby*. http://www.dunneandraby.co.uk/content/bydandr/13/0.

[7] Dunne, A. and Raby, F. A/B. *Dunne & Raby*. http://www.dunneandraby.co.uk/content/projects/476/0.

[8] Dunne, A. and Raby, F. Fictional Functions & Functional Fictions. *Dunne & Raby*. http://www.dunneandraby.co.uk/content/bydandr/46/0.

[9] Dunne, A. and Raby, F. Interpretation, Collaboration, and Critique. *Dunne & Raby*. http://www.dunneandraby.co.uk/content/bydandr/465/0.

[10] Lucas, G. *Star Wars: Episode IV - A New Hope*. 1977.

[11] Marks, L.E. On colored-hearing synesthesia: cross-modal translations of sensory dimensions. *Psychological bulletin 82*, 3 (1975), 303.

[12] McCarthy, T. *The Cobbler*. 2015.

[13] Michigan Interactive and Social Computing. *MISC 031015 Jeff Bardzell: Design as Inquiry*. 2015.

[14] Reprints, M.B.S. A Prosthetic Arm That Gives Amputees the Sense of Touch. *Bloomberg.com*, 2015. http://www.bloomberg.com/news/articles/2015-10-08/a-prosthetic-arm-that-gives-amputees-the-sense-of-touch.

[15] Rowling, J.K. *Harry Potter and the Sorcerer's Stone*. Scholastic, New York, 1998.

[16] Schmitz, M., Endres, C., and Butz, A. A Survey of Human-computer Interaction Design in Science Fiction Movies. *Proceedings of the 2Nd International Conference on INtelligent TEchnologies for Interactive enterTAINment*, ICST (Institute for Computer Sciences, Social-Informatics and Telecommunications Engineering) (2007), 7:1–7:10.

[17] Sterbenz, C. This question about the weight of a water glass explains the best way to deal with everyday stresses. *Business Insider Australia*, 2015. http://www.businessinsider.com.au/this-question-about-the-weight-of-a-water-glass-explains-the-best-way-to-deal-with-everyday-stresses-2015-6.

[18] Tharp, B. and Tharp, S. Marxist Fruit Bowl. *materious*.

http://www.materious.com/#/projects/marxist-fruit-bowl/.

[19] *Captain Planet and the Planeteers*. 1990.

[20] Spider-Man. *Marvel.com*. http://marvel.com/characters/54/spider-man.

[21] Uncanny X-Men (1963) #1. *Marvel.com*. http://marvel.com/comics/issue/12413/uncanny_x-men_1963_1.

[22] Cerebro - Marvel Universe Wiki: The definitive online source for Marvel super hero bios. http://marvel.com/universe/Cerebro.

[23] Poverty – ACOSS. http://www.acoss.org.au/poverty-2/.

[24] MoMA | Talk to Me | Menstruation Machine–Takashi's Take. https://www.moma.org/interactives/exhibitions/2011/talktome/objects/142590/.

Phenomenologically Augmented Reality With New Wearable LED Sequential Wave Imprinting Machines

Pete Scourboutakos
University of Toronto
Toronto, ON M5S 3G4, Canada
pete@eyetap.org

Max Hao Lu
University of Toronto
Toronto, ON M5S 3G4, Canada
max@eyetap.org

Sarang Nerker
University of Toronto
Toronto, ON M5S 3G4, Canada
sarang@eyetap.org

Steve Mann
University of Toronto /
WearTech™Foundation
Toronto, ON M5S 3G4, Canada
mann@eyetap.org

TEI'17, March 20-23, 2017, Yokohama, Japan.
 ISBN 978-1-4503-4676-4/17/03
DOI http://dx.doi.org/10.1145/3024969.3035534

Abstract

The Sequential Wave Imprinting Machine (SWIM), invented by Steve Mann in the 1970s, offers naked-eye augmented reality overlays with perfect alignment, through a Persistence of Exposure (PoE) of human vision, or photographic/videographic media.

This paper proposes a new SWIM design with only 2 transistor elements per picture elment, therefore making SWIM more wearable, miniature, and affordable. We present a SWIM for being worn on one finger, as a ring, to overlay a phenomenologically augmented reality for metaveillance (sensing sensors and sensing their capacity to sense) and HARCAD (Haptic Augmented Reality Computer Aided Design/Manufacture).

Author Keywords

Mediated Reality; Augmented Reality; Wearable Computing; Sequential Wave Imprinting Machine; WearTech, Lock-In amplifier; HARCAD/HARCAM; Haptic Augmented Reality CAD/CAM

ACM Classification Keywords

H.5.1 [Information interfaces and presentation (e.g., HCI)]: Artificial, augmented, and virtual realities

Figure 1: World's first wearable augmented reality computer system: Sequential Wave Imprinting Machine waved back-and-forth to display radio waves, sound waves, text, graphics, etc., overlaid on reality by persistence-of-exposure, so hundreds of people could see the overlay without the need to wear special eyeglasses.

Introduction

Augmediated reality is an experience where by the means of a system of technology, people are able to seamlessly modify (mediate) their perception of reality, while it is also being augmented.

Mediated reality systems may be organized into three types:

1. dB>0: Systems of augmentation, which involve amplification / enhancement / addition of information, such as the system presented here. These systems are augmented reality.
2. dB<0: Those of diminishment which involve attenuation / subtraction of vision, like dark glass or even HDR vision glass for welding [3]. These systems are useful where diminished reality is desired.
3. Those which are dynamic and can do both, as needed.

Many augmediated reality systems are of the third type, designed as a generalized platform with the intention of supporting a variety of applications [10]. These systems consist of input and output devices, respectively, with computer processing in between [9, 6, 5, 7].

The augmediated reality system in this paper is strictly additive (type 1). It is also purpose built for the specific application of the visualization of radio waves, in the same fashion as early augmediated reality experiments carried out by Steve Mann in the 1970s [8] (See Fig. 1).

Recently, with the availability of high efficiency and small SMD LEDs, the SWIM no longer relies on incandescent light bulbs and has thus become more practical.

This paper presents two new incarnations of SWIM. The first is based on surface mount version of the LM3914 (Fig. 2) and provides high resolution (10pixels/cm) at a modest board size. The second is a novel circuit which is used to make a small wearable SWIM which is unprecedented in miniaturization, making these experiments in augmediated reality ever more practical as a wearable computer, and also making it possible, if desired, to further miniaturize the apparatus into a single die chip for use in eyeglasses or contact lens displays [Mann 1999, CA2280022], with just two transistor elements per pixel (Fig. 3).

Head mounted displays [4], have been used extensively as the output device of choice for augmediated reality systems [1]. This is natural because they are usually already designed to work as computer displays. These types of devices are well suited to personal augmediated reality experiences, but do not work as easily for activities where multiple people or groups of people are involved and wish to partake in the same experience. For everyone to participate, everyone must wear their own pair of glasses, and high level software/networking systems are required to render the experience for everyone. This creates bottleneck points and opens up opportunities for delays and other issues which can strip the system of its humanistic intelligence, making the experience anything from less convincing to illness-inducing to painful [2]. SWIM eliminates the complexity imposed by the need for a general purpose system, and instead focuses as a single-purpose-built augmediated reality system which makes visible normally invisible radio waves. In order to achieve this effect, the SWIM is simply driven with the doppler return output of any low power X band microwave radar set.

SWIM works similarly to an oscilloscope with no timebase generator, by painting out a sensed/measured wave in light so that it is made visible. Instead of the effect of the oscilloscope phosphor we have the phenomenon of persistance of

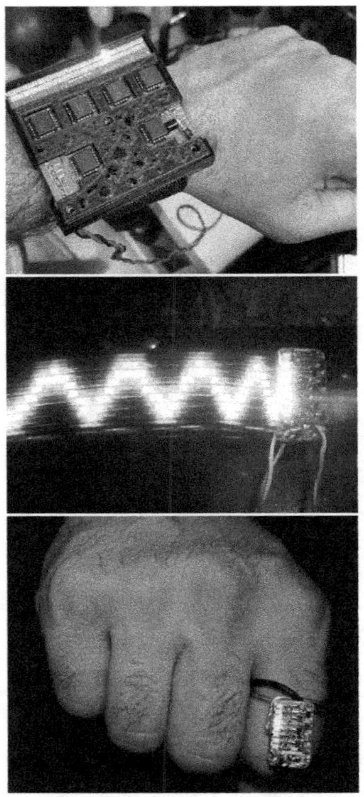

Figure 4: Wearable augmented reality without special eyeglasses. Wristworn and finger-worn. The “SWIM ring” is compact, wearable, lightweight, and easy to use. Waving the ring back and forth makes metaveillance waves visible.

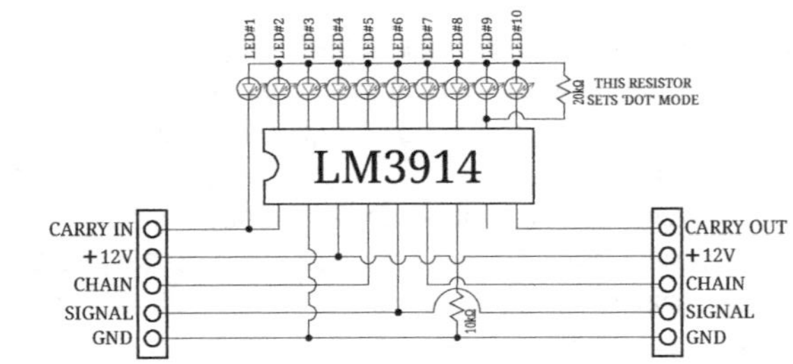

Figure 2: Schematic of modular LM-3914 based SWIM apparatus.

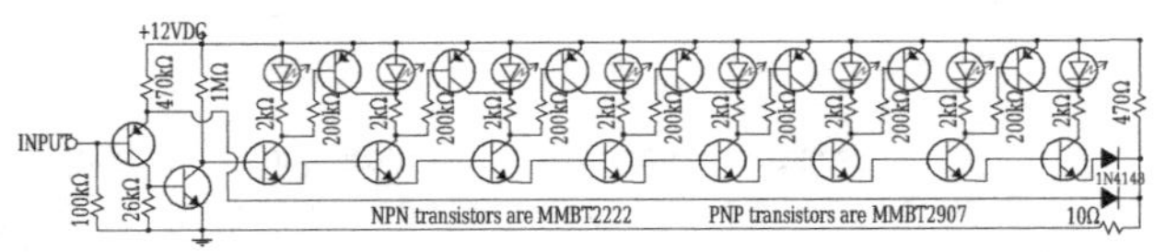

Figure 3: Schematic of novel discrete transistor LED SWIM device.

exposure [8]. An oscilloscope works in real-time but virtual-space, on its own 2D display, like most AR systems, while the SWIM uses a 1D display to produce an image like a 2D holograph, which is registered in real-time as well as in real-space, as the user sweeps the SWIM device itself through the waves in space. Last and perhaps most importantly, the augmediated reality experience SWIM creates is easily shared among a group of people, all of whom may bear witness with the naked eye, as shown in Fig. 4.

Recent Advances in SWIM

Recently SWIM (and augmented reality in general) has attracted considerable interest, and many are being built. The simplest to implement were digital, with a microcontroller driving cascaded serially programmable WS2812 RGB "neopixels", which can conveniently be purchased in a strip, but pixels are large (greater than 0.5cm) and they suffer from a limited refresh rate. SWIMs of the 1980s and 1990s were built around the LM3914 cascadable 10 segment dot/bar graph display driver IC, which produces excellent results with a high degree of accuracy, tested up to 200 cascaded ICs for HD pixel counts (2000 pixels) and large scale size. This modular design used is seen in Fig.2. The LM3914 was measured to have a bandwidth around 1.6Mhz, which translates to a very high "refresh rate" and the simple analog system controlling it approaches linear time invariancy, eliminating the possibility of any lag. Thus the system always responds instantly and the experience is seamless and convincing: humanistic integrity is maintained. LM3914 ICs were used to make a wristworn "microswim" pictured in Fig.4, which is a 60 pixel SWIM, utilizing 0603 size SMD LEDs, which fits on a 6cm square PCB (its image also shown in the same figure). A novel discrete transistor circuit has been devised, pictured in Fig.3, which makes a low pixel count SWIM smaller and cheaper than is possible with the LM3914. Pictured also in Fig. 4 is an 8 pixel discrete SWIM (fits on a 1.25cm by 1.9cm PCB small enough to be worn a ring) together with its output image.

Tactile SWIM for Haptic Augmented Reality CAD/M

Some of the early embodiments of SWIM began as electromechanical devices, which naturally lent themselves to being grasped, held, touched, etc.. One of Mann’s early experiments was to use an X-Y plotter to visualize (and feel) radio waves, sound waves, and the like (Fig. 5). This gives way to haptics for collaboratively creating physical objects: HARCAD (Fig. 7), a system to explore “Cyborg Craft”, a new kind of undigital craft: being undigital with digital computers. In this system, one or more users can grasp and touch and feel virtual objects in cyborgspace, and share the resulting haptic augmented reality experience, as a way of

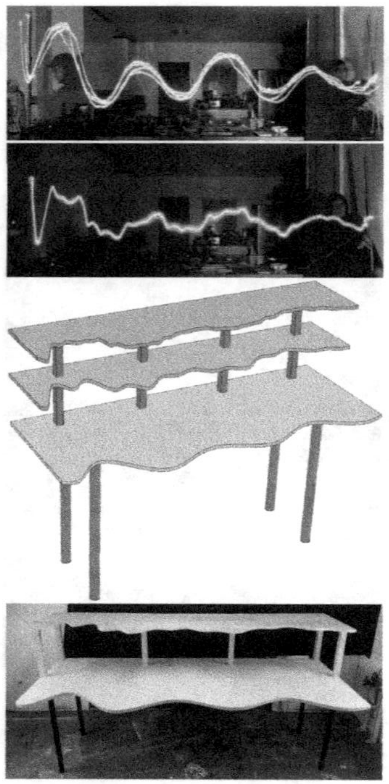

Figure 6: Furniture design with Haptic Augmented Reality CAD/CAM. A shape synthesizer generates shape information which is visualized in alignment with haptic sensation, so shapes can be seen and felt in perfect alignment. A 3D (3-dimensional) wireless position sensor comprises transducers with phase-coherent detection. Ultimately we bypass CAD altogether to directly and collaboratively interact with the manufacturing process. That's what we call "undigital cyborg craft".

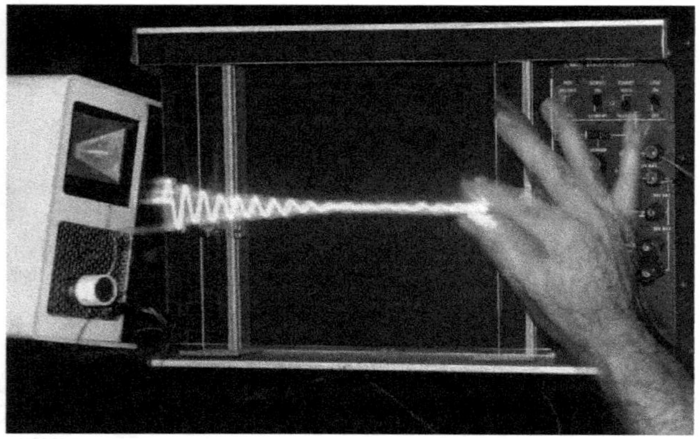

Figure 5: Mann's early haptic radio wave experiment using X-Y plotter to touch, feel, and grasp hold of radio waves in perfect alignment with reality, due to simple physical phase-coherent detection. (visuals from single light bulb + haptics).

designing and making things like cars, buildings, furniture, etc., through a collaborative design and realization process.

As a simple example, we wished to make a table with a nice curvy shape to it. A good place to begin is with waves. As a basis for synthesis, we have a shape synthesizer. In some embodiments the shape synthesizer is made in software, from simple shapes like rectangles, circles, ellipses, etc., as one might find in a computer program like Interviews idraw, Inkscape, or Autodesk Fusion 360. In other embodiments the shape synthesizer exists as a piece of hardware, as illusrated in Fig 6: Topmost is a multiple exposure, showing three exposures while moving back-and-forth, which align, approximately, with each other, while admitting a small variation. The shape is sculpted by press-pull operations. Additionally, harmonic variations are made to the shapes, to design furniture. Here a wavetable is designed in which

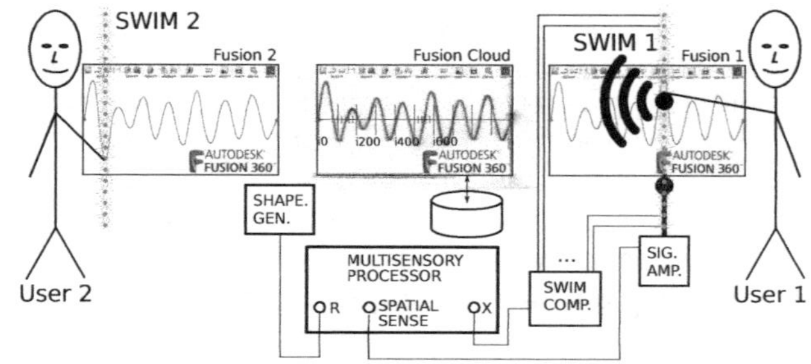

Figure 7: HARCAD system for designing furniture or other objects using two Tactile SWIMs, one held by each of two users at remote locations to press/pull on an Autodesk Fusion 360 model.

the table is the fundamental of the waveform from a musical note, and the shelf above it is the fundamental and first overtone (i.e. the first two harmonics). Here the amplitude of the waveforms decreases from left-to-right as we move further from the sound source.

Another application is PlankPoint™, a collaborative fitness system where a planking board is a pointing device for collaborative online games using HARCAD-like technology.

Conclusion

New wrist and ring worn SWIM devices make the SWIM device more wearable than ever, and LEDs allow high resultion and high luminosity with low power consumption. As a result, clear and bright AR (Augmented Reality) overlays are produced for a truly phenomenologically augmented reality. Multiple SWIMs can be used as metawands (metaveillance wands), and when equipped with haptic capability allow users to share the augmented reality with machines, for HARCAD and ultimately HARCAM.

REFERENCES

1. Thomas P Caudell and David W Mizell. 1992. Augmented reality: An application of heads-up display technology to manual manufacturing processes. In *System Sciences, 1992. Proceedings of the Twenty-Fifth Hawaii International Conference on*, Vol. 2. IEEE, 659–669.
2. David Drascic and Paul Milgram. 1996. Perceptual issues in augmented reality. In *Electronic Imaging: Science & Technology*. International Society for Optics and Photonics, 123–134.
3. Raymond Chun Hing Lo, Steve Mann, Jason Huang, Valmiki Rampersad, and Tao Ai. 2012. High dynamic range (hdr) video image processing for digital glass. In *Proceedings of the 20th ACM international conference on Multimedia*. ACM, 1477–1480.
4. Steve Mann. 1997. Wearable computing: A first step toward personal imaging. *Computer* 30, 2 (1997), 25–32.
5. Steve Mann. 1998a. Humanistic computing:"WearComp" as a new framework and application for intelligent signal processing. *Proc. IEEE* 86, 11 (1998), 2123–2151.
6. Steve Mann. 1998b. Wearable computing as means for personal empowerment. In *Proc. 3rd Int. Conf. on Wearable Computing (ICWC)*. 51–59.
7. Steve Mann. 2001. Wearable computing: Toward humanistic intelligence. *IEEE Intelligent Systems* 16, 3 (2001), 10–15.
8. Steve Mann. 2015. Phenomenal Augmented Reality: Advancing technology for the future of humanity. *IEEE Consumer Electronics Magazine* 4, 4 (2015), 92–97.
9. Steve Mann, Raymond Chun Hing Lo, Kalin Ovtcharov, Shixiang Gu, David Dai, Calvin Ngan, and Tao Ai. 2012. Realtime hdr (high dynamic range) video for eyetap wearable computers, fpga-based seeing aids, and glasseyes (eyetaps). In *Electrical & Computer Engineering (CCECE), 2012 25th IEEE Canadian Conference on*. IEEE, 1–6.
10. DWF Van Krevelen and R Poelman. 2010. A survey of augmented reality technologies, applications and limitations. *International Journal of Virtual Reality* 9, 2 (2010), 1.

MIDI Motion: Interactive Music Composition Gloves

Kristofer Klipfel
University of Colorado
Boulder, CO, 80302
krkl5448@colorado.edu

TEI '17, March 20-23, 2017, Yokohama, Japan
ACM 978-1-4503-4676-4/17/03.
http://dx.doi.org/10.1145/3024969.3035535

Abstract
Midi Motion Gloves is an interactive wearable that is used to manipulate, organize, and construct audio patterns for the purpose of composing music. Acting as an interface between the user and a Digital Audio Workspace, or DAW, the gloves give a user complete control over customization of sounds, effects, tempo, recording, looping, and other musical elements. MIDI Motion gloves utilize organic human movement like finger bending, hand rotation, and finger tapping to trigger audio clips or add effects and filters, ultimately allowing the user to efficiently compose and visualize complex musical patterns in a three-dimensional space.

Author Keywords
MIDI, music, motion, gloves, composing, tangible, patterns, sensors, pressure, flex sensor, wearable

ACM Classification Keywords
H.5.m. Information interfaces and presentation (e.g., HCI): Miscellaneous

Introduction
The techniques that an artist develops to physically interact with a musical instrument are vital to the creative composition process. Reliable research has demonstrated that areas of the brain involved in musical performance and composition may work in

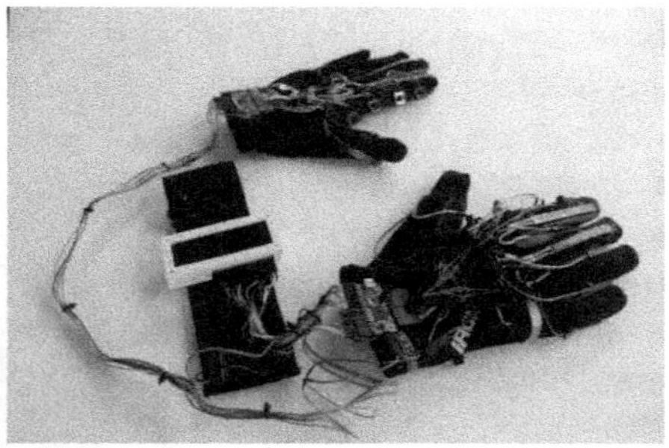

Figure 1: Working Prototype

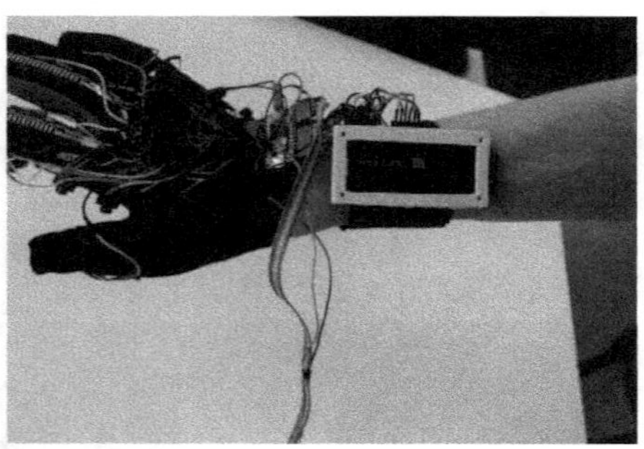

Figure 2: LCD Interface

association with other areas that are dedicated to motor skills [1]. Using a computer to create music in a Digital Audio Workspace can therefore cause a user to feel disconnected from the natural flow of musical composition, since the tactile nature of playing an instrument has then been eliminated. By constantly typing, clicking, stopping and restarting the music, the process may become tedious, choppy and end up thwarting the creative process. MIDI Motion gloves bridge the gap between user and software, in order to transform this static creation process into a more dynamic, tangible, and natural approach to digital music composition. The gloves are a functional composition tool because the link between each movement and each sound is predictable, controllable, and fully customizable. By quickly being able to toggle between a variety of sounds the user is capable of layering and composing, ultimately strengthening the artist's connection to the music as they develop musical patterns.

Technical Implementation

MIDI Motion utilizes a variety of sensors and buttons to translate tactile data into musical information interpreted by the music composition software. On each fingertip there is a force sensitive resistor (FSR) also known as a pressure sensor that registers touches and taps and in response triggers corresponding pitches and variable volume based off the speed at which the sensor collides with a surface. On the back of the index and middle fingers of each hand there are two flex sensors that, when bent, send values ranging from 0-127 to control variable effects like volume, frequency, and panning. On the side of each index finger there are four buttons that each correspond to different controls within the program such as navigation, sound toggling, undo/redo, stop/start, and up octave/down octave. To extend customization and functionality, an LCD screen (Figure 2), strapped to the wrist, acts as an interface between the gloves, the user, and the program, allowing the user to program the finger pitches to any scale in any key. (Major, Minor, Blues, Pentatonic). Lastly, a microcontroller (Teensy 3.2) on the right hand receives analog and digital signals from the sensors and then communicates with the computer through serial, keyboard, and MIDI signals.

Design Process

The design approach was developed by exploring the pros and cons of various composition and music development methods. By recognizing the major challenges and pitfalls that are present in the current music production process I was able to develop an efficient and interactive approach for making music composition a fluid, expressive, and enjoyable experience. Also, by analyzing the usage of certain commands and controls (undo, redo, up, down) I was able to make informed decisions on what features would be most valued among users.

When determining placement for sensors and controls, ergonomics was the primary consideration. Sensors on each hand are placed in locations optimal for ease of use and quick access. For example, the FSRs on the fingertips were placed just above the pads of the finger taking advantage of the natural curve of the fingers, providing a comfortable resting position and tapping angle. Control buttons were placed along the sides of the index fingers allowing easy access while simultaneously being non-intrusive to surrounding fingers. This allows the user to comfortably trigger sounds at a variety of speeds.

Related Work

While there has been a lot of research on futuristic musical interfaces, for example reacTable at TEI 2007 [2] or fabric-based multi-touch musical controllers presented at NIME [3], the most popular commercial tools for composition and performance are MIDI devices [4]. This is because of their customizability, versatility, and ease of use compared to a plain keyboard and mouse. Ableton Push is one of the most popular pieces of hardware on the market for arranging, performing, and sequencing audio [5]. Push communicates with Ableton Live, music production software, and contains velocity sensitive push pads that give the user tactile feedback while composing and arranging [5]. MIDI Motion expands upon this design by providing the user with a simpler and less constraining interface. The ability to flexibly move the hands in space allows for a more natural creative environment. Another similar technology developed by British artist Imogen Heap employs the use of three-dimensional space to manipulate pre-recorded sound. Heap's wearable presented at WIRED 2012 Conference is able to use changes in hand position to synthesize, manipulate, and alter certain sounds in a pre-recorded track. [6] MIDI Motion further expands upon this design by not only allowing the user to change sounds, but also create replicable musical patterns and rhythms.

Discussion

Interactive music gloves like MIDI Motion are the next step in tangible and interactive musical development. The ability of a musician to use their fingers to quickly layer and compose musical patterns in an unconstrained physical space allows them to be more emotionally involved and connected to the music being created. This also makes music production and performance more intuitive and less complicated for users not familiar with musical concepts. MIDI Motion immerses users into a fluid musical experience by employing natural movement to musically express and compose. While gestural MIDI gloves have a number of advantages over other forms of MIDI control and musical sequencing, there are limitations. MIDI Motion gives the user full control to program fingers to different pitches and scales but because the human hand has 10 fingers, users must track which pitches correspond to which finger as there are only 8 notes in any given scale. MIDI Motion gloves provide the user with a unique sound and motion experience combining the benefits of a traditional MIDI pad controller with those of other gestural MIDI devices on the market. In the future, allowing greater software navigation control and sequencing options will give the user more freedom to customize and control music throughout the composition process.

Acknowledgements

I would like to thank Alicia Gibb and the BTU Lab at CU Boulder for providing me with access to tools and materials throughout the build process. I would also like to thank Brielle Nickoloff for feedback and final review of the paper.

References

1. Sarwate, Avneesh, and Jeff Snyder. 2014. SkipStep: A Multi-Paradigm Touch-screen Instrument. *ICMC*.

2. Jordà, S., Geiger, G., Alonso, M. and Kaltenbrunner, M., 2007, February. The reacTable: exploring the synergy between live music performance and tabletop tangible interfaces.

Proceedings of the 1st international conference on Tangible and embedded interaction.

3. Roh, Jung-Sim, Yotam Mann, Adrian Freed, and David Wessel. Robust and Reliable Fabric, Piezoresistive Multitouch Sensing Surfaces for Musical Controllers. *NIME'2011*

4. Pedro Lopes, Alfredo Ferreira, and J. A. Madeiras Pereira. Battle of the DJs: an HCI Perspective of Traditional, Virtual, Hybrid and Multitouch DJing. *NIME'2011.*

5. Parsons, Lawrence M., et al. 2005. The brain basis of piano performance. *Neuropsychologia*, *43*(2), pp.199-215.

6. Imogen Heap. 2012. Imogen Heap Performance with Musical Gloves Demo | WIRED 2012 | WIRED. Video. Retrieved January 18, 2017 from https://www.youtube.com/watch?v=6btFObRRD9k

Star-force: A Playful Implementation of the Jedi-force

Shubham Jain
USICT, GGSIPU.
Delhi, India
shubham.jain.1994@ieee.org

Shubham Sharma
USICT, GGSIPU.
Delhi, India
Sharmashubham9800@gmail.com

Dhawal Babbar
USICT, GGSIPU.
Delhi, India
dhawal.babbar97@gmail.com

TEI '17, March 20-23, 2017, Yokohama, Japan
ACM 978-1-4503-4676-4/17/03.
http://dx.doi.org/10.1145/3024969.3041098

Abstract
We introduce *Star-force*, which is a playful implementation of sci-fi concept *The Force,* as envisioned in the Star Wars saga. This is achieved via a battle environment instantiated in mixed reality using a video see-through head-mounted display. The "weapons", i.e., the *Light-Sabers, Blasters* are based on the ESP8266 microcontroller and tracked using makers and external cameras. Through their headsets, users see the virtual Light-Sabers as beams of light emanating from their handheld controllers. Depending on the actions, such as contact between two Light-Sabers, we trigger force-feedback on the player's hands via electrical muscle stimulation. This emulates the sensation of the two powerful beams of light hitting each other.

Author Keywords
Star wars; Muscle feedback; augmented reality; mixed reality; Position tracking.

ACM Classification Keywords
H.5.1. Information interfaces and presentation (e.g., HCI): Multimedia Information Systems - Artificial, augmented, and virtual realities;

Introduction

The *Star-force* simulator builds upon the concept of Augmented Reality with additional haptic feedback to the player's hands created by means of an electrical impulse applied to the wrist muscles (via electrodes) as depicted in Figure 1. When this impulse is delivered it involuntarily contracts the target muscle and thus induces a force on the player. This feedback can be a response to player's own action, or the actions of other players. With the added muscular feedback, we aim to provide a playful but also to some degree realistic experience of the so-called *Jedi-force*.

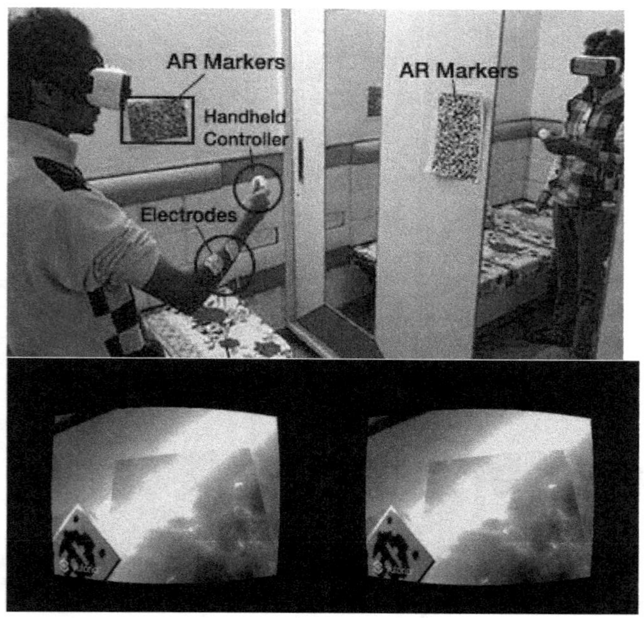

Figure 1: (Top) Setup showing the prototype (EMS hardware not shown but kept with user); (Bottom) User's AR view.

Related Work

Vibrotactile and Force feedback hardware

A popular way to simulate impact in a video game scenario is the usage of vibration feedback. In fact, most mobile or wearable commercial or research prototypes (such as [7] or [6]) feature vibration motors that deliver these sensations to the user. However, these sensations are weak when compared to what can be achieved using force-feedback hardware, such as exoskeletons [8].

On the other hand, force-feedback provides strong external forces moving the user's limbs. Here, the most popular approaches are motion platforms [15], force-feedback robotic arms [14], pulleys [12], exoskeletons [8,13] and most recently human actuators [16].

Simulating impact and force feedback with EMS

Recently, Electrical Muscle Stimulation (EMS) has been shown to be a suitable technique for force-feedback [10] and motion guidance [17]. The advantage of EMS is that it miniaturizes better than exoskeletons because the required hardware is smaller. An example of this is Muscle Plotter [11], an EMS-based interactive device that transforms the user's hand (that holds a pen) into a plotter. The hardware of such EMS devices is much smaller than their motor-based counterparts, such as the Phantom robotic arm, which can also actuate a pen [18].

EMS has been used for simulating impacts similar to those of Light-Sabers. In Impacto [9], researchers combined EMS with a solenoid to simulate the impact of collisions in VR, such as when hitting a baseball with a virtual bat. Also, Farbiz et al., used EMS to simulate the impact of a real racket with an augmented reality

Figure 2: Controller breakout board

Figure 3: Controller top with fiducial markers

tennis ball [19]. We leverage these and similar findings to design our force feedback.

Light-Sabers in popular Game concepts
Disney, Lucasfilm & Unit9 launched *Lightsaber Escape* [2], a VR experience that sensors present in the phone to control the movement of a Light-Saber. The motion of the Light-Saber is rendered via both auditory and vibration feedback. Similarly, EA Games have released *Star Wars Battlefront* for PlayStation VR where a space combat is instantiated in a VR environment, much like the one we represent with our prototype. However, in the light of TEI 2017's sci-fi topic, we opted for integrating the Light-Sabers as part of our daily experiences – hence, users can see them in mixed reality.

Implementation
We developed an AR environment based on Google Cardboard [4] and implemented in Unity3d [3]. The simulator uses live video stream from the phone's front-facing mobile camera, then processes the frames looking for AR markers (which we use for tracking) and renders 3d-objects on top of the scene. This is depicted in Figure 1.

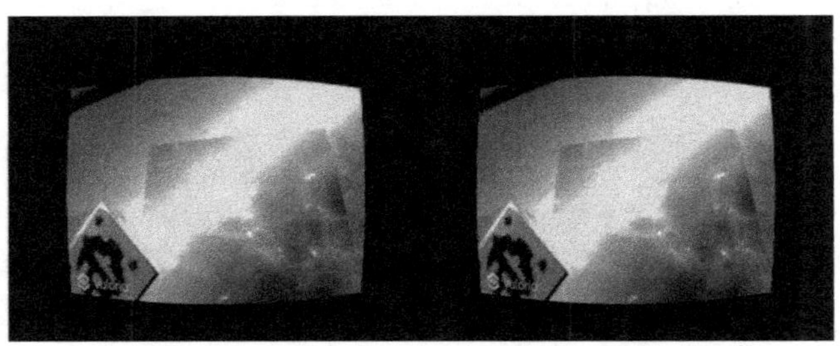

Figure 4: Augmented reality view as experienced by the player.

Hand-held Controller aka the Light-Sabers
The breakout board of hand-held controller is depicted in Figure 2. It is implemented using a microcontroller (NodeMCU development board) and an EMS control board (openEMSstim). The use of the NodeMCU allows for additional functionalities such as measuring the grip using a pressure sensitive conductive sheet (aka velostat sheet), and also tracks angular velocity and acceleration using an internal MPU-6050 IMU sensor. Tactile switches are added for additional user input. The controller transmits the sensor data using Websocket protocol. The data is sent over IP, since the controller has a built-in ESP8266 WiFi module. This sensor data is used to measure the intensity of the force-feedback, providing us with a simple closed loop system.

The hardware is packed in a 3d printed enclosure. The enclosure is strategically designed and covered with unique *fiducial* markers for object recognition as depicted in Figure 3.

Image processing for mixed reality
We use the *Vuforia SDK* [5] for Unity3d to visually map and interpret the external world. It detects the presence of an AR marker in the frame (Figure 5). Since simulating an AR environment with rendering 3d graphics is computation intensive and complex, we use a marker-based approach to reduce the complexity of detecting real-world objects. A database of distinct markers is used for performing different action:

- Weapons: The marker in this case is the controller itself. As mentioned earlier, the enclosure of the controlled is strategically designed with contrasting features, providing many points for tracking.

Figure 5: Marker recognition and overlaid Light–saber 3d graphic.

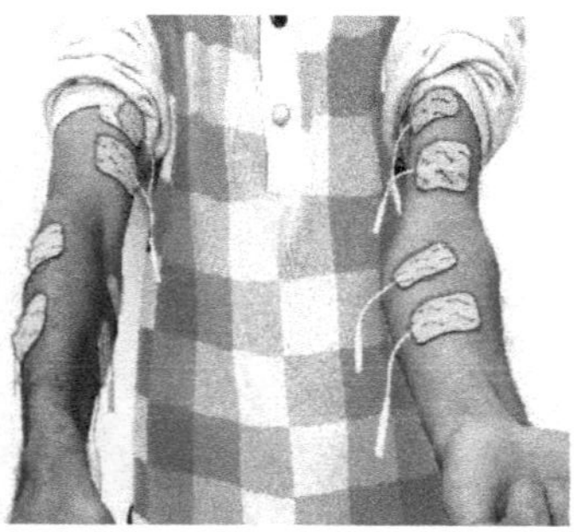

Figure 6: Electrode placement.

Whenever the controller is detected, a 3d object (Light-Saber beam) is overlaid on it.

- Force-tags: These markers are placed strategically and directly enable the force feedback on recognition. These markers are placed at specific points. A good example is a marker on the palm of opponent, which the user can use to trigger the Jedi-force on the player.
- Terrain: These markers are used to project unrealistic (but fun) surrounding such as fire, lava-flow, etc.

Designing our force-feedback using EMS

The force-feedback is provided via EMS using the openEMSstim[1] control board, which we control via Bluetooth and power via an additional 9V battery. The board was modified by adding 5 relays, to time-multiplex the EMS signal over 5 output channels (the board natively only provides two output channels). We pair this board with an off-the-shelf muscle stimulator unit, which generates the medically compliant EMS pulses.

These electrical impulses are delivered via 10 electrodes that are attached to the player's skin. Each electrode pair covers one muscle, totaling 5 muscles as depicted in Figure 6: wrist flexors (left arm only), wrist extensors (left and right arms) and biceps (left and right arms)..

Implementation considerations and limitations

We have used optical marker tracking, which resulted in computational intensive process and requires heavy CPU recourses. This limits the capabilities and form-factor of our prototypes since it requires external cameras and processing. Also, optical tracking is subject to occlusion, motion blurs and frame drops.

Furthermore, the use of EMS introduces some degree of restricted usage. The pulse intensity requires a careful calibration step and electrode placement. Lastly, the use of EMS is discouraged for people using electronic support systems such as pacemakers.

Conclusions

With Star-force, we instantiated a long dream of sci-fi, the Light-Saber. While in reality the contact of two weak light beams does not produce the exciting effects the Star-Wars saga built into our imagination, our prototype implements this in Mixed Reality. We do so by showing the light beams in the player's smartphone running the AR app, enclosed in a HMD, by producing force-feedback when two Sabers collide. The feedback is implemented via Electric Muscle Stimulation, which allows our final prototypes to be hand-held and lightweight.

We believe that our approach could be generalized, by integrating sensor data from health monitoring wearables. The application can be extended to consider pulse-rate, step-count etc., as to control the intensity of force-feedback, user health and other parameters for scoring to make the interaction interesting.

Acknowledgements

We would like to acknowledge efforts of Pedro Lopes who introduced us with openEMSstim. We would also like to acknowledge Prof. Bimlesh Wadhwa for the guidance.

[1] https://github.com/PedroLopes/openEMSstim

References

1. openEMSstim open source project by Pedro Lopes https://github.com/PedroLopes/openEMSstim
2. https://www.chromeexperiments.com/experiment/lightsaber-escape
3. Unity3d documentation https://docs.unity3d.com/Manual/index.html
4. Google VR SDK for Unity3d https://developers.google.com/vr/unity/
5. Vuforia SDK for Unity3d https://developer.vuforia.com/
6. Jerome Pasquero, Scott J. Stobbe, and Noel Stonehouse. 2011. A haptic wristwatch for eyes-free interactions. In *Proceedings of the SIGCHI Conference on Human Factors in Computing Systems*(CHI '11). ACM, New York, NY, USA, 3257-3266. DOI=http://dx.doi.org/10.1145/1978942.1979425
7. Ivan Poupyrev and Shigeaki Maruyama. 2003. Tactile interfaces for small touch screens. In*Proceedings of the 16th annual ACM symposium on User interface software and technology* (UIST '03). ACM, New York, NY, USA, 217-220. DOI=http://dx.doi.org/10.1145/964696.964721
8. Sudipto Mukherjee, Mohd. Zubair, Bhivraj Suthar, and Sachin Kansal. 2013. Exoskeleton for Tele-Operation of Industrial Robot. In *Proceedings of Conference on Advances In Robotics* (AIR '13). ACM, New York, NY, USA, , Article 108 , 5 pages. DOI=http://dx.doi.org/10.1145/2506095.2506108
9. Pedro Lopes, Alexandra Ion, and Patrick Baudisch. 2015. Impacto: Simulating Physical Impact by Combining Tactile Stimulation with Electrical Muscle Stimulation. In *Proceedings of the 28th Annual ACM Symposium on User Interface Software & Technology* (UIST '15). ACM, New York, NY, USA, 11-19. DOI: http://dx.doi.org/10.1145/2807442.2807443
10. Pedro Lopes and Patrick Baudisch. 2013. Muscle-propelled force feedback: bringing force feedback to mobile devices. In *Proceedings of the SIGCHI Conference on Human Factors in Computing Systems* (CHI '13). ACM, New York, NY, USA, 2577-2580. DOI: http://dx.doi.org/10.1145/2470654.2481355
11. Pedro Lopes, Doäa Yüksel, François Guimbretière, and Patrick Baudisch. 2016. Muscle-plotter: An Interactive System based on Electrical Muscle Stimulation that Produces Spatial Output. In*Proceedings of the 29th Annual Symposium on User Interface Software and Technology* (UIST '16). ACM, New York, NY, USA, 207-217. DOI: https://doi.org/10.1145/2984511.2984530
12. Seahak Kim, Masahiro Ishii, Yasuharu Koike, and Makoto Sato. 2000. Development of tension based haptic interface and possibility of its application to virtual reality. In *Proceedings of the ACM symposium on Virtual reality software and technology* (VRST '00). ACM, New York, NY, USA, 199-205. DOI=http://dx.doi.org/10.1145/502390.502428
13. Xiaochi Gu, Yifei Zhang, Weize Sun, Yuanzhe Bian, Dao Zhou, and Per Ola Kristensson. 2016. Dexmo: An Inexpensive and Lightweight Mechanical Exoskeleton for Motion Capture and Force Feedback in VR. In *Proceedings of the 2016 CHI Conference on Human Factors in Computing Systems* (CHI '16). ACM, New York, NY, USA, 1991-1995. DOI: https://doi.org/10.1145/2858036.2858487
14. Danieau, F., Fleureau, J., Guillotel, P., Mollet, N., Lécuyer, A., and Christie, M. HapSeat : Producing Motion Sensation with Multiple Force-feedback Devices Embedded in a Seat. Proc. VRST '12, 69–76.
15. NASA Vertical Motion Simulator. http://www.nasa.gov/centers/ames/research/technologyonepagers/vms.html

16. Lung-Pan Cheng, Patrick Lühne, Pedro Lopes, Christoph Sterz, and Patrick Baudisch. 2014. Haptic turk: a motion platform based on people. In *Proceedings of the SIGCHI Conference on Human Factors in Computing Systems* (CHI '14). ACM, New York, NY, USA, 3463-3472. DOI=http://dx.doi.org/10.1145/2556288.2557101
17. Emi Tamaki, Takashi Miyaki, and Jun Rekimoto. 2011. PossessedHand: techniques for controlling human hands using electrical muscles stimuli. In *Proceedings of the SIGCHI Conference on Human Factors in Computing Systems* (CHI '11). ACM, New York, NY, USA, 543-552. DOI=http://dx.doi.org/10.1145/1978942.1979018
18. Phantom Omni Robotic Arm, http://www.geomagic.com/en/products-landing-pages/haptic
19. Farzam Farbiz, Zhou Hao Yu, Corey Manders, and Waqas Ahmad. 2007. An electrical muscle stimulation haptic feedback for mixed reality tennis game. In *ACM SIGGRAPH 2007 posters*(SIGGRAPH '07). ACM, New York, NY, USA, , Article 140 . DOI: https://doi.org/10.1145/1280720.1280873

The Body as a Source of Aesthetic Qualities for Design: Explorations and Techniques

Claudia Núñez-Pacheco
University of Sydney
148 City Road
Sydney, NSW, Australia
claudia.nunezpacheco@sydney.edu.au

Lian Loke
University of Sydney
148 City Road
Sydney, NSW, Australia
lian.loke@sydney.edu.au

TEI '17, March 20-23, 2017, Yokohama, Japan
ACM 978-1-4503-4676-4/17/03.
http://dx.doi.org/10.1145/3024969.3025049

Abstract
Our bodily dimension plays a fundamental role in the ongoing construction of meaning. Exploring the potential of this perspective, this paper describes the structure of a one-day workshop entitled: *The body as a source of aesthetic qualities for design: Explorations and techniques.* In this workshop, participants will engage with a series of somatic exercises to get in contact with their senses, aiming to reach their tacit, less explicit dimension. Aesthetic qualities emerging from the act of filtering out ideas through the body will be used as generative tools for creativity, as well as for interrogation of subjective experience. By using a series of wearable devices and artefacts from everyday life participants will explore the nuanced differences between sensing and felt-sensing, and how the use of somatic tools and stimuli from wearables can shape the way personal narratives are expressed.

Keywords
Embodied design; Wearables; Aesthetic qualities

ACM Classification Keywords
H5.m. Information interfaces and presentation (e.g., HCI): Miscellaneous.

Figure 1: Example of wearable artefacts to be utilised in conjunction with the Focusing technique to interrogate the role of bodily self-awareness in the process of meaning-generation. These props use digital and non-technological means to generate direct sensory stimulation on the body. For instance, we use gloves with vibratory elements, and mini hot water bags to be placed in pouches of different textures. These artefacts and techniques have been previously explored in the workshop *Somatic Evaluation Methods* developed as part of the Studio component of the Master of Interaction Design and Electronic Arts at the University of Sydney [10].

Schedule

The body as a source of aesthetic qualities for design is a one-day workshop, consisting of two 3-hour sessions. Activities are divided into two main aspects, as follows:

1) Inquiring through the senses

- Introduction, overview of programme.
- Presentation: The body as a generative source - Differences between senses, feelings and felt-senses, and their relevance for design.
- Exploring inner senses and subjective experience: The homunculus exercise.
- Exploring vibrotactile patterns with microelectronics and textures: Practicing haptic-based bodily sensing and evaluation.

2) Inquiring through the felt-senses

- Evaluation of wearables through the body: Utilisation of wearable props producing direct sensory stimuli (figure 1) in conjunction with the somatic technique Focusing, to explore how personal narratives are shaped by different bodily stimuli and awareness.
- The teapot exercise: Inspired by Norman's reflective dimension of emotional engagement with objects [9], everyday objects will be interrogated through Focusing. Later, participants will re-design the object inspired by aesthetic qualities emerging from the somatic exercise.
- Group presentation of ideas.
- Closing discussion: Lessons and challenges.

Detailed proposal description

The role of the body as a generative source of creativity and meaning construction still remains as a relatively unexplored area of study. Johnson [6, p.12] points out that we have bodies that *"are acted upon by 'external' and 'internal' forces such as gravity, light, heat, wind, bodily processes, and the obtrusion of other physical objects"*. Such interaction with the environment shapes our meaning-generation process. As a result, bodily experiences are embedded in everyday representational constructions such as language [6, p.15]. Knowledge is generated by the ongoing integration of perception and action [2]. Even when design can greatly benefit from accessing the inner bodily dimension, purposely articulating its aesthetic qualities is a difficult task [4]. Within this context, we envision the potential of somatic techniques and wearable technology to elicit a process of transformation, facilitating the emergence of meaning and creativity, relevant for experience-centred design.

The workshop will explore how our bodily perception shapes the way we construct our reality, and the potential of wearable technology to assist in embodied knowledge, creativity and inquiry. We will utilise somatic techniques in combination with wearable artefacts on the self-aware body to unearth aesthetic qualities emerging from the tacit dimension. Wearable devices will be used to interrogate the role of technology in the development of personal stories. We will also explore how aesthetic qualities for apparently unremarkable artefacts can be extracted by focusing on the inner body. New ideas emerging from somatic exploration, including insights from the tacit dimension of participants will be used as components to re-design existing artefacts. Although some of the activities will be conducted in small groups and discussions will be fundamental to enrich each other's perspectives, some activities will have a strong individual focus, as observing the self to access the tacit is one of the workshop's aims.

No previous experience in somatic techniques is necessary. Although the manipulation of wearable electronics and microcontrollers is involved in some of the exercises, no previous programming experience is required.

Topics: From sensing to felt-sensing

- The importance of understanding the inner self in design research and in the practice of experience-centred design
- Focusing as a somatic technique to access the tacit dimension of experience [3].
- The role of the body in the articulation of aesthetic qualities.
- Wearable technology as scaffolding for meaning generation, and how the body "find its way" to interpret phenomena despite potentially adverse conditions.
- Transparency is not the only way: The cycle of bodily self-awareness in the interaction with wearable artefacts.

Embodied interaction as a generative tool

Recognising that the nature of embodied knowledge has a strong tacit component, we envision some strategies to unearth the potential for generative ideation existing in this dimension. As Höök [4] has discussed, there are ways of bodily knowing that cannot be translated into any form of language, but rather assimilated as part of a more holistic experience. By exploring the concept of somatic discovering through attentive self-observation, the workshop principles are situated amongst the embodied interaction agenda. Through the lens of Ross and Wensveen [12], who describe some principles of embodied interaction designs, we propose new pathways to ideate artefacts with implicit value, which acknowledge the social and ethical dimension of the self-agent individual [13], and which involve the whole somatic as well as intellectual dimensions of people's experiences. Additionally, we also aim to access the tacit dimension, as an attempt to articulate those experiences residing in our bodily knowledge.

The workshop's way of approaching wearable artefacts is meant to reveal non-reductionist ways of understanding affect, facilitating embodied articulation in a similar vein to Koefoed Hansen and Kozel's [7] use of placebo objects. A careful work of self-observation will be encouraged through the use of somatic tools, towards the generation of insights and ideas for design. Previously, Lee, Lim and Shusterman [8] have applied Somaesthetical [13] principles as a tool for design ideation through the practice of Feldenkrais, which stimulates the focus on small, but meaningful movements and their aesthetic qualities. Embodied research transfer is still an underdeveloped field recognized by Wilde et. al [14], who have experimented with ways to document, report and reflect on embodied design methods in their workshop *Embodying Embodied Research.* Contributing to the development of the field and the articulation of embodied knowledge, we introduce the Focusing technique, which has not yet been explored in depth in the area of HCI, but has been applied to different areas of knowledge, including movement-based performance [1], creative writing [11] business [5], and so on.

Learning objectives and goals

Through the use of different tools, including the somatic technique Focusing, participants will learn how, by paying attention to the inner bodily dimension, to access tacit meaning and elicit hidden aesthetic qualities. These aesthetic qualities will be explored and discussed from the standpoint of the following aspects:

- Idea generation and imagination
- Evaluation / Interrogation through the body
- The emergence of unexplored tacit needs

Additionally, participants will learn:

- A practical approach that incorporates the body in the construction of knowledge.
- Novel tools for the articulation of somatic knowledge, including some notions regarding the somatic technique Focusing and its application in design.
- How wearable technology has the potential to shape the way we perceive our personal narratives.
- Evaluation through the body: How the reflective dimension of object perception can be articulated by engaging in somatic observation.
- The differences between sensing, and felt-sensing, and how these concepts are relevant to design.
- Ways of documenting phenomenological information grounded in bodily self-observation.

References

[1] Bacon, J. Psyche moving: Active imagination and focusing in movement-based performance and psychotherapy. Body, Movement and Dance in Psychotherapy, 2, 1 2007, 17-28.

[2] Dourish, P. Where the action is: the foundations of embodied interaction, The MIT Press. 2001.

[3] Gendlin, E. T. Focusing. Random House Digital, Inc., 1978.

[4] Höök, K. Transferring qualities from horseback riding to design. In Proceedings of the 6th Nordic Conference on Human-Computer Interaction: Extending Boundaries ACM, 226-235.

[5] Ikemi, A. and Kubota, S. Humanistic Psychology in Japanese Corporations: Listening and the: Small Steps of Change. Journal of Humanistic Psychology, 36, 1 1996, 104-121.

[6] Johnson, M. The body in the mind: The bodily basis of meaning, imagination, and reason. University of Chicago Press, 2013.

[7] Koefoed Hansen, L. and Kozel, S. Embodied imagination: a hybrid method of designing for intimacy. Digital Creativity, 18, 4 2007, 207-220.

[8] Lee, W., Lim, Y.-k. and Shusterman, R. Practicing somaesthetics: exploring its impact on interactive product design ideation. In proceedings of DIS 2014.

[9] Norman, D. A. Emotional design: Why we love (or hate) everyday things. Basic books, 2004.

[10] Núñez-Pacheco, C. and Loke, L. Tacit Narratives: Surfacing aesthetic meaning by using wearable props and Focusing. In proceedings of Tangible, Embedded and Embodied Interaction TEI 2017.

[11] Perl, S. Felt sense: Writing with the body. Boynton/Cook Heinemann Portsmouth, 2004.

[12] Ross, P. R. and Wensveen, S. A. Designing behavior in interaction: Using aesthetic experience as a mechanism for design. International Journal of Design, 4, 2. 2010.

[13] Shusterman, R. Somaesthetics - Thinking Through the Body and Designing for Interactive Experience, 2011.

[14] Wilde, D., Tomico, O., Lucero, A. s., Ho ̈o ̈k, K. and Buur, J. Embodying embodied design research techniques. Aarhus Series on Human Centered Computing, 1, 2015, 4.

Paper Machines

Hyunjoo Oh
University of Colorado
Boulder, CO 80302 USA
hyunjoo.oh@colorado.edu

Kristof Klipfel
University of Colorado
Boulder, CO 80302 USA
rkl5448@colorado.edu

Sherry Hsi
Concord Consortium
Emeryville, CA USA
shsi@concord.org

Mark D. Gross
University of Colorado
Boulder, CO 80302 USA
mdgross@colorado.edu

TEI '17, March 20-23, 2017, Yokohama, Japan
ACM 978-1-4503-4676-4/17/03.
http://dx.doi.org/10.1145/3024969.3025050

Abstract

This studio invites participants to design and build machines with different kinds of paper and craft materials. We will introduce papercrafting using our design tool "FoldMecha", mechanical components, and prototyping methods for physical construction.

Participants interact with sample projects and explore a motion library, then begin the ideation process for their own working machine. During the studio, papercrafting techniques and various craft materials will be provided to further inspire participants creative process.

The goal is to provide hands-on experiences in designing and building machines with paper using design tools and prototyping techniques that we have developed. The studio will culminate in the "show & tell" demo and discussion about bottom up and bricolage design approaches as a means of creative thinking and learning. Outcomes will be showcased at the TEI events.

Keywords

Paper Mechatronics; DIY technology and techniques; bricolage design; exploratory construction

Schedule

Phase 1: Introduction & Philosophical Framing of Design

Phase 2: Motion Library; Sample Projects Decomposition; FoldMecha demo + warm-up exercise

Phase 3: Brainstorming ideas (in groups)

Phase 4: Tinkering, Concept Selection, & Prototyping

Phase 5: Fabrication

Phase 6: Presentation, Reflection, & Gallery Walk

Detailed proposal description

Conventional CAD tools are well-suited to designing physical embodiments of simple static objects. However, when the device to be designed has mechanical behavior, conventional tools challenge even experienced designers. Despite the reduced burdens of calculation, modeling, and hand skills that current CAD tools provide, designing and building mechanical models still remains demanding. It requires understanding mechanical movements, visualizing relationships between component mechanisms, and accurately predicting the behavior of these mechanical systems.

We developed FoldMecha, a computer-aided design (CAD) system for exploratory construction of mechanical papercraft [1]. Exploratory construction is a springboard for creative learning [3], and FoldMecha supports this type of playful construction. FoldMecha enables users to (a) experiment with and design movements by modifying individual components; (b) download parts to cut and build mechanical prototypes; and (c) apply those prototypes in their own creations. Paper is a flexible, creative medium with different thicknesses, colors, and textures that can be cut, folded, or combined in traditional and whimsical ways with simple craft tools. We choose paper because of its ubiquity and accessibility in design studios and classrooms. Additional layers with electronics, paper circuits, motors, and sensors can extend the existing creative possibilities of paper.

This hands-on studio invites participants to design and build machines with different kinds of paper and craft materials. We will introduce "FoldMecha", then give participants time to engage in physical and digital bricolage, experimentation with movement, and share associated prototyping methods for creative exploration and construction. Our goal is to enable participants to experiment with mechanical movement design using paper and —as Schön poetically puts it—to engage in a "reflective conversation with the materials of a design situation" [4]. During the studio, we will encourage participants to begin with ideation and search for dynamic inspirations in their surrounding environment. Using combined hands-on and simulated modeling, participants conceptualize a movement, then prototype a working machine, advancing to more complicated levels of design and engineering. Video design examples from prior workshops created by school teachers, young adults, and children are shared as examples and inspirations.

This TEI workshop will also engage users in active testing of our design tool and techniques. The feedback gathered will help improve this creative learning activity that is intended to encourage all users to understand basics of mechanical movements by playful, tangible, and exploratory construction, ultimately for creative thinking.

The workshop is open to participants from every discipline. Regardless of experience everyone is invited to work with the materials provided to tinker, work as individuals or in teams, to invent and create a paper machine.

Topics to be covered

1. Bricolage, tinkering, and constructionist approaches to design learning
2. Idea generation and iteration by design and engineering
3. Mechanical engineering automata (mechanical toys)

A positioning in the continuum of practical and theoretical skills

Although we plan to mention some basic theories of learning from tinkering, play, and design, this studio will focus primarily on direct hands-on experiences with software, tools, practical design activities, and explorations that are done with tangible materials. Participants will have better insights into mechanical motions and stronger confidence in working with papercrafts as a creative medium for design.

Learning goals/Discussion objectives

Our primary goal is to provide a hands-on experience on exploratory construction for paper machines as a means of learning mechanical movements. This will lead to valuing bricolage design, an experimental and playful assembling of components, for creative thinking and learning. A secondary goal is to demonstrate the power and utility of paper, cardboard, and papercraft as design prototyping tool.

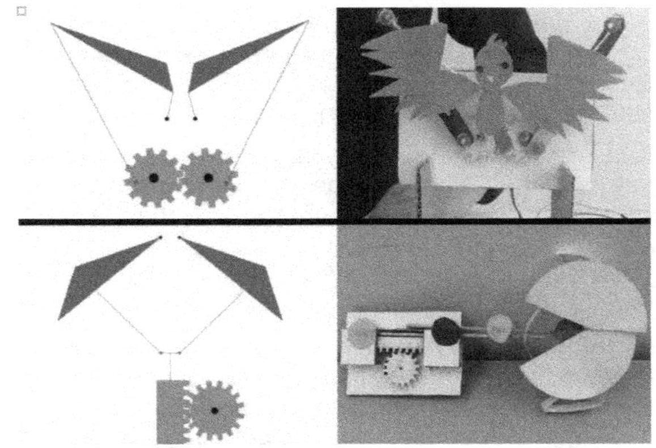

Figure 1. FoldMecha helps users design mechanical movements and construct paper machines: FoldMecha simulation snapshots (left) and paper machines using them as bare-bone structures (right). Both are created by participants in a prior workshop using FoldMecha.

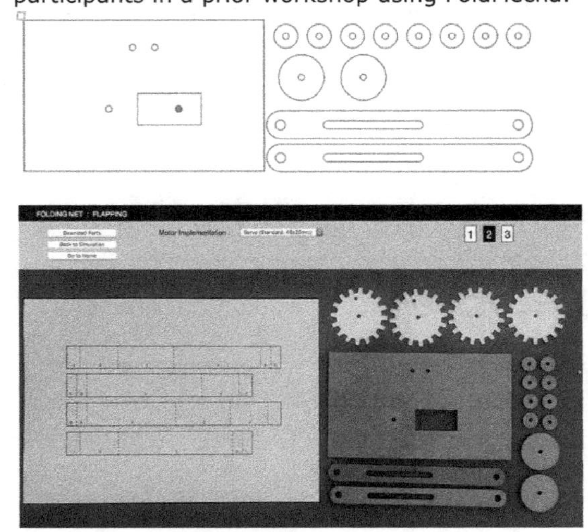

Figure 2. FoldMecha supports users to generate parts for the mechanical movement they designed and customize based on the prototyping plans: FoldMecha screen showing parts to customize and download (top) and printed and cut parts (right).

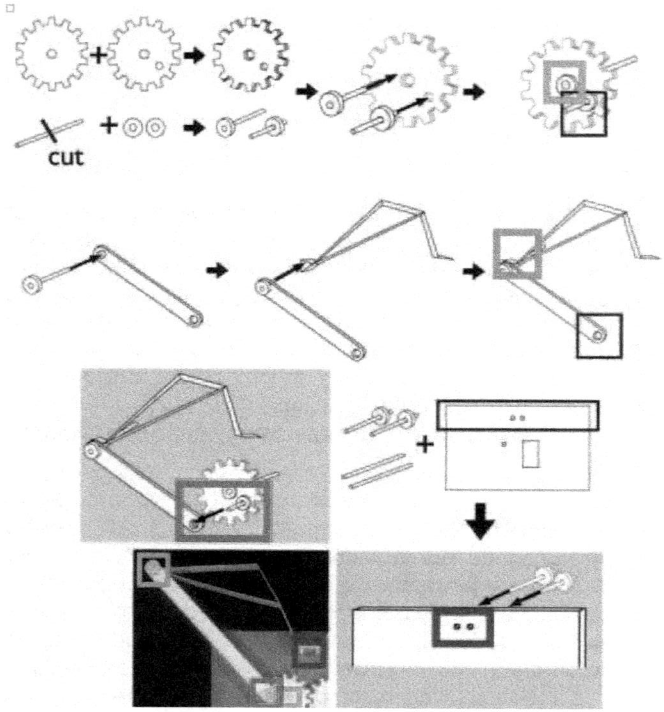

Figure 3. This studio will introduce associate prototyping methods using craft materials with the generated parts. This figure shows how to use lollipop sticks as axles to mount gears and linkages to the stand.

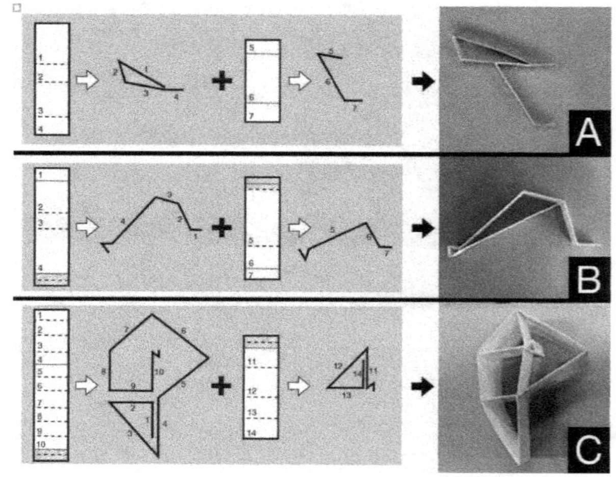

Figure 4. Dashed and dotted lines indicate mountain and valley folds respectively. Folding generates moving joints and unfolded faces become linkages [1,2].

References

1. Oh, H., Gross, M.D., and Eisenberg, H. 2015. FoldMecha: Design for Linkage-Based Paper Toys. In *Adjunct Proceedings of the 28th ACM Symposium on User Interface Software & Technology* (UIST '15 Adjunct). ACM, New York, NY, USA, 91-92.
2. Oh, H., Eisenberg, H., Gross, M.D., and Hsi, S. 2015. Paper mechatronics: a design case study for a young medium. In Proceedings of the 14th International Conference on Interaction Design and Children (IDC '15). ACM, New York, NY, USA, 371-374.
3. Resnick, M. 2007. All I really need to know (about creative thinking) I learned (by studying how children learn) in kindergarten. In *Proceedings of the 6th ACM SIGCHI conference on Creativity & cognition* (C&C '07). ACM, New York, NY, USA, 1-6.
4. Schön, D.A. 1992. Designing as reflective conversation with the materials of a design situation. *Knowledge-Based Systems* 5(1):3-14, March.

We-Coupling! Designing New Forms of Embodied Interpersonal Connection

Robb Mitchell
Univ. of Southern Denmark,
Kolding DK 6000
robb@sdu.dk

Shunichi Kasahara
Sony CSL / Tokyo University
Tokyo, Japan
kasahara@csl.sony.co.jp

Jun Nishida
Artificial Intelligence Lab
University of Tsukuba, Japan
jun.nishida@acm.org

Enrique Encinas
University of Northumbria,
Newcastle, UK
enrique.encinas@northumbria.ac.uk

TEI '17, March 20-23, 2017, Yokohama, Japan
ACM 978-1-4503-4676-4/17/03.
http://dx.doi.org/10.1145/3024969.3025051

Abstract
Positive social and collaborative effects are hailed as a major advantage of embodied and tangible approaches to interaction. This studio offers a hands-on exploration of potentially extreme versions of such benefits - systems and techniques that somehow share or transfer embodiment between two or more people. Through participatory demos, studio attendees will explore and compare a variety of approaches to experiencing the perspectives of another body, and controlling bodies other than their own. These comparisons will be a launch pad for collaboratively combining existing "body sharing" systems and mocking up new design concepts. By bringing together ideas and approaches in an actionable manner, this studio will share and develop imagination, theory, and skills relevant to the design and study of interactive systems in which the body plays a central role.

Keywords
Embodied interaction; empathy; collaboration

ACM Classification Keywords
H.5.3 Group and Organization Interfaces: Synchronous interaction

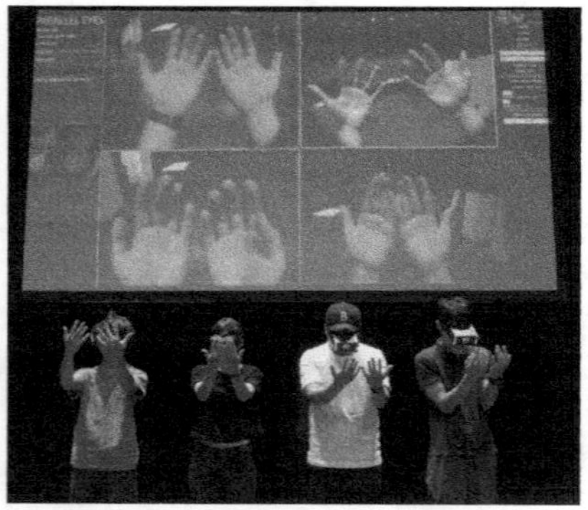

Figure 1. In "Parallel Eyes" four persons can see four shared first person videos from each other.

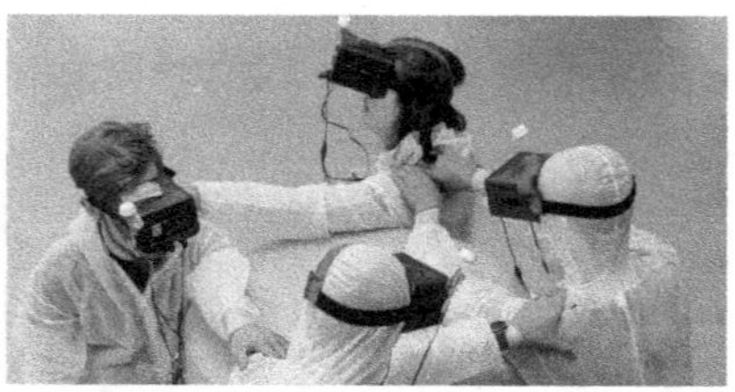

Figure 2. The Channel Surfers experimented with constant rapid switching between 2nd and 3rd person live camera perspectives.

Figure 3. The JackIn headset serves immersive omnidirectional video streams from one person to a virtual reality headset worn by another.

Introduction

In the world of fiction there are many plotlines concerning embodiment being shared or transferred between characters. This takes three main, often overlapping forms: either a character inhabits the body of another person; a character feels like they are inhabiting the body of another; and/or a character is able to directly control another person's body.
These abilities appear in not only in sci-fi [33] [6] but also in many different genres from comedy [11] to action [10], and manga [39]. In early examples e.g. [38] such body "swaps" were the result of magic or supernatural powers. However, the trend in fiction seems increasingly towards transferred or shared embodiment being due to scientific or technological progress e.g. [30] [33] [34], or special training [37].

Outside of fiction, full body swapping appears a long way off becoming reality. However, in many fields there are projects that seem to be experimenting with closely related themes. That is, developing systems and techniques to give participants experiences of taking the position or perspective of another person and other forms of providing a feeling of what it is like to inhabit and act in, or through the body of another person.

One of the most prevalent approaches has been transferring or sharing visual perspectives between two or more people. Such view swopping has taken forms both mutual such as Hachiya's seminal Inter Dis-Communication Machine [12] or the more recent Parallel Eyes [14] (figure 1) or Channel Surfers (figure 2) [36] and unidirectional e.g [26] [27] [29] (figure 3). There are also many kinds of voice controlled human tele-actors [3] that act in social situations through being a form of physical avatar that relays the voices [20] and even faces [18] of persons not present. Other senses and formats have also been explored, for instance balance [35] haptic connections and biosignals [13], pairs of handheld shape changing objects [23] and electrical stimulation for synchronising muscular activity [24] (figure 4). Digital technologies are not necessarily essential for fostering such experiences - artfully choreographed facilitation in performance practices also offer powerful means of embodied interpersonal awareness [32].

Motivations for these efforts are also manifold and various. They include practical application areas such as rehabilitation [24], sports training [22], entertainment and games [1] [19] and supporting collaborative work [14] and skill acquisition [23]. Other projects have been driven by artistic motivations [12] or a wish to foster various forms of empathy such as adults gaining insight into the embodied lives of children [26] students acting as surrogates for absent teachers [31] or sharing spatial awareness [13]. These sort of set-ups have also been explored as research tool e.g. for design [21] and in more laboratory like settings for various neurological and psychological topics such as understanding how a brain creates an image of its body [29], reducing prejudice [17] and mediating stereotyping [2].

We tentatively suggest "we-coupling" as an umbrella term for bringing together this diversity of experimentation. We choose the word "coupling" as per Paul Dourish's sense of establishing and breaking relationships between entities [5] and "we" to emphasise our interest in couplings that require and connect two or more people - together.

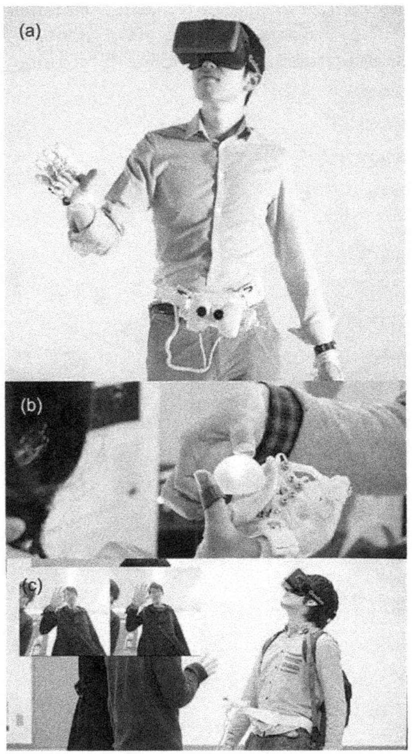
Figure 4. Video streamed from user's belt plus (b) wearing small hand exoskeletons enables the adult wearer of "CHILDHOOD SUIT" to see the world and grasp like an infant.

Studio Proposal

We propose a studio that will be an international multidisciplinary gathering around and *through* sharing and transferring embodiment. "Through" in the sense that all participants will experience several varieties of inhabiting or acting through the bodies of each other. We shall widely circulate a call for relevant contributions. Then we shall facilitate a studio that draws upon these submissions and our own experiments (see all figures). This studio will develop through the following main phases:

1) Experience & Capture

2) Share & Analyse

3) Generate & Embodied Experiments

In small groups, participants will explore existing systems and techniques related to sharing and transferring embodiment. This will include those selected from open call those provided by studio organisers (e.g. [14] [25] [26] [36]. Participants will systematically document their hands on experience during the studio to enable a set of cross case comparisons.

These comparisons of embodied experiences and systems will be enriched through a visual aids supported theoretical shared sense-making session. Currently we imagine drawing upon key concepts from three or four papers such as [7] [8] [9] [16]. However, our selection of theory sources will be finalised in response to the eventual line up of demos we curate from solicited contributions.

Then, fuelled by such mapping activities, participants will collaborate to devise new application areas and ideas for systems and techniques. The emphasis in this creative session will be on hands on experimentation. This may include modification and/or repurposing of the systems in the room, combining different systems, and/or quick and dirty prototyping with craft materials, and/or any equipment participants bring with them (whether everyday devices like smartphones and laptops or more esoteric materials).

All backgrounds and levels welcome

Participants may join this workshop either with or without contributing a demo. We will circulate a call for researchers and practitioners with relevant systems or techniques to submit a brief note of interest in an interactive demonstrating of their approach. From these submissions we will curate a balanced programme that we will announce in December 2017. Registration is also open to all TEI delegates on a first-come, first-served basis. No special skills or knowledge are required from participants joining - just a willingness to try some novel co-body experiences!

Studio Topics to be covered

- A broad range of approaches to sharing or transferring senses of embodiment. For instance: physiological muscular synchronization based on biosignal measurement and electrical muscle stimulation [25] (figure 4); immersive visual perspective sharing and swapping [14][15] (figure 1 & 3) [36] (figure 2); voice guided and speech relaying human surrogates [20]; verbal shadowing [5]; and viewpoint translation and

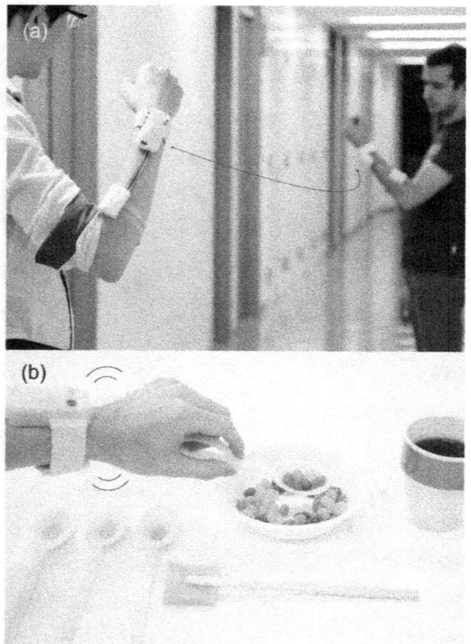

Figure 5. BioSync enables kinesthetic "swapping" via biosignal driven electrical muscular synchronization. This aids designing for differently abled users – for instance through transmitting the tremors of a Parkinson disease patient to a healthy person (lower image).

hand exoskeletons combining to give adults an experience of being a child [26] (figure 4). Contributions selected from submissions will further broaden the palette of experiences.

- Capturing, documenting, and comparing "we-coupling" related experiences.
- How several embodied interaction frameworks or theories may help explain, articulate, and be challenged by "we-coupling" experiences
- Collaborative designing of novel co-bodied experiences and application areas.

Studio Learning Goals

We shall facilitate a supportive atmosphere in which the learning will be largely "bottom up" i.e. it will occur through the hands-on experience of systems and activities, and the physical, visual, and conversational interactions between attendees. In terms of learning goals, we anticipate that participants shall:

- Experience, appreciate and critique a broad range of approaches related to fostering shared and transferred embodiment.
- Appreciate a diversity of perspectives concerning the desirability and feasibility of sharing and transferring embodiment.
- Acquire insights and practice in documenting and analyzing "we-coupling" experiences.
- Become familiar with how "body swapping" related experimentation may relate to, extend or challenge several key frameworks for the TEI community.
- Uncover, and argue for potential new application areas or other new directions for shared embodiment design and research.
- Gain an appreciation of contextual factors that may influence the impact of different shared embodiment approaches.

Studio Positioning

On the continuum of theoretical to practical skills, this studio is positioned approximately three quarters towards the practical end of the spectrum. The emphasis will be on hands-on experiences and designing, but we will strive to put theory to work in helping participants to analyze, articulate and innovate unusual embodied experiences. However, we do imagine that participants with strong inclinations towards theoretical matters will find the studio rather provoking – and we would very much welcome their participation too.

Possible Outputs

Currently we anticipate collaborating with studio participants to create an annotated portfolio submission for an international design conference on the basis of submissions received. We also believe that insights from experiential comparison of different approaches may be developed into a journal article. However, we are more excited by the interpersonal engagements that may be achieved through an intense day of "we-coupling" – we anticipate that this may result in some very rich collaborative outcomes from participants in forms and fields we can neither predict nor control.

References

[1] Albara Alohali, Kai Kunze, and Robert Earle. 2016. Run with me: designing storytelling tools for runners. *Adjunct UbiComp '16*. 5-8. http://dx.doi.org/10.1145/2968219.2971452

[2] Kevin Corti and Alex Gillespie. 2015. Revisiting Milgram's cyranoid method: experimenting with hybrid human agents. *The Journal of social psychology*,155(1), pp.30-56.

[3] Judith Donath. 2014. The social machine: designs for living online. MIT Press.

[4] Paul Dourish. 2001. *Where The Action Is.* MIT Press.

[5] Enrique Encinas. 2015. Cyrafour: How Two Human Avatars Communicate With Each Other. *CHI EA '15.* 109-114. http://dx.doi.org/10.1145/2702613.2726962

[6] William Gibson. 2014. *The Peripheral*. Penguin.

[7] Eva Hornecker and Jacob Buur. 2006. Getting a grip on tangible interaction: a framework on physical space and social interaction. *CHI '06*. 437-446. http://dx.doi.org/10.1145/1124772.1124838

[8] Caroline Hummels and Jelle van Dijk. 2015. Seven Principles to Design for Embodied Sensemaking. *TEI '15.* 21-28 http://dx.doi.org/10.1145/2677199.2680577

[9] Robert J.K. Jacob, Audrey Girouard, Leanne M. Hirshfield, Michael S. Horn, Orit Shaer, Erin Treacy Solovey, and Jamie Zigelbaum. 2008. Reality-based interaction: a framework for post-WIMP interfaces. *CHI '08.* 201-210. http://dx.doi.org/10.1145/1357054.1357089

[10] Duncan Jones. 2011. *Source Code.* Summit Entertainment.

[11] Spike Jonze. 1999. *Being John Malkovich*. USA Films.

[12] Larissa Hjorth and Olivia Khoo. 2015. *Routledge Handbook of New Media in Asia*. Routledge.

[13] Leah Heiss., 2007. Enabled apparel: the role of digitally enhanced apparel in promoting remote empathic connection. *Ai & Society*.15-24. http://dx.doi.org/10.1007/s00146-006-0076-z

[14] Shunichi Kasahara, Mitsuhito Ando, Kiyoshi Suganuma, and Jun Rekimoto. 2016. Parallel Eyes: Exploring Human Capability and Behaviors with Paralleled First Person View Sharing. *CHI '16*. 1561-1572. http://dx.doi.org/10.1145/2858036.2858495

[15] Shunichi Kasahara and Jun Rekimoto. 2015. JackIn head: immersive visual telepresence system with omnidirectional wearable camera for remote collaboration. *VRST '15*. 217-225. http://dx.doi.org/10.1145/2821592.2821608

[16] Scott R. Klemmer, Björn Hartmann, and Leila Takayama. 2006. How bodies matter: five themes for interaction design. *DIS '06*. 140-149. http://dx.doi.org/10.1145/1142405.1142429

[17] Lara Maister, Mel Slater, Maria V. Sanchez-Vives, M.V. and Manos. 2015. Changing bodies changes minds: owning another body affects social cognition. *Trends in cognitive sciences*, 6-12.

[18] Kana Misawa and Jun Rekimoto. 2015. Wearing another's personality: a human-surrogate system with a telepresence face. *ISWC '15.* 125-132. http://dx.doi.org/10.1145/2802083.2808392

[19] Robb Mitchell, Cynthia S.B. Bravo, Andreas Heiberg Skouby, and Ragna Lisa Möller. 2015. Blind Running: Perceptual Team Interdependency for Self-less Play. *CHI PLAY '15.* 649-654. http://dx.doi.org/10.1145/2793107.2810308

[20] Robb Mitchell. 2009. An in your face interface: revisiting cyranoids as a revealing medium for interpersonal interaction. In *Proceedings of SIDeR: Flirting with the Future*. 56-59.

[21] Robb Mitchell, Alex Gillespie, and Brian O'Neill. 2011. Cyranic contraptions: using personality surrogates to explore ontologically and socially dynamic

contexts. *DESIRE '11.* 199-210. http://dx.doi.org/10.1145/2079216.2079246

[22] Florian 'Floyd' Mueller, Shannon O'Brien, and Alex Thorogood. 2007. Jogging over a distance: supporting a "jogging together" experience although being apart. *CHI EA '07.* http://dx.doi.org/10.1145/1240866.1240937

[23] Ken Nakagaki, Chikara Inamura, Pasquale Totaro, Thariq Shihipar, Chantine Akikyama, Yin Shuang, and Hiroshi Ishii. 2015. Linked-Stick: Conveying a Physical Experience using a Shape-Shifting Stick. *CHI EA '15.* 1609-1614. http://dx.doi.org/10.1145/2702613.2732712

[24] Jun Nishida and Kenji Suzuki. 2016. BioSync: Synchronous Kinesthetic Experience among People. *CHI EA '16*. 3742-3745. http://dx.doi.org/10.1145/2851581.2890244

[25] Nishida, J., Takatori, H., Sato, K. and Suzuki, K., 2015. Childhood: Wearable suit for augmented child experience. In *ACM SIGGRAPH 2015 Posters* (p. 18). ACM.

[26] Jun Nishida, Hikaru Takatori, Kosuke Sato, and Kenji Suzuki. 2015. CHILDHOOD: wearable suit for augmented child experience. *SIGGRAPH '15*. http://dx.doi.org/10.1145/2782782.2792501

[27] Ellen Collaco De Oliveira, Philippe Bertrand Marta E.R. Lesur, Priscila Palomo, Marcelo Demarzo, Ausias Cebolla, Rosa Baños, and Romero Tori. 2016. Virtual Body Swap: A New Feasible Tool to be Explored in Health and Education. In *2016 XVIII Symposium on Virtual and Augmented Reality (SVR)* 81-89.

[28] Mamoru Oshii. 1995. *Ghost In The Shell*. Manga Entertainment.

[29] Valeria Petkova, and Henrik Ehrsson, 2008. If I were you: perceptual illusion of body swapping. *PloS one*, *3*(12), p.e3832.

[30] Jennifer Phang. 2015. *Advantageous*. Netflix.

[31] Pirkko Raudaskoski and Robb Mitchell. 2013. The situated accomplishment (aesthetics) of being a cyranoid. In *Proceedings of the Participatory Innovation Conference: PIN-C 2013.* 126-129.

[32] Thecla Schiphorst. 2009. The varieties of user experience bridging embodied methodologies from somatics and performance to human computer interaction. *PhD Dissertation*, School of Computing, Plymouth, United Kingdom: CAiiA Star at the University of Plymouth

[33] Singh, Tarsem. 2015. *Self/less*. Endgame Entertainment.

[34] Trumbull, Douglas. 1983. *Brainstorm*. Metro-Goldwyn-Mayer.

[35] Nobuya Suzuki, Takahiro Kobayashi, and Hiroshi Yasuda. 2005. Networked equilibrium sharing system "balance seat". ACE'05. 188-191. http://dx.doi.org/10.1145/1178477.1178504

[36] *The Channel Surfers*. 2016. www.channelsurfers.wordpress.com. Accessed 28/10/2016.

[37] Akira Toriyam. 1988-1995. *Dragon Ball Z.* Toei Animation. Fuji TV.

[38] Ustinov, Peter. 1948. *Vice Versa*. Two Cities Films.

[39] Miki Yoshikawa. 2012-2016. Yamada-kun and the Seven Witches. *Weekly Shonen Magazine.* Kondasha

Participatory Design 101: Co-Creating Tangible User Interfaces to Enrich a Business Trip Experience

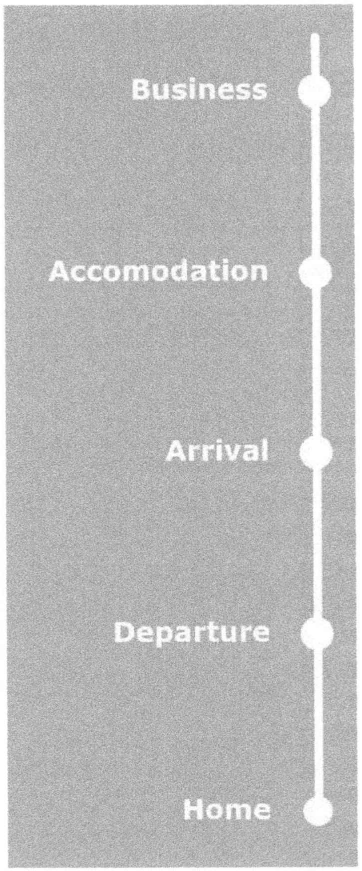

Figure 1. Guided by a timeline the participants will pinpoint situations, events and experiences of a business trip.

Marie Beuthel
Design Research Lab
Berlin University of the Arts
Einsteinufer 43, 10587 Berlin,
Germany
marie.beuthel@udk-berlin.de

Anne Wohlauf
Design Research Lab
Berlin University of the Arts
Einsteinufer 43, 10587 Berlin,
Germany
anne.wohlauf@udk-berlin.de

TEI '17, March 20-23, 2017, Yokohama, Japan
ACM 978-1-4503-4676-4/17/03.
http://dx.doi.org/10.1145/3024969.3025052

Abstract
In this studio session, the attendees develop an initial sense for participatory design (PD) by running through a co-creation process. This process enables a Tangible User Interface (TUI) design that involves potential users and other stakeholders with or without technical background. The studio participants will play the role of a user group they all can relate to: business travelers. Based on the users' expert knowledge that we will collect during the research and exploration phase, they will form ideas and visualize TUI concepts that can enrich a business trip experience. During the session, participants will apply eight hands-on methods. These derive from the PD approach that we introduce in the studio. In a reflection round, we will discuss the co-creation process and resulting concepts, and provide advice for transferring the methods learned to their own projects.

Keywords
Co-Creation; Workshop Tools; Participatory Design Methods; Prototyping; Tangible Interaction

ACM Classification Keywords
D.2.2 Design Tools and Techniques: Object-oriented design methods; D.2.10 Design: Methodologies

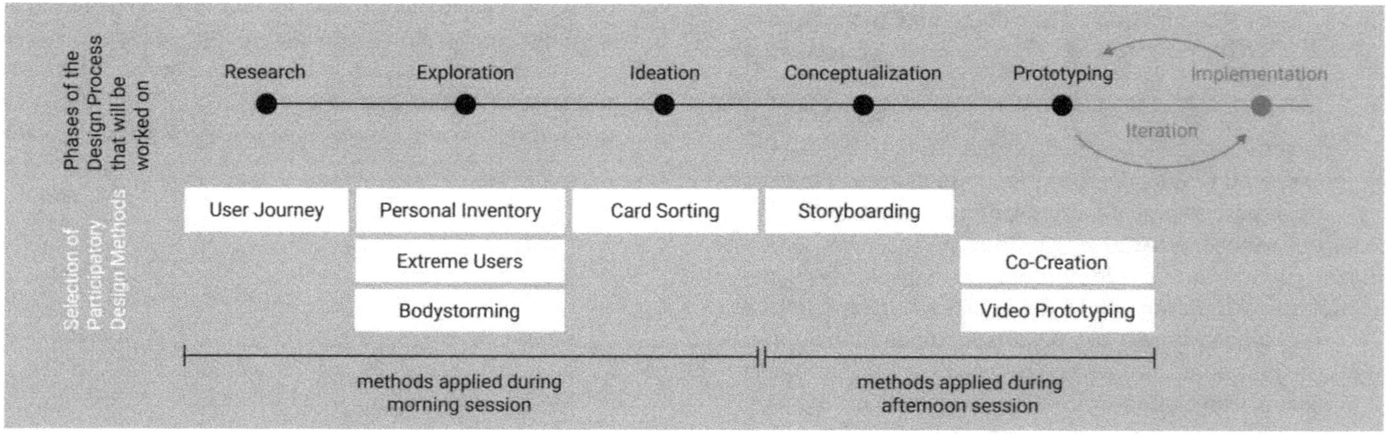

Figure 2. Studio Roadmap: After an introduction to PD, the attendees will develop TUI concepts by using eight PD methods. Reflection at the end of the studio aims to provide guidance to the participants, and how to involve users in their own work.

Introduction

User-driven participatory design processes can generate results with a higher customer acceptance than technology-driven development processes [13]. Utilizing PD methods improves the usability of products and services and increases their market success [15]. This is why the use of collaborative methods is valuable for the usability of tangible user interfaces. We will introduce the participants to the PD approach and equip them with an initiate set of methods they can reuse in future TUI development. In order to convey an understanding for PD, the attendees will go through a co-creation process while slipping into the role of a potential user group. As conference visitors most participants are able to identify themselves with the user group of business travelers and can provide empathic insights [6] for the context of a business trip.

Studio Participants

Participants of the studio should be curious about ways to involve user groups and other stakeholders in a TUI development. They will be asked to actively take part in the co-creation process, in which people from different backgrounds work together. No particular skills are required to take part.

Studio Procedure

The studio is divided into five parts, which follow a co-creation design process [12]: Research, Exploration, Ideation, Conceptualization and Prototyping (see Fig. 2). The participants will go through each part in the role as a user and later analyze the outcomes and learnings of each part.

Before the hands-on part, the participants will be introduced to the PD approach. Some examples of previous and ongoing work (e.g. [4], [2]) will be shown to give them an overview and understanding of

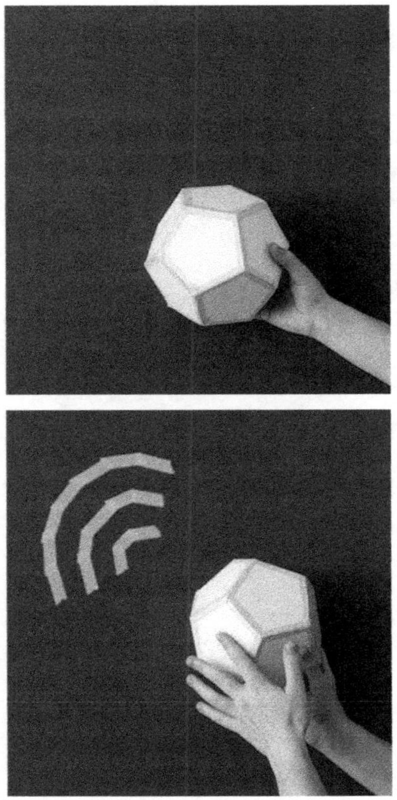

Figure 3. In the *Prototyping* phase the participants will create video prototypes using paper and tape (see example video stills above) to present tangible user interface concepts in motion.

participatory thinking and working in the field of tangible interaction.

Research
We will define the user group (business travelers), the context (business trip) and purpose (enrichment of experience) of the session's design process. Guided by a timeline the participants will first collaboratively discuss the user journey [10] of business travelers, and highlight situations, events and experiences of particular interest (see Fig. 1) that will lead towards one specific use case.

Exploration
To explore the use case practically, three participatory hands-on methods will be applied: *personal inventory, extreme users* and *bodystorming*. The *personal inventory method* [9] will raise awareness for the business travelers' personal belongings and emotional attachment towards them. The participants will define *extreme users* [3] collaboratively. This will support the investigation of the behavioral patterns business travelers perform during a journey. The *bodystorming* activity [11] is aligned with an "expressive-movement view" [14]. In this phase, the participants will act out relevant scenarios and business trip experiences, and analyze expressive body movements on human-(object-)interactions.

Ideation
The outcomes of the exploration will be the basis for an ideation phase. By collecting and clustering the findings in a *card-sorting* activity [8], the main results will become visible. We will use pictorial and linguistic comparisons and metaphors [1] in order to prepare the conceptualization phase.

Conceptualization
The results of the ideation phase will lead to concepts that explore different ways of enriching a business trip experience. By describing and visualizing the concepts, the participants will create the foundation for the prototyping phase in form of storyboards [7].

Prototyping
Using paper and adhesive tape, the participants will rapidly prototype [5] and *co-create* [12] the TUI-concepts in groups. Each group will act out scenarios taken from the storyboards that show the main features of the prototypical concepts. By filming these human-TUI-interactions [7], each concept will be recorded as *Video-Prototypes* (Fig. 3). To complete the exemplary design process, the implementation phase (as seen on the right in Fig. 2) would be the next phase, in which prototypes could be developed iteratively including intensive user testing.

After finalizing the TUI prototypes, the participants will reflect on and analyze the studio session by reviewing the applied participatory methods. We will discuss the advantages and disadvantages and share best-practices, so that the participants can easily transfer and apply the methods afterwards in their own tangible interaction projects. By discussing and comparing discoveries of the session, new insights and skills will derive for all parties involved.

Studio Learning Goals

- Participatory design approach overview
- Eight participatory design methods
  - Transfer and application
  - Best practice

References

[1] Bakker, S., Antle, A.N., and Van Den Hoven, E. Embodied metaphors in tangible interaction design. *Personal and Ubiquitous Computing 16*, 4 (2012), 433–449.

[2] Beuthel, M., Wohlauf, A., and Zach, E. Your Finger is the Key. 2016. http://www.design-research-lab.org/projects/your-finger-is-the-key-2/.

[3] Djajadiningrat, J.P., Gaver, W.W., and Frens, J.W. Interaction Relabelling and Extreme Characters: Methods for Exploring Aesthetic Interactions. *Proceedings of the Conference on Designing Interactive Systems: Processes, Practices, Methods, and Techniques, DIS 2000*, (2000), 66–71.

[4] Gaver, W.W., Bowers, J., Boucher, A., et al. The Drift Table : Designing for Ludic Engagement. *Proceeding, CHI EA '04. ACM Press*, (2004), 885–900.

[5] Hudson, S.E. and Mankoff, J. Rapid Construction of Functioning Physical Interfaces from Cardboard, Thumbtacks, Tin Foil and Masking Tape. *Proceedings of the 19th annual ACM symposium on User interface software and technology - UIST '06*, (2006), 289–298.

[6] Lindsay, S., Brittain, K., Jackson, D., Ladha, C., Ladha, K., and Olivier, P. Empathy, participatory design and people with dementia. *the 2012 ACM annual conference*, (2012), 521–530.

[7] Mackay, W. Using Video to Support Interaction Design. *DVD Tutorial, CHI*, (2002).

[8] Martin, B. and Hanington, B. *Universal methods of design: 100 ways to research complex problems, develop innovative ideas, and design effective solutions*. Rockport Publishers, 2012.

[9] Moggridge, B. and Atkinson, B. *Designing Interactions*. Cambridge, MA: MIT press, 2007.

[10] Nenonen, S., Rasila, H., Matti, J., and Karna, S. Customer Journey–a method to investigate user experience. *Proceedings of the Euro FM Conference Manchester*, Schmitt 1999 (2008), 54–63.

[11] Oulasvirta, A., Kurvinen, E., and Kankainen, T. Understanding contexts by being there: Case studies in bodystorming. *Personal and Ubiquitous Computing*, (2003), 125–134.

[12] Sanders, E.B.-N. and Stappers, P.J. Co-creation and the new landscapes of design. *CoDesign 4*, 1 (2008), 5–18.

[13] Schuler, D., Namioka, A., and Blomberg, J. Participatory Design: Principles and Practices. *System*, (1993), 319.

[14] Shaer, O. and Hornecker, E. Tangible User Interfaces: Past, Present, and Future Directions. *Foundations and Trends in Human-Computer Interaction 3*, 1-2 (2010), 1–137.

[15] Wilkinson, C.R. and De Angeli, A. Applying user centred and participatory design approaches to commercial product development. *Design Studies 35*, 6 (2014), 614–631.

Author Index

www.ingramcontent.com/pod-product-compliance
Lightning Source LLC
LaVergne TN
LVHW080104011026
849160LV00013B/1029